The Routledge International Encyclopedia of Education

The Routledge International Encyclopedia of Education is a unique and major resource for the field of education. It is a comprehensive, single-volume work, arranged alphabetically and comprising around 600 entries.

The entries range from definitions of key educational concepts and terms to biographies of key educators and specially written substantial essays on major educational topics. The volume includes authoritative and critical commentary on historical and contemporary themes; examinations of continuities, changes and emerging issues; and discussions of the educational traditions and features of major countries and continents. The following special features are also included:

- Unrivalled coverage of education in a single volume
- Entries by leading international educational researchers
- Contributors drawn from all over the globe, including Australia, Brazil, Canada, China, Finland, India, Israel, Japan, New Zealand, South Africa, the United Kingdom and the United States
- A distinguished international advisory board
- Fully cross-referenced and indexed
- Suggestions for further reading

Offering insight into the world of education in an interesting, informed and sometimes provocative way, *The Routledge International Encyclopedia of Education* is an invaluable work of reference for educators, students, researchers and policy makers in education and related fields internationally.

Gary McCulloch is Dean of Research and Consultancy and Brian Simon Professor of the History of Education at the Institute of Education, University of London, UK.

David Crook is Senior Lecturer in History of Education at the Institute of Education, University of London, UK.

Related titles

Routledge International Companion to Education
Edited by Miriam Ben-Peretz, Sally Brown and Bob Moon

The Routledge Companion to Education
Edited by Harry Daniels, Hugh Lauder and Jill Porter

Fifty Modern Thinkers on Education
Edited by Joy A. Palmer

Fifty Major Thinkers on Education
Edited by Joy A. Palmer

Philosophy of Education: Major Themes in the Analytic Tradition
Edited by Paul Hurst and Patricia White
Volume 1: Philosophy and Education
Volume 2: Education and Human Being
Volume 3: Society and Education
Volume 4: Problems of Educational Content and Practices

History of Education
Edited by Roy Lowe
Volume 1: Debates on the History of Education
Volume 2: Education in its Social Context
Volume 3: Studies in Learning and Teaching
Volume 4: Studies of Education Systems

The Sociology of Education
Edited by Stephen J. Ball
Volume 1: Theories and Methods
Volume 2: Inequalities and Oppressions
Volume 3: Institutions and Processes
Volume 4: Politics and Policies

Psychology of Education
Edited by Peter K. Smith and Anthony D. Pellegrini
Volume 1: Schools, teachers and parents
Volume 2: Pupils and Learning
Volume 3: The school curriculum
Volume 4: Social behaviour and the school peer group

Adult and Continuing Education
Edited by Peter Jarvis
Volume 1: Liberal Adult Education, Part I
Volume 2: Liberal Adult Education, Part II
Volume 3: Vocational Education
Volume 4: Teaching, Learning and Research
Volume 5: Adult Education – Viewed from the Disciplines

Curriculum Studies
Edited by David Scott
Volume 1: Curriculum Knowledge
Volume 2: Curriculum Forms
Volume 3: Pedagogy
Volume 4: Boundaries: Subjects, Assessment and Evaluation

Literacy
Edited by David Wray
Volume 1: Literacy – Its Nature and its Teaching
Volume 2: Reading – Processes and Teaching
Volume 3: Writing – Processes and Teaching
Volume 4: New Literacies - The Impact of Technologies

Special Educational Needs and Inclusive Education

Edited by David Mitchell

Volume 1: Systems and Contexts
Volume 2: Inclusive Education
Volume 3: Assessment and Teaching Strategies
Volume 4: Effective Practices

Educational Management

Edited by Harry Tomlinson

Volume 1: History and Development of Educational Management Theory
Volume 2: Leadership, Managing People and Professional Development
Volume 3: Managing Teaching and Learning
Volume 4: Current Trends and Changing Policy

Science Education

Edited by John K. Gilbert

Volume 1: Science, Education, and the Formal Curriculum
Volume 2: Science Education and Assessment in the Formal Curriculum
Volume 3: Teaching and Learning in Science Education
Volume 4: Conceptual and Teacher Development in Science Education

Early Years Education

Edited by Rod Parker-Rees and Jenny Willan

Volume 1: Histories and Traditions
Volume 2: Curriculum Issues in Early Childhood Education
Volume 3: Policy and Practice in Early Education and Care
Volume 4: Researching Early Education: Challenges and Futures

Teacher Education

Edited by David Hartley and Maurice Whitehead

Volume 1: Historical Aspects of Teacher Education from 1797 to 1905
Volume 2: Historical Aspects of Teacher Education from 1905 to 1990
Volume 3: Curriculum and Change
Volume 4: Professionalism, Social Justice and Teacher Education
Volume 5: Globalisation, Standards and Teacher Education

A History of Western Education

by James Bowen

Volume 1: The Ancient World: Orient and Mediterranean 2000 B.C – A.D. 1054
Volume 2: Civilization of Europe: Sixth to Sixteenth Century
Volume 3: The Modern West: Europe and the New World

The Routledge International Encyclopedia of Education

Edited by
Gary McCulloch
David Crook

Routledge
Taylor & Francis Group

LONDON AND NEW YORK

First published 2008
by Routledge
2 Park Square, Milton Park, Abingdon, Oxon OX14 4RN

Simultaneously published in the USA and Canada
by Routledge
270 Madison Ave, New York, NY 10016

Routledge is an imprint of the Taylor & Francis Group, an informa business

© 2008 Gary McCulloch and David Crook for editorial selection and material;
individual contributors, their own contribution

Typeset in Bembo and Helvetica by
Taylor & Francis Books
Printed and bound in Great Britain by
MPG Books Ltd, Bodmin

British Library Cataloguing in Publication Data
A catalogue record for this book is available from the British Library

Library of Congress Cataloging in Publication Data
The Routledge international encyclopedia of education / edited by Gary McCulloch
and David Crook.
    p. cm.
  Includes bibliographical references and index.
  1. Education–Encyclopedias. I. McCulloch, Gary. II. Crook, David. III. Title:
International encyclopedia of education.
  LB15R633 2008
  370.3–dc22
                        2007037744

ISBN10: 0-415-27747-7 (hbk)
ISBN13: 978-0-415-27747-1 (hbk)

Contents

Consultant Editors   viii

List of contributors   ix

Alphabetical List of Entries   xvi

Editors' introduction   xxxi

Acknowledgements   xxxvii

Entries A–Z   1

Index   653

Consultant Editors

Sandra Acker
University of Toronto, Canada

Miriam Ben-Peretz
University of Haifa, Israel

Barry Franklin
Utah State University, USA

Bob Lingard
University of Edinburgh, UK

Reba Page
University of California–Riverside, USA

Richard Pring
University of Oxford, UK

Sheldon Rothblatt
University of California–Berkeley, USA

Manabu Sato
University of Tokyo, Japan

Hannu Simola
University of Helsinki, Finland

Lorna Unwin
Institute of Education, London, UK

Contributors

Patrick Ainley
University of Greenwich, UK

Richard Aldrich
Institute of Education, University of London, UK

Huda Al-Khaizaran
Institute of Education, University of London, UK

Christian K. Anderson
Penn State University, USA

Jo Anne Anderson
Education Oversight Committee, South Carolina, USA

Ann Cheryl Armstrong
University of Sydney, Australia

Felicity Armstrong
Institute of Education, University of London, UK

David Ashton
University of Cardiff, UK

Paul Axelrod
York University, Canada

Fatemeh Bagherian
University of Tehran, Iran

Bill Bailey
University of Greenwich, UK

James A. Banks
University of Washington, USA

Ronald Barnett
Institute of Education, University of London, UK

Roger Beard
Institute of Education, University of London, UK

Charlotte Beaudoin
University of Ottawa, Canada

Kevin M. Beaver
Florida State University, USA

Miriam Ben-Peretz
University of Haifa, Israel

Raksha Bhalsod
Institute of Education, University of London, UK

Jason Blokhuis
University of Rochester, USA

Christine Brabant
University of Sherbrooke, Canada

Julia Brannen
Institute of Education, University of London, UK

Jacek Brant
Institute of Education, University of London, UK

Kevin J. Brehony
Roehampton University, UK

Harry Brighouse
University of Wisconsin–Madison, USA

Phillip Brown
University of Cardiff, UK

Lesley Burgess
Institute of Education, University of London, UK

Catherine Burke
University of Leeds, UK

Neil Burtonwood
University of Leeds, UK

Craig Campbell
University of Sydney, Australia

Roy Canning
University of Stirling, UK

Vincent Carpentier
Institute of Education, University of London, UK

David Carr
University of Edinburgh, UK

Anne Chapman
University of Western Australia, Australia

Linda Clarke
University of Westminster, UK

Mike Cole
University of Brighton, UK

Paul Collins
University of Rochester, USA

Paul M. Collins
University of Chichester, UK

Harris Cooper
Duke University, North Carolina, USA

Robert Cowen
Institute of Education, University of London, UK

Steven Cowan
Institute of Education, University of London, UK

Eve Coxon
University of Auckland, New Zealand

Anna Craft
Open University, UK

David Crook
Institute of Education, University of London, UK

Bryan Cunningham
Institute of Education, University of London, UK

Randall Curren
University of Rochester, USA

P. A. Danaher
University of Southern Queensland, Australia

Tara Davidson
Rutgers University, USA

Scott Davies
McMaster University, Canada

Malcolm Dick
University of Birmingham, UK

H. W. Dickinson
King's College, University of London, UK

Thomas Duff
Dublin Institute of Technology, Ireland

Peter Earley
Institute of Education, University of London, UK

Billie Eilam
Haifa University, Israel

Edmund T. Emmer
University of Texas, USA

Karen Evans
Institute of Education, University of London, UK

Michael W. Eysenck
Royal Holloway, University of London, UK

Michel Ferrari
Ontario Institute for Studies in Education (OISE), University of Toronto, Canada

Maria de Figueiredo-Cowen
Institute of Education, University of London, UK

Maria Isabel Figueiredo Sobreira
Historical and Geographical Institute of Clear Mounts, Brazil

Kara S. Finnigan
University of Rochester, USA

Roy Fisher
University of Huddersfield, UK

Tanya Fitzgerald
UNITEC, New Zealand

Stuart Foster
Institute of Education, University of London, UK

Barry M. Franklin
Utah State University, USA

Rob Freathy
University of Exeter, UK

Thomas N. Garavan
University of Limerick, Ireland

Jim Garrison
Virginia Tech, USA

Anne Gaskell
Open University, UK

Dianne Gereluk
Roehampton University, UK

Elizabeth T. Gershoff
University of Michigan, USA

Suresh C. Ghosh
Jawaharlal Nehru University, India

Marina-Stefania Giannakaki
Athens Institute for Education and Research, Greece

Ian Gilbert
Independent Thinking Ltd, UK

Tal Gilead
Hebrew University, Israel

Kenneth S. Goodman
University of Arizona, USA

Yetta Goodman
University of Arizona, USA

Stephen Gorard
University of Birmingham, UK

David Gough
Institute of Education, University of London, UK

Edith Aurora Graf
Educational Testing Service, USA

Andy Green
Institute of Education, University of London, UK

Patrick Groff
State University of San Diego, USA

David Guile
Institute of Education, University of London, UK

Helen Gunter
University of Manchester, UK

Susan Hallam
Institute of Education, University of London, UK

Maureen T. Hallinan
University of Notre Dame, USA

Ronald K. Hambleton
University of Massachusetts, USA

Martyn Hammersley
Open University, UK

Gregory E. Hamot
University of Iowa, USA

Peter Hannon
University of Sheffield, UK

Eleanore Hargreaves
Institute of Education, University of London, UK

Sophie Haroutunian-Gordon
Northwestern University, USA

Catherine Harris
Deakin University, Australia

Donna Marie Harris
University of Rochester, USA

Robert Hattam
University of South Australia, Australia

Terry Haydn
University of East Anglia, UK

Ruth Hayhoe
Ontario Institute for Studies in Education (OISE),
University of Toronto, Canada

Natalie Heath
Institute of Education, University of London, UK

Anja Heikkinen
University of Tampere, Finland

Jeremy Higham
University of Leeds, UK

Phil Hodkinson
University of Leeds, UK

Teruhisa Horio
Tokyo University, Japan

Peter Hunt
University of Cardiff, UK

Knud Illeris
Danish University of Education, Denmark

Michael Imber
University of Kansas, USA

Judith Ireson
Institute of Education, University of London, UK

Benjamin M. Jacobs
University of Minnesota, USA

Jennifer Jenson
York University, Canada

Kathleen W. Jones
Virginia Tech, USA

Peter Kallaway
University of Western Cape, South Africa

Pearl Rock Kane
Teachers College, Columbia University, USA

Anthony Kelly
University of Southampton, UK

W. Ashley Kent
Institute of Education, University of London, UK

Jeremy Kilpatrick
University of Georgia, USA

Geeta Kingdon
Institute of Education, University of London, UK

Steven J. Klees
University of Maryland, USA

Peter Knight
Open University, UK

Marie Lall
Institute of Education, University of London, UK

John LaNear
University of Wisconsin–Madison, USA

Hugh Lauder
University of Bath, UK

John Lesko
Saginaw Valley State University, USA

Geoff Lindsay
University of Warwick, UK

Robert W. Lissitz
University of Maryland, USA

Angela Little
Institute of Education, University of London, UK

Bernard Longden
Liverpool Hope University, UK

Roy Lowe
Institute of Education, University of London, UK

David McCallum
Victoria University, Australia

Gary McCulloch
Institute of Education, University of London, UK

Rose M. McNeese
University of Southern Mississippi, USA

Dawn B. Male
Institute of Education, University of London, UK

Tricia Maynard
University of Swansea, UK

Pam Meecham
Institute of Education, University of London, UK

Harvey Mellar
Institute of Education, University of London, UK

Edward Mifsud
Institute of Education, University of London, UK

Carlton Mills
Turks and Caicos College, Turks and Caicos Islands

Ka-Ho Mok
University of Hong Kong, Hong Kong

Kay Morris Matthews
Victoria University of Wellington, New Zealand

Roger Murphy
University of Nottingham, UK

Paul Narguizian
California State University, USA

Kristen Nawrotzki
Roehampton University, UK

David Nicholas
University of Oxford, UK

Jason Nicholls
Institute of Education, University of London, UK

Amy Nitza
University of Indiana, USA

Jon Nixon
University of Sheffield, UK

Tom O'Donoghue
University of Western Australia, Australia

John Oliphant
Waseda University, Japan

Mark Olssen
University of Surrey, UK

Marnie O'Neill
University of Western Australia, Australia

Norbert Pachler
Institute of Education, University of London, UK

Anthony Paré
McGill University, USA

Gareth Parry
University of Sheffield, UK

Lee T. Pearcy
Episcopal Academy, USA

Jo Peat
Roehampton University, UK

Michael A. Peters
University of Glasgow, UK

W. James Popham
University of California, USA

Anthony Potts
Liverpool Hope University, UK

David Seth Preston
University of East London, UK

Gareth Rees
University of Cardiff, UK

William J. Reese
University of Wisconsin–Madison, USA

Jost Reischmann
University of Bamberg, Germany

Michael J. Reiss
Institute of Education, University of London, UK

Colin Richards
University of Cumbria, UK

Mary Richardson
Roehampton University, UK

Jeni Riley
Institute of Education, University of London, UK

Geoff Riordan
University of Technology, Sydney, Australia

Fazal Rizvi
University of Illinois–Urbana–Champaign, USA

Sue Rogers
Institute of Education, University of London, UK

Christine H. Rossell
Boston University, USA

John L. Rury
University of Kansas, USA

John Rust
City University, UK

David Rutkowski
University of Illinois–Urbana–Champaign, USA

Alan Sadovnik
Rutgers University, USA

Luciola L. Santos
Universidade Federal de Minas Gerais/Federal University of Minas Gerais, Brazil

Vilma Seeberg
Kent State University, USA

Paul Sharp
University of Leeds, UK

Geoffrey Sherington
University of Sydney, Australia

Richard Siaciwena
University of Zambia, Zambia

Robert Slavin
Johns Hopkins University, USA

Harry Smaller
York University, Canada

Claire Smetherham
University of Bristol, UK

Clive Smith
Rhodes University, South Africa

Mark K. Smith
YMCA George Williams College, UK

Richard Smith
University of Durham, UK

Crain Soudien
University of Cape Town, South Africa

Amy Stambach
University of Wisconsin–Madison, USA

William B. Stanley
Monmouth University, USA

Rex Stockton
University of Indiana, USA

Louise Stoll
Institute of Education, University of London, UK

Steve Strand
University of Warwick, UK

Shinichi Suzuki
Waseda University, Japan

Alison Taysum
University of Leicester, UK

Lyn Tett
University of Edinburgh, UK

Konai Thaman
University of the South Pacific, Fiji

John B. Thomas
Loughborough University, UK

Warren Thorngate
Carleton University, Canada

Martin Thrupp
Waikato University, New Zealand

Paul Tractenberg
Rutgers University, USA

Lynne Vernon-Feagans
University of North Carolina, USA

Carol Vincent
Institute of Education, University of London, UK

Catherine Wallace
Institute of Education, University of London, UK

Jerry Wellington
University of Sheffield, UK

John White
Institute of Education, University of London, UK

Maurice Whitehead
University of Swansea, UK

Susanne Wiborg
Institute of Education, University of London, UK

Keith Williams
Edge Hill University, UK

Kimberly Williams
Plymouth State University, USA

Christopher Winch
King's College, University of London, UK

Carrie Winstanley
Roehampton University, UK

Patrick J. Wolf
University of Arkansas, USA

Tom Woodin
Institute of Education, University of London, UK

William G. Wraga
University of Georgia, USA

Michael F. D. Young
Institute of Education, University of London, UK

Joseph Zajda
Australian Catholic University, Australia

Rea Zajda
James Nicholas Publishers, Australia

David Zarifa
McMaster University, Canada

Qiang Zha
Ontario Institute for Studies in Education (OISE), University of Toronto, Canada

Alphabetical List of Entries

Abacus
Gary McCulloch

Abelard, Peter (1079–1142)
Steven Cowan

Ability
Judith Ireson

Ability grouping
Susan Hallam

Academic/academic profession
Ronald Barnett

Academic freedom
John LaNear

Academy
Gary McCulloch

Accountability
Jo Anne Anderson

Accreditation
David Crook

Accreditation of prior achievement/learning
Raksha Bhalsod

Action research
Jerry Wellington

Activity theory
Anthony Paré

Addams, Jane (1860–1935)
Steven Cowan

Adult education
Tom Woodin

Africa
Peter Kallaway and Crain Soudien

Alternative education
Rose M. McNeese

Alumni
David Crook

American Educational Research Association (AERA)
Tom Woodin

Andragogy
Jost Reischmann

Anthropology of education
Neil Burtonwood

Antiracist education
Mike Cole

Apprenticeship
Anja Heikkinen and Tom Woodin

Approved school
David Crook

Aptitude
Joseph Zajda and Rea Zajda

Aristotle (384–322 BCE)
Steven Cowan

Arithmetic
David Crook

Armed forces
H. W. Dickinson

Arnold, Matthew (1822–88)
Steven Cowan

Arnold, Thomas (1795–1842)
Steven Cowan

Art
Lesley Burgess

Ascham, Roger (1515–68)
Steven Cowan

Assessment
Eleanore Hargreaves

Athenaeum
David Crook

Attainment
Joseph Zajda and Rea Zajda

Australia
Anthony Potts and Tom O'Donoghue

Australian Association for Research in Education (AARE)
Tom Woodin

Autism
Dawn B. Male

Autodidact
Tom Woodin

Autonomy
Randall Curren

Baseline assessment
Geoff Lindsay

Basic skills
David Crook

Beecher, Catharine (1800–78)
Steven Cowan

Behaviourism
Paul Collins

Bell curve
Gary McCulloch

Benchmarking
Anthony Kelly

Bernstein, Basil (1925–2000)
Steven Cowan

Bicultural education
David Crook

Bilingual education
Catherine Wallace

Binary system
Paul Sharp

Binet, Alfred (1857–1911)
Steven Cowan

Biology
Paul Narguizian

Blind, teaching of
John Oliphant

Bloom, Benjamin (1913–99)
Steven Cowan

Boarding school/education
David Nicholas

Bourdieu, Pierre (1930–2000)
Steven Cowan

Brain drain
Gary McCulloch

Brazil
Maria Isabel Figueiredo Sobreira and Maria de Figueiredo-Cowen

British Council
Tom Woodin

British Educational Research Association (BERA)
Tom Woodin

Bruner, Jerome (1915–)
Steven Cowan

Bullying
Gary McCulloch

Burt, Cyril (1883–1971)
Steven Cowan

Business school/education
Jacek Brant

Canada
Tal Gilead

Career guidance
David Crook

Caribbean
Carlton Mills

Carnegie Foundation for the Advancement of Teaching
Tom Woodin

Case study
Jerry Wellington

Catchment area
Natalie Heath

Catholic school/education
Tom O'Donoghue

Centralisation/decentralisation
Joseph Zajda

Centre for Educational Research and Innovation (CERI)
Tom Woodin

Certificate/certification
Michael Imber

Chancellor
David Crook

Charities, educational
Mary Richardson

Charter school
Amy Stambach

Chemistry
Paul Narguizian

Child development
Jo Peat

Child guidance
Kathleen W. Jones

Child-centred education
Gary McCulloch

Children's literature
Peter Hunt

China
Ruth Hayhoe and Qiang Zha

Church
David Nicholas

Citizenship/civics
Gregory E. Hamot

Class size
David Crook

Classical education
Gary McCulloch

Classical studies
Lee T. Pearcy

Classroom
Gary McCulloch

Classroom management
Edmund T. Emmer

Classroom observation
Jerry Wellington

Coeducation
Gary McCulloch

Cognition
Michael W. Eysenck

Colet, John (1467–1519)
Steven Cowan

Collaborative/cooperative learning
Robert Slavin

College
David Crook

Comenius, Jan Amos (1592–1670)
Steven Cowan

Common school
William G. Wraga

Community education
Lyn Tett

Comparative education
Robert Cowen

Compensatory education
Gary McCulloch

Comprehension
Kenneth S. Goodman

Comprehensive school/education
Geoffrey Sherington and Craig Campbell

Compulsory education
David Crook

Computer-assisted learning
David Seth Preston

Computer studies
David Seth Preston

Conant, James Bryant (1893–1978)
Steven Cowan

Condorcet, Marie-Jean (1743–94)
Steven Cowan

Constructivism
Jerry Wellington

Continued/continuing professional development
Tom Woodin

Continuing education
Tom Woodin

Continuous assessment
Thomas N. Garavan

Core curriculum/national curriculum
Gary McCulloch

Core skills/core competencies
Roy Canning

Corporal punishment
Elizabeth T. Gershoff

Correspondence course
David Crook

Correspondence theory
Mike Cole

Counselling
Rex Stockton and Amy Nitza

Coursework
Gary McCulloch

Crafts
David Crook

Cramming
Tom Woodin

Creativity
Anna Craft

Crèche
David Crook

Credential society
Gary McCulloch

Credentials/credentialing
Claire Smetherham

Criterion-referenced tests
Ronald K. Hambleton

Critical pedagogy
Catherine Wallace

Critical theory
Mark Olssen

Cuba
Luciola L. Santos and Tom Woodin

Cultural capital
Helen Gunter

Cultural studies
Tom Woodin

Cultural transmission
Ann Cheryl Armstrong

Culture
Gary McCulloch

Curriculum
Barry M. Franklin

Curriculum development
William G. Wraga

Curriculum differentiation
Carrie Winstanley

Curriculum policy and implementation
Gary McCulloch

Curriculum standards/programmes of study
David Crook

Day release
David Crook

Dean
Gary McCulloch

Degree
David Crook

Delinquency
Kevin M. Beaver

Department
David Crook

Department for International Development (DfID)
Tom Woodin

Deschooling
Gary McCulloch

Detention
David Crook

Development plan
Paul Sharp

Dewey, John (1859–1952)
Jim Garrison

Diagnostic assessment
Edith Aurora Graf

Didactics/didacticism
Joseph Zajda and Rea Zajda

Diploma
David Crook

Diploma disease
Gary McCulloch

Disaffection
Terry Haydn

Discipline
David Crook and Tom Woodin

Discovery method/learning
Kevin J. Brehony

Distance education/learning
Richard Siaciwena

Doctorate
David Crook

Don
Gary McCulloch

Drama
David Crook

Dropouts
Gary McCulloch

Dual system
Richard Aldrich

DuBois, William E. B. (1868–1963)
Steven Cowan

Durkheim, Emile (1858–1917)
Steven Cowan

Dyslexia
Carrie Winstanley

Early childhood education
Jeni Riley

Early school leaving
Robert Hattam

East Asia
Shinichi Suzuki

Economics
Jacek Brant

Economics of education
Geeta Kingdon

Edgeworth, Maria (1767–1849)
Steven Cowan

Education
John White

Education For All
Vilma Seeberg

Education policy
Mark Olssen

Education/educational studies
David Crook

Educational broadcasting
David Crook

Educational leadership and management
Helen Gunter

Educational priority area
Keith Williams

Educational publishing
Jon Nixon

Educational research
Martyn Hammersley

Educational Resources Information Center (ERIC)
Tom Woodin

Educational targets
Steven J. Klees

Educational technology
Michel Ferrari

Educational theory
Michael A. Peters

Educationist/educationalist
Richard Aldrich

Egalitarianism
Harry Brighouse

Egypt
David Crook

E-learning
Harvey Mellar

Elementary school
David Crook

Eliot, Charles William (1834–1926)
Steven Cowan

Elitism
Carrie Winstanley

Elyot, Sir Thomas (c.1490–1546)
Steven Cowan

Emotional and behavioural difficulties/ disorders (EBD)
John B. Thomas

Endowment
David Crook

Engineering
David Crook

English
Yetta Goodman

Environmental education
David Crook and Tom Woodin

Equality of opportunity
Tom Woodin

Equity
Randall Curren

Ethnography
Ann Cheryl Armstrong

Europe
Andy Green

European Educational Research Association (EERA)
Tom Woodin

Evaluation
Jerry Wellington

Evidence-based policy/practice
David Gough

Examinations
Roger Murphy

Excellence
Michel Ferrari

Exclusion/expulsion
David Crook

Experiential learning
Joseph Zajda and Rea Zajda

Experimental research
Jerry Wellington

Extracurriculum
Keith Williams

Extra-mural class
Tom Woodin

Faculty
David Crook

Faculty psychology
David Crook

Family
Julia Brannen

Feminist theory
Tanya Fitzgerald

Ferry, Jules François Camille (1832–93)
Steven Cowan

Finland
David Crook

Formative assessment
Eleanore Hargreaves

Forster, William Edward (1818–86)
Steven Cowan

Foucault, Michel (1926–84)
Steven Cowan

Foundation degree
Keith Williams

France
Tal Gilead

Franchising
Roy Fisher

Freinet, Celestin (1896–1966)
Steven Cowan

Freire, Paolo (1921–97)
Steven Cowan

Freud, Sigmund (1856–1939)
Steven Cowan

Froebel, Friedrich (1782–1852)
Steven Cowan

Functionalism
Kevin Brehony

Further education
Bryan Cunningham

Galton, Francis (1822–1911)
Steven Cowan

Gandhi, Mohandas Karamchand (Mahatma) (1869–1948)
Tom Woodin

Gardner, Howard (1943–)
Steven Cowan

Gate-keeping
Gary McCulloch

Gender studies
Gary McCulloch

Geography
W. Ashley Kent

Germany
Tal Gilead

Giftedness
Carrie Winstanley

Globalisation
Hugh Lauder, Phillip Brown and David Ashton

Grades
Gary McCulloch

Graduate/graduation
Thomas Duff

Grammar
David Crook

Grammar of schooling
Gary McCulloch

Grammar school
David Crook

Greece
Marina-Stefania Giannakaki

Guizot, François Pierre Guillaume (1787–1874)
Steven Cowan

Habermas, Jürgen (1929–)
Steven Cowan

Habitus
Helen Gunter

Hall, Granville Stanley (1844–1924)
Steven Cowan

Harris, William Torrey (1835–1909)
Steven Cowan

Head teacher/principal
Gary McCulloch

Health education
David Crook

Herbart, Johann Friedrich (1776–1841)
Steven Cowan

Hidden curriculum
Gary McCulloch

High school
Gary McCulloch

High-stakes testing
Donna Marie Harris

Higher education
Scott Davies and David Zarifa

History
Stuart Foster

History of education
Gary McCulloch

Home economics/domestic science
David Crook

Home schooling
Christine Brabant

Homework
Harris Cooper

Hyperactivity
Jason Blokhuis

Illich, Ivan (1926–2002)
Steven Cowan

Inclusive education
Felicity Armstrong

Independent/private school/education
Pearl Rock Kane

India
Suresh C. Ghosh

Indigenous education
Tanya Fitzgerald

Individualised instruction/personalised learning
David Crook

Indoctrination
Randall Curren

Indonesia
David Crook

Industrial training
Thomas N. Garavan

Informal/nonformal learning
David Guile

In-service education
Keith Williams

Inspection
Martin Thrupp**

Instruction
Gary McCulloch

Integration
Gary McCulloch

Intelligence/intelligence tests
Steven Cowan

Intermediate/middle school
Gary McCulloch

International Association for the Evaluation of Educational Achievement (IEA)
Tom Woodin

International Bureau of Education (IBE)
Tom Woodin

International Council for Adult Education (ICAE)
Tom Woodin

International education
Angela Little

International Institute for Educational Planning (IIEP)
Tom Woodin

Iran
Fatemah Bagherian and Warren Thorngate

Iraq
Huda Al-Khaizaran

Isaacs, Susan Sutherland (1885–1948)
Steven Cowan

Israel
Tal Gilead

Italy
John Oliphant

Japan
Teruhisa Horio

Jesuit education
Maurice Whitehead

John of Salisbury (c.1115–80)
Steven Cowan

Jowett, Benjamin (1817–93)
Steven Cowan

Junior school
David Crook

Kay-Shuttleworth, Sir James (1804–77)
Steven Cowan

Keate, John (1773–1852)
Steven Cowan

Kerr, Clark (1911–2003)
Steven Cowan

Kindergarten
Kristen Nawrotzki

Knowledge economy
Claire Smetherham

Knox, John (1505–72)
Steven Cowan

Kohlberg, Lawrence (1927–87)
Steven Cowan

Lancaster, Joseph (1778–1838)
Steven Cowan

Lane, Homer (1875–1925)
Steven Cowan

Latin America
Maria de Figueiredo-Cowen and Robert Cowen

Law
Paul Tractenberg

Learning
Knud Illeris

Learning career
Phil Hodkinson

Learning community
Bryan Cunningham

Learning curve
Tom Woodin

Learning disabilities/difficulties
Felicity Armstrong

Learning society
Gareth Rees

Learning styles
David Crook

Lecture/lecturer
David Crook

Lesson
David Crook

Liberal education
Gary McCulloch

Lifelong learning
Karen Evans

Literacy
Roger Beard

Locke, John (1632–1704)
Tal Gilead

Lowe, Robert (1811–92)
Steven Cowan

Lyceum
Gary McCulloch

Magnet school
Christine H. Rossell

Makarenko, Anton Simeonovitch (1888–1939)
Steven Cowan

Makiguchi, Tsunesaburo (1871–1944)
Tom Woodin

Malaysia
Ka Ho Mok

Managerialism
Tom Woodin

Mann, Horace (1796–1859)
Steven Cowan

Mannheim, Karl (1893–1947)
Steven Cowan

Marking
David Crook

Maslow, Abraham Harold (1908–70)
David Crook

Master's
David Crook

Mathematics
Jeremy Kilpatrick

Matriculation
Gary McCulloch

Mature student
Keith Williams

McMillan, Margaret (1860–1931)
Steven Cowan

Mead, George Herbert (1863–1931)
Steven Cowan

Mead, Margaret (1901–78)
Steven Cowan

Mechanics' institute
David Crook

Medicine
Paul Narguizian

Mediterranean
Edward Mifsud

Mentor/mentoring
Tricia Maynard

Merit
David McCallum

Meritocracy
Gary McCulloch

Metropolitanism
Gary McCulloch

Mill, John Stuart (1806–73)
Steven Cowan

Mission statement
Christian K. Anderson

Mixed-ability teaching
Carrie Winstanley

Modern languages
Norbert Pachler

Modular/module
Tom Woodin

Monitor
David Crook

Monitorial system
Gary McCulloch

Montessori, Maria (1870–1952)
Steven Cowan

Moral education
David Carr

Motivation
Ian Gilbert

Mulcaster, Richard (c.1530–1611)
Steven Cowan

Multicultural education
James A. Banks

Multigrade education
Gary McCulloch

Multiple-choice tests
Jason Blokhuis**

Museum education
Pam Meecham

Music
Susan Hallam

Nature study
Paul Narguizian

Neill, Alexander Sutherland (1883–1973)
Steven Cowan

Newman, John Henry (1801–90)
Steven Cowan

New Zealand/Aotearoa
Kay Morris Matthews

Nigeria
David Crook

Nordic Educational Research Association (NERA)/Nordisk Förening för Pedagogiska Forskning (NFPF)
Tom Woodin

Normal school
Paul Axelrod

Norm-referenced tests
Ronald K. Hambleton

Numeracy
Anne Chapman

Nursery school
Kristen D. Nawrotzki and Sue Rogers

Objective tests
David Crook

Oceania
Konai Thaman

Open learning
Anne Gaskell

Open plan
Catherine Burke

Open University
Gary McCulloch

Oral examinations
David Crook

Organisation for Economic Cooperation and Development (OECD)
Fazal Rizvi and David Rutkowski

Owen, Robert (1771–1858)
Steven Cowan

Pakistan
Marie Lall

Parental choice
Carol Vincent

Parity of esteem
David Crook

Parkhurst, Helen (1887–1973)
Steven Cowan

Partnerships, educational
Barry M. Franklin

Pastoral care
Ann Cheryl Armstrong

Pedagogy
Marnie O'Neill

Peer group
David Crook

Performance indicators
Bernard Longden

Performance-related pay
Peter Earley

Pestalozzi, Johann Heinrich (1746–1827)
Steven Cowan

Philosophy of education
John White

Phonics
Patrick Groff

Phrenology
Gary McCulloch

Physical education/training
Charlotte Beaudoin

Physics
Anthony Kelly

Piaget, Jean (1896–1980)
Steven Cowan

Plagiarism
John Lesko

Plato
Richard Smith

Playground
David Crook

Politics of education
Gary McCulloch

Polynesia
Eve Coxon

Polytechnic
Patrick Ainley

Positive discrimination/affirmative action
Paul Tractenberg

Postgraduate
David Crook

Postmodernism
Kevin J. Brehony

Practitioner research
Ann Cheryl Armstrong

Prefect
Gary McCulloch

Primary school/education
Colin Richards

Privatisation/marketisation
Gary McCulloch

Proctor
David Crook

Profession/professionalism/professionalisation
Gary McCulloch

Professional education
David Crook

Professor
Gary McCulloch

Programmed learning
Paul Collins

Progression
David Crook

Progressive education
William J. Reese

Project method
Kevin J. Brehony

Psychology
David Crook

Psychology of education
John B. Thomas

Psychometrics
John Rust

Public library
Malcolm Dick

Public school
David Crook

Pupil
David Crook

Pupil mobility
Steve Strand

Qualifications
David Crook

Qualitative research
Tom O'Donoghue

Quantitative research
Stephen Gorard

Quintilian (35–95 CE)
Steven Cowan

Reader
David Crook

Reading
Peter Hannon

Reception class
Sue Rogers

Recruitment
David Crook

Rector
Gary McCulloch

Recurrent education
David Crook

Reddie, Cecil (1858–1932)
Steven Cowan

Reflective practitioner
Gary McCulloch

Religious assembly
Rob Freathy

Religious education
Rob Freathy

Religious school
Rob Freathy

Restructuring
Kara S. Finnigan

Retention
Dianne Gereluk

Rhodes Trust
Tom Woodin

Rice, Joseph Mayer (1857–1934)
Steven Cowan

Riesman, David (1909–2002)
Steven Cowan

Robbins, Lionel (1898–1984)
Steven Cowan

Rogers, Carl (1902–87)
Steven Cowan

Rousseau, Jean-Jacques (1712–78)
Tal Gilead

Rugg, Harold (1886–1960)
Steven Cowan

Rural education
Lynne Vernon-Feagans

Russia
Joseph Zajda and Rea Zajda

Sabbatical
Gary McCulloch

Sadler, Michael (1780–1835)
Steven Cowan

Sadler, Michael Ernest (1861–1943)
Steven Cowan

Sandwich course
David Crook

Sarason, Seymour (1919–)
Steven Cowan

Scandinavia
Susanne Wiborg

Scholar
David Crook

Scholarship
Richard Aldrich

Scholasticism
Paul M. Collins

Schön, Donald (1930–97)
Steven Cowan

School
Gary McCulloch

School-based management
Alison Taysum

School change
Clive Smith

School culture
Rose M. McNeese

School effectiveness
Anthony Kelly

School improvement
Anthony Kelly

School journeys
David Crook

School knowledge
Michael F. D. Young

School leadership
Alison Taysum

School reform
Donna Marie Harris

School reports
Natalie Heath

School security
Kimberly Williams

School violence
Kimberly Williams

Science/science education
Jerry Wellington

Scout Association
Tom Woodin

Secondary school/education
Gary McCulloch

Segregation/desegregation
Christine H. Rossell

Selection
Tom Woodin

Self-directed learning
Paul Collins

Semester/term
Tom Woodin

Seminar
Gary McCulloch

Seminary
Gary McCulloch

Setting
David Crook

Sex education
Michael J. Reiss

Singapore
Ka Ho Mok

Situated cognition/learning
Jerry Wellington

Sixth form
David Crook

Skills
Karen Evans

Skinner, Burrhus Fredric (1904–90)
Steven Cowan

Social capital
Mark K. Smith

Social constructivism
Gary McCulloch

Social control
Tom Woodin

Social exclusion/inclusion
Ann Cheryl Armstrong

Social promotion
Gary McCulloch

Social reconstructionism
William B. Stanley

Social reproduction
Tom Woodin

Social studies
Benjamin M. Jacobs

Sociology
David Crook

Sociology of education
Maureen T. Hallinan

Socratic method
Sophie Haroutunian-Gordon

South Africa
Clive Smith

Spearman, Charles (1863–1945)
Steven Cowan

**Special education/special educational needs/
special needs**
Felicity Armstrong

Specialisation
Jeremy Higham

Spelling
David Crook

Spencer, Herbert (1802–1903)
Steven Cowan

Spiral curriculum
Paul Collins

Sponsored and contest mobility
Gary McCulloch

Standardised tests
W. James Popham

Standards
David Crook

Steiner, Rudolf (1861–1925)
Steven Cowan

Stenhouse, Lawrence (1927–82)
Steven Cowan

Streaming/tracking
David Crook

Student
David Crook

Student finance/loans
Vincent Carpentier

Subjects
Gary McCulloch

Summative assessment
Peter Knight

Summer school
David Crook

Sunday school
Malcolm Dick

Supply/substitute teaching
Natalie Heath

Suspension
Geoff Riordan

Sweden
Jo Peat

Syllabus
Gary McCulloch

Systemic reform
Tara Davidson and Alan Sadovnik

Tanzania
David Crook

Tawney, Richard Henry (1880–1962)
Steven Cowan

Teacher
Billie Eilam

Teacher cultures
Catherine Harris

Teacher education/training
Miriam Ben-Peretz and Billie Eilam

Teacher unions
Harry Smaller

Teaching/teaching methods
David Crook

Teaching assistant
David Crook

Teaching profession
Harry Smaller

Technical education/school/college
Bill Bailey

Technocrat/technocratic/technocracy
Joseph Zajda and Rea Zajda

Technology
Jennifer Jenson

Terman, Lewis Madison (1877–1956)
Steven Cowan

Tertiary education
Bryan Cunningham

Test/testing
David Crook

Textbook
Stuart Foster and Jason Nicholls

Thelwall, John (1764–1834)
Steven Cowan

Theology
Paul M. Collins

Thesis/dissertation
Gary McCulloch

Thorndike, Edward Lee (1874–1949)
Steven Cowan

Training
Christopher Winch and Linda Clarke

Transition education
Karen Evans

Travellers, education of
P. A. Danaher

Truancy
Kimberly Williams

Tuition/tutor/tutorial
David Crook

Tyler, Ralph (1902–94)
Steven Cowan

Underachievement
Ann Cheryl Armstrong

Undergraduate
Gary McCulloch

Underperforming/failing school
Louise Stoll

United Kingdom
Roy Lowe

United Nations Children's Fund (UNICEF)
Carlton Mills

United Nations Educational, Scientific and Cultural Organization (UNESCO)
Tom Woodin

United States
Michael Imber and John L. Rury

Universal education/mass education
Vilma Seeberg

University
Gareth Parry

University extension
Tom Woodin

Urban education
Gary McCulloch

Value added
Robert W. Lissitz

Vice-chancellor
David Crook

Virtual learning
David Seth Preston

Visual aids
David Crook

Vocational education
Gary McCulloch

Voluntarism
Paul Sharp

Vouchers
Patrick J. Wolf

Vygotsky, Lev (1896–1934)
Steven Cowan

Washington, Booker T. (1856–1915)
Steven Cowan

Web-based learning
David Crook

Weber, Max (1864–1920)
Steven Cowan

Whole-class teaching
Natalie Heath

William of Wykeham (1324–1404)
Steven Cowan

Wollstonecraft, Mary (1759–97)
Steven Cowan

Work-based/work-located/workplace/work-related learning
David Crook

Work experience
Natalie Heath

Workers' education
Tom Woodin

Workers' Educational Association (WEA)
Tom Woodin

World Bank
Carlton Mills

World Education Fellowship (WEF)
Tom Woodin

Wrangler/wooden spoon
Gary McCulloch

Writing
Tom Woodin

Young, Michael (1915–2002)
Steven Cowan

Youth club/work
Mark K. Smith

Zone of proximal development
Jason Blokhuis

Zoning
Christine H. Rossell

Editors' introduction

The *International Encyclopedia of Education* constitutes a single-volume, comprehensive, international reference work relating to the practice and theory of education. It offers information on a wide range of educational matters, from abacus to zoning. It also provides a source of authoritative and critical commentary on major educational issues. It offers insight into specific areas of education in an interesting and informed way that is designed for both a specialised and a general readership, with original short entries contributed by over 200 specialists from around the world on around 600 different educational topics.

This is a unique undertaking in the contemporary field of scholarship in education. There are many works that run into a number of volumes on specialised fields such as childhood (Fass 2004), and higher education (Clark 1992; Altbach 1991; Knowles 1977). These are each substantial contributions to the area of study concerned. The present work is a synoptic survey of a wide range of topics relating to education as a whole, and so seeks to encourage greater breadth of understanding.

Examples of encyclopedias covering education as a whole that run into several volumes include Guthrie (2003), Alkin (1992), and Husen and Postlethwaite (1984). Recent specialist and extended encyclopedias that would be useful in particular areas relating to education include notably Arnett's encyclopedia of children, adolescents and the media (Arnett 2007), Reynolds' encyclopedia

of special education (Reynolds 2007), New's international encyclopedia of early childhood education, English's encyclopedia of educational leadership and administration, Lee's encyclopedia of school psychology, Matheson's encyclopedia of evaluation (Mathison 2005), English's international encyclopedia of adult education (English 2005), Farenga's encyclopedia of education and human development (Farenga 2005), Hopkins' encyclopedia of child development (Hopkins 2005), Marlow-Ferguson's survey of education systems worldwide (Marlow-Ferguson 2002), Martinez Aleman's encyclopedia of women in higher education (Martinez Aleman 2002), Grinstein's encyclopedia of mathematics education (Grinstein 2001), and Byram's encyclopedia of language teaching and learning (Byram 2000).

There are also a number of encyclopedias in related areas of study that are helpful resources for education. These include in the area of social theory, Ritzer (2005); in the social and behavioural sciences, Baites (2001); in sociology, Borgatta (1992); and in the social sciences in general, Kuper (1996).

Dictionaries perform a complementary role through their emphasis on shorter entries that define specific topics. Among these are Roeckelein (2006) on psychological theories, Alcock *et al.* (2002) on social policy, Gordon and Lawton (2003) on British education, and Turner (2006) and Abercrombie (2002) on sociology. Wellington's survey of key concepts in secondary education (2006) and

Hayes' similar contribution on primary education (2006) are also shorter introductory works in particular areas.

A number of more specialist historical and biographical dictionaries and encyclopedias are also available. These include Palmer's two volumes on major and modern thinkers in education (Palmer 2001a; 2001b), Eisenmann's historical dictionary of women's education in the United States (Eisenmann 1998), and Aldrich and Gordon's contributions on British, European and American educationists (Aldrich and Gordon 1989; Gordon and Aldrich 1997).

Finally, many handbooks have been produced which provide collections of extended essays arranged around a particular area or issue. The most substantial handbook covering education as a whole is that of Moon, Ben-Peretz and Brown (Moon *et al.* 2000). There are also several other useful resources of this kind in specific areas, such as Bursztyn's on special education (Bursztyn 2007), Townsend's on teacher education (Townsend 2007), Feinstein's on learning and the brain (2006), Abell's on research in science education (Abell 2006), Grace's on Catholic education (Grace 2006), Maclean's on education for the world of work (Maclean 2006), Pink's on urban education (Pink 2006), Hanusheck's on the economics of education (Hanusheck 2006), Skelton's on gender and education (Skelton 2006), Forest's on higher education (Forest 2006), Zajda's on globalisation, education and policy research (Zajda 2005), and Torres' on the sociology of education (Torres 2003). A number of substantial readers on aspects of education are also relevant, for example three major readers in the sociology of education in which A. H. Halsey has been involved over a number of years (Halsey *et al.* 1961; Halsey *et al.* 1997; Lauder *et al.* 2006).

There are four key dimensions to the present work as a whole. It is concerned with both the practice and theory of education, it is international in scope, it links the historical with the contemporary, and it is cross-sectoral in its approach.

In terms of *practice and theory* this work encompasses the practice of education in terms of learning and teaching, whether in schools or other educational institutions, formal and informal in nature. It also considers educational theory developed in order to understand, interpret and improve education. Research methodology and findings cited in relation to the practice and theory of education are also included.

As an *international* study, the work provides detailed reference to a number of national systems and local differences as well as to broader regional and global trends. Areas and issues that are deemed to be of interest to a broad international audience are covered in greater depth. At the same time, in common with Husen and Postlethwaite's ten-volume international encyclopedia of education (1984), there are a number of restrictions on this international design. To paraphrase Husen and Postlethwaite (volume 1, preface), the first of these arises from the nature of personal and professional contacts of the editors, although in our case certainly these have become increasingly diverse and international in character as a result of this current enterprise. Our affiliation to the Institute of Education, University of London, itself gives us access to a unique and world-class resource base of international researchers in education. The second is that the Encyclopedia is published in English. The third is that no single author could be aware of all of the dimensions of particular educational topics in all parts of the world. The fourth is that the Encyclopedia to a large extent reflects the metropolitan and Western interests and biases of much previous research on education, although an effort has been made to correct this tendency with the topics selected for entry.

The Encyclopedia seeks to connect *historical and contemporary* dimensions. The work represents changes and continuities in the nature of education during recorded history, with an emphasis in terms of proportions on the developments over the past 200 years and especially the past twenty years. It provides detailed and up-to-date appraisals of the contemporary educational scene and of issues for the future.

The work is *cross-sectoral* in that it embraces different sectors and phases of education, including schools, further education, higher education, lifelong learning and informal education

The Routledge International Encyclopedia of Education is designed to be concise, convenient, and committed to education. In these respects its rationale is similar to previous single-volume encyclopedias of education with an international dimension, in particular *Sonnenschein's Cyclopaedia of Education*, edited by Alfred Ewen Fletcher in 1889, and *Blond's Encyclopaedia of Education*, edited by Edward Blishen in 1969. Fletcher warned that 'Within the limits of a small Cyclopaedia an exhaustive treatment of the great variety of subjects dealt with is not to be expected'. He therefore aimed 'to give a telescopic rather than a microscopic view of the educational facts and questions discussed, and to bring their purely pedagogic features into clear outline' (1889: preface). Blishen also had a clear sense of what he was seeking to provide. He tried to pack into his volume

> as much information as it would hold about educational administration, teaching methods, legislation and reports, examinations, teaching aids, the primary schools, the secondary schools, further and higher education, the history and philosophy of education, and the scores of other topics into which education divides itself.

In doing so he hoped to provide a convenient handbook for a wide range of interests and a broad readership. Moreover, he was conscious of the importance of bringing together a highly diverse field, to give a 'common platform' to the many 'uncommunicating parts of education', as 'a means of bringing about contact between educational workers too often out of earshot of each other, and between them and the community they serve' (1969: introduction).

The American historian Paul Monroe expressed similar aspirations, albeit that his encyclopedia of education was spread over five volumes. He pointed out that the need for his work lay in the 'vast and varied character of educational literature', which was 'indicative of a corresponding variety in educational ideas and practices'. He saw education as growing in importance as a social process, and that teachers and educationists were increasing in numbers and significance in contemporary society. He argued that his encyclopedia would not simply provide a work of reference, but would help to systematise educational ideas and unify educational thought (1911: preface).

Such worthy ideals as these are as valid and relevant as ever in the early years of the twenty-first century. In the same spirit, the present work aims to combine breadth and depth in an accessible format, or as William Rose Benet described his *Reader's Encyclopedia*, 'a well-organised supplementary memory, in one volume' (preface, 1948/1998 4th edn). It also seeks to provide a convenient link between research, theory and practice, a link needed now even more than in Blishen's day in an area where these aspects are often divorced from each other, and where specialists have their own language and jargon. Moreover, in surveying the rapidly changing field of education in the new millennium it also reflects how current theories and practices rest, often uneasily, on the foundations established over many centuries.

New technological resources such as electronic mail, online bibliographic databases and search engines have made it possible to bring together an international group of scholars in a common pursuit in a way that Fletcher and even Blishen could hardly have dreamt of. We have been able to invite contributions from leading scholars in education from around the world, and to develop conversations with them. Nevertheless, this has remained a highly challenging task, both for authors whom we requested to distil their often extensive contributions to the literature into brief overviews and commentaries, and also editorially, as we tried to bring some balance and order to this richness.

The Encyclopedia should be suitable for library acquisition as a reference work in universities, colleges, schools, educational associations and government departments in the English-speaking world. It is designed for use also by students, scholars, and researchers in education, as an up-to-date work of general reference, and also for reliable and critical commentary on specific topics by leading writers. It will also be relevant to students and teachers across the related disciplines of social policy, sociology, politics, history, philosophy, psychology, economics, social work and law, who incorporate aspects of education into their teaching or research. Moreover, it will be suitable for teachers, practitioners and policy makers who are seeking access to information and clear and straightforward discussion of educational themes. It should also be useful for members of the public who wish to gain convenient access to familiar terms and concepts that are often mentioned without further explanation in educational debates in the media.

Entries have been organised alphabetically for general ease of access. These entries are self-contained but they are extensively cross-referenced, and the longer entries include a list of suggested further readings. The work as a whole is of approximately 400,000 words with over 600 individual entries. These entries fall broadly into three types. Longer entries of about 1,500 words, contributed by leading international scholars, provide general discussion of major topics in education. Standard entries of some 750 words each give information and detail on more specific areas. Finally, short entries of 200 to 300 words each convey thumbnail definitions and descriptions of a wide range of items, including brief biographical details of leading educators. The Encyclopedia offers a good starting point for those pursuing in-depth research, as well as for others who require rapid reference and orientation on an educational topic.

The longer entries offer generally 6–10 suggestions of further reading on the topic, with shorter pieces giving up to three or four. Suggestions for further reading include authored books, articles in journals, chapters and edited collections. Priority is generally given to work that is currently in print and available.

There are eight general types or fields of entry, although individual entries may overlap between two or more.

The first concerns *national systems and regions*. In the case of individual nations, this introduces the historical development of the system, key Acts and legislation, recent and contemporary policy reports and issues, overarching traditions, and a general appraisal. For regions, it conveys something of the historical development of the region as a whole with local comparisons and contrasts, and national differences.

The second consists of historical *biographies* of leading educational theorists, politicians and practitioners. These are lives in their social and historical contexts, with an account of their key work/s, and a critical appraisal of their significance and the nature and extent of their continuing relevance to education in the twenty-first century.

The third considers *educational institutions, phases and types*. These include the types of forum in which learning and teaching take place, in formal schooling, in different parts of life and society, in different phases and sectors, and in different formats. Entries provide information on the key aims and purposes of the institution, their origins, their national and international incidence, and prominent examples as appropriate.

The fourth examines a large number of *educational terms*. These are familiar words and phrases with a specifically educational meaning. Entries provide definitions of the term, discussion of its usages, and examples of its application as appropriate.

The fifth type of entry focuses on *educational societies and associations*. These are the major societies and associations related to education, especially international in scope, or else national with international relevance. The key aims and purposes of the society/ association, origins and development, and their contemporary contributions, are discussed, and a general appraisal is provided.

Sixth, there are entries on *subjects*. These are areas of study, whether disciplines or fields of knowledge, in the curriculum of schools and other educational institutions. Entries of this type consider the aims and scope of the subject at different levels, its historical development and incidence, the type of student involved, and contemporary issues and prospects.

The seventh type of entry covers aspects of *educational research*, with key approaches to research of specific relevance to education, and types of research developed by educationists. These give an outline of the aim and purpose, a brief explanation, and some examples of researchers and work of the type.

Eighth is a species of entry on *educational concepts*: issues and theories with a specific application to education. These entries provide a brief explanation, and some discussion of origins, historical development, and contemporary importance.

Each of these classes is global in scope and aspires to be representative in nature but not necessarily exhaustive. Cutting across each of these are both contemporary and historical dimensions, the balance of which varies according to the entry in question.

Full cross-referencing is provided between entries, in order to connect discussions of related topics. The index at the end of the work provides details of where particular topics are mentioned and addressed in more detail in the course of the work.

References

Abell, S. (ed.) (2006) *Handbook of Research on Science Education*, Holland: Lawrence Erlbaum

Abercrombie, N. (2002) *The Penguin Dictionary of Sociology*, 4th edn, London: Penguin.

Alcock, R., Erskine, A. and May, M. (eds) (2002) *The Blackwell Dictionary of Social Policy*, London: Blackwell.

Aldrich, R. and Gordon, P. (1989) *Dictionary of British Educationists*, London: Woburn.

Alkin, M. (ed.) (1992) *Encyclopedia of Educational Research*, 6th edn, New York: American Educational Research Association, 4 vols.

Altbach, P. (ed.) (1991) *International Higher Education: An Encyclopedia*, London: Garland, 2 vols.

Arnett, J. (ed.) (2007) *Encyclopedia of Children, Adolescents, and the Media*, London: Sage, 2 vols.

Baites, P. (ed.) (2001) *International Encyclopedia of the Social and Behavioral Sciences*, New York: Elsevier, 26 vols.

Benet, W. R. (ed.) (1998) [1948] *The Reader's Encyclopedia*, 4th edn, London: A&C Black.

Blishen, E. (ed.) (1969) *Blond's Encyclopaedia of Education*, London: Blond Educational.

Borgatta, E. (ed.) (1992) *Encyclopedia of Sociology*, New York: Macmillan, 4 vols.

Bursztyn, A. (ed.) (2007) *The Praeger Handbook of Special Education*, London: Praeger.

Byram, M. (ed.) (2000) *The Routledge Encyclopedia of Language Teaching and Learning*, London: Routledge.

Clark, B. (ed.) (1992) *Encyclopedia of Higher Education*, London: Pergamon, 4 vols.

Eisenmann, L. (1998) *Historical Dictionary of Women's Education in the United States*, New York: Greenwood Press.

English, F. (ed.) (2006) *Encyclopedia of Educational Leadership and Administration*, London: Sage, 2 vols.

English, L. (ed.) (2005) *International Encyclopedia of Adult Education*, London: Palgrave Macmillan.

Farenga, S. (ed.) (2005) *Encyclopedia of Education and Human Development*, London: M. E. Sharpe, 3 vols.

Fass, P. (ed.) (2004) *Encyclopedia of Children and Childhood in History and Society*, New York: Thomson, 3 vols.

Feinstein, S. (ed.) (2006) *The Praeger Handbook of Learning and the Brain*, Praeger, 2 vols.

Fletcher, A. E. (ed.) (1889) *Sonnenschein's Cyclopaedia of Education: A Handbook of Reference on All Subjects Connected with Education ... Comprising Articles by Eminent Educational Specialists*, London: Swan Sonnenschein and Co.

Forest, J. (ed.) (2006) *International Handbook of Higher Education*, Holland: Springer, 2 vols.

Gordon, P. and Aldrich, R. (1997) *Biographical Dictionary of North American and European Educationists*, London: Woburn.

Gordon, P. and Lawton, D. (2003) *Dictionary of British Education*, London: Woburn.

Grace, G. (ed.) (2006) *International Handbook of Catholic Education: Challenges for School Systems in the 21st Century*, Holland: Kluwer.

Grinstein, L. (ed.) (2001) *Encyclopedia of Mathematics Education*, London: RoutledgeFalmer.

Guthrie, J. (ed.) (2003) *Encyclopedia of Education*, New York: Macmillan, 8 vols.

Halsey, A. H., Floud, J. and Anderson, C. A. (eds) (1961) *Education, Economy, and Society: A Reader in the Sociology of Education*, New York: Free Press of Glencoe.

Halsey, A. H., Lauder, H., Brown, P. and Wells, A. (eds) (1997) *Education: Culture, Economy, Society*, Oxford: Oxford University Press.

Hanusheck, E. (ed.) (2006) *Handbook of the Economics of Education*, Holland: Elsevier, 2 vols.

Hayes, D. (2006) *Primary Education: The Key Concepts*, London: Routledge.

Hopkins, B. (ed.) (2005) *The Cambridge Encyclopedia of Child Development*, Cambridge: Cambridge University Press.

Husen, T. and Postlethwaite, T. N. (eds) (1984) *The International Encyclopedia of Education Research and Studies*, London: Pergamon, 10 vols.

Knowles, A. (ed.) (1977) *The International Encyclopedia of Higher Education*, London: Jossey-Bass, 10 vols.

Kuper, A. (ed.) (1996) *The Social Science Encyclopedia*, London: Routledge.

Lauder, H., Brown, P., Dillabough, J. and Halsey, A. H. (eds) (2006) *Education, Globalisation and Social Change*, Oxford: Oxford University Press.

Lee, S. (ed.) (2005) *Encyclopedia of School Psychology*, London: Sage.

Maclean, R. (ed.) (2006) *International Handbook on Education for the World of Work: Bridging Academic and Vocational Education*, Holland: Springer.

Marlow-Ferguson, R. (ed.) (2002) *World Education Encyclopedia: A Survey of Educational Systems Worldwide*, New York: Gale Group, 3 vols.

Martinez Aleman, A. (ed.) (2002) *Women in Higher Education: An Encyclopedia*, Oxford: ABC-CLIO.

Mathison, S. (2005) *Encyclopedia of Evaluation*, London: Sage.

Monroe, P. (ed.) (1911–13) *A Cyclopedia of Education*, New York: Macmillan, 5 vols.

Moon, B., Ben-Peretz, M. and Brown, S. (eds) (2000) *Routledge International Companion to Education*, London: Routledge.

New, R. (ed.) (2007) *Early Childhood Education: An International Encyclopedia*, London: Praeger, 4 vols.

Palmer, J. (ed.) (2001a) *Fifty Major Thinkers on Education: From Confucius to Dewey*, London: Routledge.

——(2001b) *Fifty Modern Thinkers on Education: From Piaget to the Present*, London: Routledge.

Pink, W. (ed.) (2006) *International Handbook of Urban Education*, Holland: Springer.

Reynolds, C. (ed.) (2007) *Encyclopedia of Special Education: A Reference Book for the Education of Children, Adolescents, and Adults with Disabilities and other Exceptional Individuals*, London: John Wiley, 3 vols.

Ritzer, G. (ed.) (2005) *Encyclopedia of Social Theory*, London: Sage, 2 vols.

Roeckelein, J. (ed.) (2006) *Elsevier's Dictionary of Psychological Theories*, Holland: Elsevier.

Skelton, C. (ed.) (2006) *The Sage Handbook of Gender and Education*, London: Sage.

Torres, C. (ed.) (2003) *The International Handbook on the Sociology of Education: An International Assessment of New Research and Theory*, London: Rowman and Littlefield.

Townsend, T. (ed.) (2007) *Handbook of Teacher Education: Globalisation, Standards and Professionalism in Times of Change*, Holland: Springer.

Turner, B. (ed.) (2006) *The Cambridge Dictionary of Sociology*, Cambridge: Cambridge University Press.

Wellington, J. (2006) *Secondary Education: The Key Concepts*, London: Routledge.

Zajda, J. (ed.) (2005) *International Handbook on Globalisation, Education and Policy Research: Global Pedagogies and Policies*, Holland: Springer.

Acknowledgements

So many colleagues from around the world have helped and advised us in the course of this project that it seems unjust to pick out just a few. With all the technological resources at our disposal, it is still this collegial support that has helped us through and ensured completion of the current work. Nevertheless, we should take this opportunity to thank especially our colleagues at the Institute of Education, University of London, and in particular Richard Aldrich who gave us valuable advice throughout, Tom Woodin, who supported the final stage before the submission of the work, and Steven Cowan, who provided some major input. We also thank Karen and Hugh Crook for helping to collate the material. Our colleagues at Routledge have helped us through many technical and organisational problems, and in particular Anna Clarkson, who suggested this idea in the first place and has been closely involved as we reached the end, has been unfailingly supportive.

Gary McCulloch
David Crook
August 2007

ABACUS

The abacus is a traditional counting device or 'counting tray' with a frame and board, and beads or counters to calculate numbers. It was in common use in ancient societies to add and subtract large numbers, and might be said to be a mechanical calculator that is an early predecessor of electronic calculators. There were different styles of construction in operation in China, Japan, Greece and Rome, although it was perhaps originally invented in ancient China. The Chinese abacus has thirteen vertical wires, with seven beads on each wire. The abacus has been widely used in schools to help to teach numbers and arithmetic.

See also: arithmetic

GARY McCULLOCH

ABELARD, PETER (1079–1142)

Abelard, whose name derives from Latin terms for 'bee' and 'tutor', renounced inheritance in order to devote his life to study. He was famed for developing a dialectical method of discourse and credited with founding the University of Paris. He initially taught within the Cathedral School under William of Champeaux, but soon broke away to set up his own schools at Melun and later at Corbeil. He eventually became Chair of the Cathedral school in 1113. His stance that, through doubt, one can arrive at true knowledge, inevitably led him into dispute with ecclesiastic authorities.

A follower of Plato and Aristotle, Abelard promoted the idea of intellectual reflection as being a route to knowledge of universal and religious truth. He influenced Thomas Aquinas and for some came to be seen as a harbinger of Protestantism.

A prolific author, books such as *Yes and No* challenged the view that Church authorities were to be followed, leading to most of his works being included in the infamous Index of Forbidden Books. He was denounced for his thoughts on the Holy Trinity in 1121 and condemned for heresy in 1140. His belief in openness of discussion was reflected in his reputation as a brilliant and charismatic teacher. From 1136 to 1138, whilst lecturing in Paris, one of his pupils was John of Salisbury. Another source for his universal fame derives from the correspondence between himself and his lover, Heloise, who bore his child. This became a popular classic translated into every European vernacular.

See also: Aristotle; church; John of Salisbury; Plato; scholasticism

STEVEN COWAN

ABILITY

A wide variety of human abilities has been recognised throughout recorded history, including physical, mental, creative and interpersonal abilities. Particular abilities are valued in different cultures and may be reflected in educational aims and curriculum content. Within education, the notion of ability generally relates to competence in the performance of tasks that form part of the curriculum. Mental abilities have been the subject of debate and controversy for over a hundred years. Early tests of cognitive ability were developed to identify children in need of additional help in school and were calibrated against children's typical achievement at different ages. Since then, many aptitude and ability tests have been developed for selection and recruitment, and tests of non-verbal and verbal ability are frequently used in education. There is ongoing debate about the extent to which abilities are inborn and learned. Recent developments in cognitive psychology suggest that learning plays a more important role than previously acknowledged. Children's notions of ability and effort develop with age and these conceptions influence their motivation to learn.

The term ability is used to refer to the possession of skills and competence required to perform a particular task or activity. It encompasses abilities such as those required for success in sports, reasoning, mathematics, problem solving, designing and conflict resolution. Particular abilities are valued within different cultures and while contemporary Western cultures tend to value logical, mathematical and linguistic abilities, in other historical periods and cultures greater value may be placed on other abilities, such as social conduct. Differences between the ideals and aims in education systems promote diverse abilities, especially in secondary schools.

Abilities have been the subject of assessment throughout history but the use of standardised ability tests in education began early in the twentieth century when the Paris schools approached Alfred Binet for assistance. The schools wanted tests that would help them identify children who had learning difficulties and could be educated with additional help. Binet noticed that as children grew older and progressed through school there were commonalities in the abilities they acquired, such as naming objects, defining words, reasoning

and remembering. He developed tests that sampled the kinds of tasks that were typical for each age group and calibrated the test items so that the average child in each age group was able to answer half of the items correctly.

Binet and Simon's task sampling approach was later used by many others to develop tests of ability and aptitude in a wide variety of occupations. Tests developed for use by the military during World War I and World War II included verbal and quantitative abilities, technical knowledge, and psychomotor abilities. Tests of manual dexterity, clerical skills and aptitude for working in environments such as information technology or customer services are used today to assess an individual's ability to do a particular type of work. Careers advisers may use results of such tests to give individuals advice about suitable jobs.

Many existing tests of cognitive ability are based on a statistical assumption that if a large number of people are tested, their scores form a normal distribution, similar to those for height or weight. The distribution resembles a bell shape and the curve is symmetrical so half the scores fall above the mean (average) and half below it. By convention, this distribution has a mean of 100 and 95 per cent of scores lie between 70 and 130, so individuals who score less than 70 have unusually low abilities and those who score above 130 have exceptionally high abilities. Statistical methods have also been used to clarify relationships between the different cognitive abilities sampled by test items. Theorists such as Vernon and Spearman proposed that the structure of intelligence is hierarchical, with specific and more general abilities.

Standardised test batteries contain tests of a range of cognitive abilities and may be used to assist in the identification of children with special educational needs. The use of these tests is restricted to individuals who have been trained to administer them. Some secondary schools use tests of general cognitive ability and tests of verbal and non-verbal ability for purposes of selection. For example, the eleven-plus is used for this purpose in areas of England and Northern Ireland where grammar schools operate.

Critics argue that an emphasis on cognitive abilities omits many other abilities that are important for success in life. Sternberg and Gardner both suggest that too much emphasis is given to analytic, linguistic and mathematical abilities, and Sternberg proposes that creativity and practical abilities play an important role. Gardner identified seven relatively autonomous intelligences, and his theory has generated considerable controversy on the grounds of limited evidence to justify the abilities selected and his failure to acknowledge a general cognitive ability. Nevertheless, some educators find Gardner's ideas helpful as they draw attention to a variety of ways in which young people's abilities might be recognised and developed.

Vygotsky argued that tests of mental ability were of limited value as they only assessed capabilities that a child had already acquired. In his view, useful information was provided by the child's ability to perform the same test with assistance from a capable adult. He observed that children with the same test scores did not benefit equally from assistance and proposed that the difference between performance alone and after help indicated a child's zone of proximal development. This theoretical insight inspired a generation of research into methods of dynamic assessment and the effects of adult–child interactions on children's cognitive growth.

Developments in cognitive science provide a different perspective on abilities. In this view, abilities are thought to develop as individuals learn and acquire greater knowledge and skill. Individuals who become accomplished in any domain, such as music, medicine, history, chess or sport, devote many years of practice to their chosen field. During this time they build up extensive knowledge and skill that enables them to remember and process information very efficiently. As an individual accumulates knowledge and uses it to solve problems, the organisation of knowledge in the brain becomes more closely connected with knowledge about actions and their consequences. For example, given a realistic array of chess pieces on a board, such as might be seen during a game, an expert chess player is able to recall the positions of the pieces far more accurately than a beginner. If the pieces are then arranged randomly on the board, beginners recall the positions just as accurately as experts. Furthermore, a child who is good at chess is able to recall the realistic configurations more accurately than an adult who does not play chess, even though the adult recalls the random array more accurately. This indicates that experts do not have a superior ability to remember information, but their memory for realistic configurations improves because they play a great deal of chess. Adults are usually better than children at remembering unrelated information, as they have greater knowledge of the world and are able to deploy effective strategies for remembering. Experts in many domains, including radiology and teaching, are able to perceive patterns and meaning in information that appears random to a beginner. This more efficient representation of information also facilitates further learning in the domain.

Children's conceptions of ability change during childhood and are related to other conceptions of the self. Before starting school, children do not seem to have a clear notion of ability as an internal quality and they do not think of effort and ability as separate entities. Around seven to eight years of age the notion of ability becomes more clearly delineated from the notion of effort. Children start to compare themselves with others and to see abilities as more stable and, therefore, constraining future possibilities. At around 10–12 years of age, effort and ability become differentiated as separate entities and children begin to view ability as a capacity, rather than a developing set of skills and knowledge. An important difference emerges between children who retain an 'incremental' conception and see their abilities as open to further development, and those who see their abilities as relatively fixed, an 'entity' conception. Young people who see ability as incremental appear to be more resilient in the face of challenge and more likely to expend greater effort when they encounter failure.

See also: ability grouping; aptitude; Binet, Alfred; cognition; Gardner, Howard; intelligence/intelligence tests; Spearman, Charles; streaming/tracking; test/testing; Vygotsky, Lev; zone of proximal development

Further reading

Dweck, C. S. (2002) 'The development of ability conceptions'. In A. Wigfield and J. Eccles (eds) *The Development of Achievement Motivation*, London: Academic Press.

Gardner, H., Kornhaber, M. L. and Wake, W. K. (1995) *Intelligence: Multiple Perspectives*, New York: Harcourt Brace.

Howe, M. J. A. (1998) *Principles of Abilities and Human Learning*, Hove: Psychology Press.

Ireson, J. and Hallam, S. (2001) *Ability Grouping in Education*, London: Sage.

Vygotsky, L. (1978) *Mind in Society*, London: Harvard University Press.

JUDITH IRESON

ABILITY GROUPING

Ability grouping refers to the practice of grouping students by some measure of attainment or perceived ability. This may occur at the level of the school, class, or within the class. Pupils may be selected to attend particular schools on the basis of their academic performance. Within schools, classes may be grouped on the basis of pupil attainment. These groupings take different forms. Pupils may be placed in classes on the basis of their general ability, remaining in those classes for all subjects; they may be placed in broad bands containing several classes and can be regrouped within these bands for different subjects; or they can be grouped according to attainment separately for all or some subjects. Whatever the school's structured ability grouping system, some teachers also group pupils within the class to work together

regularly or to undertake particular tasks. Internationally, over time, with increasing concerns for equality of opportunity, there has been a tendency for the level of structured ability grouping in schools to decrease, although depending on the political philosophy pertaining at the time particular systems may be favoured. For reviews of the literature see Ireson and Hallam (2001), Hallam *et al.* (2002), and Hallam (2002).

Ability grouping and its effects was the subject of extensive research for most of the twentieth century. Despite the increasing body of empirical evidence to support decision making, the field has been characterised by controversy and polemic. This is in part because there has been no clear definition of what constitutes 'effective' educational outcomes. Reviews of the international literature have shown that ability grouping has little effect on attainment when pupils' prior learning is taken into account. It is differential access to the curriculum *between* ability groups that is key. As the allocation of pupils to ability groups is a somewhat arbitrary affair and tends not to be based entirely on prior academic achievement or ability, sizeable proportions of pupils are inappropriately allocated. Once placed in a particular group it is very difficult to move out of it. Where groupings restrict access to the curriculum this has serious implications for the future educational attainment of those pupils.

Structured ability grouping affects pupils' social and personal development. Low-ability groups include disproportionate numbers of pupils of low socio-economic status, some ethnic minorities, boys, and those born in the summer. Procedures where pupils regroup for different subjects as they progress through school can split friendship groups, create anxiety, and reduce the social support that pupils have developed. The effects on self-esteem are complex. Whatever the nature of the grouping structures, high-ability pupils, boys and those of higher socio-economic status have higher self-esteem. Structured groupings legitimise the differential treatment of pupils and those in the lower or higher sets can become the targets of teasing or stigmatisation. Those pupils who find themselves in the lowest groups tend to develop negative attitudes towards school and where whole peer groups feel alienated, anti-school cultures can develop. Pupils are generally accepting of the grouping structures operating within their school and become socialised into them. The majority prefer ability grouping to mixed-ability classes because work is matched more closely to their needs, although those in the lowest groups prefer mixed-ability classes. Many pupils are unhappy with their ability group placement, most wanting to move to a higher set to be given harder work, improve their examination and career prospects, and their status within school. However, some students want to move down to have easier work and a less-pressured environment.

Teachers generally hold positive attitudes towards ability grouping, tend to prefer teaching high-ability groups, and demonstrate higher levels of efficacy and enthusiasm when doing so. High-ability groups tend to be taught by more experienced and better-qualified teachers. The activities undertaken in the classrooms of low-, middle- and high-attaining groups differ, as does the curriculum. The quality of instruction for lower-ability groups is conceptually simplified, proceeds more slowly, with more structured written work, a concentration on basic skills, worksheets and repetition, with fewer opportunities for independent learning, discussion and activities which promote critique, analysis and creativity. Teachers believe that they are matching instruction to the level of the students' ability, but the evidence suggests that many pupils find that the work they are given is inappropriate. Often, it is too easy.

See also: ability; attainment; giftedness; mixed-ability teaching; setting; streaming/ tracking; underachievement

Further reading

Hallam, S. (2002) *Ability Grouping in Schools*, London: Institute of Education.
Hallam, S., Ireson, J. and Davies, J. (2002) *Effective Pupil Grouping in the Primary School*, London: Fulton.
Ireson, J. and Hallam, S. (2001) *Ability Grouping in Education*, London: Sage.

SUSAN HALLAM

ACADEMIC/ACADEMIC PROFESSION

Perhaps, at one time, the categories of 'academic' and 'academic profession' were worn lightly: they stood for an identity and an occupational grouping that were relatively well defined. Terms such as 'knowledge', 'truth' and 'academic community' helped to identify the location of the collectivity, to confirm that it had an internal unity and stood off with its own concerns somewhat from the wider world. In the contemporary world, the categories of 'academic' and 'academic profession' have, however, become problematic.

The immediate causes of these categories becoming problematic are clear enough. Around the world, higher education has experienced a near-explosion with the arrival of 'mass higher education'. In its wake, institutions of higher education take a variety of forms, as 'mass' and 'elite' forms of higher education jostle with each other. Students, courses and relationships between research and teaching all vary; and, in turn, academic identity varies. So there can be no unity that comprises 'academic profession' and there can be no definite sense as to what constitutes 'academic'; and no assurance that there is a boundary between the 'academic' world and the wider world.

But beneath the arrival of mass higher education, and the consequent diversity across the system, lie other reasons that render the idea of 'academic profession' problematic. Three stand out. First, academic life remains structured by disciplines: 'knowledge' is itself undergoing changes and is even fragmenting and undergoing transformations, but the separateness of the disciplines remains as so many different 'tribes and territories' (Becher and Trowler 2001). As such, the idea that there can be a single 'academic profession' has to be in difficulty. Second, across the world, governments have invested more in higher education but, in return, have exacted claims on the academic community. The emergence of national quality systems, with their emphasis on 'accountability', is but one example. This has led to a process in which academics are no longer professionals in control of the conditions of their own working lives, a process that A. H. Halsey (1992) has termed 'proletarianization'. An indicator of this diminution of professional power and autonomy is the appointment of part-time staff as a significant proportion of the academic 'workforce'. Third, too, across the world, even if unevenly, the academic world has been obliged to take on a market orientation as it finds customers for its knowledge services: in this neo-liberal turn, amidst 'academic capitalism' (Slaughter and Leslie 1997), the sense of an academic profession with values of its own is challenged.

Taken together, these considerations indicate that the idea of the 'academic profession' is a problematic concept, but they add a twist: it has always been problematic and it is becoming more problematic still. Academic identity itself has fractured, there being little in the way of a connecting tissue that runs right across 'academics' and academic institutions. Academic professionalism may have always been a myth but it now – on some readings at least – seems further away than ever. Three further considerations here open up.

First, there is an issue as to power and control. The idea of 'profession', we may take it, refers to a social group in command of some body of knowledge that it puts in the service of clients; and it does so in a trustworthy manner. 'Knowledge', 'service', 'clients' and 'trust' are key concepts in the idea of 'profession'; but this set of concepts poses awkward questions in relation to the academic world. An academic teaches a student a subject, over which that academic has some command; and, characteristically, in higher education, that command over a body of knowledge is achieved partly through the academic's own primary research and scholarship. But under conditions of mass higher education, with its diversity of institutions, and selectivity in the allocation of resources for conducting research, it is clear that not every academic is going to be afforded the wherewithal to conduct their own research. It follows that the power and control over knowledge production exerted by the academic profession will at best be uneven and, to a significant extent, will be largely absent. And, to that extent, the academic profession – *as* a profession – will be diminished.

Second, given that there are two subjects in the pedagogical relationship – the academic's discipline and her students – it follows that professional responsibilities attach to the student and her learning. Academic professionalism must entail some knowledge of students as learners, of pedagogy and of curriculum design. The academic profession, until recently, however, has been a profession lacking formal training for the activities that comprise 'teaching'; and, to that extent, has been found wanting as a profession.

Third, the category of 'academic' is itself in difficulty. Indeed, many members of staffs of universities find difficulty in attributing to themselves the term 'academic'. Partly, this is a reflection of there being many identities among the staff of a university, with staff variously giving their priorities to teaching, to administration and even management and leadership, to outreach and service, both to the university itself and in and to the wider community, and to professional life beyond the university as a doctor, a business person and so on (Taylor 1999). Partly, it is because the idea of 'academic' may conjure up connotations of arcane scholarship or research with its own standards and demands cut adrift from those of the broader society.

6

If, then, the idea of the 'academic profession' is to be reclaimed, a way has to be found of finding a body of knowledge and understanding and a set of values – an ethos – around which a professional unity might be formed. Across the world, efforts are underway to locate such a professionalism in 'the scholarship of learning and teaching': the hope is that academics may become knowledgeable about learning and teaching as such and, as a result, be able to offer an ever more effective educational experience for their students.

This effort is not lightly to be dismissed but there is just another possibility, namely that the academic community might become more reflective systematically about academic life itself. What is striking about the academic profession, after all, is that despite its own rhetoric about knowledge, critique and the value of the examined life, the academic profession knows rather little about the nature of its own form of life. That enterprise has just been siphoned off to the small but fast-growing sub-set of academics whose 'subject' is that of the study of higher education. Until there is a more widespread acknowledgement across the academy that there is a collective responsibility to become systematically knowledgeable about academic life itself, it is difficult to see how the academic profession can gain legitimacy *as* a profession.

See also: dean; don; higher education; lecture/lecturer; profession/professionalism/professionalisation; professor; reader; university

Further reading

Becher, T. and Trowler, P. (2001, 2nd edn) *Academic Tribes and Territories*, Maidenhead: McGraw-Hill/Open University Press.
Halsey, A. H. (1992) *Decline of Donnish Dominion: The British Academic Profession in the Twentieth Century*, Oxford: Clarendon Press.
Slaughter, S. and Leslie, L. L. (1997) *Academic Capitalism: Politics, Policies and the Entrepreneurial University*, Baltimore MD: Johns Hopkins University Press.

Taylor, P. G. (1999) *Making Sense of Academic Life: Academics, Universities and Change*, Buckingham: Open University Press.

RONALD BARNETT

ACADEMIC FREEDOM

Academic freedom can be defined as the freedom to teach, research, publish, and engage in academic discourse, subject to the norms and standards of scholarly inquiry, without interference, wherever the search for truth may lead. Its existence is commonly regarded as the central identifying attribute of the modern university.

Contemporary notions of academic freedom are rooted in nineteenth-century German university traditions, which embodied three interrelated principles: *Lehrfreiheit*, *Lernfreiheit*, and *Freiheit der Wissenschaft*.

Lehrfreiheit, literally translated, means the freedom to inquire and to teach. The German conception protected the academic's right to examine a body of evidence and to present his conclusions in publications and lectures:

> This freedom was not, as the Germans conceived it, an inalienable endowment of all men, nor was it a superadded attraction of certain universities and not of others; rather, it was the distinctive prerogative of the academic profession, and the essential condition of all universities. Without it, no institution had the right to call itself a 'university'.
>
> (Hofstadter and Metzger 1955: 387)

Lernfreiheit means, literally, learning freedom. It translated loosely into a student's right to choose her own course of study at her own choice of university.

Metzger defined and explained the more complex *Freiheit der Wissenschaft* as

> the university's right, under the direction of its senior professors organized into separate faculties and a common senate, to control its internal affairs. Academic self-government – the heart of the somewhat cryptic phrase *Freiheit der Wissenschaft* – was acclaimed by German theorists not only for

its own sake, but also for the essential protection it accorded to freedom of teaching and research. Unless divorced from public administration and permitted to live a corporate life apart, the university, it was thought, would be dangerously vulnerable to government or religious censorship.

(1988: 1270)

These three general principles persevere as components of contemporary academic freedom. Two broad, and sometimes competing, conceptualisations now generally encapsulate the three predecessors: individual academic freedom and institutional autonomy.

Throughout the latter portion of the twentieth and into the twenty-first century, academic freedom has generally referred to a scholar's freedom to pursue the core endeavours of scholarship within their field of study without governmental, political, or ecclesiastical interference. Academic freedom, however, is not (and never has been) absolute. It is bounded by vague, and often fluid, margins that are shaped by socio-political context, the character of the sovereign authority in question, and the nature of the threat to academic freedom.

Moreover, academic freedom is bounded by responsibilities of the scholar. The American Association of University Professors (AAUP) has articulated the responsibilities of scholars thus:

> As scholars and educational officers, they should remember that the public may judge their profession and their institution by their utterances. Hence they should at all times be accurate, should exercise appropriate restraint, should show respect for the opinions of others, and should make every effort to indicate that they are not speaking for the institution.
>
> (AAUP 1940)

Institutional autonomy generally refers to the freedom of universities to be free from influences external to the university community. This autonomy was succinctly defined as 'the four essential freedoms of a university' in a leading United States Supreme Court case, *Sweezy v. New Hampshire*. Since that time, the concept has been mistakenly equated with academic freedom, though it is better considered a condition precedent for the academic freedom of scholars within the university:

> It is the business of a university to provide that atmosphere which is most conducive to speculation, experiment and creation. It is an atmosphere in which there prevail 'the four essential freedoms' of a university – to determine for itself on academic grounds who may teach, what may be taught, how it shall be taught, and who may be admitted to study.
>
> (*Sweezy v. New Hampshire* 1957: 262–63)

See also: academic/academic profession; autonomy; university

Further reading

American Association of University Professors (1940) *1940 Statement of Principles on Academic Freedom and Tenure*.

Hofstadter, R. and Metzger, W. P. (1955) *The Development of Academic Freedom in the United States*, New York: Columbia University Press.

Metzger, W. P. (1988) 'Profession and constitution: two definitions of academic freedom in America', *Texas Law Review*, 66: 1265–1322.

Sweezy v. New Hampshire (1957) 354 U.S. 234, 77 S.Ct. 1203.

Van Alstyne, W. (ed.) (1993) *Freedom and Tenure in the Academy*, Durham NC: Duke University Press.

JOHN LANEAR

ACADEMY

In ancient Athens, Plato set up his own school in 387 BCE, close to the Academy, a famous gymnasium. This Platonic heritage has encouraged the continued use of this term up to the present day, although schools and colleges entitled as an academy may now have their own particular orientations or specialisms. The Royal Academy of Arts, founded in London in 1769, is a world-famous art institution.

The term is also used in a different sense to convey the values and ethos of higher education. It tends to suggest a certain kind of peer pressure or value system within the university that encourages certain kinds of study or approach but hampers others. There is often reference to the 'divided academy', or a culture of higher education that is split between different ideals or interests. Certain kinds of subject may find it difficult to establish themselves in the environment of the academy alongside the entrenched disciplines. Women have also frequently been at odds with the prevailing ethos of the academy that has favoured male dominance. The academy therefore evokes a somewhat conservative notion of traditions in higher education, removed from or above the turmoil of everyday life, and reminiscent of the rarified atmosphere of the 'ivory tower'.

See also: higher education; Plato; university

GARY McCULLOCH

ACCOUNTABILITY

Accountability is being responsible to a higher authority. In the context of education, accountability is associated with reform intent on improving student achievement. Over time, policy makers and educators have redefined 'who is accountable for what and to whom' by shifting from the educator's personal characteristics to institutional inputs and processes and, recently, student results. Today's accountability systems are characterised by five aligned elements: performance expectations, measurements, capacity building, consequences and public engagement. The systemic approach integrates core elements with a *results*, rather than *compliance*, focus and the school/college/university is the unit of improvement (Fuhrman 1999). The United States' *No Child Left Behind* legislation

and the Australian National Education Performance Monitoring Task Force are examples of aligned systems.

Accountability systems accept variations in processes to achieve standardised results. But what are the desired results? Constituencies differ on what students are expected to know and do, including the level of proficiency students must exhibit, the groups of students included and the amount of time in which the expectation is to be met. By defining the performance expectation, greater importance is placed on one academic discipline or group of students over another. Most systems emphasise literacy and mathematical reasoning. Criticisms that the curriculum narrows through shifts in school time, materials and personnel to the areas measured at the expense of the broader school experience are not uncommon.

Once the expectation is established, the system must determine if the expectation is met. Advances in assessment techniques have broadened the array of technically defensible measures. Comprehensive measurement programmes incorporate formative, benchmark and summative testing, each serving a different purpose (Rothman 2006). Formative or diagnostic assessments are useful in adjusting instruction to the needs of individual students. These provide skill or content-specific data to indicate what the student knows or does not know at defined points in the instructional calendar. Benchmark tests measure performance against expectations for attainment or progress at defined interims. Finally, the summative test, given under standardised conditions, measures goal attainment. With these 'high stakes' assessments, adherence to professional principles that ensure reliability, validity and freedom from bias is essential. Some state or provincial systems have attempted to collect summative performance data by means other than objective tests, although data reliability, administrative complications and fiscal restraints often restrict the use of observational, portfolio and juried assessments.

Accountability systems should empower communities to solve problems. The popular media often reports on the heroic school triumphing over a constellation of barriers, many outside the classroom and school environment. The challenge to an effective accountability system is to make the heroic common. Within the greater societal context, the results of accountability efforts highlight broad social and contextual issues that impact upon school performance and generate urgency to eliminate detractors from higher achievement. Comprehensive systems incorporate the realignment of curriculum materials and practices with the expected goals, educator professional development, and ancillary investments in data collection, quality and analysis. Most US states provide additional services to students and schools not meeting benchmark and summative accountability standards.

Accountability systems assign positive or negative status to the unit evaluated. Recognition for positive accomplishments, including public displays and monetary rewards, is frequently given. *No Child Left Behind* incorporates a series of transformational actions for underperforming schools, including student supplemental (tutorial) services, choice in school assignment, and reorganisation or restructuring of the school

Using accountability data in personnel evaluations has been limited. Questions about the validity or reliability of data drawn from student assessments administered over a short time period and the variability in student gains attributable to a student's entry characteristics have deterred reliance solely on student results for educator evaluation. Policy makers and researchers in Tennessee (USA) built a value-added model for individual teachers. The Tennessee system provides informs teacher professional development, but is restricted from use in summative evaluations. Other systems continue to explore the use of student performance for judgements about individual professionals.

Education accountability systems are intended to promote attainment of specified goals through realignment of resources and establishment of consistent policy and practice frameworks. The objectives, drawn from broader societal goals, include garnering positive return on the investment of public resources and achieving economic and social justice. Whether in capacity building or in application of consequences, parents, professionals and policy makers must understand the meaning of the data and work with one another to address the problems the accountability system reveals. The most successful systems are able to integrate remedies across community responsibilities.

Cursory examinations of educational accountability systems suggest that they are about student test scores and public information. In reality, these systems are the foundation for changes in governance, resource allocation, professional practice and the quality of young people's lives. When successful the data inform changes in practices from the classroom to the government centre.

See also: assessment; benchmarking; high-stakes testing; performance indicators; standardised tests; summative assessment; underperforming/failing school

Further reading

Committee for Economic Development (2000) *Measuring What Matters: Using Assessment and Accountability to Improve Student Learning*, New York: Committee for Economic Development.

Fuhrman, S. H. (1999) *The New Accountability*. CPRE Policy Briefs, RB-27 (January).

Rothman, R. (2006) '(In) formative assessments', *Harvard Education Letter*, 22(6).

JO ANNE ANDERSON

ACCREDITATION

Accreditation is the procedure by which an authoritative body formally recognises another body or person as being competent to carry out certain tasks. In education, an accredited course or programme provider is one that has submitted itself to external scrutiny and has satisfied quality assurance standards. The accrediting body may be a local or central government department, a qualifications body, a professional council, a university or some other third party. In the United States educational accreditation rests with not-for-profit membership associations. Courses in health care or teacher education are among those that will normally be accredited.

In order to gain accreditation, a provider will normally have to provide clear evidence of the course's length, curriculum, assessment, quality, compliance with relevant legislation, arrangements for monitoring and strategy for continuous improvement. In many instances the accrediting body accredits courses for a fixed time period – three years, for example – and providers are subject to inspection visits. In some instances non-accredited courses may be of high quality, but institutions that do not submit themselves to external scrutiny are likely to be regarded with suspicion. Regrettably, disreputable private institutions describing themselves as colleges or universities operate in many countries, sometimes via the internet. Efforts to regulate such providers of bogus awards are not always successful and institutional 'blacklists' are sometimes maintained. Where public financial support is available to students, this is invariably restricted to those enrolling on accredited courses offered by providers of good standing in their particular sector.

See also: accountability; inspection; qualifications

DAVID CROOK

ACCREDITATION OF PRIOR ACHIEVEMENT/LEARNING

Universities and other institutions of higher education will normally specify minimum academic requirements before offering a place to a prospective student. In most cases, entry will be conditional upon providing evidence of lower-level certification, but situations are sometimes encountered where the paper qualifications of an applicant fall short of the expected standard but there are compensatory factors which, nevertheless, make the application a strong one. For example, let us consider the hypothetical mature applicant for a university course in business management who left school without qualifications but, since that time, has ten years' successful experience of running a private company. In such circumstances the university admissions department, in consultation with the relevant academic department, may decide to partially waive the usual entry qualifications in order to accredit the applicant's prior achievement and/or learning. Alternative terminology is sometimes applied: the British term is often 'accreditation of prior experiential learning' (APEL); Recognition of Prior Experiential Learning (RPEL) is encountered in Australia and South Africa; Validation de l'Experience (VAE) in France; and Prior Learning Assessment (PLA) in the United States.

Traditional academic approaches to learning have been challenged by such objectives as 'social inclusion' and 'widening participation'. The engagement of further and higher education with the concepts of lifelong and work-based learning has been an important catalyst for the accreditation of prior learning occurring in non-formal education settings, including the workplace. Accrediting past learning experiences has a dual role: first, it can be taken into account in relation to entry to a programme of study; second, it may permit a student to be exempted from an otherwise compulsory element of the course.

Accrediting prior achievement or learning can be a way of fast-tracking skilled workers through a qualification route. It has proved useful in the United Kingdom where shortages of public sector workers – including nurses and teachers – have necessitated recruitment from overseas. In some countries targeted for recruitment the minimum qualification levels required to practise may be below those expected in the UK. Even the most experienced teacher, or even a head teacher, from a country where teaching is not a graduate profession, cannot make progress in their career in the UK until they gain a degree and/or achieve 'qualified teacher status' (as specified by the central Department for Education and Skills). Recognising an overseas-trained teacher's past achievement and/or learning takes the form of partial training exemption and will hopefully make it possible for that person to secure career advancement in their country of settlement.

While the accreditation of prior achievement and/or learning is widely presented as an instrument for social inclusion and promotion, enabling marginalised groups with few or no formal qualifications to access education or to gain credit, European research indicates that it has been colonised disproportionately by already-advantaged groups to gain exemption from credits, largely at graduate and postgraduate level. Aspiring learners with less 'cultural capital' may therefore be disadvantaged by not knowing the 'invisible' rules and codes of the academy.

At a global level, the accreditation of prior achievement/learning movement has developed unevenly. In France and South Africa, for example, it is a prominent feature, underpinned by legislation supporting citizen rights. In such countries as South Africa, where politics has previously imported barriers to formal learning, efforts to accredit work-based experience without additional expense and time are being undertaken on a large scale. Elsewhere, policies and practices are frequently inconsistent across regions or institutions: in the UK, for example, the 'new' universities which developed out of the former industry-oriented polytechnics have embraced the concept more readily than their ancient and 'redbrick' counterparts. From a power perspective, the 'de-institutionalisation of knowledge' (Solomon and McIntyre 2000) with which the accreditation of prior learning is associated may be seen as a threat to traditional learning. Others see great benefits, though these must be balanced against the bureaucratic and complex nature of the accreditation process.

See also: accreditation; higher education; recruitment; university; work-based/work-located/workplace/work-related learning

Further reading

Solomon, N. and McIntyre, J. (2000) 'Deschooling vocational knowledge: work-based learning and the politics of the curriculum'. In C. Symes and J. McIntyre (eds) *Working Knowledge: New Vocationalism in Higher Education,* Milton Keynes: Open University Press.

Garnett, J., Portwood, D. and Costley, C. (2004) *Bridging Rhetoric and Reality: Accreditation of Prior and Experiential Learning (APEL) in the UK,* Bolton: Universities Vocational Awards Council.

Armsby, P., Costley, C. and Garnett, J. (2006) 'The legitimisation of knowledge: a work-based learning perspective of APEL', *International Journal of Lifelong Education,* 25(4): 369–83.

RAKSHA BHALSOD

ACTION RESEARCH

This concept originated when Kurt Lewin (1935; 1936 and many subsequent publications) put the approach forward as a means of researching social issues and problems. He suggested a four-phase, continuous cycle of: planning, acting, observing and reflecting, then re-planning and so on. This was later adapted by Kolb (1984) in his cyclical model of experiential learning:

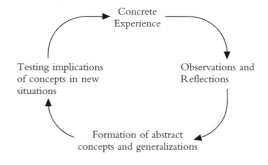

In 1975 Lawrence Stenhouse applied the idea of action research to education with his

concept of the 'teacher as researcher'. It is still associated with the idea of teacher researchers or indeed any practitioner reflecting upon and researching their own practice in order to improve it. John Elliott later expressed the idea in terms of enabling teachers to 'act more intelligently and skilfully' (1992: 69). This notion relates to the idea of the 'reflective practitioner' put forward by Donald Schön (1983). For a teacher, reflective practice starts with critical reflection on and examination of their own implicit ideas about education: reflective practitioners question their deeply held 'taken-for-granted assumptions'. In a real situation, such as a school, reflective practitioners continually evaluate the effects of their choices and actions on others (especially the pupils) and actively take advantage of opportunities to develop professionally.

Since Lewin and Kolb's time, various models of action research have been suggested: for example, several advocates have taken Lewin's cycle and adapted it into an action research spiral, a model adapted by Elliott in terms of a series of successive cycles. The spiral begins when those involved identify or 'diagnose' a particular problem, situation or issue that needs addressing. Discussion and planning follow and this leads to action or 'intervention', which is then monitored and evaluated. After the first cycle of diagnosing, planning, implementing and evaluating, the team will discuss the next stage of the spiral in the light of what has been learnt in the previous phase.

There is no one agreed definition of 'action research'. Carr and Kemmis described it as follows:

> Action Research is a form of self-reflective enquiry undertaken by participants (teachers, students or principals) in social (including educational) situations in order to improve the rationality and justice of: (a) their own social or educational practices (b) their understanding of these practices and (c) the situations (and institutions) in which these practices are carried out.
>
> (1986: 2)

This has often been used as a working definition. Perhaps the key elements of action research are that it aims:

- to improve practice (as opposed to, say, simply studying it or describing it);
- to raise practitioners' awareness of their own practice;
- to bring about change as its primary aim, rather than just collecting research data and reporting on it;
- to monitor and evaluate any change and then to re-assess and modify the intervention or innovation;
- to be a collaborative effort amongst people working in the same setting: if 'outsiders' are involved they should work in partnership with insiders;
- to bridge the gap between theory and practice.

Action researchers are more than just external observers (though they may be 'participant observers', a term coined by ethnographers to show the importance in ethnography of observing one's own working environment and questioning its practices and taken-for-granted assumptions).

Action research has been used to focus on many different areas of education including the curriculum, pedagogy (teaching and learning), policy making, management of educational institutions and staff development. It is said to have several advantages over 'traditional' approaches to research done by outsiders: the researcher may often be an 'insider' and will know and understand the situation and context of the situation being studied; action research may solve some of the traditional problems associated with the validity of research by allowing triangulation as a result of working collaboratively with others in the situation and reflecting on the process over time; and action research may solve certain ethical problems as it is likely to include those 'being researched' and will show sensitivity towards them. However, it could be argued that other approaches to research can be equally attentive to issues of triangulation and ethics; and also that action research faces as many problems as it solves, such as the possibility of the researcher becoming intimately involved in the research situation and therefore biased or failing to question or 'see' things that an outsider might ('going native' as it is sometimes termed). There can also be ethical difficulties and power issues in researching one's own colleagues or institution.

See also: educational research; ethnography; experiential learning; practitioner research; reflective practitioner; Schön, Donald; Stenhouse, Lawrence

Further reading

Carr, W. and Kemmis, S. (1986) *Becoming Critical*, Lewes: Falmer Press.

Elliott, J. (1992) *Action Research for Educational Change*, Buckingham: Open University Press.

Kemmis, S. and McTaggart, R. (1988) *The Action Research Planner*, Geelong, VIC: Deakin University Press.

Kolb, D. (1984) *Experiential Learning: Experience as the Source of Learning and Development*, Englewood Cliffs NJ: Prentice-Hall.

Lewin, K. (1935) *A Dynamic Theory of Personality*, New York: McGraw-Hill.

——(1936) *Principles of Topological Psychology*, New York: McGraw-Hill.

McNiff, J. (1997) *Action Research: Principles and Practice*, London: Routledge.

Schön, D. A. (1983) *The Reflective Practitioner: How Professionals Think in Action*, New York: Basic Books.

JERRY WELLINGTON

ACTIVITY THEORY

Activity theory originated in the revolutionary work of Russian psychologists in the 1920s and 1930s, primarily Lev Vygotsky and his colleagues A. N. Leont'ev and A. R. Luria. Their efforts to identify the social origins of human consciousness countered the established psychological perspectives of the day, including behaviourism and psychoanalysis, and brought philosophical and sociological ideas to the study of human thinking and knowing. Although activity theory has been much discussed in Russian psychology since then, it first appeared in the West in the 1970s.

Along with theories of distributed cognition, situated learning and communities of practice, activity theory belongs to a sub-discipline known as 'cultural psychology' (Cole 1996) which challenges mainstream conceptions of the genesis and nature of human consciousness. A chief assumption of cultural psychology is that consciousness is not the innate property of individuals but, rather, a socially shared phenomenon particular to localities, time periods and social practices. Human development proceeds in two stages: first inter-psychologically, in relations between and among people, and then intra-psychologically, as individuals internalise collective ways of knowing.

Another key belief in sociocultural approaches is the central role played by the activity-specific artefacts (tools and signs) that humans employ in their interactions with and construction of objective reality. Artefacts include all cultural products: physical tools like hammers and saws, semiotic tools like language and gesture, and conceptual tools like theories and laws. As Engeström *et al.* put it in the introduction to *Perspectives on Activity Theory*, 'Human nature is not found within the human individual but in the movement between the inside and the outside, in the world of artifact use and artifact creation' (1999: 5).

There have been three discernible stages to the historical development of activity theory. The first started with Vygotsky's proposition that human experience of the external world is mediated – that is, shaped or influenced – through tools and signs. The second stage grew from Leont'ev's belief, based on Marx, that consciousness and meaning are formed in collective activity or shared labour directed towards a common object (entity or objective). Leont'ev argued that the full collective activity – the activity system – is the appropriate unit of analysis for the study of human consciousness. To understand what and how people think and know, researchers must go beyond the individual mind to the collaborative projects in which that mind participates.

Following Leont'ev, later activity theorists itemised the components of activity systems: the subject or actor (person or persons engaged in activity); the object (the thing or problem to which activity is directed); the tools and signs used in the activity; the rules governing engagement in the activity; the divisions of labour within the activity; and the community or collective within which the activity functions. An activity theory analysis of a classroom might consider the ways in which artefacts (texts, lectures, educational software and so forth), classroom regulations, divisions of labour between teacher and students, among students in small groups, and the nature and dynamics of the classroom community itself influence the subjects' (students') orientation to the object of study – a foreign language, for example.

A third stage of development – initiated primarily by Engeström and colleagues at the Centre for Activity Theory and Developmental Work Research (www.edu. helsinki.fi/activity/pages/chatanddwr/chat) and Cole and colleagues at the Laboratory of Comparative Human Cognition (www.lchc. ucsd.edu) – recognises the multiplicity of perspectives within activity systems, as well as inequities in a system's division of labour, application of rules and access to artefacts. Contemporary versions of activity theory also acknowledge that activity systems function in networks – that is, two or more systems work in concert and conflict with each other. A chief focus of studies employing activity theory has been the contradictions operating within and across systems: the conflicts and disjunctures that create dissatisfaction in individuals and groups and that motivate change.

Activity theory has been widely used both for the analysis of collective practice and for intervention studies that use a form of participatory action research to engage members of an activity system in reflection on and revision of their joint practices. It is the focus of an international conference (www.iscar. org), a journal, *Mind, Culture and Activity*, and an internet discussion group (http://communication. ucsd.edu/MCA).

See also: action research; Vygotsky, Lev

Further reading

Cole, M. (1996) *Cultural Psychology: A Once and Future Discipline*, Cambridge MA: The Belknap Press of Harvard University Press.
Cole, M., Engeström, Y. and Vasquez, O. (eds) (1997) *Mind, Culture, and Activity*, Cambridge: Cambridge University Press.
Engeström, Y., Miettinen, R. and Punamäki, R.-L. (eds) (1999) *Perspectives on Activity Theory*, Cambridge: Cambridge University Press.

ANTHONY PARÉ

ADDAMS, JANE (1860–1935)

Born in Illinois, Addams was the first American woman to win a Nobel Peace Prize. She was one of the first graduates of the Rockford Female Seminary (1881), where the course she took was the same as for male students. After a tour of Europe and a fortuitous visit to Toynbee Hall in the East End of London, Addams decided to establish a similar 'settlement' to support families experiencing extremes of urban deprivation. Hull House, in Chicago, became an internationally recognised initiative where the care of children within their neighbourhood, family and social setting was seen as the appropriate context for educational support. Addams institutionalised ideas of the necessary linkage between social and educational dimensions of care of the young. Hull House established a model of holistic care, which became the framework for local authority social, cultural and educational services in the United States and elsewhere. She was appointed to the Chicago Board of Education in 1905, with lead responsibility for schools in the city.

Addams became involved in a broad range of progressive activities, including child labour, race relations, women's rights, youth justice, and health and safety at work, and was particularly supported by women. A resolute peace activist during World War I, she was a founder member of the National Association for the Advancement of Colored People and the American Civil Liberties Union. Few Americans have ever been as influential in educating succeeding generations as Addams, and her impact and inspiration live on.

See also: equality of opportunity

STEVEN COWAN

ADULT EDUCATION

Adult education is a broad-based concept that usually refers to the structured and purposeful education and training of adults that may be carried out by a number of organisations. It is generally considered to be something that adults do in addition to their normal work, and usually after an initial period of education, although not always in the case of adult literacy. The idea of an 'adult' has itself been an historically variable one, which developed gradually in relation to the specification of the education of children. For instance, J. W. Hudson's *Adult Education* (1851) included examples of what, today, would be viewed as children's education. Definitions of adult education are confused by the range of institutions that deliver it, as well as by the functions that may be ascribed to it. For instance, public service, national independence, leisure, emancipatory and economic development impulses can all be identified within the orbit of adult education.

Although adult education has been traced back to the Middle Ages, its origins are usually linked to emerging social and labour movements, which contested dominant forms of learning and knowledge from the late eighteenth century. It is possible to connect these early initiatives to the educational work of more 'mature' class-based formations in the early twentieth century in trades

unions, labour colleges and cooperatives, for example. In a similar vein, from the 1970s, radical adult education initiatives conceived of education in terms of bringing about social change by working with marginalised groups such as working classes, women or black students. This development, often referred to as 'radical' and 'critical pedagogy' or 'transformatory education', has drawn upon the work of Paolo Freire.

Alongside this strand of adult education can be found forms of provision that have been arranged 'from above' and motivated by social concern and an interest in harmonising social class relations. In Britain this is apparent in adult schools and the development of 'university extension' in which staff went out to deliver lectures and classes in industrial centres, contrasting with the recent focus upon 'access' and 'widening participation' that aims to bring students into universities. Many of these ideas would also be 'exported', for instance, to African countries, where different impulses such as nation building would come into play.

While these tendencies operated in tension, there was also considerable overlap between them in terms of students, curriculum, pedagogy and motivations. Historically, both streams of adult education responded to the imperatives of expanding democracy and the need to support the participation of marginalised groups of people. In addition, cultural independence has been a motivating factor in rural folk schools in Denmark and cooperative schools in Trentino. Furthermore, it is difficult to disentangle the range of bodies that have delivered adult education: universities, local government, voluntary organisations and social movements, to name but a few. Each of these has developed adult education in new directions.

Liberal adult education, 'well rounded' and politically neutral, was a significant element of adult education for much of the twentieth century. In reality, a range of educational courses was developed under the liberal banner, contributing to the ragged patchwork of adult education in the twentieth and twenty-first centuries. These have included leisure-based short courses and 'community education', provided by professionals working in a range of settings. Vocational education has been carried out by trades unions, employers and other agencies, a practice which has been expanded considerably in recent years. Very different versions of vocational education can be found in Mahatma Gandhi's educational work in India, which aimed to foster self-sufficient rural communities and rejected Western liberal education. From yet another standpoint, social and labour movements developed educational practices in relation to their own organisational imperatives and to help foster social change.

Since the 1980s, adult education has received increasing recognition from mainstream educational policy and practice, in part summed up by the notion of 'lifelong learning' and continuing education, which, in some cases, have replaced adult education and demoted it in value. Human capital theories have emphasised the importance of 'learning through life' in order to respond to wider economic and social changes. Vocational and distance learning have been incorporated into an assessment and certification framework that is connected to mainstream educational systems. A range of multilateral agencies, such as the World Bank and the United Nations, have paid increasing attention to adult education, comparing national systems. However, tensions alluded to above find a continuing presence in the ambiguous feelings of many adult educators who are wary of such developments. For instance, the University of the Third Age (U3A) has continued to emphasise leisure and the social aspects of learning, while the International Council for Adult Education (ICAE) has itself expressed concerns about economic globalisation and the need for 'social justice'.

See also: andragogy; athenaeum; continuing education; extra-mural class; International Council for Adult Education (ICAE); liberal education; lifelong learning; mechanics' institute; university extension; workers' education; Workers' Educational Association (WEA)

Further reading

Freire, P. (1970) *Pedagogy of the Oppressed*, Harmondsworth: Penguin.

Harrison, J. F. C. (1960) *Learning and Living 1790–1960: A Study in the History of the Adult Education Movement*, London: Routledge and Kegan Paul.

Jarvis, P. (ed) (2003) *Adult and Continuing Education: Major Themes in Education*, vols 1–5, London: Routledge.

Titmus, C. and Steele, T. (1995) *Adult Education for Independence*, Leeds: University of Leeds Press.

TOM WOODIN

AFRICA

Given Africa's diversity, attempts at surveying its social and cultural character run the risk of homogenising and essentialising its complexity. This is especially so in education, where the particular danger exists of conflating countries and their experiences before and after the 1970s. The continent's experience of education is highly complex and varied. It is now necessary to write South Africa back into the story of African educational history and to ask, on the one hand, to what extent the new South African government has been willing to learn from the experience of educational policy development in the post-colonial era, and on the other, to what extent the radical policy departures of the new government since 1994, the establishment of the African Union (AU) and the New Economic Partnership for Africa (NEPAD) offer a framework for the revival of education in what is currently being termed 'the African century'.

There is a rich heritage of indigenous and traditional education which lives on in Africa, despite the dominant presence of religious education (Christian and Muslim) and secular forms of education. Mostly in the form of oral education and folklore, it retains a social significance in traditional religious practices and initiation schools across the continent. Yet formal research and writing on this area is limited. Despite the increasing interest in pre-colonial history and the nature of indigenous knowledge systems (IKS), there is little sign that major curriculum shifts will be influenced by these developments.

Colonial education in the nineteenth century, following examples in the imperial heartlands, was dominated by the influence of Christian missionary organisations. While it sought to proselytise, its larger purpose was to engage Africans in a variety of ways with the deep cultural, social and economic practices of modernity. This modernisation favoured the new African elite entering the flagship mission schools networks such as Achimota, Livingstonia, Domboshawa, Zomba, Marianhill, Lovedale, Healdtown and Tigerkloof. Mastery of the language of the coloniser bestowed on them a new status and provided opportunities for social and economic mobility. For the majority of the population, who either attended thousands of 'bush schools' or failed to gain entry, the institution of schooling had more limited advantages.

In the early years of colonisation it was often difficult to persuade communities, parents or youth to attend schools, but by the end of the colonial period in the mid-twentieth century there was such a flood of applicants that the missions could no longer cope and governments were forced to take a much more active role in the provision of education.

The kind of education – the curriculum – felt to be appropriate to Africans was a topic of intense debate among colonial administrators, missionaries and educators, as at the great missionary councils held in Edinburgh (1910) and Le Zoute, Switzerland (1923). African opinion was seldom sought on the matter until the middle of the twentieth century. The classic liberal curriculum imported from Europe was initially taken for granted despite many arguments against its dominant role and its apparent lack of relevance to the life of the rural poor. Yet the emergent African elite was very sensitive to any attempt to reform such an education in the progressive mould – to make it 'relevant to life' – for fear that it would be watered down in ways that would exclude Africans from equal economic and social status and opportunity. (See the Phelps Stokes report on *Education in Africa* (1922) and (1924) and the British Colonial Office's document *Education Policy in British Tropical Africa* (1925) and A.V. Murray (1929).)

During the final stages of the colonial period the provision of mass schooling, tertiary education and technical training of various kinds, as well as engagement with issues of literacy and non-formal education, came to prominence as the colonial powers attempted to remedy the neglect of the past. Yet enrolments remained low.

The years of independence (Uhuru), after World War II, were characterised by an unusual optimism in the history of African education with the establishment of new schooling systems and the obligatory university in each country. The Addis Ababa Plan for African Education (1961) captured the essence of this era of expansion, as did Nyerere's *Education for Self Reliance* in Tanzania and Patrick van Rensburg's *Education with Production* in Botswana and Zimbabwe.

But there were also voices of warning that all was not well. Many saw enormous dangers in the often-haphazard expansion of African education systems and the economic problems posed by an over-commitment to an area that was often criticised for failing to meet the needs of economic growth and development. The question, at first timidly asked but later taken up more strongly, was 'Does schooling promote or retard development?' This led back to further questions about the *kind* of education that needed to be emphasised.

In that context African thinkers framed a critique of the colonial situation that would long outlive the circumstances of the time. Fanon, Memmi, Achebe, Ngugi Wa Thiogo and Paolo Freire, and a host of political, autobiographical and fiction writers all commented in various ways on the significance and the limits of the educational experience under colonialism. The relevance of this writing lies in its capacity to capture the voice of the poor and the marginalised – something that has often been lost in later 'policy' debates. By the time the economies of many African countries began to fail in the 1970s, education entered a new period of crisis.

Globalisation is often presented as being full of promise and possibility both in the economic and the political/social sphere. (Groupe de Lisbonne 1995). It is said to be liberating to the individual and society. Yet viewed from the perspective of the development of African education, the advent of globalisation has been little short of disastrous. The prosperous years of the Long Boom were brought to an end by the oil crisis and debt crises. Banks and lending agencies linked to the World Bank or the International Monetary Fund-devised Structural Adjustment Programmes (SAPs), which tied governments to the monetarist principles of the North. In the process, low priority was given to the areas of health, welfare and education. The ascendancy of the principle of cost recovery in public education meant the introduction of school and health service charges. Aside from a small class of beneficiaries, globalisation and neo-liberalism/free market policy brought intense hardship such as increased and direct costs to families and communities, this further restricting access to the children of the poor (Rajani 2003).

In the context of this, the *Education for All* (EFA) campaign and notion of lifelong education were promoted by a number of international organisations. Yet by 2000 the Dakar conference on EFA demonstrated that over 113 million children still lacked access to primary school and 880 million adults were illiterate globally, and that a significant proportion of these were in Africa (Ruperez 2003: 259). Also, while near gender parity appeared to have been achieved at the primary school level, this was distinctly not the case in secondary schools. In countries such as Uganda and Kenya, for example, four times as many boys were enrolled than girls in the upper grades of the secondary school (Rajani 2003: 6). Retention rates to grade five varied from 38 per cent in Guinea-Bissau to 99 per cent in the Seychelles.

The implications for education were that SAP policies led to an expansion of inequalities despite the efforts of the EFA campaign. Where there was policy development it tended to be centred rather narrowly around notions of skills development – Vocational and Technical Education (VET) – or human resource development (HRD) for competitiveness in a global market place.

Globally new social movements evident in Seattle and Cancun are demonstrating a will for reform to challenge what has come to be called the new Washington Consensus and to demonstrate a concern for the politics of poverty. But in Africa there have been few signs of that trend, with even relatively debt-free countries such as South Africa undergoing their own 'voluntary structural adjustment', and the African Renaissance or NEPAD, and the African Union showing every sign of continuity with previous policies, which sought to create a friendly environment for international capital.

The challenge is for research and policy development, which seeks to negotiate a changed economic, political and social order in Africa. This kind of research would of necessity need to take account of the economic needs of skilled and productive labour to ensure a degree of readiness for engagement with the labour markets of the twenty-first century, but it would also of necessity have to face the daunting challenges of an education for social equity and cultural stability.

In seeking education policies suitable for sustainable development, Barboza (2000) outlines the following issues as central to future reform:

- curricula more directly relevant to social and economic 'competencies';

19

- values necessary for survival;
- an integrated approach to development problems;
- a 'proactive education approach' which places the pupil and experimental methods at the centre of educational planning.

In pursuing those goals African education decision makers across the continent will have to think systemically and to anticipate the ravages of poverty and diseases such as HIV/AIDS, but at the same time think holistically about creating systems that will enable their young to grow with dignity and a sense of their place in the world.

See also: Education for All; globalisation; indigenous education; literacy; Nigeria; rural education; South Africa; Tanzania; World Bank

Further reading

Barboza, Nathalie (2000) 'Educating for a sustainable future: Africa in action', *Prospects*, 30(1): 71–85. Paris: UNESCO.

Barratt Brown, M. (1996) *Africa's Choices: After Thirty Years of the World Bank*, London: Penguin.

Groupe de Lisbonne (1995) *Limites à la Compétitivité*, Paris: La Découverte.

King, K. and Buchert, L. (1999) *Changing International Aid to Education*, Paris: UNESCO.

Murray, A. V. (1929) *The School in the Bush: A Critical Study of the Theory and Practice of Native Education in Africa*, London: Longmans, Green and Company.

Rajani, R. (2003) *The Education Pipeline in East Africa. A Research Report and Synthesis of Consultations in Kenya, Tanzania and Uganda*, Nairobi, Kenya: Ford Foundation.

Ruperez, F. L. (2003) 'Globalization and education', *Prospects*, 33(3): 249–61.

PETER KALLAWAY AND CRAIN SOUDIEN

ALTERNATIVE EDUCATION

Alternative education is used to describe teaching and learning in non-traditional, new, or non-standard settings, or the teaching of an unorthodox curriculum. Some institutions, generally outside the traditional or regular public school setting, promote themselves as alternative schools, perhaps on the grounds of their political or ideological stance, small size or use of particular teaching methods. Since there is no common definition for an alternative school, the term may vary from state to state or country to country. Alternative programmes may be found within a mainstream school or in such settings as a separate school building, community or recreation centre, correction or detention centre, medical facility or homeless shelter.

The purpose of education has modified over time in response to cultural changes, workforce needs, and technological developments. With each generation, the demand has increased for schools to educate students with more rigorous knowledge and skills to address the advancements of society. While increased expectations within the traditional settings of school benefit college-bound students, many non-traditional students have reacted with disruptive or violent behaviours or by dropping out of school. Consequently, alternative schools were developed to address the needs of disconnected or vulnerable students.

'Alternative education' is a perspective based upon a belief that all people can be educated, and that education may be delivered in many ways and many different environments and structures. The alternative school may be private or public. Teachers in alternative schools employ varying approaches, teaching strategies, beliefs, and support services that facilitate growth in academic, social, and career development initiatives.

Most alternative schools are innovatively structured to educate students with discipline or behavioural problems, students with specific academic or developmental needs, or those in danger of dropping out of school. Students in danger of dropping out of school are at risk of educational failure as indicated by poor grades, truancy, disruptive behaviour, suspension, pregnancy, or similar factors. In the United States of America, the high school dropout rate is approximately 25 per cent.

Examples of alternative education programmes with an academic focus include General Educational Development (GED) programmes, magnet schools, charter schools, or maths and science schools.

Basic educational accountability standards for regular education programmes usually apply to the alternative education schools within the same school district. Consequently, the curriculum for alternative schools focuses on continuing the basic academic expectations of the student's regular school with modifications and the utilisation of a variety of instructional strategies to meet the individual student's academic needs and interests. Additionally, to address the social development component of the alternative school programme, students may engage in positive social skills development, community service projects, goal setting, problem-solving, and/or peer mediation.

Faculty and staff employed in an alternative education school/programme must focus on developing and maintaining a positive school culture. At-risk youth need positive adults to serve as their mentors and to advocate their needs. School structures key to the success of alternative education programmes include building positive teacher–student relationships, incorporating cognitive-behavioural discipline practices, and providing a smaller pupil/teacher ratio (usually 15 or less students per teacher) for each class.

Many public alternative schools or programmes return the individual students to their regular schools when the students have achieved their academic and/or behavioural goals. Some students return to the alternative school after a period of time at the regular school. The rate of students returning to the alternative school determines the 'recidivism rate' for the alternative school. The recidivism rate is an indicator used to measure the success of an alternative school in meeting the needs of individual alternative school students. Some alternative school programmes allow the students to graduate from their particular settings with a regular high school diploma, a GED diploma, or an occupational or skills certification. Funding for alternative education programmes varies with the purpose of the programme.

As accountability standards for academic achievement increase, it appears that the need for dynamic alternative schools will continue to soar.

See also: autodidact; charter school; delinquency; discipline; dropouts; emotional and behavioural difficulties (EBD); exclusion/ expulsion; home schooling; magnet school; school culture; suspension; truancy

Further reading

Cox, S. and Davidson, W. (1995) 'A meta-analytic assessment of delinquency-related outcomes of alternative education programs', *Crime and Delinquency*, 41: 219–35.

Guerin, G. and Denti, L. (1999) 'Alternative education support for youth at-risk', *The Clearing House*, 73(2): 76–79.

Tobin, T. and Sprague, J. (2000) 'Alternative education strategies: reducing violence in school and the community', *Journal of Emotional and Behavioral Disorders*, 8(3): 177–87.

ROSE M. McNEESE

ALUMNI

An alumnus is a former pupil or student of a school, college or university, alumni being the collective noun. While some adults show no inclination to re-visit the scenes of their childhood or youth, others may retain some affection for one or more of their *alma mater* institutions, whether out of a sense of gratitude, pride or pity. Alumni wishing to renew peer acquaintances, sometimes after many years, may meet with success by posting contact details on a website linked to a former place of learning or by creating an entry on a commercial site. Throughout the world, many schools maintain 'old boy' or 'old girl' associations, while colleges and universities frequently maintain an alumni association. Such bodies send out regular mailings inviting past students, for example, to share their memories, to make contact with former tutors and peers, and to attend special events, dinners and weekend reunions. Glossy articles remind readers of celebrated fellow alumni: politicians, business leaders, artists, performers and others in the public eye. Additional invitations to buy, for example, commemorative ties, mugs and cufflinks and to sign up for credit cards bearing their former institution's inscription betray another, and perhaps the major, objective of alumni associations: fundraising. Institutions typically encourage tax-efficient donations and legacies from alumni to finance student bursaries and to replace or enhance computing and recreational facilities. In countries such as the United States and Japan it is usual for graduates to maintain contact with their former college or university. The response of alumni from leading institutions in these and other countries to fundraising appeals is sometimes evident from the inscriptions on new campus buildings.

See also: endowment

DAVID CROOK

AMERICAN EDUCATIONAL RESEARCH ASSOCIATION (AERA)

The American Educational Research Association (AERA) claims to be the most prominent international educational professional organisation, with the primary goal of advancing educational research and its practical application. In the words of its mission statement, AERA 'strives to advance knowledge about education, to encourage scholarly inquiry related to education, and to promote the use of research to improve education and serve the public good'. It was founded in 1915 as the National Association of Directors of Educational Research, and held its first meeting in 1916. Its current title was instituted in the 1920s, reflecting a desire to encourage a broader membership.

The Association has 25,000 members, including educators, administrators, directors of research, people working in testing and evaluation, counsellors, evaluators and graduate students. These members represent a range of academic disciplines including education, psychology, statistics, sociology, history, economics, philosophy, anthropology, and political science. Although it is primarily an American organisation, it also attracts members and participation from across the world.

AERA is divided into twelve divisions as follows: administration, organisation and leadership; curriculum studies; learning and instruction; measurement and research methodology; counselling and human development; history and historiography; social context of education; school evaluation and programme development; education in the professions; postsecondary education; teaching and teacher education; educational policy and politics. There are also well over 100 special interest groups (SIGs) which enable groups of researchers to network and focus on particular concerns. Examples include adult literacy and adult education, indigenous peoples of the Americas, religion and education, research in mathematics education, and teacher as researcher.

AERA publishes the *Educational Researcher* nine times a year. Other journals include the *American Educational Research Journal*; *Educational Evaluation and Policy Analysis*; *Journal of Educational and Behavioural Statistics*; *Review of Educational Research* and *Review of Research in Education*. Throughout its history AERA has published occasional books and monographs, and in 2004 a conscious commitment was made to a new Handbook series, overseen by an editorial board. AERA has developed its own ethical standards applicable to researchers operating in an educational context and has published books on the subject. Policies have been developed in areas such as conflicts of interest, social justice and harassment.

AERA also plays a lobbying role by representing and explaining research findings to politicians and policy makers. It communicates with a wider constituency of educationalists,

media and the general public through a programme of outreach activities which include
press releases, public policy debates and an
information service.

An awards programme serves to recognise
and stimulate high-quality scholarship in
education. These include awards related to
outstanding contributions in educational
research, to social justice, early career development, public service, gender equity and
scholars of colour. AERA also offers a number
of small grants related to educational research
to support student participation and early
career development.

AERA is an independent and democratic
organisation which reflects and serves the
needs of its members, who elect many of the
key leadership positions. Its governance
structure is made up of a Council, Executive
Board, standing committees, and annual
committees. It is governed by a legislative
and policy making body, the Council. The
President appoints members and chairs of
standing committees. The Executive Board
serves as an advisory group to the AERA
president and executive director. AERA
standing committees have been set up to
carry out and develop specific areas of business; for instance, professional development,
social justice and policies and procedures. Ad
hoc committees, task forces and working
groups are also established for particular purposes and for limited periods. A Graduate
Student Council helps to facilitate and promote the transition from graduate student to
professional researcher and/or practitioner by
providing opportunities within AERA for
growth, development and advancement.

See also: educational research

Further reading

Cochran-Smith, M. and Zeichner, K. M. (2005)
*Studying Teacher Education: The Report of the
AERA Panel on Research and Teacher Education*,
Mahwah NJ: AERA and Lawrence Erlbaum.
Green, J. L. (2006) *Review of Research in Education*,
Washington DC: AERA.
——(2006) *Handbook of Complementary Methods in
Education Research*, Mahwah NJ: AERA and
Lawrence Erlbaum.

TOM WOODIN

ANDRAGOGY

The term *andragogy* has been used in different
times and countries with various connotations.
Nowadays there exist three main understandings:

1 In many countries there is a growing
   conception of 'andragogy' as the scholarly approach and science of understanding and supporting the lifelong
   and lifewide education of adults;
2 In the United States of America especially, 'andragogy', in the tradition of
   Malcolm Knowles (discussed below),
   labels a specific theoretical and practical
   approach, based on a humanistic conception of self-directed and autonomous learners and teachers as facilitators
   of learning;
3 A further but less clear use of andragogy can be found, which goes beyond
   the limited notion of 'adult education',
   focusing on 'desirable values', 'specific
   teaching methods', 'reflections', 'academic discipline' and/or 'opposition to
   childish pedagogy'.

Literally translated, *andragogy* means the
'guiding of men', being analogous to *pedagogy*
(the 'guiding of boys'), both inappropriate
understandings in the context of sexual
equality.

The first use of the term *Andragogik* is
attributed to the German high school teacher
Alexander Kapp in 1833. In *Platons Erzie-
hungslehre* ('Plato's Educational Ideas'), Kapp
describes the lifelong necessity to learn. He
justifies Andragogik as the necessitous cultivation of adults, a concept that could also be
applied to 'adult education'.

From the 1920s adult education became
subject to greater theorising. Some German

authors rediscovered the term Andragogik to reflect upon adult education in respect of 'why', 'what for' and 'how'? Academic reflection occurred on a plane 'above' practical adult education, though the idea of a distinct discipline was not yet born. In the 1950s Andragogik can be found in publications from Switzerland (Hanselmann), Yugoslavia (Ogrizovic), the Netherlands (ten Have), Germany (Poeggeler) and other European countries, but the term was known only to insiders. Understandings of adult education continued to be located in a mixture of practice, commitment, ideologies, reflections, theories, mostly local institutions and individuals, and a clarifying term to differentiate between 'doing' and 'reflecting' was required.

The key period for the term 'andragogy' in English-language adult education accompanied the work of Malcolm Knowles (1913–97). *Andragogy, Not Pedagogy!* was the provocative title of his 1968 book. Knowles' concept of andragogy built on a conception of learners being self-directed and autonomous, and of teachers being facilitators of learning. Constructing andragogy, in opposition to pedagogy, added to the attraction of the concept: it provided an opportunity to be on the 'good side', not a 'pedagogue' (defined in 1982 by *Webster's Dictionary* as 'a teacher, especially a pedantic one'). In a short time, the term andragogy, now labelling Knowles' concept, received general recognition throughout North America and other English-speaking countries. Andragogy was attractive to adult educators and offered the promise of strengthening their sense of professionalism. Andragogy appealed because it was associated with understandable, humanistic values and beliefs, for its emphasis upon expertise, 'experience', 'mission', specific methods and a unifying idea. Criticism of Knowles' understanding of andragogy maintained that it is not a general, descriptive approach, but rather a specific, prescriptive one, born, like all educational theories, into one specific historic and societal context.

Thus, attaching andragogy exclusively to Knowles' specific approach means that the term is a relic of the past.

Since 1970 andragogy has been used in Europe in the context of evolving academic and professional institutions employing trained professionals. In 1969 the Yugoslavian Society for Andragogy launched a journal entitled *Andragogija*, and Slovenia's Andragoski Center Republike Slovenije founded *Andragoska Spoznanja* in 1993. Prague University (Czech Republic) has a 'Katedra Andragogiky', while Bamberg University (Germany) founded a 'Lehrstuhl Andragogik' in 1995. The term andragogy has a currency in other parts of the world, too: Venezuela has an 'Instituto Internacional de Andragogia', and, since 1998, the Adult Education Society of Korea has published *Andragogy Today*.

In recent decades andragogy has expanded as academic discipline, with university programmes, professors, and students in many countries, documenting a new reality of (places of) systematic reflection and professional action 'above' practice and specific teaching approaches. In this context, andragogy has become increasingly understood as an educational discipline, the subject of which is the study of lifelong and lifewide education and learning of adults. According to this understanding, andragogy is distinctive from adult education, 'further education' and 'adult pedagogy', though these are more widely used terms. Future developments in knowledge, institutions, functions and roles may require further clarification of the meaning of andragogy.

See also: adult education; further education; learning; lifelong learning; pedagogy

Further reading

Knowles, M. (1968) *Andragogy, Not Pedagogy!*, New York: Association Press.
www.andragogy.net
www.umsl.edu/~henschke

JOST REISCHMANN

ANTHROPOLOGY OF EDUCATION

Anthropology of education is concerned with how the concepts, methods and findings of social and cultural anthropology contribute to analyses of the educational process. Anthropologists focus on the process of cultural transmission and the nature of human learning in different societies and their insights, gained from extensive field studies, have helped educationalists to better understand the experiences of learners from different cultures in North American and European classrooms. Comparative education has been a feature of educational anthropology ever since Margaret Mead drew on her investigations into adolescence in Samoa in the 1920s to critique aspects of American schooling. A more recent account of schooling in Japan provides a more contemporary example of ethnographic description abroad being used as a basis for a critique of schooling at home (Benjamin 1997).

By the 1950s American anthropologists and educators were sharing conferences and writing joint publications to explore the benefits of interdisciplinary collaboration (see Spindler 1955). This kind of collaboration has provided American teachers and their trainers with materials designed to improve their understanding of the cultures of their minority group students. By juxtaposing cultures this process makes explicit some of the cultural understandings often taken for granted by both majority and minority group members. This appreciation of cultural difference and alternative competencies developed into a critique of compensatory education initiatives grounded in explanations of educational failure that described working–class and minority groups in terms of cultural deprivation. Anthropological accounts of the different learning styles preferred by members of particular groups have increasingly been employed to make the case for culturally relevant pedagogies and curricula, as in the Afro-centric school, for example.

In his 1982 book *Education and Anthropology* the English sociologist of education Frank Musgrove, somewhat heretically for the time, saw this project of culturally contexted learning as a disastrous consequence of uncritically importing the anthropological concept of culture into education. For Musgrove, the job of schools is always to transcend, rather than transmit, any particular culture. These reservations are symptomatic of a rather more reluctant collaboration between anthropologists and educationalists in the United Kingdom. Despite the early impact of a 1960s research project on school ethnographies based in the Department of Anthropology and Sociology at the University of Manchester (see, for example, Lacey's classic study of *Hightown Grammar*), Delamont and Atkinson (1995) concluded their survey of anthropological approaches in education by noting the continuing dominance of North American work; they urged a rapprochement between sociological and anthropological approaches in the UK. Their demand for more ethnographic studies of the educational careers of ethnic minority children in British schools is now increasingly being met, and ethnographic methods borrowed from anthropological fieldwork are now regularly employed by sociologists of education.

Until recently anthropologists have shown less interest in formal schooling than in a range of more informal learning contexts. This reflects the earlier focus on traditional and non-literate societies without formal educational sectors. Schools, however, have played a major role in the cultural transformation of traditional societies through the colonial and post-colonial eras, and anthropologists have increasingly turned their attention to the relationship between indigenous epistemologies and the nationalist agendas of newly independent countries.

There are a number of organisations supporting academic studies in anthropology of education. Since 1970 the American Anthropological Association (AAA) has included a specialised Council on Anthropology and Education (CAE) which has a website (www.aaanet.org/cae/AcademicPrograms.html)

which lists American universities with research programmes in educational anthropology. *Anthropology and Education Quarterly* is the journal of the CAE, and it publishes articles on schooling in different cultural contexts and on learning both inside and outside schools. In the UK *Discovering Anthropology* (http://therai.org.uk/pubs/resguide/discovering_contents.html) is a resource guide for teachers and students published by the Royal Anthropological Institute, the National Network for Teaching and Learning, and the University of Durham. It includes several specialist sections relevant to educational anthropology.

See also: comparative education; cultural transmission; culture; ethnography; informal/nonformal learning; learning; Mead, Margaret; sociology of education

Further reading

Benjamin, G. (1997) *Japanese Lessons: A Year in a Japanese School Through The Eyes of an American Anthropologist and Her Children*, New York: New York University Press.

Delamont, S. and Atkinson, P. (1995) *Fighting Familiarity: Essays on Education and Ethnography*, Cresskill NJ: Hampton Press.

Lacey, C. (1970) *Hightown Grammar*, Manchester: University of Manchester Press.

Levinson, B., Borman, K. M., Eisenhart, M., Foster, M., Fox, A. E. and Sutton, M. (2000) *Schooling the Symbolic Animal: Social and Cultural Dimensions of Education*, Lanham MD: Rowman and Littlefield.

Musgrove, F. (1982) *Education and Anthropology: Other Cultures and the Teacher*, Chichester: John Wiley.

Spindler, G. D. (1955) *Education and Anthropology*, Stanford CA: Stanford University Press

NEIL BURTONWOOD

ANTIRACIST EDUCATION

Throughout the 1970s and 1980s and into the 1990s in Britain, there was an ongoing debate between those, broadly liberals, who wished to promote multicultural education (celebrating the diversity of cultures which make up British society), and those, mainly the radical left, who advocated antiracist education (viewing the institutional racism of British society as the fundamental problem).

In other parts of the English-speaking world, issues and concerns, and in particular terminology, were somewhat different. In North America, the debate was between multicultural educationists and critical multicultural educationists, the former predominantly politically liberal, the latter politically left and intent on challenging the dominant Eurocentric ideology of US education. More recently, Marxists Peter McLaren and Ramin Farahmandpur (2005: 147) have advocated revolutionary multiculturalism, as opposed to 'critical multicultural education', as a framework

for developing a pedagogical praxis ... [which] opens up social and political spaces for the oppressed to challenge on their own terms and in their own ways the various forms of class, race, and gender oppression that are reproduced by dominant social relations.

For a number of years Critical Race Theory (CRT), which sees 'race' as the overriding form of oppression rather than social class, has been a dominant force in a number of fields as well as education in the USA. Critical race theory has recently (e.g. Gillborn 2005) been adopted in the British education context (for a Marxist critique, see Cole 2007).

In Australasia, the left has tended to advocate an antiracist multiculturalism against 'the "spaghetti and polka" approach [of the 'simple pluralist model of multicultural education'] accompanied by anti-racist strategies to reduce discrimination in the school system and address the issues of racism and cultural identity to all students throughout mainstream curricula' (Cope and Poynting 1989: 234–35). In Britain, in terms of actual hegemonic practice in schools, most schools have remained monocultural (promoting so-called 'British culture and values'), some have practised multicultural education, and only a few have actually put antiracist education into practice.

The antiracist critique of monocultural education is that, in denying the existence of, or marginalising, the cultures of minority ethnic communities, it was and is profoundly racist. The antiracist critique of multicultural education is that it was and is patronising and superficial. It was often characterised as the three 'Ss': 'saris, samosas and steel drums' (for a discussion, see Cole 1992). Up until the late 1990s, with their prognoses that Britain is an institutionally racist society, antiracists were branded as 'loony lefties' and ostracised by the mainstream. It took the *Stephen Lawrence Inquiry Report* (Macpherson 1999) to change this.

While the report could have gone further in its castigation of the inherent racism in British society, for antiracists it is nevertheless a milestone in being the first acknowledgement by the British state of the existence of widespread institutional racism. Sivanandan rightly describes the Stephen Lawrence Inquiry as 'not just a result but a learning process for the country at large' (2000: 1). He argues that, through the course of the Inquiry, 'the gravitational centre of race relations discourse was shifted from individual prejudice and ethnic need to systemic, institutional racial inequality and injustice' (ibid.).

The (2000) UK Race Relations (Amendment) Act requires each school in England and Wales to eliminate unlawful racial discrimination; to promote equality of opportunity; and to promote good relations between people of different racial groups. Specifically, schools must prepare a written 'race' equality policy; implement the policy; and monitor and evaluate its impact on pupils/students, staff and parents/carers of different ethnic groups, in particular with respect to attainment. All racist incidents, whoever perceives them to be racist, irrespective of whether they are on the receiving end, must be investigated. The provisions of this Act provide excellent ammunition for antiracists to argue their case, and antiracists would welcome similar Acts in other countries.

Modern technology provides an ample opportunity for antiracists to modify their position to include multicultural education. The way forward is to promote both antiracism and antiracist multiculturalism. This should avoid simplistic versions of 'Racist Awareness Training', practised in the past, whereby *all* white people were considered to be infected with a racist virus which could be cured by the right therapy (for a critique of RAT, see Sivanandan 1985), and patronising and offensive multicultural education. Using the Web creatively, multicultural antiracist education should be about the importance of antiracism as an underlying principle, and about the promotion of respect and non-exploitative difference in a multicultural world.

In the light of escalating racism, Islamophobia, xenophobia and xeno-racism (directed at asylum seekers and refugees; Sivanandan 2001), in society in general and in education throughout the world, the mandatory implementation of measures to undermine institutional racism is more urgent than ever. These measures must include major changes to the curriculum and to the ethos of schools and other institutions, accompanied by policies to combat racist practices in the classroom and beyond.

See also: equality of opportunity; multicultural education

Further reading

Cole, M. (1992) 'British values, liberal values or values of justice and equality: three approaches to education in multicultural Britain'. In J. Lynch, C. Modgil and S. Modgil (eds) *Cultural Diversity and the Schools, Volume 3: Equity or Excellence? Education and Cultural Reproduction*, London: Falmer Press.

——(2007) *Marxism and Educational Theory: Origins and Issues,* London: Routledge.

Cope, B. and Poynting, S. (1989) '"Race" and gender: a comparative example'. In M. Cole (ed.) *The Social Contexts of Schooling*, Lewes: Falmer Press.

Gillborn, D. (2005) 'Education policy as an act of white supremacy: whiteness, critical race theory and education reform', *Journal of Education Policy*, 20(4): 485–505.

McLaren, P. and Farahmandpur, R. (2005) *Teaching Against Global Capitalism and the New Imperialism: A Critical Pedagogy*, Oxford: Rowman and Littlefield.

Macpherson, W. (1999) *The Stephen Lawrence Inquiry: Report of an Inquiry by Sir William Macpherson*, London: HMSO.

Sivanandan, A. (1985) 'RAT and the degradation of black struggle', *Race and Class*, 25(4): 1–33.

——(2000) 'UK: reclaiming the struggle', *Race and Class*, 42(2): 67–73.

——(2001) 'Poverty is the new black', *Race and Class*, 43(2): 1–5.

MIKE COLE

APPRENTICESHIP

Apprenticeship is a term that has endured over hundreds of years and across many different countries and cultures. Unsurprisingly, it has acquired a variety of meanings in these various contexts. In common usage, it refers to the process of learning a skilled trade, usually involving 'on the job' training and at lower than normal wages for the period of learning. More generically, apprenticeship describes a general process of learning and development, for instance, in Beatrice Webb's autobiography *My Apprenticeship* (1926). The term is historically associated with learning a craft, although apprenticeships can now be found in a variety of occupations. Models of apprenticeship have also infused training practices in other areas such as medicine, the university degree and teacher education.

The longevity of the apprenticeship results from its role at the centre of human existence and in serving social, occupational, legal, educational, religious and family needs (Aldrich 2004). Originally, apprenticeship was meaningful as a learning phase in a hierarchical career structure. Apprenticeships first developed in the Middle Ages and were partly controlled by guilds. Apprentices were indentured, often for a fee, to master craftsmen, with whom they lived while learning a trade for a period of about seven years.

Apprentices aspired to become journeymen from which some, in turn, would become master craftsmen. With industrialisation, apprenticeships tended to move gradually from the single master model towards working for larger companies and in areas such as shipbuilding, engineering, woodworking and printing. In Britain, the term has been associated with skilled trades, although the historical practices of low-skilled 'parish apprenticeships' designed to deal with illegitimate and orphaned children, as well as the use of apprentices as cheap labour, connects with elements of more recent initiatives in vocational education (Aldrich 2004).

By the 1980s, in many countries, apprenticeship was considered an anachronism that was in terminal decline. More recently, it has been revitalised as an element of vocational education and training (VET). The global expansion of school systems of education came under scrutiny in the 1990s; increasingly, they were perceived as costly and unable to respond flexibly to the needs of industry and labour markets. As a result, vocational, informal and work-based learning became highly attractive to policy makers and educationalists. In this process, the previously disregarded concept of apprenticeship was rejuvenated as part of the new discourse of reform. In 'new' and 'modern' apprenticeships, the learner is typically situated in an 'authentic' work context, acquires skills experientially and holds a work contract with an employer. Apprenticeship has been one way of making explicit the connections between education and the economy, politics and social policy. Calling learners 'apprentices' has helped to locate them within the context of a globalising economy and new configurations of work. Apprenticeship as a concept has also been utilised by international bodies such as the Organisation for Economic Co-operation and Development and European Union, which is working to develop pan-European policies in this area.

Many popular classifications of different ways of organising vocational education and training have come from Germany. Greinert (2003) distinguishes school-based, state-controlled, work-based, market- and state-controlled, market-based and mixed models. Deissinger (1995) separates 'qualification styles' according to three criteria: political and organisational regulatory frameworks; didactic-curricular aspects; and vocational training in the context of socialisation.

Tracing the various functions of apprenticeship also helps one to appreciate its diverse meanings. Firstly, by controlling access to apprenticeships, economic leaders may be able to influence the labour market and help to steer production, consumption and exchange in different industries. Secondly, apprenticeship relates to divisions and hierarchies of work among various industrial and occupational groups. Historically, the notion of 'skilled' and 'unskilled' are not only connected to owning certain competencies but also to processes of collectively-controlled learning from which some groups of people may be virtually excluded. For instance, women and minority ethnic groups have traditionally found it more difficult to enter apprenticeships, while other groups have used them to enhance their power within a given hierarchy. Apprenticeship may also have a socio-political function in relation to national, regional and local political formations. They tend to be associated with skilled and high wage sectors of the economy (Gangl 2003), a fact that make apprenticeships appealing to governments eager to widen their country's employment portfolio. Apprenticeship may also be closely connected to youth work and plays an important role in controlling youth unemployment, a problem that may have an on-going impact later in life. Finally, apprenticeship may be considered as a pedagogical concept. Forms of learning can be identified in apprenticeship systems, which may be either 'person centred' between individuals or 'decentred' in a broader community of learners (Nielson and Kvale 1997). Similarly, apprenticeships tend to involve personal and social aspects of

knowledge beyond the codified forms found in formal educational systems (Eraut 2004). These pedagogical understandings of apprenticeships tend to be overshadowed by the wider economic and political context, for instance the need to raise qualification levels and promote entrepreneurship.

Despite a growing international agenda on vocational education, apprenticeships have developed differently in a number of countries where they have taken on specific features. The so-called 'dual system' has operated in Germany, Austria, Denmark and Switzerland, where employers, government and unions have been active partners. Young people have the chance to learn a number of occupations, spending three or four days a week in the workplace and the remainder in a school or training institution. These apprenticeships may last for approximately three or four years. In Germany, up to half of young people may take an apprenticeship in which they attend the well-established vocational schools, *berufsshule*, where training is carried out according to national standards. Enterprise-based training is agreed by government, trades unions and employers, although some flexibility is allowed according to changing conditions. Costs are shared between government and employers. In recent years, countries operating a dual system have had to adapt to an increasingly erratic and less-predictable economy, which has resulted in a decreasing number of opportunities for aspiring apprentices. Also, the growing specialisation of certain companies can mean that they are unable to provide the broad based training required by the apprenticeship system. As a result of falling places, the National Pact for Training and Young Skilled Staff was introduced in Germany in 1994. Employers agreed to offer apprenticeships while the government undertook to ensure a supply of quality applicants and to respond more flexibly to the changing needs of business.

In contrast to Germany, with the onset of industrialisation in Britain, apprenticeship developed towards a model of lower-status supervision. 'Learning by doing' became the predominant mode within heavy industry and specialist crafts, although this would decline in the later twentieth century. In 1994, 'modern apprenticeships' were introduced in England and they now cover a wide range of areas, including the service sector with no previous history of apprenticeships. They are based on guidelines devised by employers organised into Sector Skills Councils. Although apprentices have a contract with an employer, formal training and assessment is state funded and delivered through various contracted agencies that work according to frameworks which include National Vocational Qualifications, technical learning and key skills. Although the period of training tends to be less than two years, the system is not yet embedded or widely understood and valued: in 2001 only about a third of apprentices completed their frameworks.

Other countries have a variety of systems in place. Norway resembles the dual system, where students have the opportunity to spend two years in education and two years as an apprentice, with the onus on schools to find appropriate apprenticeship places. Countries such as Finland have a strong school-based VET system and this has led to the bizarre rhetoric of bringing back the forgotten educational potential of the workplace. In France, the state, trades unions and business have traditionally operated apprenticeships. The recent proposals of the 'first employment contract' to allow 14-year olds to leave school in order to take up an apprenticeship proved controversial. In the United States apprenticeship programmes can also be found in skilled and unionised trades such as bricklaying and sheet metal production.

The future of apprenticeships must be placed in the context of economic, industrial, occupational and educational developments within a globalising world. Generalisations are possible, despite the multi-layered and contested meanings of apprenticeship. Increasingly, orders of skills and competencies are becoming integrated into a global labour market place.

See also: crafts; dual system; skills; training; vocational education; work-based/work-located/workplace/work-related learning

Further reading

Aldrich, R. (2006) 'Apprenticeship in England: an historical perspective'. In R. Aldrich (ed.) *Lessons from History*, London: Routledge.

Deissinger, T. (1995) 'Das Konzept der "Qualifizierungsstile" als kategoriale Basis idealtypischer Ordnungsschemata zur Charakterisierung und Unterscheidung von "Berufsbildungssystemen"', *Zeitschrift für Berufs-und Wirtschaftspädagogik*, 91(4): 367–87.

Eraut, M. (2004) 'Deconstructing apprenticeship learning: what factors affect its quality?' In R. H. Mulder and P. F. E. Sloane (eds) *New Approaches to Vocational Education in Europe*, Oxford: Symposium.

Greinert, W. D. (1994) *The 'German System' of Vocational Education*, Baden-Baden: Nomos Verlagsgesellschaft.

——(2003) *A Theoretical Framework Proposal for a History of the Development of Vocational Training in Europe*, Berlin: Institut fur Berufliche Bildung und Arbeitslehre. Available at http://history.cedefop.eu.int/framework.asp

Heikkenen, A. and Sultana, R. G. (1997) *Vocational Education and Apprenticeships in Europe: Challenges for Practice and Research*, Tampere, Finland: Tampereen Yliopisto.

Nielson, K. and Kvale, S. (1997) 'Current issues of apprenticeship', *Nordisk Pedagogik*, 17(3): 130–39.

Quintini, G., Martin, J. P. and Martin, S. (2007) *The Changing Nature of the School-to-Work Transition Process in OECD Countries*, Bonn: Institute for the Study of Labour.

Stratmann, K. and Schlosser, M. (1990) *Das duale System der Berufsbildung: Ein historische Analyse seiner Reformdebatten*, Frankfurt am Main: Gesellschaft zur Foerderung Arbeitsorientierter Forschung und Bildung.

ANJA HEIKKINEN AND TOM WOODIN

APPROVED SCHOOL

Chiefly a British term now consigned to the past, an approved school was a secure institution for young offenders, typically above the age of ten. It was a successor to Victorian 'reformatory' and 'industrial' schools and a precursor of today's 'young offender institutions'. Like the British 'public school' model, approved schools – to which many more boys than girls were sent – were often organised on house system, with rigid discipline and corporal punishment routinely administered. Those committed to approved schools experienced a curriculum that bore some similarity to early secondary modern schools, though typically with less weekly instruction, with an emphasis upon rehabilitating delinquents though practical training in bricklaying, metalwork, carpentry and gardening. During the 1950s and 1960s reports of brutality and ill treatment towards juveniles led to a number of 'public inquiries, political contrition, and a stated commitment to improving conditions for young offenders' (Wills 2007). The concept of the approved school bears a similarity with the 'reform school', found in other parts of the world.

See also: delinquency

Further reading

Wills, A. (2007) 'Historical myth-making in juvenile justice policy', *History and Policy*, Policy Paper 60.

DAVID CROOK

APTITUDE

Aptitude can be defined as innate or learned ability or skill, which reflects an individual's intellectual capacity to learn and attain a level of performance or academic achievement in a particular field/discipline. Some view it in respect of quickness of learning, having a particular talent or demonstrating potential and capability for further learning. For example some young children may be said to have 'an aptitude for music' or older students 'an aptitude for computer programming'.

Aptitude is a key dimension in all definitions of intelligence. Within the domain of the heredity/environment nexus, intelligence has been defined as a 'general aptitude for learning or an ability to acquire and use knowledge and skills' (Slavin 2003: 125). Slavin argues that scholars do not share a consensus on the precise meaning of intelligence. They do agree, however, that intelligence is the ability to deal with abstractions, to solve problems, and to learn new knowledge, skills, and values.

In rethinking the concept of aptitude, we need to refer to the legacy of Richard E. Snow (1936–97), who researched extensively human aptitudes and learning environments. In his work, Snow provided a new definition of aptitude, which differed from the cognitive abilities, as it included cognitive (motivational) and affective (emotional) characteristics. He also articulated the 'aptitude complexes' theory, which explained the nexus between personal aptitudes and situational demands. These interact to determine the level of performance. Aptitude, together with metacognition and reflection, plays an important role in problem solving.

There are two opposing views of aptitude, associated with those who maintain that aptitude is innate and those who believe that aptitude can be acquired over the years. Those subscribing to the cognitive theory of learning hold the latter view. Aptitude and ability are closely related concepts. Indeed, critics of schooling in such countries as the United Kingdom – where recent governments have promoted the selection to specialist secondary schools on the grounds of aptitude while not sanctioning the further extension of selection by ability – have queried the distinction between them.

Aptitude tests are specifically designed to measure 'abilities developed over many years and predict how well a student will do in the future at learning unfamiliar material' (Woolfolk and Margetts 2007: 520). For example, colleges, universities and employers may set tests – sometimes of the multiple-choice variety – to demonstrate aptitude for verbal, numerical reasoning or diagrammatic reasoning. The colleges of Oxford University (United Kingdom) have recently introduced a History Aptitude Test (HAT) for use in the selection of candidates for all history degree courses. This test, which aims to examine the skills and potentialities required for the study of history at university, gives us an objective basis for comparing candidates from different backgrounds, including mature applicants and those from different countries. It is designed to be challenging, in order to differentiate effectively between the most able applicants for university courses, including those who may have achieved or can be expected to achieve the highest possible grades in their examinations. In consequence of such developments there is a multitude of 'how to pass' and 'test yourself' aptitude publications aimed at those seeking to enter higher education and at those entering or wishing to change employment.

See also: ability; intelligence/intelligence tests

Further reading

Slavin, R. (2003) *Education Psychology: Theory and Practice*, 7th edn, Boston MA: Allyn and Bacon.
Woolfolk, A. and Margetts, K. (2007) *Educational Psychology*, French's Forest NSW: Pearson.

JOSEPH ZAJDA AND REA ZAJDA

ARISTOTLE (384–322 BCE)

Aristotle of Stagirus was born in Macedonia and learned about medicine through his father. He was a student at Plato's Academy, later becoming tutor to Alexander. When Alexander became king, Aristotle returned to Athens where he established a new school at the Lyceum. The Lyceum used the widest possible range of teaching aids to support learning through observation and deduction. He believed that knowledge only became real when it was exchanged through teaching. He challenged the idealism of Plato, arguing that reality can be known only through experience of observation of physical objects. Thirty books survive of the 150 that he was reputed to have authored. Many are the first treatises of their sort concerning subjects such as zoology, anatomy and economics. It is believed that his books developed through a process of redrafting courses of lectures delivered at the Lyceum. Their rediscovery and shipment to Rome in 83 BCE ensured that his influence was reborn and assimilated into the culture of the expanding empire. His system of logic, including syllogistic deduction, continues to influence critical approaches within science. A second rediscovery in the later Middle Ages by monastic scholars such as Thomas Aquinas, led to the reconciling of his ideas with Christian doctrine and Aristotelian scholasticism became the dogma of the Catholic Church. This was possible because of his monotheistic beliefs. Aristotle is the principal thinker within both Christian and Islamic traditions whose mathematical and philosophical thought structured scientific approaches and content until the seventeenth century.

See also: lyceum; Plato

STEVEN COWAN

ARITHMETIC

Arithmetic, a subject that was once part of the *quadrivium* taught in medieval universities, is usually understood to be the most elementary branch of mathematics, dealing with integers or numerical computation. From an everyday perspective, the most common arithmetical operations are those of addition, subtraction, multiplication and division. In the nineteenth century arithmetic was frequently referred to as one of the vital 'three Rs' (together with reading and writing). An over-reliance on electronic calculators, it is sometimes argued, has led to a decline in children's mental arithmetic skills. In the primary school, children typically develop skills in addition and subtraction, counting and ordering before proceeding to multiplication and division, fractions and decimals. This approach is aimed at building confidence and preparing them for more advanced mathematical work in the secondary school.

See also: mathematics; numeracy

DAVID CROOK

ARMED FORCES

Education in the armed forces covers a range of activities varying in complexity from the acquisition of basic military skills to higher degree studies in specialist technical institutions, staff colleges and universities. Its origins lay with the development of armies and navies as standing professional forces with retained leaders and formal rank structures. From 1670, naval schools were opened in France at Toulon and Rochefort to teach young officers the rudiments of seamanship and navigation, and other European countries also established technical institutions teaching mathematics, artillery and engineering, often run along French or Prussian lines. In Britain, a naval academy was established at Portsmouth in 1733 and the Royal Military Academy was founded at Woolwich eight years later, but most young officers received the bulk of their education in the field or at sea, where it was common for boys to join ships as apprentices and receive a basic mathematical education from sea-going schoolmasters.

The influence of Napoleon on the training and education process was felt both within France, where the concept of military education for all officers, including the cavalry and infantry, was established with opening of a school at St Cyr in 1803, but also in Britain where the expansion of the army to meet the French challenge fostered the Royal Military College, Sandhurst, in the same year. By contrast, the United States Congress still opposed the notion of a standing professional army and was only willing to sanction training and education for a professional corps of military engineers at an academy established at West Point, New York. Nevertheless, by 1815, although they were somewhat different in nature, Britain, France and the United States, together with most European countries, possessed military establishments educating young officers. As the nineteenth century progressed, interest also grew in the concept of professional education for higher command and Prussian practice, which stressed

the study of history as a means of understanding future conflict, was widely admired, particularly in the United States. These wider professional concerns, and the technical challenges posed by an industrial revolution in the world's principal navies, led to the establishment of influential centres of technical and higher education, including the Royal Naval College Greenwich (1873) and the United States Naval War College (1884).

Progress in the education of soldiers and sailors was slower, and for many years restricted to the acquisition of basic skills. In Britain, in 1846, the War Office established an Inspector General of Army Schools whose task was to coordinate the efforts of various regimental schoolmasters, but advances were modest and some twelve years later it was reported that more than 50 per cent of soldiers were still unable to read and write. In the Royal Navy, while some shipboard education had always been available, the advent of harbour training ships for young boys in the 1850s provided a dedicated teaching environment and they were overseen by Her Majesty's Inspectors of Schools. Again, it was advances in the nature of warfare that demanded higher educational standards. The technical transformation of the world's armies and navies, and the establishment of airforces in the early years of the twentieth century, implied a need for better educated personnel. The mass mobilisation required by two world wars also provided an impetus to identify and instil basic skills via professionally designed and accelerated courses. The processes of recruitment and resettlement gave thousands of servicemen exposure to adult education programmes conducted in civilian colleges and universities.

The second half of the twentieth century saw far-reaching changes in armed forces education and many countries invested heavily in 'systematic' approaches, originally pursued in the United States Army, which seemed to promise shorter, cheaper courses with more measurable outcomes. While these had some success in basic training, they were

33

soon shown to have little broader application, and the advent of higher entry standards and better qualified candidates at all levels led, conversely, to less prescriptive courses often linked to civilian accreditation and validation. Trends towards military operations conducted on an international coalition basis seem likely to confirm this inclination and, while professional issues will undoubtedly continue to dominate armed forces' education, the study of the broader social, political and economic context for future military activity will undoubtedly increase in the future.

See also: professional education; technical education/school/college

Further reading

Dickinson, H. W. (2007) *Educating the Navy*, London: Taylor and Francis.
Simons, W. E. (ed.) (2000) *Professional Military Education in the United States – A Historical Dictionary*, Westport CT: Greenwood Press.
H. W. DICKINSON

ARNOLD, MATTHEW (1822–88)

Like his father, Thomas Arnold, Matthew was educated at Winchester College and then at Oxford University. After university, he spent a short time teaching at Rugby School and, despite only moderate success in his degree, he was elected to a fellowship at Oriel College, Oxford in 1845. After two years he was appointed private secretary to Lord Lansdowne, who, as Lord President of the Council in the 1830s, had argued strongly for extending state involvement in schooling. It was through Lansdowne that Arnold secured the post of Inspector of Schools in 1851.

From this time onwards, his life was to take a twin-track, with sustained visiting of schools and teacher training colleges combined with a regular output of poetry and literary criticism. In 1859 Arnold was sent to inspect and report upon education in

Switzerland, Holland and France as part of the Newcastle Report. He opposed the introduction of the 'Revised Code' in 1862, which established a direct link between government grants to schools and tested pupil performance. Arnold is most famous for *Culture and Anarchy* (1869), in which he advocated a view of high culture as setting a standard to resist the advance of a 'philistine' commercial culture. This work was to shape literary criticism and analysis in the English-speaking world for almost a century afterwards. The teaching of literature in schools became dominated by his idea that its purpose was to expose pupils to 'the best that has been thought and said'.

See also: Arnold, Thomas; culture; inspection
STEVEN COWAN

ARNOLD, THOMAS (1795–1842)

Thomas Arnold, headmaster of Rugby School, was a product of an elite education at Winchester College and Corpus Christi, Oxford, where he proved to be an outstanding scholar. His academic achievements led to the award of a fellowship at Oriel College. He was ordained in 1818, becoming deacon at Laleham, Middlesex. Here he opened a small private school designed to prepare boys for entry to university. In 1827 he became headmaster of Rugby School, one of the principal English 'public schools' for the sons of gentlemen. From this position he transformed the social and educational organisation of Rugby and, by transmission, all other such public schools, thus extorting a decisive influence over an entire generation of national leaders during the height of Victorian political and economic expansion. Arnold's work became universally famous through *Tom Brown's Schooldays* (1857) written by Thomas Hughes, an old boy of Rugby. It was during his time as headmaster that the school code used for 'football' was agreed, eventually giving its name to the sport that was codified in distinction to 'soccer'. A famous biography by A. P. Stanley, future dean of Westminster Cathedral, further deepened Arnold's influence amongst clerics, teachers and dons. He believed that the classics had a relevance to the modern world, but whilst at Rugby Arnold also introduced modern subjects like European languages, gave history teaching a more recent focus, made mathematics compulsory and timetabled organised games to build strength and resilience of character. The introduction of a prefect-based pastoral system organised within houses was copied elsewhere and is widely found in schools today.

See also: Arnold, Matthew; public school

STEVEN COWAN

ART

As a curriculum subject in education institutions, art is still relatively young. In Europe, the United States and some other Western countries art instruction was introduced into elementary and secondary schools during the nineteenth century in consequence of the Industrial Revolution. Vocational institutions also developed, including dedicated art schools, trade schools focusing on drawing and schools of decorative arts. Since that time, the boundaries of the subject – often referred to more broadly as 'art and design' or the 'visual arts' – in schools have enlarged to include the dimensions of appreciation, criticism, history, aesthetics and all manner of practical production skills. The emphasis of art (and design) programmes varies between and within countries, but skills widely taught include: drawing (expressive and technical); calligraphy and lettering; ceramics; painting; print-making; sculpture; bricolage; fibre arts; jewellery-making and digital imaging (see Boughton 2000: 956).

As a subject in nineteenth-century Western mass schooling systems, art tended to be an 'additional' or optional subject, though Pestalozzian influences upon elementary education favoured observational drawings of natural and everyday objects to complement the skills of describing, naming and sometimes touching items. At a more advanced level, technical drawing – invariably for boys only – was promoted for practical purposes, such as ship, railway and bridge design. Echoing Plato, Herbert Read, the British founder of the International Society for Education through Art, famously stated that 'art should be the basis of education. ... The aim of education is the creation of artists – of people efficient in the various modes of expression' (Read 1958: 1, 11), but for much of the twentieth century there were as many views about the subject's essential components as there were teachers. Some secondary school art departments emphasised observational drawing and the formal elements of basic design, but others prioritised an issues-based approach – often influenced by cross-curricular teaching with social science and humanities departments – where pupils were encouraged to explore personal responses and social concerns. The subject struggled for status and curriculum time, and continues to do so in some contexts.

Since the 1950s, teachers and practitioners of art have been 'professionalised' by the formation of associations and a body of research literature, communicated in learned journals, focusing on how art is understood, produced and valued. Recognition that human creativity, imagination and expression are reflections of personality, values, philosophies and tastes has helped to challenge the past view that some children 'can't do' art (see Addison and Burgess 2003: 15). But aspects of the subject continue to be contentious. The emphasis sometimes placed on art history tends to reinforce the existing 'heritage' canon and can lead to politicised debates about the relative merits of high, 'pop' and 'street' culture and the reiteration of patriarchal and Western practices. In consequence, subject curricula have sought to better reflect multiculturalism, folk art and the creative traditions of indigenous peoples.

Today, in many countries, the teaching of art is a mandatory subject, with a specified or recommended curriculum. Prior to the introduction of the English National Curriculum, in the early 1990s, inspectors criticised schools' preoccupation with a narrow range of activities, such as still life painting, narrative composition and simple print-making, and their uncritical reliance on 'self-expression', a legacy of nineteenth-century modernist theories. The National Curriculum – which has been subject to two revisions, both times reducing the specified content, and will change again in 2008 – has sought to give more emphasis to education's relationship with the ideas and technologies of contemporary visual culture. Four 'strands' are currently identified in respect of art teaching for 5–14 year-olds: exploring and developing ideas; investigating and making art, craft and design; evaluating and developing work; and knowledge and understanding.

At a global level, there are many higher education institutions teaching undergraduate and postgraduate programmes in art (including fine art, design and art history). Many teacher education institutions have specialist programmes for trainees wishing to work in secondary or high schools and provide training in art education for elementary or primary teachers. Professional art teachers very frequently organise 'real' or 'virtual' public exhibitions of students' – and sometimes their own – creative outputs and, formally or informally, they may influence the way in which their school, college or university markets itself in publicity materials.

See also: crafts; creativity; subjects

Further reading

Addison, N. and Burgess, L. (eds) (2003) *Issues in Art and Design Teaching*, London: Routledge-Falmer.
Boughton, D. G. (2000) 'The shaping of visual arts in education'. In M. Ben-Peretz, S. Brown and B. Moon (eds) *Routledge International Companion to Education*, London: Routledge.

Read, H. (1958) *Education Through Art*, 3rd edn, London: Faber and Faber.

LESLEY BURGESS

ASCHAM, ROGER (1515–68)

Ascham was educated in the home of Sir Humphry Wingfield, a barrister who later became speaker of the House of Commons. He proceeded to St John's College, Cambridge, aged fifteen, graduated three years later, then lectured in mathematics and developed musical skills at Cambridge, thus embodying the Christian humanist ideal. He became the Cambridge regius professor of Greek in 1540, aged twenty-five. He published *Toxophilus*, on the art of bowmanship, in 1543, as much a treatise on character and behaviour as on technical skills. As the country's leading scholar, he was called to the royal court, tutoring Henry VIII's children Prince Edward and Princess Elizabeth. He subsequently served as Latin secretary to both Edward VI and Mary I and became secretary to Queen Elizabeth I in 1559.

His best known publication was *The Scholemaster*, written in the mid-1560s and published posthumously by his wife in 1570. This book was a landmark in the formation of accessible English prose. Ascham argues for praise, rather than punishment, as the incentive for learning. He outlined a double translation method for use by individual tutors and pupils engaged in learning Latin. Although his ideas were derivative of other contemporaries and classical writers, he gave a prominence to the spoken vernacular that was to have lasting influence. Due to repeated re-publication, *The Scholemaster* exerted continuous influence, gaining a new lease of life in 1771 when Samuel Johnson published a revised edition of his works and a biography. *The Scholemaster* shares the distinction with Elyot's *The Governour* of defining, and then influencing, ideas about education and teaching in England for the sons of gentlemen.

See also: Elyot, Sir Thomas

STEVEN COWAN

ASSESSMENT

The root of the word assessment comes from the Latin word meaning 'to sit by', presumably referring to the teacher sitting by the pupil to find out about the pupil's responses. Assessment is now frequently associated with tests or examinations which in turn are used to classify a student by numerical means such as percentages, levels, grades or marks. In this case, assessment can be equated with measurement. Reporting is an essential aspect of measuring, which is why measurement allows for comparisons among students and for standardisations. Measurements can also be made, using assessment instruments such as observation, informal chat, course work, essays, peer assessment, self-assessment, or portfolio collection. If the belief is that ultimately the information can be used to report the amount, extent or level of a student's 'learning', then all these assessments can be equated with measurements. The most common means of measurement, however, is the test (or examination).

Assessments as measurements are most likely to be carried out by the teacher for the pupil, although pupils might measure themselves or each other with reference to a marking key or predetermined set of criteria. In this model of assessment, feedback is based on information usually collected by the teacher about a pupil's current achievement, and the assumption is that the measurement data are complete and valid and remain so outside the measurement situation. In this paradigm, assessment is seen as something external to and unaffected by the assessor. Consequently, results will be considered objective and context-free, available and accessible to a variety of possible audiences.

It is a belief in the fairness accompanying this objectivity that has contributed to the triumph of the examination as the world's most favoured passport to higher education and ultimately employment, as a welcome successor to nepotism and corruption. However, an unquestioning faith in the fairness of examinations has also resulted in the distortion of curricula and classroom learning to accommodate the examinations, and a new discrimination against those examination takers who are unfamiliar with the culture or language of examinations or who are denied access to teachers who can 'teach to the test'.

Traditionally, test developers needed to make sure tests had the qualities of reliability and validity. Reliability meant that the test would produce similar results if administered in similar conditions again. Validity, on the other hand, was about the test articulating appropriately the construct it sampled, which was essentially about fitness for purpose. However, more recently, validity has ceased to be seen as an inherent property of a test. Rather, as Gipps (1994: 62) reminds us, an assessment is only considered valid if the 'consequences of test interpretation and use are not only supportive of intended purposes but also consistent with other social values'.

Intended purposes for assessment can include certification or selection of individuals (served by summative assessment); accountability or improvement for systems or institutions (served by evaluative assessment); and the enhancement of learners' learning (formative assessment). Summative assessments in the form of examinations may be norm referenced or criterion referenced.

As well as meaning 'measurement', assessment can also have the meaning of inquiry. Inquiry means making a search or investigation and suggests an exploratory and sensitive venture, with no clear end points except the assessor's heightened awareness of current developments. Within this paradigm, the purpose of the assessments is a deeper understanding of individuals as learners. Assessment is viewed as part of the learning process, not as separate from it. It is not the *techniques* of assessing that are different from the measurement paradigm, but rather the *beliefs* about how the required knowledge comes about. In this model, the emphasis is not only on what or who is being assessed, but also on the assessor, the inquirer. Serafini (2001: 387) has written that, when assessment is used as inquiry, 'teachers are no longer simply test administrators. Rather, teachers and students are viewed as active creators of knowledge rather than as passive recipients'. Self-assessment and collaborative assessments that are inquiries are also likely to involve learners in reflecting on – and having dialogue about – their learning activities, rather than activities being the final stage of the assessment.

See also: accountability; criterion-referenced tests; evaluation; examinations; formative assessment; norm-referenced tests; summative assessment; test/testing

Further reading

Filer, A. (ed.) (2000) *Assessment: Social Practice, Social Product*, London: RoutledgeFalmer.
Gipps, C. (1994) *Beyond Testing: Towards a Theory of Educational Assessment*, Lewes: Falmer Press.
Serafini, F. (2001) 'Three paradigms of assessment: measurement, procedure, and inquiry', *The Reading Teacher*, 54(4): 384–93.

ELEANORE HARGREAVES

ATHENAEUM

Athenaeum is a term encountered in different contexts across the world. It may be loosely or closely associated with education. In Belgium and the Netherlands, for example, an athenaeum describes a secondary school, one that teaches Latin and Greek in the former country but one that specifically does not in the latter. A different meaning is attached to the Wadsworth Athenaeum, in Hartford, Connecticut. This was built in the early 1840s as the first public art museum in the United States. There are many examples of athenaeums functioning today as public libraries, performing arts centres and meeting rooms for community groups. Others, founded long ago, have long since disappeared.

In Britain, the term athenaeum most commonly refers to a late eighteenth- or early nineteenth-century municipal building where a male membership – typically restricted to a hundred or so men of letters, science and

law – could read, discuss and dine in pleasant surroundings. The Liverpool Athenaeum was opened in 1797, for example. The Glasgow Athenaeum, which now houses the Royal Scottish Academy of Music, was modelled on Manchester's and opened in 1847. In the same year Wolverhampton developed a less socially exclusive institution, the Wolverhampton Athenaeum and Mechanics' Library. One constant at the heart of the municipal British athenaeum was a fine library, but some institutions also organised lecture programmes.

See also: adult education; mechanics' institute; public library

DAVID CROOK

ATTAINMENT

Attainment can be understood as the acquisition of socially desirable knowledge and skills. This is typically defined by the school, by the school curriculum, by an examining body; by a local education body, or by a ministry of education. The term also relates to individual academic achievement in school, perhaps following the marking of students' exercise books, homework assignments, test or examination results. The level of student attainment may be communicated by a teacher's words (spoken or written, briefly or at length), or by marks or grades. At the level of the primary school, however, the teachers' marking criteria may not be solely focused on attainment. It is not uncommon for young children's work to be awarded, for example, 'A for effort', but 'C for attainment'.

Educational attainment is one of the primary indicators of how institutions are compared and measured, both within and across countries. In England, for example, the Department for Education and Skills produces attainment or performance tables ranking schools and colleges. In these circumstances, schools may identify a need to 'raise attainment' levels in one or several areas of the curriculum, perhaps making use of particular strategies and materials devised for school leaders (e.g. Goldsworthy 2000). Inspection outcomes may also specify such objectives. Dissatisfaction with the 'raw data' – founded mostly or solely upon attainment measures – has led, in some instances, to more refined league tables, taking account of 'value-added' measures.

Several Western countries publish official tables setting out the attainment of higher education institutions. Newspapers and student unions may additionally produce unofficial tables, sometimes drawing upon alternative measures, including student satisfaction. The 'league table' culture has had significant implications for the institutional funding formulae and resource distribution mechanisms. Higher education institutions are frequently categorised and ranked according to attainment measures for research and teaching, and there has been particular interest in using such measures to identify an elite of 'world class' universities. The political, social and economic value of attainment can govern and define the future well being and success of both the individual and the institution.

Variables affecting attainment include income, relative poverty, remoteness, and economic inactivity. Any one of these, or some combination of them, may offer an explanation as to why the attainment levels in one institution or among one group of students may appear better or worse than another. In many countries the unequal access to education of girls impacts upon attainment inequality. This is very pronounced, for example, in parts of Sub-Saharan Africa, Latin America and in some states that were formerly part of the Soviet Union. Social, cultural and economic dimensions influencing levels of attainment in schools include such personal factors as wealth, social class, parental level of education and ethnicity. The geographical location of learners can also be an important factor: a recent American publication (Beaulieu et al. 2006) stresses the importance of community collective action to raise educational attainment in rural areas.

See also: accountability; core curriculum/ national curriculum; marking; school effectiveness; school improvement; standards; value added

Further reading

Beaulieu, L. J., Israel, G. D. and Wimberley, R. C. (2006) *Improving Rural Educational Attainment*, Columbia MO: Rural Sociological Society.
Davies, P. (2002) 'Levels of attainment in geography', *Assessment in Education: Principles, Policy and Practice*, 9(2): 185–204.
Goldsworthy, A. (2000) *Raising Attainment in Primary Science*, London: Heinemann.

JOSEPH ZAJDA AND REA ZAJDA

AUSTRALIA

Australia is comprised of 7.7 million square kilometres, most of which is arid or semi-arid. The population is 19 million persons, with an annual increase of approximately 1.8 per cent. In excess of 85 per cent of Australians live in urban areas. People first occupied the landmass about 50,000 years ago. By the time of European contact the Aborigines had spread across the continent. Soon after the establishment of the first penal colony by Britain in 1788, migration of free settlers also began. In 1900, the colonies formed the Federation of the Commonwealth of Australia. Australia, however, remained very much tied to 'the mother country', and 330,000 men fought 'for King and country' in World War I. Australia also fought on the side of the Allies in the World War II. The Australia Act of 1986 gave the nation full legal independence from Britain, but with the monarch still retaining the status of sovereign. Nevertheless, a strong movement for an independent republic exists.

By the middle of the nineteenth century, the Christian churches and the individual colonies were providing education. Between 1872 and 1893, all colonies passed legislation establishing government-controlled school systems and withdrew state aid to church schools. The state schools were to be 'free, compulsory and secular'. Catholics fiercely opposed the Acts and continued to maintain and develop a separate school sector without much state aid until the 1970s.

The churches had instituted secondary education from the middle of the nineteenth century. However, it was not until the end of that century that public sector provision in this area developed. Legislation provided day schooling in what were termed 'high schools'. These provided the base for the secondary systems, which developed in each of the states after federation in 1901. The tyranny of distance provided a great challenge. Travelling teachers' schemes were implemented for students in the outback. Such developments eventually led to the establishment of correspondence schools, which function today as schools of distance education.

A major reason for the control of public schooling in Australia by state education authorities was the desire to give equal educational opportunities to all children. Indeed, until very recently, the education department in each of the six states and two territories was centrally responsible for curriculum, school buildings and supplies, leaving examinations, teachers' salaries, staffing appointments and transfers between schools. Since the 1980s there has been a move towards devolved systems. Nevertheless, very great differences persist in the context of eight autonomous public education systems with varying histories and traditions, varying political parties and priorities, and different stages of development.

Australia has forty, mainly public, universities. The majority were established by Acts of state parliament. The Commonwealth government, however, has acquired the major role in higher education policy and administration due to its key responsibility for funding. The universities were established with professional and practical objectives in mind, looking to the University of London and the Scottish universities for appropriate models. However, 'Oxbridge' and the Irish universities were also influential. By 1914, every state capital had a university. The period 1960–75 was the 'heyday of higher education'. Massive growth in the system was driven by the goals of economic development, equity and access. Since 1993, universities have been subjected to 'quality' reviews and have been required to become more market driven and more entrepreneurial.

Early technical and vocational education developed from mechanics' institutes and schools of art and was the sole responsibility of the states and territories, but, by the 1970s, the federal government began to take a greater interest in the sector as it became clear that traditional industries were beginning to decline and new ones were emerging. By the late 1980s more commonality across the states and territories began to manifest itself with the introduction of national award terminology and an increase in demands for training to meet changing national needs within industry. In 1992, the Australian National Training Authority (ANTA) was established, leading to the national system of Vocational Education and Training (VET) which operates through the cooperation of all states and territories.

Amongst the major educational issues regularly highlighted in Australia at the present time are inequities resulting from the significant increase in financial assistance to the private schools over the last decade, poor retention rates of Aboriginal students, changes in teachers' work, decrease in government funding to universities at a time of large growth in student numbers, and the over-reliance of universities on the fees paid by their large cohorts of foreign students.

See also: indigenous education

Further reading

Coaldrake, P. and Stedman, L. (1998) *On the Brink: Australia's Universities Confronting Their Future*, St Lucia: University of Queensland Press.

Department of Employment, Education, Training and Youth Affairs (1998) *Learning for Life: Final*

Report – *Review of Higher Education Financing and Policy*, Canberra ACT: Australian Government Publishing Service.

Marginson, S. (1997) *Educating Australia: Government, Economy and Citizen since 1960*, Cambridge: Cambridge University Press.

ANTHONY POTTS AND TOM O'DONOGHUE

AUSTRALIAN ASSOCIATION FOR RESEARCH IN EDUCATION (AARE)

The Australian Association for Research in Education (AARE) is a network of researchers which fosters educational research in Australia. It is a membership organisation with an elected executive committee that runs the organisation. It was formed in 1970 as a forum for discussion among researchers and a pressure group for educational research. At this time members were predominantly male, although most of the approximately 1,000 members are now female. AARE organises annual conferences and workshops and supports regional research groupings which help to forge communities of researchers. International contacts exist with other educational research associations. Special interest groups (SIGs) are organised by members on areas of interest such as assessment, early childhood, and educational philosophy and theory; each SIG will usually organise a session(s) at the annual conference.

AARE presents awards for outstanding research as well as for doctoral and early career researchers which helps to encourage student participation. It publishes professional and general publications including the peer reviewed journal, the *Australian Educational Researcher*, as well as a newsletter, the *AARE News*. Under the title of *Review of Australian Research in Education* (*RARE*) it has published a number of monographs relating to Australian education and research. It also influences educational policy in Australia by making submissions to government and policy makers and lobbying in order to strengthen the position of educational research. It has developed a code of ethics applicable to educational research.

See also: Australia; educational research

TOM WOODIN

AUTISM

Autism is a pervasive developmental disorder in which development is not only delayed but is also deviant. The term 'autistic spectrum disorder' (ASD) is used to indicate the variation of manifestations of autism between and within individuals.

Autism was first defined as a syndrome in 1943 by Leo Kanner in America. Kanner described the defining features of autism as being an inability to develop social relationships; obsessive insistence on the maintenance of sameness; repetitive and stereotyped play activities; mutism, or non-communicative use of speech; good rote memory; 'normal' physical appearance; oversensitivity to stimuli. A year later, in Austria, Hans Asperger identified a similar group of children as having autism. He proposed the following criteria: borderline, average or above-average intellectual functioning; naive, inappropriate social approaches to others; intense, circumscribed or 'special' interest in particular subjects; good spoken language, but monotonous speech and a lack of two-way conversation; lack of 'common sense'.

In 1979 Lorna Wing and Judith Gould examined all children aged under fifteen in one London borough who had any physical, behavioural or learning disability. They identified a group of children with 'classic' Kanner autism but also a further discrete group who were different from the group of children with severe learning disabilities. The shared characteristics of this discrete group were difficulties in social behaviour, in language and communication, and in the ability to think and behave flexibly. These difficulties became known as 'the triad of impairments'.

Autism is present from birth or very early in development. It can also appear after a period of around thirty months of apparently typical development. The average age of diagnosis is around five years for autism and around eleven years for Asperger's syndrome. The major diagnostic criteria are the *International Statistical Classification of Diseases and Related Health Problems, Tenth Edition* (ICD-10) and the *Diagnostic and Statistical Manual of Mental Disorders, Fourth Edition* – revised (DSMIV-R). Male to female ratios vary from 2:1 to around 5:1. About 75–85 per cent of children diagnosed with autism have learning disabilities, with a greater likelihood of females experiencing severe learning disabilities. IQ scores tend to be very stable over time. About one third of individuals with autism develop epilepsy, with early childhood and adolescence being peak times.

Individuals with autism are better at non-verbal, visual-spatial tasks than verbal ones. Some individuals with autism have been found to have excellent rote memory or to show particular abilities in – and affinity for – the world of physical objects. Psychological theories on the nature of autism include theory of mind (TOM) theories which suggest that many of the difficulties experienced by individuals with autism result from their difficulty in understanding their own, and others' mental states. The early psychoanalytic view of 'refrigerator' (cold, unfeeling) parents causing autism has been found to have no basis in fact. There is now overwhelming evidence for a biological basis and a strong genetic component (Medical Research Council 2001). Epidemiological data indicate that the incidence of ASD is in the order of 30 to 60 cases per 10,000, as compared with estimates of 4 per 10,000 made in the 1960s (Rutter 2005). There is general consensus that this increase in the rate of individuals diagnosed with ASD is largely due to better ascertainment and a broadening of the diagnostic concept.

Autism has not been found to be associated with socio-economic status, parents' IQ scores, or any particular ethnic group. The majority of children diagnosed with autism are eligible for special education services. A typical placement in the UK for children with autism who are at the lower end of the IQ scale is a special school for children with severe learning disabilities. For children with 'higher functioning autism' and Asperger's syndrome a typical placement is a mainstream school with additional support. Early intervention is seen as crucial. Education is the primary form of intervention. Educational interventions which have been particularly associated with autism include Treatment and Education of Autistic and related Communication-handicapped Children (TEACCH), Daily Life Therapy, Picture Exchange Communication System (PECS) and behavioural approaches such as the 'Lovaas method'. Evaluations of educational interventions generally have concluded that no one approach has been found to be superior to others.

See also: inclusive education; learning disabilities; special education/special educational needs/special needs

Further reading

Frith, U. (2003) *Autism: Explaining the Enigma*, Oxford: Blackwell.
Jones, G. (2002) *Educational Provision for Children with Autism and Asperger Syndrome: Meeting their Needs*, London: David Fulton.
Medical Research Council (2001) *Review of Autism Research: Epidemiology and Causes*, London: MRC.
Rutter, M. (2005) 'Aetiology of autism: findings and questions', *Journal of Intellectual Disability Research*, 49(4): 231–38.

DAWN B. MALE

AUTODIDACT

The common definition of an autodidact is one who is self-taught. It is often used to describe anyone who has directed his or her own learning for a significant duration of time. Well known examples include such people as William Blake or F. Scott Fitzgerald, who dropped out of college to pursue writing.

Autodidact implies that someone has educated him or herself and generally refers to self-directed learning away from existing educational institutions. This is something of a misnomer, given that autodidacts tend to have actively participated in collective forms of domestic, private and other associations and movements from which they received a form of education. Many also receive support from significant others in families, networks and, more recently, through the internet.

In many countries, notably Britain, historians have traced a working-class autodidactic tradition from the late eighteenth century until the early or mid-twentieth century. Some of these autodidacts wrote autobiographies in which they outlined their own learning and development, which, while being erratic and eclectic, was also considerable, exemplified in the life of radicals such as Thomas Cooper and William Lovett. Many, but by no means all, were men closely allied with social and labour movements, including adult education, where they found a home.

See also: adult education; home schooling; informal/nonformal learning

TOM WOODIN

AUTONOMY

The word 'autonomy' derives from the Greek roots *autos* (self) and *nomos* (law) and signifies a right or capacity of *self-governance*. The right to manage one's own affairs and the related right of citizens to participate in the collective self-governance of their society are generally understood to rest on possession of the capacities essential to prudent self-governance. Children, whose capacities have not fully matured, are understood to possess autonomy rights in a prospective, or forward-looking, way that places responsible adults under an obligation to nurture the development of their abilities and judgement. The idea of autonomy rights is, in this way, a starting point for an important tradition of theory concerning the aims of education and the moral dimensions of educational authority.

That tradition began in Greek antiquity and is manifested in the work of Plato (428–

347/8 BCE) and Aristotle (384–322 BCE) in a cluster of related ideas: that respect for persons as rational beings creates a collective responsibility to provide education that promotes the development and free exercise of good judgement and other intellectual virtues; that such education is fundamental to enabling persons to rationally govern themselves and participate in constitutional rule; that such education is foundational to enabling persons to live flourishing lives, because the exercise of intellectual virtues is intrinsic to living well and the possession of good judgement is instrumental to living well.

Similar ideas were advanced by John Locke (1632–1704) and other modern liberal political philosophers. Locke held that a parent's authority to govern a child derives from, and is limited by, a duty to provide care and an education preparatory to rational self-governance in accordance with moral and human law. Laying great emphasis on the active exercise of one's rational capacities, both in learning and in life, he held that, in order to act freely, we must learn to withhold judgement until we have thoroughly examined the rational basis for the beliefs we act from. This Enlightenment embrace of personal autonomy was aptly captured by Immanuel Kant (1724–1804) in the imperative, 'Have the courage to use your own understanding!'

Many contemporary educational theorists associate the idea of autonomy almost exclusively with Kant and contend that autonomy presupposes a disembodied and metaphysically problematic 'liberal self'. An alternative view is that the specific contemporary meanings of the term 'autonomy' reflect a variety of concerns quite different from Kant's, and do not presuppose his theory of 'autonomy of the will'. A concern that animates most discussions of autonomy in educational philosophy is the inclination of some parents and defenders of cultural group rights to restrict the education of children in ways that unjustifiably limit their opportunities to lead fulfilling lives or diminish their ability to engage fellow citizens in respectful and productive dialogue. In this context, those who advocate autonomy-facilitating education envision schools that would provide a modest counterweight to the power of home and culture in shaping identity, values, and options. A second concern is that governments may violate liberty rights themselves by procuring the cooperation of citizens through deception and seductive ritual. Legitimate governance is transacted primarily through reasoned and truthful persuasion, predicated on education that enables citizens to exercise their own reasoned and informed judgement about public affairs.

Contemporary political philosophers typically associate the idea of living autonomously with John Stuart Mill (1806–73), a champion of individuality and free experimentation in unconventional ways of life, but they disavow Mill's ideal as a guiding aim of education. Society must act in defence of a 'right of exit', or right to opt out of one's parents' or community's way of life. It may do this by insisting that all children receive instruction in critical thinking and exposure to diverse conceptions of how to live; but respect for legitimate diversity of opinion about the good life precludes the endorsement of any particular conception of how to live, including Mill's. Children's futures must be reasonably 'open' in order for their adult rights of self-determination to have meaning and a good prospect of yielding flourishing lives; but educational preparation for meaningful life choices must recognise that many young people will reflectively endorse the lives of faith and community commitment they have grown up with. The literature on schooling and autonomy explores the significance of these themes for multicultural education, parental choice, religious education and other matters.

See also: Aristotle; Locke, John; Mill, John Stuart; philosophy of education; Plato

Further reading

Callan, E. (1997) *Creating Citizens*, Oxford: Clarendon Press.
Curren, R. (2006) 'Developmental liberalism', *Educational Theory*, 56(4): 451–68.
Levinson, M. (1999) *The Demands of Liberal Education*, Oxford: Oxford University Press.

RANDALL CURREN

B

BASELINE ASSESSMENT

Baseline assessment (BA) refers to school entry assessment at ages 4–5, a process which became popular in the UK in the 1990s. Lindsay and Desforges (1998) identified nine purposes of BA, which can be grouped into two major categories: child-focused (pedagogic) and school-focused (managerial). The former concerns the identification of children with difficulties at an early age in order to remediate or at least ameliorate their problems by appropriate teaching. This approach, often called screening, has a long tradition in developmental paediatrics. Educationists initially developed systems to assess 7–8 year-olds when significant problems learning to read were apparent, but subsequently changed focus onto children entering school in order to identify those 'at risk' of developing such difficulties.

The second purpose is to provide a baseline against which to measure children's progress and hence to measure 'value added' by the school over Key Stage One (5–7 years). This process was initially developed to support the examination of secondary schools' effectiveness and later became a variable in constructing league tables of schools.

In 1998 statutory requirements were laid down requiring all state schools in England to assess children within seven weeks of school entry using an accredited BA scheme. Criteria for accreditation specified the domains (language, literacy, numeracy and personal and social development) but not their detail;

a requirement to provide a report of findings to parents; and the time to be spent assessing each child (20 minutes maximum). Ninety-one schemes were approved: a small number were carefully developed and evaluated schemes with technical data, but many were 'home grown' LEA schemes often lacking such evidence.

A study of the national baseline assessment scheme (Lindsay and Lewis 2003) identified several strengths. Reception teachers saw its value in helping to understand the child's developmental status during their first term in school, facilitating target setting, identification of special educational needs and setting by ability. Head teachers, however, welcomed its use for 'value added' analysis, especially in schools where pupils had low skill levels on entry, as the children's progress over Key Stage One might allow a more positive representation than absolute levels of attainment at seven years. Limitations with the national scheme included inability to compare children or schools because of the ninety-one different schemes. Also, as children could improve within the seven weeks, different scores could be obtained depending on when BA was administered: schools realised that to optimise 'value added' the lowest initial score (week one) was preferable, producing the greatest difference with later scores and so greatest 'value added'.

Because of these limitations the UK government decided to limit statutory BA to a single scheme (QCA and DfES 2003) administered during the reception year with the final scores being required at the end of

45

this period. This improved conformity but at the loss of the primary pedagogic purposes: early identification of SEN and informing teaching targets and methods at school entry.

Research undertaken on BA has also produced interesting findings about children's educational development. Girls are consistently superior at five years on both learning/educational and social/behavioural factors. The lack of difference between white and African Caribbean children has raised important questions about why the latter have relatively lower attainment later during their schooling. The importance of English language competence has been shown by the significantly lower levels of BA by children whose first language is not English, but who then demonstrate steeper growth curves between five and seven years as they gain English competence, and have similar levels of reading and numeracy at the end of Key Stage One.

Baseline assessment is an interesting example of a government building upon the work of practitioners, using this expertise and then changing the system in the light of research. The statutory system has compromises and requires evaluation of its technical quality. The major challenge, however, remains and is inherent in the attempts to construct an assessment programme with two quite different purposes. The evidence to date suggests this has not been achieved and that the pedagogic benefits may have lost out to a system that is more consistent for 'value added' but less useful for teachers. The pedagogic, child focus has given way to the managerial, school focus, holding schools to account, but it is not clear that the technical quality of the single scheme introduced is adequate for this purpose or superior to other methods available.

See also: assessment; literacy; numeracy; primary school/education; special education/ special educational needs/special needs; value added

Further reading

Lindsay, G. and Desforges, M. (1998) *Baseline Assessment: Practice, Problems and Possibilities*, London: David Fulton.
Lindsay, G. and Lewis, A. (2003) 'An evaluation of the use of accredited baseline assessment schemes in England', *British Educational Research Journal*, 29(2): 149–67.
Qualifications and Curriculum Authority and Department for Education and Skills (2003) *Foundation Stage Profile*, London: QCA.

GEOFF LINDSAY

BASIC SKILLS

The basic skills – sometimes termed 'basic skills for employability' – of learning are traditionally thought to mean the '3 Rs' of reading, writing and arithmetic. The concept is derived from the nineteenth-century utilitarian view of education, summed up by the Reverend James Fraser's view, in England, that, by the age of ten,

> the peasant boy ... shall be able to spell correctly the words that he will ordinarily have to use; he shall read a common narrative – the paragraph in the newspaper that he cares to read – with sufficient ease to be a pleasure to himself and to convey information to listeners; if gone to live at a distance from home, he shall write his mother a letter that shall be both legible and intelligible; he knows enough of ciphering to make out, or test the correctness of, a common shop bill; if he hears talk of foreign countries he has some notions as to the part of the habitable globe in which they lie; and underlying all ... he has acquaintance enough with the Holy Scriptures to follow the allusions and the arguments of a plain Saxon sermon, and a sufficient recollection of the truths taught him in his catechism, to know what are the duties required of him towards his Maker and his fellow man.

Literacy and numeracy are regarded as the key basic skills, but information and communications technology is sometimes identified as a third area of adult basic skills.

See also: arithmetic; literacy; numeracy; reading; skills; writing

DAVID CROOK

BEECHER, CATHARINE (1800–78)

Catharine Beecher was born in New York but lived and worked in Connecticut and Cincinnati. Beecher was an early American feminist and pioneer woman educationist. She believed that women's roles as carers and nurturers of the following generation fitted them well for the role of teaching, extending their influence from the home into the public sphere of the school. As the mother was so important, women ought to be educated in order to completely fulfil this crucial role. She believed that women should have access to higher learning and gave expression to this when she established the Hartford Female Seminary at the age of twenty-three. Her idea was to challenge women's thinking through education.

Beecher established another school in Cincinnati, where she introduced systematic physical exercise as part of the curriculum, known as calisthenics. Beecher influenced Dio Lewis (1823–86), a pioneer of American physical education. Beecher's publications include *The Moral Instructor for Schools and Families: Containing Lessons on the Duties of Life* (1838), where the book's female subject is cast in a political and civic light and not seen solely in domestic terms, and *A Treatise on Domestic Economy* (1841), which relates the girls' curriculum to the aspiration of improving health. An example of her organisational drive and wider influence was the establishment of the American Women's Educational Association (1850). Several women's colleges around the United States were founded in response to her ideas and support.

See also: health education; physical education/ training

STEVEN COWAN

BEHAVIOURISM

Arising in the early part of the twentieth century, behaviourism is a school of psychology based on the belief that studying behaviour – as overt and visible action – is either the best method of investigation for psychology or, in fact, the only true subject of psychology. Directly countering the mentalist psychologists of the late nineteenth century and their appeal to introspection, memory, reasoning, and will, behaviourism sought to create an objective and verifiable science of psychology that was grounded in the understanding that measurable and observable data must serve as the primary basis for both experimentation and theory. The early period, known as 'classical behaviourism', included behaviourists such as John Watson, Ivan Pavlov, and Edward Lee Thorndike. Particularly important in this period was the stimulus-response model of behaviour. Behaviourism dominated psychological theory after World War I and a variety of behaviourist approaches began to evolve. Neo-behaviourism became the best known of these derivative approaches and, as practised by B. F. Skinner and Clark L. Hull, included attempts to incorporate notions of the internal states of mind, such as feelings and perception, while still maintaining the objective nature of investigation. Skinner's development of the concept of 'operant conditioning' emphasised the consequences of behaviour as informing a subject's response.

Behaviourism continued to evolve and have relevance for psychological theory well into the 1950s and later, being basic to the development of what is known as behaviour therapy or behaviour modification. Criticism of behaviourism generally focuses on its deterministic paradigm, where all behaviour is simply a product of external stimuli, and the concern that the so-called *inner life* of the mind is ignored and ultimately devalued.

See also: psychology; Skinner, Burrhus Fredric; Thorndike, Edward L.

PAUL COLLINS

BELL CURVE

The term 'bell curve', first coined in the 1870s, describes the pattern of a statistical normal distribution, in this case that of IQ scores. It created a major controversy in the United States of America in the 1990s when Herrnstein and Murray published a book of this name that claimed that Americans with high intelligence, and their children, comprised a cognitive elite in society. It also suggested that black people tended to be less intelligent than whites and Asians, partly due to genetic factors, an argument that followed that of the psychologist Arthur Jensen. It concluded with proposals including the ending of welfare programmes. Critiques of this work attacked the psychological assumptions that underlay it, such as the supposed link between intelligence and genetics and the reduction of intelligence to a single number. They also refuted the elitism suggested by the image of the bell curve, and the fatalistic attitude that it represented in relation to the inequalities in American society, portending the maintenance of social hierarchy and potentially the rebirth of eugenics. It was a controversy that reflected in acute form the tensions that have grown around meritocratic ideals, and the antagonisms that have developed between many psychological understandings of education and those of other social scientists.

See also: elitism; intelligence/intelligence tests; meritocracy

Further reading

Fraser, S. (ed.) (1995) *The Bell Curve Wars*, New York: Basic Books.

Herrnstein, R. and Murray, C. (1994) *The Bell Curve: Intelligence and Class Structure in American Life*, New York: Free Press.

GARY McCULLOCH

BENCHMARKING

Benchmarking is defined as the analysis of performance across organisations or parts of an organisation with a view to improvement. Kelly (2001) suggests that there are two types: one relying on a comparison of outcomes against an average statistical attainment; the other on a comparison of critical processes against those in another organisation acknowledged to be more effective. The latter is prevalent in the world of business; the former in not-for-profit sectors like education.

Comparative process benchmarking began in 1959 in the Xerox Corporation, when analysis revealed a large disparity in terms of performance between the corporation's different subsidiaries. Thus a comparative process was born that focuses on how 'critical processes' (defined as ones which, if done badly, result in the organisation failing to achieve its primary purpose) as opposed to 'functional processes' (ones undertaken merely to fulfil legal or statutory obligations) can best be performed.

In the United Kingdom, the Department for Children, Schools and Families defines benchmarking in schools as a process of measuring performance against that achieved by others with broadly similar characteristics (DfES 2006a), and it requires education managers to use benchmarking data (contained in the annual 'Autumn Package') to assist them in planning school improvement. Some schools are more successful than others in helping pupils to achieve their potential; schools with different intakes achieve different results, but so too do schools with similar intakes. The 'Autumn Package' presents benchmarking data in such a way as to highlight the differences in performance of *similar* schools, taking into account factors such as prior attainment and the proportion of pupils eligible for free school meals, which research suggests are both strongly correlated with examination performance. Head teachers are expected to use the tables to 'probe for the reasons that lie behind the numbers' (DfES 2006a) and to identify priorities for school improvement and set challenging targets for pupils.

Schools also use benchmarking in their financial management. In the United Kingdom, all maintained schools are required to submit Consistent Financial Reporting (CFR) returns, using a framework of income and expenditure developed by the DfES, the Audit Commission and the schools inspectorate (Ofsted). Financial benchmarking data allow managers to identify significant differences in the way schools manage their resources. Through comparison with the income and expenditure profile for other similar (in terms of size, type, percentage of pupils with special needs, and so on) schools, managers can determine whether or not there is scope for improving efficiency (DfES 2006b).

Statistical benchmarking in education is based on a comparison of schools with similar socio-economic characteristics. Upper quartile figures represent the standards that the best performing schools are achieving and the median marks the benchmark for under-performance. While the process of benchmarking is helpful in many ways, not least because it adds structure and uniformity to how and when school managers think about improvement, statistical benchmarking as an approach is deficient in some major respects:

(i) It focuses on *what* is achieved (output) and not *how* it is achieved (process). Processes can be planned but outcomes can only be hoped for, so statistical benchmarking devalues strategic planning as a management tool.

(ii) It encourages schools towards a median performance rather than excellence per se, and in a normative way guarantees

that there will always be 'failing' schools no matter how good they are.

(iii) It ignores individual critical processes and focuses instead on whole-school attainment. In doing so, it supposes that schools are single organic entities rather than networks of sometimes conflicting and sometimes cooperating professionals.

(iv) It discourages cooperation between schools, which are only judged successful if others are judged failures. An effective school helping a less effective school guarantees only to threaten its own position by being pulled back towards the average.

(v) It encourages schools to benchmark only against others operating in similar socio-economic circumstances, which is self-contradictory as it supposes that socio-economic circumstance is the major determinant of pupil achievement while at the same time acknowledging that there is a wide range of achievement within any catchment.

See also: economics of education; educational targets; performance indicators; school effectiveness; school improvement; under-achievement

Further reading

DfES (2006a) www.teachernet.gov.uk/management/atoz/b/benchmarking/
—— (2006b) www.teachernet.gov.uk/management/atoz/f/financialbenchmarking/
Kelly, A. (2001) *Benchmarking for School Improvement: A Practical Guide for Comparing and Improving Effectiveness*, London: RoutledgeFalmer.

ANTHONY KELLY

BERNSTEIN, BASIL (1925–2000)

Bernstein came from the poor Jewish community of the East End of London, studied sociology at the London School of Economics and then qualified as a teacher at Kingsway Day College. He taught classes of post

49

office messenger boys and dockers at the City Day College between 1954 and 1960. His background, which included a period in the army towards the end of World War II, having volunteered under-age for the Royal Air Force, provided the personal basis for an interest in phonetics and linguistics. He was especially interested in the ways that speech patterns reflect social origins. Bernstein joined University College, London as a research assistant in 1960 and, within seven years, had become professor and head of the Sociology Department of the University of London Institute of Education. His impact on education and linguistics began in the mid-1960s: his publications argued that socially determined and mediated linguistic codes restrict success in formal education. This 'deficit model' of forms of speech exerted a major influence upon teacher training and resource development. He wrote of privileged 'elaborated codes' and disadvantaged 'restricted codes', suggesting a determinism and critical attitude towards the working classes that he had never intended. During the final thirty years of his life he published five landmark elaborations of his ideas about language, power, control, social positioning and discourse, which abandoned earlier suggestions of inherent deficits. The last of these volumes, *Pedagogy, Symbolic Control and Identity* (1996) encapsulated the fruits of the critical dialogue that Bernstein engaged in over many years with Pierre Bourdieu. For Bernstein, one of the powers of speech was its ability to produce symbolic resources that created community identities.

See also: Bourdieu, Pierre; sociology of education

STEVEN COWAN

BICULTURAL EDUCATION

Bicultural education suggests curricula and pedagogies for learners who experience life in two cultures, rather than a monoculture. Since the late 1960s there have been some notable policies to promote bicultural education, in the United States especially. In many instances bicultural education initiatives represent a belated recognition that, in the past, indigenous languages and cultures have not been respected by education system planners and policy makers. This has been so for the indigenous Maori people of New Zealand, for example. The promotion of bicultural education is allied to bilingual education, so many initiatives take the form of 'bilingual-bicultural' education programmes. The nature of human migration and immigration determines that multicultural education is an objective in many Western societies.

See also: bilingual education; indigenous education; multicultural education

DAVID CROOK

BILINGUAL EDUCATION

Bilingual education is educational provision in which two languages play some role as media of instruction. It aims to support both the maintenance of an existing language and the learning of a new one, with the overall goal of enabling learners to operate in two languages with a high degree of proficiency. The design of the programmes varies widely. Some involve total immersion in the second language for either the first few years or the whole period of schooling; others are known as 'dual language immersion', where both languages are used as media of instruction for varying lengths of time. In a further model, known as 'transitional bilingualism', the mother tongue is used as instructional medium only as a transition to a monolingual curriculum in the target language, often English.

The first extensive bilingual education programmes were developed in the 1970s in francophone Quebec in Canada, initially for anglophone learners of French. Later, similar programmes were developed in English-speaking areas of Toronto. In each case the model was total immersion. In these programmes the mother tongue was not threatened and research found that children gained a second language with no risk to the maintenance of the first. The end result was competence in both languages at a high cognitive level. More recently, the term 'elite bilingualism' has come to be used to describe this model, typified by cases where parents, usually from the middle classes, opt for instruction through the medium of a high-prestige language, most often English or French, or a valued heritage language, such as Welsh.

A contrasting model was developed in the context of the teaching of immigrants in the United States. Here, bilingual education programmes were designed for those whose bilingualism was a consequence of necessity, rather than choice. Frequently children were educated through transitional programmes where the first language was maintained only until it was judged feasible for them to benefit from English monolingual programmes.

The success of bilingual educational programmes, most of which are documented in North America, is variably interpreted, largely because of the widely differing circumstances of the educational provision. One of the most influential research studies is that by Thomas and Collier (1997), who investigated the outcomes of different kinds of bilingual programmes over ten years. Their findings, along with those of other studies, support the effectiveness of dual language bilingual programmes for traditionally low-achieving groups in the US. A crucial factor in the eventual success of such programmes is the opportunity for students to draw on existing linguistic resources. If the first language is developed to a high level there is cross-linguistic transfer so that time spent developing one language is not at the expense of the second. This is on the basis of what Cummins and Swain (1986) call a 'common underlying proficiency' or CUP. On the basis of the CUP principle, literacy abilities in particular, developed in one language, will support literacy acquisition in the second.

A major turning point in the development of bilingual education came with Proposition 227 in California, which voted to ban public-school bilingual education. The debate around Proposition 227 has become intense, fuelled in part by the fear that English, as the national language, might be neglected in bilingual education programmes, although the professed goal of most of these is high levels of literacy and oracy in two languages.

Overall, while transitional bilingual education programmes, especially of short duration, have been relatively less successful, there appears to be an emerging consensus among language researchers that dual language programmes are effective in developing English language academic skills among linguistic minority learners (see Cummins 2000 for a full analysis of the research studies).

While educators continue to debate the educational consequences of the different models of bilingual education, politicians tend to see minority language education largely in terms of the need to integrate minority groups around a common national language, frequently English. For the foreseeable future, while elite bilingual education programmes mushroom worldwide for linguistic majority students, particularly through the medium of English, possibilities for disadvantaged linguistic minorities to maintain their first language at the same time as acquiring a second, prestigious, one, diminish.

See also: bicultural education; curriculum; indigenous education; literacy; modern languages

Further reading

Cummins, J. (2000) *Language, Power and Pedagogy: Bilingual Children in the Crossfire*, Clevedon: Multilingual Matters.
Cummins, J. and Swain (1986) *Bilingualism and Education*, London: Longman.
Thomas, W. P. and Collier, V. (1997) *School Effectiveness for Language Minority Students*, Washington DC: National Clearinghouse for Bilingual Education.

CATHERINE WALLACE

BINARY SYSTEM

The term 'binary system' is very well known internationally. In mathematics it refers to a numeral system with only two digits: 0 and 1. It is widely used in magnetic storage devices and can be easily applied to electronic circuitry. It is almost universally employed in modern computers. In astronomy the term refers to a system of two stars that revolve around each other under the influence of mutual attraction.

In British higher education 'binary system' has a specialised meaning. As the name suggests, it refers to a system with two distinct and separate strands. Such arrangements were in place in Britain for about a quarter of a century from the mid-1960s until the early 1990s.

After the report of the Robbins Committee (1963) it was clear that the university sector which formed one of the strands of the binary system would expand, but in terms of structure and organisation would continue much as before. The bulk of the funds for the universities came from central government but were distributed through the University Grants Committee, which had been set up as early as 1919. It was intended to form a buffer between autonomous higher education institutions on the one hand and central government funding on the other, protecting the academic freedom of the universities from potential political interference. This sector concentrated on research and on teaching postgraduate and honours degree courses.

On the other side of the binary line was the local authority sector (later often referred to as the public sector) of higher education. This concept was developed in the mid-1960s. The Robbins Committee recognised the existence of important provisions for higher education in several local authority technical colleges but did not map out a clear future for these institutions, leaving them in limbo. Interest groups, led by the local education authorities and followed by the technical college teachers' union, began to suggest that there should be a new and distinct local authority sector of higher education set up. Toby Weaver, the deputy secretary at the Ministry of Education, (later Department of Education and Science), quickly took up these ideas, proposing a local authority sector of higher education to be led by newly designated polytechnics. There was much less emphasis on research in the polytechnics than in the universities, and they were developed primarily as teaching institutions. During the 1970s the local education authority traditions in advanced work – technical colleges and teacher training – were merged in several of the growing polytechnics and new institutes of higher education.

From the outset, central government was interested in expanding but controlling the costs of the local authority sector of higher education. The local education authorities maintained that, as the providing bodies, they should be permitted to develop their own institutions in their own ways. At the same time there were regular tensions between polytechnic directors and their local authorities, which were often held in very low regard. In addition, senior civil servants, with varying support from different ministers, stressed the need for more effective national leadership, planning and management in this expensive sector.

During the 1980s, student numbers increased dramatically on this side of the binary line, but institutions expanded at the price of an ever-reducing unit of resource. In 1981, the National Advisory Body (NAB) for Local Authority Higher Education was set up. NAB gave central government a greater steer over the planning, development and funding of this sector, and it was increasingly clear that the rationale for having two separate sectors of higher education in a small country was being questioned. The first step towards new arrangements was taken in 1988, when the Education Reform Act removed the polytechnics and colleges from local authority control and made them into independent corporations. Polytechnic directors, however, continued to question why their institutions were denied the title 'university', which they believed brought status and gave advantage in an increasingly competitive higher education market. Further legislation, in 1992, gave most institutions in the public sector the right to use the term 'university' in their names. From 1993 the pre- and post-1992 universities and some colleges were placed together under the auspices of either the Higher Education Funding Council England or Wales, as appropriate. Thus, a unitary structure for higher education replaced the binary system.

See also: dual system; higher education; mathematics; polytechnic

Further reading

Pratt, J. (1997) *The Polytechnic Experiment 1965–1992*, Buckingham: Open University Press.
Sharp, P. (1987) *The Creation of the Local Authority Sector of Higher Education*, Lewes: Falmer Press.
PAUL SHARP

BINET, ALFRED (1857–1911)

Binet, the French psychologist, trained in law and, after graduating in 1878, went on to study the natural sciences at the Sorbonne. He developed a personal interest in psychology, becoming a researcher in a Parisian neurological clinic in the 1880s. The birth of his two daughters redirected his interests towards child development. He was successively a researcher, associate director and director of the Sorbonne Laboratory of Experimental Psychology until 1911. Binet wrote widely on all psychological areas, but is most remembered for his work on measuring intelligence.

He developed, with his colleague Theodore Simon – who co-authored with Binet the influential *Mentally Defective Children* (1914) – an ascending scale of tasks which they thought were representative of the abilities of typical children at certain ages. The idea was to measure a child's attainment against a normative scale. The resulting score was described as the child's 'mental age'. Binet never believed that this measure was sufficient and stressed the importance of other qualitative evidence being used when assessing a child's abilities or development. From his work the term 'Intelligence Quotient' (or IQ) entered the language.

The Binet-Simon scale was appropriated by the American eugenicist H. Goddard and by Lewis Terman, who sought to use the test as an instrument for sterilisation, leading Binet to denounce this misuse of his work. Revised versions of the test were also applied to the United States Army. Concern about the low mental age of recruits heightened fears about the 'menace of the feebleminded'.

See also: intelligence/intelligence tests; psychology; psychology of education
STEVEN COWAN

BIOLOGY

Biology can be defined as a component of the natural sciences which focuses on the study of life. It investigates the functioning and biodiversity of life on Earth over time, whether in the recent, or more distant, past, to establish scientific explanations for the various kinds of organisms, including humans, that have evolved, and the biological relationships between organisms and the ecosystems in which they live. In particular, biology bases its explanations on empirical evidence gathered through the processes and mechanisms involved in the nature and methodology of science in order to better understand, explain, and make predictions about the origin, evolution, growth and development, structure and function, and distribution of life on multiple levels. These levels include the atomic and molecular basis of life, individual cells, tissues, organs, organ systems, organisms, and populations.

Biology encompasses both the ancient and most current scientific disciplines; however, its historical roots reside in the study of natural philosophy and history. The term biology was not used until the early part of the nineteenth century when naturalists, reacting against eighteenth-century natural historians' and philosophers' preoccupation with the anatomy and physiology of humans, the domestication of plants and animals, and cataloguing of different plants, animals, and minerals found in nature, wanted to redefine this area of science to include a focus on the study of life and the functioning of living things. It wasn't until the mid-nineteenth century, when two British naturalists, Charles Darwin (1809–82) and Alfred Russel Wallace (1823–1913), working independently of each other, developed the theory of evolution by natural selection, which for the first time in history provided the scientific community with a natural explanation for the biodiversity and geographical distribution of life on Earth. Up until this time, the primary explanation for the various forms of life on Earth, past and present, relied solely upon philosophical and supernatural explanations. The Darwin-Wallace theory of evolution by natural selection provided the field of biology with a unified scientific theory on the biological relationships and common ancestry among various species of organisms and how populations of organisms have evolved over time. This theory also provided scientists with an opportunity to further redefine the field of biology to include the role of the natural environment in shaping the proliferation, extinction, and geographic distribution of populations of organisms on Earth over time. Thus, in order to better understand and explain the scientific concepts and contextual underpinnings within the study of life, the field of biology incorporates and utilises the theory of evolution by natural selection as its foundation and unifying theme.

A major focus of biology in the twentieth and twenty-first centuries has been the investigation of the molecular and genetic basis of life. In doing so, major discoveries in the biology of the cell, coupled with the chemical and molecular structures of life, helped propel the field of biology further by providing a scientific explanation for the genetic mechanisms involved in reproduction, heredity, and natural selection. The incorporation of the study of genes and heredity in biology allowed for the further unification of some of the major concepts in biology, such as the role and function of genes and traits coupled with the mechanisms involved in the evolution of life on Earth.

The advancement of technological and scientific tools since the early 1800s has allowed the field of biology to gather vast amounts of empirical data on the microscopic and macroscopic world of life. In doing so, the field of biology has expanded into a variety of sub-disciplines, each with a specific focus on a particular aspect on the study of living things. These sub-disciplines include, but are not limited to, genetics, cell biology, microbiology, botany, zoology, ecology, and marine biology. The field of biology continues to evolve while at the same time adding to our current and future understanding of the study of life.

See also: chemistry; curriculum; medicine; science/science education; subjects

Further reading

Dobzhansky, T. (1973) 'Nothing in biology makes sense except in the light of evolution', *The American Biology Teacher*, 35: 125–29.
Mayr, E. (1997) *This Is Biology: The Science of the Living World*, Cambridge MA: Harvard University Press.
Narguizian, P. (2004) 'Understanding the nature of science through evolution: how to effectively blend discussions of science content with process', *The Science Teacher*, 71(9): 40–45.

PAUL NARGUIZIAN

BLIND, TEACHING OF

Despite the considerable progress made in educating blind and severely visually disabled persons since Valentin Haüy opened the

Institution des Jeunes Aveugles in Paris in 1784 for that purpose, barely 10 per cent of the world's estimated 6 million blind pre-school and school age children today receive any education at all, according to the World Health Authority.

Early Western societies generally considered the blind poor uneducable but, in the Enlightenment spirit, Diderot's essay *On Blindness* (1749) argued that the capacity to reason was not destroyed by blindness. Paris subsequently became the centre of attempts to make blind persons literate. Haüy's school inspired the creation of others across Europe, and British cities in particular embraced charitable institutions as the best setting to offer moral improvement, religious consolation, and industrial training for self-sufficiency. Liverpool (1791) and Edinburgh (1793) started schools which were widely imitated. Cultural stimulation and literacy were at first minor considerations in Britain, where more utilitarian priorities emerged. Reading was rarely taught and oral religious instruction and the teaching of basketwork and other crafts predominated. James Gall at Edinburgh produced the first British raised type, but publications were limited and predominantly religious. Under the influence of pioneers like John Alston in Glasgow, the curriculum expanded in some schools, but from the 1850s, critics condemned the typical institution for its unwelcoming, custodial atmosphere, where corporal punishment was common, and for its concentration on chapel and workshop.

In Britain, unlike France, Germany and the United States, the state remained inactive and private initiatives abounded. In 1886, Worcester College for the Blind, today's New College Worcester, was created exclusively for young boys of the upper classes. Offering a classical education, it championed Braille type, perfected by Louis Braille in Paris, and by 1951 fifteen boys had gone on to university.

England's 1870 Education Act led to short-lived School Board experiments, notably in London and Glasgow, in integrating blind children in ordinary schools. Meanwhile, Thomas Armitage's British and Foreign Blind Association, forerunner of the Royal National Institute for the Blind (RNIB), proposed Braille as the standard type and pressed for state participation in education and publication. Despite the US Printing House for the Blind having received Congressional grants from 1868, and the success of state-run blind education in Germany, Britain's 1889 royal commission report on disability in the nation recommended that control of both institutions and publishing for the blind remain in private hands. Following England's Education Act of 1893, private institutions were subject to government inspection, but the charity institution model prevailed on both sides of the Atlantic.

Although even Samuel Howe, renowned director of Boston's Perkins Institution, alma mater of Laura Bridgeman and Helen Keller, warned of the dangers of institutionalisation, special schools were equated with progress until the mid-twentieth century. Britain's 1944 Education Act facilitated their expansion, and between 1945 and 1972 the number of disabled children in institutional education almost trebled. Subsequently, growing disillusionment among the disabled and their families and the influence of Erving Goffman and Michel Foucault's anti-institutional critiques on health professionals and educators turned the tide. Since the 1978 Warnock Report and the 1981 Education Act, British mainstream schools have increasingly offered special provisions to include the disabled, but, as in other Organisation for Economic Co-operation and Development nations, lack of resources, inadequate staff training and public indifference have hindered improvements.

The benefits of integration are widely accepted, and enrolment in secondary and higher education has multiplied in Europe, the USA and Japan. Elite schools, such as the Perkins Institute, demonstrate the possible. There, on-campus speech and mobility specialists and audiologists supplement a team of educators who, in Massachusetts, work to an adjusted state curriculum. Translation software, computerised Braille embossers and talking compasses are freely available, and new software for composing mathematical texts is in development.

However, blind educators are concerned that new technology may have a divisive effect. In most British schools, with limited curricular options and low teacher expectations, even obtaining texts for exam courses remains a fundamental problem, as the RNIB's current *Where's My Book?* campaign shows.

The International Council for Education of People with Visual Impairment (ICEVI) actively promotes international initiatives to expand educational opportunities. ICEVI, through its journal *The Educator*, stresses the importance of facilitating international agency activity and fostering community and parental involvement in the quest for social and intellectual empowerment of the visually disabled.

See also: inclusive education; learning disabilities/difficulties; special education/special educational needs/special needs

Further reading

Borsay, A. (2005) *Disability and Social Policy in Britain Since 1750*, Basingstoke: Palgrave Macmillan.
Koestler, F. (1976) *The Unseen Minority: A Social History of Blindness in America*, New York: Mackay.

JOHN OLIPHANT

BLOOM, BENJAMIN (1913–99)

Bloom was born in Pennsylvania and graduated from that university. While working for his doctorate in education from Chicago University – which he obtained in 1942 – he worked in the university's board of examinations office, where he continued to work until 1959. He also taught within the education faculty, where he inspired students over four decades. His *Taxonomy of Educational Objectives* (1956) outlined a hierarchy of cognitive levels, and this approach to objective-based assessment was strongly influential in subsequent decades. A development from this practical tool for assessment, was an interest in how higher levels of cognition could be nurtured. With Lois J. Broder he undertook a study of the thought processes of undergraduate students, publishing *Problem-Solving Processes of College Students* in 1958.

As an advocate of the view that the physical and social environment of a child fundamentally affects their opportunities with regard to cognitive abilities, Bloom was an influential Congressional inquiry witness prior to the launch of the Head Start early years' programme. Bloom argued against the assumption that performance followed natural, predetermined paths. He advocated direct intervention through structured learning programmes, supported by continuous assessment and individualised learning, believing that this would challenge the normal distribution of outcomes. *Developing Talent in Young People* (1985) sought to demonstrate that the highest achievers were the product of social and environmental inputs, rather than genetic dispositions. Bloom's message was that schools can be agencies to enhance learning opportunities and can challenge such socially determining factors such as economic privilege.

See also: assessment; continuous assessment; individualised instruction/personalised learning

STEVEN COWAN

BOARDING SCHOOL/EDUCATION

The essential feature of a boarding school is regular provision of overnight accommodation for some or all of its pupils. Boarding education is the total educational experience (formal and informal) at such schools, especially with regard to any distinctive aspects that may be less evident in day schools.

The practice of sending children to live away from home for educational purposes appears in diverse historical and cultural contexts. Ethnographers have noted analogous patterns in African tribal traditions, where adolescent boys (sometimes girls) live in 'bush schools' to acquire lore and skills necessary for adult societal roles. The 2,000-year-old Jewish custom of boys residing at a *yeshiva*, in which studies encapsulate religious life, survives in modern Israel. Christian monasteries and cathedrals in medieval Europe often boarded and taught boys, who did duty as choristers, and English nunneries took girls. More commonly, day-school masters lodged boys in their houses, a practice which flourished into the nineteenth century among clergymen with scholastic interests.

The first large, purpose-built English boarding schools – Winchester (founded in 1382) and Eton (1440) – prepared boys for university education at Oxford and Cambridge. By the eighteenth century, some Tudor grammar schools had added boarding houses, thereby permanently changing their character from day schools, the more successful (e.g. Harrow and Rugby) becoming prestigious 'great schools' and exemplars of the nineteenth-century boys' public-school tradition. Small private boarding schools for girls appeared in major towns from the seventeenth century, their number increasing until the much larger proprietary girls' schools (e.g. Cheltenham Ladies' College) opened boarding houses from the 1860s. Both boys' and girls' public schools generally admitted pupils at thirteen years of age, so very many preparatory schools (frequently also offering boarding) for younger boys and, less commonly, girls were established in the second half of the nineteenth century.

The Victorian public-school ethos – associated with Thomas Arnold (headmaster of Rugby, 1828–42) – emphasised character-building, depending for effectiveness on boarding arrangements as much as on curriculum, and was replicated in the British colonies and the United States. Distinguishing features, like sport, prefects and house systems, were eventually absorbed into English day schools. Early twentieth-century 'progressive' boarding schools adopted liberal child psychology and democratic organisation (in some cases notoriously), subsequently influencing practice in many state-maintained primary schools.

The Boarding Schools' Association (BSA), founded in 1965, cites the following circumstances of potential 'boarding need': parents working overseas, remote homes, chronic family problems, pupils with special needs (disabilities, ill health, dysfunctional behaviour, learning difficulties, or exceptional talents), and religious requirements. UK independent-school fees being generally prohibitive, some thirty-five state-maintained boarding schools (accommodating 4,000 students in 2005) provide free education. Of 65,000 independent-school boarders, over 18,000 are from overseas. Full termly board has been largely superseded by weekly and flexi-board, in which pupils return home at weekends or simply sleep at school according to need.

Although Gottesman (1991) has described the UK as 'the cradle of residential education', boarders are less than 1 per cent of its school population, which is typical of almost all countries. A notable exception is Israel, where 15 per cent of secondary-school children board away from home. In Russia, government policy created a sixteenfold increase in boarding-school population between 1956 and 1966, its state-maintained schools educating all social groups and 2 per cent of the total school population. The international community is widely served by residential schools: in 2005, the Council of International Schools listed 167 boarding schools in sixty-four countries across all continents.

Most countries have a spectrum of institutions for residential or boarding education and care, some with primary focus on formal education and others on social, health, or custodial care: crucially all provide an informal-learning environment. Anderson (2005) has developed a research-based generic model for analysing boarding schools (and other residential settings), with a view to eliciting theoretical insights into their working, promoting good practice, and stimulating effective management. Embracing an array of factors in four interrelated dimensions – physical and human environment, legal and philosophical framework, personal and social development, and time (daily living and long-term transitions) – this important and comprehensive model has global application for future action research into boarding schools.

See also: Arnold, Thomas; independent/ private school/education; public school

Further reading

Anderson, E. W. (2005) *Residential and Boarding Education and Care for Young People: A Model for Good Practice*, London: Routledge.
Gottesman, M. (ed.) (1991) *Residential Child Care: An International Reader*, London: Whiting and Birch.
McLachlan, J. (1970) *American Boarding Schools: A Historical Study*, New York: Scribner.

DAVID NICHOLAS

BOURDIEU, PIERRE (1930–2000)

Bourdieu was a French academic and intellectual, notable for linking the fields of sociology, cultural studies and politics. He was identified with the post-structuralist movement in critical cultural and educational thinking. Bourdieu became famous with his first published book, an examination of the effects of French dominance over the Berber culture in Algeria (1960). This provided a grounding for much subsequent thinking and writing, in which he expanded the concept of *cultural capital*, a concept that was to become hugely influential in critiques of social formations. He established the Centre for the Sociology of Education and Culture in Paris in 1964, from where he sought to create a social theory that overcame subjectivist and objectivist approaches to social phenomena. He argued instead for an integrated approach to social practices and experiences that take place within cultural settings or 'fields'. He was a major contributor to the idea that social and natural scientists should become 'reflexive' in their own practices. Bourdieu developed the concept of *habitus*, a system of dispositions within a person that allows them to improvise actions and practices. The implications of this for learning and schooling are considerable, because it expands the notion of a learner acquiring differing types of understanding and awareness. Educational practices are viewed as a contested 'field' formed for the reproduction and allocation of intellectual and cultural capital. Bourdieu described how the state and its educational apparatuses create 'unified linguistic markets', in which one form of speech becomes legitimated as the norm. This historicised approach challenged much of Bernstein's earlier work.

See also: Bernstein, Basil; cultural capital; cultural studies; educational theory; habitus; sociology; sociology of education

STEVEN COWAN

BRAIN DRAIN

The brain drain, a term that emerged first in the early 1960s in the context of British scientists emigrating to the United States, signifies the loss of talent and expertise from one centre or region to another. Its most common usage is national and geographical, as it conveys the process by which the experts and intellectuals of one society are attracted to another. In some cases this may be due to superior resources, salaries and other incentives in the nation that is attracting the most able scientists of their generation to emigrate. In other instances, this is due much more to the insecurities of the nation that is losing its talent, as for example the Jewish scientists who left Nazi Germany in the 1930s and the Soviet Union in the post-war decades in favour of the United States. It includes the phenomenon of young people studying at university in another country and then preferring in large numbers not to return to their home country. For example, a large proportion of students from China and from different African countries who have studied abroad have chosen not to return. The brain drain is also an occupational issue, occurring when one occupation or career becomes less attractive to graduates than others. One instance of this is that research has often lost many of its most promising new recruits to careers in the City or industry which may be more lucrative and secure.

See also: globalisation; knowledge economy; recruitment

GARY McCULLOCH

BRAZIL

Brazil is the twelfth largest economy in the world, and the largest in Latin America. With a population of around 178 million, Brazil is changing steadily: the gross national product and foreign investments are rising; competition in the job market is increasing; and there is a rise in productivity with a modern industrial base for the economy.

The Brazilian educational system resulted from the impact of three major cultures in different periods. During the colonial period, the Portuguese implemented the metropolitan system, highly centralised, and geared to the training of elites. Later, the impact of French culture and educational models became visible, especially in the nineteenth and early twentieth centuries: the school curriculum was encyclopedic and emphasis was upon intellectual training. Later, from the 1950s, US political influence in Latin America affected educational as well as economic and political affairs. Two major educational reforms (to higher education in 1968 and to primary and secondary education in 1971) are examples of such influence.

The educational system is organised on two levels: basic education encompassing infant education (nursery school, ages 0–3, and pre-school, ages 4–5), compulsory fundamental education (ages 6–14) and secondary education

Table 1 Organisation of the Brazilian system of education

Level	Age	Responsibility
Basic education		
• Infant education		Municipal government
Nursery school	0–4	
Pre-School	4–5	
• Fundamental education	6–14	Municipal government
• Secondary education	15–17	State government
Higher education		
• Undergraduate education	18–	Federal government
• Graduate education		

(ages 15–17); and higher education (age 18–), including graduate education (see Table 1).

The latest educational reform (Law 9,394 of 1996) produced significant changes in the system: for example, the introduction of sequential courses in higher education with a vocational and complementary purposes; the provision of a percentage of places (45 per cent) in higher education for minority groups (blacks, native Indians, pupils with special needs); and compulsory teacher training at higher education level.

The public sector schools, with a few exceptions, lack quality, schools are poorly equipped, teachers are not well trained, and salaries are low. Private sector schools offer better equipment, better educational tools, and better trained teachers. Usually children from the middle and upper classes go to private schools.

Higher education is expanding considerably, especially in the private sector. In 1985 there were 859 higher education institutions in Brazil. In 2005 this number reached 2,165 – 89 per cent of them private.

The implementation of a national system of assessment has been an important improvement in education. Since 1993, the Ministry of Education has been assessing nationally pupils' performance in all state and private schools, through the System of Assessment of Basic Education (SAEB). Other instruments for assessing school children's performance include the National Exam of Secondary Education (ENEM), whilst the National Performance Exam (ENADE) assesses undergraduate students. Graduate education is evaluated through the Coordination for the Development of Higher Education Staff (CAPES), linked to the Ministry of Education.

In fundamental education, the 2004 census showed a significant development regarding children with special needs. In the last five years, the number of disabled children in normal schools has increased by 229 per cent.

Long-distance education has also developed in the last ten years. Schools television serves 47,000 schools, 1.3 million teachers and 28 million pupils. It covers the training of teachers and the support of classroom activities.

Education in Brazil has significantly improved in the last five years. Under Fernando Henrique Cardoso's presidency, 97 per cent of children in the 7–14 age group were enrolled in school, compared to 86 per cent in 1999. However, there are still a number of problems to be dealt with. Christovam Buarque, the first minister of education in the present Labour Party government, pointed out in 2002 that only 42 per cent of Brazilians reach year eight in elementary education at the expected age (15); 4.3 million children between 4 and 14 years of age are outside schools; 3.3 million Brazilians aged fifteen or over are unable to read and write properly; around 73 per cent of the population aged eighteen or over do not finish secondary education.

Presently, one national issue is university reform. A higher education bill has been debated in Congress, which aims to enhance university autonomy, reduce student 'drop outs', and increase technological courses. A *Plan for the Development of Education* was launched in 2007. It includes major goals such as the expansion of the federal system of higher education, the expansion of nursery schools and pre-school buildings, career

development for school teachers, and digital inclusion. But the greatest challenge is the total abolition of illiteracy in the next four years.

See also: Latin America

Further reading

Brock, C. and Schwartzman, S. (eds) (2004) *The Challenges of Education in Brazil*, Cambridge: Cambridge University Press.

Lopes, E. M. T., Faria Filho, L. M. and Veiga, C. G. (eds) (2001) *500 Anos de Educação no Brasil*, Belo Horizonte: Autêntica Editora.

Renato, P. (2004) *A Revolução Gerenciada – Educação no Brasil 1995–2002*, São Paulo: Prentice Hall.

MARIA ISABEL FIGUEIREDO SOBREIRA AND
MARIA DE FIGUEIREDO-COWEN

BRITISH COUNCIL

The British Council aims 'to build mutually beneficial relationships between people in the UK and other countries and to increase appreciation of the UK's creative ideas and achievements'. It is a non-departmental public body and registered charity which operates at arm's length from the British government although it is ultimately answerable to it.

It works in a broad number of cultural areas including the arts, popular and classical music, art and architecture, cultural diversity, science, cultural industries, training, dance, drama, film and digital technologies. The Council promotes British achievements abroad by organising collaborations and supporting networks in Britain and abroad. It also engages in income-generating work, notably through English teaching. The Council has also been sponsored by governments and businesses to deliver specific projects. In 2005–6 the Council worked in over 100 countries, and employed over 2,000 teachers who taught 325,000 learners. This equated to £25 million in earnings for British examinations boards. It also worked on 141 development contracts in over forty countries. Recent developments have included internet-based 'knowledge and learning centres', the first of which was established in Delhi in 2002. In 1999 British Visitor Centres were established in twelve countries.

Recently the Council's *Strategy 2010* has focused attention on improved perceptions of the UK and greater 'mutual understanding' between the UK and other countries. Other stated themes are mutual respect and learning, gender inclusion, democracy, governance, law and human rights. Income-generating and sponsored work has also increased.

It was established in 1934 and started life as the 'British Committee for Relations with Other Countries', although the name was changed to the 'British Council' in 1936. The Foreign Office was keen to promote British culture, education, science, technology and the English language abroad in the face of declining British imperialism, the growth of European totalitarianism and the emergence of similar cultural organisations in France, Germany and Italy. Sir Reginald Leeper, widely considered to be the founder of the Council, was keen to develop what he called 'cultural propaganda'.

Although established under the auspices of the Foreign Office, it has enjoyed a high degree of independence with its own committee and chairperson. In its early years the Council supported British Institutes such as that set up in Cairo in 1938, as well as English schools, lecture tours, music performances, art exhibitions and other cultural events. Development work focused on the Middle East and Mediterranean, Europe and Latin America. It helped to establish the Edinburgh Festival in 1947 and supported the careers of artists such as Henry Moore. Work was cut back during World War II when educational and cultural services were organised for refugees and Allied forces in Britain. During the 1950s there was a gradual move towards training local English teachers and the Council's work was expanded in Africa and Asia, where it also developed educational programmes and student training schemes supported by the Department for Technical Co-operation from 1961.

In the 1970s and 1980s reductions in funding from the British government led to the growth of teaching English to fee-paying students, initiatives funded by the host countries such as the English Language Centre in Jeddah, Saudi Arabia, and also by project management services charged to overseas partners. Youth exchanges and advice centres for those who wished to study in Britain were also established. However, after many years of cuts the government grant was increased in 1988 in part to develop work in Eastern Europe, especially on English language teaching and training in areas such as law. In 1994 a British Investment Scheme was developed to support the transformations taking place in South Africa.

The closeness to British foreign policy has also been debated and some critics have accused it of cultural imperialism. Throughout the life of the British Council wider political developments have impacted upon its educational and cultural work. For instance, work in Cairo and the Middle East was disrupted in the 1950s following the Suez crisis. A Soviet Relations Committee was set up to develop cultural relations with the Soviet Union. Similarly, in the 1960s operations were adversely affected by conflict in Vietnam, the Middle East and Nigeria. In the 1960s the Vosper Review was influential in fostering relations in Europe following Britain's failure to join the European Common Market. Following the discovery of oil in the Persian Gulf, development also took place in that region and centres were soon established in Oman and Qatar. Services were evacuated from Iran in 1979, Afghanistan in 1980, and Argentina and Lebanon in 1982.

The events of 11 September 2001 and the 'war on terror' also increased interest in the work of the British Council with its focus on inter-cultural communication and networks. Indeed, the United States of America has paid more attention to the activities of the Council's 'soft' work in promoting Britain throughout the world.

See also: culture; international education

Further reading

British Council (2006) *Making a World of Difference: Strategy 2010*, London: British Council.

Donaldson, F. (1984) *The British Council: The First 50 Years*, London: Jonathan Cape.

Taylor, P. M. (1981) *The Projection of Britain*, Cambridge: Cambridge University Press.

TOM WOODIN

BRITISH EDUCATIONAL RESEARCH ASSOCIATION (BERA)

The British Educational Research Association (BERA) is a network of educational researchers and educationalists in the United Kingdom which aims 'to sustain and promote a vital research culture in education'. This is achieved by nurturing an independent and critical body of researchers committed to enhancing education. Accordingly BERA fosters debate on the nature, quality, purpose and methodologies of educational research and it provides a range of support services for its members including training, networking and other forms of dialogue. BERA also engages in discussion and collaboration with policy makers, funding agencies, other research associations, researchers working in related fields, teachers and lecturers. BERA argues that these activities that are 'desperately needed if the educational systems of the UK (and the world) are to meet the aspirations and needs of society'.

BERA was set up in 1974. Initially psychologists predominated, although sociologists and action researchers would later emerge in significant numbers. Members also engage from disciplinary backgrounds such as history, economics and philosophy, while others have interests in curriculum, pedagogy, management and assessment. Within the Association research interests are diverse and may vary from policy and practical issues to wider theoretical, philosophical and historical understandings.

The Association is also responsible for a number of publications. *The British Educational Research Journal* is an academic peer-reviewed learned journal which publishes articles on a range of issues from around the world including reports, surveys, conceptual and methodological work, as well as book reviews. *Research Intelligence* serves as a newsletter with shorter articles and is distributed to members. Occasional papers are also published and these have covered topics such as teacher activism, employing contract researchers and drawing practice-based conclusions from educational research. A number of research reviews have been published for both academic and professional audiences on topics such as citizenship, music and pedagogy, geography education and teaching and learning. Guidelines for ethics in research have also been developed to support and improve educational research.

Each year BERA holds a major annual conference which attracts a significant number of researchers and educationalists. Since 2006 it has also held an overlapping practitioner day conference aimed at teachers and others working in education. BERA members also operate a number of special interest groups (SIGs), which focus on shared interests and concerns. These specialise in areas such as race, ethnicity and education; practitioner research; science education; and sexualities. Summer schools, seminars and 'masterclasses' have been run on a range of issues in educational research to support the research capacity of its members. Students enjoy special membership rates of the Association, and a student conference offers the opportunity to present papers, improve skills and develop networks. A number of annual awards are offered for the best dissertations, for putting research into practice as well as a Brian Simon fellowship. 'Associated societies', having similar aims to BERA, include the British Association for Applied Linguistics, the Educational Studies Association of Ireland and the British Society for Research into Learning Mathematics.

As a democratic organisation, BERA has an executive council with three elected officers, nine elected members and six co-opted members; each of these have special duties such as conference organising, nominations and awards, ethics, publications and training and development. As a registered charity, council members also serve as trustees of the charity.

See also: charities, educational; educational research

Further reading

David, T. (2003) *What Do We Know About Teaching Young Children?* Macclesfield: BERA.

Osler, A. and Starkey, H. (2005) *Education for Democratic Citizenship: A Review of Research, Policy and Practice 1995–2005*, Macclesfield: BERA.

TOM WOODIN

BRUNER, JEROME (1915–)

Bruner, the American educational psychologist, was a leading figure in the creation of the 1960s 'cognitive revolution' within psychology. Bruner was the founder of the Harvard Center for Cognitive Studies and his early work focused on the cognitive development of children. In more recent years Bruner has concentrated upon cultural aspects of psychology, through an examination of the textuality of narratives in various spheres. This was stimulated by his reading the socio-historical psychology of Vygotsky. The relationship of this 'socio-cultural turn' was elaborated in *The Culture of Education* (1996). His earlier book *Toward a Theory of Instruction* (1966), exerted widespread international influence, and his cross-curricular programme *Man: A Course of Study* (MACOS) has been extensively used in schools and teacher training programmes. Bruner chaired the Woods Hole Conference for the National Academy of Sciences and National Science Foundation (1959), which led to his writing *The Process of Education* (1960). For Bruner, children were viewed as active problem solvers, who learned by tackling new and difficult fields. Controversially, Bruner argued that children were ready at any age to engage in some aspects of any subject or field and to delay was a mistake. He argued that children learned more readily when extrinsic motives were removed and replaced by intrinsic ones such as personal interest and enjoyment. He became an adviser on education to presidents Kennedy and Johnson.

See also: psychology of education; Vygotsky, Lev

STEVEN COWAN

BULLYING

Bullying is the exercise of power by one individual or group over another through undue coercion, mental or physical torment, threats, manipulation, blackmail, or harassment. It may be based on gender, ethnic, religious or social differences, or on physical characteristics, or on financial or other gain, or a wide range of other motivations. It may take place in personal confrontations or in correspondence, including on the internet. Bullying is a common occurrence in educational institutions of all kinds. In schools, bullying often takes place between pupils, frequently leaving the victims in a highly vulnerable and traumatised state, either emotionally or physically. Elite schools may have a tradition of rites of passage, initiation or hazing for new pupils that amount to bullying behaviour. In some cases, teachers may be responsible for bullying individual pupils, and teachers and other staff members may themselves be bullied by senior or other staff. In institutions of higher education also, many students may be bullied by other students, or by lecturing staff. In other cases, students may be responsible for bullying university staff, while bullying is also common among staff, for example against new, inexperienced or insecure staff members. The stereotype bully is a familiar figure from popular culture such as Thomas Hughes' *Tom Brown's Schooldays*, but bullies may be more subtle and less visible than such a stereotype would suggest, and may in many cases exert a major and baleful influence on the everyday life of the institution involved.

See also: discipline; school violence

GARY McCULLOCH

BURT, CYRIL (1883–1971)

Burt, the British educational psychologist, developed an early knowledge of medicine through his father, who was doctor to the Darwin and Galton families. At Oxford, Burt pursued philosophy with psychology, specialising in psychometrics. In 1901 Burt became part of a research team which included Charles Spearman, on a nationwide survey of mental and physical characteristics of the population. He became a lecturer in physiology and psychology at Liverpool University, eventually being appointed as school psychologist to the London County Council in 1913, the first position of its kind. In 1931 he became Professor of Psychology at University College, London. His early works included *The Young Delinquent* (1925) and *The Subnormal Mind* (1935), where his hereditary eugenicist ideas began to emerge. These were followed by *Intelligence and Fertility* (1946). Burt's major impact upon the British educational systems came through his advocacy of the use of IQ tests for selection at the age of eleven to determine what sort of school a child would proceed to. Burt advocated a view that intelligence was primarily inherited, not socially determined, and contributed to three official education reports in the 1930s. Soon after his death, the research he claimed to have undertaken on twins was subjected to serious questioning. The exposé strengthened campaigns to change the way that eleven-year olds were assessed and challenged the basis for selection in British secondary schooling. Some of Burt's followers, such as Eysenck and Jensen, were to develop his interests in hereditary factors, to argue that genetics determined educational abilities of different ethnic groups.

See also: intelligence/intelligence tests; psychometrics; selection; Spearman, Charles

STEVEN COWAN

BUSINESS SCHOOL/EDUCATION

Business schools are higher education institutions that offer a range of courses in fields such as marketing, finance, accounting, organisational structures, and management. Business schools are probably best known for their MBA (Master of Business Administration) degrees, but they normally also offer undergraduate degrees, specialist Master's degrees and research degrees, as well as short courses and company-specific executive education. Most business schools are actually faculties of universities. Before 1965 there were no business schools in British universities, but by 2007 there were approximately 120; by 2007, business and management courses accounted for approximately one in seven of all students in British universities and one in five of all postgraduates. Part of the growth in demand for degrees in financial subjects in the 1980s and 1990s was the belief that they would enhance graduates' earning potential and career prospects. As a result, some business schools charge in excess of £10,000 for MSc degrees in finance and more than double that for MBA programmes.

Whilst a relatively new phenomenon in Europe, business schools have a long heritage in North America, some dating back to the late nineteenth century. One of the most famous and prestigious, Harvard Business School, was founded in 1908 and offered MBAs from 1910. In the 1920s, Harvard Business School pioneered the case study approach as an effective teaching technique in developing management expertise. This approach is still one of the principle ways of teaching about businesses and management issues and it is now a popular teaching technique in secondary school business education. The case method immerses students in business scenarios and offers them the opportunity to make decisions and confront dilemmas that real managers meet in their day-to-day work. The case study approach encourages a pedagogy that is atypical in traditional higher education teaching: one that is student-centred, encourages participation, and develops decision making skills and an ability to deal with uncertainty.

A fundamental question that is often asked is of the *purpose* of business schools. Are they places for academic study? Are they places for academic research? Or is their raison d'être for preparing students for effective management? Historically, in Britain, business schools appeared to be a response to the perceived failings of British management, but recent criticism argues that, while Master's courses are academically rigorous, they are somewhat irrelevant for practising managers. With a decline in students enrolling on MBA programmes, this conundrum needs to be addressed.

At the level of secondary education, business education provides a general understanding of business and the economic environment in which businesses operate. Business education is typically the realm of the 14–19 curriculum area, leading to qualifications in business, business studies and economics. In such countries as the UK, there remains a perceived academic–vocational divide, with many 'old' universities preferring students who have followed a traditional academic route, one that additionally privileges the subject of economics to business studies. Applied business qualifications, by contrast, have a more practical approach and include the study of the business sector: people, finances, marketing strategy and product planning. With the development and implementation in the UK of new specialist diplomas that have been developed in partnership with business, the perceived academic–vocational divide may be narrowed in the future.

Since 2002, the government policy of encouraging secondary schools in England to become 'specialist colleges' has introduced a new status and a new set of opportunities for business education. 'Business and enterprise' has become established as a popular specialism for schools and, by January 2007, there were already 226 such colleges. Their existence enhances the status of business education and it encourages the development of curriculum innovations that would otherwise be unlikely to happen. A typical innovation has been the introduction of business courses from age eleven, and another has been the development of enterprise education courses. There is, however, a longstanding problem of definition with enterprise education and its learning outcomes. There are three broad types of definition: one sees enterprise as teaching entrepreneurship; another sees it as more generic project development, and a final conceptualisation is the development of personal 'enterprising' dispositions, such as creativity, problem solving, and flexibility. Clearly, these three definitions have drastically different implications for teaching and the organisation of the curriculum.

See also: economics; higher education; Master's; secondary school/education; specialisation

Further reading

Davies, P. and Brant, J. (2006) *Teaching School Subjects 11–19: Business, Economics and Enterprise*, London: Routledge.

Teaching Business and Economics (journal of the Economics and Business Education Association).

JACEK BRANT

C

CANADA

From the middle of the seventeenth century, French Catholic orders, headed by the Jesuits, provided some elementary, secondary and women's education in the northern parts of New France. Following the 1763 English takeover of Canada, numerous new elementary schools were privately erected in order to serve the growing population of, predominantly, Protestant-anglophone immigrants that settled in different parts of the country. The first four decades of the eighteenth century saw failed attempts to develop a state education system in English-speaking Upper Canada, and in the predominantly French-speaking Lower Canada. Nevertheless, after the 1841 Act of Union and subsequent legislation, which created an office of Superintendent of Education for each province, locally administered systems of education emerged. In Lower Canada, then known as Canada East, a dual system of education, one for Catholics and one for Protestants, was established, leaving the two groups completely separated. In Upper Canada, then renamed Canada West, a system of free and universal elementary education was erected, a uniform system of secondary school developed, and teachers' education and certification were standardised. Nonetheless, separate schools for Catholics were maintained.

The British North American Act (1867) had long-term educational implications that are still evident today. First, the Act left the control and direction of education to the provinces coming under confederation. Consequently, although the federal government plays an indirect role in funding education, functions as the guarantor of minority educational rights, and provides education for Canadians who fall outside the provinces' jurisdiction (such as some Inuit), it has no formal role in delivering education and a national department of education does not exist. Each province has its own Department, or Ministry of Education, responsible for educational legislation, setting educational policies, school inspections, curriculum design, maintaining standards, and, normally, teachers' certification. Most provinces, however, entrust the operation of the school systems to locally elected school boards. These have wide ranging responsibilities, from setting annual budgets to hiring teachers, but in recent years there has been a trend to reduce the number of, and powers of, school boards, while centralising power at the provincial level. Second, the 1867 Act promised to safeguard the educational rights of minorities. Initially, this guaranteed that both Catholics and Protestants, whenever being a minority, could receive suitable education. The preservation of minority rights has played a key role in the development of Canadian education ever since. The 1982 Canadian Charter of Rights and Freedoms extended these rights by recognising language minorities. It asserts that English- and French-speaking Canadians have the right to be educated in their own language when there is a sufficient demand for it.

For the Canadian education system, the last decades of the nineteenth century and the early twentieth were a time of consolidation, expansion and improvement. Following the strengthening of Humanitarianism, child labour was restricted by legislation, the first kindergartens opened, the content of the curriculum broadened, manual, technical and special needs education were more readily offered and greater educational opportunities were given to women. In addition, in 1871, Ontario introduced compulsory elementary schooling, and most other provinces quickly followed. Today, the length of compulsory schooling varies according to the provinces, but it normally begins around the age of six and terminates at 16/17. In the 1930s and 1940s, there began a restructuring of secondary education, aimed at making it more accessible and practical. This reconstruction also provided the Canadian education system with its current shape. At present, most provinces offer one or two years of kindergarten education, five or six years of elementary education, three or four years of middle/ intermediate/junior high school and three or four years of academic or vocational senior high school education. In Ontario and Quebec, there is no intermediate education. Quebec also provides two years of pre-university education or three years of professional education. Graduation requirements and examination arrangements vary from province to province.

The educational hardships of the post-World War II era were met by a major investment in education in the 1960s. By the end of this decade, the Canadian per capita investment in education was higher than in any other industrial country. This investment was accompanied by the spread of progressive and child-centred approaches to education that lay more emphasis on the individual's well-being and educational pluralism. It was ensured that diverse cultural groups, such as aboriginal Canadians, would receive an education that better suits their special needs.

The economic slowdown of the 1970s and 1980s resulted in demands to reduce spending and to reform education so that it could better meet the requirements of the emerging global economy. Since the 1990s, greater focus has been placed on educational accountability and performance. Standardised tests were introduced, and new bodies responsible for measuring educational performance were formed, such as Ontario's Education Quality and Accountability office. In addition, curricula were reshaped to better answer the new economic needs, and more emphasis was given to the use of technology and technological education. Finally, there is a will to prolong education. The attendance in kindergarten, which was relatively low, is being encouraged and is found to be on the rise. There is also an attempt to raise levels of participation in higher education. This, however, is despite the relative underfunding of Canadian universities, which face fierce competition from their US counterparts.

At start of the twenty-first century, Canadian education still faces numerous challenges arising from Canada's unique historical and cultural heritage, its proximity to the USA, and the changing world economy.

See also: Catholic school/education; church; indigenous education

Further reading

Audet, L. P., Stamp, R. M. and Wilson, D. (eds) (1970) *Canadian Education: a History,* Scarborough: Prentice-Hall of Canada.

Beach, C. M., Boadway, R. W. and McInnis, R. M. (eds) (2005) *Higher Education in Canada,* Ithaca NY: John Deutsch Institute for the Study of Economic Policy Queen's University.

Dunning, P. (1997) *Education in Canada – An Overview,* Toronto: Canadian Education Association.

Johnson, F. H. (1968) *A Brief History of Canadian Education,* Toronto: McGraw-Hill Company of Canada Limited.

Mazner, R. (1994) *Public Schools and Political Ideas: Canadian Educational Policy in Historical Perspective,* Toronto: Toronto University Press.

Wotherspoon, T. (2004) *The Sociology of Education in Canada – Critical Perspective*, Oxford: Oxford University Press.

TAL GILEAD

CAREER GUIDANCE

The global shift to support lifelong learning strategies and the advent of new technologies has heightened the importance of providing learners with career guidance. Originally seen as having relevance only to the young, youth employment and careers services frequently struggled for funding and status, attracting more resources during times of recession in order to assuage unemployment statistics.

The United States was a pioneer in developing 'guidance', including career guidance, in the public school curriculum from the 1920s. Subsequently, federal funds were made available in 1946 for the appointment of vocational counsellors in schools (Gysbers 2005: 205–6). This strategic approach has determined that, today, 'Career guidance is alive and flourishing in the schools of the United States' (Gysbers 2005: 210), but this is not so everywhere. As recently as 1997 a spokesperson for the British National Association of Careers and Guidance Teachers observed that responsibility for career guidance in secondary schools too frequently rested with teachers with no special training, such as 'the Latin teacher after Latin became defunct' or 'an ageing PE [physical education] teacher' (Aldrich *et al.* 2000: 194). The continuing dependence upon untrained career advisers continues to be of concern at an international level (OECD 2004: 19).

According to the Organisation for Economic Co-operation and Development,

> Career guidance refers to services and activities intended to assist individuals of any age and at any point throughout their lives, to make educational, training and occupational choices and to manage their careers. Such services may be found in schools, universities and colleges, in training institutions, in public employment services, in the workplace, in the voluntary and community sector and in the private sector.
> (OECD 2004: 10)

In many Western countries career guidance services are fully funded by the state or employers. These are available free of charge to learners at school, in post-compulsory or higher education, to the unemployed and to those depending on welfare benefits. Notwithstanding the discourses of ongoing skills acquisition and 'no more jobs for life', those in employment are often expected to pay for impartial and professional career guidance. In their 2004 survey of thirty-four states, Watts and Sultana (2004) identified a limited market model for career guidance in several countries, including Australia, Canada, Germany, the Netherlands and the United Kingdom.

Once dependent on the accuracy of ageing brochures produced by employers and professional bodies, career guidance today normally involves the use of computer programs, which test individual aptitudes and skills. The interactive capabilities of careers guidance software are demonstrated at the website of Australia's career information service, *myfuture* (www.myfuture.edu.au).

Further reading
Aldrich, R., Crook, D. and Watson, D. (2000) *Education and Employment: The DfEE and its Place in History*, London: Institute of Education.
Gysbers, N. (2005) 'Comprehensive school guidance programs in the United States: a career profile', *International Journal for Educational and Vocational Guidance*, 5(2): 203–15.
Organisation for Economic Co-operation and Development (2004) *Career Guidance and Public Policy: Bridging the Gap*, Paris: Organisation for Economic Co-operation and Development.
Watts, A. and Sultana, R. (2004) 'Career guidance policies in 37 countries: contrasts and common themes', *International Journal for Educational and Vocational Guidance*, 4(2, 3): 105–22.

See also: counselling; lifelong learning; work experience

DAVID CROOK

CARIBBEAN

The Caribbean is generally divided into what is termed the English, French, Spanish and Dutch Caribbean since these colonial powers were primarily responsible for the conquest, domination, subjugation and degradation of the peoples of the Caribbean. As a result of this contact, they thrust their political, economic and social will on these territories. During the period of slavery the education of blacks occurred only through missionaries' efforts to provide basic literacy skills for the purpose of converting 'heathens' to Christianity. The British, who were the most dominant group, established their influence in 1655 with the capture of Jamaica from the Spanish. This influence lasted for well over three centuries.

Changes in the education system took place after emancipation in 1838. Campbell (1992) views this as the real beginning of public education. The system of education that the Caribbean inherited was not designed to promote upward social mobility. The aim of the colonial government was not the advancement of the black population, but rather to instil Christian morals, standards and principles to cement denominational loyalty.

The British structured the education system in such a way that, in order for students to be labelled as achievers, they had to sit and pass British-based examinations. This was further encouraged by the local governments as a matter of policy. This practice was used to further perpetuate the class system which is a prominent feature of the legacy of colonialism. It was not only selective but also geared towards failing students since success is primarily determined by student performance in examinations. Evans (2001) argues that this system is responsible for widening social class differences and academic abilities and lowering self-esteem. As a result, teachers and students tend to emphasise preparation for examinations since this is the measuring stick of success. Campbell (1992) argues that this

practice has become so entrenched in the veins of Caribbean people that they fear the risk of going in another direction. Furthermore, he explains that schools slowly laid the foundation for education to become a serious factor in social stratification. It can also be argued that the colonists implemented a philosophy of education and plantation values that was responsible for wasting the true wealth of the Indies, the creativity and intellectual ability of the people. In order to maintain their control over the system, the colonists also practised a policy of exclusion which was also supported and encouraged by the Church of England.

According to Chevanne (2003), religion and philanthropy were important in the evolution of higher education in the Caribbean. The first institution of higher education in the English-speaking Caribbean was Codrington College, which was established in Barbados by the Anglicans in 1743 to train priests. In the later half of the nineteenth century, a number of teacher training colleges emerged in response to the provision of a Negro Education Grant by the British government to assist missionary societies in the education of the newly freed slaves. A Commission of Higher Education was also appointed by the British government. In 1948, the sub-committee recommended the opening of the University College of the West Indies (UCWI), which was affiliated with the University of London. This institution was initially criticised for limiting access to higher education, thus reinforcing the colonial elite class system. With the Royal Charter in 1962, the UCWI developed into the University of the West Indies (UWI), with campuses in Jamaica, Barbados and Trinidad. The UWI now has sites throughout the English-speaking Caribbean.

In 1972, an effort was made to make Caribbean education more relevant to meeting the needs of its people, when Caribbean governments encouraged the development of the Caribbean Examinations Council (CXC) to replace the traditional British examinations. CXC has also introduced the Caribbean Advanced Proficiency Examinations (CAPE) to replace the traditional British Advanced Level programme. Despite this nationalisation of the education system, it continues to fail a number of students. Furthermore, a limited number of students go to high school and fewer still go on to tertiary education, a practice accepted by some on the grounds of maintaining quality and defending excellence. In their report, the task force with responsibility for reviewing the education system in Jamaica noted that performance at all levels of the system has been well below the target for that country.

The 1980s and 1990s saw a number of Caribbean countries establishing their own institutions of higher learning, offering qualifications at the tertiary level. Some of these proceeded in collaboration with the UWI and also with foreign providers. In the past fifteen years the Caribbean has witnessed a rise in offshore universities working independently or in collaboration with local institutions to offer undergraduate and postgraduate programmes. In response to this development, Chevanne (2003) recognises that the UWI is attempting to preserve its regional character by further collaborating with community colleges in the region to offer the first year of some of its degree programmes through these institutions. It is also felt in some circles that the UWI should leave the undergraduate work to the community colleges and the other colleges and concentrate on postgraduate studies. Only time will be the judge in this situation.

See also: Latin America

Further reading

Campbell, C. C. (1992) *Colony and Nation: A Short History of Education in Trinidad and Tobago*, Kingston: Ian Randle

Chevanne, B. (2003) *Legislation of Tertiary Education in the Caribbean*, Caracas, Venezuela: The International Institute for Higher Education in Latin America and the Caribbean.

Evans, H. L. (2001) *Inside Jamaican Schools: Higher Education in the Caribbean, Past, Present and Future Direction*, Kingston: University of the West Indies Press.

Foner, N. (1973) *Status and Power in Rural Jamaica: A Study of Educational and Political Change*, New York: Teachers College Press.

Miller, E. (ed.) (1991) *Education and Society in the Commonwealth Caribbean*, Mona, Jamaica: Institute of Social and Economic Research, University of the West Indies.

CARLTON MILLS

CARNEGIE FOUNDATION FOR THE ADVANCEMENT OF TEACHING

The Carnegie Foundation for the Advancement of Teaching is an independent policy and research centre in education which aims 'to do and perform all things necessary to encourage, uphold, and dignify the profession of the teacher and the cause of higher education'. The Foundation brings together researchers, teachers, policy makers and educational organisations to develop and disseminate knowledge and practices in order to improve teaching and learning in the United States of America. Research is explicitly linked to a process of 'moral action' and cultural transformation; the Foundation strives to act as 'an inspiration and a catalyst' to change at all levels of the educational system. It believes that teachers and educational leaders 'would act far more intelligently and purposefully' if they had 'a better sense of what they were really doing' and a vision about what is possible.

As an independent charitable organisation, the Carnegie Foundation develops partnerships with educational institutions, policy makers and other philanthropic foundations. It conceives of education as a holistic system of interlocking institutions. Accordingly, programmes are developed to impact not only on specific classrooms but also the wider educational context. The duration of research projects tends to be five or more years so that initial research can feed into analysis and action. The Foundation brings together networks, conferences and meetings to help foster interdisciplinarity around teaching and learning. Its staff and supporters come from many backgrounds including philosophy, psychology and law, and they also span the education system, from early childhood through to higher education.

The Foundation's work is divided into a number of strands. Research funds are devoted to undergraduate education and teaching and learning in universities. Recent initiatives in this area have addressed the political engagement of young people, how business students might receive a more rounded liberal education and the role of universities in developing moral and civic education. Continuing the early work of the Foundation, a second priority is researching the nature and scope of professional and graduate education encompassing a range of professions such as law, engineering, medicine, nursing and teaching itself. The nature and structure of doctoral programmes have also been examined.

Teacher education is a third major concern, and the Foundation strives to foster understanding and stimulate improvements by establishing models of good practice. Resources produced include videos, publications and websites, one of which assesses the pedagogical value of the oral traditions of African-American and Latino students. Under the heading of 'knowledge sharing' the Foundation creates dialogue between researchers, teachers and policy makers in order to improve knowledge of education as well as teaching and practice. This is also facilitated through projects which utilise a range of new technologies. Under this strand the Foundation includes its work on the classification of higher education institutions, the 'Carnegie Classification', which is widely used and has been continually updated since 1970.

Carnegie also publishes and supports a range of books, discussion papers, reports and magazines. *Change* is a bi-monthly magazine which covers contemporary issues in education and emerging trends. *Carnegie Perspectives* is a series of discussion papers which aims to stimulate debate on educational issues. These include titles such as 'The case for common examinations' (2007), 'Turning good intentions into educational capital' (2007) and 'Learning about student learning from community colleges' (2006).

The Foundation was founded by Andrew Carnegie in 1905, although it is independent of other Carnegie organisations. Since then it has influenced policies and helped to define many educational programmes. For instance, the Flexner Report (1910) helped to establish the nature of medical education in the USA. The Foundation also helped to create the Educational Testing Service and campaigned in favour of federal grants for higher education. In 1997 it moved its headquarters from Princeton, New Jersey to Stanford University in California. It is governed by a board of trustees who are leaders in education, business and government.

See also: academic/academic profession; profession/professionalism/professionalisation; teacher; teaching/teaching methods; teaching profession

Further reading

Golde, C. and Walker, G. (2006) *Envisioning the Future of Doctoral Education: Preparing Stewards of the Discipline*, San Francisco CA: Jossey-Bass.

Reed, A. Z. (1921) *Training for the Public Profession of the Law*, New York: The Carnegie Foundation for the Advancement of Teaching.

Sullivan, W. M., Shulman, L. S., Colby, A., Bond, L. and Wegner, J. W. (2007) *Educating Lawyers: Preparation for the Profession of Law*, San Francisco CA: Jossey-Bass.

The Carnegie Foundation for the Advancement of Teaching (1971) *Less Time, More Options: Education Beyond High School*, New York: McGraw-Hill.

——(1972) *Institutional Aid: Federal Support to Colleges and Universities*, New York: McGraw-Hill.

TOM WOODIN

CASE STUDY

One important approach used in education and educational research is the case study. A case study is a detailed examination of one person, one setting, one single set of documents or one particular event. It focuses on one 'unit': the unit may be a school (or even a classroom within it); it could even be one student in a school or college; it could be one course; in a study of employers' needs, each 'employing organisation' could make up a single case. This is at once the strength and, as some may argue, the weakness of case study, i.e. the importance of the context of the unit and the consequent problem of generalisation.

Bogdan and Biklen (1982) provide the major classifications of case study: historical-organisational case studies; observational case studies and the life history form of case study. The first involves studies of a unit, e.g. an organisation such as a school, perhaps tracing its development over time. This may involve interviews with people involved with the organisation and a study of written records. The second category involves largely participant observation of an organisation. Observational case studies will often include an historical aspect but the main concern is the contemporary scene. Finally, a life-history form of case study will involve extensive interviews with one person for the purpose of collecting a first-person narrative.

Stake (1995) made a useful distinction between three types of case study:

- *The intrinsic case study*: undertaken in order to gain a better understanding of this particular case, not because the case is unique or typical but because it is of interest in itself;
- *The instrumental case study*: used to provide insight into a particular issue or to clarify a hypothesis. The actual case is secondary: its aim is to develop our understanding and knowledge of something else;

- *The collective case study*: the study of a number of different cases. The cases may have similar or dissimilar characteristics, but they are chosen in order that theories can be generated about a larger collection of cases. In this way they employ a very different mode of thinking from the single-case study.

A case study may well involve a wide range of methods or 'tools', including:

Observation, including:

- *Participant observation*, where the researcher is more than a passive observer and participates in the events being studied;
- *Systematic observation* using a standardised observation instrument;
- *Simple observation*, involving passive unobtrusive observation (e.g. of facial expression; language use; behaviour).

Interview, including:

- *Structured interview*, using a set of pre-determined questions in a set order;
- *Focused/semi-structured interview*, using an interview schedule specifying key areas, but in no fixed order;
- *Open-ended interview*, where there is no pre-specified schedule or order of questions and little direction from interviewer.

Use of documents and records, including:

- written or recorded materials, e.g. minutes of meetings, pupil records, diaries, school brochures, reports.

Other techniques, including:

- questionnaires, standardised tests (e.g. of intelligence, personality or attainment), scales (e.g. of attitude). repertory grids, life histories, role play, simulation and gaming.

A vast amount of material is likely to be built up in developing a case study. Although only a part of it is likely to be presented in a final report, thesis or publication, it provides an important framework and evidence base for the study.

Case-study research has a large number of attractions and advantages and can be enjoyable, illuminating and insightful. If well written, case studies can be attention holding and exude a strong sense of reality. They are often accessible and engaging for readers: case studies derived from research can be of great value in teaching and learning and can identify future research agendas (Bassey 1999)

On the other hand, the main problem faced by case study is the problem of 'generalisability'. How far can lessons be learnt and generalisations made from studying just one case or one unit? 'All we can' is Wolcott's (1995) bullish answer: 'each case study is unique, but not so unique that we cannot learn from it and apply its lessons more generally' (Wolcott 1995: 17, 175). A similar point, albeit in gendered language, was made almost sixty years ago by Kluckhohn and Murray, when they wrote 'Every man is in certain respects, like all men, like some men, like no other man' (1948: 35).

Despite the inherent difficulties of judging whether case studies underline similarities to or differences from other examples, a problem faced in other forms of research, too, the study of cases is surely a valuable tool. Lessons can be learned from relating to case studies. This criterion of *relatability* is potentially more valuable even than *generalisability* or *validity*.

See also: classroom observation; educational research

Further reading

Bassey, M. (1999) *Case Study Research in Educational Settings*, Buckingham: Open University Press.

Bogdan, R. and Biklen, S. (1982) *Qualitative Research for Education*, Boston MA: Alleyn and Bacon.

Kluckhohn, C. and Murray, H. (eds) (1948) *Personality in Nature, Society and Culture*, New York: Alfred A. Knopf.

Stake, R. (1995) *The Art of Case Research*, Thousand Oaks CA: Sage Publications.

Wellington, J. (2000) *Educational Research: Contemporary Issues and Practical Approaches*, London: Continuum.

Wolcott, H. F. (1995) *The Art of Fieldwork*, London: Sage.

Yin, R. (1994) *Case Study Research: Design and Methods*, 2nd edn, Beverley Hills CA: Sage.

JERRY WELLINGTON

CATCHMENT AREA

In the United Kingdom the term 'catchment area' relates to a geographical area surrounding a nursery, primary or secondary school, from which students are drawn. Catchment areas are peculiar to each school and form a part of the institution's admission arrangements. It will normally be transparent and publicly available to parents.

Schools and the local education authorities have traditionally identified catchment areas so that all areas of housing had a designated local school, attended by the local children. Main roads normally define catchment areas, but in exceptional circumstances can be drawn part way up a multi-story apartment block. In contexts of neighbourhood or comprehensive schooling, students living within the school's catchment area may be offered a guaranteed place at their local school. Those living outside may be added to a waiting list for a place. But this has not been so in contexts where selection on the grounds of aptitude or ability has been – or continues to be – officially sanctioned. Moreover, the notion of catchment areas has been somewhat superseded by the greater emphasis now placed upon on parental choice or preference.

It has been the British experience – over many decades – that homes located within the catchment area of a highly regarded school will be subject to a price premium. The particulars for houses on the market often state the school catchment area within which the house falls and it is not uncommon for parents to 'buy' a state school place by relocating and adding significant sums to their mortgage debt. Recent research conducted on both sides of the Atlantic has pointed to a positive relationship between average house prices and the perceived quality of the local school (Haurin and Brassington 1996; Holme 2002).

The existence of catchment areas may not prevent parents from applying for places in schools beyond their locality. Current English education policy emphasises parental rights to state in-order preferences of schools, which may include some distant ones, and schools with a religious character. The local authority then undertakes a pupil allocation process, which is open to appeal. Sociological research questions the extent to which parents living in some areas are able to exercise their choice or even their preference in a meaningful way. Such factors as social class, local housing and geography may restrict parents with the least cultural capital to the school serving their catchment area (Gewirtz *et al.* 1995).

See also: comprehensive school/education; parental choice; privatisation/marketisation; pupil mobility

Further reading

Clark, J., Dyson, A. and Millward, A. (1999) *Housing and Schooling: A Case-Study in Joined up Problems*, York: York Publishing Services.
Gerwitz, S., Ball, S. and Bowe, R. (1995) *Markets, Choice and Equity in Education*, Buckingham: Open University Press.
Haurin, D. and Brassington, D. (1996) 'School quality and real house prices: inter-and intra-metropolitan effects', *Journal of Housing Economics*, 5: 351–68.
Holme, J. (2002) 'Buying homes, buying schools: school choice and the social construction of school quality', *Harvard Educational Review*, 72(2): 177–205.

NATALIE HEATH

CATHOLIC SCHOOL/EDUCATION

The Catholic Church became intimately involved in education from the early days of Christianity. During the Middle Ages Church and state cooperated in the provision of education for the clergy in cathedral schools and for the laity in parochial schools. The emphasis was primarily on religion, although some instruction was also based on the 'trivium' and the 'quadrivium'. The monasteries also devoted considerable time to the study of the scriptures. The development of scholasticism led to a synthesis between Greek philosophy and the ideas of St Thomas Aquinas. Associated with this development was training in systematic thought aimed at harmonising the findings of reason and the 'truths' of divine revelation. The outcome was an approach to learning which permeated the medieval universities until it became seriously fractured by the Renaissance and the growth of Protestantism. Following the Reformation, the Catholic Church adopted a fortress mentality. The ultimate humiliation was the loss of the papal states in 1870. Concurrently, however, a great revival took place in Catholic education internationally. Associated with this was the rapid growth in both old and new religious teaching orders of nuns, brothers and priests.

With the loss of its temporal empire the Catholic Church engaged in a massive project aimed at re-establishing its spiritual power. Schools played a central role in this project. As with the state, the Church sought to use schools to pacify and regulate the 'lower classes'. However, it also insisted on the creation of an all-pervasive religious atmosphere in the schools. This led to the emergence of various levels of tension between the Church and successive governments in various parts of the world. At the same time, the Church largely accepted state-prescribed syllabi in many countries. Throughout much of the English-speaking world this allowed Catholic schools to break down the link between being Catholic and being poor. There was also a growth in the number of secondary schools run by the Catholic Church aimed at providing education for the children of the Catholic upper and middle classes.

The religious orders constituted a large unpaid and totally dedicated workforce that could be trusted absolutely in the continual expansion of Catholic education. While this expansion was often at the expense of maintaining the highest pedagogical standards, there were plenty of exceptions, with the situation varying both between and within countries. Furthermore, by the end of the 1950s the situation in many countries demonstrated that the Catholic Church's use of its schools to accelerate Catholics through the social ranks had been very successful.

The Second Vatican Council (Vatican II), which deliberated between 1962 and 1965, opened up a new era. In Catholic education the call now was for schooling to meet the challenges of a modern and secular culture, although ironically over the next fifteen years there was also a dramatic decline in the number of nuns, brothers and priests. The new openness in thought encouraged some Catholic educationalists to question the very existence of Catholic education, while others argued for common schools in which children from all Christian denominations would be educated side by side. Yet, such radical views presented no serious threat to the Catholic Church's commitment to schooling.

Currently there are over 167,000 Catholic primary schools with 50 million students worldwide, along with nearly 200 Catholic universities. The expectation of the Vatican Congregation for Catholic Education is that they should be reviewing the vitality of their religious ethos. These are also challenging times for Catholic lay teachers who now occupy key leadership roles. Not least amongst the challenges have been those arising out of a decline in the proportion of Catholics attending Catholic schools and the increase in the number of non-Catholic teachers. Also, there are those who argue that Catholic schools have become more concerned with adopting pecuniary values than following through on the challenges posed by Vatican II, while there have been exchanges in the USA on the 'eliting' of the Catholic school. There are also those who consider that Catholic schools have been overly influenced by the contemporary education industry which tends to see knowledge as utilitarian and students as products. These are challenging times for the laity in Catholic education.

See also: church; Jesuit education; religious education; scholasticism

Further reading

Grace, G. (2002) *Catholic Schools: Mission, Markets and Morality*, London: RoutledgeFalmer.
Judge, H. (2002) *Faith-based Schools and the State: Catholics in America, France and England*, Oxford: Symposium Books.
O'Donoghue, T. (2004) *Upholding the Faith: Catholic Schools and the Recruitment and Retention of Teachers for Religious Teaching Orders, 1922–1965*, Bern: Peter Lang

TOM O'DONOGHUE

CENTRALISATION/DECENTRALISATION

Centralisation in education refers to a degree of power, control and domination, exercised by political and educational decision making authorities over all aspects of education. Centralised decision making processes, controlled by the state, affect all educational institutions, curriculum, administration, finances, educational standards and assessment. The state prefers to control, rather than delegate, decision making power over the wide spectrum of education. Centralisation in education is commonly used to refer to the administration and financing of education. The degree of centralisation in education and policy making has historically varied among nations.

The role of the state is a paradoxical one. On the one hand, the concept of the 'nation-state' necessitates the centralisation of certain functions, including provision for mass education. Current educational policy reforms designed to achieve competitiveness and diversity by means of standardised curricula, national standards and standardised assessment suggest an increasing centralisation. On the other hand, the state-defined policies of educational restructuring in response to demands for equity, participation and diversity have the effect of encouraging decentralised schooling. The tightening of state control over the curriculum was prompted by the need to 'return to basics', and to 'improve standards'. These slogans represented the policy rhetoric of neo-liberalism. There are many reasons for this: at the macro-political and macro-economic levels such a policy shift can be linked to global economic competitiveness and global markets in education.

Decentralisation in education, by contrast, can be defined as the process of delegating power and responsibility concerning resources (e.g. finance, human resources, and curriculum) by the central government to local educational institutions (Zajda 2006). Decentralisation in education potentially challenges the ubiquitous and central role of the state in education. It involves the transfer of power and decision making processes from central authorities to municipal and school-based management structures.

Over the last few decades, there has been a preoccupation with decentralisation in education policy discourses focusing on the quality and standards of education, particularly among the developing nations of Latin America, South Asia, and Eastern Europe. Neo-liberal policies, which advocated decentralised and privatised school systems, claimed the following virtues: (1) being democratic, efficient, and accountable; (2) being more responsive to the community and to local needs; (3) empowering teachers, parents, and others in the education community while improving the effectiveness of school reform; and (4) improving school quality and increasing funds available for teachers' salaries through competition.

One of the key issues in decentralisation is the necessity to understand who controls, and who ought to control, educational administration, financing and curriculum planning. Another issue relates to which of the many functions in the system to decentralise. It has been demonstrated that there is no total political and administrative decentralisation, since all policy decisions concerning finance, personnel and staffing retain varying degrees of centralisation and decentralisation (Zajda 2003). Hence, the real policy issue is one of finding the necessary balance. Some recent studies have focused on the link between globalisation, education policy and curriculum implementation. One of the key issues is the degree to which globalisation has influenced reforms for decentralising school governance and the classroom consequences of this trend.

We can distinguish between three different modes of decentralisation:

- *Deconcentration*: the spatial relocation of decision making, transferring some administrative responsibility or authority to lower levels *within* central government ministries or agencies;
- *Delegation*: the assignment of specific managerial or decision making authority to local governments;
- *Devolution*: the transfer of responsibility for governing, creating or strengthening – financially or legally – sub-national units of governments, whose activities are substantially *outside* the direct control of central government.

Weiler (1993) also divides decentralisation into three models: 'redistributive', 'effectiveness' and 'learning cultures'. The redistributive model deals with the top-down distribution of power, the effectiveness model focuses on the financial aspects and cost effectiveness of decentralisation, and the 'learning culture' model addresses cultural diversity and the adaptability of curricula to local needs. At a global level, the centralisation–decentralisation policy debate focuses on the power and control of school curricula, of defining, selecting

77

and implementing curricular content and the deployment of assessment instruments.

See also: accountability; core curriculum/ national curriculum; educational policy; educational reform; marketisation/privatisation; school-based management; standards

Further reading

Weiler, H. (1993) 'Control versus legitimation: the politics of ambivalence'. In J. Hannaway and M. Carnoy (eds) *Decentralization and School Improvement: Can We Fulfill the Promise?*, San Francisco CA: Jossey-Bass.

Zajda, J. (2003) 'Why do education reforms fail?', *European Education*, 35(1): 58–88.

——(2006) (ed.) *Decentralisation and Privatisation in Education: The Role of the State*, Dordrecht, the Netherlands: Springer.

JOSEPH ZAJDA

CENTRE FOR EDUCATIONAL RESEARCH AND INNOVATION (CERI)

The Centre for Educational Research and Innovation (CERI) is a research and dissemination centre for education across the member countries of the Organisation for Economic Co-operation and Development (OECD). It was set up in 1968 by the OECD, of which it remains a part, although it is also independently funded by member countries. OECD is itself an international organisation of developed and industrialised countries which support liberal democracy and a free market economy. It is based in Paris and directly employs a group of analysts, statisticians and support staff, but it also draws on experts and research networks from member countries.

CERI focuses on trends in education systems in the developed world. Its work is organised around four themes: education in the future, education and globalisation, innovative practices for education, and education and research. The Centre is known for its statistical work on education, and this contributes to the international indicators on education published annually in *Education at a Glance*; the *Teaching and Learning International Survey* (TALIS) which assesses the learning and teaching conditions in schools; and the *Programme for the International Assessment of Adult Competencies* (PIAAC) which measures adult competencies in terms of skills, attitudes and knowledge.

Its work is concerned with emerging trends and long-term strategies such as the impact of globalisation, internationalisation and trade in education, demographic change and markets. It has assessed the implications of such factors for various countries in terms of access, cost and quality as well as linguistic diversity and cultural understanding. For instance, the *Schooling for Tomorrow* programme aims to overcome 'short-term thinking' in lifelong education and has assessed how the demand for education might be met in the future. In partnership with the Mexican ministry of education it has worked to identify emerging models of learning. CERI has developed models of education in order to challenge what are seen as 'traditional', state-dominated and top-down models. Similarly, 'university futures' identifies key changes in higher education and has developed scenarios relevant to the next 15–20 years. *New Millennium Learners* has examined the implications for education and the 'knowledge society' of the emergence of a younger generation of learners whose lives have been strongly influenced by digital technologies. The development of 'open educational resources' which are freely available electronically has also been supported by CERI, as has incorporating e-learning into the curriculum. Formative assessment for adults linked to personalised learning has been researched in relation to both secondary schools and adult literacy and numeracy.

The Centre works to foster better links between research, policy and practice and to involve educational researchers, practitioners and government officials in cross-national discussions. It supports strategic policy development through a programme of research analyses and syntheses and by identifying, supporting and stimulating innovation in education. The practice of educational research itself has also been examined, for instance in considering the role of neuroscientific research in helping to understand learning processes and in the relationship of research to the 'users' of that research, particularly policy makers,

CERI creates international networking opportunities through a programme of national and international meetings and conferences, discussion groups and exchanges on educational policy, strategies and innovations. Internet-based forums have allowed a wider diversity of people to contribute to these. It disseminates ideas through publications, workshops and conferences and nurtures international exchanges of knowledge and experience. The audience for CERI's work comprises researchers, policy makers and practitioners to whom it disseminates policy briefs, publications and reports. The titles of its many publications help to illustrate the work of CERI. These include *Demand-Sensitive Schooling* (2006); *Think Scenarios, Rethink Education* (2006); *Personalising Education* (2006); *E-Learning in Tertiary Education and Internationalisation* (2005); and *Trade in Higher Education: Opportunities and Challenges* (2004).

Criticisms of CERI match those of its mother organisation, the OECD. Critics portray it as a members' club of wealthy nations. It is seen to further these interests by arguing for internationalisation and market-based reforms, harmonising national educational systems in line with the interests of international capital.

See also: educational research; globalisation; Organisation for Economic Co-operation and Development (OECD)

Further reading

CERI (2001) *The Well-Being of Nations: The Role of Human and Social Capital*, Paris: OECD.
Keeley, B. (2007) *Human Capital: How What You Know Shapes Your Life*, Paris: OECD.

Papadopoulos, G. S. (1994) *Education 1960–1990: The OECD Perspective*, Paris: OECD.

TOM WOODIN

CERTIFICATE/CERTIFICATION

A certificate is a document attesting that the holder has completed a particular course of training or study or possesses a particular set of qualifications. 'Certification' is an imprecise term with a variety of uses. Some certificates are similar to a diploma or degree in that they indicate attainment of a specified level of education. Some certificates have a legal status similar to that of a licence in that they grant permission to engage in a profession or other activity that would be illegal without the certificate. Other certificates have only symbolic or representational value; they are designed to indicate particular competence or expertise but afford no legally recognised privilege. Certificates may be granted directly by government bodies or agencies, by schools or other educational institutions under authority of a government agency, or by self-appointed professional or trade groups or schools with no government authority.

Certificates are often employed by business and industry to indicate completion of a training programme or competence in a certain aspect of the business. A wide range of professions and trades – including accountancy, law, financial planning, building trades, and mechanics, among many others – employ certification in this way. In every case, the issuer of the certificate attests that the holder of the certificate possesses the stated competencies, but the attestation does not normally create a legally enforceable contract or legal recourse against the issuer in the event that the holder does not possess the stated competencies. Certification is frequently employed in the computer and information technology industries. Certificates relating to specific technologies may be issued by the manufacturers and sellers of the specific technologies or by third-party groups.

The profession that has made the most extensive use of certification, both historically and contemporarily, is education. In all fifty states of the United States and many other countries, teachers and school administrators may only be hired if they possess a governmentally issued or recognised certificate or licence (the term used in some jurisdictions). Certification requirements may include a college degree, specified courses, practice teaching or other practicum or internship, good moral character or disposition, and passing one or more examinations. Depending on the rules of the particular country, state, or issuing jurisdiction, certification may be relatively broad (e.g. teacher, school administrator) or specific (e.g. middle-school teacher, chemistry teacher, high school principal).

The most common route to obtaining certification as a teacher is through a university-based programme, which itself has been accredited or otherwise authorised by a government authority to grant certificates. In the US and several other countries traditional university-based teacher certification programmes generally require four years of study, with emphasis on coursework in pedagogy, as well as the specific subjects that the certificate grants license to teach. Elementary and primary school programmes generally focus on methods of teaching, child development and classroom management. There is usually particular emphasis on the teaching of reading and other literacy skills. Secondary programmes may require more coursework in the area of certification – most often history, mathematics, language arts, or science – with less study of general pedagogy and methods of teaching. Certification programmes at both levels usually lead to a bachelor's degree in education granted along with the certificate upon completion of the programme.

In recent years in the United States there has been a movement to create non-traditional paths to teacher certification. Proponents of 'alternative' teacher certification argue that the requirements of traditional programmes are too rigid and serve to exclude potentially valuable teachers, especially in areas of chronic teacher shortage such as mathematics, science, and urban schools. Proponents of alternative certification often also question the value of much of the content of traditional programmes. Alternative certification programmes vary quite a bit, but they usually permit individuals with a bachelor's degree or experience working in a particular field to obtain certification in that field by completing a limited number of courses in methods and pedagogy and one or more supervised practicums or internships. Programmes may be university-based or organised by a school district or other education agency. Currently, almost all states have some form of alternative certification.

Obtaining a certificate grants eligibility for, but does not guarantee, employment. Some jurisdictions issue lifetime certificates to educators, whereas others require that certificates be renewed periodically. Renewal usually requires additional formal training or experience designed to ensure that the knowledge and skills of the educator remain current. Educational governing bodies may revoke the certification of educators for good cause after following procedures specified in law. Good cause may include criminal behaviour or other serious malfeasance, breach of an employment contract with a public school, or failure to meet current certification requirements.

See also: diploma; examinations; qualifications; teacher education/training; training

Further reading

Angus, D. L. (2001) *Professionalism and the Public Good: A Brief History of Teacher Certification*, Washington DC: Thomas B. Fordham Foundation.

Boyd, D., Goldhaber, D., Lankford, H. and Wyckoff, J. (2007) 'The effect of certification and preparation on teacher quality', *The Future of Children*, 17(1): 45–68.

Lucas, C. J. (1997) *Teacher Education in America: Reform Agendas for the Twenty-First Century*, New York: St Martin's Press.

MICHAEL IMBER

CHANCELLOR

In the United States, university chancellors, where that title is used, are hands-on chief executives, often former scholars with a talent for administration, business and fundraising. This is in contrast to the position in the United Kingdom and countries such as Australia, Canada and New Zealand. In these Commonwealth countries the position of university chancellor is an honorary one, though at one time the post was vested with wide administrative powers. The chancellor is the formal head of the university, appointed or elected, according to local regulations, to preside over the university's ceremonial occasions and to act as its ambassador.

Members of the British royal family and other eminent persons serve as university chancellors. For example, Princess Anne and Prince Charles are respectively chancellors of the Universities of London and Wales, while lords David Owen and Christopher Patten, both former frontline politicians, head Liverpool and Oxford universities. Some British and Commonwealth universities have a tradition of installing local business leaders as chancellors but others have demonstrated a more popular touch. In 2004 Greg Dyke, then director-general of the British Broadcasting Corporation and an alumnus of the University of York, replaced the retired opera singer Dame Janet Baker as chancellor of that university. Three years earlier, another media figure, the newsreader Anna Ford, was installed as the first female chancellor of Manchester University, from which she graduated in 1966. The former cricketer, now a Pakistani politician and charity fundraiser, Imran Khan, became chancellor of Bradford University in 2005. Atypically, the University of Huddersfield's current chancellor, the *Star Trek* actor Patrick Stewart, is not a graduate of any university, though he

was born locally. In view of the fact that, in the British and Commonwealth university contexts, chancellors are essentially figureheads, the day-to-day leadership of universities rests with a vice-chancellor, normally a distinguished academic-turned-administrator, who is frequently assisted by one or more pro vice-chancellors.

See also: university; vice-chancellor

DAVID CROOK

CHARITIES, EDUCATIONAL

A charity is a trust, company or unincorporated association established to support an area of public concern for non-commercial purposes. It is common for schools, colleges and universities operating in the private, as well as public sector of education, to hold charitable status – sometimes conferring benefits of taxation exemption – if they can demonstrate a public benefit. Learned societies representing educational professionals, too, may be charities. Historically, charities have often provided services that a state or government has failed to supply. The advancement of education is generally accepted as an important object of charity, therefore educational charities, and those with an interest in education, provide a wide range of support for organisations and individuals across all sectors of education from primary/elementary to higher education and beyond.

From the seventeenth century onwards, evidence of the involvement of charities with education in Europe became noticeable through the establishment of charity schools for the poorest children in society. In 1699, the Society for Promoting Christian Knowledge founded charity schools in England with the aim of promoting knowledge and practice of the Christian religion, together with limited tuition in reading and writing. The finances of English endowed schools were susceptible to fraud, and 1869 saw the creation of the endowed schools act and the formation of an endowments commission (later to become the UK's Charity Commission) to regulate and monitor the work of charities linked to education. Similar schools, again prompted by religion, began to open across France during the eighteenth century to provide 'instruction in decency and morality and reading and writing' (Aries 1996: 291). The founding of charity schools in America began in the early decades of the nineteenth century (Nasaw 1979), but, in contrast to Europe, philanthropic individuals or organisations, rather than the church usually led provision. Charity schools often received additional funding through local subscriptions or endowments (where income is generated through dividends from invested funds derived from donations). Charity schools – some of which continue to exist as independent schools – are still in existence, but their autonomous status means that the institutions are often required to charge fees which, ironically, means excluding children from poorer backgrounds. This problem can be overcome by the awarding of scholarships or grants to assist children whose families are unable to afford fees.

Charities that support educational projects usually offer a range of services dependent upon their budget and the scope of the charity's donation policies. There are some charities that actually provide education via schools, whereas another charity will give others the opportunity to provide educational resources where they are needed. In some countries, particularly those in the developing world, where a state-funded system of education is not in place, it is charities that often provide basic education for school-aged children and sometimes run literacy or technical programmes for adults. In contrast, educational charities working in Europe, Australia and North America tend to focus support on the development of educational practice and research, rather than allocating funds for aspects of education that are usually provided by the state.

International relief organisations such as the United Nations Children's Fund (UNICEF) or Oxfam provide emergency support and charitable assistance in many countries around the world, but educational work is a small part of their remit. Wealthy charitable trusts, for example the Esmée Fairbairn foundation (UK) and the Rockefeller foundation (USA) – both of which give to a range of causes, but with education central to their interests – require organisations and individuals to make formal applications for financial support. Applications for funding are measured against criteria and advice on applications is available through numerous books on trusts and charities. Alongside the major trusts there are numerous national charities that focus upon education. In the UK for example, the Nuffield Foundation provides financial support to facilitate the development of research into educational practice and offers other resources such as training and policy development. Some educational charities have very specific criteria, for example the Rhodes Trust only provides funding for students from Africa, India, Australia and the USA to study as undergraduates at Oxford University in the UK; other trusts or charities might only support students of a certain age, or fund research within one particular area of education.

Educational practices are constantly changing and evolving and so the need for further research and resources increases. The role of charities in supporting the process and practice of education will continue to be vital, given that governments or states have limited funding resources.

See also: church; endowment; Rhodes Trust; scholarship; voluntarism

Further reading

Aries, P. (1996) *Centuries of Childhood*, London: Random House.
Nasaw, D. (1979) *Schooled to Order. A Social History of Public Schooling in the United States*, New York: Oxford University Press.

MARY RICHARDSON

CHARTER SCHOOL

Charter schools are non-sectarian, publicly funded schools organised around a particular teaching philosophy or programmatic objective. The first charter school opened in 1991 in Minnesota, United States. Its purpose was to provide parents with selection in public schooling beyond what fell to them by default of residence. Since 1991, more than 3,600 charter schools in forty states, plus the District of Columbia, have been registered in the United States, and approximately fifteen charter schools have been registered in Alberta Province, Canada (where the first charter school opened in 1994). Historically, the concept of charter schools is attributable to a suggestion made by Ray Budde in the mid-1970s, and later supported by the American Federation of Teachers, that teachers be given contracts or 'charters' to develop pedagogically innovative schools. However, Budde's charter school concept took the form of school district- and school board-led magnet schools until it was combined in the 1990s with the concept of parental choice. Across much of the 1990s, charter schools were conceived as an option open equally to parents, whose selection of schools would inject an element of market competition into a public system thought to be dysfunctional because state-controlled. More recently, the language of parental choice in support of charter schools has shifted to one of accountability and student outcomes for reasons that charter schools have affected uneven market feedback on traditional schools and are available to parents differentially.

In the USA and Canada, charter schools range widely in curricular focus. Many carry a special programme emphasis such as direct instruction, back-to-basics, child-centred education, environmental education, bilingual or language immersion instruction. Some serve students with special needs, including students who may be pregnant or parenting, or who may be at risk of dropping out of school. Few operate with a charter to serve students with disabilities. Most charter schools are granted three-to-five-year renewable contracts by a school district or a state board of education. Universities or city councils sponsor a few charter schools. Most are located in urban areas. In the USA, state policy plays a significant role in shaping admissions policies, funding, programming, and outcomes. Some states allow for-profit organisations to initiate and manage charter schools. Most allow for the conversion of traditional and private schools to charter schools and for the initiation of new start-up charter schools. In Canada, charter schools operate under provincial legislation and must teach the provincial curriculum.

Opponents of charter schools argue that such schools promote the siphoning off of many of the best students found in traditional schools, for reasons that charter school admissions policies, although regulated, may include sibling preferences that indirectly promote segregation based on race, class, and achievement. Supporters argue that charter schools enable parents to circumvent de facto segregation by choosing, rather than having their children assigned to a particular school. Opponents contend charter schools drain funds from traditional schools and are academy-like schools within a public system. Supporters point to the fact that most charter schools receive per-pupil district funding, as do traditional schools, and offset additional expenses (particularly administrative and school maintenance expenses) with private-sector grants for which some charter schools qualify. Supporters also maintain that the academic focus of charter schools (sometimes) is a reflection of a charter school's particular curriculum and, in some cases, smaller class size.

Research points to a more complicated picture than either opponents' or supporters' visions. Case-based and statistical analyses indicate that enrolment, funding, and student outcome patterns vary across charter schools and are more directly a function of school-level characteristics and state- or provincial-level policies than overarching status as a charter school.

Outside North America, discussion is underway in the United Kingdom about whether proposed 'trust schools', which are related to grant-maintained and foundation schools, are charter-like in quality; and some groups argue that New Zealand's system of independent schooling mirrors an ideal of charter schools. As in North America, debate elsewhere revolves around funding and enrolment, and whether charter schools enable parental choice or reflect the dismantling of a comprehensive system of public education. Less frequently, both possibilities are considered in the same argument.

See also: alternative education, magnet school; marketisation; parental choice; specialisation

Further reading

Buckley, K. E. and Wohlstetter, P. (eds) (2004) *Taking Account of Charter Schools: What's Happened and What's Next?*, New York: Teachers College Press.

Lacireno-Paquet, N. (2006) 'Charter school enrollments in context: an exploration of organization and policy influences', *Peabody Journal of Education*, 81(1): 79–102.

Miron, G. and Nelson, C. (2002) *What's Public about Charter Schools? Lessons Learned about Choice and Accountability*, Thousand Oaks CA: Corwin.

AMY STAMBACH

CHEMISTRY

Chemistry can be defined as a component of the natural sciences which focuses on the study of the properties, specific characteristics and behaviour, composition, and structure of matter, which includes anything in the universe that has mass and occupies space. A significant component of the study of chemistry also includes the structural and compositional changes matter undergoes along with its corresponding energy changes. It investigates the properties of matter in terms of atoms, which include the infinitesimally small building blocks of matter that constitute the basic unit of any chemical element. In doing so, chemistry seeks to establish scientific explanations for the behaviour and characteristics of various types of individual chemical elements found in nature, including the definite composition, chemical structure, mass and weight, and how these chemical elements combine and react with each other in specific ways under various physical conditions. In particular, chemistry bases its explanations on empirical evidence gathered through the processes and mechanisms involved in the nature and methodology of science in order to better understand, explain, and make predictions about the structural and behavioural relationships of the atomic origin, chemical evolution, and the distribution of energy or atomic charges within and between the various chemical elements on multiple levels. These energy levels or atomic charges include the three fundamental particles that make up atoms, such as the protons, which contain a positive charge, and the neutrons, which are neutral and contain no charge, both found in the nucleus of an atom, and the electrons, which contain a negative charge surrounding the nucleus.

Chemistry encompasses both the ancient and most current scientific disciplines; however, its historical roots reside in the study of natural philosophy and history. Various cultures throughout time, including but not limited to the Greeks, Egyptians, Assyrians, Babylonians, Europeans, Indians, Chinese, Incans, Mayans, and Native Americans have been interested in asking questions and seeking answers about the cosmos through the study of alchemy. Early on in these ancient civilisations, the universe was seen as essentially containing two parts, the living or material world and the spiritual or immortal world. In essence, early philosophers and alchemists were concerned with incorporating the knowledge and technologies of metallurgists, brewers, dyers, tanners, and the pathology of animals in understanding the material and immortal world and whether or not matter found in nature was unchangeable or transformable. If metals were mutable, alchemists hoped to use that knowledge to be able to transform metals such as lead or copper into more valuable metals such as silver and gold while at the same time developing a potable version of the gold product in order to achieve some form of immortality.

The term chemistry was not fully understood in its current form until the early part of the nineteenth century when an English school teacher, John Dalton (1766–1844), developed the atomic theory (1803–7) in order to better explain several natural and experimental observations made throughout the field of chemistry over time. Coupled with technological advances in gas chemistry, inorganic and organic chemistry, chemists during and after Dalton's time were able to build upon the atomic theory through empirical and conceptual foundations allowing for scientific explanations of chemical reactions in terms of atoms. With the discovery of new elements and their corresponding atomic weights, Russian chemist Dmitri Mendeleev (1834–1907), in 1869, further refined the atomic theory by developing the idea of periodicity which classified the known elements based on their atomic weights, which in turn helped explain their chemical structure and behaviour, while at the same time predicting the existence of elements that were yet to be discovered. In order to better explain periodicity and the atomic theory of elements, the work of English physicist H. G. J. Moseley (1887–1915) demonstrated, in 1913, that the critical property of chemical behaviour and reactions among and between individual elements were based not on the atomic weights but on the atomic number or the number of protons found in the nucleus of the atom. To this day, all the known elements found naturally or synthesised in the laboratory are classified based on their respective atomic numbers. Thus, in order to better understand and explain the scientific concepts and contextual underpinnings

within the study of matter, the field of chemistry incorporates and utilises the atomic theory of matter and periodicity as its foundation and unifying theme.

See also: biology; curriculum; science/ science education; subjects

Further reading

Brown, T., LeMay, H. and Bursten, E. (1997) *Chemistry: The Central Science*, 7th edn, Upper Saddle River NJ: Prentice Hall.

PAUL NARGUIZIAN

CHILD DEVELOPMENT

Child development is an umbrella term, encompassing all aspects of human growth from birth to adolescence and integrating several, interrelated domains of equal importance. It is a recent phenomenon to consider development as having a lifespan nature and, until the late Middle Ages, many agree (Aries 1962) that childhood was not considered a separate and distinct stage in human development. Research into child development has only been seriously considered since the end of the nineteenth century: originally most information about child development was anecdotal, based on opinion with little scientific underpinning. Through observation and experiment, however, knowledge about this area has grown and changed.

Traditionally, inflexible age-related models of development were preferred. These stage model conceptualisations consider that the development of competencies is fixed, universal and unidirectional, with achievement at one stage being greatly dependent on the successful completion of the previous level. Although these models do appear to provide explanations for development in certain domains or at certain periods in the lifespan, they are considered to lack context and to be over-generalised. Now, therefore, child development is considered more an interplay between biological, environmental and socio-cultural factors (Baltes *et al.* 1980) with no single trajectory followed by each and every child.

Information on physical development in childhood is often presented as age-related, developmental milestones. These are expressed in terms of typical development; however, large individual differences exist. Physical development is particularly closely linked to motor development, describing the physical competencies a child will develop as s/he grows.

A child's cognitive development encompasses all psychological activities involved in the acquisition, processing, organisation and use of information. Different theories emphasise specific aspects seen as affecting cognitive development: cognitive developmental theorists, such as Piaget prioritise the active, problem-solving nature of child, contrasting with the social constructivist view of Vygotsky and Bruner, which stresses the importance of social interaction for development.

In the early twentieth century psycho-analytic theory (see Freud) had a great effect on views of child development, centring on children's emotions and the impact of their close relationships on development. Learning theorists, in contrast, believe that cognition is influenced mainly by external, environmental factors: everyone is similar at birth and has potential to develop in a similar way but different experiences affect development, resulting in different outcomes.

Constructivist theories in other domains (e.g. moral, social) were also generated, helping to explain a child's social and emotional development. Erik Erikson developed an influential life span model of development, proposing eight psychosocial developmental stages through which a healthily developing human should pass from infancy to late adulthood. Moral development theory primarily stems from Lawrence Kohlberg, who advanced a series of stages to explain the development of moral reasoning.

Socialisation is also an intrinsic part of child development, explaining how children acquire behaviour which enables them to fit in with their culture. Very early signs of sociali-sation behaviour are usually considered to have ethological value, however, as the child matures, these become more sophisticated and have different ends, such as the skills and knowledge to function successfully in society.

The domains of social and emotional development, physical development and cognitive development are inextricably linked. There are wide, individual variations in terms of children's biological makeup, their everyday experiences and contexts. The impact of culture and context on child development is now fully acknowledged and an interdisciplinary approach includes psy-chological, sociological, anthropological and biological theories. Stronger links are there-fore being forged between different fields and disciplines to study child development more holistically.

There is no ultimate theory of child development. Theorists' views diverge and children's development is affected by factors that change, such as improved nutrition or more widespread access to education. No single theory can explain the physical, cogni-tive and social aspects and their interrelation-ships. Elements which mould development are many-layered and complex with human variance influenced not only by age but by constitutive features of the environment, both physical and social. The environmental context, from familial setting to wider com-munity and culture combines with personal facets of development, in terms of heredity and biological makeup to influence the development of the whole child.

Whilst there is some common theoretical ground among all these diverse approaches to child development, precisely how a child is seen to develop depends largely on the lens through which the child is viewed. Different research disciplines will have varying emphases, but there is a clear consensus that all domains of development are interrelated.

See also: Bruner, Jerome; cognition; constructivism; Freud, Sigmund; Kohlberg Lawrence; Isaacs, Susan; Piaget, Jean; Vygotsky, Lev

Further reading

Aries, P. (1962) *L'enfant et la vie familiale sous l'ancien regime*, Paris: Plon.

Baltes, P. B., Reese, H. W. and Lipsitt, L. P. (1980) 'Life-span developmental psychology', *Annual Review of Psychology*, 31: 65–100.

Isaacs, S. (1930) *Intellectual Growth in Young Children*, London: Routledge and Kegan Paul.

JO PEAT

CHILD GUIDANCE

'Child guidance' is a twentieth-century concept describing the psychological diagnosis and treatment of juvenile emotional and behavioural issues by a multidisciplinary team of specialists including psychiatrists, psychologists, and social workers. Child guidance originated in the United States during the early twentieth-century progressive reform era as a practical programme to address the problem of juvenile delinquency. The child guidance movement brought together child savers, or progressive reformers who shared an interest in the welfare of poor urban youths; mental hygienists, a group of psychiatrists and their allies looking for ways to avoid institutionalisation for mental disorders by intervening before symptoms became acute; and private philanthropic interests with money to invest in child advocacy programmes. The proponents of child guidance believed that psychiatric intervention during childhood would address youthful misbehaviour and also circumvent the development of more severe emotional problems in adulthood. This emphasis on prevention led child guiders to extend the focus of their work from the delinquent to the 'pre-delinquent' and the non-delinquent troublesome child whose behaviour disrupted school or family life, and as early as the 1930s the work of child guidance was synonymous with a broad range of mental health services for young people.

The institutional base of child guidance was the child guidance clinic, staffed by the multidisciplinary team of professionals. The first clinic – the Juvenile Psychopathic Institute – opened in 1909 as an adjunct of the Chicago Juvenile Court to address the problem of recidivism. With funding from the wealthy Chicagoan Ethel Sturgis Dummer, these reformers hired a local physician, William Healy, to assist the court judge by providing medical and psychological assessments of delinquents. Healy created the team of physician/psychiatrist, psychologist trained to administer intelligence and mental aptitude tests, and social worker, the staff member who investigated the family life of the delinquent. Together these specialists produced a report intended to guide sentencing. The clinic and the court brought together the legal and medical approaches to juvenile crime and established treatment rather than punishment as the goal of the juvenile justice system.

The child guidance movement began in 1922 when the Commonwealth Fund, one of several philanthropic organisations specialising in the welfare of children, provided seed money for eight clinics modelled on the Chicago prototype. By the mid-1930s more than 600 clinics were in operation throughout the United States. During the inter-war years child guidance became an international phenomenon. The Commonwealth Fund supported clinics in Canada and England; specialists in Germany and the Netherlands also established clinics on the child guidance model. After World War II, American personnel brought the idea to Japan, where a child guidance movement soon flourished in the wake of the Occupation.

While the roots of child guidance lay in efforts to prevent juvenile delinquency, the clinics quickly transformed from agencies for diagnosing the causes of delinquency among the lower classes to programmes for assessing and treating emotional and behavioural problems of children from all social classes. These problems included family and school issues as well as juvenile delinquency, and collectively the behaviours seen at the child guidance clinic were labelled symptoms of 'personality maladjustment'. Child guiders also set out to educate parents and teachers about the prevention of conduct disorders. In the United States, their efforts led to an association with the federal Children's Bureau and with the Child Study Association of America, a private organisation dedicated to parent training. Teacher education, too, was influenced by the child guidance movement as mental hygienists identified the school as an important gatekeeper for the clinic. As Americans and Europeans entered the post-World War II Baby Boom era, child guidance structured childrearing advice and framed the prevention and treatment programmes for behavioural and emotional problems in young people.

Initially child guidance was marked by an eclectic approach to behavioural problems. Healy's study, *The Individual Delinquent* (1915), represented the view that a unique combination of social, intellectual, and psychological factors determined each child's behaviour. The environment in which the child lived, as well as the innate intellectual capabilities and psychodynamic elements, shaped the child's personality and determined the level of adjustment. By mid-century, however, child guidance had become synonymous with a psychoanalytic understanding of the problem child. Although clinics continued to investigate the child's environment, diagnosis narrowly centred on family dynamics rather than socio-economic issues and child guiders increasingly focused on the problem parent of the problem child. The parent most often found at fault was the child's mother. Mother-blaming, the emphasis on maternal overprotection or maternal rejection as a cause of problem behaviour, structured child guidance work for much of the twentieth century.

The phrase 'child guidance' is no longer widely used in the United States. As separate child disciplines – child psychiatry, child psychology, special education, etc. – professionalised and established specialised clinical practices over the century and beginning in the 1960s with federal funding for community mental health clinics followed by legislation mandating individualised educational programmes, child guidance ceased to be the umbrella term for age-specific psychotherapeutic services. In England, Germany, and Japan, however, 'child guidance' continues to designate mental health services for the young.

See also: behaviourism; child development; delinquency; emotional and behavioural difficulties/disorders (EBD); psychology of education

Further reading

Cohen, S. (1983) 'The mental hygiene movement, the development of personality, and the school: the medicalization of American Education', *History of Education Quarterly*, 23: 123–49.

Jones, K. W. (1999) *Taming the Troublesome Child: American Families, Child Guidance, and the Limits of Psychiatric Authority*, Cambridge MA: Harvard University Press.

Richardson, T. (1989) *The Century of the Child: The Mental Hygiene Movement and Social Policy in the United States and Canada*, Albany NY: State University of New York Press.

Thom, D. (1992) 'Wishes, anxieties, play and gestures: child guidance in inter-war England'. In R. Cooter (ed.) *In the Name of the Child: Health and Welfare, 1880–1940*, London: Routledge.

KATHLEEN W. JONES

CHILD-CENTRED EDUCATION

Child-centred education seeks to put the child first, fitting schools and other learning environments for children rather than the other way around, and building education from the needs and interests expressed by the child. A classic statement of this approach was the Plowden Report, *Children and Their*

Primary Schools, published in Britain in 1967. It has been closely associated with the ideals of progressive education, Rousseau and Dewey, and with the World Education Fellowship of the twentieth century. As such, it has attracted many fervent advocates, but also has a large number of critics who argue that education should prepare the child for adult society without undue regard for the preferences of children themselves. Internationally, it is at the heart of a number of major initiatives designed to promote the interests of children. For example, UNESCO's Convention on the Rights of the Child (2001) emphasised a child-centred approach to learning and teaching. Initiatives have been developed in many countries to promote students' learning through their active participation. UNICEF has developed a 'child friendly' approach to schooling in countries such as Pakistan, while Save the Children has similarly encouraged learner-centred teaching methods in China and elsewhere.

See also: Dewey, John; progressive education; Rousseau, Jean-Jacques; United Nations Children's Fund (UNICEF); United Nations Educational, Scientific and Cultural Organization (UNESCO); World Education Fellowship

GARY McCULLOCH

CHILDREN'S LITERATURE

Because of the inevitable power imbalance between adult writers and child readers, children's literature has been part of education – formal and informal – arguably from its earliest appearance *c*.2400 BC in Sumer (Adams 1986: 2004). The first books in English for children were courtesy books (guides to manners), such as Hugh Rhodes's *Boke of Nurture* (*c*.1545); the first major illustrated text for children, Comenius' *Orbis Sensualium Pictus* (translated 1659) was an encyclopedia. The first book produced for American children (imported from England) was John Cotton's *Spiritual Milk for Boston Babes* (1646), a catechism and school text.

Children's literature is closely linked to cultural and political education: it was central to Australian romantic nationalism in the first part of the twentieth century; after the October Revolution in 1917 in Russia it served communist ideology; in Korea it contributed to maintaining national identity during the Japanese occupation. It is often influenced by education policy: in Brazil, a major factor in the revival of children's literature was legislation in 1971, making compulsory the study of fiction by Brazilian authors in primary schools; in France, the growth of children's magazines such as *Le journal des jeunes personnes* (*The Young People's Journal*) (1833–94) may be seen as a response to the Guizot primary education law of 1833; in 1918, when the three Baltic states became independent, children's literature was needed to promote language teaching. In many places, where children's literature remains synonymous with education, the situation can be complex: in some Arab states, where modern education systems evolved only in the twentieth century, it is seen as a supplement to textbooks, and suffers from 'limitations imposed by formal education'; in Africa, children's literature exists only in countries whose education systems guarantee sufficient sales – often countries where there is strong political control over content (Hunt 2004: 947–48, 955, 991, 1007, 1050, 1124, 1178).

The Sunday School movements in the United Kingdom and United States of America in the nineteenth century were supported by millions of cheap tracts from the Religious Tract Society (1799) and the American Sunday School Union (1817), and educationally focused series by authors such as 'Peter Parley' and 'Oliver Optic' dominated children's reading in the USA until the 1860s. In the UK, school stories, from Harriet Martineau's *The Crofton Boys* (1841), had a symbiotic relationship with the 'public' schools, mirroring and producing codes of behaviour and reinforcing gender roles. They may well have contributed to the schools' survival in an increasingly democratic society (Hunt 2001: 299).

Until the 1980s, schools faded out of children's literature and children's literature faded out of schools. How far children should have access to 'their' literature in school, as opposed to acquiring 'functional literacy' has been argued for a century (Meek 1993: 90), and since the 1950s the pendulum in Western education has swung between highly structured language acquisition techniques backed by graded readers, and the 'whole language' or 'real books' approach. Ironically, the texts that require the most advanced skills in decoding and intertextual knowledge – picture books – are widely used in primary school classrooms.

In the twenty-first century, with the output of children's books at record levels internationally, and with the return of 'crossover' books which (as in the nineteenth century) are read by both children and adults, such as those by Philip Pullman and J. K. Rowling, the 'leakage' across the membrane between reading in-school and outside school is increasing. Children's literature has pioneered 'postmodern' and multimedia texts and has expanded concepts of literature to include oral storytelling (Zipes 2004), computer games and Web-based authoring – all of which have huge implications for educational practice.

There are many thousands of courses on children's literature from undergraduate to doctoral level across the world, notably in the USA, Australia, and Germany: in Thailand in 1989, eight of the ten universities and twenty-one of the thirty-six teacher training colleges ran courses (Hunt 2004: 1211). From the academic thesis to the playground rhyme, and from work with children with special needs to political propaganda, texts for children are inextricably entwined with education.

See also: Comenius, Johann Amos; literacy; reading

Further reading

Adams, G. (1986) 'The first children's literature: the case for Sumer', *Children's Literature*, 14: 1–30.
Hunt, P. (2001) *Children's Literature*, Oxford: Blackwell.

——(ed.) (2004) *International Companion Encyclopedia of Children's Literature*, 2nd edn, London and New York: Routledge.
Meek, M. (1993) 'What will literacy be like?'. In M. Styles and M-J. Drummond (eds) *The Politics of Reading*, Cambridge: University of Cambridge Institute of Education and Homerton College.
Zipes, J. (2004) *Speaking Out: Storytelling and Creative Drama for Children*, London and New York: Routledge.

PETER HUNT

CHINA

Chinese education traditions can be traced back to the Confucian philosophy emerging in the Spring and Autumn Period (770–476 BCE). The Confucian view of knowledge put emphasis on knowledge as a process of absorbing and interacting with experience, on classical teachings and on a commitment to nurturing good governance (Schwartz 1985). The Confucian tradition dominated Chinese education up to the Tang dynasty (618–907 CE), when Taoism and Buddhism flourished, and became a dominant force in education (De Bary 1982).

In contrast to the Confucian concern for human relationships, Taoism stressed attachment to nature, whose spontaneity belies deliberate planning. The Taoist view of knowledge involved intense observation of nature on one hand, and a distrust of formal compilations of knowledge on the other. Taoism was thought to provide the soil where Buddhism, introduced from India, could flourish. Buddhism emphasised democratic equality, and the Buddhist tradition of education envisioned a society without cultural or social identities among its members.

Towards the end of the Tang dynasty, Confucian thought began to reassert itself, as society became increasingly sophisticated, and Taoism and Buddhism were seen as unable to address core issues of good government and societal development. From the Song dynasty (960–1279 CE), the Confucian classics became essential readings for all those who aspired to be scholar-officials through the imperial examination system, which integrated education with the selection of officials. The Confucian approach to knowledge was now rationalist and secular, emphasising a cumulative study of the classical texts, and the education of all to find their appropriate place within the social order and live out the various rituals that gave visual form to a society of harmony and order. It was also enlivened by the progressive ideas of the sixteenth-century scholar Wang Yangming, who integrated Buddhist and Taoist insights into Confucianism and emphasised the unity of action and knowledge. By the late nineteenth century, however, the conservatism, rigidity and conformity of the imperial examination system and its associated institutions led many to believe China's weakness and humiliation in face of the Western forces was a direct result of the Confucian heritage. The last imperial dynasty was overthrown in the Revolution of 1911, and the May 4th Movement of 1919 is often seen as the beginning of China's cultural transformation.

Although the imperial examinations had been abolished in 1905, Confucian ideas continued to exert an influence over people's minds and hearts, such that a series of foreign influences were shaped by its persisting values. The broad phases and sources of influence are Meiji Japan in the early 1900s, Continental Europe between 1912 and 1919 (also in the 1930s), America in the 1920s, and the Soviet Union in the 1950s (Reynolds 2001). The first modern school system was modelled on the Japanese education system of the time, which seemed to offer a modernisation that would preserve Confucian values. Japanese patterns were soon abandoned, however, when Japanese imperialism emerged as a serious threat.

The May 4th Movement of 1919, sometimes called 'China's Enlightenment', opened the door to democratic theories of education, associated with John Dewey, which resonated with aspects of the Ming dynasty (1368–1644) neo-Confucianism of Wang Yangming (Ding 2001). However, the nationalist government which came to power in 1928 adopted European patterns of greater centralisation and standardisation in the 1930s in their efforts to build a modern state. When the Communist Party came to power in 1949, the new government chose to reform the education system in a close imitation of Soviet patterns. On the surface, this reflected a shared political commitment to socialism; but on a deeper level one can see an affinity between Soviet centralisation and the Confucian penchant for control through the regimentation of knowledge. An internal contradiction between the hierarchy and rigidity of state Confucianism and the Taoist attachment to anarchic spontaneity was thus exacerbated by Soviet patterns of extreme specialisation. A passionately radical critique of 'Soviet social imperialism' sparked the Cultural Revolution which began in 1966 (Hayhoe 1989)

When China opened its doors to the world in 1978, educational reform was seen as essential to economic modernisation. China's leading scholar in comparative education, Professor Gu Mingyuan, published a series of influential essays which convinced the new pragmatic leadership of the importance of investment in human capital (Gu 2001). This can be contrasted with the emphasis on the political function of education that had dominated since 1949. The tendency for education to be regarded as a tool of class struggle had reached its peak during the Cultural Revolution (1966–76), when young people were sent to the countryside to learn from the peasants, and universities were open only to students from peasant and working-class backgrounds.

By the late 1980s attention began to move in turn from the economic to the cultural function of education. Pioneering work on school reform by a younger generation of scholars highlighted education's role in nurturing individuality and encouraging creativity and criticised the instrumentalist obsession with economic and social goals (Ye 1989).

There was a call for attention to students' individual needs, respect for their dignity, and cultivation of their subjectivity. This reflected external currents of educational thought, yet also had roots in progressive aspects of the Confucian tradition. It gradually led the reform programme to a deeper level.

The progress of educational reform in China can be seen in a series of government documents. It was first initiated by the *Resolution on Reform of Education System* (1985), then promoted by the *Outline for Educational Reform and Development in China* (1993), and further advanced by the *Programme of Educational Revitalisation for the Twenty-first Century* (1998) and the *Resolution on Deepening Educational Reform and Promoting Quality-oriented Education* (1999). The 1985 document called for a commitment to provide nine-year compulsory education by 2000, restructuring secondary education, expanding technical education, and granting more autonomy to higher education institutions. A Compulsory Education Law followed in 1986, mandating six years of primary education and three years of junior secondary education.

The 1993 document called for the implementation of nine-year compulsory education, the improvement of education quality, and the raising of 100 top universities to world standards. The 1998 and 1999 documents have revealed China's intention to build its own innovation system, and embrace a knowledge economy. Quality is given high priority and seen in terms of encouraging students' independent thinking and creativity. Quantitative goals include ensuring that compulsory education reaches the most remote rural areas, expanding upper levels of enrolment to achieve mass higher education by 2010, and allowing private education to complement the public system. Most of these points can be found in the *Education Law* (1995), and *Higher Education Law* (1998).

Following the transfer of the sovereignty from the United Kingdom to China, in 1997, education in Hong Kong (now a Special Administrative Region of the People's Republic) retained many of its British influences. A far-reaching reform programme is now underway to achieve greater harmonisation with mainland education, including measures for Mandarin Chinese to be the linguistic vehicle of instruction.

China now has a comprehensive and diverse education system, comprised of four sectors: basic education (K–12), vocational and technical education, higher education, and adult education. By 2003, the basic education sector had 116,400 kindergartens, 425,800 primary schools, and 80,500 secondary schools. There were 11,835 vocational high schools, specialised/professional high schools, and technical schools. Formal higher education institutions numbered 1,552. At the same time, the adult education sector offered literacy programmes, and various educational opportunities from primary to tertiary levels in 31,498 schools and institutions. There was a total of 70,165 private institutions spanning all sectors. These 667,585 educational institutions enrolled a student population of 300 million, making China's education system the largest in the world. Of particular note, China stepped over the threshold of mass higher education nearly a decade ahead of its original schedule, with about 17 per cent of China's population between 18 and 22 in some sort of post-secondary education by 2003. (Ministry of Education of China 2004).

While Chinese education has achieved remarkable quantitative expansion in the past two decades, quality remains a serious concern. Educational investment is thought to be inadequate and there is a shortage of qualified teachers. There is also an imbalance in development between urban and rural areas, formal and non-formal education systems, elite and non–elite schools. There are striking inequalities in educational opportunity, as well as disparities between education and the labour market.

Nevertheless, the remarkable achievements of the past twenty-five years presage a bright future. A recent renaissance in Confucian thought suggests that the solutions to Chinese education problems may lie in some of its traditions. Education at the local level always emphasised values such as self-reliance and individual responsibility in China's past, and Confucian learning was a 'learning for one's self', as suggested by the eminent Sinologist, William Theodore de Bary (1996). Harvard-based Confucian scholar Tu Weiming has noted that 'learning to be human in the Confucian spirit is to engage oneself in a ceaseless, unending process of creative self-transformation' (Tu 1998: 13).

Chinese education traditions and China's modern development thus seem to have both a conflictual and a complementary relationship (Gu 2001). Traditional culture definitely needs to be scrutinised critically. Yet, a self-knowledge that reaches back to embrace the rich heritage of traditional thought, as well as the hard won achievements of modern development, will enable Chinese educators to make unique and valuable contributions to the world community in future (Hayhoe 2002).

See also: centralisation/decentralisation; compulsory education; Japan; rural education

Further reading

De Bary, W. T. (1982) *Three Ways of Thought in Ancient China*, Stanford CA: Stanford University Press.

——(1996) 'Confucian education in premodern Asia'. In W.-M. Tu (ed.) *Confucian Traditions in East Asian Modernity*, Cambridge MA: Harvard University Press.

Ding, G. (2001) 'Nationalization and internationalization: two turning points in China's education in the twentieth century'. In G. Peterson, R. Hayhoe and Y. Lu (eds) *Education, Culture and Identity in Twentieth-Century China*, Ann Arbor MI: University of Michigan Press.

Gu, M. (2001) *Education in China and Abroad: Perspectives from a Lifetime in Comparative Education*. Hong Kong: Comparative Education Research Centre, University of Hong Kong.

Hayhoe, R. (1989) 'China's universities and Western academic models'. In P. G. Altbach and V. Selvaratnam (eds) *From Dependence to Autonomy: The Development of Asian Universities*, Dordrecht, the Netherlands: Kluwer Academic Publishers.

——(2002) 'Wei shenme yanjiu Zhongguo jiaoyu [Why study Chinese education]?', *Zhongguo jiaoyu: yanjiu yu pinglun [China's Education: Research and Review]*, 3: 1–15.

Ministry of Education of China (2004) *2003 nian quanguo jiaoyu shiye fazhan tongji gongbao [2003 National Education Development Statistics Bulletin]*. China Education and Research Network, www.edu.cn/20040527/3106677.shtml

Reynolds, D. R. (2001) 'Sino-Foreign interactions in education'. In G. Peterson, R. Hayhoe and Y. Lu (eds) *Education, Culture, and Identity in Twentieth-Century China*, Ann Arbor MI: University of Michigan Press.

Schwartz, B. I. (1985) *The World of Thought in Ancient China*, Cambridge MA: The Belknap Press of Harvard University Press.

Tu, W.-M. (1998) 'Beyond the Enlightenment Mentality'. In M. E. Tucker and J. Berthrong (eds) *Confucianism and Ecology: The Interrelation of Heaven, Earth and Humans*, Cambridge MA: Harvard University Centre for the Study of World Religions.

Ye, Lan (1989) 'Shi lun dangdai zhongguo jiaoyu jiazhi quxiang zhi piancha [Probing errors in value orientation of contemporary Chinese education]', *Educational Research*, 5.

RUTH HAYHOE AND QIANG ZHA

CHURCH

The church is a worldwide body of Christian believers, whose members form local churches (or congregations) for worship and religious activities, usually meeting in buildings (also known as churches) dedicated for that purpose. Early missionary activity led to rapid growth throughout the Roman empire. Various socio-political factors, as well as differences in doctrinal emphasis, explain the later development of Roman Catholic, Orthodox, and (from the sixteenth-century Reformation) Protestant traditions in southern, eastern, and northern Europe. Colonisation, emigration, and missionary enterprise spread these major church groups to other continents. Political reaction to the church throughout its 2,000-year history has ranged from protection to suppression. The complex church–state relationships are of immense historical importance, but interpretation is often contested.

Education has always concerned the church, not least in teaching Christianity to converts, although the first schools were the medieval cathedral song schools, which taught boys to read and sing the choral services, and grammar schools, which gave a classical education. In a range of early modern Christian societies, schools and higher education institutions were founded and staffed by the clergy. Later, from the early eighteenth century, congregations and benefactors took an interest in providing basic education for the lower classes. At the end of the eighteenth century, the Sunday School movement spread overseas from Britain and the early nineteenth century saw the more systematic development of schools maintained by Anglican, Nonconformist and Roman Catholic bodies.

International missionary activity has often been associated with education and developing literacy. Roman Catholic teaching orders (e.g. Jesuits and Christian Brothers) made notable advances in the nineteenth century, whilst Anglican, Methodist and Baptist missions (among others) established schools throughout the British empire and elsewhere. Many religious schools in such countries as Australia, England and the United States have developed as elite, fee-paying institutions, but churches also operate schools in public education frameworks and are responsible for initiatives to bring basic education to many poor, often rural, communities in the developing world. The critique of cultural imperialism has been applied generally to missionary education, but since the late twentieth century revisionist historians have urged greater sensitivity to the different approaches adopted by missionary teachers and sharper discrimination between the actual circumstances in which they taught.

Advanced communications technology, such as digital satellite television broadcasting, is extensively utilised by the church for educational purposes in the Middle East and North Africa. Programming aims to be culturally, politically and religiously sensitive, complementing other public information channels with its holistic stance on human life and society, including needs of marginalised people and environmental issues.

See also: Catholic school/education; dual system; Jesuit education; religious education; religious school; Sunday school

Further reading

Elias, J. (2002) *A History of Christian Education: Protestant, Catholic, and Orthodox Perspectives*, Malabar FL: Krieger.
Tulasiewicz, W. and Brock, C. (eds) (1988) *Christianity and Educational Provision in International Perspective*, London: Routledge.

DAVID NICHOLAS

CITIZENSHIP/CIVICS

Citizenship/civics entails the knowledge, skills, and dispositions needed to function socially within the parameters of a nation's political and legal boundaries. Schools translate these goals into knowledge of the community, nation, and world; skills required to participate effectively in society while promoting and protecting one's interests; and dispositions that form the bases for decisions to act on one's behalf while keeping the common good in mind. Citizenship/civics education is the fundamental premise on which the whole school experience functions.

Subject matter that cultivates citizenship in students has long been discussed and debated in democratic societies. This discussion does not centre on the importance of knowledge in the life of a citizen, but on what knowledge students should apply effectively to life situations. A curriculum fostering citizenship can approach the question of 'What subject matter is most worth considering?' through various perspectives. These perspectives include the disciplines of history and the social and behavioural sciences, interdisciplinary approaches exemplified by global and multicultural education and issues-centred curricula, and the local community.

An additional source exists in the life of the school itself, such as student governance and extracurricular activities. These various disciplinary and social perspectives form the foundation of citizenship education subject matter. Each offers a unique insight into what students should both know and consider when acting as citizens.

The most common subject matter approach to learning about citizenship is the academic, compartmentalised study of history and the social and behavioural sciences. Traditionally, these subject matter sources emerge from the disciplines of world and national history, political science, geography, economics, sociology, anthropology, and psychology. Each of these disciplines plays a different role in the curriculum concerned with citizenship education, and each of them offers different ways of looking at the decisions citizens face. Interdisciplinary approaches to citizenship/civics content invert the traditional disciplinary approach by turning local, national, and global issues, trends, and problems into subject matter. Citizenship/civic education using the school and community as subject matter focuses on the life of the child as it intertwines inextricably with the curriculum. All of these approaches can work together – and, ideally, should be employed as such – in the development of responsible citizens.

Learning activities that promote citizenship/civics skills form the basis for operationalising sources of subject matter for citizenship/civic education. These learning activities include cooperative learning; concept learning; values clarification, moral development, and character education; thinking skills; role playing, simulations, and games; service learning; structured questioning; and digital technology. These learning activities can be employed in all of the subject matter approaches to citizenship development in schools. Similar to the subject matter approaches, these activities can and do overlap in practice.

Dispositions promoted in citizenship/civics education stem primarily from the form of associated living, political philosophy, and legal system in each country. Totalitarian societies, by definition, hold a utopian view of society. Therefore, dispositions are prescribed and based on the type of society deemed as most ideologically admirable. Democratic societies, on the other hand, view citizenship as a work in progress that deals with change through dispositions based on John Dewey's three moral traits of character: open-mindedness, wholeheartedness, and responsibility. However, teaching methods in a democracy may vary from citizenship transmission very similar to that found in totalitarian societies to reflective inquiry, where the method of intelligence is based on the best available evidence in order to make the most warranted decisions concerned with civic life.

Internationally, citizenship/civic education varies from a specific, mandated course of study to a more generalised approach through the disciplinary fields. In most democracies and totalitarian societies, citizenship/civics curricula are nationally centralised. However, approaches will vary widely. For example, Danish curricula for citizenship/civic education are student centred and focused on deliberative and independent decision making. In Japan, by contrast, citizenship/civic education fosters the established beliefs of the society developed over generations and valued under any form of government. States or provinces in federal democracies offer distinct but related curricula that do not emanate from a central office or ministry of education.

See also: collaborative/cooperative learning; curriculum; history; social studies

Further reading

Dewey, J. (1933) *How We Think*, Boston MA: Houghton Mifflin.

Hahn, C. (1998) *Becoming Political: Comparative Perspectives on Citizenship Education*, Albany NY: State University of New York Press.

Torney-Purta, J., Lehmann, R., Oswald, H. and Schulz, W. (2001) *Citizenship and Education in*

Twenty-Eight Countries: Civic Knowledge and Engagement at Age Fourteen, Amsterdam: IEA.

GREGORY E. HAMOT

CLASS SIZE

Teachers and lecturers frequently express a preference for teaching smaller, rather than larger, groups. Small classes are less burdensome when it comes to marking and, if there are spare desks to isolate a disruptive student, it may be easier to maintain a purposeful working atmosphere. Fee-paying schools frequently make a point of advertising to parents their low student/teacher ratios, but very small classes are thought by some to discourage student independence. Reductions in school class sizes are frequently justified to combat overcrowding and to improve student attainment, but economists and educationists are sometimes at odds about the costs and benefits of appointing additional teachers.

During the late 1980s the Student/Teacher Achievement Ratio (STAR) project, which tracked some 7,000 children in Tennessee, concluded that students in the early primary grades benefited from being placed in classes of 13–17. A British longitudinal study, based at the Institute of Education, University of London, similarly found that children aged 5–7 performed better in mathematics and reading when the class size was below twenty. Eight-to-eleven-year-olds taught in smaller classes for mathematics, English and science performed no better than their peers, however. A follow-up to Project Star suggests that there may, nevertheless, be long-term gains. In 2005 researchers at the University of Buffalo reported that the attainment of Tennessee high school graduates who had experienced small classes for a sustained period exceeded that of students confined to larger groups throughout their school lives. At an international level, research evidence of this kind has underpinned the funding of class size reduction programmes by national and local government bodies. In higher education institutions it is not uncommon for several hundred students to attend certain lectures, but seminar group sizes are typically less than twenty and may be smaller still.

See also: classroom

DAVID CROOK

CLASSICAL EDUCATION

A classical education is designed to draw on the ancient civilisations of Greece and Rome, or alternatively on the Confucian traditions of China. The Western tradition is organised in three stages. The first is the *trivium*, consisting of grammar, logic and rhetoric, to provide the foundations of learning. Grammar involves reading and writing, including through the study of Greek and Latin. Logic provides the means of reasoning and analysis of arguments, often based on the dialectic methods of the Greek philosopher Aristotle. These insights are then applied to persuasion and argument, or rhetoric. The second stage is the *quadrivium*, including arithmetic, astronomy, geometry and music, with a strongly historical approach, and making use where possible of the Socratic method. Finally, the student is prepared to go into an educated profession, for example in the law, medicine or science.

More broadly, a classical education denotes immersion in the values and heritage associated with the classical civilisations. When interpreted in this way, a classical education represents a kind of humane learning or liberal education. It may also be regarded as a refuge against aspects of modern education in which history is disregarded, and in which science, technology and vocational education are elevated above a study of the classics. For many, it would represent a defence of particular kinds of humane values, and has been developed in this way by scholars such as Sir Richard Livingstone and Alfred Whitehead in the twentieth century.

See also: classical studies; grammar; liberal education; Socratic method; vocational education

GARY McCULLOCH

CLASSICAL STUDIES

Classical studies is an academic subject embracing all aspects of the ancient Greek and Roman world, including its literary, historical, philosophical, and material remains. It retains some of the pre-disciplinary character of the classical education from which it developed. At the secondary and primary levels, students may encounter elements of classical studies in literature or social studies programmes, but specific instruction by classicists occurs for the most part in courses in Latin, or occasionally Greek, languages. In post-secondary education classical studies includes classical archaeology, ancient history, and ancillary disciplines like papyrology, epigraphy, and numismatics in addition to the core discipline of classical philology. Specialists in these areas may be grouped in a single department of classics, or there may be separate departments of archaeology or classical languages. Ancient historians may teach in a department of history, classical linguists in a department of linguistics, and other specialists in appropriate units. The distinguishing feature of a course in classical studies is instruction in the Latin and Greek languages, although the lack of any shared understanding of what else constitutes classical studies has led some to speak of a crisis of definition in the subject.

Although forerunners of modern classical studies can be found in the work of scholars of Hellenistic Alexandria, Renaissance humanists and their early-modern successors, and early-modern scholars like J. J. Scaliger (1540–1609) and Isaac Casaubon (1559–1614), classical studies as a separate academic subject originated in the nineteenth-century German educational system reformed by Karl Wilhelm von Humboldt (1767–1835) during his tenure as Prussian minister of public instruction. The classical secondary school or *Gymnasium* prepared students for university-level studies and provided philological training that equalled that in many universities of the English-speaking world. At the universities of Halle and Berlin, Friedrich Augustus Wolf (1759–1824) and his pupil August Böckh (1785–1867) developed the ideal of *Altertumswissenschaft*, the comprehensive, scientific study of antiquity.

In Great Britain and America, graduate education in classical studies modelled itself on nineteenth-century *Altertumswissenschaft* and on the seminar-based pedagogy, culminating in a dissertation of the Humboldtian university. As founding professor of Greek at Johns Hopkins University, Basil Lanneau Gildersleeve (1831–1924) dominated American classical studies for fifty years after the Civil War. He earned his Ph.D. from Göttingen in 1853, heard Böckh lecture at Berlin, and based his teaching and scholarship on German models. In England, the influence of *Altertumswissenschaft* began to be felt in mid-century, when dons like Henry Nettleship (1839–93) introduced German methods to Oxford and Cambridge. The creation of chairs of Latin at the University of London and later at Oxford (1854) and Cambridge (1869) marked the change from an essentially humanist classical education to an academic system in which classical studies was one among many distinct subjects or disciplines.

As it developed into an academic subject under the influence of Germanic *Altertumswissenschaft*, classical studies also continued and developed the humanist tradition of philological and antiquarian study of texts. Manuscripts of ancient authors, which had been copied and recopied since antiquity, had to be evaluated and used to establish the best possible form of each text. Although textual scholars like Richard Bentley (1662–1742) and Richard Porson (1759–1808) used wide reading, sensitivity to an author's style and historical good sense to produce important editions of ancient authors, textual criticism remained on an empirical basis until Karl Lachmann (1793–1851), in editions of Propertius, the New Testament and Lucretius, demonstrated that by analysing variant readings, manuscripts could be grouped into families and placed on a tree diagram or *stemma* showing their relationships, and that on the basis of this relationship it was possible to reach the earliest knowable state of the text. Lachmann's method enabled scholars to put the texts of the many Greek and Latin authors on a sounder basis than they had been since late antiquity. Great critics like A. E. Housman (1859–1936) insisted that textual criticism was an art, not a science of mechanical rules, and that it was the foundation, not the summit, of classical study, but others, especially in the English-speaking world, held up textual criticism as the be-all and end-all of philology. This exaggerated valuation led to an inevitable counter-reaction, but the principles of textual criticism continue to be an indispensable part of classical studies.

A third tradition, older than either *Altertumswissenschaft* or textual criticism, also shaped modern classical studies. Liberal education, which was from its beginnings synonymous with classical education, sought to shape the tastes, values, and attitudes first of aristocratic governing classes and, later, of the professional and managerial classes of modern Europe and America. This education used Greek and Latin languages and literature as instruments for the formation of personality and as emblems of class solidarity. Although many who experienced this education retained no more than a few classical tags and scraps of grammatical knowledge, for more than a few Europeans and Americans classical education provided a well of knowledge and understanding from which they drew throughout their lives.

The current state of classical studies reflects its inheritances from liberal or classical education, textual scholarship and comprehensive *Altertumswissenschaft*. In primary and secondary education, classical studies emphasises study of the Latin language and a small number of Latin texts. Greek is rarely found in American secondary schools and has nearly disappeared from state-supported secondary education in Great Britain. A few canonical authors, often those endorsed by examining bodies like the Advanced Placement programme in the United States, form the core of advanced courses at the secondary level, and they are usually read through the lens of rhetorical, philological, and ethical criticism in a tradition going back to the liberal, classical education of the Renaissance. In colleges and universities, in contrast, classical studies often positions itself as an interdisciplinary field. To some extent this positioning represents the lingering survival of the ideal of a comprehensive study of antiquity espoused in the works of Wolf, Böckh, and Ulrich von Wilamowitz-Moellendorff (1848–1931), perhaps the greatest practitioner of developed *Altertumswissenschaft*, but classical studies in contemporary higher education lacks the explicit humanistic purpose that lay at the core of Wilamowitz' scholarship.

Many contemporary classicists, in fact, feel the lack of any common understanding of classical studies among those who consider themselves classicists. This epistemological crisis parallels a similar crisis in the humanities generally, but it also reflects the withdrawal of classical studies to the margins of the humanities themselves over the course of the twentieth century. The abolition of compulsory Greek and Latin as a requirement for university admission early in the twentieth century, the rise of the elective system in American universities, and the multiplication of degree courses in British universities caused as much as reflected a shift in the centre of intellectual gravity away from Greek and Latin studies. Contemporary classical scholarship draws on newer fields for concepts and models to apply to the ancient world, while classroom practice in both schools and universities continues to emphasise the kind of grammatical, rhetorical, and historical knowledge that characterised traditional classical education. The divide between archaeology and philological studies, and between classical archaeologists and their colleagues who work on other cultures, continues to grow. Postmodernism has cast doubt on the idea of enduring truth implicit in the idea of a classical canon.

Despite these uncertainties and the loss of its dominant place in education and culture, classical studies remains a vital academic subject. Although the fortune of classical studies varies from country to country and from one sector of education to another, the United States and Germany showed absolute growth in numbers of primary and secondary students taking Latin during the 1990s and into the early years of the twenty-first century. Teachers of classical studies have become effective advocates for their subject through organisations like the American Classical League, the Joint Association of Classical Teachers, and the *Deutscher Altphilologenverband*. In post-secondary education, American colleges and universities in particular have taken the lead in developing ways to teach students who begin classical languages only in adulthood and in creating courses in Greek and Latin literature in translation and in ancient culture that make the results of classical scholarship accessible to a wide audience without requiring knowledge of classical languages. Advanced scholarship continues and expands the traditions of *Altertumswissenschaft* and textual and linguistic criticism, and classical scholars draw on insights and practices from other fields in the humanities and social sciences to reshape the twenty-first century's vision of antiquity.

See also: classical education; curriculum; Greece; liberal education; subject

Further reading

Beard, M. and Henderson, J. (1995) *Classics: A Very Short Introduction*, Oxford: Oxford University Press.

Calder, W. M. III and Kramer, D. J. (1992) *An Introductory Bibliography to the History of Classical Scholarship, Chiefly in the XIXth and XXth Centuries*, Hildesheim and New York: Olms.

Pfeiffer, R. (1968, 1976) *History of Classical Scholarship*, 2 vols, Oxford: Oxford University Press.

Stray, C. (1998) *Classics Transformed: Schools, Universities, and Society in England, 1830–1960*, Oxford: Clarendon Press.

Wilamowitz-Moellendorff, U. von (1927/1982) *History of Classical Scholarship (Geschichte der Philologie)*, Baltimore MD: Johns Hopkins University Press.

LEE T. PEARCY

CLASSROOM

Classrooms are locations for teaching and learning in schools and other organised educational institutions. They provide a shared space and environment for pupils and students to learn. They are designed in various ways to support different kinds of teaching methods, and indeed have changed greatly as pedagogical ideas have developed over the longer term.

Although it is often taken for granted in contemporary schools that classrooms are a basic component of the school building, design and organisation, classrooms are a relatively recent invention. Until the nineteenth century schools often had a single schoolroom for teaching and learning, and even when there were different groups being taught they might be separated only by a curtain rather than being in different rooms. Aries has documented the origins of the school class as dating back only to the late fifteenth or sixteenth century, and taking on a modern form at the start of the seventeenth century. It was used as a term for the first time in the early sixteenth century, for example in 1519 in a letter from Erasmus describing St Paul's School in London, England. The classroom developed many of its modern characteristics in the Jesuits' *ratio studiorum* and the *leges et statuta* of the University of Paris, where the curriculum was taught in specialist classes. Aries argues that the provision of specific premises for each class represented 'a realization of the special nature of childhood or youth and of the idea that within that childhood or youth a variety of categories existed' (Aries 1960: 182). The emergence of the classroom also provided a means of identifying subdivisions within schools, linking schooling more clearly with bureaucratic and social control. In modern systems of schooling, the role of the classroom was strengthened with the development of individual school subjects taught simultaneously and sequentially to different groups of pupils and students categorised by age, ability and often gender within the same institution. As schools became larger and increasingly diverse, classrooms were increasingly necessary for the efficient delivery of the curriculum. Indeed, the classroom can be viewed as an 'invention' that was designed to address the changing needs of schooling, while at the same time fitting with theories of practice and social relations and conventions (Reid 1990).

In Japan, for example, the classroom was organised to promote individual learning at the inception of modern schooling in the late nineteenth century. The concept of 'class' did not appear in Japanese pedagogy before 1886. The government mandate no. 8 in 1886 established the single-room school but also regulated the number of students in a class, with a maximum enrolment of eighty students at the lower elementary level and sixty students at the upper elementary level. The concepts of 'class' and 'classroom' were defined in decree no. 12 issued in 1891 under the title 'Rules of classroom arrangement'. Following the Elementary School Law of 1900, the modern group-based classroom developed. According to Sato, this process also mirrored the formation of the Japanese nation-state: 'As the nation-state was characterized by a homogeneous space of power relations, so the homogeneity of educational space highlighted the national education.' (Sato 1998: 194–95). Although half of Japanese schools were still single-room schools in 1900, the classroom gradually became a place where the subjects of the nation-state were socialised in a highly controlled community with a common culture. The stereotyped Japanese culture shaped in the 1920s remained dominant for the rest of the twentieth century.

Classroom life has therefore become central to the experience of school. It provides not only a stable physical environment, but also a constant social context, often with assigned seats for each student, and fixtures such as the blackboard or whiteboard at the front of the class. It is a very busy place of work, and a 'densely populated social world' (Jackson 1990: 19), which tends to be very crowded and intimate, and often noisy. Everyday exchanges within the classroom are clearly visible to everyone present. There are rules of engagement over when to talk and how to take part in discussions. There may be a number of different kinds of activity going on in the classroom at the same time. Pupils may spend almost the whole of their time during a school year in the same classroom, or may move around the school throughout the school day to take their lessons in different classrooms assigned to a particular subject and teacher. The kinds of use made of a classroom will be reflected in the pictures and schoolwork that are often pinned up on the walls of the classroom.

Classrooms may be arranged in different ways. One standard image is of rows of fixed desks with the teacher addressing the class from the front of the classroom. More progressive and child-centred approaches have encouraged the flexible use of desks and tables for group work. Open-plan classrooms with only partial divisions between groups rather than classroom walls are designed to be flexible and to encourage the sharing of resources and working spaces. There might well be a combination of traditional and progressive arrangements within the same classroom, often dictated by the age of the school and its overall design. Classroom organisation, however, appears to have changed relatively little over the past twenty years beyond adaptations to new forms of technology (Galton et al. 1999).

The position of power and authority enjoyed by teachers behind the classroom door has also become a key dimension of teachers' professionalism. Within the classroom, the teacher may practise his or her craft undisturbed and unobserved, and may well resent being inspected or being obliged to seek assistance from others. They will plan classroom lessons and discussions in advance, but will also take account of the informal, fast-moving and spontaneous character of classroom life. In England, there has been a widespread recognition, at least since the 1940s, that teachers should have the right to exercise their own judgement within the classroom domain. Since the 1970s, however, there has been an increasing tendency for the state to become fully and publicly involved in classroom activities. This trend has appeared to threaten teachers' autonomy within the classroom, which had formerly been closely associated with their professionalism, especially after the introduction of a National Curriculum in 1988 (McCulloch 1998).

The world of the classroom is therefore at the heart of educational practice. It is strongly influenced by changing social and political ideals, and yet represents a haven from the world outside. It is a place of protection and also of guidance, where pupils and students spend the majority of their waking time during their years at school. It is also where teachers engage with their pupils on an everyday basis. The classroom is the defining workplace context that provides the conditions for learning and teaching.

See also: class size; classroom management; open plan; reflective practitioner

Further reading

Aries, P. (1960) *Centuries of Childhood*, London: Penguin.

Galton, M., Hargreaves, L., Comber, C. and Wall, D. (1999) *Inside the Primary Classroom, 20 Years On*, London: Routledge.

Jackson, P. (1990) *Life in Classrooms*, New York: Teachers College Press.

McCulloch, G. (1998) 'Classroom management in England: theoretical and historical approaches to control and discipline'. In K. Shimahara (ed.) *Politics of Classroom Life: Classroom Management in International Perspective*, New York: Garland.

Reid, W. (1990) 'Strange curricula: origins and development of the institutional categories of schooling', *Journal of Curriculum Studies*, 22(3): 203–16.

Sato, M. (1998) 'Classroom management in Japan: a social history of teachers and learning'. In K. Shimahara (ed.) *Politics of Classroom Life: Classroom Management in International Perspective*, New York: Garland.

GARY McCULLOCH

CLASSROOM MANAGEMENT

Classroom management is the set of actions used by a teacher to establish and maintain an environment conducive to student learning. These actions have facilitative, preventive, and interactive features. Teacher actions that promote desirable student behaviour and engagement in class activities are facilitative; such actions are also preventive in that they tend to steer students away from inappropriate behaviours. Many aspects of classroom management occur interactively, requiring the teacher simultaneously to instruct students and to deal with those who are disengaged from an activity or whose behaviour might interfere with their own or other students' learning. The smoothly running classroom of the expert teacher masks the complexity of coordinating instructional activities for a large number of children or adolescents, working in a small space, with varying abilities, interests, and motivations.

The phases of classroom management include preparation, implementation, and maintenance. Teachers must plan how their classroom space should be arranged and they must think through the types of behaviours that are crucial for the activities in which they and their students will engage. These behavioural expectations are translated into routines and procedures that help the teacher and students cope with the complexities of the classroom environment. Although students enter a new term or class with behavioural expectations that are the residual of prior experiences, each teacher and classroom constitutes a new social setting. Thus a crucial time for classroom management occurs at the beginning of the school year or term when teachers have an opportunity to define new expectations. A principle underlying effective implementation is to teach students the procedures and routines that are needed to navigate the activity structure of the class. This means, for example, that if a teacher plans to use collaborative learning activities, students need to be taught what to do in groups, including talk and movement expectations, work procedures, and desirable group behaviour; in contrast, the use of whole class teaching methods requires teaching students different expectations for behaviour. Other common formats for which routines are helpful include transitions (for example at the beginning and end of class periods) and individual seatwork. In some subject areas, careful attention must be given to common activities (for example the use of laboratory work in science lessons). Older students may need only brief explanations and feedback to establish suitable procedures in simple formats; younger children or complex activities often require demonstration, rehearsal, and reinforcement over several weeks to establish routines.

The maintenance phase of classroom management includes techniques that teachers use to promote student engagement as well as strategies to manage inappropriate behaviours. Student engagement is promoted by keeping activities moving without interruptions, following routines and procedures consistently, by maintaining a positive tone, and using activities that are interesting, varied, and that encourage student participation. Management of inappropriate behaviours is aided by good monitoring of student behaviour, which allows the teacher to detect problems before they escalate or spread. Early detection permits the use of simple interventions such as redirection, eye contact, or proximity control. The goal of such interventions is to correct the problem promptly without interfering with the ongoing activity, giving the student centre stage, or becoming a power struggle. When simpler strategies fail, the classroom management plan needs to include effective use of communications skills, problem-solving conferences, consequences and, when needed, use of a school-wide plan for discipline.

Student perspectives on classroom management reveal the importance of relational factors as well as the teacher's ability to establish a good learning environment. Students appreciate teachers who show concern and support for their academic and personal lives; who maintain order without being punitive or arbitrary; and who teach lessons that are engaging and varied. An expanded view of classroom management's goals, beyond establishing orderly conditions for learning, is to view it as integral to the social development of children and adolescents. From this perspective, social skills and attitudes are taught by bringing students into the circle of conversation and decision making about the norms and consequences essential to the social order of the school and classroom. When teachers engage students in age-appropriate discussions of the basis for rules and procedures and the appropriateness of consequences for behaviour, student cooperation is enhanced because it reduces the appearance of arbitrariness, increases student acceptance of norms, and improves behaviour.

See also: classroom; collaborative/cooperative learning; corporal punishment; discipline; practitioner research; whole-class teaching

Further reading

Doyle, W. (1986) 'Classroom organization and management'. In M. C. Wittrock (ed.) *Handbook of Research on Teaching*, New York: Macmillan.

Evertson, C. M. and Weinstein, C. S. (eds) (2006) *Handbook of Classroom Management: Research, Practice, and Contemporary Issues*, Mahwah NJ: Lawrence Erlbaum.

EDMUND T. EMMER

CLASSROOM OBSERVATION

Classroom observation is a widely used method in educational research. It is an attractive and enjoyable method as it affords the opportunity for a researcher to see education (e.g. small group work, practical work, discussion, didactic teaching) in its natural setting. The 'whole picture' can be gained, including not only the human activity and interaction, but also the physical setting in terms of resources, environment (e.g. temperature and lighting), seating layout, equipment and so on.

It varies along two continua: in its degree of structure; and in the extent to which it may be qualitative (e.g. observations looking for different kinds of event or occurrence) or quantitative (e.g. observations of the number of times – the frequency – of certain categories or events, which are decided prior to observation).

In terms of structure, classroom observation could conceivably be totally open-ended and unstructured, i.e. the observer simply goes in to observe the natural setting. Arguably, this is impossible to achieve, as every researcher has some prior concepts or frameworks through which we observe and understand the world (all observation can be said to be 'theory-laden', or as Immanuel Kant put it: 'perceptions without concepts are blind'). At the other extreme, classroom observation in the past has sometimes been totally structured and predetermined, sometimes called 'systematic'. Classroom observers are trained in observation techniques, using a shared schedule, and instructed in exactly what to look for and how often. For example, frequencies of certain events or interactions in the class have been recorded over set time periods (e.g. four seconds), in order to analyse quantitatively the nature of classroom dialogue (see, for example, Flanders' interaction analysis). Of course, semi-structured observation lies somewhere along the continuum between these two poles.

There are several questions that can be posed of observation, which cannot be fully explored here: to what extent are data from observation valid and reliable? Since they depend on the observer, can we be sure that a similar observer would make the same observations? The answer is 'no', of course. One response has been to adopt triangulation, by employing both other methods and other researchers. Second, to what extent does the presence of an observer affect the situation being observed? This would negate claims that the situation being observed is a 'natural' one, unless the observation is covert, which would raise new questions about ethics. One suggested way around some of these issues involves the use of participant observation but it could be said that no observer could ever be non-intrusive. Ethical considerations must always be a central element in a research study involving classroom observation.

The nature and extent to which observers become part of the situation they are observing has been widely discussed, particularly by commentators on ethnography. The key phrase often associated with ethnography is 'participant observation' (e.g. Spradley 1980). This may be possible to achieve in some settings, but some classroom observation may inevitably involve the perception of an 'outsider'. In a long-term study of an organisation, such as a school, an observer may gradually become more and more of a participant. He or she is 'sucked into' the life of the organisation being studied, as an anthropologist would be in studying a tribe by living amongst them. Participant observation requires time, acceptance, carefully negotiated access, and tact.

The role of 'complete participant' has often occurred where the researcher's activities are wholly concealed from the group being studied, as happened in studies of a Glasgow gang (Patrick 1973), the police force (Holdaway 1985) and studies of the army, alcoholics and a mental hospital mentioned in Hammersley and Atkinson (1983).

Shorter studies, on the other hand, are likely to entail far more observation than participation. This could be part of a case study that might also involve visits to an organisation, a study of their documentation, interviews and discussions with staff (and/or students), and other sources of 'evidence'.

Debate is certain to continue over the reliability and validity of observation and its role in research. But, clearly, observation, with whatever degree of structure or participation, is an important part of educational inquiry and especially case study. It is a valuable 'tool', enjoyable to use, for developing insight into what goes on in classrooms: arguably, there could be no better way of gaining the 'whole picture' of school or classroom life.

See also: anthropology of education; educational research; ethnography; qualitative research; quantitative research

Further reading

Hammersley, M. and Atkinson, P. (1983) *Ethnography: Principles in Practice*, London: Routledge.
Holdaway, S. (1985) *Inside the Police Force*, Oxford: Basil Blackwell.
Patrick, J. (1973) *A Glasgow Gang Observed*, London: Eyre Methuen.
Spradley, J. P. (1980) *Participant Observation*, New York: Holt, Rhinehart and Winston.

JERRY WELLINGTON

COEDUCATION

Coeducation involves the education of both males and females in an integrated way in the same educational facilities, as opposed to single-sex education in which they are educated separately. Single-sex arrangements are more traditional, reflecting the separate spheres for men and women in society in past centuries. However, coeducation has become the norm in most countries round the world, except where it is discouraged for religious or cultural reasons. There are continuing debates about whether coeducation is more effective than single-sex education, and whether boys, or girls, might benefit from being educated in a single-sex environment.

In the United States, coeducation became established from an early stage to a greater extent than was common in other countries in the nineteenth century. Coeducation was found to be expedient, practical, and educationally appropriate in the United States in elementary and in high schools, and in both rural and urban areas. American coeducational high schools provided access to higher numbers of girls than was the case in Europe where secondary education for girls was generally separate and inferior to that of boys (Tyack and Hansot 1990: 116). Boys and girls studied mainly the same academic subjects in the same classrooms. This was unlike England, for example, where traditional elite schools were for boys only, and where secondary education for boys and girls developed in different institutions and with pressures for different curricula.

Oberlin College, founded in Ohio, USA, in 1833, was the prototype for coeducational college education, with an emphasis on propriety and the retention of traditional roles for men and women; and the University of Iowa in 1855 became the first public university to admit men and women on an equal basis. Single-sex education became confined to a minority of institutions, and in the late twentieth century coeducation made many further advances, with nearly all single-sex colleges and universities, including all of the prestigious Ivy League colleges, going coeducational at this time (Lasser 1987). In England, where resistance was stronger, often amounting to a siege mentality on the part of elite male institutions, women were not admitted to take full degrees at the University of Cambridge until 1948, and separate male and female colleges were the dominant model. Nevertheless, here too there was a decisive movement towards coeducation on the grounds of educational equity, and there were very few single-sex colleges remaining at either Oxford or Cambridge by the end of the century (Dyhouse 2006).

Despite coeducation becoming increasingly well established on both educational and social grounds, arguments about the educational merits of coeducational and single-sex education have increased rather than diminished over the past decade. Some studies have indicated that single-sex education can help students to learn more effectively, and is less distracting than coeducational environments, although evidence is so far equivocal. In some cases, it has been suggested that girls benefit from being educated separately from boys, while in others it appears that boys may gain some advantage from being educated separately from girls (US Department of Education 2005; Miller-Bernal 1993). Within the classroom, sex-role socialisation in a coeducational environment has continued to foster disruptive behaviour on the part of boys and passivity with respect to girls. The growth of coeducation has not always led to the democratic and egalitarian societies that its early proponents hoped for, and other forms of gender discrimination have continued to exist. Nevertheless, coeducation remains a key instrument for many educators intent on promoting social integration and gender equity.

See also: equality of opportunity; feminist theory

Further reading

Dyhouse, C. (2006) *Students: A Gendered History*, London: Routledge.
Lasser, C. (ed.) (1987) *Educating Men and Women Together: Coeducation in a Changing World*, Chicago IL: University of Illinois Press.
Miller-Bernal, L. (1993) 'Single-sex versus coeducational environments: a comparison of women students' experiences at four colleges', *American Journal of Education*, 102(1): 23–54.
Tyack, D. and Hansot, E. (1990) *Learning Together: A History of Coeducation in American Schools*, New Haven CT: Yale University Press.
US Department of Education (2005) *Single-Sex versus Coeducational Schooling: A Systematic Review*, Washington DC: Department of Education.

GARY McCULLOCH

COGNITION

Cognition is a general term referring to a wide range of mental processes that are used in acquiring and processing information. Cognitive processes include attention, perception, learning, retrieval, thinking, and reasoning. These processes are often used to make sense of the environment and to make appropriate plans for the future.

There are two major issues that have confronted cognitive psychologists endeavouring to understand human cognition. First, cognitive processes are nearly all internal, and thus not directly open to observation. As a consequence, considerable ingenuity is required to use indirect measures that shed light on human cognition. The development of brain-imaging techniques has been of use in this connection, but patterns of brain activation often fail to identify with clarity the details of processing. Second, human cognition is extremely complex and typically involves several different processes occurring concurrently or in rapid succession. There has been much progress in developing theoretical models that reveal some of the main interconnections within the overall information-processing system.

There is overwhelming evidence for substantial individual differences in human cognition, and many of these differences relate fairly directly to intelligence. In spite of this, it was only comparatively recently that cognitive psychologists started to consider individual differences in cognition in a systematic way. The argument that cognitive psychologists have sometimes put forward for ignoring individual differences is that the same processes are used by those of higher and lower ability. The two groups differ mainly in speed of cognitive functioning, but such a difference is not of central importance in understanding human cognition. That argument is fallacious as has been shown, for example, by the very different strategies of problem-solving used by individuals of differing levels of ability. One of the most important differences in cognitive functioning between individuals of differing levels of cognitive ability is that those with higher levels exhibit superior attentional control and focus more on the current task than those with lesser ability.

There are strong arguments for combining the approaches of cognitive psychologists and of psychologists interested in intelligence. The former study cognitive processes in great detail but sometimes fail to incorporate their findings into a broad theoretical perspective. In contrast, many psychologists working on intelligence adopt a broad theoretical approach but fail to consider the processes underlying major aspects of intelligent functioning (e.g. mathematical ability). It has increasingly been the case that the strengths of the two approaches have been combined to the mutual benefit of both.

Research into human cognition by psychologists has clear relevance for education, because it is of central importance to education to teach children to use their cognitive abilities to the full. What is required is a detailed understanding of the learning processes leading children to perform complex tasks increasingly effectively. Some of the major stages of cognitive development undergone by children have been known for several decades starting with the seminal research and theorising of Jean Piaget. However, it is only comparatively recently that there have been systematic attempts to investigate the cognitive processes underlying cognitive development and the usage of more effective strategies. Siegler (e.g. Siegler *et al.* 2003) has been instrumental in using an approach in which children are provided with concentrated training over a relatively short period of time so that important cognitive changes can be observed as they happen. This type of longitudinal approach to understanding cognitive development is known as the microgenetic method.

Siegler has played a major role in showing that children's cognitive development is less smooth and straightforward than used to be believed. For example, children who start to tackle a given type of problem with an effective strategy nevertheless tend for some time afterwards to use their previous and less effective strategies on occasion. What can be done to speed up the learning process? One possibility (often utilised) is for teachers to monitor closely the cognitive strategies used by children so that they can be encouraged to abandon less effective ones in favour of more effective ones. Alternatively, Siegler has identified several ways an appropriate choice of training problems can facilitate children's rapid adoption of effective cognitive strategies.

See also: intelligence/intelligence tests; learning; Piaget, Jean; psychology; psychology of education

Further reading

Eysenck, M. W. (2006) *Fundamentals of Cognition*, Hove: Psychology Press.
Eysenck, M. W. and Keane, M. T. (2005) *Cognitive Psychology: A Student's Handbook*, Hove: Psychology Press.
Siegler, R. S., DeLoache, J. S. and Eisenberg, N. (2003) *How Children Develop*, New York: Worth.
MICHAEL W. EYSENCK

COLET, JOHN (1467–1519)

As Dean of St Paul's Cathedral, London, Colet personally translated into English and read passages of the Bible to massive, popular congregations. A key intellectual and educational figure in the early Tudor period, he was a friend of Erasmus, whom he first met whilst studying in Italy, having previously studied in Paris. Colet was a key figure within the European Renaissance, advocating the use of translations of Biblical texts from the Greek, thus, revolutionising thinking about Catholic orthodoxy within the Christian world. Colet argued that the teachings of Jesus and St Paul could be explained to ordinary people in plain language.

Erasmus visited Colet at Oxford in the late 1490s in order to imbibe fully this outlook. Colet instituted a continuous series of Biblical lectures, open to the public, within St Paul's Cathedral which took place three days a week. The idea that anyone could understand the word of God was implicit in such a commitment. Whilst doing this, he placed himself in great personal danger, despite his prominent public position. His lasting legacy was the re-foundation of St Paul's School (1520), which survives today as one of England's elite, 'public', fee-paying schools, catering for an elite, international clientele. Colet was appointed by King Henry VIII as preacher at the service to install Cardinal Wolsey in 1515, an indication of his status and importance.

See also: church; public school; theology

STEVEN COWAN

COLLABORATIVE/COOPERATIVE LEARNING

Collaborative/cooperative learning refers to a set of instructional methods in which students work in small groups to learn academic content. These learning methods vary widely. Group sizes may range from pairs to groups of four or more. Children may be asked to work on projects, to tutor each other, or just to help each other as needed. Each group member may be responsible for a unique part of a task, or all may have the same assignments.

There are four major theoretical traditions that attempt to explain why collaborative/cooperative learning should improve student learning (Slavin *et al.* 2003). Each envisions and recommends different forms of cooperative learning.

Motivational theories focus on the reward structure surrounding group work. Motivational theorists (e.g. Johnson and Johnson 1998; Slavin *et al.* 2003) advocate the use of cooperative learning methods in which there is a group reward (such as recognition for successful groups) that the group can achieve only if all group members learn the academic content. For example, in Student Teams-Achievement Divisions (STAD) children work in four-member teams to help each other master a well defined objective, such as adding fractions, using commas correctly, or balancing chemical equations. Each week, group members take a brief quiz, and teams whose members show the greatest gains receive certificates or other recognition. The only way the team can succeed is for the group members to learn, so this is where the group's energies are focused. A key element of such methods is individual accountability, which means that the group is rewarded based on the sum or average of individual children's performance, not on an overall group task. The rationale is that if there is one group task (such as solving a single problem or completing a common project without distinct roles), some children may do the thinking part of the work while others watch or do clerical or art work (as when one child makes a bar graph and team mates colour it).

The evidence favouring cooperative learning methods that use group goals and individual accountability is strong. Slavin (1995) identified sixty-four studies of at least two weeks' duration that evaluated programmes incorporating group goals and individual accountability. These studies involved grade levels from 2 to 12 and a wide variety of academic subjects. Some fifty of these found significantly positive effects and the remainder found no differences, for an effect size of +0.32. In contrast, studies of programmes that did not use group goals and individual accountability have found few differences, with an overall effect size of +0.07. Other reviews have also supported the idea that group goals and individual accountability are essential to the effectiveness of cooperative learning (e.g. Webb and Palincsar, 1996; Chapman 2001; Rohrbeck *et al.* 2003).

Social cohesion theories provide a second major perspective on cooperative learning. These emphasise the idea that because students identify with their group, and want each other to succeed, they will work effectively to help their group mates learn (e.g. Sharan and Shachar 1982; Cohen 1994). A hallmark of such methods is an emphasis on teambuilding activities to create an *espirit de corps* within groups, but a de-emphasis on the use of external rewards.

107

Evidence for achievement outcomes of programmes based on the social cohesion perspective is mixed. Such methods can be effective if they provide well structured individual tasks within a group project.

A *developmental* perspective, based on the theories of Piaget and Vygotsky, holds that interaction among peers enhances their mastery of critical concepts, and theorists in this tradition recommend against rewards or structure (e.g. Bell *et al.* 1985). There is much evidence from brief laboratory studies to support the idea that cognitive change can come from interaction itself, but longer-term evaluations in classroom settings have been rare and inconclusive.

A related perspective is called cognitive elaboration, which posits that cooperative learning enhances achievement by giving children an opportunity to master information by summarising and restating their current understandings in working with peers (O'Donnell 2000). Methods in this category often involve pairs of students taking turns teaching each other discrete skills or content. Methods based on this theory, such as reciprocal teaching, cooperative scripts and reciprocal peer tutoring have strong evidence of effectiveness (Rohrbeck *et al.* 2003).

Collaborative/cooperative learning can be broadly applied to improve student learning, but research supports the idea that to be effective, cooperative methods should incorporate group goals, individual accountability, and task structures to emphasise the cognitive elaboration of academic content.

See also: cognition; individualised instruction/personalised learning; learning; learning styles; motivation; Piaget, Jean; Vygotsky, Lev

Further reading

Bell, N., Grossen, M. and Perret-Clermont, A.-N. (1985) 'Socio-cognitive conflict and intellectual growth'. In M. Berkowitz (ed.) *Peer Conflict and Psychological Growth*, San Francisco CA: Jossey-Bass.

Chapman, E. (2001) 'More on moderators in cooperative learning outcomes', paper presented at the annual meeting of the American Educational Research Association, Atlanta GA.

Cohen, E. (1994) *Designing Groupwork: Strategies for the Heterogeneous Classroom*, New York: Teachers College Press.

Johnson, D. W. and Johnson, R. T. (1998) *Learning Together and Alone: Cooperative, Competitive, and Individualistic Learning*, 5th edn, Boston MA: Allyn and Bacon.

O'Donnell, A. M. (2000) 'Interactive effects of prior knowledge and material format on cooperative teaching', *Journal of Experimental Education*, 68(2): 101–8.

Rohrbeck, C. A., Ginsburg-Block, M. D., Fantuzzo, J. W. and Miller, T. R. (2003) 'Peer-assisted learning interventions with elementary school students: a meta-analytic review', *Journal of Educational Psychology*, 94(2): 240–57.

Sharan, S. and Shachar, C. (1982) *Language and Learning in the Cooperative Classroom*, New York: Springer-Verlag.

Slavin, R. E. (1995) *Cooperative Learning: Theory, Research, and Practice*, 2nd edn, Boston MA: Allyn and Bacon.

Slavin, R. E., Hurley, E. A. and Chamberlain, A. M. (2003) 'Cooperative learning and achievement: theory and research'. In W. M. Reynolds and G. E. Miller (eds) *Handbook of Psychology*, vol. 7, Hoboken NJ: Wiley.

Webb, N. M. and Palincsar, A. S. (1996) 'Group processes in the classroom'. In N. D. C. Berliner and R. C. Calfee (eds) *Handbook of Educational Psychology*, New York: Simon and Schuster Macmillan.

ROBERT SLAVIN

COLLEGE

A college is an organisation that teaches students and supports their learning. Conventionally, a college is a physical entity, comprising one building or a collection of buildings, but the growth of e-learning has spawned 'virtual colleges' operating via the internet.

Across the world, the casual use of the term 'college' invariably demands further explanation. In the realm of higher education, some large universities are divided into specialist colleges. Sometimes institutions called colleges are, in fact, universities. Conversely, though, 'going to college' can sometimes be shorthand for going to university. Colleges in the higher education sector may teach a very broad range of programmes, but some – a college of law or a teacher training college, for example – may not.

Diversity is also the watchword in the adult, tertiary and further education sectors. Here, a college (e.g. a horticultural college) may have a very specific vocational focus. Other colleges predominantly teach young school-leavers in attendance every weekday, and some focus on the provision of weekly classes for adults in employment. To complicate the picture further, 'colleges' are sometimes schools. This is true, for example, of many elite British 'public schools', including Eton College.

See also: adult education; further education; higher education; public school; school; tertiary education; university

DAVID CROOK

COMENIUS, JAN AMOS (1592–1670)

Born in Moravia and educated at Heidelberg University, Comenius was exiled with Moravians during the Thirty Years War and acted as bishop during that period. He exerted direct influence in Sweden, England, Holland, Hungary and Poland, where he either lived or visited and advised upon schooling. In 1631 he published *Janua Linguarum Reserata*, which placed the learning and teaching of Latin in the context of broadening access to knowledge, rather than facilitating learning of the classics. Possibly his most celebrated publication was *Orbis Pictus*, credited as the first illustrated school book. In translation it was available in all European languages a century after its publication in 1658. It was this continent-wide influence that has led some to ascribe the name 'Father of modern education' to Comenius.

The *Didactica Magna* (1549) covered all aspects of teaching from the infant to the university undergraduate. Comenius argued in this seminal work that there was a natural state in which people yearned for knowledge. The duty of the schoolmaster was to nurture

this tendency. He felt that much schooling achieved the opposite. Many of Comenius' themes strike a chord three centuries later, such as his concerns with continuing learning, breaking up instruction into age-appropriate segments, providing financial assistance to schools and recognising the importance of the informal curriculum. Comenius is the major influence upon the worldwide Moravian movement. His ideas about childhood influenced Rousseau, Pestalozzi and Froebel. The European Community 'Comenius Project' aims to link schools across the continent.

STEVEN COWAN

COMMON SCHOOL

The common school emerged during the Antebellum period (1820–50) in the United States and during the next fifty years in Europe as an effort to establish various forms of centralised, state-supported primary education. Part of a prevailing impulse for social reform in response to rapid expansion and industrialisation of the United States, the common school movement there sought to foster social order and cohesion through a standardised public system of education. By no means a uniform movement nationally, or even within states, by the 1850s Northeastern and Midwestern states had adopted common school systems, while Southern and new Western states would adopt similar systems by the early twentieth century.

In the United States, common schools developed in part from charity schools, which catered to urban poor children, and which Americans had imported from England to North America. Compared to England, however, in the United States charity schools met little resistance and in fact were widely favoured, paving the way for universal primary education that common schools would provide. Advocacy of common schools began in New England states, especially Massachusetts, and spread through an organised network of common school reformers to the Midwest and South. Common school reformers advocated an array of education reforms, including increased local support of schools, regular attendance and a longer school year for children, improved buildings, extended terms of employment and increased wages for teachers, improved hiring practices and methods of instruction, early forms of professional preparation for teachers, professional education journals and associations, and age-gradation of students. Reformers sought state legislation for tax-supported common schools and establishment of state-level school officials. Historian Lawrence Cremin noted that reformers such as Horace Mann, who in 1843 had examined infant schooling in England and Prussia, envisioned the common school 'not as a school for the common people ... but rather as a school common to all people' (1982: 138).

Despite considerable support in the United States, the common school met with resistance. Opponents attacked the common school on the grounds of resisting taxation and of maintaining local control of schools in the face of state legislation. And despite the intent of reformers such as Mann, who saw common schools as a way to unify future citizens from diverse religious backgrounds, common schools were resisted, by Catholics in particular, when states would not also provide public support for denominational schools. Despite such resistance, by the 1850s, tax-supported common schools were generally accepted and widely legislated for in the United States.

During the three decades following the establishment of common schools in the United States, exigencies of industrialisation, urbanisation, and nationalism conditioned the development of various forms of state-supported elementary education in Europe. Consistent with constitutional principles, educational systems in Europe tended towards national centralisation and tended to retain social class and religious distinctions to a greater extent than common schools in the United States, though generally these reforms were driven largely by middle-class values. In the long run, common schooling in the West was characterised by increased centralisation of administration, state financing, secularisation, and compulsory attendance. The common school was precursor to elementary education and universal secondary education through the comprehensive high school.

See also: comprehensive school/education; elementary school; Mann, Horace; secondary school/education

Further reading

Cremin, L. A. (1982) *American Education: The National Experience, 1783–1876*, New York: Harper Colophon.
Gutek, G. L. (1995) *A History of the Western Educational Experience*, 2nd edn, Prospect Hights IL: Waveland Press.
Kaestle, C. F. (1983) *Pillars of the Republic: Common Schools and American Society, 1780–1860*, New York: Hill and Wang.

WILLIAM G. WRAGA

COMMUNITY EDUCATION

Community education is about the development of human relationships, knowledge and skills, and the engagement of people in learning to understand the wider social forces that impact on them and their communities. It provides a localised focus for social purpose education whose key values are a commitment to social justice, greater social and economic equality, and a more participatory democracy.

It is one of the newer forms of educational development but its conceptual origins stem from much older traditions. One of these traditions originates in the eighteenth-century radical working-class organisations that developed educational activities and a curriculum that involved acting and educating against the status quo in order to develop knowledge that was 'calculated to make them free' (Johnson 1988). Another tradition is derived from the provision of opportunities for community members to become partners in addressing community needs often based in community schools 'devoted to improving the quality of life for young people and adults through academic and recreational programs' (NCCE 2004). Much of this work has been inspired by the American educator John Dewey (1963) who argued that 'education is not preparation for life: education is life itself', and saw schools as having the potential to create democratic, caring communities. This approach to community education sought to address the issue of the perceived alienation of schools from the communities they served, through rebuilding and restoring community ties.

The different assumptions about the purpose, role and focus of education and learning derived from these traditions are still present today. The first, more *radical*, tradition within community education is committed to progressive social and political change and attempts, wherever possible, to forge a direct link between education and social action. The second, *reformist*, tradition leads to a community education that is concerned to solve the problems that impact on the quality of life for people, particularly those that are socio-economically disadvantaged, but is not committed to challenging dominant ways of thinking and acting. Similarly different understandings of how engaging in learning can improve people's social and economic conditions and bring about positive change lead to different practices. Within the reformist tradition, for example, there is an emphasis on the improvement of people's skills and individual capabilities whilst, within the radical model, there is a wider focus on the economic and social forces that exclude people.

Community education responds to the notion of 'community', which is used with many different shades of meaning in education and is a concept that is difficult to pin down. However, it can be broadly divided into three main areas of meaning:

- *Place* – this is the most common meaning and refers to people living in a particular geographical community such as a neighbourhood or village;
- *Interest* – this refers to people who share the same interest or activity such as community activists or environmentalists or members of the same religious or ethnic group;
- *Function* – this refers to groups with the same profession, such as teachers, or the same role, such as community representatives, who acquire a common sense of identity despite not having the same physical locus.

Community education tends to mainly focus on communities of place but, more broadly, a community is seen as a group of people who perceive common needs and problems, have a sense of identity and a common sense of objectives. Not everyone will be fully engaged in these different types of community and the perceived strength of a sense of community will vary. Within any group this sense of being part of a community will be determined by the degree to which its members experience both a sense of solidarity and a sense of significance within it.

Community education, which grows out of the experiences of ordinary people and the social interests that are generated within communities, has a different focus from mainstream education, both in its curriculum and in its methods. It is about encouraging and engaging people throughout life into learning that is based on their interests. Education is developed that is enjoyable and relevant to the participating learners and is responsive to community priorities and needs identified *with* people rather than *for* them. The motivation and purpose for learning of the participants will change over time but if education is rooted in the community 'it will allow genuinely alternative and democratic agendas to emerge at the local level' (Martin 1996:140). This enables citizens to voice their values and preferences as a means of shaping society.

Paolo Freire (1972) had a strong influence on radical community education. He argued that such education is unequivocally and explicitly political, combining critical understanding of the ideological function of the education system in maintaining cultural reproduction, with a dynamic theory of oppositional cultural action. He has exposed the dominant status of culturally valued knowledge in maintaining existing social relations. Freire offered a new paradigm of knowledge in distinguishing between the 'banking' concept of education and 'problem posing' education. In 'banking education', 'knowledge is a gift bestowed by those who consider themselves knowledgeable upon those whom they consider know nothing'. In contrast a 'problem posing' approach was intended to help people to 'develop their power to perceive critically the way they come to exist in the world in which they find themselves'. 'They come to see the world not as a static reality, but as a reality in process, in transformation ... Education is thus constantly remade in praxis' (Freire 1972: 56–57).

It is at the level of the communities in which they live that people often get their first active experience of democracy. Therefore, community education has looked to expand opportunities for democratic life here, since this is where many people can engage directly in issues that affect their everyday lives. In this sense, education can contribute to the extension of social democracy but this requires the valuing of difference in communities as well as the need for shared understanding and agreement. The experiences of marginalised communities and their own definition of their needs are central to the organisation and delivery of appropriate learning and other services. People themselves can develop their own forms of knowledge and this challenges the power of expert knowledge to monopolise the definition of what is wrong in their communities and what is needed to set problems right. It requires a democratising of the relationship between users and providers of education and learning, and a sharing of expert and lay knowledges.

Community education can contribute to greater social inclusion through an approach to knowledge and the development of the curriculum that starts from the issues and concerns of people rather than from externally imposed outcomes. This is because such learning involves the active engagement by citizens in the construction, interpretation, and, often, the re-shaping of their own social identity and social reality. The engagement of people in creating their own knowledge involves developing a capacity for self-determination and evolution and emphasises the social embeddedness of learning rather than its individual focus. Community-based knowledge learnt from experience is a valuable asset because it is derived from the issues that are important to people and builds on their experience. It emphasises the wealth of people's knowledge, rather than their deficits and values, the knowledge that people bring from their own family and community contexts.

A community education approach is designed to support and foster associations where people learn to respect and trust others, fulfil obligations and press their claims communicatively. Community education methodology and epistemology can engage with and respond to excluded groups in civil society. Such an approach to knowledge recognises that learning is located in social participation and dialogue as well as in the heads of individuals and treats teaching and learning not as two distinct activities, but as elements of a single, reciprocal process. The challenge for community educators is to forge more genuinely popular and democratic forms of education that will reconnect communities with the vision of a common culture that simultaneously respects diversity and promotes solidarity.

See also: adult education; culture; Dewey, John; Freire, Paolo; lifelong learning; workers' education

Further reading

Dewey, J. (1963) [1938] *Experience and Education*, New York: Collier Books.

Freire, P. (1972) *Pedagogy of the Oppressed*, Harmondsworth: Penguin.

Johnson, R. (1988) 'Really useful knowledge, 1790–1850'. In T. Lovett (ed.) *Radical Approaches to Adult Education: A Reader*, London: Routledge.

——(2000) 'Community education and lifelong learning: local spice for global fare'. In J. Field and M. Leicester (eds) *Lifelong Learning: Education across the Life-span*, London: Routledge.

Martin, I. (1996) 'Community education: the dialectics of development'. In R. Fieldhouse (ed.) *A History of Modern British Adult Education*, Leicester: NIACE.

Merz, C. and Furman, G. (1997) *Community and Schools: Promise and Paradox*, New York: Teachers College Press.

NCCE (National Center for Community Education) (2004) 'Evolution of the community school concept', www.nccenet.org/MissionHistory/Index.cfm

Tett, L. (2006) *Community Education, Lifelong Learning and Social Inclusion*, 2nd edn, Edinburgh: Dunedin Academic Press.

Welton, M. (1995) In defence of the lifeworld: critical perspectives on adult learning, New York: State University of New York Press.

LYN TETT

COMPARATIVE EDUCATION

The beginnings of modern comparative education are normally dated from 1817 by invoking the name of Marc Antoine Jullien of Paris. He argued that *éducation comparée* would be part of the new classificatory and positive sciences; and that such a fact-based science would rescue educational decision making from the whims of administrators. Unfortunately, Jullien did not anticipate the whims of modern politicians.

Originally, then, modern comparative education was part of the late blossoming of principles of rationality, 'order and progress' and the search for a social physics, which marked the late eighteenth and early nineteenth centuries. Quickly, 'comparative education' became a practical necessity for practical men (*sic*) as they struggled to invent various forms of the elementary school in France and the United States of America or later in England, influenced by the practices of other countries.

The gradual shift of comparative education into the universities began before the end of the nineteenth century and its intellectual motifs were initially stabilised in the inter-war period. It was the reflections of the comparative educationists of that time which came to be called the 'forces and factors school'. Several university scholars such as Nicholas Hans, Joseph Lauwerys, Friederich Schneider, Isaac Kandel and Robert Ulich paid serious attention to major historical forces such as language and religion and political philosophies as constraints on educational policies and as definers of what we might now call 'cultures'.

Both in the United Kingdom and in the USA, the rejection of these perspectives in the search for a contemporary science of comparative education marked the new positivism of the 1960s, when the field became dominated by a search for a powerful method, notably methods of prediction through the social sciences. Thus, in the major centres of comparative education in the University of London, in Teachers' College Columbia, in the Universities of Wisconsin or Chicago, scholars such as Edmund King and Brian Holmes, George Bereday, Andreas Kazamias and Arnold Anderson debated strenuously the virtues (or otherwise) of retaining an emphasis on historical perspective, or using sociological or economic modes of approach to comparative education. Similar debates were occurring in France and Germany, in Italy and Spain and Australia and Canada.

However the practical motif, always changing shape and emphasis but always re-emerging, has been a permanent part of comparative education discourse. The theme is sharp in Sir Michael Sadler's famous question in 1900: 'How far may we learn anything of practical value from the study of foreign educational systems?' The first

113

volumes of the *Yearbook of Education* (which began to be published again in the late 1940s by Evans Brothers) were on the difficulties of the reconstruction of European educational systems. Many of the discussions about 'scientific methodologies' that were very visible in the academic writing in comparative education in the 1960s were on the need to influence policy and to facilitate the transfer of educational practices from one country to another.

Currently, 'comparative education' has taken on two new emphases. One form of contemporary comparative education emphasises 'solutions': for example, the Organisation for Economic Co-operation and Development (OECD) stresses the usefulness and necessity of lifelong learning in times of economic globalisation, and the World Bank offers this kind of universal solution whenever it emphasises the necessity to construct educational systems as competitive markets in an era of knowledge economies. Another, increasingly fashionable, form of 'big science' comparative education emphasises the identification of 'successful' educational systems through tests. An international testing movement was established in the time of the Cold War (the International Education Achievement Study of Mathematics was the first major effort); but the testing industry has grown dramatically since the early 1960s, and among the most publicised studies recently have been TIMMS and PISA (The Trends in International Mathematics and Science Study and the Programme for International Student Assessment). Universities themselves – and their world league table position – have now become part of such measurement and testing (and media excitement). In other words, an area of work loosely called 'comparative education' has grown rapidly and taken on many different forms.

There is not one comparative education, but several. There is a comparative education-of-action (conducted, or contracted out, by, for example, the World Bank, national ministries of education or the OECD). There

is 'policy-driven' comparative education, which takes its working agenda from salient issues of educational policy, and carries through its work by contract research or through consultancies or even by specialising in certain areas of continuing policy importance, such as higher education. There is the 'comparative education' of the professional societies, with their annual or bi-annual conferences and their mix of theoretical and policy-driven work and the reporting of empirical research. Thus, a variety of 'comparative educations' have different sociologies of knowledge and their politics of action are also different. The only simplistic unifier that they have is a trivial notion of what it is to compare: to juxtapose descriptions of educational institutions or educational processes or educational results in two or more places, separated by an international boundary.

However, such descriptions offer little understanding of 'the causes of things', or even the contextualisation of things, and it is in those forms of understanding that the intellectual challenge of comparative education begins.

Max Weber's brilliant essay on the Chinese literati, and the changing forms of education in the agrarian economies of classical China and Egypt, as compared with nineteenth-century France or Prussia and legal-bureaucratic rationality and industrial societies, shows some of the possibilities of thinking comparatively. Rolland Paulston's rather difficult recent work on visual mapping shows some of the ways forward in a time when we are exploring a variety of 'posts' (post-industrialisation, post-colonialism and so on). The old certainties have disintegrated. However, the obvious immediacy and visibility of 'the global' has re-stimulated academic comparative education.

There is important theoretical work being done, for example, by David Phillips at Oxford University and by Juergen Schriewer at Humboldt University in Berlin; by Tony Welch in Sydney University, Australia and by Gita Steiner-Khamsi in Teachers' College

Columbia. In the UK, two important and energetic departments are offering a major stream of publication in comparative education: the comparative parts of the Institute of Education in London and the School of Education in Bristol. Similarly comparative education remains a significant area of study in Southern Europe: in Spain, not least with the work Garcia Garrido in Madrid and Miguel Pereyra in Granada; in Italy (which has a long comparative tradition) through the efforts of Donatella Palomba in Rome; and the comparative tradition in Greece, much strengthened by Andreas Kazamias (in addition to his work in the USA), is continued by Dimitris Mattheou in Athens; and, of course, the French tradition since Jullien has been a major one.

This university subject – academic comparative education – in such centres and through such scholars still retains its major historical theme of 'transfer', that is, the analysis of the movement of educational ideas and practices from one country to another. But this old theme is now the subject of considerable re-theorisation.

The question is how do things 'translate' and then 'transform' in the new contexts. How do they change shape – what are the theories on that?

A second major question, which is slowly receiving more and more attention, is what is the comparative education of times of extreme change – revolution, coups d'état, or the disintegration of polities? These historical moments of extreme drama are frequent, for example the transformation of Meiji Japan or the transformations of Turkey under Attaturk or the changed Germany of the 1930s. Currently also we have seen moments of bitter violence and human tragedy, as in East Timor or in the end of Yugoslavia or in the redefinitions of Afghanistan or Iraq. These are all historical moments when the compression of socio-economic, cultural and political power into changed educational forms takes place before our eyes.

It is this compression of power into educational forms that makes comparative education not merely interesting but academically and theoretically important. It is a problematique that Weber and others addressed as industrialised societies and modern states took shape: how does education shift its shape and how does the definition of 'educated identity' change? Weber's answer was stark. The question in our own age remains about the same. Suggesting the answers is no less theoretically difficult, and the answers which are beginning to emerge, comparatively, are equally stark.

See also: education; education/educational studies; Organisation for Economic Co-operation and Development (OECD); World Bank

Further reading

Cowen, R. (2006) 'Acting comparatively upon the educational world: puzzles and possibilities', *Oxford Review of Education*, 32(5): 561–73.

Cowen, R. and Kazamias, A. (eds) (2008, forthcoming) *International Handbook of Comparative Education*, The Hague: Springer.

Crossley, M., Broadfoot, P. and Schweisfurth, M. (eds) (2007) *Changing Educational Contexts, Issues and Identities: 40 Years of Comparative Education*, London: Routledge.

Gerth, H. and Mills, C. W. (eds) (1974) *From Max Weber: Essays in Sociology*, London: Routledge and Kegan Paul.

Ninnes, P. and Mehta, S. (eds) (2004) *Re-Imagining Comparative Education: Postfoundational Ideas and Applications for Critical Times*, New York and London: RoutledgeFalmer.

Phillips, D. and Schweisfurth, M. (2007) *Comparative and International Education: An Introduction to Theory, Method, and Practice*, London: Continuum.

Schriewer, J. (ed.) (2000) *Discourse Formation in Comparative Education*, Frankfurt am Main: Peter Lang.

ROBERT COWEN

COMPENSATORY EDUCATION

The aim of compensatory education is to enhance the educational provision of a relatively deprived group, area or community in order to improve its social and economic prospects. It has often been associated with compensating for 'cultural deprivation', but

115

this has tended to create a deficit model in which the individuals and groups involved are viewed as somehow lacking in culture – 'a euphemism for saying that working-class and ethnic groups have cultures which are at least dissonant with, if not inferior to, the "mainstream" culture of the society at large' (Keddie 1973: 8). It has also generated schemes to promote 'affirmative action' and 'positive discrimination', for example on behalf of minority ethnic groups and women. These initiatives have also been criticised where they have been based on quotas for particular groups, for instance to enter institutions of higher education. The underlying idea that education can compensate for society has also been widely challenged, notably by the British sociologist Basil Bernstein. Major educational programmes designed to support disadvantaged students and communities have continued to be developed in many countries.

One especially influential initiative in compensatory education has been *Project Head Start* in the United States, begun in 1965 as part of the 'War on Poverty' under President Lyndon B. Johnson. The Economic Opportunity Act of 1964 enabled the development of programmes to support the needs of disadvantaged pre-school children, leading to the establishment of Project Head Start. It was intended to provide pre-school children from low-income families with a special programme to support their development. The project, originally intended to be an eight-week summer programme, has survived many social and political changes over more than forty years. It is now a programme within the Administration on Children, Youth and Families in the Department of Health and Human Services, locally administered by community-based non-profit organisations and school systems. It has clearly had a major effect on communities and early childhood programmes, although its effects on educational outcomes continue to be widely debated. For many children, the early positive effects achieved through participating in Head Start may fade out during later education (Silver and Silver 1991).

A major approach of this type in Britain was the Educational Priority Areas (EPAs) programme established following the publication of the Plowden Report, *Children and Their Primary Schools*, in 1967 to give additional resources to schools in the most deprived areas of the country. Four areas of England were selected to take part in the programme. It emphasised in particular the importance of preschools and community schools. A national programme was developed but not sustained (Smith 1987). At the end of the century, Tony Blair's Labour government introduced a programme with many similar characteristics, the Education Action Zones (EAZs), which were intended to improve educational achievement and to promote social inclusion in disadvantaged areas of cities. Again, in spite of high-level support and extensive investment, this programme did not survive for long.

Meanwhile, an influential lobby pressed the claim that individual schools, rather than education in general, might be able to compensate for society depending on their levels of effectiveness. Peter Mortimore, for example, argued that school effectiveness provided an opportunity to change economically advanced Western societies, although he conceded that it should not be viewed as a panacea. According to Mortimore,

> For families whose lives are disadvantaged in relation to their peers, schools remain one of the few mechanisms that are able to provide a compensating boost. The more effective the school, the higher the proportion of students that will get to the starting-line in the competition for favourable life-chances.
>
> (Mortimore 1997: 483)

This is a further version of the continuing and widespread aim to improve the relative fortunes of disadvantaged individuals and groups through enhanced educational provision, and is likely to be pursued further in many different contexts around the world.

See also: Bernstein, Basil; educational priority areas; equality of opportunity; positive discrimination/affirmative action

Further reading

Keddie, N. (ed.) (1973) *Tinker, Tailor . . . : The Myth of Cultural Deprivation*, London: Penguin.

Mortimore, P. (1997) 'Can effective schools compensate for society?' In A. H. Halsey, H. Lauder, P. Brown and A. S. Wells (eds) *Education: Culture, Economy, Society*, Oxford: Oxford University Press.

Silver, H. and Silver, P. (1991) *An Educational War on Poverty: American and British Policy-Making, 1960–1980*, Cambridge: Cambridge University Press.

Smith, G. (1987) 'Whatever happened to Educational Priority Areas?', *Oxford Review of Education*, 13(1): 23–38.

GARY McCULLOCH

COMPREHENSION

Comprehension is the sense we make of the world around us and our experiences with it. Another way of saying this is that comprehension is *constructing* meaning. Meaning does not simply flow into the brain through the senses. Comprehension is an active process. Our brains build schemas of the world we are transacting with and then use these schemas to perceive the world and understand it. The brain tells the eyes, ears, nose, tongue, and skin what it expects to see, hear, smell, taste and feel and the senses supply inputs which either confirm what the brain expects – what it predicts – or disconfirm causing the brain to reconsider and make new predictions. Piaget, the Swiss cognitive psychologist, says that when input fits our schemas we easily assimilate it. When it does not fit we either reject it or we must accommodate, that is modify the schema so that the new input can be comprehended.

The word comprehension itself is most often used in education in connection with reading or perhaps listening. In either case we are talking about how we make sense of written or oral language. It is impossible to think of human comprehension without language since language becomes the means by which we express our understandings of our experiences. Language becomes the medium of thought itself.

Brain scientists are beginning to understand how the brain functions in constructing meaning. The cortex forms predictions based on memory. It sends signals through the thalamus to the sensory organs telling them what it expects to find. And the brain selects minimal information from the sensory input it receives to construct perceptions used to confirm what it expects. Hawkins, in his book *On Intelligence* calls this a *memory-prediction* model: 'What we perceive is a combination of what we sense and our memory-derived predictions' (2004: 87). Brain theory is coming to match theories of oral and written language comprehension. Goodman (1967) characterises reading as a psycholinguistic guessing game. Tom Bever, a psycholinguistic researcher, says that 'the model . . . to explain many puzzling and creative aspects about reading actually obtains for the fundamental processes of all language comprehension' (2006).

Comprehension is the goal of reading that drives the process. The brain is actively making sense of print. It makes predictions and inferences and tells the eyes what to look for. It then selectively samples the visual input, constructing perceptions to test its predictions. If it finds what it is looking for meaning is constructed and further predictions are made. If not, the brain seeks more input from the eyes, perhaps scanning backwards until it has resolved the problem. Reading starts with visual input. As the eyes traverse the print, jumping from fixation to fixation, the brain forms perceptions based on what it expects. In reading an alphabetic language the eye proceeds in general from left to right but at times it moves back from right to left as instructed by the brain to clarify what isn't making sense. Predictions are so useful that the eye fixates on only about 60–70 per cent of the words in a text.

In comprehension, the brain treats the text as meaningful language. Information comes from memory as well as from the senses. What the brain knows about the syntax and wording of the language is used to construct meaning.

Comprehending is the process of constructing meaning. Comprehension is what is understood. Comprehension will always be limited by what the reader or listener knew before reading or listening. Since meaning is constructed in listening and reading, there can never be an exact match of what the reader or listener understands and what the speaker or writer intends to say.

Effective reading is success in making sense of a particular text. Nothing less than that is reading, so there is no reading without comprehension. Efficient reading is getting to meaning with the least amount of input and effort. Proficient reading, by definition, is both effective and efficient. In this meaning the reader is constructing a text, parallel to, but not identical with, the published text being read. It is this reader's text that is comprehended.

See also: cognition; English; Piaget, Jean; reading; writing

Further reading

Bever, T. G. (2006) 'All language understanding is a psycholinguistic guessing game', paper presented at the Goodman Festschrift Conference, University of Arizona, 12 October.

Goodman, K. S. (1967) 'Reading: a psycholinguistic guessing game', *Journal of the Reading Specialist*, 6: 126–35.

——(1984) 'Reading, writing, and written texts: a transactional sociopsycholinguistic view'. In M. R. Ruddell and H. Singer (eds) *Theoretical Models and Processes of Reading*, Newark DE: International Reading Association.

Hawkins, J. (2004) *On Intelligence*, New York: Henry Holt and Co.

Piaget, J. (1970) *Structuralism*, New York: Harper and Row.

KENNETH S. GOODMAN

COMPREHENSIVE SCHOOL/EDUCATION

Designed to serve all in a local neighbourhood or community, the comprehensive secondary school has an open enrolment policy and does not discriminate on such grounds as social, religious or ethnic background. While students are sometimes placed in streams, tracks or sets, according to ability or interest, most comprehensive secondary schools provide a common core of studies and an extra-curriculum. In the later years of secondary education, the number of elective subjects usually increases. Comprehensive secondary education seeks to serve individual educational aspirations while also providing a common schooling experience, as a foundation for social life in democracies.

The aims of the comprehensive secondary school are thus multifaceted. As the former president of Harvard University, James Conant, wrote in his famous report, the 'three main objectives' of a comprehensive secondary education are: 'to provide a good general education for all the future citizens'; 'to provide good elective programs for those who wish to use their acquired skills immediately on graduation'; and 'to provide satisfactory programs whose vocations will depend on their subsequent education in a college or university' (Conant 1959: 17). Balancing these aims has often proved difficult. In part, this can be explained by reference to the history of the comprehensive secondary school, as well as its current dilemmas.

The ideal of the comprehensive secondary school emerged in the twentieth century as part of the movement towards secondary education for all, and was closely attached to the idea of 'adolescence' as a significant part of the life cycle: a view that came to prominence in educational thought and practice in the twentieth century (Gillis 1981). In the USA the comprehensive secondary school was often seen as a logical extension of the provision of a common school for all; thus continuing to pursue the aims of American public education in the nineteenth century.

The introduction of the American comprehensive high school in the early twentieth century was also associated with the progressive education movement which sought to relate the curriculum to the interests of pupils rather than to the older elite tradition of secondary education based upon academic subjects and disciplines. The famous 'Cardinal Principles', that the American Commission on the Reorganisation of Secondary Education published in 1918, focused on the development of the individual student as a future citizen. As such, it provided a progressive legacy for the American high school that lasted for the next forty years and beyond (Wraga 2001).

The idea that secondary schooling should be available to all was a radical development for Western traditions of post-elementary education. The American comprehensive high school was internationally significant for its particular solution to the development of mass or universal secondary education. Part of its mission was to assimilate the children of generations of European immigrants who had arrived in American cities in the late nineteenth and early twentieth centuries. With the decline of unskilled occupations for young workers by the 1930s, the great majority of America's young people remained in secondary school until at least age fifteen. Unlike most other forms of secondary schooling in the West, the modern comprehensive high school was coeducational, affording different educational experiences and new opportunities to women (Tyack and Hansot 1990). Conversely, the normalisation of prolonged high school attendance led to a new youth problem: the problem of the 'dropout' student (Dorn 1996).

By the 1940s and 1950s, the large comprehensive coeducational school of more than 2,000 students became common. It usually offered a wide range of different subjects and courses as part of the curriculum. This eventually led to criticism that academic standards were in decline and students were simply being 'warehoused' rather than prepared for life as had been claimed by promoters of comprehensive schools (Angus and Mirel 1999).

Despite these and other criticisms, such as inadequate science curricula leading to the Sputnik crisis, the American comprehensive high school provided a highly significant model for possible adaptation as 'secondary schooling for all' spread as an aim through many nations of the world.

In the wake of World War II, comprehensive secondary education was associated with a new democratic settlement and the rise of the welfare state in Britain, Europe and elsewhere. The ideal of the comprehensive school came to be seen as an educational 'wave of the future', promising to end early selection for secondary schools and extend educational opportunities. The actual introduction of comprehensive schools was often impaired by the strength of more elite traditions in secondary education that selected students on the basis of academic ability. The effort to introduce comprehensive schools in Germany generally failed because of the continuing commitment to the tripartite system of academic, technical and 'general' secondary schools. (Leschinsky and Mayer 1999). But the developing argument that selection on the basis of academic achievement and intelligence testing were practices which helped maintain social class division and privilege furthered the cause of the comprehensive secondary school. By the 1970s, new systems of comprehensive secondary schools were being established in Britain and parts of Western and Northern Europe (Henkens 2004).

The comprehensive secondary school thus has a distinctive history. It also faces an uncertain future. Even in the 1960s there was a clear difference between the secondary schools of the urban slums of America where many poor and black children lived and the neighbourhood comprehensive schools of the white middle-class suburbs where most students aspired to go to college or university (Conant 1961). In recent years the social and racial segregation of American cities has become more pronounced, while in Britain and Europe many recent immigrant arrivals from Asia and North Africa are educated in older comprehensive secondary schools, in areas of urban deprivation along with others of the urban poor (McCulloch 1998).

Critics of the comprehensive secondary school often claim that it has failed the poor. As the skilled and unskilled jobs of older industrial economies have begun to disappear in the developed world, the comprehensive school may be placed at a disadvantage where a premium is placed on gaining the credentials essential for white collar and professional occupations (Thomson 2002). This has often led to attacks on public education and the educational bureaucracies that managed the development of the comprehensive secondary schools. In the USA there are new movements supporting 'school choice' and the establishment of 'charter schools' funded by the public purse but pursuing a specific educational agenda designed to appeal to particular communities or interest groups. In American cities such as New York, large comprehensive high schools are being broken up into smaller units in an effort to provide a more coherent and often more specialised curriculum. As the former 'democracy's high school', the local comprehensive school is being subjected to continuing pressures for change (Hammack 2004).

By the end of the twentieth century, the comprehensive secondary school ideal appeared to be in decline. Some suggest that the earlier campaign for comprehensive schools to end early selection and differentiation of pupils had been replaced by later selection for higher education and increasing differentiation of secondary schools. In contrast to the view of 'one comprehensive school for all' there is a renewed focus on separate schools often based on gender, ethnic communities and religious faith as well as the older forms of 'academic merit'. In much of the English-speaking world, neo-liberal approaches to schooling have ele-

vated the importance of the interests of individual families and their strategies of school choice which may lead to private advantage; these aims now outweigh the more collective ethos and common citizenship goals which characterised the early comprehensive secondary school movement (Ball 2003).

These recent changes notwithstanding, at the beginning of the twenty-first century the comprehensive high school remains the predominant form of secondary school in much of the world. In such areas as Scandinavia, the comprehensive school stands unrivalled as the most acceptable form of secondary education for youth. Elsewhere, with the increased pressures arising from competitive tertiary educational entrance and the scarcity of well-paid secure employment, the problem for the comprehensive ideal is how it may continue to adapt, and in the process reconcile individual needs and aspirations with more collective ends (Chitty and Simon 2001).

See also: common school; high school; secondary school/education; selection

Further reading

Angus, D. L. and Mirel, J. E. (1999) *The Failed Promise of the American High School*, New York: Teachers' College Press.

Ball, S. (2003) *Class Strategies and the Education Market: The Middle Classes and Social Advantage*, London: Falmer.

Chitty, C. and Simon, B. (eds) (2001) *Promoting Comprehensive Education in the 21st Century*, Stoke-on-Trent: Trentham Books.

Conant, J. (1959) *The American High School Today*, New York: McGraw Hill.

——(1961) *Slums and Suburbs*, New York: McGraw Hill.

Dorn, S. (1996) *Creating the Dropout: An Institutional and Social History of School Failure*, Westport CT: Praeger.

Gillis, J. R. (1981) *Youth and History: Tradition and Change in European Age Relations 1770–present*, New York: Academic Press.

Hammack. F. M. (2004) *The Comprehensive High School Today*, New York: Teachers College Press.

Henkens, B. (2004) 'The rise and decline of comprehensive education: key factors in the history of reformed secondary education in Belgium', *Paedagogica Historica*, 40(1–2): 193–210.

Leschinsky, A. and Mayer, K.U. (1999) *The Comprehensive School Experiment Revisited: Evidence from Western Europe*, New York: Peter Lang.

McCulloch, G. (1998) *Failing the Ordinary Child? The Theory and Practice of Working Class Secondary Education*, Buckingham: Open University Press.

Pring, R. and Walford, G. (eds) (1997) *Affirming the Comprehensive Ideal*, London: Falmer.

Thomson, P. (2002) *Schooling the Rustbelt Kids: Making the Difference in Changing Times*, Sydney NSW: Allen and Unwin.

Tyack, D. and Hansot, E. (1990) *Learning Together: A History of Coeducation in American Schools*, New Haven CT: Yale University Press.

Wraga, W. (2001) 'A progressive legacy squandered: The Cardinal Principles Report reconsidered', *History of Education Quarterly*, 41(4): 494–519.

GEOFFREY SHERINGTON AND CRAIG CAMPBELL

COMPULSORY EDUCATION

Compulsory education refers to a form and/or length of education required by law. Compulsory education and compulsory schooling are sometimes treated as synonymous terms, yet strictly they are not. In many countries a minimum period of education is compulsory, but some or all of the instruction received by children may occur at home or in some other place, as long as the authorities can be satisfied of its quality. Governments requiring compulsory education are normally also providers of schools, though the presence of church and private schools may mean that there is no state monopoly.

The case for compulsory education is frequently traced back to the Protestant Reformation. Martin Luther proposed that it was a duty of the state to ensure that all citizens could read the Bible for themselves, and similar ideas are attributed to Jean Calvin, John Knox and French Protestants of the sixteenth century. With the development of mass schooling systems from the late eighteenth century, free tuition and compulsory attendance were frequently identified as the logical 'next steps' for governments to enforce. As Andy Green (1990) has shown, the degree of enthusiasm with which the major European countries and American states set about this was variable. National systems featuring compulsory education 'occurred first and fastest in countries where the process of state formation was most intensive' (Green 1990: 310). The path to compulsion was trodden especially slowly in England, where compulsory schooling from ages 5–10 was finally secured in 1880. A succession of minimum leaving-age extensions followed – to 11 (1893), 12 (1899), 14 (1918), 15 (1947) and 16 (1972) – but each advance was contested by a lobby opposing the measure on the grounds of necessity and expense (Crook 2005).

Today, in developed countries compulsory school systems commonly require attendance from around age six, though schooling begins at four in Northern Ireland. Attendance beyond the age of around sixteen typically requires a commitment to 'stay on' in education (and not to 'drop out'), but incentives – in the form of monetary maintenance payments to continuing students or their parents – are playing an increasingly important part in extending by stealth the years of compulsory education. In the United States this tendency to keep young people in education for longer has been driven by the *A Nation at Risk* report (1983) and the *No Child Left Behind* (NCLB) legislation (2001). In Canada and some American states it is not possible for young people under the age of eighteen to secure a driving licence if they are deemed to be high school dropouts. As Christie (2007) has recently written:

> NCLB establishes graduation rates as one of the measures that determine whether a school makes adequate yearly progress. While each state sets its own graduation rate target, the law holds schools accountable for meeting that state-set target. This in turn

121

puts on pressure to make sure students graduate. They can't graduate if they don't attend, and many won't attend unless we 'make 'em'.

(Christie 2007: 341)

Compulsory education is frequently accompanied by discourses of personal opportunity and empowerment. David Halpin (2003) has identified a still more utopian aspiration: compulsory education can be the instrument for children to live a full and good life. But the agendas of individual governments are likely to be driven more by economics. Setting an early starting age for compulsory education may be seen as a means of drawing back mothers into the labour market, simultaneously reducing the demand for preschool welfare benefit payments and increasing government taxation revenues. Extending the requirement for all young people to participate in full-time schooling, training or workplace learning to age eighteen, on the other hand, as the British government proposes to do by 2013, will reduce unemployment statistics and welfare benefits while demonstrating a commitment to the knowledge and skills economy.

The sociological functions of compulsory education may also be significant. Schools can serve as agencies of socialisation or social control, keeping the young under surveillance, subjecting them to rules, discipline and approved curricula and learning approaches (Ramirez and Boli 1994). A section of American society – including representatives of school districts, teachers' associations, parents and pupils – remained unconvinced for decades about the merits and legality of compulsory education. Mark Twain's fictional character, Huckleberry Finn, gains his education from the river and the environment around him and boasts of playing 'hooky' from school. Time and again, as Provasnik (2006) has shown, the legal basis for compulsory schooling was tested in the United States during the late nineteenth and early twentieth centuries.

In the 1960s and 1970s radical free-schoolers and deschoolers, including Ivan Illich, John Holt and Paul Goodman, likened schools governed by compulsory education laws to the Spanish Inquisition, prisons and concentration camps (Kleinberger 1975: 219). Others libertarians challenged the conservatism and hidden curricula of public school systems, while E. G. West, the free-market economist, argued that the English experience of compulsory state education was inefficient in comparison to nineteenth-century voluntarist and private education enterprises (West 1965). One provocatively titled collection of essays to emerge from such thinking was *The Twelve Year Sentence*, edited by William F. Rickenbacker in 1974.

In poorer countries, such Western attitudes towards compulsory education might be viewed as ingratitude. Some sixty years after Article 26 of the United Nations Universal Declaration of Human Rights stated that 'Everyone has the right to education' and 'Education shall be free, at least in the elementary and fundamental stages', this aspiration is yet to be realised in some parts of the globe. Since the mid-1980s, when China enacted a nine-year compulsory education law and India signified similar intentions, there has been notable progress, but the vastness of these countries, together with the factors of rural poverty, difficult terrain and unpredictable weather continue to be major impediments to rapid progress, notwithstanding their emergence as twenty-first century economic superpowers. The aspiration for universal compulsory elementary education has been sustained by the Education for All initiative (launched in 1990) and by the United Nations' eight Millennium Development Goals, one of which is to 'ensure that, by 2015, children everywhere, boys and girls alike, will be able to complete a full course of primary schooling'. A 2001 survey (Tomaschevski 2001) identified thirty-seven countries that provide free and compulsory education only to citizens or legal residents and forty-three having no national or constitutional guarantees regarding education. In these countries and others, a picture of exclusion for minority groups and persistent inequality for girls emerges (Lewis and Lockheed 2006).

See also: deschooling; Education for All; equality of opportunity; home schooling; Illich, Ivan; primary school/education; universal education/mass education; voluntarism

Further reading

Christie, K. (2007) 'The complexity of compulsory attendance', *Phi Delta Kappen*, 88(5): 341–42.

Crook, D. (2005) 'Compulsory education in the United Kingdom: historical, comparative and contemporary perspectives', *Journal of Educational Administration and Planning*, 19(3): 397–414.

Green, A. (1990), *Education and State Formation: The Rise of Education Systems in England, France and the USA*, Basingstoke: Macmillan.

Halpin, D. (2003) *Hope and Education: The Role of Utopian Imagination*, London: RoutledgeFalmer.

Kleinberger, A. H. (1975) 'A comparative analysis of compulsory education laws', *Comparative Education*, 11(3): 219–30.

Lewis, M. and Lockheed, M. (2006) *Inexcusable Absence: Why 60 million Girls still Aren't in School and what to Do about It*, Washington DC: Center for Global Development.

Provasnik, S. (2006) 'Judicial activism and the origins of parental choice: the court's role in the institutionalisation of compulsory education in the United States, 1891–1925', *History of Education Quarterly*, 46(3): 311–47.

Ramirez, F. O. and Boli, J. (1994) 'The political institutionalisation of compulsory education: the rise of compulsory schooling in the Western cultural context'. In J. A. Mangan (ed.) *A Significant Social Revolution: Cross-Cultural Aspects of the Evolution of Compulsory Education*, London: Woburn.

Rickenbacker, W. F. (1974) *The Twelve Year Sentence: Radical Views of Compulsory Education*, New York: Delta Books Company.

Tomaschevski, K. (2001) *Annual Report to the UN Commission on Human Rights by the Special Rapporteur on Education*, Geneva: Commission on Human Rights.

West, E. G. (1965) *Education and the State: A Study in Political Economy*, London: Institute of Economic Affairs.

DAVID CROOK

COMPUTER-ASSISTED LEARNING

Computer-assisted learning (CAL) is the use of some element(s) of information and communications technology (ICT) to offer automated aid to learning within an education or training setting.

CAL may involve standalone software running on a single computer, institution-wide networked packages or internet-based, globally distributed, systems. Until the early 1980s these were largely restricted to engineering or science disciplines, but in the last thirty years CAL packages have been developed for a wide range of subjects and disciplines. For example, they are commonplace in such areas as driving instruction and language teaching.

Recent ICT developments have seen the development of multimedia systems combining sound, video, graphics, text and so forth, and a hybridisation of technology has seen computer games interfaces being increasingly used within CAL. Modern CAL systems can offer a rich, enjoyable learning experience with their 24/7 capacity for 'vitual reality', replay and assessment of achievement. CAL is often mixed or 'blended' with other learning paradigms such as virtual learning or more traditional modes.

See also: educational technology; e-learning; learning; virtual learning; Web-based learning

DAVID SETH PRESTON

COMPUTER STUDIES

Computer studies is the study of computer systems in terms of their development and the people who use them, as well as an attempt to trace the patterns of their short but significant history. It may be studied as an award-bearing curriculum subject at school or in further or higher education.

Within industrial economies one finds many standardised practices and a plethora of tools to support efficient large-scale production of highly regulated quality. One such tool has been the computer, the main characteristic of which is its ability to carry out highly repetitive tasks at speed and accuracy levels far beyond the capability of any human.

The early history of computing is associated with industrialised activity, and, in particular, mass factory output. Within garment manufacturing the pattern and associated operations were stored, interpreted and implemented by a computerised system. However, despite standardisation of individual units of production, the computer system was often non-standardised: one factory often used a different system from any other. Early computing was highly specialised, restricted to tasks requiring transparent repetition and very few people understood it.

With World War II came the first truly collaborative and highly funded attempt to harness computers for a common goal. Whilst the aim was to pass 'secret', recoverable encoded signals across enemy lines, a major side effect was the understanding that computers needed an improved interface.

Prior to World War II, computers had been basically a raw machine, termed *hardware*, with little or no intermediate program, termed *software*, to communicate with the user. Often, the only way to communicate with the computer was for a human to repeatedly set a series of binary switches into the desired pattern or *code*, then send or 'upload' this to the computer. Even the most basic of instructions, such as adding two numbers, involved a long sequence of codes to be uploaded. Such wartime figures as Alan Turing found this an extremely onerous and error-prone process. Software was needed that would take some of these repetitive tasks, such as saving or printing, away from the individual project, making these available to all computer users. This set of standardised user tools for communicating and controlling the hardware became known as the *operating system*.

With the development of sophisticated operating systems, software became much easier to write within an expanded set of domains. Whereas previously computers had been used for highly specialised purposes, *application software*, with a data repository, or *database*, at its centre, became available in a vast array of areas. For example, business application software was developed to undertake all manner of increasingly sophisticated tasks.

Computers developed a utility beyond science and engineering, also becoming smaller and more powerful. Information and communications technology (ICT) is unique in its exponential performance growth: roughly every fifteen months it doubles in power per unit cost. Consequently, in around thirteen years it improves by a factor of 1,000 (or is reduced in cost by the same figure), and in twenty-five years by a factor of one million. As a result, the connected or *networked* combination of hardware and software that became known as a *computer system* became extremely affordable and compact within a generation. This computer revolution has impacted significantly upon homes and all manner of institutions of learning. For example, the internet has spawned new forms of learning, discussed elsewhere in this volume.

See also: computer-assisted learning; curriculum; educational technology; e-learning; subjects; technology; virtual learning; Web-based learning

Further reading

Leavitt, D. (2006) *The Man Who Knew too much: Alan Turing and the Invention of the Computer*, New York: W. W. Norton.
Wainwright, S. (2002) *Teaching and Assessing Skills in Computer Studies*, Cambridge: Cambridge University Press.

DAVID SETH PRESTON

CONANT, JAMES BRYANT (1893–1978)

Conant, the American chemist and educator, led the transformation of Harvard University into a world-class centre for academic excellence. He spent seventeen years teaching chemistry and then leading the department at Harvard. Whilst president of the University (1933–53), he was chairperson of the National Defense Research Committee, (1940–46), which developed the atomic bomb.

Conant became increasingly absorbed by wider social questions in relation to education. One of his innovations at Harvard was the introduction of aptitude tests for aspiring entrants, a reflection of his belief in a meritocratic society. He also ensured that the curriculum at Harvard was modernised, a move which was followed by most US universities. Changes included opening courses to women, insisting upon teaching and scholastic ability for academic appointments, provision for compulsory general studies for all students, the creation of Harvard scholarships designed to broaden the social base of the student body, and the creation of cross-departmental research and leadership. This theme was expanded upon in his *Education and Liberty* (1953). His growing concern with social questions in relation to education were expressed in *Slums and Suburbs* (1961) and *The Comprehensive High School* (1967), where earlier ideas about the relation between science and society were applied to a school context. Conant played a leading role in a number of government-sponsored investigations into education, and served as an education adviser for the Ford Foundation in Berlin in 1964. The title of his autobiography distils his multifaceted contribution in sixty years of active public life: *Several Lives* (1970).

See also: higher education; meritocracy; metropolitanism

STEVEN COWAN

CONDORCET, MARIE-JEAN (1743–94)

Condorcet, the French philosopher and educationist, was educated by Jesuits and was most remembered for his *Sketch of the Intellectual Progress of Mankind* (1795), in which he

argued that, for society to move forwards and progress to a higher level, it was necessary for education to be made more widely available. It was a secular and progressive history, tracing development from primitive states to the modern. He is seen as one of the founders of modern sociology, especially because of his concerns to connect the moral and physical sciences. Condorcet was pioneer in the use of calculus, becoming one of France's major intellectual and academic figures. He was a pioneer positivist who influenced Saint-Simon and Comte. His specialist area was mathematics and he published several important works, including *Essay on the Application of Analysis to the Probability of Majority Decisions* (1785). Condorcet became secretary to the Academy of Sciences in 1777. Under the patronage of Turgot, the finance minister, he became inspector general of the Mint. Biographies of Turgot and Voltaire established his literary reputation.

Condorcet became secretary to the Legislative Assembly after the French Revolution and was elected as a representative for Paris. He believed that education was an essential element in the creation of a democratic society. He stressed the link between education and the practical achievement of equality for all and was an advocate of moral, rather than political, education for children. His 1792 *Report and Decree on the General Organisation of Public Education* elaborated ideas for a tiered national system spanning from nursery to university. He was either murdered or committed suicide whilst imprisoned by the Jacobins in 1794.

See also: France

STEVEN COWAN

CONSTRUCTIVISM

The basic principle of constructivism is that learners *construct* or build their own knowledge and meaning as opposed to having it 'given' or 'delivered' to them. Human learning is constructed by building new knowledge upon the foundation of previous learning. This view of learning sharply contrasts with one in which learning and teaching involve the transmission of information from one individual to another, a view in which *reception*, not construction, is central. Two important practical points follow: the first is that learners construct new knowledge and understanding using *what they already know*. There is no empty vessel into which new knowledge is poured: as a result, students come to learning situations with knowledge constructed from previous experience, and that prior knowledge influences the new knowledge they will construct from any future learning experiences.

In a sense, the notion that we all construct our own knowledge for ourselves could hardly be challenged: how could it be otherwise if we are talking about 'my knowledge', 'my interpretation' or 'my meaning'? But the idea of constructivism becomes more contentious and radical if it is taken a stage further. If it is argued that all knowledge is 'in the mind' or is constructed by the learner then the debate really begins. Would this rule out the idea of shared knowledge and understanding? How might this relate to the notion of a 'body of knowledge' – scientific knowledge, for example – accumulated over a period of time? The philosopher of science Karl Popper, for example, talked of a kind of 'third world' of accumulated knowledge stored in books, libraries and now the internet, which has some sort of existence outside the human mind.

Some versions of radical constructivism can certainly be contested, especially if they lead to a kind of 'anything goes' view of knowledge. This is often termed 'epistemic relativism'. Its basic idea is that any way of knowing is as good as any other: no one form of knowing about the world should be 'privileged' above another. Thus, science is no better than astrology and one person's or one group's knowledge of the world – and their way of knowing and their epistemology – is not superior to another's.

However, a constructivist approach to learning need not imply a constructivist approach to epistemology (see Solomon

1994). One of the radical constructivists, von Glasersfeld (1984) talked in his later writing of constructivism as a theory of *knowing rather than knowledge*. And the opposite position – the so-called 'realist' view – that knowledge is independent of the learner and that knowledge is either true or false, depending on whether it corresponds with reality, is easily pulled apart. It depends on a naive view of reality, the idea that something exists 'out there', independently; and a correspondence theory of 'truth' (i.e. that knowledge is only true if it 'corresponds with' external reality). This theory of truth begs the question: how can we know if our knowledge corresponds with reality? Thus, a kind of infinite regress is set up.

One of the key messages for the classroom, seminar room or lecture theatre from constructivist thinking is the statement that learning requires some *mental* activity on the part of the learner. Physical activity on its own is not sufficient for 'active learning', the learner must be mentally active too: evidence of the first (behavioural activity) does not always imply the presence of the second. For learning to be *active*, it must lead to restructuring of the learner's mind. This is in contrast to the view of the mind as a tabula rasa onto which knowledge is etched or 'delivered' (Driver and Easley 1978).

Two other points about learning are centrally important for education:

1 New learning depends on the existing knowledge of the learner: meaningful learning must to 'start from it'. This implies that teachers/lecturers need to use some strategy for finding out where students are, by eliciting their prior knowledge;
2 New learning involves learners in constructing meaning. Knowledge is actively constructed by the learner, and is not passively received from the environment or the teacher.

See also: accreditation of prior achievement/ learning; correspondence theory; learning; postmodernism

Further reading

Driver, R. and Easley, J. (1978) 'Pupils and paradigms: a review of literature related to concept development in adolescent science students', *Studies in Science Education*, 5: 61–84.
Solomon, J. (1994) 'The rise and fall of constructivism', *Studies in Science Education*, 23: 1–19.
von Glasersfeld, E. (1984) 'An introduction to radical constructivism'. In P. Watzlawick (ed.) *The Invented Reality*, London: W. W. Norton.

JERRY WELLINGTON

CONTINUED/CONTINUING PROFESSIONAL DEVELOPMENT

Continued or continuing professional development (CPD) refers to the ongoing development, maintenance and updating of expertise, skills and knowledge that are needed to contribute to changing workplaces. In recent years CPD has been an expanding component of continuing education and lifelong learning. It is a key concern of individual practitioners and professional bodies, as well as a range of educational organisations. Many professional occupations, including doctors, lawyers, accountants, teachers and financial advisers, participate in CPD, and the term is rapidly being extended to a wider number of occupations. Some professional bodies make participation compulsory for all members in order to maintain standards.

CPD focuses upon the core skills that people need to keep abreast of social, economic, legal and cultural changes. It may encompass not just hard information such as knowledge of legal change and information technology skills, but also softer skills such as interpersonal communication and personal qualities. CPD may help individuals to fulfil their work roles effectively, demonstrate a professional standing among clients and employers, and change their careers. CPD is delivered by a diverse number of organisations including universities, charities, training agencies and others. It may involve short training courses, longer periods of study at a formal institution or personal study and development.

See also: continuing education, lifelong learning

TOM WOODIN

CONTINUING EDUCATION

Continuing education is an ambiguous concept with a number of definitions. At its broadest it refers to all forms of post-initial education and is defined by the European Universities Continuing Education Network as, 'Any form of education, both vocational or general, resumed after an interval following continuous education'. It may be considered to be one element of lifelong learning, a notion that would include both compulsory schooling and, in some definitions, any sort of informal learning beyond educational institutions. By contrast continuing education tends to refer to post-initial structured forms of learning through universities and other agencies. It is also closely connected to recent developments in vocational education, specifically continuing vocational education (CVE) and continuing professional development (CPD), which are tied into the requirements of particular jobs and the economy more generally. Specifically it has been linked to training, staff development and human resources.

In some accounts continuing education encompasses the notion of liberal adult education and non-certified forms of humanistic learning for its own sake. It may also embrace education for leisure activities, personal fulfilment and social development, second-chance education and third-age education. It can be debated whether basic skills and literacy come under the ambit of continuing education, given that they may be seen as initial, rather than continuing forms of education. However, given that adult literacy is perceived as essential to economic development, it is often placed within continuing education, especially in developing countries such as Nigeria.

Continuing education has been dated back to the late eighteenth century, although Nottingham University in the United Kingdom would not employ the term until the 1930s. In the United States of America, in 1904, the 'Madison idea' expressed the belief that the University of Madison–Wisconsin should be closely connected into the wider community. In the 1970s scholars associated with UNESCO developed notions of permanent and recurrent education, which also fed into the idea of continuing education. However, continuing education became more pervasive in the 1980s and the 1990s as education has become increasingly linked to the needs of the economy. Employees were required to upgrade and update their skills in order to respond to the rapid pace of social and technological change. This approach relied on theories of human capital in which education and training are seen as resources that countries must nurture and develop in order to benefit from economic globalisation. At the same time, governments have taken a step back from earlier interventionist stances towards a coordinating role and encouraged employers and individuals to take greater responsibility for identifying needs and paying for training.

The apparent neutrality of the term continuing education has helped to ensure its popularity across the political spectrum and in different countries where it has been a feature of the transformation of many different educational systems, many of which are beginning to bear a closer resemblance to one another. For instance, in Europe the Bologna Declaration has speeded up a trend towards comparability across national boundaries through accreditation, modularisation, credit accumulation and transfer in higher education.

The economic functions of continuing education tend to be emphasised where unemployment is high, such as in Poland and Romania. In some countries, such as the UK, there has been support for increasing access to universities, known as widening participation. Here, government funding led to the growth of vocational forms of continuing education at the expense of liberal adult education and extra-mural departments. A similar change has taken place in Finland where there was a smoother and voluntary transition towards vocational continuing education. In the USA, where community colleges and universities offer flexible modular degrees, such forms of continuing education have a longer history.

A wide array of institutional forms is responsible for continuing education. These include university departments, which took over from those specialising in adult education, stand-alone departments of continuing education, as well as initiatives that are intended to influence universities as a whole. In turn, universities find themselves competing with a range of agencies, especially those which provide CVE and CPD. In countries such as Germany, Italy, the Netherlands and Spain a significant element of continuing education is delivered through institutions outside universities. In part, this is because CPD is delivered in different ways, for instance as training, distance learning, through the internet, conferences and seminars. Networks have also adopted the title, for instance the European Union Continuing Education Network (EUCEN), in the UK, the National Institute of Adult Continuing Education (NIACE) and the American Association for Adult and Continuing Education.

See also: compulsory education; continued/continuing professional development; informal/nonformal learning; lifelong learning; recurrent education; vocational education

Further reading

Jarvis, P. (1995) *Adult and Continuing Education: Theory and Practice*, 2nd edn, London: Routledge.

Jarvis, P. and Griffin, C. (2003) *Adult and Continuing Education: Major Themes in Education*, vols 1–5, London: Routledge.

Osborne, M. and Thomas, E. (2003) *Lifelong Learning in a Changing Continent. Continuing Education in the Cities of Europe*, Leicester: National Institute for Adult Continuing Education.

TOM WOODIN

CONTINUOUS ASSESSMENT

Continuous assessment represents an assessment strategy implemented by teachers to ascertain the knowledge, skill and understanding attained by students on an ongoing basis. It differs from terminal assessment, which is carried out at the end of a course or unit of study. Terminal assessment is invariably carried out for summative purposes, whereas continuous assessment can be either summative or formative in nature. Continuous assessment represents a radically different approach to the assessment process. It is based on the premise that the most effective and fairest way to assess students' performance is to do so as soon as it has been completed or while the work is actually being carried out. This is an educationally more effective approach because it provides the student with ongoing feedback on their performance. It helps them to be more self-critical and it enhances students' mastery of the material as they work through the course, rather than leaving everything to the end of the programme of study.

Utilising a continuous assessment strategy, teachers administer assessments in a variety of ways over the duration of the programme of study. It allows the teacher the opportunity to observe multiple tasks and to collect information about what students know, understand and are able to do. The assessments, to be effective, are based on tasks or activities previously taught to students. Continuous assessment is considered to be much fairer to students who work steadily and consistently but are not effective at sitting examinations. It is considered more in tune with trends in tertiary education, where there is a move to make assessment an integral part of the learning process. There is also a desire to move away from the assessment of 'content' to the assessment of 'processes'.

Continuous assessment can take many forms and can be implemented in a number of ways. Students may be required to carry out ongoing self-assessments of their progress. This may involve students carrying out an assessment of the extent to which they have achieved specific learning outcomes. It may also involve students keeping a record of their personal development and/or completing a skills profile. A commonly used form of continuous assessment involves the administration of a series of short tests as learners proceed through the programme of study. The results of these tests may be used for formative and summative purposes and the tests can include short-answer questions, class quizzes or brief written papers. Another frequently used continuous assessment strategy involves setting students coursework, essays, and other more detailed forms of assessment, such as mini-projects of seminar papers. Students may also be asked to assemble a portfolio of work while progressing through a course. These portfolios are frequently used on competency-based courses. Some courses incorporate work-based experience. This work placement element is frequently judged using some form of continuous assessment.

Continuous assessment is considered to be more than an assessment of students' achievement. It is also a diagnostic tool, which enables students to understand areas of the course in which they are experiencing difficulty. It is useful to the teacher because it facilitates the monitoring of student understanding. The teacher can then modify his/her teaching strategies to include revision and a repeat of elements that have not been mastered by the student. The feedback component of the assessment process helps foster a strong teacher-student relationship. It can help motivate the student to continue to work hard and achieve higher levels of mastery.

Continuous assessment does, however, have disadvantages. Students may perceive that they are under constant surveillance and they may feel that they are over-assessed. This requires that teachers need to carefully plan the assessment schedule to ensure that students do not suffer from assessment overload. Continuous assessment may, if not properly managed, adversely impact the relationship between teacher and student. This is more likely to occur when the student continues to perform poorly on the assessment. Students may suffer from unequal availability of resources and the teacher needs to ensure that uniform procedures such as completion dates are observed. Teachers may experience difficulties in dealing with students who do not comply with the rules set out at the beginning of the programme of study. Teachers need to be experienced in the use of continuous assessment to ensure that the assessments have variety, use different approaches and assess the broad spectrum of learning objectives set out for the programme of study.

See also: assessment; formative assessment; summative assessment; work-based/work-located/workplace/work-related learning

Further reading

Biggs, J. (2001) *Teaching for Quality Learning at University*, Buckingham: SRHE and Open University Press.

Knight, P. T. (2002) *Being a Teacher in Higher Education*, Buckingham: SRHE and Open University Press

Purvis, R. (1990) *Continuous Assessment*, Aberdeen: CICED Publications.

Race, P. (1996) 'The art of assessing 2', *New Academic*, 5(1): 3–6.

THOMAS N. GARAVAN

CORE CURRICULUM/NATIONAL CURRICULUM

The curriculum studied by pupils and students has often been divided in terms of what should be essential for all to learn, and what should be regarded as optional. One common means of identifying these two types of curriculum is to define a core curriculum that is deemed to constitute the most fundamental knowledge. Within educational institutions and programmes of study it is not unusual to develop a core module or course which all must follow, and a number of electives or options. A well known and traditional notion of a core curriculum is the combination of reading, writing and arithmetic, or the so-called 'three Rs' (literally, reading, 'riting and 'rithmetic, a coinage widely attributed to Sir William Curtis, a London alderman, in the late eighteenth century). More recently this kind of core curriculum has often been seen as outdated for the needs of rapidly changing societies. Another kind of core curriculum is established in a number of education systems through the development of detailed national curricula, which may comprise a few or a large number of key subjects. Citizenship or civics is often regarded as an essential feature of a national curriculum, but some societies have given special privilege to areas of knowledge such as religious education, the study of ancient cultures, and many others.

See also: curriculum

GARY McCULLOCH

CORE SKILLS/CORE COMPETENCIES

The terms core and key skills are generally taken to mean the clusters of foundation generic work-related skills identified by either the Qualifications and Curriculum Authority in England (key skills) or the Scottish Qualifications Authority in Scotland (core skills). Although nuanced in different ways these skills cover: Communication, Application of Numbers (numeracy), Information and Communication Technology, Working with Others, Problem Solving and Improving Own Learning and Performance. These generic skills are normally offered at five levels of ability within the National Qualification Frameworks for each country and can be taken as certificated or stand-alone awards, although typically they are 'embedded' or 'signposted' within national qualifications

The concept of 'core competencies' has been more widely adopted in the English-speaking countries from around the world, all of which have introduced some notion of employability skills within the curriculum. However, the concept of 'competencies' is usually much more broadly defined in terms of citizenship and social responsibilities in these countries in comparison with the more narrowly defined 'skills' focus within the United Kingdom.

It should be acknowledged at the outset that core/key skills as a concept is socially constructed. Over the years, the meaning of generic skills has continually changed, reflecting social, political and economic trends. For instance, in the 1980s language education was central to any discourse on core skills, while in the 1990s enterprise education became much more prominent. Both have subsequently been eclipsed by the softer skills of teamwork and improving own learning. Indeed, in many ways the 'concept of skill has become bigger, broader and much fuzzier around the edges'. Definitions of core competencies are, therefore, contested and the concept has increasingly become imbued with notions of 'emotive and aesthetic labour' and, in turn, tangled up with attributes and dispositions.

More recent policy developments have seen a movement away from the external testing of key skills in Wales, the separation and accreditation of the 'wider' key skills in England and the further contextualisation and integration of core skills within the curriculum in Scotland. However, there is little doubt that the 'skills' agenda is at a crossroads in the UK. The notion of 'functional' skills has gained considerable ground in recent years. Employers would also seem to have a shifting agenda and are pressing instead for the development of 'work-readiness' skills. This is reflected in the recent changes in the 14–18 curriculum in both England and Scotland. The priority in policy development is now towards extending the compulsory school years for young people not in education, training or work with a view to engaging them in pre-vocational courses offered from a variety of partnership institutions.

Looking to the future, the difficulty with the debate on core skills and competencies is that it is often predicated upon a very narrow definition of the concept of employability. The communitarian aspects of participating in a social democracy are rarely addressed within this discourse. In fact, the neo-liberal economic rhetoric of the 'knowledge economy', 'lifelong learning' and 'skills' dominates the debate. Other stakeholder 'voices' are rarely heard, including those of young people. It is not surprising therefore that 'skills' have come to be revered and worshipped as the solution to all economic ills, notwithstanding that skills account for less than one fifth of the productivity gap between the UK and other rich countries. In reality, capital investment is recognised as being the 'major drag on performance' in terms of international competitiveness.

A second major obstacle to expanding the core skills and competencies of the next generation of working people is the apparent lack of a shared understanding of exactly what 'skills' are and how they can be developed. Recent research has demonstrated that the concept of skills is culturally determined and differs significantly between nation-states. For instance, the German concept of skill is much broader than that of the UK and includes notions of identity, standards of education and training and nationally negotiated agreements on working conditions.

The 'technical rationalist' approach to education and skills as exemplified within the core competencies literature has often reduced the concept of skills to basic replicative tasks devoid of professional or moral judgement. Thus instead of taking the 'high road' to a knowledge-based economy, much of the discourse on core skills has become overly concerned with skill deficits, the unemployed and the needs of industry for low paid labour.

See also: knowledge economy; lifelong learning; literacy; numeracy; skills

Further reading

Canning, R. (2007) 'Re-conceptualisng core skills', *Journal of Education and Work*, 20(1):17–26.

Clarke, L. (2006) 'A European skills framework? – but what are skills? Anglo-Saxon versus German concepts', *Journal of Education and Work*, 19(3): 255–69

Hayward, G. and Fernandez, R. (2004) 'From core skills to key skills: fast forward or back to the future?', *Oxford Review of Education*, 30(1): 117–45.

McSkeane, M. (2007) 'Core skills: towards policy and practice', unpublished Ph.D. thesis, Department of Adult Education, Maynooth: The National University of Ireland Maynooth.

Warhurst, C., Grugulis, I. and Keep, E. (2004) *The Skills that Matter*, London: Palgrave.

ROY CANNING

CORPORAL PUNISHMENT

Corporal punishment is the use of physical force, no matter how light, with the intention of causing children to experience bodily pain so as to correct or punish the child's behaviour. Corporal punishment is used by parents and teachers throughout the world as a means of punishing children for their mis-behaviours. Such physical force typically includes hitting children either with a hand or with an object, such as a wooden paddle. However, corporal punishment does not refer only to hitting children as a form of discipline; it also includes other practices that involve purposefully causing the child to experience pain in order to punish them, including washing a child's mouth out with soap, making a child kneel on sharp or painful objects (e.g. rice, a floor grate), placing hot sauce on a child's tongue, and forcing a child to engage in excessive exercise or physical exertion. The term 'corporal punishment' is often used interchangeably with the terms physical punishment or physical discipline.

There is very little data available on the international prevalence of corporal punishment in schools. Informal surveys of children in countries throughout the world and compiled by the Global Initiative to End Corporal Punishment suggest that it is quite prevalent in schools throughout the world. In the United States, the federal Department of Education (2005) reported that in the 2001–2 school year 301,016 incidents of corporal punishment occurred in schools throughout the country. Because more than half of the states have banned school corporal punishment, this prevalence of corporal punishment amounts to less than 1 per cent of the total number of school children in the entire country. It is thus more appropriate to look at prevalence within the states that allow it; such prevalence rates are as high as 9.1 per cent of all school children in Mississippi and 7.6 per cent of all school children in Arkansas.

There has been almost no empirical research on the impact of school corporal punishment on children's behaviour or mental health. The little that there is suggests that experience with school corporal punishment is associated with poor mental health and behaviour among children. In contrast, several hundred studies have been conducted that examine whether and how parents' use of corporal punishment affects their children's behaviour and mental health. Taken together, these studies indicate that the more children are spanked by their parents, the less likely they are to behave appropriately and the more likely they are to be aggressive and to have elevated mental health symptoms such as depression or anxiety.

There is a growing international consensus that corporal punishment of children by parents and teachers is a violation of international human rights law, specifically the United Nations Convention on the Rights of the Child. The United Nations Committee on the Rights of the Child has concluded that all corporal punishment of children violates children's right to protection from physical and mental violence (per Article 19 of the

Convention on the Rights of the Child) and should be banned.

There are now seventeen countries that have banned all corporal punishment of children, be it by parents, teachers, or others. They are (in order from earliest ban to most recent): Sweden, Finland, Norway, Austria, Croatia, Cyprus, Denmark, Latvia, Bulgaria, Germany, Israel, Iceland, Romania, Ukraine, Hungary, Greece, and the Netherlands. Corporal punishment of children by teachers or school administrators has been specifically banned in at least 109 of the world's 230 countries. In the United States, corporal punishment in public schools is banned in twenty-nine states, yet corporal punishment in private schools is banned in only two states (Iowa and New Jersey).

See also: classroom management; discipline; school violence

Further reading

Committee on the Rights of the Child (2006) General Comment no. 8 (2006): 'The right of the child to protection from corporal punishment and or cruelor degrading forms of punishment' (articles 1, 28(2) and 37, inter alia) (CRC/C/GC/8), Geneva: United Nations.
Gershoff, E. T. (2002) 'Corporal punishment by parents and associated child behaviors and experiences: a meta-analytic and theoretical review', *Psychological Bulletin*, 128(4): 539–79.
Global Initiative to End All Corporal Punishment of Children (2007) Online Global Table: Legality of Corporal Punishment. Available at www.endcorporalpunishment.org
United States Department of Education, Office for Civil Rights. (2005) *2002 Elementary and Secondary School Civil Rights Compliance Report.* Washington DC: US Department of Education.

ELIZABETH T. GERSHOFF

CORRESPONDENCE COURSE

A correspondence course is a programme of study, most often offered today by private tutorial colleges, in which the student and tutor interact with each other by post. Upon registering for the programme, learners are typically sent a course pack, which may include key readings, commentaries by lecturers, guidance on study skills and details of formative and summative assignment requirements. They may also receive accompanying audio or video materials. Students then work through the material within a specified period of time, complete the set assignments and post them to their tutor. After reading the work, the tutor then posts feedback and advice to the learner. The University of Chicago offered its first correspondence course in 1891 and this manifestation of distance learning became particularly popular in the 1960s in response to demand from non-traditional learners to prepare for examinations without taking on the commitment of attending regular classes. The advent of educational broadcasting and, more recently, Web-based learning, permitting more instant tutor feedback by email, has significantly reduced the demand for correspondence courses. Nevertheless, they continue to be offered by some organisations, especially in such areas of languages and religious studies.

See also: distance education/learning; Open University; Web-based learning

DAVID CROOK

CORRESPONDENCE THEORY

1976 saw the publication of Sam Bowles and Herb Gintis' seminal *Schooling in Capitalist America* (*SCA*). Its release represented a revolutionary moment in the sociology of education. Following on from the *New Sociology of Education*, which centralised notions of power and control but could not link the micro (the classroom and the school) to the macro (the economy), the strength of *SCA* lay in its focus on the capitalist economy itself. As was suggested some twelve years later, '[t]o the discipline as a whole, political radicalism became central' (Cole 1988: 8). The guiding paradigm in *SCA* is 'the correspondence principle'.

According to the correspondence principle, there is a structural correspondence between the social relations of schooling (a narrower process than *education*, signifying a compulsory period of state- and capitalist-controlled induction, rather than the opening of minds) and those of production. In other words, young people are integrated into the economic system (what goes on in the capitalist workplace) by what goes on in schooling. This includes discipline, types of personal demeanour, modes of self-presentation, self-image, and social-class identification. Specifically, according to the correspondence principle, the social relationships of education replicate the hierarchical division of labour in the capitalist economy (Bowles and Gintis 1976). Hierarchical relations are reflected in the vertical authority lines in schools (e.g. head teachers, teachers, students/pupils; just as in the capitalist economy, the students/pupils have no control over their education (Bowles and Gintis 1976)).

By attuning young people to a set of social relationships similar to those to the workplace, schooling, according to Bowles and Gintis, attempts to gear the development of personal needs to the requirements of the capitalist economy (Bowles and Gintis 1976).

One of the most trenchant critiques of Bowles and Gintis' thesis is provided, within the Marxist tradition, by Glenn Rikowski (1997: 551–74), who has identified five interlinked 'debilitating problematics' associated with the correspondence principle, and the Marxist educational theory, which it spawned. The first problematic concerns the *base/superstructure* model, where the economic base determines the superstructure (e.g. the political, legal, and, in this case, the schooling system). As Rikowski (1997: 556) points out, such determinism leaves no theoretical space for class struggle and engenders fatalism.

Second, and leading on from this, the correspondence principle is essentially functionalist. Functionalism is a branch of sociology, which is concerned with how various parts of society function in order to keep that society going. At its crudest, it makes an analogy between the organs of society and the organs

of the human body. Since functionalism is not concerned with challenges to the status quo, it is, in essence, conservative. Marxism, on the other hand, while also centrally concerned with how societies function, is not just a theory *of* society, but also a theory against society: a theory that moves beyond presently-existing society, in the pursuit of a socialist future (Rikowski 1997: 557).

Third, in order to escape the *base/superstructure* dilemma, a number of commentators (e.g. Apple 1985) have drawn on relative autonomy theory, derived from the work of the Marxist writer Louis Althusser and others, where there is a degree of autonomy or separateness between the requirements of the base and the superstructure. Relative autonomy theorists talk about determination 'in the last instance'. This was seen to offer the best of both worlds: a weak form of determination; and a space for resistance (Rikowski 1997: 558). Problems with relative autonomy theory include determining when 'the last instance' actually arrives; and the tendency for relative autonomy to slide into complete autonomy, thus deserting the Marxist project altogether.

Fourth, the seeming lack of space for resistance in *SCA* led some (e.g. Willis 1977; Apple 1985) to concentrate on the ways in which pupils/students *resist* capitalist schooling. The problem with these writings on resistance, however, is the unspecificity of the term, which, Rikowski (1997: 561) argues, thus renders it redundant. Resistance, in the work of the resistance theorists, has included fucking, fighting, farting, fiddling, anti-intelletualism, racism and sexism (Rikowski 1997: 561). Significantly, the conclusions of Paul Willis (1977), perhaps the theorist most cited to refute the functionalism of correspondence theory, are that the culture created by the resistance of 'the lads' in school is ultimately conducive to the culture of factory life.

Rikowski's (1997) fifth and final point is the dichotomy between *education for autonomy* and *social revolution*, his argument being that there is a danger that, at the expense of enhancing the individual's capacity for independent thinking, we may lose sight of Marxism's stress on social revolution. But while this dichotomy may be true of other (Marxist) writings in the 1970s and 1980s, in the final two chapters of *SCA* Bowles and Gintis make it perfectly clear that their overriding concern is with social revolution. That this is the case needs to be born in mind when considering Rikowski's very valid points above (see Cole 2007).

Rikowski's solution to the dilemmas of the correspondence principle and its legacy is to dissolve Marxist sociology of education altogether and to make the concept of labour power the starting point for an analysis of the relationship between schooling and capitalism. It is well known that the starting point of Marx's major work, *Capital*, is an analysis of commodities, the accumulation of which underpins the capitalist mode of production (Marx 1965 [1887]: 35).

Citing Marx (1969 [1863]: 167), Rikowski (2000: 20) makes it clear that there are two classes of commodities: first, labour power; second, commodities distinct from labour power. Labour power is unique in that it is the only commodity that produces a value greater than itself (when workers engage in capitalist production, they get paid less than the value they produce, the surplus being appropriated or hived off by the capitalist; in Marxist theory this is referred to as the labour theory of value). What characterises the capitalist mode of production is that education and training socially produces labour power.

The 'intentionality and social drive to reduce education and training to the social production of labour power in capitalism', as Rikowski (2000: 23) argues, grows 'stronger with time'. This growth in strength is apparent in the global drive to privatise schooling, both in order to increase profits from the schooling process itself, and in the attempt to massively increase capitalist control over the form and content (surprisingly, Bowles and Gintis rejected content as instrumental in upholding capitalism) of schooling (see Cole 2007).

SCA and the correspondence principle were, indeed, revolutionary moments in the sociology of education. Sociology of education is now mainly underpinned by postmodernism (Cole 2007), in many ways a natural progression from the slide into full autonomy.

While a focus on the capitalist economy, provided by the correspondence principle, is welcome, and while Marxists must laud Bowles and Gintis' uncompromising commitment to social revolution, the task, as I have argued following Rikowski (1997; 2000), is to dissolve Marxist sociology of education altogether and to build and to develop an understanding of the schooling/capitalist economy relation around the material concept of labour power, a task still in it its infancy (for some starting points, see Rikowski 2000)

See also: autonomy; educational theory; sociology of education

Further reading

Apple, M. (1985) *Education and Power*, London: Ark Paperbacks.

Bowles, S. and Gintis, H. (1976) *Schooling in Capitalist America: Educational Reform and the Contradictions of Economic Life*, London: Routledge and Kegan Paul.

Cole, M. (1988) 'Preface'. In M. Cole (ed.) *Bowles and Gintis Revisited: Correspondence and Contradiction in Educational Theory*, London: Falmer Press.

——(2007) *Marxism and Educational Theory: Origins and Issues*, London: Routledge.

Marx, K. (1965) [1887] *Capital Vol. 1*, Moscow: Progress Publishers.

——(1969) [1863] *Theories of Surplus Value: Part One*, London: Lawrence & Wishart.

Rikowski, G. (1997) 'Scorched earth: prelude to rebuilding Marxist educational theory', *British Journal of Sociology of Education*, 18: 551–74.

—— (2000) *That Other Great Class of Commodities: Repositioning Marxist Educational Theory*, a paper presented at the British Educational Research Association Conference, Cardiff University, 7–10 September. Available online at: www.leeds. ac.uk/educol/documents/00001624.htm

Willis, P. (1977) *Learning to Labour: How Working Class Kids Get Working Class Jobs*, Farnborough: Saxon House.

MIKE COLE

135

COUNSELLING

Counselling, in an international context, has been defined as

> a method of relating and responding to others with the aim of providing them with opportunities to explore, clarify, and work towards living in a more personally satisfying and resourceful way. Counselling may be applied to individuals, couples, families, or groups and may be used in widely different contexts and settings.
>
> (Hoxter 1998: 29)

While counselling as a profession has its origins in the United States, it now exists worldwide.

The American Counseling Association defines professional counselling as 'the applications of mental health, psychological, or human development principles, through cognitive, affective, behavioural or systematic intervention strategies, that address wellness, personal growth, or career development, as well as pathology' (American Counseling Association 2007). Counselling generally takes a developmental and preventative orientation, and focuses on understanding individuals within their environmental contexts. Counselling thus aims to help individuals define and achieve goals, and to assist them in overcoming barriers to doing so.

Professional counsellors work in schools and colleges, as well as a variety of other settings including community and government agencies, schools and colleges, business, and private practice. In addition to the traditional roles of providing direct counselling services and supervision, counsellors also perform a number of other functions related to prevention and promoting healthy development, including consultation, outreach, education, and other indirect services.

The development of professional counselling in the United States was largely influenced by the vocational and career guidance movement of the early twentieth century. As the country shifted from being primarily an agrarian society to a primarily industrial one, this movement developed as a means of helping individuals adapt to the major lifestyle changes associated with this shift. The work of Frank Parsons, including the establishment of the Vocational Bureau of Boston in 1908, and the publication of his book *Choosing a Vocation* in 1909, is largely credited as being the foundation of this movement (Gibson and Mitchell 1995). In addition to Parsons' work, other movements arose near the same time that facilitated the development of the counselling profession. The development of specialised clinics to assist children with emotional and behavioural problems, and the creation of assessment instruments to measure abilities both began around this same time as well.

Other social demands drove the advancement of the counselling profession during the twentieth century. For example, the need for counselling services rose sharply following the end of World War II to assist with the vocational and personal adjustment of returning veterans. Additionally, counselling in schools was given a major boost in the late 1950s when the arms race with the Soviet Union spurred the passage of the National Defense Education Act (NDEA). The NDEA funded programmes to train guidance counsellors with the intent of establishing a national cadre of counsellors to help students plan for post-high school education, specifically in maths and sciences (Stockton *et al.* 2002). However, the Act had a much broader impact than intended. Counsellor training proliferated, and has continued to do so. Today counsellors serve a much broader role in schools than envisioned by the NDEA.

Individual countries have adapted the profession to their unique cultural identities and needs; however, the course of its development has some general elements that are universal. As globalisation and changing economic and social forces impact a society, the need for counselling arises as a means of helping individuals adapt to these changes. This adaptation often first occurs vocationally, but is then often accompanied by needs for adapting socially and emotionally. Additionally, the problems that arise in societies as they change are consistently reflected in schools, making the role of counselling in schools a crucial one. Much as in the rest of a society, the recognition of the need for vocational guidance in schools is often followed by recognition of the importance of addressing the related social and emotional needs of students as well.

Much like the changes that surrounded the industrial revolution at the turn of the twentieth century, the twenty-first century has brought a host of changes associated with globalisation, including immigration and the changing nature of the job market, among others. These changes have resulted in the need for individuals and societies to adapt in terms of how students are prepared to enter the workforce, how they go about career planning and decision making, and how they adjust socially and emotionally to these changes. Thus, the need for counselling in schools and communities is almost certain to increase throughout the twenty-first century.

See also: careers guidance; pastoral care

Further reading

American Counseling Association, website at www.aca.org

Gibson, R. and Mitchell, M. (1995) *Introduction to Counseling and Guidance*, 4th edn, Upper Saddle River NJ: Merrill/Prentice-Hall.

Hoxter, H. (1998) 'In counselling as a profession', paper presented at the meeting for the International Association for Counselling, Paris, France.

Stockton, R., Garbelman, J., Kaladow, J., Clawson, T. and Smith, C. (2002) 'Mental health practitioners and trainees'. In R. Manderscheid and M. Henderson (eds) *Mental Health, United States 2002*, Washington DC: United States Department of Health and Human Services.

REX STOCKTON AND AMY NITZA

COURSEWORK

Coursework is work produced by pupils or students as part of their course that is assessed and included in their overall grade for the course. In this way it is unlike homework (or 'prep' which is a traditional term for this), which is often expected as part of the course but is not counted towards the final grade. The assessment for the course may be a combination of coursework and a final examination, or else based fully on coursework. The use of coursework has been widely encouraged as an alternative or supplement to examinations to avoid the stress of depending on the examination result, to minimise the role of memorisation and examination technique, and to promote independent study and research skills. On the other hand, it can give greater scope to plagiarism. Coursework may take the form of individual projects, often conducted over weeks or months, with a deadline for final submission and assessment. It can also involve group work, which can promote cooperation and social skills, although ensuring appropriate credit for individuals and full and active participation by all members of a group or team can be problematic.

See also: assessment; examinations; plagiarism

GARY McCULLOCH

CRAFTS

In the context of the curriculum, crafts is an umbrella term for the making of hand-made items. In the nursery and primary school, especially, appeals to parents for shoeboxes, yoghurt pots, wool and the like frequently provide the raw materials for imaginative creations, which children may proudly display in the classroom or bring home. In former times 'handicraft' or 'manual training' teachers were appointed to secondary schools to teach such subjects as basketry, bookbinding, ceramics, metalwork, textiles and woodwork. Today, at an international level, crafts tend to be included within secondary school art and design or design and technology curricula. These creative subjects, like music, regularly feel 'squeezed' by the greater national priority given to language, mathematics and science. The teaching of craft subjects has a prominent place in post-compulsory and adult education, although such programmes are frequently funded less generously than basic skills programmes. Specialist institutions, such as colleges of design, sewing schools and institutions specialising in blacksmithing, jewellery and silversmithing are to be found in many countries.

See also: art

DAVID CROOK

CRAMMING

Cramming refers to intensive periods of study, usually over a short period of time, in order to prepare for an examination. Cramming often involves memorisation of a large amount of factual information. It is generally considered to be a less effective mode of learning and preparing for exams than longer-term and structured forms of learning and preparation. The expansion of coursework as a replacement for exams has lessened the need for cramming, although few courses are assessed entirely in this way.

In many countries 'cram schools' are a feature of life for many students who must perform well in a competitive educational system in order to achieve and progress. The prevalence of multiple-choice examinations and the need to digest a great amount of information creates an environment conducive to the formation of such schools. They are particularly associated with East Asian countries such as China, Japan and South Korea, where they play a significant role in the education system.

They may also be found in other countries. For instance, in Britain, a 'crammer' refers to an educational organisation that prepares students for public examinations in a short period of time. Often the student will have previously failed to get the required grades and may be retaking examinations. Alternatively, they may wish to avoid prolonged study and progress to higher education more rapidly.

See also: examinations

TOM WOODIN

CREATIVITY

Creativity has been defined variously over time, within different cultures and in different domain areas. Most involve seeing creativity as involving shaping novel possibilities using imagination, and recognising originality and value of outcomes.

The idea of creativity as 'inspiration', produced by a higher power, is found in Greek, Judaic, Christian and Muslim traditions. The Romantic era in Europe spawned a view of inspiration expressed artistically, emerging from human creative genius; subjectivity of feeling playing a core role. Many disciplinary areas have contributed, the one perhaps most relevant to education being psychology.

In psychology, from the late nineteenth century, explorations focused initially on genius. Twentieth-century research was located in a number of psychological traditions, including psychoanalytic, cognitive, behaviourist and humanistic. From the 1950s, work on the limitations of intelligence testing and the role of 'divergent thinking' led to the exploration of personality traits among creative persons and psychodynamic approaches to understanding creativity. Later, from the 1980s, there was a focus on the role of the domain, which saw creativity as rooted in social systems, and inherently collaborative. Researchers in Europe and America sought to contribute to developing the 'creative organisation' (e.g. Ekvall 1996).

Since the mid-1990s, creativity in education has experienced unprecedented resurgence globally as an area of scholarship, policy making and classroom practice. It has involved exploration of conceptual frameworks, pupil and teacher perspectives, teaching creatively and for creativity and classroom practicalities in schools and universities, and examination of purpose (Craft 2005; Craft *et al.* 2007a; 2007b). Embedded is the assumption of everyday creativity as necessary and feasible, life-wide and lifelong; a distinctly different perspective to previous ones which had emphasised the extraordinary, 'big c' or 'high' creativity.

The resurgence spans Northern, Central and Southern Europe, the Middle and Far East and Australasia and North America. It reflects the relationship perceived at policy level between fostering everyday creativity within education, and economic competitiveness (Craft 2005). Research methodology shifted from positivist, large-scale studies aiming to measure creativity, towards ethnographic, qualitative research. Early twenty-first century studies of creativity in education increasingly emphasise the cultural dimensions of creativity, in particular discontinuities between 'universalised' and 'marketised' Westernised creativity discourse and Eastern perspectives (Craft *et al.* 2007a; 2007b).

In England, in particular, creativity in education is increasingly linked both to the economy, and to 'cultural development', reflecting several 'rhetorics' (Banaji and Burn 2007). Pedagogical developments include working in partnership with those beyond the classroom, initially recommended by the National Advisory Committee on Creative and Cultural Education and then by later government reviews (Roberts 2006; Department for Culture, Media and Sport 2006).

Knotty problems, yet to be adequately tackled, include how creativity is assessed and how schools handle the spectrum of creative and cultural education in the learning age. Perhaps most significant is how creativity engages with wisdom, as we face unprecedented global problems. On this latter point, Craft *et al.* (2007b) argue the urgent need for creativity to be seen as integral with wisdom and trusteeship, located in a larger system, and with attention paid to ends as well as means.

See also: art; culture; curriculum; giftedness; literacy; psychology

Further reading

Banaji, S. and Burn, A. (2007) 'Creativity through a rhetorical lens: implications for schooling, literacy and media education', *Literacy*, 41(2): 62–70.

Craft, A. (2005) *Creativity in Schools: Tensions and Dilemmas*, Oxford: RoutledgeFalmer.

Craft, A., Cremin, T. and Burnard, P. (eds) (2007a) *Creative Learning 3–11 and How to Document It*, Stoke-on-Trent: Trentham Books

Craft, A., Gardner, H. and Claxton, G. (eds) (2007b) *Creativity, Wisdom and Trusteeship: Exploring the Role of Education*, Thousand Oaks CA: Corwin Press.

Department for Culture, Media and Sport (2006) *Government Response to Paul Roberts' Report on Nurturing Creativity in Young People*, London: Department of Culture, Media and Sport.

Ekvall, G. (1996) 'Organizational climate for creativity and innovation', *European Work and Organizational Psychology*, 5: 105–23.

Roberts, P. (2006) *Nurturing Creativity in Young People. A Report to Government to Inform Future Policy*, London: Department of Culture, Media and Sport.

ANNA CRAFT

CRÈCHE

As the festival of Christmas approaches it is a tradition, particularly strong in North America and continental Europe, to exhibit a nativity scene, known as a crèche, representing the birth of Jesus Christ in the town of Bethlehem. Many Christian churches and other organisations celebrate the festival by inviting exhibits from professional and amateur craftspersons and especially from children. Thus, crèche exhibitions may display a wide range of nativity scenes, ranging from simple cardboard representations to elaborate scenes with porcelain figures or models of Jesus, his parents, shepherds, animals and the Wise Men crafted from wood or other materials.

In Eire, the United Kingdom and other countries including Australia and New Zealand the term crèche has a different meaning. In these countries it more commonly refers to a physical place, situated in or close to a parent's workplace or place of study, where childcare arrangements, normally supervised by qualified staff and subject to inspection, are available for pre-school children. A recent trend is for gymnasia and large shopping centres also to offer short-stay nurseries of this kind. A small, but increasing number, of employers provide no-cost all-day crèche facilities as an employment benefit to their workers, but it is more usual for a charge, sometimes at a subsidised rate, to be made. Universities and other adult education environments have been leaders in offering crèche facilities to staff and students. A crèche may simply comprise a room for children to listen to stories, play or paint. Others may include an outdoor play area, normally fenced. In an historical sense the term crèche may also be used to describe a foundling hospital, accommodating child orphans.

DAVID CROOK

CREDENTIAL SOCIETY

The American sociologist Randall Collins' book *The Credential Society* (1979) argues that in the United States during the twentieth century the major change in the social structure was in the rise of a large 'sinecure sector' of government employment, very large educational institutions, and the growth of the tertiary sector. The most significant factor that encouraged the growth of this sector, according to Collins, was the growth of the educational credential system. Educational credentials had served to monopolise jobs for specialised groups of workers, and so isolated them from pressures for work that was directly productive. In Collins' view, the United States has become the most credentialised society in the world. Indeed, he continued, 'The rise of a competitive system for producing an abstract cultural currency in the form of educational credentials has been the major new force shaping stratification in twentieth century America.' (Collins 1979: 94). Thus, credentials which first became established in the school system, had permeated the occupational structure

itself, and might well become even more powerful in the future in twenty-first century society. Collins' analysis, like that of the British sociologists Dore and Young, highlighted the potential contradictions beneath the rhetoric of competitive examinations and their potentially divisive role in social change.

See also: credentials/credentialing; diploma disease; meritocracy; United States

Further reading

Collins, R. (1979) *The Credential Society: An Historical Sociology of Education and Stratification*, New York: Academic Press.

GARY McCULLOCH

CREDENTIALS/CREDENTIALING

Credentials are formal documents issued by an institution once a student has met the requirements for completion of a particular programme of instruction and passed an evaluative component (for example an examination). They include certificates, diplomas and degrees. Credentials therefore constitute evidence of the training, skills and knowledge of an individual, acquired through authentication after passage through a period of education or training. Credentialing refers to the action of supplying an individual with credentials. The possession of a formal educational credential is typically seen to entitle the holder to continue with further education, to enter higher-level jobs or to receive rewards and status within the labour market. Those who do not possess credentials are often seen as excluded from such opportunities.

Historically, within the context of a more elite system of education, credentials were awarded only to a minority of the population. However, as national systems of education have expanded, credentials have been awarded on a much wider scale. At the level of higher education, this process has made the relationship between different credentials and the occupational structure of the labour market more problematic. It has led, for instance, to uncertainty about how a large number of graduates with the same credentials might stand out from others when competing for jobs and rewards. It has also meant that competition for the more elite credentials (i.e. those from higher-status institutions and/or courses) has become fierce, particularly among the middle classes.

Such massification of education, and the consequent rise in the number of credentials being awarded, has occurred in many different countries including Australia, France, the UK and the USA. Countries such as India, China and those in Eastern Europe are also rapidly taking this route. Within contemporary society, credentials are being issued by an increasing number of different bodies, including not just educational institutions but also private (often corporate) providers. They are also increasingly being provided through online and virtual learning environments.

A number of theorists have attempted to understand and map the relationships between credentials and the wider society/occupational structure and how they have changed over time. A landmark book was Randall Collins' *The Credential Society* (1979), in which he identified a trend towards what he termed credentialism. This refers to a situation where ever more individuals are chasing and being awarded credentials, so that the greater supply leads to a devaluation of the credential itself. In a more recent piece, Collins argues that:

> As educational attainment has expanded, the social distinctiveness of the bachelor's degree and its value on the marketplace have declined ... in turn, increasing the demand for still higher levels of education.
>
> (Collins 2002: B20)

This is linked to credential inflation where education both costs more and promises less of a payoff for given levels of credentials than once was so.

There are, therefore, new challenges in the face of international policies to open up credentials to more of the population. The first concerns the status or value of different credentials, including the institution that they come from (elite or lower ranking); their level (high/secondary school, further or higher education); subject; grade and type (academic, vocational or technical education). High-grade credentials awarded by elite institutions of higher education in academic subjects are typically seen to represent the greatest value within the labour market.

The second, related, issue concerns the relationship between different educational credentials and the broader social and occupational structure. Assumptions that the hierarchy of achievement within education, embodied in the form of credentials, corresponds neatly with the hierarchy of jobs in the labour market have increasingly been called into question. Due to differences in the status of credentials, evidence has shown that the reality is often less clear-cut at the start of the twenty-first century (Smetherham 2006). The future relationship between credentials and the structure of society will continue to evolve as educational policies, processes and awards, and the competition for credentials, changes.

See also: certificate/certification; credential society; degree; diploma; examinations

Further reading

Collins, R. (1979) *The Credential Society: An Historical Sociology of Education and Stratification*, London: Academic Press.
——(2002) 'The dirty little secret of credential inflation', *Chronicle of Higher Education*, 49(5): 27 September (online).
Smetherham, C. (2006) 'Firsts among equals? Evidence on the contemporary relationship between educational credentials and the occupational structure', *Journal of Education and Work*, 19(1): 27–46.

CLAIRE SMETHERHAM

CRITERION-REFERENCED TESTS

Criterion-referenced tests (CRTs) are used by teachers and other educators to assess what examinees are learning or have learned about a well defined domain of content that the test is measuring. The course might be laid out in terms of major content strands (e.g. numeration, measurement, geometry, problem-solving, etc.) and each content strand might be further defined by a set of learning outcomes, expectations, objectives, or standards (e.g. the student can solve linear equations with two unknowns; the student can solve word problems involving at least two steps). The test itself would consist of a set of test items that cover, in a representative way, the domain of content. The extent of the representativeness is a judgement that must be made by the test developer (see, for example, Hambleton and Zenisky 2003).

An examinee scoring 70 per cent on a criterion-referenced test might be considered to have mastered about 70 per cent of the material in the content domain. This type of score interpretation, known as a criterion-referenced test score interpretation, can be contrasted to the more common and better known norm-referenced test (NRT) score interpretation, in which score meaning is obtained by referencing an examinee score to the performance of other examinees. A typical NRT score interpretation might be that 'the examinee scored at the 80th percentile among tenth-grade high school students on the test' (see, for example, Hambleton and Zenisky 2003).

A test that is ideal to facilitate norm-referenced score interpretations will not be best for facilitating criterion-referenced score interpretations, and vice-versa, and so it is best to know the intended use of the test, and then the test can be constructed in a way that optimises the intended test use. Criterion-referenced and norm-referenced tests have fundamentally different purposes: CRTs are intended to provide a valid basis for describing what an examinee knows and can do; in contrast, NRTs are intended to provide a basis for interpreting test scores measuring a construct of interest by comparing examinees with each other, usually through the use of

test score norms established for groups of persons for whom the test is intended (e.g. high school graduates, community college students, college graduates). CRTs require that the domain of content be clearly spelled out, more clearly than is necessary with NRTs because of the nature of the intended interpretations: CRT scores are referenced to content domains and NRT scores are referenced to norm groups. CRT item selection is accomplished primarily by choosing test items that are judged as technically sound, and measure the domain of content in a representative way. In contrast, NRT item selection requires evidence that the test items measure the content domain of interest, but item statistics are also important: items that are too easy or too difficult, or items that do not have moderate to high discriminating power, would not normally be selected for a NRT.

Criterion-referenced tests are not limited to any particular item format. Historically, multiple-choice test items have been common, but today, many criterion-referenced tests include not only multiple-choice items, but also what are called constructed response items and these include short and long essays, and performance tasks to assess higher level thinking skills. Because examinee scores are interpreted in relation to test content, it is especially important that the evidence is strong that the test items, whatever the item format, are judged to be 'valid indicators' of the content itself. For this reason, considerable attention is given in developing criterion-referenced tests to the clarity of the domain of content and the preparation of test items so that they are valid indicators of the learning standards to which they are matched. In developing criterion-referenced tests, it is very common to commit considerable resources to using professional item writers, and reviewing items carefully for their match to the learning standards, for their technical soundness, and for their fairness to all examinees taking the test.

Though it may be of interest to be able to estimate the percentage of a domain of content that examinees have mastered, it is more common to establish 'cutscores' along the test score scale so that examinees can be sorted into performance categories such as 'failing', 'basic', 'proficient', and 'advanced'. With, for example, a 100-point score scale, these cutscores might be set at 40, 65, and 80. How these cutscores are set is often the source of great debate (Hambleton and Pitoniak 2006). Typically a group of teachers, curriculum specialists and administrators meet, define the expectations for examinees at each proficiency level, and then work through a process involving review of item content and their statistics, discussion, and consideration of consequences (e.g. failing a certain percentage of examinees), and eventually the group recommends a set of cutscores for use in interpreting the test scores. Validity evidence for the cutscores and resulting classifications of examinees comes from the characteristics of the panel itself, their perceptions and evaluation of the process, the process that the panel went through, and the reasonableness of the final cutscores (see, for example, Hambleton and Pitoniak 2006).

Criterion-referenced tests are known by many names today: basic skills tests, competency tests, standards-based tests, to name three, and they are finding many uses. They are the kinds of assessments that are valued in the schools. Teachers need to know what their students can do and cannot do in relation to the curriculum the students are being taught. At the district, state/province and national levels of education, many of the same interests are present: what do students know and what can they do? Tests that focus on the content of instruction are often viewed as much more important to teachers, educators, policy makers and parents than tests that provide a basis for comparing students with each other or to a national sample of students (i.e. norm-referenced tests). Criterion-referenced tests have also become valuable in the context of credentialing exams. Here too, interest in the scores is focused on what examinees can and cannot do in relation to a domain of content. Normally, only one cutscore is needed to separate those who are judged to have achieved a sufficiently high score to be credentialed, and those who fall short of the cutscore and should fail.

See also: examinations; multiple-choice tests; norm-referenced tests; test/testing

Further reading

Hambleton, R. and Pitoniak, M. (2006) 'Setting performance standards'. In R. Brennan (ed.) *Educational Measurement*, 4th edn, Westport CT: American Council on Education.
Hambleton, R. and Zenisky, A. (2003) 'Issues and practices of performance assessment'. In C. Reynolds and R. Kampaus (eds) *Handbook of Psychological and Educational Assessment of Children*, 2nd edn, New York: The Guilford Press.

RONALD K. HAMBLETON

CRITICAL PEDAGOGY

Critical pedagogy is committed to the promotion of social justice and emancipatory possibilities. Whether at a societal, institutional or local classroom level, the concern is to examine first how relations of power mediate in educational policy, processes and practices; once these are critically scrutinised the goal is then to pursue an agenda for social change.

Scholars such as Apple (1996) talk of the wider context of schooling and society, what Apple calls the 'cultural politics of education'. The major question addressed is: how far does the school reproduce the dominant ideologies of society? Reproduction theories point to the manner in which schooling serves the status quo, making dominant ideologies appear natural and legitimate. Apple (1996) exemplifies this through the notion of a national curriculum, such as in Britain, in which an assumed monolithic culture is embedded, thereby ignoring complex cultural realities in contemporary societies. Resistance theories, on the other hand, look to transformative possibilities, emphasising how learners can be empowered to resist and change dominating social practices, which privilege currently powerful social groups. The two models offer different dimensions to a critical pedagogy: the first providing a language of critique to deconstruct dominant schooling processes, the second offering a language of possibility to promote social change.

At the micro level, critical practitioners might ask how students and teachers can be empowered within specific classroom settings to pursue matters of social justice and, in doing so, challenge orthodox social arrangements. Feminist critiques might, for instance, consider how wider patriarchal and dominating practices are played out in specific classrooms and the forms of action available to dismantle these.

Many critical pedagogues are indebted to the Brazilian educator Paolo Freire. Freire's landmark work *The Pedagogy of the Oppressed* (Freire 1972) theorised education as consciousness raising, initially in the context of literacy programmes for the poor and dispossessed people of Brazil. The educational goal is to encourage participants in the educational process, both teachers and learners, to become more critically aware of their world, with the eventual aim of gaining creative control over it. In terms of practical pedagogy, Freire and his associates drew on the notion of 'culture circles' in which an image or key word is presented to act as a prompt to invite participants to reflect on and gain greater critical distance on an aspect of their daily lives.

Freire's work continues to be interpreted in different ways round the world, both in developing countries and in First-World contexts. It is usually pursued with disempowered groups of people and may take the form of workplace materials for new immigrants in the USA or Canada or literacy material for rural communities in countries of the South. In each case the aim is to encourage the course participants to find a voice to articulate areas of daily experience with a view to eventual challenge of iniquitous social arrangements.

One relatively recent version of critical pedagogy is centred on textual analysis. Educators use texts in the classroom 'to construct and negotiate identity, power and capital (Luke 2004: 21). Fine-tuned textual analysis may be used to unpick the discourse selections within texts and to debate their ideological significance. Texts might, for instance, conceal agency and therefore disguise responsibility for action, or they might make use of heavily persuasive strategies which only close textual critique can uncover.

A different strand of current critical pedagogy attends more to identity construction than ideology critique. The emphasis is on the manner in which learners construct identities, linked to gender, race and class. The thrust in identity focused critical pedagogy is to privilege the local over the global, in the spirit of a postmodern tendency to mistrust the grand narratives of the modernist era. The emphasis is on a response to the local and contingent. In seeking to resist what is called 'totalising discourses' the plural 'critical pedagogies' may be favoured over the singular version of the term.

To conclude, there is a tension between those arguing the case for empowerment as localised, strongly linked to particularities of voice and identity, and those seeking to maintain a sense of the bigger picture, by looking at universalist aspirations of critical pedagogy. At the same time, what different 'takes on the critical' share is constructive resistance to what is currently taken for granted, whether this is seen as the ideological givens of texts or the assumed identities and dispositions of learners.

See also: culture; Freire, Paolo; pedagogy; postmodernism

Further reading

Apple, M. (1996) *Cultural Politics and Education*, Buckingham: Open University Press.
Freire, P. (1972) *The Pedagogy of the Oppressed*, London: Penguin.

Luke, A. (2004) 'Two takes on the critical'. In B. Norton and K. Toohey (eds) *Critical Pedagogies and Language Learning*, Cambridge: Cambridge University Press.

CATHERINE WALLACE

CRITICAL THEORY

Critical theory emerged in Germany in the 1920s with the establishment of the Institute for Social Research at Frankfurt am Main in 1923. The term *critical theory* was originally coined and used by Max Horkheimer in 1937 to describe the theoretical programme of the school. Known as the 'Frankfurt School', the group became exiled to France then to the United States in the early 1930s until 1941 when it closed down. After World War II, in 1950, it was re-established in Frankfurt where it attracted new members such as Jürgen Habermas and Alfred Schmidt.

Although informed by multiple perspectives, the work of the Frankfurt School began primarily as a Marxist critique of capitalist society. In 1930, Horkheimer became director of the school, and moved its emphasis away from orthodox, scientific Marxism to become the mouthpiece for a more humanistic, philosophical Marxism. The frame of reference shifted away from a focus on the economy and exploitation towards a critique of culture and a concern with alienation.

In relation to method, Kellner (1989: 7) points out that, from the beginning to the present, critical theory has disregarded divisions between existing disciplines of knowledge, stressing the interconnectedness between them. This 'supradisciplinary' approach involves not just collaboration between researchers from different disciplines but the criticism of 'the validity claims of the separate disciplines'. Fundamentally, this is an educational approach, conceiving education as unbounded by disciplinary affiliations. In this sense, critical theory provides an overarching approach to the present age which links the study of educational institutions and processes to philosophy, politics, and economics in its critique of culture and philosophy. Linking theory and practice, it seeks to isolate and expose the relationships between cultural elements, economic and social processes, and the historical context.

Although initially conceived as a Marxist critique of capitalist society, the theoretical base of critical theory was soon to broaden, incorporating ideas drawn selectively from Neitzsche, Marx, Weber, Heidegger, Lukács, Korsch and Hegel. These influences were increasingly incorporated as critical theory sought to challenge the traditions of modernity, a core theme which it had been concerned with from the start in its opposition to the forces of modernisation and representations of modernity which saw it as a purely positive force linked to the development and progress of science, technology and industry, and instrumental conceptions of education.

Foucault's more pluralist form of critique manifests its profound educational relevance in that critique becomes manifested as a general educational and epistemological approach to knowledge, and practical politics. For Foucault, knowledge and change are achieved not through collection of the data positivistically, or the rational discussion and implementation of policy, but through criticism. Criticism is practical in that it leads to a transformation of structures and helps to demystify the ideological fog surrounding contemporary historically contingent conceptions of the real (Foucault 1988: 154). Critique, for Foucault, aims at identifying and exposing the unrecognised forms of power in people's lives, to expose and move beyond the forms in which we are entrapped in relation to the diverse ways that we act and think. Thus, the primary function of education is in teaching the skills, the *technē*, and the strategies of criticism. In this sense, critique aims to free us from the historically transitory constraints of contemporary consciousness as realised in and through discursive practices. His commitment is to a form of 'permanent criticism' that must be seen as linked to his broader programme of freedom of thought. It is the freedom to think differently than what we already know.

Critique in this sense is not a 'pure' method that is free-floating in history, but a series of practices that arise from specific historical struggles. As there can be no final transcendence, or absolute enlightenment, however, any progress through criticism can be only provisional. It is always a question of beginning again. For Foucault, then, education as criticism is thus a permanent interrogation of limits. Today, Foucauldian-inspired research in education is interrogating a whole range of phenomena, ranging from concepts such as autonomy to neo-liberal models of governmentality.

See also: educational theory; Foucault, Michel; Habermas, Jurgen; sociology; sociology of education

Further reading

Foucault, M. (1984) 'What is enlightenment?' (trans. C. Porter). In P. Rabinow (ed.) *The Foucault Reader*, New York: Pantheon.
——(1988) 'Practicing criticism' (trans. A. Sheridan). In L. D. Kritzman (ed.) *Politics, Philosophy, Culture: Interviews and Other Writings, 1977–1984*, New York: Routledge.
Kellner, D. (1989) *Critical Theory, Marxism and Modernity*, Cambridge: Polity Press.

MARK OLSSEN

CUBA

Cuba is an archipelago located in the Caribbean Sea with 11 million inhabitants. For almost four centuries it was a Spanish colony before becoming independent in 1898, following the Spanish-American War. Catholicism infused much of Cuban education during this period and the Jesuits were active in promoting religious training. From 1574, schools were created and, in 1729, the University of Havana was established. During the occupation by the United States from 1898–1902 American influences were brought to bear on the educational system and new primary schools built. However, education

continued to be marked by significant inequalities and the system helped to reproduce an entrenched class structure. In the 1930s a dictatorship was established and this was overthrown by the 1959 socialist revolution.

Education and health have been important priorities since the revolution. Schools were envisioned as places to nurture the new nation based on participation, access, economic development, self-reliance and the creation of what Che Guevara called a 'New Man' motivated by *conciencia* and the good of all. In 1961 the Nationalisation of Education Law was passed and a literacy campaign was initiated in which 250,000 volunteers were trained to help educate the wider population. Although the educational results of this initiative were mixed, it served to mobilise the population on behalf of the revolution and did improve literacy rates and school attendance, both of which have remained consistently high in comparison with similar countries. Private schooling was also nationalised in the early 1960s.

The Cuban Ministry of Education plays a central role in the provision of scientific, ideological, technical, cultural and physical formation. Education is free for all and general education is organised in kindergartens, followed by six years of primary education, three years of secondary, three years of pre-university and higher education of varying duration. According to Lopez (2000) 99 per cent of children of school age attend and finish primary school. There are approximately 1,000 nurseries for children up to five years. In addition to primary and secondary schools, there are 388 polytechnics, 428 schools for children with special needs and 61 universities. There are 230,000 teachers and 87,000 teaching assistants.

Since the 1959 revolution, education has been closely allied to economic development. Students may take different routes including the learning of vocational skills taught in technical schools and institutes. Educational institutions have built partnerships with agricultural and industrial enterprises as well as the wider community. Accordingly, both academic subjects and vocational skills infuse the educational system and pupils carry out productive work in factories or on the land as part of their schooling. Boarding schools in rural areas helped to bring together rural and urban students in a communal environment.

Higher education is controlled by the Ministry for Higher Education and graduates also carry out 'social service' for three years. Given the national priority for quality health care, Cuba has developed expertise in the training of medical experts and a number of fee-paying foreign students are educated in Cuba. Distance education and correspondence courses are offered to mature students who may be in employment. Adult education, known as 'popular education', also plays an important role in fostering participation more generally. Science and culture circles were established to foster participation in Cuban education.

In the early 1990s, following the break-up of the Soviet Union and subsequent loss of support and cooperation in addition to the ongoing US embargo, an economic crisis intensified and increased pressure was put upon the educational system. Since then the 'Struggle for Ideas' initiative has emphasised reducing pupil–teacher ratios, training more teachers and the increased use of technology including televisions, videos and computers. Cooperative educational initiatives have also been developed with Venezuela and some European universities.

The system has been criticised for stipulating that pupils must commit themselves to the revolution and for monitoring students and their families in terms of their revolutionary integration. Those without a suitable 'moral and political' background may find it more difficult to progress through the system. Others point to the need to develop a national collective consciousness as a basis for independence and survival. Cuban educationalists are proud of the fact that their education is of a high quality, despite the paucity of physical resources.

See also: Caribbean

Further reading

Carnoy, M. (2007) *Cuba's Academic Advantage: Why Students in Cuba Do Better in School*, Stanford CA: Stanford University Press.
Chavez Rodriguez, J. A. (1982) *The Democratization of Education in Present Day Cuba*, Paris: UNESCO.
Lopez, P. Meluza (2000) 'Um mestre para cada 42 habitantes'. In J. Bello and J. L. de Paiva, *Pedagogia em Foco*, Havana: Petrópolis.
MacDonald, T. (1985) *Making a New People: Education in Revolutionary Cuba*, Vancouver: New Star Books.

LUCIOLA L. SANTOS AND TOM WOODIN

CULTURAL CAPITAL

Pierre Bourdieu's relational concept of capital has made a significant contribution to the sociology of education, and, in particular, understandings of social reproduction. Of note are his two chapters in Michael F. D. Young's collection *Knowledge and Control* (1971), and, with J.-C. Passeron, *Reproduction in Education, Society and Culture* (1977). The impact of this work was strong in the 1970s and 1980s, with Connell's *Which Way Is Up?* (1983), and remains of value: in *Degrees of Choice*, Reay et al. (2005) use it to explain class, gender and race in higher education.

Bourdieu works with four capitals in order to explain how and why differentiation in social practice is structured and works:

- Cultural: legitimate knowledge goods;
- Economic: trading of material goods;
- Social: valuable social connections;
- Symbolic: recognition of prestige and taste.

Capital is integral to the competitive arena where agents struggle for position and to position others. In *An Invitation to Reflexive Sociology*, Bourdieu and Wacquant (1992) describe how

> social agents are not 'particles' that are mechanically pushed and pulled about by external forces. They are, rather, bearers of capitals and, depending on their trajectory

147

and on the position they occupy in the field by virtue of their endowment (volume and structure) in capital, they have a propensity to orient themselves actively either toward the preservation of the distribution of capital or toward the subversion of this distribution.
(Bourdieu and Wacquant 1992: 108–9, original emphasis)

Entrance is related to the specific interests of the field that agents stake claims over, combined with strategies for capital accumulation. Cultural capital enables recognition of how value is 'embodied' and 'objectified', and is underpinned by networks generating capital of 'more or less institutionalized relationships of mutual acquaintance and recognition' (Bourdieu and Wacquant 1992: 119). Such a conceptualisation of a territory, boundaries, position, strategising and valuing creates opportunities for understanding practice across disciplines, and this has relevance to connoisseurship and distinction in art, literature and culture. As Johnson, in his introduction to Bourdieu's text *The Field of Cultural Production* (1993) states:

> To enter a field, to play the game, one must possess the habitus which predisposes one to enter that field, that game, and not another. One must also possess at least the minimum amount of knowledge, or skill, or 'talent' to be accepted as a legitimate player. Entering the game, furthermore, means attempting to use that knowledge, or skill, or 'talent' in the most advantageous way possible.
>
> (8)

Education awards agents with capital through the objects they have and by virtue of the educational institution they have attended. In *Homo Academicus* (1988) Bourdieu studies biographical information (e.g. obituaries, interviews) to identify the indicators of cultural capital that are inherited or acquired such as 'academic success or precociousness' (231) from school attended and qualifications obtained; indicators of university and scientific power, such as membership of prestigious committees and awards; and indicators

of intellectual celebrity through publication and media appearances. This capital is public through revealed dispositions (voice, body, character), secular goods (credentials, dress, computers), and 'how they know' and 'are known'.

Cultural capital is cumulative because capital attracts capital. The message from the school transmitted through pedagogy is amplified by family socialisation that facilities effective reception and action. The amount and use of capital fluctuates through the staking of claims for recognition and legitimacy within a field, because 'one person's pedigree can be another's mark of infamy' (1988: 11). Where there is an acknowledgement of value and status is awarded, this is known as reconnaissance. Inequality is perpetuated because the agent's understanding of how social differentiation is produced can be lost through a process of forgetting known as misrecognition. For example, if a parent makes a judgement about a child's achievement in school, this needs to be seen within the context that has generated and articulated the judgement. Otherwise, inequality is reproduced through the unreflexive normality of how that child's achievement is accepted. Seeking to dominate and accepting domination through the symbolic capital of what is valued (taste, accent, deportment) is a form of violence through which advantage and disadvantage are reproduced.

See also: Bourdieu, Pierre; habitus; social reproduction; sociology of education

Further reading

Bourdieu, P. (1971) 'Intellectual field and creative project'. In M. F. D. Young (ed.) *Knowledge and Control: New Directions for the Sociology of Education*, London: Cassell and Collier Macmillan.

Bourdieu, P. and Wacquant, L. J. D. (1992) *An Invitation to Reflexive Sociology*, Cambridge: Polity Press.

HELEN GUNTER

CULTURAL STUDIES

Cultural studies refers to the study of culture in its widest sense to include institutions, practices, forms of classification, communication and media, values, beliefs and behaviour. It also analyses these in relation to power within and across any given societies. In this sense, it rejects the notion of culture as an exclusive preserve of 'the arts' or the Arnoldian notion of the 'best that has been thought and said'. Cultural studies is strongly interdisciplinary and borrows especially from sociology, literature, history, psychology and anthropology. Practitioners, teachers and researchers tend to be located within higher education.

In Britain, the origins of cultural studies are often traced back to the work of intellectuals involved in the post-war adult education movement, although its origins can be stretched back even further. Three texts of the late 1950s and early 1960s are seen as seminal in the development of cultural studies: Richard Hoggart's *The Uses of Literacy* (1957), Raymond Williams' *Culture and Society* (1958) and E. P. Thompson's *Making of the English Working Class* (1963). The Centre for Contemporary Cultural Studies at Birmingham University was particularly influential in developing the field of study. Under the leadership of Stuart Hall it engaged with Gramscian theory to develop original and provocative work in a number of areas. Since then, it has been closely allied with developments in gender, post-colonialism and post-structuralism. Practitioners debate whether cultural studies constitutes an intervention in favour of subordinate groups, how far it should relate to policy and how it intersects with traditional academic studies. Today, cultural studies can be identified in many different countries, including significant practices in the United States of America, Spain, Germany and Italy.

See also: culture; discipline; subjects

TOM WOODIN

CULTURAL TRANSMISSION

Cultural transmission is studied across such social sciences as sociology, social psychology, socio-biology, economics, anthropology, and education. Generally, it can be defined as the process of passing on preferences, beliefs, norms, knowledge, skills, attitudes, and values across and within generations. Culture persists over time as a result of social transmission, and the transmission of values is viewed by some as central to the maintenance of culture and cultural change: values provide a yardstick of standards against which important decisions are made and behaviours measured.

Culture is transmitted through formal education and social interactions. The most common means of cultural transmission are through child-rearing practices by parents, educators, carers and mentors. This concept presupposes a special task for the school in transmitting well defined and rather formal elements of a culture and in producing generations of pupils who think and behave in a manner deemed to be appropriate by those who develop the various curricula across the education systems of the world. The textbooks and other supplementary learning materials used in the process of schooling constitute literate socialisation aimed at developing cultural identity.

While the role of formal education is pivotal to cultural transmission, other agents, such as family, rituals, festivities, games, the narratives of oral culture, children's books, self-teaching, and recently also computer communication are formidable rivals of traditional schooling in promoting cultural transmission.

Youth cultures have also been considered important agents of cultural transmission. Sometimes youths resist traditions by creating alternative cultures and sharing them with others through cultural transmission using some of the same media as the mainstream. Examples of this expression can been seen in their music, fashion and use of language. On the one hand, this can be seen as a counter-culture but, on the other, it can also be seen as an expansion or development of a common culture. In this sense, youth actively participate in the construction of the culture and are not simply recipients of transmitted values, beliefs and norms.

Sociologists have examined transmission issues from a cultural capital perspective. Bourdieu (1984), for example, is well known for his view that schools and families work together to ensure the educational advantages of some groups while perpetuating the disadvantages of others.

In the developed countries of the West that have been built and developed through the efforts of many separate immigrant communities, socially transmitted culture becomes a little more difficult to define. The homogeneity of culture is challenged by the presence in a single society of various groups with significantly different traditions and histories. However, throughout history the dominant groups within developed industrialised societies have exerted their influence through the transmission of a preferred system of beliefs and values.

Some argue that globalisation can be an oppressive force that transforms everything and can therefore undermine cultural traditions and their transmission by presenting images that represent a new globalised culture. The power of this transmission lies in its technological appeal, utilising the glamour of the latest communication devices. Other argue that it provides greater opportunities to present new material, thus allowing others to recreate their identities and resist traditions which are considered oppressive.

Cultural transmission has also been referred to as cultural imperialism. The view is that, within a global village, everyone who is 'plugged in' is subjected to the same culture as a result of the worldwide communication networks. The process becomes somewhat like a Trojan horse: cultural goods are accompanied by 'hidden' values and beliefs that may challenge and undermine local customs and culture. It is argued that, when the perceived 'universal culture' is introduced

into a less-dominant local culture, the process of cultural transmission becomes very invasive. An alternative view is that, when one culture is influenced by another, there is not an absolute takeover, but that, rather, a new meaning emerges within that new cultural context. Cultural transmission, along with its counterpart, multiculturalism, have been intensified in some of the large cities of the world because they have become great melting pots where peoples from different cultures have been encouraged to understand and tolerate the ways of life of the various immigrant communities who now live and work there.

See also: cultural capital; culture; multicultural education; textbook

Further reading

Bourdieu, P. (1984) *Distinction: A Social Critique of the Judgement of Taste*, Cambridge MA: Harvard University Press.
Sturm, J., Dekker, J., Aldrich, R. and Simon, F. (eds) *Education and Cultural Transmission*, Ghent, Belgium: CSHP.

ANN CHERYL ARMSTRONG

CULTURE

The culture of a community encompasses its beliefs and morality as well as its artistic, scientific and technological achievements. It is represented in books, paintings, plays, buildings and other artefacts, and is also expressed through its language and media. A group may have a dominant culture and also a number of sub-cultures and a counter-culture that resists or protests against majority views. An institution might have a specific corporate or organisational culture. The elite of a society may share a high culture, while the masses have a mass or popular culture, and young people have a youth culture. The association of individuals and groups with shared values and beliefs is expressed in terms of cultural identity. A culture is passed on or transmitted to the next generation or to other cultures in large part through education, both formal and informal.

Notions of culture have been articulated most famously by Matthew Arnold in the nineteenth century, and, more recently, by T. S. Eliot, Pierre Bourdieu, Ernst Gellner and Clifford Geertz. Arnold's work *Culture and Anarchy* (1869) proposed that society was divided into Barbarians (the aristocratic class), the Philistines (or middle class), and the Populace (or working class). However, these were all infused with culture, which he defined as 'the disinterested endeavour after man's perfection', in order 'to make the best that has been thought and known in the world current everywhere; to make all men [*sic*] live in an atmosphere of sweetness and light' (Wilson 1932: 27). A broader conception was developed by the American anthropologist Clifford Geertz, who defined culture as 'a system of inherited conceptions expressed in symbolic forms by means of which people communicate, perpetuate, and develop their knowledge about and attitudes toward life' (Geertz 1973: 89).

The idea of cultural imperialism suggests that the culture of one nation or group may be imposed on another, by force or in some formulations through the systematic marginalisation of cultural practice and language. The education system has a major part to play here, as for example in cases where the indigenous culture is subjugated to imperial values. As Mac an Ghaill and Haywood note, 'from a cultural imperialist approach, the privileging of one set of values over another takes place not only as part of economic or colonial militaristic relations but also through the transference of culture' (2007: 199). From this point of view, culture may include not only American television but also a wide range of practices such as shopping centres, theme parks, music, news agencies, children's toys and fast food (Mac an Ghaill and Haywood 2007: 199). Edward Said's major work *Culture and Imperialism* (1993) also proposes that the Western literary canon has been integral both to colonial rule and to postcolonial societies.

Furthermore, this conflict of cultures gives rise to the notion of the politics of culture. This involves an often highly complex set of contests and debates around the character and position of cultures, both within specific societies and on a global scale. This may be evidenced for example in the everyday social interactions of British Sikhs growing up in Leeds in the north of England, as with the children of migrant peoples elsewhere. Second-generation British Sikhs constantly negotiate the forces of race, class and gender, and the many forms of cultural identity that are open to them in their homes and communities, at school, and in popular culture (Hall 1995). The expansion of schooling in the Arab states and in other contexts may also be viewed as a site of cultural politics, in which the modernising and globalising effects of school systems contend with attempts by local communities and marginalised groups to uphold their cultural frames of reference through a range of available means (Mazawi 2006).

See also: Arnold, Matthew; cultural capital; cultural transmission; indigenous education

Further reading

Geertz, C. (1973) *The Interpretation of Cultures*, New York: Basic Books.

Hall, K. (1995) '"There's a time to act English and a time to act Indian": the politics of identity among British Sikh teenagers'. In S. Stephens (ed.) *Children and the Politics of Culture*, Princeton NJ: Princeton University Press.

Mac an Ghaill, M. and Haywood, C. (2007) *Gender, Culture and Society: Contemporary Femininities and Masculinities*, London: Palgrave Macmillan.

Mazawi, A. E. (2006) 'Educational expansion and the mediation of discontent: the cultural politics of schooling in the Arab states'. In H. Lauder, P. Brown, J. Dillabough and A. H. Halsey (eds) *Education, Globalisation and Social Change*, Oxford: Oxford University Press.

Said, E. W. (1993) *Culture and Imperialism*, London: Chatto and Windus.

Wilson, J. Dover (ed.) (1932) *Culture and Anarchy*, Cambridge: Cambridge University Press.

GARY McCULLOCH

CURRICULUM

Curriculum is a term that has been defined variously since at least the seventeenth century, or perhaps as early as the sixteenth, by different individuals or groups on the basis of different beliefs about the nature of knowledge and the purposes of schooling. Its most common definition refers to the subjects that schools teach. Typically, this includes such recognised bodies of disciplined knowledge as history, mathematics, English, or biology. It can also include other designations for subject matter that have appeared on the scene as educators have sought to reorganise disciplinary knowledge for purposes of teaching and learning. These additional categories can represent combinations of traditional disciplines under such rubrics as social studies and language arts as well as such applications of knowledge and skills to day-to-day living as home economics and vocational education. This, however, represents only one meaning of the term. There have been numerous educators who have seen the school's role as being broader than conveying organised knowledge. They have defined the curriculum in terms of what teachers intend children to learn in school or what in fact children do learn in school, inside and outside the classroom and formal instruction, whether intended or not (Hamilton 1989; Walker 1980; Jackson 1992).

Any definition of curriculum has to recognise that there is often a critical difference between what someone thinks the curriculum should be and what actually occurs in schools. David Labaree (1999) captures this distinction by talking about four kinds of curriculum. There is the rhetorical curriculum or the recommendations that the state as well as influential groups and individuals offer concerning what the schools should teach. The adoption of those recommendations by such government bodies as school districts or individual schools produces a formal curriculum. What teachers actually do once they shut their classroom doors may in fact be

different than is dictated by policy. The result is the curriculum-in-use, which refers to the actual content that is implemented in the classroom. Finally, we know that there is often a difference between what schools and teachers intend to occur in classrooms and what children actually learn. So ultimately there is the received curriculum that points to the actual learning of children. Why these distinctions between different forms of curriculum exist has to do with the presence within social settings of what we might think of as 'mediating factors' that have affected the ability of schools to introduce curriculum recommendations in anything approaching their pristine form. Among these factors are the interplay between political parties, the influence of powerful individuals and groups, the availability of financial resources, the force of popular pressure, and the influence of class, religion, and race (Kliebard and Franklin 1983).

The question of what the term curriculum encompasses has in fact been a longstanding source of debate among those who undertake curriculum work for a livelihood. A good starting place for considering this debate is the editorial that Wilfred Carr penned for the first issue of a new journal, *Curriculum Studies* (now *Pedagogy, Culture, and Society*). Carr argues that many people, particularly practising educators, equate the concept of curriculum with the content or subjects that are being taught. This, for Carr, is a narrow definition that reduces curriculum work to the technical and practical problems of designing or planning a course or a number of courses. It is, in other words, the process of constructing lesson and unit plans and the identification of assignments, readings, and activities that support these plans. Carr is not satisfied with this narrow, and for him outdated, understanding of what curriculum work is all about.

Carr prefers to link curriculum work to larger societal issues. He talks in this vein about a hidden curriculum to refer to those tacit and unstated things, intended and unintended, that schools convey to students. Such efforts are part of the socialising role of schools. For Carr, they are often instruments of cultural reproduction, social control, or hegemony for perpetuating the values, beliefs, skills, knowledge as well as patterns of class power and privilege that exist within a culture from generation to generation (1993). Looking at the broader social role of the curriculum, but on a somewhat more positive note, Frederick Rudolph has defined the curriculum as 'one of the places where we have told ourselves who we are' (1977). As Rudolph sees it, the curriculum is a cultural artefact that describes those things that a people or a culture cherish and wish to pass on to future generations. The story of the Glorious Revolution or the American Civil War is not a part of the school curriculum by accident. They are there, Rudolph maintains, because these events are embedded with things of value that we wish to pass on to future generations. For Carr and Rudolph, then, the curriculum suggests more than an array of technical processes for selecting, organising, conveying, and evaluating subject matter. It includes a moral and political terrain.

There are a number of persistent issues that have continually been associated with the domain of curriculum. Two such issues, the relationship between curriculum and society and the question of curriculum organisation and selection, have been contentious and account for much of the disagreement among those who work in curriculum. Curriculum has been one of the instruments within the larger institution of schooling that groups, large and small, historically have used to cope with social dislocations of one sort or another. Early twentieth-century American intellectuals, concerned about smoothing the nation's transformation from a rural, agrarian society to an urban, industrial one, saw the curriculum as a means of promoting orderly change and maintaining social order. How they approached that work ran a continuum from using the school's course of study to change individuals to allow for their smoother adjustment to societal demands, to altering society itself. During the last hundred or so years the curriculum has been used variously to promote the building of a new social order, to encourage the adjustment of individuals to the existing order and for much that is in between (Franklin 1986).

One of the most persistent conflicts among those who work in the area of curriculum has involved that old Spencerian question of what knowledge is of most worth. On one side of the struggle have been those individuals and groups that have defended traditional academic disciplines as the principal organising element of the curriculum. Pitted against them have been other individuals and groups that have called for their replacement by any of a number of things that they deemed to be more functional in the day-to-day lives of children. Some of these opponents argued for broader units that bring together the content of several disciplines. Others proposed a curriculum that is not composed of academic subjects but rather of instructional units derived from the social or personal problems of youth, key experiences in the lives of young people, and virtually anything that was thought to be appealing and interesting to children (Kliebard 2004). In the United States, the struggle during the 1950s between the proponents of life adjustment education and those favouring a curriculum organised around the traditional academic disciplines is a good example of this conflict.

Despite these conflicts, there does seem to be one issue that has persistently been raised by those involved in curriculum work but always seems to receive something of a similar answer. This is the question of how one goes about constructing curriculum. Throughout the twentieth century those involved in the making of curriculum have had a penchant, it seems, for expressing the process in terms of a series of steps or procedures. For some, it is four steps, for others nine, and for still others it was some other number. Despite this number, however, it seems that there has been a broad consensus over time as to the components involved. Somewhere at the beginning of the process, the curriculum makers identify their intentions in the form of aims, goals, objectives, or some other end state. Having done that they go through a number of procedures that involve the selection and organisation of what is to be taught, which is typically expressed in terms of academic disciplines, problem areas, or experiences. Whatever unit is used, it then needs to be distributed through some sort of pedagogical or instructional activity. And finally the results of this teaching have to be assessed in terms of their success and failure. This is not to say that this process has been universally accepted. There have been quarrels concerning the advisability of initiating the process with the identification of ends and objectives. And there have been conflicts concerning the order in which the procedures of curriculum making are to be undertaken. Yet, despite these disagreements, this view of how curriculum is constructed has prevailed as something of a conventional wisdom (Franklin 1999).

See also: core curriculum/national curriculum; curriculum development; curriculum differentiation; curriculum policy and implementation; curriculum standards; extracurriculum; hidden curriculum; subjects

Further reading

Carr, W. (1993) 'Reconstructing the curriculum debate: an editorial introduction', *Curriculum Studies*, 1(1): 1–4.

Franklin, B. M. (1986) *Building the American Community: The School Curriculum and the Search for Social Control*, London: Falmer Press.

——(1999) 'Discourse, rationality, and educational research: a historical perspective of *RER*', *Review of Educational Research*, 69(4): 347–63.

Hamilton, D. (1989) *Toward a Theory of Schooling*, London: Falmer Press.

Jackson, P. (1992) 'Conceptions of curriculum and curriculum specialists'. In P. Jackson (ed.) *Handbook of Research on Curriculum*, New York: Macmillan.

Kliebard, H. M. (2004) *The Struggle for the American Curriculum, 1893–1958*, 3rd edn, New York: RoutledgeFalmer.

Kliebard, H. M. and Franklin, B. M. (1983) 'The course of the course of study: history of curriculum', pp. 138–57 in J. Hardin Best (ed.) *Historical Inquiry in Education: A Research Agenda*, Washington DC: American Educational Research Association.

Labaree, D. (1999) 'The chronic failure of curriculum reform', *Education Week*, 18 (19 May): 42–44.

Rudolph, F. (1977) *Curriculum: A History of the Undergraduate Course of Study since 1636*, San Francisco CA: Jossey Bass.

Walker, D. (1980) *Fundamentals of Curriculum*, San Diego CA: Harcourt Brace Jovanovich.

BARRY M. FRANKLIN

CURRICULUM DEVELOPMENT

Curriculum development, in its broadest sense, involves the selection, organisation, realisation, and evaluation of educational purposes in institutional settings. National constitutional provisions governing educational systems influence the nature of these tasks, especially in terms of the extent to which they are centralised or decentralised, the various levels at which tasks occur, the participants involved, and the tangible products produced.

Because curriculum is concerned fundamentally with identifying the knowledge and abilities considered of most worth for students to learn, the selection of educational purposes represents the definitive task of curriculum development. Approaches to selecting educational purposes range from a complex examination and synthesis of multiple sources, namely the nature of the students, of disciplinary subject matter, and of the society for which students are prepared to live in, to privileging one of those sources, usually subject matter, over the other two, to, most recently, simply aligning curriculum to extant standardised tests. Differing perspectives on the nature of the learner, the nature of subject matter, and the nature of society also influence and potentially complicate the task of selecting educational purposes.

Curriculum development also involves the organisation of the selected educational purposes. Educational purposes can be organised in a variety of fashions, such as by age-grade, by level of schooling, by academic or vocational education, by courses of study or diploma classifications, or by type of school.

Curriculum development involves identifying educational experiences that will provide students opportunities to learn the educational purposes. Various criteria have been proposed for identifying appropriate experiences, including consideration of the nature of targeted educational purposes, the nature of the students, and school and classroom contexts. Experiences must also be organised so as to complement each other. Educational experiences can be organised similar to educational purposes, and also often consider vertical and horizontal organisation so that educational experiences that students have at various points complement each other.

Curriculum development in its broadest sense also involves the evaluation of the educational programme to determine the extent to which the educational experiences provided to students have resulted in the attainment of the selected educational purposes, although curriculum evaluation is sometimes considered a separate phase from curriculum development. Curriculum evaluation involves selecting or developing instruments for gathering valid and reliable information about the extent and quality of student learning, as well as organising, interpreting, reporting, and using that information. The complexity of human behaviour and the relative sophistication of educational purposes require the use of a variety of sources of information about learning, including those that provide proxy inferences and those with face validity. Paper and pencil tests, especially standardised, provide proxy information about student learning, while observation of student performances and products provide relatively valid information about student learning. The more valid and reliable sources of information consulted, the more accurate the portrait of the quantity and quality of student learning.

The higher the stakes placed on student performance on any given instrument, the less valid that instrument becomes.

These curriculum development tasks occur at various levels of decision making, involve various participants, and yield various tangible products. Curriculum development occurs on national, state or provincial, school district, school and classroom levels. For example, while the selection and organisation of educational purposes more often happen at the national or state or provincial levels, selection and organisation of educational experiences occur more commonly at the system or building level. Evaluation commonly occurs on all levels named, as well as on the international level. Since the 1980s, curriculum development worldwide has become increasingly decentralised, though in most nations curriculum development is characterised by a mix of centralised and decentralised decision making.

Participants in the curriculum development process range from teachers, administrators, parents, other community members, and even students on the building and district levels, to government agencies or ministries, university faculty members, elected and appointed officials, private foundations, test publishers, and special interest lobbyists on the state and national levels. The degree of centralisation/decentralisation and the levels to which curriculum decisions are dedicated determine the participants in curriculum development. Tangible products that result from curriculum development efforts range from legislation to national, state, and district curriculum guides and tests, to teacher unit and lesson plans.

Curriculum development tasks also are influenced by local, national, regional, and even international historical, cultural, social, and political forces.

See also: assessment; centralisation/decentralisation; curriculum; curriculum policy and implementation; evaluation; subjects; test/testing

155

Further reading

Baker, D. P. and Letendre, G. K. (2005) *National Differences, Global Similarities: World Culture and the Future of Schooling*, Stanford CA: Stanford Social Sciences.

Rosenmund, M., Fries, A-V. and Heller, W. (2002) *Comparing Curriculum-making Processes*, Bern: Peter Lang.

Tanner, D. and Tanner, L. (2007) *Curriculum Development: Theory Into Practice*, Upper Saddle River NJ: Pearson.

WILLIAM G. WRAGA

CURRICULUM DIFFERENTIATION

The notion of the differentiated curriculum exists at different levels in education. In terms of policy, arguments concern the value of nationalised or standardised curricula over locally generated curricula. In schools, differentiated curricula reflect the aims and ethos of the school and how the school leadership interprets the curriculum demands made by local and/or central policy makers. More specific curriculum differentiation is found at classroom level where teachers need to decide how to teach the pupils in their care: what tasks to set, resources to provide and which groupings to utilise.

The aims of national curricula generally concern the need to raise standards and to ensure that all school-age children have the same entitlement to learning. These apparent advantages could be outweighed, however, by the lack of diversity that results from requiring similar outcomes from a wide-ranging population. Some schools may not have the capacity to deliver the national curriculum effectively if their population is particularly challenging, as there would have to be significant support to ensure that pupils reached minimum levels of achievement.

Schools that are not funded by the state are generally allowed to determine their own curricula, within certain restrictions and guidelines. This results in differentiated curricula reflecting particular views and beliefs, such as faith schools based on religious foundations or those with a particular subject focus, such as specialist dance or music schools. Some curricula are based on the writings of particular educational theorists, for example Maria Montessori, A. S. Neill and Rudolf Steiner.

More restrictions are placed on state-funded schools, but within the stipulated curriculum there is some freedom to match requirements to pupils. Probably the most common ways of differentiating the curriculum at school level is through setting, where pupils are grouped for subjects (typically mathematics and languages) with the rationale that experience and skill level would make teaching a mixed group very inefficient. A more extreme version is streaming, where pupils are grouped across all subjects according to general abilities. Pupils in the same institution can receive quite different instruction and experiences.

At the classroom level there are myriad ways to differentiate the curriculum to suit the needs of learners. In order for this to be effective, the teacher needs to have a good understanding of pupil needs and interests. Three main areas are commonly adapted: the content of what is being taught, the pedagogy by which it is delivered and expected pupil outcomes.

Content can be adapted to match abilities and preferred learning styles, where students with learning difficulties are presented with less material to cover and with activities that are easier to accomplish. These would incorporate fewer concepts and simpler skills. Able pupils would be allowed to omit repetitive practice exercises, completing more complex and abstract class and homework, at a brisker pace. This has implications for task outcomes, reflecting lower or higher expectations based on the complexity of learning experiences.

Arguments against this notion of a watered-down curriculum for pupils with problems show that it has the long-term effect of increasing the gap between pupils of different abilities, thus highlighting individual differences and perpetuating inequalities (Westwood 2001: 208).

A fairer approach than differentiating content and outcomes in this way, would be to differentiate pedagogy. By offering as much assistance as required to meet the same objectives, pupils will benefit from differentiated instruction that will encourage them to learn in ways that need their learning profiles (MacNamara and Moreton 1997). For example, teachers should use targeted assessment to identify gaps in pupil learning and provide opportunities for direct instruction or practice to fill these gaps. Structured concrete activities are likely to help and all teaching for children with difficulties is effectively accomplished through individualised instruction. Best practice suggests that pupils themselves should be involved in creating an Individualised Education Plan (IEP), which serves as a kind of contract between pupil, parents, schoolteachers and local authorities providing support services.

Pupils with severe learning problems or disabilities will require more strictly differentiated curricula. For most teachers and pupils, however, differentiating the curriculum means fairly simple adaptation of resources, tasks, assessment and grouping. Different activities and outcomes would not affect the intellectual complexity of work, but allow learning to retain interest through matching pupil interests and learning profiles.

See also: ability grouping; curriculum; curriculum policy and implementation; individualised instruction/personalised learning; learning disabilities; learning styles; pedagogy; setting; specialisation; streaming/tracking

Further reading

Clune, W. H. (1993) 'The best path to systemic educational policy: standard/centralized or differentiated/decentralized?', *Educational Evaluation and Policy Analysis*, 15(3): 233–54.
McNamara, S. and Moreton, G. (1997) *Understanding Differentiation. A Teacher's Guide*, London: David Fulton.

Tomlinson, C. A. (2004) *The Differentiated Classroom: Responding to the Needs of All Learners*, Upper Saddle River NJ: Prentice Hall.
Westwood, P. (2001) '"Differentiation" as a strategy for inclusive classroom practice: Some difficulties identified', *Australian Journal of Learning Disabilities*, 6(1): 5–11.

CARRIE WINSTANLEY

CURRICULUM POLICY AND IMPLEMENTATION

Curriculum policy and curriculum implementation are often considered as separate and distinct sets of processes. On the one hand, policy is widely regarded as something to be developed by an elite group of policy makers; on the other, implementation is something for teachers in the classroom. This is unsatisfactory if viewed as a rigid division of labour in a number of ways. First, curriculum policy needs to have a clear sense of the issues involved in implementation in order to have a prospect of success, and so there needs to be some direct input by teachers and other educators into the policy making. Second, curriculum is not simply implemented, but interpreted by practitioners as is suitable in particular circumstances. Third, some element of interaction between 'policy' and 'implementation' is necessary in order to develop and improve the curriculum further over the medium term. These issues in themselves require consideration of the nature of teachers as professionals and reflective practitioners, and of the character of education policy in being broadly dispersed and responsive.

See also: curriculum; education policy; profession/professionalism/professionalisation; reflective practitioner

GARY McCULLOCH

CURRICULUM STANDARDS/ PROGRAMMES OF STUDY

'Curriculum standards' is a term used widely in the United States of America and Canada, specifying what students should know and be

157

able to do at particular points during their thirteen years in K-12 schools (i.e. kindergarten through 12th grade, normally covering the experiences of 5–18 year-olds). The concept is familiar beyond North America, though terminology differs: in England, for example, specified national curriculum subjects are divided into 'programmes of study' and linked to 'attainment targets'.

American curriculum standards are developed at the state level, through consultation with teachers, professional organisations and parents. Such distinguished subject teaching associations as the National Academy of Sciences and the National Center for History in the Schools, among others, have developed their own national standards with the aim that these will be adopted by – or significantly influence – state governments. Curriculum standards adopted by state boards of education are communicated to school districts, classroom teachers, parents, and students via documentation and staff training. It is a very common practice for American states to publish their individual curriculum standards on the internet. These are typically similar in content, but the exact wording of standards can occasionally cause controversy: for example, in specifying that students should be aware of alternatives to the theory of biological evolution, the Kansas Board of Education's science standards have been criticised for promoting 'intelligent design'. Curriculum standards are matched to assessment strategies and can best be understood within the context of the global drive towards standards-based reform.

See also: core curriculum/national curriculum; curriculum; standards; subjects

DAVID CROOK

D

DAY RELEASE

Colleges and universities sometimes form partnerships with employers to provide one-day-a-week courses for apprentices and trainees. Day release is rarely considered to be an employee right, but employers frequently view it as an investment, both in their workers and in their business. College-based day release programmes, with employers normally meeting course costs, may focus on general literacy or numeracy support or be tailored to the particular training needs of those working in service sector industries. Colleges typically provide a theoretical input complementing the practical workplace experience, though it is not uncommon for such institutions to be equipped with workshops, kitchens, salons and so forth for the purposes of advanced practical training. Day release courses are popular in such areas as catering, beauty therapy, hairdressing, motor vehicle maintenance and social care. In the United Kingdom a new type of day release training opportunity has emerged from closer links between employers and higher education providers. For example, Balfour Beatty, a leading construction company, permits its trainees to work four days a week on a construction site and one day a week at university, with tuition fees paid by the employer. Trainees complete a succession of national vocational qualifications over a five-year period, at the end of which they graduate with a bachelor's degree in an area such as architectural technology, civil engineering or quantity surveying.

See also: apprenticeship; college; training; work-based/work-located/workplace/work-related learning

DAVID CROOK

DEAN

The title of dean is often used for a person with authority in a specific area, most commonly in higher education but also sometimes in schools. The deanship is the office and the deanery is the location of the office within the institution. The term is drawn from historical religious practice with the organisation of monks and priests. The dean may have particular responsibility for a department or faculty, or for learning and teaching, for research, for student welfare and discipline, or for other areas. In many cases assistant, associate or sub-deans may be appointed to support the dean in particular aspects of their work.

See also: faculty; higher education

GARY McCULLOCH

DEGREE

Degrees are qualifications granted by universities and other institutions of higher education, officially recognising the successful completion of a programme of study. First, or undergraduate, degrees are generally known as bachelor's degrees, examples being the Bachelor of Arts and Bachelor of Science awards. Master's degrees, the most common being the Master of Arts or Master of Science awards, are generally referred to as higher or postgraduate degrees. These are normally awarded in recognition of completing a taught programme, but some, such as the Master of Philosophy degree, are awarded for the completion of research. Doctorates are usually awarded on the basis of a thesis, although 'professional' doctorate programmes include a substantial taught element as part of the degree. Students are traditionally invited to receive their degree scrolls or certificates at a ceremony or congregation. Possession of a first degree is a requirement for some types of employment and for further academic study. Those registering for postgraduate degree programmes have often recently completed first degrees or are part-time students already in employment. Doctoral students are often those working in, or wishing to work in, the higher education sector.

See also: doctorate; graduate/graduation; higher education; Master's; postgraduate; qualifications; student; undergraduate; university

DAVID CROOK

DELINQUENCY

Delinquency refers to the deviant behaviours and sometimes-unlawful actions committed by children and adolescents. The acts that comprise delinquency are wide-ranging and variable, but can include mundane behaviours such as smoking cigarettes, drinking alcohol, and experimenting with minor forms of drug use. At the other end of the spectrum are acts of serious violence including robbery, assault, and even rape and murder. Although delinquent involvement is a relatively common feature during adolescence, rates of delinquency are not invariant between males and females. At every stage of the life course, males are much more likely than females to engage in aberrant and wayward behaviours. Gender differences in delinquent involvement, however, can vary drastically depending upon the type of crime committed. Males, for example, are disproportionately over-involved in the most physically aggressive types of delinquency, whereas the gender gap is much less marked for rates of drug and alcohol abuse and indirect aggression (e.g. verbal assaults).

Juvenile delinquency has long fascinated criminologists and other social scientists investigating the aetiology of offending behaviours. Part of the reason for focusing on delinquency is because of the firmly established age-crime curve. The age-crime curve captures the ebb and flow of delinquent involvement over the life course. According to a wealth of published research findings, delinquent involvement is a relatively rare occurrence very early in life. In early adolescence, around the ages of 12 and 13, delinquency begins to increase until 18 or 19. During this period of adolescent development, experimenting with minor acts of misconduct is a relatively normal occurrence. Shortly thereafter, during late adolescence and early adulthood, participation in offending behaviours declines sharply where it continues on a downward trend throughout adulthood. This general pattern of involvement in anti-social behaviours is one of the most consistent and robust criminological findings; it has been replicated across nations, across time periods, and using very different measures of delinquency.

Although most adolescents will not engage in criminal offending during adulthood, there exits a small pool of juvenile delinquents that will persist with offending behaviours throughout their life. Typically, these chronic criminals begin displaying signs of anti-social behaviour very early in life and persist with anti-social behaviours well into adulthood. For example, as children, chronic offenders may exhibit violent tendencies, they may physically hurt their siblings, and they may lie, steal, and cheat. As adolescents, they are apt to have frequent contact with the criminal justice system, they are likely to be suspended and expelled from school, and they are at risk for committing serious acts of violence, such as torturing animals and bullying. During adulthood, chronic offenders continue with their criminal behaviour and will likely spend time in prison or jail. Adult offenders, in short, display a relatively stable pattern of anti-social acts that can be traced back into childhood. These lifelong criminals are often referred to as chronic criminals, career criminals, habitual offenders, and life-course persistent offenders.

Most traditional delinquency theories argue that social and environmental factors are the causes of delinquent involvement. The dominant explanations of delinquency, for example, maintain that living in disadvantaged neighbourhoods, being raised by uncaring parents, and associating with anti-social peers all are potential causes of misconduct. At the same time, most of these theories downplay or reject the possibility that biological and genetic factors are associated with adolescent delinquency. However, with the recent mapping of the human genome, and with an abundance of empirical research documenting the importance of brain functioning in the aetiology of certain disorders, there has been a growing interest in the biological bases of juvenile offending. The most cutting-edge research suggests that a complex arrangement of genetic factors and social forces provides the most plausible explanation to the development of anti-social behaviours.

The importance of identifying the causes and correlates of adolescent delinquency is vitally important to crime-prevention efforts. One of the most promising ways to reduce crime and delinquency is to develop successful intervention programmes that can blunt or counteract the emergence of anti-social behaviours in at-risk youths. In order to achieve measurable and significant reductions in crime, a comprehensive understanding of the causes of youthful delinquency needs to be realised.

See also: disaffection; emotional and behavioural difficulties (EBD); exclusion/expulsion; suspension

Further reading

Moffitt, T. E. (1993) 'Adolescence-limited and life-course persistent antisocial behavior: a developmental taxonomy,' *Psychological Review*, 100: 674–701.

Rowe, D. C. (2002) *Biology and Crime*, Los Angeles CA: Roxbury Press.

Walsh, A. (2002) *Biosocial Criminology: Introduction and Integration*, Cincinnati OH: Anderson Publishing Company.

KEVIN M. BEAVER

DEPARTMENT

Department is a term with multiple applications in the field of education. National education ministries are frequently departments of state; for example, the United States Department of Education, and the Department for Children, Schools and Families in England. In many parts of the world state governments and local councils maintain an education service – or department – that organises and provides training, support and resources for local schools. Secondary school, college and university teaching staff are normally attached to an academic department, where the head of department allocates responsibilities to each team member. Each of the above type of teaching institution is likely to have a mathematics or languages department, but specialist subject departments such as management or oceanography are likely to be found only in the higher education sector. In a university graduate medical school there may be departments of anatomy, pathology, dermatology and so forth. Teaching institutions may also maintain support departments to provide, for example, catering, cleaning, reprographics and security services. Organisations having no students of their own, in both the public and private sectors and also professional bodies, may have an education department to liaise with schools, colleges and universities and to provide careers advice. Museums frequently maintain an education department to produce materials about their collections, and they may employ teachers and lecturers to lead sessions for visiting schoolchildren and adult students.

See also: college; faculty; higher education; school; subjects; university

DAVID CROOK

DEPARTMENT FOR INTERNATIONAL DEVELOPMENT (DFID)

The United Kingdom's Department for International Development (DfID) is a government department that manages Britain's aid to poorer countries in order 'to promote sustainable development and eliminate world poverty'. Since 1997 it has been headed by a cabinet minister and has two headquarters – in London and East Kilbride – in addition to sixty-four offices around the world. Almost half of the 2,500 staff work abroad. DfID works directly in over 150 countries and, in 2004, had a budget of nearly £4 billion.

It supports long-term programmes to help tackle the underlying causes of poverty but also responds to emergencies where aid may be required. Approximately 1 billion people live in extreme poverty and over 113 million children do not go to school. DfID's work is structured around supporting the eight 'Millennium Development Goals' that were agreed in 2000 with a target date of 2015. These are to

- halve the number of people living in extreme poverty and hunger;
- ensure that all children receive primary education;
- promote gender equality and give women a stronger voice;
- reduce child death rates;
- improve the health of mothers;
- combat HIV and AIDS, malaria and other diseases;

- make sure the environment is protected;
- build a global partnership for those working in development.

These were agreed by the United Nations, and approximately 190 countries have signed up to them. Although each goal has measurable targets, it is unlikely that all of these targets will be met, especially in some areas of sub-Saharan Africa.

Education is a key aspect of this work and the millennium goal is to achieve universal primary provision by 2015. DfID's work is mainly focused on sub-Saharan Africa and South Asia. It aims to foster the development of indigenous educational systems and has funded initiatives which have removed school fees, provided books, equipment, safe water and sanitation, built new schools, paid teachers' salaries and trained teachers. The Development Partnerships Programme in Higher Education funds scholarships and initiatives working with civil society organisations and non-governmental organisations (NGOs) such as the Forum for African Women Educationalists and the Global Campaign for Education. The DfID Schools Partnership was created in 2003 to create partnerships between schools in Britain and developing countries.

DfID works in close collaboration with the World Bank, United Nations, World Trade Organization and the European Commission, as well as governments, civil society, the private sector and other agencies. Almost half of DfID's funding is channelled through multilateral agencies working on behalf of many different countries. This work has supported countries like Uganda and Malawi where the number of children enrolling in primary school doubled in five years and is now over 90 per cent.

The Colonial Development Act (1929) first recognised the responsibility of the UK government for the development of its colonies. The Ministry of Overseas Development was first set up as a separate ministry in 1964, headed by a minister. It integrated the work of the former Department of Technical Co-operation, established in 1961, and the overseas aid functions of other departments such as the Foreign, Commonwealth Relations and Colonial offices. In 1970 these functions were transferred to the Foreign and Commonwealth Office with the establishment of the Overseas Development Administration (ODA). In 1974 it regained its own minister but reverted back to the Foreign Office in 1979 with the election of Margaret Thatcher.

During this time a key purpose was to nurture UK exports to the developing world. There were also allegations of a close connection between the giving of aid and wider UK foreign policy and business objectives, notably the claim that funding of the Pergau Dam in Malaysia was linked to an arms deal. Critics claim that aid is often used to discipline and channel receiving countries to accept the views and priorities of wealthy ones. Where aid is well used its value may be undermined by a wider set of issues such as trading arrangements, conflict, migration, disease and corruption.

See also: globalisation; international education; United Nations Educational, Scientific and Cultural Organization (UNESCO); World Bank

Further reading

Department for International Development (2001) *The Challenge of Universal Primary Education. Strategies for Achieving the International Development Targets*, London: DfID.

TOM WOODIN

DESCHOOLING

The concept of deschooling was developed by the philosopher Ivan Illich in his widely influential treatise *Deschooling Society* (1971). He argued that schools and schooling tended to undermine the values of a true education, and that, therefore, the 'schooled society' should be deschooled. According to Illich,

systems of compulsory schooling were much too expensive, inevitably polarised societies, and graded the nations of the world 'according to an international caste system', in which, as he put it, 'Countries are rated like castes whose international dignity is determined by the average years of schooling of its citizens, a rating which is closely related to per capita gross national product, and much more painful' (Illich 1971: 17). School itself was 'the world religion of a modernized proletariat', making 'futile promises of salvation to the poor of the technological age' (Illich 1971: 18). Like the church, it should be disestablished, and to make this effective there should be a law forbidding discrimination in employment or admission to centres of learning based on previous attendance at school. He insisted that schools could not teach skills or provide education.

In a deschooled society, by contrast, there would be new formal mechanisms for the acquisition of skills and their educational use, and also a new approach to incidental or informal education. Self-motivated learning would become more important, supported by learning webs or networks to spread equal opportunity for learning and teaching. These might include reference services to educational objects, skill exchanges, peer matching, and reference services to educators-at-large. The educational path of each student would be his or her own to follow, and only in retrospect would it take on the features of a recognised programme. Such a deschooled society, Illich concluded, could liberate individuals and resources.

Illich's denunciation of schools and schooling reflected a crisis of faith in schooling in the 1960s and early 1970s. In spite of decades of investment in schools, society remained unequal, there was still poverty and war, and there was widespread public discontent about the standards and outcomes of schooling. Educational reform appeared to have failed as, for example, Charles Silberman declared in his work *Crisis in the Classroom* (1970). Revolutionary critics of schooling

163

flourished in these conditions. Other examples of this included Paul Goodman's earlier work *Compulsory Miseducation* (1961) and Everitt Reimer's *School is Dead* (1971). The lyrics of popular music also reflected this trend, from Alice Cooper's song 'School's out' to Pink Floyd's 'We don't need no educashun, we don't want no thought control … hey teacher, leave those kids alone'.

The deschooling argument was itself widely criticised for being exaggerated in its critique of schooling and limited in its proposed alternatives (Lister 1974). Michael Huberman noted that while schools tended to be inequitable, there was little evidence to support the view that Illich's proposed alternatives would be any more equitable. On the other hand, he suggested, secondary schools might usefully be reformed so that young people could leave and re-enter the school system and complete their education at their own pace (Huberman 1974). Meanwhile, the Marxist economist Herbert Gintis suggested that Illich did not fully understand how the educational system served the capitalist system, and that his analysis was simplistic, leading him to a superficial set of proposals (Gintis 1972). Since the 1970s, the concept of deschooling has received less attention despite the continued problems of educational systems around the world, largely because of its utopian and anarchistic overtones.

See also: alternative education; Illich, Ivan; informal/nonformal learning; school

Further reading

Gintis, H. (1972) 'Towards a political economy of education: a radical critique of Ivan Illich's *Deschooling Society*', *Harvard Educational Review*, 42(1): 70–96.

Goodman, P. (1961) *Compulsory Miseducation*, London: Penguin.

Huberman, M. (1974) 'Learning, democratizing and deschooling'. In I. Lister (ed.) *Deschooling*, Cambridge: Cambridge University Press.

Illich, I. (1971) *Deschooling Society*, New York: Harper and Row.

Lister, I. (ed.) (1974) *Deschooling*, Cambridge: Cambridge University Press.

Reimer, E. (1971) *School is Dead: An Essay on Alternatives in Education*, London: Penguin.

Silberman, C. (1970) *Crisis in the Classroom*, New York: Random House.

GARY McCULLOCH

DETENTION

Convicted juvenile offenders, child immigrants and asylum seekers with cases pending may be placed in detention centres whose staffs include teachers or instructors. More typically in educational contexts, however, detention describes a school disciplinary procedure that involves the pupil being kept in school beyond the usual hours. This may occur during the lunch break, at the end of the timetabled day or, more exceptionally, at a weekend or in a school holiday. Generally issued for less serious transgressions than those leading to suspension or expulsion, receiving a detention, or notice of one, can nevertheless induce in today's children that same sinking feeling experienced by generations of previous school pupils. For a child, even a 30-minute detention – some may be longer, others shorter – can seem a lifetime when served in the company of a dour teacher and in the confines of a classroom devoid of other children. The detention period may be used to catch up with uncompleted schoolwork, but may also have a community service focus: picking up litter in the playground or shelving library books, for example.

The setting of detentions can be subject to national and state legislative frameworks, which may require schools to give parents a set period of written notice of a detention and an explanation of the circumstances leading to it. In reporting the misdemeanour, schools may unwittingly precipitate further, domestic, sanctions against the child. Equally, though, the family may sometimes take the view that a detention is too severe a penalty or altogether unfounded. The school may come under particular pressure to reconsider if the detention falls on a day of religious significance to the child's family or if it raises concerns about the child's safety in getting home.

See also: approved school; discipline

DAVID CROOK

DEVELOPMENT PLAN

This term is commonly used throughout the world in human resource management. Employees are encouraged to consider the requirements of their jobs and record their individual training needs in personal development plans. Around the world, various governments have national education development plans, and some corporations, local authorities, universities, colleges and schools have also put in place development plans for their own organisations. Educational development plans generally set out objectives alongside timescales and estimates of the resources required to implement change. Plans may address all manner of aspirations, including improving literacy attainment, raising students' test and examination scores or widening participation in higher education.

In the context of English educational history, development plan has a much more specific meaning. In the wake of the 1944 Education Act every local education authority was required to prepare and submit to the Ministry of Education a development plan for its primary and secondary schools. Each authority had to estimate immediate and prospective needs and set out the action it proposed to take to ensure that there would be sufficient primary and secondary schools for its area. Alterations to school premises had to be specified and costs estimated. Requirements for additional new schools had to be included, as did any proposals for school closures. In addition, the development plan had to indicate how the needs of children under five and those requiring special educational treatment were to be met. Proposed provisions for boarding education and for school transport also had to be included. Before submitting its development plan, a local education authority was required to consult the managers and governors of all voluntary schools affected by it and, in practice, many authorities consulted other interested parties as well. The need to produce development plans quickly led to a period of intense pressurised activity. Initially, the ministry requested that plans should be submitted by April 1946, but this deadline proved far too optimistic and had to be extended into the following decade. Several studies (e.g. Gosden and Sharp 1978; Vowles 2003) have illustrated the contentiousness of policy making in this period. The preparation of these plans was a mammoth task involving vast amounts of work, but they provided very useful local surveys of schooling. The development plans of the 1940s became outdated, but provided a blueprint for subsequent planning exercises in education.

See also: economics of education; education policy; school change; school reform

Further reading

Education Act 1944, London: HMSO.
Gosden, P. (1983) *The Educational System Since 1944*, Oxford: Martin Robertson.
Gosden, P. H. J. H. and Sharp, P. R. (1978) *The Development of an Education Service: The West Riding 1889–1974*, Oxford: Martin Robertson.
Vowles, G. (2003) *A Century of Achievement: A History of Local Education Authorities in Bedfordshire 1903–203*, Hertford: Bedfordshire County Council.

PAUL SHARP

DEWEY, JOHN (1859–1952)

John Dewey was a pragmatist philosopher, psychologist, and educator. Many regard him as the founder of progressive education with its stresses on educating the reflective democratic citizen, anti-authoritarianism, individual development that emphasises student need and interest, the social construction of knowledge, social justice, and the school as the driving force of social reconstruction. Educational institutions were important for

Dewey's personal intellectual development. He held a biologically based emergent theory of mind that emphasised learning in the context of satisfying embodied needs, desires, and interests, a theory that helped him overcome his personal struggle with a host of dualisms he found self-alienating. Learning to creatively critique such satisfactions allows us to discriminate the desirable from the merely desired, the valuable from the valued. He thought social institutions (e.g. schools) and practices (e.g. teaching) supervene on our innate biology to impart the meanings that constitute the individual mind and collective ethos of a culture. In an autobiographical essay, he identifies education, dualism, the biological basis of mind, and social constructivism as crucial to his 'intellectual development' (1930, LW 5: 156). These four points provide an excellent entry into his theory of education.

The first point, 'the importance that the practice and theory of education have had for me' holds a central synthetic place in Dewey's philosophy. For him, 'This interest fused with and brought together what might otherwise have been separate interests – that in psychology and that in social institutions and social life'. Dewey asserts that 'philosophizing should focus about education as the supreme human interest in which, moreover, other problems, cosmological, moral, logical, come to a head' (Dewey 1930, LW 5: 156). Dewey was concerned with the practical dimensions of education and served as a school inspector as a young professor at the University of Michigan where he wrote *My Pedagogic Creed* (1887, EW 5: 84–95). In 1894, he departed Michigan for the University of Chicago, where he chaired the department of philosophy and founded the Laboratory School in 1896, which become the model for many such schools around the world. The Laboratory School was a place for educational experimentation. For Dewey, experiments were not only falsifiable, but also contingent in an ever-evolving world. Two of his most important educational works, *The*

School and Society (1899, MW 1: 1–109), and *The Child and the Curriculum* (1902, MW: 271–91) report results from the Laboratory School.

Two major educational works, written by Dewey after moving to Columbia University, are the famous *Democracy and Education* (1916, MW 9) and *Experience and Education* (1938, LW 13: 1–62), a work devoted to clarifying his position between proponents of traditional 'curriculum-centered' pedagogy and the new 'child-centered' pedagogy championed by Dewey's former teacher G. Stanley Hall. Dewey's view is best thought of as an organic, functional, and holistic coordination of student, teacher, and subject matter within a social context. His answer to the classical question: 'What is the aim of education?' is stunning: 'Since growth is the characteristic of life, education is all one with growing; it has no end beyond itself' (MW 9: 58). By growth, Dewey means an ever-expanding ability to make subtle discriminations and richer connections within experience, thereby establishing continuity among otherwise durationally-extensionally detached events while at the same time refining our powers of response with regard to ever more remote consequences. The capacity to cultivate growth is, for Dewey, the criterion for evaluating the quality of any educational programme.

The second influence Dewey acknowledged is 'the intellectual scandal of dualism in logical standpoint and method between something called "science" on the one hand and something called "morals" on the other' (LW 5: 156). This led to his elaborating a position he called 'instrumentalism', which educators usually learn from his *How We Think* (1910, MW 6: 177–356; revised, 1933, LW: 105–352), although he offers a far more complete account in his *Logic: The Theory of Inquiry* (LW 12). All inquiry, including scientific inquiry, is, for Dewey, means–ends reasoning whereby we seek means for securing valued ideal ends wherein the means constitute the end obtained. Inquiry is simply an instrument of intelligence, an *organum* in the Aristotelian sense, for resolving disruptions to the unity of thought and feeling in action.

As noted, Dewey's philosophy denies a host of dualisms including: mind versus body, knower versus known, self versus society, and theory versus fact. At best, such dualisms are simply useful practical distinctions among sub-functions within a larger mutually transacting functional unity. The reticulated structure of his emergent organic holism makes Dewey's philosophy of education difficult to sum up briefly, which has caused much misunderstanding. Another dualism Dewey rejects is that between method and subject matter. For him, method, or form, is structure for a purpose: 'Method means that arrangement *of* subject matter which makes it most effective in use. Never is method something outside of the material' (MW 9: 172). When the use is pedagogical, we should arrange the subject matter to make it most effective for teaching. That is, 'the teacher should be occupied not with subject matter in itself but in its interaction with the pupils' present needs and capacities' (p. 191). Beyond subject matter knowledge, a good teacher has the pedagogical knowledge necessary to organise the subject matter as a means to the end of facilitating learning.

The third influence is the 'biological conception of the *psyche*', especially as Dewey found it in the functionalist psychology of fellow pragmatist William James (LW 5: 157). Along with Darwin and T. H. Huxley, James confirmed Dewey's organic and empirical naturalism. From his reflections on habit, James (1890/1950) drew a valuable pedagogical principle: 'The great thing, then, in all education, is to make our nervous system our ally instead of our enemy. ... For this we must make automatic and habitual, as early as possible as many useful actions as we can' (vol. I: 122). For Dewey, habits are embodied dispositions to act evincing emotion; they constitute belief while performing all the basic mental functions. Reflective, imaginative, and rational inquiry, however,

occurs when habits of response fail to rectify some problematic situation. Dewey did not understand habits mechanically: 'Rationality ... is not a force to evoke against impulse and habit. It is the attainment of a working harmony among diverse desires. "Reason" as a noun signifies the happy cooperation of a multitude of dispositions' (MW 14: 136).

Regarding the fourth influence, Dewey observes: 'The objective biological approach of the Jamesian psychology led straight to the perception of the importance of distinctive social categories, especially communication and participation' (LW 5: 159). We acquire our habits from our habitat, especially our socio-linguistic habitat. Dewey titled the first chapter of his (1922) *Human Nature and Conduct*, 'Habits as social functions' (MW 14: 15). For him, to have a mind is to participate in the socio-linguistic practices and institutions of a community. Language is crucial to Dewey's naturalised account of the *emergence* of mind: 'Through speech a person dramatically identifies himself with potential acts and deeds; he plays many roles, not in successive stages of life but in a contemporaneously enacted drama. Thus mind emerges' (LW 1: 135). Dewey worked out his social constructivist theory of mind with his friend and colleague George Herbert Mead.

Because of his commitment to the social construction of the self, Dewey was a strong advocate of participatory democracy. He understood democracy as moral, economic, and educational, not just political, hence the following definition:

> A democracy is more than a form of government; it is primarily a mode of associated living, of conjoint communicated experience. The extension in space of the number of individuals who participate in an interest so that each has to refer his own action to that of others, and to consider the action of others to give point and direction to his own, is equivalent to breaking down barriers of class, race, and national territory

which kept men from perceiving the full import of their activity.

(MW 9: 93)

The governmental structure assumed by a democracy is of secondary concern. It does not matter as long as it promotes communication. Conversation for Dewey is about creating and sharing meaning, i.e. growth. For him, the aim of society and the aim of education are identical.

In education, Dewey's influence and significanc ebbs and wanes with the fortunes of progressivism. That means that in the contemporary era of market-driven educational reform with its emphasis on normalised tests, curriculum, and standards of learning as tools for the refinement of human resources as capital for the global production function, Deweyan ideals serve largely as an alternative voice to the dominant educational discourse. Meanwhile, the John Dewey Society remains a thriving organisation. There has been tremendous international renaissance in Deweyan pragmatism among academic philosophers. This has led to a large number of new books on Dewey's philosophy. The best book for the beginner is by Raymond D. Boisvert (1998).

See also: child-centred education; educational theory; Hall, Granville Stanley; learning; Mead, George Herbert; philosophy of education; progressive education; social constructivism

Further reading

Boisvert, R. D. (1998) *John Dewey: Rethinking Our Time*, Albany NY: State University of New York Press.
Dewey, J. (1969–91) *The Collected Works of John Dewey, 1882–1953*, ed. Jo Ann Boydston, Carbondale IL: Southern Illinois University Press. Published in three series as *The Early Works* (EW), *The Middle Works* (MW) and *The Later Works* (LW). Volume and page number follow these designations.
James, W. (1890/1950) *The Principles of Psychology*, vols I and II, New York: Dover.
Westbrook, R. B. (1991) *John Dewey and American Democracy*, Ithaca NY: Cornell University Press.

JIM GARRISON

DIAGNOSTIC ASSESSMENT

The term is sometimes used to describe the practice of eliciting diagnostic information; alternatively, it may refer to the instrument used to elicit that information. The purpose of diagnostic assessment is to characterise students' levels of knowledge, skill, or understanding with respect to a domain, at a level of detail appropriate to inform the intended course of action.

Diagnosis may be used for different purposes under a variety of circumstances: as examples, an instructor may ask specific questions to pinpoint the source of a student's misunderstanding, a computer tutor may analyse a student's solution strategy, or a large-scale assessment may be administered to detect different skill patterns among students with identical scores. In the first two examples, diagnosis is focused on the individual, and the intent is to identify very specific evidence that can be used to guide the student in solving a task or in understanding a challenging concept. In the last example, diagnostic information might be provided at the individual level or at the group level, but the goal is almost always to identify weak areas at a higher level of description.

Ideally, diagnostic assessment is developed in accordance with an underlying framework that specifies how to interpret student responses. The underlying framework may be based on any combination of the following: (1) a model of component skills; (2) a model of student progress in the domain; or (3) a theory of naive ideas and procedural errors. The best applications of diagnostic assessment may represent a combination of perspectives. As pointed out by Bejar (1984: 175): 'the traditional approach to the specification of content in terms of static taxonomies may not be appropriate given the dynamic and sequential nature of diagnostic assessment'.

Only a few examples from the extensive literature on diagnostic assessment will be highlighted here. The work of Jim Minstrell and Earl Hunt on *facets* (e.g. Minstrell 2001) is an example of a student-centred approach. Facets are student ideas that are roughly ordered from more correct to more problematic, and were introduced to characterise students' developing ideas in physics. Once an interpretative framework for diagnosis has been formulated, it can guide subsequent task development. Bart *et al.* (1994) introduced the notion of a *semi-dense* item. Each possible response to a semi-dense item is interpretable with respect to a cognitive rule, and each relevant cognitive rule is represented by a possible response. Student responses to semi-dense items may provide evidence about which cognitive rules they are using.

As mentioned earlier, one application of diagnosis is to characterise student performances on large-scale assessments. There are many psychometric methods that may be applied to the diagnostic interpretation of student response patterns. In a recent review, von Davier *et al.* (2006) compared the assumptions and mathematical relationships among psychometric models for cognitive diagnosis.

Diagnostic frameworks are most useful when they link student difficulties to learning expectations. Minstrell (2001: 426) described how facets can support standards interpretation: 'Standards say what we *want students to know and be able to do*. Facets describe the sorts of things that students *do seem to know and do*'. Briggs *et al.* (2006) presented an approach where task development is based on a theory of student progress in the domain, which is in turn is linked to national standards. Each option in the items they developed corresponds to a developmental level. They also suggested an accompanying psychometric model (Wilson's Ordered Partition model), which could be used in a large-scale implementation of their approach.

Formative applications of diagnostic assessment can be used flexibly by teachers to positively affect student learning, and are an alternative to traditional tests (as shown by the work of Paul Black, Dylan William and others).

See also: assessment; cognition; formative assessment; psychometrics; standards; test/testing

Further reading

Bart, W. M., Post, T., Behr, M. J. and Lesh, R. (1994) 'A diagnostic analysis of a proportional reasoning test item: an introduction to the properties of a semi-dense item', *Focus on Learning Problems in Mathematics*, 16(3): 1–11.

Bejar, I. I. (1984) 'Educational diagnostic assessment', *Journal of Educational Measurement*, 21(2): 175–89.

Briggs, D. C., Alonzo, A. C., Schwab, C. and Wilson, M. (2006) 'Diagnostic assessment with ordered multiple-choice items', *Educational Assessment*, 11(1): 33–63.

Davier, M. von, DiBello, L. and Yamamoto, K. (2006) *Reporting Test Outcomes Using Models for Cognitive Diagnosis* (ETS RR–06–28) Princeton NJ: Educational Testing Service.

Minstrell, J. (2001) 'Facets of students' thinking: designing to cross the gap from research to standards-based practice'. In K. Crowley (ed.) *Designing For Science: Implications from Everyday, Classroom, and Professional Settings*, Mahwah NJ: Lawrence Erlbaum.

EDITH AURORA GRAF

DIDACTICS/DIDACTICISM

Didactics can be defined as a methodical study of pedagogical sciences. It is concerned with teaching and learning processes in different cultural and cross-cultural settings. Didacticism refers to the practice or quality of being didactic. Teaching described, for example by a school inspector, as being 'didactic' in one country might be deemed a great compliment to the teacher's subject knowledge. In other contexts, though, to describe a teacher as being 'didactic' might signify a dry, unimaginative approach to transmitting information without explanation or opportunities for class discussion.

The construct didactics can be traced to the German *die Didaktik*. The term is used very widely, but also very generally, throughout Europe, Russia and the Nordic countries, so it has numerous contested usages. Kron

(1993) lists thirty different definitions and explanations of didactics.

In Germany, the term *Didaktik* is used a traditional sense to refer to educational philosophy, and the contemporary usage of German didactics refers to the *geisteswissenschaftliche Didaktik* (pertaining to the humanities), with a hermeneutic approach. According to Kansanen (2002), major models of didactics are based on curricular contexts, defined by values and ideologies. Traditional models of German didactics are grounded in the social sciences and employ ideological constructions of the teaching and learning. In Norway, Finland and Denmark, on the other hand, didactics refers to a descriptive, rather than empirically based, discipline. In Sweden, didactics concentrates on curriculum and teaching research.

Didactics is linked to *Bildung*, the societal process denoting a particular pattern of existence in a constructed human culture (Kansanen 2002). The focus for didactics research tends to be on the instructional process, where earlier linear models of behaviouristic, cognitive, and process–product learning have given way to more sophisticated models of perception, intelligence, retention, learning modes and styles. Such multiple perspectives in learning have influenced theoretical shifts in didactics in order to reflect cultural diversity and pluralistic pedagogies.

'Didactic studies' is sometimes used to denote research dealing with curriculum and teaching. In Anglo-American usage, the term refers to research on the teaching and learning process, relating, for example, to

- goals – to construct models of the teaching and learning process;
- philosophy/ideology – focusing on totality and hermeneutics;
- objectives – achieving curricular outcomes;
- focus – selecting desired curriculum content for teaching;
- content – selecting desired topics and learning experiences in the curriculum.

All major models of didactics have an ideological dimension and a teleological goal – to provide quality education for all. Didactics is legitimated by its constant search for factors and variables contributing to 'good teaching'.

See also: curriculum; learning; pedagogy; teaching/teaching methods

Further reading

Kansanen, P. (2002) 'Didactics and its relation to educational psychology: problems in translating a key concept across research communities', *International Review of Education*, 48(6): 427–41.

Kron, F. (1993) *Grundwissen Didaktik*, Munich: Reinhardt.

Zajda, J. (2004) 'Learning multiple perspectives in studies of society and environment: a curriculum model', *Curriculum and Teaching*, 19(2): 41–59.

JOSEPH ZAJDA AND REA ZAJDA

DIPLOMA

Understandings of what a diploma is vary between countries. It is sometimes used in the sense of an official document or certificate, which testifies that the recipient has successfully completed a course of study. Early diplomas were made from sheepskin and, later, from parchment or fine-grade paper. A diploma may be awarded to children in recognition of completing high school, or to adult students for successfully finishing a programme of vocational training or a university degree.

A diploma may also be a qualification in its own right. In the German education system a diploma has equivalence to a standard academic degree, but this is not the case everywhere. In such countries as Australia, Hong Kong and India a diploma is a sub-degree award. In some contexts, a university diploma serves as a consolation award for students who have completed a significant amount of work for a degree but failed to complete the course, perhaps in consequence of circumstances beyond their control. There are examples, however, of vocationally oriented higher-level diplomas for which a first degree is a prerequisite.

See also: certificate/certification; degree; qualification

DAVID CROOK

DIPLOMA DISEASE

The concept of diploma disease was developed by Professor Ronald Dore, in the book of this name originally published in 1976. As a member of a delegation of the International Labour Office to inquire into large-scale unemployment in Sri Lanka, he found a clear division between 'a modern sector offering salaries and security far superior to life in the traditional peasant economy'. At the same time there was severe strain imposed due to the slow growth of the modern sector, with the school system expanding at a much more rapid rate. It was this set of processes, which he saw as common to all modern societies, for which Dore coined the arresting phrase 'the diploma disease' (Dore 1997: viii).

Dore pointed out that because of the attractions of the modern sector, the examinations that provided the entry point into it came under pressure to escalate the number of qualifications, but that this tended to create more educated people than the system required. The result was that people with high qualifications began to take jobs at a lower level, leading, for example, to those with BA degrees taking positions as bus conductors. This 'educational inflation' took place at different rates of speed and with different social effects from one country to another, but Dore insisted that it was present to some extent everywhere, and that it was especially evident in developing countries. In Britain, he proposed, a process of qualification inflation had taken place throughout the twentieth century, augmented by competition between professional groups for status. In Japan, he saw this basic issue as being largely responsible for fierce competition for examination success and for posts. In Sri Lanka (formerly Ceylon), the later growth of educational opportunities encouraged a labour market qualifications spiral so severe that Dore could see

> no prospect for Ceylon's schools and their pupils except continuous pressure for expansion of facilities, increasing intense competition at every entry port and selection post, increasingly anxious dominance of the curriculum by examinations, and an increasing experience of individual failure within the school system, and of the frustrations of unemployment on leaving it.
>
> (Dore 1997: 65)

A country like Kenya, he added for good measure, was some way behind Sri Lanka in this process, but was catching up fast. He acknowledged the possibility of reform, but emphasised that there was not likely to be any effective cure to the diploma disease that fell short of 'decoupling the institutions of occupational selection from the institutions of education' (Dore 1997: xxxi).

Dore's basic thesis was controversial, and has been much debated over the past thirty years in relation to a wide range of countries (Oxenham 1984; Little 1997a), but overall has shown much substance. Little has suggested that the novelty of the original thesis lay in the 'creative combination of ideas about assessment and education on the one hand, and about employment allocation and creation on the other' (Little 1997b: 8). She noted also the contemporary growth of internationalisation and globalisation, and asked whether the diploma disease might develop on a global scale in the next century. Furthermore, Little acknowledged that current trends in test tyranny, exam league tables, the explosion of qualifications and associated developments 'all point to the possibility that some of the fundamental tenets of the thesis hold good in the industrialised countries of the North as well as the so-called "developing countries" of the South' (Little 1997b: 6). Brown (2006) goes even further to propose that since Dore's original diagnosis of the diploma disease in the 1970s, the symptoms have worsened, so that acquisitive learning for the purposes of passing examinations is widely believed to define the purposes of education. This process appears to demean and undermine the ideal of the meritocracy. According to Brown, 'If the diploma disease signifies a shift in the purpose of education, employability is a shift in the meaning of life' (Brown 2006: 393). Opportunity had itself become a 'trap', a virulent source of the diploma disease.

See also: certificate/certification; credentials/ credentialing; diploma; examinations; meritocracy; qualifications

Further reading

Brown, P. (2006) 'The opportunity trap'. In H. Lauder, P. Brown, J. Dillabough and A. H. Halsey (eds) *Education, Globalisation and Social Change*, Oxford: Oxford University Press.

Dore, R. (1997) *The Diploma Disease: Education, Qualification and Development*, 2nd edn, London: Institute of Education, University of London.

Little, A. (ed.) (1997a) *Assessment in Education: Principles, Policy and Practice*, 4(1), special issue, 'The diploma disease twenty years on'.

Little, A. (1997b) 'The Diploma Disease twenty years on: an introduction', *Assessment in Education*, 4(1): 5–21.

Oxenham, J. (ed.) (1984) *Education versus Qualifications? A Study of the Relations between Education, Selection for Employment and the Productivity of Labour*, London: Allen and Unwin.

GARY McCULLOCH

DISAFFECTION

Disaffection is a term used to describe pupils who are, to at least some degree, not committed to the process of learning, either in particular aspects of their education, or to the project of education more generally.

The term became widely used in the 1990s and the first decade of the twenty-first century in response to the phenomenon of learners whose failure to fully realise their educational potential was caused not by lack of aptitude,

intelligence or educational opportunity, but by a reluctance to engage with the aims and processes of formal education, or the challenge of learning in particular school subjects. A major body of international research evidence about disaffection may now be found (see, for example, the websites for 'Descol: an Anglo-French-Catalan study of the pedagogical dimensions of disaffection in schools', at www.cnefei.fr/descol/anglais/navigationan. htm; and 'Teachers researching disaffection: an online dataset about pupil disaffection in seven English secondary schools', www.uea. ac.uk/~m242/nasc/welcome.htm).

Disaffection can take different forms and can be thought of in terms of a continuum, between those learners who are actively resistant to learning and being in schools and classrooms, to those who are bored with school and school subjects, and who simply lack enthusiasm and commitment to the school curriculum as it is presented to them. In the late twentieth century, attention focused principally on those pupils at the 'severe' end of the spectrum, where disaffection manifested itself in school refusal, truancy, or disruptive behaviour. More recently, attention has also focused on pupils who are quietly and passively disengaged from learning. Research suggests that such pupils have developed sophisticated strategies for disguising their lack of commitment, such as 'coasting' (consistently producing work which is below the standard they are capable of), calculating the minimum of work which is deemed to be acceptable by the teacher, and trying to render themselves 'invisible' to the teacher by not drawing attention to themselves. Such pupils have been described as 'playing truant in mind', or as 'RHINOs': 'Really here in name only'.

The public profile of disaffection as an important educational problem has grown as increasing state concern with the effectiveness of education systems led many developed nations to intensify their focus on educational measurement. This included attempts to gain greater insights into deficits in learners' attainment in relation to their educational potential. Such interventions revealed that many pupils did not fulfil their potential because of lack of effort and commitment. For many young people, there was a difference between what the state education system wanted them to achieve, and what they saw as their own priorities.

The reconceptualisation of disaffection to include pupils who were quietly disengaged from learning led to a realisation that disaffection, in its broadest sense of those not fully committed to learning, was a major cause of educational underachievement, with almost all schools in systems of compulsory state education possessing at least some pupils who were disaffected, and in many cases, large numbers of such pupils.

Attempts to explain the causes, and possible solutions to the problem of disaffection are contested and wide-ranging. The fact that many learners who are viewed as 'disaffected' display high levels of engagement in learning with respect to extra-curricular and out-of-school activities has focused attention on the prescriptive nature of the contemporary school curriculum as a potential cause of learner disaffection. Elliott and Zamorski (2002) question whether the imposition of a compulsory national curriculum in the United Kingdom in 1991 gave teachers sufficient freedom to represent knowledge in a way that would enable them to engage and motivate their pupils. Other commentators pointed to the intensive regime of assessment and testing in UK schools as contributing to pupil disaffection. The suggestion has also been made that disaffection is a result of poor teacher pedagogy, with weak systems of teacher education failing to produce teachers who are able to teach their subjects in a way that motivates and engages their pupils, and which have failed to keep abreast of recent developments in the availability and use of new media and new technology by young people. Others have looked to developments outside the school system to explain learner disaffection, such as the phenomenon of graduate unem-

ployment, and the shortage of graduate-level jobs for those qualifying from universities. The problem of disaffection has, however, brought about a consensus that developing insights into learner attitudes to education is an important issue in contemporary education.

See also: learning; learning disabilities/difficulties; motivation; truancy; underachievement

Further reading

Elliott, J. and Zamorski, B. (eds) (2002) 'Researching disaffection with teachers', *Pedagogy, Culture and Society*, 10(2): 157–67.
Klein, R. (2000) *Defying Disaffection: How Schools are Winning the Hearts and Minds of Reluctant Pupils*, Stoke: Trentham.

TERRY HAYDN

DISCIPLINE

Discipline is a term encountered in several educational contexts with varying meanings. It is sometimes used to denote a branch or body of knowledge. Disciplines are closely related to subjects of study: law, economics or biology, for example, may be regarded as disciplines. The meanings and boundaries of curriculum disciplines are rarely fixed for long, and tend to respond to the wider social, economic, political and cultural contexts. Some areas are considered to be interdisciplinary, such as biochemistry or cultural studies, working across traditional disciplinary boundaries. There are debates as to whether some disciplines have a coherent core knowledge base and methodology or whether they simply borrow from others. For example, it is often said that educational studies is defined by the application of the 'foundation' disciplines of history, psychology, sociology and philosophy to issues of teaching and learning. Recreational pursuits such as fencing, or relaxation techniques like meditation, may also be referred to as disciplines.

In respect of vocational training, the term may refer to a system of rules of conduct or method of practice. For employers, the ideal (self-)disciplined worker is punctual, conscientious, constructive, loyal, well mannered and so forth. Hardworking students may also acquire the self-discipline needed to achieve educational success through sustained concentration and work. The upbringing of the well known nineteenth-century liberal John Stuart Mill may be a case in point. Such self-discipline may be gained not only from family upbringing but also political commitment, religious participation, an interest in learning and discovery and the threat of punishment, as well as perceived financial and moral rewards later in life.

A common understanding of the term refers to the ability of a teacher to keep order or control in the classroom. As a verb, 'discipline' is sometimes understood to be synonymous with 'punish'. Corporal punishment is no longer permitted in many countries and school systems, but those who perceive a 'crisis' in children's behavioural standards frequently advocate the use of strong disciplinary sanctions, including the temporary exclusion or permanent expulsion of disruptive students.

A school's disciplinary approach is frequently to be found in its 'school rules' or 'code of pupil conduct'. While frequently specifying such unacceptable practices as bullying, racial and sexual harassment, such documents often emphasise a 'positive discipline' approach. Indeed, discipline does not necessarily imply coerciveness and may be achieved through discussion, modelling and more collective means. Posters on classroom walls sometimes carry messages about the necessity of politeness, cooperation, consideration and respect for others. It is very common, too, to encounter reward systems that promote and commend good behaviour. This may take the form of merit stars and good conduct certificates. Well behaved students may be exclusively eligible to participate in certain school events and visits. Schools frequently assert that good discipline is a two-way street and, at an international level, home–school agreements are gaining in

popularity. These contract parents to support school policies and set out the rewards and sanctions. Most educational organisations may also have a disciplinary procedure, a formal and structured way of enforcing institutional rules.

See also: bullying; classroom management; corporal punishment; exclusion/expulsion; Mill, John Stuart; suspension

DAVID CROOK AND TOM WOODIN

DISCOVERY METHOD/LEARNING

Discovery learning is a contested and controversial concept that holds that learning is more effective if a learner discovers, or finds out, something for themselves rather than being told by a teacher. Among its claimed benefits is an increase in intrinsic motivation. Like most notions in education, a search for its origins leads to an almost infinite regression. The position, in modern times, appeared, amongst other texts, in *Emile*, written by the Genevan Enlightenment philosopher Jean-Jacques Rousseau (1712–78), who, in a summation of the ideology of discovery learning, wrote regarding the ideal education of a child:

> let him know nothing because you have told him, but because he has learnt it for himself. Let him not be taught science, let him invent it. If ever you substitute in his mind authority for reason, he will cease to reason.
>
> (Rousseau 1974: 131)

Further on in his book, Rousseau wrote about how it was important for Emile to find things out for himself rather than having him taught the truth of the matter by a teacher.

Rousseau's distrust of telling, or 'transmission pedagogy', was also present in the educational theories and practice of the Zurich educationalist Johann Heinrich Pestalozzi (1746–1847) and possibly even more so in the work of the German founder of the kindergarten, Friedrich Wilhelm August Froebel

(1782–1852), in whose work it appears in connection with active learning and self-activity. Something similar is present also in the 'method' of Maria Montessori (1870–1952), but it is the American pragmatist philosopher and educationalist John Dewey (1859–1952), who gave the notion legitimacy in more recent times. Dewey's pragmatism contained a good deal of reverence for the experimental methods of natural science and for their application to human societies and to education, in particular. In his book *How We Think*, Dewey argued for the scientific method and for induction. Schools, he thought, needed to provide activities for pupils in order to modify their physical conditions. This he contrasted to the passive observation of pictures and books. In *Democracy and Education* he discussed learning from experience and concluded that this involved acting on the world to find out what it is like.

Dewey's ideas resonated later with those of the American psychologist Jerome Bruner (b. 1915). Like the Swiss philosopher and psychologist Jean Piaget (1896–1980), Bruner's is a constructivist psychology in which learners construct their own view of the world. For him, discovery learning allowed learners to organise what they encountered in terms of its regularity and relatedness. Furthermore, it allowed learners to rearrange evidence in order to reach new insights. The Estonian-born curriculum theorist Hilda Taba (1904–67) also stressed content not simply as something to be absorbed, but something requiring reorganisation. Like most of its academic advocates, she cautioned that not everything could be learned by discovery.

Discovery learning, historically, has found most support among mathematics and science educators, and in recent decades has interested advocates of information technology, including pioneers such as the educationalist and computer scientist who invented the programming language Logo, Seymour Papert (b. 1928).

Outside these fields, discovery learning is frequently criticised as devaluing canonical knowledge and promoting the reinvention of the wheel. This was the burden of the critique of the American Piagetian, David Ausubel (b. 1918), who argued that it was inefficient. In the United Kingdom in 1967, the Plowden Report on primary schooling in England and Wales sanctioned discovery learning, supported by teacher intervention, in the teaching of science. Like endorsements in other societies, this generated a backlash in the form of the *Black Papers*, a right-wing critique of child-centred education, of which discovery learning was seen to be a central element.

Nevertheless, variants of discovery learning persist, as for example in the problem-solving approach of many Masters in Business Administration programmes that emphasise the formation of specific skills, rather than the inculcation of fixed bodies of knowledge. Computer games, simulations and discovery learning virtual environments are just some of the ways in which a relatively old idea has been implemented and developed in the context of new technologies.

See also: Bruner, Jerome; child-centred education; Dewey, John; learning; progressive education; Rousseau, Jean-Jacques; teaching/teaching methods

Further reading

Bruner, J. S. (1962) *On Knowing: Essays for the Left Hand*, Cambridge MA: Harvard University Press.
Papert, S. (1980) *Mindstorms: Children, Computers and Powerful Ideas*, New York: Basic Books.
Rousseau, J-J. (1974) *Emile*, trans. B. Foxley, London: Dent.

KEVIN J. BREHONY

DISTANCE EDUCATION/LEARNING

Despite its wide use and increasing popularity, distance education does not have any single, universally accepted definition. This is probably because of the multiplicity of purposes it serves, the variety of media utilised and the different institutional/organisational and operational structures that characterise its delivery. Its definition has evolved with time and there are now many alternative terminologies, such as open learning, flexible learning, online or e-learning, and virtual education. While 'distance education' remains the more usual term, especially in developing countries, the European Commission has adopted the term 'open and distance learning'.

Distance education has been characterised by the late development of any theory relating to its practice and, to date, a lack of a unanimously accepted theory. A number of distance educators have made various contributions towards a theory of distance education. However, there is still a need for special attempts to examine the feasibility of a theory for distance education as well as a description of what could constitute a more comprehensive theory. A theory of distance education is one which can provide a foundation on which structures of need, purpose and administration can be built upon, and against which decisions can be taken with confidence.

Some of the theories, such as those of autonomy and independence, in distance education which advocate individualisation of study and the theory of industrialisation, which is based on the argument that the structure of distance education should be analysed and interpreted by using principles of industrialisation, and attempts to show that it is different from traditional face-to-face teaching, are among theories that have received wider attention. Some of the theories are directly related to, or have been influenced by, the different models and institutional structures that were developing as distance education evolved. Some theories appear to be related to, or influenced by, the growth and development of andragogy as a model of instruction which is predicated on some basic assumptions about learners which have some relationship to notions about a learner's ability, need, and desire to take responsibility for learning.

Distance education dates back to the nineteenth century, when many educational institutions (including universities) in Sweden, Germany, the United Kingdom and the United States of America were offering print-based courses. During the early twentieth century, countries such as Australia, France, New Zealand and the Soviet Union started developing distance teaching institutions or programmes. During that period, distance education enjoyed low esteem and was on the periphery of the education system. It was associated with high dropout rates and was in the main the business of private, profit-making institutions. At that time distance education served as a route to social mobility for socially and educationally disadvantaged people in the West and was about the only means of gaining a qualification in the colonial world where foreign-based profit-making private colleges also operated.

There was unprecedented and increased participation by governments in its provision worldwide during the 1960s and 1970s, and this enhanced its visibility, credibility and legitimacy. Distance education offered the possibility of extending educational opportunities more cost-effectively than conventional education. There were also ideological reasons. The establishment of the UK's Open University in 1969 was driven by an ideological imperative to widen opportunities for adults. This was reinforced by an ideological argument that university education should open its doors to adults regardless of their previous education or lack of it (Perraton 2000).

In the developing world the philosophy of equal opportunity for all in mass education was one of the main considerations in the promotion of distance education. It was also believed that distance education supported the desire for achieving greater equity and equality of opportunities to access learning. Governments established distance education institutions or programmes principally geared towards human resources development required for, especially, the public sector, which had to be indigenised as a means of consolidating political independence. But the most compelling factor was perhaps the desire for learning on the part of tens of thousands of individuals, for many reasons. Further, there was a strong belief that distance education would greatly increase access while maintaining costs at manageable levels. It has therefore been argued by some proponents that distance education is a product of democratic societies.

The development of communications technology has been the foundation or prerequisite of distance education. It was made feasible by the invention of 'post' and print and was almost solely dependent on them for many decades. As it evolved distance education began to integrate new communications and information technologies. As early as the 1960s and 1970s, particularly, broadcast capabilities helped to revolutionise its scope and capability despite the huge financial cost and the restrictions they tended to impose on learners. The new computer and satellite technologies now offer new ways of expanding the range of education and training, and have generally enhanced the attractiveness, quality, effectiveness and efficiency of distance education.

The support of international agencies and intergovernmental organisations also has had a positive influence. The World Bank, the UK Department for International Development, the United Nations Scientific and Cultural Organisation (UNESCO) and the Commonwealth Secretariat are notable examples. Perhaps more prominent is the Commonwealth of Learning (COL), which was created by Commonwealth Heads of Government in 1988 specifically to advocate and promote the use of distance education in the Commonwealth to improve access to education and training among member states.

The worldwide development of distance education has necessitated the development of global, regional and national enabling structures for networking and professional interaction among distance education practitioners, academics and policy makers. The International Council for Distance Education and Open Learning (ICDE) and regional and national professional associations in all geographical regions have contributed markedly to its growth.

There is a substantial amount of evidence that distance education has enjoyed a reasonable amount of success in both industrialised and developing countries. For example, it has contributed to equity by widening access to education to millions of people for whom it would not otherwise have been available. It has contributed to: the transmission of values; the empowerment of learners; the teaching of job skills; learners getting better jobs; an improvement in learners' lifestyles; the enhancement of non-formal education to socio-economic development; and rural development, especially in developing countries.

The recorded and perceived successes have, however, not erased the perceptions of some sections of both learners and governments, especially in developing countries, that it is a second-rate system of education, which is also perceived by some people as being used to offer a shadow of education while withholding its substance (Perraton 2000). According to Perraton, distance education is also considered by its critics to be an inefficient and cheap way of meeting educational demand, yet does not meet it. He further observes that critics point out that 'through its existence it helps insulate the elite system from pressures that might otherwise threaten its status or its ways of working' (Perraton 2000: 199). However, from his extensive and detailed analysis of distance education in developing countries, the author concluded that there was evidence to suggest that distance education can bring social and educational benefits.

Perhaps this is why the contribution of distance education to the attainment of Millennium Development Goals is as strongly and widely recognised as is the promotion of lifelong learning. The Dakar Framework for Action on Education for All (2000) also recognises the important role of distance education in widening access to education (as did the Jomtien Declaration on Education for All ten years earlier) – only if it can be improved.

It is noteworthy in this regard that the rapid development of information and communications technologies (ICTs) enhance the capacity of educational institutions to increase access to all types of education and training, at all levels and at all stages of people's lives. They can help to develop learning systems that are flexible and adaptable to all circumstances; and to change or improve the old, existing models of distance education.

But innovation theory suggests that the new technologies must show a high level of comparative advantage over current, old technologies; and this raises a variety of issues about their possible wider application. Institutional policies, curriculum structures, staff attitudes and perceptions must change to accommodate the new approaches to teaching dictated by new technologies. Second, in developing countries there are challenges presented by inadequate telecommunications infrastructure, especially outside major cities, a lack of properly trained teachers for integrating ICT into the learning process, and often poorly formulated and inadequately implemented policy frameworks and limited access to connectivity. Other challenges are shortage of financial resources and cultural biases premised on the notion that distance education is a Western social/cultural/educational construct. Third, many ethical issues intervene in the widespread use of ICT, such as questions of ownership of knowledge and exchange of education as a commodity.

The potential for distance education is huge and the challenges are not insurmountable It must be improved by, among other strategies, using both old and new technologies, especially in the developing world.

See also: andragogy; educational broadcasting; educational technology; e-learning; open learning; Open University; Web-based learning

Further reading

Bates, A. W. (1995) *Technology, Open Learning and Distance Education*, London: Routledge.

Daniel, S. J. (1996) *Mega Universities and Knowledge Media: Technology Strategies for Further Education*, London: Kogan Page.

Perraton, H. (2000) *Open and Distance Learning in the Developing World*, London: Routledge.

Yates, C. and Bradley, J. (2000) *Basic Education at a Distance*, London: Routledge and The Commonwealth of Learning.

RICHARD SIACIWENA

DOCTORATE

A doctorate is an academic degree of the highest level, deriving from the Latin *doctor*, meaning teacher. The most widely known doctorate, the Doctor of Philosophy (Ph.D., sometimes D.Phil.), is generally awarded following at least three years of personal research. Part-time students in employment may take much longer than this to complete their doctorate. Candidates following this pathway encapsulate their research and conclusions in a thesis that satisfies their institution's word-length requirement – often around 80,000–100,000 words – and are subjected to an examination process that normally includes an oral element, the viva voce. Some universities, notably in Europe and the British Commonwealth, offer an alternative pathway to the research doctorate, taking into account the overall research contribution of an academic, usually over a long period. Examiners consider a portfolio of the individual's major scholarly outputs and, if judged satisfactory, a doctorate 'by publication' may be awarded. Some universities award 'higher doctorates', such as the Doctor of Laws (LL.D.) or Doctor of Literature (D.Litt.), in recognition of the work of outstanding scholars.

The 'professional doctorate' is an alternative to conventional research doctorates. Such programmes target established practitioners wishing to reflect on and improve their existing skills through the application of research and theory. Professional doctorates, which are especially popular in the field of health care, typically require candidates to complete coursework assignments, plus a dissertation or thesis which is shorter than that required for research doctorates. The first professional doctorate in education (Ed.D.) was awarded by Harvard University in 1921 and this qualification was, for many years, largely unknown outside the United States of America. Since the 1990s, however, many British, European and Australian universities have commenced Ed.D. programmes aimed at practising education professionals.

Many universities bestow honorary doctorates upon individuals who have made a significant contribution to public life, perhaps in the field of the arts, science or international affairs. Such decisions can arouse opposition. Many people disapprove altogether of 'unearned' university degrees, and the nomination of certain individuals may give rise to controversy. In 1985, for example, academics at the University of Oxford voted against awarding an honorary doctorate to a graduate of that university, the then prime minister Margaret Thatcher.

See also: coursework; degree; examinations; higher education; oral examinations; qualifications; thesis/dissertation; university

DAVID CROOK

DON

A don is an academic member of university staff or faculty, especially in the male elite tradition of higher education until recently epitomised by Oxford and Cambridge in Britain. The term belongs mainly to an ideal of teachers in higher education described by A. H. Halsey as 'the cultivated member of a governing class as opposed to the highly trained professional expert', with an expectation of 'an intimate relation between teacher and taught, maintained through the tutorial method, the shared domestic life of a college, and the separation of the roles of teacher and examiner' (Halsey 1995: 81). According to Halsey, this ideal, and the 'donnish dominion'

that it accompanied, has gone into decline with the rise of mass higher education, the increasing access of women to university staff positions, the rise of applied, vocational and modern studies, and a general loss of prestige, salaries, autonomy and resources. The decline of the donnish hierarchy is significant in terms of being the inverse process to the rise of a meritocracy, at least in prevailing ideals of the university (Halsey 2006).

See also: higher education; meritocracy; university

Further reading

Halsey, A. H. (1995) *Decline of Donnish Dominion: The British Academic Professions in the 20th Century*, Oxford: Oxford University Press.
——(2006) 'The European university'. In H. Lauder, P. Brown, J. Dillenbaugh and A. H. Halsey (eds) *Education, Globalisation and Social Change*, Oxford: Oxford University Press.

GARY McCULLOCH

DRAMA

Drama is derived from the Greek for 'action'. Within schools, drama is sometimes timetabled as a distinct lesson, but it is also common for it to feature as an extracurricular or cross-curricular subject. After-school drama clubs feature in some schools, sometimes directed towards rehearsing and staging an annual school play or participating in an inter-schools competition. In the primary school, drama is frequently a cross-curricular outcome of physical education and music lessons encouraging creativity, self-expression, imagination and improvisation through movement. In the secondary school, literature syllabuses may include well known plays which learners engage with best when they can see, or participate in, a performance. Language lessons may also sometimes require students to script and/or present a dramatic dialogue. Drama is sometimes taught with the aim of preparing students for public examinations. Such courses typically involve a critical examination of specified plays and playwrights and an examination of issues relating to staging, lighting, props and so forth. There may also be a performance dimension to the students' assessment. Beyond the school, many colleges and universities offer programmes in drama, leading to diploma, undergraduate and postgraduate awards. Specialist drama schools, both for children and adults, are to be found in many countries.

See also: creativity; extracurriculum; music; physical education

DAVID CROOK

DROPOUTS

Pupils and students who leave their school or course before graduating or completing the programme on which they are enrolled are often described as dropouts. At secondary/high school level a high incidence of dropouts may be a symptom of courses that are not appropriate for a wide range of students, or of highly competitive examinations that induce stress and failure. Grade retention often leads to dropping out of school. Insecurity of family finances may help to encourage pupils to drop out, although there is often a high incidence of middle-class dropouts. The later consequences of dropping out may be severe; in the United States in the later twentieth century, high school graduates earned on average about 30 per cent more than high school dropouts. In higher education, dropping out may be related to a broad or inclusive entrance policy, as an aspect of trends towards mass higher education. In individual cases there may be social, academic or financial reasons for dropping out from higher education. Members of particular social and cultural groups and students with disabilities may be especially at risk of dropping out from educational institutions that are not sympathetic to specific needs.

See also: early school leaving; grade retention; higher education; secondary school/education

GARY McCULLOCH

DUAL SYSTEM

Dual system is a term variously applied to two separate elements or approaches to education. For example, these may be the control and provision of education by church or state, public or private schooling, or academic or vocational curricula.

In the United Kingdom the term is particularly applied to the dual system of school provision that dates from the Education Act of 1870. Although this legislation provided for locally elected school boards and rate-aided schools, central government continued to supply financial assistance to many church and other voluntary schools. The nature and extent of this assistance and the concessions required from the voluntary bodies in return were modified under subsequent acts of 1902 and 1944. This latter legislation extended the dual system to secondary schools. Three types of voluntary schools were then designated: controlled, aided and special agreement. Controlled schools received all of their finance from the state, while aided and special agreement schools had to provide 50 per cent of building and repair costs. In the United Kingdom the term dual system is also applied, though less commonly, to the division between state maintained and assisted schools (the two elements of the dual system referred to above) and independent schools that receive no state aid. About 7 per cent of children currently attend independent schools. A further complexity within this duality is that the leading independent schools for boys, such as Eton and Westminster, have traditionally been referred to as public schools.

In Germany the dual system refers to the two elements in a programme of vocational training. About 70 per cent of all school leavers take part in this training, which is provided by a combination of central government, state- and employers' associations and lasts for two to three years depending on the occupation. Learning takes place on two sites: vocational schools provided by the individual states and workplace training overseen by central government and employers. Trainees spend one or two days per week in vocational schools and the remaining three or four days in the workplace. Two thirds of the time in school is spent on specialised training and one third on general education. The dual system is constantly being adapted in order to include new forms of employment, such as the media, and to make use of the latest technology.

In the United States the term dual system may also be used in at least two respects. The first is with reference to separate school streams – academic and vocational – particularly in high schools as they emerged in the early twentieth century. For example, in 1918 a report entitled *Cardinal Principles of Secondary Education* highlighted the need for more non-academic education. The second application is to differences between publicly and privately funded systems of education. Early American education had a mixed private and public character, but during the nineteenth century a system of public schools came to predominate. Supporters emphasised the democratic nature of these schools as against the elitist dimensions of private education.

In recent years the idea of the 'One Best System', an education monopoly controlled and financed by central and/or local government, has come under attack. Dual public and private systems already exist in higher education in many countries. Critics have drawn attention to low standards of attainment and behaviour in some public schools and have called for a return to a dual system in which religious and other private schools have a greater role. In the United Kingdom voluntary schools have remained popular with parents, largely on the grounds of their perceived superiority over local authority schools in terms of pupil attendance, behaviour and academic achievement. One recent central government initiative has been to replace poorly performing local authority schools with academies. These are sponsored by independent individuals or bodies who contribute to the capital cost and provide significant input into how the academy is run. The government's intention is to establish 200 academies (sixty of them in London) by 2010. In the United States, similar disillusion with inner-city public schools has led to demands for increased school choice. Some 10 per cent of children in elementary and secondary education currently attend private schools, most of which have a religious affiliation. The 2002 US Supreme Court ruling in favour of a voucher plan in Cleveland, Ohio, whereby public money could be used to support students in private religious schools, indicates that this type of dual system is still very much alive.

See also: church; vocational education; voluntarism

Further reading

Greinert, W-D. (1994) *The 'German System' of Vocational Education*, Baden-Baden: Nomos.
Murphy, J. (1970) *Church, State and Schools in Britain, 1800–1970*, London: Routledge and Kegan Paul.

RICHARD ALDRICH

DUBOIS, WILLIAM E. B. (1868–1963)

DuBois graduated from Fisk University, Nashville in 1885, proceeding to a second bachelor of arts degree and a master's at Harvard in 1890 and 1891 respectively. From there, with the support of former American president Rutherford B. Hayes he obtained a scholarship to study in Berlin, though he was forced to return after two years due to financial problems. DuBois became the first African-American to receive a doctorate from Harvard, having written a thesis on the suppression of the African slave trade in America. This became the first volume of the Harvard *Historical Studies* series. His interest in issues of race and discrimination led him to develop interests in other social science approaches; his study of black communities living in the Philadelphia slums is an early example of a sociological study. This work, and numerous further studies undertaken at Atlanta

University, which he joined in 1896, secured his position as a pioneer of American sociology. DuBois wrote about contemporary Africa as a varied and complex continent, overturning widely held misconceptions about the educational capacities of Americans of African descent. He also challenged conservative approaches to race and education and confronted Booker T. Washington's formidable influence and organisation. DuBois and William Monroe Trotter co-founded the Niagara Movement, which transmuted into the National Association for the Advancement of Colored People (NAACP). The NAACP campaigned for equality of educational provision, and supported the movements for black civil and political rights. DuBois founded the NAACP's official magazine *The Crisis* in 1910 and edited it personally until 1934, and was a leading figure in the Pan-African movement.

See also: antiracist education; multicultural education

STEVEN COWAN

DURKHEIM, EMILE (1858–1917)

Durkheim, the French sociologist of education, entered the Ecole Normale Supérieure in 1879, where he met his lifelong friend Jean Jaurès. He became a fervent republican, inspired by figures such as Léon Gambetta and Jules Ferry. Durkheim started teaching philosophy in 1882 and was appointed to take charge of the social science element of the new pedagogy course at Bordeaux. He immediately began to press for a sociological input into the other humanities being taught at the university. Between 1887 and 1902 Durkheim's principal work related to education. At the same time, through a series of lectures, he elaborated ideas about a range of social phenomena that were to make him an influential international figure in the development of the social sciences. He founded the *Année Sociologique* in 1898, thus placing himself at the centre of academic debate in the humanities. He moved to the Sorbonne

in 1902, becoming Professor of Education and Sociology in 1906. His course was compulsory for all humanities students, so his impact upon a future generation was enormous. Durkheim applied sociology to new fields through studies of suicide, incest and crime. He developed key concepts within the field such as *anomie* and used his position to advance a secular, scientific rationalism in the humanities, so offending many religious, academic and political figures. Later he was heavily involved in developing propaganda during World War I, but the devastating news of his son's death precipitated a stroke and Durkheim's own death at the age of fifty-nine. He is regarded as a founding father of modern educational and sociological studies.

See also: sociology of education

STEVEN COWAN

DYSLEXIA

Contrary to common belief, dyslexia is a processing difficulty, rather than merely a spelling and/or reading problem. Developmental dyslexia is present from birth and different from acquired dyslexia, a condition brought on by accident or disease causing brain trauma or sensory impairment. The population of people with dyslexia demonstrates the same distribution of intelligence (as measured by intelligence tests) as found in the wider population of people without dyslexia. Around 5–15 per cent of people are thought to have the condition.

Controversy has characterised all aspects of dyslexia, from doubts about its existence, through arguments about possible causes, to various strategies and 'cures'. Dyslexia is summarised by the World Health Organization (WHO) as a disorder caused by constitutional cognitive disabilities, and falls within the developmental disorder of scholastic skills section. The WHO also observes that children can be dismissed as lazy and their propensity to avoid repeated failure through unrewarding schoolwork compounds this issue (Girimaji *et al.* 2001: 16). Dyslexia generally becomes apparent when children begin formal learning. Some have argued that people with dyslexia are differently able in a way that improves creativity (Davis and Braun 1993).

Dyslexia is commonly used as an umbrella term for a range of learning problems. For example, the UK-based Dyslexia Institute includes associates dyslexia with difficulties with short-term memory, mathematics, concentration, personal organisation and sequencing, as well as the more usual reading, writing and spelling. There is disagreement as to the value of this approach, with some suggesting that more specific identification should lead to better remediation. Separating other conditions from dyslexia can be useful for the practitioner, who may identify various problems in mathematics (dyscalculia), kinaesthetic development (dyspraxia), spelling (dysorthographia) and handwriting (dysgraphia) (Montgomery 1998). Some theorists are more doubtful of the value of such 'pseudo-medical terms'.

In the late nineteenth century various neurological discoveries and investigations into people with language difficulties led to the terminologies of 'reading blindness', 'dyslexia' and 'word blindness'. As neuroscience and psychology developed, studies uncovered more complexities (e.g. some evidence for a dyslexia gene). It is now accepted that the gender incidence of dyslexia is equal. The previous emphasis on boys is explained as increased reporting, not occurrence. Internationally, prevalence of dyslexia is varied as it relates closely to reading and writing demands across languages. Phonic languages, such as Spanish, cause fewer problems than, for example, English and French.

Strategies for managing dyslexia are wide-ranging and of variable quality and efficacy. If the overriding difficulty is visual, sometimes transparent overlays or coloured spectacle lenses can make text more readable. Dyslexia as an auditory difficulty is ameliorated through phonological awareness therapy and in some cases dietary changes can result in reduced symptoms (e.g. where dyslexia accompanies Attention Deficit Disorder (ADD) or Hyperactivity Disorder (HD; known together as AD/HD)).

The most valuable approach is generally agreed to be classroom management and pedagogy. Adopting a systematic and explicit approach makes an enormous positive difference (see Westwood 2003: 1–17). This provides a sound basis for useful learning strategies and experiences, leading to independence. The following characteristics of effective teachers have been found to support the learning of children with dyslexia in the mainstream classroom:

- a well managed classroom;
- showing respect for all pupils;
- having high expectations;
- using explicit instruction;
- employing high rates of questioning to check understanding;
- providing frequent feedback;
- using a variety of resources;
- encouraging a cursive handwriting style;
- presenting content with a coherent structure;
- monitoring students closely;
- presenting material in a step-by-step manner but also providing a general overview;
- close marking only a section of written work (content only marked for the remainder);
- emphasising content over presentation;
- allowing technology such as spelling and grammar checkers in class;
- not neglecting teaching of language mechanics, but de-emphasising where the focus is on ideas or argument;
- not forcing children to read aloud in large group situations;
- giving short and frequent spelling tests (not long and infrequent ones).

See also: cognition; learning disabilities/
difficulties; psychology of education; reading;
spelling; underachievement

Further reading

Davis, R. D. and Braun, E. M. (1993) *The Gift of
Dyslexia*, Burlingame CA: Ability Workshop
Press.

Girimaji, S., Zaman, S. S., Wijetunga, P. M. and
Pejarasangharn, U. (2001) *Mental Retardation:
From Knowledge to Action*, New Delhi: WHO
Regional Office for Southeast Asia.

Montgomery, D. (1998) *Reversing Lower Attainment*, London: David Fulton.

Westwood, P. (2003) *Commonsense Methods for
Children with Special Educational Needs*, London:
RoutledgeFalmer.

CARRIE WINSTANLEY

EARLY CHILDHOOD EDUCATION

The term 'early childhood education' (ECE) is open to wide interpretation. The 'global early childhood landscape' (Hayden 2000) is shaped by the social, economic, political, professional and philosophical context of each individual nation's culture. The term ECE itself embraces much that is the province of childcare services (hence the comparatively recent coining of the word 'educare'). The form and content of the education available to very young children is varied. In addition, there is no universally recognised consensus on the age-phase to which 'early childhood' refers within an individual's life span. The World Organisation for Early Childhood Education (widely known as OMEP, the Organisation Mondiale pour l'Education Prescolaire/Organizacion Mundial para la Educacion Preescolar) and the National Association for the Education of Young Children (NAEYC) define 'early childhood' as the period from birth to eight years of age. But, for example, in New Zealand it refers to children from birth to five, in Canada the focus is on the age phase immediately prior to mainstream compulsory schooling (kindergarten) and in the United Kingdom, the main focus of the present government has moved from the education of children of 3–5 years to encompass the period between birth and five years of age.

The expansion of ECE, in developed countries, at least, is due to two powerful influences. First, demand for increased childcare provision has arisen in response to the needs of parents in employment. Second, it derives from governments' growing awareness of the importance and benefit of preschool education for every child. The Audit Commission for the United Kingdom (1996) concluded that 'Children's early educational experience is crucial for developing the socialisation and learning skills that they will need throughout their lives'.

Changing historical contexts and different concepts of childhood inform the purpose of ECE. In the seventeenth century, Locke suggested that the child is born as a tabula rasa, a blank tablet or empty vessel waiting passively to be filled with a predetermined body of knowledge, and is receptive to receiving a defined range of skills and existing cultural values. This view assumes that the period of childhood must be capitalised upon in order to equip, through training, the child for the rigours of later education and the demands of adulthood. An alternative view is Rousseau's idea of the child as *an innocent* rather than an asset to society. The intrinsic goodness of Rousseau's child is regarded as something to be protected by adults from the evils of life. A third, and later, view portrayed the child as the product of science. The child in this paradigm is claimed to possess from birth inherent fixed characteristics that develop through a series of predetermined biological stages which leads to full physical, social and intellectual maturity.

Many individuals have influenced the form and content of ECE. Some are theorists, some philanthropists and others psychologists. Whilst the details of each individual's impact differs, the belief which each of the pioneers held dear is that the early years of life are formative and have an important role in enabling the individual to achieve their potential. Froebel, Montessori and Steiner were internationally renowned scholars and practitioners who founded schools, nurseries and training colleges espousing their beliefs and theories. The impact of their ideas can still be witnessed in preschools today. In the UK, Margaret McMillan and Susan Isaacs progressed Froebel's theories through the twentieth century, basing much of their practice on the study of child development. Ten principles of practice evolved from the ideas of the pioneers, which centre around the notion of childhood being a life phase in its own right, and not merely a preparation for later life. The idea that the child needs to be considered holistically is fundamental.

These ideas have formed the bedrock of what goes on in the name of ECE today, but other influences are to be found also. Psychologists such as Piaget, Vygotsky, Bruner and Donaldson have contributed to understanding about how very young children can learn most effectively. A brief summary is that children's thinking is qualitatively different in different phases of their development. The social context of learning is considered to be crucial and children learn most successfully when supported by more experienced learners and if the experience is set within a meaningful and interesting context.

Childhood is a time of rich individuality, but is also a social and cultural construct, so different skills and competencies are valued by particular societies. For example, physical skills, agility, grace and stamina are highly prized in African countries, along with the expectation that children will care for the very young. Curiosity, and self-directed and self-motivated activity are encouraged in nurseries in the UK, but obedience and passive,

receptive behaviour are considered desirable attributes in the Indian subcontinent. Pre-school or early childhood institutions (which more accurately include settings involved with mainly childcare) have many labels and each has its own connotation across the world: nursery, crèche, childcare centre, *daghem, asilo nido*, nursery school, kindergarten, *école maternelle, scuola d'infanzia*, and so on (Dahlberg *et al.* 1999). The programmes within these many settings offer a continuum of educational experience from overtly academically orientated provision and didactic teaching through to play-based learning opportunities with greater or lesser emphasis on curriculum content and predetermined outcomes.

The potential benefit of ECE appears to be supported by recent research evidence derived from neurobiological studies of the brain. Recent techniques, such as functional magnetic resonance imaging and positive emission topography, which measure the activity in the brain as tasks are performed, show that the brain is plastic and capable of continued development when stimulated and used extensively. Babies' brains are especially active. The brain of a two-year-old child has an energy consumption at the full adult level; by three years old it is twice as active as an adult's brain, at which level it remains until nine or ten years of age, when activity starts to decline. Three implications arise from this work for ECE:

- There is a very rapid increase in the development of the number of synapses (the wiring of nerve connections) between neurons (brain cells) in infancy and childhood.
- It has been suggested that there are 'critical periods' when sensory and motor systems in the brain require experience for maximum development. It is as if the brain can only develop optimally in this time span.
- In some mammals it has been shown that the more enriched and complex their environment, the greater number of synapses will form.

The findings of this research appear to offer sufficient evidence to support the case for an enriched environment and sensitive adult support in the early years of life. Gopnik *et al.* build on this notion of the child's amazing capacity by describing her/him as 'literally an alien genius' and suggest that 'Children can take advantage of an innately determined foundation, powerful learning abilities and implicit tuition from other people' (1999: 186).

Whilst there have been many intervention studies in ECE (see Ramey and Ramey 1998), one longitudinal study undertaken in the USA provides convincing evidence on the long-lasting value of preschool education. The High/Scope Perry Pre-school Evaluation (Schweinhart *et al.* 1993) is a robustly designed intervention programme and associated evaluation over a long period, with a random sample of 123 participants living in deprived circumstances. With regard to educational determinants, the programme participants compared with the control group were:

- less likely to be placed in programmes for mental impairment;
- more likely to have higher average school grades;
- graduating on time from high school more successfully;
- having higher levels of literacy by the end of secondary education.

And with regard to quality of life determinants, the participants:

- were earning a higher salary;
- were more likely to own their homes;
- were less likely to receive social services support;
- had a lower rate of involvement with crime.

More recent British evidence comes from the ongoing Effective Provision of Pre-school Education study (1997–2008) at the Institute of Education, University of London. This study has monitored approximately 2,800 children from 141 widely different types of preschool centres and 300-plus 'home' children since they were three years old. It assesses each of the participants on a range of measures of social and intellectual functioning, both prior to, and at intervals throughout, the project. It collects data on both the home environment and parental characteristics of these children, and also assesses the type and quality of the settings and the educational provision offered to the children for the duration of the project.

The main findings to date are as follows:

- high-quality settings boosted children's developmental progress over the preschool period;
- higher quality was found in integrated settings and nursery schools;
- the quality of provision was higher in settings with more qualified staff especially teachers;
- the relative influence of social class and poverty is reduced at school entry as a result of preschool experience;
- high-quality preschool reduces the risk of children having special educational needs from one in three to one in five.

The growing evidence of the benefit of ECE has spurred many governments to expand provision. This, in turn, presents challenges that are both financial and logistical, regarding such issues as managing the level and quality of training for early years practitioners. However, the commitment appears to be there with general support for the following statement:

A society can be judged by its attitude to its very youngest children, not only in what is said about them but how this attitude is expressed in what is offered to them as they grow up.

(Goldschmied and Jackson 1994, cited in Abbott and Gillen 1997)

See also: Bruner, Jerome; child development; crèche; Froebel, Friedrich; Isaacs, Susan;

kindergarten; Locke, John; McMillan, Margaret; Montessori, Maria; nursery school; Piaget, Jean; Rousseau, Jean-Jacques; Steiner, Rudolf; Vygotsky, Lev

Further reading

Abbott, L. and Gillen, J. (1997) (eds) *Educare for the Under Threes: Identifying Need and Opportunity.* Report of the research study by the Manchester Metropolitan University jointly funded with the Esmee Fairbairn Charitable Trust. Manchester: Manchester Metropolitan University.

Audit Commission (1996) *Counting to Five: Education of Children under Five*, London: HMSO.

Brannen, J. and O'Brien, M. (1995) *Childhood and Parenthood. Proceedings of the International Sociological Association Committee for Family Research Conference, 1994*, London: Institute of Education.

Chan, K. S. and Mellor, E. J. (eds) (2002) *International Developments in Early Childhood Services*, New York: Peter Lang.

Dahlberg, G. Moss, P. and Pence, A. (1999) *Beyond Quality in Early Childhood Education and Care*, Hong Kong: Routledge.

Goldschmied, E. and Jackson, S. (1994) *People under Three: Young Children in Daycare*, London: Routledge.

Gopnik, A., Meltzoff, A. and Kuhl, P. (1999) *How Babies Think*, London: Phoenix Paperback.

Hayden, J. (2000) *Landscapes in Early Childhood Education: Cross-national Perspectives on Empowerment. A Guide for the New Millennium*, New York: Peter Lang.

Penn, H. (1997) *Comparing Nurseries: Staff and Children in Italy, Spain and the UK*, London: Paul Chapman Publishing.

Ramey, C. and Ramey, S. L. (1998) 'Early intervention and early experience', *American Psychologist*, 27: 243–69.

Riley, J. L. (ed.) (2004) *Learning in the Early Years: A Guide for Teachers of Children 3–7*, London: Paul Chapman Publishing.

Schweinhart, L. J., Barnes, H. V. and Weikart, D. P. (1993) *Significant Benefits: The High/Scope Perry Pre-School Study through Age 27*, Ypsilanti MI: High/Scope Educational Research Foundation.

JENI RILEY

EARLY SCHOOL LEAVING

The aim of universal provision of post-compulsory schooling was established during the post-World War II reconstruction, especially in so-called 'developed' countries. But such an aim has been impossible to realise in practice, as significant numbers of young people leave before completing their high school years and hence 'fail' to achieve that reputable credential that often acts as an entry into further forms of education, especially university. As a consequence, schooling policy in this area suffers an ongoing legitimation crisis that continues today. In essence, the nation-state argues that its schooling system is universally good for all young people but then can't deliver. Explanations are needed for the development of policy interventions that might help, which establishes a field for educational research that has mostly been dominated by large-scale quantitative surveys that track young people through their schooling. Governments measure the problem by such means as retention rates: a measure of the percentage of students who stay on during their high school years. One of the significant narratives in this research has been an account of why young people 'drop out' of school. This term 'dropout' is now widely accepted in the literature and in the public culture, and sustains its currency as common sense through drawing on the moral panic of youth as trouble (Roman 1996).

But in Fine's (1991) words, we have been 'framing dropouts'. The term framing is being used here to refer to a 'frame-up' or a deliberate attempt to misrepresent. Fine calls attention to the way 'dropouts' are too often (mis)represented, as 'depressed, helpless, and even without options . . . as losers' (1991: 4–5). For Fine, the frame-up obscures the 'structures, ideologies, and practices that exile them systematically' (1991: 5) and hence pushes all the responsibility for leaving school early onto those young people who engage in that 'tactic'. The frame-up lets the system off the hook: we don't have to continue to work at improving curriculum, pedagogy, school structures, or school culture, and the policies that make things possible. Instead, as the argument goes, the system is working well enough: all we need to do is tinker at the edges, and provide alternatives for those who can't make it in the mainstream. Of course, what gets laminated over in such a framing is that school 'dropouts' are predominantly from working-class or underclass families, or from communities that have been historically disenfranchised or colonised within the nation-state. Young people from these communities are grossly under-represented in universities.

As a counter to this derogatory framing there are other terms competing for the attention of policy and research, such as 'early school leavers', 'early exitors', or 'students at risk of not completing schooling'. The term 'early school leaving' has been in use for many decades and provides a framing that is descriptive, carries the policy imperative of universal provision, and does not overtly blame young people for leaving school. The category provides a frame for more sociological explanations and ones that are based on qualitative forms of research that involve listening to young people who have left school early (Smyth and Hattam 2004), and that provide interpretations that do justice to the complex lives of early school leavers. The concept of 'early school leaving' confronts the moral economy that operates in these debates that pretends that it is possible to distinguish between those young people who are deserving and neglect honourably those who don't try hard enough. Unfortunately, such views still dominate the logic of schooling systems worldwide and, as a consequence, many nations have 'low equity' (McGaw 2004) education systems, understood here to mean that their schooling systems produce a small, highly educated elite and a long tail of educational underachievement.

Research that takes early school leaving seriously and ponders how schooling might be transformed around the interests of the least advantaged (Connell 1993), proposes a complex explanation for why young people leave school early. Very briefly, this theory brings into play investigations into:

- the nature of the cultural geography of school;
- how school policy and policy about youth constitute what happens in schools and especially what counts as 'good' teaching;
- the distorting effects of credentialing on what happens in schools, especially how sorting and selecting practices get to undermine assessment practices and hence learning;
- the changing nature of the interface between schooling and the labour market and how the purposes of schooling get overwhelmed by the imperatives of international economic competitiveness, and being entrepreneurial; and
- the nature of processes of identity formation of young people and the ways in which they work with their own class location, racial signification, sexuality and gender to make decisions about staying on or leaving school.

The problem of 'early school leaving' does not look like it will go away in the near future, and hence the legitimation crisis underlying the problem will only intensify because of the increasing disparity of educational outcomes. More research is required that brings together quantitative and qualitative methods, that is longitudinal and helps us to understand the ways in which young people's identities are being constituted with and without school (McLeod and Yates 2006).

See also: compulsory education; retention; underachievement; universal education

Further reading

Connell, R. (1993) *Schools and Social Justice*, Leichhardt NSW: Pluto.

Fine, M. (1991) *Framing Dropouts: Notes on the Politics of an Urban High School*, Albany NY: State University of New York Press.

McLeod, J. and Yates, L. (2006) *Making Modern Lives: Subjectivity, Schooling, and Social Change*, New York: SUNY Press.

McGaw, B. (2004) 'Learning power of PISA', *Times Educational Supplement*, 12, March.

Roman, L. (1996) 'Spectacle in the dark: youth as transgression, display, and repression', *Educational Theory*, 46(1): 1–22.

Smyth, J. and Hattam, R. (2004) *'Dropping Out', Drifting Off, being Excluded: Becoming Somebody Without School*, New York: Peter Lang.

Wexler, P. (1992) *Becoming Somebody: Towards a Social Psychology of the School*, London: Falmer Press.

ROBERT HATTAM

EAST ASIA

East Asia as a term may be used to define both a geographical area and a group of people. In particular, it refers to the countries of China, Japan and Korea. In terms of a broader historical and educational perspective, the nineteenth century was a turning point. The region faced the influx of new political powers and cultures from the West, especially following the first Opium War (1839–42). Modernising impulses swept across many parts of the region with political, industrial, philosophical and epistemological awakening from the mid-century. A number of Western thinkers also impacted upon educational ideas in East Asia, including Jean-Jacques Rousseau (1712–78), Immanuel Kant (1724–1804), Johann Heinrich Pestalozzi (1746–1827), Friedrich Froebel (1782–1852) and Johann Friedrich Herbart (1776–1841). During the 1920s the influence of John Dewey would also be felt.

The emergence of nation-states required highly qualified personnel, as well as a wider mass of people with sufficient literacy. Accordingly, new initiatives in mass schooling were introduced alongside elite learning institutions for the selected few. Although there are significant national differences, each country developed universal popular education, including vocational training, with advanced learning for a minority. These systems borrowed from European and American models. As the first imperial power in the region, Japan also introduced elements of its own educational system into its new territories.

World War II further stimulated educational reform. After 1945, civil wars broke out in China and Korea, while a US-Allied force occupied Japan. In 1948 Korea was split into the Democratic People's Republic of Korea in the north and the Republic of Korea in the south; in 1949 the People's Republic of China was established; finally, Japan became independent in 1951.

US education missions were sent to Japan in 1946 and 1950, and their recommendations were influential in setting up post-war educational systems. Compulsory education, from ages 6–13, was lengthened to nine years; co-education became obligatory in public sector; a 6–3–3 system of schooling was initiated with six years of elementary school and three years of junior high school followed by three years of senior high school; 'social study' was introduced, replacing 'shushin' or moral education; and the education of teachers and social workers was entrusted to new universities. Democratisation of Japanese society through education was a key impulse behind post-war reconstruction. These innovative educational ideas were prescribed in the Japanese Constitution (1946), the Fundamental Law of Education (1947), the Laws of School Education (1947) and others.

From the 1960s, with the recovery of Japanese capitalism, educational reform continued in line with a broadly conservative public climate. Government and business were both influenced by the *Sputnik* shock and rapid technological changes that were taking place. Increasingly a subject-centred curriculum replaced the child-centred one. In quick succession, there were calls for the diversification of the school system and the introduction of advanced vocational differentiation. During the 1980s, new educational doctrines, influenced by neo-liberal philosophy, would become increasingly popular, based on individualisation, internationalisation, lifelong learning and adaptation to the information age. After the 1990s, market principles became dominant and post-war principles were uprooted. For example, in 2004 all national and public universities became independent administrative corporations, which enjoy considerable autonomy despite some continuing accountability to the state.

After 1949, educational innovation in China was closely linked to constitutional and legal change. In 1954, the first Chinese Constitution proclaimed education for all people and a 5–3–3–4 school system was established. Significant reforms have followed on from the revised Constitution (1982) as well as legislative changes such as the Compulsory Education Act (1986), the Law of Teachers (1993), the Education Law of the People's Republic of China (1995) and the Vocational Education Act (1996). The periods of 'Great Leap Forward' from 1958 and 'Re-Adjustment' from 1960 were expected to bring steady progress in Chinese society and education. However, the Great Proletarian Cultural Revolution (1966–76) prevented Chinese education from progressing. After the Revolution, a gradual recovery and modification of the education system took place along socialistic lines. From the 1970s – and particularly during the 1980s and 1990s – Chinese society and education shifted towards modernisation, 'market socialism' and 'deregulation for reconstruction'. Education was under constant scrutiny and assessment, given the recognition that it played a crucial role in the development of the country. More recently, a national educational infrastructure has been developed and education is currently enmeshed in the explosive economic growth now taking place.

After bitter struggles against Japanese colonialism, the Korean people achieved victory in 1945. The 1948 general election marked the birth of the first Republic of Korea in the south. In the same year, the new Constitution and the Law of Education were enacted, the latter declaring that people have the right to free primary compulsory education. The aims of public education were precisely described. The Korean War (1950–53),

however, hindered the first Republic from implementing the goals of educational development. After the demise of the military regime, the second Republic (1960–61) and third Republic (1963–72) strove for educational development. The National Charter of Education (1968) reflected the emphasis on modernisation, economic and social development and national and spiritual independence. From the 1980s, educational policy has become increasingly attuned to international and global interests.

Modernisation in East Asia has taken place in the context of an encounter between East and West. Growth has not simply followed a Western model but has also been influenced by persistent endogenous cultures, which, to some extent, have also been encouraged by globalisation, market principles and information technology. A number of hidden cultural idioms can be discovered. First, the notion of literacy has changed considerably in East Asia, although the early practices of the Chinese 'keju' examination system (587–1905) continue to have an influence. Keju was a way of selecting public servants, the essence of which is to let candidates compete by memorising selected classics and composing essays or poems on given topics, relying on the prose and poems memorised. Thus, those in political authority authenticated the practice of literacy. Today, rote learning, controlled by those in power, continues to exert a significant influence on educational systems in East Asia. Second, East Asian countries share spatial and national senses of being. The names of bodies politic in East Asia suggest prototype images of nation and ethnicity. *Chunghua Jenmin Kungho Kuo* (Peoples Republic of China) places China at the centre of the world (this being the literal meaning of *Chunghua*). During the Li dynasty in Korea, the dynasty (body politic) identified itself as a subordinate political body to the Chinese dynasties, but at the same time it viewed itself a minor centre of the Korean peninsula. Japan, or *Nippon*, also suggests the origin of the rising sun, another image of the centre of

191

the world. In these senses, 'being centred' is a key intuition in the context of East Asian world-views. They relate to a form of nationalism that, at times, rejects outsiders. Third, East Asian cultures tend to view time cyclically – rather than in the Western linear way – which affects planning and accountability in education.

Despite national differences, the attempts to develop popular education in the twentieth century among East Asian countries reflect common issues and problems. Although compulsory school enrolment is nearly 100 per cent in Korea and Japan, these countries also suffer from school-phobia and excessive competition among school children; the 'eclipse' of childhood has even been observed in Japan. The 'one child per family' policy in China has also wrought many problems. In addition, low levels of literacy among adults, women and minority groups remain unsolved obstacles to progress. The practice of teacher education is often far from the ideal and teachers are excessively controlled. Discrepancies between the 'haves' and the 'have-nots', and between highly urbanised areas and rural locations, are also reflected in the unequal provision of educational services. Privatisation in education has also further increased inequality. Although the nation-state as provider of popular education has served to enlighten many people, the role of the state is increasingly coming under scrutiny. Globalisation is fostering internationalisation across borders and, in time, new bodies may appear which require new forms of education in a context of rapid social and economic change.

See also: China; Japan

Further reading

Bray, M. (ed.) (2003) *Comparative Education: Continuing Traditions, New Challenges and New Paradigms*, Dordrecht, the Netherlands: Kluwer.

Fagerlind, I. and Saha, L. J. (1989), *Education and National Development: A Comparative Perspective*, 2nd edn, Oxford: Pergamon.

Hayhoe, R. (ed.) (1984) *Contemporary Chinese Education*, Beckenham: Croom Helm.

Keeves, J. and Watanabe, R. (eds) (2003) *International Handbook of Educational Research in the Asia-Pacific Region*, Dordrecht, the Netherlands: Kluwer.

Sullivan, K. (ed.) (1998) *Education and Change in the Pacific Rim: Meeting the Challenges*, Oxford: Triangle.

Thomas, E. (ed.) (2002) *Teacher Education: Dilemmas and Prospects. World Yearbook of Education 2002*, London: Kogan Page.

Umakoshi, T. (ed.) (1989) *Education in Contemporary Asia: Tradition and Innovation* (Japanese version), Tokyo: Toshindo.

SHINICHI SUZUKI

ECONOMICS

Economics, a subject taught in higher education institutions and to pupils in the upper school age ranges, concerns the study of the production, distribution and consumption of goods and services. Most contemporary definitions of mainstream economics involve notions of scarcity and choice; the economic problem being the concern of allocating finite resources amongst competing ends. Consumers, business and governments must all make choices and the cost of their decisions may be measured in monetary terms (price) or in terms of foregone alternatives (opportunity cost).

Economics was famously defined by Alfred Marshall (1842–1924) as the 'study of man's actions in the ordinary business of life'. Whilst Adam Smith is often described as 'the Father of Economics' and references are made to the 'invisible hand' he wrote about in *The Wealth of Nations* (1776), it is Marshall who is the founder of modern economics as we know it. Marshall's *The Principles of Economics* (1890) brought together the concepts of supply and demand, costs of production and the idea of the *margin*, which is the cornerstone of modern microeconomics.

Whilst microeconomics is concerned about how individuals and businesses make decisions about resource allocation, macroeconomics deals with the economy as a whole and how government policy may influence it. Macro-economics concerns the study of unemployment, inflation, economic growth and the balance of payments. A longstanding tension exists between monetarists and Keynesians on how to best manage the economy. Keynesians advocate government interventions to positively influence employment and growth through changes in the levels of taxation and public spending. Monetarists worry that financing public expenditure through excessive borrowing may be inflationary.

See also: curriculum; economics of education; subjects

JACEK BRANT

ECONOMICS OF EDUCATION

While economics of education was initially concerned mostly with estimating economic returns to schooling and the relationship of education to economic growth, more recently it has increasingly encompassed issues of school effectiveness and analysis of the institutional conditions most conducive to the efficient provision of education.

Economics of education is sometimes regarded as a sub-discipline of labour economics, since it started in the 1960s by asking whether and to what extent education improves labour quality, in terms of increased worker productivity. Theodore Schultz's (1963) work on the economic value of education started what came to be known as the 'human capital revolution' in economics. Jacob Mincer (1974) subsequently made seminal theoretical contributions, including devising a way to estimate the economic rate of return to (an extra year of) education. A further major theoretical thrust was the enunciation of endogenous growth theory in the late 1980s, which suggested that sustained economic growth comes from spillovers ('positive externalities') in learning and knowledge from one worker to other nearby workers, and this placed education and learning at the centre of the explanation for economic growth. More recently, theoretical work has pushed frontiers in various ways, for example, by allowing economic returns to education to vary across individuals and specifying the conditions under which school voucher schemes can lead to equitable outcomes, among others (Hanushek and Welch 2006).

While economics of education involves the study of theoretical aspects, applied work has become more and more important over time. This reflects in part a greatly increased policy interest in the analysis of education. This is evident in both developed and developing countries, the latter spurred by the fact that universalisation of basic education and removal of gender disparities in educational access are two of the eight Millennium Development Goals. However, the increase in applied work in education economics also partly reflects the progressively greater availability of appropriate data over time. For instance, the compilation of cross-country data spanning 1960 to the present times has enabled empirical research on the relationship between education and economic growth. Similarly, from the early 1990s, reliable household datasets began to be available in many developing countries, permitting analysis of educational access and research on the relationship between education, on the one hand, and labour market and social outcomes, on the other. In many developed countries datasets have also become available on schools and teachers linked to student achievement test scores (sometimes on the same student, over time), allowing analysis of school quality and students' learning outcomes.

The availability of more and better data means that education economics is currently the subject of a great deal of applied research and discussion. Some of the topics of interest have been:

- Can the effect of education on earnings be separated from the effect of innate ability on earnings?
- Does education enhance economic growth?

- Should policy makers be concerned with expanding schooling supply or improving the quality of existing schools? This is known as the quantity versus quality debate.
- What teacher and school factors determine schooling participation of children and achievement levels of students?
- The relative efficiency, cost-effectiveness and equity effects of alternative delivery mechanisms in education.
- Impact evaluation of educational policy interventions, using methods that permit causal inferences

Much empirical work in economics of education has been concerned with measurement of returns to education, also termed the 'external efficiency' of schooling. Estimates of economic returns to different types of education are often used to inform public policy on budgetary allocations and on fee rates for different university subjects. However, empirical education economics is increasingly concerned with the internal efficiency of the schooling system, i.e. with the extent to which inputs into schooling lead to good educational outcomes, including in learning achievement levels. Controversy continues in 'school effectiveness research' over what school and teacher factors raise school participation and student achievement, and whether inputs-based (as opposed to incentives-based) policies are an effective means of improving school quality.

The role of the private sector in education, public–private partnerships in education and the role of incentives in motivating local level accountability have interested education economists. One way of introducing accountability within schools, namely through school voucher schemes, has been extensively analysed, both theoretically and through applied research. There has also been interest in examining the efficiency and equity implications of the pattern of intra-sectoral allocation of public education expenditure as between the different levels of education, the equity implications often being assessed by examining benefit incidence and the effectiveness of targeting of educational subsidies.

Studies based on randomised experiments are increasingly recognised by leading education economists as more reliable in permitting causal inferences, though other statistical techniques used in the discipline are also those shared with other disciplines, such as regression analysis, panel data analysis, propensity score matching methods, selectivity correction modelling and models to deal with 'endogeneity' biases.

See also: economics; educational studies; quantitative research; school effectiveness; vouchers

Further reading

Hanushek, E. and Welch, F. (eds) (2006) *Handbook on the Economics of Education*, Amsterdam: Elsevier.
Mincer, J. (1974) *Schooling, Experience and Earnings*, New York: National Bureau of Economic Research.
Schultz, T. (1963) *The Economic Value of Education*, New York: Columbia University Press.

GEETA KINGDON

EDGEWORTH, MARIA (1767–1849)

Edgeworth was brought up under the influence of her father, Richard Lovell Edgeworth (1744–1817), who was a member of the Anglo-Irish gentry. She was privately schooled in Derby and London, developing a gift for the French and Italian languages. Maria was the second of her father's twenty-two children, born to four wives, so her earliest practical involvement as an educator came with teaching her younger siblings. During her father's absence abroad Maria managed his estates and became well networked within the Unitarian movement, meeting Erasmus Darwin and others. There is some debate about whether her early writings were collaborations with her father, but she rose to prominence following publication of *Letters to Literary Ladies* (1795), a strong defence of a liberal education for women. Edgeworth's two-volume *Practical Education* (1798) and her six-part *The Parent's Assistant*, completed between 1796 and 1800, present in English an applied and adapted version of Rousseau's ideas, also reflecting the progressive characteristics of late eighteenth-century Unitarianism. She presented an alternative approach to teaching and learning to that advocated by followers of Sarah Trimmer and Joseph Lancaster. Her commitment to 'associationism' promoted a commitment to children learning through discovery, and she is therefore an early supporter of what came to be known as 'progressivism' in education. Edgeworth's influence was extended by the popularity of her fiction writing.

See also: progressive education

STEVEN COWAN

EDUCATION

Issues about the meaning of the term 'education' should be distinguished from issues about what the aims of education should be. The latter are much more interesting than the former. Radical child-centred notions that adults should not impose their own aims on children are deeply problematic: education cannot but be a kind of socialisation. Liberal democratic societies may be expected to have educational aims not shared more universally. These go beyond the traditional notion of inculcating a love of knowledge for its own sake, to embrace equipping young people with the understanding and dispositions to lead autonomous lives within a framework of civic virtues and responsibilities. This account still leaves unresolved various philosophical and practical problems.

A lot has been written about the nature of education (Peters 1966, chs 1, 2): about whether education is about 'leading out' or 'leading in'; whether it is essentially about encouraging mental growth or initiation into intrinsically worthwhile activities; what demarcates education from training or indoctrination.

As some of these examples show, apparently factual statements about what education essentially is can conceal recommendations about what it should be aiming at. But it is better to address this latter question for what it is and disentangle it from attempts at definition. 'Education' has no single meaning. In a broad sense, it can refer to upbringing. More narrowly, it has to do with institutional learning, in schools or colleges. Travel can also be called educational, and so can the mores of a society.

A more interesting question about education is about what we should be aiming at in the upbringing of young people. Some would say that this already begs the question, since it is not for us — as parents, teachers, policy makers — to impose goals on children. For developmentalists, children, like plants, are organisms with inbuilt directionality; for liberationists, children should be as free as anyone else to set their own goals.

There are problems with both positions (Hirst and Peters 1970: ch. 3; Dearden 1976: ch. 4). That children grow physically is indisputable, but there is no good reason to extrapolate the idea of growth — in the same biological sense — to minds. To say that children should be autonomous goal-setters presupposes that they already have an understanding of the goals from which they are to choose. But this understanding cannot be spun out of themselves.

Upbringing can only be induction. Children need to become language-users. This involves learning concepts, and learning concepts involves coming to know in what circumstances it is *correct* to use words like 'dog' or 'because'. Children have to learn how to operate within public rules of this sort, as well as public expectations in more specific areas — moral norms, for instance, or those which are constitutive features of games and intellectual activities like the pursuit of science. In these and other areas, children have to get things *right*. They have to be corrected when they make mistakes, develop habits of acting in accordance with what is expected of them. None of this could happen if they were left to their own – or nature's – devices. They can only learn via interaction with those already adept at operating within the norms.

So upbringing is induction into social practices. But *which*? What goals should educators follow? Is there a universal answer to this question, applicable to any human society?

One would expect *some* common practices. Every society will want children to learn their mother tongue. All will want them to regulate their physical desires – for food, drink, sex – as well as basic emotions like anger and fear. Probably all will be looking to build up some minimal concern for others' interests. Beyond such commonalities there is room for great diversity.

Many of us would say that educators should want children to learn to think for themselves, to question received opinion. But in nearly all human societies this must have been, and for many still is, out of the question. The aim reflects the values of a specifically liberal culture, in which intellectual and personal autonomy are central ideals. For its adherents, it may come naturally to oppose education to indoctrination – to favour opening minds rather than closing them. But in the tradition-bound societies that have almost always existed, upbringing must have been based on unreflective conformity to social customs; and in a world like our own, where people know of alternatives, religious and political authorities can still try to inoculate children against them.

Young people can be brought up to obey God, to know their – usually lowly – place in the social structure, to follow their leaders towards the Revolution. The aims of their education are derived from the values of their social group. The same is true of children brought up under aims deriving from the values of a liberal-democratic society. Whether this makes them culture-relative in a permissive sense is a further question. It is not unproblematic to say that liberal aims are all right in a liberal society, while fascist aims are all right in a fascist one.

Suppose we focus now on the aims of upbringing in a liberal-democratic society – or at least among parents and teachers of a liberal outlook, even if their wider society does not share it. What should they be (White 1990; Levinson 1999)?

Thinking for oneself has already been mentioned. We want children to be intellectually autonomous, to accept beliefs only on the basis of appropriate evidence. Why?

One answer is that the pursuit of truth in its various forms – scientific, historical, mathematical, etc. – is something worthwhile in itself. This view has been influential over the last century, especially in elite schooling. It has provided the rationale for a curriculum based on a range of academic disciplines to be engaged in for their own sake.

But it is hard to justify as a central educational aim. *Scholars* are interested in the pursuit of truth for its own sake, but there is no warrant for imposing this life-ideal on schoolchildren, only few of whom will become scholars. Three hundred years ago, when this broad academic curriculum was seen as providing the knowledge about God's world required for personal salvation, the aim was more understandable. Today it lacks foundation.

Embedded in the last paragraph is the thought that individuals should follow their own ideals of how to live a human life. As autonomous choosers, they should be made aware of all sorts of possible ingredients of a worthwhile life – not only scholarship, but also social service, intimate personal relationships, raising children, aesthetic pursuits, sport, self-knowledge, entrepreneurship. ... For this their school curriculum will need to provide a broad range of understanding and experience, by no means only in traditional disciplines. Thinking for oneself now gets a different rationale from the scholarly one: it becomes a necessary condition of putting together an autonomous life.

The liberal ideal is not to bring children up to be autonomous atoms, but to equip them with cooperative dispositions as citizens – not only of their immediate political communities, but also more globally (Callan 1997). In addition to the more self-regarding virtues they will need to lead a flourishing personal life – such things as self-control, confidence, practical intelligence, financial capability, self-regulation of physical desires – this also means encouraging them to be attentive to others' needs, both in their day-to-day interactions and within larger communities. Vocational aims are part of this picture. As autonomous persons in the making, young people will not be expected to follow their parents' occupations but to choose their own form of personally and communally valuable work. For this they will need a good understanding of the whole range of work available to them.

This account of educational aims brings with it implications for radical curriculum reform. It urges us not to start and finish, as we often lazily do, with an array of traditional school subjects, but to go back to fundamental goals and work out from there what curricular vehicles are best suited to realise them.

There are unresolved philosophical issues in this account: about the nature of personal well-being and whether its ingredients are merely dependent on informed individual preferences; about the relationship between individuals' own flourishing and moral demands on them; about the place of work in the good life; about the status of autonomy aims in multicultural societies, not all groups in which are attached to the autonomy ideal.

There are also unresolved practical issues – not only about the curriculum, but also about realising the liberal value of equality of respect in countries where the more affluent use educational systems to create personal, vocational and financial advantages for their children and so reduce opportunities for others (Swift 2003).

See also: curriculum; educational research; educational studies; educational theory; subjects

Further reading

Callan, E. (1997) *Creating Citizens*, Oxford: Oxford University Press
Dearden, R. F. (1976) *Problems of Primary Education*, London: Routledge and Kegan Paul.
Hirst, P. H. and Peters, R. S. (1970) *The Logic of Education*, London: Routledge and Kegan Paul.
Levinson, M. (1999) *The Demands of Liberal Education*, Oxford: Oxford University Press.
Peters, R. S. (1966) *Ethics and Education*, London: Allen and Unwin.
Swift, A. (2003) *How Not to Be a Hypocrite*, London: Routledge.
White, J. (1990) *Education and the Good Life*, London: Kogan Page.

JOHN WHITE

EDUCATION FOR ALL

Education For All (EFA) is a concerted international effort for universal education to mobilise funding by governments, multilateral agencies and non-governmental organisations that was first launched in Jomtien, Thailand, in 1990. In 2000, the United Nations included among its eight Millennium Development Goals (MDGs) two EFA goals to 'ensure that, by 2015, children everywhere, boys and girls alike, will be able to complete a full course of primary schooling' and 'eliminate gender disparity in primary and secondary education preferably by 2005 and in all levels of education no later than 2015'. EFA further promised to expand early childhood education, ensure free and compulsory primary education by 2015, promote learning and life skills programmes for young people and adults, expand adult literacy by 50 per cent by 2015, and enhance educational quality.

In 2002, major development banks and government funders followed up with the Fast Track Initiative (FTI), 'to accelerate progress', realising the centrality of education to the other MDGs and the sobering fact that more than eighty developing countries were unlikely to achieve the EFA goals. The FTI rests on a set of education policy and financing parameters, which tie receiving countries into a strict panel of controls.

EFA progress counts a reduction in out-of-school primary school-age children by around 21 million to 77 million, including 44 million girls between 1999 and 2004, and the doubling of Official Development Assistance for education between 2000 and 2006, which remained far below the estimated needs.

See also: compulsory education; educational targets; equality of opportunity; international education; primary school/education; universal education/mass education

VILMA SEEBERG

EDUCATION POLICY

Mainstream understandings of how educational policy making occurs in a democracy arose out of the dominant intellectual traditions of the social sciences. In the first half of the twentieth century general academic perspectives such as structural functionalist sociology and general systems theory were applied to educational problems. Functional explanations of education were strongly influenced by the ideas of writers like Emile Durkheim, who argued that education systems exist for the purpose of socialisation, that is to nurture and develop in individuals those abilities and capacities necessary for the maintenance of society, and the American sociologist Talcott Parsons, whose work represents an attempt to combine both 'holistic' and 'individualistic' theories of social action inspired by Durkheim and Weber respectively.

The functionalist paradigm entailed a liberal conception of the educational process as that of the 'black box' (Apple 1979). Early definitions of policy process highlighted the procedural and implementational aspects of understanding policy as 'whatever governments choose to do or not to do' (Dye 1978: 3). Policy in this sense was implicitly seen as a

form of system support. An overview of definitions offered by early theorists, however, led one writer to conclude that the 'term policy has no standard usage, and it is riddled with ambiguity' (Prunty 1984: 4).

Policy analysis can also be framed with reference to perspectives of power. Pluralism was one such perspective, and dominated the functionalist era of policy analysis. It has emerged as a response to the modernisation of Western societies, so that it provides both a way of interpreting the social and political workings of such societies as well as legitimating them. It represented the policy making process in terms of two basic assumptions. First, all power was deemed to be legitimate. Second, the state was perceived as a non-problematic, neutral arbiter, whose function was to distribute social and material goods to competing groups.

In contrast to traditional pluralist or functionalist analyses, the last thirty years has seen the emergence of what is now referred to as a critical policy analysis. While much of the early work in this tradition took its impetus from radical versions of sociology, in the last decade a growing number have utilised the works of the French post-structuralist writer Michel Foucault (Olssen *et al.* 2004). Although there are some aspects of Foucault's work that are not accepted – his neutralism over ends and values – there is within Foucault's work the basis for a broad commitment to a democratic and ethical vision of a new welfare community. Rather than employ him in a one-sided negative way that can be found in some readings of his work, these seek to utilise Foucault as an ally, sometimes going beyond the literal canon of his texts, but keeping within his general conception of critique in order to re-articulate and re-theorise a new understanding of a social-democratic polity.

Foucault's methodological insights contribute to a critical policy analysis and are thus compatible with the contributions of writers like Ball (1990), Dale (1999) and Ozga (2000). Utilising Foucault in this way, policy sociology is represented as a form of critical policy analysis with no particular affinity or attachment to the discipline of sociology. Because Foucauldianism is not located within any existing discipline, it is more genuinely able to be multi-disciplinary. In such a view, the Foucauldian perspective permits the incorporation of a form of 'critical policy analysis' within a more grounded and theoretically worked-out critical social science approach. It is not a totalising conception of critique, in the tradition of the Frankfurt School, or Marxism, or a reconstructive conception, in the tradition of Habermas. Rather, it is a form of critique which sees the possibilities of a purely rational dialogue as always mixed with heteronomous considerations of power and interest, and always supported by the imperatives of survival and well-being. Nevertheless, on this basis, and within such limitations, it struggles against oppressive social structures.

See also: Durkheim, Emile; education; Foucault, Michel; sociology of education

Further reading

Apple, M. (1979) *Ideology and Curriculum*, London: Routledge and Kegan Paul.

Ball, S. (1990) *Politics and Policy Making in Education: Explorations in Policy Sociology*, London: Routledge.

Dale, R. (1999) 'Specifying globalisation effects on national policy: a focus on the mechanisms', *Journal of Education Policy*, 14(1): 1–17.

Dye, T.R. (1978) *Understanding Public Policy*, Englewood Cliffs NJ: Prentice Hall.

Olssen, M., Codd, J. and O'Neill, A.-M. (2004) *Education Policy: Globalisation, Citizenship, Democracy*, London: Sage.

Ozga, J. (2000) *Policy Research in Educational Settings: Contested Terrain*, Buckingham: Open University Press.

Prunty, J. (1984) *A Critical Reformulation of Educational Policy Analysis*, Geelong VIC: Deakin University Press.

MARK OLSSEN

EDUCATION/EDUCATIONAL STUDIES

Education studies or educational studies may be defined as the academic study of education within the domain of higher education. It is a subject of study that, historically, has principally been undertaken by those preparing for careers as teachers, or by practising teachers registered for a higher qualification. In recent years, however, a grounding in education studies has been seen as a suitable academic preparation for a more specialist vocational course or career, in social work or corporate training, for example.

Within the institution of the university, education is a relatively new subject of academic study. Although university faculties or schools of education may be long established, the status of education is rarely thought to be on a par with such prestigious fields as engineering, law or science. Academic staff working in education departments of higher education institutions may frequently experience professional tensions inherent in their duties. The specialist in sociology of education, for example, may self-identify as an educationist specialising in sociology when teaching on education studies courses, but as a sociologist specialising in education when applying for funded research or submitting writing for publication.

Individually, the 'foundation disciplines' of education – most frequently represented as the history, philosophy, psychology and sociology of education, though others, including comparative education, economics of education and educational administration have sometimes staked an equal claim – can point to notable contributions in respect of educational methodologies, research, scholarship, publications and teaching. When it was launched in 1952, the *British Journal of Educational Studies* stated that existing journals in the field 'provide a medium for the publication of psychological and statistical research into some problems of education' and that it aimed to be broader, 'viz. to explain the significance of new thought, to provide philosophical discussion at a high level, and to deepen existing interest in the purposes and problems of current educational policy' (*BJES*, 1(1): 67). It might be argued, however, that this journal and others with similar titles have done little to actually define 'educational studies' (see Richardson 2002).

During the 1960s and 1970s, education studies became more prominent in Britain following the establishment of Bachelor of Education (B.Ed.) degrees and the association of formerly impoverished teacher training colleges with universities. But education studies was thought by many to amount to less than the sum of its parts – 'undifferentiated mush' in the words of the philosopher Richard Peters of London University Institute of Education – leading to a concentration on approaching education through its distinct foundation disciplines, rather than via an interdisciplinary approach (Aldrich and Crook 1998: 131). This had the effect of strengthening disciplinary research identities, but new questions were raised about whether trainee teachers might benefit more from extended teaching practice placements and more 'survival' advice, rather than lectures in the history or philosophy of education.

From the 1980s, from their positions of isolation – frequently in university 'departments of educational studies' – some academic voices called for new approaches to the academic study of education. Wilson (1982) lamented the absence of clear thinking about educational studies in universities where 'the problems are not properly confronted – partly, perhaps, for the quite straightforward reason that it is nobody's business to do so' (Wilson 1982: 15). He acknowledged also, however, that many working in education departments were of the view that 'education is not and could never be a serious subject or respectable intellectual enterprise'. He also observed that 'most of what passes for educational theory' is 'rubbish' (Wilson 1982: 15). The absence of a satisfactory dialectic for education studies, and, in particular, the case for developing more prominent and robust educational theory also featured in Stephen J. Ball's 1995 critique of educational studies.

Undergraduate courses in education studies – many of which do not now bear 'qualified teacher status' or carry expectations that graduates will proceed to teacher training courses – have proliferated over the past fifteen years, as British higher education has moved to a more inclusive, mass model. This has led to programme leaders addressing the challenge of developing a twenty-first century subject identity for education studies (for example Bartlett *et al.* 2001; Tubbs and Grimes 2001). Interesting materials for education studies courses are emerging (for example Kassem *et al.* 2006) and optimism within the field is stronger than it was, say, twenty years ago.

See also: education; educational theory; history of education; philosophy of education; psychology of education; sociology of education

Further reading

Aldrich, R. and Crook, D. (1998) 'Education as a university subject in England: an historical interpretation'. In P. Drewek and C. Lüth (eds) *History of Educational Studies, Geschichte der Erziehungswissenschaft, Histoire des Sciences de l'Education*, Ghent, Belgium: CSHP.

Ball, S. J. (1995) 'Intellectuals or technicians? The urgent role of theory in educational studies', *British Journal of Educational Studies*, 43(3): 255-71.

Bartlett, S., Burton, D. and Peim, N. (2001) *Introduction to Education Studies*, London: Paul Chapman Publishing.

Kassem, D., Mufti, E. and Robinson, J. (2006) *Rducation Studies: Issues and Critical Perspectives*, Maidenhead: Open University Press.

Richardson, W. (2002) 'Educational studies in the United Kingdom, 1940–2002', *British Journal of Educational Studies*, 50(1): 3–56.

Tubbs, N. and Grimes, J. (2001) 'What is educational studies', *Educational Studies*, 27(1): 3–15.

Wilson, J. (1982) 'The credibility of educational studies', *Oxford Review of Education*, 8(1): 3–19.

DAVID CROOK

EDUCATIONAL BROADCASTING

Educational broadcasting describes the transmission of audio or visual programmes to support teachers, students and other learners. In many parts of the world schools and colleges make extensive use of radio and television programmes, transmitted both by public service and commercial broadcasters. Broadcasts also service the requirements of home and distance learners studying for university or other qualifications and enhance the training of teachers and instructors when preparing to teach new or modified courses or curricula. In the home, too, those seeking to develop new skills or simply to increase their general knowledge and understanding may derive benefits from educational broadcasts.

The first authenticated radio transmission for schools was broadcast in the United Kingdom in 1924. Over the next fifteen years the British Broadcasting Corporation (BBC) pioneered talks for schools by expert speakers, including eminent historians, musicians, poets, politicians and travellers. Until the 1960s radio transmissions were broadcast live. The BBC's pioneering work in this area was greatly admired overseas, not least because the League of Nations identified school broadcasting as an area for international co-operation (League of Nations 1933). World War II slowed the development of educational broadcasting, but a variety of countries championed its growing potential from the late 1940s. One well known example occurred in Australia, where a 'School of the Air', using the Flying Doctors radio network, commenced in 1951, transmitting to school-children in isolated areas.

The first regular schools television service was launched in the United States of America by the Philco Corporation of Philadelphia in 1948, with other countries, including Canada, Japan and many European countries, following soon afterwards. As with radio broadcasts, the objectives and approaches of schools television broadcasters have displayed international variance, with American broadcasters, for example, tending to favour the transmission of packaged lessons, while their European counterparts leaned towards presenting material for teachers to select for use in the classroom (Mayer 1992). Recording technologies advanced rapidly in the 1960s and 1970s, permitting broadcasters to repeat and revise programmes (Cuban 1986). The increased affordability of audio – and later

video – tape recorders in schools, meanwhile, permitted teachers to stop and replay programmes at will and to obtain copyright clearance to maintain tape libraries. In some countries, schools themselves saw opportunities to develop broadcasting services. The Inner London Education Authority, for example, launched a closed-circuit television service for schools to share ideas and resources. Educational broadcasters have also sometimes worked together on projects, under the auspices of such international organisations as the European Broadcasting Union.

From the earliest days of school broadcasting, programme schedulers faced calls for additional or repeated transmissions in the evenings or at weekends for adults. Although this generally proved difficult to realise, the concept of educational broadcasting broadened during the 1970s, when self-supported and distance learning approaches became popular. In the UK, the Open University (OU), originally to be called the 'University of the Air' offered its first courses in 1971. Traditionally broadcast in the early mornings, late at night and at weekends, the OU's radio and television programmes, produced in partnership with the BBC, have long attracted devoted audiences from beyond the register of course participants. Now adopted in many countries throughout the world, the OU model of study promotes access to higher education for individuals and groups otherwise disadvantaged by geography, distance from a traditional university, disability, family commitments, or engagement in the workforce.

Educational broadcasting is continuing to evolve in the early twenty-first century. Digital technologies are opening new possibilities for television channels dedicated to educational content, sometimes incorporating interactive experiences for the learner. At an international level, educational broadcasters are now investing heavily in DVDs, computer CD-ROMs, Web-based learning packages and even digital curricula. The content of radio and television programmes for schools, colleges, universities and other adult learners is now invariably supplemented by dedicated websites with interactive exercises or games, downloadable worksheets and revision guides. As high-speed Web connections become more popular, it is likely that more broadcasts will be made available online, with more learners accessing these materials in the home, as well as in traditional classroom settings.

See also: distance education/learning; home schooling; Open University

Further reading

Cuban, L. (1986) *Teachers and Machines: The Classroom Use of Technology since 1920*, New York: Teachers College Press.
League of Nations (1933) *School Broadcasting*, Paris: League of Nations.
Mayer, M. (1992) *Aspects of School Television in Europe*, Munich: K. G. Saur.

DAVID CROOK

EDUCATIONAL LEADERSHIP AND MANAGEMENT

Organisational activity within educational institutions is concerned with: first, a division of labour secured by roles, responsibilities and remuneration; second, processes such as decision making and delivery through meetings and planning; third, development or the balance between maintenance (keeping things going) and innovation (strategy and futuring); fourth, people and their skills, knowledge and behaviour through deployment, performance and training; and fifth, purposes or what the organisation exists to do (e.g. curriculum, citizenship, credentials). What this activity, and the actions (talking, listening, walking) embedded within it, has been labelled varies in context and over time. The research and theorising of this practice has its origins in the United States of America, Canada and Australia, where the label used is 'educational administration'. Internationally, the field continues to use this label, as evidenced by the title of Hodgkinson's

Towards a Philosophy of Administration (1978). Some relabelling has gone on within particular countries (e.g. England shifted to 'educational management' in the 1970s and to 'leadership' in the 1990s), and within networks (e.g. the Commonwealth Council for Educational Administration is now the Commonwealth Council for Educational Administration and Management).

An interesting way to understand labelling is through the changes to the title of the British Educational Leadership, Management and Administration Society (BELMAS). It was founded in 1971 as the British Educational Administration Society (BEAS), and in 1980 inserted 'management' into the title to become the British Educational Management and Administration Society (BEMAS). 'Leadership' was added in 2002. The struggle over this shift from administration to management to leadership is based on characterising activity in particular ways, and establishing the primacy of the head teacher as the leader. In the 1960s, educational administration was regarded as the best way of describing the work of the head teacher, as both the leading policy maker and professional. Illustrative of this is Baron and Taylor's edited collection *Educational Administration and the Social Sciences* (1969), where field members used an internationally respected title and located knowledge claims within the social sciences. The challenge to this came mainly from practitioners who wanted strategy, purposes and motivating people labelled as 'management' – and head teachers as managing directors – while maintenance and clerical work was to be known as 'administration'. Illustrative of this position is Everard and Morris' book *Effective School Management* (1990), with chapters on teams and change, and, from the late 1980s, the emphasis was on the operationalising of site-based management through budgets and staffing.

In the 1990s, management faced downgrading to technical implementation. Bennis and Nanus, in their book *Leaders* (1985), stated that managers 'do things right' while leaders 'do the right things'. This private sector model of transformational leadership, based on charismatic commitment-building with followers to change practice is now globally popular, with management regarded as necessary, but transactional in nature. Illustrative of this position in education is Leithwood, Jantzi and Steinbach's book *Changing Leadership for Changing Times* (1999), which presents transformational leadership as essential for securing schools as high-reliability organisations. The head teacher or principal as organisational leader currently dominates policy in Western-style democracies, and has become associated with creating the conditions for school improvement and delivering school effectiveness. This is illustrated by Stoll and Fink's book *Changing Our Schools* (1996) where they argue for the modernisation of schools through integrating organisational processes with the measurement of impact on outcomes. Such an approach is currently dominating the licensing of head teachers to practise, and in England the central government has directly intervened and defined head teacher training and accreditation according to national standards through the creation of a National College for School Leadership.

There has been some hybridisation of the head or principal as transformational leader: first, an acknowledgement that the leader cannot, and does not, do work alone, so acknowledging the contribution of others; and, second, that the emphasis should be shifted towards the core purposes with the head teacher as an instructional leader. The leader, as the distributor of leadership through delegation, or licensing agent to act through empowerment, is a popular modification of the transformational model. While there is no direct research evidence in support of this hybrid, distributed leadership remains normatively attractive through integrating the work of others, and, in particular, by reinforcing the place of teachers in delivering organisational and systemic goals. Consistent with this is instructional leadership,

where the emphasis is on the head teacher creating the organisational conditions in which teaching and learning are delivered according to nationally determined norms.

The current characterisation of the work of head teachers and principals as transformational leaders who work with others to deliver policy requirements is highly contested. Professional researchers in higher education and practitioner researchers not only challenge this model, they are actively creating alternatives through practice and projects. There are two main areas of such work: first, work that questions the hierarchical power structures that transformational leadership reinforces; and, second, work that focuses on the educational aspects of leading and learning. Both of these critiques present leadership not as the privilege of a formal organisational role related to the functions of a post-holder, but as a relational and communal social practice where all can lead, be leaders and engage in leadership. In this way, the process is educative, and inclusive of parents and students. Leadership of the self and of others' learning provides a focus for cognitive and affective processes.

The identification of some work as being more important than others provides a central critique of transformational leadership. Organisational work regarding strategic direction and development is presented as more important than educational work around teaching and learning, and particular forms of activity such as vision and mission have been given a higher status than delivery and maintenance. The separation of a leadership cadre from the rank-and-file, through the elevation of leader activity, has faced a range of criticisms. It can be viewed as the product of North American private-sector thinking and practice, and could be damaging to the national cultures and systems onto which it is being grafted. It sustains traditional hierarchies and legitimises centralised control and authority. While the language of empowerment and cultural change may sound benign, it is a form of seduction that seeks to maintain domination by elites. Consequently, it undermines knowledgeable people, who are relegated to a follower role and must submit to the superior know-how of the leader. It is blind to the diversity of the people who work in educational organisations, so issues of gender, ethnicity, sexuality, age, and wider lives, such as parent and partner, are elided from the model. In short, transformational leadership is not transformational.

Illustrative of these arguments are Smyth's edited collection of papers *Critical Perspectives on Educational Leadership* (1989) and Blackmore's *Troubling Women* (1999), which both challenge the normality of the leader role and present alternative insights about power and social justice. Such understandings of leadership begin with the assumption that the head teacher is not the causal agent of all work, and so individuals and groups within the organisation can generate activity. This requires a different form of distributed leadership, based on notions of dispersal, and the potential generation of opportunities for democratic participation and emancipation. Notably, it is about inclusively regarding how students are positioned in their own and others' learning.

The second type of critique of transformational leadership and its hybrids is located in issues around teaching and learning. This type of work focuses on the underlying purposes of an educational organisation, and, in particular, on the nature of teaching and learning within a diverse society. The emphasis is not so much on *how* we deliver outcomes but on *what learning is about*, and *why we learn*. This adopts the view that decisions about the purposes of education are not in the hands of legislators, but are located in schools and colleges, and that dialogue within these is essential. Hence, leadership is not transformational by being contingent upon learning through organisational arrangements but is educational by being integral within how, why and what is learned. Illustrative of this position is Lingard, Hayes, Mills and Christie's book *Leading Learning* (2003),

where the authors present productive pedagogies and assessment, interrelated with leadership as a social practice.

See also: head teacher/principal; school-based management; school effectiveness; school improvement; school leadership

Further Reading

Grace, G. (1995) *School Leadership: Beyond Education Management*, London: Falmer.
Gronn, P. (2003) *The New Work of Educational Leaders*, London: Sage.
Gunter, H. (2004) 'Labels and labelling in the field of educational leadership', *Discourse*, 25(1): 21–42.
Gunter, H. and Ribbins, P. (2003) 'The field of educational leadership: studying maps and mapping studies', *British Journal of Educational Studies*, 51(3): 254–81.

HELEN GUNTER

EDUCATIONAL PRIORITY AREA

An educational priority area (EPA) is a locality where a government has deemed the provision or outcomes of education to be problematic. EPAs provide examples of area-based initiatives targeting persistent underachievement. Additional funding is designated and special educational action taken to remedy the situation.

Area-based responses to disadvantage can be found from the 1960s. Longitudinal studies dating from the 1950s suggested that environmental factors influenced educational performance more than intelligence: the close correlation between poverty and low educational attainment made targeted responses an attractive policy choice.

Setting EPA boundaries is invariably difficult. Sometimes the most severely deprived children may not actually live, or go to school, in the designated EPA. However, the availability of ever-more-detailed data, based on social and economic indices, means that governments can confidently identify areas where poverty and disadvantage persist.

In 1965 the United States launched the massive Head Start programme. This 'war on poverty' was a policy of positive discrimination.

Area-based compensatory strategies aimed to overcome perceived deficits in children, but results suggested only short-term gains. In the UK, following the Plowden Report of 1967, experimental action research in five EPAs was used to identify what strategies had the greatest impact on education. The resulting report acknowledged that the impact of education policies would be limited unless they were complemented by wider social reforms.

In the United Kingdom, the failure of the original EPA conception to generate national policies to combat inequality has not prevented their continued use. For example, inter-agency approaches have underpinned such initiatives as Education Action Zones and the London Challenge.

See also: positive discrimination/affirmative action; urban education

KEITH WILLIAMS

EDUCATIONAL PUBLISHING

Educational publishing includes a wide variety of communicative forms, organisational structures, and modes of transmission. The term is perhaps most readily associated with the major international publishing houses that continue to publish a variety of marketable educational texts. However, the term also covers the wide array of academic and professional journals and periodicals, state and regional policy documents, as well as smaller independent and/or campaigning presses and national newspapers and their relevant 'supplements'. Each of these outlets is likely to specialise in different communicative forms: for example, books for specialist academic and professional readerships, school and university textbooks for use by pupils and students, research-based and scholarly articles circulated within the educational research community, reflective essays by educational professionals relating to their own practice, research-based reports and policy guidelines, and more polemical pieces on contemporary educational issues.

A number of general trends in the publishing industry have had a specific impact on educational publishing. The rise of the international publishing conglomerates has swallowed up many of the smaller specialist educational publishing outlets. It has also resulted in an increased emphasis on market values (in this case judging the value of a book primarily by its saleability). This emphasis has in turn led to a greatly reduced shelf-life for, and turnover of, published books; a speeding up of the publication process (from commissioning through to point of publication); greater priority being given to marketing generally and niche marketing in particular; and increased in-house accountability regarding the profit-making capacity of educational publishing within organisations with a much broader publishing remit. Similarly, recent changes in retailing mechanisms (for example competitive pricing by retailers, the rise of large corporate retail outlets, and the increasing reliance on internet sales) has led to the closure or takeover of many smaller, local retailers and independent bookshops and put others at serious risk of closure.

The increased reliance on market values has led to a reduction in the variety, choice and sometimes quality of education books, with some publishers focusing on titles for professional practitioners. Very few educational books are produced for the discriminating reader with a general interest in education, perhaps because any such general readership is difficult to identify.

The proliferation of academic journals within the field of educational studies might be seen as filling this quality gap. Such journals select articles by a rigorous process of peer review and editorial oversight, and pride themselves on the quality of the articles they publish. While a few of these journals are wide ranging, most focus on specific subfields of educational practice and research. Publication in such journals has become a necessary requirement for academic career advancement by educational specialists based in universities and is used, by central government and other funding agencies, as a means of assessing research quality and allocating research funds. These journals are now instrumental in structuring the academic field of educational studies, defining career routes and professional trajectories within that field, and providing indirect evidence of the quality and quantity of research conducted across the field. While some of these academic journals place a strong emphasis on communicating to policy makers and practitioners, they have undoubtedly intensified the trend towards increased specialisation.

See also: education/educational studies; educational broadcasting; educational research, educational technology; specialisation

Further reading

Gee, J., Hull, G. and Lankshear, C. (1996) *The New Work Order: Behind the Language of the New Capitalism*, Boulder CO: Westview/Harper-Collins.

Nixon, J. and Wellington, J. (2005) '"Good books": is there a future for academic writing within the educational publishing industry?', *British Journal of Sociology of Education*, 26(1): 91–103.

Schiffrin, A. (2000) *The Business of Books: How International Conglomerates Took Over Publishing and Changed the Way We Read*, New York: Verso.

JON NIXON

EDUCATIONAL RESEARCH

The history of educational research is generally traced from the end of the nineteenth century, since only at that time did systematic inquiry begin on a significant scale (de Landsheere 1988). Over the course of the twentieth century this grew considerably in volume, and also in diversity. Partly as a result, both what counts as *research* and what counts as *educational* research have become subject to dispute. So, interpreting 'educational research' in the broadest terms, it covers a complex network of areas of work traversed by conflicting theoretical-cum-methodological approaches.

Several dimensions structure this diversity. First, there is tension between, on the one hand, those who wish to tie research closely to educational practice or policy making and, on the other, those who see it as properly operating under the auspices of an academic discipline such as one of the social sciences. And, often, this involves a difference in view about the immediate goal of inquiry. Thus, while some define it as being concerned with 'producing valid knowledge about teaching, learning and the institutional frameworks in which they occur' (Foster 1997: 14), others regard its function as extending beyond this, for example so as 'critically to inform educational judgements and decisions in order to improve educational action' (Bassey 1995: 39). The second of these definitions implies that educational research should aim at having a beneficial effect on educational policy making or practice; indeed that without this commitment it does not deserve the adjective 'educational'.

Some versions of this second position portray the task of research as directly to *serve* educational policy makers and practitioners, taking their concerns as the starting point. Others are informed by views that challenge existing institutions or forms of practice, whether on educational or political grounds. From this latter point of view, the task for research is to transform some aspect of the status quo. There are also variations in ideas about the nature of the relationship between research and policy making or practice, with some commentators seeing the function of inquiry as instrumental, for example concerned with demonstrating what does and does not 'work' (Oakley 2000), while others view its role as one of enlightenment, or perhaps even of consciousness-raising (see Hammersley 2002). There are also those who argue that educational research must be carried out by practitioners themselves, and be focused on their own practice and context (in the form of practitioner research or action research), if it is to serve its function (for a discussion of divergent examples see Elliott 2004).

In line with a policy- or practice-focused orientation, much research has been concerned with investigating effective teaching, identifying the contextual factors determining the extent and quality of learning, or assessing the consequences of various educational policies or practices. Often this has been governed by a relatively narrow frame of reference, for example evaluating effectiveness in terms of standard educational outcomes, such as national test or examination results. But there has also been work with different foci, for example concerned with equity; and this has sometimes extended to include outcomes such as changes in motivation, attitudes, social skills, or life chances. Of course, at the more disciplinary end of the spectrum, there has been much research looking at psychological and social processes operating in educational settings, at the ways in which schools, colleges, and universities function within societies, and at the history of these institutions and what has shaped their development.

A second important tension within the field of educational research is among different academic disciplines, notably sociology, philosophy, psychology, history, and economics. Psychology and sociology have generally been the most influential, and at one time there was a sharp conflict between the two. However, work in these disciplines has changed in character over the past few decades, and in part this has involved a blurring of the boundaries between them: *methodological* differences have been weakened greatly by the rise in influence of qualitative method; differences in *theoretical* orientation have also been reduced because many psychologists now give more attention to socio-cultural context. This has been reinforced by the tendency for some educational researchers to identify themselves with transdisciplinary fields, whether specifically educational ones like curriculum studies, educational administration and management, etc., or broader ones like feminist scholarship, critical research, or postmodernism. Nevertheless, the influence of disciplinary affiliation

remains important. For example, philosophers and historians tend to have rather different conceptions of the nature of inquiry from those in other disciplines.

This blurring of boundaries between the disciplines has not led to increased integration within educational research. One of the reasons is that social science disciplines themselves have become internally more heterogeneous in theoretical and methodological orientation; and this is reflected within the field of education. Initially, one of the main lines of conflict was between advocates of quantitative and qualitative methodology, this increasingly reflecting not simply differences in the practice of research but in fundamental assumptions about the nature of the social world and how it can and ought to be represented. In the first half of the twentieth century, most educational research was modelled on natural science, using experiments, tests, questionnaires, structured interviews, or systematic observation. However, during the second half of that century qualitative approaches came to be more influential. Moreover, as qualitative work became more popular, it differentiated into competing approaches, based on the use of specific methods (various kinds of interviewing or observation; different forms of analysis, such as those focusing on behaviour or on narrative/discourse; and so on) along with appeals to distinctive theoretical or philosophical orientations (pragmatism, symbolic interactionism, phenomenology, hermeneutics, constructivism, post-structuralism, postmodernism, etc.). And, in recent years, a significant trend within qualitative research, across the social sciences generally, has been away from the idea that research should aim to be scientific, parallels being drawn instead with art, imaginative literature, and literary theory (see Denzin and Lincoln 2000). At the same time, quantitative research has not disappeared from educational research or the social sciences; and in some quarters there has been increasing emphasis on the value of combining the two approaches.

Aside from these three sets of fault-lines across educational research, there is also diversity arising from researchers focusing on different parts of the education system (primary, secondary, further and higher education); on different subjects taught (both practical topics and academic disciplines); or on lifelong learning and/or learning in settings outside of educational institutions. Most research has tended to focus on schooling, and on what we might call mainstream schools; there has been rather less study of the teaching of children or students with various kinds of severe disability or giftedness, of private schools, of specialist (for instance, music or military) schools, or of those organised by specific ethnic groups or religions for their children. Furthermore, there has been a tendency for researchers to focus on educational institutions within their own society; and since a great deal more educational research is done in the West than elsewhere, coverage is biased towards these societies. The main counters to this tendency have been work in anthropology and comparative and development education. Up until the 1970s, there was a predominant tendency for educational research to take over the values and priorities embedded in Western education systems as an unquestioned framework; and much work continues to display this orientation. However, since that time there has been diversification in perspective, driven for instance by increasing interest in children's and students' experiences of schooling and/or by the application of critical orientations deriving from previously marginalised educational values or from social theories that view schooling as reproducing inequalities in social class, ethnic, gender, and ability/disability in both national and global relations. Equally important in this respect has been increased recognition of the value of research carried out by anthropologists, cultural psychologists and some sociologists on educational processes outside the context of educational institutions, whether in workplaces, families, health centres, drop-in centres, play groups, citizens' advice bureaux, or peer groups (see e.g. Lave and Wenger 1991).

That educational research is now a diverse and contested domain cannot be denied. However, there is disagreement about whether this is to be applauded, tolerated, bemoaned, or remedied. For some, a new order is required, based on greater methodological and theoretical consensus, designed to serve evidence-based policy making and practice. Others regard any attempt to generate such consensus as an unnecessary and counterproductive imposition, seeing pluralism as desirable in itself, or as reflecting the global society in which educational inquiry now operates. A third view holds that while some of the differences in orientation are probably inevitable or desirable, others are not.

See also: action research; American Educational Research Association; Australian Association for Research in Education; British Educational Research Association; critical theory; European Educational Research Association; experimental research; objective tests; practitioner research; qualitative research; quantitative research

Further reading

Bassey, M. (1995) *Creating Education through Research*, Edinburgh and Newark: Kirklington Moor Press, in conjunction with the British Educational Research Association.

De Landsheere, G. (1988) 'History of educational research'. In J. P. Keeves (ed.) *Educational Research, Methodology and Measurement: An International Handbook*, Oxford: Pergamon.

Denzin, N. K. and Lincoln, Y. S. (eds) (2000) *Handbook of Qualitative Research*, 2nd edn, Thousand Oaks CA: Sage.

Elliott, J. (2004) 'Making evidence-based practice educational'. In G. Thomas and R. Pring (eds) *Evidence-Based Practice in Education*, Maidenhead: Open University Press.

Foster, P. (1997) 'How should we judge the usefulness of educational research?', *Times Educational Supplement*, 21 November: 14.

Hammersley, M. (2002) *Educational Research, Policymaking and Practice*, London: Paul Chapman Publishing.

Lave, J. and Wenger, E. (1991) *Situated Learning: Legitimate Peripheral Participation*, Cambridge: Cambridge University Press.

Oakley, A. (2000) *Experiments in Knowing*, Cambridge: Polity Press.

MARTYN HAMMERSLEY

EDUCATIONAL RESOURCES INFORMATION CENTER (ERIC)

ERIC is an internet-based digital library of educational research and information. It provides free access to over 1.2 million education-related items, some with links to full text versions. These include bibliographic records of literature from 1966 to the present such as journal articles, books, research syntheses, conference papers, technical reports, policy papers and other educational materials. More than 600 journals are indexed regularly. ERIC also offers over 115,000 full-text PDF versions of 'grey literature' such as conference papers and reports, again freely available. Many older materials, for instance those available on microfiche, have been digitised.

The Center is used by educational researchers, teachers, policy makers, students, librarians, media and business as well as the general public. Individuals and organisations are encouraged to index their materials on ERIC. Over 6 million searches take place each month.

It is sponsored by the Institute of Education Sciences (IES) of the US Department of Education. Computer Sciences Corporation (CSC) runs ERIC under contract by developing and managing the digital collection, website, and associated technologies, as well as outreach to ERIC users. Two advisory panels of experts, a steering committee and content experts support the work of ERIC.

See also: educational publishing; educational research

TOM WOODIN

EDUCATIONAL TARGETS

Educational targets refer to setting specific educational goals, often measurable and with timelines for their achievement. They may, for example, be applied to individual children's progress at school, to institutional or national performance improvements and to the delivery of policy milestones.

After World War II, developing such targets became a common approach to directing international educational planning (as well as planning in other sectors like health and the economy as a whole). International agencies, most particularly UNESCO, convened national and regional meetings to set educational targets, often in the area of literacy and primary schooling, such as reducing a nation's illiteracy rate to 40 per cent or increasing its net enrolment ratio to 60 per cent. Globally, much attention was focused on the target of attaining universal primary education (UPE). UNESCO initiated a series of regional meetings in the early 1960s that called for UPE to be attained worldwide by 1980 (Chabbott 2003; Clemens 2004).

Although this target was not achieved, that did not dampen the enthusiasm for the approach. Indeed, a considerable amount of global educational planning today has been shaped by two initiatives that focus on educational targets. The first is the Education for All (EFA) initiative that resulted from a meeting in 1990 in Jomtien, Thailand, of representatives from 155 nations as well as from many international agencies and NGOs. The resulting Jomtien Declaration called for, among other things, universal access to and completion of primary or basic education by 2000; reduction of adult illiteracy, and expansion of early childhood education.

Halfway through the decade, it became apparent that the targets were unreachable by 2000, so the date set for their attainment was postponed. This became further institutionalised at the EFA follow-up meeting held in Dakar, Senegal. Dates were changed and targets modified. For example, the Dakar agreement called for access to and completion of free, compulsory, good quality primary education by 2015; the elimination of gender disparities in primary and secondary education by 2005;

a 50 per cent improvement in adult literacy by 2015; and expansion and improvement of early childhood education.

The second initiative that is shaping much education (and other sector) planning today is the Millennium Development Goals (MDGs). The MDGs are a broad set of targets related to education, health, poverty, gender, and the environment that were agreed upon by the largest gathering ever of world leaders at the United Nations Millennium Summit in New York in 2000. In education, the goals are very similar to two of the Dakar targets, calling for universal primary school completion by 2015 and eliminating gender disparities in primary and secondary schooling, 'preferably by 2005'.

Despite the long history of using targets for educational planning, the approach has been subject to considerable criticism. Economists have generally considered this type of 'social demand' approach to planning as fundamentally flawed. To an economist, it substitutes a political judgement for what should be an economic one. That is, for example, the expansion of primary schooling, like any resource investment, involves costs and benefits. To make a rational decision means evaluating the specific tradeoffs involved, not simply substituting a political decision that everyone must have primary schooling (Psacharopoulos and Woodhall 1985). While this has been a longstanding criticism, it is interesting to note that it is rarely directed to EFA or the MDGs, perhaps because economists have become resigned to the appeal of targets or perhaps they believe that the benefits outweigh the costs of achieving these specific targets.

One of the most common criticisms of educational targets is that they seem almost never to be achieved. The 2005 gender disparity targets above were missed and there is widespread consensus that the rest of the EFA and MDG targets will not be reached by 2015. A major question then becomes why are these targets not achieved. Aid providers and aid recipients tend to blame each other. Developing countries point to the lack of sufficient aid, despite promises, that would be necessary to achieve the targets. Donors point to a country's lack of political will, efficient management, and earmarking of national resources that would be necessary to achieve the targets. An alternative explanation, posited by Clemens (2004), is that most nations are moving to achieve UPE at a very rapid pace by historical standards, but the targets are simply unrealistic about what policy can achieve since expansion is really driven by economic development and the associated slowly increasing payoff to more education.

Repeated failures raise the related question as to why setting such targets is still so widely used for planning. Is it simply planner ignorance, or hope endlessly triumphing over experience? Some critics have offered a more structural explanation. Despite planners' good intentions, the record of endless failure points to how setting such targets is simply a legitimating mechanism, delivering a pretence of progress that is very necessary to justify a set of social arrangements in which poverty and inequality are entrenched. Regardless of the explanation, it is likely that setting educational targets will continue to constitute a major approach to educational planning.

See also: compulsory education; Education for All (EFA); performance indicators; school improvement; universal education/mass education

Further reading

Chabbott, C. (2003) *Constructing Education for Development: International Organizations and Education for All*, New York: RoutledgeFalmer.
Clemens, M. A. (2004) *The Long Walk to School: International Educational Goals in Historical Perspective*, Working Paper 37, Washington DC: Center for Global Development.
Psacharopoulos, G. and Woodhall, M. (1985) *Education for Development: An Analysis of Investment Choices*, New York: Oxford University Press.

STEVEN J. KLEES

EDUCATIONAL TECHNOLOGY

The word technology comes from the Greek *technologia*, referring to the systematic treatment of some art or craft. Now, technology in education most commonly refers to the practical arts generally, and in particular to mechanical aids to learning.

The oldest technologies, pen and paper, are in some ways still the most robust. Oxford's Bodleian Library has some of original copies of Plato's dialogues due to the dedicated work of scribes who faithfully copied them from antiquity and throughout the Middle Ages. Plato was one of the first to use writing as an educational technology to portray conversations that might inspire those seeking to become wiser. Likewise, Homer's *Odyssey* or the *Epic of Gilgamesh* show the transition between spoken and written forms. Ironically, we may now find ourselves at another juncture where new voice recognition, video, and simulation technologies allow students to rely less on literacy and return to the spoken word.

These educational technologies often support or implement a particular model of learning. This may either be at a high level, for example when simulations implement a model of business training for professionals, or at a more content-specific level, as in the physics tutoring programs designed by Kurt VanLehn (see VanLehn et al. 2005). More basically, technology developed by David Rose at the Center for Applied Special Technology (CAST) (www.cast.org) allows students to overcome impediments to reading and comprehension. Recent efforts in educational technology have expanded beyond the individual student or laptop to engage networks of students on the internet.

There can be many reasons why a technology is successfully implemented in one classroom and rejected in another, even if the model implemented is correct and important for students to learn. We need to consider one's needs and what technologies can help with them (see Rose et al. 2005; Ashburn and Floden 2006).

Educational technology will always be subservient to the educational tasks required and the values that underlie them. Gardner (1999) proposes three main orientations for educational tasks: truth, beauty, and goodness. For his part, Sternberg (1996) proposes three others: analysis, creativity, and practicality. Epictetus sought peace of mind. Clearly, different technologies will support these various educational aims differently (for eaxample, perhaps a music composition program for creativity and beauty; a science simulation for truth and analysis; and contemplative practice for goodness and peace of mind).

See also: computer-assisted learning; learning; technology; visual aids

Further reading

Ashburn, E. A. and Floden, R. E. (eds) (2006) *Meaningful Learning Using Technology: What Educators Need to Know and to Do*, New York: Teachers College Press.

Gardner, H. (1999) *The Disciplined Mind: What all Students Should Understand*, New York: Simon and Schuster.

Rose, D. H., Meyer, A. and Hitchcock, C. (eds) (2005) *The Universally Designed Classroom: Accessible Curriculum and Digital Technologies*, Cambridge MA: Harvard Education Press.

Sternberg, R. J. (1996) *Successful Intelligence*, New York: Simon & Schuster.

VanLehn, K., Lynch, C., Schulze, K., Shapiro, J. A., Shelby, R., Taylor, L., Treacy, D., Weinstein, A. and Wintersgill, M. (2005) 'The Andes physics tutoring system: five years of evaluations'. In G. McCalla, C. K. Looi, B. Bredeweg and J. Breuker (eds) *Artificial Intelligence in Education*, Amsterdam: IOS Press.

MICHEL FERRARI

EDUCATIONAL THEORY

While educational theory aspires to provide a coherent set of principles that arise from practice and are tested through research, currently there is no systematic or unified theory of education, nor is there ever likely to be one, for at least three reasons. First, education is a radically trans-disciplinary endeavour and any potential unified theory will exhaust the resources of any one discipline, although historical stages in the emergence of the concept of educational theory can be traced in terms of the dominance of particular disciplines. Second, early accounts of education that sought to provide a theory of education by giving a philosophical account of human nature or the human mind, such as those provided by Locke or Hume, for instance, have given way to scientific theories which purport to offer empirical analyses and descriptions of the operation of the mind or brain. Third, insofar as education entails reference to aims or purposes and pertains to a distinct domain of practice involving the conduct of human affairs, scholars have argued that education necessarily involves *normative* aspects as well as purely descriptive or scientific inquiry. In this regard, then, the practical problems of education that arise in education necessarily involve issues of ethics and politics concerning contestable concepts such as equality, freedom, justice, authority and responsibility. As David Hume suggested in *A Treatise of Human Nature*, 'We ourselves are not only the beings, that reason but also one of the objects, concerning which we reason'.

Understanding the concept of educational theory depends upon recognising that historically there have been different views of 'science' (and 'research') and each has contributed to the development of educational research, defining the different research traditions. In short, educational theory is a contested term insofar as it involves accounts of 'science' and 'research'. Education as a form of philosophical theory figured largely in the works of Plato and thereafter in those of the Renaissance scholars. Modern Western traditions of pedagogy and education were inaugurated and shaped by Renaissance humanism, not only in terms of its adoption of the model of Latin letters, the revival of classical literature and the reproduction of its literary forms as the basis for the 'new learning', but also, in a more deeply cultural sense, in terms of the underlying philosophical assumptions constituting notions of human nature and human inquiry, and the relations of human beings to the natural world. This

was the essence of the humanities approach to educational theory.

The term 'science' and its more recent cousin, 'research', are historically recent notions. *Scientia* was the term used in the Latin culture of late medieval Europe simply to mean systematic knowledge. It was in the eighteenth century that two clearly different approaches (or epistemologies) developed in relation to the attainment of scientific knowledge and to human beings: René Descartes' rationalism and John Locke's empiricism. Descartes' rationalism was based upon the belief that reason, rather than sense experience, is the most reliable source of knowledge. By contrast, Locke's empiricism maintained that sense experience is the only reliable source of knowledge. The distinction between the *rationalists* (Descartes, Spinoza, Leibniz) and the *empiricists* (Locke, Berkeley, Hume) has played a major role in framing our understanding of the history of science, played a significant role in our understanding of the emergence of both the social sciences and education as a science.

This philosophical distinction helped shape the distinction in the emergent social sciences between a positivist tradition, dating from the social theories of Saint-Simon and August Comte, which insisted that there is only one scientific method, common to all the sciences whether they be natural or human, and what in German is called *Geisteswissenschaften*, which was an attempt to translate John Stuart Mill's notion of 'the moral sciences'. Positivism or empiricism became the mainstream Anglo-American view of science and the dominant paradigm in the social sciences and educational research. It informed both the paradigms of educational psychology and sociology of education, at least the strand that springs from the founders of sociology, Durkheim, Marx and Weber. It insisted that there is an objective, independent, reality we call the world; that truth is correspondence to reality; and that scientists discover truth, as spectators of a world which is essentially a given. In addition, this view of science postulated that there is a methodological unity of the sciences; that facts can be distinguished from values; and that reductionism, in principle, is both possible and desirable. The positivist view of educational theory and research, especially in psychology, has tended to emphasise quantitative data and rigorous experimental or quasi-experimental methods over forms of qualitative and especially ethnographic research. Historically, it adopted the principles of methodological individualism and also been associated with the doctrines of behaviourism and operationalism (see Phillips and Burbules 2000). Both doctrines have been historically significant for educational theory. Indeed, the tradition of experimental psychology was established in Germany by Wundt at the end of the nineteenth century, and extended to education by Edward Bradford Titchener at Cornell University, while James and Dewey initiated a pragmatist strand, and Thorndike completed his massive, three-volume *Educational Psychology* in 1914, setting up the stimulus-response model that dominated education until the mid-1950s when cognitive and information-processing models of learning gained ascendancy in the work of Piaget, Vygotsky, Bruner and others. Scientific educational psychology was epitomised in the work of Cronbach (1957; 1975) who called for the merging of correlational and experimental traditions to understand the individual learner in context. Cognitive psychology in education has experienced several waves of development, including the development of the *culturalist* model of educational psychology (see Bruner 1996), and constructivist, social and discursive variants of educational psychology. As one prominent educational psychologist recently claimed:

> From William James at the end of the 19th century, and by means of E. L. Thorndike's influence during much of the 20th century, educational psychologists dominated research in education. We won the battle for 'rigorous scientific thinking' in education, over objections of philosophers and educationalists, around 1915 ... After that, educational psychologists became the 'scientists' in America's schools of education.
> (Berliner 2003: 1)

He goes on to say that as the twentieth century closed, educational psychology's influence waned and educational sociologists and anthropologists supplanted psychology's disciplinary dominance. The social philosophy represented by Dewey (1966 [1916]) that emphasised equally the importance of the social lives of both teachers and students, and the close links between education and democracy, began to reassert its influence with the acknowledgement of the importance of socio-cultural factors in education.

The view of education as a moral, human or cultural science, by contrast, holds that there is a methodological difference from the natural sciences in that cultural products or manifestations can only be grasped through *verstehen* or 'understanding', as opposed to *erklärung* (or 'explanation') in the natural sciences. Where the former relies on 'understanding' of the meaning of human action by reference to human intentions, the latter seeks 'explanation' of natural phenomena and aims at the establishment of causal laws. The former falls under the *ideographic* (or individualising) sciences, the latter, under the *monothetic* (or generalising) sciences.

It is claimed that the human sciences treat social phenomena in terms of the linguistic and symbolic representation of meaning and value. The various forms of *phenomenological*, *existential* and *hermeneutical* inquiry belong to this broad tradition and characterise the neo-Marxist work of the Brazilian educational theorist Paolo Freire (2001), who with Henry Giroux established the tradition of critical pedagogy (see Giroux 1997), economists such as Samuel Bowles and Herbert Gintis (1976), and sociologists like Pierre Bourdieu (Bourdieu and Passeron 1990) and Michael Apple (1982). Analytic philosophy of education shares with this general approach the emphasis on understanding human actions and speech-acts by reference to intentions but, in addition, it holds that philosophy of education can do no more than clarify concepts (Peters 1966). The model of the foundation disciplines in education (philosophy, history, sociology, psychology), which was common in the 1970s has now given way to faculties of education that emphasise more applied forms of education such as management, leadership, curriculum and policy, and/or departments of adult, continuing, primary secondary, higher and teacher education, each with their own distinctive focus, concepts and developing body of theory.

Recently, that has been the attempt to use structuralist and post-structuralist approaches in educational theory (Peters and Burbules 2004). Structuralism, while emphasising a mathematical formalisation and analytical rigour, differs from positivism in insisting upon the concept of wholeness, of the *system*, and of the importance of relations of constituent elements that comprise structures or systems. To this extent it stands against the analytical, reductionistic procedures of positivism and its linear conception of causality. With the human sciences structuralism shares the emphasis upon linguistic methods and the symbolic representation of value; it differs by recognising the means for accessing such meaning. On this view meaning or value exists not as a result of the individual knowing subject, construed as the author of its own semantic intentions and historical agency, but rather by virtue of a set of rules or conventions that structure language, culture and institutions.

See also: activity theory; constructivism; correspondence theory; critical theory; education; educational research; feminist theory; pedagogy

Further reading

Apple, M. W. (1982) *Education and Power*, Boston MA: Routledge and Kegan Paul.
Berliner, D. C. (2003) *Toward a Future as Rich as our Past*, Carnegie Essays on the Doctorate, Menlo Park CA: Carnegie Foundation for the Advancement of Teaching.

Bourdieu, P. and Passeron, J-C. (1990) *Reproduction in Education, Society and Culture*, trans. Richard Nice, London: Sage.
Bowles, S. and Gintis, H. (1976) *Schooling in Capitalist America: Educational Reform and the Contradictions of Economic Life*, London: Routledge and Kegan Paul.
Bruner, J. (1996) *The Culture of Education*, Cambridge MA and London: Harvard University Press.
Cronbach, L. J. (1957) 'The two disciplines of scientific psychology', *American Psychologist*, 12: 671–84.
——(1975) 'Beyond two disciplines of scientific psychology', *American Psychologist*, 30, 116–27.
Dewey, J. (1966) *Democracy and Education: An Introduction to the Philosophy of Education*, New York: Free Press and London: Collier Macmillan. First published by Macmillan, 1916.
Freire, P. (2001) [1972] *Pedagogy of the Oppressed*, trans. M. Bergman Ramos, New York: Continuum.
Giroux, H. (1997) *Pedagogy and the Politics of Hope: Theory, Culture, and Schooling: A Critical Reader*, Boulder CO: Westview Press.
Peters, M. A. and Burbules, N. (2004) *Post-structuralism and Educational Research*, Lanham MD: Rowman and Littlefield.
Peters, R. S. (1966) *Ethics and Education*, London: Allen and Unwin.
Phillips, D. C. and Burbules, N. C. (2000) *Post-positivism and Educational Research*, Lanham MD: Rowman and Littlefield.

MICHAEL A. PETERS

EDUCATIONIST/EDUCATIONALIST

Educationist/educationalist is a term used to describe a specialist in the subject of education, a person who makes a study of the science and art, theories and practices of education. The word may be used as a synonym for 'educator' in a neutral or positive way, but also can have negative connotations. Inasmuch as educationists further the growth of education, their contribution to society may be well regarded. On the other hand, teachers in schools may see educationists as theorists rather than practitioners. Colleagues in universities may regard the subject of education (and those who research and teach it) as being less rigorous and prestigious than other areas of knowledge such as history or physics.

Most educationists pursue professional careers within the formal sphere of education; the profession of educationist grew with the growth of formal education. The work of Andrew Bell and Joseph Lancaster, inventors and promoters of monitorial systems of teaching, led to the establishment of the National Society and the British and Foreign School Society respectively, bodies which provided schools and teacher training establishments for the rapidly expanding population of nineteenth-century Britain. By the middle of the century administrators such as James Kay-Shuttleworth, Horace Mann and Egerton Ryerson were laying the foundations of national systems of public education in Britain, the USA and Canada. The first professor of education in England was Joseph Payne, appointed by the College of Preceptors in 1872, but the first British university appointments were made four years later in Scotland, of S. S. Laurie at Edinburgh and J. M. D. Meiklejohn at St Andrews. The first professor of education in the USA was William H. Payne, appointed in 1879 to a chair in education at the University of Michigan.

While the majority of educationists are now educational professionals, many of the most influential thinkers and writers about education achieved greatness in other fields. For example, philosophers such as Plato and Aristotle from the Ancient World and John Locke and Jean-Jacques Rousseau from the early modern period exercised considerable influence upon educational thought and practice and are regularly included in works on 'educationists'. Plato founded the Academy in Athens while his celebrated work, the *Republic*, which provides a blueprint for Utopia, is also a major educational treatise. Plato's student, Aristotle, himself established a school of rhetoric and for three years was tutor to the young Alexander the Great. John Locke was principally a political philosopher, but he was also a doctor and scientist, and a tutor, first at Oxford and then in the families of the Earl of Shaftesbury and Sir John Banks.

In the eighteenth century his influential *Some Thoughts Concerning Education*, first published in 1693, appeared in some twenty-five English and sixteen French editions with others in Dutch, German, Italian and Swedish. Another political philosopher, Jean-Jacques Rousseau, is best known as the author of *The Social Contract*, published in 1762, but his novel, *Emile*, which appeared in the same year, with its advice to 'leave childhood to ripen in your children' has a principal place in the history of progressive education and influenced many 'specialist' educationists including Friedrich Froebel, the founder of kindergarten schools. John Dewey, arguably the most influential educationist of the twentieth century, was also a philosopher and held the chair of philosophy at Columbia University, 1904–30.

In the twentieth century, groups of educationists could be identified by their commitment to certain philosophies, methods or areas of education. For example, European advocates of child-centred education included Ellen Key, the Swedish author of *The Century of the Child*, first published in 1900 and translated into a dozen languages, A. S. Neill, the Scottish-born founder of Summerhill School and Roger Cousinet, co-founder of the Ecole Nouvelle Française. The World Library of Educationalists series, published by Routledge, provides volumes of selected writings from leading contemporary educationists. Volumes to date (2006) include those by Richard Aldrich (history of education), Stephen Ball (education policy and social class), James Banks (race and culture), Jerome Bruner (pedagogical theory and practice), John Elliott (education research), Elliot Eisner (art education and school reform), Howard Gardner (psychology of education), John Gilbert (science education), Ivor Goodson (curriculum and life politics), David Labaree (education, markets and the public good), John White (philosophy of education) and Ted Wragg (teaching and learning).

See also: education; teacher education/training

Further reading

Aldrich, R. and Gordon, P. (1989) *Dictionary of British Educationists*, London: Woburn.

Flanagan, F. M. (2006) *The Greatest Educators Ever*, London: Continuum.

Gordon, P. and Aldrich, R. (1997) *Biographical Dictionary of North American and European Educationists*, London: Woburn.

RICHARD ALDRICH

EGALITARIANISM

Even politicians and theorists who would reject egalitarianism *tout court* often invoke some sort of educational egalitarianism in justification of policy initiatives. Unlike demands to equalise overall conditions, educational egalitarianism is closely associated with meritocracy; the idea that inequality of outcomes is justified as long as the competition for those outcomes is fair, and rewards some combination of talent and effort. The principle of educational equality does the work of ensuring that, despite unequal social starting points, children have equal opportunities to develop the talents that the competitions are structured to reward. So, whereas there is nothing wrong, according to the educational egalitarian, in having a wide wage gap, there is something wrong if some children have much better chances of getting the jobs to which high wages are attached because they got superior chances to develop their talents.

But what, exactly, is the principle of educational equality? There are several versions; the dominant one is the meritocratic version which states, consistently with the motivation set out above, that:

> An individual's prospects for educational achievement should be a function only of that individual's effort and talent, not of his or her social class background.

This principle, or something like it, lies behind a good deal of contemporary rhetoric about the need to 'close the achievement gap' or to 'reduce the effect of family background on higher education uptake'.

The principle, as stated, faces several challenges, of which three bear closer investigation. The first is that it is unstable. In singling out social background as an unacceptable source of influence on outcomes the principle arbitrarily favours the talented, who merit no more credit for their natural advantages than the well-born do for their social advantages. Why should the naturally talented get special access to unequally distributed rewards? This line of reasoning suggests a much more radical principle of educational equality, one which attempts to compensate for inequality of talent, as well as for inequality of social class background.

The second challenge objects that the means that would be needed to realise the principle are unacceptable because they would undermine other values. For example, some people think that prohibiting, or imposing punitive taxes on, elite private schooling would violate parental liberty. Perfectly realising the principle would probably require even more intrusive measures: interfering with the ordinary child-rearing practices of middle-class parents that prepare their children to take good advantage of the opportunities presented in school (like teaching them to read at home, reading them bedtime stories, and teaching them middle-class manners).

In fact, observing a conflict between two values in particular circumstances does not establish that either principle is wrong. Even radical educational egalitarians tend to agree that when the principle comes into conflict with ordinary child-rearing practices that lie at the heart of family life, it should give way to the value of the family. But this does not render it inert. Those radicals will usually maintain that although parental liberty is important, it is not so important that it requires us to permit parents to purchase elite private schooling for their children. And, even if a successful argument could be given for why that was so important, the principle

216

of educational equality might still require governments to take other measures, like improving state schools so that they were effectively competing with elite private schools, or limiting inequality of wealth, or reducing child poverty, concentrations of which are a major barrier to providing good educational opportunities for less-advantaged children.

The third objection appeals to efficiency. It is, or at least can be, socially inefficient to do what would be required to produce merito-cratic educational equality, because it would result in a levelling down of educational provision and, consequently, reduced invest-ment in the total stock of human capital and, ultimately, social wealth. At least in some circumstances this seems likely, and egalitarians are unlikely to dispute it. But social wealth is only one value; fairness in the competitions to access it, and how it is distributed, also matter. Educational egalitarianism describes a principle of fairness concerning access to the stock of social wealth, and egalitarians accept that justice will sometimes conflict with growth. Depending how much weight is placed on the principle, different judgements will be made concerning the likely tradeoffs.

A corollary of the motivation for the mer-itocratic principle is the idea that as inequal-ities of outcome narrow, educational equality becomes less important, because education has a less important role in allocating people to advantages in the labour force. But educa-tion is not only valuable because it helps its recipients in social competitions; it is also intrinsically valuable, contributing as it does to personal growth and flourishing. So most egalitarians have a residual concern about the unfairness of getting more of the benefits intrinsic to education than others through no effort or merit of one's own, which concern has force even if non-educational outcomes are equalised.

See also: elitism; equality of opportunity; equity; meritocracy; moral education; par-ental choice; underachievement

Further reading

Brighouse, H. (2000) *School Choice and Social Justice*, Oxford: Oxford University Press.
Cooper, D. E. (1980) *Illusions of Equality*, London: Routledge and Kegan Paul.
Gutmann, A. (1989) *Democratic Equality*, Princeton NJ: Princeton University Press.
Jencks, C. (1988) 'Whom must we treat equally for educational opportunity to be equal?', *Ethics*, 98(3): 518–33.
Swift, A. (2003) *How Not to Be a Hypocrite: School Choice for the Morally Perplexed*, London: Routledge.

HARRY BRIGHOUSE

EGYPT

The Arab Republic of Egypt is a country of 1 million square kilometres and 79 million people, located in the Northeastern and Southwestern corners of Africa and Asia respectively. It is bounded in the north by the Mediterranean Sea, in the east by Palestine and Israel, in the south by Sudan, and in the west by Libya. Accessibility and resources made Egypt a desirable acquisition, and in ancient times the country variously formed part of five different empires. These political transitions did not inhibit the development of Ancient Egypt's rich cultural traditions, including the hieroglyphic alphabet from around 3000 BCE.

In 642 CE Egypt fell to Muslim troops from Arabia. Subsequently, Cairo was founded, developing as the capital city and the home since 983 of Al-Azhar, the world's oldest university. Under Ottoman rule, from 1517, Egypt was a traditional Muslim society, largely isolated from Western culture. Poor children were unschooled, but boys from families with resources could proceed from a *kuttab* (elementary private mosque school) to a craft or trade apprenticeship or profession. Those belonging to the *ulama* would often transfer to Al-Azhar and become religious leaders, like their fathers, or enter business.

The French invasion of Egypt (1798–99) was critical in opening up the country to Western secular influences. A 'modernisation' programme created an elaborate military school system and, subsequently, lower grade schools were developed, but they catered for a tiny majority of children. The masses, meanwhile, continued to experience rudimentary Islamic education. From 1882 Egypt was under British colonial rule, but a 1920 commission criticised 'the failure of the administration to establish any system of education which extends to the mass of the people' (Faksh 1976: 235–37). When the occupation ended two years later, there remained a dysfunctional and divided pattern of schooling.

From 1922 to 1952, under nationalist governments, there was strong pressure for expansion, increased spending and secularisation. A 1923 law provided for free and compulsory education between the ages of 6 and 12, but ambition ran well ahead of reality and resources. It was only after the abolition of school fees in the 1940s that enrolments significantly increased. Even so, it seems likely that, in 1950, fewer than 36 per cent of Egyptian school-age children were in attendance. Spending on secondary and higher education was also a priority in this period: Cairo University was founded in 1925 and the universities of Alexandria and Ain Shams followed in 1925 and 1942 respectively (Faksh 1976: 238–39).

In 1952 the Egyptian army seized control of the country and, in spite of political turbulence, including the Suez Crisis (1956) and military clashes with Israel, under General Nasser (1954–70) and his successor Anwar al-Sadat (1970–81), there was a renewed commitment to educational advance. During the 1960s Al-Azhar was converted to a modern-style university, higher education tuition became free, and, in the following decade, several new Egyptian universities opened.

Under president Husni Mubarak (1981–present), Egypt has been an influential and moderate Arab state. The entitlement to 'basic education' was extended to age fifteen in 1981, with three-year primary, preparatory and secondary stages, the latter being organised into general, technical and vocational strands. Possession of a general secondary education certificate, similar to an American high school diploma, provides entitlement to a university education. The legacy of Egypt's past remains evident in a parallel primary, preparatory and secondary school structure supervised by the Supreme Council of the Al-Azhar Institution and in the survival of a number of private schools, language schools and alternative Muslim religious schools. The Cairo American College and the American University in Cairo are the most prestigious international education institutions located in Egypt.

Since the early 1990s the Ministry of Education has been committed to achieving universal basic education and economic competitiveness. A major construction programme increased by 53 per cent the number of school classrooms between 1992 and 1996, and primary education is now accessible to 99 per cent of all villages. In 1996 a Basic Education Enhancement Programme was launched with the intention of targeting disadvantaged groups, particularly girls, and to raise the quality of teacher training and school instruction. Regional and gender disparities and class sizes have been reduced, the length of the typical school day has been extended and new instructional technologies have been introduced. Today, Egypt has one of the largest education systems in the world, with 15.5 million students – 91.7 per cent of the age cohort compared with 61.3 per cent 30 years earlier – enrolled in 37,000 public schools staffed by 807,000 teachers (United Nations 2005: 26).

There remain some key challenges for Egyptian education. The overall illiteracy rate for adults (aged fifteen and over) remains high at around 30 per cent – 40 per cent for women – with significantly higher rates found in the poorest rural districts of Upper Egypt. According to the United Nations, the inflexibility of Egypt's centralised education system prevents those regions of the country with the lowest literacy rates building capacity and offering greater incentives for teachers. Although basic schooling is compulsory and free in Egypt, families nevertheless incur costs for stationery, transport, and ministry 'user charges'. There is also a tradition for households to additionally pay for a private tutor to complement public school instruction. Families unable to meet these costs are most likely to keep their children out of school altogether. Another difficulty relates to the perceived quality of Egyptian education: many young people are dissatisfied with their learning experiences and feel unprepared for entry into the job market, particularly overseas (United Nations 2005: 26–28).

See also: dropouts; Israel; literacy; religious school; World Bank

Further reading

El-Saharty, S., Richardson, G. and Chase, S. (2005) *Egypt and the Millennium Development Goals: Challenges and Opportunities*, Washington DC: World Bank.
Faksh, M. A. (1976) 'An historical survey of the educational system in Egypt', *International Review of Education*, 22(2): 234–44.
United Nations (2005) *Embracing the Spirit of the Millennium Declaration*, Cairo: United Nations.
World Bank (2002) *Arab Republic of Egypt Education Sector Review: Progress and Priorities for the Future*, 2 vols, Washington DC: World Bank.

DAVID CROOK

E-LEARNING

The term e-learning is used by some authors to refer to any learning that uses information and communications technology, though for others it has a narrower meaning, referring specifically to online learning via the World Wide Web. The term first came into use in the late 1990s, replacing earlier terms such as computer-assisted learning and computer-based training. E-learning is based on the use of personal computers and computer networks, CD-ROMs, and the internet, but as changing technologies have begun to question the dominance of the desktop personal computer so side-by-side with e-learning we now have such terms as *t-learning* (using interactive digital television) and *m-learning* (using mobile phones and personal digital assistants). The design of e-learning involves many disciplines and has spawned a large international research effort with commercial companies, universities and government bodies all actively involved in researching and promoting e-learning, seen in many government policy documents as one of the key elements of the information society. E-learning is now used in all sectors of education, and whilst richer countries have easier access to technology, and have therefore taken the lead, e-learning is also increasingly used in education for development (see, for example, the IMFUNDO project which supports ICT educational projects in sub-Saharan Africa: www.imfundo.org).

The use of technology in education goes back some thirty years, and over the last ten years e-learning has become firmly entrenched in schools, with many governments making large investments in hardware, software and teacher training. An earlier emphasis on office software and drill and practice exercises is now beginning to be balanced by the wider use of technology in art, music, and film. In higher education, commercial training and distance education earlier models of purely online learning have now largely given way to a more complex picture of mixed and blended learning, incorporating elements of both face-to-face and online learning, with greater choice for students as to how they wish to study. Initial high hopes for e-universities have been moderated by experience and there is no sign of traditional universities disappearing. The internet has had a significant and much-agonised-over impact on ownership of materials in higher education, illustrated on the one hand by phenomena such as the MIT Open-CourseWare project (http://ocw.mit.edu/index.html) which is making course materials freely available on the internet, and on the other hand by the increasing widespread use of the internet by students to plagiarise materials for their assignments.

Earlier e-learning designs, inspired by behaviourism and cognitivism, emphasised 'interaction' with the computer as the key element, though the level of interaction offered by many systems was in fact quite limited. Later designs, inspired by constructivism and social constructivism, saw much of the value of e-learning deriving from the way in which it can facilitate interaction between people (for example through computer networks). Though the importance of interaction has not diminished, recently there has been an increased additional emphasis on 'personalisation', the aspiration to adapt learning to the specific needs of individuals. Research evidence shows that impact of e-learning on student achievement is very dependent on the teaching context, but for many proponents of e-learning it is not the impact on traditional learning, but the possibilities for new forms of learning and creative expression that justify its use. An equally important aspect of e-learning is the promise of easier access to learning: freer of the constraints of time and place than face-to-face education. Undoubtedly many students have benefited from this greater flexibility, and there has been some blurring of the boundaries between formal learning environments and more informal learning, but the hopes that this might lead to a more equitable access to education for presently excluded groups seem so far not to have been realised to any great degree.

The use of technology within teaching and learning looks set to continue to grow, though the dominance of the desktop PC is likely to diminish and we may see technology become more and more embedded into the environment of teaching and learning, and as this happens the term e-leaning may well disappear, to be replaced simply by the term 'learning'.

See also: computer-assisted learning; educational technology; learning; technology; Web-based learning

Further reading

Collis, B. and Moonen, J. (2001) *Flexible Learning in a Digital World: Experiences and Expectations*, London: Kogan Page.

Leask, M. (ed.) (2001) *Issues in Teaching using ICT*, London: RoutledgeFalmer.

Lynch, M. M. (2002) *The Online Educator: A Guide to Creating the Virtual Classroom*, London: Routledge Falmer.

HARVEY MELLAR

ELEMENTARY SCHOOL

An elementary school is where children receive their first stage of compulsory schooling. Thus, in the North American 'K-12' – i.e. kindergarten to twelfth grade – public school system, children enrol in the first grade of their elementary school at the age of six. The American elementary school normally caters for the first six grades, after which students normally proceed to a 'junior high school' or 'middle school' for grades seven, eight and sometimes nine. High schools educate children in the upper grades. To all intents and purposes, the terms 'elementary school' and 'primary school' are interchangeable today throughout the world, with a majority of countries outside North America favouring the latter term.

In the context of British education, the elementary school describes the type of school attended by the majority of British children prior to 1944. Children typically entered an elementary school at the age of five and remained there until they left school. The minimum leaving-age was set as 11 in 1893, rising to 12 in 1899 and 14 in 1918. The campaign for universal secondary schooling from age eleven helped to define the primary school as a preferable alternative to elementary schooling, which, in the British context, was equated with cheapness and a basic, utilitarian curriculum.

See also: primary school/education; public school; school

DAVID CROOK

ELIOT, CHARLES WILLIAM (1834–1926)

Eliot was a distinguished lecturer in mathematics and chemistry at Harvard University between 1854 and 1863. After a teaching tour of Europe he returned to the United States to take up a position at the new Massachusetts Institute of Technology, where he began to write about broadening the scope and purpose of higher education. He was particularly concerned with organisational and governance questions. Several of his innovations became widely accepted, including the raising of student entry standards, and broader curricula with electives and written assessments.

He became president of Harvard in 1869 and held the post for forty years. During this time Harvard changed from being essentially a finishing school for gentlemen to become the leading academic institution in America. He relaxed the previously restrictive social regime for students and adopted instead a more open, liberal and relaxed approach. This was, however, counterbalanced by ensuring that courses were modernised and demanding. Several new schools were established at Harvard during his presidency, including those of business administration and agriculture. Eliot was instrumental in establishing Radcliffe College in 1879, a degree-granting college affiliated to Harvard. Through his chairmanship of the 'Committee of Ten' he helped to secure greater standardisation of the American high school curriculum after 1892. He also served on the General Education Board, which was influential in accrediting colleges and medical schools, and the Carnegie Foundation for the Advancement of Teaching.

See also: higher education; university

STEVEN COWAN

ELITISM

Elitism is a complex and contentious term. In common use, it describes the best or top quality provision or achievement in any field (e.g. elite fighting force, elite athlete) but is more commonly employed as a negative to imply assumed superiority for spurious reasons such as wealth and class.

People comprising the social elite have access to political and media influence and their views can affect and shape society. For some, this power is achieved through high achievements in a valued field. This can be won through a combination of hard work and excellence by making best use of intellectual or physical abilities, but can also be endowed on those born into a fortuitous social position, or through inherited wealth. Such luck perpetuates elitism in turn by guaranteeing advantageous educational experiences and support for any difficulties. The perpetuation of educational, cultural and social elitsm implies exclusion of people lacking the entitlement to belong to the elite, and the corollary of this is increased inequality in society. People from disadvantaged groups are underrepresented among the social elite, demonstrating the inegalitarian nature of society and education.

Some developing countries continue to run education in ways that support notions of elitism, often based on the argument that the best educated and most able people should be resourced in such a way that will encourage them to lead their countries and reward them for such responsibilities. This is considered an outdated notion in Western democracies, where a key educational aim (not often realised) is often to limit inequality, allowing people from difficult backgrounds to play important and influential roles in society.

Intellectual elitism concerns the propensity of valuing some areas of endeavour and curriculum studies above others. More abstract and traditionally favoured subjects such as physics and mathematics have a higher status than newer and more practical additions to the curriculum such as drama. Subjects that are more highly regarded become passports to higher levels of education regardless of their use in the workplace or the value of other subjects.

Educational elitism is exemplified by schools funded through pupil fees, entrance to which is restricted to those able to pay. This excludes any pupil unable to afford tuition and, by implication, children from certain class and cultural backgrounds. Many such schools provide occasional bursaries to allow attendance for talented pupils from less advantageous backgrounds. Such schools claim that pupils' abilities are recognised and developed, allowing for social mobility and increasing opportunity. Critics suggest that this merely reinforces the extant structural elitism, serving only to alienate such pupils from their home backgrounds and never affording a genuine opportunity to join the cultural elite. They would consider a better solution is to change the social system rather than allowing access to an outdated system for a privileged few.

Elitism involves the concentration of resources on pupils demonstrating promise as potentially able to make a significant contribution to the field in which they are talented. Other pupils consequently receive less funds and attention, which undermines the commonly held educational aims of egalitarianism in provision and equality of opportunity. Programmes for pupils with identified gifts and talents are controversial for this reason.

Some supporters suggest that such pupils are likely to make a significant contribution to society, economically and otherwise, making investment worthwhile. However, research demonstrates that pupils taking up provision for the gifted and talented tend to emanate from privileged backgrounds and those with disadvantages fail to benefit from the provision. Repeatedly, it is demonstrated that pupils from poorer homes are less likely to participate in such programmes for financial and cultural reasons. Some programmes have been established to specifically address these charges of elitism by conducting talent searches in areas of underprivilege, and by constructing programmes that replicate the values and interests of the target pupils.

Advocates of specialist provision who rail against charges of elitism postulate that specifically designed activities are necessary to meet the needs of able pupils whatever their backgrounds. Such pupils are entitled to equality of challenge (Winstanley 2004) and should be provided with education that encourages their development even where this goes beyond the general offer for most school-age pupils. This implies that the apparently opposite view of egalitarianism is, in fact, compatible with differentiated provision where this is understood as fairness and not 'same-ness'.

See also: egalitarianism; equality of opportunity; excellence; giftedness; independent/private school/education

Further reading

Swift, A. (2001) *Political Philosophy: A Guide for Students and Politicians*, Cambridge: Polity Press.
Winstanley, C. (2004) *Too Clever by Half: A Fair Deal for Gifted Children*, Stoke: Trentham Books.

CARRIE WINSTANLEY

ELYOT, SIR THOMAS (*c.*1490–1546)

Elyot was a formidable European Renaissance scholar. He was largely self-educated, but studied medicine privately under Thomas Linacre. His father ensured that, from early boyhood, Elyot became involved in consideration of court and state affairs, but throughout his life he resisted consistent attempts to appoint him to high public office. The royal printer, Thomas Berthelet, published his famous *The Boke Named the Governour* in 1531. This work, influenced by Elyot's reading of Erasmus and Francesco Patrizzi, Bishop of Gaeta, was the first wholly educational work written in modern English. It exerted considerable influence as a result of many officially sanctioned reprints. In *The Boke Named the Governour* Elyot outlines the characteristics of good teachers, and presents a detailed curriculum for the education and upbringing of gentlemen. Reading, hunting, dancing and music, central to Elyot's curriculum, were all interests of King Henry VIII. Elyot compiled the first Latin–English dictionary or 'wordbook', introduced many new words into the English language, including 'encyclopaedia', and was a key figure in the development of sixteenth-century 'standard English'. He specified an acceptable and authorised usage of the vernacular within schooling and higher education, and made a major contribution to popular medical education as the author of *The Castel of Helth* (1539), written in English. Elyot also translated into English Plutarch's, *Moralia, I, The Education of Children* (1535).

See also: scholar; scholarship

STEVEN COWAN

EMOTIONAL AND BEHAVIOURAL DIFFICULTIES/DISORDERS (EBD)

The term emotional and behavioural disorders (EBD) is defined as an abnormality of behaviour, emotions or relationships and has largely replaced the older term *maladjustment*. There are differences in international usage with *difficulties* replacing *disorders* in some countries. The term is contentious but serves as more than an administrative educational category: it has the advantage of focusing attention on the behaviour of the child and possible reasons for it. The concepts used are global and interchangeable. The child is considered to have EBD when behaviour becomes either a problem to the individual or to others, causing concern to parents and teachers.

Considerable challenges arise in giving a definition of EBD acceptable to all professionals. A range of descriptive terms is used, terms often theoretically presumptive and reflecting differences in medical, psychological or educational orientation towards various disorders. Conceptual differences often have implications for educational and other provision.

The term EBD is often subjective with people, including professionals, having different tolerances for behaviour. Socially defined differences of definition occur both historically and geographically and the term has a 'catch-all' nature, covering everything from nail biting to severe autism. EBD can be situation-specific, with abnormal behaviour exhibited only at home or at school. In context, behaviour may be normal, such as anxiety before examinations or grief after a family bereavement. There are dangers of social labelling in over-emphasis on behaviour that disturbs other people, rather than the individual. The key to professional intervention is the intensity and frequency of the condition.

Emotional and behavioural disorders have been categorised in different ways. Child divided into nervous disorders, habit disorders, organic disorders, psychotic disorders, and educational and vocational difficulties. A simple division used by Chazan *et al.* (1994) is to regard disorders as externalised or internalised, the former including aggression, disruption, bullying and the latter timidity, inhibition, and social withdrawal.

Problems of definition and categorisation influence how reliably we estimate the prevalence or incidence of EBD, particularly as EBD is not homogeneous. Estimates are based on a variety of screening and diagnostic measures, and depend on the context of screening and the samples used: for example, more seriously disturbed pupils with psychotic and severe personality disorders are rarely encountered in ordinary schools, whilst teachers are more threatened by externalised behaviours than by internalised ones, and may under-estimate the latter.

Estimates vary with the condition. For example, approximately 7 per cent of children suffer anxiety disorders and about 2 per cent experience school phobia. In general, the incidence of EBD appears from epidemiological and educational surveys to be increasing, though this may be explained by conceptual refinements, better diagnosis and earlier intervention, especially as, over the years, the emphasis has moved from medical to educational models of special needs provision. It should be remembered that EBD behaviours lie on a continuum from normality to severe abnormality, that pupils often present learning and developmental problems, and that there are conceptual arguments about such issues as the validity of psychoticism in young children and the extent to which problems of childhood and adolescence continue into adulthood.

How one deals with EBD problems is determined largely by the causes in each case. Causes include faulty personality dynamics, failure to adapt to the environment, child rearing, learning failure, cycles of neuroses, and organic damage. Professionals either try to change the environment or change the child, sometimes both. We are still uncertain about the causes of some conditions and the interplay of environmental and genetic factors. EBD can be the cumulative effect of longstanding adverse circumstances, and it is rare for one factor to produce behaviour reactions. It may be necessary to place a child in a special unit or a special school, with varying degrees of expert specialist teaching and psychological and psychiatric support. Medical approaches may involve drug treatment and/or a variety of behavioural therapies, for example cognitive therapies in the case of compulsions. Where the family may be a causative factor, family therapy may be the approach of choice using the concept of the 'therapeutic school' (Smith 2000). Inclusive schooling deals with the child in a mainstream school environment, integrating him or her with the peer group (see Barratt and Thomas 1999).

EBD is a major area of developmental research for educationalists and other professionals, which presents continuing challenges in theory and practice. These challenges are succinctly reviewed by Rutter and Sroufe (2000) and in the multi-authored work edited by Clough *et al.* (2004).

See also: autism; bullying; delinquency; learning disabilities/difficulties; psychology of

education; special education/special educational needs/special needs

Further reading

Barratt, P. and Thomas, B. (1999) 'The inclusion of students with Asperger syndrome in a mainstream secondary school'. In G. Jones and H. Morgan (eds) *Good Autism Practice*, Birmingham: University of Birmingham Press.
Chazan, M., Laing, A. F. and Davies, D. (1994) *Emotional and Behavioural Difficulties in Middle Childhood*, London and Washington DC: Falmer Press.
Clough, P., Garner, P., Pardeck, J. T. and Yuen, F. (2004) *Handbook of Emotional and Behavioural Difficulties*, London: Sage.
Rutter, M. and Sroufe, L. A.(2000) 'Developmental psychopathology: concepts and challenges', *Developmental Psychopathology*, 12(3): 265–96.
Smith A. (2000) 'An integrated model of good practice'. In M. Brundrett and N. Burton (eds) *The Beacon School Experience: Case Studies in Excellence*, London: Peter Francis.

JOHN B. THOMAS

ENDOWMENT

In the context of education, an endowment is a financial gift intended to generate income for the continued support of the institution. It is normally the expectation, and sometimes a stipulation of the bequest, that the gift itself will never be spent, but rather that the compound interest should be used to support scholarships and prizes. Many schools, colleges and institutions of higher education owe their foundation to a benefactor's endowment. For example, in 1566 Sir William Harpur, a tailor from Bedford, England, created an endowment to sustain Bedford School, now a leading fee-paying English 'public' school. Many private grammar schools, subsequently absorbed into British state education, were similarly endowed around this time. As the 'Harpur Trust' fund swelled, money was subsequently used, in the eighteenth and nineteenth centuries, to found three further schools in the town.

Many educational institutions maintain an endowment fund and invite financial contributions from alumni and the private sector, perhaps as an outright gift, a memorial gift (sometimes creating a sub-fund to facilitate specific causes or activities supported by the deceased), a bequest to be paid upon the donor's death or through planned, regular giving. An endowment fund is typically managed by a board of trustees, whose membership may include professional fund managers appointed with the aim of maximising growth through investment in equities, bonds and cash savings accounts.

The nature of endowments determined that older institutions are likely to boast the largest endowments. Yet, with respective endowments of £3.1 billion and £2.7 billion, the two ancient English universities, Cambridge and Oxford, fall well short of Harvard University's fund, the world's largest, of £14.8 billion or $25.9 billion (2005 figures). In the context of restricted public funding, many universities are now seeking to spend endowment income on staff costs and equipment, as well as on support for students. For example, the London School of Economics has applied income from endowment gifts to create professorships and enhance salaries in order to compete in the employment market for world-class academics.

See also: alumni; scholarship

DAVID CROOK

ENGINEERING

The history of engineering may be traced back to the pre-scientific age of cathedral builders, military engineers and such great inventors as Leonardo da Vinci. The first Industrial Revolution saw civil and mechanical engineers harness new understandings of science to develop plant machinery, railways and roads, water supply and irrigation, while the second saw the emergence of new branches of the subject: aeronautical, chemical, electrical, mass production, motor vehicle and weapons engineering, for example. More recently, engineering has broadened further to encompass microelectronics, computers and telecommunications.

The first engineering chair in the English-speaking world was established at the University of Glasgow in 1840, and engineering faculties became established and respected components of the modern Western university. The United States Military Academy at West Point was the first school to offer an engineering education, but, in general, at a global level, the subject has, until recently, been seen as one not studied at the sub-higher education level. This is beginning to change: in the United States, for example, there have been many recent initiatives to involve the academic and corporate engineering community in the development of K-12 curricula, while in England several specialist secondary engineering schools have been designated. Some schools now offer public examination courses in engineering.

Important future challenges remain, some of which are of long standing. One is to attract more girls and women into engineering. Another is to acknowledge that engineering education is expensive, demanding the regular replacement and acquisition of new resources. As a school subject, responsibility for developing the teaching of engineering is not something that can simply be loaded upon existing science or technology teachers. At the university level, if engineering education is to be an attractive career option for top graduates, salaries will need to become more competitive.

See also: subjects; technical education/ school/college; technology

DAVID CROOK

ENGLISH

English refers to the ethnic group and national identity associated with England and to the language spoken by hundreds of millions of people around the world as a first language, second, third or further. Such widespread use has resulted in English being known as the world's unofficial lingua franca, as well as the term *world Englishes*. However, for the purposes of this entry, the focus is on the teaching and learning of English, which also involves the previously stated references to English.

English is used as a subject matter term and as a label for departments of English in secondary schools, in colleges and at universities. The content of what is taught in these courses and departments varies considerably. They include: (1) the history and development of the English language across time, in individuals and groups of readers, writers, speakers and listeners; (2) the linguistics of English, including its systems of phonology, orthography, syntax, semantics, pragmatics and their relationships to each other; (3) descriptions of English usage and how it is learned by individuals as they read, write, speak, listen and think (also known as psycholinguistics); (4) descriptions of how English language users speak, write and read in different ways (dialects and registers) depending on the social context and function of the language (also known as sociolinguistics); (5) the teaching and learning of English as a second or more language; (6) teacher education programmes that explore curriculum, methodology and instruction of teaching English as a mother tongue or second language; and (7) understanding the stated and unstated status and power of English and its policies within and between nations. English departments include courses in rhetoric, linguistics, composition, literature, speech and drama. In elementary schools, English is the focus of study under the term 'language arts' and the curriculum is planned for students to explore how English is used to speak, read, write, listen and view their worlds.

There is general agreement that children learn oral English easily by being immersed in English-speaking contexts and that children surrounded by literacy practices in English learn to read and write. However, a major controversy surrounds the teaching of English. In many classes and instructional materials the teaching of English language is on prescriptive teaching of grammar, phonics, spelling and vocabulary isolated from the context of its use based on a transmission model of teaching. However, there is a great deal of research that shows little relationship between such direct teaching and the ability to read with understanding and to develop writing proficiency. Research also shows that readers, writers, speakers and listeners expand their language abilities through continuous use. English language users get better in the areas in which they use their language the most for real and authentic purposes. The websites below provide references to such works.

English language arts programmes at all levels would be enhanced if the community of educators were more involved in explorations of the complexities that are faced in English teaching and learning. These controversies are often the focus of professional English organisations that run conferences to explore these issues. These organisations publish print and online journals, books, pamphlets and a wide range of research and knowledge about English teaching and learning for both students and teachers. Such information is accessible at the following websites: Canadian Council of Teachers of English Language Arts (www.cctela.ca); New Zealand Association for the Teaching of English (www.nzate.co.nz); Australian Association for the Teaching of English (www.aate.org.au); National Association for the Teaching of English (www.nate.org.uk); National Council of the Teaching of English (www.ncte.org).

The topic 'English' in old encyclopedias of education provides insights into the history of the issues raised above. As a result of a 1966 conference at Dartmouth, Massachusetts, John Dixon wrote *Growth through English* (1967), which remains relevant to today's concerns. The international scholarly community who assembled at that conference established an International Federation for the Teaching of English (www.ifte.net).

The need still remains for the English teaching and learning community to come together to continue to explore and develop a curriculum for teachers and students that includes the range and richness of the study of English.

See also: curriculum; literacy; phonics; reading; spelling; writing

Further reading

Appleby, A. (1974) *Tradition and Reform in Teaching English*, Urbana IL: National Council of Teachers of English.

Clark, U. (2001) *War Words: Language, History and the Disciplining of English*, New York: Elsevier.

Dixon, J. (1967) *Growth through English*, Oxford: Oxford University Press.

Goodman, Y. (2003) *Valuing Language Study: Inquiry into Language for Elementary and Middle Schools*, Urbana IL: National Council of Teachers of English.

Hillocks, G. Jr and Smith, M. W. (1991) 'Grammar and usage'. In J. Flood, J. M. Jensen, D. Lapp and J. R. Squire (eds) *Handbook of Research on Teaching the English Language Arts*, New York: Macmillan.

Hogg, R. M. and Denison, D. (2006) *A History of the English Language*, Cambridge: Cambridge University Press.

YETTA GOODMAN

ENVIRONMENTAL EDUCATION

Environmental education has grown significantly in recent decades, especially in industrialised countries. It aims to educate people about the natural environment and the interaction of humans, with a strong focus on sustainable living and ecosystems. It focuses not only upon understanding the environment but also on change, and encourages members of society to lead 'greener' lifestyles by exercising responsibility for their local and global environments. The growing interest in environmental education has been fed by environmental disasters, depleted natural and wildlife habitats, climate change and poverty. The field is a broad one, at the interface of many disciplines, including agriculture, biology, botany, chemistry, ecology, geography, oceanography and meteorology. Environmental educationists are frequently specialists in at least one of these fields.

In schools it rarely features as a subject in itself but is now an important part of science curricula around the world. It is also taught in subjects such as geography. Students may also experience school journeys or field trips to places of environmental interest, including forests, parks and rural environmental education centres. It may be studied more directly in higher education, for example, as part of environmental science and ecology. A number of scholarly journals serve the global community of environmental educationists: one such journal is appropriately titled *Applied Environmental Education and Communication*.

Environmental education is also carried out by a wider variety of agencies and non-governmental organisations, including the North American Association for Environmental Education or the Polish Centre for Environmental Activities, *Zrodla*. Many voluntary organisations carry out environmental education in diverse ways, for instance by encouraging public participation in preservation and recycling projects, living sustainably through personal choice or in alternative communities, high-profile media campaigns, consumer action, demonstrations, lobbying and other methods. Many of these initiatives started as grass-roots campaigns, but, more recently, governments and longer established voluntary organisations have supported environmental education, a development not always welcomed by activists.

See also: biology; chemistry; geography; school journeys; science/science education

DAVID CROOK AND TOM WOODIN

EQUALITY OF OPPORTUNITY

Equality of opportunity is a driving force behind much education policy and practice. It is endorsed by people from many different political positions and is widely invoked as a means to evaluate and justify educational systems. However, the ubiquity of the term hides a number of differences in the arguments and meanings employed.

Equality of opportunity in education is usually related to wider social and economic factors. For instance, it may be viewed as a means of achieving fairness in the labour market, given that there is a significant connection between educational qualifications and the type of employment for which people are eligible. Education is not only something that is valued in itself in terms of learning knowledge, it is also a positional and instrumental good that can determine one's standing in any given social hierarchy. Of course, this does not preclude the possibility that educational equality might increase while the social and economic spheres experience widening inequality.

Three broad clusters of opinion can be identified which support equality (of opportunity) in different ways. It is widely agreed that immutable personal characteristics, such as gender, race and disability, should not influence the type of education people receive. The assumption that all people share a common humanity underlines equal opportunities legislation and policies aimed at ensuring, for example, that individuals are not prevented unfairly from receiving an education. Rather, it is widely held that impartial judgements of merit, such as skills, personal ability and effort, should determine success in education and social mobility. This perspective is generally seen as a 'negative' conception insofar as it holds that individuals should have 'freedom from' unjust and unfair interference, rather than 'freedom to'. The role of the state and educational institutions is limited to monitoring and regulation.

Others argue for more active liberal versions of equality and may point to such documents as the Universal Declaration of Human Rights. Persistent inequalities have undermined policies for equal opportunities and educational goods are not equally 'available' to groups of students in any meaningful sense. Accordingly, it is argued that everyone should have an equal chance of gaining the skills and abilities that are valued in the education system. Although widely accepted in

theory, this idea could potentially have quite radical implications; for instance, in terms of redistributive policies and the prevention of private forms of education. 'Affirmative action' in the United States of America has attempted to overcome the historical exclusion of African Americans by actively supporting individuals from that group to enter educational institutions and gain jobs. This can be a difficult path to take, as highlighted by the Supreme Court decision on *University of California v. Bakke* (1978). This judgment held that student quotas were inadmissible and had served to discriminate against a white student, Allan Bakke, who had been turned down despite having higher grade scores than some ethnic minority students who had been accepted.

More radical approaches tend to focus on wider structural factors that perpetuate educational inequalities. Individuals are perceived as part of social classes and groups rather than freestanding rational beings who are able to make the choices that suit them best. For instance, Marxists have pointed to the structural class relations endemic to capitalist relations of production as playing a determining role in educational outcomes. This perspective is committed to a wider societal change that would help to eliminate inequalities themselves rather than redistribute the amount of inequality across different social groups. Advocates of this approach are likely to highlight equality of outcomes in contrast to the meritocratic argument in which equality of opportunity enables people to pursue unequal ends. In practice, though, the two can be hard to separate.

Not everyone agrees that equality of opportunity is a worthwhile objective. For example, one group of mainly right-wing libertarian thinkers argue that attempts to pursue equality of opportunity constitute an unfair attack on individual liberty. Attempts to equalise differences in ability, motivation, interest and willingness to work hard are portrayed as misguided and impractical. Policies for equality may also reduce the competitive impulse to produce wealth and to achieve to the best of one's ability. According to this line of thinking, inequality can increase the total amount of wealth and achievement, even though it is not shared equally. Fostering equality is also deemed to involve an unnecessary degree of state action, which undermines individual choice and freedom as well as the role of the family. The danger of focusing on the most disadvantaged is that a large amount of resources are doled out for very little benefit.

The notion of equality of opportunity is further confused by the tension between focusing upon individuals, on the one hand, and social classes and groups on the other. Issues of class, race, gender, disability and sexuality have all added levels of complexity to these debates and revealed how the differences contributing to educational success are socially constructed, rather than innate. For many years social class was a key theme in discussions and debates on equality of opportunity and it was clear that working-class people achieved less in educational institutions. This was borne out by research projects that examined large datasets on achievement at school and complemented by ethnographic research that revealed the ways in which working-class students came to 'fail'. A range of other factors would come to inform the discourse on equal opportunities and, in doing so, dislodge class from its dominant position. Second-wave feminism pointed to the unequal treatment of girls, whose education was infused with male-centred assumptions. Gender would become an important concept and discussions on equality have come to orbit around the construction of masculinity and femininity in education. In addition, sexuality in schools remains a contested area in which 'normal' human relations are often presented as excluding gay and lesbian people. Others have pointed to the 'racialisation' of educational systems, particularly in countries such as the USA and South Africa, and the notion of 'institutional racism' has come to refer to the ways in which

schools and other organisations racialise and exclude groups of people through their everyday organisational processes and assumptions. Similarly, the 'social model' of disability has shifted attention from the shortcomings of the individual and onto the exclusionary practices of institutions that marginalise disabled people. Finally, the significant rift between so-called 'developed' and 'developing' countries also thwarts equality of opportunity by highlighting the damaging effects of extreme forms of poverty. It has also been recognised that inequality creates its own problems in terms of the self-respect, participation and health of the most excluded.

Thus, it is clear that there are multiple and contradictory understandings of inequality. These have not always been easy to comprehend holistically, although initial attempts to do so have analysed the way in which multiple oppressions 'intersect' with one another. A further way of addressing this issue is to consider the role of those with power and wealth: the apparent winners. In a context where there is a limited amount of a perceived educational good, it is unsurprising that upper- and middle-class groups bring their power and influence to bear in acquiring it for their children, most notably through private schools and elite universities. Furthermore, within particular institutions, staff assumptions, language, organisational structures and ethos can all serve to include and exclude certain groups. Given that it is widely recognised that children are a very diverse group, an important question arises. Should education be tailored to meet specific needs or should it consist of the same contents and methods for all? The difficulty here is that, in an unequal society, 'differences' rapidly become judged to be of higher or lower value according to a wider set of societal standards.

In educational policy the 'positions' and perspectives on equality may compete with other priorities, such as the quantity and quality of educational provision. Developing nations facing a severe shortage of resources have sometimes chosen to educate an elite leadership for government and industry while restricting primary and secondary education. Although the wider population may eventually benefit from such a policy, a counter-argument for equality might focus upon the importance of helping all people to improve their level of education, for instance through adult literacy programmes. While it is generally recognised that attempts to equalise outcomes of education, if desirable, may be impossible to achieve, one policy direction has been to work towards minimum standards for all, as advocated by the Education for All movement and the Millennium Development Goals.

Dilemmas over the nature of provision are also apparent in developed liberal democracies. European countries such as Sweden have engineered greater levels of equality than in the USA, where schools in wealthy areas are more generously funded than those in poorer ones. The current interest in developing the 'human capital' of a nation to its fullest extent can also be seen to operate in tension with the competitive international trend to create 'world class' institutions, thus introducing significant levels of inequality into education systems.

Proponents of equality have argued that an inequality of resources may be required if all children are to be educated 'equally'. This has given rise to debates over whether increased resources make a difference to educational performance. Just because certain groups benefit from greater resources it does not necessarily follow that their performance will be enhanced. Such arguments have bolstered the case for 'school improvement', which emphasises that expectations, strong leadership and good teachers can make a considerable difference to pupil's success in schools. Action has also been directed at the use of education made by children and families, for instance through family learning programmes and support with reading or mentoring schemes.

Building an educational environment that welcomes and supports all students still eludes most educational systems, and equality of opportunity is likely to continue to preoccupy educational institutions, policy makers, researchers and the general public. Inequalities are likely to become more complex and contested in the future, given the tensions between ideas of human capital on the one hand and growing economic and international inequalities on the other. It is also possible that research into genetics, which is pointing to differences in dispositions across population groups, may divert debates about equality away from their social aspects.

See also: antiracist education; egalitarianism; learning disabilities/difficulties; merit; meritocracy; positive discrimination/affirmative action; social exclusion/inclusion

Further reading

Brighouse, H. (2000) *School Choice and Social Justice*, Oxford: Oxford University Press.
Cole, M. (ed.) (2006) *Education, Equality and Human Rights: Issues of Gender, 'Race', Sexuality, Disability and Social Class*, 2nd edn, London: Routledge.
Swift, A. (2001) *Political Philosophy*, Cambridge: Polity.

TOM WOODIN

EQUITY

The word 'equity' signifies what is fair and right, or what is just. Equity in personal and legal decisions requires an application of principles mediated by sensitivity to the particulars of the situation and persons involved. It requires that those who are similar in relevant respects be treated similarly, and those who are different in relevant respects be treated differently. Those who do comparable work should receive comparable pay, for instance, while one who differs from another in committing a worse crime deserves a different and greater penalty. Because it is not always clear which similarities and differences are the relevant ones, or how tensions between multiple relevant factors are to be resolved, it is not always clear what is equitable.

Aristotle (384–322 BCE) noted these facts about equity and thought it evident that education should be public and the same for all, despite the nearly complete absence of public education in his world. No one can live well without education, and he theorised that the aim of a true or just political community must be to enable all its citizens to live well. Yet the 'all' he regarded as relevantly similar did not include females, resident aliens, or slaves, and it was not until the nineteenth century CE that political and educational theorists revisited the idea that societies have an obligation to act through their governments to provide all citizens with the educational prerequisites of a good life.

The public school movements of the late nineteenth century aimed to create systems of schools that were free, universal, compulsory at both the primary and secondary levels, and second to none. Their successes were dramatic but not complete, and by the 1960s the failure of public schools to be the 'Great Equaliser' became an object of inquiry and theoretical dispute. Was it somehow inherent in the *function* of schools that they perpetuate socio-economic inequality? Was it instead a simple consequence of the nature of markets that the advantages of a high school diploma would disappear as labour markets became saturated with high school graduates? Or might a more comprehensive system succeed in creating equal opportunity? The significance of early childhood experience for educational achievement suggests that any prospect of success in creating a fair competition for subsequent economic and social rewards would require unprecedented public investments in the well being and learning of preschool children.

The difficulties inherent in creating a fair competition for access to higher learning and socio-economic success have contributed to theoretical disputes over the form of educational equality. Least disputed is the idea that certain morally irrelevant factors should not be barriers to obtaining an adequate or equally good education. Race, ethnic origin, language, gender, learning disabilities and other impairments are widely considered to be in this category, and educational policy in many countries has taken steps to make these factors irrelevant to the quality of education obtained. There is little consensus beyond this, however, and theorists remain divided over how best to conceptualise educational equity or equality. Does equity demand simple ('lot-regarding') equality of educational investments in each child? If so, is that to be measured by per-pupil expenditures or in some other way? Would it apply ('globally') to all educational investments or only ('marginally') to the investments made through public school systems? Or is educational equity more appropriately conceived not in terms of comparable 'inputs' but of comparable outcomes or (more precisely) *prospects* of success in school or in life? Furthermore, should we think of equity in terms of absolute *equality* in one of these senses, or in terms of educational *adequacy*, which seems more achievable? How would adequacy be measured?

There are many debates concerning specific aspects of educational equity. These include the use of standardised tests that may be discriminatory in their content or impact, fair access to tertiary instruction, equity in public school funding, tracking and ability grouping, the advantages conferred by private tuition schools, the ethics of affirmative action, and the gender inequities entailed by accommodating the educational preferences of some minority cultural groups.

See also: Aristotle; egalitarianism; equality of opportunity; meritocracy; positive discrimination/affirmative action; segregation/desegregation

Further reading

Barry, B. (2005) *Why Social Justice Matters*, Cambridge: Polity Press.

Brighouse, H. (2000) *A Level Playing Field: Reforming Private Schools*, London: Fabian Society.

Curren, R. (2007) *Philosophy of Education: An Anthology*, Oxford: Blackwell.

Fullinwider, R. and Lichtenberg, J. (2004) *Leveling the Playing Field: Justice, Politics, and College Admissions*, Lanham MD: Rowman and Littlefield.

RANDALL CURREN

ETHNOGRAPHY

Ethnography has its origins in social and cultural anthropology. In the 1920s and 1930s the concept was introduced into sociology by the Chicago School of Sociology, where the early work focused on the study of the city and the 'community study', and involved the application of anthropological methods to the study of Western societies. In the 1960s there was a growth in ethnographic studies, especially notable in the study of deviant groups. In Britain this was influenced by the theoretical perspectives of symbolic interactionism, phenomenology and ethnomethodology. Between the late 1960s to the early 1980s there was considerable interest focused upon school ethnographies. Included in these are: Philip Jackson (1968) *Life in Classrooms*; Stephen Ball (1981) *Beachside Comprehensive*; David Hargreaves (1967) *Social Relations in a Secondary School*; David Hargreaves *et al.* (1975) *Deviance in Classrooms*. The latter two studies, in particular, reflected the continuing influence of both symbolic interactionism and the sociology of deviance on ethnography.

Ethnographic research is qualitative in nature and has most of the following features: people's behaviour is studied in everyday natural contexts; the approach to data collection is unstructured and the main sources of data are usually participant observation and relatively informal conversations. Immersion in the setting could be absolute where the researcher participates in all the activities of the group being studied and is an observer at the same time. Non-participant ethnography, by contrast, occurs where there is limited participation and the role of the researcher in the setting under study is more focused on observation. Other methods of data collec-

tion could include unstructured interviewing, personal documents and vignettes. The categories used for interpreting what people say and do are not entirely pre-given or fixed but this does not mean that the research is unsystematic. The intention is to capture the social meanings of human interactions and the seemingly ordinary activities of people in an attempt to understand their shared meanings and any assumptions which they may take for granted without imposing meaning on them externally. The focus of an ethnographic study, therefore, is usually on a small number of cases and the analysis of data involves interpretation of the meanings and functions of human actions. This approach is problematic, however, since the interpretation of data involves a process of selection based on judgements which themselves represent a subjective construction of the experience and actions of others. Ultimately, evaluation of situations and data leads to some sort of judgement since, as researchers, we never enter a research situation with innocence. We situate these based on our particular philosophical persuasions as well as through the personal filters that we develop over our lifetimes.

With these considerations in mind, ethnographies tend to include methodological triangulation because one method of data collection can only offer a partial view of the complexity of human nature without regard to different emotional situations and variables such as time and place. Triangulation offers an opportunity to use two or more methods of data collection to study the richness and complexity of human behaviour from more than one viewpoint.

Debates about ethnography have been broadly divided into two types. There are those centring on criticisms of ethnography for not meeting the criteria assumed to be characteristic of science, and those concerned with arguments that ethnography has not broken sharply enough with the model of natural science. Quantitative researchers have criticised the scientific status of ethnography on the grounds of lack of precision, subjectivity, and non-generalisability. On the other hand, ethnographers frequently criticise quantitative research for failing to capture the true nature of human social behaviour, reifying social phenomena by treating them as more clearly defined and static than they are. There have also been some criticisms of ethnography as naturalistic; that is, too embedded in an outdated model of scientific enquiry; a model that claims to represent things as they are or as they appear to the people studied, only capturing surface appearances and not the underlying reality.

The field of ethnography has expanded over the years to include several genres, such as: the biography or life history, the memoir, short stories, diaries, the narrative. Alternative topics and styles of expression and representations have also been developed. These include feminist, native, indigenous and critical ethnographies. For example, feminist ethnography has criticised the masculine bias in Western thinking. Critical ethnography, by contrast, has set out to dispel ideology and promote emancipation by unpacking dominant social constructions and the interests they represent.

See also: classroom observation; educational research; qualitative research; sociology; sociology of education

Further reading

Atkinson, P. Coffey, A., Delamont, S., Lofland, J. and Lofland, L. (2001) *Handbook of Ethnography*, London: Sage.
Hammersley, M. (1992) *What's Wrong with Ethnography? Methodological Explorations*, London: Routledge.
Brewer, J. D. (2000) *Ethnography*, Buckingham: Open University Press.

ANN CHERYL ARMSTRONG

EUROPE

Education in Europe is characterised by its diversity. It has been influenced historically by dominant traditions that have shaped Europe as a whole: the Greco-Roman-Judaic legacy of the ancient world, the rise of Enlightenment rationalism and science, the development of capitalism which Europe incubated and disseminated across the globe, and the emphasis on individual cultivation which runs through European educational thought.

However, Europe is not, and has never been, a single entity. It is in part a geographical expression but mainly an intellectual construction whose definition has changed over time. The classical civilisation of ancient Greece and Rome, from which the idea of Europe originates, included the northern shores of Africa, fusing Hellenic, Persian, Jewish and Egyptian cultures. The rise of Islam, which divided the southern and eastern shores of the Mediterranean from the north, thus making a geographical idea of Europe possible, also added to the cultural mix of the continent. Christianity, though central to historical ideas of Europe, has been a source of both unity and division, split first between eastern Orthodoxy and western Catholicism and later between Catholicism and Protestantism. Modern Europe, and particularly its more globalised western part, has become increasingly diverse. Although the European Union now helps to define what Europe is to its current twenty-seven member states, Europe as a whole extends beyond this, its eastern boundary still disputed, and remains as culturally varied as ever. Defining European education is no easier than defining Europe itself.

According to traditional historiography, it was in ancient Greece, and particularly in the Athens of Socrates and Plato, that the first recognisably European schools emerged, teaching gymnastics, music and poetry to children and the art of oratory to young men through Socratic dialogue. The Romans, who organised schools throughout their empire, later codified the liberal arts of Greece into the 'trivium' of grammar, rhetoric and philosophy and the 'quadrivium' of arithmetic, geometry, astronomy and music, and these became one of the bases of school curricula in subsequent ages. After the collapse of the empire the Roman traditions waned in medieval Europe, not least under the weight of Catholic scholasticism, but they were again decisively revived with the Renaissance, whose new humanistic thought drew on classical traditions of learning, later modernising them through the influence, at first only partial, of Galilean and Baconian empirical scientific thought.

It was the sixteenth-century Reformation, however, which provided the first crucial catalyst for the development of popular literacy in Europe. The Protestant faith stressed individual religious enlightenment through reading of the scriptures, and with these now increasingly available in the vernacular since the invention of moveable-type printing, the wider spread of literacy was encouraged. Protestantism was also an early form of nationalism, and it was the role of education in nation-building that lay behind the early promotion of popular education by the Lutheran princes in the German states of the sixteenth and seventeenth centuries. Throughout early modern Europe, Protestant states tended to be more widely literate than Catholic states, although the Counter-Reformation also produced powerful movements for the development of education, not least through the widespread promotion of secondary schools by the Jesuits, once dubbed the 'schoolmen of Europe'.

The religious schools and universities which proliferated gradually in seventeenth and eighteenth-century Europe were the antecedents of popular education, but it was the development from the late eighteenth century of national education systems, under state auspices, which marked the beginning of modern universal schooling. These systems, first conceptualised in the blueprints of La Chalotais and Condorcet and the other radical philosophers in pre-revolutionary France, owed much the cultural humus of Enlightenment with its celebration of reason and scientific thought, the 'Rights of Man' and the primacy of nurture over nature in

human development, a notion which gave credence to the advocacy of universal human educability. However, the actual construction of education systems in post-revolutionary Europe can be seen as part of a broader process of state formation in new or reconstructed states now based on notions of national sovereignty where the nation – or the people – were part of what legitimated the state. Governments advocated mass education to furnish the bureaucrats, engineers and military recruits required by the burgeoning state apparatus, but also to promote national identity, disseminate national languages and laws and generally to explain the ways of state to the people and the duties of the people to the state.

National education systems developed during the nineteenth century, albeit at different rates, in all the more developed parts of Europe, from Victorian Britain to Romanov Russia, and have subsequently spread across the globe. They have included national networks of elementary and lower secondary schools, funded, licensed and inspected by the state, which provide usually free and compulsory education to all children up to the age of fifteen or sixteen. They have also included general and vocational upper secondary schools and higher education institutions, the majority again publicly provided in most countries, for increasingly large proportions of young people. National curricula and assessment have also been developed along with national systems of examinations and teacher training, and certification has also been formalised in most countries. Such are the broad contours of public education provision in European states and, indeed, across most of the world. However, notable regional variations are apparent across Europe, which derive from the distinctive histories and cultures in the different regions.

Southern Europe, including France and the Mediterranean states, has considerable variety in its national traditions, not least resulting from the different influences of Orthodox Christianity in Greece and the Balkans and of

Catholicism in the west. Nevertheless there are common characteristics deriving from classical traditions and from French Revolutionary and Napoleonic influences. Southern European states tend to have more centralised systems of educational administration than elsewhere in Western Europe, even after the considerable shifts towards greater regional control in France, Italy and Spain during the last two decades. Leaving aside the Balkan states, currently in a process of transition, they all now have comprehensive and non-selective systems of lower secondary schooling but have retained the practice of grade repeating (whereby children failing to reach the standard for promotion to the next grade are often required to retake a year). Many Southern European states are also notable for their relatively formalised and structured forms of classroom teaching, sometimes portrayed as 'didactic' by educationalists from elsewhere, and for their advocacy of a broad science and arts school curriculum, often seen as a legacy of classical 'encyclopedism'.

German-speaking states, including Germany, Austria and parts of Switzerland, and some proximate countries, such as the Netherlands and Belgium, also have distinctive common characteristics. They all have selective systems of secondary education and, in most cases, strong apprenticeship systems. The apprenticeship dominates at the upper secondary level to a degree not known elsewhere and is often attributed to the particular forms of social partnership operating in the labour markets in these areas. Education is typically organised on a federal basis, with the regional governments retaining the majority of powers. Also, in contrast with Southern Europe, they tend to have rather more curricular specialisation in upper secondary education. English-speaking countries (both within and outside Europe) tend to have even earlier curricular specialisation than in the German-speaking countries and with a distinctive tradition of child-centred pedagogy. They are also singular in the degree to which they have promoted school choice and

diversity and the local management of schools.

The Nordic countries probably have the most distinctive common regional characteristics. In addition to widespread provision of adult liberal education, deriving from the folk high school tradition instigated by Grundtvig in Denmark, they also have unique systems of all-through, neighbourhood comprehensive schools. These combine the primary and lower secondary phases in one institution and have virtually eliminated all forms of tracking. Both institutions have been seen as manifestations of the specific political and cultural traditions in the region, which place a strong emphasis on the promotion of equality and social solidarity through education and the welfare state more generally.

The historical pattern of differentiation in European education may be altered somewhat by existence of the European Union. According to its constitution the EU has no competency in school education and the European Commission recognises that here principle of 'subsidiarity' should prevail. However, in recent years there has been a number of initiatives within the EU which have sought greater convergence within European education and training. These include: the promotion of lifelong learning; the 'Bologna Process' for harmonising the structures of higher education; and the Lisbon goals which set targets for improvement of various areas. These have all been actively promoted by the European Commission although through a procedure, known as the 'open method of coordination', based on the voluntary agreement of the member states. These kinds of initiative, combined with the common socio-economic changes affecting all of Europe, may indeed bring some convergence in European education in years to come. However, at the same time, the accession of new states to the EU, including those still in transition from former communist rule, brings new educational traditions into the EU. It seems unlikely, therefore, that education within the European Union, or for that matter in the broader Europe, will cease to be a diverse patchwork of traditions as it has been for the past two millennia.

See also: European Educational Research Association; Finland; France; Germany; Greece; Italy; Sweden; United Kingdom

Further reading

Bowen, J. (1972) *A History of Western Education*, vols 1–3, London: Methuen.
Green, A. (1990) *Education and State Formation: The Rise of Education Systems in England, France and the USA*, London: Macmillan.

ANDY GREEN

EUROPEAN EDUCATIONAL RESEARCH ASSOCIATION (EERA)

The European Educational Research Association (EERA) is an umbrella body of national educational research associations. Current members of EERA include research associations from Belgium, the Czech Republic, Denmark, Estonia, Finland, France, Germany, Iceland, Ireland, Lithuania, the Netherlands, Norway, Portugal, Spain, Sweden, Switzerland and the United Kingdom. EERA also has an accession membership to support the development of new national associations.

It was founded in 1994 as a result of growing collaboration among national educational research associations and research institutes throughout Europe. They identified the need for researchers to exchange ideas, collaborate and offer independent advice to European policy makers and practitioners. The aims of EERA are to

- encourage collaboration amongst educational researchers in Europe;
- promote communication between educational researchers and international governmental organisations such as the European Commission, Council of Europe, Organisation for Economic

Co-operation and Development (OECD) and United Nations Educational, Scientific and Cultural Organization (UNESCO);
- improve communication amongst educational research associations and institutes within Europe.
- disseminate the findings of educational research and highlight their contribution to policy and practice.

EERA holds an annual conference, the European Conference on Educational Research, and publishes the quarterly *European Research Journal*. The Association is divided into over twenty network groups including inclusive education, teacher education, histories of education, social justice and intercultural education, economics of education, and ethnography. A postgraduate research association supports the career development and training of students and new researchers.

See also: educational research

TOM WOODIN

EVALUATION

Evaluation research can be defined as the systematic assessment or investigation of the worth, merit or value of an innovation, an initiative, a policy or a programme. As well as gauging the worth or value of an innovation, evaluations have been used to measure the 'efficacy', 'effectiveness' 'efficiency' or 'impact' of interventions or initiatives. Each of these terms is problematic.

Several types and models of evaluation have been noted in the literature. For example, 'democratic' (sometimes called 'participative') evaluation has been distinguished from non-democratic. Roughly speaking, the former involves the participants in a full and active way in the evaluation itself, its design, its conduct and even its dissemination. The latter will not really involve the people who are the 'object' of the evaluation. As with any distinction, the difference between democratic and non-democratic evaluation is a matter of *degree* rather than kind.

A second distinction is between 'scientific' or experimental evaluation and a more 'naturalistic' or 'anthropological' approach, which involves studying an innovation, a new practice or policy in situ, i.e. in its natural setting. The experimental approach may involve setting up two parallel groups in a controlled way, then providing the innovation or intervention to one group but not the other (the control group). After a suitable time, the 'impact' of the intervention can be measured. As many commentators on methodology have noted, this can be fraught with issues (see Wellington 2000). This approach, and particularly the 'gold standard' within it, the randomised controlled trial, is sometimes said to be the only way to either test or to demonstrate what 'really works' in education. Its critics though, will say that it may show *what works* but can never look behind this to show *why something works* or *how it works*, i.e. the focus in experimental evaluation is on *outcomes* rather than *processes*.

A useful distinction is often made between *formative* and *summative evaluation*. The former involves *evaluation* carried out in the early or intermediate stages of a programme, a course or an intervention while changes can still be made; thus the formative evaluation shapes and informs those changes. In contrast, summative evaluation is carried out at the end of a programme or intervention to assess its 'impact'.

Finally, a distinction was made by Janet Finch (1986) between the 'engineering model' of evaluation and the 'enlightenment model'; this distinction is still valuable in today's educational context. The former is linked totally to action, problem solving and change (hopefully improvement); while the aim of the latter is to bring about understanding, illumination and enlightenment. As mentioned above, such a distinction should be seen as labelling two poles of a continuum, rather than presenting a sharp dichotomy, i.e. all evaluations will have an 'illuminative'

aspect (Parlett and Hamilton 1976); and all evaluations will be linked to some action or other. It has been said that an evaluation is but one of the factors in determining action and many other factors will be taken into account in implementing change and action (e.g. political and economic factors, ethical considerations), but there is no reason why any evaluation should not *inform future action*, even if it does not fully determine it.

The link between evaluation and action will always be a problematic one, however: as David Hume pointed out, we can never derive an 'ought from an is'. To do so would be to commit the 'naturalistic fallacy' (the label given by the Cambridge philosopher G. E. Moore to Hume's separation). Incidentally, the 'ought' versus 'is' distinction poses a similar problem for 'evidence-based practice'.

It hardly needs saying that there will always be a political and economic dimension to every evaluation, especially if the evaluation research has been funded and sponsored by a body or a government department. This implies that the organisational and political context of every evaluation is of vital importance.

Dissemination and reporting of evaluation research is equally important and sensitive. The goal of evaluation is often to provide feedback to certain audiences (e.g. government departments, funders, teachers, curriculum developers, policy makers). Thus, the use of language and the presentation of research is a key consideration in the final stages. This may involve 'getting the message across' to a variety of audiences, perhaps using different language and presentation in different cases (e.g. visual, auditory, textual). A variety of outlets for publication, from the government report or full academic article to the newspaper report or the radio interview, may be necessary.

Evaluation research is characterised by having numerous stakeholders. For some of these people, the outcome and presentation of the evaluation may have far-reaching effects, possibly involving the promotion, demotion, prestige, status, salary or even job of the stakeholders who may be 'subject' to the evaluation.

Multiple methods are likely to be used in evaluations. If the research follows a naturalistic approach, the methods of case study work may be used (e.g. focus groups, observations, documentary research, the Delphi method, interviews, etc.). If a more experimental approach is taken, a more quantitative stance might be followed, involving randomisation, pre- and post-testing and questionnaires perhaps. Evaluation research seems to be characterised by an eclectic choice of methods.

In summary, evaluative research can have many purposes: informing decisions, improving action, illumination and understanding, informed action, 'better' practice. In a sense, however, all educational research is evaluative as it inevitably involves values and, for most people, its goal is to improve the human situation.

See also: case study; educational research; evidence-based policy/practice; experimental research; qualitative research; quantitative research

Further reading

Eisner, E. (1985) *The Art of Educational Evaluation*, London: Falmer.
Finch, J. (1986) *Research and Policy*, London: Falmer.
Parlett, M. and Hamilton, D. (1976) 'Evaluation as illumination'. In D. Tawney (ed.) *Curriculum Evaluation Today*, London: Macmillan.
Wellington, J. (2000) *Educational Research: Contemporary Issues and Practical Approaches*, London: Continuum.

JERRY WELLINGTON

EVIDENCE-BASED POLICY/PRACTICE

Evidence-based (or informed) policy and practice (EBPP or EIPP) is the idea that research evidence should have an explicit and central role in developing policy and practice. The research evidence should be identified, and then combined, in an explicit way with other legitimate factors influencing decision making, such as values, resources, and professional skills. Decision making that ignores research evidence can be unethical when social interventions may have no beneficial effect or cause more harm than good.

The need for evidence-based polices was a central part of the 1999 White Paper on 'Modernising Government' in the United Kingdom. In the United States, the Education Sciences Reform Act of 2002 had the goal of transforming education into an evidence-based field in which the best available research and data is used to inform choice of programmes or practices. For educational practice, it has been argued that professionals are too dependent on (procedural) craft knowledge, and that this should be balanced with (declarative) research knowledge, as in other professions such as medicine (Hargreaves 1996). Evidence-based medicine is the integration of best research evidence with clinical expertise and patient values (Sackett *et al.* 2000).

Before policy makers and practitioners can use research evidence, it needs to be available to them in an appropriate and useful form. Individual studies may be misleading, yet policy makers and practitioners have difficulty in directly accessing all relevant research because of the quantity of research produced, the diversity of places in which it is published, and the difficulty in assessing the quality and relevance of each study (Hillage *et al.* 1998; Towne *et al.* 2005).

Literature reviews provide one way of bringing together research findings for different audiences, but traditionally there has not been an agreed methodology for undertaking such reviews or a requirement for reviews to state their methods. EBPP requires explicit rigorous methods of review to ensure accountability of the conclusions and knowledge accumulation, with specification of:

1 the nature of the review question and its values and other conceptual assumptions;

2 clear criteria for determining which research should be included in the review and an explicit search strategy for identifying the studies meeting these criteria;

3 a method for extracting information about the results from each study and their relevance and value to answering the review question;

4 a method for synthesising this information in terms of (i) what is known; (ii) what is not known and requires further study.

Experts and expert panels are another method for synthesising knowledge for policy and practice, but can have the same limitations as traditional non-systematic literature reviews. It may also not be clear if an expert opinion is a synthesis of practice or research knowledge or some combination of the two.

Systematic methods of synthesis enable policy makers, practitioners, and all other users of research to have an active involvement in determining the review questions and, thus, research agendas. It provides the potential for a dynamic relationship between the users and producers of research, rather than the traditional passive model of dissemination of research findings.

EBPP has been used extensively in health to answer questions of efficacy ('what works') using statistical meta analysis to synthesise the findings of randomised controlled trials, and this approach is also being applied in education (for example, the What Works Clearinghouse at http://w-w-c.org). This has led some to fear that EBPP favours particular types of knowledge and has a narrow instrumental view of the purpose of education and educational research and could lead to unthinking empricism (Thomas and Pring 2004). For others, the logic of using systematic methods of synthesised research knowledge should be applied to all policy and practice questions, including issues of need, prevalence, consumer views, and conceptual and process questions about how things

'work'. For this reason, methods are being developed for systematic narrative and conceptual synthesis as in meta ethnography and mixed methods synthesis (see for example, the EPPI-Centre at http://eppi.ioe.ac.uk).

See also: educational research

Further reading

Hargreaves, D. (1996) *Teaching as a Research-Based Profession: Possibilities and Prospects*, Teacher Training Agency Annual Lecture, London: TTA.

Hillage, J., Pearson, R., Anderson, A. and Tamkin, P. (1998) *Excellence in Research in Schools*, London: Department for Education and Employment/ Institute of Employment Studies.

Sackett, D. L., Straus, S. E., Richardson, W. S., Rosenberg, W. and Haynes, R. B. (2000) *Evidence-Based Medicine: How to Practice and Teach EBM*, 2nd edn, London: Churchill-Livingstone.

Thomas, G. and Pring, R. (eds) (2004) *Evidence-Based Practice*, Buckingham: Open University Press.

Towne, L., Wise, L. and Winters, T. M. (eds) (2005) *Advancing Scientific Research in Education*, Washington DC: National Research Council, National Academy Press.

DAVID GOUGH

EXAMINATIONS

Examinations can be written, oral, or taken onscreen electronically, and can involve the observation of activities undertaken by the examination candidate. 'Traditional examinations' tended to involve the production of written answers under 'examination conditions' in a tightly controlled 'examination room' setting, where there are restrictions in relation to ensuring that the examination questions are not known in advance, that candidates work on their own, and that they are supervised to ensure that they do not 'cheat' or gain an unfair advantage through any other form of assistance. In 'high stakes examination' situations candidates, their teachers and their families may go to considerable lengths to gain an advantage over other candidates. Cramming and coaching in examination techniques may be seen as the acceptable end of a continuum which may also include bribery, copying from others, getting advice from others outside the examination room, impersonation and other forms of subterfuge.

Examinations may be pass/fail or may lead to marks, grades or other kinds of reports. In some instances students may be able to see their work after it has been assessed in order to get a detailed understanding of how it has been judged. More frequently, examination-marking procedures are tightly guarded and secretive and all that becomes public is a final result.

In recent years the variety of ways in which individuals can be examined has expanded. Onscreen *e-assessments* are becoming more common and in some cases those being examined in this way may get their results almost immediately after they complete their examination. 'Open book examinations' allow candidates to take reference texts into the exam room and 'open question examinations' allow candidates to know what questions they are going to be asked in advance of sitting the examination. Also candidates may be invited to present evidence of their learning in the form of a 'portfolio of evidence', which may draw together artefacts produced over a considerable period. To some extent there has been a move towards reducing the artificiality of examinations, bringing the conduct of assessments closer to everyday situations. In some areas of education 'continuous assessments' have replaced 'end of course examinations'. In such a situation the role of assessor may be performed by those teaching the student, and there have been many debates about the advantages and disadvantages of assessments carried out by teachers in learning situations, as opposed to external marking of formal examinations.

A great deal of work has gone into developing different types of 'written examinations'. In some parts of the world, and in some subjects, multiple-choice tests have been favoured, because they can cover many questions very quickly and can also, if necessary, be machine marked without there being any need for examiners to form a judgement about each candidate's work. In addition, sophisticated statistical techniques, some imported from the field of psychometrics, have been employed to try to improve examination marking, scaling, and equating procedures. Critics of such systems point out that educational achievements cannot satisfactorily be reduced to simple grades and marks, and sophisticated statistical procedures may give the impression of considerable accuracy of measurement inappropriately. There are many other forms of examination questions, including free-response and short-answer questions, which allow candidates more varied opportunities to show what they know and can do.

Since their first recorded use in China some 2,000 years ago, examinations have often been used as a means of attempting to avoid nepotism, or other unfair practices, in relation to providing access to scarce resources either in employment or education. However, there is always a question of how fair they really are in performing that task. Alongside concerns over fairness and bias, there are also issues in relation to fitness for purpose in relation to decisions that are made on the basis of examination results. Examinations generally cover a sample of the total number of questions/topics that could be covered, and candidates can therefore be more or less fortunate in terms of what comes up in the papers they take. Examination results are rarely able to be more than rough estimates of the achievements of individual students, and that can be discomforting in social situations where much hangs on the results. For this reason, most examination systems have appeals procedures and are frequently the subject of public debates about whether they can be improved.

See also: assessment; continuous assessment; formative assessment; high-stakes testing; oral examination; qualifications; selection; summative assessment; test/testing

Further reading

Murphy, R. and Broadfoot, P. (1995) *Effective Assessment and the Improvement of Education*, Lewes: Falmer Press.

Wood, R (1991) *Assessment and Testing: A Survey of Research*, Cambridge: Cambridge University Press.

ROGER MURPHY

EXCELLENCE

The word 'excellence' was coined in the sixteenth century from the Latin *excellentia* to refer to the state or fact of excelling; that is to say having a high degree of (usually good) qualities such as merit, skill, virtue, worth, dignity, eminence. There are several different viewpoints among educational psychologists on what constitutes excellence in education. Some say excellence is something fostered in individuals by enhancing their inherent mental abilities, their knowledge, their self-regulation, or their own personal efforts to excel. Others say that excellence is a product of particular institutional practices.

Excellence may result from some biological feature of individuals, for example, 'g', thought to be genetic inherited ability. Of course, g is necessarily expressed within particular cultural environments, thus a distinction is often made between fluid intelligence (e.g. pattern recognition) and crystallised intelligence that involves knowledge as a product of learning (e.g. vocabulary). Excellence of knowledge is typically called expertise. Research in cognitive science shows that expertise is not just more knowledge, but better organised knowledge that identifies principles and patterns, not just surface features of problems. Experts monitor their performance through self-regulation, which has three main moments: planning, monitoring, and evaluation. Effective self-regulators quickly become expert and perform in ways that are excellent.

Excellence also involves character, including authenticity in how knowledge is engaged. Recent research on education to develop character shows no consensus on how to do so. A major discussion is whether to teach specific kinds of values or attitudes (for example, generosity) until they become habitual, or whether students should engage in general practices like mindfulness meditation or journaling, that allow them to articulate truths about their own mind and character. Ultimately, excellent character should promote a moral self that expresses personal excellence. Excellence of knowledge and character are both required before someone is thought wise (what Baltes calls the coordination of mind and virtue). Wisdom is thus an excellence that engages not merely the conceptual aspects of a task, but also its personal and emotional implications. For example, one may be an expert in biomedical research that uses the great apes to study human disease, but wisdom requires that one carefully consider, articulate and personally engage with the ethical ramifications of using these apes for research, given that they are our closest biological relatives.

Excellence is a term also applied to institutions. From an institutional point of view, excellence is promoted as much in particular social and cultural settings as it is through individual activity. For example, Oxford or Harvard are considered excellent universities and produce excellent students in many disciplines. Likewise, Julliard's music school is renowned as one of the best places to learn music. The question then becomes not, 'Who is gifted or exceptional?' but 'What sort of social and personal conditions promote excellence, and what sort of actions can educators take to assure that students will learn to become excellent in ways that both they and society value?'

Excellence is developed, as are all other kinds of learning, through direct experience, emulation, or specific practices and exercises. These may, or may not, be part of an institution that itself is famed for excellence. Anders Ericsson emphasises the crucial role of the quality and amount of 'deliberate practice' in achieving the highest levels of expertise (influenced by motivation and meta-cognitive experiences, including self-efficacy beliefs and self-attributions). Rosa Pinkus and Ryan Sauder trace the emergence of a new medical sub-discipline, neurosurgery, at the turn of the century. In particular, they show how the emergence of neurosurgery was shaped by the technical and verbal rivalry between two key figures in medicine at that time, Harvey Cushing and his student Walter Dandy. Education for wisdom has been attempted by programmes that engage the whole school (like Project Wisdom), or by infusing a particular theory of wisdom into the curriculum, like Philosophy for Children, or Robert Sternberg's Balanced Theory of Wisdom.

But for Howard Gardner, any discussion of excellence must coordinate three vantage points: the individual, the knowledge domain, and the professional field. Excellent individuals are those who make a significant impact on a domain. Thus, excellence becomes something said of those who do good professional work, or can educate individuals who can do even better.

See also: ability; behaviourism; cognition; Gardner, Howard; giftedness; intelligence/ intelligence tests; moral education; psychology of education

Further reading

Ferrari, M. (ed.) (2001) *The Pursuit of Excellence through Education*, Mahwah NJ: Erlbaum.
Gardner, J. (1961) *Excellence: Can We Be Equal and Excellent Too?*, New York: Harper and Row.
MICHEL FERRARI

EXCLUSION/EXPULSION

Pupil or student exclusion or expulsion from school, resulting from unacceptable conduct breaching the discipline policy, is a more severe sanction than suspension. In the United States of America, for example, it is common for suspension to last up to ten days, during which the student remains on the school roll. By contrast, expulsion lasts for a period longer than twenty days and involves the removal of the student from the register. Such decisions are never taken lightly and may be subject to legal challenge, especially if the exclusion or expulsion is specified as permanent. A school excluding or expelling a student may be required to set and mark work initially. This applies for the first fifteen school days of the exclusion in England, for example, where it is specified that pupil exclusion should not be the sanction applied for any of the following: minor incidents such as not doing homework or not bringing dinner money; poor academic performance; lateness or truancy; pregnancy; breaking school uniform rules or rules on appearance including jewellery, body piercings or hairstyle (except possibly where persistent and in open defiance of these rules and when all other avenues have been exhausted); the behaviour of parents; parents' refusal to come to a meeting.

In the severest cases of misconduct a student may be removed to a secure juvenile institution where some teaching is provided. Otherwise, in order to comply with its legal duties to provide compulsory education, it may fall upon the state government or local education authority to make arrangements for the student to transfer to another school, or to be educated at home or in another setting. In the United Kingdom pupil referral units exist for this purpose, though they also accommodate children who cannot attend school because of medical problems, teenage mothers and pregnant schoolgirls, pupils who have been assessed as being school phobic, and pupils awaiting a school place. They also provide short placements for those who are at risk of exclusion.

See also: discipline; suspension
DAVID CROOK

EXPERIENTIAL LEARNING

Experiential learning, as opposed to traditional and rote learning, denotes knowledge acquired from experience, rather than formal schooling and is student-centred. Experiential learning theory (ELT) defines learning as 'the process whereby knowledge is created through the transformation of experience' and knowledge 'results from the combination of grasping and transforming experience' (Kolb 1984). ELT offers a pragmatic and holistic perspective of the learning process. It is called 'experiential learning' to stress the significance of life experience in learning. According to Carl Rogers, a humanistic psychologist, meaningful learning is facilitated when the student participates completely in the learning process and has control over its nature and direction. To Rogers, experiential learning is equivalent to personal change and growth, as all human beings have a natural propensity to learn. Hence, the role of the teacher is to facilitate such learning, including setting a positive climate for learning, balancing intellectual and emotional components of learning, and sharing feelings and thoughts with learners. The essence of experiential learning, as the cornerstone of learner-centred pedagogy, is the notion that experience itself is an invaluable source of learning and is 'the foundation of and the stimulus for learning' (Boud et al. 1993).

Experiential learning is the mode and process of actively engaging students in a worthwhile and authentic learning experience that will result in quality learning. Due to its mode of delivery, students engage in various constructivist and metacognitivist experiences, such as problem-solving, critical thinking, analysis and evaluation. Students, working on collaborative groups, are encouraged, within reason, to discover principles, deconstruct knowledge and reflect on their experience, thus developing higher-order thinking skills. As such, it is useful to differentiate ELT from behavioural and cognitive learning perspectives on learning, which stress the role of operant conditioning and cognitive development.

Experiential learning is also a classroom strategy where pedagogues create a cooperative learning environment, engaging learners in a meaning-making process as a direct, but guided and structured, classroom experience.

Experiential learning differs from traditional, fundamentalist and 'back to basics' approaches to classroom learning, in so far as pedagogues first immerse students in activities and then ask them to reflect on their experience. It is designed to encourage deeper thinking (generic rather than surface learning), reflection and metacognition, in order to facilitate meaningful learning.

Some scholars argue that ELT helps to understand learning at a deeper, more comprehensive level than previously, that it guidance for helping people to improve their learning, and that it offers an authentic and worthwhile pedagogy for the inclusive curriculum and individual differences in the classroom.

The concept is used to refer to experience from life and work that may be recognised, in the case of mature students, for granting life experience credits for college or university entry.

Experiential learning can be traced to the experimental pedagogy of John Dewey, Jean Piaget, Kurt Hahn, Carl Rogers, Ivan Illich, Paolo Freire and others. Experiential learning is also linked to constructivism, social constructivism, metacognition, reflection and critical thinking. John Dewey was one of the first educators to recognise that 'all genuine education comes about through experience' (Dewey 1938). ELT can be used in computer simulations of learning experiences in the classroom, and has great potential to transform schools. It offers to students a meaningful learning, personally relevant to their needs and aspirations, and it is likely to motivate and empower them to take responsibility for their own learning.

See also: accreditation of prior achievement/learning; collaborative/cooperative learning; constructivism; Dewey, John; learning; Piaget, Jean; reflective practitioner; Rogers, Carl; social constructivism

Further reading

Boud, D., Cohen, R. and Walker, D. (1993) 'Introduction: understanding learning from experience'. In D. Boud, R. Cohen and D. Walker (eds) *Using Experience for Learning*, Bristol: Society for Research in Higher Education and Open University Press.

Dewey, J. (1938) *Experience and Education,* New York: Collier Books.

Kolb, D. (1984) *Experiential Learning: Experience as the Source of Learning and Development*, Englewood Cliffs NJ: Prentice Hall.

Kolb, D., Boyatzis, R. and Mainemelis, C. (2000) 'Experiential learning theory: previous research and new directions'. In R. J. Sternberg and L. Zhang (eds) *Perspectives on Thinking, Learning and Cognitive Styles*, Mahwah NJ: Lawrence Erlbaum.

JOSEPH ZAJDA AND REA ZAJDA

EXPERIMENTAL RESEARCH

Experimental research is often contrasted with the 'naturalistic approach', although in practice the distinction is not always clear-cut and is often a matter of degree, rather than kind.

The main features of a naturalistic approach to research are:

- *Setting*: Research is carried out in the natural setting or context, e.g. workplace, home, classroom, playground.
- *Primary data-gathering instrument*: The researcher.
- *Background knowledge*: Personal, tacit, intuitive knowledge is a valuable addition to other types of knowledge.
- *Methods*: Qualitative rather than quantitative methods will be used, but not exclusively.
- *Sampling*: Purposive sampling is likely to be preferred over representative or random sampling.
- *Design*: The research design tends to unfold/emerge as the study progresses and data are collected.
- *Theory*: Theory tends to emerge from (be grounded in) the data, as opposed to being based on an initial hypothesis, which the research sets out to support (it can never be verified) or on the other hand to falsify.

Thus, naturalistic research is conducted in a natural context, as opposed to a controlled or clinical setting. The experimental approach is in direct contrast. In the traditional experimental study a control group is set up with features supposedly identical in all relevant respects (a difficult goal to achieve) to an experimental group. Things are 'done' or given to the experimental group, but not the control group. For example, they may be taught with an item of new technology, experience a different teaching or learning approach which makes them learn more efficiently while the control group are given a placebo.

If an experimental study is a genuinely randomised and controlled trial (RCT for short) then it has been said by some authors (e.g. Torgerson 2003) to be the 'gold standard' in education and medical research. To meet this 'standard', the two groups would have to be truly randomised, i.e. the groups would have to be selected by a genuinely randomised mechanism such as a random number table. In this way participants are then truly randomly assigned, from a large potential population to either the experimental group or the control group. Random allocation to groups should avoid any of the possible selection bias which might arise if other methods of allocation are used.

Torgerson (2003: 50) points out that, in reviewing the literature on an area, it is often difficult to determine whether a study is truly an RCT or not. The notion of an RCT is important to certain advocates of systematic reviewing in education, who maintain the strict and highly restrictive criterion that only RCTs should be included in a rigorous, systematic review. This criterion is not as tightly adhered to by many advocates of systematic reviewing.

Although the experimental approach and its ideal form, the RCT, may have enormous value in exploring 'what works' in both education and medicine, there are certain issues that must at least be guarded against:

- *Practical issues*: The creation of genuinely randomised groups is often very

244

different in practice. It can require a large amount of funding to achieve good sample sizes and from that lead to properly randomised control and experiment groups. Without a decent sized sample, researchers often have to resort to selecting and allocating groups in some other way, e.g. by matching like with like, and this can lead to selection bias. Equally, any intervention (whether it be a drug or a new style of teaching) needs to be given full time to work and to have an impact, i.e. to make a difference in the hope that this difference can be measured. This requires adequate time and in turn may need proper funding. There is a great danger for a researcher, who may have great belief or even faith in an intervention, to rush the 'experiment' and attempt to find an effect or an impact where there really is none.

- The 'placebo effect': This is a well documented effect in medicine, in which the placebo (i.e. the drug or medicine designed and expected to have no effect) actually makes a difference.
- The Hawthorne effect: This is a similar effect in some ways, with its history in social science rather than medicine. It can be defined as any initial improvement in performance following any newly introduced change: this is an effect or problem which researchers need to be wary of if making an intervention, e.g. introducing new teaching methods to assess their impact. The name is based on a 1924 study of productivity at the Hawthorne factory in Chicago. Two carefully matched groups (experimental and control) were isolated from other factory workers. Factors in the working conditions of the experimental group were varied, e.g. illumination, humidity, temperature, rest periods. No matter what changes were made, including negative ones such as reduced illumination or

shorter rest periods, their productivity showed an upward trend. Just as surprisingly, although no changes were made to the conditions of the control group, their output increased steadily.
- Ethical issues: Educational (and medical) interventions can sometimes be accused of being unethical if they treat one group more favourably than another, e.g. if one group is given a new laptop computer whilst the other are not.

A final comment in the experimental approach is that it can explore what works, i.e. it can test efficacy or effectiveness, but does not really look at the process of why something works or the causal factors behind it: critics say that it treats the process as a black box.

In summary, although the experimental approach and the 'gold standard' within it (the RCT) are often upheld as the best way of conducting social science research, they do have their problems and critics. Equally, however, a naturalistic approach can be messy, complex and open to criticism.

See also: educational research; qualitiative research; quantitative research

Further reading

Robson, C. (1993) Real World Research: A Resource for Social Scientists and Practitioner-Researchers, Oxford: Basil Blackwell.
Torgerson, C. (2003) Systematic Reviews, London: Continuum.
Wellington, J. (2000) Educational Research: Contemporary Issues and Practical Approaches, London: Continuum.

JERRY WELLINGTON

EXTRACURRICULUM

Extracurriculum (or extra curriculum) describes all activities or experiences beyond the official, formal curriculum. Extracurricular activities have been part of school and college life since the nineteenth century. They are voluntary, often free and are normally open to all ages and both sexes. The extra curriculum is an opportunity for academic advancement, for the transmission of certain values and for nurturing a particular ethos. For example, English public schools stressed the value of public service, organising philanthropic activities to help local poor children.

At secondary/high school, college and university levels, students participate in, and often themselves organise, clubs, meetings and societies. In the United States of America, literary and debating societies appeared in universities during the nineteenth century, later supplemented by intercollegiate athletics competitions. Here, and elsewhere, famous sporting traditions developed, such as the annual English 'Boat Race' between Oxford and Cambridge universities. Colleges were also keen to ensure their students were not tempted to spend their time on less appropriate activities. Meaningful extracurricular experiences would develop the healthy balance of intellect and social competence required of a rounded individual.

During the twentieth century, children experienced increased opportunity to engage in extracurricular activities as schools attempted to complement and enhance their curriculum. Sports and expressive arts remain particularly popular with children, and with parents hoping to enrich their child's education or discover a hidden talent. Employers may sometimes consider a student's extracurricular record as a means for determining their suitability for jobs. Accordingly, college websites frequently offer advice on how best to use extracurricular activities to increase employability.

See also: summer school

KEITH WILLIAMS

EXTRA-MURAL CLASS

Literally meaning 'beyond the wall', extra-mural educational work usually takes place outside of normal institutional parameters. The term is encountered mainly, though not exclusively, in British contexts associated with the development of university adult education. It may also be used more generically to refer to out-of-school classes and clubs and time spent learning away from a university.

In Britain, tutorial classes developed out of a partnership between the Workers' Educational Association (WEA) and universities. The WEA was established in the 1903 as a democratic voluntary organisation whose members formed classes, chose subjects and requested staff from universities. Three-year classes were intended to bring students up to university standard, and some of the first ones took place in Staffordshire, Reading and Rochdale. These classes tended to eschew certification and vocational learning in favour of liberal and social studies: economics, political economy and literature were popular early subjects. Education was conceived as valuable in itself and would contribute to personal development as well as the wider social and economic world. Academics such as R. H. Tawney were keen to engage with the world beyond universities and aimed to educate a wider working-class constituency. During the inter-war period there was a great expansion of this work among universities, which set up specific extra-mural departments. Many of politicians associated with the 1945 Labour government had themselves been active in extra-mural classes.

This development drew on the previous history of the extension movement in the late nineteenth century, when social liberal followers of T. H. Green aimed to lessen the impact of industrialism and foster a sense of civic citizenship among working-class people. It was also felt that the universities were out of touch with contemporary developments and needed to reform themselves. The extension movement was also instrumental in the foundation of several local university colleges, among them Exeter, Nottingham, Leeds and Sheffield.

From the beginning, a number of tensions became clear in university extra-mural work.

Funding was provided by the Board of Education, a fact that led critics to accuse the WEA of being led by the government towards liberal studies and away from the class struggle. However, as the role of universities became more prominent, voluntary effort would become correspondingly less significant. Increasingly, the proportion of working-class students declined as the better educated came to occupy classes: at different times academics such as G. D. H. Cole and Raymond Williams would attempt to hold on to a notion of workers' education. Over time, the interest in subjects changed gradually from social sciences to the humanities, arts and sciences. Shorter courses also became more popular and more relaxed in terms of standards. This led critics such as Sidney Raybould, from Leeds University, to vigorously defend standards in extra-mural work against leisure-based provision of a short duration.

In the 1980s many, but not all, departments of extra-mural studies would begin to change their name to 'continuing education', although some had already dropped the title in favour of 'adult education'. This shift reflected a move away from liberal studies and leisure courses towards a greater focus upon work-based learning and education directly related to the needs of the economy.

The Oxford Delegacy for Extra-Mural Studies also helped to establish extra-mural departments in African colonies after 1945, including Ghana (formerly the Gold Coast), Nigeria and East Africa. In part, this was seen as a necessary step to prepare countries for independence, although the transference of an English model of education based on an industrial democracy was not always entirely appropriate to rural societies with little experience of democracy. Over time, especially following independence, liberal education would also give way to shorter vocational courses.

Although less in use today, the extra-mural class has retained a generic use in describing educational work beyond institutional boundaries. It may also refer to a period of work experience related to a course of university study. In the United States of America some universities may also use the term to refer to years studying abroad and exchange programmes. In some schools, for instance in African countries such as Namibia, sports clubs and other societies are described as extra-mural activities.

See also: adult education; continuing education; Tawney, R. H.; university extension; workers' education; Workers' Educational Association (WEA)

Further reading

Goldman, L. (1995) *Dons and Workers: Oxford and Adult Education Since 1850*, Oxford: Clarendon Press.

Kelly, T. (1992) *A History of Adult Education in Great Britain*, 3rd edn, Liverpool: Liverpool University Press.

Titmus, C. and Steele, T. (1995) *Adult Education for Independence*, Leeds: Study of Continuing Education Unit, Leeds University.

TOM WOODIN

FACULTY

The term 'faculty' may be encountered in several educational contexts. Psychologists – sometimes termed faculty psychologists – are interested in such faculties of the mind as memory, imagination and reason. It may also be used in the plural, and perhaps inexpertly, by tutors advising students to 'sharpen' or 'apply' their 'critical faculties' to deconstruct texts or develop arguments more effectively.

In the university, a faculty describes an academic division. The University of Paris was the first university to establish faculties – these being of arts, law, medicine and theology – and the idea was widely copied by other medieval universities. Modern universities frequently have many more than four faculties and these may include education and sciences, for example. Within each faculty there may be a range of departments, schools centres, institutes or clinics, some of which may have their own structural sub-divisions. A faculty of engineering may house distinct departments of civil engineering, electrical engineering and mechanical engineering, for example. In some parts of the world – the United States, in particular – 'faculty' is used in an additional way, as a collective noun to describe all the academic staff of a university, from its most senior to most junior members. A university faculty will normally be led by a head, chair or dean, who will be a senior person – probably a professor – within the wider organisation, and there will also be a team of faculty administrators. There are likely to be faculty committees and sub-committees devoted to all manner of issues, and members of the faculty will sometimes represent their colleagues at cross-university meetings.

See also: dean; department; faculty psychology; professor; university

DAVID CROOK

FACULTY PSYCHOLOGY

The first chapter of Jerry Fodor's influential book, *The Modularity of Mind* (1983) opens with the words 'Faculty psychology is getting to be respectable again after centuries of hanging around with phrenologists and other dubious types'. Faculty psychology is founded on the hypothesis that the human mind comprises a range of psychological mechanisms, faculties or modules with specific mental functions. Some writers have traced faculty psychology back to the writings of the medieval theologian Thomas Aquinas. Later, during the early modern period, such writers as David Hume and John Locke identified a collection of cognitive faculties – reason, understanding, judgement, imagination, memory and the senses, for example – which were subjected to investigation. The concept of faculty psychology was developed by the German psychologist Christian von Wolff (1679–1754) and the Scot, Thomas Reid (1710–96), but was then misappropriated by

Franz Joseph Gall (1758–1828), the pioneer of the pseudo-scientific phrenology, who attributed personality traits to the size and shape of the human skull. Jerry Fodor's writings, though controversial, have led to renewed interest in faculty psychology during the past twenty-five years and there have been some significant recent writings.

See also: faculty; phrenology; psychology; psychology of education

DAVID CROOK

FAMILY

'The family' has been, and continues, to be an *ideological concept*, even if it is no longer seen as a single homogeneous social institution. Typifications that usually emanate from the political moral right see divorce as leading to the fragmentation of families. This notion depends upon the idea that families were once complete and stable entities and that family breakdown creates a state of moral collapse. Even sociological notions about 'the family' used to carry connotations of ideology: how family life ought to be lived according to one set of cultural principles (Barrett and McIntosh 1982).

In the late 1980s this concept of family life was subject to a great deal of critique. Families were conceptualised in terms of *households*. They were defined according to the criteria of co-residence and members' employment status. These conceptualisations were particularly amenable to study in large-scale surveys that pointed to a number of social trends: the growth of lone parent households, especially the growth at that time in low-educated lone mothers on benefit, and the rise in dual earner parent households due to rising employment of mothers with young children who had higher levels of education. At the same time, some social scientists were concerned not to treat households as a 'black box' and to keep in view gender divisions, albeit at that time the main focus was on heterosexuality. Households were conceptualised as sites for resource distribution between men and women: money, child care, domestic work and other material resources (Brannen and Wilson 1987; Pahl 1989). Much of this early research on intra-household processes drew upon qualitative methods of data collection.

The focus on the household as the unit of analysis omitted from the frame that families are *networks of kin relations* in which resources of different kinds are transmitted across the generations and that when parental separation takes place children usually maintain contact with both parents and remain part of a wider network of kin-like ties. Moreover, taking a life course perspective, it neglected to recognise that each family member moves through a variety of household forms and relationships within the generational hierarchy. The methodological challenges of studying families defined in this way were greater for survey researchers than for those working with more intensive methods, a fact reflected in the fact that the study of kinship was largely the province of social anthropologists than of other social scientists.

The failure to take an *intergenerational view of family life* led to a public policy bias that viewed families in particular ways that are only now being widely discussed. One such bias has been to ignore children: to see them as passive dependents of their parents rather than as active agents, contributors to and citizens of society beyond their families. A second bias has been to see families largely as recipients of, or a drain upon, state welfare, rather than as contributors to welfare. The argument that state welfare has 'crowded out' the ways in which family generations provide for one another is extremely tenuous. Moreover, with increased longevity in the population, families increasingly have three generations or even four of kin alive simultaneously (Grundy *et al.* 1999; Brannen *et al.* 2004). There is, therefore, the possibility that with the weakening of horizontal household ties via divorce vertical intergenerational transfers and transmission are becoming more, rather than less, important. (Bengston 2001). On the other hand, with the fall in the birth rate, some members of society are likely to lack intergenerational ties altogether, making it important therefore to take a wider definition of people's social networks than those of consanguinity.

The 1990s saw a change in how family life was understood: not so much as a form but as *relational* (Smart and Neale 1999). With the questioning of heterosexism, new family forms and relationships were being created (Weekes *et al.* 1999). Social theorists like Ulrich Beck and Beck-Gernsheim (1996) argued that the onus was now on individuals to construct their own lives. In short the growth of individualism and the detraditionalisation of society were said to fracture family ties and turn them into atomised individuals. The trend towards atomisation has been countered by a body of empirical research concerning family processes: that practices in families are a matter for *negotiation* informed by guidelines rather than rules. There is, therefore, no automatic right way to behave. Nonetheless negotiation practices carry a moral dimension concerning what is the 'proper thing to do' in families (Finch 1989; Finch and Mason 1993). But moral norms no longer draw upon one set of values, as many parts of the society have become more secular and as society has modernised and developed.

However, structural change may also be as instrumental as the agency of family members in negotiating 'new' modes of family living. Mention may be made here of the new generation of fathers with low levels of education, whose traditional role as breadwinners may be as much undermined by the changes taking place in the labour market as by changes within families themselves (Brannen *et al.* 2004).

A further example of structural change shaping family life is young people's later entry into the labour market as they spend more time in education, leading to the deferral of childbirth and to fewer children.

One consequence is the rise in *consumption expectations* concerning the appropriate conditions for having children today: to be a house buyer, to have two good incomes, and the acquisition of material possessions. A major new consumer market focuses on children themselves: with fewer children being born companies must try to sell more products to each family and each child. Children's own significance in families is also changing as greater emphasis is placed upon children's *emotional* significance to family life. Thus while families create their own conditions and relationships these are reproduced in the context of wider social changes.

From seeing the family as a single social institution, families today are what families 'do' (Morgan 1996). They are not static structures; they are the *practices* in which people engage over time. These practices vary across time and across social groups. Families are sites of social relations – whether this is within the household or between different generations living in separate households. Families involve transmission, provision and exchange of resources of different kinds: care, love, goods, money, affection, information, sociability, education, values.

See also: child guidance; cultural transmission; home schooling

Further reading

Barrett, M. and McIntosh, M. (1982) *The Anti-Social Family*, London: Verso.

Beck, U. and Beck-Gernsheim, E. (1996) 'Individualization and "precarious freedoms": perspectives and controversies of a subject-orientated sociology'. In P. Heelas, S. Lash and P. Morris (eds) *Detrationalization: Critical Reflections on Authority and Identity*, Oxford: Blackwell.

Bengston, V. (2001) 'Beyond the nuclear family: the increasing importance of intergenerational bonds', *Journal of Marriage and the Family*, 63: 1–16.

Brannen, J. and Wilson, G. (1987) *Give and Take in Families: Studies in Resource Distribution*, London: Unwin Hyman.

Brannen, J., Moss, P. and Mooney, A. (2004) *Working and Caring Over the Twentieth Century:*

Change and Continuity in Four-generation Families, Basingstoke: Palgrave.

Finch, J. (1989) *Family Obligations and Social Change*, Cambridge: Polity Press.

Finch, J. and Mason, J. (1993) *Negotiating Family Obligation*, London: Routledge.

Grundy, E., Murphy, M. and Shelton, N. (1999) 'Looking beyond the household: intergenerational perspectives on living kin and contacts with kin in Great Britain', *Population Trends*, 97: 19–27.

Morgan, D. H. J. (1996) *Family Connections*, Cambridge: Polity Press.

Pahl, J. (1989) *Money and Marriage*, Basingstoke: Macmillan.

Smart, C. and Neale, B. (1999) *Family Fragments*, Cambridge: Polity Press

Weekes, J., Donovan, C. and Heapy, B. (1999) 'Everyday experiments: narratives of non-heterosexual relationships'. In E. Silva and C. Smart (eds) *The New Family?* London: Sage.

JULIA BRANNEN

FEMINIST THEORY

In essence, feminism is both an intellectual commitment and a political movement that seeks justice for women and the end of sexism in all forms. Feminist theory, in its broadest sense, aims to understand the nature of inequalities and focuses on gender politics, power relations and sexuality. While generally providing a critique of social relations, much of feminist theory also focuses on analysing gender inequality and the promotion of women's rights, interests, and issues. Themes explored across a broad range of disciplines include women's roles and lives, discrimination, stereotyping, identities and image, objectification (especially sexual objectification), oppression, and patriarchy (see, for example, the work of Gilligan 1982). Feminist inquiry provides a wide range of perspectives on social, cultural, and political phenomena. Important topics for feminist theory and politics include: the body, class and work, disability, the family, globalisation, human rights, popular culture, race and racism, reproduction, science, the self, sex work and sexuality.

Feminist theory has developed over three distinctive phases that simultaneously illuminate the genealogy of the field and the complex theorisation across multiple disciplines (such as education, history, politics, philosophy, sociology, the sciences, human rights, media and literary studies, economics, psychology, health and legal studies and so forth). Feminism and feminist theory is deeply concerned with issues of social justice and across the three broad historical phases has adopted the tenets of social and political movements.

In the first instance, a period of feminist activity during the nineteenth century and early twentieth century that focused primarily on social, political and economic inequalities and the securing of the right to vote, has been termed the 'first wave' and the primary concern was the abolition of mandated inequalities. This focus on achieving equality shaped the concerns of liberal feminists who did not argue for revolutionary change but for women's equality with men. One of the most influential texts of this period was Simone de Beauvoir's *The Second Sex* (1949).

Second-wave feminism is generally identified with a period beginning in the early 1960s and extending through the late 1980s. This period was characterised by movements that encouraged women to understand aspects of their own personal lives as deeply politicised, and reflective of a sexist structure of power. Second-wave feminism was largely concerned with other issues of equality, discrimination and oppression, and works such as Betty Friedan's *The Feminine Mystique* (1963) that contested prevailing ideas and attitudes about women's role and status are illustrative of contemporary second-wave feminist theory This period was marked by campaigns for equal rights and affirmative action, access to contraception, legalising abortion, consciousness raising about domestic abuse and the establishment of a proliferation of women's organisations in national and international settings (for example the National Organization for Women that originated in the United States). Historical events such as the Civil Rights

Movement in the USA gave rise to radical feminism, which advocated that patriarchy was the primary cause of the social, political and economic oppression of women. Within radical feminism, Marxist feminists argued that class inequalities lay at the root of women's oppression, while social feminists focused on the social and cultural aspects of women's public and private lives.

Third-wave feminism that emerged in the 1990s (but began in the 1980s) was a response to assumptions of a 'fixed' and universal female identity that was shaped accruing to white, middle-class and heterosexual notions. Feminist theory is therefore inextricably linked with post-structuralism that emphasises the discursive power and fundamental ambiguity inherent in all gender terms and categories. Third-wave theory has expanded debates and includes queer theory, theories for/about women of colour, post-colonial theory, critical theory and new subjectivities in feminist voice. Thus, third-wave feminism seeks to challenge any universal definition of femininity and is centrally concerned with consciousness raising, activism and widespread education (the work of bell hooks is an instructive example).

Over the past two decades, advances in theory have emerged that have highlighted fragmented and non-homogeneous approaches. Accordingly, particular attention to contestations surrounding the political theorising of gender, identity, and subjectivity has framed current debates concerning the 'construction' of the female subject, the nature of sexual difference(s), the relation between sex and gender, the intersection of gender, race, class, sexuality, and so forth; and the significance of 'woman' as a political category in feminism. Intense debates have surfaced across a number of academic disciplines that have centred on gender differences, cultural rights, citizenship, feminism and multiculturalism, democracy and difference.

See also: critical theory; educational theory; family; Wollstonecraft, Mary

Further reading

Butler, J. (1999) *Gender Trouble: Feminism and the Subversion of Identity*, New York: Routledge.

Firestone, S. (1970) *The Dialectic of Sex: The Case for Feminist Revolution*, New York: Bantam Books

Gilligan, C. (1982) *In a Different Voice: Psychological Theory and Women's Development*, Cambridge MA: Harvard University Press.

hooks, bell (1980) *Talking Back: Thinking Feminist, Thinking Black*, Boston MA: South End Press.

Irigaray, L. (1985) *Speculum of the Other Woman*, trans. G. C. Gill, Ithaca NY: Cornell University Press.

Wollstonecraft, M. (1997) *The Vindications: The Rights of Men and the Rights of Woman*, eds D. L. Macdonald and K. Scherf, Toronto: Broadview Literary Texts.

TANYA FITZGERALD

FERRY, JULES FRANÇOIS CAMILLE (1832–93)

Ferry was a major force for secularising trends within the French education system and a supporter of French colonial expansion, a central feature of which was the learning and adoption of the French language and culture. Elected mayor of Paris in 1869, he immediately declared that 'the problem of the education of the people' would be his priority, even though it was the period of the Commune and Prussian siege. He served as prime minister of France, 1880–81 and 1883–85, also holding the position of Minister of Public Instruction and Fine Arts to confirm the importance that he attached to public education. From 1880 he unsuccessfully set about secularising the universities and banning clerics from teaching in them. He was more successful with legislation in 1882, making schooling compulsory between the ages of six and thirteen. Controversially, he also banned members of a range of clerical orders from practising as teachers in state-supported schools, a measure that was especially significant in relation to the schooling of girls. He gave impetus for the establishment of a training college for teachers of girls in Sèvres. He became president of the French senate in 1893 but was assassinated shortly afterwards by a Catholic fanatic. His most lasting impact lay in linking French colonial expansion with the institution of French educational practice around the globe.

See also: France; politics of education

STEVEN COWAN

FINLAND

Finland comprises a land mass of 338,144 square kilometres and, at the beginning of 2007, had a population of 5.278 million. Economists and educationists alike have marvelled at the late twentieth-century Finnish 'miracle', which saw the country transformed over a generation from a mostly agricultural economy with a barely noticed education system into the leading competitive economy with, according to the Programme for International Student Assessment (PISA), the best school system in the world. Finnish children and young people score highly on such measures as literacy, problem solving and mathematics.

From the 1970s, the Finnish government invested heavily in information and communications technology and higher education, when it became evident that economic and industrial growth could not be achieved unless the country looked beyond its historic trading links with the Soviet Union and gained access to European markets. By the early 1990s, several Finnish companies – benefiting from public–private investment and pioneering university research and development – had emerged as leading-edge businesses, including Nokia, the world's biggest manufacturer of mobile phones.

According to the Finnish ministry of education, the country's education system sets out to ensure that every citizen 'is guaranteed an equal opportunity to obtain education and develop themselves, according to their abilities and needs and irrespective of their financial means' (Ministry of Education

2006: 5). It is an egalitarian system: no tuition fees are charged for those in full-time education and all children receive free meals at school.

During the period of the 'miracle', Finland invested heavily in education to create a three-level system of basic primary- and lower secondary-age education (in a single school), upper secondary education and training, and higher education. Finland has a nine-year system of education for 7–16-year-olds in comprehensive schools, of which there were 3,579 in 2005. These schools are maintained by local authorities, which must also provide one-year pre-primary schools for six-year-olds. Attendance at pre-primary schools is voluntary, but most children now attend such a school. Upper secondary education is influenced by the German model, and comprises vocational education and training in a trade school or general education in an upper secondary school. Both forms take three years and provide a preparation for those proceeding to further study at a university or polytechnic, though students proceeding to a trade school are more likely to enter the workforce upon graduating. The status of the teaching profession in Finland is high: entry to teacher training courses is a fiercely competitive and open only to those already holding master's degrees. The esteem in which state schools are held determines that the private school sector is small.

Legislation in 1966 laid a foundation for the expansion of Finnish higher education and, since the 1980s, universities have played a major part in supporting the state's objective for technical and technological innovation. Higher education – or tertiary education, as it is generally known – is offered in universities, which emphasise research and more theoretical programmes of study, and in the more work-orientated polytechnics, which have been operating on a permanent basis since 1996.

See also: comprehensive school/education; polytechnic; Scandinavia; tertiary education; vocational education

Further reading

Raivola, R. (2000) 'Finland'. In C. Brock (ed.) *Education in a Single Europe*, London: Routledge.
Ministry of Education (2006) *Education and Science in Finland*, Helsinki: Ministry of Education.

DAVID CROOK

FORMATIVE ASSESSMENT

Formative assessment is often contrasted with summative assessment, in that their respective purposes are different. The purpose of summative assessment is to summarise a student's performance or learning at a given point in time. The purpose of formative assessment is to form or shape the student's future performance or learning. The tools for making summative and formative assessments may be the same, because the content of what is assessed may be the same: the difference lies in how the assessment is used, both at the time of assessing and subsequently. However, summative assessment is more often associated with external or high-stakes examinations/testing and formative assessment is associated with classroom assessments of different varieties because immediate classroom feedback is considered to be important in improving performance and learning (whether the feedback comes from the teacher or the students themselves).

Any assessment has to be fit for purpose if it is a valid assessment and the nature of the assessment will affect the outcome. If formative assessment is designed to be formative of good performances by the student, this will come about differently than if the assessment is formative of learning processes. Where good performances are the desired outcome, then a test may be used to inform the teacher of what he or she needs to do to help the student do better (hence a misunderstanding of formative assessment as 'informative' assessment). Where formation of good learning processes is the purpose of formative assessment, then the actual process of assessing may be the agent that enhances learning. The assessment may only be termed 'formative' if some of the desired good impact is actually forthcoming.

In the United Kingdom, as well as other countries, formative assessment has become known more often as 'Assessment for Learning'. Black and Wiliam's *Inside the Black Box* (1998), has been one of the most powerful vehicles for urging teachers and policy makers that Assessment for Learning is beneficial for students. However, although the word 'learning' is used, 'learning' in the context of the title Assessment for Learning is commonly used to include 'performing' as well as actively 'learning'.

In terms of improving students' performances, formative assessment or Assessment for Learning can mean monitoring learners' performance against targets or objectives, or closing the 'gap' between desired performance and actual performance. The British Assessment Reform Group (2002) wrote:

> Assessment for Learning [or formative assessment] is the process of seeking and interpreting evidence for use by learners and their teachers to decide where the learners are in their learning, where they need to go and how best to get there.

Some conceptions of formative assessment stress the teacher's role in assessing the learner's performance and giving directions to the student through feedback about what they need to do to improve. Other definitions focus on the importance of the student being involved in self-assessment and in decisions about what they need to do to improve performance.

When formative assessment is focused on forming or shaping learning processes themselves, it can mean teachers and students focusing on how a student learns as well as what he or she can do, knows or understands. The teacher can inquire about what helps or hinders the student's learning in order to provide the most appropriate support. This emphasis on (often internal) processes rather than observable performances makes self-assessment a very useful process in formative assessment, by which learners reflect on and make sense of their own learning in order to have more control over their own future learning processes. In this case, feedback is likely to be self-regulatory activity on the part of the learner and may even be productive helping among members of a group of learners who support each other's inquiry into learning. For some educators, all learning that does not include this process of reflection is in any case likely to be superficial learning.

See also: assessment; continuous assessment; high-stakes testing; learning; summative assessment; test/testing

Further reading

Assessment Reform Group (2002) *Assessment for Learning: 10 Principles*, London: Assessment Reform Group.
Black, P. and Wiliam, D. (1998) *Inside the Black Box*, London: King's College.
Dann, R. (2002) *Promoting Assessment as Learning: Improving the Learning Process*, London: Routledge Falmer.
Torrance, H. and Pryor, J. (1998) *Investigating Formative Assessment*, Buckingham: Open University Press.

ELEANORE HARGREAVES

FORSTER, WILLIAM EDWARD (1818–86)

Forster, the British Liberal politician, received a Quaker education in Bristol and London. Despite initially training as a lawyer, he decided to enter the wool trade, becoming a manufacturer in 1842. He married the eldest daughter of Thomas Arnold, which meant he had to leave the Society of Friends as his wife was an Anglican. Forster was elected to Parliament as a Liberal member in 1861. He held office within government from 1865 and introduced, with Edward Cardwell, education bills in 1867 and 1868. He served as vice-president of the Committee of Council on Education from 1868–74 and was charged by prime minister William Gladstone with preparing a further education bill. This

became the Elementary Schools Act, which was passed in 1870. The 'Forster' Act laid the basis for the establishment of school boards in local authority districts. These boards were empowered to make additional provision of schooling where deficiencies in provision were identified, financed by a local rate. Forster described this as 'filling up the gaps' in order not to alienate vested Anglican interests. The school boards were to be elected, with women being able to stand as candidates and vote for the first time. Controversy arose from proposals that school boards could financially support provision within denominational schools, a situation resolved by the formation of local education authorities in 1902. The Act of 1870 marks the beginning of the provision of universal elementary schooling and is, therefore, viewed as one of the major landmarks in British educational history.

See also: Arnold, Thomas; politics of education
STEVEN COWAN

FOUCAULT, MICHEL (1926–84)

Foucault was a French philosopher and cultural historian. Whilst at university he specialised in philosophy, psychology and psychopathology. He taught French at Uppsala University, Sweden from 1954 to 1958, moving to brief appointments at Warsaw and Hamburg. He was appointed head of the philosophy department at Clermont-Ferrand in 1960, shortly before publication of his *Madness and Civilization* (1961), based on his doctoral thesis, in which he argued that sanity and madness were products of the Enlightenment. In *The Order of Things* (1966), Foucault analysed the historical relationship between the development of economics, natural sciences and linguistics in the eighteenth and nineteenth centuries. He argued that everything that is normally taken as being universally valid must be tested and analysed to examine how, as knowledge, it was historically constituted. This perspective was developed further in *The Archaeology of Knowledge* (1969), which became a bestseller and established his international reputation. In this, he advocated examination of the relationship of power to discursive formations in society, in order to see how knowledge becomes possible. Subsequent studies of the clinic, the prison and mental asylums have become central reference points for post-modernist thinking. Foucault's impact has been immense, directing researchers for example, to examine how teachers or pupils are 'constituted' by regulatory regimes designed to sustain relations of authority through mono-polising definitions of knowledge.

See also: educational theory; postmodernism

STEVEN COWAN

FOUNDATION DEGREE

A foundation degree is an intermediate, work-related, higher educational qualification. Launched by the United Kingdom govern-ment in 2001, it was the first new British higher education qualification for twenty-five years. Developed in local partnerships between higher education institutions, fur-ther education colleges and employers, foun-dation degrees aim to guarantee the supply of technicians and associate professionals. Foun-dation degrees stand between the Higher National Diploma and a full undergraduate honours degree at bachelor level. A normal course of study is two years' full time or three to four years' part-time. On completion, the holder should have the opportunity to progress to a full honours degree with a further year of full-time study. Consequently, all foundation degrees carry a common value of 240 Credit Accumulation and Transfer (CATS) points, guaranteeing their currency.

To encourage lifelong learning and to increase the degree-holding percentage of the British population, foundation degree courses are easy to access. Flexible delivery encourages the enrolment of full-time employees, those seeking a career change and the unemployed.

There are no set entry requirements: providers decide on a candidate's eligibility and may value work-based experience more highly than educational qualifications.

Foundation degrees claim to offer improved business performance and flexible, profes-sional development for workers. Drawing on further education colleges' expertise of working with vocationally oriented students, pro-grammes of study combine practical experi-ence with theoretical perspectives. Similar to the American associates degree, foundation degrees face the same potential problem: will their status as a stand-alone qualification hold up?

See also: degree; further education; higher education; qualifications; undergraduate; uni-versity; work-based/work-located/workplace/work-related learning

KEITH WILLIAMS

FRANCE

Medieval France was a leading centre of educational activity: there were attempts to a school system as early as the eighth century and the Sorbonne, the first university in Northern Europe, was founded in Paris in 1257. During the early modern period of the sixteenth and seventeenth centuries, the Counter-Reformation and the Jesuit's efforts led to a significant expansion in the provision of Catholic education, but there were unsuccessful efforts to shift the control of education from Church to state after the 1789 Revolution. In 1802, Napoleon offi-cially placed the control of elementary edu-cation with the Church, but at the same time he established a system of state secondary schools for the elites. In 1806, higher educa-tion was also placed under the state's com-mand and then reordered and expanded. France was moving towards creating its highly uniformed and highly centralised national education system.

In 1828 a ministry of education was cre-ated. In 1833 the *Guizot Law* made primary education open to all, as every community was required to sustain a fixed number of schools. Continuing power struggles between the state and religious establishments, however, hindered the development of French education. The constitution of the Third Republic in 1870 shifted the balance of power in the state's favour. During the 1880s, under the leadership of minister Jules Ferry, the state took full command over education and it became secular. A highly centralised public system was erected, regulating the curriculum, examinations and the selection of teachers. Through massive state investment, thousands of schools were opened; in 1881 education was made free; and in 1882 it became compulsory from age 6–13. Today, compulsory education in France lasts from age 6–16. The 1905 legal separation of state and Church consolidated the secular nature of public education and it has been further reinforced: for example in 2004 French public schools were forbidden to display any conspicuous religious symbol.

These developments brought to the fore-front the status of private schools, particularly Catholic ones. At various points in modern French history there have been attempts to weaken, regulate or even abolish these schools, while at others there were measures to preserve their autonomy and endurance. At present, private schools – the overwhelming majority of which are still Catholic – account for around 20 per cent of all French secondary schools. Today, private schools can choose whether to receive financial support from the state, on the understanding that they must then accept a measure of central control and supervision. Private schools are unable to award nationally recognised certificates and diplomas to students.

After the 1880s reforms, pre-elementary education began to spread and elementary schooling became accessible to all. Nevertheless, two separate systems were in place: one that restricted pupils to elementary education and one for the middle and higher

classes, which provided a track leading to secondary schooling and university. Following World War I, steps were taken to create a more open-ended and egalitarian education system. Comprehensive change, however, came only after the unification of the two systems during the 1960s and 1970s. At present, practically all French pupils enter the educational system at the age of four and complete two years of pre-elementary education (*Maternelle*). Primary school begins at the age of six and lasts for five years. Normally, pupils are allocated to schools according to their place of residence. The *collège*, which became an integral part of the French system during the 1960s and 1970s reforms, provides the first four years of secondary education. The last year of the collège is an orientation year and offers both technological and academic tracks. Upon completion, pupils can either attend the *lycée professionnel*, which lasts for two to four years and leads to a professional diploma, or the *lycée d'enseignement général et technologique*, which lasts for three years and leads to a technological or academic baccalaureate. The latter is divided into three tracks: the literary, the social/economic and the scientific. Completing the baccalaureate is a necessary condition for entering higher education.

French higher education has been experiencing significant changes since the 1980s: higher education has become more accessible and diversified; the traditional faculty-based structure of French universities has become more multidisciplinary; and the universities are becoming more compatible with the general model of European higher education. Alongside reforming universities, however, are *grandes écoles*, the small, highly-prestigious and selective institutions which continue to train an elite.

At the start of the twenty-first century the major themes in French education are traditionalism, secularisation and the position of private education, equality issues and the role of the state. New challenges have been presented by France's increasing ethnic diversity, its place in the European Union and by the changing global economy.

See also: Catholic school/education; Europe; Ferry, Jules

Further reading

Corbett, A. and Moon, B. (eds) (1996) *Education in France: Continuity and Change in the Mitterrand Years, 1981–1995*, London: Routledge.
Halls, W. D. (1976) *Education, Culture and Politics in Modern France*, Oxford: Pergamon Press.
Lewis, H. D. (1985) *The French Education System*, London: Croom Helm.
Male, G. A. (1963) *Education in France*, Washington DC: US Department of Health, Education, and Welfare.
Musselin, C. (2004) *The Long March of French Universities*, London: RoutledgeFalmer.

TAL GILEAD

FRANCHISING

In franchising, a service or product is offered through an arrangement whereby the franchisor supplies expertise and/or establishes fixed standards, and the franchisee then 'delivers' as specified. Educational franchising, based on this business model, was pioneered in relations between North American universities and community colleges, and is now widespread.

Franchising, in the context of education, has been defined as 'the delivery of the whole or parts of a course in an institution other than the centre in which it is developed and validated' (Woodrow 1993: 207). Typically, the franchisee acknowledges that the award is that of the franchisor, but operates the provision under its own name. Franchising in education has become very diverse and is now practised in a range of institutions, at many levels, and over geographical distances from local to global. The archetypical franchise is one where a higher education (HE) institution franchises a course to a further education (FE) or community college. Franchising is also conducted from FE colleges to community partners; this is generally referred to as Outward Collaborative Provision (OCP). More recently, franchising of 'whole institutions' has developed within specialist college and schools systems, including instances of charter schools in the USA. Some British public (i.e. private) schools (notably Harrow) have established international franchises in Southeast Asia. The idea of franchising by leading state schools within the United Kingdom has been mooted.

A key rationale for franchising in education is that it can widen participation by making provision available to those who would otherwise be unable or reluctant to access it (e.g. ethnic minorities). There are powerful economic incentives attached to franchising: it enables participating institutions to increase their income. Other potential benefits include development opportunities for academics, curriculum diversification, internationalisation, and the sharing of expertise.

Franchising may be seen as a symptom of the commodification of education (sometimes, following the work of George Ritzer, explained as a process of *McDonaldisation*). Franchising provides a cheap way to realise the 'massification' of HE (Hayes and Wynyard 2002). Globalisation and the development of new learning technologies broadened the scope of educational franchising and opened possibilities for the franchising of learning technologies as well as global educational 'brands' (that is, institutions with marketable reputations).

There are trends towards differentiation between universities and FE/community colleges, and between universities. Strong links have developed between FE/community colleges and newer vocationally orientated universities, whilst elite universities have been slower to explore franchising or have withdrawn from franchise relationships work which may not articulate well with research-orientated missions, teaching aimed at high achievers drawn from the middle classes, or the deployment of advanced e-learning technologies.

Questions have arisen in relation to the quality assurance and regulation of franchises. Problems reported in HE to FE franchising in the UK in the 1990s included isolated students, sub-standard teaching, limited library and computing resources, inadequate facilities for students, and poor communication between partner institutions, all compounded by neglectful management. Instability resulted from colleges switching their HE partners based on perceptions of quality or straightforward 'price' factors. The Higher Education Funding Council for England issued codes of practice for 'indirectly funded partnerships' including franchise and consortia arrangements that encouraged 'transparency' and made clear that the franchising institution is responsible for quality and retains responsibility for the students. There was a requirement for the production of a statement (memorandum of cooperation) setting out the purpose and operation of the arrangement.

As universities strengthened regional links, some attempted to impose exclusivity clauses on franchise partners (that is, a condition to work with a single HE partner). This has been resisted by many colleges on the basis that they prefer different partners for different provision, as well as to protect their strategic autonomy. Most formal curriculum partnerships between HE and FE are franchises, including many that are referred to as consortia. A consortium normally involves a group of partners with a designated lead institution: the funded student numbers are managed on a basis formally agreed between the members and funding flows through the lead institution.

There is every indication that educational franchising will continue both to diversify and to grow in popularity.

See also: community education; further education; higher education

Further reading

Fisher, R., Bridge, F. and Webb, K. (2003) 'From franchise network to consortium: the evolution of a new kind of further and higher education partnership', *Journal of Vocational Education and Training*, 55(3): 301–18.

Hayes, D. and Wynyard, R. (eds) (2002) *The McDonaldization of Higher Education*, Westport CT: Greenwood Press.

Woodrow, M. (1993) 'Franchising: the quiet revolution', *Higher Education Quarterly*, 47(3): 207–20.

ROY FISHER

FREINET, CELESTIN (1896–1966)

Freinet started his teaching career in France late in 1921, after a lengthy period of convalescence arising from war injuries. He immediately joined a radical teacher union and then the Communist Party in 1927. Freinet developed the *texte libre* approach, whereby free writing by a child was shared with classmates and collectively edited before being self-printed by the whole class. These class printings were then assembled into whole-school publications, again presented by the children as a collective. A major extension of this work came with the exchange of such productions between schools where like-minded teachers practised. By 1928 the Public Educators' Cooperative (PEC) had been formed. This movement challenged traditional school books, advocating instead use of self-produced accounts of the world and life within it. Freinet encouraged pupils to create their own schedules for independent investigations out of which arose reports to share with the class and other schools. The PEC developed self-correcting sheets covering a range of basic skills and knowledge, which pupils integrated into their self-devised learning schedules. Issues that affected everyone were discussed and decided upon by the class assembly. He was forced to leave the public education system and furthered his practical teaching at a private school until his arrest and detention by the Vichy government. It was during this period of isolation and forced inactivity from teaching (1940–42) that he wrote his major works on teaching styles, cooperative and investigative learning, learning through experience and nature and child–centred development.

See also: child-centred education; collaborative/cooperative learning; writing

STEVEN COWAN

FREIRE, PAOLO (1921–97)

The writings of Freire, the Brazilian educator, have influenced academic discourse in areas as broad and diverse as pedagogy, linguistics, cultural and media studies, politics, sociology and theology. Freire's earliest experiments relating to adult literacy came to an abrupt end after the military coup in Brazil in 1964. From then he worked in exile in Bolivia for the United Nations Educational, Scientific and Cultural Organization, then for the Institute for Agrarian Reform in Chile. His main work, *Pedagogy of the Oppressed* (1970) was written whilst working in Mexico. He briefly lectured at Harvard's Centre for Studies in Social Development and then for the World Council of Churches in Switzerland as director of education.

Freire believed that teaching the word ought to be based within the world and life experience of the learner. By connecting with the common sense knowledge of the learner, literacy assumed a liberating and self-developing character. The learning process needed to become a 'communion' between the teacher and the learner. Freire advocated that people should learn about people who were different from oneself, in order to overcome divisions of race, religion, gender and class. Students and teachers should discuss and negotiate themes for study that were significant within the context of the student's life. For Freire, genuine education amounted to 'the practice of freedom'. His outlook and work echoed and influenced major developments within Latin American liberation theology and remains the major influence behind

numerous progressive schooling initiatives, especially in the Portuguese-speaking world. His approach to teaching literacy to adults has informed practice internationally.

See also: pedagogy; progressive education

STEVEN COWAN

FREUD, SIGMUND (1856–1939)

Freud, the founder of psychoanalysis, was educated in Vienna. As a medical student he became interested in the structure of the nervous system, graduating in 1881. After this he specialised in neurology, leading to a lectureship in neuropathology, and produced an important study of aphasia in children in 1891. Two important periods of study in Paris (1886) and Nancy (1889) led him to develop an interest in the subconscious mind. His first major publication with Josef Breuer, in 1893, identified emotions as the key factor in determining subconscious mental acts. Freud's identification of the *Oedipus complex*, whereby adults transfer desires from infanthood, and repressed desires rising from the unconscious mind in the form of dreams, created international recognition.

In 1910, along with Carl Jung, infants were seen as developing a structure to their mental system characterised by an *id*, which supplies energy to the system, an *ego*, which enables the child to face reality and a *superego*, which embodies self-control and rational decision making. The child was viewed as moving through stages of development towards maturity. If these stages are not followed or fulfilled the adult will display signs of pathological conduct and neuroses will become evident. His work and ideas became universally recognised and they transformed psychiatric approaches towards the young. They also gave a uniquely important place to infancy events in a person's life. Freud was forced to leave Austria in 1939, coming to London for his last few months.

See also: child development; psychology

STEVEN COWAN

261

FROEBEL, FRIEDRICH (1782–1852)

Froebel, the German psychologist, stimulated an international movement for early-years schooling. His own mother died during his first year and his father neglected him. Froebel had little formal schooling but developed his learning and knowledge through a series of jobs. He interrupted his training in architecture to take a position as teacher in Frankfurt in 1805. Three years later, he visited Pestalozzi with three boys and imbibed much of the theory and method from what he saw. He spent a year in Göttingen (1811) studying 'scientific teaching methods'. After a time in Berlin, Froebel opened his first school in Griesham, the Universal German Educational Institute, in 1816. He spent much of the 1820s writing and publishing, most notably *The Education of Man* in 1826. Another school was opened in Wartensee in 1831, followed by a scheme for training teachers in Burgdorf in 1833. The first *kindergarten* was opened in Liebenstein in 1849, with ten others following in less than eight years. He believed in children's natural goodness and argued for combining observation from nature with play activity to encourage self-development. Through this, an appreciation of spiritual wholeness with nature could be realised. His principal influences, along with Pestalozzi were Rousseau, Fichte and Schelling. Such pantheistic teaching and practice was seen as potentially seditious by the state, and in 1851 the kindergarten was made illegal. His book, *Mother Play* (1844), expounds upon his philosophy of personal growth and development of children. After his death, kindergartens spread around the world. In Germany the legislation banning them was repealed a decade later.

See also: early childhood education; kindergarten; Pestalozzi, Johann Heinrich; Rousseau, Jean-Jacques

STEVEN COWAN

FUNCTIONALISM

Functionalism is a sociological perspective that employs a biological, organic metaphor for society. Just as a human body has organs, without which it could not exist, functionalists hold that societies have institutions such as the family, schools and law courts which provide necessary functions for them in an equivalent manner to the way the heart or the lungs provide essential functions for a human being. Related to this is the view that society is a harmonious whole and its parts interact in such a way as to maintain social stability and order and restore it if that order is disturbed. This emphasis on value consensus has sometimes led to the charge that essentially it is a conservative perspective.

Functionalist analyses are to be found in the work of the prominent English Victorian thinker Herbert Spencer (1820–1903) but perhaps more explicitly in the work of the French 'founding father' of sociology, Emile Durkheim (1858–1917). That Durkheim appropriated some of Spencer's notions is undisputed. Durkheim, a positivist, hypostasised society, elevating it as an entity existing over and above the individuals that comprised it. Thus, as befitted a professor of pedagogy, he saw society as needing to recreate the conditions of its own existence through the socialisation of the young. Socialisation has a central place in functionalist theory, as it is the process by means of which individuals are attached to society through the inculcation of norms and values. Typically, socialisation takes place in the family and increasingly, since the nineteenth century, in school systems.

After Durkheim, the most prominent functionalist theorist was Talcott Parsons (1902–79) who taught at Harvard University. Parsons began publishing his main work in the early 1950s and his approach, known as structural-functionalism, dominated sociology until the 1970s when Marxist and radical sociologists criticised it on the grounds that it could not account for social change or conflict. In Parsons' grand theoretical system, which was firmly on the structure end of the structure/agency continuum, people enacted roles in differentiated social sub-systems. In *The School Class as a Social System*, his major contribution to the sociology of education, he argued that the prime functions of schooling were socialisation and selection. Within the family children had ascribed status but in schools, status is distributed by achievement which also fits pupils into their allocated roles in society.

Robert K. Merton (1910–2003) was another prominent functionalist theorist who also wrote on education in his work on the sociology of science and his study of *Puritanism, Pietism and Science*, which commenced in the 1930s. Merton advocated for the purposes of analysis the division of functions into manifest consequences which are conscious and intended and latent which are unintended and not expected. The one-time functionalist Neil J. Smelser also dealt with education in its broadest sense in his *Social Change in the Industrial Revolution: An Application of Theory to The British Cotton Industry*. Early in his career Smelser collaborated with Parsons but later departed from functionalism. When he came to write on British working-class education in the nineteenth century he adopted a more eclectic approach.

In addition to socialisation, functionalists examined the functions education systems performed for the economy, society and the political system. Among the most prominent to do this were P. W. Musgrave and Olive Banks. Both wrote both sociological and historical works.

Paradoxically, given that the revival of Marxist theory in the 1970s has been cited widely as one of the currents that were critical of functionalism, in the form of structuralist Marxism, associated with the French Marxist, Louis Althusser (1918–90), it came close to functionalist analyses. In Althusser's work, education systems met the needs of the capitalist mode of production for variously skilled labour power and they functioned to support the state by producing people imbued with ideologies aligned with the requirements of the state. As in other varieties of functionalism, the emphasis on structures, while useful for explaining certain aspects of education systems, does so by ignoring the actions of humans in conflicts over resources and policies and turns those same humans into mere bearers of structures. A similar objection may be raised to the most recent reworking of Parsonian structural functionalism, the sociological systems theory of the German sociologist Niklas Luhmann (1927–98).

Finally, functionalism is not a substitute for historical explanation. Because an institution, like an education system, functions in a particular way this is not sufficient for an explanation of how it came to be or how its purposes were conceived.

See also: Durkheim, Emile; sociology; sociology of education; Spencer, Herbert

Further reading

Alexander, J. C. (1998) *Neofunctionalism and After*, Oxford: Blackwell.

Brehony, K. J. (2001) 'Developments in the sociology of education since 1950: from structural functionalism to "policy sociology"'. In R. G. Burgess and A. Murcott (eds) *Developments in Sociology*, London: Prentice Hall.

Demaine, J. (2003) 'Social reproduction and education policy', *International Studies in Sociology of Education*, 13(2): 125–40.

KEVIN BREHONY

FURTHER EDUCATION

In some countries, 'further education' may encompass all post-school learning up to and including university study, but it does not have this connotation in the United Kingdom, where the term is most frequently encountered sometimes as an alternative to 'tertiary' education or 'post-compulsory education'.

In the seminal report of a committee on widening participation in British FE, chaired by Dame Helena Kennedy (FEFC 1997), there are two particularly insightful introductory comments. The first is that 'Defining further education exhaustively would be God's own challenge because it is such a fertile section of the education world'. The second is that

> It is further education which has invariably given second chances to those who were forced by necessity to make unfulfilling choices. It said 'try again' to those who were labelled as failures and who had decided that education was not for the likes of them.
>
> (FEFC 1997: 1–2)

The ethos of the UK sector is well captured here, and the 'second chance' dimension of much of the work of American community colleges provides a parallel.

So, what exactly may take place in this sector, comprising diverse institutions responsible for meeting the needs of millions of individuals, both teenagers and adults? Where a 'further education' sector actually exists in a national setting, certain groups of learners are likely to be prominent:

- School leavers, frequently with few existing qualifications, who have chosen to continue their studies (whether academic or vocational) in the more adult environment of a college.
- Adult returners to study, sometimes individuals who wish to progress to university as mature students and who are using FE 'access' courses as preparation for this step.
- Learners who are disadvantaged by virtue of their low basic skills levels – especially in literacy and numeracy – and/or through being non–native speakers of English. Recent immigration into the UK has boosted FE college enrolments, while in the USA commu-

nity colleges have accommodated large numbers of Hispanic speakers aiming to integrate within the host society.
- Younger learners, who have been accommodated either because they have been excluded from school or because the breadth of the college curriculum is judged more suitable for their needs.

The above list is in no sense comprehensive, and there exist, for instance, FE colleges whose mission lies specifically in meeting employers' or national needs for a skilled workforce. Australian colleges have this distinctive emphasis, offering technical and further education (TAFE), often at a very high level.

In the UK, formerly 'general' colleges are increasingly abandoning academic curriculum components in favour of enhanced vocationalism. The UK's 'land-based' colleges specialise wholly in preparing learners for careers in horticulture, arboriculture, agriculture and rural crafts. But by way of contrast, other US and UK colleges have pursued a route by which they have sought to align themselves more closely with higher education institutions, rather than employers, offering 'franchised' undergraduate degree programmes. The '2 + 2' system in the USA would exemplify this trend well, wherein a four-year programme of study has been divided into two segments, each offered by, respectively, a college and a university.

In – usually developed – countries where incomes are relatively high and fees (if any) for FE are low, demand tends to be buoyant, sustaining the existence of a large sector. If the reverse applies, FE tends to be restricted in consequence of being 'rationed by price'.

See also: community education; franchising; higher education; technical education/school/college; tertiary education; vocational education

Further reading

Department for Education and Skills (2002) *Success for All: Reforming Further Education and Training*, Nottingham: DfES.

FEFC (Further Education Funding Council) (1997) *Learning Works: Widening Participation in Further Education*. 'Kennedy Report'. Coventry: FEFC.

Green, A. and Lucas, N. (eds) (1999) *FE and Life-long Learning: Realigning the Sector for the 21st Century*, London: Institute of Education, University of London.

Lucas, N. (2004) *Teaching in Further Education: New Perspectives for a Changing Context*, London: Institute of Education, University of London.

BRYAN CUNNINGHAM

G

GALTON, FRANCIS (1822–1911)

Galton, the British polymath and scientist, studied medicine and mathematics. He was elected to the Royal Society in 1856 and was General Secretary to the British Association from 1863–67. Among his many credits were the pioneering of weather forecasting and invention of fingerprinting. He developed an interest in heredity, pioneering the systematic collection of data concerning human attributes and abilities. His cousin, Charles Darwin, was a major influence upon his thinking. Galton introduced statistical correlation and regression methods into the scientific study of humans, calling it the biometric approach. This work was taken further by his student, Karl Pearson. Galton's studies led him to the conclusion that environment had little impact upon a person's physical and educational attributes. In *Hereditary Genius* (1869), *Inquiries into Human Faculty* (1883) and *Natural Inheritance* (1889) Galton developed ideas about the limits of education for people from certain family backgrounds. His world-renowned stature as a scientist gave his ideas enormous credence during his times. He also expounded his theories of eugenics as a means of racial and social improvement. His ideas were used to support differential schooling for different 'types' of child. To further the eugenicist cause he established a laboratory and research fellowship at University College, London, along with a specialist journal. Galton helped to establish local eugenics associations all over Britain. He was the dominant influence upon a succeeding generation of British and American educational psychologists, such as Cyril Burt and B. F. Skinner, who were interested in investigating the capacities of children.

See also: Burt, Cyril; intelligence/intelligence tests; psychometrics; Skinner, Burrhus Fredric

STEVEN COWAN

GANDHI, MOHANDAS KARAMCHAND (MAHATMA) (1869–1948)

Mahatma Gandhi's educational ideas were based on the notions of *swaraj* and *swadeshi*, which implied independence, self-rule and self-reliance. He believed that education should focus on the training of the character and help to foster non-violence and an ethical way of life for all.

In 1937, at the Wardha National Education Conference, Gandhi explained his notion of 'basic education', which was to be compulsory, free and continuous for seven years, with instruction taking place in the mother tongue. Although a variety of subjects were envisaged, these would be taught through learning handicrafts and local skills, which would help to generate an income and enable education to become self-financing and sustainable. This would ensure that education was locally controlled and independent from the state, features also adapted to the needs of the rural villages. Education was to contribute to a wider collective community and would help to bring about social transformation. Gandhi implemented some of these ideas at an experimental coeducational school at Sevagram in 1938, where literacy and learning focused upon cotton production and other practical skills. The school was run democratically and connections were made with the local people.

His educational ideas were closely intertwined with his anti-colonialist stance against the British empire and Western intellectual ideas more generally. He was sceptical of both liberal education and education tied into modernisation and economic progress, which, he felt, would repeat the mistakes of the British and lead to inequality and violence in which the mass of rural villages suffered at the expense of urban areas. However, the nationalists under Nehru pursued a more modernising agenda and were able to utilise Gandhi's popularity in rural areas while sidelining his key educational ideas.

See also: India

TOM WOODIN

GARDNER, HOWARD (1943–)

An educational psychologist and Professor of Cognition and Education at Harvard Graduate School, Gardner developed a critique of the notion of a single human intelligence that is measurable by standardised psychometric testing and is in essence hereditary. Instead, Gardner posited a theory of *multiple intelligences*, which could be identified, and which are distinct although they operate in conjunction with each other in certain conditions. Amongst the eight 'intelligences' that Gardner identified are the bodily-kinaesthetic, spatial, intrapersonal and naturalist intelligences. Whilst his ideas may not have been received uncritically within traditional academic, educational psychology, Gardner's impact amongst educators and policy makers has been considerable.

Gardner was influenced by Erik Erikson, his tutor, and Jerome Bruner, with whom he worked on the *Man: A Course of Study* (MACOS) project. He questioned Piaget's idea that knowledge and understanding necessarily occur in coherent, structured forms. A further, important influence was Norman Geschwind, the neurologist. Gardner was amongst the first to investigate the role of the right hemisphere in linguistic and paralinguistic areas of cognition. He was a founder member and co-director for over twenty years of *Project Zero*, an institute set up to investigate higher cognitive processes.

A prolific author, Gardner has produced several landmark works including *The Arts and Human Development* (1973), *Frames of Mind* (1983), *The Unschooled Mind* (1991) and *Multiple Intelligences* (1993). One of the most important effects of Gardner's theoretical contribution has been to stimulate interest in interdisciplinary approaches to teaching and learning across the student age range. He has also stimulated thinking amongst educators of all kinds, about broader ways of conceptualising abilities, capacities and intelligences.

See also: Bruner, Jerome; cognition; creativity; intelligence/intelligence tests; learning styles; psychology of education

STEVEN COWAN

GATE-KEEPING

Gate-keeping in relation to education refers to the propensity of educational institutions and of powerful groups and individuals to regulate access to higher levels of education, or to particular types and areas of knowledge. The process involves selection of individuals to go through to the next level based on a particular set of criteria. Often it can carry with it a number of assumptions and values about the individuals who should be granted entry. One key point where gate-keeping is an issue is entry to higher education institutions, where there may be formal mechanisms but also informal and tacit notions that affect whether individuals will succeed in their application. Gate-keeping in this sense may be a role or post assigned to particular individuals within an educational institution, who will be guided by their experience and values, as well as the general aspirations of the institution. There is also an important aspect of gate-keeping in relation to research in education, as researchers of schools and other educational institutions generally need to acquire permission to carry out their research. In this instance, the institution or the individual within it who has this role acts as the gate-keeper to the knowledge that is being sought, whether it be archives held at the institution, or teachers and students for interviewing.

See also: educational research; selection

GARY McCULLOCH

GENDER STUDIES

Gender studies are concerned with the nature and role of gender, considered from a wide range of disciplinary and interdisciplinary perspectives. In higher education courses devoted to this subject, gender is appraised in terms of its social, cultural and political dynamics, in relation both to structural relationships and changes, and individual and group experience. Its study has generated an extensive literature and body of theory, often emanating from and engaging with feminist writers. It has often been associated especially with women's studies, which focus principally on women, including their history, contemporary changes, future prospects, and writings and other work produced by women. Such courses might commonly investigate the inequalities of a patriarchal society, and the extent to which women have achieved equality in relation to men, or where influenced by postmodernism they might develop issues around multiple identities. In recent years there has also been a growth in men's studies, which have sought to understand the nature of masculinities and how these have been expressed and represented in a changing society. These would often be included within a broad prospectus of gender studies.

See also: feminist theory; postmodernism

GARY McCULLOCH

GEOGRAPHY

There is no one clear-cut definition for geography, but the one proposed by the International Geographical Union (IGU) in 1992 is broad enough to be acceptable to most geographers:

> Geography is the science which seeks to explain the character of places and the distribution of people, features and events as they occur and develop over the surface of the earth. Geography is concerned with human-environment interactions in the context of specific places and locations. Its special characteristics are its breadth of study; its span of methodology; its synthesis of work from other disciplines including the physical sciences and the humanities and its interest in the future management of people-environment inter-relationships.

Some of the central concepts of geographical studies are: location and distribution; place; people-environment relationships; spatial interaction; and region. Geographers ask the following questions: Where is it? What is it like? Why is it there? What impact doest it have? How should it be managed for the mutual benefit of humanity and environments?

It has been argued for years (not always successfully) that a geographical education is an essential prerequisite for an educated person. As far back as 1885, Peter Kropotkin wrote that it was 'the task of geography to interest the child in the great phenomena of nature, to awaken the desire of knowing and explaining them'. Similarly Fairgrieve in 1926 wrote that

> Geography enables man to place himself on the world and to know where he stands with regard to his fellows. By a study of geography we are enabled to understand

269

facts without a knowledge of which it is impossible to do our duty as citizens of this very confusing and contradictory world.

Kropotkin and Fairgrieve are as relevant today as they were in previous centuries.

Internationally there are big differences in the nature, status and role of geography education. In countries like Finland, Germany and the UK, geography per se is well represented from the early years through to the upper secondary school (16–19 age range) and has a relatively high status. In contrast in other countries such as the USA, it is part of an integrated social studies or humanities curriculum with relatively low status. In general, geography curricula are usually structured as regional studies or thematic studies. Thematic studies are either systematic or issues-based.

Although there is an active international community of geography educators, mainly related to the IGU's Geography Education Commission and its activities – publications, symposia, conferences and its academic journal, *International Research in Geographical and Environmental Education* – the membership is predominantly white, English speaking and from the developed world.

Even so it is possible to identify certain common elements in geography education across the world and that is supported by recent international surveys conducted by Haubrich (1996) and Gerber (2003). Geography is shown to occupy an uneasy place in the curricula of nations. In some instances it is found in curriculum frameworks in which the word geography itself does not exist; in several countries the number of students taking the subject is on the decline; 'making the case for geography' to politicians has not always been successful; it faces severe competition from established subjects such as history and newer subjects as business studies and information technology (ICT). Underlying some of these concerns is that geography has an image of being outdated and inaccurate. At times too it does not

sufficiently 'grab' students' interest and enthusiasm and so needs to be made more meaningful to their lives. Related to this is the need to raise the quality of students' thinking in geography classrooms and much has now been achieved to address this. Another related concern is that the 'worlds' of school geography and higher education geography have drifted apart. Indeed Goudie (1993) has argued that a 'chasm' has appeared with two-way communications and mutual benefit being lost. A final challenge is to maintain, hopefully strengthen, the fieldwork traditions of geography where it is well established; and in other countries the case for fieldwork needs be more effectively made.

However a number of major opportunities exist for future geography educators. These include: geography being the natural vehicle for educating young people about the environment and sustainable development; the huge potential of ICT and geographical information systems; and the vibrancy and relevance of higher education geography. The future of geography looks bright.

See also: curriculum; environmental education; subjects

Further reading

Fairgrieve, J. H. (1926) *Geography in School*, London: University of London Press.

Gerber, R. (2003) 'The global scene for geographical education'. In R. Gerber (ed.) *International Handbook on Geographical Education*, Dordrecht, the Netherlands: Kluwer.

Goudie, A. (1993) 'Schools and universities – the great divide', *Geography*, 78(4): 338–39.

Haubrich, H. (1996) 'Geographical education 1996: results of a survey in 38 countries', *International Geographical Union Commission of Geographical Education Newsletter*, 32: 1–28.

Kent, W. A. (2000) 'Geography: changes and challenges'. In W. A. Kent (ed.) *School Subject Teaching*, London: Kogan Page.

Kropotkin, P. (1885) 'What geography ought to be', *The Nineteenth Century*, 18: 940–56.

W. ASHLEY KENT

GERMANY

The Reformation and Counter-Reformation led to significant educational advances in Germany. Yet education, as in previous centuries, remained essentially the Church's concern. In the eighteenth century, however, the German states started to take interest in education. In 1763, Fredrick the Great of Prussia mandated compulsory school attendance from the age of five to 13–14. In the early nineteenth century, a new national concept of education emerged in Germany. The emphasis was placed, on the one hand, on personal and individual developments, and on the other, on classical studies and German culture, language and nationhood. This concept of *Bildung* had a defining influence on the development of the academically rigorous secondary school, the *Gymnasium*, the form of its leaving certificate, the *Abitur*, and the general nature of the German *Universität*.

In the latter stages of the nineteenth century, the industrial revolution and the 1871 unification of Germany resulted in greater emphasis being placed on meeting the educational needs of the state. New forms of professional, technological and vocational education developed, and increased importance was given to fostering a sense of belongingness, obedience and loyalty to the state. The 1871 unification, nevertheless, left the control of education in the hands of the member states. Today, the main responsibility for education still remains with the sixteen states (*Länder*) that compose the federal state. Within its jurisdiction, each state is in command of educational legislation, school inspection, curriculum development and the administration and financing of schools and higher education. Although the state governments cooperate among themselves in order to assure a certain degree of national uniformity, significant regional differences can still be found. The actual running of a school is generally entrusted to local municipalities. Federal involvement in education is restricted to matters such as partly financing higher education and the regulation of teacher training.

After the defeat of imperial Germany in World War I, measures were taken by the new Weimar Republic to make the education system more accessible and egalitarian: a public school system which provided all children with unified four years of elementary education was established; the age of compulsory education was raised to eighteen; participation in higher education rose; progressive methods of education were introduced and women received greater educational opportunities. The education of the Republic, however, failed to create the foundations necessary for the subsistence of a stable democracy. With the 1933 coming to power of the National Socialist Party, education became an instrument for achieving the party's goals and spreading its ideology. Nazi Germany secularised the still-predominantly denominational education, instilled nationalistic, racist and anti-democratic educational practices and doctrines, limited the education of women and placed the educational emphasis on physical instruction, the development of youth movements, obedience to the Führer and German nationalism.

After World War II, defeated Germany was divided into East and West. In the East, under Soviet supervision, a secular and highly centralised education system was erected. This system, which cherished equality, provided all children with a single ten-year track of compulsory education in a polytechnic school emphasising communist values and practical work. East Germany's technological advancement was slow, however, partly because of low higher education progression rates. In the West, the Weimer education system, with its denominational, three-track nature, was restored almost unchanged. In the 1960s and 1970s reforms sought to make the education system more egalitarian, accessible and meritocratic.

Today, education for the vast majority of children begins between the ages of three and five in the kindergarten. These institutions, which focus mainly on play, are not seen as an integral part of the state system. They are normally run by non-governmental bodies and charge fees. Full-time compulsory education starts at the age of six and lasts for nine or ten years, depending on the state. Compulsory part-time education continues until the age of eighteen. At the age of six, most children enter a state's *Grundschule*. Although fee-paying primary and secondary schools exist, including church schools and Montessori and Waldorf schools, the private sector accounts for less than 10 per cent of all German schools. Primary education lasts between four and six years, according to the state. At the end of this phase, based on teachers' recommendations and parents' requests, the pupil enters one of three secondary education tracks. Those entering the vocational track receive in the *Hauptschule* a general education until age 15–16, after which they can complete a further two or three years of full-time training or combine part-time training with an apprenticeship, leading to a vocational qualification. Those entering the professional track in the *Realschule* receive an extended general education until the age of sixteen. This leads to two further years of specialised instruction, leading to a professional leaving certificate. Those entering the academic track in the *Gymnasium* receive a general education until the age of 18–19, when they sit the *Abitur*, which serves as a matriculation examination for university education. Some mobility between the three tracks is possible: indeed, some schools offer more than one track and even provide a dual qualification pathway.

In German universities students are, to a considerable extent, able to design their own course of studies. Traditionally, students graduate with a *Diplom* or *Magister* after five or six years of studies. Presently, however, German universities are adapting the unified European system of three-year bachelor's and two-year master's degrees. Additionally, Germany offers other forms of vocational, technical and scientific higher education, leading to degrees and other qualifications.

Following the 1990 unification, the East, while preserving a slightly more egalitarian orientation, basically adopted the educational system of the West. At the start of the twenty-first century the German education system faces various challenges: there remain some geographical, gender and social class disparities; German universities have to adapt to the predominant European model of higher education; and the increasing number of immigrants demands inclusive education strategies which do not compromise the finest traditions of academic excellence.

See also: Europe

Further reading

Ash, G. M. (1997) *German Universities Past and Future: Crisis or Renewal*, Oxford: Berghahn Books.

Blackburn, G. W. (1985) *Education in the Third Reich: A Study of Race and History in Nazi Textbooks*, Albany NY: State University of New York Press.

Fuhr, C. (1997) *The German Education System Since 1945*, Bonn: Inter Nationes.

Hearnden, A. (1974) *Education in the Two Germanys*, Oxford: Blackwell.

Hahn, H. J. (1998) *Education and Society and Germany*, Oxford: Berg.

TAL GILEAD

GIFTEDNESS

People whose abilities are significantly greater than average are described as gifted. For children, this would cover advanced development and for adults, exceptional accomplishments. The word 'giftedness' is sometimes presented as synonymous with other related terms such as *talent*, *high* or *exceptional ability* and *genius*.

Worldwide, the understanding of giftedness is varied and sometimes imbued with a moral or religious dimension. This demonstrates the complexity of the concept and the importance of understanding its meaning within its particular context. An example is the French word for giftedness (*surdoué*) that translates as *endow*, echoing the English concept that abilities are bestowed either through genetics or from something more mysterious. Non-Western societies tend to have different views on the nature of giftedness, with models emphasising high achievement as a result of hard work, rather than through the luck of being bequeathed with superior faculties. Developments discussed here focus on the Western models, as these have the longest education research history and are the most influential in the field.

One of the first relevant publications in England set the controversial tone of the field in 1894, when Galton proclaimed that high ability was hereditary and the preserve of people from certain classes and races. In France, for reasons of determining appropriate education for children with complex learning needs, Binet was developing a range of testing tools to measure intelligence. This embryonic measure of Intelligence Quotient (IQ) was adopted by a range of educationists and psychologists (including Terman and Burt) and employed to prove popular views that intelligence is genetic, fixed and is a capacity with which people are differently bestowed. These ideas have been very significant in the field and have influenced policy makers, for example in the introduction of examinations for children at age eleven to determine the future of their schooling.

It took a further sixty years (until around the 1970s) for these views to shift in the popular consciousness. As psycho-sociological developments lent clarity to debates about nature–nurture, researchers and practitioners began to take increasing notice of variables affecting test performance and the value of broadening definitions of high ability to reflect all fields of human endeavour, rather than intellectual spheres only. Since the 1980s, Gardner's notion of *multiple intelligences* has affected gifted education, and other theorists (e.g. Sternberg, Renzulli) have also advocated a more inclusive approach.

Contemporary definitions allow for giftedness to apply to children with abilities in non-academic fields or those unable to achieve well due to factors such as disability, poor backgrounds or lack of fluency in the dominant language. Such children tend to underachieve in school and, where this is not addressed, middle-class children of educated parents dominate gifted education programmes.

The number of influential longitudinal studies in giftedness is necessarily relatively small. Early studies (1920s–1950s) reinforced notions that giftedness is genetic and children are predisposed to depression and difficulties with normal social development. Some believe that the gifted feel and experience life more intensely than others and this can lead to social isolation. Recent studies (1970s–present) have shown that much of this is falsely conceived and gifted children are generally popular in school with a normal array of friends.

In terms of education provision, recommendations differ depending on the extent and nature of the giftedness. In some cases accelerating the pupil out of their age range is the best option available, but care must be taken to avoid social problems. Generally, enriching the curriculum is a key recommendation, together with ensuring that pupils spend some time with an intellectual peer group based on shared interests and abilities, as well as with children of their own chronological age. Research is starting to show that a general rise in achievement is noted when the gifted population of a school are encouraged to demonstrate their full abilities (Reis and Renzulli 2004).

Giftedness is a contentious term describing a controversial topic and the field continues to be dogged by charges of elitism. Further research is required to determine the optimum pedagogies and policies.

See also: ability; ability grouping; Binet, Alfred; Burt, Cyril; elitism; excellence; Galton, Francis; intelligence/intelligence tests; streaming/tracking; Terman, Lewis M.

Further reading

Heller, K. A., Monks, F. J., Sternberg, R. J. and Subotnik, R. F. (eds) (2000) *International Handbook of Research and Development of Giftedness and Talent*, Oxford: Elsevier Science.

Reis, S. M. and Renzulli, J. S. (2004) 'Current research on the social and emotional development of gifted and talented students: good news and future possibilities'. In *Psychology in the Schools*, 41, published online in Wiley InterScience.

Sternberg, R. J. (1990) *Metaphors of Mind: Conceptions of the Nature of Intelligence*, New York: Cambridge University Press.

CARRIE WINSTANLEY

GLOBALISATION

In the past twenty years two theories, *human capital* and *skill formation* have dominated our understanding of the education–economy relationship. These rival theories have sought to explain the generation and use of education and skill with respect to the economy. However, in the light of changes in the global economy, neither theory is now adequate and a new theory, that of *skills capture*, is sketched here. In order to understand its significance, it is important to outline human capital and skill formation theories to explain what have been considered their theoretical and empirical strengths and weaknesses, before explaining why they are now both under threat in the face of new skill developments arising out of globalisation: in particular the global skill strategies of multinational companies (MNCs).

Human capital theory (HCT) starts from the neo-classical economic assumption that human beings are calculating pleasure machines; that is, that they are capable of reasoning instrumentally from means to ends. However, the ends are set in terms of the pursuit of self-interest defined in terms of the acquisition of income and wealth. In this context investment in education is seen as a function of a basic human drive to secure income and wealth since it is a fundamental tenet of human capital theory that investment in education does, over time, lead to greater income. Hence, to act rationally, human beings will invest in education.

A further key assumption made by human capital theorists is that a notional equilibrium between the supply and demand for skilled labour can be achieved. The mechanism which enables this equilibrium is that employers will respond to the greater productive potential of educated labour by making the appropriate investments to utilise their potential. The increase in productive potential is in turn rewarded with higher incomes. In other words, however much the supply of educated labour increases, employers, over time, will respond by matching supply with demand.

When looking at the issue of globalisation, and especially with respect to skills capture theory, this assumption turns out to be the Achilles heel of the theory.

Human capital has been specifically applied to economic globalisation by Becker (2006) and Reich (1991). For Becker, the doyen of human capital theorists, the new technological revolution has placed human capital at the centre of economic productivity:

> Human capital refers to the knowledge, information, ideas, skills, and health of individuals. This is the 'age of human capital' ... the economic success of individuals, and also whole economies, depends on how extensively and effectively people invest in themselves.
>
> (Becker 2006: 290)

Reich (1991) has applied this view to globalisation, assuming that the creation of global labour markets will lead to a closer match between human capital, productivity and incomes. The underlying view of all these theorists is that differences in income are increasingly based on the skills workers posses and apply. The policy prescription that follows from this is precisely that which we see applied in many countries to increase the length and participation of students in education and then to lay down paths for lifelong learning.

It will be seen from the discussion of globalisation that in a variety of ways human capital's fundamental assumptions have been reproduced and simply applied to a new economic environment – globalisation. But one of the problems of HCT is that beyond the general prescription to increase educational opportunities, it can tell us very little about why some societies use skill sets in ways that make them more competitive than others. When we examine the trajectories of education and skill that different countries structure for individuals we find they are quite different and that they can have a significant impact on a nation's competitiveness (Hall and Soskice 2001). HCT tells us little about the institutions that structure the choices that individuals make and the nature of the education and training they receive. Under these circumstances the policy assumption that can be inferred from human capital theory, that more education is a 'good' tells us nothing about how such a general injunction should be translated into policies that are beneficial for both the individual and the society.

It is at this point that skill formation theory (SFT) enters the picture because it seeks to explain the relationship between institutional structures, power and reward in relation to skill.

SFT introduces a key set of concepts to enable us to understand the institutional, social and political determinants of skill. The first major statement in this tradition was that of Maurice *et al.* (1986) who compared the institutional and labour market basis for the development and rewards for skill in Germany and France. Skill is inevitably a political issue because it stands at the centre of the conflict between capital and labour. Where workers have skills that cannot be substituted by machines or routinisation they can, in principle, command a higher return in the labour market. In some countries, such as Germany through the dual system of training,

cooperation between workers and employers replaced conflict for much of the post-war era because there were advantages for both sides. The high level of skill, especially in German engineering, commanded high wages because there is a premium on German products in the global market place (Estevez-Abe *et al.* 2001). Equally, issues to do with motivation to achieve a level of skill can be seen to be socially structured. In theory, then, different countries can gain a comparative advantage because of the skill sets they develop as a result of their unique institutional structures. However, this theory also needs substantial revision in the light of globalisation.

We have coined the term skills capture theory (SCT) to draw attention to several dimensions to what may be termed a new global skills regime. The notion of capture focuses on who has the power to determine the nature of skills, where they are generated and how they are to be rewarded. In the past, as we have seen, if highly valued skills were embedded in particular contexts then that gave workers and their unions a degree of bargaining power over work conditions and wages. However, once skills can be disembedded and constructed more or less anywhere, then the bargaining power of workers is greatly reduced. In this sense we can talk of skills capture.

Several processes related to globalisation have brought about this state of affairs. First, where once skills were generated in particular social contexts and then used by corporations in what may be called an outside-in process (from society to the economy), now the reverse is true. Corporations have the social technologies of production, standardisation, quality control and benchmarking to create oases of production in areas where it was previously thought it would be impossible to create high-quality products. All that is required is a motivated workforce and the basic infrastructure. Hence high-quality manufactured goods are being produced not only in China but also in countries like India,

Brazil and Vietnam: in fact, wherever, cost savings can be achieved. This even applies to German products. For example, ten years ago we interviewed a senior human resources executive of a high-end German automobile manufacturer. At that time, when we asked whether the cars they produced could be made anywhere, his answer was 'no', only in Germany. We interviewed the same person for our current project and this time he did not give the same response. Rather, he pointed to the 24-hour design team that was situated in southern Germany, Mumbai and California. The team worked on the same design tasks and problems: when one team ended their day, the next team began.

Second, processes of standardisation, what we call digital Taylorism, have enabled innovations to be translated into sets of routines that might require some degree of education but not the kind of creativity and independence of judgement that is often associated with the knowledge economy. Standardisation is of particular importance in relation to outsourcing because once standard processes have been established they can be 'shipped' abroad and integrated into the MNC's organisation across the globe (Brown *et al.* 2008).

Third, universities in developing and redeveloping nations such as China, India and Russia, have maintained high standards despite poverty and social upheaval. There is now a significant supply of graduate labour, which enables MNCs to engage in a skills arbitrage where if the costs are too high in one location they can simply 'buy in' from another. The key to this possibility is that the quality of graduates, especially in technical areas such as science, engineering and information technology, is equal to those found in the West (Brown and Lauder 2006).

Finally, what brings these processes together are electronic communications, in particular the internet and intranets. These enable MNCs to standardise the judgements they make in relation to graduates and to place them where they can be most effective.

It may be considered that the role of MNCs in this process has been given too much importance, because although they may dominate economies in terms of innovation, they do not in relation to employment. However, that would be to misunderstand the increasing participation of small and medium-sized companies in economic globalisation.

The implications of this analysis for the education-economy relationship and the way it is theorised by SCT for both HCT and SFT theories are profound. First, HCT predicts that we should see increasing returns to education on the basis of the increased productivity that education enables. However, that is not what longitudinal data on graduate earnings in either the United States or Britain show (Lauder *et al.* 2007). The reason for this is that the development of economic globalisation is premised on disequilibrium: that is given the quality of graduates from countries like India and China and the income differentials between them and Western graduates, it makes sense for MNCs to invest in the former. In turn, this raises the stakes in the positional competition for credentials in Western societies because MNCs will only recruit from what are considered the elite universities. Since elite universities largely recruit from higher income and wealth groups, the implications for equality of opportunity also need to be considered.

See also: economics of education; educational theory; knowledge economy; lifelong learning; skills

Further reading

Becker, G., (2006) 'The age of human capital'. In H. Lauder, P. Brown, J. Dillabough and A. H. Halsey (eds) *Education, Globalization and Social Change*, Oxford: Oxford University Press.

Brown, P. and Lauder, H. (2006) 'Globalization, knowledge and the myth of the magnet economy', *Globalization, Societies and Education*, 4(1): 25–57.

Brown, P., Lauder, H. and Ashton, D. (2008, forthcoming) 'Towards a high skills economy:

higher education and the new realities of global capitalism'. In R. Boden, R. Deem, D. Epstein, F. Rizvi and S. Wright (eds) *World Year Book of Education 2008. Geographies of Knowledge, Geometries of Power: Higher Education in the 21st Century*. London: Routledge.

Estevez-Abe, M., Iversen, T. and Soskice, D. (2001) 'Social protection and the formation of skills: a reinterpretation of the welfare state'. In P. Hall and D. Soskice (eds) *Varieties of Capitalism*, Oxford: Oxford University Press.

Hall, P., and Soskice, D. (eds) (2001) *Varieties of Capitalism*, Oxford: Oxford University Press.

Lauder, H., Egerton, M., Brown, P. and Ashton, D. (2007) *Education, Skill Bias Theory and Graduate Earnings: A Critique and Alternative*, Bath: Education Department, University of Bath.

Maurice, M., Sellier, F. and Silvestre, J.-J. (1986) *The Social Foundations of Industrial Power*, Cambridge MA: MIT Press.

Reich, R. (1991) *The Work of Nations*, New York: Simon and Schuster.

Acknowledgement

This entry relies on our current study, the Global Skill Strategies of Multinational Companies (ESRC: RES–000–023–0287).

HUGH LAUDER, PHILLIP BROWN AND DAVID ASHTON

GRADES

A grade awarded to a pupil or student signifies the evaluation or score given for a piece of work during an examination. This may be numerical, often out of 10, 20 or 100. Marks might be allocated to particular questions or features of the work, and added up to provide the grade as a whole, or might be based on a set of guidelines or criteria to be assessed. In many cases the numerical scores are translated into classifications that are expressed as a letter. The top grade is often an A or alpha, with a number of further classifications to denote lesser grades that are considered to have succeeded or passed. There will usually be one or more further classifications or grades to denote lack of success, or failure. Often in higher education institutions for the purposes of awarding degrees, these grades are presented in terms of classes, thus a first

class is the most successful, with second class (often divided into upper second and lower second) and third class following, and then the fail grade. The first class or A grade is commonly based on a numerical score or percentage of 70, while a pass grade might be based on a score of 40 or 50. In considering overall grades from a set of examinations or modules taken, the scores of each will be assessed with any particular circumstances or weightings to arrive at a combined grade.

See also: assessment; examinations

GARY McCULLOCH

GRADUATE/GRADUATION

A graduate is described as a person who has successfully completed a programme of study in a university or college and has been awarded a first degree from that institution. In the United States and Canada, the definition applies to a student who has completed a programme of study at a high school and received a diploma.

The term graduate is also a verb, used in the sense of receiving or causing to receive a degree or diploma. The act of graduation deems the graduate to be a member of the alumni of the institution and they normally have certain electoral rights and access to the institution's library, for example. A graduand is a person about to receive a degree or other such award.

Graduation is the act of graduating at a ceremony at which university, college or high school diplomas, degrees or other academic awards are conferred or awarded. Sometimes referred to as a rite of passage, it dates back to the twelfth century.

Prior to graduation, registered students are required to undertake such examinations/assessments as may be prescribed for the programme of study, and these are normally specified in a programme document setting out the curriculum, scheduled teaching hours, scheme of assessments and the allocation of marks to each element of each subject or module. The programme document would also normally set out the level of performance required by the student in terms of achieving a pass or higher-level grade. The purpose of assessment is to establish the extent to which students have fulfilled the objectives of their programme of study and demonstrated their knowledge and understanding of the various components that constitute the programme.

University/college examination board meetings, comprising internal and external examiners, consider the results achieved by students following programmes of study and determine the result and level of performance in respect of each candidate. Such boards then make recommendations to the institution's academic council as to the awards to be made to students who have successfully completed the university's or college's programme of study. Examinations and assessments are conducted in accordance with the institution's regulations and marks and standards. Ratification of examination/assessment results by the academic council deems examination candidates eligible for an institute degree or other academic award, which will be conferred at an institute graduation ceremony.

At the higher education graduation ceremony, each graduand wears a gown with sleeves and a hood. The shape of sleeves and the colour of both the gown and the hood varies by institution, the level of the academic award – bachelor, master or doctor – and by the academic discipline or field of study. In high schools in the USA and Canada there is a tradition that graduates wear a class ring on the third finger of their right hand or on a chain around their neck.

Universities or colleges normally charge a ceremonial fee. The fee helps to defray some of the costs to the institute associated with the graduation event. If a student is not in 'good standing' (if they owe money to the institution or have library fines outstanding or unreturned books) they are not permitted to graduate. Each graduand is normally permitted to invite perhaps two guests to the graduation ceremony.

Graduation ceremonies are very special annual ritual events in a university or college calendar and entail a good deal of pomp and ceremony. A declaration is normally read out by a senior university/college officer confirming that the graduands have successfully completed the programme of study for the award being presented to them. Each graduand's name is read out and they are invited to a platform and the institute's president, rector or vice-chancellor presents the award to them. Institutions normally provide for a photographer to record the graduate's happy event.

See also: alumni; degree; diploma; high school; higher education; university

THOMAS DUFF

GRAMMAR

Grammar refers to the correct use of words to form sentences and convey meaning, covering both spoken and written language use. Studied formally, it involves paying close attention to such matters as linguistic history, syntax, inflexions and pronunciation. The ancient Greeks pioneered the classification and codification of language, also an interest of scholars throughout the Roman empire. Medieval European writers were influenced by this Greco-Roman tradition, and Latin grammar was applied to the vernacular European languages that evolved from Latin. Teutonic languages, such as German, were a stronger influence upon the development of English grammar.

Since the Middle Ages the teaching of traditional grammar was a vital function of school work. As the name suggests, early grammar schools offered formal, technical instruction in this field. The modern schoolchild's experience will normally include some instruction in the 'rules of grammar', and particularly in the application of the 'parts of speech', namely nouns, verbs, adjectives, adverbs, pronouns, conjunctions, prepositions and interjections. With the rise of sociolingistics, especially since the 1960s, there has been much contestation over how, or even whether, traditional grammar should be taught in schools. The global drive for high standards in education has, however, reinforced the importance of literacy and communication skills. A proportion of the marks available in some formal examinations and tests are devoted to the correct usage of grammar, spelling and punctuation, providing an incentive for teachers and students to pay attention to the received rules of grammar.

See also: literacy; spelling; standards; writing

DAVID CROOK

GRAMMAR OF SCHOOLING

The American historians of curriculum and pedagogy, Tyack and Cuban, define the grammar of schooling in terms of the organisational forms that govern instruction. They argue that these have persisted over time relatively unchanged, while challenges to this basic grammar have generally been only transitory (Tyack and Cuban 1995: 5). Indeed, they argue, 'Little has changed in the ways that schools divide time and space, classify students and allocate them to classrooms, splinter knowledge into "subjects", and award grades and "credits" as evidence of learning' (Tyack and Cuban 1995: 85). Such features tend to be taken for granted, while departures from customary or conventional school practice attract attention. They see the grammar of schooling as a whole as being a product of history, established as part of the 'standard institutional template' of modern schooling in the nineteenth century. These views have a number of significant implications for initiatives to reform educational institutions and practices. They help to explain the durability and strength of established approaches, not so much through a 'conscious conservatism' as through 'unexamined institutional habits and widespread cultural beliefs about what constitutes a "real school"' (Tyack and Cuban 1995: 88). Innovations in schooling can therefore be only temporary or left on the periphery of the system, often in spite of major investment and high-level political support for change.

See also: pedagogy; school; school change; school reform

Further reading

Tyack, D. and Cuban, L. (1995) *Tinkering toward Utopia: A Century of Public School Reform*, Cambridge MA: Harvard University Press.

GARY McCULLOCH

GRAMMAR SCHOOL

As Foster Watson (1916) noted, the term grammar school is found predominantly in English-speaking contexts, but some scholars attribute its provenance to Charlemagne, the eighth-century king of the Franks and founder of Court School under Alcuin of York. Grammar was central to the curriculum of the school and Charlemagne issued capitularies to abbots of monasteries and bishops of dioceses, requiring them to promote the 'study of letters' throughout the Holy Roman empire. By the second half of the eleventh century, some English church and cathedral schools offering free or cheap education to local poor boys were referred to as *scola grammatice*. The first actual use of 'gramer scole' appears in a fourteenth-century English text, though this refers to a school in Alexandria, Greece (Watson 1916: 1–2).

By the fifteenth century, the term had become a familiar one, describing a school established by a pious person by means of an endowment. The earliest grammar schools were established to provide free instruction to the children of a particular locality, and it was the centrality of Latin as a curriculum subject in such schools that gave the term a currency in England and beyond. The first American Latin Grammar School was established in Boston in 1635, as an elite institution for sons destined for leadership positions in the Church, state or courts, and also for entrance to Harvard College, founded in the following year. In England, too, the grammar school

279

curriculum, based on Latin, stood for academic excellence, but as the demand for Latin declined in the eighteenth century some grammar schools developed into elite 'public' schools, while others broadened their curricula in response to local needs. Grammar schools in English coastal towns 'added such subjects as arithmetic, astronomy, natural philosophy and writing' (Aldrich 1996: 27), while others reverted to elementary subjects. By the nineteenth century, many grammar schools were on the verge of extinction: endowments had diminished in value, and a legal ruling by Lord Eldon relating to Leeds Grammar School, in 1805, had decided that no money of a grammar school trust might be used for purposes other than classical studies (Sanderson 1962: 29). This principle was reversed in 1840, when a Grammar School Act permitted curriculum diversification. Something of an English grammar school revival then followed.

When the state moved, in 1902, to establish its own secondary schools, the endowed schools provided a model for local education authorities to emulate. The first decade of the twentieth century saw the establishment of a new wave of municipal grammar schools for eleven-year-old boys and girls that were seen both as the symbols of educational advance and the guardians of cultural excellence. For the working-class child, the acquisition of a highly competitive grammar school scholarship or free place, achieved as a result of success in the 'eleven-plus' examination, represented a considerable success, although families sometimes experienced difficulties in meeting the costs of a uniform and books, and in some instances fees, as well as adjusting to the loss of assumed juvenile earnings. From 1917, grammar school courses were linked to School Certificate accreditation, strengthening links with the universities, and reinforcing the widely held perception that a grammar school education could open doors that would otherwise remain firmly shut. Grammar schools provided an academic education for a minority destined for white-collar work or for university, followed by a professional career. The majority of children, by contrast, received only a basic education in an elementary school, occasionally followed by a short period in a lower status secondary institution (Crook et al. 1999: 9–10).

Following World War II, the English grammar school took its place alongside technical and secondary modern schools in a tripartite system in which they supposedly enjoyed 'parity of esteem'. When it became clear, both on grounds of cost and uncertainty over how technical aptitudes might be identified, that the number of technical schools would be negligible, however, the eleven-plus became a pass/fail examination. Those who passed won the prize of being taught courses leading to public examinations, superior employment and possibly a university place by graduates in a grammar school that boasted a library, laboratories and playing fields. Those who failed would enjoy none of these advantages.

As secondary modern schools gradually began to imitate the grammar school curriculum and non-selective, comprehensive education was advanced as a more socially just alternative to selection, the grammar school came under fire. From the late 1950s, selective systems around the world became subject to change, and grammar schools found themselves susceptible to closure or merger. In the United Kingdom, the process of 'going comprehensive' was largely a grass roots one, emanating from the local education authorities. In most places, grammar schools disappeared, some joining the fee-paying sector, but a small number – 164 in England (2007 figures) – remain within state education. For the past forty years grammar schools have been the subject of calls, on the one hand, for a revival, and, on the other, for their final extinction. Prestigious grammar schools are found in the public and private sectors of other countries, too: Auckland Grammar School, New Zealand, is a state school, for example, while Sydney Grammar School, Australia, is independent.

See also: church; classical studies; comprehensive school/education; endowment; examinations; excellence; grammar; parity of esteem; public school; scholarship; secondary school/education; selection; technical education/school/college

Further reading

Aldrich, R. (1996) *Education for the Nation*, London: Cassell.
Crook, D., Power, S. and Whitty, G. (1999) *The Grammar School Question: A Review of Research on Comprehensive and Selective Education*, London: Institute of Education.
Sanderson, J. M. (1962) 'The grammar school and the education of the poor, 1786–1840', *British Journal of Educational Studies*, 11(1): 28–43.
Watson, F. (1916) *The Old Grammar Schools*, Cambridge: Cambridge University Press.

DAVID CROOK

GREECE

Ancient Greek civilisation exerted a widespread influence upon Western languages, politics, philosophy, science, and culture. In respect of education, Athenian boys' public and private schools promoted the teaching of poetry and literature. They were pioneers of education for citizenship, and higher-level schooling was provided in military schools. Importance was also placed upon the education of females in Athens, but girls were educated at home rather than in schools, as was the case in Sparta. The Spartan emphasis upon physical fitness, self-discipline and military training provided an important model for later schools around the world.

Today, formal education in Greece is organised into three levels: primary, secondary, and tertiary. Compulsory education includes the six-year primary school (starting at the age of six years) and the three-year *gymnasium*, which is the lower level of secondary education. Pre-school education is not compulsory and can start at the age of two-and-a-half years. Upper secondary education includes the *unified lyceum* (three years) and the technical and vocational educational institutions (two or three years).

Special schools operate, at both primary and secondary levels, for children with special needs. More often, these children attend 'special classes' in comprehensive schools and gradually integrate into normal classes. Intercultural schools are in operation for foreign immigrants, cultural minority children or repatriated Greeks. 'Tutorial' and 'reception' classes are provided for these children if they opt to attend comprehensive schools.

Tertiary education encompasses universities and technological educational institutions. The latter are oriented to the application of knowledge. Upper secondary school graduates are admitted to these institutions through national examinations. The competitiveness for entrance has led to a proliferation of private 'cram schools' offering preparatory courses for these examinations. Many students who do not succeed study abroad. An exception to this system is the Hellenic Open University, where students aged twenty-two or over are admitted after a process of drawing lots. This is the only state university charging fees for undergraduate studies.

Another, post-secondary, level exists, consisting of institutes of initial vocational training (IEKs). These provide a formal, but unclassified, level of education. They accept both lower and upper secondary school graduates. Studies last one or two years, depending on the specialisation.

Formal education is provided for free by the state at all levels. Exceptions are the state IEKs and some postgraduate courses. In parallel with the state sector, a relatively small number of private schools operate at both primary and secondary levels and private IEKs. The education ministry supervises all such education institutions, public and private.

At tertiary level, the operation of private institutions is prohibited by the Constitution. Nevertheless, many private institutions, often franchises of foreign universities, operate under the auspices of the ministry of commerce. Their academic status is not officially recognised. A constitutional amendment is being promoted to allow the function of non-profit, private universities from 2007. These will operate under the same regulations as state universities, but will not be publicly subsidised.

Greek formal education is characterised by high degree of centralisation and a percentage of GDP spending that ranks amongst the lowest in OECD countries. The most strictly regulated institutions are primary and secondary schools. The ministry of education controls curricula, textbooks, as well as the appointment, salaries and promotion of teachers. Private schools enjoy greater autonomy in terms of staff selection and promotion. However, their curricula, textbooks, and baseline salaries and minimum qualifications of their teachers, are those prescribed by the ministry. Tertiary education establishments enjoy greater autonomy, although the academic community demands more decision making responsibilities.

The centralised curriculum of formal education has an ethnocentric and denominational character. It emphasises the continuity of the Greek culture over the centuries and codifies the Greek Orthodox religion as an integral element of Greek identity. This curriculum has been criticised for contributing to xenophobia in schools (yet, limited to non-European immigrants) and for promoting assimilation practices in the context of intercultural education.

Since 2000, the curriculum content of basic education has been decentralised, with teachers encouraged to develop their own syllabus for 30 per cent of the available teaching time. Further initiatives to modernise school knowledge include: a new, thematic curriculum in compulsory education promoting cross-disciplinary learning and new methodologies; promotion of entrepreneurial attitudes; and cultivation of a European perspective. Yet, issues relating to ethnic identity and religious education have undergone marginal changes, due to resistance from the Greek Orthodox Church and

the public. New measures have also been introduced for the evaluation of education at all levels. These do not, however, equate to the strict accountability criteria and performance-related rewards found in other countries.

Besides formal education, non-formal adult education grew rapidly in Greece during the 1990s, under European structural fund support. Its largest part consists of private centres of continuing vocational training (KEKs), controlled by the ministry of labour and operating under rigid accreditation and monitoring procedures.

Nowadays, the main problems of Greek education can be summarised as follows: absence of holistic policy-planning covering all education levels; shortage and inefficient use of resources; non-implementation of reforms (often due to grass-roots resistance and the associated political cost); lack of systematic research to inform policy; inadequate practitioner training to implement policies; reproduction of social inequalities; and high unemployment rates of graduates (often attributed to the weak business sector). The EU plays an important role in overcoming such problems, through structural fund support that extends up to 2013.

See also: classical studies; Europe; Mediterranean; Organisation for Economic Co-operation and Development (OECD)

Further reading

Damanakis, M. (2005) 'European and intercultural dimension in Greek education', *European Educational Research Journal*, 4(1): 79–88.
EURYBASE (www.eurydice.org).
Giamouridis, A. and Bagley, C. (2006) 'Policy, politics, and social inequality in the educational system of Greece', *Journal of Modern Greek Studies*, 24(1): 1–20.

MARINA-STEFANIA GIANNAKAKI

GUIZOT, FRANÇOIS PIERRE GUILLAUME (1787–1874)

Guizot, the French minister for education, was born into a Huguenot family. After studying at Geneva and Paris, he became Professor of Modern History at the Sorbonne in 1812, aged twenty-five. Due to political turmoil and affiliations he was prohibited from lecturing or holding academic posts from 1822–28. He was the elected to the Chamber of Deputies in 1830 and was Minister of Public Instruction from 1833 to 1837. Many of his educational ideas came from his first wife, the author Pauline Meulan. In 1833 he secured legislation to establish a system of primary schooling covering the entire nation. Under this law, every community with over 500 residents was to establish a boy's primary school, whilst each town with over 6,000 residents was required to establish a higher primary school. The legislation also brought in a school inspectorate and the creation of local school boards, consisting of lay and cle-

rical members. Each regional department was required to create a teacher training college and teaching qualifications were systematised and strengthened. Another reform was the institution of a minimum wage for teachers. These reforms were extended to include girls' education in 1836. One of Guizot's favoured methods was the issuing of ministerial circulars to those responsible for the school system at different levels. His *Manuel général de l'instruction primaire* codified expectations and kept the profession updated with current developments. Guizot briefly became premier in 1847/48, but fled Paris on the overthrow of Louis Philippe. He devoted the rest of his life to academic historical writing.

See also: France; politics of education

STEVEN COWAN

HABERMAS, JÜRGEN (1929–)

Habermas, the German philosopher, studied in Göttingen, Zurich and Bonn and became research assistant under Theodore Adorno at the University of Frankfurt. He held professorships at Frankfurt, Heidelberg and Starnberg. *Knowledge and Human Interests* (1968) placed him at the forefront of European critical theory. Habermas argued that rationality was located in the structures of interpersonal linguistic communication, rather than within cosmological models or within individuals. Education should have as its primary aim the realisation and development of the human potential for rationality. This manifests itself through speech acts, which have a *telos* or purpose: mutual understanding. All humans have communicative competence to bring about such understandings. In *Theory of Communicative Action* (1981) Habermas identifies the origin of modern social and political crises in the one-sided processes of rationalisation, directed by financial, administrative and bureaucratic interests. These interfere with purposeful and meaningful acts of communication in the public sphere by interposing instrumental rationalism, reflecting the interests of social formations such as the market or the state. Open and undisturbed linguistic interaction was essential for human development, hence the need to institutionalise the enhancement of communication within the education system. Emancipation and self-determination were other necessary aims for education to ensure that the public sphere – which is the meeting point for free individuals interacting through myriad communicative acts – is strengthened. Habermas' defence of modern, civil society relates also to ideas of the creation of identities through a person's ability to engage within a lifeworld that is free from instrumentalist distortions.

See also: critical theory

STEVEN COWAN

HABITUS

Pierre Bourdieu's thinking tool of *habitus* has been developed through empirical work, so its conceptualisation and use has developed over time and in context. It has been developed in texts such as Bourdieu's *The Logic of Practice* (1989), *In Other Words* (1990), and *Pascalian Meditations* (2000). The starting point in his sociology is to ask: 'how can behaviour be regulated without being the product of obedience to rules?' (1990: 65). Habitus 'as social life incorporated' (1990: 31) is meant to bridge the opposition between the individual and society, and is described as a system of

> durable, transposable dispositions, structured structures predisposed to function as structuring structures, that is, as principles which generate and organize practices and representations that can be objectively adapted to their outcomes without presupposing a conscious aiming at ends or an

express mastery of the operations necessary in order to attain them.

(1989: 53)

The agent is predisposed to do certain things that are revealed within a social arena or field of practice, such as a cultural field, university field or economic field. It encompasses ways of talking, moving and making things, and regularities in social actions:

> The habitus as the feel for the game is the social game embodied and turned into a second nature. Nothing is simultaneously freer and more constrained than the action of the good player. He quite naturally materializes at just the place the ball is about to fall, as if the ball were in command of him – but by that very fact, he is in command of the ball.
>
> (1990: 63)

Dispositions are a socio-historical conditioning about actions that are regarded as reasonable by those who occupy the same social space: 'habitus is that presence of the past in the present which makes possible the presence in the present of the forth-coming' (2000: 210). Bourdieu's aim is to reintroduce the socialising and socialised agent, and within practice the objective social conditions in which the agent lives is inculcated as 'structured structures'. As the agent develops practice within different contexts then dispositions are 'structuring structures'. Hence habitus,

> goes hand in hand with vagueness and indeterminacy. As a generative spontaneity which asserts itself in an improvised confrontation with ever-renewed situations, it obeys a practical logic, that of vagueness, of the more-or-less, which defines one's ordinary relation to the world.
>
> (1990: 77–78, author's emphasis)

In *Masculine Domination* (2001), Bourdieu talks about 'the genesis of the female habitus' (63), and argues that matters of body image and self-esteem that focus on the individual objectifies rather than socialises the agent. In particular, the representations of the self and reactions to this are relational and constructed, and are based on the use and acceptance of 'schemes of perception' such as 'thin/fat, big/small, elegant/coarse, delicate/gross' (64–65). The female habitus is formed through the interplay of agency and structure, and where 'masculine domination ... constitutes women as symbolic objects ... [and] ... has the effect of keeping them in a permanent state of bodily insecurity', and what is feminine is 'a form of indulgence towards real or supposed male expectations ... [and so] dependence on others tends to become constitutive of their being' (66).

Within education, habitus has been used by researchers to describe, understand and explain a range of practice. In *Bourdieu and Education* (1998) Grenfell and James provide an overview of Bourdieu's thinking tools and show how they can be used. Of note is work on social class and educational choice, such as Ball's *Class Strategies and the Education Market* (2003). In the field of educational leadership, Gunter, in *Leaders and Leadership in Education* (2001) has used habitus to think through knowledge production, and Lingard *et al.*'s book *Leading Learning* (2003) focuses on leadership as a relational social practice. The challenge for such work is how the revealing of habitus within a field such as a classroom, a school, a family, can illustrate both the reproduction of education and the possibilities of social change.

See also: Bourdieu, Pierre; cultural capital; sociology of education

Further reading

Bourdieu, P. (1990) *In Other Words: Essays Towards a Reflexive Sociology*, trans. Matthew Adamson, Cambridge: Polity Press.

Grenfell, M. and James, D., with Hodkinson, P., Reay, D. and Robbins, D. (1998) *Bourdieu and Education*, London: Falmer Press.

Reay, D. (1995) '"They employ cleaners to do that": habitus in the primary classroom', *British Journal of Sociology of Education*, 16(3): 353–71.

HELEN GUNTER

HALL, GRANVILLE STANLEY (1844–1924)

Hall was educated at Williams College, Massachusetts. From 1868 to 1871 he studied philosophy in Germany, returning to Antioch College, Yellow Springs, Ohio to teach literature and philosophy for five years. He then taught English at Harvard University, while studying for a doctorate – which he gained in 1878 – under the supervision of William James, who was developing psychological studies. Hall returned to Germany under the influence of Wündt, the pioneer in physiological psychology who established the first university laboratory in Leipzig. In 1883 Hall established his own experimental psychological laboratory at the new Johns Hopkins University in Baltimore, Maryland, where John Dewey became his student. In the same year Hall published *The Study of Children* and *The Content of Children's Minds*. His work in establishing the Child Study Association of America (1888) and the American Psychological Association, of which he became president in 1892, did much to create the academic field of educational psychology, as well as create a link between research and those who worked with children. He was a popular lecturer and doctoral supervisor. Many of his students went on to develop the field in other universities. In his later career Hall's interests shifted away from education and towards mainstream psychology: his two-volume *Adolescence* (1904) was a seminal publication.

See also: Dewey, John; psychology of education

STEVEN COWAN

HARRIS, WILLIAM TORREY (1835–1909)

Harris was an American educational administrator and philosopher. He left Yale after two years without graduating and began private tutoring and teaching in public schools in 1856. He was an early supporter of Froebel's ideas and established, with Susan Blow, the first permanent kindergarten in the USA in St Louis in 1873. Founder of the St Louis Philosophical Society in 1866, Harris became editor of the *Journal of Speculative Philosophy* in 1867, editing it until 1893. The *Journal* broadened awareness of the Hegelian tradition within the USA and offered many thinkers – including Pierce, Dewey and James – early publication opportunities. Harris was an admirer of the transcendentalist Amos Bronson Alcott, a notable superintendent of the public school system in St Louis, a position that Harris was later to occupy (1868–80). After Alcott's death in 1888, Harris coauthored a two-volume biography (1893).

Harris served as US Commissioner for Education from 1889 to 1906 under presidents Cleveland, Harrison, McKinlay and Roosevelt. He was editor of a new edition (1901) of *Webster's International Dictionary of the English Language*. A prolific author, with over 400 articles to his name, Harris' educational ideas were summarised in *The Psychologic Foundations of Education* (1898). He was a believer in schooling for individualism, with self-development of the child as the primary aim of education. He argued for a clear separation between religion and public schooling in order to protect personal freedom.

See also: kindergarten

STEVEN COWAN

HEAD TEACHER/PRINCIPAL

The head teacher, often known simply as the head, is commonly responsible not only for the teaching conducted at a school, but also for the overall efficiency, quality, discipline and standards that are attained by the institution. The nature and extent of these duties vary considerably. The traditional titles of headmaster and headmistress have been generally superseded by the inclusive title of head teacher. In some countries including the United States of America, 'principal' is the more familiar usage. He or she may be accountable to a governing body at the school, and to local and national officials, as well as to the parents of pupils attending the school. In many cases the managerial and pastoral duties involved in maintaining and developing the school may leave little or no scope for taking an active part in teaching activities. The workload of the head teacher may be increased further by the need to respond effectively to new requirements and policy initiatives at a national level, and these pressures have grown greatly in many parts of the world in recent years. Nevertheless, heads often prefer to teach at least one class or subject to retain an everyday involvement with pupils at the school. Most schools also have a deputy or assistant head, or more as required, who support the work of the head teacher.

See also: educational leadership and management; school-based management; school leadership

GARY McCULLOCH

HEALTH EDUCATION

In schools, the theme of health education is frequently taught in a cross-curricular way, rather than as a distinct, timetabled subject, for example in programmes of 'personal, social and health education', sometimes dubbed 'sex, drugs and rock and roll'.

Education and health are linked, with research studies pointing to the existence of a 'virtuous circle': individuals with higher levels of education take better care of their health, and those in good health produce the best outcomes in the education system. Programmes of health education are designed to enable learners to understand how their bodies function, to promote exercise, relaxation, a balanced diet and the avoidance of unhealthy habits. In the early part of the twentieth century it was common for students to learn more prescriptively about 'health and hygiene' and to be set textbook exercises relating to body circulation, nutrition, sleep and so forth. After Britain's disastrous Boer War (1899–1902) an inquiry attributed its

dismal military performances to the poor health and fitness of the troops. In the schools, medical and dental inspections and hot meals were introduced during the first decade of the twentieth century and there was new thinking about school design, emphasising the health benefits of well lit and ventilated buildings. Briefly, North American and European educators developed an 'open air' model of schooling, sometimes for sickly children suffering from tuberculosis, though in some places the model was applied more widely, falling out of favour only when drug treatments were acknowledged to be a more proven means of combating the illness.

Both in the past and today, many national school systems have prioritised child nutrition by making available milk and health snacks, as well as a lunchtime meal. In some countries – Finland, for example – this is provided free of charge. Elsewhere, there is sometimes dismay about the implications of privatising school catering contracts, the proliferation of 'junk food' and the selling off of school playing fields. To many professionals working in the field, the presence of school vending machines, stocked with crisps and chocolate bars undermine efforts to promote children's healthy eating and physical activity.

In the developing world, charities and international agencies such as the United Nations Children's Fund (UNICEF) have led health education programmes promoting fresh water, sanitation and disease reduction, with HIV/AIDS providing a particular focus for this work. In the West, songs about physical exercise, brushing teeth and washing are frequently taught to young children, both in the home and the nursery. Slightly older children sometimes experience talks and demonstrations in school by nurses or health education professionals, with the emphasis still upon an association between fitness and fun. The kind of health education directed at secondary-age children and post-compulsory students may be starker, focusing on obesity, sexually transmitted diseases, unplanned pregnancies and alcohol and drug abuse. Evidence suggests that the 'live for today' generation remains reluctant to heed 'nannying' advice, creating research agendas for those who work in the field about how best to promote health through education.

See also: curriculum; sex education; subjects; United Nations Children's Fund (UNICEF)

Further reading

Glanz, K., Lewis, F. M. and Rimer, B. K. (2002) *Health Behavior and Health Education: Theory, Research, and Practice*, 3rd edn, San Francisco CA: Jossey-Bass.

Weare, K. 'The contribution of education to health promotion'. In G. Macdonald (ed.) *The Disciplines of Health Promotion*, 2nd edn, London: Routledge.

DAVID CROOK

HERBART, JOHANN FRIEDRICH (1776–1841)

Herbart was a seminal German philosopher and educationalist. He studied under Fichte at Jena University from 1794 to 1797, where he imbibed elements of idealism alongside a 'practical' approach to scientific research. Herbart was appointed to the chair of philosophy at Königsburg in 1809, after authoring some major publications during the previous decade. Wilhelm III sanctioned the appointment, having recognised Herbart's potential for introducing Pestolozzian influences into national education and schooling. Herbart identified links between teaching as a scientific field and education, which was central to character formation, personal morality and social improvement. He was interested in mental capabilities, arguing that teacher training should focus more on *how* pupils learned, as well as on teaching methods. His major writings include *Aesthetic Revelation of the World as the Chief Work of Education* (1804) and *General Pedagogy Deduced from the Purpose of Education* (1806). Herbart established an experimental school and trained teachers in his methods and approach. Although a major

figure, his direct contemporary influence was less than others, such as von Humboldt, partly because much of his thinking was for advanced grammar schools, whereas the 1809 German reforms focused upon extending the reach of schooling much further. Nevertheless, Herbart's ideas and influence grew in the decades immediately following his death, with several teacher training institutions being established and organised around his principles. Educational associations and journals, along with reprints of his works, ensured and enhanced his impact.

See also: psychology of education; teacher education/training

STEVEN COWAN

HIDDEN CURRICULUM

As well as the formal curriculum expressed in the knowledge codified in the subjects and syllabus, it is common to refer to the 'hidden curriculum'. By this is meant the values and ideals that are tacitly and perhaps unconsciously conveyed to learners on an everyday basis. The term was first coined by Jackson (1968), but although Jackson was especially interested in the implications of the hidden curriculum in classroom life, it has implications for teaching and learning processes throughout the school and in other educational institutions. It is often invoked to help explain the way in which dominant ideas about social class, gender, ethnicity and other key cultural and political issues are passed on or reproduced through education. It also raises significant issues about why certain groups are less successful than others at school. In these ways it has lent itself to neo-Marxist theories about the reproduction of inequality and resistance to dominant groups and ideologies.

Lynch (1989) explores an empirical case in the processes involved in the hidden curriculum in Ireland, that is, how particular cultural practices are both disseminated and legitimated through the educational system. She demonstrates that schooling primes students to be competent in the scientific, technological and commercial spheres, and also to compete with others in the acquisition of high-level credentials. Prize-giving is a significant feature in this process according to Lynch: 'By awarding prizes for academic or extracurricular successes, the school both reinforces the importance of the particular activity involved, and encourages pupils to compete with each other even more strongly to gain the designated prize' (Lynch 1989: 74–75). In her study, prizes are awarded for achievement in approved activities in a wide range of types of school, tending to reinforce the competitive individualism of the formal school system, with girls' secondary schools being the most competitive. Another example is the mode of dress of pupils in school. This was not specified by any state regulation in this national context, and so schools had a high level of autonomy in this respect, but nearly 70 per cent of Irish second-level schools required pupils to wear a uniform, and of these 75 per cent required all pupils to wear it at all times.

In the case of Latin America, too, the hidden curriculum is a potent factor in demanding conformity to a particular set of ideals and norms, and in restricting the extent to which equality is achieved between different social groups. Stromquist's study of poverty and the education of girls in this context argues that while boys and girls have largely equal access to schooling, the hidden curriculum disadvantages girls by reproducing gender-based power relations. She complains that schooling as a fundamental site for the formation of gender ideologies tends to pass unquestioned, and thus that governments fail to seek to reform either the formal or the hidden curriculum, or to train teachers for non-sexist or anti-sexist practices (Stromquist 2007).

Nor is the hidden curriculum by any means confined to schools. In higher education also, its processes are pervasive although, as has been noted, not particularly hidden. Margolis and Romero, for example, suggest that graduate schools tend to reproduce 'academia itself with its ivory tower, valorization of theoretical knowledge, disciplinary structures, emphasis on discourse and method, and hierarchies of knowledge and rank'. Indeed, they contend, mentoring in this context is perhaps the most important single element of the hidden curriculum in higher education, being 'the process whereby people of power embedded in the system personally select and groom their successors – successors who will in their turn safeguard the noble house' (Margolis and Romero 2001: 81). In educational institutions in general, then, the nature and effects of the hidden curriculum is a key issue for investigation and discussion.

See also: classroom; culture; curriculum

Further reading

Jackson, P. (1968) *Life in Classrooms*, New York: Holt, Rinehart and Winston.
Lynch, K. (1989) *The Hidden Curriculum: Reproduction in Education, a Reappraisal*, London: Falmer Press.
Margolis, E. and Romero, M. (2001) '"In the image and likeness. . .": how mentoring functions in the hidden curriculum'. In E. Margolis (ed.) *The Hidden Curriculum in Higher Education*, London: Routledge.
Stromquist, N. (2007) 'What poverty does to girls' education: the intersection of class, gender and policy in Latin America'. In H. Lauder, P. Brown, J. Dillabough and A. H. Halsey (eds) *Education, Globalisation and Social Change*, Oxford: Oxford University Press.

GARY McCULLOCH

HIGH SCHOOL

High school is an alternative or more commonly used term for secondary education in some countries, that is, it denotes the schooling that takes place following elementary or primary school and before tertiary or higher education. In Australia, Canada and the United States, for example, high school is the usual terminology. It varies markedly in its length, in its age of entry and in its leaving age from one place to another. In some locations, such as the United States, it is compulsory until the final leaving age, while in many others the first years are compulsory and the later or senior years are optional or based on selection or specialisation. The relationship between the compulsory and optional periods also varies from place to place. In Israel high school is attended for a three-year period, with only the first year compulsory. This term is also often used in the titles of many individual institutions around the world. The high school is often divided into different sections or types, in particular the junior high school, the senior high school, and the vocational high school. The junior high school in the United States is usually attended for three years up to the age of 13 or 14, before transfer to the high school and senior high school.

See also: secondary school/education

GARY McCULLOCH

HIGH-STAKES TESTING

High-stakes testing serves various purposes in primary through secondary schools in industrialised nations. The purposes of high-stakes tests include promoting accountability among schools, teachers, and students; initiating change in curriculum and instruction; and improving student achievement. Outcomes from these tests may be used to determine student retention and grade-level promotion; inform decisions about student placement in primary, secondary, and higher education institutions; and determine the rank and status of a school.

Since the late 1980s, testing has been used to promote school accountability in order to increase educational quality and promote student outcomes in England and the United States. In England, the Education Reform Act of 1988 established a national curriculum and required subject-specific testing in government-supported schools because of concerns about the decline in education. At the ages of seven, eleven, and fourteen students are tested in English and mathematics and/or

science. The No Child Left Behind Act of 2001 has been the United States federal government's response to educational inequality among students and schools. This legislation requires that all public schools test students in reading and mathematics from grades three through eight. Schools are required to meet annual yearly progress targets for its students in aggregate and by racial, socio-economic, and special education status. It is anticipated that this testing will provide the motivation and common expectations to close the academic achievement gaps that exist among students by 2014. Since the United States lacks a national curriculum and assessment system, individual states determine both the annual tests and yearly performance targets. This fact makes it difficult to formulate school performance comparisons between states.

In most countries, including England and the United States, testing tends to be aligned with national or state curricula in order to provide teachers with clear instructional goals that are applicable to the majority of students. Common educational goals provide students and their parents with clear expectations about learning outcomes. There are concerns among opponents in the United States that high-stakes testing narrows the curriculum taught by focusing on tested content. Non-tested subject areas including social studies, foreign language, art and music are often excluded from instruction. However, in countries with centralised curricula and assessment systems, such as Japan and England, the test helps drive curriculum and instruction because it represents valued knowledge. Although high-stakes testing helps to improve content coverage, it does not necessarily remedy pedagogical problems that must be addressed in order to meet the learning needs of students that vary academically in the United States.

There are various consequences for poor high-stakes testing outcomes. In certain states in the USA students may be retained in a grade if they do not meet prescribed outcomes. Test outcomes can affect secondary school options and post-secondary career and educational opportunities because students may be denied a diploma in some states if they do not meet required performance standards. Performance in primary school examinations in Singapore determines students' academic ability-stream placement in secondary schools. This placement determines the level of secondary school examination that students prepare for and the type of post-secondary programme they can pursue. Similarly, in Japan, test performance determines entrance to both secondary schools and universities. Schools with chronic low performance may confront negative consequences as well. Low-performing schools in the USA may be required to develop and implement improvement plans and/or they may be assigned a school improvement team. In extreme cases, there are some states that allow for either a school takeover or school reconstitution where the entire staff is terminated and replaced with newly hired personnel, including administrators and teachers. Both the USA and England have provisions that allow students and their parents the choice of transferring from a chronically low-performing school to one that is relatively better. However, these options may be limited because schools may not accept students because of enrolment limits. Others may deny student enrolment out of the concern that those arriving from low-performing schools may depress future school-wide test performance and affect their rank and status.

See also: ability grouping; accountability; curriculum; streaming/tracking

Further reading

Gregory, K. and Clarke, M. (2003) 'High-stakes assessment in England and Singapore', *Theory Into Practice*, 42(1): 66–74.

Heubert, J. P. and Hauser, R. M. (1999) *High Stakes: Testing for Tracking, Promotion, and Graduation*, Washington DC: National Academy Press.

Levinson, C. Y. (2000) 'Student assessment in eight countries', *Educational Leadership*, 57(5): 58–61.

DONNA MARIE HARRIS

HIGHER EDUCATION

What is known as 'higher education' today has medieval roots. Some of the world's oldest surviving organisations are, indeed, European universities. Most of those entities were originally small, reclusive, religious-based organisations that taught theology, medicine, or law to relatively few students. But over the course of centuries, the basic form of the university was transformed from these idiosyncratic origins. In the nineteenth century, the German research university emerged as a model of grand reputation, while over the twentieth century the American comprehensive university grew in size and stature, and has since been imitated internationally. Today, universities and colleges in most nations are secular, rationalised and comprehensive institutions that are embedded within coordinated systems and are formally sequenced after primary and secondary levels.

Contemporary higher education is massively growing in two ways. First, enrolments have greatly expanded. Between the 1960s and 1980s, scholars such as Clark Kerr, Martin Trow, and Burton Clark ably described the transformation from 'elite' to 'mass' levels of enrolment in North America and Europe, and since then, others have documented worldwide growth (Schofer and Meyer 2005). Second, universities and colleges have also expanded laterally, assuming a multitude of diverse tasks, teaching an astounding range of subjects and investigating an even broader array of research topics. Today, community colleges, polytechnics, and universities are codifying an ever-expanding array of knowledge into formal programmes of research and instruction. In many nations, post-secondary systems are divided into two broad sectors: degree-granting and vocational sectors. Typically, graduates from the former sector enter broad academic programmes or professional training, while the latter obtain more technical skills for immediate use in the labour market.

Why is this transformation of higher education occurring? Various social science theories have been advanced to account for both forms of expansion. *Political* theories typically cite the tendency of state officials to expand enrolments in response to popular demand for avenues for upward social mobility. Likewise, *credentialists* see ever-tightening forms of labour market competition and dynamics of credential inflation as continually fuelling the demand for higher education. *Critical* theories, in contrast, view higher education as a tool of elite domination and as an engine of capitalist development. *Human capital* theories highlight states' and individuals' mutual interest in using formal knowledge to create wealth-enhancing skills and nurture the technical innovation that is seen to be vital in today's economy. Finally, *institutionalists* step outside these economic rationales, and instead conceptualise enrolment expansion and diversification as products of institutionalisation. They emphasise that education in all forms has become increasingly valorised in modern culture and connected to other social institutions. Institutionalists see these processes as buttressed by processes of isomorphism, wherein post-secondary organisations mirror the structures and strategies of their most reputable peers in an attempt to garner legitimacy.

The changing nature of higher education is creating several frontiers for contemporary research. Scholars are noting how enrolment growth is bringing new types of students into universities and colleges. In most countries, a reverse gender gap has emerged, with women typically enrolling in higher education at greater rates than men (OECD 2006). While males still comprise the majority of professors, graduate students, and enrolees in many scientific fields, the latter-day story of enrolment expansion is one of feminisation. Other researchers are investigating how norms of the life course are being re-imagined as a result of higher education expansion. Talk of the new 'k-16' norm and the necessity of 'lifelong learning' are attracting rising numbers of non-traditional students, including part-timers, second career students, older students with families, and commuters. As these students enter the system, more institutions are accommodating them through part-time hours, branch campuses, and online learning.

Expansion is also altering the organisational form and governance of higher education. Researchers are examining pressures for public higher education institutions to be both more entrepreneurial and more accountable to states. The former trend is strengthening relationships between research universities and for-profit industries, decried by some as 'academic capitalism' (Slaughter and Leslie 1997). The latter trend is giving rise to quality assurance programmes that are becoming international in scope. Other researchers are examining how similar pressures are intensifying patterns of competition and stratification in higher education. For instance, domestic and world rankings of universities – once an American exception – are becoming ubiquitous, and are fuelling inter-organisational competition for faculty, admissions, and research funds (Davies and Zarifa 2006). Finally, expansion is triggering the emergence of greater organisational variety in higher education, marked by new types of private and for-profit universities, international branch campuses, transnational enrolments, corporate universities, and online institutions. Overall, higher education has moved far from its origins as a scattering of cloistered institutions in medieval Europe into its present state – a highly differentiated and mass global industry that is increasingly interconnected with other societal institutions.

See also: academic/academic profession; credentials/credentialing; degree; graduate/graduation; lifelong learning; polytechnic; university; vocational education

Further reading

Clark, B. (1983) *The Higher Education System: Academic Organization in Cross-National Perspective*, Berkeley CA: University of California Press.

Davies, S. and Zarifa, D. (2006) 'The stratification of universities: comparing Canada and the United States'. Paper presented at the annual meetings of the American Educational Research Association, San Francisco.

Kerr, C. (2001) *The Uses of the University*, 5th edn, Cambridge MA: Harvard University Press.

OECD (2006) *Education Policy Analysis: Focus on Higher Education, 2005–2006*, Paris: OECD.

Schofer, E. and Meyer, J. W. (2005) 'The worldwide expansion of higher education in the twentieth century', *American Sociological Review*, 70(6): 898–920.

Slaughter, S. and Leslie, L. (1997) *Academic Capitalism: Politics, Policies and the Entrepreneurial University*, Baltimore MD: Johns Hopkins University Press.

Trow, M. A. (1984) 'The analysis of status'. In B. R. Clark (ed.) *Perpectives on Higher Education: Eight Disciplinary and Comparative Views*, Berkeley CA: University of California Press.

SCOTT DAVIES AND DAVID ZARIFA

HISTORY

History as a curriculum subject refers to the status, place and organisational structure accorded to the study of the past in formal educational settings. History commonly is mandated in education systems throughout the world. For example, history is a curriculum certainty throughout Europe, in China, Japan, North America, and among the states of the former Soviet Union. Moreover, in countries such as the USA and England history has existed as a school subject for more than 100 years. Despite history's widespread acceptance in the curriculum, four factors determine that history's place in the curriculum differs in international settings.

Firstly, history often experiences different forms of curriculum. For example, Japan and Greece have highly centralised systems in which governments determine historical content, resources, and assessment. By contrast, in Sweden and Germany, curriculum decisions are made at regional and local levels. Second, differences occur in how history is organised within the school structure. For example, in the United States history exists under the social studies umbrella, which includes geography and political science; other nations use the humanities to unite related subject areas including citizenship and religious education. As such, levels of subject integration vary considerably. In secondary schools in England, for example, history remains a separate subject, whereas in other countries it is subsumed into social studies and loses individual identity.

The third factor influencing history's place in the curriculum relates to the internal organisation of the subject. Given that it is impossible for any curriculum to cover the vast sweep of human history, the selection and arrangement of content must be addressed. The most common format employed is to teach history chronologically. Typically courses begin with the Stone Age or ancient civilisations and progress through to the modern era. Alternative curriculum structures include attention to enduring themes such as war and peace, technology and transport, a 'patch' approach which focuses on particular historical periods in sequence, such as Renaissance, Industrial Revolution, or indepth studies. Curriculum designers also have to consider the balance between local, national and international history.

The fourth factor influencing history in the curriculum centres on enduring and controversial debates over the subject's nature and purpose (Aldrich 1991). Differences of opinion have resulted in fierce ideological battles in many nations (for example England, Japan and the USA) (Phillips 2000; Nash *et al.* 2001). On the one hand, some view history as valuable in inculcating in the young a sense of national pride, in forging national unity, and in socialising future citizens. On the other hand, advocates of what is commonly termed 'new history' view the subject as interpretive and complex with few absolute truths. Accordingly, they argue, students should appreciate how history is constructed and focus on the intelligent analysis and critical application of historical evidence, on historical research, and on narrative construction.

In most nations across the globe the former view of history dominates. Routinely, classroom history is based on traditional methods of textbook recitation and teacher lecture in which students largely remain passive receivers of historical facts to be memorised and regurgitated. However, since the early 1970s advocates of *new history* have challenged traditional practice in many nations across the world. Arguably the most influential curriculum innovation was the Schools Council History Project (SCHP) that began in England in 1972 (Shemilt 1980).

Fundamentally, new history encouraged students to appreciate history not as a body of content but as a form of knowledge. New history's vigorous challenge to accepted practice also offered schools an alternative curriculum structure. Rather than pursue a chronological sweep of national history, new history advocates proposed dividing curriculum time into units of study that focused on themes or structures. Accordingly, through the SCHP students were introduced to in-depth studies, local research and fieldwork and, through an exploration of 'medicine through time', a study in development. In many respects the current national curriculum history for England and Wales is an unlikely compromise between traditional and new approaches. An intriguing aspect of history's future development in international settings will be the extent to which nations adhere to these two alternative traditions.

To some extent history's place in the school curriculum faces significant challenges. Moves to subject integration, increased curriculum emphasis on literacy and numeracy and on technological and scientific knowledge, threaten the amount of curriculum time devoted to history as a discrete subject. Nevertheless because history largely remains a political construct seen by governments as an instrument to forge national identities, its continued curriculum presence appears assured.

See also: citizenship/civics; core curriculum/ national curriculum; curriculum; social studies; subjects

Further reading

Aldrich, R. (ed.) (1991) *History in the National Curriculum*, London: Kogan Page.

Nash, G., Crabtree, C. and Dunn, R. (2001) *History on Trial: Culture Wars and the Teaching of the Past*, New York: Vintage Books.

Phillips, R. (2000) *History Teaching, Nationhood, and the State: A Study in Educational Politics*, London: Cassell.

Shemilt, D. (1980) *History 13–16 Evaluation Study*, Edinburgh: Holmes McDougall.

STUART FOSTER

HISTORY OF EDUCATION

History of education is the study of the educational provision, policies, ideas, institutions, and experiences of past times. It investigates education over time, whether in the recent or the more distant past, to establish patterns of explanation for the kinds of education that have developed, and the relationship between education and the broader society. In particular, it considers the nature of historical continuities, the character and extent of change, the types of context within which education has developed, and the kinds of contestation over education that have arisen between different ideals and groups in society. It seeks also to understand the origins of current institutions and of contemporary problems and issues in education.

The nature of the relationship between education and society has engendered a number of historical debates. In the first half of the twentieth century a liberal model of modern systems of schooling developed that emphasised the value of such systems for the gradual progress of society and for improved economic productivity and individual prosperity. Over the past half century, revisionist approaches have explored different kinds of educational provision and experience, while radical revisionists, influenced by Marxism, have emphasised issues of social class conflict and control involved in modern schooling. Recent contributions have begun to examine the position of marginalised groups in education, international, comparative and global approaches, the historical characteristics of the curriculum, the nature of teachers and teaching, and other issues. These developments have encouraged the application of a range of methods and theoretical perspectives in historical study (McCulloch and Richardson 2000).

A major focus of the history of education has concerned the origins, nature and effects of the systems of compulsory mass schooling organised by national states that developed around the world during the nineteenth century. These became established in many different societies, urban and rural, well established and newly founded, within a relatively short time. They shared many characteristics in common, including recognisable similarities in their timetables, architecture, teaching practices and curriculum (see, for example, Miller 1989). They became consolidated and expanded during the twentieth century, but by the 1970s began to experience increasing difficulties, leading to attempts to reform and restructure them. More broadly, the history of education has embraced informal educational practices and processes, including those of the family and Church, not only for the young but also throughout life and society (see also McCulloch 2005 for examples of historical study in relation to schooling and to more informal aspects of education).

In the early years of the twenty-first century, there are unresolved questions around the future of the field and how it should relate to contemporary educational issues. Once regarded as one of the key foundation disciplines in educational studies, it has tended to be marginalised in recent developments in educational research. Its former place in the teacher training curriculum has been contested in many countries. The education policies of the past thirty years have often lacked the historical awareness evident in earlier reforms, even to the extent that they may ignore the implications of relatively recent initiatives or problems. The ways in which historians of education engage with other educators at the same time that they try to build a common agenda with historians and social scientists in other fields, will be central to the survival and further development of the field at a time of turbulence and rapid change.

A number of societies specialising in the history of education have developed in many countries since the 1960s. In several cases these have also generated academic journals devoted to research in this field, such as *History of Education* (UK), *History of Education Quarterly* (USA), *Histoire de l'Education* (France) and *History of Education Review* (Australia and New Zealand). *Paedagogica Historica* is produced by the International Standing Conference on the History of Education (www.inrp.fr/she/ische). An example of a leading national society, with international links, is the History of Education Society (UK), founded in 1967, with regular conferences and support for teaching and research in the field (www.historyofeducation. org.uk).

See also: curriculum; education/educational studies; education policy; educational research

Further reading

McCulloch, G. (ed.) (2005) *The RoutledgeFalmer Reader in the History of Education*, London: RoutledgeFalmer.
McCulloch, G. and Richardson, W. (2000) *Historical Research In Educational Settings*, Buckingham: Open University Press.
Miller, P. (1989) 'Historiography of compulsory schooling: what is the problem?', *History of Education*, 18(2): 123–44.

GARY McCULLOCH

HOME ECONOMICS/DOMESTIC SCIENCE

The term 'domestic science' is attributed to the American author Christine Frederick (1883–1970), who published widely in women's magazines and popular books on the topic of 'domestic efficiency' during the first part of the twentieth century. Women were advised to apply scientific principles to the household economy and the concept of 'domestic science' was born. Some knowledge of budgeting, shopping, cleaning, cooking, design and laundry will provide a head start for any young person, male or female, preparing to lead a more independent life. A subject covering these topics surely merits an assured place on the school curriculum. The 'problem' for domestic science and home economics (which, by the 1960s was seen as a preferred term) has historically been to demonstrate its usefulness to all, and to challenge the stereotypical and patronising view that this is a 'girls' subject'. As a term, 'home economics' also now seems to be in decline, with 'technology' – food technology, in particular – and art and design subsuming some of the themes associated with the subject. A reaction has set in against modern dependencies upon 'fast', pre-packaged or microwave food and many people are looking to lead cleaner, greener, less wasteful and more ethical lifestyles. Current interests, fuelled by television programmes, have encouraged interest in mending, recycling, organic gardening, 'proper' cooking and managing money better. These objectives, which are sometimes promoted in schools, are in the best traditions of home economics/ domestic science.

See also: curriculum; health education; subjects

DAVID CROOK

HOME SCHOOLING

Home schooling can be defined as the education of school-aged children under their parents' supervision, in and around the home, and in place of full-time school attendance. This broad definition only mentions school-aged children, then specifies no more than a shift in the monitoring of the education of those children from the state onto parents,

and from schools to homes. This type of education might occur for a short period of time or for all of childhood. These are, indeed, the only clear parameters bordering a practice that is otherwise very diverse in terms of teaching and learning settings, physical settings, and social settings.

The teaching and learning settings home schooled children experience differ tremendously depending on the family's educational preferences. The degrees of structure imposed on children for example, range widely. At one end of the spectrum, children can be enrolled in distance learning programmes executed on a strict daily schedule; at the other end of the spectrum is a "freer" version of education called 'child-led learning' or 'unschooling', where the only framework for learning is a child's natural curiosity and adaptation to their environment, with parental intervention in the form of facilitation only. In between these extremes lies a wide array of possibilities and hybrid settings, which might include learning from regular textbooks, educational games, the internet and instructional software, dialogue and discussion, autodidactic learning, private tutoring, project-based learning, excursions and hands-on experimentation.

Contrary to what the term suggests, home schooling does not always try to reproduce the school model; neither is it generally restricted to the home. Therefore, the physical settings where the learning takes place vary. There might be a classroom in the home, or not. The weekly schedule might include visits to the town library, cultural centres and parks, as well as the use of community sport facilities.

As for the social setting, the home and family are considered the natural locus for education, since one of the grounding principles of this practice is that the building of sustained family relationships is primordial for a child's development. The dynamic of home schooling has been described as a 'community of learning practice' by Barratt-Peacock (2003), where socialisation of the children occurs 'through the ongoing family conversation, experiences gained from domestic occupation and accompanied excursions into the field of authentic adult practice', like specialised clubs and societies, local businesses and community volunteering. In addition, most parents tend to reach out to other home schooling families in their areas in order to introduce children to their peers and meet like-minded 'colleagues' themselves, thus forming local 'support groups'. These groups might organise activities such as cultural outings, outdoor excursions, group learning of particular topics and larger events like concerts or science fairs. Parents meet regularly to compare methods and discuss pedagogical achievements and problems. State or provincial associations can also offer legal advice, political representation, internet discussion forums, conferences and book fairs.

Home schooling is present on all continents and its diffusion is increasingly facilitated by modern communications technologies. Its value is debated in both the academic literature and popular press. The debate is largely centred on political, social and moral issues such as the formation of citizens, parental and children's rights, the value of schooling, the evolution of educational institutions, the transmission of values and the moral development of the child. While research on this practice is limited, available evidence to date suggests that home schooled children perform as well or better than their schooled peers in terms of academic and social outcomes.

Legislation and policies relating to home schooling vary according to country. In the United States and Canada, home schooling has developed significantly since the 1960s and is now considered a modern educational and social movement. Home schooling is legal, and many states sponsor and collaborate with home schoolers through offers like access to distance learning resources, part-time school attendance and specialised home schooling centres. In Europe and Oceania, home schooling practices and their legality are in flux (Petrie 2001). Some countries such as Germany have been known to prosecute home schoolers, although they sometimes permit individual cases. Some, like France, exercise strict control over the curriculum. Others, like the United Kingdom, accommodate home schoolers with only light supervision, sometimes relying on the expertise of specialists employed solely for the monitoring of home schooling.

See also: distance education/learning; independent/private school/education; individualised instruction/personalised learning; informal/nonformal learning; parental choice

Further reading

Barratt-Peacock, J. (2003) 'Australian home education: a model', *Evaluation and Research in Education*, 17 (2, 3): 101–11.

Petrie, A. (2001) 'Home education in Europe and the implementation of changes to the law', *International Review of Education*, 47(5): 477–500.

Stevens, M. L. (2001) *Kingdom of Children: Culture and Controversy in the Homeschooling Movement*, Princeton NJ: Princeton University Press.

CHRISTINE BRABANT

HOMEWORK

Homework can be defined as tasks assigned to students by school teachers that are intended to be carried out during out-of-school hours, although homework might also be done during in-school study periods (Cooper *et al.* 2006). This definition explicitly excludes (a) in-school or out-of-school guided study such as test preparation classes or tutoring; (b) home study courses delivered through the mail, television, on audio or video cassette, or over the internet; and (c) extracurricular activities such as sports teams and clubs. Homework practices vary across cultures. Studies indicate that the amount of time students spend on homework varies from country to country, as does the amount of time students spend in school (Baker and Letendre 2005).

Assignments set as homework can be classified according to their amount, skill area, level of difficulty, purpose, choice for the student, completion deadline, degree of individualisation and social context. The amount of homework students do can be expressed as the total amount of time spent on assignments per night or per week but is best thought of in terms of, first, the frequency with which homework is assigned and, second, the duration of each assignment. Evidence suggests that more frequent but shorter assignments are more effective than fewer but longer ones.

Homework can call for the use of different skill areas. Students may be asked to read, to submit written products, or to perform practice exercises to enhance memory or retention of material. The difficulty level of homework assignments can vary, while their purposes can be divided into instructional and non-instructional objectives. Practice assignments are meant to reinforce the learning of material already presented in class and to help the student master specific skills. Preparation assignments introduce material to be presented in future lessons. Evidence suggests that assignments that incorporate practice and/or preparation material are most effective. Extension homework involves the transfer of previously learned skills to new situations. Integrative homework requires the student to apply many separately learned skills and concepts to produce a single product. There are other purposes of homework beyond enhancing classroom instruction. Homework can be used to (a) inform parents about what is going on in school; (b) facilitate communication between parent and child; (c) fulfil directives from school administrators; and (d) punish students. Homework assignments rarely reflect a single purpose. Instead, most assignments have elements of several different purposes.

Individualised assignments occur when teachers tailor the set work to meet the needs of each student or when different assignments are presented to groups of students smaller than the class as a whole. Assignments that take into consideration the learning styles of students may be most effective. The degree of choice afforded a student refers to whether the homework assignment is compulsory or voluntary. Within compulsory homework assignments, students can be given different degrees of discretion concerning which or how many parts of the assignment to complete. Providing choice among assignments may produce the most positive effects on learning. Homework completion deadlines also can vary. Some assignments are short-term and meant to be completed for the next class meeting. Other assignments are long-term, with students given extended periods of time to complete the task. Finally, homework assignments can vary according to the social context in which they are carried out. Some assignments are meant to be completed by the student alone. Assisted homework explicitly calls for the involvement of another person, typically a parent or other adult. Still other assignments involve groups of students working cooperatively to produce a single product.

The value of homework has been vigorously debated in both the educational literature and popular press. Proponents of homework suggest that it can (a) hasten and strengthen learning; and (b) teach positive character traits, such as self-discipline and time management. Opponents of homework suggest that it can extinguish the desire for learning, deny children access to leisure time, and lead to parental interference in the learning process.

See also: coursework; pupil; student

Further reading

Baker, D. P. and Letendre, G. K. (2005) *National Differences, Global Similarities: World Culture and The Future Of Schooling*, Stanford CA: Stanford University Press.

Cooper, H., Robinson, J. C. and Patall, E. A. (2006) 'Does homework improve academic achievement?: a synthesis of research, 1987–2003', *Review of Educational Research*, 76: 1–62.

Cooper, Harris (2007) *The Battle over Homework: Common Ground for Administrators, Teachers, and Parents*, 3rd edn, Thousand Oaks CA: Corwin.

HARRIS COOPER

HYPERACTIVITY

Hyperactivity refers to disruptive behavioural patterns commonly associated with attention deficit hyperactive disorder (ADHD), a condition characterised by excessive levels of motor activity, impulsivity and/or inattentiveness diagnosed more often in males than in females. Based on differences in symptomatic manifestation, the American Psychiatric Association has identified a number of subtypes of ADHD, including a predominantly inattentive subtype, a predominantly hyperactive-impulsive subtype and a combined subtype. Hyperactivity may be a significant feature of the predominantly inattentive subtype, while inattention may be a significant feature of the predominantly hyperactive-impulsive subtype. The majority of children diagnosed with ADHD have the combined subtype, manifesting at least six symptoms of inattention and at least six symptoms of hyperactivity-impulsivity.

Diagnostic criteria for hyperactivity include an inability to remain seated, difficulty working quietly and excessive chatter. Diagnostic criteria for impulsivity include an inability to take turns and a tendency to interrupt classroom discussions or activities. Diagnostic criteria for inattentiveness include an inability to focus or sustain effort and forgetfulness or absent-mindedness. Some scholars have argued that ADHD does not exist, while others have claimed it is overly inclusive. It has also been posited that response inhibition may be the primary cause of distinct hyperactive-impulsive and inattentive conditions. According to this theory, poor impulse control may result from some dysfunction of the neurotransmitters within a child's central nervous system. Considerations of appropriateness, which normally control behaviours considered hyperactive (blurting or fidgeting, for example) may be precluded to some extent by this underlying neurological impairment.

See also: behaviourism; classroom management; discipline; emotional and behavioural difficulties/disorders (EBD); learning disabilities/difficulties; special education/special educational needs/special needs

JASON BLOKHUIS

I

ILLICH, IVAN (1926–2002)

Illich, the social critic, was born in Vienna. His family was forced to leave Austria in 1941 because of his mother's Jewish ancestry. From 1943–46 he studied for the priesthood in Rome. His doctorate from Salzburg, in 1951, specialised in the nature of historical knowledge. Illich became a priest in a mixed Irish-Puerto Rican district of New York from 1953–56, where he learned Spanish and became an advocate for Puerto Rican culture. He was Rector of the Catholic University of Ponce in Puerto Rico from 1956–60, but was forced to leave because of his opposition to the bishop's decree against birth control. He then moved on to establish the Centre for Inter-Cultural Formation, sending Catholic missionaries to Latin America. After a series of disputes with the Church, he left the priesthood in 1969.

In *Deschooling Society* (1973) he argued that the institutional structures of schools, and the form of education they offered, reinforced models of exploitation that were symptomatic of industrialised capitalism. Schooling, he argued, achieved the reverse of what its stated aims were and closed children's minds from social reality. For Illich, learning had become commodified into a thing to enable it to be measured and controlled, rather than being a liberating and self-determining process which enabled children to grow as autonomous and creative people engaging in free social exchange. Illich was a prolific author until his death, becoming explicitly concerned once again with education and forms of literacy in his *The Alphabetization of the Popular Mind* (1988) and *Vineyard of the Mind* (1993).

See also: deschooling; Latin America; school
STEVEN COWAN

INCLUSIVE EDUCATION

Inclusive education is a term that has emerged since the early 1990s and has become associated with a global movement in support of widening access to education. In general, inclusive education refers to the widening of participation in mainstream education, often with particular reference to disabled children and young people and those identified as having special educational needs. More broadly, inclusive education is the term used to refer to the right of all to participate in education on a basis of equality, regardless of differences of status, gender, ethnicity or impairment. While it has become part of current international discourse, inclusive education is interpreted in diverse ways in response to particular cultures, policies, structures, practices and available resources in different settings. The origins of the term are associated with the Salamanca Statement, which came out of the United Nations Educational, Scientific and Cultural Organization's (UNESCO) World Conference on Special Needs Education: Access and Quality, held in Spain in 1994, which built on the United Nations Convention on the Rights of the Child (1989). The Statement declared the fundamental right of all children to education and the importance of recognising diversity and that every child has 'unique characteristics, interests and learning needs' which education systems need to take into account. The Salamanca Statement asserted the importance of mainstream schools adopting an 'inclusive orientation' as the 'most effective way of combating discriminatory attitudes, creating welcoming communities, building an inclusive society and achieving education for all'. The statement, which was adopted by ninety-four governments and twenty non-governmental organisations, called for the adoption of the principle of inclusive education as law, and the enrolling of all children in mainstream schools 'unless there are compelling reasons for doing otherwise'.

Although the term inclusion was not used widely before the 1990s, the principles of inclusive education were already emerging internationally. UNESCO's World Declaration on 'Education for All', adopted in Jomtien, 1990, called for 'a learning environment in which everyone would have the chance to acquire the basic elements which serve as a foundation for further learning and enable full participation in society'. The Education for All programme is also informed by the Salamanca Statement (1994) and the Dakar Framework for Action (2000). A number of countries had already introduced legislation in support of widening participation of disabled children in mainstream education, such as Laws n.118 (1971) and n.517 (1977) in Italy, the Education of All Handicapped Children Act (1975) (reauthorised as the Individuals with Disabilities Act in 1997) in the United States, and the 1981 Education Act in the United Kingdom.

Inclusive education is based on the right of all to attend their local school or college on an equal basis. It involves establishing unconditional access for all people and the valuing of difference and identity (Corbett

and Slee 2000). The concept of inclusive education should be understood as a terrain in which competing and sometimes contradictory values, policies and processes are involved. Legislation and policy statements concerning barriers to participation, which may, or may not, adopt the term of 'inclusive education', frequently focus on disabled students, rather than on *all* learners. The British Special Educational Needs and Disability Act (2001) is designed to remove physical, curricular and pedagogical barriers to participation for disabled students in schools, colleges and universities. While such legislation contributes to the development of inclusive education, it refers specifically to disability and learning difficulty. In contrast, the Irish Education Act (1998) sought to enact legislation to ensure that the education system is accountable to all for the education provided, and 'respects the diversity of values, beliefs, languages and traditions in Irish society and is conducted in a spirit of partnership ... '. Similarly, The Irish Equal Status Act (2000) treats different forms of injustice and exclusion as part of one struggle to overcome inequality in society and in education, prohibiting discrimination on nine grounds, including gender, marital status, family status, sexual orientation, religion, age, disability, race, and membership of the traveller community.

In addition to UNESCO, another organisation that supports the development of inclusive education and takes into account contextual variations is the Centre for Studies in Inclusive Education.

See also: Education for All (EFA); equality of opportunity; learning disabilities/difficulties; special education/special educational needs/special needs; United Nations Educational, Scientific and Cultural Organization (UNESCO)

Further reading

Allan, J. (2003) *Inclusion, Participation and Democracy: What is the Purpose?*, Dordrecht, the Netherlands: Kluwer Academic.

Booth, T. and Ainscow, M. (2002) *The Index for Inclusion*, 2nd edn, Bristol: Centre for Studies on Inclusive Education.

Corbett, J. and Slee, R. (2000) 'An international conversation in inclusive education'. In F. Armstrong, D. Armstrong and L. Barton (eds) *Inclusive Education: Policy, Contexts and Comparative Perspectives*, London: David Fulton.

FELICITY ARMSTRONG

INDEPENDENT/PRIVATE SCHOOL/ EDUCATION

At an international level, private schools – which, confusingly, include British 'public schools', whose high fees determine that they are not accessible to the general public – are often defined by what they are not. Characteristically, the schools do not have to conform to government mandates and they do not have to teach a state-determined curriculum. They are neither obliged to appeal to a wide audience, nor do they have to accept all students who apply. At a fundamental level, private schools do not have to serve the interests of the state; instead, they exist to serve the religious orientation or values of families. Estelle James refers to these motivations as 'differentiated demands' (James 1989).

The term *private school* encompasses three kinds of schools: religious-affiliated schools (though in some countries these are also to be found in the state sector), for-profit or proprietary schools, and independent schools. Despite their differences, these schools share common threads. They are usually self-governed, often by a board or religious order. With the exception of countries that provide government funding or government subsidies, private schools are supported largely by tuition that is supplemented by private donations and/or institutional affiliations such as a church or foundation. Because they are selected on the basis of family choice, private schools respond in a market-like fashion most acutely to their constituent's needs (Kane 1992).

Although private schools differ in many ways, their role of fulfilling the peculiar educational needs of various sub-groups has been consistent. Before most developed nations enacted compulsory schooling laws in the late nineteenth- and early twentieth century, schooling outside of the home was predominantly private in that it was primarily church-sponsored and access was often restricted by gender or social class, and it was fee-based. However, since this was generally the only formal schooling option, it was often referred to as 'public' school. Churches and charities played (and still do) an important role in providing free or low-cost schooling to socially disadvantaged students. Even with the advent of an active state role in providing compulsory education, families still seek private education to fulfil their educational needs. When preferences for education are more diverse than government provides, private schools emerge to fill these unmet needs.

The prevalence of private education varies widely around the world, and reflects family values as well as the political, economic and social conditions of nations. In the Republic of Ireland, for example, where nearly the entire population is Catholic, more than 90 per cent of primary and secondary pupils are enrolled in 'private' schools. Irish private schools are run by the Catholic Church but funded by the government. In strongly socialist-oriented Sweden, on the other hand, where student achievement in the state schools ranks highly in international tests, only about 1 per cent of students attend private schools. In the United States, an economically and religiously diverse nation, about 10 per cent of all students attend private schools, mostly religiously affiliated, and only 1 per cent of all students attend secular schools. In China, since the advent of free enterprise and rapid economic development in the early 1980s, there has been a massive increase in the number of private for-profit or proprietary schools, estimated at about 60,000 primary and secondary schools serving 1.5 million students (Kwong 1997). These nations provide examples of how the evolution of private schools is best described as 'contextual'.

The most prevalent form of private schooling today is religiously affiliated. Religious schools generally owe their origins to beleaguered minorities who found state-run schools inhospitable to their religious beliefs. For example, the growth of Catholic schools in the United States was fuelled by Irish Catholic immigrants who were estranged in the government or 'common' schools of the early twentieth century (Ravitch 1974: 9–17). Predominantly Protestant clergy taught in these schools, using the King James version of the Bible and, not surprisingly, the curriculum was a Protestant *paideia* (Stewart *et al.* 2003). In the Netherlands, full state support for religious private schools emerged because Dutch society was comprised 'of minorities that were already sharply segmented along religious lines' (Walford 2001).

For-profit private schools are increasing today in China and other rapidly developing countries. Governments cannot keep pace with the educational needs of their fast-developing economies, which fuels an 'excess demand' for education (James 1989). This rapid privatisation is unique in China, where the school system was entirely government controlled by the Communist Party until reforms were enacted in 1978 (Tsang 2003). Given the long history of state control in China, it is likely that the government will begin to exert more control over these proprietary schools as economic expansion slows to a manageable pace. On the whole, proprietary schools are a relatively new phenomenon of the developing world, and it remains to be seen whether governments will exercise more control to limit their growth.

Independent private schools comprise the smallest segment of private schools, but they are perhaps the most pedagogically diverse. Within their ranks are the elite boarding schools such as Phillips Academy in Andover, Massachusetts, and independent day schools. In the United States boarding schools grew out of the academy movement and were shaped by the European model of education for the upper classes. Emphasising physical, intellectual and moral education, they included both classical and modern curriculum as well as physical exercise and play. Independent day schools have their antecedents in proprietary, town and church schools and the country day schools that were designed to provide an education comparable to that offered in the best Eastern boarding schools.

The prestigious elite independent schools in England, such as Rugby School in Warwickshire, grew out of church-run charity schools for the poor in the seventeenth century. Over time these charitable origins transformed dramatically. The minimal charitable support was supplemented by fees charged to lodge, clothe and otherwise maintain the students, to the private profit of the trustees or headmaster. After a time, such fees eclipsed the original charitable income, and the raising of endowments became a minor, and later a major, source of the overall revenue to subsidise the high costs of running these boarding schools.

Beginning in the seventeenth century, a variety of quasi-private schools existed in the United States. These schools had private governance and ownership but most depended on public funds for their survival. Some were maintained by churches as direct adjuncts of their religious programmes, others were run as private ventures by individuals or groups of teachers. Still others known as academies were founded by self-perpetuating boards of trustees to offer instruction beyond rudimentary literacy and computation, providing models for secondary education in this country. In addition to receiving public funds, most schools were also public in that they were open to all children who had the desire and means to attend (Cremin 1957: 23–25; Sizer 1964: 1–48).

Today, independent boarding and day schools reflect the wide range of diversity of origins and ownership: some traditional, some progressive, some single sex, some coeducational, some highly academic and selective, others second-chance schools for students who have failed elsewhere, some with impressive financial endowments and others with recourse only to tuition, and some fully reliant on philanthropy to cover the cost of educating children from low-income families.

The defining characteristic of an independent school is its 'self-selecting and thus self-perpetuating board of trustees [which] bears ultimate responsibility for an independent school's philosophy, resources, and program' (Kane 1992: 7). In addition, most independent schools are financially self-supporting, determine their own curriculum and select faculty and students whom they feel will best fit with the school's mission. To protect their freedom from government interference, independent schools tend to avoid accepting public monies (Kane 1992: 8–12). Small schools, intimate class size, and a personalised environment characterise most independent schools.

In countries having strong independent/private education sectors, the most costly and well known schools have membership of prestigious organisations, such as the National Association of Independent Schools (USA), the Headmasters' and Headmistresses Conference, and the Girls' School Association (both UK). Elite independent schools typically include in their mission the development of mind, body and character. They emphasise academic rigour and character development, and many have a strong athletic, sports or arts component. Independent schools enjoy an influence disproportionate to their actual numbers, sometimes due to the quality of the academic programme, extended teaching hours, superior student/teacher ratios, successful higher education progression rates and the substantial social, economic, and political capital of their alumni.

Today, independent schools around the world face substantial challenges. Governments are increasingly viewing education as central to economic competitiveness and are prioritising quality improvement in state schools. Successful reform efforts mean that families may be more likely to choose a free state school over an expensive day or boarding school, though in the UK it is interesting that after ten years of Labour government reforms focused on improving the quality of state schooling, parental applications to the independent school sector are at a record high.

Even if government schools improve, private schools are likely to continue to attract families committed to distinct values or religious beliefs, or who feel that bureaucratic government schools are not sufficiently responsive to their needs.

See also: boarding school/education; Catholic school/education; endowment; privatisation; public school; religious school

Further reading

Cremin, L. A. (ed.) (1957) *The Republic and the School: Horace Mann on the Education of Free Men*, New York: Teachers College Press.
James, E. (1989) *Comparing Public and Private Schools*, Philadelphia PA: Falmer Press.
Kane, P. (ed.) (1992) *Independent Schools, Independent Thinkers*, San Francisco CA: Jossey-Bass.
Kwong, J. (1997) 'The reemergence of private schools in socialist China', *Comparative Education Review*, 41(3): 244–59.
Ravitch, D. (1974) *The Great School War, New York City, 1805–1973: A History of the Public Schools as Battlefields of Social Change*, New York: Basic Books.
Sizer, T. R. (ed.) (1964) *The Age of the Academies*, New York: Teachers College, Columbia University.
Stewart, D., Kane, P. and Scruggs, L. (2003) 'Education and training'. In L. Solomon (ed.) *The State of America's Nonprofit Sector*, Baltimore MD: Johns Hopkins University Press and Aspen Institute.
Tsang, M. C. (2003) 'School choice in the People's Republic of China'. In D. Plank and G. Sykes (eds) *Choosing Choice*, New York: Teachers College Press.
Walford, G. (2001) 'Privatization in industrialized countries'. In H. Levin (ed.) *Privatizing Education*, Boulder CO: Westview Press.

PEARL ROCK KANE

INDIA

'Education', observes F. W. Thomas, 'is no exotic in India. There is no country where the love of learning has so early an origin or has exercised so lasting and powerful influence' (1891: 1). The early origin of education in India could be traced back to the centuries before the beginning of the Christian era to the Vedic scriptures of the four *Vedas* (Riga, Yajur, Sama and Atharva). Each Veda comprised four components, known as *Samhitas*, *Brahmanas*, *Aranyakas* and *Upanishads*. The scriptures were composed and transmitted orally by the *brahmanas* – the priestly class of the Aryan invaders – who gave shape to the history and culture of the sub-continent.

The recipients of this learning were mostly the children of the *brahmanas* who gathered at the residences of their *gurus* or teachers, and were provided free board and lodging in lieu of service to the latter. The students or *shisyas* observed *brahmacharya* or celibacy during the period of their studies, often lasting more than a decade, and set up their own schools when they returned home, thereby facilitating the transfer of knowledge to the prosperity through *guru-shisya parampara*, or succession of teachers through students.

While the *brahmanas* took care of the spiritual needs of the people, including acquisition of knowledge to liberate oneself from the *samsara* or transmigration, the cycle of birth and death, the other three classes – the *kshatriyas* (warriors), the *vaisyas* (traders) and the *sudras* (slaves), usually the people of the Indus Valley Civilisation vanquished by the Aryans – looked after their basic, needs and requirements. As with the study of the Vedas, the student had to live with his guru to learn the secrets of his work, assimilate his spirit and method, not revealed in any final manner at all.

The shaping of the Aryan schools of learning and of its various disciplines was conterminous with the shaping of the Aryan political organisation, from tribal to monarchical, between 1500 BCE and 600 BCE. These were the years that saw the composition of Indian religious scriptures, as well as the coming into existence of a variety of ascetic movements, the most of important of

which was Buddhism, which offered a serious challenge through its *viharas* or monasteries to Brahmanism, in achieving *nirvana* or salvation. The Brahmanism rejuvenated itself through the works of *sutrakaras* or compilers like Panini and Patanjali, Manu and Yajnavalkya, Kapila and Gautama, Kanada and Kautilya to meet the challenge of Buddhism, but in the process they canonised learning which adversely affected the growth and development of original and creative ideas in future. And so the succeeding centuries after the beginning of the Christian era were characterised more by a desire to preserve and explain than by any serious attempt to broaden and widen the horizon of past learning.

When Islam came to India and established its own rule in the twelfth century, the Muslim rulers imported their own system of education, consisting of maktabs, madrasahs, mosques and khanqahs, which revolved upon the patronage provided by the Muslim rulers from Qutab-ud-din-Aibak onwards, as well as on the Muslim nobles and officials, both at the centre and in the provinces. While Islamic education – through maktabs with Arabic medium, to teach Quran and madrasahs with Persian medium to teach Persian literature, culture and jurisprudence – spread to the remote parts of their extensive dominion, vedic learning survived in Muslim India through Guru-Shisya Parampara, thriving in the Hindu kingdoms in the north and in those across the Vindhyas. While in many respects Islamic education emphasised continuities with the past, it also created new conditions for the further development of vernaculars and *patshalas* (village schools), as well as for the birth of a new language, Urdu, which was soon to become the lingua franca of the Muslim community in India.

By the time the British came to India as traders of the East India Company and settled down in Calcutta (Kolkata) in the late seventeenth century, only the Islamic and the vedic education were in existence, while the Buddhist education disappeared following the demolition of the viharas by the Muslim rulers. In the beginning, the British, though interested in the existing higher education, were reluctant to take a part in the education of the people of the country. However, events at home, including a fresh demand for raw materials for a booming industrial revolution and pressures from the utilitarians for a modern education in India, as well as the transformation of the British from traders to rulers in India, forced their hands. In 1813 the Charter Act of India provided one lakh rupee (then worth £10,000) annually for the education of the people and, after a bitter Anglo-Oriental controversy, English was introduced as the official language, replacing Persian in 1835. And in 1854 an education dispatch from London laid down the foundation of a modern system of education, with provisions for universities on the London model at Calcutta (Kolkata), Bombay (Mumbai) and Madras (Chennai), for departments of education in the provinces and for grants-in-aid to encourage private enterprise in education.

However, Indians educated under this new system soon found that the British administration was unable to meet their hopes and aspirations and they became increasingly disillusioned. In 1885 Allan Octavium Hume founded the Indian National Congress to create a platform for disgruntled Indians to voice their discontent, but soon a section of them was drawn to militant nationalism. By the time British officials had realised their blunder of spreading higher education and took several steps – including the Indian Universities Act of 1904–5 – to control it, it was too late. With the freedom movement in full flow in the early twentieth century, the British had hardly any time to think about Indian education. With the outbreak of World War II in 1939, the British found it increasingly difficult to resist the freedom struggle led by Gandhi. After the war, despite preparing plans for post-war development, including the Sergeant Plan for education, the British decided to withdraw following a

change of government at home: in August 1947 the sub-continent was bifurcated into India and Pakistan.

The nascent Indian nation was occupied with too many problems after the departure of the British to effectively address the area of education. Yet the Congress government realised the need to renovate the educational structure of the country to suit national needs and aspirations. Over time it appointed three commissions – Radhakrishnan (1948–49), Mudaliar (1952–53), and Kothari (1964–66) – to investigate the problems of education.

Based on the Kothari Commission's recommendations, the Congress government issued its first education policy resolution in 1968. But by that time India had started witnessing great changes in the political scene, with the rise of the leaders from the socio-economic backward classes who, since 1947, had benefited from the expansion of non-vocational and liberal education. While many of the educated unemployed were members of radical social groups, many became members of newly formed political parties. These forces of disintegration added to the tensions of a society already suffering from casteism, linguism and communalism. In 1986 the Congress government at the centre, despite its loss of power in many states, was bold enough to issue a new education policy, replacing the 1968 one, to tackle these problems. However, a non-Congress government halted its implementation and appointed a review committee to look into the problem of education in May 1990.

In the final decade of the twentieth century education in India experienced a critical phase, hampered by the absence of a stable government at the centre. While globalisation has certainly reduced pressures upon higher education, the elite social groups living in the metropolitan cities have mostly reaped its benefits. Despite the passing of parliamentary Acts in 1995 and 2003, offering equal opportunities in education to disabled children and an entitlement to elementary education, the country has not been able to greatly increase its literacy rate, which stands at a little above 60 per cent. With a population exceeding 1 billion, India is now one of the most illiterate countries in the world.

See also: Pakistan

Further reading

Ghosh, S. C. (1989) *Education Policy in India since Warren Hastings*, Calcutta: Naya Prokash.
——(1995/2000) *The History of Education in Modern India*, New Delhi: Orient Longman.
——(2002) *Civilization, Education and School in Ancient and Medieval India*, Frankfurt: Peter Lang.
Thomas, F. W. (1891) *History and Prospects of British Education in India*, London: George Bell and Sons.

SURESH C. GHOSH

INDIGENOUS EDUCATION

Indigenous populations are distributed in regions across the globe. The numbers, condition and experience of indigenous groups is not uniform, and consequently, there is no one fixed or universal definition of what it means to be indigenous or belong to an indigenous group. Across these disparate nations there are shared experiences of a legacy with the land and of the long-term effects of colonisation. Despite the diversity of indigenous peoples, they share common problems and issues in dealing with the prevailing, or invading, society.

Nations have constantly sought to acquire social, political, military, religious and economic resources, status and power that have required active acquisition of land both from neighbouring states and beyond. These acts of conquest, synonymously termed as either colonialism or imperialism, subjugated indigenous peoples to the domination and sovereignty of their conquerors. One of the enduring legacies of colonialism (the transfer of a population to a new territory) and imperialism (exercising indirect and direct control over a nation) has been the subjugation of indigenous knowledge, rights, histories,

language, culture, spirituality, values and beliefs. The central concern, therefore, is that the cultures of indigenous peoples are being lost and that indigenous peoples suffer both discrimination and pressure to assimilate and conform to the prevailing demands of non-indigenous societies.

Historically, indigenous peoples have insisted upon the right of access to education. Invariably the nature, and consequently the outcome, of this education has been constructed through and measured by non-indigenous standards, values and philosophies. Ultimately the purpose of this education has been to assimilate indigenous peoples into non-indigenous cultures and societies.

Indigenous education is inextricably linked with the histories, knowledge and rights of indigenous peoples as the original occupants of the land. Most indigenous peoples, and, in particular, those who have suffered the impact and effects of colonisation, have struggled to access education that acknowledges, respects and promotes the right of indigenous peoples to be indigenous (see Smith 1999).

The *Coolangatta Statement on Indigenous Rights on Education* (1999) fundamentally stated the inherent belief that indigenous people have the right to be indigenous. The Coolangatta Statement represented the collective voices of indigenous peoples from many nations who advocated the reform and transformation of education for indigenous peoples. Indigenous peoples argued that they have been denied equity in non-indigenous education systems, which have systematically and systemically failed to provide educational services that nurture the whole indigenous person. Non-indigenous education has not been cognisant of indigenous scholarship, language, traditions, culture, spirituality and self-determination. Indigenous peoples therefore assert the following:

- Indigenous peoples have the right to all levels and forms of education and have the right to establish and control their educational systems and institutions providing education in their own language (*kohanga reo* and *kura kaupapa* Maori schools in New Zealand and tribal/First Nations universities in the United States, Canada and New Zealand, for example). The use of existing indigenous languages is a fundamental right and must be protected.

- Indigenous peoples have the right to have the dignity and diversity of their cultures, traditions, histories and aspirations appropriately reflected in all forms of education and public information.
- Indigenous peoples have the right to their own knowledge, languages and culturally appropriate education, including bicultural and bilingual education. Through recognising both formal and informal ways the participation of family and community is guaranteed.
- Indigenous peoples must have the necessary resources and control over their own education systems and dissemination of knowledge. Elders must be recognised and respected as teachers of the young people. Indigenous wisdom must be recognised and encouraged.
- Indigenous peoples have the right to revitalise, use, develop and transmit to future generations their histories, languages, oral traditions, philosophies, writing systems and literatures, and any research conducted with/for/about indigenous peoples and communities.

The right of indigenous peoples to education is often mistakenly interpreted in terms of access to non-indigenous education. As a result, educational materials providing accurate and fair information on their cultures and ways of life are all too rare, and history textbooks frequently depict them in negative terms. In many cases, educational programmes fail to offer indigenous peoples the possibility of participating in decision making, in the design of curricula, the selection of teachers and teaching methods, and the definition of standards. Indigenous communities across the world are today demanding educational provision that respects their diverse cultures and languages, while not excluding them from broader participation in national education systems.

See also: bicultural education; bilingual education; culture; equality of opportunity

Further reading

Marker, M. (2000) 'Ethnohistory and indigenous education: a moment of uncertainty', *History of Education*, 29(1): 79–85.

May, S. (1999) *Indigenous Community Based Education*, Clevedon: Multilingual Matters Ltd.

Smith, L. Tuhiwai (1999) *Decolonizing Methodologies: Research and Indigenous Peoples*, London: Zed Books.

TANYA FITZGERALD

INDIVIDUALISED INSTRUCTION/ PERSONALISED LEARNING

These terms are broadly synonymous, with individualised instruction being the more common usage, especially in the United States of America. 'Personalised learning' is used principally in the United Kingdom. Despite being current 'buzzwords' in education, their reference to a method of learning in which the lesson style, pace, materials and resources reflect individual learners' abilities and interests owes something to the tradition of progressive education. Many teachers, past and present, might maintain that their teaching has always instinctively been sensitive to individual learners' needs and preferred learning styles. In the early twentieth century, for example, the 'Dalton Plan', developed by Helen Parkhurst in Massachusetts, placed importance upon high school students and teachers agreeing individual learning goals.

Individualised instruction and personalised learning are endorsed as mechanisms to reinforce the understanding of 'below-average' learners and those with special educational needs, and to extend that of gifted students.

The approaches may involve some one-to-one teaching and the keeping of extensive teacher records, so that learners do not unnecessarily repeat work. They are, perhaps naturally, popular with parents and are seen as essential in order to realise aspirations conveyed in such national strategies as *No Child Left Behind* (USA) and *Every Child Matters* (UK). Attention to individualisation and personalisation has informed, and continues to inform, initiatives intended to make schools more accountable to parents, teacher training reforms and the use of technology, both in the classroom and for the recording of individual students' learning achievements and targets.

See also: accountability; giftedness; instruction; learning; learning styles; Parkhurst, Helen; progressive education; special education/special educational needs/special needs

DAVID CROOK

INDOCTRINATION

From its origins in Latin (*indoctrināre, -īnāt*), the word 'indoctrinate' and its cognate, 'doctrinate', meant to teach, instruct in a subject, or imbue with learning or knowledge. The 'doctrina' in *De Doctrina Christiana* refers to an education primarily in the liberal arts, which Augustine (354–430) advocated as preparation for the Christian teacher's work in interpreting scripture and conveying its truths. To 'indoctrinate' could also mean to imbue with, or induce commitment to, a doctrine or article of faith. This sub-meaning became dominant and acquired negative connotations in the early decades of the twentieth century.

The presumption of Augustine's *De Catechisandis Rudibus* (*Catechising the Uninstructed*) was that few people can achieve genuine knowledge of matters divine, and everyone must in any case be induced to accept Christian beliefs and live without sin. The focus of instruction was belief in the service of salvation, and Augustine held that belief provides a necessary foundation for any later employment of reason in achieving knowledge.

The aims and methods of religious and political (ideological) indoctrination are similar, and more or less forceful or psychologically coercive. Lutheran reformers in sixteenth-century Germany created a form of religious indoctrination and schooling that involved systematic efforts to implant fear and shame, frequent and unvarying repetition of material to be committed to memory, and corporal punishment which took to heart the Dominican Giovanni Dominici's admonishment that children be trained to beg for punishment and give thanks for whippings received. Chinese communist 're-education' after 1950 similarly involved manipulations of guilt, shame and fear, systematic repetition of morally charged language, and intense psychological pressures towards conformity of belief created by immersion in residential 'revolutionary colleges' where all communication was monitored and public confession of 'sins' and rituals of submission were required. Similar techniques of forceful indoctrination continue to be used in fundamentalist Bible camps.

The terms 'education' and 'indoctrination' remained synonymous into the twentieth century, and only acquired distinct meanings with the advent of non-sectarian public school systems and the progressive education movement. John Dewey objected to the 'submission' and 'passivity' engendered by 'authoritarian education' – the 'traditional' education of schools developed on the German model – and called for student-centred learning that would be more consistent with the political ideals of individual freedom and democratic self-governance. The forms of intelligence essential to a democratic culture could not be imposed, but only acquired through free participation in a community of inquiry, Dewey argued.

Since the middle of the twentieth century, educational philosophers have expended much effort on characterising and defining indoctrination. The clearest instances of it share the purpose of inducing commitment to beliefs or doctrines, sometimes through conversion, 'rebirth', or 'emptying' of competing beliefs, and employ methods that are to some extent psychologically seductive or coercive. Appeals to reason may be one of the methods used, but the overall choice of methods rests on a conviction that appeals to reasons and evidence are insufficient to the task of ensuring 'correct' belief. This conviction may rest on assumptions about the insufficiency of evidence for the beliefs, the learner's immaturity, the limits of human rationality generally, or the presence of corrupting factors, such as the learner's social class origins, the enticements of 'Satan', or a competing worldview. Indeed, it is characteristic of indoctrination that it suppresses exercises of critical reason, often through manipulations that associate doubt, questioning, and contrary evidence with evil, weakness, and danger. There have been numerous efforts to analyse and define indoctrination more precisely, but controversy continues. The various proposed definitions have put more or less weight on the role of doctrines, intentions, methods, and outcomes.

There are a number of ongoing debates arising from uncertainties about the conceptual boundaries of indoctrination: If the education of children must begin before they have become critical thinkers and can evaluate what they are taught, is indoctrination unavoidable? Would that not undermine the very ideal of accepting beliefs just to the extent that it is rational to do so? Is some indoctrination present in all teaching or education? Is all indoctrination bad? Is religious education inherently indoctrinating? Is political education inherently indoctrinating, even in the service of an open society?

See also: autonomy; Dewey, John; education; philosophy of education; progressive education; theology

Further reading

Speicker, B. and Straughan, R. (eds) (1991) *Freedom and Indoctrination in Education: International Perspectives*, London: Cassell.

Strauss, G. (1978) *Luther's House of Learning: Indoctrination of the Young in the German Reformation*, Baltimore MD: Johns Hopkins University Press.

Winn, D. (1983) *The Manipulated Mind: Brainwashing, Conditioning and Indoctrination*, London: Octagon Press.

RANDALL CURREN

INDONESIA

Indonesia, in Southeast Asia, comprises more than 17,000 islands, making it the world's largest archipelagic state. It is also the world's fourth most populous country, with around 220 million inhabitants, of which more than 85 per cent are Muslims.

The Dutch colonial power withdrew in 1949, but its legacy is still to be found in Indonesia's three-tier structure of primary, middle and high schools. In the eastern part of the country, where Christian missionaries were once active, Catholic and Protestant schools predominate and, overall, the country's school provision demonstrates a balance between the public and private sectors. Running parallel to Indonesia's mainstream schools is a network of Islamic madrasahs, also organised on a three-tier model by student age. Public schools are generally more popular with parents than private or religious schools, and educational standards are widely thought to be higher in the state schools. The twenty-first century has seen the growth of some elite Indonesian private schools, however.

The first significant move towards Indonesian public education came when the colonial government established a system of village schools in 1906. There were around 3,500 public schools by 1913 and a similar number of private, religious schools, serving a population of 40 million (Kristiansen and Pratikno 2006: 514). Only a few natives, drawn exclusively from the Javanese elite groups, were permitted to study in the Dutch schools up to university level. Less than 6 per cent of the population was literate when, in 1945, a constitution stipulated that every citizen had the right to education and that the government had a duty to provide a national education system (Brojonegro 2001).

Lack of money initially thwarted progress. New post-war schools were predominantly private and based on religious teaching and funding, these being mostly Islamic in Sumatra and Java, and Christian in the eastern parts of the country. The 1970s and 1980s saw the expansion of national, secular education, under the authoritarian regime of President Suharto, partly in consequence of increasing oil revenues. The number of primary schools increased from 65,000 in 1973 to 130,000 in 1984 and the number of children enrolled in them doubled to 26 million (Kristiansen and Pratikno 2006: 515), partly in consequence of the abolition of school fees in 1977.

Universal primary education was achieved in the mid-1980s, and nine years of schooling became mandatory in the mid-1990s after secondary fees were officially abolished. There was a commitment, made concrete in 1994, to extend compulsory schooling from six to nine years: six years in *sekolah dasar*, a primary/elementary school followed by three in *sekolah menengah pertama*, a middle/junior secondary school. Junior secondary school enrolment rates quadrupled between the mid-1970s and 1997, but an ambitious target – that 95 per cent of the school-age population would receive nine years of schooling by 2004 – is yet to be achieved. Against a backdrop of recent economic crises, this target has been postponed to 2008.

At the age of 15 or 16, some students proceed to a national senior secondary/high school, of which there are two sorts: academic track and technical/vocational track. Graduation from the former type provides a preparation for university, while students leaving the latter enter employment as skilled workers. Enrolments after 1994 were held back, however, by the persistence of some secondary schools levying fees after their supposed abolition. Indonesia's economic crisis of the late 1990s presented a further setback for the expansion of secondary education: many families found themselves unable to meet the costs of books, stationery, uniforms and transport, on top of irregular school fees (Kristiansen and Pratikno 2006: 516).

Since 2001 there has been a significant decentralisation of education services to 440 districts, partly funded by international organisations in partnership with the Ministry of National Education. The World Bank and International Monetary Fund have pressed for greater privatisation, deregulation and devolution in Indonesian education, arguing that this will make the country more attractive to overseas investors (Leigh 1999). Critics have regularly argued that rote learning and memorisation dominate Indonesia's highly centralised education system, and that more appropriate pedagogies are needed to compete in the global marketplace. One recent school improvement initiative has been the appointment of 'master teacher trainers' to work as agents of change with clusters of schools, helping teachers to implement more student-centred learning approaches in the classroom.

Following the Indian Ocean tsunami of December 2004, which claimed the lives of an estimated 160,000 Indonesians, the government entered into many partnerships with charities, non-governmental agencies and other organisations to rebuild schools and develop educational provision. The outcomes of these arrangements are likely to become evident over the next few years.

See also: centralisation/decentralisation; East Asia; privatisation/marketisation; religious school; school improvement

Further reading

Brojonegro, S. (2001) *National Education Profile, Indonesia*, Bangkok: UNESCO Asia and Pacific Region Bureau for Education.

Kristiansen, S. and Pratikno, S. (2006) 'Decentralising education in Indonesia', *International Journal of Educational Development*, 26: 513–31.

Leigh, B. (1999) 'Learning and knowing boundaries: schooling in New Order Indonesia', *Journal of Social Issues in Southeast Asia*, 14(1): 34–56.

DAVID CROOK

INDUSTRIAL TRAINING

The term 'training' has its origins in an industrial context. The *Oxford English Dictionary* definition, for example, defines training as a practical education in any profession, art or craft. More broadly, training refers to the acquisition of knowledge, skills and competencies that come about as a result of the teaching of vocational or practical skills and knowledge that relates to specific practical skills. Training traditionally formed a core component of apprenticeships and was usually considered to take place on the job.

The term training has, however, taken on a broader meaning within the context of human resource management and development. In this context it is viewed as a strategy to enhance employee performance. Training in organisations – which may be termed industrial training – is generally categorised as on-the-job or off-the-job. On-the-job training focuses on training given in the day-to-day work situation using the actual tools, equipment, documents and materials that employees will use when fully trained. On-the-job training, if undertaken in a structured way, is considered to be the most effective way to acquire vocational skills. Off-the-job training takes place away from the normal work situation, usually in a classroom setting. However, it may take place out of doors or in the employee's home using computer technology. Off-the-job training is frequently held to involve a waste of resources because the employee is not considered to be productive when the training is taking place. It does, however, allow the employee to get away from the work situation and concentrate on developing specialist skills, understanding key issues or ideas.

Industrial training focuses on job knowledge, skill or attitude. It tends to be provided over relatively short periods and has a more practical purpose than concepts such as education and development. It focuses particularly on the skills, knowledge and attitudes required to perform a job to optimum levels of performance. By contrast, development focuses on experience and personal insight. Industrial training is an activity applicable to all, from senior managers to junior employees, and it tends to span the continuum of formal to informal. Informal training may be derived from work experience, while other aspects of industrial training may aim to impart skills that are useful in particular situations.

In the context of industrial training distinctions are made between initial, continued skill or refresher training and retraining. Initial training focuses on the newcomer to a job. The aim is to provide the employee with the specific skills required to achieve experienced worker standard. Continued skill or refresher training emphasises the acquisition of new knowledge and skills by an experienced employee. These skill requirements may come about due to changes in technology or external regulations. Retraining emphasises the acquisition of a totally new knowledge and skill set by an experienced employee. The need for retraining may come about due to job obsolescence of job loss. Becker (1962), writing in an academic context, has made an important distinction between general and specific training. He argued that training could be distinguished by it portability between firms. General training is highly portable. It has application to many employees. On the other hand, specific training focuses on the application of skills that are valuable to a particular employer.

See also: apprenticeship; skills; training; vocational education; work-based/work-located/workplace/work-related learning; work experience

Further reading

Garavan, T. N. (1997) 'Training, development, education and learning: different or the same?', *Journal of European Industrial Training*, 21(2): 39–50.

Gibbs, S. (2002) *Learning and Development: Processes, Practices and Perspectives at Work*, Basingstoke: Palgrave Macmillan.

Sloman, M. (2003) *Training in the Age of the Learner*, London: CIPD.

Truelove, S. (1997) *Training in Practice*, Oxford: Blackwell Business.

THOMAS N. GARAVAN

INFORMAL/NONFORMAL LEARNING

The concept of informal/nonformal learning has received considerable attention worldwide as the debate about lifelong learning has increasingly drawn attention to the value of forms of learning that occur outside educational institutions, including in the home and workplace. The term informal learning, however, has an interesting genealogy, politically and intellectually (Colley *et al.* 2003; Straka 2004). Interest in the idea of nonformal education spread during the 1970s through Freire's movement for literacy and 'conscientisation' (i.e. a combination of consciousness-raising and politicisation). This initially resulted in the development of radical social-democratic models of non-formal education in the Southern hemisphere, and subsequently gave rise in the North to the development of radical education projects associated with various – feminist, antiracist, post-colonial – 'new social movements' (Colley *et al.* 2003).

'Informal learning' is strongly associated with Lauren Resnick's (1987) 'Learning in school and out', a presidential address to the American Educational Research Association. Resnick criticised schools for concentrating too much on the development of individualised and decontextualised forms of knowledge and competence, which only educated people to be good learners in school settings. She argued in favour of aspects of many informal modes of learning such as apprenticeship to be incorporated into the school curriculum, so as to bring a greater degree of 'authenticity' to the learning experience. The legacy of this critique resonated in the global educational and policy making communities long after her address.

Many recent writers (e.g. Coffield 2000; Eraut 2000; Hager 2001) have written about informal learning, with some providing definitions. For example, Colardyn and Bjornavöld (2004) distinguish between 'intention to learn' and the 'structure in which the learning takes place'. They define informal learning as

> learning resulting from daily life activities related to work, family or leisure. It is often referred to as experiential learning and can to a certain degree be understood as accidental learning. It is not structured in terms of learning objectives, learning times and/or learning support. Typically, it does not lead to certification.
>
> (Colardyn and Bjornavöld 2004: 4)

To some, drawing a distinction between formal and informal learning is questionable. Billett (2004) has argued that policy makers have unproblematically taken concepts and assumptions associated with formal learning as premises for what constitutes the formalisms and structure of legitimate learning experiences, with the result that informal learning is defined by what it is not, rather than attempting to illuminate its qualities or characteristics.

See also: alternative education; Freire, Paolo; home schooling; lifelong learning; work-based/work-located/workplace/work-related learning

Further reading

Billett, S. (2004) 'Workplace participatory practices: conceptualising workplaces as learning environments', *Journal of Workplace Learning*, 16(6): 312–24.

Coffield, F. (ed.) (2000) *The Necessity of Informal Learning*, Bristol: Policy Press.

Colardyn, D. and Bjornavöld, J. (2004) 'Validation of formal, non-formal and informal learning: policy and practices in EU Member States', *European Journal of Education*, 39(1): 69–89.

Colley, H., Hodkinson, P. and Malcolm, J. (2003) *Informality and Formality in Learning: A Report for the Learning and Skills Research Centre*, London: Learning and Skills Research Centre.

Eraut, M. (2000) 'Non-formal learning, implicit learning and tacit knowledge'. In F. Coffield (ed.) *The Necessity of Informal Learning*, Bristol: Policy Press.

Hager, P. (2001) 'Lifelong learning and the contribution of informal learning'. In D. Aspin, J. Chapman, M. Hatton and Y. Sawano (eds) *International Handbook of Lifelong Learning*, Dordrecht, the Netherlands: Kluwer.

Resnick, L. B. (1987) 'Learning in school and out', *Educational Researcher*, 16(9): 13–20.

Straka, G. A. (2004) *Informal Learning: Genealogy, Concepts, Antagonisms and Questions*, Bremen: Institut Technik und Bildung, University of Bremen.

DAVID GUILE

IN-SERVICE EDUCATION

In-service education refers to all education and training undertaken by teachers during service. It is often collective and work-based, enabling teachers to broaden and develop their knowledge and skills, enhancing their professional lives and effectiveness. In-service education covers the formal learning experienced between initial training and retirement. In nineteenth-century England local teacher associations emerged, allowing teachers to meet, share experiences and defend teaching methods against criticisms arising from the 'payment by results' system. The National Society employed peripatetic masters and mistresses offering demonstrations of teaching and organisational skill. Many teachers took no courses after their initial training and were reliant on outdated pedagogical knowledge. Consequently, in the United Kingdom and many other countries, provision increased throughout the twentieth century. Central governments, professional associations and local authorities are, singly or together, providers of in-service courses for teachers, often lasting just a single day or half day, but sometimes running over several weeks. Secondment opportunities for teachers to study for higher degrees are generally less available today than they once were, somewhat marginalising the role of higher education institutions as in-service providers. Criticisms of in-service education have focused on its piecemeal approach, the dominance of award-bearing courses and subsequent absence of a clearly defined concept of teacher development. Work-based in-service programmes can focus on organisational and management problems more than pedagogical issues. Since provision is tied to resources, this suggests a role as a management tool delivering the agenda of the budget holder, which raises the issue of defining the teacher's role. Are teachers as professionals capable of identifying their own training needs or are they vocational workers undertaking training programmes designed by others?

See also: continued/continuing professional development; professional education; workers' education

KEITH WILLIAMS

INSPECTION

Inspection is one of the two means commonly used to evaluate schools and other educational institutions, the other being performance indicators. Although direct inspection and the use of performance indicators may be regarded as complementary (OECD 1995), they are used to greatly varying extents in different countries. Until the last decade, the United Kingdom and New Zealand mainly used school inspection. By contrast, the USA, where there is no tradition of inspection, has relied almost entirely on performance indicators, particularly standardised test scores (Wilson 1995). European countries have tended to rely on a mixture of inspection and performance indicators. While advances in computing are making performance indicator data increasingly easy to collect, it is likely that direct inspection will remain an important form of educational evaluation in many countries in the future. Indeed, China, which has only been developing its school inspection system since the mid-1980s, now has a workforce of over 23,000 inspection personnel (Department of International Co-operation and Exchanges 2000).

Inspection involves the collection, interpretation and reporting of evidence to do with educational standards and quality and the efficiency of educational institutions (Richards 2001). Collection of evidence often starts prior to inspection. In England, once notified of an inspection by the Office for Standards in Education (Ofsted) school leaders are required to complete forms which provide Ofsted with information about their school and matters of potential significance to the inspection team and the school. On arrival in the school, inspection teams then observe lessons and meet with staff, parents and pupils. Judgements are made against a seven-point scale and findings reported back to school staff, parents and the general public, since reports on every school in England are made available to the public on the Ofsted website (www.ofsted.gov.uk).

Public reporting of inspection findings has been a development reflecting the changing role of inspection in neo-liberal economies over the last two decades. Public reporting serves to provide consumers of education with information about school quality to inform their choice of school. It also reflects a shift from 'friendly' (i.e. advisory) inspections to an external form of inspection which in turn reflects the managerial intent to separate regulation of the public sector from policy advice and delivery, in order to prevent 'provider capture'. Under an external model of inspection, inspectors can therefore require schools to be shut down while not being themselves required to provide the advice on how schools can get out of their predicament.

Such 'high stakes' inspections raise the question whether inspectors take enough account of local social, economic and political contexts when they make inspection judgements. Schools and other educational institutions serving diverse communities and student intakes face significantly different constraints and possibilities which inspectors need to take into account if inspections findings are to be fair and credible. Unfortunately educational politics have not always allowed

contextualisation of inspection findings. For instance, during the 1990s Ofsted argued that any contextualisation of findings would encourage the use of pupil's backgrounds as an excuse for poor performance. Inspection methodology and public discourses have subsequently shifted to take more account of context, although the development of genuinely contextualised inspection findings remains a continuing challenge (Thrupp 2005).

The response of teachers and school leaders to inspection also reflects how 'high stakes' the outcomes of inspection are. Although inspection can lead to genuine improvement in schools, it can also distract from teaching and learning and lead to fabrication through the creation of artefacts and the stage managing of events. For instance in England the period between schools hearing they are going to be inspected and the inspection team arriving has been well known for the frenetic level of activity generated as schools attempt to shore up areas thought to be weak and get a full raft of Ofsted-sanctioned policies in place, though Ofsted has responded by reducing the notice period given for inspections. Along with the problem of contextualising inspection findings, these often perverse and unintended effects of inspection point to the advantages of advisory over external inspection. The latter model has fallen out of favour in some countries: for instance New Zealand's Education Review Office developed a model of external inspection over the 1990s but since 2001 has adopted a more consultative and inclusive approach.

See also: accountability; performance indicators; school effectiveness; school improvement

Further reading

Department of International Co-operation and Exchanges (2000) *Educational Inspection System in China*, Beijing: Department of International Co-operation and Exchanges, Ministry of Education.

Organisation for Economic Co-operation and Development (1995) *Schools Under Scrutiny*, Paris: OECD.

Richards, C. (2001) *School Inspection in England: A Reappraisal*, Southend-on-Sea: Impact.

Thrupp, M. (2005) *School Improvement: An Unofficial Approach*, London: Continuum.

Wilson, T. A. (1995) 'Notes on the American fascination with the English tradition of school inspection', *Cambridge Journal of Education* 25(1): 89–96.

MARTIN THRUPP

INSTRUCTION

An instruction is a requirement, either written or oral in form, with which the recipient is expected to comply, for example when a teacher tells a pupil or class to complete an exercise or to stop working. Instruction more broadly is the passing of knowledge from a teacher or lecturer to an individual or group. Public instruction is equivalent to schooling or organised educational provision under the auspices of a state or department. The directive element in instruction obviates against debate, discussion and interaction. In this sense it is teacher-centred rather than pupil-centred, and tends to emphasise the passing on of received or established knowledge rather than critical approaches to issues or ideas. Thus 'religious instruction' is an especially common phrase when referring to the teaching of established religious doctrine and practices.

See also: individualised instruction/personalised learning; pedagogy; teaching/teaching methods

GARY McCULLOCH

INTEGRATION

Integration in relation to social issues involves ensuring that pupils and students are assimilated into a larger group, and that they are able to participate in educational activities and programmes. This is often relevant to the needs of disabled children and students, and also to pupils from minority cultures. Integration has an affinity with ideals of inclusion in which social barriers to full participation are confronted and addressed; it might be viewed as an outcome of an effective policy of inclusion. It is also contrary to practices of segregation in that it emphasises bringing individuals and groups together from different traditions and backgrounds. Integration would therefore be an outcome of desegregation.

In terms of calculus and mathematics, integration is based on the principle of combining or accumulating, as opposed to differentiation, and is encountered in more advanced courses of mathematics in secondary schools and higher education.

See also: inclusive education; mathematics; segregation/desegregation; social exclusion/inclusion

GARY McCULLOCH

INTELLIGENCE/INTELLIGENCE TESTS

Intelligence is a concept that has become difficult to define, partly due to the multiplicity of uses to which it has been put. Despite the ambiguities of the meaning of the term it is, nevertheless, very important because of the popular currency it enjoys in describing certain states of mind and thinking, as well as of knowledge and understanding. In particular, the term crosses the boundaries of psychology and educational discourses and practices. This popular currency for the term was reinforced throughout the whole of the twentieth century through the almost universalised application of intelligence testing in schools and other institutional contexts, such as the military and personnel selection. Arising from the purposes of such tests – to define grades and levels of ability or cognitive potential – a concept of intelligence, describing something approximating to a general mental capacity, has emerged.

During the first decade of the twentieth century, Alfred Binet (1857–1911), along with Theodore Simon (1872–1961), produced versions of an 'intelligence scale'.

From these beginnings, Lewis Terman (1877–1956) developed the notion of measuring intelligence as a quotient, hence IQ tests. David Weschler (1896–1981) refined the work of Binet and Simon by devising a test in which an arbitrary value of 100 was ascribed to the mean intelligence. Weschler also sought to question what he saw as the simplistic notion of 'general intelligence' that had been current since Charles Spearman's research from the 1890s. He subdivided intelligence into non-verbal (performance) and verbal areas, which were then further subdivided, tested and measured separately.

Cyril Burt (1883–1971), following Galton (1822–1911), argued that general intelligence – defined as 'cognitive ability' – was predominantly an inherited trait. Due to Burt's powerful and influential institutional positions during his professional career – as the first school psychologist within the London County Council, and then as professor of psychology at University College, London – his hereditary and eugenicist philosophy became widely embedded within child development discourses, almost the common sense of his time, and exerting substantial influence upon educationalists and policy makers.

A major challenge to the Galton-Spearman-Binet-Weschler-Burt psychometric tradition, came from Howard Gardner (1943–), who proposed a theory of 'multiple intelligences' in his book *Frames of Mind* (1983). Gardner proposed eight dimensions of intelligence, amongst which are the kinaesthetic, verbal, logical, natural and spatial. This broadening of the concept of intelligence became popularly current during the 1990s within educational and schooling discourses and practices, but failed to be viewed as a positive contribution within mainstream educational psychometrics. Another trenchant critic of the notion of hereditary intelligence has been S. J. Gould, whose book *The Mismeasure of Man* (1981) strengthened the scepticism amongst educators about the ideology of testing for intelligence.

Yet the history of the term predates the late nineteenth-century psychological appropriations. In the Middle Ages 'intelligence' was used to refer to the faculty of understanding the soul and the term was later used to signify perception or insight. During the seventeenth century the term became associated with notions of a pervasive and powerful presence – of being 'an intelligence'. Yet, concurrent with these varied usages in early modern English, we find the word being used to describe a quality of thinking. Additionally, the word came to refer to knowledge, information and factual matter: more than one early eighteenth-century newspaper was called *The Intelligencer*, implying an exchange of information. Another current and popular use of the term is to describe a particular type of privileged, secret or private information obtained through espionage, dating from the times of Tudor court intrigues.

For historians of education and culture, cognates of the concept – 'intellectual', for example – are of considerable importance, as they describe particular types of people in relation to their acquisition of learning. Ever since Byron coined the term intellectual, in 1819, it has been used pejoratively, but thanks to sociological and political thinkers like Karl Mannheim (1893–1947) and Antonio Gramsci (1891–1937), it has been reclaimed in a more positive sense.

See also: ability; ability grouping; Binet, Alfred; Burt, Cyril; cognition; Galton, Francis; Gardner, Howard; psychometrics; Spearman, Charles; Terman, Lewis M.; test/testing

Further reading

Gardner, H. (1983) *Frames of Mind: The Theory of Multiple Intelligences*, New York: Basic Books.
Gould, S. J. (1981) *The Mismeasure of Man*, New York: W.W. Norton and Co.
Mackintosh, N. J. (1998) *IQ and Human Intelligence*, Oxford: Oxford University Press.
Sternberg, R. J. (1991) 'Death, taxes and bad intelligence tests', *Intelligence*, 15: 257–69

STEVEN COWAN

INTERMEDIATE/MIDDLE SCHOOL

An intermediate or middle school occupies a position between the primary or elementary school, on the one hand, and the secondary or high school, on the other, in a number of educational systems around the world. Organisationally, it provides for a distinct phase of education for pupils of about 9–13 years of age, although the precise period and age-range varies. It reflects a view that the educational needs and interests of adolescents are distinct from those of both children and youths, and should be nurtured in a separate environment. In Canada, Japan and the United States, for example, such schools have commonly been known as junior high schools. Middle schools have also developed in the United States, and in other countries including Australia, and in some parts of England following the Plowden Report of 1967. Intermediate schools have been a feature of education in New Zealand and elsewhere. However, this kind of organisational arrangement has not always been popular or convenient. Many education systems have found it more straightforward to allow for a single change of school, most commonly from primary to secondary, as a key dividing line between the stages of compulsory schooling.

See also: elementary school; high school; primary school/education; secondary school/education

GARY McCULLOCH

INTERNATIONAL ASSOCIATION FOR THE EVALUATION OF EDUCATIONAL ACHIEVEMENT (IEA)

The International Association for the Evaluation of Educational Achievement (IEA) is an independent and international cooperative of national research institutions and governmental research agencies. It carries out comparative research projects to assist policy makers in identifying strengths and weaknesses of educational systems especially in relation to teaching and learning, assessment and educational improvement. Its headquarters is in Amsterdam, having previously been located in The Hague, Hamburg and Stockholm.

The IEA was established in 1958 by a group of scholars who came together through the United Nations Educational, Scientific and Cultural Organisation (UNESCO). Following this a number of research centres developed large scale cross-national surveys across different cultures and languages. The first of these examined the teaching of mathematics and highlighted the influence of teachers and teaching methods. More than twenty-three evaluations have been conducted including surveys of learning in basic school subjects such as the Progress in International Reading Literacy Study, while other projects have focused on civic education, information technology in education and pre-primary education. Many of these studies are repeated over time and are used to monitor the implementation of policies and change in education. Participating countries are expected to fund and appoint a national study centre and contribute to the international costs.

Since the late 1950s, membership of the IEA has grown from an initial twelve to sixty-two educational research institutes, universities and ministries of education, although non-member countries also take part in IEA projects. In 2003 more than fifty educational systems participated in the Trends in Mathematics and Science Study, twelve of them from Arabic countries and Africa. The involvement of these new participants has required a reconsideration of the ways in which data are conceived and collected, and has resulted in increased training for new members.

See also: educational research; evaluation

TOM WOODIN

INTERNATIONAL BUREAU OF EDUCATION (IBE)

The International Bureau of Education (IBE) is a United Nations Educational, Scientific and Cultural Organisation (UNESCO) institute

319

which specialises in curriculum development. It carries out capacity building, analyses educational trends, undertakes surveys on comparative education and disseminates educational information, focusing on innovations in curricula and teaching methods. It fosters dialogue on education policies through the International Conference on Education. IBE maintains an international educational information centre, manages a databank on comparative education, 'World data on education', and through 'INNODATA' it disseminates information on educational innovations. The Bureau coordinates national reports on the development of education and produces a number of publications including *Prospects*, a review of comparative education, and its newsletter, *Educational Innovation and Information*. IBE works towards the *Education for All* strategy adopted at the Dakar Forum in 2000

IBE is the oldest UNESCO institute, having been established in 1925 as a non-governmental organisation to collect information and act as a coordinating centre for institutions and societies interested in education. In 1929 membership was extended to governments and it became the first intergovernmental organisation in education. For forty years it was led by Jean Piaget, professor of psychology at the University of Geneva. In 1969, the IBE joined UNESCO as an autonomous institution. It is governed by a council composed of representatives of twenty-eight member states elected by the general conference of UNESCO.

See also: comparative education; Education for All (EFA); international education; Piaget, Jean; United Nations Educational, Scientific and Cultural Organization (UNESCO)

TOM WOODIN

INTERNATIONAL COUNCIL FOR ADULT EDUCATION (ICAE)

The International Council for Adult Education (ICAE) was established in 1973 as a worldwide network of adult educators and their organisations. It promotes 'lifelong learning as a necessary component for people to contribute creatively to their communities and live in independent and democratic societies'. Adult learning is conceived as closely interconnected with social justice, human rights, cultural diversity and democratic participation. It is committed to supporting the 'voiceless', for example, the Ocho Rios Declaration (2001) called for 'justice, democracy and respect for difference' and criticised the growing inequality resulting from economic globalisation. Given that adult learning is broadly conceived, initiatives which have been supported include opposing violence against women, youth camps, literacy and HIV related strategies.

The ICAE is striving to reposition itself in terms of global adult education favouring multi-national and multi-sectoral interventions. This involves monitoring the right to education and lifelong learning, building alliances and fostering cooperation to help strengthen civil society, developing research on new developments, constructing 'learning spaces' which connect theoretical and practical issues, and strengthening communication among members in order to share knowledge, for instance, through networks, seminars and conferences. ICAE publishes a quarterly journal, *Convergence, an International Journal of Adult Education*, which assesses developments in adult and nonformal education as well as the newsletter, *Voices Rising*.

ICAE is run by an elected executive committee which represents the wider membership of more than 700 literacy, adult and lifelong learning associations; seven regional member organisations as well as national and sectoral members in over fifty countries. Members are located across Africa, Asia, the Caribbean, Europe, Latin America and North America.

See also: adult education; informal/nonformal learning; lifelong learning

TOM WOODIN

INTERNATIONAL EDUCATION

International education and comparative education are closely related fields of study. Halls (1989) classified international education as a subfield of comparative education, and focused on international pedagogy. Others (as below) locate comparative education as a subfield of international education. While some in comparative education have promoted a particular method of enquiry, most of those who contribute to the international and comparative education literature employ theories and methods from a range of social sciences, including economics, development studies, post-colonial studies, (comparative) sociology, cross-cultural psychology, planning and management, political science and anthropology, as well as history and philosophy (Rust *et al.* 1999; Little 2000). At its simplest, international education extends the boundaries of knowledge about education beyond single nations and cultures. International education embraces the practices of analysis, advocacy and activity.

Those who study international education focus, *inter alia*, on:

- *'Other' education systems, policies, practices and philosophies.* This type of study was common throughout the twentieth century. The 'other' is relative to the author's and/or institution's identity, the 'our'. Hence 'other' education systems from the standpoint of an English university might include studies of French, Chinese, US and Kenyan education. From the standpoint of a Chinese university, the 'other' might include studies of education in France, Russia, Japan and Brazil. The focus of these studies may be single or multi-country. They may or may not include systematic comparisons with other countries and may or may not include comparison with the education system of which the author most closely identifies. Examples of this type of study are provided by Edmund King's *Other Schools and Ours* (1958) and, more recently, Alexander's *Culture and Pedagogy* (2000).

- *Educational borrowing and lending.* These studies identify how educational ideas, policies and practices are borrowed or lent between two or more national or cultural contexts (i.e. *international* or *intercultural exchange*). Borrowing and lending may be more or less voluntary, wholesale and planned/organised. In today's world education policy makers borrow and adapt policies on a range of issues including class size, privatisation, decentralisation, assessment styles and outcomes-based curricula. Studies examine why and how ideas, policies and practices are borrowed, how they are implemented/adapted and to what effect. Borrowing and lending is conditioned by economic, political and cultural relations between countries. In the years following World War II the reconstruction of education systems in Japan and the Philippines was heavily guided by American interests and finance. In the recent history of many developing countries colonial relations (especially British and French) have imposed the direction of policy and practice.

- *The contribution of education to development.* In the second half of the twentieth century education systems in newly independent countries expanded quickly. Education became part of the political project to 'modernise' economy and society and to create strong and unified national political identities among peoples, many of whom had constituted separate societies or communities prior to colonisation. 'Development studies', influenced strongly by economists, political scientists and sociologists, emerged during this period. The role of education in the 'development' of societies, defined variously as economic growth, nation–building and social equality, became the focus for many classic collections of work (e.g. Anderson and Bowman 1965; Coleman 1965). In many studies, the country is the unit of analysis, treated either holistically/systemically or comparatively/contrastively. In others, intranational social groups differentiated by ethnicity, gender, language, religion, region, economic and social status for the analysis of the reciprocal impacts of education access, quality and outcomes on development.

- *Education, dependency and globalisation.* During the 1970s Marxist–Leninist writings on exploitation and imperialism influenced conceptualisation of development. Dependency theory addressed the economic, political and cultural dependency of poor countries on rich countries, the mechanisms through which these were maintained and the resultant 'underdevelopment'. This perspective encouraged social scientists to abandon the national economy, the nation–state and national society as a central unit of analysis and to refocus on the economic, political and cultural relations between economies, states and societies. Globalisation emerged during the 1990s as a framework for exploring these relations in the wake of the end of the Cold War and the widespread adoption of neoliberal economic policies. The globalisation framework positions the role of national and 'local' economic and political forces in the determination of educational policy and practice alongside the global.

- *International education practices and organisations.* These include studies of school curricula that adopt an explicitly international or intercultural orientation in curriculum (e.g. comparative religion, citizenship, development studies, comparative history); of assessments and examinations that are geared to an international curriculum (e.g. the International Baccalaureate); of institutions that enrol an international student body (e.g. World Colleges); and of organisations whose purpose is the furtherance of international understanding (e.g. UNESCO) or educational development across the world (e.g. the World Bank, UNICEF).

- *International education comparisons.* International education comparisons provide 'snapshots', 'at-a-glance summaries' and 'league tables' of education systems worldwide. Many multi-lateral agencies (e.g. UNESCO, OECD, UNICEF, World Bank, UNDP) include comparisons of economic and social development indicators alongside the educational. International comparisons are frequently used (or 'cherry-picked') by policy makers to justify education reform at home; or by 'development' agencies to promote and urge reform elsewhere. Researchers use international data sets on education to identify factors that explain inter- and intranational variations in achievement. Multi-country data sets are particularly useful in the identification of factors which differentiate national systems of education and which are not usually captured through single country studies.

A second broad category of work is oriented towards the *advocacy* of education goals, targets, policies and practices and the promotion of international understanding and peace. In the contemporary world much of this advocacy work is undertaken by intergovernmental and international non-governmental organisations. Contemporary examples include the world wide movement on Education for All, led by UNESCO, the Global Campaign for Education (an alliance of non–governmental agencies), the United Nations Literacy Decade and the United Nations Decade of

Education for Sustainable Development. These contemporary examples have a long history dating back at least as far as the 1960s and the UNESCO-sponsored regional conferences on Universal Primary Education, held in Addis Ababa, Karachi and Santiago. International advocacies in education are more or less informed by systematic analysis and more or less inclusive of the educational ideas, policies and practices of all 'stakeholders' in education. In Europe, international education as advocacy has a very long history. In the wake of the Thirty Years War (1618–48), Comenius promoted the establishment of a pansophic college to promote understanding among Christians and nations involved in the war. In the wake of the Napoleonic wars (1803–15), Marc-Antoine Julien, a French educator, promoted the systematic collection of information about education ideas and practices as a means of promoting trust among educators and politicians. In the wake of World War I the League of Nations gave renewed impetus to the work of the International Bureau of Education. Towards the end of World War II, the Allies set up the United Nations Organisation for Educational and Cultural Reconstruction which became the United Nations Educational, Social and Cultural Organization (UNESCO). UNESCO is designed to encourage international peace and universal respect by promoting collaboration among nations.

Many more people are involved in the activities of international education than in the practices of analysis or advocacy. Key activities include student and faculty exchange, study abroad, conferences and networks attracting international participation, books and journals attracting international authorships and readerships, strategies for internationalising the curricula and pedagogy of educational institutions, cross-border transactions and trade, and international cooperation programmes of various kinds.

See also: comparative education; Department for International Development (DFID); Education for All (EFA); globalisation; Organisation for Economic Co-operation and Development (OECD); United Nations Children's Fund (UNICEF); United Nations Educational, Scientific and Cultural Organization (UNESCO); World Bank

Further reading

Alexander, R. (2000) *Culture and Pedagogy*, Oxford: Blackwell.

Anderson, C.A. and Bowman, M. J. (eds) (1965) *Education and Economic Development*, Chicago IL: Aldine Publishing Company

Coleman, J. S. (ed.) (1965) *Education and Political Development*, Princeton NJ: Princeton University Press.

Halls, W. (ed.) (1989) *Comparative Education: Contemporary issues*, London: Kingsley, and Paris: UNESCO.

King, E. J. (1958) *Other Schools and Ours*, London: Methuen.

Little, A. W. (2000) 'Development studies and comparative education: context, content, comparison and contributors', *Comparative Education*, 36(3): 279–96.

Rust, V., Soumare, A., Pescador, O. and Shibuya, M. (1999) 'Research strategies in comparative education', *Comparative Education Review*, 43(1): 86–109.

ANGELA LITTLE

INTERNATIONAL INSTITUTE FOR EDUCATIONAL PLANNING (IIEP)

The International Institute for Educational Planning (IIEP) is a United Nations Educational, Scientific and Cultural Organization (UNESCO) institute specialising in educational planning and management. It aims to support countries in planning their educational systems. This is achieved through the training of educational leaders and personnel through a mix of year-long courses, distance learning, intensive and customised courses. Since its formation in 1963, over 5,000 people have been trained by IIEP. Educational institutions are also supported in developing appropriate administrative procedures.

Policy forums, networks and international cooperation are fostered to build the capacity to respond to the long-term developmental needs of countries as well as emergency situations. The Institute encourages communication and exchanges between countries, especially those in the South. For instance, it has supported the development of consortia such as the Southern African Consortium for Monitoring Educational Quality (SACMEQ), the Asian Network of Training and Research Institutions in Educational Planning (ANTRIEP), the International Working Group on Education (IWGE) and ForGestion, a network of education specialists in Latin America. In supporting these networks IIEP solicits the active collaboration of national governments and international organisations, including UNICEF and the World Bank, professional associations and educational agencies. IIEP engages in research in order to support and advise policy makers on issues such as international competition, the brain drain, equitable access, new technologies and decentralisation. Ideas and practices are communicated through and a quarterly newsletter which outlines the activities of the Institute and is published in a range of languages.

IIEP was established by UNESCO although it enjoys considerable autonomy and receives grants from member states and elsewhere. It is run by a governing board of educational experts and specialists.

See also: comparative education; United Nations Educational, Scientific and Cultural Organization (UNESCO)

TOM WOODIN

IRAN

Education in Iran covers three historical eras: the pre-Islamic era (until 642 CE), the early Islamic era, from 642 until the 1907 Constitutional Revolution, and the current era, from 1907 until today.

During the pre-Islamic era, only aristocrats were allowed to receive education. In the Achaemenid period (c.550–330 BCE), formal education in law was offered at schools established at Zoroastrian religious centres in order to train professionals for governing the country. During the Sasanid empire (226–642 CE), Jondi-Shapour University was established to train professionals in medicine, mathematics, astronomy, logic, and religion.

From the beginning of the early Islamic era, all citizens were allowed to receive education if they could afford it. Primary schools were established in mosques or *maktabkhaneh* (a home usually belonging to a teacher). Advanced education was taught at mosques or scientific centres near them, and citizens assisted in the establishment and management of educational institutes (Safavi 2004).

The third era was born from the establishment of Tehran's Darolfonoon School in the 1850s, which marked the beginning of modern education in Iran. After the Constitutional Revolution, the government became responsible for providing public education, free of charge, for all Iranians in order to accelerate the development and modernisation of Iran. The Ministry of Knowledge directed education from primary to higher levels until the 1960s, when the government made two ministries responsible for education, one for pre-university education and one for universities and related institutes.

Today, the Ministry of Education and Training in Tehran manages pre-university education throughout the country. The ministry determines educational goals and policies, introduces programmes and projects, prepares and distributes textbooks, employs staff, makes rules for the management and evaluation of education for the country. Pre-university education has three levels:

- Primary school (public education) is a five-year programme that teaches students reading, writing, calculation, social skills through subjects such as literature, mathematics and geometry, science and hygiene, social sciences, arts, and physical activities.
- Intermediate school is a three-year programme teaching students academic

and practical subjects such as religion, social sciences, literature, Arabic language, English language, mathematics, sciences, career and technology (vocational skills), history and geography, physical education, and arts.

- High school offers two types of three-year programme, one academic and another vocational. Students in the academic programme pursue one of three majors: mathematics and physics, sciences, or social sciences to prepare them for university studies. The vocational programme offers practical training, such as computer programming, mechanics, electricity, industrial design, dress design, physical education, woodwork and painting, to prepare students for entering the labour market after graduation.

The Ministry of Science, Research and Technology governs Iran's fifty-plus public universities and related institutes. In order to be admitted to university, students with an academic high school diploma must pass a university preparation year, then take a national university entrance examination called the *konkour*. During the past decade, over 1 million students have taken the konkour each year, far more than can be accommodated by public universities. A ministerial committee assigns students to different universities across the country according to konkour marks and preferred majors. Students study four years to graduate with a bachelor's degree. If they apply for a postgraduate degree, they must take an advanced national konkour in their area of specialisation. For some programmes, they must also pass an oral examination or interview in Farsi or English, or both.

Students with a vocational high school diploma must also pass a national konkour; if passed, they may enter a two-year programme and receive a diploma similar to a college degree. To receive a bachelor's degree, they must pass another national examination to enter the last two years of a bachelor's degree programme.

Private education was re-established in 1998 for those who could afford it, in part to accommodate the students who were not selected for public universities. The largest private university in Iran is the Islamic Azad University, with campuses across the country and a total enrolment of over 500,000. The majority of Iranians still prefer public university education, which is free of charge and considered to be of better quality.

Further reading

Ravandi, M. (1967) *History of Education and Training in Iran and Europe*, Tehran: Gooya.
Safavi, A. (2004) *History of Education and Training in Iran, from Ancient Iran to Today*, Tehran: Roshd.
Safi, A. (2000) *Organization and Laws of Education in Iran*, Tehran: Samt.
Soltanzadeh, H. (1985) *History of Schools in Iran*, Tehran: Agah.

FATEMAH BAGHERIAN AND WARREN THORNGATE

IRAQ

Modern education in Iraq emerged in the middle of the nineteenth century and was shaped by two distinct modernity projects of the Ottoman empire: the *Tanzimāt* (reform) system (1839–76) and, as a reaction to this, the Sunni Islamisation of the education system led by the last sultan, Abdülhamid II (1876–1909) (Fortna 2002). In the three Mesopotamian provinces, the Ottoman empire established new military and civilian schools to teach people the skills required to build modern states. Following World War I, a new Iraqi state emerged in 1921. The school system and the College of Law, instituted under Ottoman rule, began slowly to expand under British supervision. The educational structure was set at six years of compulsory primary schooling, three years of intermediate secondary schooling, and three years of preparatory secondary schooling for higher education. When Iraq became independent in 1932, the country inherited two main forms of Islam, Sunni and Shi'a, a strong Ottoman legacy in its state education system, and the British legacy of the legitimation of Arab tribal tradition.

During the 1920s and 1930s, three types of modern educational projects, namely Arabisation, Islamisation and the militarisation of education, were established by three Arab nationalist directors-general of education, though these projects conflicted with each other. What was counted as good knowledge was based on the Arab-Islamic ethic of unity and loyalty but was transformed in a militaristic and pragmatic way in the education system. The effect of these projects was the emergence of an authoritarian leadership. The military was used as a political means for gaining power over opposition movements. (Tripp 2000; Simon 2004). The moral code for the education of the new Iraqi was framed by national education. The Ottoman legacy of 'The Guide to Morals' was transformed into the textbooks called *Civic Ethics* during the monarchy and *National and Social Education* during the republic after 1958. During the Ba'thist regime of Saddam Hussain, study of the textbook called *National Education* at the secondary school, and of *Pan-Arab Culture* for students from the first to the third year at the university was compulsory. In 1993, examinations in Islamic education, followed by 'the Great National Religious Campaign' for teaching the Qur'an (recitation and interpretation) for all educational levels, were introduced at the intermediate and preparatory levels.

The minister of education accredits programmes for the training of teachers for Iraqi primary and secondary schools. A higher teacher training college was established in the 1920s, offering four-year courses for prospective secondary school teachers. This college, and the teacher training facilities within the University of Baghdad, established in 1958, included specialist English and science departments.

By 2003, twenty state universities, including semi-private institutions (financially supported by the state) were established in Iraq. Research projects in the colleges of agriculture, arts, engineering, medicine and science were under the surveillance of the Ba'th Party and access to universities remained unequal and different for urban and rural areas, for the north and the south and for different religious groups and regions.

In northern regions such as Salahaddin and Sulaimaniya, education is rapidly expanding, but in the central regions and the south problems in the aftermath of the 2003 war increased the 'brain drain', and provision is persistently disturbed by cross-border terrorist networks and activity, and by political, social and educational insecurity. The impact of the conflicts on the education system has had a devastating effect upon all children and adults and it is difficult, at the time of writing, to predict the future of education in Iraq.

Further reading

Fortna, B. C. (2002) *Imperial Classroom: Islam, the State, and Education in the Late Ottoman Empire*, Oxford: Oxford University Press.
Simon, R. S. (2004) [1986] *Iraq: Between the Two World Wars: The Militarist Origins of Tyranny*, New York: Columbia University Press.
Tripp, C. (2000) *A History of Iraq*, Cambridge: Cambridge University Press.

HUDA AL-KHAIZARAN

ISAACS, SUSAN SUTHERLAND (1885–1948)

Isaacs, the child psychologist, was the daughter of a Methodist lay preacher, who removed her out of school, aged fourteen, when she professed to agnosticism. Isaacs nevertheless went on to train as a nursery teacher and so impressed her teachers that they persuaded her to take a degree at Manchester University. She gained a B.A. from Manchester in 1912 and an M.A. in the following year, then becoming a research assistant at the Psychological Laboratory in Cambridge, where she specialised in child development, and a lecturer at Darlington and Manchester from 1913 to 1915. She married Nathan Isaacs, a famous metallurgist, in 1922, who shared her enthusiasm for the ideas of Froebel. Appointed principal of the Malting House School in Cambridge in 1924, she developed liberal, progressive approaches to teaching and learning over the next three years, influencing such later publications as *Intellectual Growth of Young Children* (1930), *The Children We Teach* (1932) and *Social Development in Young Children* (1933). She received her doctorate from Manchester in 1931 and held the post of Head of the Child Development Department at the University of London Institute of Education from 1933 to 1943. She transformed the small department into a major educational centre with an international reputation for excellence. Under her leadership, it became a meeting point for different academic specialisms, encouraging cross-disciplinary approaches to the study of child development.

See also: child development; Froebel, Friedrich

STEVEN COWAN

ISRAEL

The state of Israel was established on 15 May 1948, but wealthy European Jews erected the first modern schools in pre-state Israel in the second half of the eighteenth century. These schools, which taught in the major European languages and combined secular subjects with religious studies, provided the small Jewish community with an alternative to long-existing forms of religious education. The arrival of growing numbers of Jewish immigrants from Germany, Eastern Europe and Russia in the late nineteenth- and early twentieth centuries brought with it an expansion of the educational system, which ignited a debate regarding the preferable language of instruction. Eventually, Hebrew predominated: Hebrew elementary schools and kindergartens were opened first, then Hebrew secondary schools and, finally,

Hebrew institutes of higher education. This education system played a major role in the revival of the Hebrew language. During the British mandate over Israel, which commenced in 1917, three separate trends in Jewish–Zionist education evolved: a 'general' trend based on already existing Hebrew schools; a religious trend that gave greater emphasis to Jewish studies; and a trend founded by the labour movement that was grounded in socialist ideals and progressive methods.

In the first years of Israel's independence, the state's educational efforts were concentrated on two major fronts. First, it worked to consolidate its control over education. In 1949 a ministry of education was created and a law passed ordering all citizens to partake in nine years of free, compulsory education. In 1953 the State Education Law introduced a highly centralised state system comprising three types of schools: state schools, state-religious schools and Arab state schools (teaching in Arabic and placing greater emphasis on Arab history and culture). Outside the state system were found Jewish religious ultra-orthodox schools that were, nevertheless, subsidised and supervised by the state, and a few church schools. This basic structure of the educational system remains unchanged today. The second front on which early state efforts focused was absorbing the influx of Jewish immigrants coming mainly from North Africa and the Middle East. In the first three years of its existence Israel's population more than doubled. The state's position was that the new immigrants, who came from a very different cultural and religious heritage, should adopt local patterns of thought. The educational system was envisaged as a melting pot that would enable immigrants to be assimilated into existing Israeli society, embracing a more Westernised and secular identity that better fitted the classical socialist-Zionist vision. The echoes of this forced assimilation are still felt in contemporary Israel.

In the 1950s and 1960s, Israel's education system, in general, and programmes of vocational secondary education, in particular, evolved at a rapid pace. The state provided three years of free kindergarten education, of which one was compulsory, eight years of compulsory and free elementary schooling, and three years of free secondary education. In 1968 the organisation of schools was reformed and the length of compulsory education extended to eleven years. Today, following the 1968 reform, state schooling mostly comprises of six years of elementary education, three years of comprehensive junior high school and three years of senior high school, of which the last two are free but not compulsory. The introduction of comprehensive junior high schools, which brought together pupils from diverse social and economic backgrounds, resulted partly from policies of social integration aiming at bridging cultural gaps within Israeli society. The educational value of these policies, however, is still being debated. Israel's senior high schools offer either vocational training or academic studies that lead to a matriculation certificate, which is a prerequisite for attending higher education.

The turbulent 1970s prepared the ground for fundamental changes in education. Since that time, Israeli education has been moving away from the ideologies that underlay the first phases of its development. The socialist-Zionist ideal has lost its hegemony, as Israel has become a more pluralistic state. This change is clearly manifest in educational attitudes towards the immigrants – approximately 1 million of them – who arrived in Israel in the 1990s, mainly from the former Soviet Union. Unlike their predecessors, they were not required to adopt a new identity but were rather expected to slowly adapt to existing Israeli culture while making their own contribution to it. A second significant change is a move towards a more standardised model of contemporary Western education. Since the 1980s, education in Israel has focused increasingly on the welfare of individuals; greater emphasis has been placed upon a scientific, modern curriculum; decentralisation

has promoted concepts of educational choice; teachers have lost some of their previous social status; and higher education has become more diversified, with the formation of some private establishments.

At the start of the twenty-first century, Israeli education faces complicated challenges: it has to bridge some deep social, cultural, economic, religious and ethnic rifts; it has to respond to constant regional developments, especially those arising from Israeli–Palestinian relationships; and it has to adjust to the new individualistic and materialistic trends in society, while simultaneously trying to satisfy demands presented by globalisation.

Further reading

Bentwich, J. S. (1965) *Education in Israel*, London: Routledge and Kegan Paul.

Elazar, D. (1997) 'Education in a society at a crossroads: an historical perspective on Israeli schooling', *Israel Studies*, 2(2): 40–65.

Gur-Ze'ev, I. (ed.) (2000) *Conflicting Philosophies of Education in Israel/Palestine*, Boston MA: Kluwer.

Iram, Y. and Schmida, M. (1998) *The Educational System of Israel*, Westport CT: Greenwood Press.

Kalekin-Fishman, D. (2004) *Ideology, Policy and Practice. Education for Immigrants and Minorities in Israel Today*, Boston MA: Kluwer.

TAL GILEAD

ITALY

The history of education in Italy begins with ancient Rome, where, from the fourth century BCE, wealthy families sent their boys, and sometimes girls, to schools where learning was underpinned by savage corporal punishment regimes. Such families also employed tutors for children of both sexes. Schools for students up to the age of 11 or 12 focused on reading, writing and mathematics: children worked on an abacus for learning arithmetic and they used a stylus and a wax tablet for writing. During the period of the later Roman empire a system of tiered schooling developed, with the *ludus* offering education for socialisation to children under the age of seven, the *grammaticus* teaching a curriculum based on language, poetry and public speaking to the children up to the age of around fifteen, while the *rhetor* offered high-level education for elite Roman males prior to entering politics.

In modern times, following unification in 1861, Massimo d'Azeglio observed, 'We have made Italy, now we must make Italians'. Public education has since played a vital role in creating a national identity. Piedmont's 1859 *Lex Casati* was adopted to frame a system of Napoleonic inspiration, based on principles of universalism and meritocracy, in which municipalities provided free, compulsory elementary education to spread the language chosen to symbolise unity. The ministry of education in Rome became the nation's conscience on educational issues, and defined a lasting pattern, setting the school-leaving age at nine in 1877 and raising it subsequently. The lyceum offered secondary school education, and a path to university. Legislation in the fascist years (1923–43) fundamentally changed little, but formalised the teaching of the Catholic religion, provided teacher training for elementary school teachers and introduced sanctions for non-attendance.

In 1945, one in three Italians communicated only in dialect, but post-war prosperity and faith in education saw secondary attendance quadruple and university undergraduate numbers treble by 1970. Egalitarian moves to liberalise university admission from 1969 and groundbreaking laws to include children with special educational needs (Law 77/517) created optimism. However, momentum was lost from the 1980s due to recession, political instability, a declining birth rate and shrinking resources, and critics increasingly condemned the system as over-centralised, lacking transparency and irresponsive to social and economic change. By the late 1990s, extensive structural reforms had begun.

Currently, universal availability of pre-school education is a government goal. Compulsory schooling starts at age six in primary school. Exams to enter early secondary schooling at eleven have been discontinued and children spend three years there before being examined for the middle school diploma at fourteen years old.

For their second cycle of education, students choose either the *liceo,* the *istituto tecnico* or the *istituto professionale.* The *liceo classico* emphasises Greek and Latin while the *liceo scientifico* offers chemistry, physics and some Latin. The *liceo linguistico* concentrates on modern languages, and the *liceo artistico* provides courses in art. The *istituto tecnico* focuses on subjects such as aeronautics, business studies and information technology, while the *istituto professionale* is more vocational and might, for example, prepare students for careers in the hospitality sector. At nineteen, state exams for the *maturità* diploma complete the above paths of study, and a pass grade enables students to enter tertiary education. Students may leave school at fifteen.

Universities, technical universities and academies provide the third cycle of education. Other institutions provide instruction in such fields as commerce, fashion and industry. The Ministry of Education, Universities and Research runs universities. In a rationalised, three-level model of higher education, first-level degree courses last three years. Second-level postgraduate courses normally require two further years and an original dissertation for a specialised degree. First degrees in dentistry and medicine are considered equivalent. Third-level studies may be at *scuole di specializzazione* offering professional training usually for three or four years, or in doctoral research programmes of a minimum three years and requiring original dissertations, or in training courses for highly specialised professions. Infant and elementary school teachers now follow a four-year university curriculum. Secondary school teachers either complete a two-year postgraduate training or pass state exams to teach particular subjects at specified levels.

It is early to evaluate recent changes, but certain obstacles are being defined, and there is little evidence so far of increased community, teacher and parental involvement in decentralised decision making. Schools' autonomy in personnel management and resource deployment remains far below the OECD average (OECD 2004). Teacher pay and prestige remain low and the costs of obtaining the new qualifications will deter less privileged students, as will the expenses of postgraduate education.

In 2004, Italian universities, some among the earliest founded in Europe, had a dropout rate of 60 per cent, the highest in the OECD, indicating a failure to match student needs and aspirations. Female undergraduates have outnumbered male since 1997, but few women hold the highest faculty positions. Continued discrimination against foreign lecturers indicates a deep resistance to forsaking protectionism in academic life.

Formal delegation of decision making alone will not suffice. Leading administrators and senior professional figures need to create transparency and promote genuine community involvement at every stage.

See also: abacus; Catholic school/education; classical education; corporal punishment; dropout; Europe

Further reading

De Mauro, T. (1991) *Storia linguistica dell'Italia unita*, Rome: Laterza.

Ginsburg, P. (2003) *Italy and its Discontents: Family, Civil Society and State, 1980–2000*, New York and Basingstoke: Palgrave Macmillan.

Organisation for Economic Co-operation and Development (2004) *Reviews of National Policies for Education – Italy*, Paris: OECD Publishing.

JOHN OLIPHANT

J

JAPAN

In terms of modern Japanese history, 1945 marks a significant turning point, which saw the implementation of significant educational reforms. These precipitated a dramatic transformation of educational ideals and of the entire school system. Before World War II Japanese education emphasised indoctrination in 'national morality', fidelity and obedience, as set out in the Imperial Rescript on Education or *Kyoiku Chokugo* of 1890. A new constitution and *Fundamental Law* of education were formulated in 1947, establishing new ideals and principles. Democracy and pacifism now became the leading ideals, replacing ultra-nationalism and militarism. The contrast between the old and new order was marked: education became a right, rather than a duty, and freedom, respect for individuality, egalitarianism and internationalism were now emphasised in place of control, conformism, elitism and nationalism.

The school system was changed from a multi-track one to a simple comprehensive 6–3–3–4 pattern (i.e. six years of primary, three years of junior high school, three years of senior high school, and four years of university education, including two years at a junior college). Overall, the changes introduced the democratisation and demilitarisation of Japanese education.

During the 1950s however, when the occupation of the Allied powers ended, the trend towards 'hyper-democratisation' in social reform, including education, was reversed. The Local Education Administration Law, promulgated in 1956, led to local boards of education being nominated, rather than elected, and in the following year a system for controlling teachers through the apparatus of appraisal was introduced. The content of textbooks also became subject to screening (from 1958) and a nationwide achievement test, encouraging student competition, began in 1961. These measures and others undermined the post-war educational ideals and returned power to the state.

Government education policy became strongly linked to plans to develop the Japanese economy and there was a significant increase in student progression to senior high school and university from the 1960s and 1970s. In 1960, 42.5 per cent of the relevant age cohort proceeded to senior high school and just 6.2 per cent reached university. By 1970 the equivalent figures were 82.1 per cent and 23.6 per cent, and in 2000 these were 95.9 per cent and 49.1 per cent.

In 1984, Prime Minister Nakasone inaugurated the *Rinkyoshin* (Council on Educational Reform), with the support of financial and business groups. Nakasone intended to replace the Japanese post-war settlement, as represented by the 1947 Constitution and Fundamental Law, with an education system emphasising neo-liberalism (Hood 2001). The *Rinkyoshin* maintained support for traditionalism and patriotism, but also for deregulation and privatisation, strongly encouraging, for example, the further development of private pre-paratory schools or *juku*, for example.

As the Organisation for Economic Co-operation and Development (OECD) has noted, Japan is a prominent player in the global knowledge economy and has an impressive student graduation rate from upper secondary education. Japan has per-formed strongly in large-scale surveys of international pupil attainment in mathematics and science and Japanese people, in general, are engaging in study over longer periods, but tertiary graduation rates remain variable and for advanced research programmes – such as doctorates – they are lower than in several comparable countries. A 'gender gap', evi-denced by low progression rates of females to high-level qualifications also remains of con-cern (OECD 2005), as are such issues as 'school phobia', school violence and bullying. Teachers' professional identity is challenged by intensive inspection, strict state control of textbooks, large class sizes and the imposition of punishments for failing to respectfully observe ceremonies involving the national anthem and flag (Horio 1997).

On 15 December 2006 the 1947 Funda-mental Law was revised to emphasise the teaching of such values as 'love of country', 'public spirit' and 'tradition' and to extend the control of politicians over schools. The situation is very controversial: critics fear that this may precipitate militaristic thinking in schools and undermine such twenty-first century objectives as peace, human rights and international friendship.

See also: China; East Asia

Further reading

Cave, P. (2001) 'Educational reform in Japan in the 1990s: "individuality" and other uncertainties', *Comparative Education*, 37(2): 173–91.
Hood, C. P. (2001) *Japanese Education Reform: Nakasone's Legacy*, London: Routledge.
Horio, T. (1997) *Gendai-syakai to Kyoiku [Modern Society and Education]*, Tokyo: Iwanami Shoten.
OECD (2005) *Education at a Glance 2005: OECD Briefing Notes for Japan*, Paris: OECD.

TERUHISA HORIO

JESUIT EDUCATION

Jesuit education developed through Ignatius Loyola's realisation that his new Society of Jesus, founded in 1540, required the highest levels of learning: the Society's *Constitutions* sought 'to aid its own members and their fellow men to attain the ultimate end for which they were created' and education was seen as a means of achieving this and of helping to promote post-Reformation Roman Catholicism.

The first Jesuit school for lay students opened in Messina in Sicily in 1548. By Loyola's death in 1556, there were forty Jesuit schools worldwide. These cost the Society nothing, apart from time and man-power, and students of the Jesuits received free tuition: princes and bishops requesting Jesuit educational support were expected to endow new foundations.

Key priorities in the formation of Jesuits became the priorities of Jesuit education more generally. Lay students up to the age of eighteen were grounded in the humanities through the study of grammar, syntax, poetry and rhetoric. Older students, clerical and lay, studied philosophy (including natural science) and theology, while the *ideal* Jesuit university offered education in civil law and medicine, both provided by lay professors.

The early Jesuits built on Loyola's *Spiritual Exercises* and on the Society's *Constitutions* by codifying Jesuit educational theory and prac-tice. A *Ratio Studiorum*, or universal plan of studies, first published in 1599, effectively created an international network of schools, colleges and universities, both for Jesuits and for young lay men. Many features of Jesuit educational philosophy and practice were later applied to girls' education by Mary Ward (1585–1645) and Madeleine Sophie Barat (1779–1865) (Duminuco 2000).

In Jesuit colleges and universities, the rec-tor delegated curricular responsibility to a *prefect of studies* and managerial and dis-ciplinary matters to a *prefect general*. The superior of each Jesuit province was required to undertake regular appraisal of the progress of educational institutions under his jurisdiction and to submit an annual, written report of his findings to the Jesuit superior general in Rome. Using a range of management and reporting techniques that became common universally in education only in the late twentieth century, Jesuit education provided the first educational 'system' in the Western world.

Jesuit educational emphases on public speaking, debating, drama and literary studies played a formative role in the subsequent careers of a host of men of letters: Calderón, Corneille, Goldoni, Molière, Racine and Voltaire and, at a later period, Arthur Conan Doyle and James Joyce, all received a Jesuit education. Equally, the Jesuits' encouragement of scholarship in mathematics and the sciences, particularly in higher education, helped foster the outstanding talent of Boscovich, Clavius, Descartes, Kircher, Mesmer, Torricelli and Volta, among others. All these successes earned the Jesuits a formidable reputation as the 'schoolmasters of Europe'.

By the mid-eighteenth century, the *Ratio Studiorum*, unreformed since 1599, was no longer keeping Jesuit education in the vanguard position that it had earlier enjoyed. Nevertheless, the universal suppression of the Jesuits by the papacy in 1773 had a profound effect on educational provision generally: many nation-states had to take urgent measures to try and fill the educational vacuum created by the closure then of more than 700 colleges and universities educating some 250,000 students worldwide.

Following the restoration of the Jesuits in 1814, the *Ratio Studiorum* was revised and updated in 1832. Though Jesuit education thereafter was disrupted by political hostility, particularly in France and Germany, the work of the Jesuits greatly expanded globally. A period of unprecedented growth from 1914 to 1965 witnessed 10,000 Jesuits – 30 per cent of the Society of Jesus – engaged in education by the 1960s (Sauvé *et al.* 2001).

Since 1965, rapid change in the educational world, international decline in the number of Jesuits and new priorities within the Society, including a *preferential option for the poor* and emphasis on *education for justice*, have led to radical changes in Jesuit education. Though many Jesuit educational institutions have closed since the mid-1960s, new Jesuit ventures, not least in the field of informal education, have been opened. For those educational institutions remaining in Jesuit trusteeship, the formation of committed lay men and women prepared to carry forward Jesuit educational ideals is a major challenge for the twenty-first century.

See also: Catholic school/education; church; religious education; religious school; theology

Further reading

Duminuco, V. J. (ed.) (2000) *The Jesuit Ratio Studiorum: 400th Anniversary Perspectives*, New York: Fordham University Press.
Sauvé, J., Codina, G. and Escalera, J. (2001) 'Educación'. In C. E. O'Neill and J. M. Domínguez (eds) *Diccionario Histórico de la Compañía de Jesús*, 4 vols, Rome: Institutum Historicum Societatis Iesu; Madrid: Universidad Pontificia Comillas.

MAURICE WHITEHEAD

JOHN OF SALISBURY (*c*.1115–80)

John of Salisbury was a pupil of Peter Abelard in Paris from 1136–38 and then spent a further three years studying Latin literature and language at Chartres. He returned to Paris for further study until at least 1145, when he became clerk to Pope Eugene III. He returned to England in 1150 to act as clerk to Theobald, Archbishop of Canterbury, a position that required acting as emissary to the papal court. John of Salisbury personally knew the Englishman, Nicholas Brekespear, who became Pope Adrian IV (pope, 1154–59) and stayed with him in 1156. From this visit John secured a papal grant which enabled King Henry II (king, 1154–89) to conquer Ireland.

John was the first medieval writer to emphasise the importance of studying of history within philosophy and other branches of learning. His *Metalogicus* (in four volumes, 1159) is the earliest medieval work to show a thorough and first-hand acquaintance with all of Aristotle's work. In it, John argues in defence of grammar and logic as the foundations for learning. His *Policraticus* (1159), although a miscellany, attempts to outline what a statesman ought to learn. It also contains a satire upon scholastic practices of the times. John is now seen as an early forerunner of later humanism, seeking to reconcile Christian teachings with the best classical writings. John became secretary to Thomas à Becket when the latter became Archbishop of Canterbury in 1162, but, like Becket, was forced into exile until 1170, when they made an ill fated return to Canterbury. During the murder of the archbishop in Canterbury cathedral some of Becket's blood spattered on to John's clothing.

See also: Aristotle; grammar; scholar

STEVEN COWAN

JOWETT, BENJAMIN (1817–93)

Jowett, the English scholar, cleric and translator, was educated at Baliol College, Oxford, where he became a tutor in 1842. He was ordained deacon in 1842, priest in 1845 and was appointed Master of Balliol in 1870, holding the position until his death. He was famous for his personal attention to students, many of whom were to become senior figures in their professions and political life. Jowett was Regius professor of Greek (1855–93) and served a term as vice-chancellor of Oxford University (1882–86). He supported competitive examinations for the Indian civil service based on merit and was a contributor, alongside other notable Church of England intellectuals, to *Essays and Reviews* (1860), a collection of Broad Church statements. This created a furore and led to him being tried for heresy, of which he was acquitted. Jowett believed that the Bible expressed religious truth through metaphor and myth, rather

than through literal accounts. This liberal position allied him with other leading educators including Thomas Arnold, A. P. Stanley and F. D. Maurice, who argued that the revelations of modern natural science should be seen as the unfolding of God's divine plan. He was a major influence in the repeal of religious tests for university positions in 1871 and influenced the university extension movement. Whilst at Baliol he considerably expanded the buildings and range of departments. Another major contribution was his translations of writings by Plato, Aristotle and Thucydides.

See also: classical studies; university extension

STEVEN COWAN

JUNIOR SCHOOL

The British state junior school is not to be confused with the 'junior high school' (for an older age range of students extensively in the United States). In the British context, the junior years of schooling are normally recognised as lasting from ages 7–11. From the late nineteenth century, extensions to the period of compulsory schooling and increased understandings of child development brought demands for children's school experiences to contain distinctive, age-related phases. The principal distinction was between primary and secondary schooling, with age eleven as the normal age of transfer, but a further subdivision within elementary/primary schooling distinguished between the infant and junior stages. Infant education was taken to mean schooling for the under sevens and junior schooling for those aged 7–11.

Under the overall umbrella of primary education, distinct junior schools developed in some districts, very frequently adjacent to a feeder infant school. It is common for a state primary school under a single head teacher to cater for the full 5–11 age range, but some primaries nevertheless embody the infant and junior distinction in their organisational structure. Like other types of school in the

United Kingdom, junior schools may be either denominational or secular, and subject to, or independent from, local education authority control. A junior school is organised into year groups (known as years three to six in England) and the work of the school is focused on key stage two of the national curriculum (again in England). Upon reaching the age of eleven, junior school children proceed to a secondary school to continue their education. The currency of the term 'junior school' is quite different within the independent sector, where large fee-paying schools sometimes have a separate junior and senior 'school' under separate head teachers. The age ranges covered by such 'junior schools' in the private sector varies according to the pupils' ages covered by the parent school.

See also: elementary school; primary school/education

DAVID CROOK

K

KAY-SHUTTLEWORTH, SIR JAMES (1804–77)

Kay-Shuttleworth, the English educational administrator, studied medicine in Edinburgh, qualifying in 1827. From there he secured a post as secretary to the Board of Health in Manchester. As Dr James Kay – the suffix Shuttleworth was added upon marriage, later – his publication *Moral and Physical Condition of the Working Class in Manchester in 1832* (1833) brought him to national prominence after linking the city's inadequate schooling with the destitution and degradation of the poor. In 1835 he was appointed as an assistant Poor Law commissioner, working in East Anglia and London. His talents as an administrator and author of reports led to his appointment, in 1839, as the first secretary to the new committee of the Privy Council on Education, which had been established to administer the first government grants for schooling. He held this post for ten years, during which he developed the administrative framework for the future Department of Education and school inspection system. He worked unbearably long hours and retired through ill health in 1849. As a private venture, Kay-Shuttleworth established the first English teacher training college in Battersea, London, in 1839–40. This became a model for later colleges, recruiting local pupils as trainee teachers. Two important publications were *Public Education* (1853) and *Four Periods of Public Education* (1862). To the end, Kay-Shuttleworth retained his belief that the state should not unnecessarily supplant the parent in provision of schooling.

See also: teacher education/training

STEVEN COWAN

KEATE, JOHN (1773–1852)

Keate was a notable headmaster of Eton College, England, where he worked from 1797 to 1834. His background was somewhat typical, being the son of a senior cleric, attending Eton himself, studying at King's College, Cambridge, specialising in classics and becoming a cleric himself before rejoining Eton as a master. He was short in stature and an admirable scholar. Fellow masters of the previously lawless institution welcomed his harsh disciplinarian approach, including his frequent 'floggings'.

Keate's leadership helped Eton to re-establish itself as the leading elite private school for the sons of the gentry and aristocracy. His insistence upon self-discipline and instilling physical toughness into young men became a hallmark of later developments at schools such as Rugby, under the direction of Thomas Arnold. As a 'feeder' school for King's College, Keate's improvements at Eton were to have a positive effect upon student standards in Cambridge. Keate became a Canon of Windsor in 1820, indicating royal approval of his work. Many of his former pupils became leading authority figures in Britain and its empire. By the time of his death, Keate had become an almost legendary figure and a model for fictional renditions of archetypal headmasters.

See also: Arnold, Thomas; corporal punishment; public school

STEVEN COWAN

KERR, CLARK (1911–2003)

Kerr was an economist, academic in the field of industrial relations and the founding director of the Institute of Industrial Relations. He came to prominence when in 1949, at the height of McCarthyism, employees of the University of California–Berkeley were required to sign an oath of loyalty. Kerr supported colleagues who refused to sign and campaigned for their reinstatement. He gained popularity with the governing regents of the university, becoming the first chancellor of UC Berkeley in 1952 and first president from 1958 to 1967. As chancellor, he commenced a building and development programme that was to transform Berkeley into what Kerr termed a 'multiversity'. The changes included new landscaping, high-rise buildings housing centres for university schools and residences for students, a theatre and concert hall. Three further campuses were opened. Kerr's expansion plans were underpinned by egalitarian ideas about broadening access to higher education, which he expounded in *The Uses of the University* (1963). Another innovation was the involvement of students in university policy issues. Kerr became internationally prominent when the Free Speech Movement, centred upon the Berkeley campus, led to protests and arrests in 1964. Some thought he was too tolerant of student political demonstrations, others that he was too authoritarian. Following the election of Ronald Reagan as governor of California, the regents dismissed Clark in 1967, but he remained a public figure as a leading member of the Carnegie Commission on Higher Education, which influenced Congress to introduce the federal Pell Grant Program to support economically disadvantaged students.

See also: higher education; university

STEVEN COWAN

KINDERGARTEN

Kindergarten is a name used for various types of preschool or pre-compulsory education or childcare in many parts of the world. Developed by the German educationalist Friedrich Froebel in the mid-nineteenth century, the kindergarten was initially both a philosophy of education and a specific set of practices and materials for use in the education of young children. Although few twenty-first century institutions reflect Froebel's original philosophy or pedagogy, the continued use of the kindergarten name in some places is a testament to the importance of Froebel's nineteenth-century work and to that of his dedicated international followers.

Froebel's philosophy developed out of his own teaching and learning experiences and incorporated aspects of panentheism, natural philosophy, Romanticism, German idealism and nationalism, and is connected to the ideas of Johann Amos Comenius and Jean-Jacques Rousseau and Johann Pestalozzi. He believed that children were born with innate skills and interests, which would unfold over time, resulting in harmonious intellectual, spiritual and physical development. Like Rousseau and Pestalozzi, Froebel believed that this development happened in stages brought about through activity and experience. However, Froebel went further, asserting that child's play had both educational value and social and spiritual significance. He thought that interaction with symbolic materials, with nature and with other people would encourage and strengthen young children's development at different stages.

In 1837, Froebel opened his first educational institution for very young children in Bad Blankenburg, Germany, renaming it *kindergarten* (garden of children) three years later. Froebel's kindergarten focused on holistic development, eschewing traditional lessons in reading, writing, or arithmetic. Its three key elements were the gifts, occupations, and songs and games. The gifts were a set of simple, unadorned geometric solids (mostly wooden blocks) for exploratory and symbolic play. The occupations, tasks such as paper folding, weaving, parquetry, or clay work, were intended to meet children's need for focused activity and to channel their creative energies. Froebel wrote the songs and games to be used by mothers with their own infants and by specially trained female teachers, called kindergartners ('child-gardeners'), in educational institutions.

Froebel's kindergarten was radically different from the academic rote learning common in his day. From the time of the abortive revolution of 1848, political, educational and religious leaders were increasingly suspicious of the kindergarten, fearing it would promote social upheaval. In 1851, the Prussian Ministry of Education banned kindergartens from 1851 to 1860, an act which had knock-on effects in other German states.

Well educated, politically liberal middle- and upper-class women played a large part in expanding kindergarten education before, during and after the ban. Some of Froebel's students began kindergartens outside of Germany after emigrating as political refugees in 1848, but most influential of all was the Baroness Bertha von Marenholtz-Bülow (1810–93), who toured Europe as an emissary and exegete of the kindergarten. Marenholtz-Bülow's portrayal of the kindergarten as a means of liberating women through education attracted interest in many parts of the West in particular. By the end of the nineteenth century, her efforts and those of other kindergarten missionaries led to the formation of kindergartens and supporting organisations in places as diverse as Argentina, Australia, Belgium, England, India, Japan, Russia, the USA and Turkey.

In the twentieth century they expanded even further.

In general, local and national movements sought to promote kindergartens as independent, philanthropic, or state-sector institutions, to reform extant schooling along Froebelian lines and to professionalise the training and work of kindergartners. Their reasons for doing so and the strategies they employed varied with their political, social and cultural contexts and the forms of early education already in place. The transfer of the kindergarten to new contexts required the translation of Froebelian texts and the adaptation of the ideas and methods to meet local conditions. In many cases these processes left the Froebelian kindergarten utterly transformed. In the twentieth century, impetus for further change came from the fields of child guidance and child development, from early childhood educators such as Maria Montessori and Margaret McMillan, and from political and social changes which altered beliefs about childhood and about schooling in general. Many twenty-first-century kindergartens have little in common with Froebelian philosophy and methods, whilst institutions with pedagogical, philosophical, or historical connections to Froebel's kindergarten may be known by other names, such as preschool or nursery school.

See also: early childhood education; Froebel, Friedrich; nursery school

Further reading

Froebel, F. (1897) *Friedrich Froebel's Pedagogics of the Kindergarten*, trans. J. Jarvis, London: Edward Arnold.
Wollons, R. (ed.) (2000) *Kindergartens and Cultures: The Global Diffusion of an Idea*, New Haven CT: Yale University Press.

KRISTEN NAWROTZKI

KNOWLEDGE ECONOMY

A number of definitions and understandings of the term knowledge economy exist, many of which simply emphasise information and high technology. A broader definition includes recognition of knowledge as the key factor in production, diminishing the importance of capital, labour and natural resources.

The concept denotes a shift from the relatively low-skilled industrial economies of the twentieth century, based on the mass production of goods, to economies based on knowledge, creative industries and a profusion of jobs requiring highly educated workers. The generation, use and exploitation of knowledge are the predominant players in the creation of wealth. Education, therefore, has a key role.

The image of a knowledge economy has appeared in the work of many popular writers on economic and social trends, including Robert Reich (1991) and Peter Drucker (1993). The term came to prominence in the 1990s as a means of referring to the way in which high technology businesses, especially computer software and telecoms, as well as educational and research institutions, could contribute to a country's economy. Because it crystallised an important feature of the national interest in education, the theme began to form part of wider political discourse.

The idea that we are now living and working in economies that are increasingly knowledge-based has formed a key element driving forward educational policies across both industrialised and developing nations. This is closely linked with processes of globalisation, since in a global economy the prosperity of countries is seen to depend on the skills, knowledge and intellectual capital of individuals.

Education is seen to have a critical role both in terms of producing the highly skilled workers required and in enhancing national economic competitiveness, social cohesion and social justice through the development of human capital. It is through education that the knowledge and creativity necessary for innovation, expansion and growth are developed. In turn, policies reflect such priorities as raising standards, facilitating and widening access to higher education, upgrading skills, encouraging lifelong learning and creativity.

Global agencies including the World Bank, International Finance Corporation (IFC) and Organisation for Economic Co-operation and Development (OECD), as well as national governments, have stressed the importance of investing in education. They have argued that developed, developing and transition economies face significant new challenges in the global environment, affecting not only the shape and mode of operation, but also the purpose, of higher education systems. In a 2002 World Bank report, it is stated that:

> Knowledge accumulation and application has become one of the major factors in economic development and is increasingly at the core of a country's competitive advantage in the global economy ... Tertiary education is central to the creation of the intellectual capacity on which knowledge production and utilization depend and to the promotion of lifelong learning practices necessary to update one's knowledge and skills.
>
> (World Bank 2002: vii)

There are, however, two contested issues associated with the links between education and the development of knowledge economies. The first concerns the role of education and what is deemed to be 'useful' knowledge. The second concerns the emphasis placed in discourses of the knowledge economy upon the sufficiency of highly skilled jobs. Data from the United Kingdom and United States of America, for example, show a high degree of over-qualification among university leavers, suggesting that many are not able to find jobs commensurate with their skills and abilities (Brown and Lauder 2003).

The idea that individuals will earn what they are worth, as reflected in their credentials, is not supported by evidence, which points to increased disparities in the incomes of university graduates, including those based on gender and ethnicity. As Brown and Lauder

(2003) argue, the policies of educational expansion in developing countries, particularly at university level, enables knowledge industries to compete for highly skilled workers with lower wage costs. A further issue, therefore, relates to the creation of new inequalities within and between nations on a global scale. The future impact upon the global knowledge economy of rapidly developing economies such as China, India or Russia, and how universities and education policies develop in response, remains to be seen.

See also: credentials/credentialing; globalisation; lifelong learning; Organisation for Economic Co-operation and Development (OECD); qualifications; skills; World Bank

Further reading

Brown, P. and Lauder, H. (2003) *Globalisation and the Knowledge Economy: Some Observations on Recent Trends in Employment, Education and the Labour Market*, Working Paper 43, Cardiff: Cardiff University School of Social Sciences.

Drucker, P. F. (1993) *Post-Capitalist Society*, New York: Harper Business.

Reich, R. (1991) *The Work of Nations: Preparing Ourselves for 21st Century Capitalism*, New York: Knopf.

World Bank (2002) *Constructing Knowledge Societies: New Challenges for Tertiary Education*, Washington DC: World Bank.

CLAIRE SMETHERHAM

KNOX, JOHN (1505–72)

Knox, the Scottish Protestant reformer, was self-educated, acquiring competence in Latin and French with some elements of Hebrew and Greek. He was ordained as a Catholic priest but became a follower of the Scottish schoolmaster George Wishart, who was burned alive in 1546 for preaching the doctrines of Reformation. Knox suffered imprisonment on a galley, after which he spent time in Switzerland and met John Calvin. He spent periods preaching in Scotland, England and Switzerland again, building a reputation as the leading Protestant radical. Knox instigated and led a series of riots and ransackings

of major Catholic churches in Scotland in 1559 and, in the following year, became the leading figure of the General Assembly of the Kirk. This assembly drew up the *Book of Discipline*, which contained a scheme for an education system proposing: universal elementary schooling from ages 5–8, teaching literacy and the catechism; grammar schooling for 8–12-year-olds; high schools for 12–16-year-olds to teach Greek, Latin, rhetoric and logic; a three-year general university arts course for 16–19-year-olds; and a five-year medicine, law or divinity course leading to a doctorate. No distinction was to be made between rich or poor, with ability and merit being the factor determining progress through the levels. Parliament rejected the scheme, but the Presbyterians ensured it remained the blueprint for all later developments. Knox projected the idea of a national system that was graded, compulsory and democratic, based upon merit and entitlement, supported by state bursaries.

See also: church

STEVEN COWAN

KOHLBERG, LAWRENCE (1927–87)

An advocate of moral education, Kohlberg gained a doctorate from Chicago in 1958 for a study on developmental changes in children's moral thinking. This work became famous even before publication because it included an evaluation of children's responses to a fictional dilemma of a poor man stealing expensive medicines for his terminally ill wife. Kohlberg taught at Yale, Chicago and Harvard, where he established the Center for Moral Education. His six stages of moral development closely resembled the structure of Piaget's thinking, with its emphasis upon cognitive development and its description of a chronological series of stages. Kohlberg believed that moral development – the ability to reason using certain forms of thinking in order to arrive at judgements – was directly related to cognitive development. Much of the research work at Harvard over twenty years was concerned with identifying whether there are universal stages in moral development. He developed the *Moral Discussion Approach* and *Just Community Approach* to deal with moral issues in schools. The idea was to induce disequilibria through discussion to create the necessary conditions for cognitive development. The Just Community Approach set out to extend student responsibility for solving problems through creating forms of direct, participatory democracy. For Kohlberg, the aim was to foster universal principles of justice rather than transmitting the values of one's own culture or sub-culture. Two major works were *The Philosophy of Moral Development* (1981) and *The Psychology of Moral Development* (1984).

See also: cognition; moral education

STEVEN COWAN

L

LANCASTER, JOSEPH (1778–1838)

Lancaster was born in Southwark, England, into a Quaker family. He was to formulate and develop – simultaneously with Andrew Bell, of the Church of England's National Society – the 'monitorial system' of schooling, outlined in *Improvements in Education* (1803). Lancaster became a major figure in the history of schooling, not only in Britain, but also in the British colonies, where the monitorial system was popular, and in the United States of America, where he spent most of his last twenty years. He was known for his opposition to denominational teaching and physical punishment, but in 1814 an inquiry into the abuse of boys precipitated his resignation from the Nonconformist British and Foreign School Society (BFSS), which he had founded. The first BFSS school had been established at Borough Road, London, in 1805. By the time he arrived in America, the monitorial system was widely used, having become compulsory in Pennsylvania in 1818.

Lancaster pioneered the development of specific learning materials for the teaching of reading and arithmetic. He began a movement for training and raising the status of teachers, and planned school trips for his pupils as part of their general education. He secured broad financial patronage across the religious and social class spectrum of the British establishment and generated support for educating the poor. Lancaster believed that reading and writing should be taught together and required his teachers to keep records of student progress.

See also: monitor; monitorial system; pedagogy; religious school

STEVEN COWAN

LANE, HOMER (1875–1925)

Lane, the American-born educationist, began teaching manual skills in Massachusetts, before establishing a self-governing youth club in Detroit. He became superintendent of a home for difficult and delinquent youths from 1912–13. He was then invited to travel to Dorset, England in order to become the superintendent of the 'Little Commonwealth', where he worked between 1913 and 1918. This was a home for boys and girls, many of whom were offenders, up to late adolescence. Lane immediately introduced ideas about self-regulation and management that he had developed in the United States, almost a reverse of control and discipline approaches that were then commonplace.

At the Little Commonwealth, Lane introduced the use of group therapy, emphasising shared responsibility between residents. His approach stressed the importance of freedom, self-government, trust and mutual respect, but his use of psychoanalytical approaches proved controversial. Lane believed that children should be allowed to grow through exploring things that interested them and that

343

the teacher's role was to support the child's self-expression. The Little Commonwealth was forced to close after two female residents alleged sexual impropriety on the part of Lane. His practices presented a challenge to existing approaches towards education of offenders, and he exerted a direct influence upon later progressive educators such as James Simpson and A. S. Neill, especially through his book *Talks to Parents and Teachers* (1928).

See also: delinquency; progressive education; youth club/work

STEVEN COWAN

LATIN AMERICA

The countries of Latin America share some historical, economic and cultural motifs, and their educational systems – amid their individual differences – reflect these social processes and their long trajectories of change.

Historically, Latin America after about 1500 was colonised by the kingdoms of Spain and Portugal, although almost all these new colonies in the New World became independent in the early nineteenth century. In religion, a strong Catholic tradition was established in the colonial period and remains culturally very visible despite some current Protestant missionary movements. In politics, the secular motif of republicanism – notably from France – was influential for much of the nineteenth- and early twentieth centuries. After World War II, the political and economic influence of the United States of America became strong.

Economically, there has been some recovery from British economic domination in the nineteenth century: a number of countries such as Brazil, Chile, and Mexico have seen considerable industrial development and are now, like Argentina, trying to develop a position within the world 'knowledge economy'. However, economic differences between and within countries are marked:

socio-economic stratification is sharp, with the current exception of Cuba.

Politically, the Latin American countries as a group might be termed dramatic; there has been a pattern of oscillation between attempts at government through democratic elections, military dictatorships, coups d'état, and violent resistance movements to governmental power in both the countryside and urban areas. This is a paradox, as the independence movements at the beginning of the nineteenth century had little of the bitterness of the anti-colonial wars against the European powers in the twentieth. Radical solutions to domination by small and often corrupt elites have, however, been tried, most notably in Cuba and Nicaragua. At the moment, there are interesting political mixtures emerging – of nationalist-populist movements with neo-liberal policies – as well as a continuous sotto voce neo-Marxist discourse among intellectuals. In practical terms, the neo-populist motif takes easy shape through complaint about the role of the USA in the region – a theme which is visible in the politics of Argentina with President Néstor Kirchner; Brazil, with Luiz Inácio Lula da Silva; Chile, with Michelle Bachelet; Bolivia's Evo Morales; and with Hugo Chávez in Venezuela, who is currently the most controversial populist president.

Culturally, Latin America has been termed (by Carlos Fuentes) 'an immensely rich civilization, plural and cosmic' (Gómez-Buendía 2001). The cultural mix is complex: memories and large populations descended from the indigenous Aztec, Inca and Mayan civilisations, the Iberian migrations (including diasporic Jews) from the sixteenth century onwards, the subsequent African slave trade which markedly affected Brazil, and the major migrations of the nineteenth century from Germany and Italy for example, as well as the newer migrations from the Middle East, confirm most of Latin America as societies of migration. But these are societies of migration unified by memories and the languages of Spain and Portugal, rather than say Quechua or Italian.

In education, the most striking initial characteristic of the area is the echoes of this complex history. The policies and practices of education were influenced initially by the Catholic Church and Iberian administrative traditions, then French and – from around the mid-twentieth century – by the United States. The theme of 'dependency' and cultural imperialism are in the discourse of Latin American intellectuals before the themes penetrate educational discussion in the Northern hemisphere, and for good reason: the ideas of dependency and cultural imperialism reflect the Latin American experience.

In colonial times, the Church and the Spanish and Portuguese crowns used education as a mechanism of political, economic, and social control. Different Catholic orders, such as Augustinians, Dominicans and Jesuits, taught the indigenous population with an emphasis on their conversion to Christianity. Such 'secondary education' as was provided – scholastic in method, emphasising memorisation and 'reasoning', and with little science – was aimed at the formation of a ruling elite (i.e. administrators, priests, judges, magistrates and teachers).

The colonial universities (established in the Spanish-speaking countries as early as the sixteenth century) reflected this stance. The first university was established in Santo Domingo, in 1538, by the Dominicans, with the imprimatur of the Holy See and the official blessing of the crown. Other universities established later in Mexico, Peru, and Guatemala had as their major purpose the training of a ruling professional class for the Church and the state. In contrast, the Portuguese never exported their university system to the new colony. Brazilian colonial education remained under Jesuit control for three centuries. The first higher education institutions were created only in the nineteenth century when the Portuguese kingdom moved its locus of power to Brazil.

However, the influence of Spain and Portugal on ideas, and on ideas about education, began to weaken, affected partly by the Enlightenment and partly by the ferment of philosophical ideas in Europe in the eighteenth century. Thus, by the time of nineteenth-century efforts at educational reform, France was the dominant source of intellectual and cultural inspiration in much of Latin America: French educational institutions and practices were imported and adopted. For example, the school curriculum was – and still is – encyclopedic; the teaching of sciences was implemented under the influence of French positivism; Normal Schools, located at the secondary level for the training of teachers, followed the French model and are only now being phased out; and at the higher education level the Napoleonic model of the Université de France and the Grandes Écoles was copied or adapted, as was the administration and management of the educational systems themselves which were, until recently, heavily centralised.

From the 1920s, American influence on education became important, especially in Brazil through John Dewey and the New School movement of the Pioneers of Education, led by Anísio Teixeira and Fernando de Azevedo. However, this influence was less strong in the Spanish speaking-countries where an anti-American movement was already underway. This movement, called *arielism*, appeared first in Uruguay, with José Rodo who warned against 'US imperialism'. Nevertheless, from the 1950s to the 1970s, the American impact on educational policies and reforms became considerable. Advice and technical assistance were on offer. 'Development' was made available, not least for Cold War reasons, for all levels of education. Fellowship programmes and Latin American scholarships (both ways) were built up through US foundations and the efforts of Latin American government agencies and foundations as well. A paradoxical consequence was that the earlier academic resistance was updated, as it were, not least through new critiques via Marxist discourse and the creation of dependency theory and a search for a 'critical pedagogy', a phrase linked in the Latin American context with the names of Paolo Freire and Ivan Illich.

Thus, in the contemporary period, the struggle, in intellectual (and political) terms, has been over the direction of educational reforms.

In practical and policy (and political) terms, the struggle has been won by a range of regional and international agencies. Since the 1990s, major and numerous educational reform programmes have been undertaken with the support of international agencies such as the World Bank, the Inter-American Development Bank and the Organisation of American States. The time frame was remarkably tight: 1985 in Ecuador and Uruguay, 1993 in Argentina and Mexico; and 1994 in Bolivia and Colombia. Similarly, national systems of educational assessment were implemented in a very close time frame: Chile in 1988, Brazil in 1990, Mexico and Paraguay in 1992, Argentina, Uruguay and Bolivia in 1994, and Peru in 1996.

There has been a double rationale for these reforms: economic globalisation and knowledge economies as an imperative (and thus the reform of education in certain ways); and the elimination of social and economic inequalities. Thus, with very little variation, the educational reforms have focused on making education universally available so that – the public discourse emphasises – poverty can be reduced and groups from different socio-economic backgrounds and different ethnicities can take up their share in 'the right to education'.

However, in addition to this motif, the reforms have emphasised improvements in assessment, in teacher competencies, and the introduction of information and communications technology in schools. 'Competencies' has become a major word in the discussion about and practices of curriculum reform. Great emphasis has also been placed on 'management and leadership'. In other words, the educational discourse (and some of the practice) is like that of neo-liberal states in the Northern hemisphere. The reform frame for education has become part of the current consensus among several of the international agencies about what counts as a 'good education' and how educational systems can become well run and 'fit for purpose'.

Whether these 'solutions' will work in Latin America will take time to assess. Certainly the routine crises over both equity and quality in the Latin American educational systems are dramatic enough and deeply rooted: lack of schools, poor salaries for teachers, poor school attendance, and marked differences in quality between private and state-financed schools. Rates of dropout and grade-repetition remain high. There are major differences between poor and rich sectors in cities, in urban and rural environments, and between regions within particular countries. Even now, although across Latin America almost 100 per cent of children aged 7–10 are in schools, many go through school and leave school without learning how to write and read properly; most 15–17-year-olds are not in secondary school (in Argentina, for example, 37 per cent do not reach secondary education); one half of secondary school pupils are aged eighteen or over; and only 9 per cent of the age cohort enrol in higher education.

Nevertheless, it is clear that major efforts are being made in many Latin American countries to turn teaching into an all-graduate profession; perhaps more systematic measures of 'quality' in education systems – however crude the measures – may help to highlight problems; many of the universities of Latin America are newly confident. They are building fresh links with Spanish (and Portuguese-speaking) areas, sustaining their traditional ties with France and some English-speaking countries; and they are strengthening their research links with the European Union. There is a new alertness both to the need to provide good basic education and to change the quality of higher education rapidly.

It is probably correct to suggest that the political agenda for education, in many Latin American countries, has snapped into focus.

Perhaps there are now grounds for careful optimism that the educational systems of Latin American are beginning to develop their own trajectories.

See also: Brazil

Further reading

Braslavsky, C. (2000) *The Secondary Education Curriculum in Latin America: New Tendencies and Changes*, Geneva: International Bureau of Education.

Castro, C. de Moura (2000) *Myth, Reality and Reform: Higher Education Policy in Latin America*, Baltimore MD: Johns Hopkins University Press.

Cowen, R. (ed.) (2002) *Comparative Education*, 38(4), special issue on 'Latin America and educational transfer'.

Freire, P. and Faundez, A. (1985) *Por Uma Pedagogia da Pergunta*, 3rd edn, São Paulo: Paz e Terra.

Gómez–Buendía H. (2001) *Education in Latin America and the Caribbean: An Agenda for the Coming Century*, Bogotá: UNDP.

Torres, C. A. and Puiggrós, A. (eds) (1997) *Latin American Education: Comparative Perspectives*, Boulder CO: Westview Press.

MARIA DE FIGUEIREDO-COWEN AND
ROBERT COWEN

LAW

Law, as it relates to education, is both an academic/curricular course of study and a key element in the structure by which education is provided. As to the academic and curricular aspect, law's role is most visible and substantial in the undergraduate and graduate courses designed to equip students to qualify for the practice of law. In the United States, legal education for law practice is exclusively a graduate/professional programme. In the United Kingdom and many other countries, it is traditionally an undergraduate programme with a bridge period between those studies and the practice of law, although there has been movement in some countries toward the US graduate model. Some students, but a small minority, study law with the intention of becoming scholars and teachers. Others are attracted to legal education because of a belief that the training or the credential will enhance careers in business, medicine or other fields.

Since the UK and USA have common-law legal systems, the subject matter coverage of their legal education programmes is similar. The curricula in countries with a civil law system give more emphasis to statutes or codes. In the UK, the national requirements are more formalised than in the USA and they focus on seven foundation subjects, including contracts, torts (personal injury law), criminal law, equity and the law of trusts, the law of the European Union, property (or land) law and public law (constitutional and administrative law). Students also are expected to have expertise in legal research skills, the English legal system and another area of legal study. In the USA, individual law schools determine their curricula under broad accreditation guidelines, but virtually all law schools offer as required first-year courses contracts, torts, property, constitutional law, civil procedure, criminal law and procedure, legal method, and legal research and writing. During the two additional years of full-time legal study in the USA, a wide variety of optional courses, seminars and clinical programmes are offered.

Law courses also find their way into curricula from upper-secondary school through further education in the UK and community colleges and universities in the USA. Typically, these are independent courses rather than formal majors or specialisations. Sometimes they are specifically focused, as in business law courses, and sometimes they are much broader in their orientation and coverage. A relatively longstanding and substantial effort in both the UK and the USA involves the introduction of law-related education in elementary and secondary schools. Typically, this involves a curriculum, for teaching law-related subjects, professional development activities to enable teachers to effectively deliver the curriculum, and a series of conferences and activities involving lawyers and judges. A variant on that theme is the 'street law' programme begun in the USA at Georgetown University Law School in 1972 and now taught in more than thirty countries, including Northern Ireland. The mission is 'To provide practical, participatory education about law, democracy and human rights', mainly to students in secondary schools, juvenile justice institutions, prisons or community settings.

Law is relevant to education in another, quite different manner. In a variety of ways, law provides for the substance, structure and operation of schools, especially those denominated as public or state schools. In countries such as the USA with written constitutions, the obligation of government to provide public schools is usually explicit. In the USA, that is universally true at the state level, and education is generally regarded as a state, rather than national, function. Both the federal constitution and state constitutions afford students with educational rights – many of them enforceable through the courts – that can override statutory or regulatory provisions. In countries such as the UK without written constitutions, education is neither a constitutional obligation nor right, but international treaties or conventions may play a related role. In most countries, whether or not they have a written constitution, there are elaborate statutes, regulations and policies providing for or governing the provision of education. In the USA especially, a concern is periodically expressed that education has become too 'legalised'. On the other hand, during the past five decades legal claims on behalf of students to courts and administrative agencies have provided major impetus for enhancing both educational access and equity. In the UK and most other countries, educational claims, especially those of an institutional reform nature, are much less frequently pursued through the courts or quasi-judicial agencies, if they are pursued at all. In those countries, the adequacy of educational programmes for disabled /handicapped students is usually the issue most frequently litigated. Scholars and others regularly debate which approach – litigation or legislation/policy formulation – is more likely to lead to the provision of high-quality education for all of a nation's children.

See also: curriculum; professional education; subjects

Further reading

Glenn, H. P. (2000) *Legal Traditions of the World*, Oxford: Oxford University Press.

Moliterno, J. E. and Lederer, F. I. (1991) *An Introduction to Law, Law Study, and the Lawyer's Role*, Durham NC: Carolina Academic Press.

Yudof, M. G., Kirp, D., Levin, B. and Moran, R. (2002) *Educational Policy and the Law*, 4th edn, Belmont CA: Thomson Wadsworth.

PAUL TRACTENBERG

LEARNING

Although learning is something we all know about and practise every day, it is, at the same time, a very complex matter. Many definitions have been given, one of the most broad and open being that 'learning is any process that in living organisms leads to permanent capacity change and which is not solely due to biological maturation or aging' (Illeris 2007).

Traditionally, learning psychology has dealt with learning as an internal process of acquisition, but since the 1980s other approaches have suggested that it is rather a social process, taking place as an interaction between people. Thus, a contemporary understanding would be that any learning comprises both an external social process of interaction and an internal process of elaboration and acquisition of the impulses that are created in the interaction. These two processes are usually taking place at the same time, but in the case of reflection the elaboration and acquisition process can be taken up without any new interaction.

Further, both psychological and neurological studies imply that the acquisition process always includes two fundamentally different sides: a content side, dealing with the knowledge, skills, understandings, attitudes or whatever the learning is about, and an incentive side, dealing with the emotions, motivations and volition that raise the necessary mental energy for the process.

In this way, it is a basic condition of learning that it has three dimensions: the content dimension, the incentive dimension and the interaction dimension, and no learning can be fully understood or dealt with without considering these three dimensions.

When something is learned it becomes part of the learner's capacity, which, under certain conditions, can be recalled or reactivated. This implies that it is, somehow, maintained in the brain and nervous system. Recent research indicates that this maintenance has the character of traces or 'engrams' that lead the electro-chemical circuits in the brain to follow routes that have already been used. In psychology, the term 'mental schemes' is used, and four different kinds of schemes define four different learning types:

- *cumulative* (or mechanical) learning, by which new mental schemes are founded, which can be reactivated or 'remembered' only in situations which are subjectively parallel to the learning situation;
- *assimilative* (or additive) learning, by which new elements are added to already existing schemes. This is the type of learning we usually practise, and the outcome can be reactivated in situations when we are oriented to the content area in question;
- *accommodative* (or transcending) learning, by which (parts of) schemes are broken down and reconstructed. This happens when a motivated learner is confronted with impulses which do not fit into existing schemes, and such learning can be reactivated in all relevant situations;
- *transformative* (or expanding) learning, which implies that several schemes are reconstructed simultaneously and,

thereby, implies a change in the organisation of the self or the identity.

Good learning, according to this typology, implies that the learner is able to 'choose' and 'use' the type of learning which is most appropriate to the particular content and situation.

In connection with learning it is also important to be aware that there are many situations in which possible, demanded or intended learning does not occur or only happens in a restricted or distorted way. Such situations may just be a case of misunderstanding, lack of concentration, bad or insufficient communication or the like. But very often it will be a case of defence or resistance.

Learning defence may be of a personal nature, for example defending the individual against insights that, for some reason, are personally disagreeable or threatening. But in modern society wider defences are created to protect individuals against the enormous amount of information and influences and constant requests of changes in understandings and attitudes.

Resistance to learning is activated in response to situations and influences which the individual finds unacceptable, and can provide a very strong incentive to learn something different from that which was expected. Very often our strongest and most remarkable learning has its roots in some sort of resistance.

Finally, it shall be mentioned that a lot of general conditions influence our learning. These include: internal conditions, such as personal dispositions, age and gender; external conditions, including the learning spaces of school, the workplace and everyday life; the sort of society and subculture we belong to.

See also: informal/nonformal learning; learning career; learning community; learning styles

Further reading

Illeris, K. (2007) *How We Learn: An Introduction to Learning and Non-Learning in School and Beyond*, London: Routledge.

Jarvis, P. (2006) *Towards a Comprehensive Theory of Human Learning*, London: Routledge.

Wenger, E. (1998) *Communities of Practice: Learning, Meaning, and Identity*, New York: Cambridge University Press

KNUD ILLERIS

LEARNING CAREER

Learning career is a way of understanding the ways in which a person's relationship with, and perceptions of, learning change over time. There is general agreement that the concept has its origins in the symbolic interactionism of the Chicago School in the 1930s. In this context, 'career' simply means the partly unpredictable ways in which a person's life develops over time. The focus on learning career simply centres concerns on learning, as opposed, say, to studying a person's driving career. As Goodlad (2007) points out, the concept developed at a time of growing individualism in the United Kingdom and other Western countries.

This rise of individualism created difficulties for those concerned to recognise the significance of individual agency by learners. Much of the policy rhetoric ignored structural inequalities in relation to learning and education. The concept of learning career was an attempt to retain a genuinely individual perspective, whilst incorporating issues of social structure.

For Bloomer and Hodkinson (2000), in a study of learning within 14–19 education, the concept of learning career had four main constituent parts. They were:

(i) that individual students agentically constructed their own learning through interactions with the teaching and college-based experiences they encountered on their courses;

(ii) that this 'studentship' had a significant longitudinal dimension, so a person's approaches to learning developed and changed over time, often in ways that were non-linear and only partly unpredictable;

(iii) that all people develop a battery of dispositions (what Bourdieu termed 'habitus') which are embodied and largely tacit, and which orientate them to lived experiences and challenges. These dispositions are often enduring, but can and do change. This use of habitus has the advantage of integrating structural issues with agency in the development of a person's dispositions;

(iv) that a student's dispositions towards a college course are directly influenced by their life and experiences outside college, as well as within it.

The term 'learning career' was intended to capture all of this. Such learning careers are a complex combination of continuity and change.

Learning careers alert us to the fact that a student's engagement with learning is limited by their current dispositions. These dispositions enable some learning, but constrain or even prevent other learning. These dispositions have their origins in that person's prior life, including their (possibly changing) social position. However, a person's dispositions do not determine their learning. There is always a range of possibilities, which are influenced by many factors other than the starting dispositions. Also, dispositions can and do change over time, sometimes as a direct influence of education. For Bloomer and Hodkinson learning careers should always be understood in relation to these wider issues (Bloomer and Hodkinson 2002).

As the concept of learning career has become more popular, it has been criticised. For example, Bloomer and Hodkinson's work has seen as being too individualistic, despite their claim to be equally concerned with social structure. A further problem with the work on learning careers is that different strands of the work remain largely unrelated. Thus, work by Pollard and Filer (1999), which looks at the pupil careers of primary school children, is rarely considered by the literatures concerned with further or adult education. Another weakness is that much of the learning careers literature is only concerned with education and formal learning. Everyday informal learning is often excluded, and it is unclear how the concept would work in this wider context.

The most significant judgement about the value of the concept depends upon its ability to deal with structure as well as agency. Without the structural dimension, the concept of learning career simply reinforces the dominant obsession with individualism in education. If the structural dimension is successfully incorporated, then learning career can provide a necessary counter-narrative (Goodlad 2007).

See also: habitus; informal/nonformal learning; learning; student

Further reading

Bloomer, M. and Hodkinson, P. (2000) 'Learning careers: continuity and change in young people's dispositions to learning', *British Educational Research Journal*, 26(5): 583–98.
——(2002) 'Learning careers and cultural capital: adding a social and longitudinal dimension to our understanding of learning'. In R. Nata (ed.) *Progress in Education*, vol. 5, Hauppauge NY: Nova Science.
Goodlad, C. (2007) 'The rise and rise of learning careers: a Foucaldian genealogy', *Research in Post-Compulsory Education*, 12(1): 107–20.
Pollard, A. and Filer, A. (1999) *The Social World of Pupil Career*, London: Cassell.

PHIL HODKINSON

LEARNING COMMUNITY

In educational contexts, we can in general most usefully focus on the notion of learning communities as being desirable attributes of two specific groups, first, learners, and second, their teachers. Within such an entity as a learning community, we can discern the fact that peers engage in collaborative learning, with specific goals in mind. Rather than tackling problems – of learning or of teaching – in an insular way, individuals work together, pooling their insights, usually

through a discursive process, to arrive at agreed solutions to problems. In this model of learning there is, then, no single source of knowledge (or of power); advances in knowledge and the refinement of interpretations of knowledge take place as the result of collective, supportive, endeavour. Formal or informal peer mentoring may often be seen to be playing a part in such a learning environment.

A further important perspective on the learning community would strongly acknowledge that sometimes whole organisations – a school, for example – might legitimately be described as such. In these kinds of settings, learners, teachers, managers and administrators are all working to one common purpose (e.g. learner achievement or the prestige of the institution) in a collaborative, democratic way. Structures such as 'school councils', made up of elected learners and key staff, may also play a formal part in maintaining such learning communities. Some observers would go so far as to say that an educational institution displaying the above features probably merits being described as a 'learning organisation'.

In classroom settings, one of the classic manifestations of the learning community is the small task group organised by many teachers to work on set questions. A group of, say, five or six individual pupils or students are given a task (or tasks) to complete over a certain period of time. Each member of the group must contribute to the process of tackling what has been set; on occasion there will be an allocation of specific roles within the group, e.g. 'chair', 'timekeeper', 'recorder', etc. In certain curricular contexts, the formal assessment and accreditation of the work accomplished in such settings will be possible.

Groups of teachers, typically but not invariably organising themselves along subject-specific lines, may also function as learning communities (or in some analyses, simply as communities of practice). Changes in the content and/or structure of a curriculum can often be responded to much more efficiently

351

and constructively by a group of professionals allocating time to discussing the implications of such changes. The dissemination of good pedagogic practice provides another fairly commonly observed example of how groups of teachers may act as learning communities. In a number of UK and US colleges this activity has been enhanced by the establishment and resourcing of 'learning and teaching forums'.

It is crucial to stress that a true learning community cannot be one in which the sole purpose of a group of individuals lies in its existence to deal with specific problems in a reactive way. Learning communities are as much about a frame of mind, a set of attitudes and an ethos as they are about problem-solving. The willingness of group members to act in collegial ways to support each other, and their enthusiasm with regard to proactively seeking out new challenges (and perhaps anticipating how best to respond to these) are both also key features of an effective learning community.

One of the most highly developed variants of the learning community is the Action Learning Set, a highly 'managed' group of co-practitioners engaged in action learning within clear guidelines relating to such matters as frequency and duration of meetings, group membership, confidentiality of proceedings, etc. The distinctive features of such sets have been outlined particularly helpfully by McGill and Beaty (2001).

In recent times, increasing attention has been paid to the use of Virtual Learning Environments (VLEs) to facilitate online learning communities. Such VLEs are made possible by the use of interactive computer platforms including 'Blackboard', and are of course of special value where members of a learner group find it hard to meet for face-to-face interaction. Students enrolled on a distance learning programme, based perhaps in a number of different countries, could enjoy a far greater sense of community than might be possible using more traditional methods of communicating with tutors and peers.

It would be possible to invoke a fairly wide range of associated concepts and developments to further illuminate the notion of 'learning community'. The increasing trend towards 'inter-agency working', where, for example, educators are working more closely with social work teams to monitor the well-being and progress of individual children, would almost certainly provide us with examples of collaborative learning and action not all that dissimilar from those described above. The perspectives of writers such as Michael Young (on 'connectivity', for instance, 1993) or Michael Apple (on 'democratic professionalism', in Sachs 2001) are of great interest and value in this regard.

See also: collaborative/cooperative learning; learning; teaching/teaching methods; virtual learning

Further reading

Cullingford, C. (2006) *Mentoring in Education: An International Perspective*, Aldershot: Ashgate.

Jaques, D. (2000) *Learning in Groups*, London: Kogan Page.

McGill, I. and Beaty, L. (2001) *Action Learning: A Guide for Professional, Management and Educational Development*, London: Kogan Page

Sachs, J. (2001) 'Teacher professional identity: competing discourses, competing outcomes', *Journal of Educational Policy*, 16(2): 149–61.

Wenger, R. (1998) *Communities of Practice: Learning, Meaning and Identity*, Cambridge: Cambridge University Press.

Young, M. (1993) *Towards Connectivity: An Interim Approach to Unifying the Post-16 Curriculum*, London: Institute of Education.

BRYAN CUNNINGHAM

LEARNING CURVE

The learning curve refers to the rate of a person's progress in gaining new skills or knowledge. The term 'steep learning curve' describes the rapid progress of an individual learner or, conversely, it is also applied to a task that is perceived to be especially difficult. The latter is often seen to be a misuse of the term, given that a steep curve implies that a lot is being learnt.

Although it has entered into popular usage, it was developed in the field of cognitive psychology. The German psychologist Hermann Ebbinghaus (1850–1909) is credited with describing the term. He carried out a number of experiments in memorisation and found that adding to the amount of information to be learned increased the amount of time needed to be able to recall a list of items; repetition and association improved the ability to memorise. He also developed the notion of a 'forgetting curve', which held that one forgets information rapidly but that the rate of forgetting gradually levels out over time. In the 1930 the aircraft industry also introduced the term into engineering. It was able to plot a graph whereby increasing the number of units produced resulted in a cheaper and more efficient unit cost. Today, numerous educational businesses, media and consultancies use the term, given its association with rapid educational improvement.

See also: learning; progression

TOM WOODIN

LEARNING DISABILITIES/DIFFICULTIES

The term learning disabilities has become widely used since the last quarter of the twentieth century, but it is mainly a British term. It co-exists with 'learning difficulties'. In some situations, particularly those involving professionals such as psychologists, medical practitioners and teachers, the qualifiers 'mild', 'moderate' and 'severe' may precede both terms. Professionals use these terms to refer to an individual's intellectual impairment. In general, 'learning difficulties' is used in the context of education and 'learning disabilities' in social and health care settings, but either term may be used in both contexts.

The terms 'specific learning disabilities' and 'specific learning difficulties' refer to a difficulty experienced in a particular area, such as literacy or language processing (often referred to as dyslexia) rather than implying a broad intellectual impairment.

The term 'learning disabilities' has emerged from a long history in which different labels have been introduced and then supplanted by others, reflecting contemporary interests and discourses. In Britain, the Idiots Act of 1886 and a royal commission, set up in the same year, introduced a clearly differentiated set of categories including, in ascending order based on perceptions about intellectual functioning at the time, 'idiot', 'imbecile' and 'high-grade defectives' or 'feeble-minded children' (Armstrong 2003). The label 'mentally handicapped' was introduced in the 1940s: adults and children identified as having a mental handicap were often placed in long-stay hospitals and institutions where the emphasis was on care rather than education. Since the 1970s children can no longer be categorised as ineducable and, under the framework of special educational needs, 'students with learning difficulties' replaced such terms as 'remedial' and 'educationally subnormal'. Similarly, 'learning difficulties' became the preferred term for health professionals.

'Learning disabilities' is not automatically translatable or meaningful across all national contexts. Unlike concepts such as deafness, blindness and physical impairments, the category of learning disability is not recognised in some cultures (Safford and Safford 1996). Those concerned with issues of self-determination and empowerment contest the classification 'people with learning disabilities': it is seen as a label that imposes a homogenising and deficit-driven identity on individuals and groups. In general, therefore, the term 'learning difficulties' is preferred.

See also: blind, teaching of; dyslexia; inclusive education; special education/special educational needs/special needs

Further reading

Armstrong, D. (2003) *Experiences of Special Education: Re-evaluating Policy and Practice through Life Stories*, London: RoutledgeFalmer.
Department for Education and Science (1978) *Special Educational Needs: Report of the Committee*

of Inquiry into the Education of Handicapped Children and Young People (Warnock Report), London: HMSO.

Race, D. G. (ed.) (2002) *Learning Disability: A Social Approach*, London: Routledge.

Safford, P. L. and Safford, E. J. (1996) *A History of Childhood and Disability*, New York: Teachers College Press.

FELICITY ARMSTRONG

LEARNING SOCIETY

The essential characteristics of a learning society are twofold. First, its social institutions acknowledge that learning takes place across the full range of social settings. It occurs in families, workplaces, informal associations and other community contexts; learning is not confined to formal educational organisations, such as schools, colleges and universities. Second, learning opportunities are organised so that the citizens of a learning society are able to access them throughout the life-course, not simply in childhood and early adulthood, during which participation in compulsory education and other formal provision has usually been concentrated. Individuals are given the opportunity to continue to develop their capacities from birth right through to old age, as what John Field (2000) has called 'permanently learning subjects'.

The creation of a learning society has been widely promoted as a goal of education policy, at least since the 1960s. International organisations, such as UNESCO, the OECD and the EC, have been strong advocates. National governments have also espoused the learning society as a key policy aim. However, creating a learning society has been advocated for a wide diversity of reasons. Moreover, there have been significant differences in the institutional arrangements which have been envisaged as the means to achieve the necessary features of the learning society.

Not surprisingly, therefore, many commentators have emphasised that the learning society is a *contested* concept. Beyond the essential principles of lifelong learning across social life as a whole, there are divergent accounts of what exactly it constitutes. At least partly in consequence, it is difficult to identify concrete developments in educational provision that fulfil even its basic requirements. The learning society remains, therefore, essentially *normative*. There is a sharp disjuncture between, on the one hand, blueprints of the learning opportunities which ought to be in place to achieve a learning society and the realities of existing social institutions and practices, on the other.

Although the concept of the learning society has important antecedents in the nineteenth and early twentieth centuries, its emergence in contemporary policy debates can be traced to deliberations about the future of educational provision organised under the auspices of international organisations such as UNESCO and the OECD during the 1960s and 1970s. The focus of concern here was the inability of conventional educational systems to respond effectively to what were seen to be the challenges of contemporary economic, social and technological change. Of particular note was *Learning To Be*, a 1972 UNESCO report produced by a panel of international experts chaired by a former French prime minister (Fauré *et al.* 1972). This advanced an authoritative case for a much more flexible education system, with access to learning opportunities at all levels available to citizens throughout the whole of their lives, thereby enabling them to respond to new demands in their careers, in their engagement with the public sphere and in their personal lives. It also recognised the significance of informal and non-formal learning in a range of social settings, in addition to formal provision through established educational institutions. Technological innovations were seen to be central in this context, enabling people to access learning opportunities through distributed systems.

Equally, the implications for formal educational provision in schools and colleges were thought to be profound. This was especially emphasised in the influential writings of Torsten Husén. He recognised that the shift to the more flexible and dispersed educational systems of the learning society implied that schools would no longer be the principal source of knowledge about the social world. Accordingly, their pedagogy and curriculum should reflect this and be redirected towards developing young people's capacities to learn on their own initiative; 'learning how to learn' would provide the basis for effective participation in the learning society throughout their lives. The teacher's role would change from transmitting knowledge to diagnosing the learning needs of students and charting the progress they achieve.

These debates during the 1960s and 1970s served, therefore, to establish the core elements of the concept of the learning society. However, their influence in terms of policy development, still less of actual educational provision, was limited. Indeed, by the end of the 1970s, the learning society had even faded somewhat from the concerns of the international organisations and other commentators. When it re-emerged in the debates over education policy during the 1990s, it did so in a context which again reflected the wider circumstances of the time. In particular, under the influence of the OECD and the European Commission, the learning society came to be defined primarily in terms of the economic imperatives of the era. It was in these terms too that the concept came to be absorbed into the policy pronouncements of national governments.

Accordingly, the creation of a learning society was deemed necessary in order to meet the challenges of a globalised economy, in which the advanced industrial countries could not sustain their competitive position on the basis of low costs. Rather, given the priorities of the knowledge economy, what was required was continuous innovation in products and processes. Such innovation, in turn, required workforces which were highly skilled and able to adapt to changes in technology and the organisation of production.

Hence, all employees should be accomplished learners, able to renew and develop their skills not only by participating in formal education and training provision, but also – and equally, if not more importantly – through interacting with colleagues and other non-formal and informal means. Moreover, firms and other organisations in the economy should also be explicitly learning systems, facilitating organisational learning within and between organisations in order to promote innovation and change (OECD 1996).

It was also acknowledged, however, that this prioritisation of skills renewal and continuous learning was not wholly unproblematic. In particular, existing social inequalities could be compounded for those groups which are excluded from the new learning opportunities. The relative disadvantage of the 'learning poor' would be greater in a society in which access to learning is more significant. Clearly, the potential creation of new patterns of social inequality runs sharply counter to the ethos of the learning society, with its emphasis on widening opportunities for learning and improving the quality of life across the board. Nevertheless, these arguments do serve to emphasise that it cannot simply be taken for granted that beneficial distributional consequences will flow from a shift towards a learning society (Gorard and Rees 2002).

For many commentators, however, the problems with conceiving of the learning society in terms of economic imperatives run much deeper. For them, such a conceptualisation denies its transformative potential. Here, creating a learning society entails the wholesale restructuring of social relations. Earlier examples of this type of approach are found in the radical educational programmes of Freire and Illich. More recently, Stewart Ranson has argued that a learning society requires establishing the conditions in which individual citizens are enabled to develop the capabilities and capacities to engage with others in face-to-face participation in the life of the local community. In this way, they are empowered

355

to shift the terms on which social change is regulated within their communities and, ultimately, in society as a whole. As he puts it: 'The deep learning of the learning society is thus learning the capabilities for an active and democratic citizenship' (1998: 28)

Despite their manifest differences, each account of the learning society shares a commitment to creating radically widened access to learning opportunities and entails some redefinition of how learning is understood. In its nature, therefore, the learning society is conceived of in terms of a set of social conditions which need to be set in place in order to transcend the perceived shortcomings of presently existing educational systems. It is a concept which is partly based on *diagnosis* of current shortcomings in the organisation of learning and partly on *prognosis* in respect of the impacts of new forms of such organisations in the face of changing societal circumstances. In short, for the moment, the learning society represents a highly significant *aspiration* for education policy, rather than an objective that has been achieved.

See also: globalisation; informal/nonformal learning; knowledge economy; learning; learning career; lifelong learning

Further reading

Coffield, F. (ed.) (2000) *Differing Visions of a Learning Society: Research Findings*, vols 1 and 2, Bristol: Policy Press.
Edwards, R. (1997) *Changing Places? Flexibility, Lifelong Learning and the Learning Society*, London: Routledge.
Fauré, E., Herrera, F., Kaddowa, A., Lopes, H., Petrovsky, A., Rahmena, M. and Ward, F. (1972) *Learning To Be: The World of Education Today and Tomorrow*, Paris: UNESCO/Harrap.
Field, J. (2000) *Lifelong Learning and the New Educational Order*, Stoke on Trent: Trentham Books.
Gorard, S. and Rees, G. (2002) *Creating a Learning Society? Learning Careers and Policies for Lifelong Learning*, Bristol: Policy Press.
Husén, T. (1974) *The Learning Society*, London: Methuen.
OECD (1996) *Lifelong Learning for All*, Paris: OECD.
Ranson, S. (ed.) (1998) *Inside the Learning Society*, London: Cassell.

GARETH REES

LEARNING STYLES

When questioned, children and adults often have clear views about 'what works best' in relation to their own learning. Since publishing *Frames of Mind* in 1983, Howard Gardner, the American cognitive psychologist, has become a celebrated figure for identifying seven, now eight, different kinds of intelligence. In the following year David Kolb outlined four distinct learning styles in his model of 'experiential learning'. Kolb's model involves a four-stage cycle of learning, but recognises that some learners are naturally 'activists', while others are 'reflectors', 'theorists' or 'pragmatists'. Other learning style theorists have suggested adjustments and adaptations to Kolb's model and something of a consensus has developed around the view that there are 'visual', 'auditory' and 'kinaesthetic' learners. In the United Kingdom it is not unknown for school children, on the basis of having taken a test, to wear badges with such messages as 'I am a kinaesthetic learner' on open days, demonstrating to parents how seriously personalised learning is taken by the school. Politicians and educationists alike have latched onto Gardner's multiple intelligences model to justify, for example, inclusive education strategies, accelerated learning programmes and specialist schools. In the corporate world, learning style theory has been widely embraced as a replacement for one-size-fits-all training. At every turn, apparently, management gurus and sales leaders see in it advantages that will give their own business a competitive edge in a cut-throat marketplace. In recent years there has been a proliferation of learning styles questionnaires and profilers, many of them in the shape of pay-per-view Web-based interactive programs. Through these means, young learners, uncertain about their career aspirations, may be surprised (or not) to learn of apparent potential to excel as artists, lawyers, computer programmers, athletes, musicians, politicians or philosophers. Despite its current popularity, critics of learning style models have dismissed some aspects as mumbo-jumbo. There continue to be academic debates about the solid scientific basis for Gardner's multiple intelligence theory.

See also: experiential learning; Gardner, Howard; individualised instruction/personalised learning; intelligence/intelligence tests; learning

DAVID CROOK

LECTURE/LECTURER

A lecture is an oral presentation of factual information and interpretation by an expert before an audience of learners. In the academy, the traditional lecture takes the form of a talk, with students taking notes, sometimes in preparation for discussion in a group seminar or individual tutorial. Today, few university teachers, commonly called lecturers, adopt such a restricted approach. The term 'class' is sometimes preferred to lecture and lecturers often distribute printed handouts, draw upon audio-visual excerpts and project onto a screen pictures, diagrams, quotations and key terms. Many lecturers adopt an interactive approach, inviting their listeners to make observations and ask questions during the presentation.

The originator of the 'pure' lecture method is often said to be the French theological scholar Peter Abelard (1079–1142). The biographer of Samuel Johnson (1709–84), James Boswell, recalled his subject's view that 'Lectures were once useful; but now, when all can read, and Books are so numerous, Lectures are unnecessary'. Similarly, Cambridge's distinguished professor of philosophy, Henry Sidgwick (1838–1900), viewed the lecture as 'an antiquated survival' and 'a relic of the times before the printing-press was invented'. The development of

borrowing libraries undermined the lecturing model comparatively little, however. Even today, many universities continue to require of their students a minimum attendance level at lectures. While registered students generally comprise the audience for university lectures, inaugural and valedictory lectures, as well as guest lectures by leading public figures, are typically open to the public and news media. Conferences such as those organised by higher education institutions, learned societies and professional bodies sometimes include keynote lectures, presented by expert speakers. With the advance of video and Web-based technologies, some lecturers may now be delivered at a distance from the listening audience.

See also: Abelard, Peter; college; higher education; instruction; tuition/tutor/tutorial; university; visual aids

DAVID CROOK

LESSON

In the setting of the school a lesson is a block of time, perhaps 45 minutes or one hour, devoted to a particular curriculum activity, with pupils working under the direction of a teacher. Secondary school subjects with a practical element, such as the sciences, are frequently timetabled as 'double lessons' to allow extra time to set up and pack away the equipment used for experiments. At school, most children will experience, for example, mathematics and art lessons inside a classroom, though physical education and games lessons may, weather permitting, be held outside. Before commencing a lesson the teacher will normally have prepared any resources needed by the class and have considered the teaching objectives and intended learning outcomes. Lessons are widely thought to be most effective when careful thought has been given to the timing of each element. How much time should be spent on the introduction and conclusion? How long should be devoted to collective or individual textbook reading, to practical elements, group activities and the completion by pupils of exercises or worksheets? Teachers may devise their own lesson plan, follow or adapt one developed by a colleague, or even draw upon those available from internet resource banks. In some circumstances learners may experience lessons on a one-to-one basis. Children with special educational needs, for example, may intensively work with a teacher or teaching assistant during some or all of their weekly timetabled lessons. Lessons may also be taught in the home: as important tests and examinations loom, anxious parents with the means to do it sometimes employ private tutors to provide extra lessons in their children's weakest subjects. Children, and adults too, may also pay for one-to-one music lessons in a private music teacher's home.

See also: curriculum; instruction; school; subjects; teacher; tuition/tutor/tutorial

DAVID CROOK

LIBERAL EDUCATION

The ideal of a liberal education is one that is civilised, broad and humane, based on learning that is disinterested and cultivated for its own sake. It emerged in its modern form from the eighteenth-century Enlightenment, and developed in the nineteenth century to emphasise the search for truth by the free and critical intelligence, to 'follow the argument whithersoever it goes' (Rothblatt 1976: 197). It is not simply an academic education, for this implies a narrowness and concern with individual examination success that sits uncomfortably with a broad liberal ideal. Its roots in political liberty also create potential tensions with the modern demands of an interventionist state. Moreover, it is generally contrasted with a vocational education that is instrumental and designed primarily as a preparation for a job or career. Adult education has often been associated with a liberal ideal that attempts to divorce it from direct concerns with career advancement or materialism, and that emphasises individual, personal interest and curiosity.

Critics of liberal education would regard it as a dated and elitist notion that does too little to further industrial and economic productivity on the one side, and social justice on the other. The dominant image is that projected in Plato's *Republic*, of the philosopher-kings who disdain work and commerce. Nevertheless, the values that it represents continue to resonate in changing times, often by adapting to new challenges. In relation to technical and vocational education, for example, it may offer opportunities of intellectual enrichment. Alfred North Whitehead, a leading philosopher in the early twentieth century, suggested that liberal education was based in a 'Platonic ideal' that encouraged art, fostered a spirit of disinterested curiosity, and promoted freedom of thought, but insisted that it should not be divorced from the commercial and material considerations of the mass of humanity. According to Whitehead, action should be married to thought, and therefore, he concluded,

> The antithesis between a technical and a liberal education is fallacious. There can be no adequate technical education which is not liberal, and no liberal education which is not technical: that is, no education which does not impart both technique and intellectual vision.
>
> (Whitehead 1932: 74)

More recently, Richard Pring has also expressed the need to avoid a two-track system by including a broad vocational preparation as part of a re-examined idea of liberal education (Pring 1995: 192). Indeed, Pring argues for the vocationalisation of the liberal ideal (as others have called for the liberalising of the vocational ideal), through a questioning of 'the dualisms between thinking and doing, between theory and practice, between the world of education and the world of work, between education and training, which for too long have impoverished the educational experience of many' (Pring 1995: 193).

Revised approaches to liberal education to meet the challenges of the twenty-first century world might also develop a more inclusive rationale, broadening the scope of citizenship. The cultivation of humanity in an increasingly interlocked world might well involve a heightened sense of internationalism, and also a greater awareness of commonalities with fellow human beings of different backgrounds and orientations. Rather than being preserved for the elite, liberal education might seek to produce free citizens and critical thinkers from across the community. These kinds of values have been related to the finer aspirations of higher education, with attempts being made in some institutions of higher education to promote new courses that may inculcate international and social ideals (Nussbaum 1997). Seeking to combine intellectual virtue and moral virtue, it might also have much to contribute to debates about international conflict, cultural antagonisms, and the power of the state in a divided world (Hancock 1999).

See also: classical education; Plato; technical education/school/college; vocational education

Further reading

Hancock, R. C. (ed.) (1999) *America, the West, and Liberal Education*, Oxford: Rowman and Littlefield.

Nussbaum, M. (1997) *Cultivating Humanity: A Classical Defense of Reform in Liberal Education*, Cambridge MA: Harvard University Press.

Pring, R. (1995) *Closing the Gap: Liberal Education and Vocational Preparation*, London: Hodder and Stoughton.

Rothblatt, S. (1976) *Tradition and Change in English Liberal Education: An Essay in History and Culture*, London: Faber and Faber.

Whitehead, A. N. (1932) 'Technical education and its relation to science and literature'. In A. N. Whitehead (ed.) *The Aims of Education, and other Essays*, London: Williams and Norgate Ltd.

GARY McCULLOCH

LIFELONG LEARNING

Lifelong learning has been described as a rainbow concept, with many shades of meaning in a spectrum of purposes. The first book-length exploration of lifelong learning is usually attributed to Yeaxlee in 1929, although the significance of learning outside and beyond schooling has featured in the writings of thinkers from Plato to Dewey. From the 1990s onwards, lifelong learning has been reinvented and has assumed a new significance for educational policy making at a global level.

Historically, ideas of learning as a lifelong process countered twentieth-century tendencies to equate education with the mass schooling in the first two decades of life. While schooling for children selected and filtered for socio-economic purposes, lifelong learning was, for its proponents, a radical perspective that sought ways to re-establish the relationship between learning and real life, by emphasising

- the development of all kinds of abilities, interests, knowledge and qualifications from the pre-school years to post-retirement;
- the value of the many forms of learning that are experienced through family, work and the community, as well as educational institutions.

A variety of concepts of lifelong learning have dominated in different societies and at different times. Some concepts of lifelong learning are underpinned by the ideal of lifelong engagement with the ideas and practices of democracy. This version was important in the early 1900s, with the international sweep of emancipatory discourses, which are equal and opposite to the globalisation discourses sweeping the world we inhabit a century later. Lifelong learning was about freeing people from the slavery of ignorance, and emphasised education that was woven into the organised life of the community and rooted in the social aspirations of the democratic movements of the country.

Other versions of lifelong learning had humanistic rather than socio-political foundations. In 1972, *Learning to Be* (the Fauré Report) defined the aim of 'lifelong education' as 'the fulfilment of man, through the flexible organisation of different stages of education' and 'a process which should last the whole life for individuals and not just be tacked onto school or university for a privileged or specialised few'. Well known articulations of the concept of a learning society, emphasised not only 'second chance' conceptions of lifelong learning, but also that untapped potential has to be seen as the norm, not the exception, in the population. International bodies such as the United Nations Educational, Scientific and Cultural Organization adopted the humanistic version of lifelong learning to provide their master concepts for educational planning, but their use represented worthy ideals with relatively little to show in real advances in access to lifelong learning opportunities.

A global political consensus on lifelong learning marked the end of the twentieth century (e.g. the Delors Report, the European Competitiveness and Economic Growth Agenda, and positions adopted by the Organisation for Economic Co-operation and Development [OECD] and the G8 Delhi Declaration). This fundamentally reshaped the discourses and ideas of lifelong learning. The analysis of the 'proper relationship between education and real life' came to be driven by the notion of the knowledge-driven economy. Governments emphasise lifelong learning as the means for people to improve 'employability', as national governments can no longer guarantee employment in a global competitive environment.

Much thinking and planning for lifelong learning has focused on reorganisation of institutions of learning for more openness and flexibility. This has not given sufficient recognition to the fact that new forms of learning are superimposed on old forms that retain much of their original power. Social institutions, old and new, continue to interlock to shape typical life courses and perpetuate or even reinforce inequalities. International statistics suggest increases in participation in learning at all ages, but growing inequalities. In 1997 the OECD highlighted the need to 'counter social exclusion' as widening gaps became apparent between the sense of control over their own lives and their society of the 'learning rich' and the isolation and powerless of those who become disengaged, often in youth.

In the early twenty-first century some lifelong learning policies have been criticised as 'blame the victim' policies that have focused attention on deficits in individuals' skills and 'employability' instead of the structural conditions that are fuelling inequalities. Evans (2001) points to a radical vision of lifelong learning that can encompass work and reconnect learning to the wider purposes of citizenship. Can learning, as a lifelong process, link, rather than separate, generations and incorporate working lives without becoming human resource development in disguise?

See also: further education; knowledge economy; learning; learning society; recurrent education; skills; social exclusion/inclusion

Further reading

Aspin, D., Chapman, J., Hatton, M. and Sawano, Y. (2001) *International Handbook of Lifelong Learning*, Dordrecht, the Netherlands: Springer.
Evans, K. (2001) 'Relationships between work and life'. In B. Crick (ed.) *Towards a Citizenship Culture*, London: Political Quarterly/Blackwell.
Field J. (2002) *Lifelong Learning and the New Educational Order*, Stoke on Trent: Trentham Books.

KAREN EVANS

LITERACY

The meaning of the word literacy derives from the Latin word *litera* (letter) and is traditionally concerned with the ability to read and write. This ability is widely seen as one of the basic skills of education.

In the late twentieth century, literacy was increasingly used also to refer to more general competence, as with 'computer', 'financial' or even 'emotional' literacy. Within education, there was a similar divergence of meaning, between psychological and sociological studies.

In psychological studies, there have been several major developments, which highlight the importance of links between research, policy and practice. One development concerns models of reading and writing processes. It has long been recognised that reading is a complex process, involving a range of information sources: in particular, word recognition, decoding, anticipation and comprehension. In the middle years of the twentieth century, the models that influenced educational practice gave priority to the anticipation of written language sequences, which visual information was seen as being used to confirm or reject. Subsequent research suggested a model of reading as an 'interactive-compensatory' process, in which information sources are differentially used, according to the reader's familiarity with the subject matter and with the words and grammar used to communicate it. It is also now widely agreed that, in the reading of written English, the use of phonological skills constitutes a critical sub-process (see Stanovich 2000).

In models of the writing process, there is a long-standing recognition of the importance of composing in creating texts, on both paper and computer screens. There has also been progress in studying how the editing and re-drafting of texts is assisted by various forms of 'discourse knowledge'. The role of working memory has been established as an important factor in the effective development of writing skill (Kellogg 1994).

A second development is the use of systematic reviews of evidence. These reviews have, for example, reviewed the accumulated research on phonological development, phonics, comprehension and fluency (National Reading Panel 2000). Such reviews have also prompted critiques that highlight the limitations of the experimental research used in many of the studies reviewed.

A third development involves the use of schools' literacy attainment as an indicator of their effectiveness and the use of high-stakes testing, to monitor and 'drive up' national attainment standards. This development has also been accompanied by the compilation of international league tables that compare the educational attainment of different countries, especially in reading. Comparisons of writing attainment have proved more difficult, due to cultural factors.

To some commentators, such uses of literacy attainment have been seen as an inevitable part of the strategic management of public expenditure. Others have raised questions about the ways such managerialism may distort classroom practice and contribute to narrow, instrumental views of curricular provision.

In sociological studies of literacy, an influential distinction has been made between an 'autonomous' concept of literacy, focusing on decontextualised skills, and a 'social practice' concept of literacy, focusing on literacy as a socially, culturally and historically situated tool, used for particular purposes in particular contexts (Street 1984). 'Critical literacy' theorists have further argued that literacy is ideologically shaped by hegemonic forces that reflect the distribution of power between different social groups.

Such divergences in definition have triggered considerable debate. Some proponents of a skill-based model have questioned how far literacy is social, political or relative at the level of decoding or spelling. The case for a relative notion of literacy may be greater in relation to comprehension, in which differences in background knowledge influence the meaning that readers may construct from specific texts.

The social practice concept has been extended by interest in 'multiple literacies', especially the ways in which texts can be encrypted by electronic means. However, earlier optimistic predictions of the positive effects of, for example, word processing on students' writing attainment have not been supported in systematic reviews of evidence. Nevertheless, new theories have been developed to help explain the multi-modal transformation of traditional pen and paper communication afforded by digital technologies (see Kress 2003).

See also: basic skills; comprehension; core skills/core competencies; curriculum; phonics; reading; spelling; writing

Further reading

Kellogg, R. (1994) *The Psychology Of Writing*, New York: Oxford University Press.
Kress, G. (2003) *Literacy in the New Media Age*, London: Routledge.
National Reading Panel (2000) *Teaching Children to Read: An Evidence-Based Assessment of the Scientific Research Literature on Reading and Its Implications for Reading Instruction*, Washington DC: National Institute of Child Health and Human Development.
Stanovich, K. (2000) *Progress In Understanding Reading*, New York: Guilford.
Street, B. (1984) *Literacy In Theory And Practice*, Cambridge: Cambridge University Press.

ROGER BEARD

LOCKE, JOHN (1632–1704)

Primarily renowned for his *Essay Concerning Human Understanding* (1690) and his *Two Treatises on Government* (1690), John Locke, an Englishman, occupies a key place in the development of modern Western thought. Classical scholar by training, physician by vocation, medical researcher and writer by choice, Locke had a substantial influence on the philosophical, political, theological, ethical, economical and educational thought of his time. Locke's contribution to the latter stemmed mainly from his theory of knowledge and from his writings on education.

Locke, often regarded as the founder of British empiricism, famously argued that at birth the mind was a blank slate, a tabula rasa.

He held that there are no innate ideas and that all knowledge comes through the senses. Although Locke did not exclude the existence of natural human tendencies or inborn individual predispositions, his theory of knowledge ascribed a great forming power to education. Locke, indeed, was among the first modern-age thinkers to assert that people become what they are chiefly by their education. Locke's claim that experience is the only source of knowledge formed the basis of Enlightenment educational thought. Embracing Locke's sensualist psychology and rejecting the doctrine of original sin, the thinkers of the Enlightenment advanced the idea that education has the ability to improve all aspects of human life. The roots of our modern belief in the power of education can, therefore, be traced back to Locke.

Locke's additional contribution to educational theory came from his various works on this subject: *Some Thoughts Concerning Reading and Study for a Gentleman* (1720), a memorandum on working schools, and *On the Conduct of the Understanding* (1706), which discusses the training of the mind. Locke's most influential pedagogical treatise, however, is undoubtedly *Some Thoughts Concerning Education* (1693), which, within twelve years, saw five English editions and was translated into all the major European languages. Being based on a series of letters in which Locke advised friends about how to best rear their son, it does not provide a systematic theory of education. Instead, the book, which incorporates observations taken from Locke's personal experience, deals with different aspects of private home education provided by a tutor for a child designated to become a gentleman. Despite its seemingly limited purpose, the book has quite general applications: it provides guidelines for humanising a person by preparing him to be incorporated into civil society.

The book's emphasis was on moral education. Accepting the Christian view that human nature has a lower and passionate side and a higher and reasonable side, Locke argued that the foundation of all virtues was the subjection of the passions to reason. Scattered throughout the book are suggestions on how to develop the child's reason and bring him to accept its dictates and act accordingly. Moreover, the book also discussed specific virtues, such as generosity, humility, industry, and how they should be cultivated, as well as specific vices, such as hypocrisy, cruelty, indolence, and how they should be eradicated. Locke's understanding of virtues and vices, it should be noted, was traditional and very similar to the Christian one prevailing in his day. On a more practical level, Locke argued that in the course of the child's moral education he should be brought under the authority of his parents but that his spirit must be kept active and free, that corporal punishment must be reduced while the use of praise and blame extended, and that practice and example should be widely used.

Although Locke attributed to intellectual training only a secondary importance, he promoted some progressive principles of instruction. According to Locke, instruction was to encourage the child's learning by making it pleasurable; it was to foster curiosity; to be adapted to the child's mind; to progress from the simple to the complex; and not to overburden the child's memory. Locke's suggested curriculum, however, was typical for his time. In addition to moral education and intellectual instruction Locke also wrote about the physical aspect of child rearing.

Today, the practicalities of Locke's education are mostly outdated, but his general ideas helped to transform education. His insistence on educating man for society rather than for serving God, his belief in the power of education, his emphasis on its moral aspects, and some of his principles of instruction have, through their subsequent influence on other thinkers, such as Rousseau, shaped our view of education. But more than that, Locke's thought itself played a considerable role in constituting the ideal of modern education.

See also: child guidance; corporal punishment; home schooling; moral education; philosophy of education; progressive education; Rousseau, Jean-Jacques

Further reading

Jeffreys, M. V. C. (1967) *John Locke: Prophet of Common Sense*, London: Methuen.

Locke, J. (1989) [1693] *Some Thoughts Concerning Education*, eds J. W. Yolton and J. S. Yolton, Oxford: Clarendon Press.

Tarcov, N. (1984) *Locke's Education for Liberty*, London: University of Chicago Press.

Yolton, J. W. (1971) *John Locke and Education*, New York: Random House.

TAL GILEAD

LOWE, ROBERT (1811–92)

Lowe, who became Viscount Sherbrooke in 1880, was a British Liberal politician. He graduated from Oxford (B.A. 1833; M.A. 1836) and was elected a Fellow of Magdalen College (1835–36). He qualified as a barrister in 1842, before travelling to Sydney, Australia, where he became a member of the legislative council for New South Wales. Lowe returned to England in 1850, becoming a leader writer for *The Times* and then Member of Parliament for Kidderminster (1852–59), Calne (1859–68) and the University of London (1868–80). Lord Palmerston appointed him vice-president of the Committee of Council on Education in 1859, in which position he rejected a central recommendation of the 1858 Newcastle Commission, that county school boards should be created to promote universal elementary schooling. Instead, he introduced the 'Revised Code' in 1862, which linked government grants to schools to pupils' tested performance in reading, writing and arithmetic. This 'payment by results' system encouraged rote learning and 'teaching to the test' until it was phased out in the 1890s. As Chancellor of the Exchequer in Gladstone's 1868 administration, Lowe supported W. E. Forster's 1870 elementary schools bill. He was famous for his caustic wit, such as justifying increased government spending on the basis that there was a need 'to teach our future masters their letters'. Lowe was an albino, who suffered from very poor sight throughout his life.

See also: accountability; Forster, William; politics of education

STEVEN COWAN

LYCEUM

The *Lyceum* was the original name of the school established by the Greek philosopher Aristotle in 335 BCE. In the nineteenth century the title was adopted in the United States for a movement to promote the popular instruction of adults through lectures, concerts and other means. Lyceum groups disseminated information on a wide range of subjects, and supported the establishment of libraries, museums and public schools. The first group was based in Milbury in Massachusetts, with lectures by Josiah Holbrook. These led in 1839 to the formation of the short-lived National American Lyceum. In the 1830s, several thousand such groups were in existence, especially in the North, and they became highly familiar and influential during the rest of the century. In many ways the role of the Lyceum movement was similar to that of the mechanics' institutes which were introduced in Britain during this period, and which spread to a number of other countries around the world.

See also: adult education; Aristotle; mechanics' institute; United States

GARY McCULLOCH

M

MAGNET SCHOOL

A magnet school is a school with a special theme and other attractive characteristics, whose purpose is to *attract*, rather than force, students of different races to the same school. Magnet schools were a school desegregation tool created in the United States in the late 1960s and throughout the 1970s and 1980s as an alternative to mandatory reassignment (e.g. 'forced bussing'), which caused significant white flight and protest. With a voluntary magnet school plan, students could stay at their neighbourhood school or they could volunteer for a magnet school. Transportation was provided by the school district administration.

The process of attracting students to these schools begins with a marketing campaign. Glossy brochures are mailed to parents and to the local media. Press releases are also written for the local media. The US federal government, and sometimes the state government, funds magnet programmes so that they usually have higher expenditures. Their names also give a sense of why they might be attractive: the Thomas Pullham Creative and Performing Arts magnet (in Prince George's County, Maryland), the Copley Square International High magnet (in Boston), the School 59 Science magnet (also called the 'Zoo School' in Buffalo); the Greenfield Montessori magnet school (in Milwaukee); the Central High School Classical Greek/ Computers Unlimited magnet high school (in Kansas City).

What makes a magnet school different from a school of choice (e.g. the Bronx High School of Science) is the use of racial quotas in admissions in order to ensure a racially balanced school, usually because the school district is under a court order to desegregate its schools. The issue of whether racial quotes can be used for magnet school admission if a school district is not under such a court order will be decided in 2007 by the Supreme Court in *Parents v. Seattle School District, et al.* and *Meredith v. Jefferson County Board of Education, et al.*

The success of magnet schools in attracting white students, the limiting factor, depends not only on marketing, but on the magnet structure and the percentage minority in the programme (Rossell 2003). There are three types of magnet structures: (1) the whole school attendance zone magnet, (2) the programme-within-a-school (PWS) magnet, and (3) the dedicated magnet. The more separate the magnet programme from resident minority students and the lower the percentage minority in the programme, the more successful it is in attracting white students to a black neighbourhood. As a result, the dedicated magnet where magnet students are in a separate school is the most successful and the PWS magnet where magnet students are in a separate programme, but still in a school with a resident neighbourhood minority population the next most successful. The least successful structure is the whole-school-attendance zone magnet where all the students in the school are in the magnet programme, including neighbourhood students who did not choose the programme.

Although voluntary plans produce more interracial exposure than mandatory reassignment plans, Rossell (2003) found that there is such a thing as too many magnet schools. There is only limited demand for magnet programmes, and when there are a lot of them, they may disrupt the school district and cause white flight, disperse the limited number of whites who are willing to send their child to a magnet school in an opposite race neighbourhood, and increase the percentage minority in the magnet programmes. These factors will further reduce the number of whites willing to send their child to a magnet school in a minority neighbourhood from 21 per cent when the programme is 50 per cent white and 50 per cent minority, to 5–13 per cent when the programme is three quarters minority and one quarter white (Rossell 2003).

Although many school districts are no longer under court order, the number of magnet schools seems not to have declined. In 1981, there were about 1,000 magnet schools in the USA according to the US Department of Education. In 1991, there were about 2,400 (Rossell and Armor 1996). In 2005, the Department of Education estimates the total number is above 4,000. Magnet schools appear to be here to stay, even if they are no longer desegregation tools, as they seem to have benefited from the widespread support for school choice in the USA.

See also: parental choice; segregation/desegregation; zoning

Further reading

Rossell, C. H. (2003) 'The desegregation efficiency of magnet schools', *Urban Affairs Review*, 38: 697–725.
——(2005) 'Whatever happened to magnet schools?', *Education Next*, 5(2): 44–49.

Rossell, C. H. and Armor, D. (1996) 'The effectiveness of school desegregation plans, 1968–91', *American Politics Quarterly*, 24(3): 267–302.

CHRISTINE H. ROSSELL

MAKARENKO, ANTON SIMEONOVITCH (1888–1939)

Makarenko, the Soviet educator, started teaching in 1905, aged sixteen, joining the Poltava Teacher's Institute in 1914, where he specialised in the history of education and was influenced by the writings of Owen, Pestalozzi and Gorky. After a spell as head teacher of a primary school in Kryukov, he moved in 1920 to a settlement for orphans and youth offenders, which he named Gorky Colony. Here, he put into practice his ideas about a unified educational experience based upon active and real work. All educational activity was to be purpose-oriented and the students were to engage in community, technical and physical labour so they had experience of different types of productive labour. All decision making was collective, with power resting with an elected central council and decentralised work brigades. From 1928 to 1935 he headed another colony at Dzerzhinsky, which attracted many international visitors. His prolific publishing on educational topics placed him at the forefront of Soviet educational theory and pedagogy. His last official position, from 1935 to 1937, was as assistant director of children's labour colonies in the Ukraine. Among those he influenced was the French progressive educator Freinet, and his most prominent writings were *A Book for Parents* (1939) and a novel, *The Road to Life* (1933).

See also: collaborative/cooperative learning; Freinet, Celestin; progressive education; Russia; youth club/work

STEVEN COWAN

MAKIGUCHI, TSUNESABURO (1871–1944)

Tsunesaburo Makiguchi was a school teacher, primary school principal, educational thinker and Buddhist. In *Jinsei Chirigaku* (*Geography of Human Life*, 1903) he developed progressive ideas on the relation between people's lives and their spatial location. He also wrote the *Soka Kyoikugaku Taikei* (*The System of Value-Creation Pedagogy*, 1930–35) which reflected on his work as a teacher and developed proposals for reforming the Japanese educational system which he claimed stifled creativity and independent thinking. Makiguchi was a humanist who argued that education must be seen as the joint responsibility of school, home and community. He proposed that children's education should be divided between school, apprenticeships and learning through home and community work. This would help students to learn values and motivate them to become active learners.

He converted to *Nichiren Shoshu*, a Buddhist sect, and established *Soka Kyoiku Gakkai* (the Value-Creation Education Society) with his friend and collaborator Josei Toda. Although it started out as a small group of educationalists they attracted a wider membership believing that individual transformation was the basis for progressive social change. He opposed the military government and, during World War II, was arrested for his beliefs. He died in prison. Today his ideas are propagated by the *Soka Gakkai International* comprising soka (value creating) groups and educational institutions, from early years to universities, which can be found in many countries including Japan, the USA, Hong Kong, India, Singapore and Malaysia.

See also: Japan

TOM WOODIN

MALAYSIA

The complex and diverse history of the Malay Archipelago has impacted on contemporary forms of education in Malaysia. For instance, madrasahs and other Muslim schools left their mark, as did the missionaries who established Christian schools. By contrast, the British colonial administration supported secular education and helped to found schools such as the Penang Free School (1816). However, the British did not favour 'over-educating' the Malay population and teaching largely took place in English. Malaya gained independence in 1957 and became Malaysia in 1963. Since then, the country has embarked on a significant process of economic growth which has considerably raised living standards. This has had a symbiotic relationship with educational expansion.

Education not only contributed to the economy, it has also been implicated in the process of nation-building. A persistent and thorny issue has been the continuing inter-ethnic tensions between Malay, Chinese and Indian populations. At independence the Malay majority feared the economic and demographic dominance of the Chinese and the nation was constructed upon a compromise offering equal citizenship for all groups, while also providing for affirmative action in favour of the *bumiputras*, who comprise Malays and other indigenous groups. This was reflected in the Education Act of 1961, which stipulated that only Malay and English could be taught in secondary schools, although the teaching of English would be phased out following race riots in 1969. Chinese and Indian schools and colleges have been permitted, but all students have had to learn Malay. Under the influence of the dominant United Malays National Organisation (UMNO), governments channel the vast bulk of funding to Malay-dominated schools. Universities also operate an informal selective system which favours the Malay population. Despite debates over affirmative action and attempts to alleviate its worst effects – for instance by introducing Tamil and Chinese into national schools – segregation remains deeply engrained in the educational system.

Early years education is patchy and takes place in private schools run by business, voluntary and religious groups. By contrast, six years of primary education, divided into two levels, is compulsory for all children aged 7–12. Students must take the Ujian

367

Pencapaian Sekolah Rendah (UPSR) or Primary School Evaluation Test, which covers Malay comprehension, written Malay, English, science and mathematics. Since 2003 science and mathematics have been taught in English and other subjects in Malay. Although Chinese and Tamil schools teach in their respective languages, they have to follow the Malay curriculum of the more numerous national schools: this also helps students progress to secondary education.

Secondary education lasts for five years and tends to continue the work of national schools. A standardised test at the end of the third year is used to create a prestigious science stream and a less-prestigious arts stream. A further test, after the fifth year, Sijil Pelajaran Malaysia (SPM) or Malaysian Certificate of Education, is based on the old British 'school certificate', although students also now receive an 'O' level grade for English. Chinese independent high schools operate their own tests which are recognised by some foreign universities but not the Malaysian government. Accordingly, some Chinese students also take the SPM or gain entry to private colleges. There is much competition to do well in the tests which operate throughout school life, a fact reflected in the recent growth of private tuition. There are also a number of selective schools and international schools serving foreign populations.

During the two-year pre-university stage, students either study for the standardised Malaysian Higher School Certificate or take matriculation, a programme run by the ministry of education with exams set and marked by teachers: 90 per cent of places go to *bumiputras*, which also helps to facilitate entry to university. Private colleges also offer programmes from other countries or the international baccalaureate.

In 2004 a ministry of higher education was established to coordinate the university sector, which has traditionally been highly subsidised by the state. A large number of institutions now proliferate in comparison with one university in 1957. Polytechnics also offer diplomas and vocational study. A range of private institutions, some from abroad, such as Monash University (Australia) and the University of Nottingham (United Kingdom), have established bases in Malaysia.

In recent years the state has been moving towards a coordinating and development role in higher education. Since the late 1980s a process of *corporatisation* has taken place with the aim of developing 'world-class' institutions closely tied into globalising processes. This has meant universities are expected to raise income, for instance, through charging tuition fees, franchising, borrowing money, business ventures, establishing companies or consultancy firms and acquiring investment shares. They are becoming more 'entrepreneurial' in promoting social and economic development at the same time as fulfilling a traditional mission of research and teaching. Although public universities now enjoy more autonomy and flexibility in finance, they are still held accountable to the public through a process of 'centralised decentralisation'. Some faculty members feel that the collegial approach in university governance has gone and that academic freedom is under threat in the face of market forces.

See also: China; East Asia

Further reading

Baginda, Abdul Razak Abdullah (2005) *Education in Multicultural Societies: Perspectives on Education in Malaysia*, London: ASEAN Academic Press.

Lee, M. (2004) *Restructuring Higher Education in Malaysia*, Penang: School of Educational Studies, Universiti Sains Malaysia.

Mok, K. H. (2007) 'The search for new governance: corporatization and privatization of public universities in Singapore and Malaysia', *Asia Pacific Journal of Education*, 27(2).

Morshidi, S. (2006) 'Malaysia'. In UNESCO (ed.) *Higher Education in South-East Asia*, Bangkok: UNESCO Bangkok.

KA HO MOK

MANAGERIALISM

Managerialism refers to the over-use of managers and management techniques, especially in governing and running public services. Detractors who view it in ideological terms often employ it pejoratively. It has been closely associated with the development of 'new public management', 'entrepreneurial governance' and 'corporate managerialism'. Central to the notion of managerialism is that social, economic, political and cultural issues and problems can be defined and solved in terms of management: any organisation, for instance, a school or hospital, can be run according to key principles irrespective of its purpose. A central tenet of managerialism upholds 'the right to manage' in the face of government bureaucracy, trade union intransigency and the professionalism of teachers. Management is seen to bring about efficiency, value for money, and customer care. The influence of managerialism has infused the educational policies of many countries and a number of international bodies, such as the Organisation for Economic Co-operation and Development, International Monetary Fund and World Bank, have supported policies associated with managerialism.

Managerialism has been connected to wider social and economic changes, in particular the onset of globalisation. It has been represented not only as a specific set of ideas about management but also as an ideology closely allied to the growth of neo-liberalism. Theories of human capital have held that countries need to compete in a global market place to protect their position and improve their world ranking. This became apparent with the rise of the new right in the USA and the UK in the 1980s when markets were introduced and nurtured in welfare provision to help break up what were perceived as monolithic and 'failing' public services.

Elected politicians have argued they are unable to manage at the level of detail required and, consequently, the functions of advice, funding, delivery and regulation have been separated while budgets and authority have been devolved down to the school level. Accordingly, the role of government shifted to one of regulation, setting overall targets and auditing although, in itself, this can form a tight framework with little room for manoeuvre. Policies that foster the commodification of education through 'diversity' and 'choice' have encouraged private participation by business and third sector organisations. Service providers have had to become entrepreneurial in competing for contracts in a commodified market place and schools have had to compete for students. Teacher professionalism and trade union power have been undermined by this fragmentation as well as the introduction of performance-related pay.

These developments have resulted in a confusion of the boundaries between public and private and lines of accountability have become less clear. Responsibility has also shifted from the state to private citizens. In order for this new system to function effectively, schools, parents and communities are positioned as partners with responsibility for these changes. Marginalised groups of people may also be incorporated into collaborative and 'inclusive' management processes. Critics hold that such participation is both highly disciplined and controlled. Those influenced by Michel Foucault have argued that this development amounts to a form of self-governance through disciplinary knowledge.

However, there are also significant national and cultural differences in the meaning and practice of management. Presentations of managerialism as a unified global discourse may be wide of the mark. In different countries, managerialism may serve the interests of differing constituencies and take a number of forms. All aspects of management cannot simply be labelled as evidence of managerialism. Some managers and school heads reject managerialist discourse or may adopt its language while continuing to operate according to their existing values.

See also: educational leadership and management; performance indicators; performance-related pay; privatisation/marketisation; profession/professionalism/professionalisation; restructuring; school-based management

Further reading

Clarke, J., Gewirtz, S. and McLaughlin, E. (2000) *New Managerialism, New Welfare?* London: Sage/Open University.

Inglis, F. (2000) 'A malediction upon management', *Journal of Education Policy*, 15(4): 417–29.

Organisation for Economic Co-operation and Development (1995) *Governance in Transition: Public Management Reform in OECD Countries*, Paris: OECD.

Power, S., Halpin, D. and Whitty, G. (1997) 'Managing the state and the market: "new" education management in five countries', *British Journal of Educational Studies*, 45(4): 342–62.

TOM WOODIN

MANN, HORACE (1796–1859)

Mann graduated from Brown University, Rhode Island, in 1819, where he returned to lecture in 1821. He began studying law in 1823, developing a lucrative practice until 1837. Mann served in the Massachusetts House of Representatives for six years from 1827 and was then elected to the state senate, becoming its president in 1836. In 1837 he signed into law the Education Act establishing the state board of education, charged with expanding and improving the common school system. He accepted an offer to become the first secretary of the board, holding this position until 1848. His annual reports were descriptive and analytical, and they influenced thinking elsewhere. He expanded teacher training and raised salaries, organised education conventions and founded the *Common School Journal*, which he personally edited for ten years. Free high school provision was also massively expanded. Mann was a Unitarian, favouring non-sectarian schooling and university provision. After touring Europe, in 1843 he wrote a controversial report, influenced by von Humboldt, identifying improved teacher training as the key to improving standards. Upon the death of John Quincy Adams, Mann was elected to the vacant congressional seat in 1848, but he served for only two years before becoming the first president of Antioch College, Ohio. His principal contribution to education lay in advocating common schooling for all, irrespective of race and creed, for the goal of shared citizenship.

See also: common school; equality of opportunity

STEVEN COWAN

MANNHEIM, KARL (1893–1947)

Mannheim, the Hungarian-born sociologist, studied in Budapest, Berlin, Freiburg and Heidelberg, where his interests focused around philosophy, philology and pedagogy. He attended lectures by Georg Simmel and was influenced by Edmund Husserl, leading him to develop his own ideas about the sociology of knowledge. Mannheim was part of the intellectual group, also including Lukács, Bartok and Kodály, who established the Hungarian Free School of Arts and Social Science for adults. He moved on to lecturing posts in Budapest and Heidelberg, becoming professor of sociology in Frankfurt from 1930 to 1933, when he was forced to leave. Harold Laski invited Mannheim to come to England, where he lectured at the London School of Economics and, from 1946 until his death, at the University of London Institute of Education.

Mannheim developed the concept of 'cultural capital' as early as 1936. He believed that science, along with other academic disciplines, should be studied as a specific form of social organisation. His most famous work, *Ideology and Utopia* (1936, English version) explored the structures behind fields of knowledge. Later work expanded upon ideas of the role of intellectuals within democratic societies. During the later period of his life he was a leading exponent of the idea that education had a leading role to play in ensuring that society was freed from its inherited and disfiguring conflicts. In *Man and Society* (1940), he argued that the main aim of education was to promote personal freedom and autonomy.

See also: autonomy; cultural capital; sociology of education

STEVEN COWAN

MARKING

Marking describes the assessment process that leads examiners, assessors or teachers to form a judgement about the quality of student work before them. In public examinations a candidate's mark or, more often, a set of marks are frequently synthesised into an overall grade or classification. Aside from the demands of formal tests and examinations, the regular collection of exercise books for marking enables school teachers to ensure that pupils are making an effort in class, completing homework tasks and responding to such individualised comments as 'Please answer in full sentences' or 'More detail is required'. From their earliest experience of schooling pupils are typically introduced to simple tests, perhaps based on weekly spelling lists or mental arithmetic. The marking of formative tests with 'right' or 'wrong' answers demands relatively little teacher time and may sometimes be delegated to the children themselves. Reliable computer software applications are increasingly used by examination bodies and higher education institutions for the marking of simple tests such as multiple choice assessments. At the school gate, parents' opinions about the quality and professionalism of particular teachers are frequently based, however falsely, on the regularity and care of their marking. The marking of older students' essays and assignments is typically more time intensive, sometimes involving the application of grade-related criteria. Over an academic semester, term or year, teachers and lecturers build up a profile of individual students' strengths, areas for concern and targets for improvement in their grade books, providing an agenda for discussion with learners or their parents.

See also: assessment; examinations; grades; teaching/teaching methods; test/testing

DAVID CROOK

MASLOW, ABRAHAM HAROLD (1908–70)

Abraham Maslow, the American psychologist, was born into a Russian Jewish family in Brooklyn, New York, the eldest of seven children. He did well at school but became unhappy studying law at the City College of New York, so left the course. He subsequently commenced a psychology degree at the University of Wisconsin, studying under the behaviourist Harry Harlow. Here, Maslow completed a B.A. in 1930, an M.A. in 1931 and a doctorate in 1934. After working briefly with E. L. Thorndike at Columbia University, he obtained a teaching post at Brooklyn College in 1937, where he remained for fourteen years. In 1951 he was appointed head of the psychology department at Brandeis University, where he developed an interest in self-actualisation. Here, between 1951 and 1969, he developed his own theories in the field of humanistic psychology, referred to as the 'third force', beyond Freudian theory and behaviourism. Maslow's work identified a hierarchy of human needs, with 'instinctoid' physical needs, such as air, water, food, sleep and sex being the most basic. Safety needs – including security and stability – and psychological needs for such things as belonging, love and acceptance were of a higher order. Individuals seeking personal fulfilment, the highest-ranking human need, according to Maslow, were the most creative, motivated and self-actualising people. Among his best known publications are *Motivation and Personality* (1954), *Towards a Psychology of Being* (1962) and *Farther Reaches of Human Nature*, published posthumously in 1971.

See also: creativity; motivation; psychology of education; Thorndike, Edward L.

DAVID CROOK

MASTER'S

Programmes leading to the award of a master's degree are widely offered by institutions of higher education, normally recruiting postgraduate students who have gained a 'good' first degree. The Master of Arts (M.A.) and Master of Science (M.Sc.) awards are most common master's courses, though many other examples are to be found in the prospectuses of universities and colleges, including the Master of Education (M.Ed.) award. At a global level, one very popular variant is the Master of Business Administration degree, a graduate programme offered by many universities and business schools.

A taught master's programme comprises an approved sequence of modules or courses, with face-to-face instruction. Many institutions also offer distance learning master's programmes, where the student accesses online or broadcast curriculum materials and receives tutor support by mail, telephone or via the internet. Some master's qualifications, such as the Master of Philosophy (M.Phil.) degree, are research-based programmes, requiring students to write a thesis and defend it in an oral examination. Full-time taught master's programmes are normally of one year's duration, with part-time courses typically completed within 2–4 years. Master's degrees gained by research may be the outcome of a significantly longer period of study.

Although there have been efforts to bring greater transparency and standardisation to university awards – through the European 'Bologna Process', for example – not all master's degrees are 'earned' in the orthodox sense. For example, at Oxford and Cambridge Universities in England an M.A. is conferred by right, after a specified time period, upon holders of the universities' first degrees and certain staff members. Some universities also award honorary master's degrees to individuals who have made some notable contribution to public life, not necessarily in the academic field.

See also: degree; distance education/learning; higher education; oral examinations; postgraduate; qualifications; student; thesis/dissertation; university

DAVID CROOK

MATHEMATICS

Mathematics is both a central component of the school curriculum for all pupils and a discipline typically seen as formidable and esoteric. The core of primary school mathematics is, as it has been for centuries, numerical computation. The goal is to equip children with the mathematics they need for coping with daily affairs. By the time they reach secondary school, mathematics has typically become a formal, abstract subject whose mastery may seem out of reach. The main goal has shifted to that of training the mind to reason mathematically, although that goal is increasingly being challenged by arguments for a more practical mathematics. Despite efforts throughout the twentieth century to make school mathematics more attractive and accessible, inadequate performance in mathematics is still commonly used to deny pupils entry to further study that would lead to various career and educational opportunities. The slogan 'mathematics for all' was widely promoted in the last decades of the century, giving rise to disputes among mathematicians, educators, parents, and the public over how much attention should be given in the curriculum to practising routine procedures, solving practical problems by applying mathematics, learning about the historical and cultural sources of mathematical ideas, discussing the results of one's mathematical investigations, learning definitions and proving theorems, or even using mathematics to challenge the social order.

According to sixth-century commentaries on Aristotle, Plato's Academy had the following phrase engraved over the door: 'Let no one ignorant of geometry enter here'. Whether true or not, the story expresses a view that educators have held throughout history: The study of mathematics is prerequisite for developing learners' powers of abstraction and reasoning. Less obvious perhaps is another persistent message: Mathematics is a hurdle that learners need to surmount before their education can continue. For centuries, examinations in mathematics have been used to decide who would be admitted to entry-level jobs, vocational training schemes, or higher education institutions. Once admitted, candidates for advancement might find they were expected to pass additional mathematics examinations even though the content of those examinations might have no obvious connection to the work they would be doing. Not surprisingly, then, although mathematics is almost universally understood to be an important school subject, it often becomes increasingly disliked and even feared as learners discover that it is being used, at times arbitrarily, to control their educational progress.

Primary school mathematics typically consists of a large dose of computational arithmetic along with elementary measurement concepts and some informal geometry. As pupils reach the middle grades, algebra appears, usually as arithmetic that has been generalised to simple linear equations and functions. In secondary school, the functions become more complex – rational, exponential, and trigonometric – leading ultimately to the calculus. Secondary school mathematics also includes more attention to geometry, typically the geometry of transformations, as well as to concepts of probability and statistics. Although there are many variations across countries in the placement of topics and some variations in the topics themselves, most have a curriculum that follows this general pattern.

Although mathematics has been a fundamental school subject since well before Plato's time, mathematics education as a field of scholarly study dates back little more than a century. It appeared near the end of the nineteenth century, when the preparation of teachers began to move out of specialised colleges, seminaries, normal schools, and institutes and into universities. University professors charged with educating teachers of mathematics began to study the learning and teaching of school mathematics. They borrowed theories and techniques from the nascent field of psychology, which was becoming the 'master science' of the school. They also turned to mathematicians for assistance in studying mathematics teaching. For example, the German mathematician Felix Klein proposed that analytic geometry and calculus become part of the secondary school curriculum and that the concept of function should be the unifying theme for this reform, proposals that were widely adopted.

At the Fourth International Congress of Mathematicians in Rome in 1908, the International Commission on the Teaching of Mathematics (ICTM) was formed and almost immediately began a series of surveys on the state of mathematics teaching at all levels of schooling around the world. The work of the ICTM was halted by World War I, although its journal *L'Enseignement Mathématique* has continued publication to this day. Not until 1952 did a reconstituted International Commission on Mathematical Instruction (ICMI) appear. Since then, international activities in mathematics education have flourished. The ICMI not only holds an international congress every four years but also conducts regional meetings as well as studies and associated meetings on topics of special interest.

During the middle decades of the twentieth century, mathematicians led efforts to change the school mathematics curriculum in many countries to include greater attention to the foundational ideas of mathematics. In what became known as the 'new math' movement, the language of sets, relations, and functions was introduced to help clarify terminology and bring order to what was seen as a chaotic and unmotivated curriculum. Pupils learned about one-to-one correspondences between sets, set union and intersection, the distributive and commutative properties, number systems with bases other than ten, and functions as sets of ordered pairs. These ideas were meant to entice more pupils to the study of mathematics, but they often ended up confusing both teachers and pupils.

373

Progress in computing technology during the last half of the twentieth century began to transform the uses of mathematics in society, the way mathematics is done, and eventually the teaching and learning of school mathematics. As mathematics has become more deeply embedded in modern life, pressure has been exerted on the school mathematics curriculum to become more useful. On the one hand, people whose jobs require extensive computations have less need than previous generations for mechanical skill with paper-and-pencil calculations, since such calculations are routinely performed by computers. But on the other hand, they need good estimation skills and a keen sense of numbers and operations so they can detect situations in which incorrect numbers or operations have been employed. Mathematics itself has become a more experimental science as computers allow the proving of theorems by checking huge numbers of cases rather than offering general arguments, a development that has also helped make the subject more impenetrable. Yet the availability of calculators and computers in school classrooms enables pupils to investigate realistic problems from many domains. They are no longer confined to solving simple algebraic equations with integer roots but instead can find approximate solutions to a variety of equations. They can fit functions to data that they themselves collect and then use those functions to answer questions. They can represent functions using tables, equations, and graphs, switching easily between representations to see the effects of a change in the function. For many pupils, statistics rather than calculus has become the most useful and significant part of the mathematics curriculum.

Three decades of international surveys in which countries are ranked according to their average achievement in mathematics have convinced educators, politicians, and the public in many countries that school mathematics needs reformation. Recent videotape studies of mathematics lessons have suggested that the sources of low achievement may lie as much in the teaching as in the curriculum. Teachers of mathematics are being urged to change their pedagogy by giving pupils challenging problems to investigate on their own or in small groups. The effective management of such instruction, however, demands appropriate instructional materials and considerable mathematical sophistication. Inadequate instruments for forming and assessing pupils' ability to solve challenging mathematical problems greatly hamper the improvement of school mathematics, as do chronic shortages of well qualified teachers. Programmes of professional education to update teachers' knowledge of mathematics and of pedagogy continue to be indispensable.

Substantial issues have arisen recently because of efforts to make mathematics a more appealing school subject by introducing curriculum content that is both practical and realistic. Mathematical problems drawn from situations familiar to students from traditionally under-represented groups may be viewed as condescending or inauthentic. Teachers of mathematics are often unprepared to handle discussions of politically or socially charged issues that, although genuine, may be viewed by students and their parents as inappropriate for the mathematics class. Much of school mathematics remains embedded in a rigid social and cultural matrix whose norms are seemingly impervious to change even as the world changes drastically around it.

See also: arithmetic; curriculum; numeracy; subjects

Further reading

Bishop, A., Clements, K., Keitel, C., Kilpatrick, J. and Laborde, C. (eds) (1996) *International Handbook of Mathematics Education*, Dordrecht, the Netherlands: Kluwer.

Bishop, A., Clements, M. A., Keitel, C., Kilpatrick, J. and Leung, F. K. S. (eds) (2003) *Second International Handbook of Mathematics Education*, Dordrecht, the Netherlands: Kluwer.

Nunes, T. and Bryant, P. (eds) (1997) *Learning and Teaching Mathematics: An International Perspective*, East Sussex: Psychology Press.

Sierpinska, A. and Kilpatrick, J. (eds) (1998) *Mathematics Education as a Research Domain: A Search for Identity*, Dordrecht, the Netherlands: Kluwer.

Steffe, L. P., Nesher, P., Cobb, P., Goldin, G.A. and Greer, B. (eds) (1996) *Theories of Mathematical Learning*, Mahwah NJ: Lawrence Erlbaum.

JEREMY KILPATRICK

MATRICULATION

Matriculation, often shortened to matric, is the formal process involved in entering a university – literally being added to the list of members of the university. The prerequisites for matriculation may be the attainment of a particular grade in an entrance examination or another form of qualification. In some universities matriculation is marked through a formal ceremony, which may involve wearing academic dress or signing a membership book.

See also: examinations; qualifications; university

GARY McCULLOCH

MATURE STUDENT

Anyone over the age of twenty-one at the start of their further or higher education course is likely to be considered a mature student, though some institutions and employers have their own particular understandings of the term. Mature students may study to improve their career prospects, to acquire basic skills, for the love of their subject or to gain the certificate, diploma or degree that was not possible for them when they left school. As with other students, mature students may be studying full-time, part-time or via distance learning.

In an increasingly uncertain employment market, employees may look to improve their job prospects through the acquisition of educational qualifications, ensuring that mature students continue to make up a significant proportion of the undergraduate population. Many colleges and universities welcome mature students for their commitment and knowledge and may accept them on the basis of successful completion of an access or return-to-learn course as a substitute for normal certification requirements.

Currently, in the United Kingdom, school teaching assistants pursuing foundation degree courses are almost entirely mature, part-time and female. Many aim to progress to fully qualified teacher status, but the challenges they face are greater than those of their younger counterparts. Family commitments are often demanding, especially for those with young children or elderly relatives. Even part-time study has a big impact on family routines, and the mature student must identify opportunities for periods of quiet, uninterrupted study. Mature students should ensure their tutors are fully aware of their circumstances. Colleges and universities usually employ advisers and welfare officers and a mature students' society will offer advice, support and camaraderie.

See also: lifelong learning; student

KEITH WILLIAMS

McMILLAN, MARGARET (1860–1931)

A tireless campaigner for the improvement of children's health, McMillan was born in New York but schooled in Scotland. Her first job was as a junior superintendent in a home for young girls in London. During the late 1880s, with her sister Rachel, she became involved in progressive and trade union activity, where her ability as a speaker became apparent. The sisters moved to Bradford in 1892 in order to become full-time political tutors and activists. At the same time, McMillan undertook, with the Bradford School Medical Officer, the first complete medical inspection of elementary school children in Britain. This confirmed that child neglect and want were both widespread and endemic. The report proposed that local authorities should provide free school meals, bathing facilities and proper heating and ventilation. She was an elected

375

Independent Labour Party member of the Bradford school board between 1894 and 1902, when she returned to London to campaign for school clinics, where needy children could receive nourishment and medical attention. The sisters opened the first clinic in Bow, east London in 1908, with another following in south London two years later. Her writings condemned child labour and argued for a nurturing, caring purpose to schooling. In *The Child and the State* (1911), McMillan argued in favour of a broad curriculum, rather than a limited vocational one, for poor children. Her vision for early years education was set out in *The Nursery School* (1919) and she was to serve as president of the Nursery Schools Association from 1923. She was elected as a Labour member of the London County Council in 1919, serving until 1922.

See also: health education; nursery school

STEVEN COWAN

MEAD, GEORGE HERBERT (1863–1931)

Mead graduated from Oberlin College, Ohio in 1883 and, after a brief teaching experience, worked for four years for the Wisconsin Railway Company on a project that connected Minnesota to Saskatchewan. After two years studying at Harvard he secured his M.A. in 1888, then studied at Berlin and Leipzig universities, specialising in philosophy and psychology. He returned to teach philosophy at the University of Michigan in 1891. His next post was at University of Chicago, where he held senior academic positions from 1894 until his death in 1931. The influences of Hegelian thought and William James led Mead to adopt a radical empiricism. He believed that psychology should be based upon observable physiological phenomena, and this was to have important effects upon research into child development and education in the United States. Mead argued that mind was the natural product of the interaction of the human

organism with its social and physical environment. The gap between socially acquired reasoning and biologically driven impulse was where language operated, thus laying a basis for the emergence of self-consciousness and intelligence. Mead therefore provided a broader philosophical framework for educationists to consider issues of learning and development. He laid a theoretical basis for the emergence of the 'Chicago School' of sociology, with its emphasis upon pragmatic and empirical research approaches to life experiences and perceptions. Mead engaged in a close intellectual interaction with John Dewey but published no book during his lifetime. His *Philosophy of the Present* (1932), *Mind, Self and Society* (1934) and *The Philosophy of the Act* (1938), compiled after his death by students, using Mead's lecture notes, helped to provide theoretical foundations for later, radical social science perspectives of the 1960s and 1970s.

See also: Dewey, John; intelligence/intelligence tests; philosophy of education; psychology of education

STEVEN COWAN

MEAD, MARGARET (1901–78)

Mead, the American anthropologist, studied social sciences at Barnard College, New York and moved to Columbia University to complete her M.A. (1924) and Ph.D. (1929). In the Department of Anthropology at Columbia, Mead was greatly influenced by Professor Franz Boas and his assistant Dr Ruth Benedict. Mead's doctoral research took her to American Samoa to study adolescent girls. This produced a best-selling book, *Coming of Age In Samoa* (1928), in which she supported the idea that social conditioning, rather than biological factors, was the dominant formative influence upon sexuality. The work aroused substantial interest, altering the way that educators viewed adolescent development. During this field trip and others Mead pioneered the use of systematic photography, and later film, in social science research. In

1929 she studied children's play in New Guinea, reporting in *Growing Up in New Guinea* (1931) that this was significantly shaped by the influences of adult society. Again, the work transformed educators' ideas about children's personal and social development. The final sections of the book present a cross-cultural comparison with American child rearing practices. Her next work on gender identities and roles focused on the historical, physical and social factors shaping three separate communities. Despite serious questions about the reliability of her evidence, Mead's writing helped shape twentieth-century views about child development and socialisation. In 1974 she became the first elected president of the American Association for the Advancement of Science.

See also: anthropology of education; child development; educational research

STEVEN COWAN

MECHANICS' INSTITUTE

Chiefly a British term, the history of the mechanics' institute may be traced back to Dr George Birkbeck who, in 1800, began a series of Saturday evening lectures at Anderson's Institution, Glasgow, Scotland, where he was professor of natural philosophy, 'for persons engaged in the practical exercise of the mechanical arts'. Within a short space of time the lectures were attracting weekly audiences of 500. In 1823, by which time Birkbeck had relocated to London, this class evolved into the Glasgow Mechanics' Institute. With a similar organisation operating in Edinburgh, Birkbeck moved to extend the principle to England. He inaugurated the London Mechanics' Institute in 1824, and thereafter the movement spread very quickly to other parts of Britain. It has been estimated that, by 1851, there were at least 600 mechanics' institutes operating. In the early days lectures tended to be heavily weighted towards science and engineering, but they subsequently encompassed broader aspects of nineteenth-century culture. Like the municipal athenaeum, set up to meet demand from the wealthy male intelligentsia, mechanics' institutes often maintained a library, as well as providing instruction and opportunities for discussion. Mechanics' institute were gradually absorbed into the mainstream of British education. Some provided the nucleus of public libraries and others became technical colleges. The London Mechanics' Institute took the name of its founder, and Birkbeck College was incorporated into the University of London. The mechanics' institute movement paved the way for subsequent organisations in the field of workers' education, including the Workers' Educational Association.

See also: adult education; athenaeum; workers' education; Workers' Educational Association (WEA)

DAVID CROOK

MEDICINE

Medicine can be defined as the science devoted to explaining and coping with disease. A significant component of the study of medicine includes the science of healing. It investigates the anatomy and physiology of the human being along with focusing on *homeostasis*, which is the intra- and inter-relationships found among the various individual organs and organ systems and their respective physiological functions and responses within the body's internal and external environments. Homeostasis, coupled with the human body's natural tendency to heal itself through its various organ and physiological systems, provides the field of medicine with a unifying theoretical, contextual, and conceptual foundation in the overall treatment of human illnesses. Modern day medicine bases its findings and explanations upon scientific information and methodology in order to better understand and diagnose the causative properties, treatments, and preventative measures involved in human anatomical, physiological, and behavioural diseases.

Medicine encompasses both the ancient and most current scientific disciplines; however, its historical roots reside in the study of philosophy, theology, and pseudo-science. Various cultures throughout time, including but not limited to the Greeks, Egyptians, Assyrians, Babylonians, Europeans, Indians, Chinese, Mayans, and Native Americans have developed ways of explaining and diagnosing human diseases, although a significant amount of the diagnostic and prognostic descriptions of the past have focused on pseudo-scientific claims or fallacies. Medicine evolved significantly through the development and application of science and technology beginning in the late nineteenth and early twentieth centuries, and continues to build its knowledge base and structure to this day.

See also: biology; professional education; science/science education; subjects

PAUL NARGUIZIAN

MEDITERRANEAN

Geographically, the Mediterranean stretches from the Straits of Gibraltar to the Dardanelles, with a total area of 2.5 million square kilometres. Regionally, the Mediterranean comprises all the coastal countries of the Mediterranean Sea that may be split into three blocks: the Arab countries Algeria, Egypt, Lebanon, Libya, Morocco, Syria and Tunisia; the East European countries Albania, Bosnia and Herzegovina, Croatia, Serbia and Montenegro, Slovenia and Turkey; and the West European countries Cyprus, France, Greece, Israel, Italy, Malta and Spain. The latter (excluding Israel) are also the southern peripheral countries of the European Union (EU). The Mediterranean region is inhabited by 7 per cent of the world's population or 450 million, of which 200 million are Arabs, who by 2025 are expected to comprise 60 per cent of the Mediterranean population.

The Babylonians, Hebrews, Phoenicians, Egyptians and Greeks, in particular, were at the forefront of learning and teaching. The pursuit of knowledge in the Mediterranean dates back to ancient times of the proto-literate man in Mesopotamia (3000–2000 BCE), the emergence of the classical Babylonian written language and the Sumerian scribes. These were later followed by the establishment of the House of Wisdom (c.1500 BCE). During the same period the proto-literate man appeared in Egypt (3000–1800 BCE) as evidenced by, amongst various archaeological discoveries, the earliest school room in the palace of Mari and papyrus sheets with mathematical text. In the Greek *polis* (town), education was closely associated with daily affairs and structure of the polis. Sparta (eighth century BCE) founded an education system for military purposes and Greece (sixth century BCE) taught literacy by some unknown formal process of teaching. The Athenians (fourth century BCE) consciously dealt with the process of education through the so called *paideia* or education for good. Formal systems were established by Socrates, Plato and the Republic, and the Lyceum of Aristotle.

Since the eleventh century CE, Mediterranean universities have established networks of intellectual cooperation and, by the sixteenth century, they were overruled by the powers of the Church and state itself.

Presently, university cooperation reflects the geopolitical situation of the region, not least through EU exchange schemes such as *Erasmus* and *Eureka*. The Council of Europe has set up the Transmed Information Centre and has also established the Mediterranean Programme and Network of Mediterranean Bookshops. Important networks and communities include: the Community of Mediterranean Universities founded in Bari in 1983 that strengthened cooperation among the 129 universities; the University of the Mediterranean (UNIMED) based in Italy but branched out in Amman (Jordan), Cairo (Egypt), Valletta (Malta), Montpellier (France) and Rabat (Morocco); the Network of Mediterranean Study Centres; the *Laboratorio Mediterraneo* and South-East Mediterranean Project (SEMEP) covering Albania, Greece,

Turkey, Lebanon, Cyprus, Israel, Jordan and Egypt. In spite of such initiatives, the gap between the north and the south persists in educational standards, particularly in science and technology.

Almost all the countries have a pre-school period of two to four years, while the majority have six years of primary education. The secondary education sector is quite varied, with most countries having a lower or inter-mediate school (*gymnasium*) and upper or high school (*lyceum*) duration. The vocational or technical sector runs parallel to upper sec-ondary. Practically all Mediterranean coun-tries offer 3–6-year undergraduate courses, teacher training colleges and technical insti-tutes in over 250 universities and research centres. The Al-Azhar University in Egypt is a religious school that spans the primary, secondary and tertiary levels in one institution.

UNESCO statistics confirm that Arab countries have 8–11 years of compulsory education, Eastern European countries 8 or 9 years while the Western European states have 9–11 years. The maximum school com-mencement age is seven years and the mini-mum leaving age is fourteen (both instances being in the Eastern European bloc). The pre-primary enrolment rate is still low in Arab and Eastern European regions – for example 5 per cent in Algeria and 8 per cent in Turkey – when compared to the more developed Western European bloc, where it exceeds 85 per cent in most countries. The primary enrolment rate is over 85 per cent across the Mediterranean, but secondary rates are again lower in Arab countries – just 35 per cent in Morocco – compared to the next-lowest rates of Albania (73 per cent) and Greece (84 per cent). The highest rates of out-of-school primary children are found in Morocco (13 per cent), Turkey (11 per cent) and Malta (6 per cent). Pupil/teacher ratios are relatively low in the whole region; at primary level the highest ratios are found in Algeria (28:1), Albania (21:1) and Cyprus (19:1), while at secondary level the highest ratios are found in Algeria (21:1), Albania

(18:1) and France (12:1). The whole Medi-terranean experiences considerable student mobility, particularly at the tertiary level, with highest rates being in the regions of Morocco (15 per cent), Albania (27 per cent) and Cyprus (92 per cent). Malta and Albania have the highest proportion of graduates in edu-cation (19 per cent and 36 per cent respec-tively), probably reflecting their dependence on human capital and very limited natural resources. Public expenditure on education varies between states from 3 per cent to 8 per cent of gross domestic product, with expendi-ture per pupil as a percentage of GDP per capita being highest in Morocco (31 per cent), Croatia (26 per cent) and Cyprus (35 per cent).

See also: Egypt; Europe; France; Greece; Israel; Italy

Further reading

Postlethwaite, T. N. (ed.) (1988) *The Encyclopaedia of Comparative Education and National Systems of Education*, Oxford: Pergamon.
——(1995) *International Encyclopaedia of National Systems of Education*, 2nd edn, Oxford: Pergamon.

EDWARD MIFSUD

MENTOR/MENTORING

Mentoring has traditionally been defined as a dyadic relationship in which a more knowl-edgeable and experienced person (a mentor) befriends and works with a less knowledge-able and experienced person (a mentee or protégé) in order to support the mentee's learning and development. A mentor's role may incorporate that of guide, adviser, spon-sor, role model, counsellor, trainer or coach. Mentoring can, however, be differentiated from coaching: while coaching focuses on the development of specific skills, mentoring has a broader remit and aims to support the mentee emotionally, socially and professionally.

Over the centuries it is possible to identify examples of schemes that have resonances with mentoring. However, it was not until the late 1970s that this phenomenon experienced a rapid rise in popularity. Within the teaching profession, the growing interest in mentoring can be linked to concerns about teacher retention and to widespread reforms of initial teacher education. Mentoring is now a common feature of (pre-service and in-service) teachers' professional development in many parts of Europe as well as in, for example, North America, Australia, New Zealand, China and Japan. It is often used at times of transition: for example, in teacher preparation and in the induction of newly qualified teachers and newly appointed head teachers.

There is, however, little agreement about the exact nature of mentoring. Some researchers have noted that the word 'mentor' was first used in Homer's The Odyssey, an epic poem from Ancient Greece, in which Odysseus, king of Ithaca, entrusted the care of his household and his son Telemachus to his old friend Mentor. It has been argued, however, that Mentor's relationship with Telemachus is not consistent with modern understandings of mentoring (Roberts 2000). Other researchers have attempted to gain greater insight into the mentor's role through observing and analysing what those engaged in mentoring actually do. This has proved to be extremely complex – not least because the role of the mentor, the nature of the mentoring relationship and the mentoring skills and strategies used will change as the mentee gains what are perceived to be appropriate attitudes, understandings, knowledge and skills, demonstrates increased competence and confidence, and moves towards independence (see Maynard and Furlong 1993).

As mentoring has become more established, questions have been raised about the content of mentor training programmes; the appropriateness of mentors becoming involved in assessment procedures; and, when matching mentor and mentee, whether due consideration is given to issues such as personality, gender and ethnicity. As mentoring is centred on a relationship, however, experiences and outcomes will be difficult to predict. There is little hard evidence about the effectiveness of mentoring although it appears to enhance mentees' learning, confidence and commitment to teaching. Mentoring is also seen to benefit mentors through providing a sense of satisfaction and greater insight into their own thinking and practice.

Since the millennium, understandings about mentoring within the teaching profession have been evolving and expanding. For example, the use of computer technology as a way of enhancing the mentoring process is being explored. There have also been calls for mentoring to be reconceptualised as a collegial and collaborative activity undertaken by groups of teachers as part of the development of professional learning communities. Mentoring would thus become not so much about the enculturation of intending teachers as the 'reculturing' of schools (Hargreaves and Fullan 2000).

Within schools, pupils may also act as mentors. Peer mentoring schemes (cross-phase or cross-school mentoring), where older children support younger children who are experiencing academic or personal difficulties, are widespread in the USA and, in the UK, have increased in number since the 1980s. Youth mentoring, which aims to address social exclusion, can involve adults working with pupils in school settings as well as in the community. An example of youth mentoring is 'Big Brothers Big Sisters', a scheme which originated in the USA and has now been established in many countries around the world. In England, since 1999, a growing number of 'learning mentors' have been working in primary and secondary schools in order to help children and young people overcome 'barriers to learning' such as truancy, punctuality and disaffection.

See also: continued/continuing professional development; peer group; profession/professionalism/professionalisation; teaching profession

Further reading

Hargreaves, A. and Fullan, M. (2000) 'Mentoring in the new millennium', Theory into Practice, 39(1): 50–56.

Maynard, T. and Furlong, J. (1993) 'Learning to teach and models of mentoring'. In D. McIntyre, H. Hagger and M. Wilkin (eds) *Mentoring: Perspectives on School-based Teacher Education*, London: Kogan Page.

Roberts, A. (2000) 'Mentoring revisited: a phenomenological reading of the literature', *Mentoring and Tutoring*, 8(2): 145–70.

TRICIA MAYNARD

MERIT

The appearance of the concept of merit in relation to education is thought to have accompanied the decline of patronage in the civil service in Britain in the second half of the nineteenth century, eventually spreading through Western countries to create what Michael Young (1958) described as a new form of oligarchy. 'Meritocracy' would displace nepotism and the inheritance of social position more generally, and schooling would provide the technical means of producing a hierarchy of distinction based on educational achievement. Thus there are historical links between the rise of meritocratic thinking and the provision of popular schooling, as well as a conflation of merit with the requirements and outcomes of schooling. These associations between merit and formal education provision meant that educational distinction came to be understood as merit more readily than other kinds of achievement (Bourdieu 1986).

In some countries, completion of the compulsory years of schooling was recognised with the awarding of the 'Merit Certificate'. But larger numbers wanted to proceed to advanced education that promised increased merit and greater rewards, driving an expansion in secondary school provision along with attempts at educational selection to allow efficiencies in sorting those with merit. For the most part, selection regimes were underpinned by a political doctrine of 'equality of opportunity' that ratified particular conceptions of merit. Proponents of schooling for democracy argued that no reasonable complaint could be made in circumstances where educational arrangements allowed full opportunity for merit to express itself and be registered.

In England and most of the colonies, however, institutional provision ratified pre-existing assumptions about the social distribution of merit (or different kinds of merit). In England, for example, the 1895 'Bryce' royal commission recommended three grades of secondary school to prepare distinct groups for their life's calling. The three grades corresponded to the life trajectories of a cultured and literary class, a commercial or industrial class, and an artisan class. In Australia, many private school headmasters opposed the establishment of state secondary education on the grounds that it would soil an 'aristocracy of culture', and science began to spell out the implications of natural limits on merit, particularly as these applied to the working class, women and Aborigines (McCallum 1990).

Advances in the science of measurement and individual differences during the early twentieth century shaped new ways in which merit came to be conceptualised, as well as new techniques for achieving efficiencies in educational selection. Educational psychology sought to develop tests that would measure the capacity of children to succeed in further education, leading to the recognition of merit. Whereas its origins may lie in more general notions of excellence, honour and reward – as in the Prussian Order of Merit – now merit became specifically enmeshed with ideas about the distribution of intelligence.

One of the central organising assumptions of educational theory on selection was the belief that educational resources should be allocated to those 'best fitted' to receive them. If nature had decreed that there was a certain fixed distribution of ability throughout the population, the mission of psychological testing was to uncover it. Natural ability groups would replace social groups as the repositories of merit.

But psychological theories of intelligence also provided the groundwork for the erection of a suitable institutional structure and for the interpretation of patterns of achievement resulting from the induction of the expanding school population. On this terrain, psychology was not simply an apologetic discourse for current arrangements. The science of individual differences had scope to record the appearance of merit or talent lying in any social group. Yet psychology drew on the school system itself to sustain the fiction that there was sufficient commonality of experience in schools to permit differences to be determined as pre-social or 'natural'. It should be remembered that an existing differentiated school system was in place well before its population became an object of intelligence testing.

Current moves to produce a differentiated education system in a period of mass tertiary participation owes part of its rationale to systems of power and knowledge that underpinned stratification of the secondary school system and the determination of limits on the distribution of merit in the population (Collins 1977).

See also: ability; equality of opportunity; intelligence/intelligence tests; meritocracy; psychology of education; selection; test/testing

Further reading

Bourdieu, P. (1986) *Distinction. A Social Critique of the Judgement of Taste*, trans. R. Nice, London: Routledge and Kegan Paul.
Collins, R. (1977) 'Functional and conflict theories of educational stratification'. In J. Karabel and A. H. Halsey (eds) *Power and Ideology in Education*, New York: Oxford University Press, 118–36.
McCallum, D. (1990) *The Social Production of Merit*, London: Falmer.
Young, M. (1958) *The Rise of the Meritocracy*, Harmondsworth: Penguin.

DAVID McCALLUM

MERITOCRACY

Michael Young's classic book *The Rise of the Meritocracy* (1958) coined the word 'meritocracy', which came to express the ideals of modern societies that were based on the outcomes of competitive examinations: individual merit. This, in turn, was made up of the combination of intelligence and effort $(I + E = M)$ (Young 1958: 94). Yet, ironically, Young's work was intended fundamentally to be a satire of these ideals and a warning of what they might lead to in terms of dangerous social polarisation.

In his book, Young defined a meritocracy as a society in which promotion at work and social advancement were dependent on the individual's success in examinations. It meant also that the social elite was 'selected according to brains and educated according to deserts', rather than owing its position to either the accident of birth or to wealth. This was 'rule not so much by the people as by the cleverest people; not an aristocracy of birth, not a plutocracy of wealth, but a true meritocracy of talent' (Young 1958: 21). The book is written as a fictional history of social developments in Britain from 1870, when the first Education Act was passed to introduce mass state education, to the year 2033. Over this time, the narrator notes with approval the decline of nepotism and of aristocratic influence, and the rise of selection by merit. Comprehensive schools had threatened this process for a while, but intelligence testing and grammar schools survived and prospered. Thus, the 'workshop of the world', which Britain had been in the nineteenth century, became the 'grammar school of the world' (Young 1958: 46). Indeed, he boasts, 'the world beholds for the first time the spectacle of a brilliant class, the five per cent of the nation who know what five per cent means' (Young 1958: 103). However, those excluded from this new elite form the new lower classes, and become discontented and alienated. In the year 2034, they finally revolt, and revolution ensues. The narrator of the book is himself killed in this revolt.

Young clearly intended to draw attention to the contradictions of the notion of the meritocracy, which he felt was gaining ground in contemporary thought, and the book itself succeeds in doing so.

Subsequently, there have been many criticisms of meritocratic approaches. For example, the sociologist Goldthorpe insisted that it was not possible for any one well defined and objective conception of merit to be established. According to Goldthorpe then, attempts to provide the structure of inequality in modern societies with a meritocratic legitimation, or to argue that this kind of legitimation was becoming more appropriate as these societies evolved, would not succeed (Goldthorpe 1997: 665). Moreover, while the most straightforward version of a meritocracy would be genetic, it was clear that 'merit' was itself strongly influenced by the actions of families, schools and the wider culture in reproducing advantage and inequality (Feinstein 2006: 417). Meritocracy, indeed, appeared to be an ideology that sought to justify a new form of social inequality by means of a systematisation of a narrow view of intelligence. As the final footnote of Young's book wryly remarks, 'The failings of sociology are as illuminating as its successes.' (Young 1958: 190).

See also: elitism; equality of opportunity; examinations; excellence; merit; selection; sociology; Young, Michael

Further reading

Feinstein, L. (2006) 'Social class and cognitive development in childhood in the UK'. In H. Lauder, P. Brown, J. Dillabaugh and A. H. Halsey (eds) *Education, Globalisation and Social Change*, Oxford: Oxford University Press.
Goldthorpe, J. (1997) 'Problems of "meritocracy"'. In A. H. Halsey, H. Lauder, P. Brown and A. Wells (eds) *Education: Culture, Economy, Society*, Oxford: Oxford University Press.
Young, M. (1958) *The Rise of the Meritocracy 1870–2033: An Essay on Education and Equality*, London: Thames and Hudson.

GARY McCULLOCH

METROPOLITANISM

In one sense, metropolitanism involves the development of the planning of services for large urban areas which have fragmented into different areas and districts. It consists of a wide range of agencies cooperating to organise education and other key activities for the metropolitan area as a whole. According to Robert Havighurst, a metropolis is a new kind of community, in which large department stores, banks, schools, libraries, parks, factories, churches, play spaces, houses, highways, subways, railways, suburban villages, the central city, shopping centres and open fields are all bound together in a set of processes of action and planning. Metropolitanism might also constitute an awareness of being a citizen of a metropolitan unit (Havighurst 1968).

The American historian of education Lawrence Cremin interpreted metropolitanism in this basic sense but also proposed a further set of meanings. It did reflect the long-term development of large-scale metropolitan societies within which educational institutions were transformed and proliferated. However, in another way it was about the export of the culture and civilisation of a metropolitan society to other nations and regions of the world. This took place in part, for example, through Christian missions, but also through cultural products such as books, magazines, films, television, and even the export of entire systems of formal education (Cremin 1988). This kind of process has also been described as cultural imperialism, inasmuch as it involves the imposition of a regime of values and practices that often overwhelms or downgrades indigenous forms of culture and education in different parts of the world.

See also: indigenous education; urban education

Further reading

Cremin, L. (1988) *American Education: The Metropolitan Experience, 1876–1980*, New York: Harper and Row.
Havighurst, R. (ed.) (1968) *Metropolitanism: The Challenge to Education*, Chicago IL: University of Chicago Press.

GARY McCULLOCH

MILL, JOHN STUART (1806–73)

Mill was the eldest son of the Scottish utilitarian and East India Company official, James Mill. His father took a direct control over his education, ensuring that John Stuart was kept from the influence of other children. Taught mainly by his father, with occasional assistance from such figures as Francis Place and Jeremy Bentham, Mill learnt Greek from the age of three, Latin from age eight and was introduced as a young boy to such subjects as logic and economics. He worked in the India Office from 1823 until his retirement, as a senior official, in 1858, but he suffered a mental breakdown in his early twenties. He had a late political career, as Member of Parliament for Westminster from 1865–68 and was elected to the honorary position of Rector of St Andrews University, Scotland in 1866.

His reputation as a major thinker of his age was consolidated with his *System of Logic* (1843) and *Principles of Political Economy* (1848). But it was the publication of *On Liberty* (1859), essentially co-authored with his wife, Harriet Taylor, which brought him to the centre of public debate about the role and functions of government. Mill was a leading advocate of government support for university scholarships, public libraries and the provision of public galleries and museums. Some ideas expressed in *Representative Government* (1861) were embodied in the creation of school boards in the 1870s. Mill was equally famous for his support for women's equality, most notably expressed in *The Subjection of Women* (1869).

See also: economics of education; equality of opportunity; politics of education

STEVEN COWAN

MISSION STATEMENT

A mission statement is an institution's formal, public declaration of its purposes, explaining its current activities and characteristics, its values, and its goals for the future. Mission statements are ubiquitous among educational institutions, from preschools to graduate schools, in both public and private schools and universities. These statements may provide some context about the organisation's history and role, providing factual details about the size of the organisation and its founding date as a means to demonstrate its impact. Other educationally related organisations have mission statements including accrediting agencies, policy organisations, educational unions and lobbying groups, and governmental agencies related to education. Also, units within an educational institution (e.g. departments, service offices) have mission statements, specific to their particular roles. The process of writing or revising a mission statement can often be cyclical, automatically renewing every certain number of years. A mission statement can be as short as a sentence but within educational settings they are usually much longer as they try to cover the range of activities the institution engages in, such 'teaching, research, and service' or the specific areas of knowledge taught.

Mission statements are written as a means to articulate a shared purpose and meaning in order to increase organisational success. They are often required by accrediting bodies or governmental agencies (state school boards for public education, state governing boards for higher education) or created during a period of restructuring or strategic planning. They can serve as an important (and expected) rhetorical device. Mission statements can be used as a means to test progress or to see if new initiatives will fit within the overall mission of the institution. They are usually written collaboratively with input from various groups within the institution, but are primarily 'owned' by the institutional leaders who guide its composition and implementation. For example, they may use the statement as a public relations tool to inspire constituents to believe in the core goals of the institution and to work towards them or to show funders, such as legislative bodies, that more money is needed if the institution is to live up to its mission. Policy makers use mission statements as a tool for accountability and as a means to eliminate or prevent programme duplication. The process of writing or revisiting mission statements can be a means for self-reflection among educational leaders.

The conventional wisdom has been that mission statements all look alike as institutions imitate each other's towards an 'ideal form' in substance and style, and that they are more likely to focus on aspirations, especially among institutions wishing to rise in stature or prestige. However, recent research indicates that mission statements more often reflect the true nature of an institution (Morphew and Hartley 2006). Also, most differences among mission statements are found between public and private institutions, especially as they articulate what they mean by the type of 'service' they offer their benefactors and communities.

While schools have long had organisational missions, the trend to articulate them into mission statements grew in the 1970s, as educational organisations adopted this practice from the corporate world. While some might argue for their utility as a means to articulate values and goals, critics see them as useless, arguing that once written, they are soon forgotten and ignored. Furthermore, critics contend that they are excessively vague or overly general, not truly focusing an institution's behaviour. Creating a vague statement provides more latitude for growth and to respond to unexpected opportunities. The related phenomenon among institutions of higher education is that of 'mission creep', wherein a college or university modifies its mission (or at times only its name) as a means to gain higher status and prestige. Usually this isomorphism involves adding or enhancing a research function to the institution. Examining different versions of mission statements over time can be one means to demonstrate how an institution has (or has not) changed, although mission statements do not always accurately reflect institutional behaviour.

If the goal of a mission statement is to provide a common sense of purpose, an effective mission statement communicates that purpose, reflecting the notion of what an institution should be in the minds of its faculty, students, alumni, and the public while also providing direction for the organisation's future. The statement should reflect the institution's core mission as a means for different individuals and groups to come together to achieve shared purposes, deeply rooted in the institution's identity, providing enough specificity to provide guidance while still allowing for flexibility.

See also: accountability; college; faculty; school; university

Further reading:

Davies, G. K. (1986) 'The importance of being general: philosophy, politics, and institutional mission statements'. In J. C. Smart (ed.) *Higher Education: Handbook of Theory and Research*, New York: Agathon Press.

Meacham, J. and Gaff, J. G. (2006) 'Learning goals in mission statements: implications for educational leadership', *Liberal Education*, 92(1): 6–13.

Morphew, C. C. and Hartley, M. (2006) 'Mission statements: a thematic analysis of rhetoric across institutional type', *Journal of Higher Education*, 77(3): 456–71.

CHRISTIAN K. ANDERSON

MIXED-ABILITY TEACHING

Mixed-ability teaching is linked to ability grouping, and concerns the pedagogies required to serve groups of children in schools where neither setting or streaming have been adopted (Ireson and Hallam 2001).

No classroom can be entirely homogeneous. Pupils vary in their cultural backgrounds, attitudes, skills, knowledge and experience. Even if grouped closely in age and restricted to one gender, personality, motivation, self-esteem, propensities and interests will ensure a range of approaches to learning and different degrees of success. Ability is another factor to consider in grouping people in their learning and is one of the most common and controversial methods of differentiating pupils. Where teachers, local policy makers or governments object to this method, mixed-ability teaching arises.

Following the 1944 Education Act in the UK, an extreme example of streaming was introduced in the form of different schools for children of different measured ability. Using intelligence tests, pupils were selected for entry into schools with more or less emphasis on academic ability. Children who did not attend the academic schools were presented with fewer options to excel and their low expectations were not raised through their education. A comprehensive system was created to rectify these inequalities, emphasising fair and equal opportunities for all. This included being taught in mixed-ability groups and sharing the most effective teachers across all abilities, not preserving them for the most able.

Research demonstrates mixed findings concerning the efficacy of mixed-ability teaching. Having more able achievers together with those who may be struggling could act as encouragement to the less able, pulled up through the positive modelling of the high achievers. It could equally become a burden, constantly serving to reinforce repeated failure or mediocrity. For the high achievers, arrogance can be displayed through being unchallenged at the top of the class, or understanding can grow of different people and their abilities. Most children will have an uneven ability spread, doing better in some subjects than others, reinforcing the positive effect of not consigning some pupils to the 'bottom set' for every subject.

Mixed-ability teaching is more easily managed across the school than ability groups, which must allow a certain amount of movement between groups if they are to genuinely reflect pupils' abilities. The ease with which mixed ability teaching can be tackled depends on multiple factors including the size of the class and the teacher's knowl-

edge of pupils and their abilities. Within a mixed ability group it is necessary to differentiate provision through either individual or small group tasks (with children of different or like abilities), and through the use of different materials, tasks and/or outcomes. Basing groups on shared interests can promote friendships and increase motivation.

Varied resources also help to support diverse interests, and by teaching thematically and adapting published materials teachers can make tasks more relevant to pupils. With larger classes, establishing a mentoring scheme can help to avoid anonymity, pairing pupils who can get along but who may not always be drawn to working together.

Helping pupils set individual goals will ensure that they are working at the level that matches their ability. Familiarity with their preferred ways of approaching tasks will increase confidence both in class activities and for independent learning. Understanding learning styles could be helpful, although many teachers consider this 'movement' to be little more than a rebranding of effective pedagogy.

Tasks that have a combination of closed and open-ended factors will provide structure whilst allowing pupils to take control of their own learning, increasing and sustaining motivation. Teachers need to provide both sufficient support for the weaker pupil and extra tasks for those that finish quickly. Support should match pupil need and all tasks (for more and less able) should not be empty time-occupying activities.

In general, more formal education systems tend to employ ability-based teaching, but curiously, there is no clear trend in the development of mixed-ability teaching across the world. In 2002 for example, similar difficulties in schools in Scotland and in the United States were met with opposing policies. Where the USA was moving away from setting and streaming towards mixed-ability teaching, Scottish policy makers recommended the division of pupils by ability in some subjects.

See also: ability; ability grouping; curriculum differentiation; setting; streaming/tracking

Further reading

Boaler, J., Wiliam, D. and Brown, M. (2000) 'Students' experiences of ability grouping: disaffection, polarisation and the construction of failure', *British Educational Research Journal*, 26(5): 631–48.

Ireson, J. and Hallam, S. (2001) *Ability Grouping in Education*, London: Paul Chapman.

CARRIE WINSTANLEY

MODERN LANGUAGES

In a world characterised by globalisation and internationalisation, as well as in view of the attendant growth in importance of English as a lingua franca, the ability to speak one or more foreign language(s) has become increasingly essential, particularly in non-English speaking countries. Among other things, this has led to a growing emphasis in many countries on an early start for foreign language teaching and learning and the introduction of foreign language education as part of the primary/elementary school curriculum, as well as a growth in English-medium higher education provision.

Modern language education (as opposed to 'ancient' languages such as classical Greek or Latin) tends to be underpinned by a diverse set of rationales, normally including some reference to the importance of foreign languages as a medium of communication at an individual, interpersonal, level, as well as their contribution at a national level to a country's economic competitiveness. Foreign language education is also often promoted as a means of developing intercultural competence in increasingly multilingual and multicultural societies and as an ingredient in broad conceptualisations of citizenship. In this respect, the efforts of the European Commission to further tolerance and combat xenophobia through foreign language education initiatives and mobility programmes are particularly noteworthy.

The rationale for the inclusion of a modern language subject in the curriculum determines the aims and objectives set out for it in a national curriculum or in national framework documents. Concomitant with the nature of the rationale delineated above there has been a noticeable trend away from aims which foreground the achievement of native-speaker like proficiency at the end of what normally is only a rather short period of language study in compulsory and even in post-compulsory education – across the EU foreign language study is afforded between 9 and 34 per cent of curriculum time in secondary education – towards a laying of foundations for foreign language study in later life. What has remained relatively constant in recent years is the assumption that the learning of a foreign language combines the acquisition of a range of skills, usually in the areas of speaking, listening, reading and writing, with content knowledge from a range of areas and disciplines including – depending on the learner's level of proficiency and the educational phase – literature, culture, society, language and linguistics, politics and history. What has grown considerably, particularly in the higher education sector, is the number of non-specialist linguists who study a foreign language in addition and/or subservient to (an)other subject(s).

Also related are questions about methodology and curricular organisation. Since the 1970s Communicative Language Teaching (CLT) has emerged as the prevalent approach to foreign language teaching. It is eclectic in nature, draws on a number of foundation disciplines such as linguistics, psychology, philosophy, sociology and educational research, and has developed in many variations throughout the world. Common to all these variants is the notion of the development of 'communicative competence' in learners, in other words their ability to understand language and the functions it performs. They tend to differ in terms of the relative importance afforded to the role of grammar. In recent years the traditional subject-based model, where languages occupied separate slots on the timetable, have been called into question and challenged by cross–curricular and content-based approaches. These models are based on cross-fertilisation of curriculum content across subjects such as geography, business studies or science and provide students with an opportunity to continue their subject domain-specific development as well as concurrently work on their language proficiency. Different models of operationalisation exist according to shifting emphases on content and language.

Most recently, the characteristics and potential of new technologies have promised – or threatened as some might see it – some rather fundamental changes in the teaching and learning of foreign languages. The easy access to multimodal, authentic material as well as to communication with target language speakers from all over the world, not just from the countries where the target language is spoken, across temporal and geographical distance is in the process of redefining the landscape for foreign language and culture education.

See also: classical studies; curriculum; subjects

Further reading

Lightbown, P. and Spada, N. (1999) *How Languages are Learned*, revised edn, Oxford: Oxford University Press.

Macaro, E. (2003) *Teaching and Learning a Second Language: A Guide to Recent Research and its Applications*, London: Continuum.

Mitchell, R. and Myles, F. (1998) *Second Language Learning Theories*, London: Arnold.

NORBERT PACHLER

MODULAR/MODULE

Modular education refers to the process of dividing the curriculum into independent units or modules that can be combined in a number of flexible ways according to the needs and preferences of individual students, institutions and employers. This practice has become especially widespread in higher education, where varying numbers of credits are awarded for each module completed successfully which, in turn, contribute to a degree.

This way of organising education is also designed to allow an institution to respond rapidly to wider social and economic changes: individual modules can be replaced and adapted without harming the overall system. It is seen as beneficial for employers who will benefit from a growing diversity of potential employees, each of whom may have chosen a different modular route. In some contexts, modular education also aims to bridge the divide between academic and vocational forms of learning. More broadly, this development has fostered transference and comparability across different institutions and systems and, in theory, allows a student to move between different institutions. For instance, it forms one element in the Bologna Process, which aims to bring about closer European cooperation in higher education.

Modular also refers to a mode of building based on the amalgamation of small buildings or 'modular classrooms', which may form temporary accommodation in expanding schools.

See also: degree; higher education

TOM WOODIN

MONITOR

In education, monitor is sometimes encountered as a verb, meaning to watch or keep under surveillance. School children with a record of poor conduct may be monitored closely by their teachers in order to judge whether they have learnt from past mistakes or whether further disciplinary sanctions are necessary. The behaviour and work of learners may be monitored by teachers to assess levels of knowledge and understanding, to determine whether the student has special educational needs or may benefit from remedial or extension work. Public education institutions themselves and school districts are frequently monitored by inspection agencies interested in such matters as test and examination performance, student participation, progression, truancy and dropout rates, compliance with relevant legislation and financial viability. The areas of school effectiveness and school improvement draw heavily upon data gained from monitoring exercises.

Pupil monitors were a feature of early nineteenth-century English denominational schools. The monitorial system associated with Joseph Lancaster and Andrew Bell, which was emulated and adapted in various parts of the world, saw groups of monitors charged with teaching classes of younger children. Pupils continue to serve as monitors in many schools, and the term is sometimes synonymous with that of prefect. School monitors may have responsibility for distributing stationery, assisting in the library and greeting school visitors. They may also issue refreshments, such as fruit juice or milk, to their peers. Many adults remember with amusement their days as a school milk monitor. Nostalgic memories may also be rekindled by reading school fiction, including Enid Blyton's *The Naughtiest Girl is a Monitor* (1945).

See also: accountability; inspection; Lancaster, Joseph; monitorial system; prefect

DAVID CROOK

MONITORIAL SYSTEM

The monitorial, mutual or Madras system was developed in the late eighteenth and early nineteenth centuries as a means of instructing a large number of students at an elementary level. It was devised independently by two British educators, Andrew Bell and Joseph Lancaster, and was widely used in different parts of the world during the nineteenth century. It involved the teacher instructing a small group of advanced students who would pass on this knowledge to a much larger group of pupils. The monitors thus have a key position in the teaching scheme, more pivotal than prefects and pupil teachers in their support of instruction and discipline,

and often would go on to become teachers themselves. Lancaster opened a school in 1798 that successfully developed this approach in a mechanical form of provision. Bell also used this system in Madras, India, from 1789. The basic technique was highly popular and permitted the development of elementary education on a large scale relatively cheaply with a small teaching force. It was superseded in due course with the increasing use of a classroom system of simultaneous instruction, and a growing preference for less mechanical forms of provision.

See also: classroom; Lancaster, Joseph; monitor; prefect

GARY McCULLOCH

MONTESSORI, MARIA (1870–1952)

An Italian doctor and school innovator, in 1896 Montessori was the first woman to qualify in medicine in Italy, leading to work with mentally challenged children in a Rome psychiatric clinic. She studied in London and Paris and was influenced by ideas of Séguin and Decroly, returning to lecture in pedagogy at Rome University from 1901–7, where she was also professor of anthropology (1904–8). In 1907 she became director of the *Casa dei Bambini* (Children's House), a refuge for very poor children in a Rome slum. Here, she was able to put into effect her 'scientific method', based upon observation, experimentation and analysis. She believed in developing children's senses and basic skills in stages as a prelude to practising activities such as writing. Classroom activities were to be purposeful and designed in ascending sequences to allow for development. Her ideas were published in 1909 in *The Montessori Method*, followed by the two-volume *Advanced Montessori Method* (1917–18). A two-month public education experiment at the Panama-Pacific Exposition (1915), involving twenty-one pupils being taught using her methods, led to worldwide acclaim. She left Italy when Mussolini came to power and

389

continued to train teachers from Amsterdam. When war broke out she moved to India and Sri Lanka (Ceylon), where her influence continues to be considerable. 'Follow the child' and 'First educate the senses, then educate the intellect', were two of her famous sayings. Her students set up schools in her name around the world. Montessori was the first to design especially made classroom furniture to fit children.

See also: child development; early childhood education; Italy

STEVEN COWAN

MORAL EDUCATION

Philosophical interest in the practice of moral education reaches back to antiquity: both Plato and Aristotle were deeply exercised by questions of moral formation, and most − if not all − of their great moral philosophical successors have had something to say on this topic. That said, it is striking that modern theorising about moral education, from the beginning of the last century to the present, has been driven more from social scientific than moral philosophical perspectives. In this respect, key moments of twentieth-century theorising about moral development and education have included: (i) Emile Durkheim's (1961) sociological claim that a form of moral education grounded in autonomous obedience to some consensual conception of common good is needed to sustain civil cohesion in post-religious or secular societies; (ii) Freudian and other psychoanalytic attempts to locate the sources of good and evil and the origins of moral conscience in early psychological conflicts and in the mechanisms of repression; (iii) the efforts of psychological behaviourists to conceive moral formation in terms of (socially) conditioned responses to stimuli; and (iv) Jean Piaget's (1932) groundbreaking attempt, in the wake of gestalt and cognitivist critiques of such learning theory, to provide a cognitive-developmental account of moral reason and judgement.

Owing something to such early developments, it is possible to discern − roughly from the end of World War II to the dawn of the twenty-first century − the emergence of three fairly distinctive moral educational trends. First, directly in the wake of Piaget, Lawrence Kohlberg's (1981) highly influential cognitive stage theory may be seen as attempting to steer a liberal educational course between views of moral formation grounded in social or behavioural conditioning, and the morally relativist approaches of so-called 'values clarification. Second, by way of reaction to moral cognitivism, advocates of so-called 'care ethics' have sought to re-affirm the significance of feeling and affect in moral life, widely held to have been sidelined by the primary emphasis of Piaget, Kohlberg and others on moral reason. While some pioneers of care ethics − such as Noddings (1984) − have been philosophers, this view seems to have deeper roots in the feminist psychoanalytic theory of such psychologists as Chodorow (1989) and Gilligan (1982). Third, however, the so-called character education movement (see, for example, Kilpatrick 1992; Lickona 1992) − initially American but now steadily gaining ground in other parts of the world such as the United Kingdom − has also emerged partly by way of reaction to cognitive stage theory. Once more, while it has sometimes been politically driven, and although it has occasionally also drawn inspiration from Aristotelian virtue ethics, the main architects of character education have been social scientists, particularly psychologists.

Still, it is hard to deny that the fundamental issues of modern moral educational theory are conceptual rather than empirical. In common with such key philosophical contributors to post-war moral educational theory as R. S. Peters (1981) and John Wilson (1990), the cognitive stage theories of Piaget and Kohlberg are grounded in modified forms of Kantian ethics, taking the main aim of moral education to be the capacity for self-legislation in the light of universal justice principles. The argument of care ethicists, character educationalists and virtue ethicists with such rationalist approaches rests on a number of claims: (i) that moral agency is not centrally a matter of autonomous respect for moral principles, or, at least, any absolute or universal form of these; (ii) that such recognition of principles cannot ensure effective moral motivation; and (iii) (combining (i) and (ii)) that the practical rationality or wisdom of good moral character is a matter of context-bound refinement of more fundamental cognitive-affective dispositions and sensibilities on a basis of early moral training. For many of the new Aristotelian character educators, at any rate, moral formation aims at the cultivation of capacities for particular context-sensitive judgement in the light of appropriate experience rather than at the grasp of transcendent (Kantian or other) moral universals. While some moral theorists have also continued to seek a degree of conceptual accommodation between these alternatives, the prospects of success in this direction remain to be seen.

See also: Aristotle; Durkheim, Emile; Kohlberg, Lawrence; philosophy of education; Piaget, Jean; Plato; religious education

Further reading

Aristotle (1925) *The Nicomachean Ethics*, trans. David Ross, Oxford: Oxford University Press.

Carr, D. and Steutel, J. (eds) (1999) *Virtue Ethics and Moral Education*, London: Routledge.

Chodorow, N. (1989) *Feminism and Psychoanalytic Theory*, Cambridge: Polity Press.

Durkheim, E. (1961) *Moral Education: A Study in the Theory and Application of the Sociology of Education*, New York: Collier Macmillan.

Gilligan, C. (1982) *In a Different Voice: Psychological Theory and Women's Development*, Cambridge MA: Harvard University Press.

Halstead, M. and McLaughlin, T. (eds) (1999) *Education in Morality*, London: Routledge.

Hirst, P. H. (1974) *Moral Education in a Secular Society*, London: London University Press.

Kilpatrick, W. (1992) *Why Johnny Can't Tell Right from Wrong: Moral Illiteracy and the Case for Character Education*, New York: Simon and Schuster.

Kohlberg, L. (1981) *Essays on Moral Development (Volume I): The Philosophy of Moral Development: Moral Stages and the Idea of Justice*, New York: Harper and Row.

Lickona, T. (1992) *Educating for Character: How Our Schools Can Teach Respect and Responsibility*, New York: Bantam Doubleday Dell.

Noddings, N. (1984) *Caring: A Feminist Approach to Ethics*, Berkeley CA: University of California Press.

Peters, R. S. (1981) *Moral Development and Moral Education*, London: George Allen and Unwin.

Piaget, J. (1932) *The Moral Judgement of the Child*, New York: Free Press.

Plato (1961) *Plato: The Collected Dialogues*, eds E. Hamilton and H. Cairns, Princeton NJ: Princeton University Press

Wilson, J. (1990) *A New Introduction to Moral Education*, London: Cassell.

DAVID CARR

MOTIVATION

Motivating learners is the holy grail for teachers, just as motivating workers is for bosses. However, this desire to influence the actions of others engenders strategies leading to *external* motivation – rewards, punishments, carrots, sticks, money, chocolate. Yet it is *internal* motivation – performance driven by internal reasons – that is the key to independent working and learning.

Herzberg (1968) identifies 'hygiene factors' which, if perceived as poor, lead to job *dissatisfaction*. These include the physical environment, pay and relationships. However, addressing these does not lead to job *satisfaction*. To achieve this the worker must also enjoy (in order of importance):

- achievement;
- recognition;
- the work itself (to be motivated *by* the work; not simply to *do* the work);
- responsibility;
- a sense of growth or advancement.

These factors can be applied to learners too, for example:

- to leave a class knowing that something has been achieved;
- to be recognised as an individual, not just a student or mark on the register;

391

- to do work that is enjoyable and demanding;
- to have a sense of control and opportunities for taking responsibility;
- to feel 'better' now than on entering the classroom.

If motivation is an issue then so is *de-motivation*, the process whereby the learner enters the classroom in a positive state only to have that undermined by the antithesis of the list above. For example:

- the class ends as a learner is part way through a piece of work: they have to leave it unfinished;
- their individuality, personality and intelligence strengths are overlooked or not valued;
- the work is boring, repetitive, unchallenging and apparently pointless;
- the learner has no control of any part of a strictly regimented lesson or day;
- feedback is delayed, unhelpful or negative and any indication of growth comes from a source other than the teacher.

Herzberg talks about 'KITA motivation', where the worker is apparently 'motivated' by the intellectual equivalent of a 'kick in the ass'. The work will get done, but not because the worker wants to do the work. They just don't like being kicked.

To move beyond the school-based version of KITA motivation – 'If you do this I will look kindly upon you, reward and praise you physically and/or mentally' or 'If you don't I will punish you and make you feel guilty until one of us gives in' – it is important to consider what is known as 'the WIIFM?' or 'what's in it for me?'

According to Carter (1998), 'The brain's main function is to keep the organism of which it is a part alive and reproducing'. The culmination of six million years of evolution is not school or college examinations. When faced with the not inconsiderable deployment of precious resources needed to make new neurological connections in order to learn, the learner will be more motivated if the learning relates to our sense of survival, to real life and has a perceived point.

Helping an individual explore the benefits of the new learning contributes significantly to intrinsic motivation. Furthermore, enjoyment itself – doing something for the love of it, as is the true meaning of the word 'amateur' – can be motivational. Csikszentmihalyi (1992) states, 'Seeking pleasure is a reflex response built into our genes for the preservation of the species'. This is where 'celebration', recognising and celebrating what is being done, is better for internal motivation than 'reward', external bribery to do something that the learner wouldn't do if it weren't for the reward.

One of our key learning neurochemicals is dopamine, generated when we experience, or are about to experience, something we perceive to be positive. Giving the learner a choice – 'a sense of participation in determining the content of life' according to Csikszentmihalyi – in what is happening can help generate positive neurochemicals. Ipsative referencing strategies such as the 'personal best' approach, used in sport, can also contribute to this sense of control.

Csikszentmihalyi also points out the benefits to motivation and achievement of a state he calls 'flow', something that occurs when a task is at the limits of the learner's abilities and takes place in a risk-free, playful environment, where failure is not only tolerated, but encouraged.

The factors above, combined with positive relationships, tapping into a learner's innate curiosity (push-pull learning motivation, where the learner 'pulls' the learning towards them to help them answer their own self-generated questions) and a sense of hope – that things can get better and 'I can do something about it' – can lead to better motivation in classrooms.

See also: disaffection; learning; psychology of education

Further reading

Carter, R. (1998) *Mapping the Mind*, London: Weidenfeld and Nicolson.

Csikszentmihalyi, M. (1992) *Flow*, London: Rider.

Gilbert, I. (2002) *Essential Motivation in the Class-room*, London: RoutledegeFalmer.

——(2006) *The Big Book of Independent Thinking*, London: Crown House Publishing.

Herzberg, F. (1968) 'One more time – how do you motivate employees?' In T. Levitt, F. Herzberg, R. L. Katz, P. J. Brouwer, C. R. Rogers, F. J. Roethlisberger, D. Mayer, H. M. Greenberg, P. F. Drucker and R. L. Nolan, *Business Classics: Fifteen Key Concepts for Managerial Success*, Boston MA: Harvard Business School Publishing Corp.

IAN GILBERT

MULCASTER, RICHARD (*c.*1530–1611)

Mulcaster was a Tudor humanist and a product of an education at Eton, King's College, Cambridge, and Christ Church, Oxford. He spent most of his working life as a teacher, becoming the first head master, aged around thirty, of Merchant Taylor's School, where he remained until 1586. During his final years at the school he produced two important educational works, *The Positions* (1581) and *The Elementaries* (1582). Although both echo quite strongly the views of Roger Ascham, their most striking quality lies in their advocacy of English as the prime medium of instruction and their evident address to the merchant classes rather than the nobility. One of Mulcaster's major legacies was his call for the standardising of English orthography, spelling and meaning: 'I honour Latin but worship English'. Another was his influence upon the English writers Edmund Spenser and Thomas Kydd, his pupils at Merchant Taylor's. Moreover, no fewer than six members of the committee that produced the English Authorised Version of the Bible were former pupils of Mulcaster. A distinctive feature of Mulcaster's curriculum was the prominence he gave to physical education, especially football, which he felt toughened and conditioned pupils. After a series of financial arguments with the Merchant Taylor's trustees he resigned, becoming a cleric between 1589 and 1596 and then high master of St Paul's School, London from 1596 to 1608.

See also: Ascham, Roger; public school

STEVEN COWAN

MULTICULTURAL EDUCATION

Multicultural education is a movement designed to change schools, colleges, and universities so that students from diverse racial, ethnic, cultural, language, social class, and religious groups will experience equal educational opportunity. Multicultural education also tries to help students from all groups to develop democratic racial and ethnic attitudes needed to function effectively in culturally diverse communities, national civic cultures, and in the global community.

Most nation-states and societies around the world are characterised by cultural, ethnic, language, and religious diversity. The quests for political, cultural, and economic rights by ethnic minority groups that have intensified within the last forty years, the growth in international migration, and the increasing recognition of structural inequality within democratic nation-states have given rise to multicultural education – or *intercultural education* as it is usually called in Europe – in democratic nations around the world. The number of people living outside their country of birth or citizenship grew from 120 million in 1990 to 160 million in 2000 (Martin and Widgren 2002).

The United States has been diverse since its founding. However, the number of immigrants entering the USA, most of whom are now coming from nations in Latin America and Asia, has greatly increased within the last two decades. The US Census Bureau (2005) projects that ethnic minorities will make up 50 per cent of the US population by 2050. Ethnic and cultural diversity increased in European nations such as the United Kingdom, France, Germany, and the Netherlands after World War II when groups from their former colonies emigrated to these nations to improve their economic conditions. Significant numbers of immigrants from the West Indies, India and Pakistan settled in the United Kingdom. Many Algerian immigrants, as well as immigrants from Cambodia, Laos, and Vietnam, moved to France. People from Morocco and Surinam emigrated to the Netherlands (Eldering and Kloprogge 1989). Many migrant workers from the Mediterranean nations in Europe settled in Western European nations such as France, the United Kingdom, Germany, and Switzerland in the post-World War II period in search of greater economic opportunities. They provided unskilled labour that was needed in these nations.

One of the challenges to pluralistic democratic nation-states is to provide opportunities for cultural, ethnic, language, and religious groups to maintain components of their community cultures while at the same time constructing a nation-state in which diverse groups are structurally included and to which they feel allegiance (Kymlicka 1995). This challenge has become intensified as democratic nation-states such as the USA, Canada, Australia, Germany, France, the Netherlands and the UK become more diversified and as racial and ethnic groups within these nations push for cultural, economic and political rights. An important aim of multicultural education is to change schools, colleges, and universities so that they reflect the diverse groups within the nation who want to become structurally included while helping the nation to maintain a delicate balance between unity and diversity.

There is consensus among multicultural researchers and theorists about overarching goals (Banks 2004). However, there is less agreement, in both practice and theory, about which ethnic, social, cultural, and religious groups should be included in educational reforms related to diversity. The groups on which multicultural education focuses vary within, as well as across, nations.

When multicultural education emerged in nations such as the USA, Australia, the UK, France, and Canada in the 1970s and 1980s, the emphasis was on ethnic and language minority groups, on immigrant groups, and on groups that had been historically victimised by institutionalised discrimination and racism.

As the field of multicultural education has developed, especially within the USA, increased emphasis has been given to issues related to gender and social class. A few theorists in the United States include sexual orientation in their conceptualisation of multicultural education. However, it receives little attention in the majority of multicultural education courses, programmes, and projects. In most nations, such as the USA, Canada, Germany, Australia, and the United Kingdom, multicultural education usually focuses on racial, ethnic and language groups (Luchtenberg 2004). Other variables of diversity, including sexual orientation and disability, receive less emphasis.

Banks (2004) has conceptualised multicultural education as consisting of five dimensions: (1) content integration; (2) the knowledge construction process; (3) prejudice reduction, (4) an equity pedagogy; and (5) an empowering school culture and social structure. Although each dimension is conceptually distinct, in practice they overlap and are interrelated:

- *Content integration* deals with the extent to which teachers use examples and content from a variety of cultures and groups to illustrate key concepts, principles, generalisations, and theories in their subject area or discipline. Content in all subjects and disciplines can be integrated with ethnic and cultural content. However, more opportunities exist for the integration of ethnic and cultural content into some subject areas and disciplines, such as social studies and art, than in others, such as math and science. Content integration is frequently mistaken by school practitioners as comprising the whole of multicultural education, and is thus viewed as irrelevant to instruction in disciplines such as maths and science.

- *The knowledge construction process* describes teaching activities that help students to understand, investigate, and determine how the cultural assumptions, frames of references, perspectives, and biases of researchers and textbook writers influence the ways in which knowledge is constructed (Banks 2006). The knowledge construction process helps teachers and students to understand why the cultural identities and social positions of researchers need to be taken into account when assessing the validity of knowledge claims (Banks 2007). Multicultural education theorists believe that the values, personal histories, attitudes, and beliefs of researchers cannot be separated from the knowledge they create. In multicultural teaching and learning, paradigms, themes, and concepts that exclude or distort the life experiences, histories, and contributions of marginalised groups are challenged.

- *The prejudice reduction dimension* seeks to help students develop positive and democratic racial attitudes. It also helps students to understand how ethnic identity is influenced by the context of schooling and the attitudes and beliefs of mainstream groups. The contact theory developed by Allport (1954) has significantly influenced research and theory in intergroup relations. He hypothesised that prejudice can be reduced by interracial contact if contact situations have (1) equal status; (2) common goals; (3) intergroup cooperation; and (4) are sanctioned by authorities such as parents, principals, and teachers.

- *An equity pedagogy* exists when teachers modify their teaching in ways that will facilitate the academic achievement of students from diverse racial, cultural, social class, and language groups. This includes using a variety of teaching styles and approaches that are consistent with the range of learning styles within various cultural and ethnic groups, and being demanding but highly personalised when working with students from diverse groups. It includes using cooperative teaching techniques in maths and science instruction to enhance the academic achievement of minority students. Teachers practise culturally responsive teaching when equity pedagogy is implemented that incorporates important aspects of the family and community cultures and languages of their students into instruction.

- *An empowering school culture* involves restructuring the culture and organisation of the school so that students from diverse groups experience equality. Members of the school staff examine and change the culture and social structure of the school. Grouping and labelling practices, sports participation, gaps in achievement among groups, disproportionate rates of enrolment in gifted and special education programmes among groups, and the interaction of the staff and the students across ethnic and racial lines are important variables that are examined and reformed.

Multicultural education faces both challenges and opportunities as it enters its fourth decade. The focus on national testing and standards in Western nations such as the USA and the UK has diverted attention from issues related to diversity and social justice (Gillborn 2007; Sleeter 2007). However, the significant number of immigrants that are settling in nations such as Australia, the USA and Canada – and the low birth rate among the middle-class mainstream populations in these nations as well as in Western Europe and Japan – are factors that will make diversity and education high-priority issues around the world for the foreseeable future.

See also: antiracist education; culture; equality of opportunity; indigenous education

Further reading

Allport, G. W. (1954) *The Nature of Prejudice*, Reading MA: Addison-Wesley.

Banks, J. A. (2004) 'Multicultural education: historical development, dimensions, and practice'. In J. A. Banks and C. A. M. Banks (eds) *Handbook of Research on Multicultural Education*, 2nd edn, San Francisco CA: Jossey-Bass.

——(2006) *Race, Culture, and Education: The Selected Works of James A. Banks*, London and New York: Routledge.

——(2007) *Educating Citizens in a Multicultural Society*, 2nd edn, New York: Teachers College Press.

Eldering, L. and Kloprogge, J. (1989) *Different Cultures Same School: Ethnic Minority Children in Europe*, Amsterdam: Swets and Zeitliner.

Gillborn, D. (2007) 'Accountability, standards, and race inequity in the United Kingdom: small steps on the road of progress or the defense of White supremacy'. In C. E. Sleeter (ed.) *Facing Accountability in Education: Democracy and Equity at Risk*, New York: Teachers College Press.

Kymlicka, W. (1995) *Multicultural Citizenship: A Liberal Theory of Minority Rights*, New York: Oxford University Press.

Luchtenberg, S. (ed.) (2004). *Migration, Education, and Change*, London and New York: Routledge.

Martin, P. and Widgren, J. (2002) 'International migration: facing the challenge', *Population Reference Bulletin*, 57(1), Washington DC: Population Reference Bureau.

Sleeter, C. E. (ed.) (2007) *Facing Accountability in Education: Democracy and Equity at Risk*, New York: Teachers College Press.

US Census Bureau (2005) *Statistical Abstract of the United States: 2006*, 125th edn, Washington DC: US Government Printing Office.

JAMES A. BANKS

MULTIGRADE EDUCATION

Whereas most teaching and learning in schools around the world takes place in monograde classes, that is, classes with learners from a single curriculum grade, a significant minority is based on multigrade education in which teachers are responsible within the same time period for learners from across two or more year grades. Multigraded schooling is common in many countries with well developed education systems and high rates of participation, but is particularly widespread and significant in many developing countries. Although it is often regarded as being of lower status than monograde education, in some cases it has been transformed into a positive pedagogy. This is apparent, for example, with the *Escuela Nueva* programme, introduced in Colombia from 1976 and adapted for use in many other countries. It has been argued that in a wide range of nations around the world multigraded education can make a significant contribution to the goals of Education For All, those of access and quality. In order to do so it requires attention to curriculum, learning materials, teacher education and assessment as parts of an integrated strategy (Little 2006: 340).

See also: Education for All (EFA); progression; social promotion

Further reading

Little, A. (ed.) (2006) *Education for All and Multigrade Teaching: Challenges and Opportunities*, Dordrecht, the Netherlands: Springer.

GARY McCULLOCH

MULTIPLE-CHOICE TESTS

Multiple-choice or selective-response tests are a means by which particular competencies may be assessed. A multiple-choice test consists of a series of items, each featuring a 'stem' containing a question, an incomplete statement, or a series of words or figures followed by a number of possible responses. Examinees must identify the most appropriate response from among distracting alternatives. The optimum number of alternatives in a multiple-choice test item is four.

Multiple-choice tests are generally considered effective for assessment of relatively unsophisticated skills, particularly the ability to recall or recognise facts. Most multiple-choice tests are not designed to measure reasoning or critical thinking, though some research suggests this is possible. The relative ease with which multiple-choice tests may be scored has contributed to their popularity among educators and producers of standardised tests (which typically include multiple-choice items). Inferences about scholastic aptitude, intelligence, or suitability for higher education are frequently based on standardised test scores. In many jurisdictions, standardised multiple-choice tests administered to students have become a means by which public and private agencies purport to assess instructional, institutional or curricular quality. This is not without controversy, given the limitations of multiple-choice tests in measuring educational outcomes. Moreover, there is no generally accepted way to correct multiple-choice test results for guessing, which occurs whenever an examinee chooses a response with some degree of uncertainty. Because correct guesses are more likely in multiple-choice tests than in other test types, increased error variance and reduced validity and reliability are particularly serious problems.

See also: assessment; objective tests; test/testing

JASON BLOKHUIS

MUSEUM EDUCATION

During the last twenty years, the role of the public museum and art gallery in Western culture has undergone wholesale revision. Under the rubric of social democracy, the public museum has reappraised displays and collections in tandem with a revision of educational methodologies for museum audiences. The legacy of fixed taxonomies and chronologies and the West's development of models of scientific rationalism and hierarchies of taste, employed by museums,

products of eighteenth-century Enlightenment classificatory systems, have been scrutinised by theorists such as Foucault and Bourdieu and found wanting. Traditionally a repository of state values through the display of other cultures (a process dubbed 'trophies of empire'), the public museum has not been immune to broader social emancipation set in motion by the social unrest of the late 1960s. Collections circumscribed by a colonial past and Enlightenment philosophy have found themselves subject to criticism in a postmodern and post-colonial world impatient with perceived bias and the aspiration to present universal values at the expense of minority or alternative cultures. Under the guidance of post-structuralism – in particular alterity theory, which insists that knowing others through any accurate and impartial representation is impossible – confidence in definitive knowable truths has been eroded. The repercussions for ethnographic collections, in particular, have been far-reaching, ushering in an era of pluralistic interpretation, with primacy often given to the personal narratives of those whose artefacts and cultural practices are displayed. Display is currently likely to embrace a range of interpretive strategies and navigational devices, creating greater access and inclusion. Broadly speaking, there has been a rejection of positivistic epistemology, a recalibration of subject boundaries to interdisciplinarity, and a questioning of curatorial authority and detachment.

The educational role of the museum is not new, but after an initial impetus to focus on education in the nineteenth century there was a paradigm shift to collecting, preserving and researching artefacts, a change that erroneously misrepresents the contemporary emphasis on museum education as a new phenomena (see Hooper-Greenhill 1991; Bennett 1995). By the 1920s, the museum's pedagogic role had become ancillary to the increasingly specialised task of curatorial scholarship. However, a renaissance in the educational role of the museum is perceptible at least since David Anderson's (1997) call for a change of emphasis away from the specialisation of collection preservation and research to a searching examination of visitors' museum experiences. The interregnum in foregrounding museum education saw the consolidation of traditional teaching methods, that sits uncomfortably with the commitment to lifelong intergenerational learning and widening participation, currently favoured by policy makers and funding bodies. There has been a notable shift away from didactic learning theories employing a transmission model to widespread interest in *interpretive communities* that use common *interpretive strategies*. Interpretive educational strategies often disrupt the traditional authority of the curator as sole interpreter of meaning and history. The hierarchical view of communication is thus undermined, allowing for polysemic readings of artefacts and artworks. Furthermore, education departments are likely to deploy multimodal educational strategies that take account of multiple learning styles as diverse groups and self-directed individuals demand appropriate forms of communication. Justification for learning through material culture has gained a fillip from contemporary theories around the importance of the embodied experience. An embrace of object-based learning, the power of touch and a reinvestment in narratives and storytelling have been interwoven with the increased learning power of the internet and digital technologies. There is broad recognition that audiences are not passive recipients of knowledge, but rather are active audiences bringing prior knowledge and experience to the museum visit, creating a demand for what George Hein (1998) has referred to as a constructivist museum, where learning is negotiated.

There is another related educational issue that lies at the heart of debates about the function of museums. The museum's educational role is now to affect cultural change in the audiences' perceptions of others, replacing misunderstanding, hostility or indifference with increased levels of understanding and tolerance. This marks a significant departure from the acquisition of knowledge fuelled by curiosity about, say, Cycladic sculpture or nomadic peoples. Museums have increasingly become forums for the promotion of peaceful community relations, particularly where there are historical uncertainties and ethnic tension, acting as a regenerative social force in the promotion of cultural understanding. Museums of reconciliation and atonement that negotiate histories across divided cultures have education as their core remit to become agents of social change.

However, the role of the museum as cultural regenerator, social worker and a location for the delivery of government education directives through funding policies is not without critics. The iconic landmark building and the revamping of post-industrial power stations, textile mills or railway stations into leisure and educational venues, with smart cafes and bookshops, is also an indication of the unavoidable commodification of all spheres of culture foreseen by Georg Simmel as early as 1900. The culture of accountability, fostered by a pragmatic, instrumental political climate, has prised museums away from their other-worldliness, to enter an educational world of interactive learning across cultures and generations. The contemporary museum is a hybrid, poised between the competing demands of social regeneration, education, corporate culture and commerce.

See also: cultural transmission; culture; ethnography; history; informal/nonformal learning

Further reading

Anderson, D. (1997) *A Common Wealth: Museums in the Learning Age*, London: Department of Culture, Media and Sport.
Bennett, T. (1995) *The Birth of the Museum*, London and New York: Routledge.
Falk, J. H. and Dierking, L. D. (2000) *Learning From Museums*, Walnut Creek CA: AltaMira Press.

Hein, G. E. (1998) *Learning in the Museum*, London: Routledge.

Hooper-Greenhill, E. (1991) *Museums and Gallery Education*, Leicester: Leicester University Press

PAM MEECHAM

MUSIC

Music is a human construct. While sound may exist as an objective reality, for that sound to be defined as music requires human beings to acknowledge it as such. What is acknowledged as 'music' varies between cultures, groups, and individuals. Music, and informal tuition relating to it, has a very long history. There is evidence of the existence of musical instruments over 40,000 years ago. Informal musical tuition continues to play an important role in music education around the world today, particularly where there is little or no formal education, where music is not valued or is controlled by the state, and as an addition to what is offered by the state.

The extent to which music education is provided through state education systems, internationally, varies, as does the means by which it is offered. Provision depends on the nature of the education system, economic wealth, political factors and the perceived role and value placed on music in society. Music has a very powerful impact on human behaviour and from time to time governments have seen fit to control music in society, including removing it from the school curriculum. Central control of music education in state schools is exercised in some countries through the implementation of a national curriculum. However, as music plays an important role in the everyday life of most people around the world, informal music education through community music making continues in all cultures alongside or instead of more formal provision.

There is long-standing and continuing debate worldwide relating to the aims of music education, what should be taught, and how it should be taught. Recently, because of threats to the place of music in the curriculum of some developed countries, the benefits of music education, beyond those for its own sake, including the development of a range of personal and social skills in children, have been stressed. Claims have been made that active engagement with music can improve spatial reasoning, attainment in other school subjects, reading, listening, self-discipline, moral development, physical coordination, social cooperation, teamwork, and communication skills. There is a need for further rigorous evidence to justify these claims.

Formal music education can be approached in a range of ways. At different times and in different cultures, it has focused on listening, understanding, and appreciation of music; performance; creativity; combinations of these; or has developed within a more general arts education. Depending on the focus adopted children may learn to read musical notation; develop critical listening skills; acquire knowledge about the history of music, instruments, world musics, acoustics and the contribution of music to other art forms; learn to compose or improvise using a range of instruments or computer technology; develop technical skills in playing an instrument or singing; and develop performing and communication skills. Within general music education, there are ongoing debates as to which of these should be included and whether the curriculum should focus on traditional national musics and cultures or Western popular culture, the latter an increasingly worldwide phenomenon.

In many countries systems are in place for providing general music education for all pupils and specialised opportunities for those who show particular interest in or aptitude for music. For instance, music may become optional as pupils progress through school; specialist selective schools may offer a full-time education with music at its core; extra-curricula music schools may operate out of school hours providing tuition and ensemble opportunities; centrally or locally funded music services may provide instrumental music tuition in schools during the school day in addition to a range of out-of-school music activities. Complementary to state-funded provision, private teachers and local community groups may offer further opportunities to develop musical skills. In some cultures music is learned informally within the community through everyday life activities where it is a natural part of work, play, rituals, ceremonies, and religious and family occasions. Such informal music making occurs, to some extent, in all societies, forming an essential part of musical culture. For those who wish to pursue careers in music, universities, colleges and conservatoires provide opportunities to develop a range of academic, performing, creative and technical skills.

See also: curriculum; extracurriculum; subjects

Further reading

Colwell, R. and Richardson, C. (eds) (2002) *The New Handbook of Research on Music Teaching and Learning: A Project of the Music Educators National Conference*, Oxford: Oxford University Press.

Hargreaves, D. J. and North, A. C. (2001) *Musical Development and Learning: The International Perspective*, London: Continuum

Welch, G. (ed.) (2004) 'Mapping music education research – international perspectives', *Psychology of Music*, 32(3): 235–367.

SUSAN HALLAM

N

NATURE STUDY

Nature study can be defined as the field devoted to observing and appreciating the natural world. A significant component of nature study, which utilises human beings' incessant curiosity about nature, includes observing the natural environment. This may include organisms such as birds, insects, plants, trees, and animals. It can also include the natural non-living surroundings found in the natural environment such as rocks and minerals. Nature study also investigates the interrelationships found in nature among the corresponding non-living and living systems and the physical, chemical, biological, and behavioural effects they can have within and between each other. Through the informal study of nature, naturalists seek to gather observations, which can come in the form of written notes, pictures of organisms, and descriptions of the place the observations took place, in order to better explain the natural world around them.

The historical roots of nature study reside in the study of natural philosophy and history. In the late nineteenth and early twentieth centuries, nature study was considered a popular education movement in the United States, spearheaded by the American educator and conservationist Anna Botsford Comstock (1854–1930) who emphasised that nature should be studied through experiencing and immersing oneself in it, rather than just reading about it. Although both scientists and educators in the United States supported nature study, it was replaced by the more formal study of science in the mid-twentieth century.

See also: biology; curriculum; environmental education; science/science education; subjects

PAUL NARGUIZIAN

NEILL, ALEXANDER SUTHERLAND (1883–1973)

Neill, the progressive educator and founder of Summerhill School, graduated in English literature from Edinburgh University and qualified as a teacher. After periods teaching in London and Dresden he established his own school at Lyme Regis, Dorset in 1924, which subsequently relocated to Suffolk and became known as Summerhill. Neill believed in maximum freedom for children to grow into their identities and be free from negative and restraining adult influences. His school was run along consultative and democratic lines, ensuring maximum participation in all matters by the children. Lesson attendance and participation in activities was optional. Neill's writings became the touchstone for those who sought 'progressive' solutions and antidotes to the controlled environments of conventional schooling. *The Problem Parent* (1932), *That Dreadful School* (1937) and *Summerhill* (1962) tackled key aspects of his general outlook. His influence was enhanced in later years through the celebrity status he achieved via television documentaries about Summerhill. He received academic recognition from Newcastle and Exeter Universities, but was never welcomed by the political establishment. Nevertheless, he affected a generation of teachers by making them redefine their relationship with pupils. Neill believed that for a school to be educative it ought to embody the freedom that was essential to learning. Neill is seen as one of the leading inspirations for the home schooling movement, which criticises the way that schools institutionalise, rather than educate, young people. In addition, his example and ideas have informed the many subsequent experiments with progressive schooling around the world, often initiated by ex-pupils of Summerhill.

See also: child-centred education; home schooling; progressive education

STEVEN COWAN

NEWMAN, JOHN HENRY (1801–90)

Newman entered Oxford University in 1818, graduating from Trinity College in 1820. He was elected a fellow in 1822 and ordained in 1824, becoming vice-principal of St Alban Hall in 1825 and then vicar of St Mary's University Church in 1826. He became a leading spokesman for the Oxford Movement, an Anglo-Catholic group which questioned the basis and direction of the Anglican Church. Newman wrote twenty-six of the *Tracts for the Times*, including the last, tract 90, which argued that the thirty-nine Articles of the Church of England implied membership of the Universal Catholic family. Newman then became editor of the *British Critic*, an influential Anglo-Catholic publication. He resigned from his position at St Mary's with a famous sermon, 'The parting of friends', and set up a retreat outside of Oxford. After two years in Rome he was ordained into the Catholic priesthood in 1846. He established the Oratory of St Philip, a Catholic private

school for the sons of the wealthy in Birmingham in 1847, and a branch of the school in London shortly after. Newman became the first rector of the new Catholic university in Dublin from 1854 to 1858. In *The Idea of a University Education* (1854) Newman makes an essentially liberal restatement of the aims of higher education within a Catholic framework. Newman's fame spread with the publication of an account of his personal spiritual journey, *Apologia pro Vita Sua* (1864). He was the first person to receive an honorary fellowship at Trinity College, Oxford and he became a cardinal in 1879.

See also: higher education; religious education; religious school; theology; university

STEVEN COWAN

NEW ZEALAND/AOTEAROA

With the signing of the Treaty of Waitangi in 1840, New Zealand became a British colony and British traditions strongly influenced the development of education. Schooling for Maori was prioritised by first the British Colonial Office and then the settler government was concerned to assimilate the Maori (indigenous) population. In 1867 the Native Schools Act created the native schools system for Maori children. State-controlled village primary schools for Maori were administered centrally by the Department of Education. English was the medium of instruction and government inspectors enforced school regulations.

The 1877 Education Act established free, secular and compulsory primary schooling, and was administered by ten regional educational boards. No restrictions were placed on Maori or Pakeha (European) children attending schools in either system. However, the goal of the state was to transfer each native school into the board school system once Maori children were sufficiently 'Europeanised'. While a number of native schools (renamed Maori schools in 1947) did transfer to boards, many remained as Maori schools because Maori communities themselves preferred them. It was not until 1969 that the remaining 105 Maori schools were transferred to education board control, creating one uniform system of primary school administration.

Secondary schools in New Zealand were initially founded by the Anglican and Catholic churches, and prior to 1876, by provincial governments. Because these schools charged fees, settler demand for publicly provided state secondary schooling emerged from 1877 with the introduction of district high schools, from 1880 with the technical high schools, and from 1903 with some free places in the endowed schools. It was not until the 1914 Education Act that secondary schooling became free to all who gained the Proficiency Certificate in their final year of primary schooling. Open access to secondary schooling became available in 1937, once Proficiency was abolished.

State-provided secondary schooling dominates in New Zealand, although private schools, usually with a religious affiliation, have, since the Conditional Integration of Private Schools Act (1975), been able to have recurrent expenditure refunded by the state in exchange for certain conditions while retaining their 'special character'.

There is also a comprehensive range of education services for pre-school children and for children of all ages with disabilities and special needs. In addition, the correspondence schools provide primary, secondary and continuing education for homebound children. There are also schools offering tuition in the Maori language at early childhood (*kohanga reo*) and primary and secondary (*kura kaupapa* Maori) levels.

Current issues in New Zealand education stem from the late 1980s, when, for the first time, equality of opportunity, a central tenet of the welfare model of state, came under threat from the conception of education as a private good, a commercial investment subject to the competitive conditions of the market. In 1990, a new policy-orientated Ministry of

Education was established, replacing the former Department of Education with its all-embracing functions including its regional offices. The middle-level administrative tiers, regional education boards, were abolished. At the same time, individual schools and their new boards of trustees which administered them were given greater operational and management autonomy. These changes were legislated through the 1989 Education Act and the 1990 and 1991 Education Amendment Acts. In 1991, a 'user pays' tertiary student fees system was introduced, and laid the basis for later changes resulting in the introduction of a student loans scheme.

Administrative reform has been followed by significant changes in the areas of curriculum and qualifications. Major changes have included the New Zealand Curriculum Framework (1993) and the associated National Certificate of Educational Achievement (NCEA). Administered by the New Zealand Qualifications Authority (NZQA), seven learning areas and eight levels of skill are registered on the framework, against which students from secondary school through to postgraduate university study meet achievement standards. NZQA have also increased control over state funding to tertiary institutions and, for the first time, course approval, monitoring, examining and entry to the university is now subject to its approval. A further government monitoring authority, the Tertiary Education Commission (TEC) was established in 2000 to evaluate the research outputs of universities, polytechnics and *wananga* (Maori tertiary institutions) and to distribute state funding according to research productivity from the Performance Based Research Fund (PBRF).

Public debate currently centres upon the workability of a seamless qualifications framework, the billions of dollars owed in student loans, and how schools can cope with increasing cultural and ethnic diversity, including a 20 per cent Maori student enrolment. These will remain the main educational issues for the immediate future.

403

Further reading

Dakin, J. C. (1973) *Education in New Zealand*, Hamden CT: Archon Books.

Grant, D. (2003) *Those Who Can Teach: A History of Secondary Education in New Zealand from the Union Perspective*, Wellington: Steele Roberts.

Harrison, M. (ed.) (2004) *Education Matters: Government, Markets and New Zealand Schools*, Wellington: Education Forum.

Middleton, S., Codd, J. and Jones, A. (1990) *New Zealand Education Policy Today*, Wellington: Allen and Unwin.

KAY MORRIS MATTHEWS

NIGERIA

The Federal Republic of Nigeria, with a population of around 140 million and a land mass of more than 900 square kilometres, contains more people than any other African country. Nigeria lies on the west coast of Africa near the equator, and is bordered by the Republic of Benin to the west, Chad and Cameroon to the east, and Niger to the north. The Gulf of Guinea and the Atlantic Ocean lie to the south. Half the population is Muslim, 40 per cent is Christian and the remaining 10 per cent follow indigenous beliefs.

Prior to the period of nineteenth-century European conquests, Nigeria was home to kingdoms and city-states that were influential centres of culture and trade. The coastal enclave of Lagos became a British colony in 1861, becoming a centre for trade, missionary activity and subsequent military expansion in the region, leading to a protectorate being declared in 1900. The British dependencies of Northern and Southern Nigeria were merged into a single territory, geographically the largest in the British empire, in 1914. After World War II, the government of the colony was reorganised, with a degree of autonomy granted to three regions: the predominantly Christian east and west and the predominantly Muslim north. This approach compounded feelings of tribal separatism, and by the time political independence from Britain was gained in 1960,

Nigeria's peoples for the most part had not yet come to think of themselves as Nigerians. Ethnic loyalty took precedence over national identity. The nation's people identified themselves primarily as Hausa-Falani [in the north], Ibo [in the east], or Yoruba [in the west], for example.

> (Davis and Kalu-Nwiwu 2001: 1)

In the first half of the twentieth century Nigeria's institutions of education were principally the results of Christian missionary efforts, and also Muslim initiatives in the north. A national movement to develop free primary education – though mostly for boys – commenced in 1955, but both the colonial and Nigerian governments underestimated the costs: only two of twelve regions – the Western and Lagos states – had succeeded in establishing a primary school system by the mid-1960s and growth was slowed by civil war in the period 1967–70. During the 1970s there was a period of reconstruction: the Christian mission schools were nationalised and secularised, and opportunities for girls to receive schooling increased, though mainly in the south.

In 1977 the country's military administration launched a national education policy for free and compulsory nine-year schooling: six in a primary school and three in a junior secondary institution. At the time, there was confidence that revenues from the oil boom would make this affordable, but the resultant growth paid little attention to quality. Efforts were also undermined by corruption and mismanagement, while progress in the areas of scientific, technological and vocational education was also very limited. Although the national education policy was revised and restated in 1981 and 1990, authoritarian governments and periods of military rule, with only brief periods of democracy, were unfavourable for educational development. In the eyes of many, standards of school organisation and discipline fell significantly during this period. A further drive for nine-year schooling was launched in 1992, but advances were restricted by insufficient money for the upgrading of sub-standard school buildings, the acute shortage of qualified teachers and their poor motivation, sometimes resulting from substantial wage arrears.

In 1999 Nigeria returned to democratic rule. The new government quickly prioritised universal basic education and the implementation of the targets set out in the 1990 Jomtien Declaration. Some fundamental issues remain unresolved, however: too few classrooms and too many children determine that primary school classes in many poor areas of the country are conducted under trees. Children from deprived families very frequently have to drop out of school through being unable to meet the costs of schooling, including stationery, uniforms and equipment, and also in consequence of households needing additional labour or meagre wages. In 2004, statistics showed that around 7 million children of primary school age were not enrolled in school, of which 62 per cent – still in northern Nigeria – were girls. This led to an alliance between the Nigerian government, the United Nations Children's Fund (UNICEF), the British Department for International Development (DFID) and other organisations to launch a girls' education project. This is aimed at helping Nigeria to meet the third Millennium Development Goal: eliminating gender disparity in education no later than 2015. The initiative has brought benefits in respect of supporting teacher training, supplying pupils with books and equipment, and improving the supply of water and sanitation for schools.

There is a three-tier model of education in Nigeria: primary, secondary and higher. The system is less bounded by age grading than perhaps any other in the world: secondary-age children frequently return to primary schooling after interrupting their studies and it is not uncommon for adults in their early twenties to be enrolled in secondary schools. This presents challenges for interpreting statistics about Nigerian education. Of the

secondary schools, many private ones offer courses leading to British examination body awards. Higher education in Nigeria is offered in sixty-seven universities, of which twenty-one are private institutions, and there are 250 higher education and research institutions. Only a tiny proportion of the population experiences higher education, either in Nigeria or overseas.

See also: Africa; Department for International Development (DFID); Education for All (EFA); educational targets; multigrade education; United Nations Children's Fund (UNICEF)

Further reading

Davis, T. J. and Kalu-Nwiwu, A. (2001) 'Education, ethnicity and national integration in the history of Nigeria: continuing problems of Africa's colonial legacy', *The Journal of Negro History*, 86(1): 1–11.
Ezeani, E. (2005) *Education in Nigeria: Problems, Dilemmas and Perspectives*, London: Veritas Lumen Publishers.

DAVID CROOK

NORDIC EDUCATIONAL RESEARCH ASSOCIATION (NERA)/NORDISK FÖRENING FÖR PEDAGOGISKA FORSKNING (NFPF)

The Nordic Educational Research Association (NERA) supports and promotes educational research in the Nordic countries of Denmark, Finland, Iceland, Norway and Sweden. It organises an annual conference which brings together a wide variety of researchers to discuss and debate educational research. Members of the Association coordinate research networks that arrange conference sessions, symposia and other events. These include networks on adult education, child care, multicultural education and higher education. NERA also publishes the journal *Nordisk Pedagogik* (Nordic Educational Research) which debates and disseminates key issues in Nordic educational research.

405

NERA was founded in 1972 and is open to all with an interest in educational research in a Nordic context. Members come from a range of disciplines, although they are united by common interests in the theory and practice of education. NERA is a member of the European Educational Research Association (EERA) and those who join NERA gain automatic membership of EERA. Individuals, institutions and students are all members and in 2005 there were over 800 in total. The annual general assembly of members elects a board to run the business of NERA.

See also: educational research; European Educational Research Association (EERA); Finland; Scandinavia; Sweden

TOM WOODIN

NORMAL SCHOOL

A venue for the instruction of classroom teachers, the normal school was most prominent between the mid-nineteenth and first half of the twentieth centuries, a time of significant expansion in primary and secondary school enrolments. While it took a variety of forms in response to the local and national circumstances in which it was forged, the normal school signalled an interest by educators internationally in bringing state control, regulation, and uniformity to teacher training.

Although the first known European teacher training institute was established as a German 'seminary' in the early eighteenth century, the term 'normal school' owes its origins to developments in France following the French Revolution in 1789. Students attending the *Ecole Normale*, founded in 1795, were expected to absorb and subsequently teach the values and ideals of the republic. "'The professors will give lessons to the students in the art of teaching morality and of shaping the hearts of young republicans to the practice of public and private virtues'" (Smith 1982: 7). The school closed after a few months, but it was reopened by Napoleon in 1808 with the explicit purpose of preparing teachers for French secondary schools, the *lycées*. A normal school system emerged in the 1830s, and as a reflection of its special standing, the Paris institute was renamed the *Ecole Normale Supérieure* in 1845. The écoles normales became an important and enduring component of French education, though in the twentieth century many graduate 'normaliens' concluded their careers as university teachers.

Rooted in the German *Lehrerseminar* and the Austrian *Normalschule*, Prussian teacher training, which included a boarding school system and a practice school, proved influential on the continent, in Russia, and in North America in the nineteenth century. Under the leadership of education minister Count Dimitrii Tolstoi, Russia established more than 100 normal schools, seminaries, and other teacher training institutes between 1866 and 1880. Like educational officials in other countries, Tolstoi believed that elementary school teachers could be over-educated, particularly if their instruction included radical ideas. Instead, they should be equipped only 'with such knowledge and skills as are necessary for keeping an ordinary elementary school' (Sinel 1969: 253).

Also noteworthy was the Glasgow Normal School, established by merchant David Stow in 1837. Author of the widely read *The Methods of Teaching*, Stow criticised both the Lancasterian monitorial system, and the excessive regimentation characteristic of most prevailing pedagogical practices. He proposed, instead, 'activity centred teaching' through which students would be more stimulated and engaged. He believed, as well, that Christian values and scriptures should infuse the curriculum.

Influenced more by Prussian than Stowian pedagogy, Canada's first normal school was established by a prominent educator, Egerton Ryerson, in Toronto in 1847. Subjected to a heavy curriculum, severe behavioural codes, and strict segregation of the sexes, aspiring teachers learned by example, and were expected to replicate their own formalistic educational experiences in future classrooms.

The distinctive history of normal school development in the United States reflected the growing diversity of the American population. Persuaded that teachers required rigorous and regulated preparation, Horace Mann, secretary of the State Board of Education, established the country's first state-supported normal school in Lexington, Massachusetts in 1839. By 1898, there were 166 public and 165 private normal schools throughout the USA. Those in the East confined themselves to the subject of teacher education, but normal schools in the Midwest and the West more commonly served as stepping-stones to college education, and in some cases achieved post-secondary educational status. The Illinois State Normal University, for example, was considered a 'people's university open to young men and women from all walks of life' (Herbst 1989: 95).

Over the course of the twentieth century, normal schools, whose students were predominantly female, were generally absorbed into or replaced by university-based faculties of education, which had the effect of elevating the professional status of teachers. However, institutes of teacher education remain sites of controversy over such questions as the degree of academic versus practical training they provide, and the extent of government regulation to which they are subjected. The disputes they witness frequently flow from those which run through the world of education at large.

See also: Lancaster, Joseph; monitorial system; seminary; teacher education/training

Further reading

Herbst, J. (1989) *And Sadly Teach: Teacher Education and Professionalization in American Culture*, Madison WI: University of Wisconsin Press.
Sinel, Allen (1969) 'Count Dimitrii Tolstoi and the preparation of Russian school teachers', *Canadian Slavic Studies*, 3(2): 246–62.
Smith, R. J. (1982) *The Ecole Normale Supérieure and the Third Republic*, Albany NY: State University of New York Press.

PAUL AXELROD

NORM-REFERENCED TESTS

Norm-referenced tests are constructed to assess examinee performance on aptitude, achievement, and personality variables (e.g. verbal reasoning, intelligence, creativity, mathematics achievement, self-concept), and interpret the resulting test scores in relation to a well defined reference group (e.g. a representative sample of adults between the ages of 18 and 49). These tests can be used for accomplishing many purposes: selection, classification, diagnosis, description, and research. For example, tests might be used to select the most promising candidates for university admission or for a job, to determine intelligence, or to assess occupational personality. Examples of norm-referenced tests in the United States would be: (1) the Graduate Record Exam used for admission to graduate schools; (2) the Armed Services Vocational Aptitude Battery used in selecting candidates for the military, and for classifying them into positions to maximise their success; (3) the Stanford-Binet intelligence scale to measure the intelligence levels of special needs children; and (4) the Minnesota Multiphasic Personality Inventory used to assess the personality of job applicants. There are several thousand standardised tests in the United States and more being developed all the time. The AERA-APA-NCME Test Standards are used to evaluate these tests for technical quality, fairness, and their utility in particular applications.

Norm-referenced tests are 'standardised' so that test scores can be meaningfully interpreted in relation to the scores of a reference group (known as the norm group). Clearly, it is important that examinees and the reference group hear/read the same test directions, are given the same amount of time to complete the test, and see the same or equivalent test content. For security reasons and to maintain the validity of test scores, it is common too for test publishers to prepare 'parallel forms' of a test. Parallel forms are considered to be interchangeable with one another, and candidates would be indifferent as to the form of the test they were given. Considerable effort is needed to ensure that forms of a test are parallel: content must be carefully matched, and pre-testing is needed to obtain item statistics that can be used to ensure that the forms of a test are equivalent in their difficulty, reliability, and validity.

One of the most expensive and time-consuming aspects of norm-referenced test construction is the development of test score norms. The population of candidates for whom the test is intended is identified, a sample is drawn that represents that population, and then the test is administered to that sample of examinees. Scores obtained from this administration provide the basis for preparing test score norms. Sometimes there may be interest in compiling multiple sets of norms for a test (e.g. children under twelve, children twelve and over; males and females, persons with a high school education, persons with college degrees, etc.). Just about every aspect of the norming process is challenging. Who exactly is the intended population for the test? How can sampling be carried out to achieve the goal of a representative sample of examinees, but make the actual test administration feasible and cost effective? What statistical manipulations are needed to match the actual sample of examinees to the sample that was intended and to 'smooth out' the distribution of test scores?

The scales on which test scores are reported for users remain one of the most confusing aspects of norm-referenced testing. Percentile score norms are the most straightforward. Each possible score on the test is linked to the percentage of examinees in a well defined reference group achieving that score or lower scores. Thus, we might say that an examinee scoring 30 out of 50 on a nationally normed achievement test was at the 75 percentile in the norm group, meaning that about 75 per cent of the examinees in the norm group scored 30 or less on the test. Other popular normative frameworks for score interpretations include 'stanines', 'stens', grade-equivalent scores, age-equivalent scores, normalised z scores, T scores, and more.

Norm-referenced achievement tests are criticised by some persons because (1) they can result in a narrowing of the school curriculum to match test content; (2) examinees can be taught to raise their scores (via 'coaching') without necessarily knowing more content; (3) they are biased against minority groups; and so on. But others argue that these shortcomings, if they occur at all, are bad testing practices that can easily be fixed, or considered in test score interpretations (see Phelps 2005). For example, much of the bias in testing, if it occurs, can be handled with more diversity in the pool of item writers, sensitivity review committees, and more careful screening of item statistics during the test development process.

See also: criterion-referenced tests; examinations; standardised tests; test/testing

Further reading

Phelps, R. (ed.) (2005) *Defending Standardized Testing*, Mahwah NJ: Lawrence Erlbaum.
Thorndike, R. (2005) *Measurement and Evaluation in Psychology and Education*, 7th edn, Upper Saddle River NJ: Pearson Merrill Prentice Hall.

RONALD K. HAMBLETON

NUMERACY

Numeracy, variously referred to in the literature as 'quantitative literacy', 'mathematical literacy' and 'statistical literacy', concerns the use of mathematics for understanding, for learning and for solving problems. This involves the ability to 'do mathematics' and to deal with mathematical concepts. The current paradigm of 'critical numeracy' follows a general shift in perspectives on the basics of mathematics education since the 1950s. Very broadly, the trend has been from an emphasis on the acquisition of a predetermined set of low-level mathematic skills towards an understanding of mathematics as a tool for learning.

The term numeracy was introduced in the Crowther Report (UK) in 1959 to represent the mirror image of literacy. Numeracy was seen to include both an understanding of the scientific approach to the study of phenomena – observation, hypothesis, experiment and verification – and the need in the modern world to think quantitatively. This perspective on numeracy embodied a highly sophisticated level and type of mathematical understanding. The associations of mathematics with science and the 'modern world' were regarded as separate yet crucial facets of numeracy.

A policy document on literacy and numeracy published by the Education Department of Western Australia in 1977 stated that 'the term "numerate" is understood to mean mathematical literacy'. For numeracy, this implied: the mastery of basic number facts; competency in arithmetic operations; skills in estimation and the habit of making estimates; sound spatial concepts; skills in interpreting graphs; sound proportion concepts; and statistical literacy based on experiences with chance processes. This view of numeracy emphasised competency with number skills, which was often seen as synonymous with quite low-level written, and sometimes mental, computational skills. So, to be numerate was to know and display the correct use of standard algorithms. Similar kinds of meanings are still very prevalent with the general public and employer groups. Even in a university context, many people still equate being numerate with having a fairly low-level mathematics background. However, within the field of mathematics education there has been more recently a reassessment of what is meant by being numerate.

The Cockroft Report (UK), *Mathematics Counts*, published in 1982, equated numeracy with the ability to cope confidently with the mathematical demands of everyday life. It was proposed that these demands did not require as high a level of mathematical understanding as was suggested in the Crowther Report of 1959 and that the close association with science was no longer present. It was found that the mathematical needs of learners did not, in fact, involve a great deal of mathematical content. In particular, regarding computational skills, it was found that adults who were competent mathematically in their everyday life often did not use the standard computational procedures they learned at school. The findings of this report promoted the view that mathematical needs and demands, or basics, were variant. This was a significant first step in recognising that the basics are subject to particular cultural and other contextual factors which might influence a student's confidence, ability and recognition that mathematics is useful to their life.

An important development in conceptualisations of numeracy was the British Open University's notion of 'informed numeracy'. This term was used to distinguish numeracy from algorithmic skill or the ability to 'do sums'. Informed numeracy was defined as knowing: when to use mathematics; what mathematics to use; how to do mathematics; and how to use the results provided by the mathematics (Open University Course Team 1980). Informed numeracy was thus an important tool for understanding and learning in a range of situations pertaining to everyday problems. It involved a critical awareness of the value of mathematics in everyday life. This definition of numeracy comprised two critical dimensions: context and purpose. Foremost was the contextual emphasis underpinning informed numeracy generally. That is, the processes involved in using mathematics depend upon the particular social (and cultural) context.

The late 1980s saw another major theoretical shift in terms of the relationship between numeracy and language and literacy. This shift can be seen to underpin the relatively recent development of the term 'critical numeracy'. Critical numeracy refers to the appropriate use of mathematics to deal with real life tasks to achieve social purposes. This involves: interpreting and representing mathematical ideas in social contexts;

understanding and expressing quantitative information across a range of texts; and interpreting mathematical meaning from a critical perspective (Lee *et al.* 1994). In this sense, numeracy is concerned with using, critically analysing and culturally locating mathematics, as well as with the more traditional mathematical activities of identifying and using symbols and rules and developing conceptual understanding (Johnston 1994). Dealing with the accelerating rate of changes in media forms, information and technologies requires new and increasingly sophisticated uses of mathematics; this is the central concern of critical numeracy.

See also: arithmetic; literacy; mathematics

Further reading

Cockcroft, W. H. (1982) *Mathematics Counts*, London: HMSO.
Crowther, G. (1959) *15 to 18*, London: HMSO.
Education Department of Western Australia (1977) *Literacy and Numeracy Policy Statement no. 6*, Perth: EDWA.
Johnston, B. (1994) 'Critical numeracy?', *Fine Print*, 16(4): 32–36.
Lee, A., Chapman, A. and Roe, P. (1994) *Pedagogical Relations between Adult Literacy and Numeracy*, Canberra, ACT: DEET.
Open University Course Team (1980) *Mathematics Across the Curriculum*, Buckingham: Open University Press.

ANNE CHAPMAN

NURSERY SCHOOL

Nursery schools are institutions for the education and care of children under compulsory school age. They sometimes overlap with day nurseries, which place priority on meeting the childcare needs of working parents, and with kindergartens, pre-kindergartens, or infant schools, which tend to have a greater focus on education as such and which are more likely to be connected with primary schools. Nursery schools are known by a variety of names around the world (such as *écoles maternelles* in France, *förskola* in Sweden, *detskij sad* in Russia, and *hoiku-en* in Japan)

and there are considerable variations in how nursery schools are funded, organised and staffed. They may be independent non-profit or for-profit ventures, run by parents as cooperatives, or provided for out of government funds. They may be separate from or affiliated with other schools and educational institutions, though in the latter case they are often called nursery classes or nursery units. Based upon their levels of training and respective roles, nursery school staff may be called nursery teachers, nursery nurses or nursery assistants

Depending on their social, economic, and cultural context, nursery schools may serve young children for all or part of the day, either daily or less often. In most countries, nursery schools and the people who work in them are regulated at least to some degree by the state, even where governments do not fund or operate nursery schools themselves.

In the United Kingdom, for example, there are two main types of nursery schools may be identified: maintained nursery schools which are funded by the local authority, offering free places to children aged 3 and 4, and private fee-paying nursery schools. Both types of nursery school have to be registered with government regulatory bodies and are subject to regular inspection. Typically, nursery schools offer sessions of about two hours per day, although some may offer a full day to meet the needs of the community. The child/staff ratio for children aged 3–5 in a nursery school is set officially in the UK at between 20 and 26 children to 2 adults, where one of those adults is a qualified teacher and the other is a trained nursery nurse or classroom assistant. State-funded nursery schools in England and Wales are required to follow the National Curriculum Foundation Stage, which focuses on the distinctive needs of children from age three to the end of the reception class of primary school.

The origins of the nursery school lie in the pioneering and philanthropic work of the social reformer and industrialist Robert Owen (1771–1858). Owen's interest in

410

community and concern to provide secure and appropriate education and care for the children of his workers paved the way for the so-called English nursery school movement. He is credited with establishing the first nursery-infant school for children under the age of five in New Lanark, near Glasgow, in 1816. The British nursery school was subsequently influenced, in the later decades of the nineteenth century, by the philosophy and practice of the kindergarten movement inspired by the German educator Friedrich Froebel (1782–1852). Other key figures in the development of the nursery school include the socialist child-saver Margaret McMillan (1869–1931), who became the first president of the British Nursery Schools Association, founded in 1923; Maria Montessori (1870–1952); and Susan Isaacs (1885–1948). Each of these individuals sought to establish a curriculum specifically tailored to the needs of young children and distinct from the more formal methods of the primary school.

Nursery school movements developed in England, the United States of America and elsewhere around the start of the twentieth century. Most institutions had their roots in earlier forms of childhood education (such as the kindergartens or French *salles d'asiles*) and in the new fields of psychology, child development and child guidance. In England, McMillan and others championed the open-air nursery school in the 1910s and 1920s. She saw the nursery school as a way of improving the health and hygiene conditions of working-class children under the age of five. Although local education authorities in England were permitted to open their own nursery schools from 1918 and their development was endorsed by the 1933 Hadow Report, decades of budgetary restrictions blocked progress. The period immediately following World War II actually saw a marked decline in the number of British nursery schools as mothers were encouraged to stay at home. The Plowden Report, *Children and Their Primary Schools* (1967) supported part-time nursery education but

viewed it as being aimed principally at those in need of support on the one hand, and the children of teachers on the other. It was not until the final years of the twentieth century, by which time a large market in independent nursery schools and other early years institutions had developed, that the British state began to invest in education for the under-fives.

In contrast to the working-class focus of English nursery schools, the first US nursery schools were university-based pre-school laboratories in which the psychological, cognitive, and physiological development of young children was observed and measured by middle-class parents and by child scientists. Their rapid expansion in the 1920s was due to widespread funding from the Laura Spelman Rockefeller Memorial, a private philanthropic trust that made child development research a priority. The US federal government's Emergency and Lanham Act nursery schools of 1933–43 and its Head Start programmes from 1965 marked major efforts to expand state-sector nursery schooling specifically for the poor, but it was in the independent, mainstream sector that US nursery schooling saw its greatest growth.

In the late twentieth century, nursery schools in England, the USA and elsewhere attracted increased attention from psychologists and policy makers who saw them as a means of enhancing child development and improving countries' educational and economic competitiveness. New ideas about developmental psychology and educational sociology led to experimentation with a wide range of curricula in compensatory and mainstream nursery schools. By the start of the twenty-first century, efforts at achieving universal state-sector nursery school provision in England and the USA looked poised to bring them in line with the more comprehensive state-sector nursery provision of countries such as France and Sweden.

Nursery schools' balance of emphasis on custodial care and educational work varies greatly from place to place according to cultural and demographic circumstances, the availability of alternatives, and the extent of mothers' workforce participation. In general terms, the nursery school curriculum is based on a diet of play and active learning, emphasising the development of children's social and language skills, physical health and emotional well-being.

Many nursery schools claim an affiliation with particular pedagogical programmes such as those of Montessori or Rudolf Steiner. Some, such as Head Start programmes in the United States of America and Sure Start children's centres in England, are specifically designed to offer compensatory education to the educationally or socially disadvantaged prior to compulsory schooling. Others offer environments and activities intended to enrich or complement the home lives of children in the mainstream.

Since their inception, institutions known as nursery schools have been subject to changing perceptions of childhood, motherhood and fluctuating economic demands. At the same time nursery schooling has been championed consistently by a number of influential educators for its contribution to early learning and the well-being of the child. Some would argue that little has changed and that

contemporary debate continues to centre on these two themes.

See also: early childhood education; Froebel, Friedrich; Isaacs, Susan; kindergarten; McMillan, Margaret; Montessori, Maria; Owen, Robert; reception class; Steiner, Rudolf

Further reading

Beatty, B. (1995) *Preschool Education in America: The Culture of Young Children from the Colonial Era to the Present*, New Haven CT: Yale University Press.

Hartley, D. (1993) *Understanding the Nursery: A Sociological Analysis*, London: Cassell.

Isaacs, S. (1929) *The Nursery Years*, London: Routledge and Kegan Paul.

McMillan, M. (1930) *The Nursery School*, London: George Allen and Unwin.

Moss, P. and Penn, H. (1996) *Transforming Nursery Education*, London: Paul Chapman.

Organisation for Economic Co-operation and Development (2001) *Starting Strong: Early Childhood Education and Care*, Paris: OECD.

Whitbread, N. (1972) *The Evolution of the Nursery-Infant School: A History of Infant and Nursery Education in Britain, 1800–1970*, London: Routledge and Kegan Paul.

KRISTEN D. NAWROTZKI AND SUE ROGERS

OBJECTIVE TESTS

Objective tests often present learners with a correct answer hidden among distracting incorrect answers or possibilities. Those answering questions will be 'right' or 'wrong', and marking – which may be undertaken electronically by technologies recognising the graphite of a pencil mark in the appropriate box, identifying a mouse click in an appropriate area of a computer screen or accepting the presence of the correctly matching word(s) in a 'fill-in-the-blank' candidate response – will be standardised, removing the possibility of one examiner seeing merit in a response and another disagreeing. Objective tests may be appropriate in instances where the memorisation of facts and figures is essential, but they may also be deployed in instances where, by applying their knowledge and understanding, test candidates can logically identify an answer, sometimes by systematically discounting the alternatives. True/false and multiple-choice questions are very common forms of objective tests.

See also: multiple-choice tests; test/testing

DAVID CROOK

OCEANIA

Oceania is a geographical world region subject to various definitions. Australia and New Zealand/Aotearoa are often said to be part of Oceania, though the focus of this entry is upon the educational development of other Pacific Island countries (PICs). This essay systematically reviews early childhood education (ECE), primary, secondary and further education in Oceania.

Although all PICs acknowledge the importance of ECE in their formal education plans there is great country variation in its delivery. Most do not have a clear policy on ECE which, up until now, has been the responsibility of non-government and community organisations, especially religious ones. Many ECE teachers are untrained or retired primary school teachers, although there are now ECE training programmes offered by some teachers' colleges (such as Fiji's Lautoka Teachers' College) as well as the University of the South Pacific (USP), which has been offering a three-course certificate programme though its continuing education section since the mid-1980s, and more recently a Diploma in Early Childhood Education since the early 1990s. This latter programme is available through distance and flexible learning to all the university's twelve member countries. USP hopes to offer a degree in ECE soon. The main challenges in ECE are related to curriculum development and teacher education, as well as to the need for countries to develop clear policies because of its importance as a foundation for later school development.

With a few exceptions (such as Papua New Guinea, the Solomon Islands and Vanuatu),

413

most PICs have achieved universal primary education. The major concern now is about quality and relevance, rather than access. Teacher/pupil ratios range from approximately 1:20 in Tuvalu and Tonga to 1:35 in Fiji and Vanuatu. Most PICs have teachers' colleges which provide both pre-service and in-service training, while the USP offers an upgrading programme at undergraduate degree. While countries such as Fiji, Samoa and Tonga have close to 100 per cent of their primary teaching forces trained, there continues to be a high percentage of untrained teachers in such countries as the Solomon Islands (*c.*30 per cent), and Vanuatu (*c.*50 per cent). Challenges facing PICs in relation to primary education include: provision of training opportunities for untrained teachers; updating the teacher education curriculum to include such areas as ICT, Pacific values, cultures and pedagogies; quality assurance; and developing outcome-based student assessment. There is also a need to upgrade the physical infrastructure and resources of primary schools, especially rural ones. External donor agencies have been providing assistance towards upgrading of basic education to most PICs either through bilateral arrangements (as in Kiribati, Fiji and Tonga) or regionally, as in the current European Union/New Zealand International Aid and Development Agency-funded Pacific Regional Educational Development Initiative (PRIDE). This project is focused on strengthening the planning capabilities of PICs and assisting the implementation of their strategic plans which encompass all levels of education.

Access to secondary education continues to be an important issue in most PICs, and a shortage of secondary school places is still a problem in countries such as the Solomon Islands and Vanuatu. Competitive external assessment at the end of year six or year eight have been the normal entry route for most students, although many countries, such as those in Micronesia and increasingly in others such as Fiji, are using internal assessment methods. A feature of Pacific secondary education is the important role of non-governmental organisations, especially religious ones, which continue to be responsible for the administration of most secondary schooling in many PICs. Many more secondary teachers are now trained (over 50 per cent of the secondary teaching force in some countries), but there continues to be a substantial proportion of untrained teachers in all Pacific schools, especially in mission schools. Teacher training programmes for lower secondary levels are available in many countries, and a few such as Tonga, Fiji and Samoa now offer teacher training programmes for upper secondary teachers. USP continues to be the main teacher education institution for upper secondary and currently offers concurrent teacher education programmes for senior high teaching (B.A./B.Sc. +GCED), as well as an end-on programme (PGCE). Teacher/pupil ratios vary depending on subjects, from 1:40 in lower-level English and mathematics to 1:20 in most pre-degree (or year seven) classes. The secondary school curriculum has historically been tied (perhaps too tightly) to university requirements and it continues to be too 'academic' according to some critics. Attempts to change the school curriculum and create more technical and vocational courses have not been successful. External examinations also greatly influence the curriculum and students are subjected to many, including in year/forms 4, 5, 6 and 7. A hot issue now relates to pre-degree courses (form seven). While some countries (such as Fiji and Tonga) have been developing their own curriculum and examinations at the form seven level, others have been using the USP foundation programme, and, since 2004, a regional form seven programme offered by the South Pacific Board for Educational Assessment. Other challenges facing secondary school officials include: students' and teachers' English competence (the medium of instruction in most secondary schools is English), relevance and quality of subjects taught; inclusion of new areas such as information and communications technology, HIV/AIDS, and values education; ensuring a qualified teaching force and retaining good quality teachers. There exists a regional Forum Basic Education Plan which, among other things is targeting areas such as basic education, a regional qualification framework, technical and vocational education and training, and financing education.

Despite Pacific nations' commitment to educating their people, the fact remains that only a very small proportion of the region's population (fewer than 5 per cent) are able to access higher education institutions, either in the region or outside. Today opportunities for higher education continue to be limited. Before the establishment of the USP in 1968, most Pacific Island students had to leave home in order to attend high school and virtually all had to leave their home countries in order to pursue university and other tertiary level studies. Now there are several higher education institutions serving the region, including USP, the French University of the Pacific, the universities of Guam and Papua New Guinea and the National University of Samoa. Atenisi University and the recently established University of Fiji are private institutions.

Because of the region's geography, USP pioneered the development of distance education in 1970, using satellite communications technology. Today the USP is providing higher education to groups of students who cannot, or do not wish to, participate in conventional education, either because of an accident of geography or birth, the cost of attending schools and/or university, or simply failure to reach the cut-off points. Today, more than half of USP students study via distance and over 11,000 have received formal qualifications from USP and thousands more have been able to access its accredited, as well as non-accredited, programmes. Distance learners have included people in full-time employment and housewives, as well as school leavers. As well as the main campus in Fiji, there are two campuses in Samoa and Vanuatu and centres at all other member countries.

Higher education institutions outside of the Pacific Island region have also begun to offer university-level programmes in some PICs. The services they provide include distance education courses as well as on-site programmes supported by resident tutors. Some programmes, particularly vocational ones, are offered through existing national post-secondary institutions. Most, if not all, of these institutions are profit-oriented, targeting a small but influential and affluent clientele in areas such as business and commerce, using curricula imported from metropolitan countries, with little effort to adapt to Pacific contexts. This, plus the push for market-driven economies and educational development, awareness of and concern about issues such as cross-cultural transfer, globalised curricula and appropriate learning strategies, will become more urgent because in these trends and developments cultural diversity is being blurred and services and products standardised and homogenised. The major challenges to higher education in PICs include: bridging the gap between readily available curriculum resources from overseas universities and less readily available but more relevant and better contextualised materials produced within the region; implications for some groups of students of differential fees recently introduced by USP in high-demand areas; admission policies, especially of students with school-based qualifications; students' learning difficulties; quality assurance issues and accreditation; and matching higher education with national and regional development needs.

See also: Australia; distance education/learning; New Zealand/Aotearoa; teacher education/training; universal education

Further reading

Crocombe, R. (1992) *New Zealand's Relations with Other Pacific Islands*, Suva, Fiji and Christchurch, NZ: Institute of Pacific Studies, University of the South Pacific and University of Canterbury Press.

Guy, R., Kosuge, T. and Hayakawa, R. (eds) (2000) *Distance Education in the South Pacific: Nets and Voyages*, Suva, Fiji: USP, in association with Pacific Islands Nations Fund.

Pene, F., Taufe'ulungaki, A. and Benson, C. (eds) (2002) *The Tree of Opportunity: Re-thinking Pacific Education*, Suva, Fiji: USP.

Taufe'ulungaki, A. M. (1987) 'Educational provision and operation: regional dimensions in the South Pacific'. In K. Bacchus and C. Brock (eds) *The Challenge of Scale: Educational Development in the Small Island States of the Commonwealth*, London: Commonwealth Secretariat.

Teasdale, R. G. and Teasdale, J. (eds) (1992) *Voices in a Seashell: Education, Culture and Identity*, Suva, Fiji: UNESCO and USP.

Thaman, K. H. (1994) 'Cultural democracy for whom? A view from the Pacific Islands', *Directions: Journal of Educational Studies*, 16(1): 3–19.

KONAI THAMAN

OPEN LEARNING

Open learning is an educational philosophy that emphasises learners' choices and aims to reduce barriers to study. In its most developed form, it can be seen as a transfer of control over the learning process to the learner, and from the institution or teacher, usually through the use of various forms of technology.

Originating in the 1950s and 1960s, it is a contested term, which gained impetus from the foundation of the Open University, in the United Kingdom, in 1969, and occasioned much debate in the 1980s and 1990s. Discussion centred round boundaries with distance education, the use of 'open learning' as a slogan to describe a wide range of systems (Rumble 1989) and the discourse of 'open learning' to serve political and economic agendas (Edwards 1991). The range of educational and training initiatives included under the banner of 'open learning' at the time is well illustrated by Paine (1988).

Discussions in this period clarified the different and overlapping ways in which the term was used. In the first place, 'open learning' is used to signal a value system underpinning educational provision. This is essentially student-centred and emphasises increasing and widening access and equity through the provision of educational opportunities in a flexible manner. While always relative in application, it aims to provide students with choices about when, where, how and what to study and to enable them to overcome geographical, political, social and other constraints. In this way, it differs from distance education and e-learning, which are essentially methods of delivery, rather than value-laden. It is this sense of open learning, which has survived into the twenty-first century.

The term was also used in the 1980s to describe the delivery of in-house corporate training schemes by employers, one example being the UK's Manpower Services Commission's *Open Tech* programme. While these schemes were flexible in terms of mode and media of delivery, they were not open in access, being restricted to company employees. In this way, 'open learning' became associated with 'flexible learning', an equally contested term, but one that has its roots in work and industry, rather than educational philosophy.

The positive and 'progressive' ethos of the term 'open learning' ensured its continuing usage in a number of different contexts. One, mainly historical, use relates to organisational models and systems; institutions adopted the phrase to indicate their role or values but changed their terminology in the 1990s and early 2000s. Open Learning Australia, which jointly develops and markets courses and acts as an educational broker between institutions, became Open Universities Australia; the Open Learning Institute, Hong Kong, which began by importing and adapting courses from other institutions, gained university status and became the Open University, Hong Kong in 1997.

After early debates, the term has been particularly associated in the UK with the Open University, which is one of the very few institutions globally to operate a genuine policy of open access with no educational qualifications required for entry. The Open University has also developed a model of 'supported open learning' which includes specially designed, multimedia teaching materials underpinned by research and scholarship; personal teaching and learner support; and educational advice and guidance services. The journal *Open Learning*, which replaced its forerunner *Teaching at a Distance* in 1986, has included many debates on the international usage of the term.

Open learning is, thus, politically, historically and culturally situated, but still survives. By the turn of the century, various umbrella terms gained greater currency; 'open and distance learning' (ODL) became one of the most frequently employed, for example by the Canadian online *International Review of Research into Open and Distance Learning* (IRRODL) founded in 2000, or by UNESCO (2002). The term has since been extended to include e-learning, for instance by the online *European Journal of Open Distance and eLearning* (EURODL), relaunched in 2004. When used in its original form as 'open learning', it retains the underpinning values of an educational philosophy with a social justice agenda (Gaskell 2007).

See also: distance education/learning; educational technology; e-learning; Open University; technology

Further reading

Edwards, R. (1991) 'The inevitable future?: post-Fordism in work and learning', *Open Learning*, 6(2): 236–42.
Gaskell, A. (2007) 'Open learning and e-learning', *Open Learning*, 22(1): 1–4.
Paine, N. (ed.) (1988) *Open Learning in Transition: an Agenda for Action*, Cambridge: National Extension College.
Rumble, G. (1989) '"Open learning", "distance learning", and the misuse of language', *Open Learning*, 4(2): 28–36.
UNESCO (2002) *Open and Distance Learning: Trends, Policy and Strategy Considerations*, Paris: UNESCO.

ANNE GASKELL

OPEN PLAN

Open plan is an approach to teaching and learning that allows for diversity of configurations of time and space in a setting that lends itself to team teaching, self-directed learning and collaboration. The open plan classroom became popular in school design in Europe and the USA between the end of the 1950s and 1970s.

Open plan classrooms were pioneered by post-World War II educators and architects in Britain, concerned to harness the best and most innovative practice at a time when freedom in learning was thought to be an important component in rebuilding democracies. Having pioneered the design of infant schools during the 1940s and 1950s, the architects Mary Crowley (later, Medd) and David Medd became key players in the research and development team at the British Ministry of Education, in creating design prototypes for primary and middle schools. The schools they designed became internationally acclaimed and attracted much interest.

Open plan teaching and learning departed radically from traditional approaches to pedagogy as teachers, individually or in teams, designed and supported learning activities, rather than instruct the whole class. Ideally, open plan was achieved from close collaboration between architects and educators who paid close attention to the observed needs of children and their teachers. The design solution was complex and consisted of a range of subtle, modulated spaces, neither completely open nor closed, where groups of children might carry out different projects at different educational levels simultaneously. Finmere school in Oxfordshire, designed by Mary Medd and opened in 1960, was a classic open plan design, not simply an open space but a carefully designated set of spaces with specific intentions for use and the highest degree of flexibility. Key features included 'home bays' and spaces such as 'sitting room' and 'kitchen', reflecting a domestic realism in the educational environment. The space was divided by means of two folding partitions and a series of fixed wall partitions, creating work bays offering space for a variety of possible uses.

Where teachers were adequately prepared and trained to teach in open plan settings, the approach was popular and did allow for innovation, especially in cross-curricular learning, and a freeing up of the disciplined atmosphere of the school. However, in Britain, open plan was closely associated with progressive education and, as such, came under attack from those who did not believe that such strategies were in the best interests of the child. In 1974, a report published by the National Union of Teachers (NUT) (England) noted the most popular complaints of teachers, which more often than not included noise nuisance. In research studies that followed in the USA, where half of all schools built between 1967 and 1969 were open plan, and in Europe, it was concluded that architectural design does not fundamentally determine teacher practice but that teachers arrange their spaces in accordance with their perceived needs, habits and beliefs – hence the practice of erecting walls and other barriers in originally planned open spaces to bring about a return to a classroom environment. Malcolm Seaborne noted, in his study of primary school design, that the financial constraints placed by governments on the design of new schools during these years did not enable the full scale of the experiment to be explored. This, together with a reluctance on the part of many teachers to let go of tried and tested approaches to teaching in the classroom, made the open plan experiment difficult to sustain. By the mid-1970s, government pressure in Britain was building against the freedom of experimentation and innovation which had been enjoyed by teachers for over a decade.

Since the 1970s, open plan has been revisited within new frameworks encouraging self-directed learning and interdisciplinary work. Some schools designed in the early years of the twenty-first century have embraced open plan approaches to teaching and learning and attempted to provide settings for this. One such example in the UK is Bishops Park College in Essex, where the organisation of time for learning has been radically altered, allowing for longer periods of interdisciplinary learning supplemented by master classes. The college has open plan areas, but these come secondary to the main reconfiguration of mini-schools within the larger college. In the USA, the state of Minnesota is committed to open plan school design and linked teacher training.

See also: classroom; progressive education; teaching/teaching methods

Further reading

Department of Education and Science (1967) *Children and Their Primary Schools*, London: HMSO.
Seaborne, M. (1977) *The English School: Its Architecture and Organisation. Vol 2: 1870–1970*, London: Routledge and Kegan Paul.

CATHERINE BURKE

OPEN UNIVERSITY

The Open University, based in Milton Keynes in the United Kingdom, is a university that provides higher education courses on a part-time and distance learning basis, and is therefore 'open' for a wider range of students than traditional universities, including employed, mature and disabled people. It was established in 1969, drawing on an original idea put forward by Michael Young, and has become the largest university in the UK with nearly 200,000 students, and one of the largest universities in the world. Its distance learning methods have developed with changes in technology, but have included summer schools, radio and television lectures, and Web-based learning, leading to undergraduate and postgraduate degrees in a wide range of subjects. Its growth reflects the relative affluence of advanced regions and economies, which, as Halsey suggests, has created a regime of the 'third age' with resources and appetite for further education (Halsey 2006: 859). A number of higher education institutions in other countries also include 'open university' in their titles, and the model of the Open University is increasingly influential and prominent internationally.

See also: distance education/learning; educational broadcasting; mature student; open learning; summer school; university; Web-based learning; Young, Michael

Further reading

Halsey, A. H. (2006) 'The European university'. In H. Lauder, P. Brown, J. Dillaboug and A. H. Halsey (eds) *Education, Globalisation and Social Change*, Oxford: Oxford University Press.

GARY McCULLOCH

ORAL EXAMINATIONS

Oral examinations are formal assessments of a student's knowledge and understanding of a prescribed topic or programme and/or of the student's ideas and arguments. Its origins are to be found in the medieval European universities, where they predated written examinations by several centuries. Today, students of music are frequently subjected to an oral examination testing their understanding of musical theory, the principles of composition or the history of music. In foreign language teaching, the oral examination may require the candidate to read aloud – in order for the examiner to grade the candidate's pronunciation and accent – and/or to engage in discussion in with the examiner in the language under examination.

In the context of contemporary higher education, some programmes require all students to take an oral examination, but an 'oral' may also be invoked in exceptional or special circumstances. For example, examiners may wish to interview a student before finally deciding which classification of degree to award, or it may replace some other element of assessment that a candidate is unable to complete, perhaps as a result of illness or disability. A particular type of oral examination taken in many countries by higher degree students is the viva voce. This is an oral defence of a scholarly thesis or dissertation, involving an extended discussion between the candidate and her/his examiners. Following the viva voce the examiners reach a decision on whether they will recommend to the university that a degree or doctorate be granted. Medical or dental students may encounter an altogether different application of the term 'oral examination': the close inspection of a patient's mouth.

See also: doctorate; examinations; grades; thesis/dissertation

DAVID CROOK

ORGANISATION FOR ECONOMIC CO-OPERATION AND DEVELOPMENT (OECD)

The Organisation for Economic Co-operation and Development (OECD) is an inter-governmental organisation (IGO), which plays a highly significant role in promoting neo-liberal thinking in education, not only within its own member countries but also around the world. Founded in 1961, the OECD grew out of the Marshall Plan and superseded the Organisation for European Economic Co-operation (OEEC). The sixteen original countries that formed OEEC shared a common interest in the economic reconstruction of Europe after the devastation of World War II. Today, the OECD's brief is much broader, concerned with both economic and social policy, including education. Its membership has extended to thirty, mostly developed, countries which between them produce two thirds of the world's goods and services. Headquartered in Paris, the OECD sponsors wide-ranging policy debates and produces several highly influential publications in both French and English. Unlike other large IGOs, the OECD does not dispense money but rather concentrates its resources on data collection useful for comparative policy analysis and on investigating and disseminating policy ideas.

The OECD has always been committed to market economy and pluralistic democracy;

but over the past decade it has sought to promote a neo-liberal view of international trade and state governance around the world. According to Article 1 of the OECD Convention, its aims are:

1 to achieve the highest sustainable economic growth and employment and a rising standard of living in member countries, while maintaining financial stability, and thus to contribute to the development of the world economy;

2 to contribute to sound economic expansion in member as well as non-member countries in the process of economic development; and

3 to contribute to the expansion of world trade on a multilateral, non-discriminatory basis in accordance with international obligations.

While the OECD is primarily concerned with the economic improvement of its member countries, it insists that members must work within a global framework. It has developed a highly sophisticated view of globalisation that is concerned not only with the global expansion of market ideology but also with the development of neo-liberal state structures of public sector governance. These structures encourage re-engineering of the administrative functions of the states, designed to facilitate a new culture of bureaucratic rationalisation and perfomativity aligned to the needs of the global market economy.

The OECD's perspective on education has always been informed by versions of human capital theory. Education has been viewed as a major contributor to economic development, both of the individual as well as of the nation. The OECD has insisted upon the role education must play in producing skilled human resources considered necessary for economic growth. Over the last decade, this general sentiment has been associated with the OECD's focus on the requirements of a knowledge economy. A new human capital theory has emerged that is concerned with

individual enterprise within a globalised economy. The emphasis has been on a view of education that facilitates the global movement of capital, while it benefits the individual. Such an education stresses that a highly skilled, mobile, and flexible workforce is necessary for nations to succeed within the new knowledge economy.

For most of the 1960s, the OECD's educational work was located within its economic policy portfolio. Education did not emerge as a separate portfolio until 1968 with the creation of the Centre for Educational Research and Innovation (CERI), followed shortly by the formation of the Education Committee in 1970. For most of the 1970s and 1980s, the OECD's educational work was located within a social democratic framework, with tacit support for Keynesian economics. The Educational Committee was a forum for sharing policy ideas, with little attempt to forge a common educational agenda; and CERI's work was mostly oriented to an agenda of curriculum and pedagogic reform. The major foci of this work were on issues of access and equity, and on vocational training as well as issues of transition to work. These themes were subjected to rigorous analytical review. A range of policy options were presented that member countries could consider but were free to ignore. The same approach applied to country reviews, which involved an overall assessment of the functioning of a country's education and training system. These reviews of initially member and later non-member countries offered no formal mechanism for comparison, but were rather conducted by external examiners in terms of the country's own stated priorities. Different countries had different expectations of the reviews, and often used them as a stimulus to broaden the scope of policy debates or to institute new programmes.

This long established OECD approach to policy debates began to change during the later part of 1980s. The OECD now pursues a more activist neo-liberal policy agenda, encapsulated in the recurring discourses of quality, equity, diversity, accountability, mobility, lifelong learning, and internationalisation. Even the long established OECD programmes, such as the Programme on Educational Building (PEB) and the Programme on Institutional Management in Higher Education (IMHE) are now located within a broader framework of a neo-liberal policy agenda. PEB assists member countries in the planning, design, building and maintenance of educational facilities by establishing forums for the exchange of knowledge about matters related to educational building, focusing largely on the performative criteria of efficiency and effectiveness, often through advocacy for privatisation. IMHE is another OECD forum whose membership includes institutions, government, and non-government agencies concerned with issues in higher education. In recent years, IMHE's agenda has been dominated by concerns of reform, including ways of ensuring performance, control, accountability and quality assurance, providing responsive services, improving the management of human resources, and internationalising campuses. Central to the OECD's perspective on reform is the preference for increased competition and greater recourse to market disciplines.

Linked to this view of reform is the importance the OECD now attaches to the development of indicators. Since the creation of the Unit for Education Statistics and Indicators in 1994, the OECD has increasingly produced a large amount of comparative data that now constitutes a major bulk of its work in education. The Unit produces an annual publication, *Education at a Glance*, together with an analytical supplement which comments in greater detail on selected themes of key importance to member countries. Data is collected in three areas of interest: the demographic, economic and social context of education; resources and school processes; and outcomes of education. Some of this data is derived from international surveys, such as the indicators on achievement of thirteen-year-olds generated from the Third International

Mathematics and Science Study (TIMMS), produced in 1993–94 by the International Association of Educational Evaluators, while other indicators are based on programmes the OECD itself administers, such as the Programme for International Student Assessment (PISA), a three-yearly survey of fifteen-year-old students in selected industrialised countries, designed to measure skills the OECD deems essential for them to be able to fully participate in society.

The OECD's work on indicators functions on two levels: it assists member countries and others to clarify and compare their own policy positions, helping them to administer the public accountability of educational systems, but it simultaneously draws countries into a single comparative field that pivots around certain normative assumptions about educational provision and performance. In this way, the OECD is no longer simply a forum for policy discussion but a major international mediator of educational knowledge, a policy actor in its own right promoting a particular conception of education and its relationship to social and economic development. The OECD represents its neo-liberal conception of education as a consensus in policy which focuses on the need of member countries to benchmark their performance against the specific skills of individuals thought necessary to participate in a knowledge-based global economy. The benchmarking is considered necessary for developing educational programmes that achieve better outcomes (more effectiveness) at lower cost (more efficiency).

The OECD has sought to promote this neo-liberal ideology not only within its own member countries but also more broadly around the world. It has done this by circulating policy ideas through its publications and by working multilaterally with a number of other IGOs. It has joined, for example, UNESCO and EUROSTAT to develop a World Education Indicators project which involves each organisation in collecting data from its respective membership but working in conjunction in their compilation and dissemination. The OECD and the European Union have also worked together to develop a policy agenda on lifelong learning linked to its understanding of the demands of the knowledge economy. And in more recent years, the OECD has created the Forum on Trade in Educational Services to discuss the main issues and trends in the global trade of educational services. It has teamed up with UNESCO to create a new international initiative to enhance quality provision in cross-border higher education and to develop a system for the accreditation and recognition of qualifications at both the national and the international level. This agenda is linked to the concerns both of the WTO's General Agreement on Trade in Services (GATS) and the Bologna Process sponsored by the European Union. This multilateralism suggests that the OECD now views itself as a leading policy player on the international level, committed to re-articulating the role education must play in line with the demands of the global economy.

See also: Centre for Educational Research and Innovation (CERI); globalisation; human capital; international education; knowledge economy

Further reading

Henry, M. Lingard, B., Rizvi, F. and Taylor, S. (2001), *The OECD, Globalisation and Education Policy*, Oxford: IAU Press and Pergamon.

Keeley, B. (2007) *Human Capital: How What you Know Shapes your Life*, Paris: OECD.

Organisation for Economic Co-operation and Development (2004a) *Learning for Tomorrow's World: First Results from PISA 2003*, Paris: OECD.

——(2004b) *What Makes School Systems Perform? Seeing School Systems Through the Prism of PISA*, Paris: OECD.

——(2004c) *OECD Work on Education*, Paris: OECD.

——(2004d) *Innovation in the Knowledge Economy: Implications for Education and Learning*, Paris: OECD.

——(2007) *Qualifications Systems: Bridges to Lifelong Learning*, Paris: OECD.

Slaughter, A.-M. (2004) *A New World Order*, Princeton NJ: Princeton University Press.

FAZAL RIZVI AND DAVID RUTKOWSKI

OWEN, ROBERT (1771–1858)

Owen, the socialist educator, became the manager of a cotton mill at the age of nineteen and married the daughter of the owner of New Lanark Mills, Glasgow, Scotland in 1799. He rose to become manager and co-owner at the age of twenty-nine. He established a school at New Lanark for the employees' children under the age of twelve, laying special emphasis upon the infant section. He believed that schooling should be centred on the social welfare of the child and he emphasised kindliness, play, and cooperation. Other schools following the New Lanark example were established and his principles became fundamental to the influential Owenite movement that sprang up in most urban centres during the 1830s and 1840s. Owen strongly believed in equality of educational provision between girls and boys and ensured that the broad curriculum was available to all pupils. Owen extended his influence in the mid-1820s when he set up a colony along similar lines at New Harmony, USA. In the 1840s the establishment of Owenite 'Halls of Science', in opposition to middle-class sponsored mechanics' institutes, introduced a decisive new element into the movement for self-education amongst the working classes. Owen believed in connecting education with recreation, and at one time exerted a direct and immediate influence upon hundreds of thousands of adults. His *New View of Society* (1813–16) connected his educational philosophy with his wider political views, becoming one of the benchmark works for nineteenth-century political radicals and the labour movement.

See also: early childhood education; politics of education; workers' education

STEVEN COWAN

P

PAKISTAN

Pakistan became independent in August 1947. Historically part of British India, the regions that were to make up Pakistan did not benefit from the imperial education infrastructure as much as the core regions that went on to make up the Indian state.

Given the brutal aftermath of partition, the highest priority was that of creating a new nation after independence. The first meeting on education was held in Karachi in November 1947. It resulted in the creation of Pakistan's education infrastructure consisting of an Advisory Board of Education, an Inter-University Board and a Council of Technical Education. Islam, though central to education and politics, was in Jinnah's vision not to result in Pakistan being turned into a theocracy. Islam was going to be used to oppose identity formation on the basis of ethnicity. The inclusion of Islamic studies in the curriculum and making Urdu compulsory for all were seen as a tool to unify the diverse country, which until 1971 included East Bengal, separated from West Pakistan by 1,500 miles of Indian territory.

Whilst the state struggled to set up a countrywide education infrastructure, a parallel system of private schools, where English was the medium of instruction, and madrassas (Islamic schools) existed from the start. The government not only promoted the state education system but also continued to patronise cadet colleges and elite institutions, effectively creating a two-tier education system.

In 1949 the central goals of improving quality, achieving 80 per cent literacy in twenty years, and requiring 75 per cent of children of school age to be enrolled were formulated. The subsequent nine 5-year plans (1957–2003) set out to increase the quantity of the schooling infrastructure and increase the enrolment of children through mass literacy programmes. The targets of these plans and goals were, however, not achieved as envisaged. Literacy did go up from 16 per cent in 1951 to 51.6 per cent in 2003, but fell short of 100 per cent by 1975 as had originally been planned.

In 1959 a report indicated a significant change in government thinking, shifting the responsibility for universal education from the state to the parents, resulting in an increased number of private schools out of reach of the majority of Pakistanis. The same report also created the textbook board, whose primary task has since been to ensure that the government's policies have been reflected in the textbooks.

In 1969, when General Yahya Khan imposed martial law, the New Education Policy was formulated. At the time, Pakistan was on the verge of civil war, with Bengali nationalism leading to the secession of Bangladesh. Zulfikar Ali Bhutto announced another new education policy when coming to power in the new truncated Pakistan, which did not, however, diverge significantly from the previous policies. Adult literacy became a priority and 3,334 private educational institutions were nationalised.

Bhutto's government ended when General Zia ul Haq took over in July 1977. Zia made significant changes to the education system by introducing radical Islamisation measures. The National Education Policy and Implementation Programme set out to Islamise the youth by giving textbooks of all subjects a religious orientation. Despite this, English-medium schools were not banned and the private sector expanded rapidly to cater for the more affluent middle and upper classes. By the time Zia died, in 1988, Pakistan studies and Islamic theology were being studied in universities and the number of madrassas had increased.

The civilian governments which followed Zia's rule, led alternatively by Benazir Bhutto and Nawaz Sharif, did not reverse the Islamisation process. The National Education Policy, 1998–2010, put forward by the Sharif government, focused on the universalisation of primary education by 2010 and an increased emphasis on information technology. Islamisation and privatisation continued to be encouraged.

Under General Musharraf's government the Education Sector Reforms Action Plan 2001–4 continues to encourage private sector investment in secondary and higher education. Currently there is a major curriculum review underway. The United States Agency for International Development is supporting Pakistan's education reform with $100 million, amongst which the Education Sector Reform Assistance (ESRA) focuses on education policy issues such as teaching methods to instil democratic attitudes. A madrassa regulation board has also been created to establish a network of model madrassas and regulate others.

See also: India

Further reading

Khan Jalalzai, M. (2005) *The Crisis of Education in Pakistan: State Policies and Textbooks*, Lahore: Al Abbas International.

Rafi Khan, S. (2005) *Basic Education in Rural Pakistan: A Comparative Institutional Analysis of Government, Private and NGO Schools*, Oxford: Oxford University Press.

Rahman, T. (2004) *Denizens of Alien Worlds: A Study of Education, Inequality and Polarisation in Pakistan*, Oxford: Oxford University Press.

MARIE LALL

PARENTAL CHOICE

Throughout the 1980s, the influence of neo-liberalism in states around the world meant that an institutionalised, centralised welfare state was no longer seen as viable. Instead, 'the roles, relations, and responsibilities of state, market and society' were rearranged (Rhoten 2000: 594). The role of the central state is continuing to change as it retreats from being a direct provider, instead setting up the conditions in which competition can take place. It becomes an 'evaluative state', which focuses on implementing a regulatory system of performance outputs and indicators. The mechanisms through which the state moves towards this role of 'steering at a distance' (Ball 1994: 54) include policies of decentralisation, deregulation and, more recently, private sector involvement. Consumer choice is an integral part of these changes, and market-led systems of education (to varying degrees) are now common. As Whitty notes (2002: 11), 'such policies received particular encouragement from New Right governments in Britain and the USA in the 1980s, and were subsequently fostered by the IMF and World Bank in Latin America and Eastern Europe'. Proponents of parental choice, such as Chubb and Moe (1990) and Tooley (2000) argue that choice policies as part of a market-led system in education will increase the level of school accountability to parents, thereby discouraging 'producer capture' (control of schools by teachers and, especially, local administrators) and encouraging diversity on the supply side, that parents are best placed to know what sort of education will suit their child, and that choice schemes can result in higher standards of education and, therefore, higher levels of pupil achievement.

A variety of different choice schemes for education can be seen in developed and developing countries around the world. The World Bank website (www.worldbank.org/education) includes case studies from various countries which demonstrate the diversity of the schemes and also the particularity of nation-states, that is, the importance of countries' differing demographics, resources, and past and present patterns of educational provision and principle, in determining how choice schemes will be received and play out.

Chile's government began to provide vouchers in 1981 to any students wishing to attend private school, and the budgets of public schools were also tied to their enrolment success (or otherwise). One marked result of Chile's unlimited voucher programme has been a middle-class exodus from public schools. By contrast, in Milwaukee, one of the most well known of American choice initiatives, the scheme is aimed at students from low-income families only. Here, although it is highly contested, the scheme has a populist appeal (Whitty 2002: 59–61). Currently in the USA there appears to be growing public support for 'opportunity scholarships' (vouchers) which would allow much wider public funding for private school places.

In Britain the system is somewhat different as parents can exercise a preference for any state-funded school of their choice. The use of 'preference' here indicates that parents may not be able to access the school of their choice, and some schools manage demand by setting tests for prospective pupils, thereby 'cream-skimming' the most academically able. The degree to which the state education system in the UK and other developed countries has become polarised is disputed, but research with middle-class parents in particular demonstrates an understanding of local hierarchies of schools (Gewirtz *et al.* 1995).

This then indicates the most commonly cited concern with parental choice, that choice may increase social stratification: school choice may be advantageous for more privileged groups in society who are better prepared to exercise that choice (see OECD 1994). As Whitty argues, 'the mere provision of new choices to individual families is unlikely to overcome deep-rooted patterns of structural and cultural disadvantage' (2002: 12).

See also: catchment area; centralisation/decentralisation; privatisation/marketisation; vouchers

Further reading

Ball, S. (1994) *Education Reform*, Buckingham: Open University Press.

Chubb, J. and Moe, T. (1990) *Politics, Markets and America's Schools*, Washington DC: Brookings Institution Press.

Gewirtz, S., Ball, S. and Bowe, R. (1995) *Markets, Choice and Equity in Education*, Buckingham: Open University Press.

OECD (1994) *School: A Matter of Choice*, Paris: OECD/CERI.

Rhoten, D. (2000) 'Education decentralization in Argentina: a "global-local conditions of possibility" approach to state, market and society change', *Journal of Education Policy*, 15(6): 539–619.

Tooley, J. (2000) *Reclaiming Education*, London: Continuum Press.

Whitty, G. (2002) *Making Sense of Education Policy*, London: Paul Chapman.

CAROL VINCENT

PARITY OF ESTEEM

Parity of esteem is a term sometimes used to describe the intended equality of schools which may otherwise invite contrast in respect of, for example, location, ethos or curriculum specialism. The term had a particular currency in England and Wales in the period following the 1944 Education Act, which heralded the transfer of all state school pupils from primary to secondary school at age eleven. The mechanism for selecting pupils for one type of secondary school, rather than another was the 'eleven-plus' examination. In instances where local education authorities maintained secondary technical, as well as secondary modern and grammar schools, it was somewhat easier to argue that the schools were separate but equal, having parity of esteem. Being expensive to build and equip with workshops and specialist facilities, however, few secondary technical schools emerged after World War II. By default, therefore, the eleven-plus developed in most areas as a pass/fail instrument, with successful candidates, a minority, winning places at prestigious grammar schools. Although official rhetoric stated that the majority of eleven-year olds had been 'selected' for a secondary modern education, the relatively poor resourcing of, and limited pupil opportunities afforded by, these schools made risible the idea that they enjoyed parity of esteem with the grammars.

See also: equality of opportunity; grammar school; selection

DAVID CROOK

PARKHURST, HELEN (1887–1973)

Parkhurst qualified as a teacher from Wisconsin State College in 1907. From 1905 to 1913 she worked in a number of primary schools where overcrowding and lack of resources prevented the teacher from giving pupils individual attention. This personal experience was widened with a post within the Wisconsin State Teacher College. She worked with Maria Montessori in Rome from 1913 to 1915 and then became Montessori's representative in the USA, where she established a school in New York. Parkhurst developed her ideas whilst at the high school in Dalton, of which she was head teacher from 1920 to 1942. This school gave its name to Parkhurst's 'Laboratory Plan', outlined initially in her *Education on the Dalton Plan* (1922). In Dalton schools the youngest pupils are encouraged to make choices and later to take on responsibility for self-directed learning. Structure is provided by a home base or house, organised across pupil ages, supported by a collection of materials and resources

relevant to the topic. Teachers become facilitators and supporters in the educative process. Her subsequent books, *Work Rhythms in Education* (1947) and *Exploring the Child's World* (1951), argue that children should progress at a rate suited to their own abilities and interests. School work should consolidate experience and, by doing so, become real for the child. Dalton schools were established in places such as England, Holland and Japan. In later life Parkhurst became a regular and prominent contributor via radio and television to educational debates around the world.

See also: individualised instruction/personalised learning; Montessori, Maria; progressive education

STEVEN COWAN

PARTNERSHIPS, EDUCATIONAL

Educational partnerships represent collaborative groupings of people and/or agencies, including government, business, the voluntary sector, faith-based institutions, parents, and the community, that are working together to solve any of a number of problems related to schooling. What distinguishes partnerships from other collaborations is that its members adhere to compatible goals and are willing to assume the responsibilities and risks associated with pursuing their joint ventures (Glazer 2004).

Partnerships in the educational realm take myriad forms. At the simplest level, the notion of a partnership can be used to describe the joint efforts of schools and parents to enhance the academic success of children. There are, of course, more complex forms of partnerships. Individual schools often establish partnerships with business enterprises and voluntary organisations to secure both their financial support and their expertise in addressing pressing needs. Such associations often involve cash or in-kind donations to schools or the participation of employees in providing mentoring and tutoring to a school's students. Youth Trust, for example, is a longstanding partnership between Minneapolis' public schools and its chamber of commerce in which city firms donate money and provide volunteers to undertake projects to help school age youth develop marketable skills.

A group of schools or an entire school district can also establish partnerships with other government agencies, with non-government organisations (NGOs), and with businesses to undertake large-scale reform initiatives. In the United States, the New York Networks for School Renewal, an Annenberg Foundation-funded project, sponsored an array of different partnerships between groups of schools and intermediary organisations as well as between individual schools and voluntary and business groups to improve academic attainment through the establishment of small, more personalised schools. At about the same time in the United Kingdom, Britain's New Labour government introduced its Education Action Zone programme that promoted partnerships between clusters of schools in disadvantaged communities to transform the organisation and management of such schools and to garner private financial support and expertise for efforts to improve academic standards.

The impetus for partnerships in recent years has been the transformation of the world economy under conditions of globalisation. Such changes have resulted in the increased mobility of capital across national borders and have led governments to attempt to attract investment by reducing public expenditure and taxes and curbing state regulation. As a result, government has been less willing and able to support an array of social provisions, including education, which in turn has necessitated the establishment of mechanisms to secure private funding for these once public enterprises. Partnerships have been an increasingly popular strategy for securing this needed support (Franklin et al. 2003).

Educational partnerships, not surprisingly, bring with them benefits and liabilities. On the positive side, they provide new sources of monetary support for financially strapped state schools. Partnerships can make private and voluntary sector expertise available to schools, which in turn can improve both their managerial efficiency and student attainment. And partnerships represent a good source for securing volunteers to assist schools in their teaching and learning functions. On the downside, however, partnerships bring with them the prospect of external control. There is a persistent fear that the establishment of partnerships with business is the first step in the privatisation of state schooling. And even if it does not go that far, there is the related concern that business partners are more interested in exploiting schools for their benefit than in enhancing the academic success of children. Finally, partnerships are often short-lived ventures. Initially these programmes bring new resources into schools to allow them to enrich their curriculum and the services that they offer children. Yet available funding, changing priorities, and time limitations can lead to the quick termination of a partnership, thereby depriving a school of the financial resources necessary to continue supporting valuable initiatives and popular services (Rosenau 2000).

See also: educational priority area; privatisation/marketisation; urban education; voluntarism

Further reading

Franklin, B. M., Bloch, M.N. and Popkewitz, T. S. (2003) 'Educational partnerships: an introductory framework'. In B. M. Franklin, M. N. Bloch and T. S. Popkewitz (eds) *Educational Partnerships and the State: The Paradoxes of Governing Schools, Children and Families*, New York: Palgrave Macmillan.

Glazer, C. (2004) 'Working together: corporate and community development'. In D. Maurrasse (ed.) *A Future for Everyone: Innovative Social Responsibility and Community Partnerships*, New York: Routledge.

Rosenau, P. V. (2000) 'The strengths and weaknesses of public-private partnerships'. In P. V.

Rosenau (ed.) *Public-Private Policy Partnerships*, Cambridge MA: MIT Press.

BARRY M. FRANKLIN

PASTORAL CARE

The term pastoral care was first used in *The Educational Year Book*, published in 1954 in the UK. It later became recognised in 1970 by P. F. Smart and was popularised by Michael Marland (1974) in his book of the same name where he defined the term as 'looking after the total welfare of the pupil'. Since its emergence as a professional concept in the 1970s, there has been a proliferation of publications on the subject, which have attempted to define and professionalise this area of growing interest.

It has its roots in the teachings and structure of the Christian Church, with the notion that the Good Shepherd always tends to his flock of sheep both morally and spiritually. In the early years, when education was provided almost entirely by church schools, the application of the concept was an extension of the teachings of the Church. However, since its introduction into the secular comprehensive system, from 1965 onwards, the meaning of the term has become more elusive. Pastoral responsibilities were introduced into schools when it was felt that the latter were growing in size and organisational complexity, and thus becoming more goal-oriented and perhaps impersonal. As schools became more complex organisations, it became even more difficult to maintain caring roles and pastoral care provided a system for supporting integration within the secondary school community. It was felt that the school system should not focus entirely on tests, standards and hierarchy. Rather, it should emphasise uniqueness, human rights and social justice.

Over the years, the debates surrounding the meaning and implementation of pastoral care raged on. The Department of Education and Science (1989) in the UK advised that pastoral care is concerned with promoting pupils' personal and social development and fostering positive attitudes: through the quality of teaching and learning; through the nature of relationships amongst pupils, teachers and adults other than teachers; through arrangements for monitoring pupils' overall progress, academic, personal and social; through specific pastoral systems; and through extra curricular activities and the school ethos.

Nonetheless, pastoral care remains something of an enigma, being used to describe the intangibles like ethos, values, attitudes and relationships. It has taken on a wide range of immeasurables and is very subjective in terms of its underpinning values and its role in supporting educational success. In some schools it focuses on the non–instructional and non-academic areas of school life and is therefore perceived as complementary to the academic aspects of school life. However, the National Teaching Advisory Service website (www.ntas.org.uk) has defined pastoral care as, 'a school's arrangements for monitoring and advising pupils on their personal, career and *academic* development'. On the other hand, TeacherNet (www.teachernet.gov.uk/ teachingandlearning/socialandpastoral/), which has been developed by the English Department for Education and Skills and carries information related to social and pastoral issues, has established links to information on bullying, managing relationships, truancy and supporting pupils with medical needs.

According to Power (1996) there are two emerging perspectives. There is the view that pastoral care is the result of progressive enlightenment, supporting the integration of learning and social/emotional needs. By contrast, others perceive it as a means of increasing social control. Whatever the label used, concern for the welfare of pupils is a fairly universal practice. Countries like Australia, the Cayman Islands, Nigeria, Israel, New Zealand and Uganda have broadly followed the UK model. Other countries such as the USA have introduced specialised school counsellors, usually with a psychological background, focusing on children with problems, rather than developing a universal system of pastoral support for all children.

Further information on pastoral care can be obtained from the National Association for Pastoral Care in Education (NAPCE) in the UK and its quarterly journal, *Pastoral Care in Education*.

See also: bullying; counselling; integration; moral education; truancy

Further reading

Department for Education and Science (1989) *Report by Her Majesty's Inspectors on Pastoral Care in Secondary Schools: An Inspection of Some Aspects of Pastoral Care in 1987–8*, Stanmore: DES.

Lang, P., Best, R. and Lichtenberg, A. (1994) *Caring for Children: International Perspectives on Pastoral Care and PSE*, London: Cassell.

Marland, M. (1974) *Pastoral Care*, London: Heinemann.

Power, S. (1996) *The Pastoral and the Academic: Conflict and Contradiction in the Curriculum*, London: Cassell

ANN CHERYL ARMSTRONG

PEDAGOGY

Pedagogy can be defined as the general principles of effective teaching, entailing a complex blend of theoretical understanding, practical skills and competencies. Traditional definitions describe pedagogy as either the science (theory) or the art (practice) of teaching that makes a difference in the intellectual and social development of students.

Various pedagogical models have been based on the structure of knowledge, and how that is deployed through effective teaching strategies in different subject disciplines. Bernstein's work on the classification and framing of knowledge (1975) suggested that strong boundaries between subject disciplines promoted more highly differentiated pedagogical practices, whereas weak boundaries implied more integrated approaches to teaching and the construction of knowledge. Shulman drew these strands together, conceptualising pedagogy as consisting of subject matter knowledge, pedagogical knowledge, and pedagogical content knowledge.

Edgar Stones challenged Shulman's position, arguing that a generalised theoretical framework for pedagogy, based on developing knowledge of how human beings learn, would be a more productive approach. He argued for a pedagodical framework that unified theory and practice, laying the foundation for a theory-informed, research-informed and open-endedly dynamic approach to teaching. Such an approach would permit the identification and analysis of subject-specific aspects of each teaching problem in their relationship to the pedagogical principles.

Stones claimed that a broadly based, coherent pedagogical theory would equip teachers to address the theory/practice interface in an informed way, enabling them to construct personal models of teaching to monitor effectively their own performance. Stones' proposition had the capacity to provide a framework of pedagogical principles for mentor teachers to assist pre-service and novice teachers to consolidate their understanding of the relationships between theory and practice, and for all parties to engage in reflective practices to improve the quality of teaching and learning. Application of the general framework of pedagogical principles to classroom-based action research could generate case studies with a common theoretical base, irrespective of the demands of subject-specific disciplines to guide future research and practice to improve the quality of teaching and learning.

Pedagogy has been critiqued as the embodiment of teacher-focused education that gives insufficient attention to the interests and engagement of learners, or to individual differences in learners. Theories of learning such as experiential and constructivist approaches have influenced the development of child-centred pedagogies in which the role of the teacher is to structure experiences through which the learner will be able to construct knowledge. Cognitive psychology, such as Jerome Bruner's work, contributed to theories of instruction and theories of the human mind. Work in fields on multiple intelligences, emotional intelligence and personality dynamics has focused awareness on the differences in the ways in which individuals learn. Recognition that not all people learn equally well in the same ways has increased pressure on teachers to adapt their pedagogical theories and practices to provide multiple and varied opportunities for teaching and learning.

Since Freire's (1970) seminal work the *Pedagogy of the Oppressed*, proponents of social justice have argued for critical pedagogies and pedagogies of opposition within agendas of social reconstruction and reform, and cultural recognition and inclusivity. Culturally relevant pedagogies promote academic success, development or maintenance of cultural competence and critical consciousness to challenge the existing social order. Such approaches are frequently associated with postmodern definitions of literacy encompassing all aspects of media and multiliteracies to accommodate the influence of communications technologies in constructing information and meanings.

The knowledge explosion, combined with technological change, has led to postmodern pedagogies demanding flexible delivery and accommodation of multiple resources that cannot be controlled by the teacher. Concomitantly, rapidity of social change, including workplace and career volatility, requires pedagogies for lifelong learning, which emphasise skills and competencies, rather than specific content knowledge. In such an environment, pedagogical facilitation may be a more productive way of conceptualising the teacher role.

Different research and theories may underpin different models of pedagogy; in different contexts, differing teaching approaches work differentially with different communities of students. Research shows that expert teachers have a large repertoire of pedagogical strategies which they can deploy to meet the demands of their teaching contexts.

Excellent pedagogical practice requires the capacity to draw upon different pedagogical models and strategies to provide the most effective environment for learning.

See also: Bernstein, Basil; Bruner, Jerome; Friere, Paolo; instruction; learning; school knowledge; teacher; teaching/teaching methods

Further reading

Bernstein, B. (1975) *Class, Codes and Control vol 3: Classification and Framing*, London: Routledge and Kegan Paul.
Freire, P. (1970) *Pedagogy of the Oppressed*, New York: Herder and Herder.
Stones, E. (1992) *Quality of Teaching: A Sample of Cases*, London: Routledge.

MARNIE O'NEILL

PEER GROUP

In educational contexts, peer group typically describes a group of learners working at the same level and often of similar age. Peer groups can enhance the learning experience, offering mutual encouragement, academic and personal support. Peer groups often make arrangements to meet socially and sometimes hold informal meetings prior to making presentations or taking examinations. The group may meet to prepare for seminars, exchange feedback on draft writing and engage in collective revision for examinations, for example. Peer groups are not always be a positive influence, however. Young people sometimes experience pressure to imitate the appearance, tastes and behaviour of their peers. 'Peer group pressure' is often blamed for teenage smoking, under-age sexual intercourse and misuse of alcohol and drugs.

Workers, as well as students, often belong to peer groups. Trainee and probationary teachers, for example, are sometimes placed in – or form their own – groups for the purposes of sharing strategies and resources. They may observe their peers teaching in the classroom and engage in constructive discussion about pedagogies.

See also: collaborative/cooperative learning; pupil; student

DAVID CROOK

PERFORMANCE INDICATORS

Performance indicators (PIs) are one of many tools to help answer the question: how do you know what you are achieving? PIs are quantifiable measurements, agreed in advance, which reflect the relative success of an organisation. What is selected for measurement is governed by the nature of the organisation.

PIs are usually seen as numerical measurements of achievement that are easy to collect, interpret and use. In theory, they can only be derived for things over which direct control can be exerted to achieve outcome of the measure.

PIs are of interest to a wide range of bodies, including government, universities and colleges, and funding bodies. Increasingly PIs are being used commercially to create league tables to 'help' prospective students gain information about university choice, and through public sector funded developments to provide standardised quantitative measures alongside qualitative examiners' reports, course evaluations and other relevant documents that are deemed helpful in guiding student choice and selection.

So, for example, schools may focus on examination success rates or the number of children entitled to free school meals, while universities might focus on non-completion rates for undergraduate studies or salary levels post-qualification. Whatever PIs are selected, and in whatever sector of society, they must reflect the organisation's goals, they must be key to the success of the organisation, and they must be quantifiable (measurable).

Across developed nations, stakeholders concerned about education standards and accountability have progressively introduced

and relied on PIs to focus the education enterprise on specific goals or key targets. In higher education, the primary purposes of PIs have been refined and developed and can now be justified as a means to:

- provide reliable information on the nature and performance of the higher education sector as a whole;
- enable direct comparison between to be made;
- enable institutions to benchmark their own performance against selected universities;
- provide an evidence base for policy development; and
- finally and politically the most import aspect, to contribute to the public accountability of higher education.

In the United States an influential publication, *US News and World Reports*, annually publishes the ranked outcome of several key quality performance indicators for US universities and colleges. Seven broad categories are used to construct the rankings and are derived from key PIs. The categories are measured in relation to peer assessment; graduation and retention rate; faculty resources such as class size; student admission data (for example, average admission test scores); financial resources; alumni giving; and, only for national universities and liberal arts colleges, graduation rate performance. The PIs consist of both input and output measures, which, it is claimed, capture the education received by the individual student. The *Australian*, which is Australia's only national broadsheet, draws similarly on the PIs provided by the Department of Education Science and Training to produce national rankings.

It is clear that if a key PI is going to be of any value, there must be a way to accurately define and measure it. In Canada, the performance measures are obtained specifically for the production of league tables through the distribution of a specifically designed

431

questionnaire for the production of the ranking tables. The PIs are precisely defined and instructions for how the measure should be made are provided. In the Western world, newspaper tables have highlighted such PIs as library holdings, graduation rates and full-time enrolment numbers.

It is an important feature that key PIs remain constant from year to year to enable them to be incorporated into a trend analysis. Clearly, if the measures were inconsistent then a reflective analysis and a predictive analysis would prove difficult, if not impossible. PIs can be very useful tools in helping answer two basic questions: How do you know what you are achieving? How can your activity improve its performance?

See also: accountability; benchmarking; educational targets; managerialism; performance-related pay; school improvement; standards

Further reading

Cave, M., Hanney, S., Henkel, M. and Kogan, M. (1996) *The Use of Performance Indicators in Higher Education: The Challenge of the Quality Movement*, 3rd edn, London: Jessica Kingsley.

Draper, D. and Gittoes, M. (2004) 'Statistical analysis of performance indicators in UK higher education', *Journal of the Royal Statistical Society*, Series A (Statistics in Society), 167(3): 449–74.

Hulpia, H. and Valcke, M. (2004) 'The use of performance indicators in a school improvement policy: the theoretical and empirical context', *Evaluation and Research in Education*, 18(1, 2): 102–19.

BERNARD LONGDEN

PERFORMANCE-RELATED PAY

'Payment by results' is not new; however, relating remuneration to performance in the job – performance-related pay (PRP) – has been controversial and emotive, especially in the education sector where clear measures of an individual teacher's 'performance' are seen by many as problematic. But how important is pay anyway in motivating educational professionals? This will vary from one country to another and although there is evidence that low salaries do cause dissatisfaction, it appears that 'pay' is not a strong motivator in itself. In Herzberg's terms, it is a 'hygiene' factor, or a dissatisfier, rather than a motivator or a satisfier, such as a sense of achievement, autonomy, recognition or the challenge of the job (Evans 1999).

The process by which the performance of teachers and other educational professionals is managed has been called different things in different countries: staff appraisal, performance review or teacher evaluation being the most common. Essentially it is the process by which an employee and their superordinate (boss or line manager) meet to discuss the performance of the employee. Performance management or appraisal can be evaluative (review) or developmental (targets and objective setting) and some argue there is an inherent conflict between the two. However, analytically four separate objectives can be identified: development review, performance review, potential review, and rewards review. It is this last objective – rewards review or pay linked to performance – that has proved most controversial and led to much debate amongst policy makers and practitioners (especially the teachers' professional associations) and academics and researchers (Tomlinson 2000; Wragg *et al.* 2004).

The idea of linking pay to an individual's performance at work is a practice commonly found in the private sector, although its form may vary slightly from individual PRP, profit-related pay, team-based pay and/or competency pay (linked to skill acquisition). However, there is little evidence that it works successfully in either the private or public sectors. Research into PRP shows that it does not have a significant motivational impact on public sector workers, including teachers (Richardson 1999; Tomlinson 2000) despite the fact that employees themselves often believe that there should be a link between reward and performance on the job.

Essentially PRP involves an annual discussion between manager and employer at which a set of performance targets or objectives are agreed. A year later, an assessment is made of the extent to which that year's targets have been met, and the outcome of the assessment is an overall performance rating, which then determines pay levels and bonuses. However, before any scheme of PRP can be considered there are four questions that need answering:

- What is PRP for?
- How could a scheme operate so that it was fair and workable?
- Who should be involved and when?
- How could it be funded?

Without serious consideration of these questions any PRP scheme's chances of success in the education or other sectors are slim. So although many teachers sympathise with the notion of linking performance with pay and indeed for a minority it may make them work harder or more thoughtfully, for most education workers individual PRP goes against the grain. Richardson (1999) notes that this is unsurprising because both the private and public sectors typically do not overcome certain generic problems, such as securing goal clarity and commitment, undertaking appraisals in a fair and professional manner, removing the threat of individual PRP to team activity, and whether the rewards on offer are funded by new money.

Teachers, like many other professional workers in the public sector, have complex jobs and it is difficult to specify a set of objectives that are clear and measurable, realistic and challenging. To date there has been a tendency to measure teachers' performance in terms of pupil outcomes, which is unsatisfactory and highly problematic for numerous reasons. It is hard to establish the precise contribution of an individual teacher to students' examination or test performance, although significant developments have been made in recent years in measuring overall school performance, taking into account

context and 'value added' and looking at intra-school variation, particularly at subject department or year group level.

The typical conclusion from studies into PRP, especially in the education sector, is that individual PRP schemes have not generally been a great success. They are not great motivators, although they are for some individuals, and research suggests that antipathy is more common than enthusiasm both amongst teachers and their line managers. To work they need to be, amongst other things, fair and equitable, acceptable, provide opportunities for progression and be simple to administer.

See also: managerialism; motivation; performance indicators

Further reading

DfEE (2000) *School Performance Award Scheme*, London: DfEE.
Evans, L. (1999) *Managing to Motivate: A Guide for School Leaders*, London: Cassell.
Richardson, R. (1999) *Performance Related Pay in Schools*, London: LSE.
Tomlinson, H. (2000) *Performance Related Pay in Education*, London: Routledge.
Wragg, T., Chamberlain, R., Hayes, G. and Wragg, C. (2004) *Performance Related Pay for Teachers*, London: Routledge.

PETER EARLEY

PESTALOZZI, JOHANN HEINRICH (1746–1827)

The first steps taken by Pestalozzi, the Swiss educationist, towards developing educational ideas were recorded in a journal he wrote about the life of his infant son, Jacob. After failing as a farmer, Pestalozzi developed a cotton-spinning business that offered work to poor local children and orphans. Influenced by the writings of Rousseau, Pestalozzi sought to provide the children with a general and industrial education, but his school went bankrupt in 1780. Pestalozzi's reputation as an innovative thinker surpassed his record as a businessman, and his collection of essays,

Investigations in the Course of Nature in the Development of the Human Race (1797) is seen a pioneering work of educational sociology. By 1800 he was running a larger school in Bergdorf Castle, mainly for orphans, to which came such visitors as Froebel, Herbart and Neef, who was to spread Pestalozzi's ideas to the United States. *How Gertrude Teaches Her Children* (1801) expanded upon the idea that learning takes place through enriched sensory experiences and it commended object lessons and activity-based learning. He wanted schools to be more family-like, engendering a sense of security for the child. He also believed in extending learning beyond the classroom and school. Education needed to be holistic, linking the physical, social and psychological aspects of the child. From 1805 he ran his institute at Yverdon, beside Lake Geneva, but difficulties forced closure in 1825. Pestalozzi's later writings called for a more scientific approach to pedagogy. Fichte incorporated some of his ideas into the German educational reforms of 1809.

See also: early childhood education; Froebel, Friedrich; Herbart, Johann Friedrich

STEVEN COWAN

PHILOSOPHY OF EDUCATION

Philosophy of education is the disciplined study of philosophical issues arising in ideas, practices and policies relevant to education. It focuses, like all philosophy, on the understanding of central concepts in the field, on revealing and examining assumptions, and on the critical analysis of arguments. In this way it embraces work across a wide range: from critiques of new policy initiatives through to the study of fundamental concepts like the good life, the human mind, liberal democracy. At this deeper end of its labours it merges with ethics, philosophy of mind, political philosophy and other areas of general philosophy.

It is difficult to understand what counts as a philosophical task unless one is already immersed in the field. Understandably, those who are not inside philosophy of education often misunderstand what it is about. They may see it as operating in some stratospheric realm of abstract ideas, out of touch with what is going on, on the ground in classrooms and in families. While this is indeed a professional hazard, the best philosophy of education is very different. Take the school curriculum. Whatever its content in different situations, it should be serving wider educational aims. What should these be? The acquisition of knowledge for its own sake? Letting children develop to their full potential? Helping them and others to lead a fulfilling life? Preparation for democratic citizenship? These and other familiar aims raise questions unanswerable by empirical investigation alone, or even at all. How can the pursuit of knowledge be justified as an aim? Does the notion of development make sense outside a biological context? What counts as a fulfilling life? How defensible is liberal democracy as a political arrangement?

Much of the content of philosophy of education, as in some of these examples, is in ethics and political philosophy. Other topics in these fields include: rival accounts of moral education, notions of morality lying behind them, views about the relationship between morality and personal well-being, and between morality and religion; the promotion of personal autonomy as an educational aim and, behind that, its place in liberal thinking; education in a multicultural society based partly on common and partly on conflicting values about morality, religion, parental authority and autonomy, the place of faith schools; equality and inequality in education; about the distribution of schooling, selection, inclusion, private schooling, the role of the state and of the market.

Another branch of the subject has to do with learners and their minds. Outsiders to philosophy may think that this work belongs to psychology rather than philosophy, but there are conceptual issues here which lie outside the province of empirical investigation and which are of great relevance to teachers. Philosophy can help us to understand the concepts we use in thinking about the mind and how they are interrelated. Examples of particular significance to the educator are the concepts of: mind in general; thinking, intelligence, learning, development, imagination, creativity, concepts and concept-formation, the emotions, motivation. Work in these areas is also applied to philosophical critiques of psychological material widely used in education: nature–nurture issues about intelligence; multiple intelligences; the teaching of thinking skills; developmentalist accounts of concept-acquisition.

A related area of general philosophy is epistemology, or theory of knowledge. Again, much of its work has clear educational application. Many, perhaps most, teachers are in the business of passing on knowledge. But what exactly is it to know something, as distinct, say, from merely believing it? How do truth and evidence come into the picture? Is knowledge an objective matter or culturally relative? How is knowledge related to learning? Teachers want pupils to come to know how to do things (e.g. swim, count, use a computer) as well as to know that things are the case (e.g. that the United States of America is a federal country, that 31 is a prime number). How are knowing-how and knowing-that related? Is knowledge different from understanding? What light can philosophy throw on issues of assessment? Can one provide a taxonomy of types of knowledge harnessable to the construction of school curricula?

These are only some of the ways in which philosophy is an indispensable contributor to the study and practice of education. In a longer piece one could say more about the place of the arts in education and the ways in which philosophical aesthetics can throw light on this; and about applications of the philosophies of religion, science, social science and mathematics to teaching and learning in these areas.

See also: education/educational studies; educational research; educational theory; moral education

Further reading

Blake, N., Smeyers, P., Smith, R. and Standish, P. (eds) (2003) *The Blackwell Guide to the Philosophy of Education*, Oxford: Blackwell.
Hirst, P. H. and White, P.A (eds) (1998) *Philosophy of Education: Major Themes in the Analytic Tradition*, 4 vols, London: Routledge
'Philosophy of education: problems of'. In T. Honderich (ed.) (1995) *The Oxford Companion to Philosophy*, Oxford: Oxford University Press.
JOHN WHITE

PHONICS

The term phonics refers to the manner in which the approximately forty *phonemes* (speech sounds) in English are represented in writing by its twenty-six letters, or combinations of them. The phonemes of English are spelled in over 300 diverse ways. For example, the phoneme *i* (as in the word, *this*) is given twenty-two different spellings. Phonemes are called consonants or vowels, depending on how they are pronounced. The first and last letters in the written word *run* represent consonant speech sounds. The middle letter in this word stands for a vowel phoneme.

Children around the world acquire the ability to speak their particular languages without any conscious endeavour on their part. However, children must make deliberate efforts to become knowledgeable about phonemes and letters. These young students' conscious knowledge of speech sounds is called *phonemic* or *phonological awareness*.

The fact that the phonemes in English are not spelled in a totally predictable manner is one reason certain teacher educators reject direct, intensive, systematic, early, and comprehensive (DISEC) instruction of phonics information. The word *have* is a prime example of the peculiar style in which given English words are spelled. It has been argued that this word violates the phonics rule that the *a* in *have* and *save* should be pronounced in the same manner.

Opponents of DISEC teaching of reading and spelling contend that the relationships between letters, and the speech sounds they represent (phonics rules), are too unreliable to be of significant help in teaching children to read and spell correctly. It has been maintained that unless the concurrence between a letter and a speech sound happens at least 75 per cent of the time, it is not useful to teach children about that connection.

Experts in teacher education who reject DISEC phonics instruction contend that children best learn to read words (a) by looking at them repeatedly while saying their names, and (b) by guessing at the identities of written words through the use of *context cues*. The latter procedure involves speculations that learners make as to the identities of written words within sentences, without any application of phonics rules for that purpose.

However, there is pertinent experimental research that refutes this negative opinion about the need for phonics teaching. It is found, for example, that the use of context cues is more frequent among beginning readers than skilled ones. The usefulness of context cues also diminishes as the reading ability of children advances. These experimental findings suggest that children use context cues as a temporary crutch to compensate for their lack of phonics knowledge. It thus is held that urging youngsters to guess at the identity of words in order to read them is misleading advice.

As for students learning to spell, certain teacher educators argue that encouraging youngsters to create invented spellings of words will suffice for that purpose. Learning to spell for young students is a process much like their previous informal acquisition of speaking ability, it is maintained. The defence of non-DISEC teaching of both reading and spelling has been described as part of the whole language theory of children's literacy development.

Experimental research has revealed that the negative opinions about DISEC teaching of phonics fail to consider a unique aspect of the application of that instruction. This empirical evidence indicates that if the application of phonics information leads students to the creation of an approximate sounding of a given written word, these children often will be able to correctly infer its authentic articulation. Also, the similarity discovered between the levels of children's reading and spelling skills suggest that children's application of phonics rules when spelling words must not be underestimated.

It further has been opined that DISEC teaching of reading and spelling are improper practices, because students inherit unique learning styles, and diverse kinds of intelligences. These assumed genetic characteristics are not compatible with the DISEC form of reading and spelling instruction, it is claimed. The lack of convincing experimental data to that effect has been pointed out.

The controversy about the merit of DISEC phonics instruction, doubtless, will continue since the two parties in this dispute rely on dissimilar kinds of evidence as support for their opposing positions. Those who defend DISEC teaching of phonics information refer to experimental findings that reveal that it is an essential pedagogy. To the contrary, their opponents have produced qualitative (anecdotal) evidence for confirmation of their position. As a consequence, in the foreseeable future teachers will have to continue to make a forced choice between these two conflicting views.

See also: learning; literacy; reading; spelling; teaching/teaching methods

Further reading

Groff, P. and Seymour, D. (1987) *Word Recognition: The Why and the How*, Springfield IL: Charles C. Thomas.

Stanovich, K. E. (2000) *Progress in Understanding Reading*, New York: Guilford Press.

Venezky, R. L. (1999) *The American Way of Spelling*, New York: Guilford Press.

PATRICK GROFF

PHRENOLOGY

A popular theory in the nineteenth century, the science of phrenology (literally, knowledge of the mind) aimed to determine features of individual character and personality from the shape of the head. This was the basis of the notion, widely held even over the past century, that feeling and locating 'bumps on the skull' held the clues to a person's character and prospects. It was also supposed to reveal potential traits of aggression and criminality. Phrenology helped to support the growth of popular education in the nineteenth century, and also distinctive ideas about the education of the so-called 'feeble-minded', 'used to justify improving the mind and morals of the working classes through infant education and public schooling – albeit, within a hierarchically ordered and scientifically managed middle-class meritocracy' (Tomlinson 2005: xv). The German physician Franz Joseph Gall developed the basic thesis at the start of the nineteenth century, and it was popularised by Johann Spurzheim and George Combe. It spread from Europe to America and became a highly influential theory there also. It represented a theory about human nature and individual intelligence that was very powerful in its time, but eventually gave way to twentieth-century ideas and practices around intelligence testing.

See also: faculty psychology; intelligence/intelligence tests; meritocracy

Further reading

Tomlinson, S. (2005) *Head Masters: Phrenology, Secular Education, and Nineteenth-century Social Thought*, Tuscaloosa AL: University of Alabama Press.

GARY McCULLOCH

PHYSICAL EDUCATION/TRAINING

In most educational writings, physical education (PE) has been recognised as a field of study and a profession that contributes to physical, emotional and social development of school-aged children and youth. It is a systematic introduction to, and progression through, the skills and understandings required for lifelong involvement in physical activity, sport, and healthy practices. In addition, it involves two approaches to learning: 'learning to move' and 'moving to learn'. *Learning to move*, or education into physical activity and sport, is the approach perhaps most commonly understood, and includes learning the skills and understanding required for participation in activities, knowledge of one's body and its range of and capacity for movement. The range of learning in PE will include eye-hand and eye-foot coordination, coping with space, speed, distance, equipment, etc.; and knowing 'what?' and 'how?' about the activities. On the other hand, *moving to learn* uses physical activity and sport as a context for and a means of learning. It involves a whole range of learning outcomes which are not inherent to physical activity and sport, but which are valuable extrinsic educational lessons such as social skills, managing cooperation and competition, applying aesthetic judgements, etc.; and knowing 'when?' and 'why?" different behaviours and actions are appropriate and effective.

In most countries of the world, PE is an integral part of educational programmes for nearly all school-age children and youth. However, as reported by worldwide survey (Hardman and Marshall 2003), despite the seemingly widespread acceptance of the positive impact attributed to a physically active lifestyle and school subject itself, PE is drowning in heavy water. The justification and legitimisation of PE as a core element of educational systems has not always been too convincing. PE often finds itself in a defensive position; it is frequently marginalised and suffers from decreasing curriculum time allocation, low subject status and esteem, and budgetary controls with inadequate financial and personnel resources.

At the beginning of the twenty-first century, educational reforms gave a new mission

437

to PE in response to a worldwide phenomenon regarding two major public health problems: physical inactivity and bad nutrition both associated with obesity in school-age children and youth. In many countries and states, PE was then entitled *Health and Physical Education* (HPE), and gained a new legitimate place in school curricula. School HPE programmes were revised to address physically active and healthy lifestyle skills, knowledge and issues; aiming at empowering students with the knowledge and skills to develop a healthy and active lifestyle. In such a context, new learning outcomes were identified. For example: fitness management (the ability to develop and follow a personal fitness plan and pattern of daily practices); personal/social management (skills for developing healthy lifestyles, healthy relationships, career directions and life management); and healthy lifestyle practices (knowledge components related to today's major health issues, i.e. nutrition, alcohol, tobacco, drugs, sexual behaviours, etc.) are increasingly present in the HPE programmes.

The 1999 World Summit of PE held by the International Council of Sport Science and Physical Education (ICSSPE) addressed a number of trends regarding the future of PE. As reported (2001), *quality physical education and physical activities* was identified as a common denominator, and perceived as a key to successful future developments. In such a context, many non-governmental organisations and associations have suggested guidelines for the future development of quality physical education programmes. According to the Canadian Association for Health, Physical Education, Recreation and Dance, a 'quality daily physical education' (QPE) is a way to define a programme that is well planned, taught by qualified and enthusiastic professionals, and offers a variety of learning opportunities to all students on a daily basis throughout the entire school year, from pre-school to year twelve. The Society of State Directors of Health, Physical Education, and Recreation, having a similar interest, also recommended that: (1) QPE should be delivered in a planned, ongoing and sequential fashion by certified physical education teachers; (2) QPE should be a component of every school improvement plan and should also ensure that PE is coordinated with other components of a school health programme including health education, family-community partnerships, school environment, staff wellness, health services, mental health services, and nutrition services; and (3) all schools should provide additional opportunities for physical activity and sport that support and complement quality physical education programmes.

See also: curriculum; health education; subjects

Further reading

Hardman, K. and Marshall, J. J. (2003) 'The state and status of physical education in schools: foundation for deconstruction and reconstruction of physical education'. In: ICSSPE (ed.) *Physical Education: Deconstruction and Reconstruction – Issues and Directions*, Schorndorf: Hofmann.
Kirk, D., Macdonald, D. and O'Sullivan, M. (2006) *Handbook of Physical Education*, Thousand Oaks CA: Sage.
Puhse, U. and Gerber, M. (eds) (2005) *International Comparison of Physical Education: Concepts, Problems, Prospects*, Oxford: Meyer and Meyer Sport.
CHARLOTTE BEAUDOIN

PHYSICS

Physics is widely taught in schools, colleges and institutions of higher education throughout the world, sometimes as an independent subject and sometimes as part of the general science curriculum. Aspects of the subject have been popularised by books and television programmes, yet it continues to decline in popularity. Since developed economies are increasingly reliant on science for their success, this poses a tension for schools: to maintain challenging levels of instruction for those who aspire to scientific careers while simultaneously delivering a general science education to all.

Physics as a discipline was born of the need to supply the Industrial Revolution with engineering solutions. At that time, in many countries, secondary school examinations were administered by universities, so there was an explicit relationship between the development of the subject and what was studied in schools. This remained the case until around 1945, after which the concatenation of research and teaching was broken.

In the 1980s, the fashion was for an 'entitlement' to science for everyone, but some initiatives to 'mix and match' science and non-science subjects at senior levels did more harm than good. Research suggests that students find the transition to senior physics difficult. It is seen as dull and impenetrable (Evans and Evans 1994), too mathematical and not relevant to everyday life (Black 2000). Initiatives such as the Institute of Physics/Schlumberger 'Lab in a Lorry', developed by Jenkins, Kelly and others in 2001, is one attempt to counter such negative perceptions. Staffed by practising physicists, rather than teachers, it provides young people with the opportunity to do off-curriculum experimental physics intuitively. As an approach, it appears to offer a more promising prospect than, say, initiatives seeking to reduce the emphasis on the recollection of formulae (as recommended by the Physical Science Study Committee in the United States of America and the Science and Technology in Society project in the United Kingdom) or the amount of mathematics involved, not least because those who study physics know that they 'obviously' benefit from studying mathematics concurrently.

Early specialisation, a characteristic of education in England, Wales and some other countries with an historic link to Britain, is sometimes blamed for the decline of physics, but comparisons between post-compulsory systems are difficult to make and inconclusive because the time spent doing physics and methods of assessment vary so much: physics might be one of ten subjects studied (as in Finland), one of seven (as in the Netherlands and Ireland) or one of three (as in the UK). Some systems use structured curriculum-based questions in their assessment, as in the French Baccalauréat; others rely on multiple-choice questions and aptitude tests, as in the United States; still more use a mixture of the two, as in Japan (Black 2000). It is difficult to draw conclusions from this diversity, to find a causal link between mode of delivery and decline, but experience suggests that the road to recovery for physics is likely to be paved with partnerships between policy makers, researchers and teachers in a way that allows practitioners to share ownership of new ideas. It is also likely that as part of the recovery, schools will increasingly use 'out-of-school' initiatives to rekindle interest – to put the 'fizz' back into physics – as it rediscovers its links with cutting-edge research in the universities. From a policy making viewpoint, a strong case can be made for developing secondary schools with a specialism in physics, as well as in other science disciplines.

See also: curriculum; engineering; mathematics; science/science education; specialisation; subjects

Further reading

Black, P. (2000) 'Physics in other countries'. In A. Morris (ed.) *Shaping the Future: Revitalising Physics Education*, Bristol: IoP Publishing.

Evans, P. and Evans, S. (1994) *Anyone for Science?*, London: City Technology Colleges Trust.

Hunt, A. (2000) 'The physics curriculum'. In A. Morris (ed.) *Shaping the Future: Revitalising Physics Education*, Bristol: IoP Publishing.

ANTHONY KELLY

PIAGET, JEAN (1896–1980)

Piaget, born in Neuchatel, Switzerland, was the most influential developmental psychologist of the twentieth century, whose work became a basic starting point for teacher training courses around the world. He was a child prodigy, publishing noted biological papers before the age of sixteen. He studied under Theodore Simon, co-author of the Binet-Simon intelligence test, from 1919–21 at the Sorbonne, where he became interested in the way that children's wrong answers in tests reflected a distinct way of looking at the world, rather than simply the making of mistakes. This led Piaget to the conclusion that children constructed their view of the world in line with the stage of cognitive development they possessed, rather than simply learning from adults. These ideas found fuller expression in *The Language and Thought of the Child* (1926). Piaget held numerous senior academic positions in France and Switzerland, notably as professor of developmental psychology at the Sorbonne (1952–63) and director of the International Centre for Epistemology at Geneva (1955–80). During the 1930s and 1940s he developed his theory on the stages of childhood and adolescence, moving from non-verbal modes (age 0–2), through to intuitive operation combining with speech (age 2–6). These early stages are followed by what he called 'concrete operations', where a child (aged 7–11) develops skills with signs and symbols which enable him/her to function within networks of intellectual activities. *The Origins of Intelligence in Children* (1954) refined his earlier thinking. Piaget engaged in a creative, critical dialogue with Vygotsky and his works.

See also: cognition; early childhood education; psychology of education; Vygotsky, Lev

STEVEN COWAN

PLAGIARISM

Plagiarism, also *plagiary*, refers to various forms of derivation resulting from unacknowledged copying. Deceitful intent is the essential factor in academic definitions of plagiarism, and these definitions are closely related to the conventions for citing sources of influence. Plagiarists ignore such conventions, feigning to have composed texts they have only copied, and pretending to have originated ideas they have actually lifted from someone else.

Historically, the concept of plagiarism has

> existed alongside of imitation so that there have always been acceptable and unacceptable modes of using the work of one's predecessors. What has not changed through time is the ethic of borrowing. Throughout history the act of using the work of another with an intent to deceive has been branded as plagiarism.
>
> (Shaw 1982: 51)

In ancient Rome, the Latin word *plagiarius* ('kidnapper') from which the English 'plagiarism' derives was first used in reference to literary theft. The Roman poet Martial mocked a parroting poet: 'the page which is yours stands up against you and says, "You are a thief"'.

There is nothing inherently wrong with re-using the language or ideas of others. Humans quite naturally mimic the behaviour of others, linguistic behavioural aspects included. From a socio-linguistic perspective, such mimicry and shared forms of communication are known as *convergence*, members of a speech community having in common a repertoire of expressions and linguistic rituals.

Indeed, the human mind so easily internalises language input and other sensory stimuli that, in some cases when these memories are recalled, an individual cannot distinguish memory from inspiration; *cryptomnesia* is the technical term describing this phenomenon: 'hidden memories' lurking in the subconscious mind, later venturing forth to masquerade as original thinking. Helen Keller's *Frost King* plagiarism episode, and George Harrison's *My Sweet Lord* controversy are perhaps the most famous instances of evident cryptomnesia.

Educators recognise that students' minds are malleable, and influencing students is an integral component of the learning process. Cheating and 'cribbing' have long been recognised to be detrimental to learning, the antithesis to desired outcomes. Rather disturbingly, recent research documents an

440

apparent increase in academic dishonesty, with plagiarism being at the top of the list of observed cheating behaviours. Beginning in the 1990s, new modes of plagiarism made a debut along with the internet: 'copy-and-paste' composing from online sources; downloads of complete papers from internet-accessible databases; and 'research services' which write custom-made essays on a fee basis, the so called 'contract plagiarism'. The modern 'term paper mill industry', namely the commercialised subcontracting of research papers, has called into question the worth of academic credentials and qualifications. If students can, in effect, buy and plagiarise their way to a university degree, jobbing out their papers via the internet, even at elite schools such as Oxford and Harvard, the differences between an earned accredited degree and one bought through a 'diploma mill' become obscured.

In response to pervasive forms of academic dishonesty, educational institutions worldwide have responded in kind with technologically sophisticated means of cheat detection. A number of software programs are now available to scan student papers for matching text, alerting teachers to 'copy-and-paste' from the internet or to re-submission of the same paper as verified against other papers in a centralised database. Also, the widespread problems with plagiarism seem to have invigorated an 'academic integrity' movement (see www.academicintegrity.org) and the use of honour codes, momentum for these movements often resulting from student-led initiatives which, it should be noted, have also included student protests against the use of plagiarism detection software.

Thomas Mallon, author of *Stolen Words*, wrote that 'academics remain curiously willing to vaporise the whole phenomenon of plagiarism in a cloud of French theory', and this is certainly true of some scholars within academe. Yet as modern linguistic research has demonstrated, human communication is unbounded in scope. There are infinite possibilities for new, specific meanings which an author might choose to convey through language. Even in deconstructing a literary text after the mode of certain critical theorists, a person is essentially 'rewriting' that text through a creative and imaginative rearrangement of meaningful symbols. And this verifies, in effect, through such 'rewriting', that authorship remains a valid construct, part of 'our human destiny and its narratives' (Burke 1998: 206). As wryly noted by Mark Twain, and presciently apropos in this instance to the (supposed) Death of the Author, 'The reports of my death are greatly exaggerated'.

See also: coursework; credentials/credentialing; degree; examinations; learning; qualifications; student; writing

Further reading

www.plagiary.org
Burke, S. (1998) *The Death and Return of the Author*, 2nd edn, Edinburgh: Edinburgh University Press.
Ezell, A. and Bear, J. (2005) *Degree Mills*, Amherst NY: Prometheus Books.
Mallon, T. (2001) *Stolen Words*, San Diego CA: Harcourt.
Shaw, P. (1982) 'Plagiary', *American Scholar*, 51: 326–37.

JOHN LESKO

PLATO

Plato (428–347 BCE) was an Athenian aristocrat whose family were heavily involved in contemporary politics. After the execution in 399 BCE of his friend and teacher, Socrates, on a charge of corrupting the young and worshipping unauthorised gods, he travelled to Sicily where he became tutor to the royal family. On his return to Athens he established the philosophical school called the Academy. His pupils included Aristotle, who was to become a philosopher of the same stature as Plato himself. Plato's writings usually take the form of dialogues between Socrates and others, many of them identifiable historical figures. It is thus never certain whether the views expressed are Plato's own. The Socrates represented in the earlier dialogues appears from independent evidence to hold views similar to those of the historical person; the Socrates of the later dialogues is generally thought to be a mouthpiece for Plato's own ideas.

Despite these difficulties many writers have been, perversely enough perhaps, happy to identify Plato's views on education with the conclusions that emerge from the *Republic*, his investigation of the ideal city-state and of the human soul that it is expected will be found 'writ large' in the world of human politics. The institutional arrangements envisaged by the discussants of the *Republic* involve an elitist education for the future rulers or Guardians. The essential preliminary is to dispose of the children of inferior Guardians and any other defective offspring (460: all references are by convention to the pagination of the Stephanus edition, reproduced in most translations). The institution of the family having been abolished, surviving children are brought up in communal nurseries and trained to become philosophically inclined, feisty (no other word translates the Greek so well), quick and strong (376).

Schooling is designed to form the Guardians' aesthetic and moral sensibilities. Most poets will therefore be expelled, since they do not instil proper respect for the gods or the traditional Greek heroes, and often represent low-life characters who are poor role-models for the young. They appeal to the emotions and so fail to foster reason. Fortified by only the better kinds of poetry and music – patriotic and military, especially – the apprentice Guardians undergo two years of physical and military training between the ages of 18 and 20. Then they study mathematics for ten years before graduating to philosophy or dialectic, the science of rigorous argument including logic.

The general populace is to be persuaded that some are born with, metaphorically speaking, the gold in them that destines them to be Guardians, and others with the silver

that marks them out to be 'Auxiliaries' (we might think of these as managers, executives and higher functionaries). The 'children of iron and bronze' will become artisans or farmers: little education worth the name is planned for them. (It is commonly noted that this tripartite system startlingly resembles the grammar, technical and modern schools set up in the UK following the Butler Act of 1944). Women are to enjoy the same educational opportunities as their male counterparts, as long as they have the innate ability required.

Whatever we are to make of these utopian or dystopian flights of fancy, Plato's broader ethical and epistemological theories hold clear implications for moral learning. It seems that Plato derived from Socrates the idea that no-one does wrong willingly. Wrong-doing is a matter of lacking knowledge rather than of weakness of will. The various virtues – courage, piety, justice and so on – are to be understood as a unity and as constituting wisdom. Possession of this wisdom brings fulfilment. There is, therefore, no happiness for anyone who does not live a morally good life. In the *Republic* 'Socrates' pictures humankind as living in a vast cave. We sit in chains with our backs to a fire, which casts shadows onto the wall as onto a screen. People pass between us and the fire: unable to turn round and see them, we take their shadows and the shadows of the things they carry for reality. We become absorbed in this 'reality television', as it were. There are even prizes to be won by the prisoners for remembering the order of sequence of the shadows and for predicting which will come next (516): we might compare questions about reality television programmes or television quiz shows. Occasionally a prisoner breaks free, turns round and sees that there are things in the cave more real than the shadows. If he escapes from the cave he finds that there is a whole world beyond, which at first he cannot see directly because his eyes are unused to the light. First he looks at the shadows of things, as he is accustomed to, then at their reflections in pools and puddles, and then at the things themselves. Finally he raises his eyes and sees the source of the light that makes them visible: the sun, which in this analogy is the Good itself, the sovereign source of knowledge and morality. If he returns to the cave to release his companions they will not thank him; in fact they will probably try to kill him, as the Athenians killed Socrates.

Here education is seen as a lifelong enterprise, not without risk, consisting significantly in the learning of morality through the purification of consciousness. Our task is to struggle free of the web of illusions, fantasies, stale ideas and slogans that surrounds and comforts us: to understand and see things truly, unclouded by the demands of our own egoism. Writers such as Simone Weil and Iris Murdoch have drawn on elements of this picture, emphasising the importance in formal education of developing capacities of attention and discrimination. Good teachers and worthwhile curriculum subjects like mathematics teach accuracy and truth. In this vision thought, goodness and reality are intimately connected.

Perhaps it is Plato's use of the dialogue form that best expresses his philosophy of education. The dialogues, especially the early ones, often represent Socrates as claiming to be wise only in that he knows that he knows nothing. He questions those who claim to know what courage, goodness or justice is, and reveals their claims to knowledge as unfounded. This procedure is called *elenchus*, a combination of cross-examination and refutation. It usually leads to *aporia*, a sense of inconclusiveness and impasse, rather than to definite conclusions. The point lies less in reaching such conclusions – the timeless Platonic doctrines, about education or anything else, that some readers seek – than in illustrating how human understanding can become enlightened about its own limitations and possibilities, and how it can learn to abandon brash, hubristic certainty in favour of a proper modesty: the educated sense of one's own ignorance that Socrates possessed.

Virtually all the dialogues are carefully composed literary artefacts that describe the setting where discussion takes place and the characters of those who can properly be called the dramatis personae. Theaetetus, for example, in the dialogue that bears his name, is a fully fleshed-out young man: gifted, promising, but perhaps a little too smooth and sure (144). The dialogue is an examination of his soul (145) and thus of all our souls insofar as we share Theaetetus' faults. Phaedrus, in the dialogue named after him, seems to inspire Socrates in a way that reminds us that it is not only the pupil who learns in good education. Martha Nussbaum's comment on this dialogue applies to the dialogues in general. She writes that it displays the muses of philosophy and poetry working together, 'combining the rigor of speculative argument with sensitive responses to the particulars of human experience. It ... asks of us the full participation of all parts of our souls' (Nussbaum 1986: 227). Since these include imagination and emotion, the Plato of the *Republic*, if he is there to be taken literally, would have to ban himself from his ideal city.

Thus Plato offers a re-education of perspective through his dialogues, both to their participants and to the reader prepared to engage intellectually, emotionally and imaginatively with them. He shows education, of a peculiarly rich and powerful kind, in the process of taking place: an endless activity, demanding and exhilarating, uniting lyric joy and philosophical wisdom (Fendt and Rozema 1998: 164) in the pursuit of goodness and well-being.

See also: academy; Aristotle; Greece; moral education; philosophy of education; Socratic method

Further reading

Annas, J. (1981) *An Introduction to Plato's Republic*, Oxford: Clarendon Press.

Fendt, G. and Rozema, D. (1998) *Platonic Errors: Plato, a Kind of Poet*, Westport CT: Greenwood Press.

Hadot, P. (1995) *Philosophy as a Way of Life*, Oxford: Blackwell.

Hogan, P. and Smith, R. (2003) 'The activity of philosophy and the practice of education'. In N. Blake, P. Smeyers, R. Smith and P. Standish (eds) *The Blackwell Guide to the Philosophy of Education*, Oxford: Blackwell.

Nussbaum, M. (1986) '"This story isn't true": madness, reason, and recantation in the *Phaedrus*'. In *The Fragility of Goodness: Luck and Ethics in Greek Tragedy and Philosophy*, Cambridge: Cambridge University Press.

Plato (1961) *Collected Dialogues*, trans. E. Hamilton and H. Cairns, Princeton NJ: Princeton University Press.

RICHARD SMITH

PLAYGROUND

For young children, the school playground is a place of fun, games and fantasy. It is normally a supervised area within the boundaries of a school where children may play freely with their friends before the school day begins, during the lunch break and in other intervals between lessons. Many traditional playground games revolve around skipping ropes, balls, hoops, clapping and the recitation of rhymes. Some traditional games, including 'hopscotch', 'tag', 'kiss chase', 'oranges and lemons', 'Simon says' and 'hide and seek' have proved to be enduring international favourites. The playground provides an initiation to the world of trading and bartering: today, as in the past, it is here that children strike their first deals to exchange collectable stickers, coins and cards. The game of conkers, where children do battle with the fruits of the horse chestnut tree strung on shoelaces, continues to be a seasonal favourite, though fears of litigation have sometimes caused nervous head teachers to restrict or ban this and other playground games once thought to be harmless. The playground is a place where children inadvertently market the latest must-have pocket toys and games more effectively than commercial advertising can ever achieve. 'Beyblades', 'clackers', 'yo-yos' and 'Rubik cubes' became global crazes – more than once, in some instances – on the strength of playground popularity. In recent years it has been increasingly common for school playgrounds to feature large-scale versions of popular games such as Jenga, Connect 4 and chess and to install ropes and climbing frames. The playground may also have a more formal function: it is frequently used for timetabled outdoor physical education and games.

See also: physical education/training

DAVID CROOK

POLITICS OF EDUCATION

The politics of education concern the interests involved in debates between individuals, groups and organisations to decide the character and direction of education. Understanding these interests involves addressing the nature of the relationships between interest groups and stake holders. For example, religious groups might come into conflict over the nature of religious education in schools, and as a result might well seek to enlist support for their own views, or a compromise that might avoid outcomes that would be against their own interests. In terms of the politics, the issues would be in such a case about resolving differences and finding a means of accommodation between rival interests.

At a more profound level, a broad distinction has often been drawn between educational politics, on the one hand, and the politics of education on the other. Educational politics concern the tensions and negotiations between interest groups within the sphere of education. By contrast, the politics of education would involve taking account of connections with wider social debates, with considerations of power, and with the relationship between the state and society. This is an approach that emphasises sociological dimensions of power relationships and theoretical insights into the state. It also embraces an awareness of changes and continuities in political dynamics over the medium and long term.

See also: education policy; religious education; sociology of education

GARY McCULLOCH

POLYNESIA

For the purposes of this entry 'Polynesia', one of the three geographic-cultural regions of Oceania, includes the small island countries of Samoa, Tonga, the Cook Islands and Niue. The development of formal education in each of these countries has been strongly influenced by New Zealand.

Formal schooling was introduced to Polynesian societies in the early decades of the nineteenth century by European missionaries, intent on their objective of Christianising the indigenous people of the various islands. In this they were very successful and, throughout Polynesia, people enthusiastically learnt to read and write. By the end of the nineteenth century, the conversion of Polynesians to Christianity was complete, basic literacy in local languages was almost 100 per cent and access to mission-provided primary schooling, albeit of a limited nature, was widespread.

New Zealand's official involvement in the education systems of Polynesian countries began at the turn of the twentieth century, when the New Zealand government took control of the Cook Islands and Niue under the Pacific Islands Annexation Act (1901). Samoa, which had been a German colony since 1900, came under New Zealand administration in 1919, and New Zealand also took responsibility for educational administration in Tonga, which had become a British protectorate in 1900. While promoting the notion of state schooling, the New Zealand administrators were keen to avoid the costs involved in a fully state-funded system, so worked with the various church groups in sharing both the control and responsibility of expanding school systems. Much of what was offered in Polynesian schools was based on that practised in New Zealand's Maori schools.

In the post-World War II decades, the international move to prepare colonial territories for self-government, a process in which education was perceived to be central, resulted in primary schooling throughout Polynesia being upgraded and secondary schooling established or expanded. Many more New Zealand teachers worked in Polynesian schools and curricula and assessment were increasingly prescribed by the New Zealand Department of Education. Growing numbers (though still a very select group) of the islands' students sat New Zealand examinations and went on scholarship to New Zealand for higher secondary and tertiary education. In 1968 the University of the South Pacific was established to serve the 'manpower needs' of the newly emerging self-governing countries. Education was promoted by both the island governments and the ex-colonisers as the key to modernisation. One outcome of this was the loss of skilled workers through emigration, particularly to New Zealand.

By the early 1980s dissatisfaction with this approach led to a shift to more 'relevant' education with localised curricula and assessment methods, at the national level for primary and junior secondary and the regional level for senior secondary and tertiary. National teachers' colleges and curriculum development units, supported by multilateral and bilateral aid agencies – particularly based in New Zealand and Australia – worked together to develop programmes reflective of the sociocultural contexts in which the schools of each island country are located, and aid programmes became specifically geared to educational self-reliance.

For these small, 'developing' and aid-dependent countries, the educational issues of the last fifteen years have reflected debates within the international development community about the relationship between education and development, and how aid to education can most effectively promote economic growth. During the 1990s education development in Polynesia came under increased scrutiny from the World Bank and subject to the recommendations of the Bank's global blueprint. These countries also were affected by significant changes in the policies and procedures underpinning the aid programmes of New Zealand and Australia, both of which had moved to a more economistic 'export of educational services' approach. In the case of New Zealand, this included the marketing to Polynesian countries of its National Qualifications Framework, with the result that secondary students in three of these countries are once again doing New Zealand examinations, thus reversing the trend to localisation of the previous decade.

Since 2000, the global agenda for increased allocations of resources to basic education has focused the attention of Polynesian educators on the Education For All targets and the education Millennium Development Goals. Despite their constrained resources, vulnerability to natural disasters and the logistical difficulties of delivering education services to remote communities on tiny land areas surrounded by vast oceans, these Polynesian countries are well on track to meet the set targets. A key focus now is on raising the quality of teaching at all levels of education.

See also: Education For All (EFA); New Zealand/Aotearoa; Oceania; World Bank

Further reading

Campbell, C. and Sherington, G. (eds) (2007) *Going to School in Oceania*, New York: Greenwood Press.

Coxon, E. (2002) 'From patronage to profiteering? New Zealand's educational relationship with the small states of Oceania', *Educational Philosophy and Theory*, 34(1): 57–75.

Coxon, E. and Taufe'ulungaki, A. (eds) (2003) *Global/Local Intersections: Researching the Delivery of Aid to Pacific Education*, Auckland: Research Unit in Pacific Education, University of Auckland.

Murray, T. R. and Postlethwaite, T. N. (eds) (1984) *Schooling in the Pacific Islands*, Oxford: Pergamon Press.

EVE COXON

POLYTECHNIC

The first polytechnic was founded in Paris, in 1794, to school army officers in engineering and artillery. Emulated in Prague, Vienna, Zurich and in German technical schooling, as well as the Royal Polytechnic Institute in London patronised by Prince Albert (later the Regent Street Polytechnic, as Quintin Hogg's Young Men's Christian Institute became known), the trajectory of polytechnics was very different in the United Kingdom and countries following the same model (Australia, New Zealand, Hong Kong and Singapore) compared with elsewhere. This was because Karl Marx advocated 'polytechnic education' in a resolution adopted by the first Congress of the International Workingmen's Association in 1866 (Small 1984). Despite doubts over their translation, 'polytechnic education' subsequently became prominent in socialist countries, including China, where it embodied the principle of combining practical training with theoretical education. Marx's idea of poly-, or many-sided, technical training in the foundations of different crafts as 'the only means of producing fully developed human beings' was lost.

However, in the UK something of this socialist ideal resurfaced in attenuated form with the unexpected announcement, in 1964, by the new Labour government's education minister, Anthony Crosland, of polytechnics in England and Wales (with Central Institutions to be developed in Scotland). There are two predominant opinions on the success or failure of *The Polytechnic Experiment*, as John Pratt (1997) called it. The first of these is that the polytechnics were introduced to save money on expanding existing higher education as recommended by the 1963 Robbins Report. They thus reinserted selection into the tertiary sector as it was being phased out of comprehensive secondary schools. On this reading, the polytechnics acted as a buffer protecting the universities from changes that would have been required by the admission of more students. The other interpretation is that the polytechnics represented *A Liberal Vocationalism* (Silver and Brennan 1988) related to employment for local people and under the democratic control of local education authorities. Sydney Webb's description of polytechnics as 'the people's universities' was later to be used by Eric Robinson, director of North East London Polytechnic, to argue for a 'comprehensive system of education for adults' and to replace 'the boarding school university by that of the urban community university' (Robinson 1968).

Incorporated by the 1988 Education Reform Act under their own Polytechnic Funding Council, the polytechnics of England and Wales – thirty-four in number at that time – were educating more than half of all full-time first degree students and were to become significant players in the field of teacher training as a consequence of mergers with colleges of education. They were variable in size, the most populous, Manchester Polytechnic, with 25,000 students, being larger than Manchester University, then the largest non-federal university in England with 16,000 students. Many polytechnics had a large proportion of part-time students and sandwich and sub-degree course participants, as well as a much higher proportion of mature students than the universities, though far fewer polytechnic students were enrolled on postgraduate programmes or came from overseas.

The British polytechnics thus maintained their original brief, with increasing numbers of students taking more applied and technical subjects, though with marked 'academic drift', as Burgess and Pratt first called it, especially during the 1980s when universities raised entry requirements rather than expand on reduced resources. In consequence, polytechnics expanded their provision of arts and humanities courses, which were an attraction for women students, especially. The pioneering contribution of the polytechnics in such new areas as cultural studies and in

multidisciplinary modular degrees should be particularly celebrated.

The rapid expansion of the polytechnics on reduced per capita funding so impressed a Conservative government that was, by the end of the 1980s, moving towards an Americanised model of mass higher education, that it upgraded them to full university status in 1992, 'to disguise the fact,' as Tyrrell Burgess wittily said at the time, 'that the universities had become polytechnics' through a similar, if belated, expansion. Ironically, the end of 'the binary divide' led also to the end of what had been a shared culture of higher education between universities and polytechnics that had been maintained by the university-nominated Council for National Academic Awards, which formally approved polytechnic courses. The introduction of a market in differentiated student fees can only heighten this tendency towards a new binarism within a nominally unitary higher education.

There is still a place for the polytechnic in the twenty-first century, as evidenced by their recent introduction in Finland.

See also: binary system; Finland; higher education; mature students; sandwich course; technical education/school/college; university; vocational education

Further reading

Pratt, J. (1997) *The Polytechnic Experiment 1965–1992*, Milton Keynes: Open University Press in association with the Society for Research into Higher Education.

Robbins, D. (1988) *The Rise of Independent Study: The Politics and the Philosophy of an Educational Innovation, 1970–87*, Milton Keynes: Open University Press in association with the Society for Research into Higher Education.

Robinson, E. E. (1968) *The New Polytechnics*, Harmondsworth: Penguin.

Silver, H. and Brennan, J. (1988) *A Liberal Vocationalism*, London: Methuen.

Small, R. (1984) 'The concept of polytechnical education', *British Journal of Educational Studies*, 32(1): 27–44.

PATRICK AINLEY

POSITIVE DISCRIMINATION/ AFFIRMATIVE ACTION

Positive discrimination and affirmative action are sometimes considered to be synonymous terms relating to efforts to compensate for historic discrimination in access to education or employment, or to promote diversity in schools and the workplace. The term positive discrimination tends to be used primarily in the United Kingdom and other European countries, and the term affirmative action, although it is used to a limited extent in the UK, is primarily used in the United States.

The definition of these terms is complicated, however, by the fact that positive discrimination, in the sense of favouring one candidate for a school or job over another because of race, ethnicity, colour, national origin or gender is generally contrary to UK law. The Race Relations Act of 1976 and the Sex Discrimination Act of 1975 both have been interpreted to invalidate such positive discrimination in most cases, regardless of the stated purpose. Thus, positive discrimination in the UK is more akin to reverse discrimination in the USA than it is to affirmative action, the legality of which is still arguable. The more apt UK synonym for US affirmative action is, therefore, probably positive action.

In both countries, the law encourages or requires public entities, including those that operate or administer schools and universities, and some private entities to eliminate unlawful discrimination and promote equality of opportunity. Complexities arise, however, over precisely what those goals mean and what techniques can be used to implement them. In the US context, the original intent of both the most relevant federal constitutional principle – the 14th Amendment's Equal Protection Clause – and of federal civil rights legislation was to liberate black Americans from the vestiges of slavery. Affirmative action became the omnibus term to describe many efforts to enhance their status and their opportunities to participate in and enjoy the benefits of education, employment, housing, the political process and, more generally, public services and facilities. Because of the historic disadvantages of black Americans, many believed that they would require some special public assistance to achieve real equality. In the common vernacular, levelling the playing field would simply be insufficient to equalise opportunities in education, employment or other sectors if the players reached the starting line with dramatically disparate skills or resources.

For much of the past five decades the USA has been seeking to determine precisely what are the appropriate goals and acceptable techniques of affirmative action. Over those years, views about both goals and techniques have shifted, with the courts heavily engaged in that process. Much of the activity has resulted from the growing backlash among white males to what they have perceived to be the unfair benefits accorded to black Americans and women. The backlash has been particularly acute in connection with zero-sum decisions: admission to elite schools and universities, and employment in desirable jobs.

The relevant US law is less than entirely clear, partly because it is in a state of ongoing flux. Some important principles are relatively clear, though. Formal quotas relating to race, ethnicity, national origin or gender in education or employment are not permissible, and even specific numerical goals are suspect. These characteristics cannot be the basis for quantifiable bonus points in educational admissions or employment decisions, nor can they even serve as tie-breakers. But they can be part of a less formal, holistic approach to making admissions and employment decisions because US courts have recognised that diversity in schools and in the workplace is an important value. Additionally, special outreach to minority communities to engender knowledge about and interest in certain educational or employment opportunities is likely to be deemed appropriate. This may parallel the UK approach under which public authorities have a statutory duty to develop and implement race equality policies and codes of practice. For example, positive action in employment can include providing training, as well as special outreach, just to underrepresented racial groups.

Diversity is hardly unchallenged, however, even in situations that are not clearly zero-sum. In two cases pending before the US Supreme Court, voluntary affirmative action plans adopted by local school boards to diversify all their schools have been challenged by students who failed to gain admission to their preferred public schools and, instead, had to attend other public schools. Their claim is that this constitutes unlawful reverse discrimination based on their race.

Under UK law, their argument might well succeed in light of the interpretation given to positive discrimination. If it succeeds in the USA, the distinction between positive discrimination and affirmative action will be reduced, if it is not eliminated.

See also: equality of opportunity; law

Further reading

Edwards, J. (1995) *When Race Counts: The Morality of Racial Preference in Britain and America*, London: Routledge.
Guinier, L. and Sturm, S. (2001) *Who's Qualified?*, Boston MA: Beacon Press.
Sowell, T. (2004) *Affirmative Action around the World: An Empirical Study*, New Haven CT: Yale University Press.

PAUL TRACTENBERG

POSTGRADUATE

A postgraduate student, or simply postgraduate, is a higher education student who has already completed a first, or undergraduate, degree, normally in a related area. Postgraduate courses offer students an opportunity to further their skills and qualifications in a particular area of specialisation. This might lead to the award of a postgraduate certificate or diploma, a master's degree or a doctorate. Postgraduate students often enjoy a different status to undergraduates

within their departments. They may, for example, take on work as teaching assistants, perhaps tutoring undergraduate students or demonstrating experiments in the science laboratory. Whatever their age, by virtue of having already completed a first degree, a postgraduate is a mature student.

See also: certificate/certification; degree; diploma; higher education; master's; mature student; teaching assistant; university

DAVID CROOK

POSTMODERNISM

Postmodernism is an intellectual movement that questions everything, including philosophies, strategies and world views. It is applied to fields as disparate as architecture, history and music. Moreover, it has had a major impact on feminist thought and practice. For a movement or intellectual position that condemns essentialism, the notion that objects have a fixed essence that distinguishes them from other objects, it is perhaps unsurprising that postmodernism resists definition in anything but the broadest manner. As concepts often derive much of their meaning from their opposite, it is useful to observe that postmodernism's opposite is modernity and the Enlightenment. While the latter celebrated reason or rationality, which it installed as the ultimate test of law, society, politics, ethics and morality, postmodernism sees rationality as oppressive and the Enlightenment's reliance on knowledge as the key to human betterment and emancipation, an illusion.

Linked with this scepticism towards emancipatory strategies is a rejection of universals in favour of particularism and what the French philosopher, Jean-François Lyotard (1924–98) called an incredulity towards metanarratives, such as Christianity or Marxism, that present a story in which potentially everything is explained and legitimated. Along with the rejection of metanarratives and universals, the possibility of locating grounds upon which to base truth claims is denied by postmodernism in favour of varying degrees of relativism in which every proposition is true within the context within which it is advanced. This has the possible consequence that nothing may be held to be true, including the metanarrative of postmodernism itself.

If postmodernism is against the Enlightenment and the positivist conception of science associated with it, postmodernist thinkers are generally in favour of some of the positions that have been labelled post-structuralist. These include the notion of the 'linguistic turn', the acceptance of the view that language does not simply reflect reality but is constituent of it. This position was advanced by the French theorist Jacques Derrida (1930–2004), whose notion of deconstruction is a central one in postmodernism. Deconstruction is a strategy that attempts to open a text to show it has several possible meanings and interpretations. It does this by showing that the binary oppositions within it are unstable. The conclusion of deconstruction is that meaning is never fixed and there is no position from which interpretation can secure it.

Deconstruction is also applied to the subject in postmodernism. The unitary, conscious, acting subject of Enlightenment thought is rejected, most prominently by the French philosopher Michel Foucault (1926–84), in favour of a fragmented subject or self constituted by discourses, who does not speak but is, instead, spoken.

Another central strand in postmodernism is derived from the French philosopher Jean Baudrillard (1929–2007), who used the term 'hyperreal' to signify the distorting impact of contemporary media and consumerism upon an individual's ability to distinguish the real from the unreal. He argued that this was because of the proliferation of simulacra which are not a copy of the real, but the hyperreal, a simulation of a non-existent reality.

Despite being highly controversial and the target of many influential critiques, postmodernism has had a major impact on the teaching and study of the humanities and the social sciences in the last three decades. In education it has stimulated much debate within universities and colleges, but despite its apparently radical approach to knowledge and hierarchy it has had less impact on policies and practices in school systems concerned with the curriculum and pedagogy. Where it has had most success in changing the discourse of education is in gaining acceptance for the idea that everything, childhood for example, or the curriculum, is socially constructed and that, as a consequence, educational practices do not have to be as they are. However, postmodernism's emphasis on difference and hostility to universals weakens its ability to explain how a socially constructed world is able to resist change in the direction of the greater plurality that its proponents advocate.

See also: educational theory; feminist theory; Foucault, Michel

Further reading

Anderson, P. (1998) *The Origins of Postmodernity*, London: Verso.

Eagleton, T. (1996) *The Illusions of Postmodernism*, Oxford: Blackwell.

Jameson, F. (1991) *Postmodernism, or the Cultural Logic of Late Capitalism*, London: Verso.

Lyotard, J-F. (1984) *The Postmodern Condition: A Report on Knowledge*, Manchester: Manchester University Press.

Parker, S. (1997) *Reflective Teaching in the Postmodern World: A Manifesto for Education in Postmodernity*, Buckingham: Open University Press.

Usher, R. and Edwards, R. (1994) *Postmodernism and Education*, London: Routledge.

KEVIN J. BREHONY

PRACTITIONER RESEARCH

Practitioner research is a strategy used by professionals and practitioners in any field to examine a situation or a problem. Persons conducting practitioner research would reflect on the issues related to the situation rather than begin from a position of trying different strategies to 'fix' the problem. The idea is to arrive at a greater understanding of their own practice. Its roots are in naturalistic research where the researchers conduct research in their own setting. The philosophy is rooted in the work of Donald Schön (1983) and Lawrence Stenhouse (1975) who referred to the teacher as a researcher. Practitioner researchers claim that their interest in this type of research is not focused merely on finding results to fix a problem but more on understanding the dynamics of a situation. In this exploration, they examine themselves as part of the context because it enables them to question what is happening in teaching and learning situations. They believe that research is essential to good professional practice and are keen to explore new ideas and strategies, carefully studying the results, and making informed decisions for action.

Practitioner research is a long-term learning process that takes place over several months and offers a relatively high level of support to a relatively small group of participants who become members of a learning community. Participants are provided with an opportunity to share their research as it unfolds, to focus on individual and group issues, and create strategies for dealing with issues at various stages of the research work. An important factor in practitioner research is that it is not conducted by outside observers but by people who are involved in the situation and who are able to grow as a community through the research experience. This means that the researcher would have an insider's perspective of the situation, with insights into the various people and circumstances. The researcher would probably have easier access to the background information as well as the persons to be interviewed and/or observed. They may also have developed a healthy rapport with the community involved. Because they have all this intimate knowledge of the community, they would also have an appreciation of the dynamics involved and would be able to advise on the design of the research, the ethics involved and the reporting and dissemination of the findings.

This level of familiarity, along with prejudice, self-interest, defensiveness and insecurity may also be a disadvantage by distorting the research process. The position of the researcher, their own experiences and perspectives, may also create a familiarity with the area of study that can lead to a second-guessing of the participants' meanings. Therefore, reflexivity about the role of the researcher in these situations and the mutual interrogation of the researcher's and participants' experiences is an essential feature of qualitative research of this nature where the local researcher is asked to treat the familiar situation with a sense of freshness, as if they were experiencing it for the first time. When conducting research within one's own environment, there could be a tendency to simply add on the research as another activity to be done along with everything else. This could easily lead to the research being stretched out over an extended period of time or abandoned due to a lack of time.

Stenhouse (1975) provides some measure of support for those who engage in insider research, stating that the observer has a direct cultural link to those whom she/he is observing and researching. If within one's research paradigm, there is the understanding that no social activity is value-free, then if the observer or researcher is able to maintain a fairly objective critical stance to the project, that should present a truer reconstruction of reality than that presented by the stranger with his gaps of cultural understanding. Though some may argue that a practitioner's view would be too close to be objective, there is the argument that this view as an 'insider' researcher allows an almost immediate access to a first-hand understanding of the history, culture and nuances related to the situation.

See also: action research; educational research; learning community; qualitative research; Schön, Donald; Stenhouse, Lawrence

Further reading

Pring, R. (2000) *Philosophy of Educational Research*, London: Continuum.
Schön, D. (1983) *The Reflective Practitioner*, London: Temple Smith.

Stenhouse, L. (1975) *An Introduction to Curriculum Research and Development*, London: Heinemann.
ANN CHERYL ARMSTRONG

PREFECT

A prefect is a pupil or student who is given a measure of delegated authority in matters of discipline or in specific areas such as games, sports and administration by the head teacher in a school. In the system devised by Thomas Arnold at Rugby School in England in the early nineteenth century, prefects were given considerable powers as part of the corporate structure. They became a familiar feature of independent schools, but over the past century have often been employed in schools of different kinds in a number of countries. Recently their disciplinary powers and independence have generally been much reduced. A head prefect or head boy or girl is usually appointed to organise the work of a group of prefects. Such roles are a mark of respect and recognition and confer official status within the school.

See also: Arnold, Thomas

GARY McCULLOCH

PRIMARY SCHOOL/EDUCATION

More so than other phases, primary school/ education is context-specific, which makes generalisations across countries particularly hazardous. It is a designated stage within education systems and is aimed, in theory at least, at all children of a specified age range. That age range varies from country to country. For children, entry to primary education may be as early as age four or as late as age seven. The end point of primary education is usually age 11 or 12. Primary education is usually considered as the first compulsory stage of mass education but in practice many children in Third-World countries, especially girls, do not attend primary schools or only do so for only limited periods of time. For the most part, primary education is provided

in state-funded institutions, though in all but a small number of countries private-funded schools for a small minority of children complement this provision. Primary education may be preceded by a non-compulsory pre-school stage and it is always succeeded by a secondary phase – usually provided in separate institutions – though access to this may not always be available to all pupils.

The widespread provision of primary/ elementary education by governments in Europe and North America was a feature of the nineteenth century, though beginning somewhat earlier in a few states. It represented the systematisation of ad hoc provision provided over centuries by a wide variety of institutions and individuals, very often, but not always, associated with religious groups. In many countries that ad hoc provision has left a legacy in terms of a combination of state, voluntary (i.e. religious) and independent schools catering for children of primary-school age. The mass provision of primary/ elementary education was aimed at those social groups not receiving any formal educational provision, especially but not only workers in the newly industrialised areas. It served to provide them with basic literacy and numeracy and with 'appropriate' attitudes to work in fast industrialising societies. The late nineteenth and twentieth centuries saw the extension of primary education to children in European colonies and latterly to those in independent states.

Over time, primary education has served a variety of purposes, though the relative importance of these has changed from time to time and country to country.

One major purpose of primary education has been, and is, instruction, particularly reading and writing (less often speaking and listening) in the mother tongue along with computational arithmetic (sometimes, but not always complemented by elementary measurement and geometry). This 'basic' curriculum is common to all primary schools worldwide. However, beyond this there is considerable variation. The curriculum may include elements of science, the humanities, arts, physical education, information technology and, increasingly, a second language. In many countries the place (or absence) of religious education is a contentious issue. Looked at somewhat differently, the curriculum of primary education can be construed in terms of procedural knowledge, conceptual knowledge, skills acquisition and metacognitive knowledge. Over time, the relative importance of these components has changed. In the nineteenth century most emphasis was placed on procedural knowledge and skill acquisition, often of a very elementary kind. The latter half of the twentieth century saw an increasing emphasis on conceptual knowledge and more advanced skills acquisition, particularly in First-World states seeking to maximise human capital in an ever more competitive global economy. Currently there is a growing interest in fostering metacognitive knowledge, though in some Third-World countries the priority remains that of basic skill acquisition.

A second major purpose of primary education has been, and is, socialisation, i.e. the induction of children into the norms, values, traditions and other aspects of the culture of their societies. This is sometimes done explicitly and formally through programmes of civic or personal education, but is more often done informally and often implicitly through the rules, conventions, routines, daily interactions and assumptions in the everyday life of school and classroom. The socialisation process is often aided by the close interpersonal relationships which develop between children and 'their' class teacher, who in most educational systems is responsible for all or almost the entire curriculum for the whole of any school year or, in some cases, for several years. Socialisation has always been a major purpose of primary education, especially in the nineteenth and twentieth centuries when large numbers of children entered formal education for the first time. It has been particularly important in helping create social and political cohesion in Third-World countries after independence. It remains very significant in the First World – partly as a result of the development of increasingly complex multicultural societies where the values of tolerance and respect for others are so much needed and where they can be fostered and reinforced from the minute children enter school.

Linked to socialisation is another function of primary education. Primary school teachers are also concerned with children's welfare – physical, emotional and social. Primary schools are the most accessible 'outposts' of the state (and whatever welfare functions it is able to discharge) as far as most parents and children are concerned. Schools are crucially important points of contact, especially for economically disadvantaged families. In the late nineteenth and early twentieth centuries primary teachers in First-World countries were particularly concerned for children's physical welfare, as illustrated by the introduction of school meals and medical treatment and the emphasis placed on physical training. That concern remains a priority in many Third-World states. In very recent years there has been a resurgence of concern in the First World about children's social and emotional welfare as a result of social changes, including new patterns of family life and child-rearing and what many see as the commercialisation, even 'toxicisation', of childhood.

Traditionally, primary education has also served to classify children into various categories in order to provide differentiated educational provision at the primary and/or secondary stages. Within the primary phase, children may be identified as having different abilities or levels of ability and may be sorted into different streams, sets or other categories (such as 'special needs' or 'handicapped' pupils) or, in some states, they may be promoted early or held back in relation their peers. In some countries primary education plays a major part in preparing children for different forms of secondary education – academic, vocational, practical, etc. In others, especially in the

Third World, it selects those deemed suitable for the limited number of secondary school places that are available. This classification function involves some sort of summative examination or assessment at the end of the primary stage, which very often has a backwash effect on the teaching and the curriculum in the preceding years.

The challenges facing primary education are similar in general terms to those facing other phases. Apart from a consensus on the need for primary education to provide a basic education in terms of improved numeracy and literacy, there are ongoing debates, especially in First-World countries, about the needs and purposes it should address in the future, about the values it should embody, about the relationship between in-school and out-of-school learning, about its relationship with majority and minority cultures and about its role in introducing children to global issues such as climate change, world trade or other First-World/Third-World relationships.

There are, however, particular issues facing primary education. What should be the constituents of the primary curriculum beyond the 'basics'? What are the implications for curriculum and teaching created by widespread opportunities for e-learning? Is the class-teacher system fit for purpose? What is the role, if any, of subject specialisation in the primary phase? How should teaching groups be organised? What is the place of testing in any assessment system? How can the quality of primary education be assured? How can primary schools complement the education provided by parents? What is the relationship between education and care? Over what age range should primary education extend? What is its relationship to the phases that precede and succeed it? Should primary education be extended parity of treatment with secondary education in terms of staffing and material resources?

All of these are important issues in First-World contexts. Yet it has to be remembered that universal primary education still remains a dream to be realised in too many Third-World states, especially for girls.

See also: compulsory education; curriculum; elementary school; literacy; numeracy; secondary school/education; universal education/mass education

Further reading

Alexander, R. (2000) *Culture and Pedagogy*, Oxford: Blackwell

Benavot, A. and Karmens, D. (1989) *The Curriculum Content of Primary Education in Developing Countries*, Washington DC: World Bank.

Hayes, D. (2006) *Primary Education: the Key Concepts*, London: Routledge.

Moyles, J. and Hargreaves, L. (eds) (1998) *The Primary Curriculum: Learning from International Perspectives*, London: Routledge

Qualifications and Assessment Agency (2007) *International Review of Curriculum and Assessment Frameworks Internet Archive*, at www.inca.org.uk

COLIN RICHARDS

PRIVATISATION/MARKETISATION

The privatisation of state education systems involves opening them up to the influences of the private sector; marketisation is about opening them up to market forces. These are closely related concepts that are often employed together to analyse contemporary trends in educational policies in many countries around the world, although they may be conceived in different ways. As Marginson notes, 'privatisation' is about the transfer of production, or means of production, from government (public) sector ownership to private ownership, for example through the sale or donation of government land, buildings or equipment, the denationalisation of public enterprises, the raising of public equity in private enterprises, or the contracting out of aspects of public sector production to private agents. However, he adds, privatisation does not necessarily imply the development of markets, and markets may develop in public as well as private institutions (Marginson 1997: 36). Green (2005) points out that the privatisation of state education is part of a broader canvas of social policy and public services in which there has been an international trend towards increasing the use of the private sector in the management and delivery of public services, influenced by the desire to restrain public expenditure and increase the benefits supposedly offered by private sector expertise in a competitive environment (Green 2005: 5).

The growth of private sector participation in public sector education may be understood in terms of a wide range of types and forms of privatisation with an increasingly international and even global dimension. Those that have affected the education system in Britain most strongly include support for infrastructure: capital works such as buildings and major refurbishments of school and university buildings. A major development of this type has been the Private Finance Initiative, launched in 1992, in which private sector funding and ownership provide for new buildings and refurbishments. Privatisations also include national programmes of different kinds that are contracted out to private providers, ranging from information technology and management systems to pedagogical and curricular initiatives. They may also involve contracts to run services or provide support to local authorities or individual institutions, from school meals to childcare. The international features of such provision are reflected in the roles of American companies such as Edison in other education systems, and the buying and selling of parts of public education systems by international companies (see Ball 2007: ch. 3).

Examples of marketisation would include the dezoning of secondary schools in New Zealand at the end of the 1980s and in the early 1990s. At one stage, designated schools were permitted to control their own enrolment policies, with highly differentiated effects on different secondary schools. The marketised regime led to the destabilisation of working-class schools, while strong schools were further strengthened. According to Marginson,

Like elite private schools in Australia, the market leaders in New Zealand government schooling controlled the market, evaded the

pressure of numbers and selling, and sustained an organic relationship with their own communities that were constituted, overtly or covertly, on social-economic and ethnic lines; and all with the active compliance of government.

(Marginson 1997: 179)

In Victoria, Australia, the Schools for the Future programme, introduced in 1993 on a pilot basis, enabled school councils to manage resources and personnel, giving principals much greater power. By 1995, Schools for the Future was established in most of Victoria's government schools, controlling budgets covering more than 90 per cent of expenditure, and their principals could select staff. Parents became consumers, while neighbouring schools were competitors. The development of education vouchers in different national contexts is a recurring instance of marketisation. Higher education could also be marketised, for example through competitive bidding for funds (Marginson 1997: 194).

Both privatisation and marketisation offer radical alternatives for education systems that have struggled to provide services that satisfy a broad clientele, and appeal to the rhetoric of choice and the promotion of greater quality. By the same token, they challenge established values and ethics in schools and universities around universal and equitable provision and citizenship rights, and place strains on teachers and institutions (Whitty 1997). The debate around these different ideals and practices has become increasingly intense and politicised, generating sometimes creative but often not clearly considered and unsustainable initiatives, and giving rise to tensions that are likely to develop further in coming decades.

See also: economics of education; education policy; parental choice; vouchers; zoning

Further reading

Ball, S. (2007) *Education plc: Understanding Private Sector Participation in Public Sector Education*, London: Routledge.

455

Green, C. (2005) *The Privatisation of State Educa-tion: Public Partners, Private Dealings*, London: Routledge.

Marginson, S. (1997) *Markets in Education*, Sydney NSW: Allen and Unwin.

Whitty, G. (1997) 'Marketisation, the state, and the re-formation of the teaching profession'. In A. H. Halsey, H. Lauder, P. Brown and A. Wells (eds) *Education: Culture, Economy, Society*, Oxford: Oxford University Press.

GARY McCULLOCH

PROCTOR

A British term, proctors are found in a range of settings, generally exercising supervisory roles. In legal contexts, a proctor, or pro-curator, is a court lawyer. An ecclesiastical proctor is a representative of the clergy: when a vacancy for the most senior Church of England post, that of Archbishop of Canter-bury, is to be filled, it falls to the cathedral proctor to confirm that an election has been conducted in accordance with Church law. The Church of England General Synod (or parliament) includes among its membership several proctors representing universities with traditional Church associations.

A proctor is also a university official, typically a junior or middle-ranking staff member, with responsibility in some insti-tutions for drawing up candidate lists and invigilating student examinations. The office of proctor at the universities of Cambridge and Oxford can be traced back to medieval times. Their duties variously included reg-ulating the hours of examinations and lec-tures, punishing students dressed incorrectly or found out of college at a prohibited hour. The duties of proctors considerably dimin-ished after the development of police con-stabularies in the nineteenth century, but Oxbridge proctors continue to carry out some regulatory and disciplinary functions, as well as administrative and ceremonial duties. Today, Cambridge University appoints one senior, one junior and several pro-proctors, including a Pro-Proctor for Motor Vehicles responsible for licensing the cars and motor-bikes of student who have not reached M.A. status.

See also: examinations

DAVID CROOK

PROFESSION/PROFESSIONALISM/ PROFESSIONALISATION

Occupational groups have often been ana-lysed in relation to their aspirations to become a profession, exerting power and constituting a monopoly of specialised expertise. A useful distinction in this regard is between professionalism and professionalisa-tion. The former refers to the rights and obligations of professionals to determine their own tasks as they see fit. The latter denotes the public project of occupational groups, often over a long period of time, to acquire the status and security that will enable them to be recognised as a profession. Educators in general, and different groups of teachers in particular, have widely sought to be regarded in these terms, although there are a number of problematic issues about their significance for education.

The classic professions have been those of medicine, law and the Church, each of which has developed an area of specialist expertise and knowledge that has enjoyed authority and respect in many different societies. The nature of the knowledge base is an important feature of the claims of an occupational group to be regarded as a pro-fession, specifically whether their expertise is unique and the value placed on that expertise (Eraut 1994). Teaching has commonly been advocated as having the attributes of a pro-fession of this kind. However, these claims might be conditioned by the extent to which the knowledge involved is specialised and esoteric, such as with university teaching, or common and general, such as with different forms of mass education. The expertise or skills with which an occupational group is imbued might also be regarded as either rig-orous or relevant. Schön refers to a 'varied topography of professional practice', in which there is 'a high, hard ground where practitioners can make effective use of research-based theory and technique', and 'a swampy lowland where situations are confusing "messes" incapable of technical solution'. The problems of the high ground might be of great technical interest, Schön continues, but might be relatively unimportant to clients or to the wider society, 'while in the swamp are the problems of greatest human concern' (Schön 1983: 42). These variations lead Hargreaves and Goodson to define a number of types of teacher professionalism: practical professionalism, which emphasises the practical knowledge and judgement that people have of their own work, extended professionalism, which involves a mediation between experience and theory beyond the classroom, and complex professionalism, based on the complexity of the tasks that the work demands (Hargreaves and Goodson 1996).

A further issue with the exercise of 'professional knowledge' is the autonomy or control over that knowledge that the professional enjoys. For the sociologist of medicine Eliot Freidson, such control is the essence of professionalism. Freidson suggests that a profession is an occupation that controls its own work, organised by a special set of institutions sustained in part by a particular ideology of expertise and service (Freidson 1994: 10). Professional autonomy, on this view, entails sufficient authority over one's own work to be free exercise discretionary judgement as a matter of course, with time, equipment, assistance and other resources available to carry it out fully and well. This need not mean total autonomy over all areas of work, which would be difficult if not impossible to attain, but might involve different types of characteristics in different societies, and could relate to jurisdiction over particular areas of work more than others (Torstendahl 1990). In the case of school teachers, in England for example, the dominant tradition of professionalism in the twentieth century was that of control over what to teach (curriculum) and how to

teach it (pedagogy), even though this was never complete, being limited by the constraints of examinations, parents and other factors. This approach to professionalism was severely challenged with the introduction of a national curriculum in 1988 which curtailed such control on the part of teachers, although teachers continue to find areas within which to exercise discretion (McCulloch et al. 2000).

Professionalisation as a public project would conventionally involve the negotiation over time of certain attributes for the occupation, including self-government, pensions and salaries, conditions of service, training and qualifications. Teachers have often claimed success in this project, but doubts as to their status have often been expressed, and they have been described in the United States as 'special but shadowed' and 'only partially professionalised' – employed subordinates with only limited economic advances and prestige indicators (Lortie 1975: 22–23). The feminisation of teaching in many societies and types of educational institution in the past century has also given rise to issues of professional status because of the male domination of the 'classic' professions. Acker notes that 'professional' and 'women' have sometimes been regarded as 'virtually incompatible concepts', with the professional ideal being based on male experiences, although she also points to possible alternative bases for alternative approaches drawing on feminine experiences such as caring and service (Acker 1999). Teacher unions meanwhile would tend to emphasise the affinities between teachers and other employed workers, indicating working-class solidarity rather than middle-class and professional status.

Over the last thirty years, the role of professional groups has been much discussed in relation to the state on the one hand and the market on the other. The rise of an increased role for the state in a wider range of welfare activities such as education, health and social care led in many societies by the mid-twentieth century to a growing sector of 'caring

457

professionals' with a supporting bureaucracy under the auspices of the state. The professional ideal included trained expertise and selection by merit that would supplant previous kinds of routes to social success and respectability based on money, family and social class. According to Perkin, 'A professional society is one structured around career hierarchies rather than classes, one in which people find their place according to trained expertise and the service they provide rather than the possession or lack of inherited wealth or acquired capital.' (Perkin 1989/ 2002: 359). This set of developments came under challenge before the end of the century with criticisms of the supposedly unaccountable and monopolistic nature of the professions, and political initiatives designed to promote greater power for the consumer. The backlash against the professions has created fears of deprofessionalisation, that is, of a loss of privileges and authority for the occupational group as a whole, and of status and security for those within it. Deskilling, or a loss of the kinds of skill or expertise associated with a professional group due to changes in market demand or new requirements, might also be related to this process. Such problems have been evident with respect to teachers and other educators whose social position was far from entrenched in any case, and also generated a range of models of 'new professionalism'.

In response to these new threats, strategies involving a 'new professionalism' have become familiar in different contexts. These might seek a new balance between discretion on one hand and accountability on the other, or aim for a stronger ethic of service and responsibility to the consumer, or promote a restructuring of established work patterns in the interests of making them more flexible and responsive. Professionals themselves have in many cases tried to find fresh ways of asserting their identity, networking and appealing to their clientele through the media, marketing techniques and the new technologies. Educators have begun to respond to these challenges, leading to a wide range of debates about future strategic development at an institutional, local, national and increasingly an international level. Indeed the emergence of the global professional, taking advantage of new possibilities allowed by international transport and communications technology, takes these debates to a qualitatively different phase. At the same time, ideals and traditions relating to older and historical forms of professionalism continue to resonate strongly. The coming decades will no doubt witness the persistence and perhaps the escalation of arguments about the nature and role of professionalism, in education as in other areas of society, together with renewed efforts to attain security, status and a measure of control in the changing conditions of the twenty-first century.

See also: accountability; autonomy; church; law; medicine; Schön, Donald; teaching profession

Further reading

Acker, S. (1999) 'Caring as work for women educators'. In E. Smyth, S. Acker, P. Bourne and A. Prentice (eds) *Challenging Professions: Historical and Contemporary Perspectives on Women's Professional Work*, Toronto: University of Toronto Press.

Eraut, M. (1994) *Developing Professional Knowledge and Competence*, London: Falmer Press.

Freidson, E. (1994) *Professionalism Reborn: Theory, Prophecy and Policy*, Oxford: Blackwell.

Hargreaves, A. and Goodson, I. (1996) 'Teachers' professional lives: aspirations and actualities'. In I. Goodson and A. Hargreaves (eds) *Teachers' Professional Lives*, London: Falmer.

Lortie, D. C. (1975) *Schoolteacher: A Sociological Study*, Chicago IL: University of Chicago Press.

McCulloch, G., Helsby, G. and Knight, P. (2000) *The Politics of Professionalism: Teachers and the Curriculum*, London: Continuum.

Perkin, H. (1989/2002) *The Rise of Professional Society: England since 1880*, London: Routledge.

Schön, D. A. (1983) *The Reflective Practitioner: How Professionals Think in Action*, London: Temple Smith.

Torstendahl, R. (1990) 'Introduction: promotion and strategies of knowledge-based groups'. In R. Torstendahl and M. Burrage (eds) *The*

Formation of Professions: Knowledge, State and Strategy, London: Sage.

GARY McCULLOCH

PROFESSIONAL EDUCATION

Professional education embraces educational activities for practising professionals. These may include conferences, courses and other events. Eraut has argued that while professionals continually learn on the job in consequence of their encountering cases, problems and projects, 'case-specific learning ... may not contribute a great deal to their general professional knowledge base unless the case is regarded as special rather than routine and time is set aside to deliberate upon its significance' (Eraut 1994: 10). This has created demand among professional workers, he argues, for more opportunities to participate in off-the-job learning and to reflect upon 'critical incidents' that have shaped, and sometimes clouded, their professional lives. The global rise of the professional doctorate may be seen as one response to this demand: the Doctor in Education (Ed.D.) degree, for example, is popular among busy education professionals, including head teachers and principals, who wish to reflect upon practice, undertake research and make connections between theory and practice. In the past decade, across several countries, taught university programmes, especially at master's and doctoral levels, have sought to bring professionals from a range of backgrounds together in order that they may learn from each other, as well as from lectures and texts. Such programmes may focus on the nature of twenty-first-century professionalism and professional identity, on the similarities and differences between professional sectors and on possible blueprints for professional reform.

See also: continued/continuing professional development; doctorate; profession/professionalism/professionalisation; reflective practitioner

Further reading

Eraut, M. (1994) *Developing Professional Knowledge and Competence*, London: Falmer Press.

DAVID CROOK

PROFESSOR

A professor has qualifications and reputation that confer high academic status, usually in a university but sometimes in a school. This status will be based on a high degree of expert knowledge in a particular field or area, generally developed through research that is published in books and academic journal articles, but in some cases through teaching. In research-oriented universities the position is most likely to be awarded for outstanding research. In many countries, the position of professor is gained by only a small proportion of academic staff, either by promotion within an institution or by appointment in open competition. The holder may be awarded a Chair, whether personal (for example if the professorship is gained through promotion within the institution) or in a particular area of study. In others, including the United States, the title is held more widely and there are a number of gradations such as assistant professor. In some faculties and departments there are a number of professors and they may form a group as a professoriate.

Many universities maintain a custom and practice that new professors present a professorial lecture to set out their views on their area of study. When they retire, professors usually keep their title as a courtesy, and their university may appoint them to an emeritus professorship in honour of their service to the field. The public stereotype of a professor is of someone (generally male) who is so intensely preoccupied with their subject that they tend to have a personality disorder of some kind, for example being 'absent-minded' in everyday life (as in the 1961 film *The Absent Minded Professor*, with Professor Ned Brainard played by the actor Fred Macmurray), or 'nutty' (as in Jerry Lewis' *The Nutty Professor*, 1963), or perversely ill at ease in society (as with Professor Welch in Kingsley Amis' humorous university novel *Lucky Jim*, 1954). The stereotype may have at least a kernel of truth insofar as men have been much more likely than women to become professors, whatever their work–life balance, although this unequal gender distribution has now begun to be addressed in many countries.

See also: higher education; university

GARY McCULLOCH

PROGRAMMED LEARNING

Programmed learning is an educational technique that focuses on learning through small, incremental steps with the purpose of eliciting correct responses that can be immediately reinforced. The technique was promoted by B. F. Skinner to 'manage human learning under controlled conditions'. Each step of the technique, called a frame, typically contains information from which the student must supply a correct multiple-choice or recognition response. The student may follow the prepared and logically sequenced material in a book, on a computer, or using a 'teaching machine' that Skinner developed specifically for this purpose. Generally self-paced and self-administered, the student works independently on each frame until the correct response is achieved. If the student's response is correct then he will advance to the next level of material. In some models of the technique, an incorrect response will lead to a path that provides more background or supplementary material. Programmed learning reflects the theory of operant conditioning where the consequences of a behaviour will inform a subject's response to a stimulus, in contrast to classical conditioning where it is the stimulus itself that informs the subject's response. Ideally, the positive reinforcement a subject receives from providing a correct answer will promote increased correct responses. One difficulty with programmed learning is the limitations that such a narrow and formalised

instructional technique present with regard to the student's ability to transfer knowledge from one setting to another.

See also: learning; Skinner, Burrhus Fredric

PAUL COLLINS

PROGRESSION

In education, progression describes the process of moving forward to the next stage. Moving through elementary/primary schooling and secondary education, possibly to employment, post-compulsory or higher education demonstrates student progression through the education system. Where compulsory education is based on 'age-grading', cohorts of same-age students move to the next class or school type together, in contrast to multi-age or multigrade teaching arrangements, where there is a mixture of learner ages and abilities.

Educationists sometimes speak of students' progression through a curriculum or syllabus: in physical education, for example, there may be progression from early movement exercises to the practising of skills demonstrating control and coordination to participation in competitive team sports involving tactics. Independent learning curriculum materials are normally packaged in a way that facilitates progression, with learners perhaps working through a series of work cards or exercises as they become more proficient. Learning providers sometimes use the term in their marketing: a series of modules or courses may be advertised, for example, as a pathway of progression to higher education or to a professional qualification. Where parallel academic and vocational pathways exist in secondary or post-compulsory education, a progression route to university may be identified for each. For those in employment, participation in continuing education, professional development and training courses, attendance at conferences and at other events may enhance opportunities for career progression.

See also: continued/continuing professional development; continuing education; learning career; learning curve; multigrade education

DAVID CROOK

PROGRESSIVE EDUCATION

By the late nineteenth century, citizens in many Western nations were discussing something called the 'new' or 'progressive' impulse in education. Contemporaries could not agree about the origins, definition, or precise meaning of progressive education. Nor can historians today. Yet the concept remains useful since it helps capture an evolving critique of traditional forms of mass instruction associated with state-sponsored schooling. It also retains its resonance since it posits an alternative way of looking at the nature of children, learning, and the educational process. Never a static idea or coherent set of programmes, progressive education has informed the writings of key educationists and reformers, spawned numerous professional organisations, and has often been embraced by teacher educators in many Western nations. To the chagrin of many of its advocates, it has often shaped educational theory more than educational practice, but its appeal among liberal and radical educators remains striking.

The earliest advocates of the new education knew what they were against. While applauding the spread of literacy, mass education, and schools in the nineteenth century, they attacked the formalism of established school practices, characterised by a fixed curriculum oriented around textbooks, sing-song instructional methods, rote memorisation, and student competition. Leading progressive theorists in Europe and America shared some basic assumptions about education. They usually desired more freedom for the child; greater recognition of children's stages of development and of each individual pupil's needs, interests, and experience; new curricular innovations to make students more active learners; and learning environments that enhanced the growth of the child in harmonious relationship with peers and the natural world (Cremin 1961). By the mid-twentieth century, progressives attracted to cognitive psychology also wanted education to promote enquiry and problem solving.

United in opposition to conventional forms of discipline and instruction, early theorists of progressive education drew upon diverse strands of educational theory. Some applauded the writings of the Moravian cleric, John Amos Comenius (1592–1671), who wanted children to learn from nature, play, and tangible, real objects prior to formal instruction in textbooks; others praised the English writer John Locke (1632–1704), who famously wrote that most of what people become is due to their education. Jean-Jacques Rousseau, the eccentric genius, electrified the educational world with his great fictional work, *Emile* (1762), where he explained how to rear a child through natural methods. Rousseau's views on religion made him a persona non grata among many child-centred educators. Others liked his positive views of children and preference for experience over books in their early education. Like Locke, he emphasised the needs of the individual child (and not those of adult society). Rousseau greatly impressed Johann Heinrich Pestalozzi (1746–1827), the Swiss giant among the progressives. Pestalozzi's pedagogy, however, also reflected his own favourable views of peasant family life, particularly women's role in child-rearing, and his personal observations on how orphans and poor scholars learned in his model schools. Friedrich Froebel (1782–1852) in turn, the famous German inventor of the kindergarten, drew much inspiration from Pestalozzi, whom he apprenticed with, but was also influenced by science, evangelical Protestantism, and romanticism (Reese 2005).

Pestalozzi and Froebel were without peer in the galaxy of pedagogical stars in post-Napoleonic Europe. Today, however, John Dewey (1859–1952) remains the most familiar name associated with child-centred education, 'learning by doing', and other concepts linked with progressive education. In reality, while a critic of traditional educational practices, Dewey was also critical of Pestalozzi, Froebel, and his own followers and rejected the popular notion that he was the father of progressive education. If anyone deserved that title, he believed, it was Francis W. Parker (1837–1902). As a school administrator in Quincy, Massachusetts (1875–80) and elsewhere, Parker became the most popular advocate of the new education in America after the Civil War. In his published writings, he attacked the mind-numbing pedagogical regimen of the typical school and called for more student-friendly teaching methods. Like other American progressives, Parker visited model schools on the continent and also profited from university study in Germany, one of many examples of the intimate linkages among reformers in the Old World and New.

In numerous speeches, essays, and books, progressives everywhere rejected the traditional Christian view that children, born with original sin, needed firm if not harsh discipline to break their will. While they applauded the spread of literacy and rising state provision for schools, they attacked traditional educational norms, particularly corporal punishment and reliance upon textbooks and rote learning. Rousseau had urged his readers to learn to see the world through the child's eyes. Progressive reformers extended this claim and argued that educators should adapt the school to the child, not the child to the school. Followers of Pestalozzi, fearing the unsettling effects of the Industrial Revolution and other social changes, favoured an education that tapped and strengthened all of the senses, not just the faculty of memory. Many championed manual training, to foster eye-and-hand coordination, and object teaching, to instruct children more naturally by using familiar objects – such as peas and beans in counting – before subjecting the child to textbooks. 'Educating the hand, heart, and mind' became a familiar progressive slogan, replaced

in the twentieth century by new cliches such as 'learning by doing' and 'hands on' pedagogy.

Encountering resistance to their ideas in existing schools, progressive educators beginning in the nineteenth century often established model or experimental schools, frequently outside of the purview of state control. Whether privately or publicly funded, progressive schools defied easy characterisation, since the freedom to experiment assured curricular and pedagogical diversity. Consider the various well known expressions of the new education: *Pestalozzian schools* in *Casa dei Bambini* in San Lorenzo in Italy, Swedish *Folk Schools* and Soviet progressive schools and *platoon schools* in the 1920s and 1930s, English *infant schools* in the 1950s and 1960s, and assorted 'open classrooms' in the United States in the 1970s all wore the progressive banner. Other activists worked in the Dalton schools, Waldorf schools, and in other unique learning environments, offering an alternative to the didactic, textbook, tradition-bound school systems prevalent in most Western nations (Rohrs and Lenhart 1995). Progressive schools all exemplified a spirit of revolt against formalism and the desire to enliven instruction along more cooperative lines to enhance the freedom of the child.

With the spread of research universities in the West in the late nineteenth century, university-trained activists, often academicians, led renewed campaigns for progressive education and child-centred learning. Like earlier advocates of the new education, they tried to improve instruction and child-nurture among the very young, focusing on early childhood and elementary education. The establishment of education and psychology as university subjects gave the study of the child a more scientific and professional aura. Those trained in psychology such as G. Stanley Hall and John Dewey brought its insights to bear in understanding the educational process. In the 1880s, Hall became prominent for studying the *Contents of Children's Minds*, and Child Study Associations – some guided by romantic views of the child, others more concerned with scientific measurement and assessment of individual growth – formed in many nations. University-educated scholars studied the child in educational research bureaus and institutes in many American and European settings. Some reformers such as Montessori were trained as physicians, sharing an intense interest with early romantic poets, novelists, and other activists in discovering the best means to secure healthy human development (Rohrs and Lenhart 1995: 87–91). Few child-centred theorists paid as much attention to adolescents or secondary schools, since younger children appeared more malleable and the higher schools were especially hidebound and subject-, not student-oriented. Alternative high schools formed on the fringes of the American secondary system in the late twentieth century, but many secondary schools remained oriented around familiar subject matter and old-fashioned pedagogy.

Inspired by Dewey's example, leading American universities in the early twentieth century established model laboratory schools on campus to study children and experiment with different teaching methods. Particular schools, such as Teachers College, Columbia University, in the United States, and the Institute of Education, University of London, England, became prominently associated with the advancement of progressive education. At Columbia, William Kilpatrick, a follower of Dewey, developed the famous *project method*, a curricular innovation that challenged traditional didactic instruction (Kliebard 2004: 135–40). Similarly, Susan Isaacs and her colleagues in London championed innovative teaching practices in the English primary schools during the inter-war period (Rohrs and Lenhart 1995: 336–37).

In addition to its changing cavalcade of leaders, progressive education was kept alive and revitalised in the twentieth century through new professional organisations, which held conferences and published specialist journals that publicised new developments in child welfare and educational research. Professional groups arose to advance

the new education in many nations, from Europe to Australia. The Progressive Education Association (founded in 1919) in the United States and the New Education Fellowship (founded in 1920) in Europe became internationally famous, their members champions of educational experimentation and improvement. Progressives remained a diverse coalition of reform-minded individuals. They sometimes strongly disagreed among themselves whether their goal was the reconstruction of society or simply more freedom for the child and less teacher- and subject-centred classrooms.

Whether or not they engaged in what Dewey called sugar-coated educational practices and wallowed in childhood sentimentality, progressives knew that it was easier to espouse innovative educational ideals than to transform schools (Cuban 1984). Progressivism often captivated teacher educators, whether in early normal schools or later in schools of education, and the spread of kindergartens, infant schools, and other innovations in different times and places were tangible examples of the new education. But many progressive schools remained private and elite, out of the reach of the masses of children, whose parents often favoured traditional discipline and education in the basics. While Pestalozzi, Montessori, and other progressive educators had worked with poor children, progressive educators frequently found themselves criticised for mostly teaching advantaged, if not elite, children.

Innovative, child-centred teaching practices appeared in prestigious laboratory schools on college campuses and in exceptional suburban public schools such as Winnetka, Illinois, during the 1920s and 1930s. But working-class citizens were rarely interested in an education that aimed to promote creativity and human freedom. In the United States, the outcry against increased standardised testing in the 1990s came mostly from a handful of affluent suburban school districts that prized more flexible teaching methods in their otherwise high-status academic systems.

Even progressive innovations may be changed by the schools more than the other way around. In Japan, and increasingly in the United States, kindergarten pupils are tested to ensure their readiness for first grade and for success in educational systems based on the mastery of textbook knowledge as measured by competitive examinations. Tradition has often stood like a mighty fortress ready to absorb or repel the next wave of progressive reforms.

See also: child-centred education; Comenius, Johann Amos; Dewey, John; educational theory; Froebel, Friedrich; individualised instruction/personalised learning; Isaacs, Susan; Locke, John; Montessori, Maria; open plan; pedagogy; Pestalozzi, Johann Heinrich; project method; Rousseau, Jean-Jacques

Further reading

Cremin, L. A. (1961) *The Transformation of the School: Progressivism in American Education 1867–1957*, New York: Vintage Books.

Cuban, L. (1984) *How Teachers Taught: Constancy and Change in American Classrooms 1890–1980*, New York: Longman.

Gordon, P. and Aldrich, R. (eds) (1997) *Biographical Dictionary of North American and European Educationists*, London: The Woburn Press.

Kliebard, H. M. (2004) *The Struggle for the American Curriculum 1893–1958*, New York: Routledge-Falmer.

Reese, W. J. (2005) *America's Public Schools: From The Common School To 'No Child Left Behind'*, Baltimore MD: Johns Hopkins University Press.

Rohrs, H. and Lenhart, V. (eds) (1995) *Progressive Education Across the Continents: A Handbook*, Frankfurt am Main: Peter Lang.

WILLIAM J. REESE

PROJECT METHOD

The specification of 'projects' for school children to work on over a period of several days, and sometimes weeks, is a familiar teaching approach. Although he did not claim to have originated it, the Project Method (PM) is indissolubly linked with the name of William Heard Kilpatrick (1871–

1965), a collaborator of the American pragmatist philosopher and educationist, John Dewey. It is generally considered a means by which students can develop independent research and learning skills, gathering information from the school library, community resources, their home and so forth. Many famous educational theorists can be associated with the PM, for the ideas that underlie it have been common currency among child-centred educators for at least three centuries. Ideas such as 'learning by doing' and a relatively restricted role for the teacher may be found in the work of Jean-Jacques Rousseau (1712–78) and Johann Heinrich Pestalozzi (1746–1827). These ideas were attractive to vocational educators and manual trainers such as the Swede Otto Salomon (1849–1907) and the American agricultural educator Rufus W. Stimson (1868–1947), who developed a home project method in the first decade of the twentieth century.

Kilpatrick was appointed to teach philosophy of education at Teachers College, Columbia University, New York in 1912 and he stayed there until his retirement in 1937. In an article, described by Cremin (1961) as 'a theoretical analysis,' published in 1918, Kilpatrick defined the project as a 'whole-hearted purposeful activity proceeding in a social environment', and a 'hearty purposeful act'. As an example of a project he referred to a girl making a dress in a 'whole-hearted purposeful' way in a social environment. Projects, however, did not have to be only individual. They could also be collective; the wholehearted action of a group.

A purposeful act, he thought, was a typical unit of a worthy life, which in turn was the ideal of democratic citizenship. Moreover, it was consistent with the 'laws of learning' that Kilpatrick held to be the stimulus–response theories that the psychologist Edward L. Thorndike (1874–1949) promoted. A purposeful act also provided criteria by which to judge the ordinary school. Starting with the view that the 'child is naturally active, especially along social lines', a statement which might equally have emanated from Friedrich Froebel (1782–1852), Kilpatrick criticised the 'regime of coercion' which had often reduced schools to what he termed 'aimless dawdling' and had turned pupils into 'selfish individualists'. Wholehearted purposeful activity, in contrast, was 'the best guarantee of the utilisation of the child's native capacities now too frequently wasted'. Proper guidance by the skilful teacher would lead to character building and efficiency, an end of schooling much discussed at the time in the United States of America.

Kilpatrick's was a child-centred approach that was opposed to what he referred to as 'customary set-task alone-at-your-own-desk procedure' and also to extrinsic subject matter or school knowledge typically organised into subjects. This he felt had been rendered obsolete by the social changes wrought by industrialism. His point, which continues to resonate in contemporary debates on education, was that the future is unknowable and therefore it is best, in the words of the ubiquitous slogan to teach 'how to think rather than what to think'.

For the PM to work properly, Kilpatrick thought, changes in schooling were required, 'in room furniture and equipment, perhaps in school architecture'. It necessitated also 'the new type of text-book, the new kind of curriculum and program, possibly new plans of grading and promotion, most of all a changed attitude as to what to wish for in the way of achievement'.

This revolutionary approach appealed to educators in the Soviet Union in the early 1920s, who were trying to construct a new school in a revolutionary society. The project method was promoted there by Nadezhda K. Krupskaya (1869–1939), Lenin's wife and a prominent figure in the Commissariat of Education. Containing elements consistent with Marxist polytechnic education, it was enthusiastically advocated by Victor N. Shulgin (1894–1965), head of the Institute of Educational Research in Moscow, who proclaimed the 'withering away of the school'. Education,

he argued, during the 'cultural revolution' of 1928 to 1931, should take the form of projects organised outside school. However, in 1931, the Central Committee of the Communist Party of the Soviet Union condemned the 'ill-considered craze for the project method': teacher-directed pedagogy and a traditional subject-based curriculum were reinstated in conformity with Stalin's view of the requirements of Soviet industrialisation.

Reaction to the child-centred nature of the PM and a reassertion of the 'orderly organization of subject matter' came from Dewey at around the same period. Schools in the USA and elsewhere proved resistant to the adoption of the PM but, periodically, support for it and criticism of teacher-centred subject-based education still finds expression.

See also: child-centred education; deschooling; homework; individualised instruction/personalised learning; progressive education

Further reading

Beineke, J. A. (1998) *And There Were Giants in the Land*, New York: Peter Lang.
Cremin, L. A. (1961) *The Transformation of the School*, New York: Vintage Books.
Holmes, L. E. (1991) *The Kremlin and the Schoolhouse: Reforming Education in Soviet Russia, 1917–1931*, Bloomington IN: Indiana University Press.
Levine, D. (2001) 'The Project Method and the stubborn grammar of schooling: a Milwaukee story', *Educational Foundations*, 15(1): 5–24.
Moore, G. E. (1988) 'The forgotten leader in agricultural education: Rufus W. Stimson', *The Journal of the American Association of Teacher Educators in Agriculture*, 29(3): 50–58.

KEVIN J. BREHONY

PSYCHOLOGY

Psychology is derived from the Greek *psyche*, meaning mind or soul, and *logos*, meaning reason or study. The subject may therefore be defined as the study of the human mind – the 'science of mental life', according to William James, one of the founding fathers of psychology – although it also focuses on individual and group behaviour. An early psychologist, Hermann Ebbinghaus (1850–1909) famously wrote in 1908 that 'Psychology has a long past, but only a short history'. By this he meant that, while thinking about human feelings, emotions, intelligence and behaviour is far from new, the disciplined study of these issues only emerged from work conducted in German and American laboratories in the late nineteenth century. James, a professor at Harvard University, helped to establish the 'new' psychology with the publication of his seminal 1890 text *Principles of Psychology*.

There are several distinct approaches to the study of psychology: cognitive psychology focuses on such issues as how mental processes work; experimental psychologists may investigate learning, memory and emotions; social psychology studies the behaviour of individuals and groups; developmental psychologists are interested in child development and ageing; while clinical psychology is focused towards understanding, preventing, and relieving psychological disorders and promoting well-being. Educational psychologists and psychologists of education have many shared interests, but the former work mostly with individual learners, while the work of the latter focuses more on educational mechanisms and processes, including testing.

See also: child development; cognition; learning; motivation; psychology of education

DAVID CROOK

PSYCHOLOGY OF EDUCATION

Psychology of education may be defined as the psychological study of educational processes and systems or, more widely, as the study of educational growth and behaviour in all its aspects: intellectual, emotional, social and physical. The term is sometimes used as a synonym for educational psychology though this definition may confuse readers in that educational psychology is both study and

research in an academic discipline and a field of professional expertise in the clinical and school settings of the child guidance and school psychological services. This brief article discusses the topic as an area of educational scholarship and research. As an academic discipline, psychology of education varies internationally in the way it is organised. The American Psychological Society has a Division of Educational Psychology dealing with the academic discipline and a Division of School Psychology catering for the professional application of the subject. The British Psychological Society has equivalent provision in a Psychology of Education Section to meet the scientific concerns of members and a Division of Educational and Child Psychology to deal with professional issues. There is a separate Scottish Division of Educational Psychology. Occasional attempts by British scholars to retitle the discipline as School Psychology or Psychopedagogy have been unsuccessful.

As an academic discipline the history and development of the subject is entwined with that of child development and child psychiatry, and psychology of education can probably claim parentage from the discipline of education as well as from general psychology. Some writers trace psychology of education to classical Greece and others have argued a case for seeing historical figures such as the Valencian scholar Juan Vives (died 1540) and the Genevan philosopher Jean-Jacques Rousseau (died 1778) as fathers of the discipline. It is more conventional to see the subject as developing to meet the practical needs of teachers in the expanding mass educational systems of late nineteenth-century Europe and North America.

Drawing on the pedagogic traditions of continental Europe, men like Rein at Jena and Bain in Scotland attempted to build an educational science, the practice of which was to cross the Atlantic and dominate US development until World War I. The major figures in the USA were William James and G. Stanley Hall. Bibliographically, much psychology of education at this period was subsumed under child study, but increasingly the subject posed questions of research and practice in issues of schooling, the first area to which general psychology applied itself. The need to train large numbers of teachers for state schools created schools of education in universities, promoted education as an academic subject and encouraged the growth of research and scholarship in the psychology of education which thus became a major topic in both theory of education and in the training of teachers. Indeed, before 1944 in the United Kingdom the majority of professors of education were psychologists.

Psychology of education has evolved under a number of influences, all of which are present to various degrees today. Children and adolescents are still studied, though with much more rigour than the early Child Study movement allowed. Experimentalism and psychometrics became the major emphasis in the first half of the twentieth century, owing much to Francis Galton (died 1911) in Britain and to Alfred Binet (died 1911) in France. In the USA up to 1940, educational research was largely 'psychology and measurement' with Lewis Terman and R. B. Cattell major players. In Great Britain up to 1950, in both research councils and in universities 'psychometrics in general and mental or intelligence testing in particular held the field' (Richardson 2002) though the European influences of psychoanalysis, Gestalt psychology and the work of Piaget in Geneva and of Vygotsky in Moscow was to be increasingly reflected in British and American psychology of education from mid-century onwards, though it may be true to argue that Freud, Adler and Jung had greater impact in the USA than in Britain and that the Genevan school of Piaget was strongest in continental Europe. The work of the Tavistock Clinic in London was to place human relations and groupwork at the centre of psychology of education in Britain, and the work of Piagetian scholars was to lead to much work on the development of concepts in the subjects of the school

curriculum though a behaviourist tradition continued strongly in many countries. The 1960s in Britain saw psychology of education established as one of the four basic disciplines of educational studies, and in a period of rapid growth there developed a more eclectic psychology than the old psychometric tradition (Thomas 2007). Developments in Britain were to be exported within the English-speaking world by British psychologists who often took up appointments in the expanding higher education systems of Australia, New Zealand and Canada, for example, at the Schonell Educational Research Centre of the University of Queensland. The last half-century has seen increased volumes of research and teaching in psychology of education worldwide and a plethora of new books, journals and research projects. Not all of this work has come from schools of education, for much has been produced from schools of academic psychology and specialist research institutes like the Buros Institute of Mental Measurement in the USA or the Institute of Psychology of the Chinese Academy of Sciences, or from medical institutions such as the Institute of Psychiatry in London, witness the work of Professor H. J. Eysenck and Sir Michael Rutter.

In Britain, though psychology of education is no longer the major sub-discipline of the 1960s and has lost its former strengths in teacher training, psychologists are still making important contributions to educational studies in areas as diverse as assessment, curriculum, school effectiveness, inclusive education, gender and bilingual education, as well as established fields of previous application such as special education and counselling. Any current British or American text of the subject shows the increasing volume and complexity of research with, for example, older concepts such as self and intelligence now referring to multiple selves and multiple intelligences, and work in neuroscience and genetics influencing theory and application. Schools are no longer the only focus of attention as lifespan learning concepts have encouraged psychologists to look at teaching and learning in tertiary educational institutions and throughout adulthood. Theory and applications vary country by country. India has a psychology of education still developing a variety of topics, whilst France has no equivalent of British schools counselling (Bernard *et al.* 2007)

Though some earlier texts took a narrow cognitive view of psychology of education, most writers from the 1990s onwards have taken a broad view using other areas of theoretical and applied psychology where there is relevance to schools and other educational institutions. Such was the approach taken by Galloway and Edwards (1992) who covered work on classroom interaction and took into account work from sociology and philosophy of education. These authors recognised that their work is not value-free, is grounded in views of the aims of education and the nature of childhood and shares explicit links across the discipline of educational studies. Fontana (1995) has pointed out that it would be arrogant to believe psychology alone has all the answers to educational problems, and in the first decade of the twenty-first century there are still large gaps in our current knowledge that need to be filled. Coming back to where this article began, Galloway and Edwards also believed that the distinction made between psychology of education and educational psychology may have been unhelpful, and see the two approaches as complementary. Readers may judge this for themselves in following up the literature in books and international journals like *British Journal of Educational Psychology* (UK), *Journal of Educational Psychology* (USA), *Contemporary Educational Psychology* (USA), and *School Psychology International* (UK).

See also: Binet, Alfred; education/educational studies; Freud, Sigmund; Galton, Francis; Hall, Granville Stanley; Piaget, Jean; psychometrics; Terman, Lewis M.; Vygotsky, Lev

Further reading

Bernard, J. L., Cohen-Sculi, V. and Guichard, J. (2007) 'Counselling psychology in France: a paradoxical situation', *Applied Psychology: An International Journal*, 56(1): 131–51.
Fontana, D. (1995) *Psychology for Teachers*, London: Macmillan.
Galloway, D. and Edwards, A. (1992) *Secondary School Teaching and Educational Psychology*, London and New York: Longman.
Richardson, W. (2002) 'Educational studies in the United Kingdom, 1940–2002', *British Journal of Educational Studies*, 50(1): 3–56.
Thomas, J. B. (2007) 'Psychology of education in the UK: development in the 1960s', *Educational Studies*, 33(1): 53–65.

JOHN B. THOMAS

PSYCHOMETRICS

Psychometrics is the science of psychological assessment. It originated in ancient China during the Chan dynasty (300 BCE) with a system for the selection and advancement of the emperor's officers of state (Wainer 2000). This system survived in one form or another for hundreds of years, and was ultimately adopted for admission examinations into the Indian, French and US civil services in the nineteenth century. With the scientific revolution in the West, a more mathematical approach to psychometrics developed hand-in-hand with mathematical statistics. Both disciplines claim the early pioneers of Quetelet, Galton, Pearson and Spearman among their founders. Galton, often considered the father of psychometrics, invited visitors to the 1885 International Health Exhibition in London to have their faculties tested in his 'Anthropometric Laboratory' for three pence, the resultant dataset leading to the development of the statistical techniques of correlation and factor analysis that have continued to form the backbone of psychometric procedures ever since.

Psychometric tests can be divided into two broad categories: knowledge-based tests of optimal performance and person-based tests of typical behaviour (Rust and Golombok 2007). In tests of optimal performance, candidates are invited to demonstrate the best they can achieve, examples being school and university examinations, intelligence tests,

tests of numerical or verbal reasoning used in recruitment, and memory and concentration tests used within clinical settings. In tests of typical behaviour, candidates are required to indicate how they would usually behave. Personality and integrity tests, assessments of motivation and values, and career guidance batteries are examples. Both are of practical importance. For example, a person may be able to demonstrate a high degree of competence in accurate and complex calculations, but may have no wish whatsoever to work as an accountant.

Psychometric testing, and other forms of assessment such as interviews, are all underpinned by four psychometric principles. These are reliability, validity, standardisation and freedom from bias. Reliability is the extent to which an assessment is free from error. Test scores are treated as measurements and their degree of accuracy assessed. There is no such thing as a perfectly accurate measurement, even in the physical world, but there are techniques for calibrating and improving accuracy and these form an important part of development. Validity is the degree to which an assessment is able to achieve its purpose. Thus, if the purpose of a test is to select potential high performers for work in the public service, we should be able to call upon some evidence that those with higher scores actually do perform at a superior level. Standardisation is concerned with how decisions based on an assessment are made. A typical example is the application of a threshold or 'pass mark' to a set of results. If the pass mark for entry to a training programme or academic course is set too low, then those selected may find difficulty in handling the material they are expected to learn, while if it is set too high then potential successful achievers may have been unnecessarily excluded. Identification and reduction of bias in assessment, particularly in terms of gender, ethnicity and disability, are a legal requirement within an equal opportunities society.

Psychometricians originated intelligence (IQ) testing, something that remains highly controversial, particularly where claims are made of the innate superiority (or inferiority) of women (or men), minority groups, or inner city dwellers in this respect. Many of these arguments have been rendered sterile by recognition of the importance of the 'Flynn Effect'; the year on year rise in IQ scores over the past century. These far outweigh any differences between groups and render implausible the claim that group differences are necessarily due to genetic causes.

The twenty-first century has seen a rapid increase in the practice and sophistication of psychometric testing. Much of this has been due to developments in information technology and database management, and also to advances in statistical modelling procedures (Rao and Sinharay 2007). Today, over 70 per cent of employers use psychometric tests of ability or personality for recruitment. Tests are also used to diagnose conditions such as dyslexia, memory loss, or the ability to drive. And the psychometric principles themselves play a paramount role in the development and evaluation of the school examination system.

See also: assessment; Galton, Francis; intelligence/intelligence tests; Spearman, Charles

Further reading

Flynn, J. (2007) *What is Intelligence? Beyond the Flynn Effect*, Cambridge: Cambridge University Press.
Rao, C. R. and Sinharay, S. (2007) *Handbook of Statistics, 26: Psychometrics*, Amsterdam: Elsevier.
Rust, J. and Golombok, S. (2007) *Modern Psychometrics*, 3rd edn, London: Routledge.
Wainer, H. (2000) *Computer Adaptive Testing: A Primer*, 2nd edn, Mahwah NJ: Lawrence Erlbaum.

JOHN RUST

PUBLIC LIBRARY

Libraries are institutions providing or restricting access to information, extending the activities of schools, colleges and universities and creating opportunities for informal learning. Traditionally, libraries have been collections of books and periodicals or buildings which housed them. Public libraries are distinctive in being publicly owned and funded, staffed by civil servants and open to those who want to use them. Other libraries belong to individuals, specialist societies and religious, commercial or educational institutions. Depending upon their context, libraries have enabled their users to acquire information and develop ways of interpreting the world.

Collections of written knowledge go back to ancient Mesopotamia, Egypt and Greece, where text was recorded on clay tablets or papyri. By the second century CE, libraries began to store information in bound wooden boards called codices. These codices evolved into books. Public libraries existed in ancient Rome, but given that literacy and leisure were scarce commodities they were used by limited numbers of people. Manuscripts, moreover, had to be copied by hand to produce duplicated versions. Many ancient libraries were destroyed by war, but religious and classical texts survived in Muslim 'halls of science' and Christian monasteries.

The expansion of printing from the sixteenth century increased the production of books. They became cheaper and covered subjects such as politics, science, astrology, commerce, fiction, travel, history and topography. The spread of education in Europe and the Americas increased the demand for books and provision of libraries. They included school, college and university libraries and subscription libraries where individual subscribers bought shares in the institution which allowed them to access publications. The first public libraries emerged through donations from wealthy bibliophiles. The Francis Trigge Chained Library (1598) in Grantham, Lincolnshire, UK, is one early example. Libraries could be contested spaces, as books could threaten as well as illuminate. In Birmingham, UK, the purchase of 'controversial' theological books for the local subscription library in 1787 was a subject of dispute between members of the Anglican Church and the supporters of Joseph Priestley, the radical Unitarian philosopher and educationalist.

National libraries were linked to the growth of the independent nation-state, for example, in Athens (1828), Buenos Aires (1812), Rio de Janeiro (1810 and 1814) and Washington (1800). They were symbols of nationhood and provided, amongst other things, learning opportunities for those wanting to find out about their country's history, culture and identity. National libraries were also created by post-colonial African and Asian states in the late twentieth century.

The urban public library which emerged in nineteenth- and twentieth-century Britain and America, reflected the growth of civic culture, a belief in the civilising role of education and representative democracy, although even in the 1940s, most libraries in the southern USA were closed to blacks. Two Americans heavily influenced the twentieth-century public library: Melvil Dewey (1851–1931) and Andrew Carnegie (1835–1911). Dewey, the president of the American Library Association, provided a standardised method for cataloguing and easily locating books on shelves via the Dewey Decimal Classification System. Carnegie, a Scottish-born American industrialist, believed in making knowledge widely accessible and financed the construction of thousands of public libraries in the English-speaking world.

By the late twentieth century, many public libraries were places where books could be borrowed as well as consulted, and repositories for newspapers, magazines, archives, maps, prints, photographs, microfilm, microfiche, audio and video tapes, LPs, CDs and DVDs. They also provided resources and activities to cater for children, young people, older residents, business customers, speakers and readers of different languages, the visually impaired, family and local historians and those seeking educational courses and leisure activities. Mobile libraries emerged to provide services to the housebound and those in districts without library buildings. By the twenty-first century, many libraries extended their operations to enable users to send and receive emails, access information electronically and purchase refreshments. Websites reveal the range of services that libraries offer. Public libraries are channels for public demands, but their future is not assured; the decline of book borrowing together with financial pressures because of competing demands for public money have led to the closure of many buildings in Western countries.

See also: informal/nonformal learning; literacy

Further reading

Johnson, E. D. and Harris, M. H. (1976) *History of Libraries in the Western World*, Metuchen NJ: Scarecrow Press.

Kelly, T. (1970) *History of Public Libraries in Great Britain 1845–1975*, London: Library Association.

Stam, D. H. (ed.) (2001) *International Dictionary of Library Histories*, vols 1 and 2, Chicago IL and London: Fitzroy Dearborn.

MALCOLM DICK

PUBLIC SCHOOL

In most parts of the world the term 'public school' connotes a school of any type (e.g. elementary/primary or high/secondary) that is supported by tax revenues or other public funds. These are schools open to all without payment of additional fees. In the United States, for example, a twelve-grade system of public schooling has evolved, permitting children to continuously progress from kindergarten to college or university without payment of fees.

By contrast, British 'public schools' are decidedly not for the general public: these are the most prestigious (and expensive) private fee-paying schools. British public schools have membership of prestigious bodies, such as the Headmasters' and Headmistresses' Conference or the Girls' Schools Association, many are boarding schools and a

significant proportion serve the 13–18 age range, in contrast to most state secondary schools which recruit their youngest pupils at age eleven. Many British public schools originated from the endowments of pious founders wishing to educate poor local children, but with the passage of time the leading public schools – including Eton College, Rugby School, Westminster School and Winchester College – positioned themselves as schools for the elite.

See also: independent/private school/education; school

DAVID CROOK

PUPIL

Pupil is a term that is commonly used interchangeably with student, though the former normally denotes a younger learner enrolled in compulsory schooling. It is most widely used in Britain and the Commonwealth countries. Pupil learning typically varies by age. Once they progress from primary to secondary education, for example, pupils normally focus more on test and examination outcomes and on progression to employment or further study.

Today, pupils and teachers are located at the opposite ends of the learning and teaching spectrum, but the pupil–teacher system, exported by Victorian Britain to many parts of the British empire, was, for a period, an important element in national teacher training systems. This apprenticeship model is still to be found in the field of English law, where trainee barristers must complete a one-year supervised 'pupillage' in a set of law chambers prior to qualification.

See also: student

DAVID CROOK

PUPIL MOBILITY

Pupil mobility refers to movement between or changes of school, either once or on repeated occasions, at times other than the normal age at which pupils start or finish their education at a school. It may, or may not, be associated with geographical mobility or change of home. It is therefore important to distinguish between (a) change of school, (b) change of home, and (c) a simultaneous change of school and of home, with research indicating the latter may have the strongest association with pupils' social adjustment and attainment. It is important to distinguish between a focus on the progress of individual pupils and the calculation of summary indicators at a higher level such as a school. Some school-level aggregate measures of pupil mobility total the number of pupils entering the school (joiners) plus the number of pupils leaving the school (leavers) at non-standard times, and can create school mobility rates which exceed 100 per cent. It should be noted in literature searches that other terms such as pupil or school 'transience', 'turbulence' and 'casual admissions' have previously been used in the context of pupil mobility.

The recent increase in interest in pupil mobility among education professionals, both in the United Kingdom and United States, has centred on the adverse effects that high levels of pupil mobility may have on the interpretation of school performance data, on school funding formulas, and on strategies such as progress monitoring and school target setting. There is a widespread assumption that pupil mobility is disruptive to education, either directly by disrupting curriculum continuity and progression, or indirectly through domestic stress or poor social adjustment. However, the research evidence in relation to outcomes such as attainment tests, graduation rates, high school dropout and psychosocial adjustment is mixed. Some research supports a strong link between mobility and low attainment (see Rumberger and Larson 1998). However, research based on longitudinal analysis of pupil progress suggests the association between pupil mobility and attainment may often be explained by pupils' low prior attainment, their socio-economic circumstances and other background factors (see Strand and Demie 2006). The weight of current evidence within the primary phase (ages 4–11) is that change of school is not directly related to poor educational progress, although evidence within the secondary phase (ages 11–16) is more equivocal.

There are several factors that may moderate the impact of mobility. For example, the impact may be greater in secondary, rather than primary school; it may be greater for subjects like mathematics than English; it may be greater when allied to a simultaneous change of home; and there may be a cumulative impact of the total number of moves over a pupil's education. Other important mediating factors include parental attitudes to the school move, and the effectiveness of the schools' induction procedures and support for mobile pupils.

Overall, the reasons for the school move are vital in assessing the potential impact, if any, on attainment. Where the mobility reflects international mobility then the association with attainment is pronounced (Strand and Demie 2006). Such pupils face substantial social, cultural and linguistic adjustments, beyond a simple change of school. More generally, children of refugees, asylum seekers or labour migrants who have just entered the country directly from overseas, and pupils admitted following family breakdown, domestic difficulties, the imprisonment of a parent or school problems such as exclusion, may all be more likely to experience problems. At the same time, there is little evidence to demonstrate a negative impact of mobility for children of professional and managerial workers and other high-income groups who are mobile for career reasons, or children of military families who experience many moves but typically within a structured and supportive whole school framework. The individual circumstances of pupils, the attitudes and actions of parents and the effectiveness of school support for newcomers are all relevant to pupils' adjustment and progress.

Change of school and/or home undoubtedly involves social and emotional adjustment, but the impact on pupils' educational progress or longer-term psychosocial adjustment is less clear cut. Teachers, parents and educators should maintain high expectations for the educational progress of mobile pupils.

See also: attainment; dropouts; early school leaving; exclusion/expulsion; school

Further reading

Dobson, J. and Henthorne, K. (1999) *Pupil Mobility in Schools*, DfEE Research Report RR168, London: DfEE.

Rumberger, R. and Larson, A. (1998) 'Student mobility and the increased risk of high school dropout', *American Journal of Education*, 107(1): 1–35.

Strand, S. and Demie, F. (2006) 'Pupil mobility, attainment and progress in primary school', *British Educational Research Journal*, 32(4): 551–68.

STEVE STRAND

Q

QUALIFICATIONS

Qualifications are attained upon successful completion of a programme of education, training or work experience. The first qualifications attained by individuals typically follow the successful completion of public examinations at around the age of sixteen with others often taken around the age of eighteen. Such examinations are usually 'national', but the International Baccalaureate is recognised internationally. Initial school-level qualifications are frequently in such academic subjects as mathematics, language and science, but children, as well as adults, may embark upon vocational, or pre-vocational, qualifications too, for example in such areas as business studies, bricklaying, hairdressing or travel and tourism.

Very frequently a certificate will be awarded detailing the holder's name alongside the qualification attained. This may be shown or supplied to educational institutions or prospective employers when applying for a course of study or a job. Award-bearing programmes of study, leading to a qualification, are widely thought to motivate learners most and, although there will always be notable exceptions, there is a strong relationship between the individual's highest level of qualification and earning power in the employment market. Those applying for university ahead of sitting the examinations required for entry will normally be given some target grades: if these are achieved, the candidate is regarded as sufficiently qualified to begin their studies.

Qualifications are normally subject to hierarchies. In the university, for example, the qualifications for beginning a master's programme are likely to include the possession of an undergraduate degree. Similarly, entry to a doctoral programme may only be open to those qualified at master's level. Professional qualification routes may also require the successful completion of work experience, working alongside a mentor: in the United Kingdom trainee barristers must secure and complete a 'pupillage' with a practising member of the profession, while junior hospital doctors must accompany senior colleagues on their ward rounds as part of the qualifying process. The trainee school teacher normally completes a substantial period of school-based teaching practice before he/she is deemed qualified to teach without close supervision, and in some countries those wishing to become a deputy head or head teacher must successfully complete a further qualification.

The acquisition of higher-level qualifications, in combination with the gaining of work experience, is the normal route to professional progression: a 'fully qualified' accountant who has passed all the expected examinations and been admitted into the membership of a professional body, is likely to charge a higher hourly rate to clients than a 'part-qualified' accountant. Business clients may choose to switch to another accountant on the grounds of cost at this point, deeming that a partly qualified professional is sufficient to review the ledgers. By contrast, even if it were permitted, it seems unlikely that many would choose to board an aeroplane flown by a pilot who was less than fully qualified, and the householder employing an unqualified or apprentice electrician or plumber to undertake major works might be considered foolish.

Academic studies of international labour markets and social mobility have frequently focused on data about qualification structures and levels. The Comparative Analysis of Social Mobility in Industrial Nations (CASMIN) schema illustrates the hierarchical nature of educational qualifications and distinguishes between those that are 'academic' and others that are 'vocationally oriented'. At a global level, programmes leading to qualifications have proliferated in the past quarter of a century. A number of difficulties follow from this: some awards are not recognised by rival bodies, and universities have to be confident in the 'equivalence' of qualifications held by prospective students from overseas. Many countries have an agency with overall responsibility for a national framework of qualifications – the Qualifications and Curriculum Authority in the UK, for example – and across Europe there has been gradual convergence towards the Bologna Framework of Qualifications for the European Higher Education Area. Certain trades and professions, too, are characterised by an 'alphabet soup' of practitioner qualifications. The streamlining of qualifications is generally held to be a desirable objective.

Although paper-based qualifications are of huge significance, the qualifications required to undertake some work may be linked to personal or physical qualities and life experience, rather than educational assessment. The principal qualifications to be a bodyguard may be related to physique and strength, for example, while other work may demand that the person appointed should, above all else, be 'a good listener'.

See also: attainment; certificate/certification; degree; diploma; examinations; skills; subjects; training

Further reading

National Academic Recognition Information Centre (1996) *International Guide to Qualifications in Education*, 4th edn, London: Mansell.
Shavit, Y. and Müller, W. (1998) *From School to Work: A Comparative Study of Educational Qualifications and Occupational Destinations*, Oxford: Clarendon Press.

DAVID CROOK

QUALITATIVE RESEARCH

The field of educational studies has seen a burgeoning of research in recent years. Much of this research is conceptualised within a qualitative research framework and is reported in such areas as ethnography, action research, life history, connoisseurship and illuminative evaluation, where the most common research techniques used are participant observation and in-depth interviewing. In considering this development it is important to highlight two main research paradigms. The first paradigm is modelled on the natural sciences with an emphasis on empirical quantifiable observations, the object being to seek causal relationship leading to explanations. The other paradigm arises out of the humanities with an emphasis on qualitative data and associated interpretive approaches to analysis, the object being to seek understanding.

Various strands in qualitative inquiry can be identified. Some commence their distinctions at the epistemological level, differentiating between studies which are built upon the assumptions of continental idealism, phenomenological and hermeneutic philosophers, and the critical theory approach, particularly that of the Frankfurt School. Others discriminate between those who base their work on a positivist, post-positivist, constructivist, feminist, ethnic, Marxist or cultural studies framework. Also, one needs to ponder the difference between qualitative data and qualitative analysis. Both quantitative and qualitative researchers commence with qualitative data, whether it be in the form of interview material, observations, ticks in boxes, documents, photographs, or a multitude of other kinds of artefacts. The particular research approach adopted dictates the kind of qualitative data gathered. Nevertheless, both the quantitative and the qualitative researcher are then faced with analysing their data. The quantitative researcher quantifies the data and then analyses it mathematically, while the qualitative researcher uses non-mathematical procedures.

While the field of qualitative research is currently something of a mosaic, the literature does suggest several common features. First, qualitative researchers are essentially interested in trying to understand participants' perspectives on their situations, where perspectives are defined as the frameworks by which one makes sense of one's world. They are also interested in trying to understand actions as something in which participants engage because of the particular perspectives which they have. Furthermore, qualitative researchers are interested in trying to understand patterns which emerge in the interactions between participants' perspectives and their actions as they evolve over time. This involves the ongoing collection of data with a focus on the process of social interaction.

Qualitative researchers are also predisposed to working as far as possible in natural settings and thus to favour participant observation and semi-structured interviews over experiments and standardised interviews. Also, rather than setting out to test preconceived hypotheses, they generally aim to generate theories from the data, thus trying to avoid the imposition of inappropriate frames of reference on participants. This may cause them to change their research design and data collection at various stages of a research project, while data gathering and data analysis tend to be concurrent rather than consecutive activities.

In many qualitative research projects one does not know from the outset what kinds of

categories will emerge from the data. This is not to ignore the many codified modes of qualitative analysis which sit between two extremes. At one end there is very little analysis. Here the emphasis is on what is often referred to as 'thick description'. At the other end are such exact and in-depth methods as microanalysis and microethnography. Qualitative researchers also tend to adopt one, or a variation of two main strategies in their analyses. On the one hand, there are those who work from the ground up, fracturing the data into very small pieces, methodically coding and assembling all the lower level categories, and then moving upwards to seek larger collectives. On the other hand, there are those who 'skim the cream': they move away from the data, reflect upon the major ideas which emerged, and then work with these ideas until they identify broad topics. All of this activity results in accounts which tend to be judged according to such criteria as 'authenticity', 'trustworthiness', 'dependability' and 'credibility' rather than 'validity' and 'reliability', and which gets published in such specialised journals as *Qualitative Studies in Education*.

See also: action research; educational research; ethnography; quantitative research

Further reading

Gubrium, J. F. and Holstein, J. A. (eds) (2002) *Handbook of Interview Research: Context and Method*, Thousand Oaks CA: Sage.

Lancy, D. F. (1993) *Qualitative Research in Education: An Introduction to the Major Traditions*, New York: Longman.

O'Donoghue, T. and Punch, K. (eds) (2003) *Qualitative Educational Research in Action: Doing and Reflecting*, London: RoutledgeFalmer.

TOM O'DONOGHUE

QUANTITATIVE RESEARCH

At its simplest level, quantitative research is a form of educational research based on evidence in the form of numbers or measurements. This is to distinguish it from qualitative research, which is generally based on evidence in the form of texts and narratives. An analysis of the extent to which the current test scores of a group of students could be predicted by their earlier scores in similar tests would, therefore, be an example of quantitative research. Another example would be a consideration of the rates of participation in higher education by different social groups. The term quantitative research is often taken to refer, more narrowly, to either experimental research, or the conduct of questionnaire surveys. However, those who use this term often imply more than the simple contrast between work involving numbers and work involving narratives. In addition, much quantitative work in education uses the techniques of 'statistics', based on a well established sampling theory. This emphasis on statistics is particularly prevalent in the psychology of education, for example, but less so in the sociology of education.

Sampling theory assumes that the measurements used by a researcher are from a subset of a larger 'population', that anyone in the larger population could have been selected for the research, and that the subset (or sample) has been selected randomly. It also assumes that the purpose of analysis is to estimate the likelihood that the entire population has the same characteristics and patterns as those discovered in the sample. A further assumption is that the entire sample selected for inclusion in the research had agreed to take part. If these assumptions are met then researchers can calculate clear estimates of how much of the variability in their findings is due to the process of random sampling – using techniques such as the standard error or confidence intervals – and how much is due to substantive differences in measurements. Also, researchers can then use a significance test, such as a t-test or a chi-squared test, to help them decide whether the findings from their research sample can be safely generalised to the entire population.

An entire approach to research, sometimes referred to as a paradigm, has been built on this relatively simple base. International surveys, market research, attitude and opinion scaling, laboratory experiments, and randomised field trials, are all usually considered as being within this genre. In addition, many quantitative researchers move on to the field of statistical modelling, in which several measurements are combined in order to try and create an explanation for an educational process. Many of these explanatory models are based on the idea of regression. Where two measurements are strongly related (such as a test score at age eleven and a later test score at age thirteen) then one measurement can be 'predicted' reasonably accurately from the other. In multiple regression, several measurements are used to predict the value of another. This is one basis for the calculation of value-added school performance tables.

The methods of traditional statistics can be elegant and powerful, but they are also sometimes difficult to understand. Modelling requires substantial prior knowledge of statistics to be used effectively. This means that a considerable part of beginners' training in quantitative research is based on statistics, which can be off-putting for newcomers with anxieties about mathematics. It also means that many researchers come to believe that this is all that quantitative research is, and can be. A problem for this rather narrow view of quantitative research is that much research in education is not, in fact, based on samples drawn randomly from a pre-defined population, and the people in any selected sample rarely all agree to take part anyway.

In reality, most researchers work with incomplete samples selected for their own convenience. The careful probability calculations of sampling theory, therefore, do not apply in such situations, which means that the practice of statistics, as described above, should not be as widespread as it is. It remains popular in use for a variety of reasons – partly because the models that can be built on this basis are so powerful and appealing, partly because the practice is quite openly abused with unsuitable data, and partly because some researchers have difficulty imagining what to do instead.

One alternative, increasing in popularity, is to perform calculations on population data instead of with samples. This has become possible because of the increasing public availability of powerful datasets derived from officially collected international, national and regional statistics, or other figures originally collected for another purpose. One advantage in using population figures is that it makes the issues of generalisation and significance testing, as described above, irrelevant. This leaves analysts with the problem of deciding whether the differences or patterns they observe in their population data are robust enough to be worthy of note. Is the difference or pattern robust enough to outweigh the potential bias caused by errors in the measurement or non-response, for example? However, exactly the same problems are faced by analysts using the traditional statistical approach – where they are usually ignored in the concern over the variation caused by random sampling.

Quantitative research, therefore, faces an uncertain but exciting future. It may be that new generations of researchers will begin to focus more on real everyday numbers, such as frequencies and true measurements, on analyses not involving random sampling, and on making subjective judgements about the importance of findings. If so, quantitative research may cease to be considered a paradigm totally separated from qualitative research, cease to be considered so mathematically threatening to outsiders, and become more open to working in education that routinely mixes data of all kinds in searching for solutions to important problems for society.

See also: educational research; experimental research; qualitative research; value added

Further reading

De Vaus, D. (2002) *Analyzing Social Data*, London: Sage.

Gorard, S. (2003) *Quantitative Methods in Social Science: The Role of Numbers Made Easy*, London: Continuum.

Gorard, S. with Taylor, C. (2004) *Combining Methods in Educational and Social Research*, London: Open University Press.

STEPHEN GORARD

QUINTILIAN (35–95 CE)

The father of Quintilian, the Roman educator, was a teacher of rhetoric who ensured his son studied under the most famous teachers in the empire. Quintilian established a public school in Rome in 68 CE which was funded by an imperial grant. He had some very important students such as Pliny the Younger and members of Emperor Domitian's family. Quintilian taught at the school until he reached the age of 50.

He was follower of Cicero, many of whose ideas were incorporated in his one surviving book *Institutio Oratoria*, written for use by contemporary teachers and composed, as was usual, as a series of lectures. He argued that nurture shaped capacities for learning. Education could benefit everyone, especially those charged with caring for infants, as what the very young child heard would shape its language for the future. Quintilian argued for professional teachers. He supported the commencement of formal learning before the age of seven because memory was better in the early years. The influence of the *Institutio* came in several stages. By 800 it had been lost, only to be rediscovered in part form, 400 years later. As only mutilated texts were available the work fell out of favour and had virtually disappeared once more by the end of the twelfth century. Then, in 1416, a complete copy was discovered by Poggio in St Gall, who ensured that many copies were made. It therefore exerted a strong influence at the height of the Renaissance, becoming one of the most printed books on education in the early modern period.

See also: classical education

STEVEN COWAN

R

READER

In educational contexts, reader has at least three different meanings. First, school curricula and national education systems prioritise the objective of teaching young children to read, after inducting them through story-telling, handling books and identifying letters and sounds. Young children's reading is typically promoted as a fun activity, as well as an instrumental one. Campaigns with titles like *Every Child a Reader* – this example having a currency in both the United Kingdom and the United States – are directed at children and their parents, while older children are encouraged to maintain the reading habit by exploring new genres and authors and, in formal classes, by approaching texts critically. The recent boom in discursive book clubs, sometimes organised by libraries or adult education institutions, has provided new outlets for readers to exchange under-standings and opinions about particular texts. Second, the term reader is used to describe an edited collection of writings considered important within a particular field of scholarship or essential to those undertaking a taught course, for which the reader may be a 'set text'. Academic publishers' catalogues may therefore include readers on areas ranging from astronomy to sociolinguistics to Victorian studies. Readers can also bring together, often in a single volume, essential extracts from such prolific writers as Karl Marx or Bertrand Russell. Third, reader is an academic title, most commonly found in the UK and countries influenced by the British higher education system. A reader is a senior post-holder, someone with higher status than a lecturer or senior lecturer, but positioned below the professorial rank. Promotion to reader may be a reward for excellence in research or teaching, or may be in recognition of additional responsibilities. After serving a period as reader, an academic may be well positioned for further career advancement by being appointed to a university chair.

See also: academic/academic profession; educational publishing; literacy; professor; reading

DAVID CROOK

READING

Reading is deriving meaning from written language. Reading is to written language what understanding speech is to spoken language. However, whereas spoken language is characteristic of all human beings, written language is not found in all societies and, even where it is found, not everyone can read. Also, whereas spoken language has probably been a characteristic of human societies for hundreds of thousands of years, the archaeological record indicates that written language has existed for little more than five millennia. It is a recent cultural invention that depends heavily on education for its continuance.

Reading is fundamental to education for at least three reasons. First, if education is concerned with inducting successive generations into a shared culture, and if that culture depends upon written language, education necessarily involves teaching reading. That teaching has to include, not just symbol decoding, but also higher order, meaning-related reading skills. Second, reading has become crucial for participation and citizenship in modern societies and insofar as education is concerned with enabling such participation, it must enable people to read. That includes enabling critical reading of, say, literary or political or advertising texts, as well as more mundane reading of road signs, benefit or tax forms, or medicinal labels. Third, reading is now central to the actual conduct of learning and teaching in contemporary educational institutions. Curricula, textbooks, learning activities, assessment and the organisation of schools all involve reading, whether of print on paper or on screen or of touch systems such as Braille. Reading is the key for accessing cultural resources. There is, of course, more to education than learning to read and it is possible to posit forms of education in which reading would be unimportant, but it is hard to conceive of anyone in modern society being considered fully 'educated' if they cannot read.

Institutions to teach reading and writing must be as old as writing systems themselves, the earliest of which can be traced back to around 3300 BCE. There is evidence of quite formal schooling in written language from the Sumerian period (Robinson 1995). Although there had been precursors of written language in cave drawings, carvings and other symbols, what distinguished the emergence of written language was that the symbols represented speech and that they could be used in different combinations to make different meanings. In some systems of written language the symbols were pictograms or ideograms, that is marks having some simi-

larity to whatever was referred to in the spoken language. Over time symbols became abbreviated or stylised. Reading in such systems involves learning the meaning of hundreds, sometimes thousands, of symbols. The alphabetic system was first developed around 3,000 years ago by the Phoenicians and reached the English-speaking world via the Greeks and Romans. It is a system for representing the sounds heard in speech and, as there is only a finite number of sounds used in any language, it means that a writing system requires only a relatively small set of symbols. For example, spoken English uses around forty-four basic sounds (phonemes) and twenty-six letters used singly and in combinations can represent them. Sadly, in English, letter-sound correspondences are rather irregular and learning to read is more difficult than in most other languages using alphabets. Whatever the system, it is important from an educational perspective to recognise that reading, in evolutionary terms, is a recent human accomplishment and that learning to read is not as easy or natural as learning to understand speech.

The emergence of reading and writing has had a dramatic impact on human culture, comparable to the much earlier evolution of spoken language. It has enabled communication between people not in the same place or time. It has permitted record keeping and the storing of knowledge. It has reduced demands on memory. It has enhanced the development of spoken art forms (e.g. drama, poetry) and led to new ones (e.g. the novel). It has made science possible. It has accelerated the process whereby each generation can build upon the accumulated knowledge of previous generations. It has hastened changes in technology, such as the printing press, the production of paper, the computer and the internet that have changed the nature of reading and writing.

Reading is more than decoding symbols into the sounds of speech. People rarely read simply to decode; they generally do so to derive meaning from what is written. This means that readers bring their own purposes and their understanding of writers' purposes to the texts they read. More than that, they bring their knowledge of how social groups use certain texts in certain ways. For example, readers who encounter this text as encyclopedia users will bring to their reading certain expectations of its purpose and what they might derive from it that would be different if they encountered the same text as a newspaper article, poem or government policy document. Insofar as readers' purposes, expectations and knowledge differ, their readings of texts will differ. Theorists have conceptualised this in terms of there being different genres (Halliday and Hasan 1985), different discourses (Gee 1996), or a plurality of literacies (Barton 1994). Also, it must be remembered that writing is an imperfect system for representing speech. As Olson (1994) has pointed out, it is better at representing 'what is said' than 'how it is said'. This too requires the reader to contribute something over and above what resides in the words being read.

Education has been the means whereby reading, at first an activity restricted to very few members of society, spread, over thousands of years and particularly over the past four or five generations, to virtually all members of modern societies. One could see elite schooling of the past as teaching the young of more powerful groups in society how to read – in their own and in classical languages. The introduction of mass schooling in the industrialising societies of the nineteenth century was very much about teaching the lower classes to read, writing being considered less important, and even inappropriate, for them (Hannon 1995).

Methods of teaching reading arouse deep passions amongst educators and policy makers. This is partly because their effectiveness is both crucial to the whole educational enterprise and yet remains a matter of some uncertainty for researchers (Kamil *et al.* 2000). It also reflects the fact that reading, because it involves the orchestration of processes from visual and auditory perception to conceptual and social understanding, is one of the most complex of all human abilities to learn or to teach. Hannon (2000) has argued that reading involves skills and knowledge at five main levels – subword units (letters, strings of letters, syllables); words; sentences and other strings of words; texts; and the purposes of texts – and that teaching methods vary in which level is given priority. Some focus at the level of 'purpose', on the grounds that if learners do not understand the point of reading they are unlikely to learn. Some methods give primacy to explicit teaching at the 'subword' and 'word' levels on the grounds that without basic decoding skills learners will never be able to read. Underlying these different methods are two different conceptions of reading – either as a social practice in which learners become proficient through engagement with others' purposes and furthering their own (as is the case with children learning spoken language) or, psychologically, as an individual skill which is to be acquired through training. The two conceptions are not mutually exclusive but, because they touch on how learners, particularly children, are viewed, the contrast between them can become exaggerated. Finally, it should be noted that the learning and teaching of reading is linked to the learning and teaching of writing. Reading and writing are the two key aspects of literacy and current methods of teaching recognise their interdependence.

Reading has always been a political issue – in the sense that which groups in society should read and what they should read has been contested – but in recent decades it has become political in a new sense. There is said in many countries to be a 'reading standards' crisis – that standards are falling or at least are not high enough. These are not 'developing' countries where literacy and primary education are limited but long industrialised countries where there has been universal primary education for several generations. There is actually little evidence of falling reading standards but there is evidence of increasing need, as a consequence of global economic competitiveness, for a more skilled, more literate workforce. The result has been national policies to raise reading standards. In England, to take one example, there have been policies for primary schools (DfEE 1998) and for millions of adults said to lack reading skills (DfES 2001). What is noteworthy about these policies is that, by historical standards of educational change, they have been extremely largescale, centrally directed, well funded, politically high-profile and have affected the lives of millions of learners. Reading, once a concern of a minority of specialists, is now centre-stage in national life.

See also: basic skills; culture; literacy; phonics; spelling; standards; writing

Further reading

Barton, D. (1994) *Literacy: An Introduction to the Ecology of Written Language*, Oxford: Blackwell.

Department for Education and Employment (1998) *The National Literacy Strategy: Framework for Teaching*, London: DfEE.

Department for Education and Skills (2001) *Delivering Skills for Life: A National Strategy*, London: DfES.

Gee, J. P. (1996) *Social Linguistics and Literacies: Ideologies in Discourses*, 2nd edn, London: Falmer Press.

Halliday, M. and Hasan, R. (1985) *Language, Context and Text: Aspects of Language in a Social Semiotic Perspective*, Waurn Ponds VIC: Deakin University Press.

Hannon, P. (1995) *Literacy, Home and School: Research and Practice in Teaching Literacy with Parents*, London: Falmer Press.

——(2000) *Reflecting on Literacy in Education*, London: RoutledgeFalmer.

Kamil, M. L., Mosenthal, P. B., Pearson, P. D. and Barr, R. (2000) *Handbook of Reading Research*, vol. III, Mahwah NJ: Lawrence Erlbaum.

Olson, D. (1994) *The World on Paper*, Cambridge: Cambridge University Press.

Robinson, A. (1995) *The Story of Writing: Alphabets, Hieroglyphs and Pictograms*, London: Thames and Hudson.

PETER HANNON

RECEPTION CLASS

The 'reception class', a term with a particular currency in the United Kingdom, is the first class of primary school. It receives the new intake of children usually aged four or five. In England, Scotland and Wales, the statutory school starting age is the term after a child's fifth birthday, established originally in the Education Act of 1870. Documentary evidence indicates that the decision had little to do with educational criteria and was more closely related to a combination of child protection issues and economic pressures; an early school-starting age justified an early school-leaving age, so that children were free to join the workforce.

In practice, most children in England and Wales start school before the statutory age of five. Government figures suggest that 62 per cent of four-year-olds in England and Wales were admitted to reception classes of primary schools in 2006. Four distinct admission policies across the UK can be identified. These are: (a) at the statutory age (termly admission after the child's fifth birthday); (b) as 'rising-fives' (termly admission in the term in which the child's fifth birthday occurs); (c) from roughly four and a half (two intakes per year); and (d) from four (one intake per year). Evidence suggests that, increasingly, schools favour one intake per year for its perceived benefits for summer-born children, although increases in the number of young four-year-olds entering school can be attributed to a range of factors, including (a) falling rolls creating pressure for schools to fill places; (b) pressure from parents for their children to start school earlier because of a lack of sufficient free, pre-school provision, but also for its perceived educational benefits; (c) the demands of the national curriculum to ensure that children have sufficient time in school before formal assessment at seven.

In 2000, a foundation stage for children aged three until the end of the reception year in school was established in England and Wales, informed by the *Curriculum Guidance for the Foundation Stage*. The aim of this initiative was twofold: first, to establish a long-awaited and distinct educational phase for young children and second, to clarify for practitioners working with young children key areas of learning and appropriate progression towards Key Stage One of the National Curriculum. It provides a bridge between nursery and Key Stage One, stresses flexibility and informality in the reception year, focuses on child development, practical play and outdoor activity, and provides clear guidance for teachers. However, studies have highlighted the continued division between nursery and reception in spite of the fact that the foundation stage was designed precisely to overcome such divisions. The key elements of the debate can be summarised as follows: diverse admission policies have led to uneven quality of provision for four-year-olds in reception classes; a reduction in adult attention is due to reduced adult: child ratios in reception classes; a lack of appropriately trained staff in reception classes may lead to over-formal activities; there may be a reduction in the availability of choice of activity, outdoor play, appropriate resources and equipment and time and space for active play; changes in teaching style and classroom ethos (David 1990; Adams *et al.* 2004). Others argue that the location of the reception class in school, unlike other separately managed preschool settings, may result in features of a formal school curriculum percolating down to the teachers and children in the reception class. In turn this can result in competing discourses of school improvement versus a distinctive pedagogy for early childhood (Aubrey 2004). Overwhelmingly, studies of reception class pedagogy explicitly endorse a nursery-style provision for four-year-olds and argue that there is no compelling evidence that starting school early has lasting educational benefits (Sharp 2002). Indeed, opponents of an early school starting age warn that over formal education introduced too soon may be detrimental to children's social well-being and long-term attitude to learning. On the other hand, proponents of early school entry argue that it can enable children from disadvantaged backgrounds to make up for a deficit in their academic skills.

In the global context, the UK is unusual in its policy of admitting children to school at age four or five, rather than the more common European and international age of six and sometimes seven (Sharp 2002; Rogers and Rose 2007). It is possible to argue that educational provision for children under five in the UK is still subject to a long history of political ambivalence, some would say expediency. While there have been unprecedented developments in the pre-school sector since 1997 in the UK, the policy to admit children who are under five to reception classes of primary schools has remained unchanged and largely unchallenged.

See also: child development; early childhood education; primary school/education

Further reading

Adams, S., Alexander, E., Drummond, M. J. and Moyles, J. (2004) *Inside the Foundation Stage: Recreating the Reception Year*, London: ATL.

Aubrey, C. (2004) 'Implementing the foundation stage in reception classes', *British Educational Research Journal*, 30(5): 633–56.

David, T. (1990) *Under Five–Under Educated?*, Buckingham: Open University Press.

Sharp, C. (2002) *School Starting Age: European Policy and Recent Research*, Slough: NFER.

Rogers, S. and Rose, J. (2007) 'Ready for reception? The advantages and disadvantages of single-point entry to school', *Early Years*, 27(1): 47–63.

SUE ROGERS

RECRUITMENT

In education, recruitment describes the process of enrolling students or hiring staff. In seeking to recruit teachers, schools will normally specify that the teacher has been trained and, for a senior post, advertisements and criteria for the post may demand that the teacher appointed should be an experienced practitioner. In many countries it is easier to recruit teachers of certain secondary subjects than others. In the United Kingdom, for example, there has long been a shortage of secondary mathematics and science teachers. Financial inducements – sometimes called 'golden hellos' – have been offered to those recruited to courses of teacher training and/or those taking up first appointments.

In relation to students, less-popular schools, shunned by parents – in contexts where parental choice operates – may be said to have a 'recruitment problem' and face possible closure. Similarly, some college or university courses of study may struggle to 'recruit to target', while others may be oversubscribed.

Recruitment is a term frequently used alongside that of selection: applicants competing for a single advertised position are likely to be interviewed, and may also have to complete a psychometric, aptitude, intelligence or skills test, or make a presentation to the appointment panel. University applicants are frequently interviewed prior to receiving the offer of a place or a rejection decision, while entry to selective schools often requires the student to pass a test or examination.

See also: career guidance; intelligence/intelligence tests; selection

DAVID CROOK

RECTOR

In institutions of higher education in many countries, the rector, literally the ruler, is the most important academic position, being preferred to other terminology such as chancellor or president. While a common term for a leading official, in churches as well as in education, its usage is sporadic internationally, appearing much more frequently in some national contexts than in others. It is a highly prominent position in Scotland, for example, where it is an elected position in the ancient universities, and often attracts media interest. The rector of Edinburgh University is elected every three years by students and staff. The term is also often employed in other European countries and in different parts of the

world. The rectorship is thus a key position in such different and dispersed universities as the University of Turku in Finland, the United Nations University in Tokyo, and the National University of Rwanda. In England, the United States and Canada, on the other hand, its use is much less common, and the term chancellor or president is widely preferred. In some institutional contexts, the rector may be a leading official at school level as well as in higher education.

See also: chancellor; higher education; university

GARY McCULLOCH

RECURRENT EDUCATION

Recurrent education, a term now little mentioned, has now been subsumed into lifelong learning, which it once rivalled. It has the meaning of alternating periods of systematic post-compulsory study with such other activities as work and leisure. The Organisation for Economic Co-operation and Development (OECD) was an early champion, publishing *Recurrent Education: A Strategy for Lifelong Learning – A Clarifying Report* in 1973. Supporters of recurrent education frequently asserted that it should be a 'right' or 'entitlement' for individuals to return to learning throughout their lifetime. Once a key term, it is now often overlooked by educational dictionaries, encyclopedias and glossaries.

See also: lifelong learning

DAVID CROOK

REDDIE, CECIL (1858–1932)

Reddie, who became a progressive headmaster, obtained a bachelor of science degree from Edinburgh University in 1882 and then studied at Göttingen University for two years, where he was awarded his doctorate in 1884. Whilst there, Reddie encountered progressive ideas about teaching which were to shape his later thinking. Upon returning to

Britain he taught science at Fettes College, Edinburgh and at Clifton College, Bristol, both established private schools for boys. At Clifton, Reddie worked under J. M. Wilson, who transformed ideas about science teaching in the elite private schools in Britain. Reddie joined the Fellowship of the New Life, an ethically based socialist group which sought to realise the qualities of cooperation and equality within their chosen spheres of life, rather than leave progress to political events. He was to crystallise his ideas in a series of controversial article called *Modern Mis-education* (1888). Reddie decided to establish a new school based upon New Life principles at Abbotsholme, Derbyshire, where he combined academic and practical pursuits for the boys. All pupils worked on the estate farm doing things such as haymaking, growing vegetables and tending animals. Modern, rather than classical, languages were taught. The spirit of cooperation rather than competition was at the heart of the school ethos. Reddie emphasised the arts in the curriculum and believed in spiritual and religious freedom. Abbotsholme was the first school to introduce sex, health and hygiene education, something that caused controversy in pre-World War I England. One of Reddie's great influences was the mystic William Blake. His work influenced Kurt Hahn's school at Salem in Germany.

See also: head teacher/principal; independent/private school/education; progressive education; public school

STEVEN COWAN

REFLECTIVE PRACTITIONER

The notion of the 'reflective practitioner' portrayed in Schön (1983) is one that challenges many established ideas about expertise, curriculum and pedagogy. It responds to what Schön viewed as a growing crisis of confidence in the professions, and an emergent questioning of professionals' rights and freedoms, to assert the importance of professional approaches to knowing, as distinct from academic theorising. Reflective practices, he claimed, were based not simply on technical expertise but on knowing-in-action, knowing-in-practice, much of which was tacit and spontaneous.

In Schön's view, schools tended to enforce a stable system of rules and procedures within which teachers were expected to deliver technical expertise, transmitting knowledge in an established format, subject to a system of controls. He drew attention to the ways in which curriculum and lesson plans, as well as measures of performance and rewards and punishments, emanated from the centre and were imposed on teachers at the periphery. Supervisors ensured that teachers carried out the functions expected of them, and provided them with resources for doing so, allocating rewards and punishments to them based on their measured performance (Schön 1983: 330). This approach was based on a perspective of 'technical rationality' which located professional practice as a process of problem solving based on clear and fixed goals.

Against this set of imperatives, Schön set out a number of key issues for reflective practitioners to consider. The curriculum, for example, should be addressed as 'an inventory of *themes* of understanding and skill' (Schön 1983: 333), as opposed to a set of materials to be learned. Different students presented their own patterns for understanding and action, so needed to be appreciated individually. Moreover, besides struggling against the rigid order of lesson plans, schedules, isolated classrooms and objective measures of performance, reflective practitioners should also question and criticise the basic idea of the school as a place for transmitting 'measured doses of privileged knowledge' in a progressive way. Thus, the idea of reflective practice would in Schön's view lead to 'a vision of professionals as agents of society's reflective conversation with its situation, agents who engage in cooperative inquiry within a framework of institutionalised contention' (Schön 1983: 353).

This approach led Schön to raise issues about the kind of professional education that would be most appropriate for an epistemology of practice based on reflection-in-action. The crisis of confidence in professional knowledge, he suggested, corresponded to a similar crisis in professional education: 'If professionals are blamed for ineffectiveness and impropriety, their schools are blamed for failing to teach the rudiments of effective and ethical practice.' (Schön 1987: 8). There was a hierarchy of knowledge in professional schools, drawn from medical education, in which basic science was superior to applied science, which in turn came before and above the technical skills of day-to-day practice. He proposed as a radical alternative that professional schools based in the universities should learn from other – he described them as 'deviant' – traditions of education for practice such as studios of art and design, conservatories of music and dance, athletics coaching, and apprenticeship in the crafts, which emphasised coaching and learning by doing. In this way, according to Schön, 'Professional education should be redesigned to combine the teaching of applied science with coaching in the artistry of reflection-in-action.' (Schön 1987: xii). Architectural designing and the design studio, for example, were taken as prototypes of reflection-in-action and education for artistry in other fields of practice, so that the generalised educational setting would become what he described as a 'reflective practicum'. Students would mainly learn by doing, with the help of coaching. Other major instances of the reflective practicum were classes in musical performance, psychoanalysis supervision, and seminars in counselling and consulting skills.

Potentially, Schön argued, a reflective practicum could 'bridge the worlds of university and practice' (Schön 1987: ch. 11). It would challenge the institutionalised tension between academic rigour on the one hand and professional relevance on the other. Schön's ideals have been and continue to be highly influential, although the dynamics of the relationship between 'reflection' and 'action' remain contentious, as do the implications for the professional curriculum (Eraut 1994), forming the basis for continuing vigorous debate.

See also: curriculum; profession/professionalism/professionalisation; professional education; Schön, Donald; teacher education/training

Further reading

Eraut, M. (1994) *Developing Professional Knowledge and Competence*, London: Falmer.
Schön, D. (1983) *The Reflective Practitioner: How Professionals Think in Action*, London: Temple Smith.
——(1987) *Educating the Reflective Practitioner: Toward a New Design for Teaching and Learning in the Professions*, San Francisco CA: Jossey-Bass.

GARY McCULLOCH

RELIGIOUS ASSEMBLY

A religious assembly is an official gathering of the staff and pupils of a school for the purpose of an act of collective worship. This frequently includes some combination of the following elements: stories, prayers, music, drama, singing and an address. Religious assemblies often aim to worship God, to nurture specific values, to celebrate special occasions or to promote a corporate identity. In some national education systems, such as the United States of America and France, religious assemblies are not present in state or public schools, but in England and Wales the presence of religious assemblies is a result of the historic partnership of Church and state in school provision.

In accordance with the 1944 Education Act, the School Standards and Framework Act (1998) stated that all state-maintained schools in England and Wales should provide a daily religious assembly (act of collective worship) for all pupils. Officially, religious assemblies should provide the opportunity for pupils to revere or venerate a divine being or power, to consider spiritual and moral issues, to explore their own beliefs, to encourage pupil participation and response, and to develop a positive community spirit with a common ethos and shared values. In state-maintained schools with a religious character, religious assemblies should be provided in accordance with the school's trust deed or religious affiliation. In state-maintained schools without a religious character, religious assemblies are required to be wholly or mainly of a broadly Christian character as determined by the Education Reform Act (1988). This means that most religious assemblies that take place in a school within each term should reflect Christian traditions without being distinctive of any particular denomination. This requirement is controversial primarily because it neglects the secular and pluralist nature of school populations and the desire of many teachers to promote social cohesion, mutual understanding and tolerant cooperation. For this reason, many schools ignore the requirements or adopt alternative approaches including (i) parallel faith-based assemblies in which pupils are divided according to their religious backgrounds, (ii) multi-faith assemblies which draw on elements from a variety of faiths, (iii) assemblies which aim to develop pupils spiritually, morally, socially and culturally, but not in regard to a particular faith, and (iv) secular assemblies which emphasise secular ethical and educational issues, such as the promotion of charitable work or the reinforcement of the school ethos.

To protect the consciences of teachers (as well as their employment rights), school staffs do not have to participate in or attend religious assemblies in state-maintained schools that do not have a religious character. Similarly, parents have the right to withdraw their children from religious assemblies without explanation and schools must continue to supervise these children unless they are attending an alternative form of provision elsewhere. In 2006, pupils above the age of compulsory schooling (i.e. 16) were given the right to withdraw themselves from religious assemblies. Furthermore, the requirement for religious assemblies to be broadly Christian can be lifted in exceptional cases relating to the family background, ages and aptitudes of some or all of the pupils at a school. In such cases, schools have to apply for a 'determination' from their local Standing Advisory Council for Religious Education (SACRE). According to the Education Reform Act (1988), local education authorities have to establish a SACRE for the purpose of providing advice on matters pertaining to religious education and collective worship. A SACRE is comprised of representatives from the Church of England, Christian denominations and other religions, teacher associations and the local education authority. Each group has one vote and each must regulate its own proceedings. After a school receives a determination, it may offer alternative forms of religious assembly which may be distinctive of a particular religion, but may not be distinctive of any denomination within that religion. Nevertheless, few teachers or pupils withdraw from religious assemblies and few schools apply for determinations to lift the requirement for broadly Christian religious assemblies.

The English and Welsh experience raises important questions. How much time, space, resources and staffing should be dedicated to religious assemblies? What forms of religious assembly are appropriate in state-maintained schools in religiously heterogeneous societies? To what extent is worship a private and personal matter rather than a public and social concern of state-maintained educational institutions?

See also: church; religious education; religious school

Further reading

Copley, T. (1999) *Spiritual Development in the State School*, Exeter: University of Exeter Press.
Hull, J. M. (1975) *School Worship: An Obituary*, London: SCM.
Webster, D. (1995) *Collective Worship in Schools*, Cleethorpes: Kenelm Press.

ROB FREATHY

RELIGIOUS EDUCATION

Religious education pertains to processes of teaching and learning that relate to, or are of the nature of, religion. Religious education can be systematic or unsystematic and can take place in formal or informal settings. In formal educational contexts, religious education is used to refer either to the educational process as a whole and through it the transmission of religious beliefs and values or to describe subjects or elements of the curriculum that are concerned with religion. The nature and purpose of this curricular provision is determined by some or all of the following aims: religious nurture and faith development, the acquisition of knowledge and understanding about religion(s), the impartation of skills, the advancement of attitudes and values, and the promotion of personal morality and social cohesion. Each form of curricular provision can be located on a spectrum ranging from straightforward indoctrination as found in catechesis, to the non-committed study of religious phenomena as found in Religious Studies.

Historically and internationally, religious education has predominantly attempted to induct pupils into a particular faith, including gaining knowledge of its doctrines and practices, by requiring them to memorise and interpret sacred writings. Concerns regarding this form of provision have led to the exclusion of religious education from state or public schools in places as varied as Albania, France, India and the United States of America. In these countries, religious education is generally confined to independent schools and provision within the faith communities. By contrast, religious education that promotes a particular religion or denomination is present in state or public schools in Germany, Greece and Slovakia. In other countries, the state or public schools provide a form of religious education which does not seek to promote any one religion or denomination, for instance in Denmark, the Netherlands, Norway and Sweden.

In England and Wales, the term 'religious education' was used in the 1944 Education Act to refer to religious instruction and collective worship, but in the Education Reform Act (1988) religious education was used to describe the classroom subject only (RE). This was placed on the 'basic curriculum' rather than among the ten subjects that formed the mandatory national curriculum. In accordance with the 1944 and 1988 legislative acts, the School Standards and Framework Act (1998) stated that RE should be provided for all pupils in state-maintained schools, except those pupils who have been withdrawn by their parents. In state-maintained schools with a religious character, RE is generally under the control of the governing body and can be provided in accordance with the school's trust-deed or religious affiliation. In state-maintained schools without a religious character, RE is provided in accordance with a local education authority (LEA) agreed syllabus. Each LEA is required to establish an occasional body called an Agreed Syllabus Conference (ASC) which produces an agreed syllabus for RE. The committees on an ASC are comprised of representatives from the Church of England, Christian denominations and other religions, teacher associations and the LEA. Before the LEA can adopt it, an agreed syllabus must be unanimously supported by all of the committees. An agreed syllabus must not require teaching by means of any catechism or formulary, which is distinctive of a particular religious denomination, and it must not be designed to convert pupils or to urge particular beliefs upon them. According to the Education Reform Act (1988), the content of agreed syllabuses should reflect the fact that religious traditions in Great Britain are in the main Christian whilst taking account of the teaching and practices of other principal religions. Despite the success of ASCs in managing the acrimony caused by competing views of RE, dissatisfaction grew as a result of RE's exclusion from the national curriculum and the statutorily prescribed attainment targets, programmes of study and assessment arrangements which it incorporated. This led to the publication of central guidance by the School Curriculum and Assessment Authority and the Qualifications and Curriculum Authority. This represented the growing consensus between central government, the major religious groups and religious education professionals regarding the aims, methods and content of RE in state-maintained schools without a religious character. Nevertheless, vibrant disagreements continue in regard to what many perceive as conservative forms of religious education provided in some state-maintained and independent faith schools.

See also: curriculum; indoctrination; religious assembly; religious school; subjects

Further reading

Grimmit, M. (ed.) (2000) *Pedagogies of Religious Education*, Great Wakering: McCrimmon.
Jackson, R. (2004) *Rethinking Religious Education and Plurality*, London: RoutledgeFalmer.
Wright, A. (2004) *Religion, Education and Post-modernity*, London: RoutledgeFalmer.

ROB FREATHY

RELIGIOUS SCHOOL

Adherents of the world's religions have played a part in establishing, maintaining and managing schools in accordance with their worldviews. Religious schools may cater for all or part of a child's school life course. They can be full- or part-time, residential or day, state-maintained or independent. Examples of religious schools include Christian Sunday schools, Islamic madrasahs, Hindu ashrams and Buddhist wats. In the United States of America and France, the separation of Church and state has ensured that state or public schools are not religiously affiliated. In these countries, religious schools are either independent of the state or public school system or are provided in addition to it. However, in other countries, religious schools are wholly or partly state-maintained, such as in Denmark and the Netherlands.

In England and Wales, the Christian churches were largely responsible for mass schooling until the 1870 Education Act, which led to the creation of a dual system of non-denominational 'state' schools and voluntary (church) schools which received subsidies from central government. After the 1902 Education Act, local education authorities (LEAs) took responsibility for the 'state' schools and for the provision of maintenance grants to voluntary schools. The 1944 Education Act increased government subsidy for voluntary schools and divided them into different types depending on the level of public funding which they received and the degree of autonomy afforded to their managers. Since the School Standards and Framework Act (1998), state-maintained schools have been divided into four categories. Community schools are multi-faith or secular in character and fully funded by LEAs. Foundation schools, which have more autonomy than community schools, may or may not have a religious character depending on the nature of their trust deed. Voluntary controlled schools have a limited religious character, are allowed to appoint only a minority of their governors from the voluntary (church) body and have their building and maintenance costs fully funded by the LEA. Voluntary aided schools have a greater religious character, are allowed to appoint a majority of their governors from the voluntary (church) body and receive only partial LEA funding for building and maintenance. After coming to power in 1997 with a drive to welcome diversity, the New Labour government sought to expand the number of state-maintained religious schools where there was a clear demand from parents and communities. Thus, a number of independent schools affiliated to non-Christian religions were allowed to become voluntary aided schools (for example Islamia Primary School, Brent, London). Representatives of faith groups were also invited to become sponsors of 'academies' in disadvantaged areas and to determine the religious character and admissions policies of these schools through representation on the board of trustees.

There are numerous arguments in favour of, and in opposition to, state-maintained religious schooling. Supporters of state-maintained religious schools may claim that: (i) they provide pupils with a sense of religious identity and nourish their faith; (ii) they afford parents the right to educate their children in accordance with their own religious convictions; (iii) they protect minority cultures from being subsumed into the majority culture as disseminated, for instance, through the media; (iv) they take seriously the personal and social significance of faith; (v) they protect religious adherents who come from ethnic minority backgrounds from exposure to racism; (vi) they have special qualities, such as high-quality teaching, good attainment, excellent pupil behaviour and an ethos and curriculum permeated by religion; and (vii) they encourage representatives of religious and ethnic minorities to become socially and politically active through such means as the governing body or parent groups.

Opponents of state-maintained religious schools may claim that: (i) they promote sectarianism and social fragmentation by separating pupils according to religious background; (ii) their selective admissions procedures disadvantage other schools and encourage parental competition and deception in regard to patterns of residence and claims to religious affiliation, respectively; (iii) they indoctrinate pupils into particular worldviews, which limits their personal autonomy and privileges one worldview over another; (iv) they undermine future social cohesion and cooperation by failing to develop shared norms and values between adherents of different faiths; and (v) they use public funds to subsidise proselytisation rather than recognising that religious beliefs are a matter of private concern.

See also: academy; dual system; independent/private school/education; religious assembly; religious education; Sunday school

Further reading

Chadwick, P. (1997) *Shifting Alliances: Church and State in English Education*, London: Cassell.
Cruickshank, M. (1963) *Church and State in English Education: 1870 to the Present Day*, London: Macmillan.
Gardner, R., Lawton, D. and Cairns, J. (eds) (2005) *Faith Schools: Consensus or Conflict?*, London: RoutledgeFalmer.

ROB FREATHY

RESTRUCTURING

Restructuring refers to a systemic or comprehensive structural change at any level of the educational system. Restructuring is usually associated with the business sector because of related calls for efficiency; however, in education the approach is also implemented to improve instructional quality or educational opportunities. In theory, restructuring will allow the educational unit to become more flexible and, therefore, more responsive to student needs.

At the elementary and secondary levels, restructuring is linked to concerns about the quality of educational programmes or academic performance, encompassing a variety of reforms over several decades, including those focused on the school size; student grouping; school governance; and district oversight. For example, the small schools movement is a restructuring reform that involves breaking up large schools into smaller semi-autonomous units, referred to as houses, academies, or schools-within-schools. In theory, these structural changes will provide more cohesive, often theme-centred, learning opportunities that will result in increased engagement among students and improved academic performance. Restructuring has also involved multi-age groupings in which teams of teachers have collective responsibility for student learning and the authority to make resource and curricular decisions. School governance changes, such as site-based management, involve restructuring of authority and oversight between the school and the district. Despite the centrality of resource efficiency, site-based management primarily is designed to allow individuals at the school site increased control over resources to improve quality. Restructuring has also involved reconfiguration of schools within a district (e.g. by region) and reorganisation of district offices, sometimes involving newly defined district roles and primarily occurring in large urban districts.

Through the passage of the *No Child Left Behind Act* of 2001 (NCLB) in the United States, the term restructuring has become widespread and is associated with low performance through the law's accountability sanctions. Drawing upon select restructuring initiatives, NCLB requires that a district create and implement a restructuring plan for any school that does not make Adequate Yearly Progress (AYP) for five years. The plans must include one or more of the following:

- reopening as a charter school;
- replacing all or most of the staff (referred to as reconstitution);
- contracting with a private management company;
- turning over the operation of the school to the state (or state takeover); and
- restructuring in another way, such as adopting a comprehensive reform model or hiring an external consultant.

State policies specify which federal options are available to schools and districts.

For institutions of higher education, restructuring is primarily implemented to improve efficiency, often through a change in the governance or administrative structure. Restructuring in these situations is considered the necessary result of fiscal stress and the desire to use scarce resources more effectively. Less frequently, restructuring results from concerns around programme quality.

While restructuring in higher education institutions usually involves creating a new governing body, it may also refer to the consolidation of academic units and, in more extreme cases, elimination of courses or departments. Decisions that involve this type of reorganisation are frequently referred to as academic restructuring. Concerns about this type of restructuring focus on the investment in and valuing of some programmes or departments at the expense of others based on external resources or demands, as well as the extent to which restructuring policies change the role or function of universities and limit the scope of knowledge available to students (see Gumport 2000).

An additional, though related, area of restructuring in higher education institutions is workforce restructuring. This structural reform involves, for example, changing the division of labour between research and teaching; hiring more part-time workers; or hiring more untenured faculty.

While less common, restructuring may occur across an entire higher education system, such as a university with multiple campuses or multiple universities, for example, all public institutions in New Jersey. In these instances, restructuring results in a new administrative structure to manage and oversee these entities. In addition, institutional mergers, while rare, have occurred in some countries and enable multiple organisations to gain efficiencies in resource distribution and programme delivery.

See also: accountability; education policy; school-based management; school change; school improvement; school reform; systemic reform

Further reading

Elmore, R. F. and associates (1991) *Restructuring Schools: The Next Generation of Educational Reform*, San Francisco CA: Jossey-Bass.
Gumport, P. J. (2000) 'Academic restructuring: organizational change and institutional imperatives', *Higher Education*, 39(1): 67–91.

KARA S. FINNIGAN

493

RETENTION

Retention commonly describes students who remain in a higher education institution and successfully complete a degree. The factors which impede retention are various and they give rise to such terms as attrition, 'dropping out', failure to complete, interruption, non-completion, suspension and withdrawal (Longden 2002). The ambiguity surrounding some of this language obfuscates the reasons why students leave a programme.

One factor favouring higher education student retention is the development of positive working relationships between staff and students, achieved in such ways as being on first name terms. The development of effective monitoring systems for checking attendance and absence also has the potential to reduce student non-completion. Collaborative teaching and learning practices may help students to develop networks and social bonds within the formal structured learning environment. Staggered assessment deadlines may accommodate part-time students' family and employment circumstances, while the quality of student accommodation and diversity of extracurricular activities may also impact upon retention rates.

When considering non-completion, two sets of factors must be considered: those relating to individuals that may be internally or externally imposed, and ones applying to the policy, practice and ethos of the institution. Much of the early work on retention focused primarily on the student, with less emphasis on the complex factors occurring at the institutional level (Tinto 1975). Students whose personal qualities and dispositions are inconsistent with institutional values were identified as being largely unable to interact with others and, therefore, at risk of non-completion. Findings pointed to a strong association between students' family backgrounds, social capital and prior experiences and their prospects for successful completion of the degree course. The individual's personal commitment to the university appeared also to strongly influence their likelihood of completion.

Whilst this early work on retention was groundbreaking and instrumental, the predominant focus upon the individual has been criticised for overlooking a wider, more complex range of factors (Ozga and Sukhnandan 1997). The experiences of conventional students (i.e. those who enter university immediately after secondary school) and mature participants invite comparison in respect of student preparedness, compatibility of institution and subject choice, and time of exit. Mature students appear to do more research before deciding to enter university, improving their retention prospects in some respects, though they are more susceptible than their younger counterparts to unfavourable external circumstances such as family illness or unemployment.

Recent research on retention has concentrated upon factors embedded within the institutional setting, recognising practices that disadvantage individual students or groups of students. There is a clear tension between government 'widening participation' strategies, aimed at encouraging more non-traditional students to enter university, and the universal objective to maximise student retention rates. Financial benefits sometimes offered to higher education institutions may provide a powerful incentive to enrol more non-traditional students. On the other hand, the probability of disproportionately large numbers of these students entering the 'at risk' category will act as a deterrent for universities anxious to protect and improve their retention rates.

See also: dropouts; higher education; progression; student

Further reading

Longden, B. (2002) 'Retention rates – renewed interest but whose interest is being served?', *Research Papers in Education*, 17(1): 3–29.
Ozga, J. and Sukhnandan, L. (1997) 'Undergraduate non-completion: developing an

explanatory model', *Higher Education Quarterly*, 52(3): 316–33.

Thomas, L. (2002) 'Student retention in higher education: the role of institutional habitus', *Journal of Education Policy*, 17(4): 423–42.

Tinto, V. (1975) 'Dropout from higher education: a theoretical synthesis of recent research', *Review of Educational Research*, 45: 89–125.

Yorke, M. and Longden, B. (2004) *Retention and Student Success in Higher Education*, Maidenhead: Open University Press.

DIANNE GERELUK

RHODES TRUST

The Rhodes Trust is an educational charity that awards scholarships to study at the University of Oxford. The grants are available to selected students from Australia, Bermuda, Canada, Germany, Hong Kong, India, Jamaica and the Commonwealth Caribbean, Kenya, New Zealand, Pakistan, Southern Africa, the USA, Zambia and Zimbabwe. Scholarships are awarded annually for one, two, or three years and include fees and a monthly stipend.

The Trust was created and endowed through the will of Cecil John Rhodes after he died in 1902. The aim of the trust was to educate future leaders of the world and Rhodes felt that his own university, Oxford, nurtured broad views and personal development. He believed that progress and civilisation would be spread by the most economically advanced countries such as Britain and the USA. There were originally fifty-two scholarships although others have been added. In total there have been over 7,000 Rhodes scholars of which the Trust estimates 4,000 are still living.

Rhodes was a Briton who emigrated to South Africa in 1870 and devoted himself to expanding British imperial interests, especially in what would become Rhodesia (Zimbabwe). He became wealthy through diamond mining, becoming the head of De Beers Consolidated Mines. By contrast, in 2003, to mark the centenary of the Trust, £10 million was devoted to establishing the Mandela Rhodes Foundation in South Africa, which aimed to contribute

> to the achievement of true equality, of dignity and educational opportunity for all, to the enhancement of the cultural heritage, to the strengthening of democracy, and the rule of law, and to the alleviation of poverty and suffering, especially amongst the children of the country.

The Rhodes Scholars' Southern Africa Forum (RSSAF) is a charitable organisation established by Rhodes scholars which aims to harness the skills and resources of the 'Rhodes community' to bring about educational and social change in Southern Africa.

See also: charities, educational; scholarship

TOM WOODIN

RICE, JOSEPH MAYER (1857–1934)

Mayer graduated in Medicine from Columbia University in 1881, later becoming interested in teaching and child psychology. He studied pedagogy and psychology at Leipzig and Jena under the influence of Herbart. He believed that children learn best when taught at levels suited to their stages of natural development. On returning to the United States of America from Germany, Rice wanted to test whether this central idea was correct. He pioneered large-scale research into classroom practices and how they affected learning amongst children, sponsored by *Forum* magazine. His research exposed the routine and repetition that characterised most American public schools, and it initially ignited severe criticism from those with allegiances to the schools. His research into the organisation of teacher training was equally critical, and he undertook extensive studies of the teaching of spelling (1897), arithmetic (1902), and language (1903), comparing the performance of schools in cities where different methods were used. A conclusion from his research was that clearly defined standards could be reached with the additional gain of efficiency across the educational system. He argued that trained administrators, rather than political appointees, should run education and that standardised testing with scientific measurement was the key tool in order to improve schools. His progressive ideas were published in *Scientific Management in Schools* (1913) and *The People's Government* (1915). While Rice's ideas challenged the rigid, mechanical teaching methods that he found, in succeeding decades some of his ideas became appropriated to justify less progressive approaches in schools.

See also: classroom observation

STEVEN COWAN

RIESMAN, DAVID (1909–2002)

Riesman, the American sociologist and writer on higher education, graduated from Harvard in 1931 and took a further law degree in 1934. He taught at the law school of the University of Buffalo from 1937 to 1941 and then worked in senior legal positions for five years. As a researcher at Columbia University, he met figures such as Margaret Mead and Ruth Benedict, who encouraged him to redirect his interests towards sociology. He joined the social sciences faculty of Chicago University in 1946 and was the main author of *The Lonely Crowd* (1950), which examined conformity and individuality in modern American society. The book helped to popularise sociology to a much wider audience. He returned to Harvard in 1958 as Professor of Social Sciences, a post he held until retirement in 1980. His principal concern was with trends in higher education. In *Constraint and Variety in American Education* (1956), Riesman examined the growing fragmentation and duplication endemic within a system that was driven by market forces. He also criticised anti-intellectual interest groups which sought to compromise academic independence and disinterested enquiry. In *The Academic Revolution* (with Christopher Jencks, 1968), he identified

shifting trends towards greater control of higher education institutions by faculties. He was later to write critically of the sector's tendency to provide for the wants of student consumers. Riesman exercised active leadership as a member of the Carnegie Commission on Higher Education and its Council on Policy Studies.

See also: higher education

STEVEN COWAN

ROBBINS, LIONEL (1898–1984)

Robbins was a British economist and higher education policy maker. He studied at University College, London and at the London School of Economics (LSE). From 1924 to 1930 he held lecturing posts at New College, Oxford and at the LSE. He was appointed to a chair at the LSE aged thirty, remaining in post until 1960. During this period he established himself as a major force in economic theory. His eminence in the field was evidenced by his appointment to direct the economic section of the War Cabinet (1941–45) and his later chairmanship of *The Financial Times* (1961–63). He chaired an official inquiry into higher education from 1961 to 1963, which proposed the substantial expansion of the sector in the 'Robbins Report'. The Report institutionalised the idea that anyone with the requisite academic qualifications and desire to continue their education should be afforded a place. Another product of the Robbins Report was the creation of Colleges of Advanced Technology. Robbins' *The University in the Modern World* (1966) encapsulated his thinking about the link between economic progress and higher education. Another Robbins legacy was the increased international status of the LSE, whose governing body he chaired from 1968 to 1973. Robbins was a prolific author in the fields of theoretical and applied economics.

See also: economics of education; higher education

STEVEN COWAN

ROGERS, CARL (1902–87)

As a student, Rogers, the American psychologist, spent half of 1922 in China, which was to profoundly cement his commitment to the link between science and belief. He graduated in history in 1924, and proceeded to the Union Theological College, but in 1926 abandoned plans to train as a minister of religion in order to study clinical psychology. He obtained a doctorate at Teachers College, Columbia University in 1928 and commenced a post at the Rochester Society for the Prevention of Cruelty to Children. His experiences were encapsulated in *The Clinical Treatment of the Problem Child* (1939), in which he began to outline his thinking about 'relationship therapy', where support was offered through structured social encounters. In 1940 Rogers was elected to a chair at Ohio State University. In *Counselling and Psychotherapy* (1942), Rogers shifted the focus away from the diagnosis of problems and towards therapeutic support for the individual. The book was addressed to wider educational and childcare audiences, including school, health, medical and social services practitioners. His endorsed child-centred counselling, which was to be unconditional and value-free, a view that was to become part of professional standards in succeeding decades. Fuller expression of this approach appeared in *Client-centered Therapy* (1951), which contained detailed accounts and commentaries of actual interviews and support sessions. Rogers moved into informal, alternative and experimental settings in later life, reaching popular audiences with *On Becoming a Person* (1968) and a degree of notoriety with *Freedom to Learn: A View of What Education Might Become* (1969), in which he advocated deschooling.

See also: deschooling; progressive education; psychology of education

STEVEN COWAN

ROUSSEAU, JEAN-JACQUES (1712–78)

Jean-Jacques Rousseau was a French-Swiss thinker and musician, a prominent member of the French Enlightenment, and a forefather of the Romantic Movement. Admired, praised, followed and idolised at times, prosecuted, condemned, and discredited at others, Rousseau and his ideas are a permanent source of contention. Nevertheless, as the author of *Discourse on the Arts and the Sciences* (1750), *The New Heloise* (1761), *Emile* (1762), *The Social Contract* (1762) and the posthumous *Confessions* (1782), Rousseau has influenced, perhaps more profoundly than any of his contemporaries, literary, political, social, moral, and, above all, educational thought since the eighteenth century.

Rousseau's educational ideas, as he admitted himself, reflect his personal feelings. Losing both parents at an early age, Rousseau lived a turbulent life. Failing to find his place in society, he criticised the contemporary social conventions, and sought to reform them through education. In his *Political Economy* (1755) and *Consideration on the Government of Poland* (1772), Rousseau advanced the notion of a nationalistic education that would result in social reconstruction. In the novel *The New Heloise* (1761), he idealised the development of morals through education in a family setting, but his most comprehensive, renowned and influential treatment of education is found in *Emile*. Written partly as a romance, and partly as a philosophical treaty, this work describes the upbringing, from birth to marriage, of an ordinary child, Emile, by his tutor, Jean-Jacques. The work is divided into five books, each dealing with a different period in Emile's life. The last book also refers to the education of Emile's future wife, Sophie. The ultimate aim of Emile's education is the creation of a good and happy individual, fit to live, not in the present society, but in Rousseau's ideal one.

At the heart of Rousseau's educational theory, as set out in Emile, is a unique perception of human nature. He held that the

497

individual is born happy and good, mainly because his desires do not exceed his powers. From this starting point, he came to the conclusion that the role of education is to protect, rather than to change, human nature. Believing that contemporary society had a corrupting influence, he sought not to initiate Emile into it, but to protect him from it. Until the age of fifteen, Emile is educated in almost complete physical, social and intellectual isolation. His education takes place in the countryside and he rarely comes into contact with anyone but his tutor. Moreover, Rousseau argued that, until the age of twelve, education should be negative. No commands or punishments are to be given to the child and he is to be taught nothing directly. Emile hardly reads books or receives formal lessons. Instead, he is forced to know and accept what his tutor thinks is worthy, by being placed in situations and conditions that would necessarily lead him to that. Learning, according to Rousseau, should be based on experience. Although this idea has profoundly affected educational theory, Rousseau's approach to teaching has been severely criticised for neglecting the intellectual aspects of education and for its use of manipulative measures and hidden power.

Rousseau also held an innovative understanding of child development, which has led some to claim that he 'discovered' childhood. Unlike his educational predecessors, who thought of the child as a little adult, Rousseau recognised that, according to their age, children have distinctive needs, capabilities, and interests. Promoting the notion that development occurs in phases, he sought to adapt education and the principles of learning to the developmental stage of the child. One of Rousseau's most basic and influential ideas was that education should not try to accelerate the child's development, but rather follow its natural progress. In contrast, however, to Rousseau's progressive approach to childhood stands his attitude towards women's education. Sophie complements Emile, but she is not his equal. Her education, according

to Rousseau, was directed towards making her a competent mother and housekeeper, yet leaving her ignorant and submissive.

Rousseau's educational ideas, despite their controversial nature, have transformed modern education. They inspired the reformers of the French Revolution. They deeply influenced prominent educational thinkers, including Pestalozzi, Froebel, Neill and Tolstoy. They brought the individual and the child to the centre of attention. They also prompted the creation of a direct link between education and psychology. But, most importantly, they laid the seeds of a new educational discourse, one that is still present. The significance of Rousseau's educational thought is best indicated by the fact that, even today, almost 250 years after publication of his most influential writing, this continues to stir heated debates.

See also: child-centred education; progressive education

Further reading

Bloch, J. (1995) *Rousseauism and Education in Eighteenth-century France*, Oxford: Voltaire Foundations.
Compayré, G. (1908) *Jean-Jacques Rousseau and Education From Nature*, trans. R. P. Jago, London: Harrap.
Martin, J. R. (1985) *Reclaiming a Conversation: The Ideal of the Educated Woman*, London: Yale University Press.

TAL GILEAD

RUGG, HAROLD (1886–1960)

Rugg was born in Fitchburg, Massachusetts, the son of a carpenter. He graduated with a science degree from Dartmouth College in 1908 and qualified in the following year as an engineer. His first lecturing post was in engineering at James Millikin University, Illinois. By 1915 his interests had switched to education, and his Ph.D. thesis focused on mental discipline in school studies. This led to a post at the University of Chicago in educational studies. During World War I he collaborated with Edward Thorndike on army classification and testing. In 1920 Rugg was appointed to a professorship at Columbia University, a post he held until 1951. Rugg's 'Social Science Pamphlets' were issued in twelve volumes between 1921 and 1926. A fourteen-volume textbook series then followed, under the theme 'Man and His Changing Society' (1929–45). These were read widely in American homes, as well as in academic institutions. At the heart of Rugg's work was a belief in education as an agent for social change and social reconstruction. His practical, scientific, engineering experience combined with his progressive child-centred humanism to produce something that was in tune with the period following World War I. But in the post-1945 political climate Rugg was seen by many as a potential subversive, and in some places his writings were banned or even burned. Other principal writings include *Statistical Methods Applied to Education* (1917), *The Child-Centred School* (1926, with Ann Shumaker) and *The Teacher in School and Society* (1950, with B. Marian Brooks).

See also: child-centred education; progressive education; Thorndike, Edward L.

STEVEN COWAN

RURAL EDUCATION

Rural education is a term that refers to the formal teaching/learning environments that are located in non-urban settings. Although the term seems intuitively clear and understandable, it has been used to encompass a wide variety of non-urban environments where education is delivered to children and adults. Traditionally, rural education included education from elementary through secondary school, but recent changes around the world have broadened its scope to include pre-school as well as post-secondary rural education. Worldwide, people associate rural education *qualitatively*, as it conjures up associations linked to agrarian life, small communities and a sense of place, but also less access to resources. Policy makers and governmental agencies have used *quantitative* definitions, using population size and distance from urban centres in order to guide decision making about the allocation of resources. Thus, rural education has multiple levels of use and complexities in the definition.

A major challenge in understanding rural education is how to define 'rural'. Around the world, the *qualitative* definition is similar across both developing and developed countries, even though the scope and the depth of issues clearly differ across countries. Rural is generally associated with at least six characteristics that are agreed upon by organizations as large and global as the United Nations Educational, Scientific and Cultural Organization (UNESCO) and as small and targeted as the Rural Schools and Community Trust. These characteristics include:

- education that takes place at a distance from a large urban area, with most of formal education in developing countries considered rural;
- education that takes place in an environment that has historical roots in an agrarian culture, even though there may be recent decreases in the ties to agriculture because of out-migration and lower levels of farming in many developed countries;
- education that has access to fewer resources, including highly qualified teachers, high-quality buildings, and high-quality professional development and curricula;
- education that has been traditionally thought to take place in small schools, although in some countries there are current trends towards large consolidated schools;
- education that tries to meet the needs of the community through cooperation with other sectors of the local economy, such as support of agrarian life but with a need for children to attend school; and
- education that is grounded in a 'sense of place' and rooted in the lives of the

499

families. These qualitative attributes of rural education are reflected in the consensus definition provided by the International Research and Training Centre for Rural Education (INRULED). They provide descriptors rather than a tight definition, using phrases such as 'comprehensive change agent', 'an integral part of socio-economic development', and 'cultural centre of local community and village' (INRULED 1991).

When the above six descriptors associated with the *qualitative* definition of rural education are used in both developed and developing countries, rural people are found to be different from urban people. A few generally accepted differences include rural people being less educated, more homogeneous with respect to ethnicity and culture (although this is changing especially in developed countries with large immigrant groups changing the face of rural communities), living in more intergenerational families who have lived in the area for generations, experiencing more migration of educated youth, having higher levels of poverty and displaying higher levels of discrimination with respect to minority groups, including women.

The challenge of defining 'rural' in a *quantitative* way has proved more difficult than the qualitative definitions. There are enormous differences around the world in quantitative definitions of rural education. The United Nations has acknowledged that there is really no way to accurately compare rural education across countries because of the differing, and sometimes vague, quantitative definitions developed by different countries. For instance, the Population Division of the United Nations defined rural population as the 'population living in areas classified as rural, that is, it is the difference between the total population of a country and its urban population'. This vague definition was compounded by the definition of urban that included the 'population living in areas clas-

sified as urban according to the criteria used by each area or country' (Atchoarena and Gasperini 2003: 38). This kind of consensus definition among countries actually hinders international comparisons and the authors of the UN report call for the development of specific indicators in the definition for comparative purposes. Weisheit *et al.* (1995) found no single widely accepted definition of rural. They encouraged scholars interested in rural issues to adopt a definition that makes intuitive sense, is easy and unproblematic, and allows for comparisons with other research. Above all, they urged scholars to make their rural definition explicit. This has been harder to accomplish than many might think.

Most countries in the world depend on quantitative definitions to describe their population and draft policy for rural areas, including education policy. For instance, in the United States, the Census Bureau and the Office of Management and Budget (OMB) have used a number of definitions of rural over the years to describe the changing population in the USA and to allocate resources to schools located in rural areas. These definitions have classified counties into urban and rural depending on the size of the largest cities within the counties, using the Beale Codes or the Rural–Urban Continuum Codes developed by OMB. These systems have been criticised because some very large counties with a city may be designated as urban, even though there might be large pockets of rural communities within the county. Recently, the US Department of Education updated its own guidelines to reflect advances in technology and research in defining rural schools. In 2006 they revised the classification of schools with a system called *Rural Locales*. This system classifies areas of the USA into twelve different categories, three of which are rural. The Locale code for an area is based on the place's population size and distance from a populous area. The advantages of this new system are that it does not rely on county boundaries, it has a small city designation, it better identifies suburban areas and towns, and it has a more differentiated classification of rural areas. Rural places may be fringe, distant, or remote from an urbanised area, depending on its distance from that area. Any school within these three categories is considered rural. In contrast to these gradations from urban to rural that work for the USA, Canada (Statistics Canada 2001) has made a recommendation that 'rural and small town' include the population living in towns outside the commuting zone of large urban areas of population greater than 10,000. South Africa has an even more different and historical approach to defining rural education. It has identified traditional authorities that are community owned and formal rural areas that were commercial farms in traditionally white areas of South Africa (Ministry of Education 2005), classifying these as rural education areas. Each country's definition gives precision in defining rural education within that country, but the varied definitions make quantitative comparisons across countries impossible.

Although there are challenges to both the quantitative and qualitative definitions of rural education, there are some common emerging trends around the world. According to UNESCO, there was tremendous growth in rural education from 1960 to 1985. Developed countries dramatically increased students and institutions in the 1960s and 1970s, with a decline in population from the 1980s to the present. By contrast, developing countries have made gains since the 1990s in both population and institutions. UNESCO has highlighted the growing crisis in rural education because even though there have been great advances in education in rural areas, the gap in educational attainment and resources for education is increasing between rural and urban areas. Poverty associated with rural areas and the concomitant lack of rural political power has accentuated this gap. Yet some recent trends have helped it to close: advances in technology have reduced the psychological distance between urban and

rural education. In many developed and some developing countries, teleconferencing, distance education, Web-based professional development and the generally greater access to communication via cellphones and the internet have improved access to resources remarkably in many rural areas. For instance, it is now possible for teachers in remote areas to complete college-level classes from their home community, download curricula materials at almost no cost, and participate in long-distance consultation with the best research and development centres. Another emergent trend is the expansion of the scope of education in rural areas. No longer is rural education thought to be restricted to elementary through secondary school, but is has been expanded to include early childhood education and post-secondary education. In addition, education that was focused mostly on traditional classroom subjects such as literacy, history, social studies, and mathematics has now been expanded to include health issues, cultural history, and technological skills that can fuel the rural economy. These advances have been accomplished through the cooperation of international, national, and local agencies with the support of foundations and professional organisations that have helped mobilise the resources and the will to support rural education in the future. In the United States they include organisations such as the National Rural Education Association (NREA), the Organizations Concerned about Rural Education (OCRE), and foundations such as the Rural Schools and Community Trust. Other important organisations around the world include the Australian Rural Education Research Association; the Isolated Children's Parents Association of Australia; the Rural Development Council of Ireland; the Africa Foundation; Aga Khan Education Services; and the International Research and Training Centre for Rural Education, to name but a few. The collective will of these partners over the next decade should help develop better definitions of rural education, preserve the best features of rural education, and

501

provide more and better resources in education for the world's rural people.

See also: community education/school/college; distance education/learning; United Nations Educational, Scientific and Cultural Organization (UNESCO); urban education; virtual learning

Further reading

Atchoarena, D. and Gasperini, L. (eds) (2003) *Education for Rural Development: Towards New Policy Responses*, Paris: UNESCO.

Chatterjee, B. and Khan, Q. (eds) (2003) *Rural Education: Status and Trends*, Hebei, China: INRULED.

Geverdt, J. and Phan, T. (2006) *Documentation to the NCES Common Core of Data Public Elementary/Secondary School Locale code File: School Year 2003–2004* (NCES 2006–2332), US Department of Education, Washington DC: National Center for Educational Statistics.

IRULED (1991) *Final Report of the International Symposium on Rural Education*, Shandong, China: UNESCO.

McLauglin, D. H., Huberman, M. B. and Hawkins, E. K. (1997) *Characteristics of Small and Rural School Districts*, Washington DC: NCES, US Department of Education.

Ministry of Education (South Africa) (2005) *Education for Rural People in Africa: Policy Lessons, Options and Priorities*, South Africa: UNESCO.

Statistics Canada (2001) 'Rural and small town Canada', *Analysis Bulletin*, 3(3): 1–17.

Weisheit, R. A., Wells, L. E. and Falcon, D. N. (1995) 'Community policing in small town and rural America', *Crime and Delinquency*, 4(3): 331–61.

LYNNE VERNON-FEAGANS

RUSSIA

The Russian Federation (RF) occupies a land mass of 17 million square kilometres: it is the nation with largest surface area in the world. The RF consists of eighty-nine regions and republics, divided into the following four classes: twenty-one republics (including Chechnya); fifty-two *oblast*, or regions; ten autonomous *okrugs*, or districts; and six *krais*, or territories. The republics are titular homelands of non-Russian minorities, such as *oblast* and *krais*. Russia has eleven time zones and more than 100 languages are spoken by its various nationalities. In 2006 Russia's population was 142.9 million, yet the country is sparsely populated, with only around nine people per square kilometre. The bulk of the population, which is forecast to decline to 134 million by 2015, resides in urban areas.

In the imperial age, especially between the reigns of Peter the Great (1672–1725) and Nicholas II (1868–1918), educational policy shifted from egalitarian to elitist principles. Peter the Great promoted able men, irrespective of class, occupation, wealth, or ethnicity. Education as an agency of social transformation has been a significant feature of the Russian cultural heritage since the Westernising era of Peter the Great and the reforms of the Enlightenment under Catherine the Great (1762–96). The Russian census of 1897 indicated that only 22 per cent of the population were literate (12 per cent for females). By 1920 the literacy rate increased to 54 per cent, climbing to almost 100 per cent in 1960.

Between 1917 and 2007, Russia experienced three major politico-economic and educational transformations. The first radical ideological transformation was due to the 1917 October (Bolshevik) Revolution and the Civil War that followed. By 1922, the Union of Soviet Socialist Republics (USSR) was formed. The October 1917 revolution, which put Lenin and the Bolsheviks in power, was followed by the complete rejection of most political and educational assumptions, and the formation of a communist education system. The second transformation occurred during Stalin's rule (1924–53), which was affected by World War II, and resulted in a significant industrial output. Within less than thirty years the USSR, by means of compulsory schooling for the masses, ideology, power and control, had brought the backward, agrarian nation, which tsarist Russia had been, to a position of world hegemony. During World War II the USSR played a major part in defeating Nazi Germany and, after 1945, it was a superpower which, between the 1950s and mid-1980s posed a potential nuclear threat to the United States of America. From 1957, when the Sputnik was launched, there was renewed international interest in Soviet education, especially in regard to its influence upon modernisation, science, technology and economic progress.

The third radical ideological transformation, brought on by economic stagnation, took place under President Mikhail Gorbachev, who introduced *glasnost* (openness), and *perestroika* (restructuring). This proved to be the undoing of the state. In December 1991, the USSR collapsed, and the new Russian Federation, under President Boris Yeltsin, was born. Yeltsin became the first elected president of the RF, and ruled until 1999. The education reform challenged the excessively centralised Soviet education system by introducing Western and market-oriented models of decentralisation, privatisation, and marketisation in the economy and society.

During the 1990s, Yeltsin's government transformed Russia's communist and centrally planned economy into a capitalist, market economy. The strategies of 'shock therapy', the dismantling of the Soviet welfare state and price controls, and the introduction of privatisation devastated the living standards of many Russians (Nikandrov 2001) and the education sector was badly affected by the economic meltdown which prompted Yeltsin's resignation in 2000.

The geography of Russia has always hindered the implementation of government education reforms aimed at improving literacy, standards, curricula, and teaching programmes. Apart from the geographic isolation of some schools, for example in the far east and far north, problems have also stemmed from the size and variety of population, their nationalities and languages spoken. Some 130 languages were spoken in the USSR, with newspapers published in sixty-five different languages. Pluralism in education had been guaranteed by the Constitution of the USSR, with article 45 stressing the pupils' rights 'to attend a school where teaching is in the native language'.

The hegemonic goal of schooling in the USSR was the building of a new kind of society, conceived after the October 1917 Revolution (Zajda 1980). While Stalin's era (1924–53) and the post-Stalin system of Soviet schooling (1954–64) provided invaluable ingredients for technological, military and economic success, security and social stability, they also produced some negative outcomes, including political indoctrination, strict Party control of education and society, unwieldy meritocratic and technocratic schooling, and excessively competitive examinations at all levels of education.

By 1977, Soviet educational attainment had greatly improved. Ten-year schooling had become free and compulsory, the number of students in higher education institutions had multiplied by forty since 1914, and five times as many students were receiving a secondary education. The Soviet system, as a hybrid of Euro-Soviet schooling, had inherited a long-standing centralising tradition from imperial Russia. Its characteristic features – central control, a universal and compulsory curriculum, and political socialisation – characterised education in Russia for six decades until 1991.

A historical survey of education reforms in Russia over the last three centuries, beginning with Peter the Great's founding of a School of Mathematical and Naval Sciences in St Petersburg in 1703, through to the final years of the USSR during the late 1980s, demonstrates some unresolved tensions between the role of the state and the economic imperatives. It also depicts the dialectic between tradition and global influences, which is identifiable today. The new hybrid of higher education in Russia, for example, reflects the nexus between those aspects that were lost during the Soviet era and the Westernisation of universities. Recent years have witnessed a restoration of the Russian relationship with European academic life and the reintroduction of Russia into the international network of tertiary education.

Figures from 2006 reveal that 15 million students were attending some 62,000 schools, of which 41,000 were rural schools, 5,600 of these having fewer than twenty pupils. General education schools (*obshchaia sredniaia shkola*) provide elementary (grades 1–4) and secondary (grades 5–11/12) schooling. Recent curriculum reforms have seen a foreign language (e.g. English, French, German, or Spanish) introduced into grade 5, biology and geography into grade 6, civics into grades 6–9, and information technology in grades 8 and 9. In 2001 legislation defined four different types of secondary schools in Russia: lyceums; gymnasia; special schools with intensive courses of study; and general schools. The new state public examinations (*yedinssvenneyi gosudarstvennyi examen* – YGE) for the final year of secondary schooling are currently held in year 11, but Russia is introducing twelve-year schooling, modelled on the West.

Between 1991 and 2007 Russia attempted a major restructuring of its entire educational system. Higher education reforms included the introduction of bachelor's and master's degrees and a six-level system from diploma to doctorate. In 2006 there were 655 state higher education institutions (VUZ) and 645 private institutions, with the latter sector experiencing dramatic growth in the past fifteen years. During recent years the largest increase in the number of first-year students, of some 600 per cent, was in private colleges (from 183,000 in 1997 to 1,079,300 in 2005). There are eighty-nine private higher education institutions in Moscow alone. Efforts to limit the proportion of private students have frequently failed, because cash-strapped universities prefer to enrol full-fee paying students. In response to globalisation, market forces and the Bologna Process, Russia has introduced its own 'league tables' for universities and institutions are likely to be categorised into 'flagship', 'major' and 'other' groups (Fursenko 2006).

Since 1991 the RF has experienced an era of 'endless reforms'. The concepts of decentralisation, delegation, devolution, school-based/site-based management and self-governing schools were introduced at the height of decentralisation and privatisation during the 1990s. Recent major policy reforms in the higher education sector have resulted in the growth of private universities and fee-paying students (Zajda 2006). The impact of globalisation and market forces has produced a new dimension of social stratification and educational inequality. The application of market principles to schooling, especially in private schools, and school choice in general, reflects the new trend of concentrating cultural capital and educational privilege among the children of the privileged *Novye Russkie* (the New Russian bourgeoisie). Streaming by ability, competitive entrance examinations, elite universities, and restricted entry into the higher education sector (unless one is a full fee-paying student), typical of capitalist democracies, is the new dysfunctional outcome of a reform that is inherently inequitable, despite the proffered policy of curricular equivalence, state standards, and state exams. These developments are likely to be significant for the destiny of the RF.

See also: centralisation/decentralisation; meritocracy, privatisation/marketisation; rural education

Further reading

Fursenko, A. (2006) 'Vuzy budut pervogo, vtorogo i tretjevo sorta' (Higher education institutions will be first, second and third class), *Moskovski Komsomolets*, 6 December.

Nikandrov, N. (2001) *Rossiia: Sotsializatsiia I Vospitanie Na Rubezhe Tysiachileti* (*Russia: Socialisation and Upbringing at the Crossroads of Millennia*), Cheboksary: Chuvash University Press.

Zajda, J. (1980) *Education in the USSR*, Oxford: Pergamon Press.

——(2006) 'Schooling, education reforms and policy shifts in the Russian Federation (1991–2004)'. In K. Masurek and M. Winzer (eds) *Schooling Around the World*, Boston MA: Pearson Allyn and Bacon.

JOSEPH ZAJDA AND REA ZAJDA

S

SABBATICAL

A sabbatical gives provision for an established member of an educational institution to pursue a particular set of goals for a specified period that cannot be developed in normal working circumstances. In an institution of higher education, for example, it is often possible to apply for sabbatical for a term or a longer period to concentrate on a programme of research that may often involve travel away from the institution. In some institutions this might be arranged on a regular basis, perhaps every five years, while in others it might only be provided in particular circumstances. Usually, sabbatical leave is awarded with the usual pay for the employee involved, but on some occasions unpaid leave might be given. In most cases it is expected that a report be provided for the institution at the end of the sabbatical leave to explain the extent to which it has achieved its purposes. In schools and other educational institutions in different countries, regular sabbatical leave may also be provided for a range of purposes.

Student unions often provide for sabbatical officers of the union to take a year out of their study or remain at the institution following the end of their course. This differs from a gap year, which students may take before or after their course in higher education to gain experience of different societies and environments, often through travel and casual work.

See also: higher education; semester/term; university

GARY McCULLOCH

SADLER, MICHAEL (1780–1835)

Sadler wrote his first social pamphlet, *An Apology for the Methodists*, aged seventeen in 1797. This reflected a shift within his family from Anglicanism towards Methodism. He lived and worked in Leeds, Yorkshire, where he was to serve as honorary treasurer for the poor rates. Here, he became aware of the hardship endured by children working in cotton mills. Sadler developed ideas for the state to develop a social conscience, making it incumbent upon government to intervene where private, individual effort was ineffective. He was elected Member of Parliament in 1829 and, during the following six years, wrote about social conditions in Britain. These included his poem *The Factory Girl's Last Day* (1830) *and On the Distress of the Agricultural Labourer* (1831). In 1832 he introduced into Parliament a bill proposing to limit child labour to ten hours a day. Although this was defeated, he secured the chairmanship of a parliamentary inquiry into child labour. Some of the workers interviewed by Sadler's committee were dismissed by their employers, creating a scandal that turned public opinion. The committee report, published in 1833, had considerable impact and eventually led to a series of parliamentary Acts to restrain and regulate child labour and to make some compulsory provision of schooling. After his death, Sadler's work was taken forward by Lord Ashley, the Earl of Shaftesbury.

See also: compulsory education; workers' education

STEVEN COWAN

SADLER, MICHAEL ERNEST (1861–1943)

A pioneer of comparative education studies, Sadler was educated at Trinity College, Oxford, gaining a degree in literature and humanities in 1882. Whilst there, he became president of the student union, partly due to his powers of persuasion skills in debate. He was later appointed secretary of the Oxford University Delegacy for Local Examinations, the extension college, which allowed Sadler to tour the country giving lectures to working-class adults. He also participated in summer schools and was a central figure in the establishment of several libraries. The extension school model of Oxford, which Sadler did much to promote, eventually came to be copied by other British universities. He proposed a conference on the question of secondary education in 1893, which led to the establishment of the Bryce Commission of 1894. Sadler's ideas on secondary education – some of which were embodied in the Bryce Report (1895) and the 1902 Education Act – were influenced by the German example and the work of Kerschensteiner. These can be found in *Continuation Schools in England and Elsewhere* (1907). From 1895 to 1903 Sadler was director of the English Office of Special Inquiries and Reports. This office produced eleven volumes of detailed studies of educational practice from around the world, laying a basis for what was to become comparative education studies. From 1903 to 1911 Sadler was Professor of Education at Manchester University. During this period he wrote a series of major reports for local authorities advising them on how best to implement aspects of the 1902 Education Act. This was

followed by the vice-chancellorship of Leeds University (1911–23), a period in which he oversaw its growth into a major centre for academic research and higher studies.

See also: comparative education; extra-mural class; summer school

STEVEN COWAN

SANDWICH COURSE

In the context of higher education, a sandwich course is one that permits a student to complete a period of paid work experience part-way through their registration for a degree with a higher education institution. During the 1970s and 1980s, sandwich courses at diploma and degree levels were pioneered by British polytechnics, many of which later became universities. This was particularly so in such vocational areas as business studies and engineering. Today, certain undergraduate degrees are marketed as sandwich courses, with students completing one or more placements ahead of commencing their final year of study. The sandwich 'filling' may be 'thick', taking the form of a single placement for a year, or may include several 'thin' periods of work experience. Where a higher education provider does not formally offer a sandwich course qualification route it may nevertheless still be possible for students to take a year out in order to work, perhaps for a business sponsor. Sandwich courses encourage industry-higher education links that may offer benefits for all parties. Students have an opportunity to acquire practical, on-the-job skills that may enhance their employment prospects after graduation, while courses trade on their associations with prestigious employers. Businesses, meanwhile, may benefit from the enthusiasm and creativity of generally young and cheap-to-employ undergraduates eager to make a positive impression. Official support for sandwich courses is offered by such leading British bodies as the Royal Academy of Engineering, which runs a 'Year in Industry' scheme. Occasionally, students may follow a sandwich course route to employment in the public sector. For example, the British civil service offers sandwich placements in a range of government departments.

See also: college; degree; higher education; polytechnic; qualifications; university; vocational education; work-based/work-located/workplace/work-related learning

DAVID CROOK

SARASON, SEYMOUR (1919–)

Sarason was born in New York into a family of immigrant Jewish tailors. His writings reflect a dual concern with American identity and perceptions from the margins of institution. As a teenager he contracted polio and this informed his thinking about the processes that people with disabilities undergo and the things that are done to them in the name of care. After winning a scholarship at Clarke University, Worcester, Massachusetts, he moved in 1942 to practical work at the Southbury Training School for mentally challenged people. Here he developed his scepticism about a number of orthodoxies within clinical psychology. In 1945 he began his lifelong association with Yale University's psychology department. His *Psychological Problems in Mental Deficiency* (1949) was the first of many texts which probed and critiqued existing orthodoxies and practice within the field. This led to an expanded interest in the need for interdisciplinary thinking, research and practice, from which flowed such books as *The Clinical Interaction* (1954) and *Psychology in Community Settings* (1966). This further led to his active engagement in the field of education studies. Jointly with Davidson and Blatt he wrote *The Preparation of Teachers: an Unstudied Problem* (1962). Such work emanated from the Yale Institute of Human Relations. His interest in alternative community settings for the better realisation of the talents of mentally challenged people connected with growing concerns about

resistance to change within educational settings. He argued that traditional and entrenched political interests and values within schools negated attempts at positive change. This view found full expression in the *The Culture of the School and the Problem of Change* (1971). A further major preoccupation of Sarason's has been the lack of historical and social content within teacher training and practice. In *The Case for Change* (1993) Sarason discusses gaps in the training that teachers receive. In *Teaching as a Performing Art* (1999) he advances a view of the necessary skills and abilities for effective teaching in order to contrast with the content of existing courses.

See also: psychology; special education/special educational needs/special needs; teaching/teaching methods

STEVEN COWAN

SCANDINAVIA

The different models of education systems around the world can usually be clustered in regions in terms of their distinctiveness. This is also the case for the Scandinavian countries, Denmark, Norway and Sweden, as they share in common similar traits that distinguish themselves from other European education systems. The Scandinavian countries share the same basic institutional structure which best can be defined as an all-through, non-selective state school with mixed ability classes covering the entire compulsory school age. In contrast to other countries, such as those of the United Kingdom in particular, the private sector is also relatively weak in each country, Norway being the most extreme example with 98 per cent of children in state schools. The private schools are not selective in an elitist sense and are largely funded and controlled by the state. Upper secondary schools are differentiated in Scandinavia, Sweden being the exception with its integrated academic/vocational *gymnasieskola*, but upper secondary education has near universal enrolments in all of these countries.

School choice has been introduced in Denmark and Sweden, but the salience at the secondary level is rather limited since most children stay in their initial local school and its impact has mainly been limited to the major urban areas. Measures to increase private schools have not substantially enlarged that sector in any of these countries.

The Scandinavian countries all share an exceptionally egalitarian structure of schooling, with all kinds of selection delayed until the upper secondary phase. A number of pre-conditions existed in the nineteenth century, which helped the early introduction of a linear education system as opposed to the parallel education systems that persisted – often until the mid-twentieth century – in, for example, France, Germany and the UK. In Scandinavia, the lower secondary classes in the Latin schools were transferred in to new middle schools which then provided a single educational ladder from the primary schools through to the upper secondary schools. The middle school was introduced in Norway in 1869, Denmark in 1903 and in Sweden in 1905, and its importance cannot be underestimated as it allowed the school types to be articulated with one another so that all children, in principle, could progress as far as their abilities allowed. The Scandinavian states shared a common Lutheran religious heritage, which was favourable to the establishment of universal literacy, and they were also early to introduce state regulation of education, thus creating the basis for later systematic reforms. Furthermore, their social class systems were distinctly favourable to populist politics since they combined relative weak landowning and bourgeois classes with a strong class of independent peasant farmers who were able to form alliances with the smaller nascent working classes of the industrial areas. The relative social and political weakness of the landowning and bourgeois classes meant the secondary school was less skewed towards the upper classes than in many other countries, thus making it easier to combine the secondary school with the primary school using the middle school as a link. The strong independent peasant class was thus the major force in propelling the liberal parties in the latter part of the nineteenth century which successfully introduced the middle school.

The second major wave of reform occurred under social democratic governments in these countries, and dates largely from after World War II. Social democracy has been exceptionally powerful here, mainly due to these governments' ability to weld political alliances between the industrial working class, small farmers and sections of the middle class. It has been these parties, often in coalition with liberal allies, which have pushed through the particular radical comprehensivisation of school systems. This was done by abolishing the middle school in order to introduce, first, a seven-year – then, later, a nine-year – comprehensive school. Norway abolished its middle schools in 1936, progressively integrating them with the primary schools to create a nine-year, all-through comprehensive school by 1969. Denmark abolished its middle schools in 1958 and by 1975 had completed its own transition to a nine-year comprehensive school system. Sweden introduced its nine-year comprehensive system in 1962, after extensive trials, as in Norway, in the 1950s; and then, after 1969, started to integrate its upper secondary schools as well. Subsequently, all three countries progressively eliminated streaming and setting in all subjects, so that the schools today are almost entirely mixed ability. Neo-liberal winds have been blowing over Scandinavia in recent years, which may undermine the strong egalitarianism of the schools, but it is too early to say anything conclusively about their effects.

See also: egalitarianism; Finland; Sweden

Further reading

Tjeldvoll, A. (ed.) (1998) *Education and the Scandinavian Welfare State in the Year 2000*, New York: Garland Publishing.

Wiborg, S. (2004) 'Education and social integration: a comparative study of the comprehensive school system in Scandinavia', *London Review of Education*, 2(2): 83–93.

——(forthcoming 2007) *Education and Social Integration: The Uneven Advance of the Comprehensives*, New York: Palgrave Macmillan.

SUSANNE WIBORG

SCHOLAR

'Scholar' is frequently used to refer to a learned person, a specialist and original thinker, whose research and writings – scholarship – are held in very high regard. An academic working in a highly prescribed field, too, may be identified as, for example, a Shakespearean or Biblical scholar. Traditionally, the term scholar had a particular application in the field of arts, humanities, languages and religion, but contemporary universities are apt to describe their leading academic staff members from any faculty or department as world-class scholars. Universities sometimes confer the title of Visiting Scholar on a distinguished colleague from another university. The title sometimes carries the expectation that the visiting scholar will lecture or perform some other duties within the host institution.

'Scholar' can be used in a very broad sense to describe any schoolchild. More specifically, the recipient of a scholarship to a school, college or institution of higher education is a scholar. In Britain, for example, there is a notable tradition of leading private schools and universities appointing young music scholars. For example, cathedral schools typically offer choral scholarships and a number of colleges of Oxford and Cambridge universities fund organ scholarships. Scholarships are sometimes attached to educational charities or trusts. Former American president Bill Clinton held the title of Rhodes Scholar while studying at Oxford University between 1968 and 1970.

See also: academic/academic profession; scholarship; student

DAVID CROOK

SCHOLARSHIP

Scholarship is a term with two broad meanings. The first refers to academic achievement or a fund of knowledge; the second to a grant of money to support a student.

Scholarship in the first sense is the product of specialised research and study. Its synonyms include learning and erudition. It may be used with reference to the high levels of learning and academic achievement of an individual scholar, and in previous centuries was particularly applied to proficiency in the Greek and Latin languages and literature. The term is also used in a more general sense to encompass the collective attainments of scholars or the methods and standards characteristic of a good scholar. For example, historical scholarship might be defined in terms of the ability to consult all of the relevant primary and secondary sources, to form an independent judgement and to present the findings in a clear and accessible form.

The second meaning of scholarship is of a grant of money awarded to a student of merit by a government, foundation, college or other body to pay for her or his educational expenses such as fees, upkeep, books, etc. Scholarships are typically awarded on the results of an examination to enable meretricious students to proceed from one level of education to another, for example from elementary to secondary school, or from secondary school to university.

In England, during the twentieth century, the term 'scholarship examination' was widely applied to the examination (also known as the eleven plus) that decided which children should proceed to grammar schools and which should go to secondary technical and secondary modern schools. Another type of scholarship examination took place at the end of secondary schooling. This was in addition to the Higher School Certificate – subsequently the General Certificate of Education, Advanced Level – and was used to determine the award of State Scholarships in support of pupils proceeding to university.

Prior to 1850 the majority of scholarships to the universities of Oxford and Cambridge were confined to boys from specified schools, districts or families. They were also restricted by subject. For example, in 1909 more than half of the scholarships and exhibitions at Oxford were in classics. Although more open scholarships became available during the twentieth century, apart from the universities of Oxford and Cambridge, higher education establishments in the UK are not well endowed and there are few scholarships. This is in contrast to the USA where, in addition to scholarships offered by individual universities, there are some 6,000 competitive scholarships offered annually.

International programmes of long standing include the Rhodes Scholarships, established in 1903 by Cecil Rhodes to enable students from the English-speaking world and beyond to study at the University of Oxford. Rhodes' purpose was to promote international understanding amongst the world's leaders. His criteria for selection, therefore, included not only literary and scholastic attainments, but also leadership potential, moral qualities and sporting prowess. American scholars have featured strongly in this programme and currently comprise about a third of the ninety-two annual awards.

There are a number of contemporary international scholarship programmes that enable students to study at undergraduate and postgraduate levels in countries other than their own. Ilchman *et al.* (2004) provide a substantial overview of national and international scholarships. Major international programmes emanating from Europe currently include the ERASMUS/SOCRATES programme of the European Union which comprises nearly 2,000 participating universities, and the German Deutscher Akademischer Austauschdienst (DAAD) which in 2002 made grants to 14,687 Germans to study outside of Germany and 21,334 for non-Germans to study in Germany. The Commonwealth Scholarships and Fellowships Plan, inaugurated at the first conference of Commonwealth education ministers in 1959, makes 600 awards annually of up to three years duration. One of the best known American examples is the Fulbright Program, which funds senior scholars and other students for study abroad and supports teacher exchanges between American and foreign educators. Two recent initiatives are those of the Ford Foundation, which in 2000 made a grant of $280 million for an international fellowship programme of 300–400 awards per year; and the Bill and Melinda Gates Foundation of $210 million for the Gates Cambridge Scholarship to fund 200 students annually from around the world to study topics that relate to global problems at postgraduate level at the University of Cambridge.

See also: academic/academic profession; classical studies; elementary school; examinations; Rhodes Trust; scholar; secondary school/education; student finance/loans; university

Further reading

Ilchman, A. S., Ilchman, W. F. and Tolar, M. H. (eds) (2004) *The Lucky Few and the Worthy Many: Scholarship Competitions and the World's Future Leaders*, Bloomington IN: Indiana University Press.
Nicholls, G. (2005) *The Challenge to Scholarship: Rethinking Learning, Teaching and Research*, London: Routledge.

RICHARD ALDRICH

SCHOLASTICISM

The term scholasticism comes from the Latin *scholasticus*, meaning 'that which belongs to a school' and refers to a method of learning which schoolmen (academics) pursued in the universities of Western Europe during the Middle Ages. The transition to the Middle Ages was marked by the emergence of new ideas and learning. A catalyst for this is to be seen, for example, in the city of Toledo, where the interchange of ideas of between

Christians, Muslims and Jews allowed the teachings of the philosopher Aristotle to be reintroduced into the mainstream of European culture. A parallel movement was the desire to give a more rigorous and systematic account of Church teachings, which may be seen in interpretation of the Bible by Anselm of Laon (died 1117), the use of dialectic in the works of Peter Abelard (1079–1142) and the *Sentences* of Peter Lombard (*c.*1100–60).

Scholastic method, which emerged from these influences, has two main elements: reading (*lectio*) and disputation (*disputatio*). Disputations might take one of two forms: the first in which the topic for dispute was announced prior to the discourse and the second in which the topic was unannounced (*quodlibet*). *Disputatio* was pursued through the critical investigation of a chosen scholar's work, and the comparison of this with authoritative texts such as Bible or Conciliar documents. Where the chosen scholar and other sources disagreed, statements of the disagreement would be written down and collected: 'sentences' (*sententiae*). The disputation was continued through a dialectical process which aimed at producing a synthesis of agreement. Agreement was sought through the use of philology and logic, which were used to demonstrate that words had a variety of meanings which might be brought into harmony. The written output of this method of disputation is seen in works known as *quaestiones*, 'questions', while a more systematic output was the *summa*. A classic example of such a systematic theological disputation is the *Summa Theologiae* of Thomas Aquinas (*c.*1225–74).

During the Middle Ages there was a variety of schools of theological thought. Disputes that arose between the schools focused on the detail of doctrines and were often acrimonious. Such disputes were often between members of two of the leading religious orders, the Dominicans and the Franciscans. While earlier scholasticism focused mainly on issues of philosophy and theology, later on the schools of the universities began to widen

their brief into such areas as nature and science. This broadening of interests was also paralleled by divergent approaches to core scholastic concerns such as 'universals'. 'Realists' argued that general categories or concepts such as colours were 'real', 'nominalists' argued the contrary. The work of John Duns Scotus (*c.*1266–1308), a realist, gave rise to another theological school of thought, with a focus on human freedom of will (voluntarism); while William of Ockham (*c.*1288–1348), a nominalist, also sought to question scholastic methods, applying his 'razor' to the complexities he saw in the inherited traditions of scholastic thought. By the late fourteenth century, John Wycliffe (*c.*1320–84) took questions of change further still and is often seen as a precursor to the Protestant reformers.

The new learning of the Renaissance in Europe signalled a further challenge to the methods of scholasticism. Humanists such as Erasmus (1466–1536) were especially critical of scholasticism, and this was echoed by the Protestant reformers such as Martin Luther (1483–1546) and John Calvin (1509–64). Their theological work is as much a rejection of the schoolmen as it is the positive creation of something different. However while the Council of Trent (1545–63) did not simply reiterate the methodological assumptions of the scholastics, Roman Catholic theology remained largely committed to the paradigms of Thomas Aquinas' *Summa*. It is also the case that after the initial flowering of a new scholarship and theological method among the Protestant reformers, later generations settled into a reiteration of opinions and disputes akin to those of the medieval schoolmen.

While some Protestant theologians attempted to engage with the philosophical consequences of the Enlightenment, Roman Catholic theologians, on the whole, did not. In that tradition, scholarship during the nineteenth and early twentieth centuries was characterised by a neo-Thomism or neo-scholasticism, apart from the brief emergence of the 'Catholic modernists'. It was only with the emergence of nouvelle théologie in the mid-twentieth century in figures such as Chenu, de Lubac and Congar that the dominance of scholasticism was at last challenged, and the path to the Second Vatican Council was prepared.

See also: church; religious education; scholar; scholarship; theology

Further reading

Evans, G. R. (2001) *The Medieval Theologians*, Oxford: Blackwell.
Kenny, A. (1980) *Aquinas*, Past Masters series, New York: Oxford University Press.
Rosemann, P. W. (1999) *Understanding Scholastic Thought with Foucault*, Basingstoke: Palgrave Macmillan.

PAUL M. COLLINS

SCHÖN, DONALD (1930–97)

Schön developed such ideas as 'the learning society', 'double loop learning' and 'reflection in action'. These have been highly influential within teacher training and in respect of the organisation of educational institutions. Educated at Yale (philosophy), the Sorbonne (music) and Harvard (philosophy) between 1951 and 1955, Schön lectured at Kansas University and, between 1957 and 1973 became a leading administrator and theorist in organisational research in a variety of institutional settings. During this period he published extensively, arguing that the dominant characteristic of the modern state was instability brought about by rapid technological change. Therefore, organisations need to continually reinvent themselves in order to respond to change. They need to become learning organisations where education and training is an integral and organic function rather than a desirable add-on. People working in organisations need to become continuous learners, through active, self-reflexive practice. This had substantial implications for the training of teachers, and the models of the 'reflective practitioner' became embedded in many training models. Schön's

early publications include *Displacement of Concepts* (1963) – which later appeared as *Invention and the Evolution of Ideas* (1967) – *Technology and Change* (1967) and *Beyond the Stable State* (1971). In the following two decades Schön expanded his ideas about reflexive action perspectives and organisational learning. His empirical research on the behaviour and practice of professionals produced *The Reflective Practitioner* (1983), which transformed thinking about continuous professional development in the 1980s. Schön argued that the role of education was not to transmit knowledge and values from the centre to the periphery, but that it should become an organically functional aspect of how organisations or institutions operate.

See also: professional education; reflective practitioner

STEVEN COWAN

SCHOOL

School is a widely recognised term for an organised educational institution, and indeed, as a verb, for the process of providing instruction in a disciplined manner. It may also be used metaphorically to denote a group with common beliefs, influences or origins, such as a school of thought, or the old school, or the school of hard knocks (that is, the outside world). There are many different types of specialised schools, like vocational schools, normal schools, and schools of history.

Schools have existed in one form or another at least as far back as Ancient Greece, as a means of organising the education of the young away from their homes and families. The Greeks encouraged them, and the Romans accepted the basic Greek format and spread it throughout the Roman empire. They have often been established by churches to instil approved values and doctrine, as well as to impart whatever was deemed appropriate in the way of literacy, numeracy and skills. They may be independent and separate institutions, or else part of a wider system governed by rules and regulations from elsewhere. National systems of schooling are characterised by schools under the control of the state, inspected regularly to maintain and improve standards. In recent centuries, schools have generally become distinctive in their architecture, buildings and grounds, identified individually by title and tradition, and separated geographically from other types of institutions. In many cases, however, schools are also general resources for the local community in providing a convenient place for meetings, clubs and other activities. Community schools are especially concerned to promote a close relationship with the local neighbourhood.

School has often been unpopular for pupils, as in William Shakespeare's famous reference in *As You Like It* (1599) to the second age of man represented by 'the whining school boy, with his satchel,/And shining morning face, creeping like snail/Unwillingly to school'. It has encountered resistance from parents and families when it has meant a loss of labour, income or other support around the home. On the other hand, schools often attract nostalgia when looking back later in life, when it appears that one's school days were the best time of one's life. There is a tribal quality in the loyalty of many former pupils towards their old school, encouraged by the invention of songs, magazines and traditions designed to celebrate individual schools. One especially famous school song, 'Forty Years On', was written by Edward Ernest Bowen and John Farmer at Harrow School in England in 1872, and has since been used by many other schools around the world. In many cases, schools have also been a source of power and prestige. This is particularly true of elite schools in some societies, where the 'old school tie' or 'old boy (or girl) network' has been a passport to high-status careers and social and political influence.

In many societies and small communities, a single school might be sufficient to provide for the education of all local children. However, in large communities and where advanced instruction and specialisation are expected, schools have become increasingly differentiated. Different types of schools have been developed to cater for different age ranges, abilities and specialist interests, and to prepare for different kinds of adult roles and occupations. Technical schools, for example, have a particular kind of curriculum and seek to prepare their pupils for industrial and commercial posts. This diversification of schools has been encouraged further in many countries by attempts to promote cultural, ethnic and religious differences. On the other hand, maintaining a particular model of school for all pupils is often emphasised as part of a fostering of social cohesion. Overall, schools have become highly familiar institutions to the extent that their existence is often taken for granted, and they often become symbolic of the society to which they belong in the values that they express.

See also: deschooling; elementary school; primary school/education; public school; secondary school/education

Further reading

King, E. (1967) *Other Schools and Ours: A Comparative Study for Today*, London: Holt, Rinehart and Winston.
Spring, J. (2001) *The American School, 1642–2000*, 5th edn, New York: McGraw-Hill.
White, J. (2007) *What Schools Are For and Why*, London: Philosophy of Education Society of Great Britain.

GARY McCULLOCH

SCHOOL-BASED MANAGEMENT

School-based management is a strategy to shift the balance of power from the state to individual schools. Such a move potentially enables involvement of the school community in managerialist decisions, budgets and staffing. Head teachers become managing directors and school administration becomes maintenance and clerical work. Such a decentralisation of power might engage with place-based schooling, which Thomson (2006) argues is shaped by its context and the areas in which it is located. Even within a context of decentralisation, education policy makers at national level are positioned to potentially re-centralise the devolved power as their policies determine what can and cannot be done in schools. Moreover, policy makers are not immersed in the messiness of the day-to-day realities of the people whose personalities and identities they are shaping. This presents a constraint over school-based management, which tries to balance the requirements of national policies with the needs of the community it serves. Clearly there are tensions between school-based management serving local needs on one hand, and the state with its 'one size fits all' policy on the other (Ball 2006).

Turning to examine school management models in the contemporary literature, it appears they may have emerged as a result of the educational policies identified above. Brighouse and Woods (2003) illustrate this by identifying two school management models that focus on problem solving and compliance. In brief educational policies may have developed a culture of accountability and regulation within which schools operate. Linear and deterministic school management models have been deployed to demonstrate conformity, and in so doing have colluded in embedding a culture of accountability and regulation in schools. This leads to the necessity of scrutinising what the purpose of education is, and whether school management models engage with such purpose.

The aim of school-based management is arguably shared with the aim of 'school leadership' and 'school administration'. It may be defined as having the right teacher with the right resources, in the right place, teaching the right pupils at the right time. Whilst this approach has remained a constant, some labelling and re-labelling may have occurred, as a result of political, cultural and economic market changes since the 1970s. In the English context, such a shift is usefully signposted

by Gunter (2004). The era of school administration stretches from 1944 to 1974, when the social sciences influenced practice. The move to school management occurred between 1974 and 1988. This latter period was marked by the interplay between neo-liberalist market forces and practice. Gunter argues that, from 1988 onwards, the organisation of schools and their leadership activity was shaped by the deeply embedded cultures of the private sector. Having suggested these changes relate to the historical, cultural and economic context of the day, it is important to unpack the relationship Gunter identifies between school-based management and neo-liberalist market forces. Greenfield and Ribbins (1993) shed light on this interplay, when they suggest that the concept of 'management' has its roots in the Ford Motor Company in America in the 1980s, and is determined by the need to improve the 'bottom line'. Here, the nature of the product is irrelevant due to the sharp focus on cost accounting, where value has little or no meaning. Thus, managerialism potentially resonates with industry's need for economic production of commodities. Such a perspective sees an elite managerial group practise the higher-order thinking skills for the masses of the people. The masses are then enabled to perform the routine jobs that require little training, to satisfy the demands of the infrastructure. Thus, a managerialist approach needs only educate a small elite whilst the majority of human beings are left as undeveloped potential. The extent to which such a situation is ethically just is open to question and cannot be pursued here.

See also: centralisation/decentralisation; educational leadership and management; managerialism

Further reading

Ball, S. (2006) *Education Policy and Social Class*, London: Routledge.

Brighouse, T. and Woods, D. (2003) *How to Improve Your School*, London: Routledge.

Greenfield, T. and Ribbins, P. (1993) *Greenfield on Educational Administration: Towards a Humane Science*, London: Routledge.

Gunter, H. M. (2004) 'Labels and labelling in the field of educational leadership', *Discourse: Studies in the Cultural Politics of Education*, 25(1): 21–41.

Thomson, P. (2006) 'Miners, diggers, ferals and showmen: school–community projects that affirm and unsettle identities and place? , *British Journal of Sociology of Education*, 27(1): 81–96.

ALISON TAYSUM

SCHOOL CHANGE

School change can be regarded as a planned effort aimed at change in one or more schools that is intended to accomplish educational goals more effectively. It is popularly believed that schools are the most difficult of institutions to change. It was only in the late 1940s, when the field of educational leadership and management was in its infancy, that researchers began to take an interest in understanding school change. During the 1970s, research that focused upon successful schools showed that schools could be changed and improved such that both educators and learners benefited. By the late 1970s and early 1980s, research had also begun to identify factors, across contexts, cultures and national boundaries, that were associated with good schools. This gave impetus to the question of how to change schools.

In addition, during the 1980s factors external to schools played an increasingly influential role in promoting school change. International forces such as globalisation and decentralisation, together with increased public demands for school accountability, put pressure on school systems and schools to change. For example, in the United States of America the 1983 publication of *A Nation at Risk* resulted in profound school system change at the levels of governance, management and curriculum. In the United Kingdom two prominent traditions in school change, school effectiveness (generally referred to as school restructuring in the USA) and school improvement, emerged during the 1980s. Efforts have since been made to integrate these two traditions. These can be traced in the journal *School Effectiveness and School Improvement*. In the USA, school change has focused successively on change in the curriculum and change in the organisation of schools. School organisation development (OD) and whole-school reform have been widely used change strategies. Both have come to be associated with the idea of a 'learning school', where change is more likely to be sustained.

While the school change literature recognises certain common features of successful change, the form it will take and significance it will have for participants varies according to a particular school's context. These include the school itself, its leadership, culture, values and readiness to engage in and capacity to manage a change process. In addition, how change is introduced is as important as the change itself. By the mid-1980s the central role of leadership and management in successful school change was recognised. The principal/head teacher was identified as the single most important factor in promoting change, in developing contexts in particular. In addition, effective school change is more likely to occur in a school culture characterised by a sense of community (see, for example, Fullan 2001: 201–2) and teamwork, than one characterised by traditional bureaucratic organisation.

Research into large-scale national reform – the relation between national policy and local implementation in particular – shows that change is a local process. The focus is shifting from recipes and techniques of mass-based system change to institutional culture change processes. Nevertheless, a tension remains between increased school self-management and centralised, prescriptive management approaches, and between increased professional autonomy and national systems of accountability.

Broader political, social, economic, cultural and demographic factors, including the national education system, can either help or hinder change. Research in South Africa (see Fleisch and Christie 2004) suggests that in certain circumstances, such as states in political and social transition, school change is unlikely to succeed without basic social and political changes and support, including at a district level, outside the school. The establishment of political legitimacy and authority has been identified as a precondition for sustainable school change.

A criticism of school change is that it neglects issues of power and conflict. Its humanistic perspective places people and their interaction at the centre of organisations. Critical theory and postmodernism offer new perspectives that draw attention to the political nature of school change. They look at change in terms of power relations and their effect on race, class and gender. They ask who benefits from the change.

School change is seldom, if ever, a straightforward linear process. One never has enough knowledge to know exactly what to do. There is no one best way but research does offer some ideas to consider and principles to adopt that can help the process along.

See also: educational leadership and management; restructuring; school effectiveness; school improvement; school leadership; school reform

Further reading

Fleisch, B. and Christie, P. (2004) 'Structural change, leadership and school effectiveness/ improvement: perspectives from South Africa', *Discourse: Studies in the Cultural Politics of Education*, 25(1): 95–112.

Fullan, M. (1985) 'Change processes and strategies at the local level', *The Elementary School Journal*, 85(3), 391–422.

——(2001) *The New Meaning of Educational Change*, 3rd edn, New York: Teachers College Press.

CLIVE SMITH

SCHOOL CULTURE

'School culture' can be defined as the context in which everything else in the school takes place. It describes 'the way things are done around here'. The concept of culture helps one understand the unspoken rules and expectations within the organisation that develop over many years based on how the key players reinforce, nurture, or transform the norms, beliefs, and assumptions of the organisation. School culture is based on a complex web of traditions and rituals that build up over time and form the essence of the school. A school with a wholesome culture knows what it believes in and where it is going. It is a place with a profound focus on learning and human relationships.

The norms and values of a school define for people what is right and correct to do, what is acceptable, and what is expected. Norms are unstated expressions of certain values and beliefs held by members of the organisation that define in a basic 'taken for granted' fashion how the school views itself and its environment. Values are what a school stands for, while beliefs represent the core understandings about student capacity, teacher responsibility, teacher knowledge, and educational success. Values provide the basis for people to judge or evaluate the situations they face, the worth of their actions and activities, their priorities, and the behaviours of people when they work together.

The heart of a school's culture is its vision and purpose. The vision of a school reflects the beliefs, perceptions, and values that guide the organisation and shape the definition of success for the school. School traditions may run deeply in the community. A tradition that is tied to school's vision reinforces cultural ties. The vision may be reflected in the architecture of the school, certain symbols such as a mascot or school colours, or a hall in the building dedicated to student achievement, or school projects. The vision and traditions of a school help to weave a cohesive school identity and school culture.

Relationships form the foundation for school culture. Cooperative relationships among the community, parents, teachers, students, and administrators foster positive school culture. In well defined and strong school cultures where students know that the staff and faculty care and there is trust, respect, and strong relationships among them, teachers tend to be more satisfied with their work and enjoy teaching and students are less likely to misbehave or drop out of school.

Facilitating meaningful relationships between student needs and the instructional practices in schools may provide the key to improving student learning. Educational research supports the assumption that positive and focused school cultures lead to higher student achievement. When students feel supported and valued and the school day is structured and organised to accommodate instructional priorities and student needs, the students are more likely to actively engage in classroom activities that lead to increasing student learning. Additionally, within effective schools there is a consistently applied set of expectations that challenges teachers and students to achieve excellence with a set of symbolic activities and sanctions that encourage and reward effort, improvement, and accomplishment while discouraging disorder and complacency. The safe and orderly school with effective classroom management built on clear expectations and a positive culture for learning and behaving is based on positive relationships.

School culture can be described as the 'feeling' of the school. When one 'feels welcomed' in a positive, structured, orderly, and caring environment where learning and students are valued, student achievement increases.

See also: classroom management; culture; school knowledge

Further reading

Deal, T. E. (1985) 'The symbolism of effective schools', *The Elementary School Journal*, 85(5): 601–20.

Deal, T. E. and Peterson, K. D. (2003) *Shaping School Culture: The Heart of Leadership*, San Francisco CA: Jossey-Bass.

Marzano, R. J. (2003) *What Works in Schools*, Alexandria VA: ASCD.

Wang, M. C., Haertel, G. D. and Walberg, H. J. (1993) 'Toward a knowledge base for school learning', *Review of Educational Research*, 63(3): 249–94.

ROSE M. McNEESE

SCHOOL EFFECTIVENESS

Research into school effectiveness investigates the extent to which schools fulfil their aims efficiently. It does not look at processes or address the issue of whether or not those aims are worthwhile. It accepts that differences between student outcomes are largely determined by socio-economic status and 'natural' factors, but maintains that schools can and do make a significant difference. It attempts to explain why and to what extent those differences vary from school to school and between countries.

As a quantitative, organisation-focused movement, school effectiveness was launched in 1979 – its *annus mirabilis* – though earlier research by Coleman *et al.* (1966) and Jencks *et al.* (1972) could be included. In that year, Brookover *et al.* and Edmonds in the USA, and Rutter *et al.* in the UK, produced seminal studies which found that schools have a 'small but significant' effect on student attainment. Several school-level factors were found to impact and these included: the balance of able and less-able students attending the school; the presence or absence of reward systems; the physical environment; the opportunity for students to take responsibility; and having strong leadership with democratic decision making. Among the factors found *not* to be correlated with effectiveness were class size and school size.

In the 1980s, researchers added to the list of school factors affecting outcomes: a high proportion of students in positions of authority; low levels of institutional control; high academic expectations; a low ratio of pupils to teachers; a safe and orderly school climate; and evaluating student progress early and often (Teddlie and Reynolds 2000). Later, with the advent of more sophisticated approaches in multi-level and structural equation modelling, and paying greater attention to school improvement experience, still more SER emerged: in the UK, from Mortimore *et al.* (1988); in the USA, from Levine and Lezotte (1990) and Teddlie and Stringfield (1993). Mortimore *et al.* found that effective schools have purposeful leadership, consistent teaching and structured lessons, are intellectually challenging places where teaching is focused, have good communications between students and teachers, and have an active parent body. The American studies found additionally that effective schools spend more time on tasks, are more encouraging of independent practice, have a lower number of interruptions, have firm discipline and exude a friendly atmosphere. Yet there also emerged around this time indications from outside the English-speaking world that some findings were culture-specific and context-dependent; for example, in some countries, leadership was found to have little or no effect on student outcomes (van de Grift 1990).

School effectiveness research seeks to measure a school's output, correct for input and circumstance ('context'), and assign a scalar to the value the school adds to the learning experience of its students. Its approach can be criticised on a number of counts. First, schools are complicated palimpsests and the idea that they are homogeneous entities, while convenient for policy makers, does not ring true with parents and practitioners. Rarely do children come home from lessons and talk about the organisation that is their school; *their* paradigm is of the classroom and the curriculum as they interact with it. Second, because school effectiveness focuses on measurables, it tends to ignore 'difficult-to-measure' but important factors like the impact of competitor schools on each other; teacher satisfaction; and societal culture, the last of which makes international comparisons

like the Programme for International Student Assessment (PISA) difficult to make and sometimes nonsensical. Third, the act of measurement itself affects what is being measured. Schools learn to limit their engagement to those activities that produce the most visible 'public' effects. And last, while school effectiveness research is good at listing and ranking influencing factors – though some are so obvious as to seem de trop – it is not so good at understanding educative *processes*, without which practical efforts at improvement become futile. Nor does it provide an accurate account of the waxing and waning of everyday life in schools; only a snapshot of things as they were at the moment of measurement.

Currently, there are concerted efforts being made within school effectiveness to utilise more widely new approaches and to engage fully with (the more rigorous end of) school improvement research, even if the two fields are in some ways critiques of each other (Fidler 2001).

See also: educational leadership and management; educational measurement; educational targets; school improvement; school leadership

Further reading

Brookover, W., Beady, C., Flood, P. and Schweitzer, J. (1979) *School Systems and Student Achievement*, New York: Praeger.

Coleman, J., Campbell, E., Hobson, C., McPartland, J., Mood, A., Weinfeld, F. and York, R. (1966) *Equality of Educational Opportunity*, Washington DC: NCES-US Government Printing Office.

Edmonds, R. (1979) 'Effective schools for the urban poor', *Educational Leadership*, 37(1): 15–24.

Fidler, B. (2001) 'A structural critique of school effectiveness and school Improvement'. In: A. Harris and N. Bennett (eds) *School Effectiveness and School Improvement*, London: Continuum.

Jencks, C., Smith, M., Ackland, H., Bane, M., Cohen, D., Gintis, H., Heyns, B. and Micholson, S. (1972) *Inequality: A Reassessment of the Effect of Family and Schooling in America*, New York: Basic Books.

Levine, D. and Lezotte, L. (1990) *Unusually Effective Schools*, Madison WI: National Center for Effective Schools Research and Development.

Mortimore, P., Sammons, P., Stoll, L., Lewis, D. and Ecob, R. (1988) *School Matters*, Wells: Open Books.

Rutter, M., Maughan, B., Mortimore, P. and Ouston, J. (1979) *Fifteen Thousand Hours*, London: Open Books.

Teddlie, C. and Reynolds, D. (2000) *The International Handbook of School Effectiveness Research*, London: Falmer Press.

Teddlie, C. and Stringfield, S. (1993) *Schools Do Make a Difference*, New York: Teachers College Press.

van de Grift, W. (1990) 'Educational leadership and academic achievement in elementary education', *School Effectiveness and School Improvement*, 1(3): 26–40.

ANTHONY KELLY

SCHOOL IMPROVEMENT

School improvement is a developmental approach to understanding how and why schools change or remain static over time. Whereas school effectiveness research is cross-sectional, output-focused and empirical, school improvement is longitudinal, process-focused and evangelical. It holds that all schools *need* to be improved and that all schools *can* be improved, though they operate under different sets of circumstances, produce different outcomes and need to be judged 'effective' using different metrics. School improvement is therefore qualitative and usually small-scale in approach, and unlike school effectiveness, which is disinterested in the propriety of aims, it seeks to interpret and evaluate the appropriateness of policy and the effect of practice at different systemic levels. It seeks insights rather than correlations; it is attitudinal and tactile.

School improvement followed in the wake of school effectiveness (1979) so its provenance can be traced to the 1980s, though there was earlier work on developing curriculum resources to improve student outcomes that could be included in the genre (Hopkins and Lagerweij 1996). The early emphasis was on improvement of output

resulting from government fiat. In later years this shifted to process and out*come*-focused research, and became naturalistic, grounded and very practitioner-based, which sometimes manifested itself in obscurity and a querulous tendency that bordered on the self-destructive (Reynolds 2007).

Typically, school improvement research produces case studies, strategies and resources, but recounting success is not the same as creating it (Fullan 1991). Consequently, in the 1990s, 'leadership of change' became the nostrum, albeit in the context of a growing managerialism. Educational reform in most developed countries had been accompanied by a shift to local self-management of schools, which established new responsibilities for teachers and heads and a growing need in schools for external support. School improvement engaged with this 'change movement' because it had the potential to build in schools the capacity for organisational learning and self-generated improvement. As a result, improvement research continues to rest on a number of assumptions: that although the school is the 'load' to be moved, better classroom teaching is the 'lever' to be pulled; that 'systems thinking' is possible and desirable; that internal conditions are critical to success; that there are many perspectives to whole school improvement; and that external improvement techniques can be imported into schools from outside education (Kelly 2004).

If school effectiveness research is about *measuring* difference, then school improvement is about *generating* it. The former sees itself as 'doing the science' that allows the latter to endure. In that sense, it lights the way for school improvement, though this must additionally be guided by external influences: in society, in communities and among policy makers. Today, the emphasis within school improvement is on policy. It is more political and less managerial than previously, but its praxis still produces extremes of usefulness and benefit. At worst, it is a farrago of anecdote celebrating the folklore of charisma and the practical nous of teachers. In its solipsism, it represents a rush to action by frightened policy makers (and advisers) whose attempts at theorising from findings, when made at all, tend to be tenuous and imprecise. In fairness, school effectiveness and school improvement differ subtly but intrinsically in respect of their relationship with theory. The former is essentially experimentalist and *testing* of theory; the latter seeks to coalesce what is known and is *developing* of theory.

At its best, school improvement is an insightful and practical fugue. It has contributed to – indeed, it has *shaped* – our understandings of change as it relates to the educative process, and its best exponents are among the foremost academics working in the field of education. It is not empirical, but why should it be? It makes no attempt at proving the causality that other approaches seek but invariably fail to find. It rejects the illusion that schools are rational entities whose inmates operate with complete knowledge and certainty, but embraces schools as chaotic places and bravely attempts to capture the subtleties therein. The challenge for school improvement going forward is for it to develop a rapprochement with school effectiveness: to encourage more quantitative work in the one and greater practical empathy in the other (Reynolds and Stoll 1996), and to engage fully both approaches in schools serving disengaged constituencies.

See also: educational leadership and management; managerialism; school-based management; school effectiveness; school leadership

Further reading

Fullan, M. (1991) *The New Meaning of Educational Change*, New York: Teachers College Press.
Hopkins, D. and Lagerweij, N. (1996) 'The school improvement knowledge base'. In D. Reynolds, R. Bollen, B. Creemers, D. Hopkins, L. Stoll and N. Lagerweij (eds) *Making Good Schools: Linking School Effectiveness and School Improvement*, London: Routledge.

Kelly, A. (2004) *The Intellectual Capital of Schools*, New York: Kluwer Academic.
Reynolds, D. (2007) Closing session of the International Congress for School Effectiveness and Improvement, Portoro, Slovenia, 6 January.
Reynolds, D. and Stoll, L. (1996) 'Merging school effectiveness and school Improvement'. In D. Reynolds, R. Bollen, B. Creemers, D. Hopkins, L. Stoll and N. Lagerweij (eds) *Making Good Schools: Linking School Effectiveness and School Improvement*, London: Routledge.

ANTHONY KELLY

SCHOOL JOURNEYS

School journey is a term with two principal understandings: first, the daily two-way journey between a pupil's home and school and, second, an organised school trip or visit by children to some place of educational interest.

In developing countries it is not uncommon for children to walk several miles from their home to school and back. In other contexts, school buses, distinctively yellow in many countries, enable children to make their daily school journeys. Across the world, many children are delivered by motor car to the school gates by a parent, sometimes concerned by the hazards of busy roads or by the possibility of strangers accosting their children. This lifestyle choice is frequently criticised for being unnecessarily overprotective, unhealthy and unsustainable. Road congestion, air pollution and accidents are all unwelcome by-products of school journeys in the car. In the UK, for example, around 20 per cent of weekday child road casualties occur in the few minutes leading up to 9 a.m. Where possible, many schools encourage children to cycle to school or to walk, sometimes as a 'walking bus' following a set route with responsible adults at the front and rear to supervise the safe negotiation of busy roads.

In many countries schools offer a varied programme of school trips or journeys. Local visits may be made to theatres, shopping centres and museums, while more distant school journeys, sometimes residential, may be made to locations of historical, geographical, cultural or other interest at home or abroad. School journeys enable pupils and students to see each other and their teachers in a different and enjoyable context, but they can also present challenges for the organisers to ensure safety and security.

See also: extracurriculum; school

DAVID CROOK

SCHOOL KNOWLEDGE

The idea that both in the selection of content and in its structure, knowledge in schools or as expressed in the curriculum is different from the knowledge people draw on at work, in the home and in everyday life is as old as the institution of schooling itself. However, it was only as recently as the 1970s that the specific concept *school knowledge* was coined within the sociology of education as a way of challenging the 'taken for grantedness' of the distinction between school and non-school knowledge within the curriculum. It was argued at the time that school/non-school knowledge differences masked powerful but unspoken interests and had distributional consequences in terms of educational opportunities for different social classes. From this type of 'sociological' perspective the 'schooling' of knowledge was not the benign outcome of an evolving tradition, as most educationalists assumed, but the result of an unconscious and sometimes conscious exercise of power.

Despite the universalising claims made for schooling in democratic countries, it is difficult to deny that school knowledge represents a particular view of the world that is more likely to be explicit in subjects like history and English literature than in the natural sciences (although recent efforts to introduce creationism into school biology provides an exception to this trend). The questions 'whose literature?', 'whose history?' and even 'whose science?' inevitably followed the idea

of school knowledge together with the idea that a more 'democratic' schooling of knowledge could be achieved that took into account the perspectives of subordinate and previously neglected social groups. However, the curriculum implications of these apparently emancipatory possibilities of the critique of 'school knowledge' turned out to be less straightforward than had been hoped. Although the curriculum could be transformed, at least in theory, into a site of wider political struggles, the substantive issues of 'what to teach?' and how to distinguish school from non-school knowledge remained. The most extreme argument was that school knowledge should reflect the experiences and interests of local, and in particular cases indigenous, communities. However, it did not take long for it to be recognised that a locally based curriculum would be likely to disadvantage working-class and ethnic minority pupils even more than the curriculum that was being replaced. The consequences of such well intentioned ideas have been well documented by educational researchers; perhaps the most well known case is the 1970s programme known as *Mathematics for the Majority*. Without some criteria for distinguishing school from non-school knowledge that do not rely solely on answers to the question 'whose knowledge?' or who the pupils or teachers are, the sociology of school knowledge had little to offer teachers.

In addressing the issues raised by the sociology of school knowledge, I find it useful to distinguish between two ideas: *Knowledge of the Powerful* and *Powerful Knowledge*. The former refers to who gets the knowledge and what they use it for. Even today, it is those with more power in society who not only have a greater sense of ownership of school knowledge but have far greater access to it. It is not surprising that many sociological critiques of school knowledge have treated school knowledge as almost synonymous with *Knowledge of the Powerful*. However in these critiques school knowledge is associated with groups of knowers: those with the power to define what counts as knowledge. We learn nothing about the nature of the knowledge itself. We need, I suggest, another concept that I will call *powerful knowledge* to refer to what the knowledge can do. I am thinking, in particular, of the kind and reliability of the explanations that it provides. This was what the Chartists in the nineteenth century were seeking with their famous slogan 'really useful knowledge'; it was a critique of a curriculum based largely on the scriptures. It is also, if not always consciously, what parents hope that their children will acquire at school; powerful knowledge that is not available at home. Powerful knowledge is most straightforwardly equated with the sciences; however, a modern curriculum has to recognise the importance of a range of different kinds of knowledge offering explanations and understandings with different levels of reliability. If we accept the distinction between 'powerful' and 'non-powerful' (or powerless) knowledge, how school and non-school knowledge are differentiated is a crucial educational issue.

Powerful knowledge in modern societies is increasingly specialised and divided up into domains or fields. School knowledge, therefore, must be concerned with (a) the differences between different forms of specialist knowledge and the relations between them; (b) how this specialist knowledge differs from the knowledge people acquire in everyday life; (c) how the different domains (sciences and humanities) differ; and (d) how specialist knowledge is 'pedagogised'; in other words how it is placed, selected and sequenced in curricula for different groups of learners. Differentiation, therefore, in the sense I am using it here, refers to:

- the differences between school and everyday knowledge;
- the differences between knowledge domains, and how far they are expressed in different subjects like physics and history;

- the differences between specialist knowledge (e.g. physics) and pedagogised knowledge (i.e. school physics for different groups of learners).

Schools are of course not always successful in enabling pupils to acquire powerful knowledge. It is also true that schools are more successful with some pupils than others. The success of pupils is highly dependent on the culture that they bring to school. Elite cultures that are less constrained by the material exigencies of life are, therefore, not surprisingly, far more congruent with powerful knowledge that is relatively independent of specific contexts, than disadvantaged and subordinate cultures. This means that if schools are to play a role in promoting social equality, they have to take the knowledge base of the curriculum very seriously, even when this appears to go against the immediate demands of pupils and sometimes their parents. For children from disadvantaged homes, active participation in school may be the only chance that they have to acquire powerful knowledge and move, intellectually at least, beyond their local and particular circumstances. It does them no service to construct a curriculum around their experience and, as a result, leave them there.

The most sustained and original attempt to conceptualise school knowledge is that developed by the English sociologist Basil Bernstein (1925–2000). Bernstein begins by distinguishing between the *classification of knowledge* (or the degree of insulation between knowledge domains) and the *framing of knowledge* (the degree of insulation between school knowledge and the everyday knowledge that pupils bring to school). Second, he proposes that *classification* can be 'strong' when domains are highly insulated from each other, as in such cases as physics and history, or 'weak' when the boundaries are blurred, as in social studies or general science programmes. Likewise, *framing* can be *strong* when school and non-school knowledge are insulated from each other, or *weak* when the boundaries between school and non-school knowledge are blurred, as in the case of many programmes in adult education and some curricula designed for less able pupils. In his later work, Bernstein moved from a focus on relations between domains to the structure of the domains themselves by introducing the concepts of *vertical* and *horizontal knowledge* structures. This distinction refers to the way that different domains of knowledge embody different ideas of how knowledge progresses. In vertical knowledge structures – Bernstein's example is physics – progress takes place by moving to higher levels of abstraction (for example from Newton's laws of gravity to Einstein's theory of relativity). In horizontal knowledge structures, like the social sciences and the humanities, knowledge progresses by developing new languages which pose new problems. Bernstein's concepts provide us with a language for thinking about different curriculum possibilities and their implications. His second crucial argument is the link he makes between knowledge structures, boundaries and learner identities. His hypothesis is that strong boundaries between knowledge domains and between school and non-school knowledge play a critical role in supporting learner identities and, therefore, are a condition for learners to progress. Boundaries here refer to *relations between contents*, not the *knowledge contents* themselves. Two further points are worth making about knowledge boundaries. First, although strong boundaries have traditionally been expressed in disciplines and subjects, this is a historical fact and not necessarily the only form that strong boundaries can take. Second, acquiring powerful knowledge can not only involve *boundary maintenance* but the opportunities for *boundary crossing* and the questioning of learner identities.

In the 1970s and 1980s the sociology of school knowledge focused on the differentiation of school from non-school knowledge largely as an expression of power relations (e.g. Young and Whitty 1976). While not dismissing the importance of this view, this article has argued that the forms that this differentiation can take are equally important if schools are to enable pupils to acquire knowledge that they would be unlikely to have access to at home or in the community. I have suggested that understanding the differences between school and non-school knowledge needs to begin with the ideas of Bernstein, who conceptualised this differentiation in terms of the concepts *classification* and *framing*. Contemporary forms of accountability are tending to weaken the boundaries between school and non-school knowledge on the grounds that they inhibit a more accessible and more economically relevant curriculum. The issue that Bernstein's analysis raises is that to follow this path may be to deny the conditions for acquiring powerful knowledge to the very pupils who are already disadvantaged by their social circumstances. Resolving this tension between political demands and educational realities is, I would argue, the major educational question for our time.

See also: Bernstein, Basil; curriculum; school; school culture; sociology of education; subjects

Further reading

Bernstein, B. (2000) *Pedagogy, Symbolic Control and Identity: Theory, Research, Critique*, 2nd edn, Oxford: Rowman and Littlefield.
Moore, R. (2004) *Education and Society*, London: Polity Press.
Muller, J. (2000) *Reclaiming Knowledge: Social Theory, Curriculum and Education Policy*, London: RoutledgeFalmer.
Young, M. (2007) *Bringing Knowledge Back In: From Social Constructivism to Social Realism in the Sociology of Education*, London: Routledge.
Young, M. and Whitty, G. (1976) *Explorations in the Politics of School Knowledge*, Driffield: Nafferton Books.

MICHAEL F. D. YOUNG

SCHOOL LEADERSHIP

At an international level, school leadership is located within a complex field with contested boundaries (Lumby *et al.* 2005; Ribbins

2006), sometimes demanding negotiation between what is private and what is public in the life of the school. School leadership is located within a political framework of possibilities and limitations structured by educational policy. Cultural processes that potentially sustain social reproduction or present individuals with alternative career and life trajectories are shaped by and shape school leadership. Moreover, school leadership has a relationship with economic markets, potentially competitive in nature, that is played out at local, national and global levels. The interplay between these processes and markets influences the way(s) in which school leadership operates through relationships between members of the school community and the institution. Thus, school leaders include all those involved in school education, including local and national politicians and administrators, professional researchers and consultants, governors, parents and children, as well as educational professionals in schools. Arguably then, school leadership has the potential to influence, and be influenced by, issues of equity and social justice and may, therefore, be considered a moral and ethical praxis.

There remains an absence of clarity about criteria by which to define school leadership. However, it might be argued that school leadership is moving towards being defined by the way it is collectively understood by all those affected by it, regardless of local, national and international contexts within which it takes place.

See also: educational leadership and management; school effectiveness; school improvement

Further reading

Campbell, C., Gold, A. and Lunt, I. (2003) 'Articulating leadership values in action: conversations with school leaders', *International Journal of Leadership in Education*, 6(3): 203–21.
Lumby, J., Foskett, N. and Fidler, B. (2005) 'Researching educational leadership and management', *Educational Management, Administration and Leadership*, 33(2): 135–37.

Ribbins, P. (2006) 'History and the study of administration and leadership in education: introduction to a special issue', *Journal of Educational Administration and History*, 38(2): 113–24.
ALISON TAYSUM

SCHOOL REFORM

School reform since the 1980s reflects numerous efforts to improve educational quality and access across nations in the Americas and Europe. These efforts have been promoted by shifts in social, economic, and political factors. In the United States of America the movement towards school reform was prompted by the release of the 1983 *A Nation at Risk* report that suggested education was on the decline and this affected the country's global economic status because students were not being prepared to thrive in the emerging global economy. In response to sub-standard schools and limited access among the poor and many ethnic groups, various Latin American countries during the 1990s promoted educational change. Contemporary school improvement strategies have focused on school governance, standards-based curriculum, and school competition.

Since the 1980s, school reform efforts have focused on changing school governance from a system that has been traditionally centralised and 'top down' to one that is more decentralised. In the USA, England, and Latin America including Mexico, Chile, and Brazil, decentralisation has fostered local control over school management, including resource allocation. School-based management provides administrators and teachers more input regarding the daily operation of schools based on the rationale that they possess the professional expertise to make decisions that fit their local context. It is assumed that decentralisation allows for the dismantling of bureaucratic structures that often impede change. In the USA some school administrators are given discretion over teacher hiring. In England local administrators, such as head teachers and school governors, have control over allocated funding. In Minas Gerais, Brazil, reform efforts in 1991 gave schools discretion over administration, funding, and instruction. In addition, members of local communities were given a role in school management, including selecting school directors and providing input about the allocation of school funding.

Curriculum reform efforts emerged to improve the quality of instruction and student outcomes. The Education Reform Act of 1988 established a national curriculum in England in order to provide common educational exposure and expectations. In the USA the Goals 2000 legislation passed in 1994 promoted subject-area standards associated with curricula in order to create universal expectations between schools and classrooms regarding the breadth and depth of knowledge that students are exposed to during an academic year and grade level. In order to monitor improvements in student learning, testing has been aligned with standards-based curricula in England and the USA. As a result of England's Education Reform Act, testing is required for students at ages seven, eleven, and fourteen. In the USA the No Child Left Behind Act of 2001 (NCLB) requires student testing in grades three through eight. Test outcomes are used to examine school and student progress with a specific focus on student sub-groups by race/ethnicity, socio-economic status, and special education status. Schools that fail to meet annual yearly performance goals may be targeted for improvement and face closure if poor outcomes persist over time. Students not meeting required proficiency levels may be retained in their grade or denied a diploma at the secondary school level.

Market-based reform efforts, including school choice and vouchers, reflect strategies to promote educational improvement by letting competition for the best schools dictate school selection and funding. It is assumed that all schools, including those with poor performance, would take the necessary steps to improve and provide appealing educational programmes in order to attract students. The inability of schools to draw students would eventually close them because they would lack the necessary funds to function. School choice in England serves many purposes, including the promotion of school efficiency and parental control over schooling. In the USA students attending schools experiencing chronic low performance have the opportunity to attend a higher-performing school in their district if one exists. Proponents of school vouchers propose that parents receive per pupil expenditures to attend any school, regardless of attendance boundaries and including private schools. In the USA school vouchers have been used experimentally in cities including Milwaukee, Wisconsin, where there has been a limited choice programme for low-income students since 1990.

See also: centralisation/decentralisation; parental choice; school-based management; school change; school effectiveness; school improvement; standards

Further reading

Gordon, D. T. (ed.) (2003) *A Nation Reformed? American Education 20 Years after A Nation At Risk*, Cambridge MA: Harvard Education Press.

Grindle, M. S. (2004) *Despite the Odds: The Contentious Politics of Education Reform*, Princeton NJ: Princeton University Press

Stearns, K. (1996) *School Reform: Lessons from England*, Princeton NJ: Princeton University Press.

DONNA MARIE HARRIS

SCHOOL REPORTS

The term 'school report' may refer to two distinct kinds of report: first, and most commonly, a report which the school writes *about each student* to inform their parents or guardians about their progress, sometimes called a report card. The form of these reports differs, but in many countries it is a general practice for schools, primary and secondary, to send home a school report for each child each year. The report will contain details of the student's achievement in each of the subject areas studied and will usually comment on the student's effort and attainment. Schools may also send home interim reports, say at the end of each term, which are in less depth but provide a brief comment on the student's progress in each subject. The reports are often accompanied by an invitation for parents to visit the school to discuss their child's progress with their teachers.

The second form of school report is a *report about a school*. In England, for example, the Office for Standards in Education (Ofsted) produces a report following their inspection of each state school. The report outlines the performance of the school, highlighting strengths and weaknesses, and identifies any areas for improvement. Ofsted reports are freely available from schools and accessible via the internet. They are used by some parents as a means of gaining additional information about schools when deciding where they wish to send their children.

See also: inspection

NATALIE HEATH

SCHOOL SECURITY

School security comprises all the measures that are designed to keep school personnel and students safe. There are two major categories of school security: prevention programmes and intervention programmes. In the United States, the Hamilton Fish National Institute on School and Community Violence and the Office of Juvenile Justice have recorded many specific prevention programmes. Additionally, the US Department of Education's Safe, Disciplined and Drug-Free Schools Expert Panel has developed a list of exemplary and promising programmes.

Generally, prevention programmes include such strategies as conflict resolution, social skills training, parental involvement/parent training, empathy training, tutoring, mentoring, and after-school programmes. Structural

prevention initiatives include the use of metal detectors and video surveillance cameras, the introduction of school uniforms, improved monitoring, and a reduction in the number of entrances and exits. Environmental changes – achieved through improved lighting, increased supervision and cleaner, more welcoming spaces – can also achieve positive results (Schneider *et al.* 2000).

Intervention programmes focus on students who have demonstrated 'risk factors' associated with violence, possibly through carrying a weapon, fighting or bullying, and are increasingly acknowledging new types of external dangers to schools and children, including terrorism. The importance attached to American school security is signalled by the fact that the US Federal Bureau of Investigation has developed a practical threat assessment resource for schools. Some commentators (for example Furlong *et al.* 2001) argue that using risk factors to predict violent behaviour is inappropriate, yet this remains a very common practice. Intervention may also take the form of removing at-risk students, sometimes placing them in alternative school settings, providing intensive family therapy, case management with violent children, and gang intervention programmes.

One very popular (and often contested) intervention strategy used in school security efforts has been the implementation of 'zero tolerance' policies. In such instances the carrying of a dangerous object, possession of drugs, demonstration of violence or some less serious offence may lead to students being suspended or expelled from schools forthwith. Some contemporary thinkers (for example Shanker 1995) view zero tolerance as a necessary 'get tough' strategy, though others (for example Kohn 2004) contend that this overly aggressive strategy erodes the positive school culture of caring and safety.

School security has become a growing business around the world. Contractors and other visitors to schools are routinely required to initially report to the reception desk and to carry a badge or pass at all times.

Those who work in schools are expected to challenge people whose status is not apparent, while children's awareness of 'stranger danger' is being continually heightened. Horrific incidents, including the massacres of sixteen children and their primary school teacher at Dunblane, Scotland, in 1996 and, three years later, at Columbine High School, Colorado, where two boys killed twelve of their classmates and a teacher, have intensified efforts to increase and improve school security and also to contemplate risk management strategies to keep students and school personnel safe.

See also: bullying; discipline; exclusion/expulsion; school violence; suspension

Further reading

Furlong, M. J., Bates, M. P. and Smith, D. C. (2001) 'Predicting school weapon possession: a secondary analysis of the youth risk behavior surveillance survey', *Psychology in the Schools*, 38(2): 127–39.

Kohn, A. (2004) 'Safety from the inside out: rethinking traditional approaches', *Educational Horizons*, 83(1): 33–41.

Schneider, T., Walker, H. and Sprague, J. (2000) *Safe School Design: A Handbook for Educational Leaders Applying the Principles of Crime Prevention through Environmental Design*, University of Oregon, Portland OR: ERIC Clearinghouse on Educational Management.

Shanker, A. (1995) 'Restoring the connection between behavior and consequences', *Vital Speeches of the Day*, 15 May: 308.

KIMBERLY WILLIAMS

SCHOOL VIOLENCE

Understandings of school violence are continuing to evolve, but, broadly speaking, it encompasses any harmful behaviour that happens in schools or on school grounds. This harm may take the form of physical, emotional/psychological or sexual behaviour and may also result from deprivation. Such behaviours as bullying, hitting, fighting, attacking, using weapons or dangerous objects, stealing, arson, suicide and self-mutilation are all examples of violence that may be encountered in the school. Schools are also frequently a location for emotional or psychologically damaging behaviours by children, including ostracising, teasing, harassment, name-calling, and threatening. Sexually violent behaviours at school may include sexual harassment, sexual violence (for example inappropriate grabbing of others' bodies) and rape. Deprivation behaviours constituting violence may include unequal access to necessary resources, the underfunding of necessary programmes and the failure to provide an adequate education.

The problematics of understanding school violence mirror those of defining violence as a general term. 'Violence is the act of purposefully hurting someone' according the American Psychological Association (quoted in Stark 2006), yet almost every word in this sentence is open to questioning and interpretation. An alternative definition, provided by the US Centers for Disease Control and Prevention (CDC), defines violence as 'the threatened or actual use of physical force or power against another person, against oneself, or against a group or community which results in or has a high likelihood of resulting in injury, death, or deprivation' (para. 3). In this understanding of the term, not only is the threat of violence included, it also makes explicit that violence may be directed at another person, the self, or the community.

Elsewhere, it has been contended that violence 'occurs whenever anyone inflicts or threatens to inflict physical or emotional injury or discomfort upon another person's body, feeling, or possessions' (Remboldt 1994: 1). This offers a useful starting point for considering violence inside the school premises. Here, teachers and other adult workers are much more likely to fall victim to theft than to forms of physical violence, yet theft of – or damage to – possessions is often omitted from definitions of violence which, in schools, is most commonly recognised in its physical form.

Based on her experience of Canadian schools, Irene MacDonald offered a comprehensive definition of school violence in 1998, stating that it

> represents those actual or threatened beha-
> viours or actions, that are symptomatic of
> an unfulfilled need (e.g. to belong, have
> power, seek approval), expressed in the form
> of sexual, emotional, or physical harm, that
> has a deleterious effect on establishing and
> maintaining a safe and caring school climate.
> (MacDonald 1998: 19)

Others (for example Galtung 1969) have identified deprivation as a form of violence. Accordingly, economically poor students, or those attending under-funded schools, may be viewed as victims of violence.

Contemporary authors such as Kimberly Williams (2004) have suggested that school violence needs to be personally examined and defined because it looks different in different places for different people. She calls for an examination of the ways that school violence may be socially constructed (that is, determined and affected by one's social location in respect of age, race, gender, geographic location, and so on) to be able to examine it more effectively. Without question, school violence is a complicated issue with many facets. This must be acknowledged and addressed if schools are to meet their aspirations to provide high-quality educational experiences for all children.

See also: bullying; corporal punishment; discipline; exclusion/expulsion; school security; suspension

Further reading

Galtung, J. (1969) 'Violence, peace, and peace research', *Journal of Peace Research*, 6(3): 167–91.
MacDonald, I. (1998) 'Navigating towards a safe and caring school', paper presented at the annual meeting of the American Educational Research Association, 13–17 April, San Diego, California.
Remboldt, C. (1994) *Solving Violence in Your School: Why a Systematic Approach is Necessary*, Minneapolis MN: Johnson Institute.
Stark, J. E. (2006) 'Commentary: violence', www.gradebook.org/violence.html

Williams, K. M. (2004) *The PEACE Approach to Violence Prevention: A Handbook for Teachers and Administrators*, Lanham MD: Scarecrow Press.
KIMBERLY WILLIAMS

SCIENCE/SCIENCE EDUCATION

Science and science education have a relatively short history. School science education began in the nineteenth century, aimed mainly at an elite. Science itself became a 'profession' in the same era. A number of recurring debates have featured in the short history of science education: process versus content; science for some or science for all?; the same science for all versus a segregated curriculum pre-sixteen; separate science versus 'integrated'; and the role of practical work in comparison with theory in learning science. These could all be subsumed under the aegis of 'what is science education for?' The widely varying contexts in which science and science education have taken place have ensured that change has been the norm rather than the exception over the last 100 years.

There are several long-standing debates on the science curriculum, which have been evident internationally. Many of these stem from the worldwide curriculum reform era of the 1960s and 1970s but they have continued to simmer since that period (Jenkins 2003; 2004).

Process versus content is a recurrent debate but its impact was felt most in the 1970s and 1980s when the 'process movement' became prominent (Wellington 1989). This was founded on the view that the key aim in learning science is for students to acquire the processes of science such as inferring and hypothesising. One of its difficulties was that the true nature of science and scientific method (and hence it processes) has proved impossible to define; another is that many critics of the process movement argued that processes cannot be taught in isolation from the central theories and ideas of science, i.e. its content. The process movement saw a huge rise in process-based schemes and published resources, which are now largely of historical interest.

The debate on how practical work and learning by discovery or investigation should feature in science is over a century old and still living healthily. The early days of Armstrong (see Jenkins 1979), with his emphasis on discovery learning, reverberated in the heyday of Nuffield Science in the UK and post-Sputnik science from the 1960s to the 1980s and then the push to include Investigations as part of the compulsory national curriculum in many contexts. The Nuffield motto was 'I do and I understand', but to critics this was seen as a mantra that was adulterated to 'I do and I become confused'. There has never been a clear consensus on the role of practical work and whether it contributes to science learning or has simply confused children, especially when hands-on work does not go to plan (nature does not always behave itself) or children do not discover what they are supposed to. A more positive view of practical work is that it can be highly motivating and can aid memory; if combined with appropriate reflection and discussion (as some have put it, 'minds-on as well as hands-on': Wellington 1998) then practical work can be of great value.

Investigational work became widespread internationally in the 1990s and is still a feature of school science in most countries. Although it may have helped to improve students' enjoyment of science, the 'school version' of scientific investigation has been criticised for portraying a narrow and incomplete image of real science and scientific method (Wellington 2000).

Another of the key recurring debates on the science curriculum is the extent to which all students pre-sixteen should be given the same diet as opposed to carefully selected topics for some, according to ability and attainment. One of the main problems in offering the choice of (say) two separate sciences from three is the gender division that seemed to appear in virtually very country (except perhaps the Soviet bloc) from the 1960s and 1970s. Girls chose biology; boys chose physics, albeit with some notable and successful exceptions. More recently, Sjoberg (2003) notes that gender differences are greatest in Northern European countries. Another issue in segregating the curriculum relates to the problematic basis on which decisions on ability and attainment are made. On the other hand, the belief in the same science for all can lead to a situation where the science curriculum is neither appropriate for, nor of interest to, a large number of pupils. This would seem to be a perennial dilemma – for science and for other curriculum subjects.

Integration versus separation: the notion of 'general science' was very much part of the 1960s discourse and this transmuted into a slightly different debate in the 1970s: should students be taught science as an integrated whole (a compound) or should the sciences be separated and taught as separate entities (a mixture)? The debate was made more complex by two factors: the difference in parity of esteem between the lower status integrated version (sometimes seen as a successor to the poorly regarded 'general science') and the elite separate sciences such as physics and chemistry; and the philosophical debate, still unresolved, as to whether science is a unified whole with a continuous vein running through it of the 'scientific method'. In the twenty-first century, the term 'integrated science' is rarely used – but the key debates over how science should be divided up, how some topics are chosen and others are excluded from the curriculum, and to what extent science should be taught and learnt as a unified whole, remain unresolved.

Internationally, the overarching debate over the last century has concerned the purpose of science education. There have been three sets of arguments (that are not mutually exclusive) relating to the rationale for science teaching and learning. I will call them intrinsic value, citizenship and utilitarian arguments. The first has involved exploring the case for learning science on the basis that it allows us to make sense of natural phenomena, including our own selves; that science is interesting and intellectually stimulating; and that science is now (even if it were not 100 years ago) part of our culture and 'heritage'. The citizenship arguments, alternatively called arguments for 'scientific literacy', are based on the view that citizens in a participative democracy can only make informed decisions if they are literate in science; equally, those who run a country, the key decision makers, need to have a good grounding in science and know the limitations of scientific evidence, in order to make key policy decisions on (say) what people eat, how energy is supplied and how the environment is to be protected. Finally, the utilitarian arguments are perhaps three-pronged: science education can 'train the mind' for people in every future career, by developing generic skills that will be of value to all e.g. analysing, inferring, understanding data. Science can also be of direct vocational value to some students who will use science in their job, and to an even smaller number who will actually become 'scientists'. Third, science education can play a major role in developing key attitudes and dispositions such as wonder, curiosity, healthy scepticism, an enquiring mind and a critical disposition. Of course, this scientific attitude will be of value not only for employment but also for citizenship in a future society based on science and technology.

All of the above movements and tensions within science education have played a part internationally in its evolution, and many are certain to recur in shaping its future.

One of the main determinants of science education has been, unsurprisingly, the societal and scientific context in which it takes place. This varies from one nation to another and from one era to another. Thus, internationally, debates over the curriculum, the nature of learning in science and the avowed purposes of science education differ between the so-called 'developing world' and the 'industrialised world' (Jenkins 2003). For example, whilst countries in the latter group

are questioning the utilitarian arguments for science education and the value of practical work, those in the 'developing world' see science education as vital to their economic future and would welcome practical work if only they could afford it.

Similarly, the period between 1945 and 1965 was seen as a rich and healthy time for science and science education with the launch of Sputnik and the advent of nuclear power at sites like Calder Hall (now Sellafield) in 1956; society looked forward with optimism to a science-based future (Jenkins 2004: 33) and huge sums were invested internationally into curriculum reform. In sharp contrast, at the start of the twenty-first century, science is no longer seen as objective and certain or capable of creating a civilised world. In most contemporary scientific issues – especially those connected with genetics, climate change, diet and medicine – the underlying science is uncertain and certainly no longer value-free.

A major achievement for science education is that 'Science' is now an established part of the school curriculum throughout most of the world, and this was far from the case at the start of the last century, when it was an option for a small elite. But not all is well. In the current era, with widespread concerns over global warming and the effects of human activity on the future of the planet, young people's attitudes to science have changed. Science, as taught in schools, is often seen as lacking any connection to key issues – the struggle for relevance continues. Many young people are said to be unmotivated and uninspired by science teaching – this negative attitude is said to be far greater in the 'industrialised world' (Sjoberg 2003), where people seem to have forgotten that science is partly responsible for delivering the material wealth and comfort that most of its inhabitants enjoy. Post-sixteen, fewer students in the industrialised world are choosing to continue with science, opting instead for the so-called 'easier' subjects. Along with falling numbers, gender differences characterise this phase, especially in the physical sciences. These problems are connected (perhaps as a cause as well as an effect) with the continuing shortage of good science teachers in physics and chemistry.

The need for curriculum reform to address all these issues is as pressing now as it was in the early twentieth century and the post-Sputnik era. The trend in the early twenty-first century is towards a curriculum emphasis on scientific literacy and science for citizenship, not only to attract and enthuse more students but also to enable informed decision making on socio-scientific issues and greater participation in an advanced democracy. One thing is certain: the debate on the curriculum, the learning of science and the purposes of science education is set to continue.

See also: biology; chemistry; core curriculum/national curriculum; curriculum; engineering; physics; subjects

Further reading

Jenkins, E. (1979) *From Armstrong to Nuffield*, London: John Murray.
——(2003) *Innovations in Science and Technology Education*, vol. 8, Paris: UNESCO.
——(2004) 'From option to compulsion: school science teaching, 1954–2004', *School Science Review*, 85(313): 33–40.
Sjoberg, S. (2003) 'Science and technology education in Europe'. In E. Jenkins (ed.) *Innovations in Science and Technology Education*, vol. 8, Paris: UNESCO.
Wellington, J. (2000) *Teaching and Learning Secondary Science*, London: Routledge
Wellington, J. (ed.) (1989) *Skills and Processes in Science Education*, London: Routledge.
——(1998) *Practical Work in School Science: Which Way Now?*, London: Routledge.

JERRY WELLINGTON

SCOUT ASSOCIATION

The Scout Association organises outdoor and adventurous activities for young people aged 6–25. It aims to foster personal development which includes 'physical, intellectual, social and spiritual well-being of the individual' as a contribution to wider social citizenship. Emphasis is placed on 'learning by doing' and key activities include camping, woodcraft, hiking, backpacking, canoeing, caving, climbing and associated activities. Recently Scouts have also been involved in projects related to peace education, drug abuse prevention, renewable energies and environmental conservation. They wear distinctive uniforms with hats, neckerchiefs and merit badges.

In Britain over 400,000 young people are Scouts, approximately 10 per cent of them girls, although internationally there are over 28 million young people from 216 countries, two thirds in developing countries. Scouting is open to all young people of every faith and background. The Scout Association is made up of local groups of young people who meet weekly and pay a small subscription charge. These groups are run largely by volunteer adults. Different provision is made for various age groups, including beavers (6–8), cubs (8–10§, scouts (10§–14), explorers (14–18) and network (18–25). The World Organisation of the Scout Movement organises international events, 'moots' and 'jamborees' for different age groups. The movement is related to a female movement, the Guides, which has formed a parallel organisation and internationally, the World Association of Girl Guides and Girl Scouts (WAGGGS).

Lord Robert Baden-Powell of Gilwell (1857–1941) established scouting and drew inspiration from his experience of soldiering, particularly in the Boer War. In 1907 he tried out his ideas at a camp on Brownsea Island in the UK with a mixture of boys from different social classes. Baden-Powell wrote up his ideas into *Scouting for Boys* (1908) which, for many years, served as a manual for the movement.

See also: citizenship; youth club/work

TOM WOODIN

SECONDARY SCHOOL/EDUCATION

Secondary education forms an intermediate stage between primary or elementary education and higher or university education. It is also a distinctive phase of schooling with its own set of aims and ideals and a characteristic set of problems and tensions. These derive from the long history and traditions of the secondary school, which originate in notions of liberal education and in elite provision for the middle classes and professions. It has developed latterly into a mass institution, but is often beset with uncertainty as to its proper character and purposes. This is often reflected in continuing debates about how to reconcile the elite functions with the more general requirements of secondary education, how to relate the original liberal ideals to specialisation and preparation for work, and tensions between the terminal and the preparatory character of secondary education.

Ideals of the secondary school and secondary education are explicable only by reference to their long history and the traditions that have become attached to them along the way. This is measured in hundreds of years rather than in decades. As the English pioneer of secondary education, Matthew Arnold, pointed out in the 1860s, while elementary schools for the poor were a modern invention,

> The secondary school has a long history; through a series of changes it goes back, in every European country, to the beginnings of civilised society in that country; from the time when this society had any sort of organisation, a certain sort of schools and schooling existed, and between that schooling and the schooling which the children of the richer class of society at this day receive there is an unbroken connection.
>
> (Arnold 1964 [1865]: 35)

The origins of these ideals lay in the liberal education of the Greeks, expressed most fully by Plato and Aristotle, the fruits of which the historian I. L. Kandel summed up as 'judgment and good taste, self-control and modesty, ability to meet one's fellow men, and intellectual interests' (1930: 20). In the Middle Ages, this tradition was pursued in schools associated with the Church, such as that at Canterbury in England and Alcuin's *Ecole du Palais*, founded by Charlemagne in France. The curriculum was based on the seven liberal arts: the *trivium* of grammar, rhetoric and dialectic, and the *quadrivium* of geometry, arithmetic, astronomy and music.

There was, indeed, as Arnold averred, a direct link between this form of education and the schools attended by the 'richer class of society' in the nineteenth century. There were striking similarities in the secondary schools developed in different nations. The German *Gymnasium*, the French *lycée* and the English endowed grammar school bore a strong family resemblance. The *Gymnasium* developed on classical lines, influenced by Wilhelm von Humboldt, to develop during the nineteenth century the ideal of *Bildung* that guaranteed individuals freedom to develop their talents to the greatest possible extent, untrammelled by preparations for a future career (Albisetti 1983). At the same time, there were also significant differences. In America secondary education, dating from 1635 in Boston, became established in public high schools during the nineteenth century, but with a more practical bent than elsewhere. Nevertheless, these were all elite, middle-class institutions, clearly distinguishable from the schools of the masses and orientated towards the universities and the professions (Herbst 1996).

Over the past century, secondary education has spread from these elite origins to become a mass institution. Yet the resilience of its ideals has led to basic uncertainties as to its character and role which continue to plague its development. In Durkheim's terms, it became 'intellectually disorientated between a past which is dying and a future which is still undecided, and as a consequence lacks the vigour and vitality which it once possessed' (1977 [1938]: 8). Three closely related aspects of these unresolved issues may be identified here. The first and key question is how secondary education reconciles its elite functions with the needs of the population as a whole. This problem has been addressed in a number of ways. Selection through examination has been widely promoted as a means of identifying individual merit and potential for further study. This has permitted at least some limited access for children from poorer social backgrounds, but examinations as a device for doing so have remained problematic. In some nations, such as the United States, secondary education set out to embrace the whole school population of the neighbourhood or town in a single institution under what has become known as the comprehensive model (Conant 1959). This has been widely imitated, but inequalities of opportunity and achievement have generally remained evident. Elsewhere, different types of secondary education and schools for different types of ability or orientation have been developed, such as in the so-called 'tripartite' system of grammar, technical and modern schools in mid-twentieth-century England, but these have tended to foster inequality and stifle opportunity in an even more striking way (McCulloch 1998).

In consequence, a second issue concerns the curriculum of secondary schools. How far can the general nature of their original liberal ideals be reconciled with specialisation and direct preparation for the workforce? This has led to sharp disputes about the kinds of subjects that should be included in the secondary school curriculum, and the ways in which they should be taught and for whom. For example, there have been major differences between those who have sought to make a sharp distinction between secondary and technical instruction, and those who argue that a technical curriculum may be incorporated within secondary education. Others have argued that there should be specialist forms of secondary education based on the supposedly different requirements of boys and girls in later life. In recent years, too, there has been a widespread tendency towards specialisation in secondary education, often manifested in the development of separate, specialist institutions that encourage particular kinds of orientation. Such initiatives have commonly encountered difficulties that stem ultimately from the historical tensions underlying secondary education itself.

Thus, there remains also an unresolved tension between secondary education as a terminal phase and as a preparatory stage. This is another symptom of the conflict between the elite and mass purposes of secondary education. It also goes to the heart of the relationship between secondary and further and higher education. For many pupils, often the majority, the secondary school is the final destination of their educational career. They will leave school after completing their course, and begin their working lives. However, for others, it is only one stage in their educational development, during which they are preparing to go on to more advanced and specialised study at university or other educational institutions. Again, therefore, the key question for secondary schools is how to cater adequately for both of these types of pupil, often described as academic and non-academic, in their examinations and curriculum. For the leading New Zealand educational policy maker Clarence Beeby, this constituted 'a problem of secondary education unsolved worldwide'. According to Beeby, too (1984: 108–9),

> Only by persistently experimenting with alternative forms of secondary school, with modifications to existing curricula and methods of handling mature students, and with new methods of bridging the gap between school and industry will we inch our way towards a workable solution to this most recalcitrant of educational problems.

Experiments have not been lacking and continue to be devised, but there is little sign as yet of the doubts that have come to surround secondary education being assuaged or answered.

See also: comprehensive school/education; examinations; further education; grammar school; high school; higher education; primary school/education; selection; specialisation

Further reading

Albisetti, J. (1983) *Secondary School Reform in Imperial Germany*, Princeton NJ: Princeton University Press.

Arnold, Matthew (1964) [1865] *Schools and Universities on the Continent*, ed. R. H. Super, Ann Arbor MI: University of Michigan Press.

Beeby, C. E. (1984) 'A problem of secondary education unsolved worldwide'. In G. McDonald and A. Campbell (eds) *Looking Forward: Essays On The Future Of Education In New Zealand*, Wellington: Te Aro Press.

Conant, J. B. (1959) *The American High School Today: A First Report to Interested Citizens*, New York: McGraw-Hill.

Durkheim, E. (1977) [1938] *The Evolution of Educational Thought: Lectures on the Formation and Development of Secondary Education in France*, London: Routledge and Kegan Paul.

Herbst, J. (1996) *The Once and Future School: Three Hundred and Fifty Years of American Secondary Education*, New York: Routledge.

Kandel, I. L. (1930) *History of Secondary Education: A Study in the Development of Liberal Education*, London: Harrap.

McCulloch, G. (1998) *Failing the Ordinary Child? The Theory and Practice of Working Class Secondary Education*, Buckingham: Open University Press.

GARY McCULLOCH

SEGREGATION/DESEGREGATION

School segregation is the separation of students on the basis of a socially significant ascribed characteristic. It can be de facto (caused by individual actions) or de jure (created by law). School *de*segregation is the systematic elimination of that segregation.

The dominant rule for assigning students to schools in the United States has been residence in a contiguous attendance zone around the school called a neighbourhood attendance zone. In seventeen states in the Southern US, however, before 1954 state law required that there be a *dual* system of neighbourhood attendance zones – one for whites and one for blacks. The US Congress also required that the District of Columbia have a dual school system.

Brown v. Board of Education (1954) declared this dual system of neighbourhood schools to be in violation of the US Constitution. *Brown v. Board of Education* (1955) then declared the remedy to be a single set of 'compact' neighbourhood attendance zones. This decision began the process of desegregation in the USA. The first plans were called 'freedom of choice', implemented in Southern school districts. Students were initially assigned to the school for their race, but could transfer to other schools. Only black students – about 15 per cent of them – transferred. By the late 1960s, most Southern school districts had adopted a single set of neighbourhood school zones and freedom of choice. For the smaller school districts, this was usually sufficient to desegregate all, or almost all, of their schools. For the larger school districts, it was not.

As a result, the Supreme Court turned *Brown* on its head in *Green v. New Kent County* (1968) when it opined that Southern school districts had to achieve racially balanced schools. School desegregation plans with racial balance goals accompanied by cross-town bussing became the law of the land, although initially affecting only the South. In the North, some neighbourhood schools were racially imbalanced because of the neighbourhood's racial composition. In the 1960s, many northern school districts responded to this by voluntarily adopting M-to-M desegregation plans in which any child could leave a school in which his or her race was in the majority to go to a school in which his or her race was in the minority. As with freedom-of-choice plans, only black students volunteered. By the early 1970s, however, Northern courts began to interpret school board actions that contributed to school racial imbalance as intentional racial discrimination, even without the history of de jure segregation, and ordered plans similar to those in the South.

By 1991, 12 per cent of all districts and 59 per cent of the largest school districts in the USA had school desegregation plans (Rossell 2002). The types of school desegregation plans can be categorised into voluntary and mandatory desegregation plans, depending on whether parents have the option of keeping their child at their neighbourhood school (voluntary) or have no choice about staying at their neighbourhood school (mandatory) if they wish to keep their child in the public schools. About half of whites assigned to schools in black neighbourhoods did not show up at the school they were assigned to (Rossell 2002).

Of those districts with plans in 1991, 4 per cent had voluntary M to M plans and 23 per cent had magnet-voluntary plans for a total of 27 per cent with voluntary plans. In addition, 4 per cent had controlled choice, 17 per cent had magnet-mandatory, and 52 per cent had mandatory plans without magnets for a total of 73 per cent with mandatory plans (Rossell 2002).

There have been no new desegregation plans in the last decade, and every year a handful of school districts are released from court order. However, although no one knows for sure how many districts are still under a court ordered desegregation plan, there are undoubtedly hundreds. In addition, many of the districts that have been released from court order have maintained all or part of their plans and continue to use racial balance quotas in student assignment and/or magnet school admission. The issue of whether racial quotas can be used if a school district is not under such a desegregation court order is a contentious one that will be decided in 2007 by the Supreme Court in *Parents v. Seattle School District, et al.* and *Meredith v. Jefferson County Board of Education, et al.* Most observers predict the verdict will be to prohibit strict racial quotas.

See also: catchment area; magnet school; neighbourhood school; zoning

Further reading

Rossell, C. (2002) 'The effectiveness of desegregation plans'. In C. H. Rossell, D. J. Armor and H. J. Walberg (eds) *School Desegregation in the 21st Century*, Westport CT: Praeger.

CHRISTINE H. ROSSELL

SELECTION

Selection refers to the various ways in which educational systems channel students into what are seen as appropriate courses, schools and employment. It can take a wide variety of forms. Students may be selected according to criteria such as ability and willingness to pay, aptitude and intelligence, geographical location, lottery and ethnicity. Each of these will have varying implications. Although it is usually individuals who are selected, controversy arises from the fact that, collectively, whole groups of students tend to be affected by such processes.

One function of education is to facilitate the process of selection for employment by certifying students and nurturing skills that will be valued in the workplace. The theory of equal opportunities holds that such selection should take place according to neutral criteria such as ability and qualifications. However, less explicit factors may also play a role, such as having attended particular 'selective' educational establishments.

Selection can take place at all levels of the education system. For instance, most countries tend to have a limited and patchy provision of early years education, and nurseries may have to select according to certain criteria in addition to the ability to pay fees. By contrast, primary schools tend to operate with the least amount of selection and are more likely to be compulsory and available to all.

It is generally true that a greater degree of selection will take place as students progress through the various levels of education, although academic selection by ability underpins primary schooling in Singapore. In Britain, following the 1944 Education Act, the 'eleven-plus' examination became widespread and determined whether children attended high-status grammar schools or lower-status secondary moderns. Critics contested the assumption that these tests revealed ability, intelligence and aptitude for different 'types' of education. They pointed to the cultural bias inherent in such tests and the way in which they tended to perpetuate social class and ethnic inequalities. In many areas comprehensive schools replaced this system, although selection through setting and streaming would sometimes continue within schools.

Given the smaller number of university places available, higher education is inevitably more selective, but in recent years many systems have been expanding considerably. In the United Kingdom, over 40 per cent of 18–30-year-olds now attend university. In a context of widespread poverty, nations have made choices between developing various levels of education. Some developing countries have constructed selective forms of education in order to nurture political and economic leaders who can contribute to nation building and economic development. Selective education also plays a role in rapidly developing countries: for instance, in China selective 'key schools' were fostered following the Cultural Revolution and, more recently, higher education has been much expanded and diversified in order to enhance economic growth. These policies have tended to disproportionately benefit the urban middle classes.

The spatial aspect of school boundaries and catchment areas may also define who is selected to attend prestigious or less successful schools. In some developing countries the geographical location of certain schools may preclude the possibility of attendance. In the United States of America wealthy areas tend to have better funded schools than poorer areas: in cities such as New York this has created considerable tensions and the drawing up of boundaries has been politically contested. In England, middle-class people have generally been more able to buy expensive houses close to 'good' schools.

Market-based reforms have been introduced in many countries, by which parents are offered a 'choice'. In an unequal society, it is likely that such a diversity of educational forms will become associated with higher- and lower-status institutions. This may give rise to self-selection, although critics have shown how such policies lead to growing educational inequality, particularly according to social class and 'race'. Informal processes of institutional racism may operate to ensure that racialised groups are selected out of more prestigious educational options. This is most apparent in countries such as the USA and South Africa, which are marked by a high degree of racialisation. In Malaysia, ethnic selection in education takes place more openly, given that benefits for the indigenous *bumiputras* were written into the constitution.

Perhaps the most notable example of selective schooling can be found in the number of private schools and elite universities that have traditionally provided a route to wealth and power for a small minority of students. Notable examples would be the top British 'public' schools, as well as the Ivy League colleges in the USA, which are able to command considerable fees. Critics have alleged that ruling groups are able to exercise their economic power through these institutions while also operating informal networks to enhance the options open to their own children.

See also: ability; ability grouping; aptitude; grammar school; intelligence/intelligence tests; secondary school/education; setting; streaming/tracking

Further reading

Crook, D., Power, S. and Whitty, G. (1999) *The Grammar School Question: A Review of Research on Comprehensive and Selective Education*, London: Institute of Education, University of London.
DeSena, J. N. (2006) '"What's a mother to do?" Gentrification, school selection, and the consequences for community cohesion', *American Behavioral Scientist*, 50(2): 241–57.
Vernon, P. E. (ed.) (1957) *Secondary School Selection*, London: Methuen.

TOM WOODIN

SELF-DIRECTED LEARNING

Self-directed learning is an approach to education that relies on students taking the overall responsibility and initiative for the educational process such that the student is generally expected to determine the learning goal itself, the process to be used to reach the goal, and possibly even to provide an appropriate assessment strategy. Ideally, the student will also be able to recognise the importance of a justification for their choices as well. The practice of self-directed learning may occur at a variety of different levels and settings. On a limited scale, self-directed learning may be practised during activities with narrow time-frames and objectives, such as when primary students might use a science period to capture and investigate an insect of their choice from the school grounds. At the other end of the scale, an adult may be responsible to set goals that extend through a range of activities and subjects encompassing their entire programme, such as when universities demand that doctoral candidates create and pursue original research in their field.

The success of self-directed learning in achieving learning goals is, in general, related to the learner's ability and willingness to take ownership and control of the learning process, such as using and responding to summative and formative evaluation instruments, engaging in realistic planning with appropriate and available resources, and the ongoing modification of learning goals. Unfortunately, further and more inclusive studies are needed as the research has mostly used white, middle-class subjects.

See also: autodidact; learning

PAUL COLLINS

SEMESTER/TERM

A term or semester divides an academic year into time periods during which classes and lectures are held. Semester derives from Latin origins, and more recently German, literally meaning 'six months'. Academic years tend to be considerably shorter than calendar years, given that most institutions have long summer breaks when classes and lectures do not take place. Semesters and terms are organised in various ways. Semesters split the year into two half-yearly sections and may run for approximately 15–18 weeks. Trisemesters split the year into three, as do many terms. The academic year may also be split into quarters although teaching may take place in only three of these. Some universities may reserve part of semesters for coursework, writing and examinations, a time when classes and lectures do not take place. A 'reading week' may also offer a gap in teaching during term time. Terms and semesters may be of unequal length. For instance, an autumn term is often longer than a summer one.

In some countries the long summer break has been criticised by educationists on the grounds that the long break from teaching impacts adversely upon learning and educational progress. Instead, five or six terms a year have been suggested, with a greater number of shorter breaks to foster continuity.

See also: college; higher education; school; university

TOM WOODIN

SEMINAR

While lectures are well known for being traditional in their format, the same is also true of seminars, which involve interactive discussion in small, or sometimes larger, groups facilitated by a tutor. The basic idea is that of a Socratic dialogue, in which knowledge is advanced through conversation and the interchange of ideas. Learning is intended to be active and participative, rather than passive and reactive. Often the seminar is held in combination with a lecture that is intended to introduce a topic, and there may be a presentation of some key issues by a participant or a group of participants to start a discussion. Often it is a forum in which debates can develop that lead on to wider issues that are not necessarily intended within the course, and a skilled facilitator is normally required in order to maintain an appropriate focus and direction for the discussion. Seminars are often also held in a series to develop new research in a particular area of study, and may attract researchers in related fields to discuss their methods and findings with colleagues in their own and in other institutions for mutual benefit.

See also: lecture; Socratic method; tuition/ tutor/tutorial

GARY McCULLOCH

SEMINARY

A seminary is a specialised institution of higher education, drawn from the Latin word 'seminarium', or seedbed. It is usually designed to instruct students in a specific religious faith, in an environment conducive to such learning such as a residential college, with the aim of preparing them to become preachers or members of the clergy. Roman Catholic seminaries were established during the Counter-Reformation to educate students under the control of senior clergy, rather than in the universities. Minor seminaries have also been established in many places at secondary or high school level to prepare pupils for later entry into adult seminaries. They may also develop alongside theological colleges. In some cases, seminaries may be secular institutions with the aim of training teachers. Examples include the Princeton Theological Seminary, established by the General Assembly of the Presbyterian Church in 1812, which is a residential community that prepares men and women for the clergy, and London Theological Seminary, founded in 1977, an evangelical Protestant college for training preachers and pastors. John Cornwell's memoir *Seminary Boy* (2006) recounts his life in a minor seminary in the West Midlands, England.

See also: Jesuit education; religious education; religious school

Further reading

Cornwell, J. (2006) *Seminary Boy*, London: Fourth Estate.

GARY McCULLOCH

SETTING

'Setting' is a term with several educational meanings. The context of the school or classroom provides an educational setting for learning and teaching. 'Target-setting', meanwhile, may specify ambitions for student, teachers, institutions or even governments to aim higher and raise levels of achievement or performance.

A more specific use of 'setting' relates to the division of student cohorts into ability groupings, particularly in such subjects as mathematics and modern foreign languages. Setting on an individual subject basis is widely held to be more acceptable and flexible than 'streaming' which, in some countries, once determined that only the ablest students in secondary schools experienced an academic curriculum and the opportunity to sit public examinations. For the purposes of preparing students for formal assessments, which are sometimes differentiated by level, setting may assist teachers in their lesson preparation. In the staffroom, the discourse of 'top', 'middle' and 'bottom' sets may feature frequently in teacher discussions, but schools sometimes elect to mask their setting policies from students and parents by identifying, for example, 'blue', 'green' and 'yellow' groups. The increasing recognition of young pupils as individual learners, together with the adoption of structured learning programmes, have determined that, in recent years, setting is a feature of primary or elementary schools, as well as those serving older groups. Schools normally emphasise the flexibility of any setting arrangements and the regularity of reviews to ensure that students are learning at their own pace.

See also: ability grouping; streaming/tracking

DAVID CROOK

SEX EDUCATION

The role of schools in education about sex and personal relationships has nearly always proved controversial. For one thing, there are those who argue that sex education should not be taught in schools, maintaining that the home alone is the proper place for it. Then, the precise aims of sex education vary greatly. Other issues include the age at which school sex education should start, the teaching approaches to be used, the framework of values within which it should take place, whether or not parents should be able to withdraw their children from school sex education, whether classes should (sometimes) be single-sex, who should teach it, the training which teachers of sex education should receive and where within the school curriculum it should be taught.

The aims of school sex education have broadened over time, responding to such perceived crises as rises in sexually transmitted infections (particularly HIV) and teenage pregnancy, as well as to shifts in political agendas and the influence of organised religion. Examination of policy guidelines and the resources used for teaching school sex education indicate that the following main aims are found:

- helping young people to know about such biological topics as development, puberty and conception;
- preventing children from experiencing sexual abuse;
- decreasing guilt, embarrassment and anxiety about sexual matters;
- encouraging good relationships, including sexual relationships;
- preventing under-age teenagers from engaging in sexual intercourse (abstinence education);
- preventing under-age girls from getting pregnant;
- decreasing the incidence of sexually transmitted infections;
- helping young people question the role of women and men in society;
- encouraging people to be more tolerant of those with different sexualities from themselves (Halstead and Reiss 2003).

There are significant differences between countries in the extent to which national politics have affected school sex education. In both the UK and the USA, national politics have been extremely influential, with a small but powerful lobby believing that much school sex education is corruptive. In the Netherlands, on the other hand, sex education has remained remarkably non-political. It has been argued that this has led in the Netherlands to a much more coherent programme of school sex education in which teachers are not worried that they may be blamed for teaching something that they shouldn't be. Whether this is partly responsible for the fact that a teenage girl in the UK or USA at the start of the twenty-first century is about ten times as likely to become pregnant than in the Netherlands is controversial.

Sex education cannot be neutral. Even when teaching the 'facts' in biology, messages about values are conveyed. For example, school science textbooks often omit all mention of the clitoris and when they do refer to it, frequently talk of it as the female's equivalent of a penis. Males are rendered visible, females less so; and the female exists by virtue of comparison with the male. Emily Martin has shown that while menstruation is viewed in scientific textbooks as a failure (you should have got pregnant), sperm maturation is viewed as a wonderful achievement in which countless millions of sperm are manufactured each day (Martin 1991). Furthermore, sperm are viewed as active and streamlined whereas the egg is large and passive and just drifts along or sits there waiting. The way the egg is portrayed in science textbooks has been likened to that of the fairy tale *Sleeping Beauty*, in which a dormant, virginal bride awaits a male's magic kiss. However, since the 1980s biologists have seen both egg and sperm as active partners. Just as sperm seek out the

539

egg, so the vagina discriminates between sperm, and the egg seeks out sperm to catch.

Most sex educators agree that the best provision for sex education occurs when schools involve parents and community leaders in the development (or, at least, the approval) of a programme and then teach this across the curriculum, in a number of traditional subjects (including science, English, religious studies, history and geography), in PSE, PSHE or PSHCE (personal, social, health and citizenship education) lessons and in tutor groups or form periods.

The main journal in the field is *Sex Education* (www.tandf.co.uk/journals/carfax/14681811. html).

See also: biology; curriculum; health education; textbook

Further reading

Francoeur, R. T. and Noonan, R. J. (eds) (2004) *The Continuum Complete International Encyclopedia of Sexuality, Updated with More Countries*, New York: Continuum.

Halstead, J. M. and Reiss, M. J. (2003) *Values in Sex Education: From Principles to Practice*, London: RoutledgeFalmer.

Martin, E. (1991) 'The egg and the sperm: how science has constructed a romance based on stereotypical male-female roles', *Signs: Journal of Women in Culture and Society*, 16(3): 485–501.

MICHAEL J. REISS

SINGAPORE

The Ministry of Education (MOE) is responsible for education policy in Singapore. It controls public schools and plays an advisory role in relation to private schools. Approximately 4 per cent of the gross domestic product is devoted to education, amounting to almost 20 per cent of government expenditure. Although education has not always been compulsory, attendance figures have tended to be very high. Funding, scholarships and bursaries have supported able students from poorer families.

As part of the British empire, Singapore's education was partly shaped by its colonial history, beyond the few inherited elite educational establishments. Singapore gained increasing independence from Britain after 1945 and from Malaysia after 1965. Governments in Singapore emphasised the role of education in nation building, economic development and international competitiveness, an early practical application of 'human capital' theory. Through much of the 1960s and 1970s the education system focused upon producing a minority of highly trained university graduates alongside a much larger number of students who had failed to reach the required grade. Following reforms introduced in 1979, attempts were made to increase retention and ensure that more children left school with some skills. Students were also able to progress more slowly through school. Increasingly, vocational education was introduced to help meet the needs of industry. Children with special educational needs have tended to be educated in separate schools run by voluntary welfare organisations and are partly funded by the MOE.

A notable feature of the education system of Singapore has been the emphasis on assessment, streaming and sorting of students in order that they may make an appropriate contribution. Critics have pointed to the contradiction between the public commitment to developing all students to the best of their ability and the marked selectivity within the system. Public attention and parental concern helps to ensure that education remains highly competitive

Singapore has operated a bilingual policy in which everyone learns English alongside a mother-tongue language such as Malay, Tamil, Mandarin or non-Tamil Indian language, though no ethnic group has to learn the language of another. English was also suited to interaction in the world economy and its dominance was symbolised by the closure/integration of the Nanyang Chinese University in 1978. More recently, the popularity of madrasahs has caused concern and debate in some quarters.

Kindergartens exist for children aged 3–6 and are run by a range of civic, voluntary, business and religious groups. The curriculum focuses on play, numbers, social and language skills. Since 2003 six years of elementary schooling has been compulsory. Primary education is divided into a four-year 'foundation stage' in which students follow a common curriculum, and a two-year 'orientation stage' during which they are streamed. Subjects covered include English, maths and languages as well as civics and moral education, music, arts, health, social studies and physical education. The primary school-leaving examination is used to allocate secondary school places as well as determine whether students have reached the national standard.

The results of the examination help to determine which secondary stream students enter: 'special', 'express', 'normal (academic)' or 'normal (technical)'. For the next four years secondary schools deliver a modified British-style system in which the main qualifications are the Cambridge University-administered Ordinary Level ('O' level) and Advanced Level ('A' level) examinations, although some schools also operate the International Baccalaureate. There has been a traditional emphasis on science and language, although arts and general subjects are also taught. Students must also participate in extracurricular activities which include sports, cadet groups, clubs and performing arts. A 'gifted educational programme' and 'integrated programme' have identified an educational elite who, in some cases, are able to skip O-levels and study directly for A-levels or the baccalaureate. Given the large number of expatriate groups in Singapore, there are also a number of international schools such as the Singapore American School.

A range of grading systems is operated according to different educational routes. Broadly, those who do well may progress to junior college or a Centralised Institute where 25 per cent of students take a two-year pre-university course, usually leading to A-levels. Vocational subjects such as business and engineering can be followed at polytechnics which offer diplomas. Alternatively, colleges of the Institute of Technical Education also provide vocational courses and many students enter directly following O-levels. It is possible to continue at university via the latter two routes although only a relatively small number do so. For those who do not progress to university, short-course and technical training institutes help to develop specific skills required by employers.

The largest, and most prestigious, higher education institutions are the National University of Singapore, the Nanyang Technological University and the Singapore Management University. University enrolments have been connected to the requirements of industry, resulting in many engineering, science and vocational degrees. For those pursuing liberal arts and social science courses, the civil service and teaching are popular professions.

The Singapore government has aimed to turn the country into an exporter of high-quality higher education (Mok and Tan 2004). In 1998 the Economic Development Board (EDB) launched a plan to attract more than ten 'world class' universities. This paid dividends in 2000 with the establishment of INSEAD and the Graduate School of Business University of Chicago, which offer courses such as MBAs. The University of New South Wales (UNSW) Asia is the first foreign university wholly owned and operated by an overseas institution. It provides a wide range of undergraduate, postgraduate and research programmes targeted at both local and international students. Leading private institutions such as the Singapore Institute of Management (SIM), in collaboration with overseas partners, also provide university education. In the wider context of the corporatisation and marketisation of higher education in Singapore, it is clear that the higher education sector has experienced significant restructuring. With the growing importance of transnational higher education, a higher education market is forming in Singapore (Mok 2005).

See also: bilingual education; East Asia

Further reading

Mok, K. H. (2005) 'Pro-competition policy tools and state capacity: corporatization of public universities in Hong Kong and Singapore', *Policy and Society*, 24(3): 1–26.
Mok, K. H. and Tan, J. (2004) *Globalization and Marketization in Education: A Comparative Analysis of Hong Kong and Singapore*, Cheltenham: Edward Elgar.
Shanmugaratnam, T. (2005) 'Summary of transnational higher education in Singapore, addendum to the president's address', Singapore: Ministry of Education.
Tan, C, Wong, B., Chua, J. and Kang, T. (eds) (2006) *Critical Perspectives on Education: An Introduction*, Singapore: Prentice Hall.

KA HO MOK

SITUATED COGNITION/LEARNING

The basic principle underlying 'situated cognition' is that learning takes place, and knowledge and understanding are acquired, in different contexts and situations. The strong thesis is that all cognition (i.e. skills, ability and understanding) is dependent on the context that it was acquired in; and it does not readily transfer to other contexts or other situations. The debate over whether cognition is situated or not is linked to the debate over transfer of learning and the idea of learning communities. The key question for those who believe in situated cognition is: can skills, knowledge and understanding learnt in one context transfer to another, very different context? Or is cognition situated and context dependent?

Those who argue the case that all learning and cognition are situated base their view on the following claims:

- Learning is fundamentally social and cultural (not individual and impersonal). It is the situation that counts, not the subject matter. The focus then shifts from what is learned to *how* it is learned, *where and with or through whom*.

- The community of learners is vitally important, e.g. as in the apprenticeship model of learning. Learners become part of a community of practice; initially they are on the periphery of this community – as they learn and become socialised into it they move from this 'legitimate peripheral participation' (Lave and Wenger 1991) to more central involvement.

- As a result, the following roles become vitally important: coaching, mentoring, showing, getting 'a feel for things', trying things out and practising. The focus is on participation, not reception and transmission.

- The focus in learning should be on social and community aspects, not the individual's mind/brain (i.e. the shift is from the individual as a unit of analysis to the sociocultural setting, the community).

Protagonists such as Lave (1988) argue that there is little evidence of people's ability to apply knowledge they gain in one context to problems they encounter in another. This implies that the so-called core or key skills, e.g. problem solving, are not transferable.

Those who argue against the idea of situated learning argue for the claim that cognition (i.e. skills, knowledge and understanding) can transfer from one context to another. They argue that to teach and learn in the 'right way' can improve the chances of transfer occurring. This would involve:

- teaching and learning for understanding, as opposed to rote learning, following specific rules without knowing why, etc.;

- using lots of examples and situations in teaching and learning i.e. multiple contexts;

- helping students to reflect on their own learning, and how they achieved it, i.e. metacognition; preparation for future learning should be seen as the aim of all teaching and learning.

The debate has been alive for a long time, but the jury is still out. 'Situated cognition' is widely discussed at present, with numerous websites devoted to it and certain books and articles seemingly determined to show that all cognition is situated and context dependent. Reality may lie somewhere in the middle ground between the two poles, i.e. those at one end with an implicit belief in transfer, and those at the other pole who wish to assert that all cognition is inevitably situated.

See also: cognition; core skills/core competencies; learning; learning community

Further reading

Adey, P. (1997) '"It all depends on the context, doesn't it?" Searching for general, educable dragons', *Studies in Science Education*, 29: 45–92.
Lave, J. (1988) *Cognition in Practice*, Cambridge: Cambridge University Press.
Lave, J. and Wenger, E. (1991) *Situated Learning: Legitimate Peripheral Participation*, New York: Cambridge University Press.

JERRY WELLINGTON

SIXTH FORM

A term strongly associated with British, and British-influenced, education systems – in Hong Kong and the West Indies, for example – the sixth form comprises the oldest students in the secondary school who, having completed public examinations at age sixteen, have chosen to remain at school. The term has a currency in both maintained and independent schools. Strictly speaking, the notion of the sixth form, which was originally associated with the selective grammar school, should now be redundant. It is, however, a curiosity that while the national curriculum has embedded the idea that secondary schooling from ages 11–16 encompasses years 7, 8, 9, 10 and 11 (rather than the first, second, third, fourth and fifth years of a bygone age), reference to the 'sixth form' is often preferred to 'years 12 and 13'.

The traditional sixth-form programme, leading to General Certificate of Education Advanced Level examinations lasts for two years (and now incorporates intermediate 'Advanced Supplementary' examinations during the first year), so it is conventional to distinguish between lower sixth and upper sixth students. Traditional sixth forms are oriented towards preparation for higher education. Sixth formers are sometimes appointed as prefects and take on duties working in the school library or assisting a lower-school form tutor with pastoral work. They may have exclusive access to a common room and be exempt from the wearing of a school uniform.

The changes in British post-compulsory education over the past quarter of a century have broadened the concept of the sixth form. Students disappointed with their public examination performance at age sixteen may have an opportunity to repeat courses and follow vocational programmes in what is sometimes termed the 'new sixth'.

Between the 1960s and 1980s, especially, a number of British local education authorities reorganised their secondary education provision to created specialist sixth form colleges, catering for 16–19-year-olds. Some British sixth form colleges have continued to prioritise academic programmes for young people, while others have moved towards the model of the further education college, becoming significantly more vocational and catering for a broad range of adult learners. Specialist sixth form institutions generally have a very different character to sixth forms operating within secondary schools.

See also: further education; prefect; secondary school/education

DAVID CROOK

SKILLS

There is much controversy about what skills are and how they should be measured. Skills are commonly associated in people's minds with training, qualifications, apprenticeship, experience and high abilities. Theoretical perspectives on skill differ according to where skill is considered to reside. Some perspectives, principally rooted in psychology and economics, view skills as attributes of the person. By contrast, management and industrial relations specialists, together with occupational psychologists, see skills as residing in the job. Sociologists, anthropologists and social historians see skills as socially constructed and residing in settings. They focus on how skills are shaped by social relations.

Approaches that view skills as an individual attribute are often associated with human capital theories, which argue that in market economies a person's value as an employee is determined by their knowledge and abilities, and the extent to which their knowledge and abilities are in supply and demand in the labour market give them value as 'skills'. These approaches assume that these attributes can be measured objectively, and often rely on variables such as year of schooling and qualifications as proxy measures of skill. One of the problems with these approaches is the validity of the definitions and measures of skills that are used, since context determines the value of the skill.

In versions that focus on the job, skill is seen as an objective feature of work, is defined by the requirements of the job and can be measured through an analysis of job content. Levels of skill are often differentiated according to the complexity of the job and according to the scope of discretion that the post-holder has in making decisions and judgements. Levels of education, training and experience are also associated with the skills level of jobs. There are disparities between the skills people possess as compared with skills expected to be used at work. The nature of the skills gap is contested. Some surveys and analyses identify 'skill shortages' while others identify 'underemployment', by demonstrating that increases in educational qualifications and

in work-related knowledge have overtaken the skills levels of the jobs available.

These apparent contradictions often have their foundations in ways in which skills are identified, recognised and valued. The tacit dimensions of skill are increasingly important, as social skills, organisational skills and abilities to deal with unfamiliar situations are emphasised in job requirements. The idea of individuals being able to transfer skills between jobs in the interests of 'flexibility' has also come to the fore as an instrument of lifelong learning policies. Personal competences such as communication, interpersonal and problem-solving competences have been portrayed as generic or transferable skills that are highly significant for individual effectiveness and adaptability within the labour market. Considerable problems of definition surround the investigation of tacit dimensions of skill. While explicit knowledge and skills are easily codified and conveyed to others, tacit forms are experiential, subjective and personal, and substantially more difficult to convey. The growing interest in their codification stems from recognition that tacit skills are very important in the performance of individuals, organisations, networks and possibly whole communities. 'Know-how' involves complex links between skill formation and personal knowledge developed through experience. This is so often taken for granted that the extent to which it pervades our activities is unappreciated.

Approaches that focus on 'skill in the job' and 'skill in the individual' are often criticised for ignoring the social and historical development of the different conceptions of skill. Skill is a powerful concept since it implies a measure of the worth. The skills that are recognised and rewarded reflect the power and influence of social groupings. They are used by different interest groups to claim status, preferential treatment and higher rewards. This is illustrated, for example, in the valuing of cognitive skills over the practical and vocational, in restrictions in entry to occupational and professional groups, and in the attribution and reward of skills according to gender. Gender has been critically important in defining skill, which has often been determined by the sex of those who do the work rather than its content.

See also: ability; apprenticeship; globalisation; lifelong learning; qualifications; training

Further reading

Eraut, M., Alderton, J., Cole, G. and Senker, P. (2000) 'Development of knowledge and skills at work'. In F. Coffield (ed.) *Differing Visions of a Learning Society*, Bristol: Policy Press.
Evans, K. (2005) 'Tacit skills and occupational mobility in a global culture'. In J. Zajda (ed.) *International Handbook on Education, Globalization and Education Policy*, Dordrecht, the Netherlands: Springer.
Noon, M. and Blyton, P. (2002) *The Realities of Work*, 2nd edn, Basingstoke: Palgrave.

KAREN EVANS

SKINNER, BURRHUS FREDRIC (1904–90)

B. F. Skinner was a prominent behaviourist and iconoclast, who denied the existence of mind. He believed that human organisms could be understood through detailed, scientific observation of behaviours under controlled conditions. They could then be modified using 'operant conditioning'. The early influence of Pavlov drew him to enrol at Harvard, aged twenty-four, gaining a doctorate three years later. He spent most of his academic life at Harvard. Operant conditioning was a process of re-ordering environmental factors in order to produce desirable behaviours. Behaviour, according to Skinner, was produced by learned expectations of outcomes. Therefore, by modifying outcomes, behaviour could be changed. He developed an interest in a teaching machine, through which he developed an approach to learning that was addressed to the particular level of understanding of the individual. The researcher then broke down problems into their respective parts, providing instant feedback when the student had completed each phase. These ideas were encapsulated in *The*

Technology of Teaching (1968), which advocated programmed teaching and learning. The educational process should principally be involved in 'shaping strategies' to modify children's behaviours. The modification process was seen as removing a factor seen as a cause and substituting something (an incentive) that would condition an appropriate response. He believed in relinquishing rights in exchange for greater uniformity and social cohesion, something that made aspects of his work attractive to certain types of governments. Skinner's *Beyond Freedom and Dignity* (1971) controversially popularised many of his ideas. He argued for pharmacological and surgical interventions in children, should operant conditioning not succeed, stating that such programmes would enhance the general good.

See also: behaviourism; programmed learning

STEVEN COWAN

SOCIAL CAPITAL

The notion of social capital came into usage during the first quarter of the twentieth century. However, it was Pierre Bourdieu's (1930–2002) work on social theory, and James S. Coleman's (1926–95) around the social context of education that moved the idea into mainstream academic debates. Subsequent contributions from Robert D. Putnam (1941–) launched social capital as a popular focus for research and policy discussion.

Its central idea is that the relationships and interactions involved in social networks enable people to build communities, commit themselves to each other, and knit the social fabric. A sense of belonging and the concrete experience of social networks (and the relationships of trust and tolerance that can be involved) can, it is argued, bring great benefits to people.

For Bourdieu social capital is set alongside cultural and economic capital, and is a mechanism helping to govern access to resources and power. Actual or potential

545

resources are linked to possession of a durable network of more or less institutionalised relationships of mutual acquaintance and recognition. The basic thesis was that privileged individuals held onto their position by using their connections with others similarly advantaged. In contrast, Coleman's theorisation of social capital illuminated the processes and experiences of non-elite groups. Drawing upon rational choice theory he looked to it as part of a wider exploration of the nature of social structures. He took the view that social capital was defined by its function. It was a variety of different entities that had two characteristics in common: they consist of some aspect of a social structure, and facilitate certain actions of individuals within that structure. Coleman highlighted the role of the family and kinship networks, and religious institutions in the cultivation of reciprocity and trust. However, as some commentators have identified, defining something by its function is problematic and Coleman's concept of social capital tended to the benign.

It was into this situation that Robert Putnam's work on social capital exploded. Returning to commentators such as de Tocqueville, and drawing on some of the debates around, and insights from, Coleman's contribution, he looked to the significance of association and civic community. For him social capital referred to connections among individuals, i.e. social networks and the norms of reciprocity and trustworthiness that arise from them. Drawing upon a substantial bank of data, he was able to argue that there had been a significant decline in social capital in the United States over the last quarter of the twentieth century. He also demonstrated that child development and educational achievement is powerfully shaped by it: in high social-capital areas public spaces are cleaner, people are friendlier, streets are safer and there is a strong relationship between the possession of social capital and better health. Putnam's claims with regard to declining social capital have been disputed

and remain a matter of debate. However, there does seem to be a significant body of evidence backing up his claims with regard to the benefits.

Those concerned with social capital have looked to the density of social networks that people are involved in, the extent to which they are engaged with others in informal, social activities, and their membership of groups and associations. Many of the earlier contributions failed to discriminate between different types of social capital. Michael Woolcock (1964–) has since distinguished three types: bonding social capital, denoting ties between people in similar situations, such as immediate family, close friends and neighbours; bridging social capital, which takes in more distant ties of like persons, such as loose friendships and workmates; and linking social capital, which reaches out to unlike people in dissimilar situations.

The notion of social capital has generated important insights, and has been a useful focus for data collection and analysis. However, it is not developed theoretically. Four main issues have been commented on. First, there is a danger of skewing to the economic when we introduce notions such as 'capital' into the consideration of the social. Second, exploration has rarely been fully historically located. Third, much of the main work has failed to adequately address gender dimensions. Fourth, there needs to be work around negative aspects, including using social capital to exclude others, the scale of local surveillance, definitions of 'acceptable behaviour', and the ways in which horizons may actually be narrowed. This said, some of the empirical work that has been done linking involvement in associational life and participation in social networks to the enhancement of educational achievement, the promotion of health and the reduction of crime is of great significance.

See also: Bourdieu, Pierre; cultural capital; educational theory; family; functionalism; sociology; sociology of education

Further reading

Field, J. (2003) *Social Capital*, London: Routledge.

Putnam, R. D. (2000) *Bowling Alone: The Collapse and Revival of American Community*, New York: Simon and Schuster.

Woolcock, M. (2001) 'The place of social capital in understanding social and economic outcomes', *Isuma: Canadian Journal of Policy Research*, 2(1): 1–17.

MARK K. SMITH

SOCIAL CONSTRUCTIVISM

This term (also social constructionism) relates to how individuals and groups construct their social world in an active way, as opposed to it being imposed upon them. The social construction of reality is not therefore natural or obvious, nor is it immutable or essential, but arises from the society or culture. Gramsci's theory of hegemony is an example of this kind of approach, as it views the proletariat actively endorsing a constriction of reality that serves the interests of the bourgeoisie. Vygotsky also emphasised the importance of the social context in cognitive development. National identity may also be regarded as a social construction. In the 1960s and 1970s, this perspective was developed further in the sociology of education, influenced in particular by Berger and Luckmann's *The Social Construction of Reality* (1966) and Young's *Knowledge and Control* (1971). This standpoint is often criticised for its implication that if reality is a social construction, any explanation may be as valid or true as any other. Nevertheless, as Torres has argued (2006: 549–50), social constructions are not simply products of the imagination but the product of real people interacting in complex ways, and therefore not all explanations should be expected to have the same quality or validity.

See also: activity theory; Vygotsky, Lev

Further reading

Berger, P. and Luckmann, T. (1966) *The Social Construction of Reality*, New York: Anchor Books.

Torres, C. A. (2006) 'Democracy, education, and multiculturalism: dilemmas of citizenship in a global world'. In H. Lauder, P. Brown, S. Dillabough and A. H. Halsey (eds) *Education, Globalisation and Social Change*, Oxford: Oxford University Press, 537–56.

Young, M. F. D. (ed.) (1971) *Knowledge and Control: New Directions for the Sociology of Education*, London: Collier Macmillan.

GARY McCULLOCH

SOCIAL CONTROL

Social control usually refers to the means by which society and/or social groups ensure the conformity of members in line with a prescribed set of rules, guidelines and values. Definitions of social control are wide-ranging and often closely allied to education. The concept has been employed to describe a condition of society, a means to ensure compliance, and a method to analyse social phenomena. Social control was employed through much of the twentieth century, especially in the United States of America. In the 1970s radical theorists also adapted the term, although its use has been less frequent since the 1980s.

Sociologists developed the notion of social control in the late nineteenth century, and one of the earliest uses was in A. E. Ross' *Social Control* (1901). The concept was developed to explain how American society might be maintained in the face of urbanisation, the influx of immigrants and the breakdown of traditional communities and family structures. According to this perspective, local communities and 'primary groups' such as the family had been essential in maintaining social control but this was breaking down in the modern context. Social scientists were keen to discover how social harmony could be retained in the impersonal context of the city, and education was conceived as one institution capable of fulfilling this role. Social control was viewed as both a social process and a desired state of society. Thinkers drew on Durkheim's notion of collective conscience, which incorporated a sense of both conscience and consciousness; thus, social control resided in a set of legitimate moral principles that rendered coercive control unnecessary. Indeed, such constraints were seen as a source for individual autonomy and social stability.

Later uses of social control by functionalists broke the concept down into a set of variables, which became associated with the exercise of power and influence over particular groups of people such as criminals and 'deviants'. The focus shifted to the interdependence between a system and its component parts, a model that was applied to education. In *The Social System* (1951), Talcott Parsons viewed social control as something that enabled social systems, such as schools, to maintain order and stability. While most people internalised rule-abiding behaviour, social control helped to ensure the conformity of those who broke rules. These ideas were inherently conservative and uncritically justified the existing 'systems' of the post-war USA, or most other societies in which they were applied.

Others would challenge these normative assumptions in terms that emphasised the divisions inherent in society and the growing repression and alienation of certain groups. A lack of open conflict was not interpreted as an indication of consensus. Conflict theories also connected social control to deviance; for instance, the process of labelling school dropouts was seen as conducive to further rule breaking. Marxists identified the ways in which social control was essential in maintaining capitalist divisions of labour and imposing ruling-class norms and values, in part through the education system. For instance, writers such as C. Wright Mills in *The Power Elite* (1956) highlighted the ways in which a powerful minority maintained their position in society; social control helped to create and sustain their dominance over others. Education was viewed as one element of a broader welfare system that channelled the behaviour of the working classes and other subordinate groups by allocating roles in a system and also by inculcating particular behaviour and values. Although social control was viewed coercively, it could take on a tacit and subtle nature within education, which revealed wider power structures. For instance, in discussing progressive education Sharp and Green (1974) noted how 'the open curriculum is epiphenomenal to a latent structure of control' which gave opportunities to some while withholding it from others. Such insights would also be applied historically, for instance, to nineteenth-century British education policy that was perceived in terms of class domination and state formation. From another perspective ethnomethodologists and phenomenologists studied the construction of meaning and social control through small group interactions.

The strengths of social control lie in the insight that conformity can be produced in subtle as well as coercive ways and that education for freedom and fulfilment can also be channelled and constrained. However, a number of historical meanings are apparent. It can point to interactions between specific individuals, and between groups/institutions and individuals, as well as between whole societies and their members. For many it is a term which is both too broad in its meaning and too blunt in its focus.

See also: Durkheim, Emile; educational theory; functionalism; sociology of education

Further reading

Davies, B. (1976) *Social Control and Education*, London: Methuen.
Johnson, R. (1970) 'Educational policy and social control in early Victorian England', *Past and Present*, 49: 96–119.
Meier, R. F. (1982) 'Perspectives on the concept of social control', *Annual Review of Sociology*, 8: 35–55.
Sharp, R. and Green, A. (1974) *Education and Social Control*, London: Routledge.

TOM WOODIN

SOCIAL EXCLUSION/INCLUSION

Social exclusion is a fairly recent term that has its roots in France and was first used in 1974 by Richard Lenoir to refer to the emerging poverty that was affecting those of the working class who were considered to be social misfits and were not supported by the welfare state. This concept was embraced by the European Community. The term later expanded beyond the original understandings to include those who are disabled, aged, bed-ridden, mentally challenged, antisocial, and so on.

So popular is the concern regarding social exclusion that, in 1997, the British Government established a Social Exclusion Unit and a website (www.socialexclusionunit.gov.uk/). The new agenda was aimed at dealing with both the causes and the consequences of social exclusion by exploring opportunities to improve social justice, strengthen communities and sustain long-term economic growth. The government's campaign has focused on tackling what has been described as the problems causing social exclusion, namely unemployment, poor skills, low incomes, poor housing, high crime, poor health and family problems. Inappropriate behaviours, which include teenage pregnancies, truancies and exclusions, are tackled at the level of the school. This suggests that social exclusion is understood through the lens of a deficit model and occurs as a result of deficiencies and/or deviancy within the youth of the country.

What is not provided is a conceptual understanding of social exclusion where the term is understood in terms of poverty and the position of lowliness in relation to the centres of power, resources and the socially acceptable values of those in positions of power. Duffy (1995) perceives social exclusion as being broader than poverty, encompassing not only low material means but the inability to participate effectively in economic, social, political and cultural life, and, in some characterisations, alienation and distance from the mainstream society. In 1999, the Poverty and Social Exclusion Survey of Britain identified four significant dimensions to social exclusion: exclusion from social participation in the normal activities of society, adequate income, the labour market, and service. More recently, the concept of social exclusion has been broadened to include groups such as disabled people, those with special educational needs, advocates of multiculturalism and other movements based on the acknowledgement of diversity.

In the USA, those who are socially excluded are generally referred to as the 'underclass'. This expression, along with the term social exclusion/inclusion, spread to the developing countries of the world through its use by international agencies such as the International Labour Organization, the World Health Organization, the United Nations Education Scientific and Cultural Organization, the United Nations Development Programme, funding agencies such as the World Bank and aid agencies such as the Department for International Development. This popular expression is currently used by the World Bank in working with the poor and historically socially excluded groups to promote 'equal access to opportunities, assets and services while respecting their unique cultural heritages, identities and knowledge' (www.worldbank.org).

When the concept spread to the developing countries of the world, the definition was incongruous with the prevailing situation because the structure and conditions of societies in the South are different from those countries of the North in which the concept was originally applied. Historically, the countries of the South were mostly colonies of the countries of the North, with quite different political histories and social relations. There are the more developed systems of the coloniser versus the less developed systems of those who were colonised. For former colonies, this translated into greater budgetary constraints, a less comprehensive education support and health care system, higher levels of unemployment, lower state contributions to welfare systems and minimal recognition of the rights of disabled people and other marginalised groups. In situations like these, social services are overlooked in favour of priorities.

See also: equality of opportunity; equity; delinquency; learning disabilities/difficulties; multiculturalism; truancy

Further reading

Duffy, K. (1995) *Social Exclusion and Human Dignity in Europe*, Strasbourg: Council of Europe.
Estivill, J. (2003) *Concepts and Strategies for Combating Social Exclusion: An Overview*, Geneva: ILO-STEP.
Parsons, C. (1999) *Education, Exclusion and Citizenship*, London: Routledge.
Wolfe, M. (1995) 'Globalization and social exclusion: some paradoxes'. In G. Rodger, C. Gore and J. B. Figueireido (eds) *Social Exclusion: Rhetoric, Reality, Reponses*, Geneva: International Institute for Labour Studies.

ANN CHERYL ARMSTRONG

SOCIAL PROMOTION

Social promotion is the elevation of a pupil or student to a higher class or grade alongside other students from the same class, rather than on the basis of achieving high grades or completing the course. It is based on age or cohort, rather than on merit. It can lead to educational difficulties, especially where progress in the higher class depends on knowledge that should have been gained previously in the lower class, and potentially to dropping out or failure. The major alternative to this approach is known as grade retention, where students are held back to repeat a level of schooling. However, grade retention can lead to stress and low esteem, which themselves may also increase the risks of dropping out. In some cases, retention and promotion decisions may be made on the basis of the results of a single test, referred to as high-stakes testing. Attitudes and policies vary widely as to whether students should be held back or promoted despite poor grades.

In the United States, grade retention has been encouraged, especially since President George W. Bush's *No Child Left Behind Act*, and boys and minorities have been particularly prone to grade retention. Research has not so far clearly identified lasting gains from retention, while students who are promoted with their peers do appear to gain at least some benefit from this.

See also: high-stakes testing; learning career; peer group

GARY McCULLOCH

SOCIAL RECONSTRUCTIONISM

Social reconstructionism originated as a small left-wing faction within the much larger American progressive education reform movement in the early 1930s. While American educators representing a wide range of views are labelled reconstructionists, for example Kenneth Benne, Boyd Bode, John Childs, John Dewey, William Kilpatrick, B. O. Smith, and W. O. Stanley, the most prominent reconstructionists were George Counts, Harold Rugg, and Theodore Brameld. Reconstructionism had roots in earlier nineteenth-century American radical traditions and Dewey's educational philosophy, but the movement crystallised and gained national attention following Counts' 1932 publication *Dare the Schools Build a New Social Order?*, perhaps the clearest statement of the reconstructionist position.

Counts' call for educators to help lead the transformation of American society came at the height of America's worst depression. The reconstructionist's reaction to the apparent collapse of the economic system was amplified by the impact of modernism (for example industrialisation, technology, urbanisation, and modernist modes of thought, including scientific methodology, Darwinism, positivism, pragmatism, and quantum theory), which had undermined traditional conceptions of knowledge. The reconstructionists had a strong faith in the potential of scientific method, technology, and 'social engineering' to provide solutions to our most pressing social and economic problems. However, a scientific approach to curriculum and schooling was insufficient in the absence of a theory of social welfare.

For Counts, the 1929 depression confirmed that American society was in a state of crisis and required the construction of a new economic and social order based on a theory of social welfare aimed at the expansion of participatory democracy, social justice and the redistribution of economic and political power. Since political and economic power are held largely by a powerful elite class, Counts believed the realisation of a truly democratic social order could not happen unless the capitalist economy of the United States was either eliminated or changed radically to meet social needs. Some form of collective planning was essential if we were to achieve a democratic social order.

Counts rejected as inadequate the views of left progressives like Dewey, who supported a curriculum focused on enhancing student competence to analyse social problems with the goal of improving society. The construction of an educational programme oriented by a radical theory of social welfare requires that we free ourselves from the progressive educator's fear of indoctrination. Education, by its very nature, always contains a large element of indoctrination, which is essential to the existence and evolution of human society. In a democratic society, professional responsibility requires using education to socialise our young in ways calculated to expand and reinforce a democratic culture. Counts argued that teachers and schools were well positioned as a vanguard to challenge the dominant social order and help bring about necessary changes in our social, cultural, and economic institutions.

Dewey agreed that too much of education involved indoctrination to preserve an unjust social order. However, he rejected Counts' recommendation that we reverse the aim of indoctrination to promote the reconstructionists' conception of a preferred society. For Dewey, indoctrination of students to embrace a particular social order worked to limit the scope of student thought and was antithetical to democracy. At most, schools should impose a method of intelligence that would enable students to become competent citizens who will determine how best to solve social problems in the future. This debate between Dewey and Counts was at the core of dialogue among reconstructionists and often discussed in *The Social Frontier*, a reconstructionist journal founded in 1934. Critical educators continue to argue variations of this debate.

Although more moderate politically than Counts, Harold Rugg's social studies textbook series was successful in circulating many reconstructionist ideas throughout the nation's schools. Ironically, Rugg's popularity provoked a strong conservative backlash that gradually eliminated his textbooks from schools during the 1940s. Rugg's influence remains in many current approaches to problem-based education in American social studies.

Theodore Brameld is the educator most responsible for continuing the reconstructionist influence between 1945 and 1975. His publications and professional activism helped keep reconstructionist ideas alive as part of the continuing debates over curriculum and school reform, and contemporary proponents of critical pedagogy often draw on the reconstructionist legacy. That said, reconstructionist ideas remain on the margins of education reform debates.

See also: critical pedagogy; Dewey, John; indoctrination; progressive education

Further reading

Counts, G. S. (1932) *Dare the Schools Build a New Social Order?* New York: John Day.
James, M. E. (ed.) (1995) *Social Reconstruction Through Education*, Norwood NJ: Ablex Publishing Corporation.

Riley, K. L. (ed.) (2006) *Social Reconstruction: People, Politics, Perspectives*, Greenwich CT: Information Age Publishing.

WILLIAM B. STANLEY

SOCIAL REPRODUCTION

Social reproduction is a key concept in education. While educational institutions are often discussed in terms of social and economic changes, they also serve to reproduce society and its language, institutions, occupational structure and values. A key function of any educational institution is also to ensure its own reproduction by fulfilling individual and social needs.

A number of different approaches to social reproduction can be identified in debates that have been central to the sociology of education. Functionalist perspectives have perceived education as a social system that educates future citizens to play appropriate roles and so ensures the reproduction of society. This involves channelling students into particular work roles as well as inculcating attitudes and values conducive to a well ordered society. This approach is conservative in its focus on reproducing rather than changing society, and conflict tends to be viewed in dysfunctional terms.

Although other sociologists have contested this conservative functionalism, they have also analysed the close relation between schooling and the occupational hierarchy. In focusing upon the reproduction of social classes under capitalism in the United States of America, Samuel Bowles and Herbert Gintis (1976) argued that there existed a 'correspondence' between the educational system and the labour market; the education system prepared students for roles within a hierarchical division of labour. The French Marxist, Louis Althusser, viewed education as an 'ideological state apparatus' which ensured the reproduction of attitudes and consciousness supportive of capitalism. The broader and subtler notion of hegemony, originally developed by Antonio Gramsci, has also been used to reveal the ways in which societies reproduce dominant, albeit contested, ideas. For example, Paul Willis' *Learning to Labour* (1977), an ethnographic account of 'how working class kids get working class jobs', analysed the considerable autonomy exercised by pupils and their oppositional ideas that, ultimately, led to their 'failure'. Pierre Bourdieu (1977) also introduced the concept of 'cultural capital' to explain how the reproduction of inequalities took place in education. Stephen Ball (2003) has shown how middle-class parents are able to employ successful strategies to ensure the success of their children, a process more apparent where 'choice' and market-based reforms have been introduced.

There has been a continuing recognition of the way in which social divisions are reproduced. Surveys in Britain carried out by A. H. Halsey and others focused on the ways in which social class differences were reproduced within the education system. More recently, others have highlighted how education has contributed to the reproduction of inequalities related to disability, race and gender. For instance, proponents of inclusive education have argued that disabled people and those labelled special needs often receive inferior education to supposedly 'normal' students, both in separate and mainstream institutions. Similarly, processes of 'institutional racism' adversely affect racialised groups. Gendered assumptions also enter many educational systems and serve to reproduce inequalities, although in countries such as Britain the performance of female pupils is beginning to match and improve on that of boys.

While it is easy to recognise the ways in which these social differences are reproduced, it has proved more difficult to address this issue in terms of policy. Government policies tend to be driven by complex and contradictory impulses, so that encouraging the 'gifted' and 'more able' to thrive is a tendency which exists alongside those aiming to foster greater equality. There has been a reluctance to frame initiatives in terms of reducing inequality, although policies can be identified which have asserted the need to improve the educational outcomes of those at the bottom. For instance, the school improvement movement has pointed to the potential for enhancing the performance of 'failing' schools through effective teaching and leadership. Similarly, policies focused on early years' education have explicitly aimed to break a lifecycle of 'disadvantage' among particular groups. While such policies can lead to significant improvements, inequalities connected to structural factors have persisted. Education is not solely responsible for social reproduction but must be viewed within a wider context of family, inheritance, and workplace processes that exert autonomous influences.

See also: cultural capital; educational theory; functionalism; sociology of education

Further reading

Ball, S. (2003) *Class Strategies and the Education Market: The Middle Classes and Social Advantage*, London: Routledge.

Bourdieu, P. and Passeron, J-C. (1977) *Reproduction in Education: Society and Culture*, London: Sage.

Bowles, S. and Gintis, H. (1976) *Schooling in Capitalist America*, New York: Basic Books.

Demaine, J. (2003) 'Social reproduction and education policy', *International Studies in Sociology of Education*, 13(2): 125–40.

TOM WOODIN

SOCIAL STUDIES

Social studies, one of the core subject areas of the USA's elementary and secondary school curriculum, has been conceptualised by educational scholars, practitioners and policy makers, as well as the public at large, in so many disparate ways over time that there is, in fact, no universally accepted definition of what social studies education is, in theory or practice. Since its formal introduction into the school curriculum, in the early twentieth century, with the 1916 publication of *The Social Studies in Secondary Schools* by the National Education Association's Committee on Social Studies, the term 'social studies' has been used to describe, among other things: the teaching of history, social sciences (including geography, economics, political science, sociology, anthropology and/or psychology), civics and/or humanities; the study of social problems, controversial issues and/or current events; and more generally, social education, citizenship education, democratic education, character education, multicultural education, global education, life adjustment education and/or the core curriculum. These descriptors do not even specify what content is to be addressed (my community? my country? the world? past and/or present?); how the curriculum is to be organised (chronologically? topically? interdisciplinarily?); what instructional methods and learning modes are to be employed (inquiry? projects? source analysis? debate?); and for what purposes (knowledge acquisition? good citizenship? community service? social reform?). One critic notoriously asserted that social studies education is so muddled it should be referred to instead as 'social stew'.

Despite the apparent discord within the social studies field, there are in fact several characteristic features of social studies upon which most educators agree. First, social studies education comprises the subject or subjects in which historical and contemporary aspects of human civilisation and civil society, including political, economic, social, and cultural life, are addressed most directly in the school curriculum. As John Dewey explained in a 1938 article for *Progressive Education* entitled 'What is social study?', social studies involves answering all manner of questions that have social origin and social consequences. In this sense, Dewey argued, social studies can give direction to all other branches of study in the school, including literature, science, mathematics, languages, and the fine arts, for they all relate to the essence of human civilisation in some fashion. At a minimum, the social studies curriculum centres on understanding civic life.

In the view of the National Council for Social Studies, the leading professional organisation in the field, the primary aim of social studies is developing the knowledge, skills and attitudes necessary for participating in civic affairs.

Indeed, citizenship education has been the single most common justification for social studies education since the field's inception. How 'citizenship' is defined, politically and pedagogically, has long been a matter of contention, however. For some educators, citizenship education entails transmitting normative facts, concepts and mores to the rising generation, while for others, it involves developing critical thinking and reflective decision making among future citizens. The International Association for the Evaluation of Educational Achievement's (IEA) Civic Education Study, conducted in twenty-eight North and South American, European and Asian countries during the 1990s, found that citizenship education may also focus on national, regional or global identity, multicultural consciousness, democratic discourse and civic action. In any case, the extent to which the social studies curriculum in a given place and time tends towards cultural continuity or social transformation is highly contingent on larger public policy considerations regarding what schools are for. Perhaps no other school subject is as closely tied to the political and social purposes of schooling as social studies.

Another distinctive feature of social studies education is its multidisciplinarity. Some iterations of social studies consist of an interdisciplinary fusion of the social sciences in which disciplinary boundaries are almost entirely disregarded in favour of addressing topics head-on (more common at the elementary level), while others feature a crossdisciplinary federation of the constituent social studies disciplines in which distinct social science courses (e.g. history, economics and psychology) are offered under the aegis of the social studies programme (more common at the secondary level). Either way, social studies content and skills normally derive from various disciplinary perspectives at once.

Finally, social studies provides students opportunities to inquire formally into the society in which they live, helping them to understand its wonders and complexities, triumphs and failures, and strengths and frailties, and to make informed judgements about the way their world ought to be. In this way, social studies education is a deliberately democratic endeavour.

See also: citizenship/civics; sociology

Further reading

Social Education (practitioner journal).
Theory and Research in Social Education (academic journal).

BENJAMIN M. JACOBS

SOCIOLOGY

Sociology may defined as the scientific study of human social behaviour. Like economics, anthropology and politics, it belongs to a group of social sciences, but its scope is perhaps broader. Sociologists observe, analyse and theorise all manner of behaviours exhibited, for example, by the state, communities, families and individuals. The term sociology is believed to have first been coined in the early nineteenth century by the French philosopher Auguste Comte, who was seeking to develop a new science to understand the laws of human society. In respect of education, sociologists have demonstrated a particular commitment to inequality issues relating to social class, gender, race, disability and sexual orientation. Education policy sociologists focus on the intentions and outcomes of education reforms and of the political and policy discourses accompanying change. Sociology is frequently taught in schools with the aim of preparing students for public examinations. It is also widely taught at undergraduate and postgraduate level in institutions of higher education.

See also: sociology of education; subjects

DAVID CROOK

SOCIOLOGY OF EDUCATION

Sociology of education is the study of schools and schooling. A sociological perspective on education ranges from a broad conceptualisation of the school as a societal institution to a more focused examination of within- and between-school processes and outcomes. Institutional analyses, such as cross-national studies of the delivery of education, educational expansion, and the transition from school to work, consider how education is influenced by political, economic, and social conditions. Studies of school processes and outcomes focus on characteristics of schools and how they affect student cognitive and social development.

Over the past few decades, sociologists of education applied general sociological theories to the study of schools and the schooling process. For example, they relied on consensus theory and structural functionalism to define the goal of education as the maintenance of social order. A school's purpose was to teach students how to take their place in society and contribute to the interdependence required to sustain social order. Conflict theory was used by sociologists of education to explain how conflicting goals of students, teachers, parents, and the community result in social change. From this perspective, the privileged class used dominance and subordination in schools to preserve its power and superiority over the underprivileged. Sociologists of education adopted this viewpoint to explain educational inequalities associated with background characteristics, such as race/ethnicity, gender and class.

More recently, sociologists of education have adopted a worldview in studying education. By considering globalisation, technological advances, demographic changes, immigration and other global patterns, they are better able to explain educational expansion, the diffusion of knowledge and curricular change, advances in literacy and educational attainment, and the effects of societal interdependence on school processes and outcomes.

In addition, sociologists of education utilise theoretical perspectives within sub-disciplines in sociology to construct theories about how schools function. Social psychological theories are used to describe within school and classroom processes, such as instructional and pedagogical techniques, the formation of school norms, and peer influences on student outcomes. Organisation theory provides insights into how a school functions as a bureaucracy, a semi-professional organisation, or a loosely coupled organisation, and how the formal and informal characteristics of a school affect student opportunities to learn. Theories of social stratification and mobility inform analyses of school effects on educational achievement, aspirations, and attainment, as well as occupational status and income.

Despite these theoretical advances, most of the research in sociology of education has been empirical and somewhat atheoretical. A gap exists between theoretical ideas about how schools work and empirical studies of education. Researchers have difficulty applying grand and middle-range theories to particular school situations and problems. Schools differ in environment, governance, organisational structure, autonomy, size, and student composition, often creating challenges in applying general theories to situational educational issues.

Recent empirical work in sociology of education has gained status within the scientific community for several reasons. First, many researchers and research centres have focused on the same educational issues, such as tracking or the achievement gap, and validated and replicated these studies. They produced a systematic body of research in which researchers, educators, and policy makers can be highly confident. Second, a number of nationally representative surveys are now in the public domain. The high quality of these data has led to numerous methodologically sophisticated analyses. Third, the current level of government involvement in education in the United States has motivated studies evaluating the consequences of federal assessment and accountability requirements on student outcomes. Sociology of education research has provided a scientific analysis of the strengths and weaknesses of this and other government regulations affecting all public school children in the United States. As a result, the unique contributions of sociologists to education policy have become more obvious.

Given the recent impressive growth of sociology of education, its future as a scientific enterprise and as a tool for educators is promising. Efforts to link survey research with observational studies are likely to intensify as researchers see the benefits of these complementary methodologies for studying school effects on student outcomes. Technologies that facilitate communication among international academic communities will encourage more cross-national comparative research. State and national efforts to follow students' progress through their school careers will demonstrate long-term student outcomes. New research, building on the foundation of past and current work, should lead to theoretical formulations that will unify these studies and better explain the cognitive and social processes that lead to educational achievement and attainment.

See also: education; educational studies; equality of opportunity; school culture; school improvement; sociology

Further reading

Arum, R. and Beattie , I. (eds) (2000) *The Structure of Schooling: Readings in the Sociology of Education,* Mountain View CA: Mayfield Publishing.
Hallinan, M.T. (ed.) (2000) *Handbook of the Sociology of Education,* New York: Kluwer Academic/ Plenum.
Hedges, L. and Schneider, B. (eds) (2005) *Social Organization of Schooling,* New York: Russell Sage.
Sadovnik, A., Bohrnstedt, G., Borman, K. and O'Day, J. (eds) (2007) *No Child Left Behind and the Reduction of the Achievement Gap: Sociological Perspectives on Federal Education Policy,* New York: Routledge.

MAUREEN T. HALLINAN

SOCRATIC METHOD

Socrates, as he is presented by Plato in more than thirty dialogues composed in the years 388–347 BCE, followed no one method of investigation (Haroutunian-Gordon 1987; 1988; 1989; 1990). Why, then, do we use the phrase 'the Socratic method' instead of 'Socratic methods'? We refer to 'the Socratic method' not because Socrates followed or even espoused one method – one step-by-step procedure – for making discoveries. Rather, we use the phrase because Socrates, as Plato presents him, lived the life of an inquirer according to beliefs that he movingly articulates in the *Republic* (518). That set of beliefs, as illustrated by the life that Socrates led, is what we call 'the Socratic method'. What are those beliefs?

First, Socrates believed that every human being has the power to learn. That power is 'indwelling' (518c), which means that no person imparts it to another. To say that everyone has the 'power to learn' means that all, with a few exceptions, have the power to see what is true and to separate that from what is false. The separation of truth from falsity, or, as Socrates puts it, the recognition of knowledge, is something that the learner does for him/herself. The Socrates whom Plato presents spent his life seeking truth and treating others as though they were truth-seekers as well.

Second, Socrates believed that recognition of what is known – what is true – requires effort on the part of the learner. The effort involves looking where one ought to look in order to see what one ought to see. Socrates tells us that one ought not to look at that which is hearsay or opinion. Rather, one must use one's reason as well as one's senses (or instead of one's senses, upon occasion) so as to see (518c).

But, even using one's reason is only the beginning. Socrates says that in order see what is true, one must look with the 'whole soul'. According to Liddell and Scott's Greek-English lexicon, the Greek word for 'soul', *psyche*, refers to breath, life, and heart, as well as mind and understanding. Consequently, seeing the truth requires that one look in the right place with affection, desire, and energy, as well as reason.

Third, an artful teacher, who is analogised to a midwife in the *Theaetetus*, can help the student to look in the right place with breath, life, heart and reason so that he or she sees what is true. The artful teacher, described at 518c, is illustrated by Socrates himself.

In many of the dialogues, Plato shows Socrates questioning himself, as well as others. He asks, for example: What is friendship (*Lysis*)? What is virtue (*Meno*)? What is justice (*Republic*)? What is knowledge (*Theaetetus*)? What is piety (*Euthyphro*)? What is love (*Symposium*)? Sometimes, the questions come from the interlocutors rather than Socrates, as when Meno (*Meno*) asks whether virtue can be taught, or Glaucon (*Republic*) asks whether justice is better than injustice.

As his interlocutors respond to the questions, Socrates queries them further to see whether their answers are justified by reason and life's experience. In so doing, all may discover that not only is the answer riddled with misconception, but in addition, there is a prior question which requires resolution before the one on the table is satisfactorily addressed.

The conversations in the dialogues are not simply academic: all the characters, including Socrates, become fascinated, frustrated, flabbergasted, and furious by turns as the dialogues proceed. Most become committed to resolving the dilemma, however. While they sometimes resist Socrates' questioning, especially when confronted by contradictions in their reasoning, they generally follow the path down which he leads them. That is, they generally look where they should, and so arrive at insight and realisation. Socrates, too, reaches understanding as the dialogues proceed, which is why he chooses to live as he does.

The Socratic method is not a pre-defined series of steps towards a goal. Rather, it is a way of living, namely questioning what has been asserted until the truth or falsity of the assertion is seen and the deepest points of doubt are revealed. The path of Socratic questioning meanders, and often Socrates and his interlocutors end with more dilemmas than they had at the start. But in the course of the journey, truth is glimpsed, if only fleetingly, and that is good enough for Socrates.

See also: Greece; learning; philosophy of education; Plato

Further reading

Hamilton, E. and Cairns, H. (eds) (1961) *The Collected Dialogues of Plato*, Princeton NJ: Princeton University Press.

Haroutunian-Gordon, S. (1987) 'Evaluating teachers: the case of Socrates', *Teachers College Record*, 89(1): 117–32.

——(1988) 'Teaching in an ill-structured situation: the case of Socrates', *Educational Theory*, 38(2): 225–37.

——(1989) 'Socrates as teacher'. In P. W. Jackson and S. Haroutunian-Gordon (eds) *From Socrates to Software: The Teacher as Text and The Text as Teacher*. 88th National Society for the Study of Education Yearbook, Chicago IL: University of Chicago Press, 5–23.

——(1990) 'Statements of method in teaching: the case of Socrates', *Studies in Philosophy of Education*, 10(2): 139–56.

SOPHIE HAROUTUNIAN-GORDON

SOUTH AFRICA

Although indigenous tribal initiation 'schools' existed in traditional societies, it was the Dutch East India Company in 1658 that established the first formal school in what later became South Africa (SA). Houghton, cited in Behr's *Education in South Africa* (1988) noted that from that first school, for imported black slaves, 'The official policy and desired aims of all governments at the Cape up to 1847 were concentrated on " ... keeping the races apart"' (Behr 1988: 13). Indeed, organisation along racial lines has been the defining feature of the history of SA schooling.

Until 1900 it was mainly the Dutch Reformed Church that provided rudimentary formal schooling for white children. Besides mission schools since 1795, black schooling was largely neglected. In 1948 the new Nationalist Party government introduced its policy of *apartheid*. The now infamous 1953 Bantu Education Act for the first time provided for central government control of black schooling. Molteno, in his chapter in Kallaway's edited volume *Apartheid and Education* (1984), cites the notorious words of then Minister of Native Affairs, Verwoerd:

> 'There is no place for him (the Black African), in the European community above the level of certain forms of labour ... for that reason it is of no avail for him to receive a training which has as its aim absorption in the European community, where he cannot be absorbed'.
>
> (Molteno 1984: 92–93)

Increased opposition to this policy resulted in the outbreak of violence in schools in Soweto, southwest of Johannesburg, in 1976. In the decade of upheaval that followed, black urban schooling in SA came to a virtual standstill. After the unbanning of political organisations and the release of political prisoners, including Nelson Mandela, that followed in 1990, it was clear that a new education dispensation would be part of the new negotiated political order. Following SA's first democratic election in 1994, the 1995 Education White Paper laid out the vision for a new racially integrated education system based upon the principles of democracy, equity and the redress of past inequalities.

In the next decade, a plethora of new education policies designed to realise these principles followed. These included *Curriculum 2005*, an outcomes-based education (OBE) curriculum, a National Qualifications Framework for lifelong learning and a decentralised education system. Other policies provided for a multilingual language policy, the transfer of teacher education from the college to the higher education sector and national norms and standards for school funding. These policies connected SA to global education developments and lent political legitimacy to the new education dispensation.

However, despite these policy intentions to break with the apartheid past and the practical achievement of creating a unified and racially integrated education system, by the turn of the millennium there was little evidence of change, at school level in particular. Nowhere was this crisis in policy implementation more evident than in the Curriculum 2005 Review Committee's (2000) gloomy report on the introduction of OBE. New education policies have not yet been able to overcome the apartheid legacy of inequality in school provision or the ongoing lack of financial resources to address this, particularly in rural areas. The School Register of Needs showed that achieving equal resource distribution for schools across all race groups in the foreseeable future is a near-impossible task. Although SA spends 6 per cent of its gross domestic product on education, salaries consume 80–90 per cent of recurrent expenditure, leaving little for resource expansion. The effects of 14 per cent of SA teachers being affected by HIV/AIDS places a further strain on existing resources.

A defining and ongoing tension exists between the constitutional mandate for equity and redress and the liberal value of individual choice. From a social theory perspective, the outcome of this balancing act at a policy level is that the emerging racially integrated middle class benefits most from the changes. Policy reform has not taken adequate account of the differential race and class capacity to take advantage of the opportunities for public participation in policy development and implementation. In her edited volume *Changing Class*, Chisholm (2004) observed, 'The institutional incapacity to deliver ... [is] arguably one of the greatest challenges in post-apartheid South Africa' (Chisolm 2004: 12). In this view, rather than promoting mass democracy, policy reproduces existing asymmetrical power relations and promotes further inequity in school provision. The management of this tension will continue to be a central theme in SA schooling in the second decade of the twenty-first century.

See also: Africa

Further reading

Behr, A. (1988) *Education in South Africa: Origins, Issues and Trends: 1652–1988*, Pretoria: Academia.
Chisholm, L. (ed.) (2004) *Changing Class: Education and Social Change in Post-Apartheid South Africa*, Cape Town: HSRC Press.
Molteno, F. (1984) 'The historical foundations of the schooling of Black South Africans'. In P. Kallaway (ed.) *Apartheid and Education: The Education of Black South Africans*, Johannesburg: Ravan Press.

CLIVE SMITH

SPEARMAN, CHARLES (1863–1945)

The early career of Spearman, a British psychologist, was in the military, serving during the Boer War and World War I. During this period he undertook testing of personnel within the army. His ideas about inherent abilities were strongly influenced by Francis Galton and by the experimental approach adopted by Wundt, Kulpe and Muller, who Spearman encountered as a student in Germany, from 1897 to 1907. He secured his doctorate in Leipzig in 1904, aged forty-one, and immediately published a book, *General Intelligence Objectively Determined and Measured* (1904). In 1907 he obtained a post in experimental psychology at University College, London, where he was promoted to a chair in mind and logic in 1911, remaining there until retirement in 1928. His principal contribution to psychology stemmed from his view that intelligence was a single and identifiable factor, having specific and general characteristics, both of which were measurable. His 1923 book, *The Nature of Intelligence and the Principles of Cognition*, provided support for pupil testing in order to allocate children to secondary schools adjudged suitable for their type and level of intelligence. During the 1930s Spearman spent a considerable amount of time touring and lecturing in the United States. His 1927 book *The Abilities of Man* became a standard work and influenced a generation of educational psychologists.

See also: ability; cognition; Galton, Francis; intelligence/intelligence tests; psychology; psychology of education

STEVEN COWAN

SPECIAL EDUCATION/SPECIAL EDUCATIONAL NEEDS/SPECIAL NEEDS

Special education is a field devoted to adults and children with learning disabilities or learning difficulties. Such learners are often said to have special educational needs. The history of special education has centred around perceptions relating to the sometimes contradictory concerns of identification and categorisation of impairments, and appropriate responses to the 'needs' of disabled children and young people within the existing structures, knowledge and values of the time.

The idea of 'special' learners is not new. While early societies took the view that a small number of children with physical and mental handicaps were uneducable, specialist institutions, often maintained by voluntary subscriptions and philanthropy, notably for the deaf and blind, became a feature of Western societies from the eighteenth century. In the late nineteenth century, campaigners such as G. E. Shuttleworth in England presented papers on the 'special needs of feeble-minded children' and urged the setting up of state 'special schools' which could respond to the needs of handicapped children (Pritchard 1963).

For much of the twentieth century a 'medical model', focusing on 'handicap' dominated the sphere of special education, but the second half of the twentieth century saw more countries move towards a model of inclusiveness, supporting where possible the attendance of those with special needs or learning difficulties in mainstream institutional settings. In England, for example, the number of special schools significantly

559

declined in the decades following the Warnock Report (Department of Education and
Science 1978) and 1981 Education Act.

Such terms as 'education for the handicapped' are now infrequently encountered.
Discourses now focus of the 'disabilities',
'difficulties' and 'needs' of 'special' learners
and on how they might maximise their
engagement with learning, be motivated,
stretched and rewarded.

See also: blind, teaching of; dyslexia; giftedness; inclusive education; learning disabilities/
difficulties

Further reading

Department of Education and Science (1978) *Special
Educational Needs* (Warnock Report), London:
HMSO.
Pritchard, D. G. (1963) *Education and the Handi-
capped, 1760–1960*, London: Routledge and
Kegan Paul.

FELICITY ARMSTRONG

SPECIALISATION

Specialisation commonly refers to institutional specialisation in curricular terms, that is
to say it occurs when a school, college or
higher education institution has taken a strategic decision to specialise in an area of the
curriculum, or perhaps a particular approach
to learning, and to market itself as a specialist
institution in this area. The institution will have
specialised facilities, access to resources and
specialist staff to support the curricular area.

The approach to specialisation taken may
essentially be an exclusive one whereby the
institution only provides courses in the particular discipline or in closely related areas, for
example a college of music or a business
school (where the selection and admission of
the students is likely to be on the basis of
demonstrated achievement, capability and
interest in the specialism). This form of specialisation is more frequently found in further
or higher education but rather less so in secondary education where the approach tends

to be one of an area or areas of the curriculum being highlighted and given preferential
funding and access to resources (and where
selection by specialist aptitude tends to be
rare). An example here would be a languages
college in England where foreign and community languages are given a preferential status in terms of resources, curriculum time
and status but clearly within the context of a
secondary school providing the full range of
the secondary curriculum. A further form of
specialisation will relate not only to specific
offerings but to a more general approach to
education where technology, often information technology, will be emphasised across all
curriculum areas, or a school with a vocational specialism where a general orientation
to work-related learning may be seen in
many areas of the curriculum other than the
specific vocational courses. In primary education, specialisation is rare and where it
exists is likely to relate to an approach to
learning or a philosophy of education, for
example a Montessori school.

An educational institution may specialise
for a variety of reasons: it may be in response
to a particular local or regional context, such
as with a further education agricultural college specialising in land-based occupations in
a rural area or a maritime college in a coastal
area. It may serve to meet a particular occupational need, as with the *lycées professionels pub-
liques* in France, which are upper secondary
schools and colleges specialising in education
and training in particular vocational areas. In
other cases specialisation may derive from the
vision of the principal or head teacher and
other senior figures within a secondary
school, seeking to capitalise on existing facilities and staff expertise to develop a specialism
within the broader curriculum, to develop
market differentiation and respond to a local
educational context by focusing on a particular niche. In some cases the impetus for
specialisation may come from a systematic
analysis of the local and regional employment
context and the needs of the young people
entering this market. It may also come in

response to the opportunities to bid for additional resources and the advantage perceived in the school in presenting a case focused on a particular area of the curriculum; or more specifically there may be targeted funds for the development of a specialisation, as with the specialist schools initiative in England.

The specialist schools programme in England commands wide support across the political spectrum and forms a central plank of the government's policy to diversify secondary education, increase choice and raise standards of attainment. It commenced in 1993, focusing on technology colleges and building on the City Technology Colleges programme. The range of potential specialisms was extended in successive years first to include languages and then sports and arts specialisms, followed by science; mathematics and computing; business and enterprise; engineering; music; humanities; and special educational needs. A vocational specialism is also possible and strongly encouraged. High-performing schools may take a second specialism or add a rural dimension.

In the specialist schools programme there is a strong emphasis on raising standards and achievement, both in the specialism and the core subjects of the curriculum. Schools must raise sponsorship and present a development plan for approval. In return, they receive support and significant levels of additional per capita and capital funding, and are required to work in partnership to share their facilities and expertise with neighbouring schools and their local community. By 2006–7, 80 per cent of all maintained schools in England were designated specialist schools. The government is clearly committed to the continued expansion of the programme, which is overseen by the Specialist Schools and Academies Trust and anticipates that all maintained schools will eventually become either specialist schools or be part of the academies programme.

See also: academy; business school; curriculum; curriculum differentiation; professional education; secondary school/education

Further reading

Higham, J. J. S., Sharp, P. R. and Priestley, M. (2000) 'Developing diversity through specialisation in secondary education: comparing approaches in New Zealand and England', *Compare*, 30(2): 145–62.

Institute of Education, University of Warwick (2004) *A Study of the Specialist Schools Programme*, London: DfES.

Yeomans, D. J., Higham, J. J. S. and Sharp, P.R. (2000) *The Impact of the Specialist Schools Programme: Case Studies*, London: Department for Education and Skills.

JEREMY HIGHAM

SPELLING

Media stories regularly report employers' dissatisfaction with young people's capacity to spell words correctly. Debates about the spelling standards are invariably accompanied by contradictory evidence, however. Certainly, the advent of word processors and mobile telephones has created in Western countries a dependence upon automatic spell-checkers and text messaging, yet few, if any, educationists would argue that spelling 'doesn't matter'. Indeed, research indicates that spelling competency is a key driver for raising literacy.

For several centuries, texts for teachers and parents focused on words for children to learn, rather than on how spelling should be taught or learnt. Most books listed words according to the number of syllables or according to the similarity of speech sounds, or *phonemes*, so mixing very common words with obscure, almost-forgotten ones. According to one scholar, the words to be learned were frequently 'arranged in dreary spelling lists, unrelated to each other and utterly devoid of vital significance to the child' (Towery 1979: 23). Gradually, a less arbitrary approach to word learning emerged, with lists becoming based on frequency of use and related to age. Throughout the British Commonwealth, generations of upper-primary-age children learnt words drawn from Fred J. Schonell's *The Essential Spelling List* of 3,200 'everyday words', first published in 1932, in preparation for weekly tests. The memorisation and testing of words in 'families', sharing common letter sequences remains a feature of many schools today, but since the 1970s more educators have favoured a 'whole language' approach, where the spellings are learnt through children encountering new words in their reading and using them in their writing (Westwood 2005: 4). There has been criticism of this 'immersion' approach, particularly in Australia, and a leading advocate of whole language, Mem Fox, wrote in 1997:

> Why have some teachers stopped teaching things like spelling? I think they heard statements such as: 'You don't do spelling lists in whole language', so they stopped teaching spelling altogether. It was the wrong message. We must teach spelling. We need the power of being able to spell correctly.
>
> (quoted in Westwood 2005: 6)

As language and alphabets have changed over the centuries, so, too, have spellings of names, places and other words. English spelling began as an alphabetic or phonemic writing system, but the subsequent influx of new vocabulary from Germanic, Scandinavian, French, Latin, Greek, and Spanish influences led to alternative or replacement spellings and demands for simplification. The earliest known English spelling reformer was a thirteenth-century monk named Orm. More than 400 years later, while resident in London, the American Founding Father and polymath Benjamin Franklin published *A Scheme for a New Alphabet and Reformed Mode of Spelling* (1768), which proposed the withdrawal and replacement of some letters to bring English spelling more closely in line with pronunciation. George Bernard Shaw created an alphabet that emphasised the anomalies of conventional spelling. He was supported by Sir James Pitman, grandson of the inventor of the shorthand system and inventor of his own 'initial teaching alphabet'.

Spelling competitions have long been popular in the United States. The 2002 documentary film *Spellbound* follows the fortunes of eight under-fifteen spelling champions with an astonishing knowledge of complex and mostly unknown English language words as they compete in the Scripps Howard National Spelling Bee. The earliest *Spelling Bee* television programmes, contested by adults from British and American teams, were broadcast in the late 1930s. Since that time the format has on several occasions been revived by broadcasters on both sides of the Atlantic.

See also: basic skills; dyslexia; literacy; phonics; reading; standards; writing

Further reading

Brown, G. D. A. and Ellis, N. C. (eds) (1994) *Handbook of Spelling: Theory, Process, and Intervention*, Chichester: John Wiley.

Templeton, S. and Morris, D. (1999) 'Questions teachers ask about spelling', *Reading Research Quarterly*, 34(1): 102–12.

Towery, G. M. (1979) 'Spelling instruction through the nineteenth century', *The English Journal*, 68(4): 22–27.

Westwood, P. (2005) *Spelling: Approaches to Teaching and Assessment*, 2nd edn, Camberwell VIC: ACER Press.

DAVID CROOK

SPENCER, HERBERT (1802–1903)

Spencer's *Essays on Education* (1861) were translated and published in fifteen languages. His writings achieved massive worldwide sales, ranking him alongside Charles Darwin as the most influential British thinker of his age. It was Spencer who coined the phrase 'survival of the fittest', which encapsulated his combination of biological evolutionism with social utilitarianism. Spencer's evolutionism pre-dated Darwin's *Origin of Species* (1859). He was educated at home in a dissenting family and never studied at university. Despite this, he acquired widespread knowledge in a range of academic fields through personal inquiry. This influenced his views concerning education. Spencer opposed government intervention in schooling, believing that natural progress would be hindered by artificial amelioration. His main impact in world education, however, came through his outlining of a hierarchy of knowledge, placing that which related to self-preservation of the species (science) at the forefront. This was followed, successively, by knowledge that secured life's necessities, then child rearing and nurture, followed by reproducing and maintaining social and political organisation, and lastly recreation and leisure. This last category, Spencer felt, should not be included at all within the formal curriculum, leading many to accuse him of cultural philistinism. Additionally, he argued that learning ought to reflect natural processes. He therefore emphasised discovery and self-directed learning. He also popularised pedagogic ideas of starting from the particular and moving to the general, moving from the concrete to the abstract and from the simple to the complex. Another important contribution came in linking physical education to wider moral, social and intellectual contexts.

See also: discovery method/learning

STEVEN COWAN

SPIRAL CURRICULUM

The spiral curriculum is based on the belief that various important and fundamental ideas and subjects should be introduced early in a student's education and then revisited at increasingly advanced levels of instruction as the student matures and progresses. Ideally taking place over periods of some years or more, the recurring development of these core concepts allows students to develop an increasingly sophisticated understanding of the material, as well as helping students recognise the ongoing nature of learning and understanding. The notion of the spiral curriculum originated with Jerome Bruner, an American cognitive and educational psychologist, whose particular constructivist approach to learning

theory adopted the inquiry-discovery method. Following on from Piaget's work, Bruner understood that as children engaged in the combinatorial process of constructing new ideas from past and present knowledge and experience, that the extent of the student's ability to integrate new ideas and gain further knowledge through this method was linked to the student's familiarity with the subject itself and the specific structure of the associated discipline. The spiral curriculum also incorporated Bruner's belief that, given an appropriate level of instruction, any subject could be taught to children of any age. The spiral curriculum therefore introduces concepts and topics earlier than generally done in the schools, thus facilitating the process of knowledge construction for younger students. Criticism of the spiral curriculum generally focuses on the perceived lack of any mastery of skills that is implied in the notion of learning as an ongoing process that is never completed.

See also: Bruner, Jerome; curriculum; Piaget, Jean; psychology of education; subjects

PAUL COLLINS

SPONSORED AND CONTEST MOBILITY

The American sociologist Ralph H. Turner proposed in the early 1960s a framework for relating differences between the American and English systems of education to the norms of upward mobility that had developed in each country. He examined the way in which the accepted mode of upward mobility shaped the school system directly and indirectly through its effects on prevailing values. In England, according to Turner, sponsored mobility was dominant, whereas in America it was contest mobility that was most apparent. In contest mobility, elite status was a prize won in an open contest, though the candidate's own efforts, as in a sporting event where many compete for a few recognised rewards. In sponsored mobility on the other hand, the established elite chose recruits to the elite through a controlled selection process, as with entry to a private club. Turner himself conceded that these differences were 'ideal types', and indeed there was some evidence that undermined his claims. In America there were some trends evident towards a growth of sponsored mobility, while in England the influence of examinations and meritocratic ideals strengthened a trend towards contest mobility. In both societies indeed, as in others around the world, these two tendencies developed alongside and closely entangled with each other.

See also: meritocracy

Further reading

Turner, R. H. (1963) 'Modes of social ascent through education: sponsored and contest mobility'. In A. H. Halsey, J. Floud and C. A. Anderson (eds) *Education, Economy, and Society*, New York: Free Press.

GARY McCULLOCH

STANDARDISED TESTS

Standardised tests are assessment instruments that are administered, scored, and interpreted in a standard, predetermined manner. Although standardised tests in the field of education are employed worldwide, their use has been particularly prevalent in the USA. Indeed, during the final years of the twentieth century and the early part of the twenty-first century, almost all educational accountability programmes in the USA were based dominantly on students' standardised test performances. Although it is possible for standardised tests to be employed for small-scale assessment tasks, such as those involved in the routine classroom testing of students, almost all standardised tests are used in settings where large-scale assessments are required. A typical use of a standardised test, therefore, is to monitor the quality of tax-supported schools by annually requiring all students in those schools to complete one or more standardised tests.

Standardised tests in education are customarily classified into one of two categories, namely, aptitude tests and achievement tests. Educational aptitude tests are intended to predict how well students will perform in a subsequent academic setting. For example, students nearing the late stages of their pre-collegiate schooling might be required to take a college entrance examination whose sole purpose is to predict the grades likely to be earned by those test-takers after arriving at college. Although, for well over fifty years, such assessments have been described as aptitude tests, during the 1990s critics objected to 'aptitude' as a modifier because this descriptor tended to connote the measurement of a set of innate, unalterable capacities in students. However, even though it might be more accurate, and more politically correct, to refer to such assessments as 'predictor tests', the label 'aptitude tests' is still widely used.

In contrast, educational achievement tests are intended to assess the degree to which students possess certain skills and knowledge. Achievement tests attempt to supply answers to questions about what it is that students know and can do. In most situations where a standardised test is used as the cornerstone of an educational accountability strategy, such tests are, understandably, achievement tests rather than aptitude tests.

Standardised achievement testing in the USA commenced shortly after World War I. It was during this conflict that the *Army Alpha* was employed by military officials to predict which army recruits were likely to succeed in officer training programmes. Scores of test-takers were compared with scores of a set of previous test-takers (known as the 'norm group') so that army recruits with the highest scores could be sent to officer training programmes. The *Army Alpha*, administered to 1,750,000 men during World War I, embodied the basic assessment strategy adopted by subsequent developers not only of standardised aptitude tests such as the *Alpha*, but also by developers of standardised achievement tests. Because today's standardised tests yield scores whose interpretations must be referenced to the performance of the examinees constituting a test's norm group, these tests are often described as 'norm-referenced' tests.

During the 1980s and 1990s, a new genre of standardised achievement tests became increasingly popular, not only in the USA, but also in many other nations. These newer achievement tests were designed to measure the degree to which students had mastered official collections of curricular aims known as 'content standards'. Such assessments, typically referred to as 'standards-based' tests, are aimed less at providing comparative interpretations and more at determining the extent to which students have mastered particular content standards. Because students' score-interpretations are typically referenced to a set of targeted criterion outcomes, that is, the content standards being measured, standards-based examinations are usually characterised as 'criterion-referenced' tests.

Because of the significant role standardised achievement tests play in today's educational accountability programmes, increasing concerns have been recently registered regarding the degree to which some standardised tests are sensitive to instruction, that is, are capable of accurately discerning differences in instructional quality. Because of the way in which standardised tests are typically constructed, many of today's standardised achievement tests are so closely linked to students' socio-economic status that these tests tend to measure what students bring to school rather than what they have learned there. Clearly, an instructionally insensitive standardised test is altogether inappropriate for evaluating the quality of schooling.

Standardised tests, whether focused on aptitude or achievement, have been with us for many years. Their continued existence, however, does not necessarily signify that such tests are appropriate for the measurement missions they are currently being asked to accomplish.

See also: academic achievement; accountability; aptitude; assessment; criterion-referenced tests; norm-referenced tests; test/testing

Further reading

Lehmann, N. (1999) *The Big Test: The Secret History of the American Meritocracy*, New York: Farrar, Straus, and Giroux.

Phelps, R. P. (ed.) (2005) *Defending Standardized Testing*, Mahwah NJ: Lawrence Erlbaum.

Sacks, P. (2001) *Standardized Minds: The High Price of America's Testing Culture and what We Can Do to Change It*, Cambridge MA: Da Capo Press.

W. JAMES POPHAM

STANDARDS

In education, the term 'standards' may be encountered in several contexts. In some countries especially in the developing world, children do not move together to the next class in the school as an age cohort. Instead, only those who pass tests or examinations proceed to the next class or standard. Monograde arrangements of this type were common features of early compulsory school systems. In Victorian England, for example, elementary schools were grouped into six, later seven, standards in the 1890s, though many children left school before reaching the upper levels. Another manifestation of the term is found in North America, where 'curriculum standards', developed by state governments and sometimes professional subject associations, specify what students should know and be able to do at particular points during their school career. Additionally, standards is sometimes used as an alternative to skills or competences in vocational education: a trainee meeting certain specified standards may be eligible for a qualification or admittance into a trade or profession.

The term is also very commonly used in discussions about the quality of education, the robustness and reliability of assessment systems and the performance of local, national and international education systems.

Assessment evidence indicating year-by-year progress in meeting specified national education targets and improved statistics for examination passes often underpin declarations that 'standards are rising'. Very frequently such claims are greeted with disbelief among those who equate higher success rates with 'soft' marking and the more widespread use of coursework. Employers, for example, are regularly critical of young people's abilities in such areas as spelling and mental arithmetic.

Studies that set out to settle arguments about whether educational standards are rising or falling are themselves often susceptible to suggestions of flawed methodology and bias, though agreement that standards are 'not high enough' can generally be reached. The largest, most respected and influential comparative studies are:

- *The Program for International Student Assessment (PISA)*: Under the auspices of the Organisation for Economic Co-operation and Development (OECD), PISA is an assessment (begun in 2000) that focuses on the capabilities of fifteen-year-olds in reading literacy, mathematics literacy, and science literacy. The survey was implemented in forty-three countries in the first assessment (2000), in forty-one countries in the second assessment (2003), in fifty-seven countries in the third assessment (2006) and sixty-two countries have signed up to participate in the fourth assessment in 2009. Tests are typically administered to between 4,500 and 10,000 students in each country.
- *The Trends in International Mathematics and Science Study (TIMSS)*: Since 1995, this survey, conducted every four years under the auspices of the International Association for the Evaluation of Educational Achievement (IEA), provides data on the mathematics and science achievement of ten- and fourteen-year-old students.
- *The Progress in International Reading Literacy Study (PIRLS)*: PIRLS is the largest and most rigorous study of the reading achievement of ten-year-olds. Like TIMMS, it is conducted under the auspices of the International Association for the Evaluation of Educational Achievement. Some thirty-five countries participated in the 2001 survey and forty countries in the 2006 follow-up.

Discourses focusing on the need for 'higher standards' have driven, and are continuing to drive, educational reforms at a global level. They underpin strategies for school effectiveness and improvement, inspection, centralised and national curricula, institutional performance tables, standardised and high-stakes testing, and performance-related pay for teachers.

See also: assessment; coursework; curriculum standards/programmes of study; educational targets; examinations; inspection; numeracy; Organisation for Economic Co-operation and Development (OECD)

Further reading

Goldstein, H. and Heath, A. (eds) (2000) *Educational Standards*, New York: Oxford University Press.
Naumann, J. (2005) 'TIMSS, PISA and PIRLS and low educational achievement in world society', *Prospects*, 35(2): 229–48.
Thomas, S. and Peng, W-J. (2004) 'The use of educational standards and benchmarks in indicator publications', *European Educational Research Journal*, 3(1): 177–212.

DAVID CROOK

STEINER, RUDOLF (1861–1925)

An Austrian educator, after studying philosophy and mathematics in Vienna Steiner edited the scientific writings of Goethe (1889–96) in Weimar. He obtained his doctorate in 1894 for a study of Fichte's theory of knowledge, served as editor of the *Magazin für Literatur* and became involved with the working men's educational movement. Steiner developed what he called 'anthroposophy', which was 'knowledge produced by the higher self in man'. Annie Besant, the English educational radical and theosophist, exerted a key influence upon Steiner. His first school was opened in 1913 in Dornach, Switzerland, and other schools evolved as teachers spread Steiner's beliefs and methods. In 1919 he was invited to build a school for the children of workers of the Waldorf-Astoria cigarette factory – hence the name 'Waldorf School' – by which many Steiner schools are known. *The Story of My Life* (1924), published posthumously in 1928, further extended his influence. One of the distinctive characteristics of Steiner schools is their variety, ranging from schools for physically- and mentally challenged pupils to schools specialising in the arts or sciences. The movement became a global one, with over 500 Steiner schools existing worldwide at the end of the twentieth century. Although Steiner retained a belief in the special status of Christianity he espoused a belief in occultism and clairvoyance, arguing that humans have existed since the creation of the planet, originally as spirits and evolving to reach today's form. Steiner schools pay special attention to developmentally appropriate curricular activities and are viewed by many to be sensitive to the needs of children.

See also: special education/special educational needs/special needs

STEVEN COWAN

STENHOUSE, LAWRENCE (1927–82)

Stenhouse, a British teacher trainer and curriculum theorist, spent much of the early 1950s working as teacher in schools in Glasgow and Dunfermline, Scotland, where he developed an interest in low achievers. He lectured in psychology and education at Durham (1957–63) and Glasgow (1963–67) and in 1967 published *Culture and Education*.

This established his reputation as a leading advocate of a professional philosophy for teachers. He was also one of the first teacher educators to talk in theoretical and sociological terms about issues of 'cultural transmission'. Stenhouse became director of the Humanities Curriculum Project in 1967, which was to have considerable impact upon humanities practice in secondary schools, shifting from content-based to activity-based ideas of learning, and breaking down traditional subject barriers. For Stenhouse, the aim of education was emancipation, as opposed to acceptance of paternalism and the role of authority. He was a firm believer in the benefit of self-discovered knowledge for students. He established the Centre for Applied Research in Education at the University of East Anglia in 1972, becoming professor in 1978. His *Curriculum Research and Development in Action* (1980) and *Authority, Education and Emancipation* (1983) encapsulate his thinking upon self-reflexive practice by teachers, who are encouraged to question what they do so that they can become self-determining and self-authorising agents for learning. Stenhouse wanted teachers, by adopting a self-critical research stance towards their own practice, to be able to escape from the control situation they so often found themselves in.

See also: cultural transmission; curriculum; subjects

STEVEN COWAN

STREAMING/TRACKING

Streaming or tracking refers to the educational practice, sometimes undertaken by schools, of placing students in a series of classes, or requiring them to follow a curriculum targeted at their achievement or ability level. The process of allocating learners to streams or tracks can be contentious, particularly if there is no subsequent provision for transfer between classes. Where streaming/tracking is used as a device to prepare the 'best and brightest' students for entrance examinations to elite institutions, for example, there may be no provision to accommodate 'late developers' who might benefit from the challenge of the upper stream/track. Conversely, the inflexible use of streaming/tracking may allocate a learner judged to be academic to a pathway of dry learning that motivates them less than the vocational, hands-on experience that they desire. For these reasons, setting, an alternative mechanism for ability grouping, made on a subject-by-subject basis, is often preferred to streaming/tracking.

See also: ability; ability grouping; attainment; giftedness; mixed-ability teaching; underachievement

DAVID CROOK

STUDENT

A student is someone enrolled on a programme of study in an educational institution of some kind. Some countries have traditionally applied the term exclusively to post-compulsory learners, but it is now very common for pupil and student to be used interchangeably. Thus, there are school, college and university students. Other distinctions apply, too: universities around the world variously distinguish between undergraduates and postgraduates, freshmen and sophomores, resident and non-resident students, domestic and overseas students and orthodox and mature students, for example. Beyond the classrooms and libraries of teaching institutions, students sometimes have use of dedicated space such as a common room, bar or student union. By virtue of their age and limited finances, students frequently benefit from concessionary travel, reduced admission to public and sporting events and discounts in retail stores. They may also qualify for free or cheaper health treatment. Their membership of a union, guild or association may entitle them to vote in student elections and influence decision making in their institution of study.

The term student is also sometimes used to denote an attentive follower of ideological thought or a disciple of some influential thinker. Thus, reference may be made to students of the Frankfurt School of Social Research or to a student of Karl Marx's writings.

See also: mature student; pupil; student finance/loans

DAVID CROOK

STUDENT FINANCE/LOANS

At a global level, higher education students are facing increasing costs associated with continuing their education. The term 'student finance' typically refers to university or college tuition fees, costs of accommodation (which are predictably higher in the world's major cities), books and equipment and living expenses. A variety of student finance systems are to be found, with some central (or local) governments offering relatively generous levels of support via student grants, and others viewing this as a matter for the individual. Some countries promote student loans, typically at favourable market interest rates, while more local assistance may also be available in the shape of bursaries or interest-free loans, awarded on the basis of financial need, hardship or eligibility under the terms of an endowment by, for example, educational charities or businesses.

It is a common global practice for students to 'work their way' – perhaps by means of a term-time evening or weekend job, or vacation employment – through college or university. Students' parents or other family members may also provide significant financial support, but the arrival of mass higher education in Europe, the United States and other Western countries has determined that an increasing number of university graduates are paying off their student debts during their early years of employment, inevitably reducing their disposable income for such expenses as housing, leisure and starting a family.

Historically, state contributions to student finance systems have reflected the state of the public finances and the sensibilities of the electorate. Individuals with no experience of, or interest in, higher education may feel resentful towards a government that significantly subsidises a privileged group of higher education students. 'Why should we pay for the education of others?' might be the objection here, especially in the light of the argument that the returns from higher education may be greater for the individual – in the form of higher salaries and social status – than the returns to the wider society. On the other hand, if state assistance is not afforded to relatively poor students capable of benefiting from higher education, university recruitment and entry to graduate employment will become restricted to the already advantaged (Ainley 2005; Callender and Jackson 2005).

The transition from an elite to a more universal system of higher education after World War II was driven by wider opportunities for secondary education. In turn, this created a demand for higher education and pressure for public subsidies. In the United States, legislation in 1944 offered financial assistance for former service personnel to attend university, while in the United Kingdom the 1962 Education Act placed a duty upon local education authorities to award student grants for living expenses and tuition fees.

However, the slowdown of government expenditure that followed the international economic crisis of the 1970s impacted upon the resources allocated to universities. The stagnation of public funding collided with a dramatic increase in higher education enrolment, contributing to widespread reductions in per student funding from the 1980s. In this context of underinvestment, growing international concerns emerged about how policies of expansion and widening participation in higher education should be funded.

At a global level, higher education funding is dominated by discourses of 'cost sharing', intended to bring about a 'shift of some of the higher educational per-student costs from governments and taxpayers to parents and students' (Teixeira et al. 2006: 9). As an alternative to loans, some countries have now moved to establish new funding mechanisms, whereby university leavers begin to pay back some of the costs of their tuition once they are in employment and earning a specified minimum salary (Barr and Crawford 2005).

While there are significant disagreements about student finance matters in the West, the inequity of access to higher education is far greater in the developing world, where opportunities to commence a university education, whether at home or overseas, may be restricted to a tiny elite. Scholarships for otherwise disadvantaged applicants from developing countries to attend universities in such places as Australia, the United States and the United Kingdom have become more abundant in recent years, but the prospect of universal global access to affordable higher education in the twenty-first century is not yet in sight.

See also: charities, educational; economics of education; higher education; scholarship; student

Further reading

Ainley, P. (2005) 'For free universities', *Journal of Further and Higher Education*, 29(3): 277–85.

Barr, N. and Crawford, I. (2005) *Financing Higher Education: Answers from the UK*, London: Routledge.

Callender, C. and Jackson, J. (2005) 'Does the fear of debt deter students from higher education?', *Journal of Social Policy*, 34(4): 509–40.

Teixeira, J., Johnstone, B. D., Rosa, M. J. and Vossensteyn, H. (2006) *Cost-sharing and Accessibility in Higher Education: A Fairer Deal?*, Dordrecht, the Netherlands: Springer.

VINCENT CARPENTIER

SUBJECTS

Subjects are the basic building blocks of the modern academic curriculum. They provide a means of organising the knowledge imparted in schools and other educational institutions into particular fields or areas. They are intended to represent the current state of understanding of an area such as mathematics or geography, arranged in sequential form suitable for teaching and learning. In many ways, subjects constitute a compromise or coalition in terms of the areas and kinds of knowledge about an area that are included and excluded. They are also the basis for the organisation of schools into subject departments, which themselves are often hierarchical in nature and tend to create status differences in the school as a whole. In primary schools, individual teachers might be involved in teaching a wide range of different subjects, while in secondary schools they would tend to specialise in one or perhaps two. Often, subject areas are represented by subject associations, which promote their interests and profile and link together schools and universities.

Subjects that are associated with the most able students and examinations leading to the university tend to be of the highest status and exert most authority, both inside schools and for the public in general. Goodson identifies three distinct traditions – the academic, the utilitarian and the pedagogic – and traces their development in relation to subjects in the school curriculum. According to Goodson, since the nineteenth century academic subjects have been associated with written examinations, have been focused on content, have stressed abstract and theoretical knowledge, and have carried high status. By contrast, subjects in the utilitarian tradition have dealt with practical knowledge, while those in the pedagogic tradition are based on personal, social and commonsense knowledge (Goodson 1987: 25). He suggests that the difference in prestige that exists between these traditions establishes a clear hierarchy of status between subjects, and also within subjects. Thus, for example, pure mathematics tends to have higher status within the school than applied mathematics, and much greater prestige than handicraft or housecraft. This also extends to the status and authority of individual teachers: 'Academic subjects provide the

teacher with a career structure characterized by better promotion prospects and pay than less academic subjects.' (Goodson 1987: 34).

Subject departments have also become important features of the organisation of secondary schools, universities and many other types of educational institution. In secondary schools they often comprise the teachers' professional community, with common interests and values as well as shared problems and dilemmas in relation to the school as a whole. They can provide key contexts for teachers and teaching, but vary greatly in terms of the collegiality, technical culture, service ethic and professional commitment that they encourage from their members (Talbert 1995). Siskin has suggested that subject departments create potent dividing lines within the secondary school, boundaries which teachers rarely cross, and that they play an active and complex role in the ways in which teachers think about and conduct their practice (Siskin 1994). Indeed, it is possible for the interests and values represented by particular subject communities to be different from and even at odds with those of other subject departments in the same school, or of the school in general.

Subjects are therefore social and political in nature rather than simply abstract constructs. They change and develop over time in relation not only to advances in knowledge and understanding but also to values and interests of teachers in schools and departments. They underpin an academic curriculum oriented towards examinations. They may also give rise to differences and divisions that lead to difficulties within and across schools. Many attempts have been made to challenge the primacy of established subjects, for example by encouraging a more integrated curriculum and emphasising themes that cut across subjects. Nevertheless, in general, subjects appear to be entrenched forms of organisation within modern systems of schooling that are resilient in the face of change, and it is likely that they will continue to enforce adherence to particular areas of knowledge in the manner of rival clubs, parties, or tribes.

See also: curriculum; examinations; secondary school/education; teacher

Further reading

Goodson, I. (1987) *School Subjects and Curriculum Change: Studies in Curriculum History*, revised edn, London: Falmer.

Siskin, L. S. (1994) *Realms of Knowledge: Academic Departments in Secondary Schools*, London: Falmer.

Talbert, J. (1995) 'Boundaries of teachers' professional communities in U.S. high schools: power and precariousness of the subject department'. In L. S. Siskin and J. W. Little (eds) *The Subjects in Question: Departmental Organisation and the High School*, New York: Teachers College Press.

GARY McCULLOCH

SUMMATIVE ASSESSMENT

Summative assessment is done with the intention of summing up achievement, which is often made public, sometimes in the form of a warrant, such as certificate or declaration of fitness to practise. It is frequently contrasted with formative assessment, where the intention is to inform students and teachers in order to improve future performance. With summative assessment the public stakes tend to be high, whereas formative feedback is often private and the stakes are high only in the sense that most people fret if feedback suggests that major improvements are needed.

This simple account does not withstand close scrutiny. Formative assessment can sum up achievement and summative assessment often provides feedback for improvement; it is becoming more common to give students feedback on their exams, as well as on their coursework. Summative assessment does not have to come at the end of a module and, while formative feedback often occurs during a module, it could happen at the end. Nor is it invariably the case that formative intentions lead to private judgements and summative intentions to public ones. In other words, although people recognise 'summative assessment', it is quite an ambiguous term.

By and large, summative judgements 'count', which means that grade point averages, rankings and classifications derive from them. Consequently, assessments for summative purposes have to be highly reliable so, ideally, they should be based on several pieces of evidence (because performance on any one occasion may not be a good representation of competence); amassed over a period of time (because performances can change over time); judged by more than one person (because judges disagree); using clear criteria or rubrics (because judgements should all be made on the same basis). With the exception of assessments, such as objective tests, where the answer is straightforward and can be computer-marked, reliability is expensive and the more fine-grained we want judgements to be (for example, choosing to grade on a percentage scale, rather than make 'pass/fail' judgements), the greater the cost.

Costs can be reduced and reliability enhanced in public examinations systems where large numbers of people follow one curriculum and it is feasible to invest in examiner training, item banks and statistical analyses of marks and grades. So too in subject areas that emphasise information retention, understanding of concepts and application of algorithms. Here there is interesting work to develop on-demand computer-based assessment. Kingdon and colleagues (2005) consider some of the profound implications it has for educational practice. However, development costs tend to be high. A good example of some of the problematics of developing large-scale reliable tests is Bostrom *et al.*'s (2004) commentary on the development of a listening comprehension test.

There are also subject areas that still depend on the skilful judgements of well trained examiners and there are sectors, notably higher education, in which curriculum diversity is such that economies of scale and reliability are elusive.

571

Unfortunately, one way to reduce the costs of reliable assessment is to concentrate on assessing a simplified version of the achievement in question, putting reliability and validity at loggerheads. This is a significant problem when it comes to complex achievements (also known as higher-order skills, attributes or competencies). Employers greatly value such achievements but there are problems. Often these achievements are best assessed in practice or workplace settings. That is expensive and, because of variations in the settings, it is hard to get reliable judgements. Proxy assessments, such as simulations, in-class presentations and 'paper-and-pencil' tests tend to have restricted validity. The growing use of e-portfolio claims to achievement has attractions but the costs of reliable marking can be prohibitive.

In many systems there is a tradition of using coursework in summative assessment, although there has always been unease because some candidates have had excessive help from parents and friends. Now that 'Google knowledge' is commonplace, concerns about plagiarism are forcing reappraisals of the part coursework plays in summative assessment.

People outside the education system are consumers of summative judgements, but it is clear that they find it difficult to know what summative assessments signify. There is a major, and probably growing, problem with effectively communicating the meaning of summative assessments. There is also a concern that summative assessment can obstruct good learning and put people off lifelong learning (Boud and Falchikov 2006). Yet, regardless of the problems, summative assessment is a deeply embedded social practice that is unlikely to be dislodged by evidence alone.

See also: academic achievement; assessment; examinations; formative assessment; marking; test/testing

Further reading

Boud, D. and Falchikov, N. (2006) 'Aligning assessment with long-term learning', *Assessment and Evaluation in Higher Education*, 31(4): 399–413.

Bostrom, R. French, R. Johnson-Laird, P. and Parshall, C. (2004) *Review and Evaluation of the Development of a Listening Comprehension (LC) Section of the LSAT*, Newtown PA: Law School Assessment Council (www.uky.edu/~bostrom/listfinal!.htm)

Kingdon, M. (2005) *The Development of e-assessment 2004–14*, Hellingly: The Exam on Demand Assessment Advisory Group (www.examondemand.co.uk).

PETER KNIGHT

SUMMER SCHOOL

A summer school is a gathering of learners, typically at a school, college or university during the long vacation. Summer schools frequently combine recreation with instruction: art, foreign language, music and sport summer schools are popular with both children and adults, for example, and some programmes are targeted at families. Summer schools may be residential, making use of dormitories and halls of residence during 'downtime', or participants may perhaps camp in the grounds of the host institution. In some instances the purpose of a summer school may be for remedial or supplementary study. Schools wishing to raise pupil test scores or examination pass rates, for example, may open during the summer in order to offer extra instruction in literacy, numeracy or science. Other summer schools may bring together groups of learners for national or international workshops. For example, they may offer enrichment activities for children identified as gifted or provide opportunities for university research students to share their findings, typically in a more relaxed and informal context than the one in which they operate for the rest of the year.

See also: extracurriculum; semester/term

DAVID CROOK

SUNDAY SCHOOL

A Sunday school usually provides instruction in Christianity on a Sunday. Historically, Sunday schools have normally been linked to churches or chapels, but other organisations and individuals have also created them.

The first Sunday schools were created by Nonconformists in England, Wales and North America in the late seventeenth and early eighteenth centuries. The Sunday school movement, however, owes its origins to Robert Raikes (1735–1811), an Anglican newspaper proprietor in Gloucester, England. In 1780, shocked by the irreverent behaviour and language of local poor children on the Sabbath, he established Sunday schools where they were taught religion and reading. In 1783, Raikes advertised his achievements in his newspaper, the *Gloucester Journal*. Sunday schools spread throughout England at a time of demographic growth, political and social unrest and industrial and agricultural change. Their expansion was assisted by a proliferation of sermons and pamphlets and the activities of the interdenominational Sunday School Society (1785) and the largely Nonconformist Sunday School Union (1811). Hannah More (1745–1833) and Sarah Trimmer (1741–1810) wrote moral tales for use in teaching. In the USA, the American Sunday School Union (founded in 1817) established schools in the Eastern states and Mississippi Valley.

Sunday schools initiated mass schooling in England between 1780 and 1833, before the advent of state support for education. Prior to the establishment of Sunday schools there were few means of instruction for children of the poor. Existing schools often levied fees, which restricted their use by parents. Moreover, children started employment at a young age, thus limiting opportunities for any programme of teaching. Sunday schools provided an education on a day when paid work was not normally permitted. They were financed by subscriptions from the rich and staffed by volunteer teachers who gave their time without payment. Sunday schools taught more than religion. Other subjects included reading, though debate took place whether teaching children to read on the Sabbath was contrary to Christianity; social morality, which pro-

vided a form of citizenship education; and in some towns, such as Stockport, Cheshire, arithmetic and vocational training on weekday evenings. Adults as well as children sometimes went to classes.

Christian writers have celebrated the English Sunday school, but their approach has removed the institutions from the historical context and experiences which caused an explosive growth in their numbers after 1780. Social historians have interpreted them in different ways (see Dick 1984). Either Sunday schools promoted work discipline during the Industrial Revolution, or they subdued the radical tendencies of the working classes through religious terrorism, or they created a working-class culture of religion and respectability, or they were patriarchal institutions that taught obedience and deference. Their nature depended on the contexts in which they operated and the beliefs and commitments of those who promoted and staffed them.

Alternative socialist Sunday schools began in the 1890s, when socialist movements developed in Britain. Mary Gray (1854–1941), a member of the Social Democratic Federation, created the first in 1892. In 1909, the National Council of British Socialist Sunday Schools was formed to connect the schools and assist them in their teaching. It produced *The Socialist Commandments* (1912), *The Red Dawn: A Book of Verse for Revolutionaries and Others* (1915) and the *Proletarian Song Book* (1923). The Socialist Commandments required children to love their fellow pupils, be a friend of the weak and understand that 'all the good things of the earth are produced by labour' and 'whoever enjoys them without working for them is stealing the bread of the workers'. They reached their peak of popularity in the 1920s when over thirty towns had branches of the movement, but they faced opposition from churches and employers.

Restrictions on child employment and the advent of day schooling reduced the importance of Sunday schools. Changing patterns of leisure and the rise of a secular society also

573

contributed to a reduction of their significance. Sunday schools, nevertheless, survive in many churches for teaching Christianity to children.

See also: church; religious school

Further reading

Dick, M. (1984) 'Religion and the origins of mass schooling: the English Sunday school, *c*.1780–1840'. In V. A. McClelland (ed.) *The Churches and Education*, Leicester: History of Education Society.

Laqueur, T. W. (1976) *Religion and Respectability: Sunday Schools and Working Class Culture 1780–1850*, New Haven CT and London: Yale University Press.

Thompson, E. P. (1968) *The Making of the English Working Class*, Harmondsworth: Pelican.

MALCOLM DICK

SUPPLY/SUBSTITUTE TEACHING

Supply/substitute teaching is the term used to describe teachers who do not have a permanent contract with any one school but who instead work in schools as and when they are required to replace a teacher who is unable to teach as the result of sickness or other absence. Supply teachers are sometimes referred to as cover teachers or substitute teachers in Canada and the United States and as relief teachers in Australia and New Zealand.

In the UK, the supply teacher is paid for the time he/she works in the school. Supply teachers may obtain work by being members of an employment agency which acts as an intermediary between the teacher and schools. Alternatively, supply teachers may have individual relationships with schools that will contact them as and when a teacher is required or they will be part of a list of teachers kept by the local education authority (LEA). If teachers are employed directly by the school or LEA, their yearly salary is divided by the number of school days in the year to calculate their daily rate. Agency teachers' pay is set by the agency. In the UK, supply teachers have to be qualified teachers and usually expect to be given guidance by the

school as to the lessons they will be required to teach. In secondary schools, unqualified teaching assistants may be allowed to cover lessons for the teacher, supervising a class of students in doing work which has been set by the absent teacher.

In some other countries, supply teachers operate in slightly different ways: they do not always have to be qualified teachers and it is not always expected that lessons will be set for the supply teacher to use. Supply teachers have to be flexible, adaptable to teaching a range of different age groups at short notice and able to think on their feet. Traditionally, supply teaching is viewed as challenging, as students like to feel that they can 'get one over' a new teacher. However, some teachers rise to this, enjoying the flexibility, sense of challenge and the opportunity to work in a variety of environments.

See also: teacher; teaching/teaching methods

NATALIE HEATH

SUSPENSION

A suspension is a form of exclusion of a student from school activities as a result of a breach of a discipline policy for a specified period of time. Suspensions are either an exclusion from the school or an exclusion from regular classroom activities within a school.

A suspension from school for a set period of time may be accompanied by specific requirements on the child or the parent/caregiver regarding matters such as attendance at an alternative school setting, such as a suspension centre, involvement in counselling, mediation or some form of professional assessment of the child. Alternatively, the school or school system authority may impose requirements on itself in order for the child to be able to return to school, such as the development of an alternative programme of study or the provision of resources to manage the particular behaviour. A suspension from classroom activities within a school, sometimes called in-school suspension or 'time-out' usually requires the child to spend a set period of time in an isolated setting within the school. The child is required to complete work set by the school and is supervised by one of the staff.

Data on rates of suspension are available from different school jurisdictions, and these may include a reporting of suspension rates, causes, outcomes, and demographic data on students suspended. Typically the overall rate of suspension for a school system is low in percentage terms: for example, in Australia, suspensions of more than one week occur at rates of less than 1.5 per cent of the student population. Aggregated reports can be misleading as there is typically wide variation in suspension rates among schools. Moreover, where data are available they show that suspension rates among boys are higher than among girls and that they are often higher among minority groups. For instance in some states in Australia, suspension rates for Aboriginal students are many times higher than for non-indigenous students. Similar patterns have been reported in America, with high suspension rates for low-income and minority students. Some school system authorities report rates of recidivism, that is, the number of students who are placed on a subsequent suspension within a defined period, such as a year. The recidivism rate is posited as an indicator of the effectiveness of suspension in addressing the behaviours that lead to the suspension.

In Western countries there has been a trend towards zero-tolerance suspension polices. Up to 90 per cent of school districts in America have zero-tolerance suspension polices in relation to violence and drugs. These polices have resulted in higher rates of suspension. They have also been criticised on the grounds that they are populist in the sense that they respond to public concerns as opposed to educational concerns, and moreover that they are ultimately ineffective.

There is considerable debate about what suspension data indicate. Some school authorities argue that high rates of suspension indicate that a school system is actively and effectively responding to student misbehaviour. Others argue that rates of suspension are an indicator of the effectiveness of the educational programmes offered by the school. Yet others suggest that suspension rates are simply reflective of the socio-economic context in which the school or system of schools operates. Analyses of suspension rates of schools in comparable socio-economic areas indicate that there is wide variation in rates of suspension among schools in similar contexts, suggesting that variations in suspension rates may be more reflective of school effects as opposed to characteristics of students. Moreover, compelling arguments have been made in the literature, and school system policies often point out that suspension in itself is not a solution to a problem, but can be considered an opportunity for an intervention programme designed to address a problem.

Suspensions are a common element of a school's and school system's range of responses to serious student behaviour problems. Other students, teachers and non-teaching staff need to be protected from extreme, threatening and violent behaviour. The literature suggests that matters such as natural justice or procedural fairness in the determination of a suspension case; the involvement of parents in the management of the behaviour problem; the need to be alert to discrimination against minority groups; and constantly reviewing the school's educational programme in relation to the extent to which it engages students and therefore the role it plays in influencing student behaviour, need ongoing consideration by school and school system authorities.

See also: counselling; detention; discipline; exclusion/expulsion; truancy

Further reading

Christie, C., Nelson, C. M. and Jolivette, K. (2004) 'School characteristics related to the use of suspension', *Education and Treatment of Children*, 27(4): 509–26.

Costenbader, V. and Markson, S. (1998) 'School suspension: a study with secondary school students', *Journal of School Psychology*, 36(1): 59–82.

Riordan, G. (2006) 'Reducing student "suspension rates" and engaging students in learning: principal and teacher approaches that work', *Improving Schools*, 9: 239–50.

Stage, S. A. (1997) 'A preliminary investigation of the relationship between in-school suspension and the disruptive classroom behavior of students with behavioral disorders', *Behavioral Disorders*, 23(1): 57–76.

GEOFF RIORDAN

SWEDEN

The Swedish education system began formally in 1842 when it became the responsibility of each parish to establish a coeducational elementary school. Grammar schools and lower secondary schools flourished for boys in towns, with girls referred to separate schools. At the beginning of the twentieth century, coeducational lower secondary schools were introduced and, with the advent of the nine-year compulsory school system in 1962, separate girls' schools began to disappear.

Reforms in the 1990s transformed the Swedish education system from a heavily centralised system to one where the state, and the national and local authorities shared responsibility for education, with the state defining national objectives and local bodies responsible for ensuring that activities conformed to these guidelines. It became a requirement of both the state and local authorities that the education system was systematically monitored and evaluated.

Education in Sweden is seen as a lifelong process and legislation stipulates that all children, young people and adults in Sweden have equal access to the state education system regardless of gender, place of residence or socio-economic circumstances. Early years' education has existed in Sweden since the nineteenth century in the form of day nurseries and kindergartens. The municipalities provide childcare for all children between the ages of one and twelve, whose parents work or study and, in 2003, universal and free preschool was introduced for four- and five-year-olds. Municipalities must also provide a place in a pre-school class for children in the year they turn six, a bridge between preschool and the beginning of compulsory schooling.

School attendance is compulsory for all children between the ages of seven and sixteen living in Sweden. Included in compulsory schooling are the regular compulsory school, approved independent schools, Sami schools, special schools, and programmes for pupils with learning disabilities. Today most children with physical disabilities are taught in the regular compulsory school, whilst children with different learning disabilities attend the *särskola*, often integrated into the regular compulsory school. Children usually attend the school nearest their home, though parents may choose a different municipal or approved independent school. The home municipality bears the cost of the pupil's schooling regardless of the school chosen.

The municipalities are obliged by law to award grants to approved independent schools according to the same criteria as those applied to their own schools. Nearly half of the independent schools have a specific pedagogical orientation or are denominational. Education at an independent compulsory school receiving a public grant is free of charge and open to all.

Almost all pupils continue to upper secondary school, a single administrative unit integrating all forms of academic and vocational education. Study at this level is of one of seventeen national programmes, all of which offer a broad general education and basic eligibility to continue studies at the post-secondary level. The curriculum at this level applies to the upper secondary school (including pupils with learning disabilities) and municipal adult education (again including those with learning disabilities). New national syllabi for each subject decree what is to be achieved by the end of the fifth and ninth year of school, which allows for nationwide evaluation of school achievements. Successful completion of an upper secondary programme of study qualifies a pupil for post-secondary education.

Approximately one third of students continue to tertiary education within three years of completing upper secondary school. Most tertiary institutions in Sweden are state-run and free of charge. The government's long-term goal is that 50 per cent of young people in any given cohort start higher education by the time they reach the age of twenty-five.

Adult education in Sweden has a long history, the state education system giving adults the opportunity to supplement their education in accordance with their individual requirements. This is to enable those with limited education to strengthen their position in the labour market and in cultural and political life.

Despite the high level of participation in both formal and non-formal education in Sweden, there has been a concurrent increase in the proportion of 16–24-year-olds not in education, training or employment. The need to increase the number of immigrant children who progress to the post-compulsory stage of education or leave compulsory education with a complete set of grades is also pressing. This integration of marginalised groups back into the education system and society as a whole constitutes one of the biggest challenges in Sweden at present. There is recognition, too, that although internationally Swedish pupils compare well, there are wide discrepancies between different schools and municipalities. A current preoccupation, therefore, of the Swedish education authorities is to improve this, so that all children have access to a good quality education.

See also: Europe; Scandinavia

JO PEAT

SYLLABUS

The syllabus outlines the course to be followed by pupils or students. It defines the curriculum of the course or programme, setting out the key topics, the constituent parts, and the sequence in which they should be studied. The syllabus should also clarify the aims and objectives of the course to afford an understanding of its purpose and expectations. Other features of a detailed and well designed syllabus generally include the grading policy for the course, prerequisite and corequisite courses, locations and times for the course, contact information, materials, resources and key texts required to follow the course, and a schedule and deadlines for any work required for the course. Assessment and examinations should be clearly based on the published or circulated syllabus for the course, and draw systematically from the different areas or sections outlined in the syllabus. An examination board may be responsible for setting out the syllabus of a course. Within a school or other educational institution, a syllabus may be adapted to the strengths and aptitudes of the teachers and pupils involved in order to emphasise or focus on particular features more than others. In an institution of higher education or different kinds of adult education, the syllabus may be provided for students at the beginning of the course. The syllabus should be reviewed and updated regularly, and care is often required to ensure that the current version is being used and adapted correctly.

See also: curriculum; examinations

GARY McCULLOCH

SYSTEMIC REFORM

Systemic reform, sometimes labelled 'standards-based' reform, refers to the system-wide restructuring of large school districts in order to align all policies implemented throughout the system. It includes the establishment of high academic standards in order to increase student achievement, through the use of similar curricular and instructional programmes throughout the district (Massell *et al.* 1997). Increased alignment of all standards, practices and actors within the education system may improve the use of limited resources, therefore ensuring more sustainable reforms. In the United States, state and local governments have varied their implementation of systemic reform, with some states beginning their reform efforts at the local level such as in San Diego, California and Chicago, Illinois, and others, such as Pennsylvania, initiating their reform efforts at the state level.

Systemic reform has been carried out through technical means by adding resources to the school district; via normative means by trying to modify the beliefs, values, or norms within the district; and by political means, by developing professional networks and improving valuable political constituencies (Oakes 1992). Traditionally, systemic reform has often entailed basing curriculum frameworks and assessments on standards for learning. Standards-based reforms have resulted in the use of high-stakes tests to hold states and local districts accountable for student achievement and with curriculum and pedagogy linked to these tests. There have been two models of standards-based systemic reform, the first bureaucratic or implemented 'top down' from the state or district level; the second, professional, which is implemented from the 'bottom up' by teachers and administrators in consultation with the district and state (O'Day 2002).

In San Diego, the school district 'instantiated a content-driven, centralized, comprehensive, and fast-paced reform starting in 1998' that used a combination of technical, normative, and political means (Hubbard *et al.* 2006). This centralised approach to systemic reform included professional development for the superintendent, principals, and teachers to improve instruction and to form 'communities of practice' and accountability throughout the school system in an effort to

increase student achievement. Critics of these systemic reforms believe that teachers lose autonomy in the process of standardising the curriculum throughout the district and that the curriculum is not appropriate and inadaptable for all levels of students (Hubbard *et al.* 2006).

Systemic reform in Chicago was implemented at the local level in an attempt to involve all members of the school community in reforming the schools. Politically, power was removed from the board of education and given to the mayor, who appointed a chief executive officer of the Chicago Public School System. In addition, local school councils (LSCs) were adopted, consisting of six parents, two community representatives, two teachers, and one principal, who were given the power to spend discretionary funds, voice input or concern in school reforms, and had the ability to hire and fire principals. Although there were some positive outcomes of this reform effort, there were minimal increases in achievement (Russo 2004).

In Philadelphia, systemic reform began when the state of Pennsylvania took over the Philadelphia school system in December 2001. Using a 'diverse provider model', Philadelphia schools were governed by the School Reform Commission (SRC), a five-person panel, chosen by both the mayor of Philadelphia and the state of Pennsylvania. The SRC outsourced some of the Philadelphia schools to for-profit and non-profit Educational Management Organizations (EMOs) In addition to reducing class sizes, strengthening discipline and safety measures, reforms included mandating a standardised core curriculum in four major subjects, establishing six-week benchmark tests, and improving professional development for teachers. Although attempts to standardise and implement functional reforms have shown some positive outcomes, some issues still remain concerning the responsibility and accountability of the diverse provider model as EMOs tried to balance improving instruction and achievement under varying levels of federal, state, and local regulations (Useem 2007).

The *No Child Left Behind Law* (2001) has increased the number of school districts experimenting with systemic reform in an effort to meet accountability requirements by 2014. Supporters argue systemic reform provides districts with the organisational mechanisms to meet accountability standards; critics argue that there are significant factors outside schools, especially poverty, that limit the success of systemic reform.

See also: accountability; core curriculum/ national curriculum; educational priority area; school reform; standards; urban education

Further reading

Hubbard, L., Stein, M. K. and Mehan, H. (2006) *Reform as Learning: When School Reform Collides with School Culture and Community Politics*, New York: Routledge.

Massell, D., Kirst, M. and Hoppe, M. (1997) *Persistence and Change: Standards-Based Systemic Reform in Nine States*, Consortium for Policy Research in Education policy briefs, 21 March.

Oakes, J. (1992) 'Can tracking research inform practice? Technical, normative, and political considerations', *Educational Researcher*, 2: 12–21.

O'Day, J. (2002) 'Complexity, accountability, and school improvement', *Harvard Educational Review*, 72(3): 293–329.

Russo, A. (2004) *School Reform in Chicago: Lessons in Policy and Practice*, Cambridge MA: Harvard University Press.

Useem, E. (2007) 'Learning from Philadelphia's school reform: the impact of NCLB and Related State Legislation'. in A. R. Sadovnik, J. A. O'Day, G. W. Borhnstedt and K. M. Borman (eds) *No Child Left Behind and the Reduction of the Achievement Gap: Sociological Perspectives on Federal Educational Policy*, New York: Routledge.

TARA DAVIDSON AND ALAN SADOVNIK

T

TANZANIA

The United Republic of Tanzania is a country in East Africa, bordered by Kenya and Uganda to the north, Rwanda, Burundi and the Democratic Republic of the Congo to the west, and Zambia, Malawi and Mozambique to the south. To the east, it borders the Indian Ocean. Tanzania was formed in 1964, when, shortly after achieving independence from British colonial rule (in place since 1919), Tanganyika (the country's mainland of around 945,000 square kilometres) merged with Zanzibar (islands of around 1,658 square kilometres off the east coast). Today, Tanzania comprises twenty-six administrative regions, a population of around 39 million people (2007 figures) and over a hundred different ethnic groups. The overall population includes a balance of Christians and Muslims, but the inhabitants of Zanzibar are almost entirely Muslim.

Tanzania is one of the poorest countries in the world, with more than 50 per cent of households living in absolute poverty. The structure of the formal education and training system in Tanzania constitutes two years of pre-primary education, seven years of primary education, four years of junior secondary education, two years of senior secondary and up to three or more years of tertiary education, which covers all programmes and courses for adults, including those provided by higher education institutions. Of these stages, only primary education is compulsory and offered free of charge. Secondary education, for a minority, is directed towards taking 'ordinary' and 'advanced' examinations offered by English qualification-awarding bodies. Primary school teaching is bilingual, with students learning Kiswahili (or Swahili) and English. The latter language is the medium of instruction in post-primary education, though Kiswahili is taught as a compulsory secondary school subject and is an option for those proceeding to tertiary education.

Prior to independence, faith-based organisations and the colonial government provided primary schooling, including for disabled children, but the requirement to pay fees severely restricted school attendance. President Julius Nyerere's Arusha Declaration (1967) outlined a socialist vision to develop Tanzanian 'education for self-reliance', including a commitment to achieve universal primary education in two years. Under Nyerere, state primary schooling became compulsory and, with the exception of a small number of seminaries, the private and voluntary schools which since the 1920s had offered distinctive forms of education to communities of African, Asian and European origin, were brought into a unified national system. Cost-free secondary schools were also developed, but the state's ambitions ran far ahead of the reality: schools were poorly resourced and, in spite of massive enrolments, fewer than half of all primary-age children had been accommodated by 1973 (Samoff 1987: 336). In order to sustain educational expansion it became necessary for the government to permit private schooling initiatives. Many unofficial private schools, both primary and secondary, began to operate from the late 1960s, funded by churches and voluntary subscriptions, and in the mid-1970s the registration of private secondary schools was allowed.

Economic difficulties, which saw Tanzanian foreign debts escalate, necessitated the reintroduction of school fees for state primary and secondary education in 1984, a measure that caused attendance rates to plummet. Subsequently, in consequence of Tanzania's Basic Education Master Plan (1997) and Primary Education Development Plan (2001), and with help from international agencies including the World Bank, it became possible in 2002 to reintroduce cost-free, seven-year compulsory schooling from ages 7–14. At first glance, the results have been spectacular: according to World Bank statistics, Tanzania's primary school enrolment rate rose from 58.6 per cent in 2000 to 96.1 per cent in 2006, and the country is on track to reach the United Nations Millennium Development Goal of universal and free primary schooling by 2015. The hidden costs of schooling determine, however, that a high proportion of children living in poverty fail to complete their entitlement, and while the pass rate for the Primary School Leaving Examinations – taken by students in Standard Seven – have increased since 2000 from 22 per cent to 61.8 per cent, progression to secondary school, where fees are charged in both the public and private sectors, is low at 46.1 per cent (2005 figures). The secondary school retention rate for girls is notably poor and, overall, Tanzanian women are severely disadvantaged in terms of access to literacy and formal education, as are orphaned children, including those who have lost one or both parents to HIV/AIDS. Primary class sizes have been rising steadily since the mid-1980s and, in the five-year period from 2000 to 2005, the pupil/teacher ratio rose from 1:41 to 1:56.

A one-party socialist state from 1961 until the mid-1980s, Tanzania is now a multi-party democracy and its government is currently committed to changing its educational role from that of 'key player' to 'facilitator'. It is moving towards decentralising government funding to the ninety-nine local authorities and encouraging private investment in education. It is typical in many districts for primary schools to be predominantly funded by religious and other charities and by voluntary subscriptions. Many secondary institutions are private or church-run, with some marketing themselves as international schools.

Tanzania's first higher education institution was the University College of Tanganyika, awarding University of London external degrees, established in 1961. This became a constituent college of the University of East Africa two years later, but since 1970 has operated independently as the National University of Dar es Salaam. There are now around 200 tertiary institutions in the sector, including private universities and colleges, but the tertiary enrolment rate in 2005 was just 1.4 per cent.

See also: Africa; centralisation/decentralisation; development plan; Education for All (EFA); standards; voluntarism

Further reading

Buchert, L. (1994) *Education in the Development of Tanzania, 1919–1990*, London: James Currey.
Lwaitama, A. F., Mtalo, E. G. and Mboma, L. (eds) (2001) *The Multi-Dimensional Crisis of Education in Tanzania: Debate and Action*, Dar es Salaam: University of Dar es Salaam Convocation.
Mkude, D., Cooksey, B. and Levey, L. (2003) *Higher Education in Tanzania: A Case Study*, Oxford: James Currey
Samoff, J. (1987) 'School expansion in Tanzania: private initiatives and public policy', *Comparative Education Review*, 31(3): 333–60.

DAVID CROOK

TAWNEY, RICHARD HENRY (1880–1962)

Educated at Rugby School and Balliol College, Oxford, where he became friends with William Beveridge, the influential social reformer R. H. Tawney followed in the tradition of F. D. Maurice and Anglican socialists. This found expression in his going to work at Toynbee Hall in east London, where the Workers' Educational Association (WEA) was based alongside a number of other community improvement initiatives led by reforming members of the upper class. He was a lecturer at Glasgow University from 1908 to 1914, during which time he also led many WEA classes, leaving lasting impressions upon his students. Tawney was a member of the WEA executive committee for forty-two years, holding senior office from 1920 to 1944. For Tawney, effective learning was achieved through active fellowship, where the form of education was essentially a democratic one. This stemmed from his belief in the oneness of humanity under God, hence his social egalitarianism. *Religion and the Rise of Capitalism* (1926) was a brilliant historical analysis, while *Equality* (1931), became a major benchmark for progressive thinkers in the English-speaking world during the mid-twentieth century. Many of the ideas contained in *Secondary Education for All* (1922) were incorporated into the 1928 Labour Party manifesto, of which Tawney wrote a major part. He was a member of the Consultative Committee of the Board of Education, 1921–31, and he contributed significantly to the 'Hadow Report', *The Education of the Adolescent* (1926). This argued for the creation of universal secondary schooling. He was the foremost economic historian of his generation and a powerful social thinker, working at the London School of Economics from 1918 to 1949.

See also: equality of opportunity; politics of education; secondary school/education; Workers' Educational Association (WEA)

STEVEN COWAN

TEACHER

A teacher is a person whose profession is to teach or instruct students in educational institutions, like schools, colleges or universities, and to guide their learning experiences. In today's global, heterogeneous world, teachers prepare students for productive, equitable participation in society. Nevertheless, the population of teachers is not representative of that of students in respect of gender, ethnicity and race.

Currently, in most cultures, teaching is referred to as a profession and requires certification or a licence to practise. Licensure and certification vary widely among educational systems regarding the required period of training, institutions of training, and examinations required for elementary/primary, secondary, and university teaching. These matters are subject to criteria and standards determined by national systems designed to ensure that practising teachers have been adequately prepared. In most countries teachers will also be able to access further professional development opportunities while in post.

Professionalism leads to the expectation that teachers will continuously search for responsible courses of action in situations of uncertainty, demonstrate their commitment to students and work cooperatively with colleagues. Teachers frequently hold pastoral and managerial, as well as academic responsibilities: they contribute to and deliver curricula, influence the strategic direction of their institution, provide feedback and encouragement on work submitted and advise their students about study skills, health and other matters related to their well-being. But conforming to norms of collegiality and solidarity can sometimes collide with professional norms. The occupational status of teachers is generally related to the degree of selection involved in obtaining certification, a teaching post, and the time spent in training. At an international level, teachers have membership of a diverse range of professional organisations and unions whose raison d'être is to protect and enhance their economic status, employment rights and working conditions, as well as to promote their professional status.

Teachers' workplaces are described as 'loosely coupled systems', with formal hierarchies and specialised divisions of labour (such as subject teams being led by a head of department), but control and accountability are also exerted through the daily organisation of work. Administrators frequently support the high-order work of teachers (such as timetabling and students' examination entries) and, in some contexts, a teaching or classroom assistant may provide additional support. Nevertheless, some teachers' work may be mundane, for example supervising children and rearranging classroom furniture. The expectations that teachers have upon entering the profession, for example regarding their resources, responsibilities, power and pay, are sometimes unfulfilled.

Teachers interact and communicate with students, colleagues, parents, and administrators, and their multiple commitments to these stakeholders may conflict. Research suggests that teachers become disillusioned when they perceive that they are overworked, underpaid, over-regulated or subject to over-intrusive inspection. But their commitment to the profession is heightened by more complex, intellectually demanding and rewarding work with students. Some perceive teaching as an intelligent technique, others as a political activity or even as a moral endeavour. It is likely that teachers will transmit some of their own emotions and positions regarding morality and ethics to their students.

Teachers engage in diverse intellectual and professional activities in complex social settings characterised by uncertainty, intangibility and ambiguity. Accordingly, they draw upon their knowledge of: (a) the philosophical, social, and cultural foundations of education, which direct teachers' personal orientations and perspectives; (b) curriculum subject matter and how to make best use of it; (c) pedagogical approaches designed to make subject content accessible and engaging for all students, differentiating materials as necessary; (d) students' existing knowledge, beliefs and preferred learning styles; (e) the influences of language, culture, family, and community

on students' development and learning; and (f) how interactions may be structured to promote student learning and assess and monitor their progress.

Expert teachers possess both routine and flexibly adaptive knowledge. They apply techniques of metacognition to facilitate students' learning and critical thinking. The effectiveness of the teacher is demonstrated not only by their knowledge, but also by personal attributes like perseverance, enthusiasm, and care for students, and also by such contextual factors as class or school size and opportunities for professional cooperation with colleagues and stakeholders.

See also: continued/continuing professional development; learning; pastoral care; pedagogy; student; teacher union; teaching/teaching methods; teaching assistant; teaching profession

Further reading

Bransford, J. D., Brown, A. L. and Cocking, R.R. (eds) (2000) *How People Learn: Brain, Mind, Experience, and School*, Washington DC: National Academies Press.

Darling-Hammond, L. and Bransford, J. (eds) (2005) *Preparing Teachers for a Changing World: What Teachers Should Learn and Be Able to Do*, San Francisco CA: Jossey-Bass.

Lampert, M. (2001) *Teaching Problems and the Problems of Teaching*, New Haven CT and London: Yale University Press.

Little, J. W. (2003) 'Inside teacher community: representations of classroom practice', *Teachers College Record*, 105(6): 913–45.

Squire, G. (1999) *Teaching as a Professional Discipline*, London and Philadelphia PA: Falmer Press.

BILLIE EILAM

TEACHER CULTURES

The term 'teacher culture' came to prominence in the early 1970s, when Dan Lortie called to attention an 'odd gap' in our knowledge about teachers: 'We have too few studies which explore the subjective world of teachers in terms of *their* conceptions of what is salient' (1973: 490). The subsequent publication of *Schoolteacher: A Sociological Study* (Lortie 1975) sought to explore the world of teaching from an insider – that is, teacher – perspective. A large body of research has since sought to examine teachers' work lives (see e.g. the works of Jennifer Nias, Ivor Goodson, Judith Warren Little and Geert Kelchtermans). There has been debate about the nature of teacher culture and whether it is characterised by uniformity or pluralism. The works of Fieman-Nemser and Floden (1986), Hargreaves (1994), and Grossman and Stodolosky (1995) repeatedly document differences among teacher cultures and argue that, as teaching is characterised by diversity, the assumption that multiple, sometimes competing, teacher cultures are simultaneously in operation is justifiable.

This body of research has also focused on the *content* and *form* of teacher cultures. The *content* or *substance* 'consists of the substantive attitudes, values, beliefs, (knowledge,) habits, assumptions and ways of doing things that are shared within a particular group' (Hargreaves 1994: 218). These beliefs include, for example, beliefs about philosophy (the purpose and nature of teaching), epistemology (the nature of knowledge) and pedagogy (learners/learning and teachers/teaching) and these beliefs shape the way in which teachers perceive their work, and especially the way they see their relationships with students, teachers and people in leadership roles.

Hargreaves (1994) has identified four distinct forms of teacher culture: fragmented individualism, Balkanisation, collaborative culture and contrived collegiality; and proposes a fifth form of teacher culture, which he terms the moving mosaic. These varying forms of teacher culture evidence the adaptive nature of cultures. Indeed, Keesing (1974) refers to cultures as ecosystems that respond to systemic changes with both negative adjustive changes (that is, the culture works to protect the cultural assumptions of a group of people) or positive adjustive changes (the culture works to revise the cultural assumptions of a group of people). Thus, it may be argued that teacher cultures act to either maintain or challenge the status quo. This is most evident when we consider teachers' engagement with educational change and the tendency of teacher cultures towards negative adjustive changes that have been broadly (and perhaps unfairly) labelled as teacher resistance to change. Teacher cultures, therefore, are not merely sets of values, beliefs and representations; they are also 'regular modes of action and patterns of interaction that teachers internalise, produce and reproduce during (and as a result of) their work experiences' (De Lima 1997: 44).

See also: culture; pedagogy; school culture; teacher; teaching/teaching methods; teaching profession

Further reading

De Lima, J. (1997) 'Colleagues and friends: professional and personal relationships among teachers in two Portuguese secondary schools'. Unpublished Ph.D. thesis, Ontario Institute for Studies in Education, Toronto, Canada.

Feiman-Nemser, S. and Floden, R. E. (1986) 'The cultures of teaching'. In M. C. Wittrock (ed.) *Handbook of Research on Teaching*, New York: Macmillan Library Reference.

Grossman, P. L. and Stodolsky, S. S. (1995) 'Content as context: the role of school subjects in secondary school teaching', *Educational Researcher*, 24(8): 5–11.

Hargreaves, A. (1994) *Changing Teachers, Changing Times: Teachers' Work and Culture in the Postmodern Age*, London: Cassell.

Keesing, R. (1974) 'Theories of culture', *Annual Review of Anthropology*, 3: 72–97.

Lortie, D. C. (1973) 'Observations on teaching and work'. In R. W. M. Travers (ed.) *Second Handbook of Research on Teaching*, Chicago IL: Rand McNally.

——(1975) *Schoolteacher: A Sociological Study*, Chicago IL and London: University of Chicago Press.

CATHERINE HARRIS

TEACHER EDUCATION/TRAINING

Teacher education/training programmes generally comprise the following elements: the subject specialism to be taught by the trainee teacher (e.g. mathematics, English, geography); the foundation disciplines of educational studies which promote comprehension of teaching and learning (e.g. history, philosophy, psychology and sociology); professional studies focusing on such practical matters as classroom management; and the practicum or supervised teaching practice experience (Ben-Peretz 1994).

Courses of teacher education and training are typically either *concurrent*, where the subject specialism is studied simultaneously alongside elements of professional studies (e.g. in India and Israel), or *consecutive*, where professional training occurs after subject courses leading to a university degree have been completed (e.g. in the Netherlands and Japan). Some countries, including the United Kingdom, offer both models. The relative merits of these approaches continue to be debated, but one extensive review of American research found a positive relationship between teachers' subject knowledge, their teaching quality and the attainment levels of those they teach, especially in mathematics, science and reading. However, there is evidence of a threshold, beyond which additional subject matter courses for teachers have a minimal effect on students' knowledge (Wilson *et al.* 2001).

The value placed upon foundation disciplines and professional studies is frequently judged in regard to their relevance to practical teaching. Training programmes have, for example, frequently been criticised for being over-theoretical and insufficiently focused on the realities of urban, multicultural schooling (Zeichner 2003). The practicum, by contrast, is the course component which many countries view most favourably, though the time devoted to teaching practice varies greatly between, and sometimes within, countries.

In countries where teaching is regarded as a high-status occupation, and where the financial rewards compare well with those of other graduate professions, entry to teacher training courses is competitive. This is not the case everywhere, however. Poor professional status

and pay can be detrimental to recruitment, leaving training course places unfilled. Many countries have, for example, experienced difficulties in recruiting teachers of science, mathematics and languages, although the calibre of applicants for teacher training courses typically improves during economic downturns, when private sector graduate employment becomes more uncertain. Once widely seen as a 'job for life', Zeichner (2003) reported that a majority of teachers trained in the United States of American leave the profession within three years of completing their training, with the exodus from low-achieving schools and posts in special education being especially strong.

The role of teacher educators in relation to their students is analogous to that of teachers and pupils. Contrasting models of teacher educator have been identified (see Jackson 1975; Ducharme 1986), reflecting the ambiguity of a role which, according to Ben-Peretz (2001), is 'impossible'. Expectations that teacher educators will administer to the extensive professional and personal needs of pre-service teachers, and to the teaching profession, frequently conflict with external demands, constraints and forces of de-professionalisation.

A range of other factors influences the type and quality of teacher education. These include: the *location* in which the programme is offered (e.g. university, college of education, school); the *social context* of the training provider and programme (including course numbers, gender balance, cultural diversity, ideological perspectives and programme ethos); *administrative dimensions* (such as policies and strategies which regulate and sustain programme quality and the nature of central government influence and control); and *evaluation procedures* (relating to the course provider, its staff and the teachers emerging from the programme).

Kennedy (1999) argues that both craft knowledge, based on experience, and propositional, theoretical knowledge are necessary for teacher education and the future of teaching. 'Discourses of derision' surround teacher education at a global level, yet the once widely held view that good teachers are 'born, not made' is rarely voiced today. The argument that a high-quality teaching force can only result from investment in high-quality teacher preparation programmes remains compelling.

See also: continued/continuing professional development; education/educational studies; profession/professionalism/professionalisation; teaching profession

Further reading

Ben-Peretz, M. (1994) 'Teacher education programs: curriculum'. In T. Husen and T. N. Postworth (eds) *The International Encyclopedia of Education*, 2nd edn, vol. 10, Oxford: Pergamon Press.

——(2001) 'The impossible role of teacher educators in a changing world', *Journal of Teacher Education*, 51(1): 48–56.

Ducharme, E. R. (1986) *Teacher Educators: What Do We Know?* ERIC Digest 15. Washington DC: ERIC.

Jackson, P. (1975) 'Divided we stand: observations on the internal organization of the education professoriate'. In A. Bagely (ed.) *The Professor of Education: An Assessment of Condition*, Minneapolis MN: University of Minnesota Press.

Kennedy, M. M. (1999) 'Schools and the problem of knowledge'. In J. D. Raths and A. C. McAninch (eds) *What Counts as Knowledge in Teacher Education*, Stanford CA: Ablex.

Wilson, S. M., Floden, R. E. and Ferrini-Mundy, J. (2001) *Teacher Preparation Research: Current Knowledge, Gaps, and Recommendations*, Washington DC: Centre for the Study of Teaching and Policy.

Zeichner, K. M. (2003) 'The adequacies and inadequacies of three current strategies to recruit, prepare, and retain the best teachers for all students', *Teachers College Record*, 105(3): 490–519.

MIRIAM BEN-PERETZ AND BILLIE EILAM

TEACHER UNIONS

Similar to other public and private sector workers, teachers employed in state schooling systems in most nations also belong to associations, federations or unions, whose primary purpose (stated or otherwise) is to protect and enhance the material conditions of teachers' work (salaries and benefits, pensions, job security, working conditions, etc.). Not surprisingly perhaps, in many jurisdictions these organisations first came into existence soon after the formation of centralised schooling systems, as teachers began to feel the effects of formal control by the state (Blum 1969; Cooper 1992). Certainly by the start of the twentieth century, teacher unions were in existence in most nations, although, then and now, their mandates and capacities to engage in protective activity have largely been circumscribed by state regulation.

In some jurisdictions full labour rights are provided, requiring employers to bargain for a range of issues (salaries, benefits, hours of work, numbers and sizes of classes, etc.) and to allow for arbitration and/or industrial action (e.g. work to rule; strikes) where negotiations break down. In others, state regulations limit (or preclude) negotiation rights and access to sanctions, leaving unions to work mainly in the area of teacher professional development, supporting individual teachers in difficulty, and lobbying government for more beneficial legislation, regulation and funding.

Over the years teacher unions and their members have also debated about engagement with a number of broader themes, mandates and tensions: issues such as promoting the larger 'cause of education'; relations with other labour organisations and political parties; relations with parent and community organisations; supporting larger social movements relating to issues such as child poverty, gender/race equity, etc.; support for/opposition to government domestic and foreign policy, and so on (Peterson 1993). In many ways, the nature and level of support for/opposition to these larger themes (as well as for determining the level of militancy in negotiating contracts), can be related to the nature of the teacher membership itself, including issues of individual teacher identity (gender, race, age, class location, status in the schooling system), which in turn are not unrelated to the influences of professionalisation and its elitist affectations (Derber *et al.* 1990).

Teachers relations with the state have always been complex, particularly given the purpose of state schooling systems in promoting proper citizenship among the young, and the importance of teachers in adhering to this role (Lawn 1987). In more totalitarian regimes, teacher unions – and particularly their leadership – have typically been allied with, if not closely controlled by, the ruling regimes. However, it is important to note that, even in the most democratic nations, teacher unions exist, and exert power, largely to the extent government legislation allows them to do so. In Canada, for example, teachers in virtually all public elementary and secondary schools must belong to a specific union which is designated by provincial government legislation: a decree which also embeds the constitution, bylaws and regulations of these organisations.

More recently, teacher union leaders, activists and academics have been embroiled in debates over whether unions and their members should adopt a more professional mode of relations with their employers, rather than adhering to industrial unionism values and practices (Kerchner and Mitchell 1988; Barber 1992). Labelled third generation or new teacher unionism , advocates call for less confrontation and more collaboration with employers and their school reform initiatives, and advocate for agreements which include more individual teacher accountability and reward, peer-review of practice, and more teacher-work flexibility in school schedules. On the other hand, opponents call attention to the larger looming context of neo-liberal political economy, the overall diminution of the social aspects of the public sector, and concern for the further individualising and privatising of what should remain a truly public and

shared endeavour (Lawn 1990; Urban 1991; Stevenson 2005). Interestingly, even seeming proponents of cooperativism continue to harken on the need for continued attention to the material and social concerns of the teacher membership at large, even if union leaders are also considering venturing into these new waters (McDonnell and Pascal 1988; Meyer 2005).

See also: profession/professionalism/professionalisation; teacher; teaching profession

Further reading

Barber, M. (1992) *Education and the Teacher Unions*, London: Cassell.
Blum, A. (1969) *Teacher Unions and Associations: A Comparative Study*, Urbana IL: University of Illinois Press.
Cooper, B. C. (ed.) (1992) *Labor relations in education: An International Perspective*, Westport CT: Greenwood Press.
Derber, C., Schwartz, W. A. and Magrass, Y. (1990) *Power in the Highest Degree: Professionals and the Rise of a New Mandarin Order*, New York and Oxford: Oxford University Press.
Kerchner, C. T. and Mitchell, D. E. (1988) *The Changing Idea of A Teachers' Union*, London: Falmer Press.
Lawn, M. (1987) *Servants of the State*, Lewes: Falmer.
——(1990) 'Re-inventing the polite trade union? A new teacher unionism for the nineties in England and Wales'. Unpublished paper.
McDonnell, L. and Pascal, A. (1988) *Teacher Unions and Educational Reform*, Los Angeles CA: Rand Corporation.
Meyer, H-D. (2005) 'Trade, profession or entrepreneurs? The market faithful raise important questions about the future of teacher unions', *American Journal of Education*, 112: 138–43.
Peterson, B. (1993) 'Which side are you on? A reflection on the role of teacher unions', *Rethinking Schools*, 8(1): 12–13.
Stevenson, H. (2005) 'From "school correspondent" to workplace bargainer? The changing role of the school union representative', *British Journal of Sociology of Education*, 26(2): 219–33.
Urban, W. (1991) 'Is there a new teacher unionism?', *Educational Theory*, 41(3): 331–38.

HARRY SMALLER

TEACHING/TEACHING METHODS

Teaching describes the process of educating or instructing learners. It is sometimes represented as an art or science, in which context pedagogy is a synonym. In formal learning, teaching is undertaken by those who work as, for example, instructors, lecturers, teachers and tutors, but teaching is not only undertaken by education specialists. For example, the work of religious leaders involves doctrinal teaching and, in the course of their work, members of the emergency services teach about safety and security, sometimes addressing school children or adult community groups. It is frequently maintained that children learn more out of school than in school. For better or worse, children may learn more from the teaching of their parents, siblings and peer groups than they do from their teachers at school. Teaching also refers to the profession to which teachers belong. Many maintain that teaching is on a par with such professions as law and medicine, though the financial rewards and status attached to these latter careers are typically greater.

Classroom teaching methods may be defined as pedagogical strategies used in teaching. Such approaches may, for example, involve individualised learning, small group work and whole-class teaching. In higher education, lecturing is a teaching method used to impart information, ideas and argument to large groups of learners, while seminars and tutorials allow tutors to follow up lectures with groups and individual students. Educators, especially in schools, frequently draw up a schedule – known in schools as a lesson plan – detailing the teaching methods to be deployed during a class, their sequence, timing and respective contributions to the teaching and learning objectives. For example, the teaching methods used for a particular class may include a lecture-style introduction to the topic making use of visual aids, the posing of questions for small group discussions, plenary feedback on those discussions, student completion of a textbook exercise and concluding remarks by the teacher. In schools, such a plan may involve additional provision for learners with special educational needs and gifted students.

See also: individualised instruction/personalised learning; instruction; lecture/lecturer; lesson; pedagogy; teaching profession; visual aids

DAVID CROOK

TEACHING ASSISTANT

At an international level, higher education institutions frequently employ graduate teaching assistants. Their duties are likely to be defined by departmental needs and may include assessment and marking, assistance with laboratory experiments, leading group discussions and teaching undergraduate classes. Working as a teaching assistant may offer valuable experience for the graduate student wishing to pursue a career in the academy. For universities there are cost savings, though institutional guidelines normally limit the maximum number of weekly hours that a teaching assistant may work.

Teaching assistants, sometimes known as classroom assistants, are also to be found working, often in a part-time or sessional capacity, in schools. Here, the teaching assistant is unlikely to be a graduate, but will be expected to be of good character with a sound command of literacy and numeracy. In the school setting, a teaching assistant's duties may include reading to pupils and listening to children read, intensively working with special needs students, supervising play and mealtimes and helping the teacher with such ancillary tasks as photocopying and stapling. Unlike teachers, it is unusual for school teaching assistants to be paid during vacations, but in the United Kingdom opportunities for higher-level posts with more favourable employment conditions have recently emerged. Many countries operate teaching assistant programmes which recruit foreign language teachers from abroad, normally to work in secondary schools.

Typically, native undergraduate or graduate linguists are appointed to a one-year paid teaching assistant placement, working alongside the school's foreign language teachers.

See also: higher education; school; teacher; teaching/teaching methods; teaching profession

DAVID CROOK

TEACHING PROFESSION

'Teaching profession' is a generic label for the group of workers who are employed to educate or train students, whether in schools or other settings. More narrowly, it is sometimes used to identify a particular group of teachers who meet certain prescribed criteria, for example through possessing particular credentials, having membership of particular organisations or being employed in particular institutions. More ideologically, the term is employed in different ways to signal, extol, promote and/or enforce particular forms of status, knowledge, values, beliefs and behaviours.

Historically, the term 'profession' has been used to identify or describe occupational groups possessing a set of particular (but often shifting) 'attributes', such as extensive training, specialised knowledge and skills, certification or licensing, service to people, membership of a professional organisation or being bound by ethical codes. The so-called 'classical' professions are those such as medicine and law, which have been able to garner state support for legislation, allowing them the power to control (or 'self-regulate') such attributes as training, certification, conditions, standards of practice and workplace autonomy. A number of 'functionalist' sociologists have contended over the years that teachers also fulfil most, or all, of these 'classical attributes'. In most parts of the world, however, governments have been very reluctant to legislate for teachers' self-regulation or workplace autonomy.

Given this lack of congruence between functionalist theories and the real world of teachers, other approaches have been attempted to explain the existence, nature and power of 'professionalism'. One approach has been that of 'interactionism' (symbolic and otherwise) – attempting to understand the concept from the point of view of the actors (i.e. teachers) themselves. As Joseph Blasé has noted, 'This perspective, in brief, argues that although social factors affect behaviour, individuals act on the basis of meanings associated with social interaction' (1988: 126). Implicit in the interactionist argument is that teachers themselves are largely responsible for the construction and maintenance of 'professionalism', its powers and its contingencies.

By comparison, stratification and social conflict theorists, among others, argue that 'professionalisation' is much more structural in nature, and can be understood more completely through historical and socio-political analysis. It is no surprise, some argue, that the term 'profession' came to prominence during an era of major social unrest occasioned by the Industrial Revolution. The rise of middle-class skilled workers, including teachers as 'servants of the State' (Lawn 1987), was a means of developing state bureaucracies, and there developed a mutual dependency between the 'modern state professional' and the state itself (Ozga and Lawn 1981: 19). However, while governments were prepared to trade 'autonomy' provisions for workers in fields such as law, health and engineering, teachers constituted much more of a problem for state officials. On the one hand, given the socialisation agenda ascribed to the rise of state schooling systems, it was important that teachers should present themselves as 'professional role models' to youth. But governments have also frequently wished to exercise strong controls over teachers' training and practice. To this day, teachers in many parts of the world still struggle against these historically tight regulations and controls over their work.

Critical sociologists have noted the ways in which the discourses attached to these traditional forms of 'teacher professionalism' have encompassed very gendered and 'deracialised' interpretations (Troyna 1994; Acker 1999). It has also been argued that, with the increasing neo-liberal restructuring of state schooling in many nations, meanings of 'professionalism' have also shifted, sacrificing the collective ethos explicit in traditional professional cultures to the 'market turn' of contemporary schooling (Burbules and Torres 2000; Mahony and Hextall 2000).

See also: profession/professionalism/professionalisation; teacher; teacher education/training; teacher unions; teaching/teaching methods

Further reading

Acker, S. (1999) *Realities of Teachers' Work: Never a Dull Moment*, London: Cassell.

Blasé, J. (1988) 'The everyday political perspective of teachers: vulnerability and conservatism', *Qualitative Studies in Education*, 1(2): 125–42.

Burbules, N. and Torres, C. (2000) *Globalization and Education: Critical Perspectives*, London: Routledge.

Lawn, M. (1987) *Servants of the State: The Contested Control of Teaching, 1900–1930*, London: Falmer Press.

Mahony, P. and Hextall, I. (2000) *Reconstructing Teaching: Standards, Performance and Accountability*, London: RoutledgeFalmer.

Ozga, J. and Lawn, M. (1981) *Teachers, Professionalism and Class*, London: Hutchinson.

Troyna, B. (1994) 'The "everyday world" of teachers? Deracialized discourses in the sociology of teachers and the teaching profession', *British Journal of Sociology of Education*, 15(3): 325–39.

HARRY SMALLER

TECHNICAL EDUCATION/SCHOOL/ COLLEGE

The official aims of technical education are to promote the national economy and the development of industry and commerce by improving the efficiency of employees in branches of industry and commerce. These aims are implemented through instruction in the knowledge and skills relevant either to specific occupations or to a group of occupations in a particular industry. Thus, a technical course typically provides education in the related scientific principles and in many cases instruction in the practice of the trade or occupation. Successful completion of such courses normally leads to the award of a technical qualification by a recognised body or agency.

The courses can be attended on a full-time or a part-time basis. In England, technical education was for a long time a 'night school' affair in which workers attended classes in the evenings after the day's work, usually with no support from their employers. In these circumstances the purposes of the courses were likely to have as much to do with the workers' desire for self-improvement, making up for minimal education earlier in their lives and aspirations for social mobility through getting a better job. More recently, in the belief that the technical education of workers can contribute to the efficiency of their enterprise, employers have been willing to release employees from the workplace during the day, or in a small number of cases, release for longer periods of study.

Technical education is historically related to apprenticeship, whether in the shape of a formal indenture or an informal learnership and in that it has been seen as the means whereby some elements of education and training for skilled employment, in the changed conditions of modern industry, have been transferred from the workplace to an educational institution. Such components include the teaching of mathematics and calculations, and science as they relate to the skilled trade in question. In business studies programmes relevant aspects of economics, accounting, commercial law and marketing, for example, would make up the students' course of study.

Organised technical education was a product of the nineteenth century. Earlier institutional developments in the form of charitable provision for orphans and the children of the poor and destitute, as in Schools of Industry in England, were designed to reduce pauperism and the burdens of poor relief. These provided instruction, mainly for girls, in domestic skills and, in some cases,

591

in literacy and numeracy. The association of technical skills and education with the poor and lower social classes has been one cause of its low status and esteem in many countries.

As national systems of education developed, the range of institutions making provision for technical education increased. These tended to reflect different levels or strata within the labour force for which different courses were designed. Early provision of technical education was aimed at manual workers whose training in craft skills was believed to have been worst affected by the decline in apprenticeship resulting from industrialisation and mass production. Development of technical institutions had to wait upon the establishment of elementary schooling as a necessary and minimum foundation of technical education. The earlier development of compulsory education for all in France and Germany is shown in the creation of *écoles des arts et métiers* and *Berufschule* in the first half of the nineteenth century. The first technical colleges in England were established in the 1890s.

In many countries a form of full-time, pre-employment technical education as a part of secondary education has been developed. These, too, were presented as a means of replacing apprenticeship to some extent, or, at least, as a way of preparing pupils for entry into apprenticeship. In addition to this clearly economic justification, these schools have also been seen as providing a modern post-primary or secondary education, which was more appropriate to the realities of industrial societies than the literary curriculum of the traditional grammar school. The *Realschule* in Germany is an example of this, whereas in England the secondary technical school, as a successor to the pre-war junior technical school, was not developed in numbers sufficient to challenge the dominant position of the secondary grammar school and was lost in the reorganisation of secondary education along comprehensive lines from the 1960s onwards. In France, the technological

Baccalaureate has been introduced recently as an alternative course of study and leaving qualification for secondary school students.

A third form of technical education is its presence as part of higher education. In English-speaking contexts this has been referred to as technological education, that is, something more advanced than technical education. In European countries this provision, intended to supply qualified personnel in technology and applied science, was, like other variants of 'technical', planned into national schemes for education and training – the *Technische Hochschule* in Germany, for instance, were developed from the early nineteenth century. In England, advanced technical education has taken place alongside the other forms described above, often as part-time study, with or without the support of employers, for those already in employment. As the volume and proportion of these higher courses increased, some technical institutions in England and Wales were given a distinct status at the apex of the technical college sector; this was the case with the colleges of advanced technology designated in the 1950s, and the 'new' polytechnics designated in the late 1960s.

In this formative period of technical education, the focus of policy and provision was on identified groups of the workforce whose performance in their skilled crafts or in the applications of science to production was seen to be dependent on technical education and training. Consequently, the target population was historically relatively small in most countries. The exception to this general rule was Germany or Prussia where, from the 1890s, it has been compulsory for employers to release their young workers up to the age of eighteen to attend *Fortbildungschule* (continuation schools), the curriculum of which combines further general education with technical and job-related studies. The particular conditions which contributed to this German development were the central role accorded to education and training in the cause of nation building and the role of the active state in developing the competitive economy. Legislation requiring the participation of employers' associations (*Handelskammer*) in local arrangements required the building of the social partnership approach to economic planning, training and industrial relations which is common in Western European societies and particularly strong in Germany.

Since the 1980s technical education as a term and concept would appear to have given place to vocational education and training (VET) in policy discourse and in general usage. In England and Wales, the colleges of further education generally have ceased to refer to themselves as technical colleges and, instead, style themselves simply as college. The reasons for the decreasing use of technical education may well include the view that, as a concept, it is restrictive. Generally its beneficiaries were at the beginning of their working lives, and were those destined for skilled manual or routine clerical employment, and the majority were males. Given recent changes in the world economy, especially during the last twenty years or so, and changes in production and national labour markets leading to frequent changes of job during workers' lifetimes, governments are increasingly taking a wider view of work-related education and training. Technological development has taken away many of the old skilled occupations and created new employments not included in former systems of technical education. The new discourse of VET emphasises the need for all workers to have functional skills of literacy and numeracy as the requisite employability skills of the flexible worker in a changing economy and labour market. Rather than providing a training and a qualification for life, current policies assume the need for periods of retraining during the working life, and that access to training opportunities should be made more equal by the social inclusion of those citizens who would not in the past have participated in courses of technical education.

See also: apprenticeship; further education; higher education; polytechnic; secondary school/education; vocational education; work–based/work–located/workplace/work–related learning; workers' education

Further reading

Bailey, B. (2002) 'Further education'. In R. Aldrich (ed.) *A Century of Education*, London: Routledge.

Hayward, G. and James, S. (eds) (2004) *Balancing the Skills Equation*, Bristol: Policy Press.

Magnus, P. (1907) 'Technical education', *Encyclopaedia Britannica*, 11th edn, Cambridge: Cambridge University Press.

Millis, C. T. (1925) *Technical Education*, London: Edward Arnold.

Reeder, D. (1979) 'A recurring debate: education and industry'. In G. Bernbaum (ed.) *Schooling in Decline*, London: Macmillan.

BILL BAILEY

TECHNOCRAT/TECHNOCRATIC/ TECHNOCRACY

'Technocrat' can be defined as a technological expert in administration, management, and related leadership positions. A technocrat can be a highly trained and highly skilled bureaucrat, or a functionary in an organisation, who makes policy decisions based solely on empirical evidence and technical information, rather than personal opinion. A technocrat can be administrator who is motivated by efficiency, effectiveness and quality control. In a derogatory sense, it refers to a person with technical knowledge/skills whose strategic goal is to advance the system at the expense of the individual: someone for whom the end justifies the means.

Hence, technocratic refers to a leadership style by an individual in a position of power. One could speak of technocratic styles of governance, policy making, and technocratic behaviour by senior executives. Another usage is that of technocratic discourse in public policy, trade, foreign affairs, health, and education. Technocratic leadership may be responding more to globalisation and the markets, rather than the welfare of the people. Technocratic styles of leadership and policy making can weaken democracy, especially in some societies that have adopted efficiency-driven neo-liberal and conservative policies.

'Technocracy' can be defined as a rule and ubiquitous dominance of technology in technologically and industrially advanced societies, where technology plays a central role in every day life. 'Technocracy' comes from the Greek, and the philosophy of Aristotle, where *tekhne* (techno) is skill, or practical knowledge, and *kratos* (cracy) refers to power. The origins of technocracy can be found in Francis Bacon, who, in his *New Atlantis* (1627), predicted a futuristic society, based on the rule of scientists. Both Auguste Comte and his positivism, and Saint-Simon, argued for scientific method and approach to the study of society, and its mode of governance, and could be regarded as the first-generation 'technocrats'.

Edward Bellamy's (1899) novel, *Looking Backward*, described the future of America in 1999, where a utopian society offered the good life and work for all. This new world was governed by the scientific and technological organisation of work, and inspired the technocractic movement that followed later in the 1930s. Koestler's *The Act of Creation* (1964), like Zamiatin's *We* (1921), and Huxley's *Brave New World* (1932) are dedicated to technocracy, a futuristic world dominated by a technologically advanced culture, and where meritocracy has evolved into technocracy and the new technocratic class. Zamiatin's science fiction novel is a metaphor for 'The One State', where technology is supreme, and the citizens of a glass city are under the constant surveillance of a technocratic political elite.

The origins of the technocracy movement may be traced to Frederick W. Taylor and his *The Principles of Scientific Management* (1911). Taylor was an American engineer who sought to improve industrial efficiency. As an advocate of the 'efficiency movement', he was called by many 'The Father of Scientific Management'. The modern term was coined by an American engineer, W. H. Smith, in 1919, and was popularised in 1941 by James Burham, a management expert, in his book *Managerial Revolution*. Thorstein Veblen also believed that a technical elite could better manage society and its economy. The term was widely used to describe economics and politics, and now generally refers to an educated elite which governs through use of technology/technological knowledge. It is close to the Weberian notion of ideal type of bureaucracy, where the elite, selected by meritocratic process, on the basis of education and expertise are allocated specific roles and authority.

Technocracy, in general, refers to a system of governance, based on the rule of experts, rather than principles of democracy. Technocracy, rather than democracy, is re-emerging, as a dominant neo-conservative politico-economic ideology, in a number of countries, including the USA, Canada, Japan, China, and the Russian Federation. In this sense, technocracy is opposing democracy. Hence, the term may have either positive or negative connotations.

The teleological goal of a technocratic society is to ensure, as in utilitarianism, the greatest happiness of the greatest number, by means of technological progress, and to provide the highest standard of living possible for all in the future. Technocracy was used by Neil Postman to describe a social organisation where technological and scientific applications play a central part in the decision making process.

Modern technology can be viewed as the inevitable and 'natural' evolution of the processes in society whereby science has become the servant of technology. Taken to its extreme, technocracy can lead to 'technodeterminism', or the increasing domination of society by technology (Bowen 2005).

See also: centralisation/decentralisation; democracy; elitism; ideology; managerialism; meritocracy; science/science education; technology

Further reading

Bowen, J. (2005) 'Environmental imperatives for the twenty first century'. In J. Bowen (ed.) *Environment Education: Imperatives for the 21st Century*, Melbourne VIC: James Nicholas Publishers.

Fischer, F. (1990). *Technocracy and the Politics of Expertise*, Newbury Park CA: Sage.

McAvoy, G. E. (1999). *Controlling Technocracy: Citizen Rationality and the Nimby Syndrome*, Washington DC: Georgetown University Press.

Radaelli, C. M. (1999) *Technocracy in the European Union*, London: Longman.

JOSEPH ZAJDA AND REA ZAJDA

TECHNOLOGY

'Technology' encompasses a broad semiotic field. Applied variously to the discovery and use of fire by early humans, through mechanical innovations like the printing press, from the robotic arms used to repair satellites in outer space, through human genomic research, to digital codes for creating and inhabiting virtual worlds, 'technology' includes the tool, the activities surrounding the tool, and knowledge (cultural and social) of the tool, its communities, and its practices. However variously it has been applied, the term 'technology' has its roots in the Greek word *techne*, once referring to the art, craft or skill in the production of an object. In this sense, *techne* has always signified the larger, materially embodied and socially situated production process usually overseen by skilled craft workers, like those adept in pottery production or sword making. Most recently, however, technology seems to have become the default term for the technological subset of computers in many educational authorities' curriculum directives, and also popular magazines and newspapers.

There are many significant points of convergence between education and technology; indeed education itself has been argued to be a technology 'of the self' (Foucault 1988). That is, education has historically focused on the formation and improvement of the self.

But whether that self be a 'good citizen' or a 'good worker', education's very production of the self is a kind of technological relation which philosophers like Martin Heidegger problematised as 'a resource that aims at efficiency' driven towards 'the maximum yield at the minimum expense' (Heidegger 1977). More recently J-P. Lyotard has elaborated a thoroughgoing technologisation of education in which knowledge is commodified: 'Knowledge will be produced in order to be sold, it is and will be consumed in order to be valorised in a new production: in both cases the goal is exchange' (1984). Technology in this sense is linked closely to notions of capitalist production, whether that is school-based or workforce-based (Ford assembly lines). The blackboard was a technological innovation that allowed teachers to focus and channel students' attention in the classroom. Required under new technology-driven imperatives to maximise attentional input more efficiently, teachers themselves are constructed as a re-tooled technology of information delivery. The blackboard and the whiteboard are technologies that facilitate the administrative and managerial functions of institutionalised public schooling, in contrast to those that constitute 'tools of intellect' (Bruner and Olson 1977) such as literacy and computation, which support the development, preservation, and transmission of 'worthwhile knowledge' in education.

Most commonly, technology is understood as any tool that enables the making of something, and is in this sense primarily an artefact. But artefacts are not utilised in isolation: in fact, a whole system of practices accords them meaning and enables their use. On this view, technology is most aptly seen as a system of practice, meaning its artefacts and the uses of those artefacts are inseparable (Franklin 1999). In school settings, the narrower sense of technology as a tool persists and refers to computers and other digital artefacts (e.g. the internet, websites).

In the curriculum, technology figures in two main ways: one as an emergent subject field which has partially replaced and reconfigured traditional school subjects; the other as a way of advancing learning and teaching; and in this latter sense it is important to understand that educational technologies have existed since the pointer, blackboard, and pencil. As a subject area, technology has been present in the school curriculum for some time: in woodworking, metallurgy, mechanics, and most recently in the development of computer courses (whether hardware- or software-focused). Here, the focus is on the tool itself (computers) and on the development of skills in relation to that tool (programming) in order to prepare an individual to better participate in a skilled labour force, resulting most recently in the often-heard call for the development of 'computer literacy' or 'technological literacy' by educational policy makers. A more integrative approach calls for technology to be 'implemented across the curriculum', as a supportive and essential tool for teaching and learning, in effect a 'new literacy'. This has resulted in cross-curricular integrative approaches that have students and teachers in arts, mathematics, science, and literature making use of computer technologies to enhance subject-area learning and as a key force in the reshaping of pedagogical practice, making it more 'student centred' and 'constructivist', i.e. focused on the active creation of a product by the student.

See also: computer-assisted learning; computer studies; educational technology; virtual learning

Further Reading

Bruner, J. S. and Olson, D. R. (1977) 'Symbols and texts as tools of the intellect', *Interchange*, 8(4): 1–15.
Cuban, L. (1985) *Teachers and Machines: The Classroom of Technology Since 1920*, New York: Teachers College Press.
Foucault, M.(1988) 'Technologies of the self'. In L. H. Martin, H. Gutman and P. H. Hutton (eds) *Technologies of the Self: A Seminar with Michel Foucault*, Amherst MA: University of Massachusetts Press.
Franklin, U. (1999) *The Real World of Technology*, Toronto: House of Anansi Press.
Heidegger, M. (1977) *The Question Concerning Technology and other Essays*, trans. William Lovitt, New York: Harper Torchbooks.
Lyotard, J-P. (1984) *The Postmodern Condition: A Report on Knowledge*, Manchester: Manchester University Press.
Papert, S. (1980) *Mindstorms: Children, Computers, Powerful Ideas*, New York: Basic Books.

JENNIFER JENSON

TERMAN, LEWIS MADISON (1877–1956)

An American pioneer of intelligence testing, Terman was largely self-educated, becoming a teacher in his teens. He proceeded to teacher training college in Danville, Indiana, graduating in 1898. He became Principal of Johnson County High School immediately after graduation, aged twenty-one, and was awarded a doctorate from Clark University, Massachusetts, in 1905 for his study of test results from groups of fourteen-year-olds. He moved for health reasons to California in 1906, becoming a high school principal and then professor of psychology and pedagogy at the State Normal School in Los Angeles. Later, from 1910 to 1942, he held various academic positions within the education faculty of Stanford University, serving for twenty years as head of the psychology department.

Terman adapted the Binet-Simon tests to an American setting. In *The Measurement of Intelligence* (1916), Terman outlined his thinking on the subject, coining the term 'intelligence quotient' or 'IQ'. His tests were used internationally in succeeding decades and Terman's work developing aptitude tests for US military recruits was similarly well known. His research findings helped to legitimate the grading system adopted in US high schools. Whilst at Stanford, Terman initiated a thirty-year longitudinal study of 1,500 students who achieved high IQ scores when young. His beliefs in inherited intelligence were outlined in his five-volume *Genetic Studies of Genius*, published from 1925 to 1959.

Terman believed in providing a separate education for the top 1 per cent of gifted children.

See also: giftedness; intelligence/intelligence tests; psychology of education

STEVEN COWAN

TERTIARY EDUCATION

The term 'tertiary' derives from the division in many national contexts of the state education system into three principal phases, with tertiary being the third of these (from Latin *tertiarus*, the third part). Primary and secondary schooling precedes tertiary education – also known as post-sixteen or post-compulsory education – in Britain. In a greatly contrasting national setting such as Zambia, however, the structure can be described as a '9–3–4' one, where the first nine years offer a basic (i.e. primary) education, the following three comprising a high school (i.e secondary) phase, and the last four offering tertiary education for that segment of the population able to access it.

Tertiary is sometimes used interchangeably with the term further education (FE). In reality, there is often a notable difference between the two, as generally speaking FE accommodates a higher proportion of learners focusing on vocational options, whereas tertiary tends to carry the connotation that an institution – and more broadly, the sector – has a more academic emphasis.

In national systems evidencing a relatively high degree of choice, the school curriculum may offer learners the option of staying on to study certain specialisms that are also available at tertiary level. In such an educational environment it is therefore possible to find certain courses of an identical nature offered in both schools and colleges.

In virtually all national settings, the development of a tertiary sector has lagged behind primary and secondary education. As economies expand, diversify away from primary production, and become more knowledge-dependent, so the need for a more highly skilled workforce will tend to stimulate the growth of tertiary education. In the case of the most highly developed nations – the so-called 'post-industrial' societies – there is typically a particularly pressing need for two categories of new entrants to the labour market. The first of these is represented by such highly skilled knowledge workers as information technology consultants, product designers and the teachers/trainers needed to develop expertise in others. The second category comprises the huge number of individuals who will be involved in the kinds of service industries that are generally called into being as a result of economic development, rising affluence and growing choice. Although membership of this group can sometimes be seen to include some relatively low-skilled occupations (e.g. caring, catering, health and beauty operatives, leisure industry staff, floristry) a number of these have become increasingly certificated and state-regulated. What is important is that tertiary-level institutions and training programmes have been called into being – and continue in the developed world especially to expand – to meet the needs of both sets of individuals. An expanding and more effective public sector has been observed to be very significant in generating demand for workers educated to tertiary level, for example, for positions in the civil service and health service.

The inception and growth of a tertiary education sector is a fundamental transformative ingredient of a society moving along a development continuum, from an overwhelmingly low-skills, largely agrarian stage to an urbanised, technology-dependent and high-consuming position. The latter stage is also, importantly, one typically displaying high participation levels in formal education well beyond the statutory minimum leaving age. We might, therefore, say that there is a link between the growth of tertiary education and the growth of aspirations. Put simply, opportunities for post-secondary learning tend to be a catalyst for individuals' learning aspirations.

See also: college; further education; higher education; secondary education; vocational education; work-based/work-located/workplace/work-related learning

Further reading

Skilbeck, M., Wagner, A. and Esnault, E. (1998) *Redefining Tertiary Education*, Paris: OECD.
World Bank (2002) *Constructing Knowledge Societies: New Challenges for Tertiary Education*, Washington DC: World Bank.

BRYAN CUNNINGHAM

TEST/TESTING

A test is a procedure for critical evaluation or assessment. Tests may be used to determine capability, competence, skill, proficiency or potential. They are not only used in educational settings: individuals are likely at some point in their lives to experience eyesight, hearing or other medical tests. Tests are used to determine competence to drive a car, and tests for accuracy in shorthand notation and typing speed may determine suitability for some types of employment.

In education, learners encounter tests – and examinations – intended to assess their knowledge, skills, understandings and abilities. On the basis of testing what students know, understand or can do, they may be allocated to one particular type of school rather than another, they may be moved from one class to another, and may be encouraged or required to change or abandon their programme of studies.

Educational tests range in complexity from simple pencil and paper exercises in basic arithmetic or spelling, true or false dilemmas and multiple-choice questions to complex problem-solving or experimental tasks. Specific examples of tests and testing approaches are the subject of several entries in this volume. Intelligence testing, in particular, is fraught with controversies about validity, reliability and objectivity, and it is sometimes claimed that tests reveal more about those administering the exercise than it does about the candidates.

See also: assessment; criterion-referenced tests; examinations; high-stakes testing; intelligence/intelligence tests; multiple-choice tests; norm-referenced tests; objective tests; standardised tests

DAVID CROOK

TEXTBOOK

Textbooks are a common resource in most educational environments. Even with the emergence of new forms of electronic media, the school textbook has endured as a popular teaching and learning tool. Often combining narrative text with diagrams, pictures and photographs, charts, and end-of-section questions, modern textbooks continue to represent a practical and conveniently packaged source of knowledge and information across subject areas.

The pedagogical function of the school textbook has changed over time. Where traditionally it played the role of key syllabus tool, central to the planning and delivery of lessons, textbooks now tend to be used as one resource among several others. This development can be traced back to pedagogical and disciplinary innovations that began in the 1960s and 1970s, when traditional emphases on rote learning, in which students were encouraged to memorise knowledge, were replaced by new approaches that valued creativity, critical thinking and interpretation (Marsden 2001). These developments influenced the internal layout of many textbooks. Where a single authoritative narrative often dominated traditional schoolbooks, modern textbooks typically include far more source materials, illustrative examples, and suggestions for activities, designed to encourage students to engage with content and perspectives.

The role and function of school textbooks vary considerably across international settings. In Japan, China and many East Asian societies, for example, the textbook continues to play a central role in classes, forming the basis for syllabi in many subjects. Routinely the teacher's role is to teach the textbook. With education geared to passing university entrance examinations that emphasise knowledge retention, students are required to memorise textbook information in preparation for the all-important tests. Likewise, in the United States, high school subjects tend to be dominated by survey courses in which 'general knowledge' and breadth are emphasised. School subject textbooks in the United States are often large, some in excess of 1,000 pages. With the need to cover an extensive range of content over relatively short periods of time, teaching and learning activities are often centred on the textbook. In contrast, the use of textbooks in countries such as Sweden varies widely across classrooms. This is due in part to the highly decentralised nature of the Swedish education system, where teachers are encouraged to design their own syllabi, often in consultation with students. Swedish schoolbooks typically are small, designed to complement teaching and learning.

Textbooks are the product and effect of various political and market-driven pressures and interests. In England and Wales, for example, publishers operate in a competitive free market, with teachers free to choose books as they see fit. However, to be marketable, publications must conform to the dictates of the highly prescriptive national curriculum and the external examination boards. In Japan, curriculum guidelines are decentralised and assessment internal. However, only textbooks that have received official government approval may be used in schools. In many Southern and Western states of the USA, adoption committees are appointed to evaluate textbooks for use in local schools. Approved textbooks in large states such as Texas and California tend to dominate markets to such an extent that they become a popular choice across other states, even those in the North and East of the country where the textbook market is more liberal. As several commentators have pointed

out, textbook publishers seek to maximise profits according to demand within context-specific political constraints (Apple and Christian-Smith 1991).

Textbook research is a growing field. Work to date has been dominated by analyses of history, geography and civics textbooks across international settings. Projects supported by supra-national bodies such as UNESCO and the Council of Europe have been driven by humanitarian concerns (Pingel 1999). In 1986 the Council of Europe addressed the problem of 'misrepresentation' in school history textbooks across member states of what was then the European Economic Community (Council of Europe 1986). In the United States, researchers such as Michael Apple have attempted to construct a critical theory of the school textbook.

The Georg Eckert Institute in Braunschweig, Germany (www.gei.de) is, arguably, the world centre for school textbook research. The Institute includes a textbook library of approximately 100,000 volumes from over eighty nations and is responsible for the organisation of international conferences on a regular basis.

See also: curriculum; educational publishing; pedagogy; subjects; syllabus

Further reading

Apple, M. and Christian-Smith, L. (eds) (1991) *The Politics of the Textbook*, New York: Routledge.
Council of Europe (1986) *Against Bias and Prejudice: The Council of Europe's Work on History Teaching and History Textbooks: Recommendations on History Teaching and History Textbooks Adopted at Council of Europe Conferences and Symposia, 1953–1983*, Strasbourg: Council of Europe.
Marsden, W. E. (2001) *The School Textbook: Geography, History and Social Studies*, London: Woburn Press.
Pingel, F. (1999) *UNESCO Guidebook on Textbook Research and Textbook Revision*, Hanover: Verlag Hahnsche Buchhandlung.

STUART FOSTER AND JASON NICHOLLS

THELWALL, JOHN (1764–1834)

The founder of educational speech therapy, Thelwall became famous in 1794, after being arrested and then acquitted for treason. He was one of the most prominent speakers and leaders of the London Corresponding Society. Thelwall established a reputation from his public lectures, which were conducted from rooms off the Strand in London, which influenced a generation of working-class intellectuals, many of whom were to become the first recognisable leaders of the British labour movement. The impact of his lectures was such that Prime Minister Pitt framed the Seditious Meetings Act specifically with a view to proscribing Thelwall's educational work. A recognised poet, he influenced Wordsworth and Coleridge in their early years as writers. After attempting farming in rural Wales, he began speaking and elocution courses in Lancashire, eventually returning to London in 1806 to establish a school in Bedford Place, near the British Museum where, in addition to teaching oratory he treated clients with speech impediments. In his *Letter to Henry Cline* (1810), Thelwall outlined in detail his theory and practice of speech therapy, accompanied by case studies. In the book he outlines his arguments for the bases of speech disorders. His breakthrough came with understanding that behind speech impediments there lay a combination of physiological, psychological and educational factors and that each person presented particular combinations of these. Equally importantly, he argued for the belief that through training and 'action' most speech impediments could be treated. Thelwall was a prolific journal editor and author throughout his life.

See also: special education/special educational needs/special needs

STEVEN COWAN

THEOLOGY

'Theology' is rooted in two Greek words: *theos* and *logos*, meaning 'god' and 'word'. Literally, theology might be understood to be 'a word about God', or 'the Word of God'. It refers in customary English usage to the study of and reflection upon the teachings and practices of the Christian Church, although 'theology' is by no means the preserve of the Christian tradition, and might also be used to refer to faith communities, such as Muslims, Jews and Hindus. Within the Christian tradition, since the time of St Anselm (*c.*1033–1109) theology has been seen as the quest of 'faith seeking understanding' (*fides quaerens intellectum*). This approach distinguishes theology from the phenomenological methods of 'religious studies' or 'comparative religion', based upon the methods of anthropology and sociology. The philosophy of religion is another discipline akin to theology, which may either support or offer a critique of theological enquiry.

There are a variety of subdivisions or sub-disciplines in 'theology'. These include ethics, biblical studies, and Church history. A narrower understanding of theology focuses on Church teachings or dogmas is referred to as either 'systematic theology' or 'dogmatics'. 'Fundamental theology' a sub-discipline, particularly taught in Roman Catholic circles, refers to the study of preliminary questions of knowing (epistemology) and interpreting (hermeneutics) which frame the study of doctrine and practice. These philosophical questions have always preoccupied theologians, but following the Enlightenment such questions became key to the articulation of theology in the modern world and continue to be so in the light of postmodern philosophy.

A growing area of concern for theologians in the twentieth century was a clearer understanding of approaches to theology and their consequent methodological implications. One method relates to the desire to give an account of faith to others. This task is usually known as 'apologetics'. Famous examples of this endeavour may be seen in the first *Apologia* of Justin Martyr addressed to the Roman emperor Antonius Pius (*c*.150), John Calvin's *Institutes of the Christian Religion* (1539) addressed to Francis I, king of France, and the personal testimony of John Henry Newman's *Apologia pro vita sua* (1864). The landscape of theological method may be observed through the following brief genealogy. In 1984, George Lindbeck, in *The Nature of Doctrine*, explored the possibility of understanding doctrine not only in cognitive and propositional terms, but also as non-informative and non-discursive symbols of inner feelings or existential orientations. In this approach religious faith is understood as an aesthetic enterprise, a view which may be traced back to Schleiermacher (1768–1834). The publication of *Types of Christian Theology* in 1992 by Hans Frei highlighted differences in theologians' perspectives on and engagement with world views beyond the immediate world view of the Christian Tradition. Frei sets out a spectrum of possibilities. Thus, a conservative theologian eschews anything other than a Christian/Biblical world view, while those of a liberal or radical stance seek to engage to a greater or lesser extent with other perspectives, thus crafting their theological endeavour in relation, for example, to a particular philosophy. For instance Rudolf Bultmann (1884–1976) and John Macquarrie (1919–) explicitly craft their theological work in relation to the philosophy of Martin Heidegger (1889–1976), while Karl Barth (1886–1968) deliberately sets his face against any 'philosophical tints'. A classic theological method may be found in the works of Thomas Aquinas (*c*.1225–74) and Richard Hooker (1554–1600) in which three major resources: scripture, tradition and reason are brought together in what is sometimes referred to as a theological 'dance'. In other words, these three sources are given equal weight. This is contrary to classic Protestant method in which scripture is valued above any other resource, being understood as the revealed word of God. Eastern Orthodoxy brings

another perspective to this methodological spectrum, claiming that scripture is to be understood as 'written tradition' and tradition is 'unwritten Scripture'. John Wesley (1703–91) in the period of the Enlightenment, argued that 'experience' should be added to scripture, tradition and reason to form a 'quadrilateral'. This echoes the 'turn to the subject' in philosophy and such explicit recognition of the role of (religious) 'experience' has in the long term transformed the discipline of theology from being a discourse solely about the divine to one that also reflects upon the experience of having faith. A further transformation of the discipline occurred during the twentieth century, evinced in writers such as Jürgen Moltmann (1926–), who acknowledged the crucial role of context in the formation of theological understandings and perspectives. This recognition of context led to the emergence of liberation theologies in Latin America, South Africa, and India; and is also manifest in black and feminist theological movements.

See also: church; religious assembly; religious education; religious school; scholarship; scholasticism; subject

Further reading

Frei, H. W. (1992) *Types of Christian Theology*, New Haven CT and London: Yale University Press.

Lindbeck, G. A. (1984) *The Nature of Doctrine: Religion and Theology in a Postliberal Age*, London: SPCK.

Rahner, K. (1978) *Foundations of Christian Faith*, London: Darton Longman and Todd.

PAUL M. COLLINS

THESIS/DISSERTATION

In broad terms, a thesis may be a basic proposal or proposition intended to generate an argument. It is also a common title for a sustained piece of scholarly and academic writing produced to meet the requirements for the passing of a degree, in whole or in part. The term is often used as an alternative to 'dissertation' depending on the context. For the purposes of a doctorate, the thesis will often be made up of 80,000 words or more in the case of a Ph.D., or of 40,000 or 50,000 words if produced alongside taught coursework such as in a Doctor of Education degree. At this level, it will normally be expected to show evidence of systematic and rigorous research, and a substantive and original contribution to the literature on the chosen topic. At master's and undergraduate levels, the thesis or dissertation will be shorter, and while it is still expected to be systematic and rigorous in its approach, may be less fully developed in its methods, data, discussion, findings, and general conclusion. At doctoral level, following the submission of the thesis, it is usually defended by the student at an oral examination or viva voce before the degree may be awarded.

See also: degree; doctorate; oral examination

GARY McCULLOCH

THORNDIKE, EDWARD LEE (1874–1949)

Thorndike, the American psychologist, obtained a B.A., M.A. and Ph.D. from the Wesleyan University, Middletown, Connecticut within the space of four years, from 1895 to 1898. His doctorate focused on animal learning. Based on experiments with cats in a 'puzzle box', Thorndike developed ideas that anticipated B. F. Skinner's notions of operant conditioning. He argued that learning was aided by systems of reward and punishment, also believing that learning ought to be activity-based and the curriculum should be individualised, as far as possible. He held several senior academic positions at Columbia University from 1899 to 1942, where he pursued psychology and educational research. One of his many major public positions was as president of the American Psychological Association in 1912. Over a quarter of a century he conducted a debate with Charles Spearman about the nature of intelligence, with Thorndike arguing for 'connectionism',

a multi-faceted approach to the phenomenon, which contrasted with Spearman's conception of a single, unified factor. Thorndike developed approaches towards testing what he called 'social' and 'mechanical' intelligence, thereby laying a broader basis for later revisions of Terman's work. Thorndike was an extraordinarily prolific author who supplied a series of basic texts covering the entire range of possible applications and connections of psychology. His publications, including *The Principles of Teaching: Based on Psychology* (1906), *The Teacher's World Book* (1921), *The Fundamentals of Learning* (1932), and *Human Nature and the Social Order* (1940), gained readerships beyond academic institutions, and he also compiled dictionaries for children and adults.

See also: individualised instruction/personalised learning; intelligence/intelligence tests; psychology of education; Skinner, Burrhus Fredric; Spearman, Charles; Terman, Lewis Madison

STEVEN COWAN

TRAINING

Training is usually employed as a contrastive concept to education. It is associated either with vocational education or with the processes associated with the learning of habits and routines. So, for example, it is customary to speak of job training on the one hand and training children to brush their teeth on the other. Training is also used in the sense of *conditioning* where a repetitive process is applied to someone (or an animal) in order to achieve a desired behavioural result. Thus, rats may be conditioned to run through a maze. The position is further complicated because, while it makes sense to say of both animals and humans that they can be trained, it does not make sense to say that animals can be educated.

If training is associated only with conditioning, then it is hard to see what its educational value might be or even whether it is ethically desirable when applied to humans, given the lack of independence, let alone autonomy, that it implies. On this view, someone who is trained to do something is capable of little more than making an automatic response in appropriate circumstances. These considerations are reinforced by reflection on the human role in the workplace in many situations, where production line work practices and the division of labour require the learning of routines so repetitive that there is little scope for independence either in their learning or in their application. For these reasons, the idea that training is a desirable component of, or alternative to, education does not usually receive much favour in circles committed to liberal forms of education. Nevertheless, there are some who are prepared to allow that training has a role to play in education. Such a position has three identifiable sub-categories.

First, there are those who think that training and vocational education are largely the same. Those who take a competence-based view of the educational process are such a group, and they can be found amongst the adherents of such programmes as National Vocational Qualifications in the United Kingdom and the tradition of instrumental vocational education associated with David Snedden in the United States at the beginning of the twentieth century. Second, there are those who see the importance of training in moral education and think that the inculcation of appropriate reactions and behaviour are a precondition of the later transition to moral autonomy. Third, there are those, largely philosophers influenced by Wittgenstein, who hold that not just moral development but some of the more fundamental aspects of early human development presuppose training. Some have gone on to argue that training is not incompatible with autonomy or with a range of educational processes beyond earliest childhood, but is in fact a presupposition of their achievement.

Training is thus a complex concept that is apparently applicable to a range of human and animal activities. Its use in educational contexts is, however, contested both because of its alleged moral dubiousness and its overtones of authority (there are trainees and a trainer in an unequal relationship). Many educators in the progressive tradition, including Rousseau, who object to its apparently authoritarian overtones, have also opposed it. It is arguable, however, that those opposed to the use of training in educational contexts fail to distinguish clearly between what Ryle (1949) called *drilling*, on the one hand, and *training* on the other. To drill someone is to shape his or her behaviour like that of a rat in a maze. The goal of drilling is to produce an automatic, uniform and regular response. Thus, for example, one drills soldiers to slope arms.

Training, on the other hand, cannot be assimilated to drilling. There are many activities that not only require the confident application of routine procedures as in drilling, but also the use of independent and informed judgement in novel and unpredictable situations. To use Ryle's example, someone who is trained in map reading has got to be able to recognise and understand automatically the symbols on a map. However, the matching of the symbols to the terrain, locating oneself on the terrain and plotting a route are all activities that require interpretation, experience and judgement. One may begin such a process of training with a small amount of drilling, but it is likely to be a minor component of the process of acquiring a complex skill. If Ryle's analysis is right, then it is a mistake to think that vocational training, other than for the most basic procedures, could involve nothing more than drilling. It does, however, involve correction, repetition, explanation, interpretation and instruction, and is thus a highly complex pedagogic concept.

The development of training systems is integral to changes in the social structures in which they are embedded and has been through qualitatively different stages. Traditionally, training was associated with apprenticeship, whereby the apprentice was socialised into a craft or manual occupation. Historically, one of the most universal apprenticeship systems was found in Britain, first given formal recognition through the 1563 Statute of Artificers, in place until repealed in 1814 and followed by a laissez-faire system whereby apprenticeship was no longer statutory but regulated by free collective bargaining between employers and trades unions.

With growing recognition of the value of a formal taught element, especially in the German states under Bismarck, but also in Britain and the United States through the mechanics' institutes, skills acquisition ceased to rely only on work experience and employer goodwill, and the meaning of training changed significantly. The latter half of the twentieth century represented the culmination of this process, as the trade apprenticeship was transformed in many countries into a system of industrial training regulated through an administrative tripartite (employers' associations, trades unions and government) framework, financed through a training levy on firms, and covering most of the working population. In Britain, for example, this new system was introduced by the Industrial Training Act of 1974, which represented the first attempt to formulate a modern industrial manpower policy, and meant that training became an important dimension in the dialogue between employers, trades unions and government. As in Germany, the Netherlands and the Scandinavian countries, apprentices became 'trainees' who, though still with an employer, also attended college on a day or block release basis and were awarded a qualification having achieved a particular standard, initially after a certain period of time. However, in Britain there has been a watering down of this system of industrial training, with the result that the modern apprenticeship of today bears a greater similarity to the system of the 1950s than to the dual system in Germany.

The identity of the training system with the social structure makes for a diversity of institutional forms internationally, radically different models of skill formation and notions of training (Crouch et al. 1999). In France, for instance, training is invariably associated with a formal taught element, whereas in Britain the term may be applied to only a few hours of instruction. The relation between the state and industry and between employers and employees is critical to understanding the different approaches adopted. Models such as the dual system in Germany are built on state intervention and reflect a concern to regulate the supply of labour within the reigning industrial policy. Here, the firm and the vocational schools are jointly recognised as places of learning, vocational training is the responsibility of both the public and private sectors, and the integration of the social partners (the industrial trades unions and the employers' associations) at all levels is critical. The educational content of learning in the vocational schools is broadly defined, with general skills regarded as social and personal, as well as technical competences, and it is the social partners who devise the training regulations, specifying the occupations in the sector concerned, the length, content and stages of training, and the examinations and qualifications.

At the other extreme are the employer-led, rather than consensus-based, systems in place in, for example, Britain and the United States. Here the competitive market system unfettered by state intervention is seen as the prime mechanism for economic success, with employers and individuals free to negotiate what training is best suited for their needs. In neo-classical economic terms, employers are assumed to provide the training to meet their 'human capital' needs (Becker 1964). The limitations of this market-led approach with respect to training are: first, the problem of getting the unemployed to enter the labour market; second, that skills imparted through work-based training tend to be firm-specific rather than transferable between employers;

and, third, that 'education' tends to be distinct from 'training'. Individual employer reluctance to provide work-based training, the lack of a comprehensive system of provision and the marginalisation of trades union involvement have all contributed to the weaknesses associated with this approach, including severe skill shortages and working populations with significantly lower training and skill levels than found in 'interventionist' countries.

A higher standard of vocational training is generally recognised as essential to increasing productivity (Prais 1995). A debate focuses on how low-skill economies, dependent on basic skills and a core of highly educated professionals, can move to what is known as a 'high skill equilibrium' (Crouch *et al.* 1999). To do this, training needs to be conceived in its widest sense, as expressing the relation between education and work and as such representing not just the transmission of skills but a critical means of personal development and the realisation of human potential (Ashton and Green 1996).

See also: apprenticeship; autonomy; dual system; industrial training; instruction; moral education; qualifications; skills; vocational education; work-based/work-located/workplace/work-related learning

Further reading

Ashton, D. and Green, F. (1996) *Education, Training and the Global Economy*, Cheltenham: Edward Elgar.

Becker, G. S. (1964) *Human Capital*, New York: National Bureau of Economic Research.

Crouch, C., Finegold, D. and Sako, M. (1999) *Are Skills the Answer? The Political Economy of Skill Creation in Advanced Industrial Countries*, Oxford: Oxford University Press.

Prais, S. J. (1995) *Productivity, Education and Training: An International Perspective*, Cambridge: Cambridge University Press.

Ryle, G. (1949) *The Concept of Mind*, London: Hutchinson.

CHRISTOPHER WINCH AND LINDA CLARKE

TRANSITION EDUCATION

Studies of transition in education are of two main kinds:

- those that focus on the transitions of individuals as they move between educational stages and life situations;
- those that focus on societies and systems undergoing fundamental socio-political changes.

Individual transitions have assumed increasing importance in education with the growth of lifelong learning and greater complexity in options available to people at different stages of their lives. A transition has taken place when an event or series of events results in changed roles, relationships and expectations. Rapidly changing conditions mean people often need to take on new roles. These may be planned or unplanned, in work, education and their personal lives.

Societies and educational systems are also described as being 'in transition' when they are undergoing political transformations involving democratisation. The educational transitions, which involve all levels from the systemic to the institutional and individual, are pivotal in the change process.

Understanding and supporting individual transitions is of particular importance to guidance specialists as well as teachers and trainers. The literature on career transitions emphasises role change and movement between phases of education and into working life. Life event transitions emphasise coping strategies, relationships and emotions. Transitions of both kinds often occur together. They affect individuals differently, and people can be helped to adapt and gain from a transition.

Human life does not proceed in orderly time-bound stages and people are dealing with multiple roles and transitions at different stages of their lives. Important transitions occur within schooling, between school and later stages of the education system, between education and work, within adult and working life and at the end of working life. The dominant metaphor for education-work transitions in the mid-twentieth century was that of 'filling niches'. Research and practice in the field of education-work transitions focused on occupational choice and guiding people into 'right' occupational choices. From the 1970s education to work transitions became predominant concerns worldwide as unemployment among young people and adults grew. In the context of high unemployment, the importance of understanding the relationships between opportunity structures, the labour market, social class, family life and education became increasingly recognised. 'Pathways' and 'trajectories' became dominant metaphors for understanding transitions. Where education and labour market policies emphasise employability and lifelong learning, individuals are encouraged to invest resources in their personal development and to continue learning through their lifetime. In the early twenty-first century 'navigation' has become the emergent metaphor for transitions as the development of people's confidence and agency to navigate the different life transitions have become central features of policies and practices.

Management of personal strain and cognitive coping have been shown to be important in all transitions. This includes educational transitions between stages of schooling, and into further and higher education, where at least some of the drop out that occurs can be ascribed to personal strain in at least one of the stages, to problems in cognitive coping, or both.

At a societal level educational transition processes, the passage of one system into another over time, are linked to political transformations from the authoritarian to the democratic, according to McLeish and Phillips (1998). Educational transitions in Eastern and Central European countries and in South Africa have been the most researched. At the macro level, transition involves the design and adoption of new educational structures and practices. For changes to become implemented and embedded at the micro level

takes longer, since these processes involve changes in the expectations of teachers and learners as well as institutional processes. The individual actors are themselves going through personal transitions that involve adaptation to new environments without the benefit of the scripts and routines that worked for them in the previous system. The individual and societal versions of transition are rarely combined in research studies, which tend to focus on one or the other. An exception is the analysis of individual transitions within a societal perspective in the book *Learning and Work in the Risk Society*, which tracked young people from the German Democratic Republic through their experiences of the political changes and their individual transitions into the transformed labour market and institutions of post-communism.

See also: learning career; lifelong learning; skills; training

Further reading

Evans, K., Behrens, M. and Kaluza, J. (2000) *Learning and Work in the Risk Society*, Basingstoke: Palgrave.
McLeish, E. A. and Phillips, D. (eds) (1998) *Processes of Transition in Education Systems*, Oxford: Symposium Books.
Nicholson, N. and West, M. (1991) 'Transitions, work histories and careers'. In M. B. Arthur, D. T. Hall and B. S. Lawrence (eds) *Handbook of Career Theory*, Cambridge: Cambridge University Press.

KAREN EVANS

TRAVELLERS, EDUCATION OF

'Travellers' refers to a large number and a wide variety of individuals and groups who for reasons of culture/ethnicity, lifestyle and/or occupation are mobile for most or all of their lives or for different parts of the year. 'Travellers' is a term used mostly in Europe, and includes Gypsy Travellers, Irish and Scottish Travellers, Roma (Gypsy Travellers from Eastern Europe), New (Age) Travellers and members of bargee, circus and fairground communities. 'Migrants' is used in Central America and the Southern USA to denote seasonal agricultural workers. 'Nomads' is applied in Africa and Asia to fisherpeople and pastoralists.

Some forms of mobility (such as 'the jetset') evoke high status and wealth, and popular culture romanticises mobile communities (the idea of running away with the circus). By contrast, most Travellers experience suspicion from their settled counterparts and many endure poverty and discrimination on account of their itinerancy, as was shown by the mistreatment of Gypsies during the Holocaust. This situation has developed over centuries as fixed residence has become normalised and nomadism has become marginalised and even pathologised, particularly in the West. Consequently many Traveller communities have undergone generations of ill health and illiteracy, even though they have often diverse and rich cultural heritages and multiliteracies (for example, from cultural knowledge of the landscapes through which they pass to machinery maintenance and fairground art).

'Traveller education' denotes the provision of compulsory, formal schooling for mobile communities. The starting point for Traveller education is generally having to work against the grain of conventional schooling, predicated on learners and teachers being present together in a fixed location. Mobile students, therefore, constitute a significant challenge to educational systems to accommodate the distinctive aspirations and needs of learners who regularly move among locations.

Travellers respond to this mismatch between educational provision and learner mobility in several ways. Some families send their children to boarding school or to stay with non-mobile family members; some leave their itinerant occupations while their children are being schooled; and some keep their children with them while travelling, either sending them to the local school in each new town or enrolling them in a distance education programme.

Educational systems also engage with this mismatch with multiple responses. An ongoing debate in Traveller education is between segregation and integration; the former has prompted specialised institutions such as National Schools for Travellers in Ireland and the Queensland School for Travelling Show Children (founded in 2000) in Australia, while the latter has led to support being provided to students in regular classrooms, for example by the Traveller Education Support Services (TESSs) in England. Given wider educational changes, Traveller educators are also concerned about the most appropriate means of enhancing early childhood education, post-compulsory education and adult literacy. More broadly, Traveller education is positioned in an often-uneasy ambivalence, working to promote the interests of mobile learners and their families on the one hand and implementing state policies that are seen as uncomprehending of or even hostile to that mobility on the other.

Despite these difficulties, Traveller education has sometimes been the site of innovative educational practice. For example, several TESSs used the introduction by the Blair government of the literacy hour in England to produce and disseminate reading materials that contested negative stereotypes and circulated positive images of Travellers. Similarly the European Federation for the Education of the Children of Occupational Travellers (EFECOT) (1988–2003) funded and implemented a number of projects designed to use contemporary educational technology to enact schooling in ways that fitted the rhythms of Travellers' mobile lifestyles.

These innovations have been made possible by the formation of organisations that have provided information about, and lobbied actively for, the educational rights of Travellers. In addition to EFECOT, these have included the National Association for Teachers of Travellers (NATT) in England, the Gypsy Research Centre (established in 1979) in France, the National Commission for Nomadic Education (with its *Journal of*

Nomadic Studies, founded in 1989) in Nigeria, the Scottish Traveller Education Project in Scotland (begun in 1991) and the National Association of State Directors of Migrant Education in the United States. Likewise, some Travellers have had to become adept at representing their communities to bring home to governments and policy makers the deleterious educational and social impact of particular legislation or policy.

Traveller education is therefore contested and sometimes controversial. Conventional schooling's basis in learners and teachers being fixed residents creates both challenges and opportunities for Travellers and those who help to educate them.

See also: community education; compulsory education; culture; literacy

Further reading

Dyer, C. (ed.) (2006) *The Education of Nomadic Peoples: Current Issues, Future Prospects*, New York: Berghahn Books.
Salinas, C. and Fránquiz, M. E. (eds) (2004) *Scholars in the Field: The Challenges of Migrant Education*, Charleston WV: AEL.
Tyler, C. (ed.) (2005) *Traveller Education: Accounts of Good Practice*, Stoke on Trent: Trentham Books.

P. A. DANAHER

TRUANCY

Truancy is a by-product of compulsory education (legally mandated school attendance). As elementary/primary schools, and later secondary/high schools, were mandated in various countries, truancy came to describe the absence from these educational structures without acceptable parental excuse or permission. Typically, the following will suffice as 'acceptable' parental or legal guardian excuses for children missing school: personal illness, religious reasons/observances, suspension from school, death or illness in the family. Most schools have a body or a person who can determine if an excuse is legally acceptable or valid. Parents or legal guardians are typically held accountable for a child's school attendance, but truancy is also a major issue for schools (Reid 1999), for governments and for society at large (Carlen *et al.* 1992). In the United States, if a child persistently truants, parents/guardians may be legally prosecuted for 'educational neglect'.

The United States Department of Education created a *Manual to Combat Truancy* in 1996 in conjunction with the Department of Justice. This states that 'truancy is the first sign of trouble; the first indicator that a young person is giving up and losing his or her way' (para. 1). It is stated that chronically truant students are at higher risk of dropping out of school altogether and then put themselves at 'a long term disadvantage for becoming productive citizens' (para. 2). They also make the connection between truancy and daytime crime rates, stating that 'truancy is a gateway to crime' (para. 3) and urge that 'combating truancy is one of the first ways a community can reach out quickly to a disaffected young person and help families that may be struggling with a rebellious teenager' (para. 4). The guide offers the following solutions: 'involve parents in all truancy activities'; 'ensure that students face firm sanctions for truancy'; 'create meaningful incentives for parental responsibility'; 'establish ongoing truancy prevention programs in schools'; 'involve local law enforcement in truancy reduction efforts'. It also provides information on model truancy reduction programmes.

Studies in several countries have pointed to an increasing proportion of crimes being committed by truanting youths during school hours, and another concern relates to the impact of child labour on school attendance. A 2003 report for the International Labour Office noted that:

> Being a boy and living in a rural area increases the likelihood of working in the child labour market. Working outside the home increases with age because both physical and mental ability to do work increase with age. The higher the education of the

parents, the lower the likelihood of the child working. Speaking the language of the test at home, small family size, living with both parents and having a large number of books at home lowers the incidence of working in the labor market. Generally school attributes associated with improved school quality lower the incidence of child labour. The country-level measures also proved significant in explaining variation in child labour across countries.

(Orazem and Gunnarsson 2003: 15)

Other factors associated with truancy include consumerism (Guare and Cooper 2003) and school security. Several published research reports have shown a link between school-aged children staying at home because they are afraid of being bullied. The stress experienced by victims of bullying and harassment can also result in school absences.

Criminal involvement, lack of parental involvement or responsibility, inappropriate sanctions, child labour, and bullying/school violence are among the top reasons for truancy across the globe. In addition, some have blamed an unacceptable lack of school quality for children s absences from school. Truancy is a major concern among school officials that needs to be addressed to improve the overall education and welfare of children.

See also: bullying; compulsory education; school security; school violence; suspension

Further reading

Carlen, P., Gleeson, D. and Wardhaugh, J. (1992) *Truancy: The Politics of Compulsory Schooling*, Buckingham: Open University Press.

Guare, R. E. and Cooper, B. S. (2003) *Truancy Revisited: Students as School Consumers*, Lanham MD: Rowman and Littlefield.

Orazem, P. F. and Gunnarsson, V. (2003) *Child Labour, School Attendance and Academic Performance: A Review*, International Labour Office, Geneva: ILO.

Reid, K. (1999) *Truancy in Schools*, London: Routledge.

KIMBERLY WILLIAMS

TUITION/TUTOR/TUTORIAL

In American contexts especially, 'tuition' is used to denote the fee payable for higher education instruction. 'Tuition fees' is the preferred term in Britain and some other countries. Tuition – sometimes called tutelage – also refers to the act of instructing a student, imparting the tutor's knowledge or skill. The term is frequently encountered in the sense of a private arrangement between the instructor – or tutor – and student. 'Private tuition' involves the hiring of someone to work on a one-to-one basis with a student. For a child, this may be in preparation for a school or college entrance test (such as the 'eleven-plus' test for entry to England's small remaining number of selective grammar schools) or perhaps for the learning of a musical instrument not offered at school. Business people preparing for a high-stakes visit abroad may engage a private tutor to rapidly impart a rudimentary knowledge of the language and customs of another culture.

In the context of higher education, tutorials, like seminars, follow up lectures. Traditionally, the higher education tutorial is a one-to-one meeting between student and tutor, whereas a seminar is a group discussion. A personal tutor is a staff member assigned to advise or counsel students about general matters of course progress, while academic tutors facilitate intellectual discussion of lectures and emerging ideas, and they may also provide feedback on the student's draft writing. The shift to a mass model of higher education has put a strain on the academic tutorial system, including at the English universities of Oxford and Cambridge, where teaching in the arts traditionally rested more upon individual weekly tutorials than with attendance at lectures. Higher education institutions regularly offer 'group tutorials', using the term interchangeably with seminars.

See also: counselling; higher education; instruction; lecture/lecturer; seminar; student finance/loans

DAVID CROOK

TYLER, RALPH (1902–94)

Tyler was born into a professional family in Chicago and, after completing a bachelor's degree at Doane College in Crete, Nebraska, he worked as a high school science teacher in South Dakota. He subsequently earned an M.A. from the University of Nebraska and a Ph.D. from Chicago, with both dissertations focusing upon issues of testing. Tyler lectured at the universities of North Carolina and Ohio State between 1927 and 1932, while developing his key idea that, rather than testing in order to place an individual along a line of normal distribution, educators should be 'evaluating' performance and attributes through evidence collection based upon clear objectives. Tyler is, therefore, the progenitor of what later came to be known as 'portfolio assessment', an especially significant feature of vocational education and training. At the University of Chicago, from 1933, he led an eight-year study of schools, curriculum types and teaching styles in order to assess their effectiveness, becoming chair of the education department mid-way through the project. Tyler outlined principles for evaluating effective learning that might be seen as managerial in their approach. Certainly his ideas, set out in *Basic Principles of Curriculum Instruction* (1949), influenced school managers and administrators. He moved to Stanford University in 1953 as the founder and first director of the Centre for Behavioural Sciences.

See also: assessment; evaluation; test/testing

STEVEN COWAN

U

UNDERACHIEVEMENT

Underachievement is a very widely used term that means different things to different people. It is used by politicians, academics, journalists, teachers, psychologists, social workers and other practitioners who work with children and youth to describe the poor academic performance of equivalent students, ethnic groups, social groups, social classes, gender, sectors of the schooling community, nations and geographical regions. Teachers frequently use the term to describe pupils who have difficulties in learning and/or are difficult to teach. In general, their ability is not reflected in their performance. More recently, the term has been specifically used by some researchers in relation to the perceived under-performance of boys. Politicians on the other hand, use the term more loosely to suggest that the standards of achievement need to be raised. When reviewing the school system, they, along with other policy makers, consider whether the schools are as effective as they could be and whether they are making the maximum effort to support their charges in producing the highest academic achievement possible. Sometimes the term is used alongside social exclusion to identify socio-economic groups who have been marginalised. To complicate matters, the term underachievement does not possess a universally agreed definition.

There are two main perspectives which are used to define underachievement, that of the sociologist and that of the psychologist. Psychologists generally define educational achievement in terms of individuals. They use the term to refer to the discrepancy between a child's Intelligence Quotient (IQ) and their score on an educational test. Sociologists, by contrast, generally use the term to describe the educational outcomes of a social group. Whereas psychologists consider that the IQ score or similar test measures the mental aptitude or potential of an individual child, and that this can be measured independently of literacy skills and what is taught in the curriculum, sociologists would be interested in differences between, say, working-class pupils or middle-class pupils of the same sex or age. Given the assumption that all things being equal they should be performing at the same level, the difference between the levels of performance is what constitutes underachievement. The sociologist would be interested in the social factors that contribute to such differences in performance.

When used loosely, underachievement could mean low achievement or lower achievement if used to compare performance or achievement between one group or individual with another group or individual. This usage implies that the individual or group could perform better and that improvement is possible. Sometimes the descriptor can promote discrimination by suggesting that perceived deficiencies may lie within the individual or within the

611

social group to which the individual belongs, rather than looking more widely at educational and other social systems. This can have a negative effect on persons and groups who belong to ethnic minorities, and undermine their efforts to succeed. The term underachievement suggests some reference point in innate intellectual ability. However, using this as an absolute measure would be to take a simplistic stance, ignoring the complex interplay between individuals and the wider social groups such as families and communities, in which their identities and social outcomes are formed. Interactions in these social groups have an impact on the intangible qualities like attitude, motivation and self-esteem, and these would have an effect on pupils' general behaviours as well as performance.

Underachievement is a term that combines a range of different perspectives. Some teachers and parents would identify causes such as cultural expectations, peer pressure, or poor language skills. Other variables to consider when looking at underachievement would be degree of motivation, self-esteem, attitudes to learning, the economic conditions in which the persons live and the pedagogy used in institutions of learning. Another concern related to the psychological perspective is the reliability and validity of any such test as predictors of potential. The cultural bias of IQ tests in favour of specific power groups has also been questioned. Children in vulnerable positions, and particularly those disaffected from the mainstream, may be seriously disadvantaged by such tests because they may have little relevance or resemblance to their everyday reality. In consequence, they may lead to drastic underestimates of levels of underachievement.

See also: ability; aptitude; intelligence/intelligence tests; learning disabilities/difficulties; motivation; social exclusion/inclusion; standards

Further reading

Gorard, S. and Smith, E. (2004) 'What is "underachievement" at school?', *School Leadership and Management*, 24(2): 205–25.
Plewis, I. (1991) 'Underachievement: a case of conceptual confusion', *British Educational Research Journal*, 17(4): 377–85.
West, A. and Pennell, H. (2003) *Underachievement in Schools*, London: RoutledgeFalmer.

ANN CHERYL ARMSTRONG

UNDERGRADUATE

An undergraduate is a student taking a course in higher education leading to their first or bachelor's degree. This course is often studied full-time and over three or four years immediately or soon after leaving school, but increasingly in many cases it is taken part-time at different stages during one's life. Where the undergraduate is studying a full-time, post-school programme, it is partly to enhance an experience and appreciation of independent study, but will also be intended to maximise the prospects of going forward into a professional career in a related area. Generally the undergraduate course specialises in a particular subject or area, or may consist of two linked areas, or in some cases it is possible to choose from a number of loosely associated options to construct a broad programme of study. In some countries, a first year undergraduate is known as a 'freshman' or a 'fresher'. In the United States, a second year undergraduate is known as a 'sophomore'. The course usually involves a combination of lectures and seminars in the chosen subject, assessed either continuously or by examination on its completion, or a combination of the two. Having followed the course successfully, passed the requirements involved, and received the appropriate degree, the student becomes a graduate, and is entitled to study for a postgraduate degree.

See also: degree; higher education; postgraduate; university

GARY McCULLOCH

UNDERPERFORMING/FAILING SCHOOL

Underperforming/failing school is a term applied when a school is deemed, by external measures, not to be meeting standards set by a particular system. The term's origins come from increasing policy concerns in the 1990s that the level of knowledge and skills of the past were no longer acceptable in a changing world. This led to greater accountability of schools through an increasing focus on outcomes, measuring school effectiveness by results, and making this information widely available. Such action highlighted that some schools were not making a necessary and sufficient difference to their students' education. An Organisation for Economic Co-operation and Development (OECD 1997) project on *Combating Failure at School* in the mid-1990s brought interest in failing schools into sharper relief internationally, although at this time many country participants emphasised failure of students, rather than failure of schools. Since then, policy makers in more countries have been attracted to the idea of highlighting and 'treating' failure of schools.

Identification of an underperforming school is most often the consequence of publication of comparative tables of students' academic results or an external inspection, or both. A range of judgement criteria is applied by which the school has failed or is considered at risk of failing. In addition to students' performance, judgement criteria often include poor quality of education and care, and poor school leadership and management (including financial). School failure is generally attributed to a lack of the following: will or effort among those most closely involved; appropriate staff with necessary skills to bring about recovery; resources; and knowledge concerning what to do.

Different countries and states use a range of often highly evocative labels for such schools, relating both to their designation and subsequent action. In England, a school failing an external inspection is placed 'in special measures', while an equivalent in parts of the United States is 'on probation'. Such language can create demoralisation and is seen as unjust, even where school improvement ensues (Mintrop 2004).

A limitation of highlighting the school as being the root cause of failure and identifying failing schools is that school factors generally account for approximately 15–20 per cent of the variance in student performance. The link between achievement and social class also creates a tension because many underperforming schools are located in areas of deprivation, facing significant economic, social and inter-cultural challenges. In addition, the policy of choice in some countries allows students in low-performing schools to transfer to higher-performing ones, exacerbating the problem for underperforming schools. Failing schools can actually be characterised in many different ways; for example, in England underperformance of schools in more affluent areas is increasingly highlighted through the use of value added approaches.

External policy consequences for underperformance generally take the form of sanctions, intervention and, sometimes, incentives. At the least, there is close monitoring, an expectation that an improvement plan will be produced with commitment to action and, sometimes, support through requirement to participate in specific programmes or targeted support networks. In some jurisdictions, the approach has also included tailoring support towards different kinds of difficulty and identifying strategies to prevent failure. In more severe cases, however, and where progress is viewed as unacceptable, state takeover, closure or a form of reconstitution can ensue.

Concern about reliance on within-school approaches to turn around underperformance rests on whether failing schools have the awareness of and belief in the need for improvement, and the capacity to act on this to implement necessary changes. The knowledge base from university academics working with struggling schools to help them turn themselves around generally refers to the complexity of their challenging circumstances as well as highlighting many of the factors identified in school improvement in areas of significant deprivation. These include: focusing on teaching and learning; contextually appropriate and gradually broadening leadership; creating a positive school culture; using data for decision making; building a learning community; improving parental and community involvement; and drawing on outside support and resources.

Overall, however, current approaches to 'transform' underperforming schools have mixed results. Where deep and lasting improvement is concerned, it seems there are 'no quick fixes' (Stoll and Myers 1998).

See also: accountability; inspection; school culture; school effectiveness; school improvement; school leadership

Further reading

Mintrop, H. (2004) *Schools on Probation: How Accountability Works (and Doesn't Work)*, New York: Teachers College Press.

OECD (1997) *Combating Failure at School: Dimensions of the Problem, Country Experiences and Policy Implications*, Paris: OECD.

Stoll, L. and Myers, K. (eds) (1998) *No Quick Fixes: Perspectives on Schools in Difficulty*, London: Falmer Press.

LOUISE STOLL

UNITED KINGDOM

Education takes on slightly differing forms in different parts of the United Kingdom, although the main structure of the formal system is recognisable in each of the four constituent countries.

In the United Kingdom, formal education is provided at primary level for pupils up to age eleven, at secondary level to at least the age of sixteen, and thereafter in post-school colleges and universities, which constitute the further and higher sectors of education. There are numerous exceptions to this widely established pattern. In some localities and in some sectors, transfer to the secondary

stage occurs at 12 or 13 years of age. Some local authorities rely on middle schools to break down the strict distinction between primary and secondary sectors. After attainment of the school-leaving age of sixteen, some young people pursue their schooling in either sixth-form colleges or in colleges of further education rather than in school. There is also a very inconsistent pattern across the United Kingdom of pre-school and nursery education, despite the stated intention of successive governments to extend pre-school provision.

The education system in the United Kingdom bears clear signs of its origins. Before the involvement of the state during the nineteenth century, all schooling was privately financed, and this private sector has survived and has been supplemented by numerous new foundations during the last two centuries. Many of these private schools (those affiliated to the Headmasters' Conference are known as public schools) remain very prestigious, with fee levels and patterns of boarding education, which result in their still being restricted to the most privileged sectors of society. Under the influence of leading nineteenth-century headmasters such as Thomas Arnold of Rugby, these schools developed a distinctive curriculum, based on the classics and a distinctive ethos. Some of their characteristics, such as a house system (originally intended to allow for close supervision of residential pupils) and the sixth form, have been widely copied, and many commentators have noted the extent to which the curriculum still followed in state secondary schools is drawn from this model, although, of course, during the twentieth century other subjects were introduced alongside the original classical curriculum. Similarly, those universities founded before the first state grants in 1893 remain among the most prestigious and have proved most resistant to entrants from the lower social classes and to females.

The primary sector is similarly deeply marked by its twin origins in the nineteenth century. About 7 per cent of all pupils attend the preparatory schools, established to provide a route into the major public schools, and most of their pupils still proceed to private secondary schools of one sort or another. Thus there exists a private sector, which although subject to state inspection and oversight, retains many of its historical characteristics and exists largely separate from the state sector, catering for an identifiable clientele. This private sector is particularly strong in southeast England, although it is matched in other parts of the United Kingdom (Wales being something of an exception in this respect).

The majority of the population passes through state primary schools, many of which began as church schools during the nineteenth century. At this time the Anglican Church became the main provider of what was then called elementary schooling and most of its schools survive and retain an allegiance to the Church, although much of the funding now comes from the state. As it became increasingly clear during the nineteenth century that the churches alone could not hope to cater for the growing numbers of children of school age, the 1870 Education Act enabled the provision of board schools (so called because they were run by locally elected school boards) to fill the gaps. The 1902 Education Act confirmed this 'dual system' by which state and church schools coexisted, allowing for state funding of church schools. This system survives to the present day. Debates about the primacy of the 'three Rs', which were prevalent at that time, also survive in controversies around the 'core curriculum' and the importance of basic skills.

The secondary sector is even more complex, bearing similar marks of its origins. Many of the sixteenth-century boys' grammar schools survive, although some have been taken over by the state. There was a rash of new foundations of secondary schools in the closing years of the nineteenth century, and the 1902 Act allowed for the establishment of municipal secondary schools. This period witnessed a swift growth in girls' secondary schools: most secondary schooling remained single-sex until after World War II. At this time, the school boards were replaced by a smaller number of local education authorities (LEAs), which were given responsibility for the provision of both primary and secondary schooling in the areas under their jurisdiction. Thus there developed a school system that was centrally governed but locally administered, the LEAs having wide powers and developing contrasting patterns in different localities. It should be added that separate legislation for Scotland, Wales and Northern Ireland resulted in significant disparities of provision across the United Kingdom.

The 1944 Education Act made secondary schooling compulsory. During the post-war period arguments for the common secondary school became popular, resulting in the establishment of many comprehensive schools and the reconstitution of many existing schools. By 1980, 80 per cent of secondary pupils were being educated in mixed comprehensive schools. The abolition of direct grant status in 1976, by which many of the pre-existing grammars were funded directly by central government, resulted in a semi-permanent enhancement of the private sector, so that in recent years the contrast between the two sectors has become more, rather then less, marked.

The twentieth century also witnessed a swift growth of the post-school sector, with further education colleges being widely seen as focused on vocational training and the universities on a wider education. During the 1970s, this growth was at its swiftest and was sustained through the implementation of a 'binary policy', which involved closer designation of the vocational role of each institution. However, the continuing scramble for growth has seen this replaced by a ferocious competition for funding, with external assessments of research capacity and excellence in teaching becoming the arbiters of funding levels. In this context, the government remains committed at the time of writing to a target of 50 per cent of the population passing through full-time higher education, although this remains controversial.

Against this background, the rise of the 'New Right' during the 1970s and 1980s did much to define what remain the major areas of controversy down to the present. After 1979, the Conservative government stressed the significance of vocational education, introducing new funding sources to ensure that curricula, at every level, remained focused on the needs of employment and of the economy. The 1988 Education Reform Act was deeply influential. It brought to an end the Inner London Education Authority, in the process weakening all local authorities; it confirmed the power of the government, rather than the professionals, to determine what went on in schools. It identified four 'key stages' of a child's education. Further, it introduced a national curriculum and a testing and inspection regime designed to confirm and publicise the extent to which schools were achieving the targets set by central government. Since then, the annual publication of league tables of school performance has placed schools in a semi-permanent frenzy of marketing.

Since its election in 1997, the Labour government has appeared in some respects to alleviate the worst excesses of this legacy, introducing Education Action Zones, softening the testing regime and, through the Dearing Report, promising a lighter touch for higher education. But its resolute insistence on targets and its efforts to variegate the comprehensive sector, as well as the introduction of controversial 'top up' fees for higher education, suggest that the emphasis is on continuity of policy. The traditional Labour emphasis on hostility to private education and selection at eleven-plus has been largely abandoned in favour of school effectiveness and an attempt to offer each child, or each family, the chance to progress through the system by their own efforts.

The issues that confront education in the United Kingdom at this time are largely the legacy of its recent historical development. It remains to be seen how much the teaching profession can win back the ability to determine what goes on in schools. This will depend on the extent to which the bureaucratisation of the system and its submission to a competitive ethic can be alleviated. It remains to be seen how far the drive to focus on the needs of the child, now largely neglected, and to use schooling as an instrument for social justice (both briefly fashionable after World War II) will re-emerge in some new form. Much of this will depend on the extent of the resources allocated to education by government. At this time, despite the mantra of 'education, education, education' adopted by Tony Blair when he became prime minister, it seems most likely that the exigencies of Britain's economic situation, together with rival claims on the public purse (including the war on terrorism) will not lead to any radical change in the provision or purposes of education in the foreseeable future.

See also: Europe

Further reading

Aldrich, R. (ed.) (2002) *A Century of Education*, London: RoutledgeFalmer.

Chitty, C. (2004) *Education Policy in Britain*, Basingstoke: Palgrave Macmillan.

Dunford, J. and Sharp, P. (1990) *The Education System in England and Wales*, London: Longman.

Gearon, L. (2002) *Education in the United Kingdom: Structures and Organisation*, London: David Fulton.

Green, J. E. (2001) *Education in the United Kingdom and Ireland*, Bloomington IN: Phi Delta Kappa Foundation.

Holt, G., Andrews, C., Boyd, S., Harper, A., Loose, J., O'Donnell, S. and Sargent, C. (2002) *Education in England, Wales and Northern Ireland: A Guide to the System*, 3rd edn, Slough: National Foundation for Educational Research.

Jones, G. E. (1997) *The Education of a Nation*, Cardiff: University of Wales Press.

Kogan Page (2005) *British Qualifications: A Complete Guide to Professional, Vocational and Academic Qualifications in the UK*, 36th edn, London: Kogan Page.

ROY LOWE

UNITED NATIONS CHILDREN'S FUND (UNICEF)

The United Nations International Children's Emergency Fund (UNICEF) was a creation of the United Nations General Assembly in December 1946, following World War II. In 1953 it was restyled the United Nations Children's Fund, but the acronym was retained.

The agency was originally founded to alleviate poverty among children in Europe by providing food, clothing and healthcare. The Fund's interests subsequently broadened and, today, UNICEF is mandated by the General Assembly 'to advocate for the protection of children's rights, to help meet their basic needs and to expand their opportunities to reach their full potential'. A recent publication, *1946–2006: Sixty Years for Children* (UNICEF 2006a) recognises its achievements since being founded, against a backdrop of global social, political and economic change, while also identifying the challenges for the period to 2015, the deadline for achieving the Millennium Development Goals intended to transform the lives of millions of children

UNICEF is guided by the Convention on the Rights of the Child, a declaration comprising ten articles, which was adopted by the UN General Assembly in 1959. According to its website, UNICEF

- 'strives to establish children's rights as enduring ethical principles and international standards of behaviour towards children';
- 'insists that the survival, protection and development of children are universal development imperatives that are integral to human progress';
- 'mobilizes political will and material resources to help countries, particularly developing countries, ensure a "first call for children" and to build their capacity to form appropriate policies and deliver services for children and their families';

- 'is committed to ensuring special protection for the most disadvantaged children – victims of war, disasters, extreme poverty, all forms of violence and exploitation and those with disabilities';
- 'responds in emergencies to protect the rights of children. In coordination with United Nations partners and humanitarian agencies, UNICEF makes its unique facilities for rapid response available to its partners to relieve the suffering of children and those who provide their care';
- 'is non-partisan and its cooperation is free of discrimination. In everything it does, the most disadvantaged children and the countries in greatest need have priority';
- 'aims, through its country programmes, to promote the equal rights of women and girls and to support their full participation in the political, social, and economic development of their communities';
- 'works with all its partners towards the attainment of the sustainable human development goals adopted by the world community and the realization of the vision of peace and social progress enshrined in the Charter of the United Nations'.

UNICEF has led many educational programmes and 'supports national policies that promote free and compulsory quality education in child-friendly schools that provide safe, healthy and gender-sensitive learning environments including health and nutrition services, and safe water and sanitation'. It seeks the eradication of poverty, violence, disease and discrimination among children throughout the world. Healthcare is a particular priority and, for example, UNICEF has led a range of projects designed to support families and children affected by HIV/AIDS (see, for example UNICEF 2007). Strategic programmes have also focused on extending educational opportunities for girls.

UNICEF regularly publishes reports on *The State of the World's Children* (see, for example UNICEF 2006b) and each year, in April, it sponsors a Global Action Week campaigning to raise awareness of the importance of Education for All. The focus in 2007 was Education as a Human Right, highlighting that this right is still currently denied to millions of children across the world. The Fund has successfully brought children's issues to the forefront of the global political agenda. With this level of ongoing dedication, it is expected that further changes and improvements will take place in the lives of children.

See also: compulsory education; Education for All (EFA); globalisation; health education; universal education/mass education

Further reading

Himes, J. (1993) *The UN Convention on the Rights of the Child: Three Essays on the Challenge of Implementation*, UNICEF Innocenti Essay 5, Florence: UNICEF Innocenti Research Centre.

UNICEF (2006a) *1946–2006: Sixty Years for Children*, New York: UNICEF.

——(2006b) *The State of the World's Children 2007: Executive Summary*, New York: UNICEF.

——(2007) *Children and AIDS: A Stocktaking Report*, New York: UNICEF.

CARLTON MILLS

UNITED NATIONS EDUCATIONAL, SCIENTIFIC AND CULTURAL ORGANIZATION (UNESCO)

UNESCO is a specialised agency of the United Nations which develops ideas and nurtures international agreement in relation to education, science, culture and communication.

The right to education is enshrined in Article 26 of the Universal Declaration of Human Rights as well as the Convention on the Rights of the Child. In recent decades UNESCO believes that an international consensus on education has been forming which is giving its work greater prominence. The report of the International Commission on Education for the Twenty-first Century, *Teaching: the Treasure Within* (1996), together with a series of UNESCO world conferences (adult education, Hamburg, 1997; higher education, Paris, 1998; technical and vocational education, Seoul, 1999; science, Budapest, 1999) helped to crystallise an international agenda around the notion of lifelong learning connected to economic development, combating poverty and supporting human rights and social justice.

The framework for UNESCO is provided by a number of key documents and policies, including the Education for All goals (EFA); the UN Millennium Development Goals; the UN Literacy Decade 2003–12; the UN Decade of Education for Sustainable Development 2005–14; and the EDUCAIDS Global Initiative on Education and HIV/AIDS. The Millennium Development Goals are central to UNESCO's purpose, especially those aiming, by 2015, to halve the proportion of people living in extreme poverty in developing countries, create universal primary education, eliminate gender inequality in education, and support countries with strategies for sustainable development. In addition, three strategic objectives help to define the educational work of UNESCO: promoting education as a fundamental right; improving the quality of education through curriculum, teaching and values education; and promoting innovation, sharing of information and practices and policy dialogue in education.

UNESCO was instrumental in establishing EFA. In 1990 it organised a world conference in Jomtien, Thailand which launched the global movement to provide basic education to all children, youth and adults. In 2000 The Dakar World Education Forum committed governments to achieving six educational goals by 2015 and confirmed UNESCO as the coordinating body. These are to expand and improve comprehensive early childcare and education; ensure all children – particularly girls – have access to free and compulsory primary education; ensure that the learning needs of young people and adults are met through appropriate programmes; achieve 50 per cent improvement in levels of adult literacy and equitable access to basic and continuing education for all adults; eliminate gender disparities in education by 2005 and bring about gender equality in education; and improve the quality of education so that measurable outcomes are achieved by all especially in literacy, numeracy and life skills. There are four official partners of the EFA project: the World Bank, United Nations Population Fund, United Nations Development Programme and United Nations Children's Fund.

UNESCO also supports civic education to promote human rights, democracy, peace and citizenship. It aims to nurture curricula and teaching methods which respect cultural and linguistic diversity while promoting shared values and understanding. Particularly significant is the HIV/AIDS pandemic which is undermining long-term investment in education and is especially serious among young adults. Other key areas of development are improving access to quality science and technology education, higher education, teacher training and physical education.

UNESCO emphasises the importance of 'reaching the unreached', for instance the poor, women and girls, rural populations, minorities, refugees and victims of disasters, and people with special needs. It is an active partner in the United Nations Girls' Education Initiative (UNGEI) and aims to mobilise public opinion to support these 'victims'. Increasing recognition is being given to non-formal basic education as a means to encourage the participation of marginal groups, better social services and quality of life in general.

UNESCO's work in promoting cultural diversity, dialogue and understanding may also be construed as educational. For instance, it helped to establish the World Copyright Convention in 1952; it has preserved histor-ical monuments, especially those on the World Heritage List, as well as library and archive collections. It has published general histories of Africa, the Caribbean, Latin America, the civilisations of Central Asia, and the history of humanity. Since the 1940s, understandings of culture have been expanded from works of art to encompass anthropological meanings of the everyday and ways of living among the world's diverse populations.

Educational work is also closely interlinked with its scientific programmes, for instance, in promoting science and technology for sustainable development, a concept UNESCO helped to define in the 1960s. In the area of 'social and human sciences' work has focused upon ethics, human rights, anti-discrimination, democracy and the management of social transformation. It supports the notion of 'a knowledge society' and the dissemination of appropriate information and computer technology in education, science and culture.

Member states, acting in cooperation with civil society, have responsibility for implementing change, and they have established National Commissions to handle their relationship with the Organisation. UNESCO supports governments by mobilising finance and personnel at national and international levels of decision making. As a global coordinating body, it aims to provide 'international leadership for creating learning societies'. It works to establish frameworks for education by acting as a 'laboratory' of ideas to anticipate and respond to emerging trends and developments. For instance, it helped to develop and popularise ideas of 'functional literacy' that are widely used today. UNESCO serves as a clearing house and dissemination centre for successful and effective educational practices, and develops standards and guidelines for key areas of education. It publishes an annual Global Monitoring Report that charts the work both of individual countries and international trends. It also works through a number of specialist institutes including the International Bureau of Education, the UNESCO Institute for Education and the International Institute for Educational Planning.

UNESCO also works closer to the ground: 'downstream' rather than 'upstream'. It nurtures networks and provides expertise in order that countries can increase their capacity to offer quality education. It aims to be a trusted interlocutor among educational actors from civil society, business and governments. The Organisation initiates and promotes dialogue and information sharing to help achieve its aims, and works as a 'catalyst' for educational change. For instance, the 1960 World Conference on Adult Education contributed to the eventual formation of the International Council for Adult Education (ICAE) in 1973. Every two years it holds a general conference of member states with an executive board that carries projects forward. Since 1958 its permanent headquarters has been in Paris.

UNESCO was founded in the wake of World War II in 1945, when it declared that 'since wars begin in the minds of men, it is in the minds of men that the defences of peace must be constructed'. This would be achieved by fostering the 'intellectual and moral solidarity of mankind'. A number of earlier organisations contributed to the idea for UNESCO, such as the International Institute of Intellectual Co-operation (IICI) and the International Bureau of Education (IBE). During the war the Conference of Allied Ministers of Education (CAME) had met in England to discuss the reconstruction of systems of education, and this fed into proposals for a broad-based educational and cultural organisation. UNESCO was created following the ratification of twenty countries: Australia, Brazil, Canada, China, Czechoslovakia, Denmark, the Dominican Republic, Egypt, France, Greece, India, Lebanon, Mexico, New Zealand, Norway, Saudi Arabia, South Africa, Turkey, the United Kingdom and the United States. In 2007 there were 192 member countries.

Early initiatives coalesced around the notion of 'fundamental education', which searched for the universal common denominators of education and considered what all people should learn. Later there would be a shift of emphasis towards tackling discrimination, as in the Convention against Discrimination in Education (1960). The need for setting priorities and planning was also clearly recognised in response to the earlier phase. From the 1970s, ideas of recurrent and lifelong education focused attention on the need to learn throughout life, themes apparent in the report of the International Commission on the Development of Education, *Learning to Be* (1972). More recent developments have concentrated on education in relation to globalisation, values in the face continual social change, gender, and disability.

Inevitably the wider political and economic context has directly impinged upon UNESCO, where tensions between countries have found expression, for instance, over increased funding to support developing countries or over political allegiances during the Cold War. The dates at which different countries joined also reflects this wider political situation. After World War II Japan and the Federal Republic of Germany became members in 1951, and Spain joined in 1953. In 1956 the Republic of South Africa withdrew, claiming 'interference' in its 'racial problems', and it was not to rejoin until 1994 under Nelson Mandela. The USSR joined UNESCO in 1954 and was replaced by the Russian Federation in 1992 alongside twelve former Soviet republics which joined from 1991 to 1993. Nineteen African states became members in 1960 following independence from colonial rule. The People's Republic of China joined in 1971. In 1984 the USA withdrew from UNESCO, complaining of mismanagement and suspicious of its political motives. The UK and Singapore followed suit in 1985. These withdrawals significantly reduced the funding available to UNESCO, a fact which reflects the unequal influence of various countries within the Organisation. However, the UK returned in 1997 and the USA in 2003. In part, the USA's decision was motivated by the increase in terrorism. UNESCO argues that this development has increased the validity of its mission in working towards shared understanding, respect for the diversity of cultures and global visions of development linked to human rights and the alleviation of poverty.

See also: Education for All (EFA); globalisation; International Bureau of Education (IBE); International Council for Adult Education (ICAE); international education; International Institute for Educational Planning (IIEP); universal education/mass education

Further reading

Delors, J. (1996) *Learning: the Treasure Within*, Paris: UNESCO.
Droit, R-P. (2005) *Humanity in the Making: Overview of the Intellectual History of UNESCO, 1945–2005*, Paris: UNESCO.
Faure, E. et al (1972) *Learning to Be: the World of Education Today and Tomorrow*, Paris: UNESCO.
Lacoste, M. C. (1994) *The Story of a Grand Design: Unesco 1946–1993, People, Events and Achievements*, Paris: UNESCO.
Omolewa, M. (2007) 'UNESCO as a network', *Paedagogica Historica*, 43(2): 211–21.
UNESCO (1947) *Fundamental Education: Common Ground for All Peoples*, Paris: UNESCO.
Valderrama, F. (1995) *A History of UNESCO*, Paris: UNESCO.

TOM WOODIN

UNITED STATES

Education has served a variety of functions since the earliest European settlements in North America. Over time, schools have become more essential to the United States' social and economic development. During the nineteenth century, the creation of state school systems contributed to an emerging national identity. In the twentieth century, the scope of educational services and the level of participation increased dramatically, accompanied by debates over equity in the schools. In recent decades, these concerns have been eclipsed by a growing preoccupation with educational achievement.

Formal schooling was a notable feature of certain European colonies in the New World. In Massachusetts, legislation called for schools to ensure religious conformity and help children resist that 'old deluder Satan'. This and similar laws often were honoured in the breach, but reflected the significance that many settlers assigned to training children to read and interpret the Bible and other religious material. Similar concerns led to the development of higher education institutions. Harvard College was founded in 1636 to train Puritan ministers. Additional institutions were founded later in other colonies, principally for religious purposes.

Following the Revolution, new significance was attached to formal schooling, even if lines of responsibility were unclear. Early leaders such as Thomas Jefferson believed that an educated population was necessary for a democracy, but the constitution of the new republic made no mention of schooling, leaving it to the states. This has remained a basic principle of American federalism. States were slow in organising schools, and consequently education remained a local affair. In the northeast, district schools were established by communities, eventually dotting the countryside in large numbers and enrolling a majority of children. Thus began a longstanding tradition of local control of education (Cremin 1970).

The first major reform initiative was the common school movement, focusing on primary education. Horace Mann, appointed to oversee schools in Massachusetts in 1837, was the principal voice of this movement. His work focused on New England, but was widely influential elsewhere. Mann and fellow reformers advocated longer school terms, better trained teachers, and improved pedagogy. They offered a vision of schools uniting the nation's disparate population and prompting economic development. By the late nineteenth century, schools had changed all over the country, but especially in northern and western states. The development of public education was slower in the South, where plantation elites resisted the idea of popular schooling, attendance rates were low and illiteracy widespread.

The latter half of the nineteenth century witnessed momentous changes. The Civil War ended slavery, and millions of free blacks learned to read in schools supported by the federal government, northern philanthropists and black community members. Compulsory attendance laws were enacted in most states, although they appeared latest in the South. Average lifetime schooling increased from 210 days in 1800 to more than 1,000 days in 1900. More than 90 per cent of children received at least some formal schooling. In larger cities, Catholic immigrants established schools in reaction to nativist and Protestant influences in public education. Private secondary schools, usually called academies, became quite common. They eventually were eclipsed by public high schools, which multiplied rapidly after 1890. The vast majority were coeducational. Many colleges also were established in the nineteenth century, most by religious groups but also by state governments. Most such institutions were quite modest, and their graduates lacked career options outside the religious ministry (Kaestle 1983).

By 1900, the basic structure of a national but locally controlled system of education was in place, with near universal primary schooling and rapidly developing secondary and tertiary sectors. The United States led the world in secondary enrolment levels, as it continued to do for most of the twentieth century. This expansion was accomplished with local funding, much of it in response to a rising demand for marketable credentials. Urban growth accelerated in the wake of industrialisation and large-scale immigration, creating badly overcrowded city schools.

This era also brought progressive reform ideas, espoused by John Dewey and others, although this brand of liberal pedagogy had little immediate effect on public schooling. Administrative reforms caught on more quickly, especially the expansion of bureaucratic systems of supervision and control. Curricula became differentiated, particularly at the secondary level, as schools prepared students for various occupational strata. Schools also became responsible for providing psychological, recreational, and even medical services for students, a continuing trend (Tyack 1975).

Secondary education developed in a distinctive form. In 1918, a report entitled the 'Cardinal Principles of Education' signalled a movement to create the comprehensive high school, an institution designed to bring youth from different social backgrounds together. By the 1960s, more than half of all children aged 14–18 were enrolled in such schools. Most comprehensive high schools divided students into various tracks representing test scores or grades, but these also reflected differences in race, ethnicity, or social class. Growing numbers of high school graduates enrolled in post-secondary institutions, especially in the decades following World War II. American university enrolments began to lead those of other industrialised nations by a wide margin.

The years after 1950 were a time of rapid change in American education. It was an era of prosperity and economic growth, but one marked by conflict over equality and social justice. The Civil Rights Movement, a massive campaign against racial discrimination, had profound effects on public education. Law throughout the South and in certain other states mandated racially segregated schools, but in 1954 the Supreme Court's pivotal *Brown v. Board of Education* decision removed the legal foundations of segregated school systems. A decade later, federal civil rights legislation led to widespread desegregation in the South. As blacks moved to cities in the North, however, suburbanisation helped to preserve segregation, a process known as 'white flight'. Court-ordered bussing sought to remedy segregation, but proved widely unpopular. Despite some progress against racial inequity, significant disparities in black and white schooling remain a telling feature of American life.

The Civil Rights Movement also inspired litigation and legislation addressing equity in the education of other groups. Federal and state laws prohibiting gender discrimination in education have succeeded in vastly expanding opportunities for girls and women. Since the 1970s, America's expanding complement of students with limited English proficiency has been legally entitled to programmes to promote fluency in English, along with bilingual instruction in many subjects, and students with disabilities to programmes designed to meet their educational needs. These measures have succeeded to varying degrees, but have also consumed an increasing share of resources, creating tensions between educators and advocates of different constituent groups (Ravitch 1980; Hubert 1999).

Growing federal involvement in education led to the elevation of the US Department of Education to cabinet status in 1978. Five years later, the department published *A Nation at Risk*, a politically motivated pamphlet charging that declining academic performance in public schools made the nation economically vulnerable. This report proved a watershed in American education as policy makers began to focus less on equity and the affective development of students and more on academic achievement. During the next two decades, most state legislatures and many local school districts increased high school graduation requirements and developed new programmes of standardised testing both to assess student learning and to evaluate schools.

Also in the 1980s, post-secondary enrolment, following a slight decline in the previous decade, expanded to include the majority of high school graduates. The earning power of college graduates increased faster than less educated workers, promoting the appeal of higher education, especially to women, who were entering the workforce in increasing numbers. Inequities in education also grew as middle-class and white flight from large central cities created racially isolated and economically disadvantaged schools. As education became more important in the labour market, the poorest members of society were increasingly relegated to the weakest institutions (Rury 2002).

Recent federal initiatives have focused on boosting the academic performance of schools, but with limited success. In 2001, the Bush administration launched 'No Child Left Behind' (NCLB), a policy regime designed to compel schools to demonstrate that increasing numbers of students are academically 'proficient'. This is undertaken by linking of resources to assessment, an approach often described as 'accountability'. NCLB is proving troublesome to many schools, which face sanctions for failing to meet its escalating performance standards. Some requirements have been changed in response to local and state protests (Imber and van Geel 2004).

Today, many states are embroiled in legislative and judicial battles concerning the organisation and funding of public schools. Many schools must deal with shrinking budgets even as academic performance expectations continue to rise. Dissatisfaction with perceived failures of public schools has led some politicians and reformers to advocate programmes of school choice, sending students to private schools at public expense. Many states have created 'charter schools', publicly funded institutions exempt from customary state regulations. A small but vocal minority of parents has chosen to abandon the public and private school system in favour of home schooling, which is legal in almost all states and tacitly condoned in the others (Good and Braden 2000).

Despite these challenges, and the demands of its highly diverse and growing student population, the American educational system remains a vital source of social and economic development for the nation. While its future shape and organisation is much debated, there can be little doubt that Americans attach great importance to education. This fact, more than anything else, will undoubtedly ensure its essential role in the nation's life for the foreseeable future.

Further reading

Cremin, L. (1970) *American Education: The Colonial Experience*, New York: Harper and Row.

Good, T. and Braden, J. (2000) *The Great School Debate: Choice, Vouchers, and Charters*, Mahwah NJ: Lawrence Erlbaum.

Hubert, J. P. (ed.) (1999) *Law and School Reform: Six Strategies for Promoting Educational Equity*, New Haven CT: Yale University Press.

Imber, M. and van Geel, T. (2004) *Education Law*, 3rd edn, Mahwah NJ: Lawrence Erlbaum.

Kaestle, C. F. (1983) *Pillars of the Republic: Common Schools and American Society, 1790–1860*, New York: Hill and Wang.

Ravitch, D. (1980) *The Troubled Crusade: American Education, 1945–1980*, New York: Basic Books.

Rury, J. L. (2002) *Education and Social Change: Themes in the History of American Schooling*, Mahwah NJ: Lawrence Erlbaum.

Tyack, D. B. (1975) *The One Best System: A History of Urban Education in the United States*, Cambridge MA: Harvard University Press.

MICHAEL IMBER AND JOHN L. RURY

UNIVERSAL EDUCATION/MASS EDUCATION

Universal education (UE) expresses an ideal closely associated with the modern era. It embodies concepts such as the capacity and need of all individuals for learning, for understanding the self and the world, and for self-actualisation, as well as the community's need for preparing individuals for responsible membership and contribution to its well-being. The universal appeal of the drive for UE can be found in the child's curiosity and the adult's impetus to improve her or his life, and life chances which promise greater security and safety. UE is a popular secular drive, which belongs to the realm of civil society. UE has come to serve as the focal point of socialisation into the institutional frames of the modern state, its economic development, and social cohesion. At the philosophical level, UE involves the individual as the basic unit of action rather than a corporate group (e.g. seminarians) and by definition incorporates all individuals. Equality

of access, then, is an essential aspect of universality. UE is the abstract ideal and mass education (ME) is the institutional expression of it. Ideological and institutional pressures worldwide, across many diverse polities, produced the demand for universal and equal access to education; states and multi-state agencies have established systems of ME.

The modern state is bound to secure the rights of its citizens, including the right to education, and in return requires the citizen to perform certain duties, including the duty to become educated. For the state, ME provides the mechanism through which individuals are prepared for and selected into its political, economic and social institutions and through which individuals develop the competencies and obligations of citizenship that advance the interests of the state and national unity. Given these overriding interests, the modern state has seen the need to provide ME publicly and to make it compulsory. Based on that premise, modern citizens made the rational choice, demanding that the state provide it universally and for free.

ME is a prominent attribute of the modern world: by the year 2000, most of the world's countries had attained an estimated 70 per cent net enrolment rates of primary school age children (Education For All Global Monitoring Report 2005, 2004: 92); though the gap between the developing and developed countries was growing wider and disproportionate numbers of girls were excluded. The United Nations agencies defined UE to mean 'all children of school age participate in the school system and complete schooling,' (ibid.: 90) and predicted 'clearly universal enrolment in primary school [will not] be achieved in the short or even medium term' (ibid.: 94). In the educational literature of the twentieth century, UE was used synonymously with basic or primary education.

The expansion of ME institutions has been explained from an integrating-institutions perspective by Meyer *et al.* (1977), contending the similarity of patterns the world over.

ME arose along with the nation-state prior to the onset of the Industrial Revolution in Europe, Japan and the United States and, almost within a single decade, governments added public funding to compulsory attendance regulations, creating the public school. Over the past two centuries until World War II, systems of ME expanded at an even rate, and since then have accelerated greatly in speed. They argue in several publications that systems of ME are core institutions of integration in the rational state, are chartered to be universal, standardised, and rationalised, and commonly feature 'remarkably homogeneous aspirations throughout the world' (Boli et al. 1985: 148), which link mastery of the curriculum with individual self-actualisation and national development. Official ME charters typically address individuals across regional, ethnic, class, and gender lines.

Despite this secular ideology of universal progress, the inability of the ME systems to adequately realise their common ideals reproduces differences and inequalities among the people. Critical theorists stress that the rational mass system is designed to provide specific advantages to particular elites according to localities, and that the rise of ME reflects the increasingly differentiated division of labour required by marketisation and capital expansion. The system functions to sustain and legitimate the class order and position of dominant groups (Bourdieu and Passeron 1970; Bernstein 1971–75; Spring 1972; Bowles and Gintis 1976). ME is needed to provide the cognitive skills and affective dispositions required by modern production and by the state (Inkeles and Smith 1975) and to instil a common normative, cultural base that explains an increasingly differentiated and precarious social structure. That the system has largely failed to accomplish these goals in the advanced post-industrialised regions and states speaks to the strength of the socio-economic forces that conflict with the ideal concepts underlying ME. The precariousness of the social order produces the most difficult challenges to ME in the past two centuries.

The goal of achieving UE at the primary level was included in the Universal Declaration of Human Rights in 1948; reiterated in 1990 by 180 countries in the World Declaration on Education For All, and in the Millennium Declaration of 2000.

See also: compulsory education; Education for All (EFA); equality of opportunity

Further reading

Bernstein, B. (1971–75) *Class, Codes, and Control*, 3 vols, London: Routledge and Kegan Paul.
Boli, J., Ramirez, F. O. and Meyer, J. W. (1985) 'Explaining the origins and expansion of mass education', *Comparative Education Review*, 29(2): 145–70.
Bourdieu, P. and Passeron, J. C. (1970) *La reproduction culturelle*, Paris: Editions de Minuit.
Bowles, S. and Gintis, H. (1976) *Schooling in Capitalist America*, New York: Basic Books.
Education For All Global Monitoring Report 2005 (2004), Paris: UNESCO.
Inkeles, A. and Smith, D. (1975) *Becoming Modern: Individual Change in Six Developing Countries*, Cambridge MA: Harvard University Press.
Meyer, J. W., Ramirez, F. O., Rubinson, R. and Boli-Bennett, J. (1977) 'The world educational revolution, 1950–70', *Sociology of Education*, 50: 242–58.
Meyer, J. W., Ramirez, F. O. and Soysal, Y. N. (1992) 'World expansion of mass education, 1870–1980', *Sociology of Education*, 65(2): 128–49.
Spring, J. (1972) *Education and the Rise of the Corporate State*, Boston MA: Beacon Press.

VILMA SEEBERG

UNIVERSITY

The university is an organisation engaged with the advancement of knowledge, including its creation, conservation, interpretation, transmission and application. It is a key institution in systems of higher or tertiary education. The university teaches and examines students in a variety of academic disciplines and professional fields. Its staff, as well as some of its students, undertakes scholarship and research. The intellectual work of the university is expected to define the highest levels of knowledge, understanding and learning in a given field. Students who meet the standards and requirements of an approved programme of study are awarded the degree.

As an ideal, the university is dedicated to the disinterested pursuit of truth, undertaken across the entire span of human knowledge, and under conditions that guarantee academic freedom. As an institution, especially when part of a system or structure of higher education, the university is obliged to undertake a broader role. There is an unresolved tension between the aspirations of a self-governing community of scholars and the external demands of society and the state. The result is 'a history filled with irony and ambiguity, of a struggle between simplicity and complexity, of outrage and accommodation, of ideals lost and regained' (Rothblatt and Wittrock 1993).

The university, after the Church, is the oldest institution with a continuous history in the Western world, but it has never enjoyed a monopoly of higher education. Although Greek, Islamic, Indian and Chinese civilisations possessed important institutions of intellectual learning, these never achieved the separate, corporate and autonomous form of the medieval European university. The universities that emerged in Bologna, Paris and Oxford in the twelfth and thirteenth centuries were guilds or guild federations of master professors and student apprentices. The corporate privileges they received from papal, royal, imperial and communal authorities included jurisdiction in civil and sometimes criminal matters, the granting of degrees, and, in theory, the right to teach in all universities.

To be admitted into these small communities, a student had to be male, proficient in Latin and find the necessary finances to support his studies. What has become known as the scholastic method involved various forms of teaching. Lectures came in many different kinds – ordinary, extraordinary and cursory – and involved readings and commentaries based on prescribed texts. Alongside lectures, the universities of the Middle Ages eagerly cultivated the disputation. This active form of teaching required two or more disputants to argue for opposing solutions to a problem formulated in advance by the teacher. The disputation was also a key element in the lengthy oral examinations that led to the bachelor's degree and then the master's degree (Pedersen 1997).

Although their chief goal was to prepare men for the professions of law, theology and medicine, it was the medieval university that institutionalised concepts of pedagogy, scholarship and intellectual tradition that are still present today in the liberal university tradition (Scott 1984). The mission of the liberal university was to cultivate as well as to educate. A university, wrote Cardinal Newman in 1852, 'aims at raising the intellectual tone of society, at cultivating the public mind, at purifying the national taste'. By close and careful teaching through the medium of the general or liberal undergraduate curriculum, a university education provided young people with an initiation into the prevailing culture.

The rival model of the modern university that emerged during the nineteenth century saw the production of knowledge assume central importance. At the University of Berlin that Wilhem von Humboldt helped found in 1809, research and not only instruction was regarded as a primary duty of professors. Alongside research, there was an emphasis on philosophy and science, on graduate education, on the department and the institute, and on the freedom of professors (*Lehrfreiheit*) and students (*Lernfreiheit*). Reform of the German system along these lines produced universities of outstanding quality and established the research-centred university as the foremost model internationally. It was copied in Central and Northern Europe, adopted in Japan, and decisively influenced the development of the English and American academic systems.

It was in the United States, where the land grant movement of the 1860s had brought agriculture, engineering and business administration into the university curriculum, that the German model achieved a particular dominance during the twentieth century. Among the hundreds of universities and colleges, public and private, which contributed to growth and diversity of American higher education, those that invested most heavily in research became its most prestigious and powerful universities. These large research universities, with their graduate, professional, undergraduate and extension schools, represented a new type of institution in the world, what Clark Kerr called the multiversity. It comprised not one but several communities; its many parts held together by administrative rules; and its system of government much like a city or city state. It pursued knowledge for its own sake and it performed functions on behalf of society. As such, 'it is not really private and it is not really public; it is neither entirely of the world nor entirely apart from it' (Kerr 1995: 1).

Over the past century, and especially after World War II, the inward focus of the relatively self-contained university gave way to a larger involvement with society and the economy. On the one hand, post-war governments have come to view universities as instruments of social and economic policy. Larger sums of public money have been used to expand existing universities, create new ones, develop new courses, and align university research more closely to national priorities. On the other hand, the expansion and increasing specialisation of knowledge have required universities to respond to new sources of complexity as well as carry and cover a new range of professional and trans-disciplinary subjects. In the global economy of higher education, the oldest and the newest universities now compete for domestic and international students, for private and public funds, and for status in national and world rankings.

As the number of tasks, expectations and responsibilities of universities have multiplied with each passing decade, debates have sharpened regarding the coherence and integrity of the university; and the need for differentiation in its mission. With the shift to mass levels of participation in higher education, a question is posed about whether all universities should take on this expansion or just some. In binary systems, universities organised in a separate sector might be shielded from some of these pressures. In stratified systems, a planning framework or the market will define the academic division of labour between elite and mass functions. In the United States, and not without controversy, some of the most selective universities have operated affirmative admissions policies to secure the enrolment of under-represented groups.

Another aspect of differentiation is the extent to which a unity of research, teaching and study can or should be maintained under mass conditions. The principle that those who teach at the most advanced levels should themselves be engaged in research, and that teaching and learning should be related to research, was central to the emergence and development of the modern research university. In some cases, as in the French and former Soviet systems, this unity had been formally denied by the location of research in outside academies. Elsewhere, the relationship of research to teaching and learning has grown 'increasingly complex, ambiguous and controversial' (Clark 1995: 3). A research orientation is held to restrict or distort the general education of undergraduate students. Conversely, a commitment to research is often constrained by the other activities in which universities are engaged. The specialities and costs of science and the open boundaries of mass higher education have made integration more difficult, even within the graduate school where research and advanced education are most concentrated.

A more fundamental challenge to the link between knowledge production and dissemination is that associated with the growth of the knowledge economy. The diffusion of knowledge production beyond the university and throughout society has increased the number of potential sites where knowledge can be created. Advances in information and communications technology have brought other competitors in the form of corporate and virtual universities. One response has been for universities to turn parts of their organisation into commercial enterprises. Another has seen them enter into global alliances and strategic partnerships. Yet another has encouraged universities to invest in distributed learning, with academic programmes offered both face-to-face and online.

See also: academic/academic profession; academic freedom; degree; doctorate; higher education; knowledge economy; master's; professor; scholarship; student; tertiary education; undergraduate

Further reading

Clark, B. R. (1995) *Places of Inquiry: Research and Advanced Education in Modern Universities*, Berkeley and Los Angeles CA: University of California Press.

Kerr, C. (1995) *The Uses of the University*, 4th edn, Cambridge MA: Harvard University Press.

Pederson, O. (1997) *The First Universities: Studium Generale and the Origins of University Education in Europe*, Cambridge: Cambridge University Press.

Rothblatt, S. and Wittrock, B. (eds) (1993) *The European and American University since 1800*, Cambridge: Cambridge University Press.

Scott, P. (1984) *The Crisis of the University*, Beckenham: Croom Helm.

GARETH PARRY

UNIVERSITY EXTENSION

University extension originated in 1873 when James Stuart from Cambridge University gave lectures to the North of England Council for the Promotion of Higher Education of Women, the Crewe Mechanics' Institute and the Rochdale Equitable Pioneers Society. By lecturing to non-university students in locations far removed from the university, the movement responded to social and economic changes and the widening of democracy in the late nineteenth century. At its peak, lectures would be delivered to audiences of 1,000 and written syllabuses, writing, discussion groups and summer schools were

also introduced. Influenced by liberal intellectuals such as T. H. Green, the extension movement was perceived as one way to help reform the ancient universities, which were seen as inaccessible and archaic in their curriculum, organisation and teaching. Its activities helped to found university colleges at Sheffield, Nottingham, Reading and Exeter, which established disciplinary departments, rather than colleges. Lectures were also popular among women and helped to increase the momentum for women's education.

Subjects covered by the early university extension were very much within the area of liberal education and included history, political economy and literature. Science also featured, and there were examples of vocational study in agricultural work. This would be popularised in the United States of America with the creation of the Cooperative Extension Service in 1914, which provided instruction to farmers in agriculture and home economics. University extension was also influential in many European countries such as Scandinavia, Germany and Holland. It would be developed in colonies and newly independent African nations. In recent years the idea of university extension has been eclipsed somewhat by the emphasis on lifelong learning and continuing education.

See also: adult education; continuing education; extra-mural class; liberal education; lifelong learning; mechanics' institute

TOM WOODIN

URBAN EDUCATION

Urbanism and urbanisation are key influences on the nature of education around the world, to such an extent that urban educational institutions are significantly different from most of those elsewhere (Coulby and Jones 1992). According to Cohen and Reese, analysing urban educational issues in the United States (1992: 65), 'City schools are unique for their complex racial and ethnic mixes, vast bureaucracies and specialised functions and services.' Ravitch suggests that by any measure, student performance in United States urban schools is 'appallingly low', so that, 'While almost every urban district has some exceptionally effective schools, outcomes for most students and most schools compare unfavorably with those in nonurban districts' (Ravitch 1999: 1). Individual cities differ greatly, but they share a basic educational challenge of catering for the diverse needs and interests of large communities. Social and geographical differences within the city, from the inner city to the leafy suburbs, readily translate into educational inequality. The social geography of educational outcomes within the city is indeed very noticeable in cities all over the world. Education is also a major political issue in many cities, leading to particular pressures for reform and improvement of urban educational provision.

The processes of urbanisation have transformed the nature of educational relationships. In some cases such as the United States, Britain, Australia and Canada, this phenomenon was well recognised during the nineteenth century (Goodenow and Marsden 1992), and has become increasingly significant since. In Chicago, for example, the initial growth and spread from the city centre was followed by a growth of suburban communities, so that by the 1970s more than half of the population of the Chicago Metropolitan District lived outside the city limits, a trend evident also in other American cities. The development of private and public transport facilities sustained this pattern of growth, which was accompanied by the increasing differentiation of social groups in different areas of the same city. Educational facilities sharply reflected these emerging differences. In many others, the educational impact of urbanisation has been more recent. In the former Soviet Union, for example, a major growth of large cities such as Moscow, Leningrad, Tashkent and Kiev took place in the mid-twentieth century, with the proportion of the whole population living in urban centres passing 50 per cent during this time. In Rio de Janeiro

in Brazil, a slum population in the Gamboa area emerged between the 1920s and 1950s, with immense implications for schooling in this area to contend with the social deprivation of 'slum children'. In the major cities of India such as Bombay, Calcutta, Delhi and Madras, the population grew greatly in the middle decades of the twentieth century with migrants and refugees from the countryside, posing difficult challenges for educational services (Lauwerys and Scanlon 1970).

In Guangzhou, in southern China, with a population that grew from 1 million to 6 million between 1949 and 1990, educational development has been a key feature of recent decades. Even here, nevertheless, disparities in educational provision between the central city and other parts of Guangzhou have also emerged. These have been reflected in different levels of funding, teachers' qualifications, facilities, prestige and student performance for schools in different regions. In a very densely populated area, further building of educational facilities is expensive, although urban development has become increasingly flexible to respond to the challenges of growth (Lee and Zibiao 1994).

Urbanisation in Kenya has produced major problems of educational provision, especially in the main urban centres of Nairobi and Mombasa. In Nairobi, there is an environment of extreme poverty, poor health, limited social services and basic infrastructure which makes it difficult to sustain educational development. There are high dropout rates, especially among already disadvantaged groups, while a number of expensive private schools achieve high results for those able to pay. Striking differences exist between districts and environments within the city, as between Nairobi and elsewhere, and between the majority of primary schools and the thriving private sector (Lillis 1992).

In the very different environment of New York City, a large education budget has provided for the growth of an education system, including provision for special education. Yet here too, there is a persistently wide range of achievement among school districts, closely correlated with ethnicity and class. In disadvantaged areas of the city, schools have tended to have a high dropout rate among pupils and a high turnover of teachers. These continuing difficulties have encouraged attempts to improve educational performance across the city by means of initiatives in urban school reform. Such initiatives have included the introduction of charter school legislation, and of scholarships to the large number of non-public schools that exist in the city. There have also developed significant collaborative ventures between the urban education authority and urban interest groups. One of these, involving South Bronx Churches, led to the establishment of the Bronx Leadership Academy High School in 1991 and a number of more recent innovations of this type (Ravitch and Viteritti 2000). Similar concerns have influenced reform in other American cities like Chicago and Houston, and major European cities such as London and Rotterdam. In London, the pattern of highly differentiated achievement within the city and private schools for those parents able to afford the fees has also led to efforts to promote school improvement, close failing schools, and to establish 'Education Action Zones' and specialised academies, with the support of the national government.

The future of urban education is likely to witness many further initiatives around the world to redress the inequalities and differences found within the same city. Urban and national authorities have already been drawn in to attempt to find solutions, so far with mixed results. It may well be that with the growth of international patterns of migration and population movements, a more global perspective on the issues involved is required, taking account of the broad social, political and economic forces that are involved (Coulby and Jones 1992). As the process of urbanisation continues unabated around the world and cities grow ever more massive, the problems that have become closely associated with them have the potential to become increasingly acute. Teachers in city schools are obliged to address many difficult challenges, both inside and outside of the classroom. Their pupils, particularly in disadvantaged areas, will often struggle to achieve their potential, even in nations where equality of opportunity is a general ideal and expectation. A number of initiatives to improve and develop urban education have achieved success. Nevertheless, it is in the cities that educational reform in the twenty-first century will face its greatest test.

See also: academy; catchment area; educational priority area; metropolitanism; parental choice; rural education; zoning

Further reading

Cohen, R. D. and Reese, W. J. (1992) 'Education and America's cities'. In R. K. Goodenow and W. E. Marsden (eds) *The City and Education in Four Nations*, Cambridge: Cambridge University Press.

Coulby, D. and Jones, C. (1992) 'Theoretical approaches to urban education: an international perspective'. In D. Coulby, C. Jones and D. Harris (eds) *World Yearbook of Education 1992: Urban Education*, London: Kogan Page.

Goodenow, R. K. and Marsden, W. E. (eds) (1992) *The City and Education in Four Nations*, Cambridge: Cambridge University Press.

Lauwerys, J. A. and Scanlon, D. G. (eds) (1970) *World Yearbook of Education 1970: Education in Cities*, London: Evans.

Lee, W. O. and Li, Z. (1994) 'Disparities in educational development in a fast-developing Chinese city: the case of Guangzhou'. In N. P. Stromquist (ed.) *Education in Urban Areas: Cross-National Dimensions*, London: Praeger.

Lillis, K. (1992) 'Urbanisation and education in Nairobi'. In D. Coulby, C. Jones and D. Harris (eds) *World Yearbook of Education 1992: Urban Education*, London: Kogan Page.

Ravitch, D. (ed.) (1999) *Brookings Papers on Education Policy*, Washington DC: Brookings Institution Press.

Ravitch, D. and Viteritti, J. P. (eds) (2000) *City Schools: Lessons from New York*, Baltimore MD: Johns Hopkins University Press.

GARY McCULLOCH

V

VALUE ADDED

The term 'value added' has become very popular among educators interested in determining the importance of certain factors in school effectiveness. The term refers to a statistical analysis that investigates the contribution to a student's performance by one or more teachers, schools, programmes, or policies. When doing a value added analysis, the researcher is typically attempting to characterise the contribution of a certain factor to the changing performance that is observed in a set of students as they progress through school. For example, the contribution of different teachers to the change in school performance from fifth grade to sixth grade of a set of students might be the factor being examined. The current students' performance, relative to some previous measure of performance might be examined, on the other hand, for a consistent effect due to the impact of system policy decisions or the quality of the teaching of a school system. Sometimes the analysis is so generic that the results might not even specify what it is about the school that seems to contribute to the change in performance from one year to another.

This approach is quite different from that historically used to compare schools in terms of their students' average performance score. This status-based approach was used despite knowing that many factors can influence that performance level other than the effectiveness of the teacher or the quality of the school.

For example, we know that schools with higher social-economic status students usually outscore other schools. One of the primary motivations for the work on value added assessment models is to try to correct for such confounding input characteristics. In other words, it does not seem fair to credit or to damn a teacher or a school because of the pre-existing capabilities or advantages their students bring to school. This reasoning has led to interest in the change in performance of students, on the assumption that change from entrance to exit of the classroom after a year's teaching is a purer measure of the effect of a good school than the absolute performance level of the student measured upon leaving the classroom, ignoring where they were when they began.

Once the school system or the government has become convinced of the wisdom of such a value added approach, and the misleading nature of status-based presentations, we are faced with the difficulty of actually developing the analytic strategy to make it happen. The earliest examples of such work include that begun in 1984 by Webster and others in the Dallas school system of Texas, USA, and the work associated with Sanders begun in the early 1990s in the state of Tennessee, USA, known as the TVAAS system.

The following gives a quick appreciation of the complications in such work. What do we do about missing data? Suppose a student does not take the final examination that is going to be compared to his or her incoming test score to calculate their change score (because they are absent or they transfer). Now the complication comes when we realise that the students who are absent are not a representative sample of all the students. Instead, they are more likely to be the less able students. The usual value added study that results in comparisons of school effectiveness is what methodologists call a correlation, or field-based study. In other words, these are not experiments with random assignment of students to classrooms, but depend upon access to real data collected from the field. The assignment of students to teachers or the attendance of students in particular schools are usually very un-random. So, the effect of this is to provide conclusions that might be statistical niceties, but in fact are not 'true' representations of the school. If we believe that student characteristics interact with teacher characteristics, we have another complication that is very hard (some believe impossible) to untangle using statistical approaches, even for the best of the value added models.

See also: performance indicators; school effectiveness; school improvement

Further reading

Lissitz, R. W. (ed.) (2006) *Longitudinal and Value Added Modeling of Student Performance*, Maple Grove MN: Jam Press.
——(2005) *Value Added Models in Education: Theory and Applications*, Maple Grove MN: Jam Press.
ROBERT W. LISSITZ

VICE-CHANCELLOR

In England, Northern Ireland, Wales and the British Commonwealth a vice-chancellor is, in effect, the chief executive of a university. Technically, the vice-chancellor deputises for the chancellor, but the latter is frequently an honorary position with duties limited to ceremonial events. In these countries the vice-chancellor is ultimately responsible for the day-to-day management of the university,

heading a team of senior managers responsible for strategic and operational matters. Most, if not all, staff of the university will ultimately report (typically through line management structures) to the vice-chancellor, who is normally a professor with significant experience of administration, as well as being a distinguished scholar. Historically, women have experienced many barriers to academic promotion, but today a number of women hold vice-chancellorships, including Professor Alison Richard of Cambridge University.

Where university vice-chancellors have been notable public figures, this is usually because they have faced difficulties in spearheading managerial reforms. Benjamin Jowett, the theologian and master of Balliol College, Oxford, struggled to pursue his reformist agenda as vice-chancellor of Oxford University from 1882–86, for example. One of Jowett's successors, the present incumbent and first external appointment to the Oxford vice-chancellorship, Professor John Hood, also experienced initial resistence in advancing private sector-style reforms.

Scottish universities generally combine the post of principal and vice-chancellor, and the title signifies a different kind of university role in certain other countries, sometimes being ceremonial or as a deputy to a 'hands-on' chancellor or president.

See also: chancellor; rector; university
DAVID CROOK

VIRTUAL LEARNING

Virtual learning (VL) is the use of often highly sophisticated components of information and communications technology (ICT) to offer a remote learning experience. VL content ranges from courses in basic life skills to university award-bearing programmes. An important element of VL is *simulation*, which may take the form of learners watching streamed or downloaded videos of lectures. In sophisticated forms of VL, *artificial intelligence* may be used, for example as an assessment tool simulating tutor responses to the student's previous work.

Virtual learning environments (VLEs) are structured database shells with a set of tools such as chat rooms, space for lecture notes, quizzes, class lists and student performance analysers. Educators can upload material as and when they wish it to be made available to the learners. Many universities and schools use VLEs as a single, user-friendly and globally available source of student information.

VL may be the only education paradigm used by learners – those studying online degree programmes, for example – or it may be 'blended' with other, more traditional forms of pedagogy and learning.

See also: computer-assisted learning; educational technology; e-learning; learning; Web-based learning

DAVID SETH PRESTON

VISUAL AIDS

In the context of the classroom, visual aids are resources used by the teacher or lecturer to illustrate and reinforce the material being taught. For example, in schools maps are frequently used as visual aids by teachers of geography, diagrams and charts by teachers of science, photographs and timelines by teachers of history. Education and training activities frequently involve the use of flip charts, positioned in front of the audience, which can be especially suitable for scribing key words and ideas emerging from group work. The blackboard/whiteboard or over-head projector may be thought of as basic classroom visual aids which have been complemented, or replaced, by interactive hardware capable of displaying computer projections. During the 1960s and 1970s instructors made frequent use of reel-to-reel – and later cassette – tape recorders to play commentaries accompanying projected photographic slides, an idea fleetingly known as 'radiovision'. Classroom televisions, used for showing recorded programmes – on video

tape or, more recently, on DVD – have proved a more enduring audio-visual resource.

The effective use of visual aids should not be taken for granted and there are many manuals of do's and don'ts for instructors considering their use. For example, the Higher Education Academy for England advises that visual aids 'can reinforce learning by stimulating other senses than just the aural – the audience can see as well as listen'. However, aids 'that are gimmicky, poorly presented, difficult to read or which fail because of faulty equipment will hinder learning rather than help it'.

See also: classroom; educational broadcasting; instruction; lecture/lecturer; lesson; teaching/teaching methods

DAVID CROOK

VOCATIONAL EDUCATION

Vocational education is designed primarily to prepare pupils and students for their future work or vocation, especially in skilled industries. It may be sufficiently broad to equip the learner for a wide range of potential occupations, and to include academic subjects. It may, on the other hand, be directed specifically at a particular industry or other occupation, with little recognition for academic approaches. The curriculum of schools may incorporate a vocational emphasis, either for all pupils or for a particular group of pupils, and indeed in some countries vocational schools have developed at the level of secondary education. It may also be the focus of post-school education, and in some cases might be seen as a type of apprenticeship. Vocational education is often regarded as the antithesis of liberal education, usually with lower status, although there have been many attempts in different countries to combine features of both, and to encourage a 'liberal vocationalism' (Silver and Brennan 1988).

In some countries, including the United States, vocationalism has often been seen as a way of addressing economic and social

633

difficulties (Kantor 1982). However, many critics of vocationalism and vocationalisation emphasise the potential risks that such approaches pose to the liberal values of schools and universities. Grubb and Lazerson (2006) argue that vocationalism has become a key feature in many different education systems around the world. They contend that vocationalism has transformed the character of secondary education so that it has become pre-vocational, rather than academic and liberal, in nature, while at the same time expanding post-school education at a sub-university level. According to Grubb and Lazerson, this tends to turn education into a commodity with economic value, thus undermining the many other purposes of education such as civic, social, intellectual, nation-building, religious and other goals, potentially leading to a state they describe as 'HyperVoc':

> In this grim world, narrow work skills for routinised work are all that matter; the search among students for fast access to employment leads them to avoid other 'frills' including the arts, the humanities, or any version of general education; employers seek specific skills narrowly tailored to their production, certified through specific qualifications; and both broad occupational programmes and broad academic programmes disappear – except perhaps for elite students – because they are not seen as useful.
>
> (Grubb and Lazerson 2006: 302)

Other critics refer to the growth of a 'new vocationalism' since the 1980s, as a means of countering unemployment and undermining the academic curriculum (for example Holt 1987). In Britain, for instance, the Technical and Vocational Education Initiative (TVEI), launched in 1982, aimed to vocationalise the secondary school curriculum and thereby equip young people for the 'world of work' (Gleeson 1987).

Vocationalisation has also become a major theme in many developing nations around the world. Lauglo and Maclean, for example,

review the vocationalisation of secondary education as it has developed in African countries, specifically Botswana, Ghana, Kenya and Mozambique (Lauglo and Maclean 2005). Indeed, in many African countries vocationalisation of the curriculum has been a major policy goal over the past decade, encouraged by the World Bank. In India, also, vocationalisation of secondary education was emphasised as a priority in a national policy scheme in 1988, with the aim of enhancing individual employability, reducing a perceived mismatch between demand and supply of skilled manpower, and providing an alternative for those pursuing higher education.

See also: apprenticeship; curriculum; liberal education; professional education; qualifications; secondary school/education; training; work-based/work-located/workplace/work-related learning

Further reading

Gleeson, D. (ed.) (1987) *TVEI and Secondary Education: A Critical Appraisal*, London: Methuen.

Grubb, W. N. and Lazerson, M. (2006) 'The globalization of rhetoric and practice: the education gospel and vocationalism'. In H. Lauder, P. Brown, J. Dillabough and A. H. Halsey (eds) *Education, Globalisation and Social Change*, Oxford: Oxford University Press.

Holt, M. (1987) *Skills and Vocationalism: The Easy Answer*, Buckingham: Open University Press.

Kantor, H. (ed.) (1982) *Work, Youth and Schooling: Historical Perspectives on Vocationalism in American Education*, Stanford CA: Stanford University Press.

Lauglo, J. and Maclean, R. (eds) (2005) *Vocationalisation of Secondary Education Revisited*, Dordrecht, the Netherlands: Springer.

Silver, H. and Brennan, J. (1988) *A Liberal Vocationalism*, London: Methuen

GARY McCULLOCH

VOLUNTARISM

Voluntarism in philosophy is a theory that regards will, rather than intellect, as the fundamental principle or agency. In more general usage, it normally refers to the practice of supporting institutions – such as schools or hospitals – through voluntary contributions and permitting an unhindered private sector, rather than reliance on state aid.

In 1776 the American Founding Fathers supported the principle of voluntarism, rather than government-controlled education. The idea of a national university was rejected at this point and, even in 1860, the 300 public schools of the United States were overshadowed by its 6,000 private academies (Peterson 1983). In nineteenth-century England voluntarists believed that religion and education could not be separated. They argued that, in order to preserve religious and civil liberties, the state should have no involvement with schools at all. Most advocates of voluntarism subscribed to the economic and political doctrines of free trade and laissez-faire, which they were quite prepared to extend to education. They rejected notions that the state might give financial assistance to schools provided for the education of poor children, and resolved to build and support their own schools entirely from private resources voluntarily subscribed. There is a consensus amongst historians of education that voluntarism failed in its objectives and put back the setting up of a national system of elementary schooling in England by at least a quarter of a century.

Voluntarism is also used in the sense of volunteering. Voluntary Service Overseas (VSO), a widely known international development charity founded in the 1950s, initially focused on providing voluntary work placements for school leavers in African countries. While still promoting such opportunities for young people, the average age of VSO volunteers is now significantly older, with the majority – trained teachers among them – drawn from skilled, professional backgrounds.

Support for limiting state educational activity in favour of the private sector is still frequently advocated. In respect of the developing world and poorer countries, for example, it is sometimes claimed that for-profit businesses possess greater potential to create inward investment.

See also: charities, educational; church; economics of education; privatisation/marketisation; religious school

Further reading

Murphy, J. (1971) *Church, State and Schools in Britain, 1800–1970*, London: Routledge and Kegan Paul.
Peterson, R. A. (1983) 'Education in colonial America', *The Freeman*, 33(9): 1529–33.

PAUL SHARP

VOUCHERS

School vouchers provide government resources to parents to enable them to enrol their children in independent private schools of their choosing. Vouchers are a specific form of parental choice of schools intended to serve as an alternative to pupil assignment to public schools by residential zone.

Three defining characteristics of voucher schemes distinguish them from other more common forms of school choice. Because vouchers involve actual government funds directed to schools by parents, they differ from privately funded scholarship programmes for school-age children and from tuition tax credit policies. Voucher arrangements also are distinct from public school choice schemes (e.g. charter schools, magnet schools) in that the choice set includes privately run schools. Vouchers differ from programmes of government direct financial support of private schools, common in Canada and throughout much of Europe, because the private schools remain largely autonomous in their operations, even though they are receiving public funds.

School voucher programmes are either universal or targeted. Universal schemes, such as the longstanding programme in Chile, make vouchers available equally to all students. Begun in 1981, the Chilean voucher programme served one third of the country's 2,000,000 elementary school students by

1996. Universal voucher programmes are largely justified based upon the expectation that their creation of an education market will benefit participants, because their parents can better match them to an appropriate school, and non-participants, because the threat of losing students will motivate them to improve their services.

Targeted voucher programmes limit eligibility to students that are disadvantaged in some respect. All twelve voucher programmes fully authorised or operated by US states and localities in the spring of 2007 were targeted at students who lived in low-income families, had a disability, resided in a rural area without a public school, or were attending a public school designated in need of improvement under state or federal accountability systems. Targeted voucher programmes serve an estimated 56,000 students in eight different states in the USA. The first such programme was established in the state of Vermont in 1869. They are primarily justified in terms of extending the opportunity to exercise school choice to students with special needs for whom a private school environment might be especially important, as well as based on social justice considerations, since wealthier families always have had educational options for their children.

The effects of school voucher programmes on participants and non-participants have been fiercely debated. The best evidence so far regarding the likely participant effects of vouchers comes from random assignment studies of the Milwaukee, Wisconsin voucher programme, as well as experimental evaluations of 'voucher-like' privately funded scholarship programmes in Charlotte (North Carolina), Dayton, (Ohio), New York, and Washington DC. Seven of the eight analyses of these experimental data have reported positive and statistically significant impacts of vouchers on the achievement of either all participants, or just the sub-group of African-American students, after at least two years in the programme. Every study of parental satisfaction with school vouchers has concluded

that parents are much more satisfied with their child's school if they have used a voucher to select it.

Studies of the effects of vouchers on non-participating students and schools are more mixed in their conclusions than are the studies of participant effects. Although few empirical studies suggest that non-participating students are harmed educationally by the extension of school choice through vouchers, the dozen or so studies indicating that voucher programmes provide a healthy dose of competition that spurs public schools to improve are approximately balanced by studies that conclude vouchers themselves have no clear effect on achievement in surrounding schools. Many of the voucher programmes judged to have little or no competitive effects are highly limited in scope and duration, which may explain why public schools have not changed perceptibly in response to them.

See also: charter school; experimental research; independent/private school/education; magnet school; parental choice; privatisation/marketisation

Further reading

Friedman, M. (1955) 'The role of government in education'. In R. A. Solo (ed.) *Economics and the Public Interest*, New Brunswick NJ: Rutgers University Press.

Gill, B. P., Timpane, M., Ross, K. E., Brewer, D. and Booker, K. (2007) *Rhetoric vs. Reality: What We Know and What We Need to Know About Vouchers and Charter Schools*, 2nd edn, Santa Monica CA: Rand Corporation.

Howell, W. G. and Peterson, P. E., with Wolf, P. J. and Campbell, D. E. (2006) *The Education Gap: Vouchers and Urban Schools*, revised edn, Washington DC: Brookings Institution Press.

PATRICK J. WOLF

VYGOTSKY, LEV (1896–1934)

Vygotsky, the Russian psychologist, studied philosophy and literature, with special interests in French and German Enlightenment thinkers, at the University of Moscow. He later specialised in psychology and education. In 1924 he was appointed as a researcher at the Moscow Institute of Experimental Psychology, where he became the leading figure. His aim was to produce a unifying theoretical foundation for psychology within a Marxist framework. His work stressed the social and historical factors in cognitive development, and he pioneered research methodologies relating to children's learning. His writings were banned in the Soviet Union from 1936 to 1956, and they only began to resurface for translation in the 1970s and 1980s. Thus,

Vygotsky's influence upon linguistics, cultural studies, cognitive psychology and child development began some fifty years after his early death from tuberculosis. His major work is *Thought and Language* (published posthumously in 1934), in which he examines the cultural/psychological tools that are necessary for cognitive development in children. He was an advocate of structured learning through planned teaching.

See also: psychology; psychology of education; Russia

STEVEN COWAN

W

WASHINGTON, BOOKER T. (1856–1915)

Washington, the black American educator, was born a slave in Virginia, the son of an enslaved mother and an unknown white man. He worked in salt furnaces and coal mines before the age of ten and then as a house boy. He left work and went to school aged sixteen. Reputedly, he walked 200 miles to get to Hampton Institute, where he paid his way by working as a school janitor. Mentored by Samuel Armstrong, the anti-slavery Civil War commander who believed that African Americans should receive a practical education, in 1881 Washington became the first teacher of the Tuskegee Institute. By 1888 Tuskegee had 450 students and owned over 500 acres of land, teaching a range of vocational and craft subjects. By 1900 Tuskegee Institute owned 2,460 acres upon which stood sixty buildings, nearly all of which had been built by the students themselves as part of their practical education. During this period Washington secured the support of local white political leaders by arguing against democratic rights for African Americans. He felt that black people should show their loyalty to the United States by working hard without complaining before being granted the vote. The purpose of education for black people was to raise their moral outlook and train them for economic independence. *Working with the Hands* (1904) is an expression of his ideas about integrating industrial training within education. His views attracted substantial financial support from wealthy white magnates such as Carnegie and Huntington, who saw in Washington an acceptable leader of black opinion.

See also: equality of opportunity; politics of education

STEVEN COWAN

WEB-BASED LEARNING

Web-based learning is a sub-component of e-learning and distance education/learning. This form of learning takes place when learners use the internet to gain knowledge, acccess support or feedback from an instructor or tutor, or demonstrate understanding by completing Web-based tasks which may sometimes form part of an assessed pro- gramme of learning. Web-based learning may be of free, informal and of short duration (for example when a website is consulted for the purposes of establishing information such as a definition or fact). On the other hand, it may involve accessing password-protected inter- net resources regularly over a period of time (for example when higher education institu- tions offer accredited online courses for fee- paying students). For learners, being able to access – and sometimes interact with – edu- cational materials at any time of the day or night is a great benefit. The 'Google generation' has developed a dependency on immediate internet-supplied information that may once have necessitated a library visit. For providers of Web-based learning programmes, including universities, the Web has created possibilities to enrol, 'teach', support and assess non-traditional or distant students. High-quality Web-based study programmes do not come cheap, however and significant expenditure may be required to purchase reliable and accessible computer hardware and software.

See also: distance education/learning; e-learning

DAVID CROOK

WEBER, MAX (1864–1920)

A founding father of sociology, Weber was a precociously gifted teenager already specialising in political and religious history by the age of thirteen. He studied law at Heidelberg (1882–84) and gained a doctorate in 1889 for a study of medieval business organisation. Academic positions in Berlin, Freiburg and Göttingen established his reputation but he suffered a mental breakdown in 1898 which lasted some five years. His most important work, *The Protestant Ethic and the Spirit of Capitalism* (1905) challenged Marxist views concerning the primacy of the economic in historical development. In a series of major studies he outlined an interpretive approach to social sciences, stressing the need for careful studies of institutions in order to identify underlying processes. Weber argued for a value-free approach, which he thought could be reinforced by adopting both historical and comparative perspectives. In *Economy and Society* (1914) he developed the idea of social action and social actors engaging in interaction, the understanding of which was to be derived from identifying the meanings that participants ascribed to their actions. His studies of bureaucratisation described a shift from value orientation and action towards structures dominated by preset goals. Within such systems individuals are envisaged as being trapped in rule-based, rational forms of control. These perspectives remain potently suggestive for analysts of dominant trends within educational institutions. His linking of the Protestant work ethic to the growth of capitalism has provided an historical and theoretical framework for much research into the ideology of schooling.

See also: sociology

STEVEN COWAN

WHOLE-CLASS TEACHING

Whole-class teaching refers to the practice of teaching a class of children the same lesson altogether, rather than teaching a lesson to a smaller group of children within the class, or allowing students to work on an individualised scheme of work. The practice of whole-class teaching has gone in and out of fashion and varies across countries. In the United Kingdom, whole-class teaching takes place in most secondary schools each day along with individual and small group work. In primary schools the daily maths/numeracy and English/literacy lessons begin with a session of whole-class teaching.

Whole-class teaching requires the teacher to tailor his or her teaching to fit in with the needs of all the students in the class so that all children are challenged and stretched whilst taking part in the same lesson. Historically, whole-class teaching has involved a didactic process of the teacher imparting knowledge to the students with little interaction between students and between students and the teacher. However, whole-class teaching in the current context involves a two-way interaction between teacher and students. Often the whole-class teaching forms the basis of the lesson, providing teaching input on the learning objectives that are then reinforced by students' independent and collaborative group work. The development of modern information technology within the classroom has enabled whole-class teaching to be less didactic and more easily differentiated. For example, the introduction of interactive whiteboards into Western secondary school classrooms has enabled greater engagement between teachers and students. It has made teaching less prescriptive and allowed for increased student participation during whole-class teaching. Interactive whiteboards are connected to a computer and the teacher may write on the board or show a computer program on it. Students may come up and demonstrate answers on the board or partake in games on the board in front of the class.

See also: ability grouping; mixed-ability teaching

NATALIE HEATH

WILLIAM OF WYKEHAM (1324–1404)

William of Wykeham was thought to have been born into a commoner's family in Hampshire. Nevertheless, he rose to the highest political offices under Edward III, as well as to high clerical positions, mostly reflecting his abilities. His motto, 'Manners maketh man', is thought to reflect his experience and belief that through education anyone could rise. Wykeham amassed a considerable fortune from holding multiple offices under the Crown. As bishop of Winchester he set about purchasing land in Winchester and Oxford in order to found a school and college. His endowment founded a school in 1373 – which evolved into Winchester College – which laid the pattern for succeeding schools. Winchester served as a feeder school for New College, Oxford (founded in 1380), providing a model for the later link between Eton College and King's College, Cambridge in the reigns of Henry VI (1422–61 and 1470–71). Another Winchester school, the College of St Mary, founded by William of Wykeham in 1387, was the first to have an integral chapel, and Wykeham's expertise in the design of castles influenced the architecture of the collegiate buildings. Winchester College pupils are today still referred to as *Wykehamists* and his motto remains that of the school.

See also: public school

STEVEN COWAN

WOLLSTONECRAFT, MARY (1759–97)

Wollstonecraft was an English radical author and polemicist. She established a school with her sister in east London, from which she developed ideas about teaching that were published in *Thoughts on the Education of Daughters* (1787). Her publication *Vindication of the Rights of Man* (1790) was one of the first responses to Burke's *Reflections* and was a major inspiration for Thomas Paine's later work of the same title. This was followed in 1792 by Wollstonecraft's most famous work, *Vindication of the Rights of Women*. A major section of this work concerned the education of girls and women, which she placed within a context of civil liberties and rights. She argued for a wider curriculum than polite arts, preparations for domestic economy or motherhood. She is the first English woman to sustain the case for education as being part of the basic entitlements of a child.

Wollstonecraft was a prolific, self-supporting, professional author, thus putting her skills and knowledge to practical use. She established, more than any other, the right of an educated woman to take her place in public and political spheres rather than restricting herself to the private and domestic. This view ran counter to others of her time such as Hannah More and Sarah Trimmer. She viewed the current education of women as being principally designed to make them contented with enslavement. Reassessments in the 1970s reintroduced her work and legacy to a new, popular audience and she became something of an iconic figure for the new feminists in education.

See also: equality of opportunity; feminist theory

STEVEN COWAN

WORK-BASED/WORK-LOCATED/ WORKPLACE/WORK-RELATED LEARNING

Work-based learning (WBL), also sometimes known by similar terms, is applied to learning that is either (a) work-related, taking place *away from* but *for* work, or (b) work-located, taking place *at* work. In recent years Western governments have sought to encourage workers to enhance their skills by engaging in continuing professional development and lifelong learning, contributing to the learning society and knowledge economy. WBL is particularly associated with higher education as a mechanism for *widening participation* of learners in that sector.

In the workplace, WBL may take the form of a company in-house learning programme. This may be of short duration and functional, for example the provision of training to use a newly installed telephone system or bespoke software package. It may also cover reflective practices linked to staff appraisal or performance management, or may focus on 'hands on' problem-solving challenges, project management and collaborative tasks.

WBL is not a new idea. In many countries a *work placement* or *work experience* is an established part of schooling for upper secondary-age students and is designed to provide a 'taster' of the world of employment, introducing to them the expected codes of behaviour, punctuality, dress and language, as well as other routines and challenges of the workplace. Many higher education programmes also include an element of WBL: 'sandwich courses', in particular, offer opportunities to spend a period – often an 'industrial year' – earning, as well as learning, 'on the job'. In the United Kingdom accredited courses at university level, such as foundation degrees aimed at health workers and teaching assistants, 'professional master's' degrees and 'professional doctorates' have been developed for 'reflective practitioners' wishing to think about career progression and develop blueprints for workplace change, often including the dimensions of managing time, people, priorities and problems.

It is in the spirit of WBL that programmes are designed to fit around the needs of learners and employers and that the latter are supportive – for example by meeting courses

costs and granting study leave – of their employees. Employers may also sometimes help to shape the design of WBL curricula. Many public- and private-sector organisations have risen admirably to the challenge of supporting WBL. Investors in People UK, which reports to and receives funds from the Department for Education and Skills, has awarded a quality standard to more than 30,000 businesses demonstrating good practice. Nevertheless, for some employers WBL may be viewed as an unwarranted organisational cost, rather than an investment in the workforce.

It is often argued that accredited WBL programmes run by higher education organisations are beneficial for workers, but they also bring benefits to universities wishing to engage constructively with the local business community. WBL offers opportunities for universities to demonstrate excellence in teaching, research and knowledge transfer, and the partnerships formed with employers may enhance student recruitment. Higher education-level programmes, which sometimes give learners a 'head start' by accrediting prior learning, permit participants to encounter theoretical – as well as practical – ideas and library literature about the lives and work of others professionals, and about the diverse nature of, and the cultural practices of, the workplace (Ebbutt 1996; Foster and Stephenson 1998). Non-traditional methods of assessment are frequently used for WBL programmes, including, for example, the keeping of a reflective diary, a video journal and student presentations, though higher-level award-bearing courses are likely also to include a significant element of formal writing. Discussions with, and feedback from, tutors can generate new ideas and agendas for theoretical, applied or practice-based research, and the observations of tutors visiting the learners' place of work may lead to the identification of further training needs and targets, either for the organisation or for the individual. Additionally, the opportunity to study for a qualification may enhance learner motivation and produce a stronger commitment to career development and progression. The emergence of new professional understandings has, in some instances, seen WBL programmes contribute to revised specifications of workplace roles and the identification of competency standards (Gonczi 1999).

See also: accreditation of prior achievement/ learning; continued/continuing professional development; higher education; knowledge economy; learning society; lifelong learning; practitioner research; professional education; reflective practitioner; sandwich course; skills; vocational education; workers' education

Further reading

Ebbutt, D. (1996) 'Universities, work-based learning and issues about knowledge', *Research in Post-compulsory Education*, 3(1): 357–72.
Foster, E. and Stephenson, J. (1998) 'Work-based learning and universities in the UK: a review of current practices and trends', *Higher Education Research and Development*, 17(2): 155–70.
Gonczi, A. (1999) 'Competency-based learning: a dubious past – an assured future?' In D. Boud and J. Garrick (eds) *Understanding Learning at Work*, London: Routledge.

DAVID CROOK

WORK EXPERIENCE

'Work experience' is a term most commonly used to describe the opportunity given secondary school students to try out one or two weeks of work during the school term. Students usually arrange, with the help of their school and sometimes family, a work experience placement. During the placement students are exempt from attending school and instead attend the workplace they have chosen, keeping the same hours as other employees and observing and carrying out tasks. The aim of work experience is to give students an understanding of the world of work, which may also help them to consider the kind of career they may wish to choose. The school normally supports the work experience student, and a teacher may visit

during the placement to check how the student is doing. Work experience is not confined to the school years. University and college students and others interested in a particular career often undertake work experience as a means of deciding whether they are suited to a particular career. Many companies and organisations set aside placements each year for people to gain work experience. For some of these there is fierce competition, particularly in media organisations. People who are unemployed may also undertake a work experience programme as a means of gaining skills and preparing themselves for the world of work.

See also: career guidance; sabbatical; sixth form; voluntarism

NATALIE HEATH

WORKERS' EDUCATION

Workers' education generally applies to the education of working-class people as opposed to middle-class people who may also work. It is a term with a strong historical presence, but is less in use today. It is sometimes used interchangeably with labour education, especially in the United States of America. A number of contested definitions can be discerned which, in reality, overlap. Most obviously, it refers to the educational activities of workers' movements such as trade unions and cooperatives, which run courses and educational programmes. Independent working-class educational organisations and institutions have also emerged out of workers' movements to develop workers' education. Examples include Ruskin College in the United Kingdom, Highlander in the USA and the educational initiatives of the Mondragon cooperatives in Spain. The notion of workers' education also embraces informal learning from the experience of inequality and participation in campaigns and struggles, as well as consciousness-raising activities of various movements. It can describe the attempts of working-class movements to educate the broader public and gain new members. For many working-class 'auto-didacts', education has taken place outside of formal educational institutions: self-directed, although mediated by a wider community context and network of domestic and private associations.

A third area relates to vocational education necessary to do a job of work, sometimes through apprenticeships and training. Trade unions, in particular, have sought control over the education of workers alongside employers and the state, which tend to play more dominant roles in defining the nature of such education. Finally, workers' education may also be defined more generically in terms of mainstream education provided for working-class children and adults, primarily by the state. This is more relevant to historical developments in countries such as Britain, where class understandings have been pervasive. Working-class people were often educated separately for much of the nineteenth and twentieth centuries, and the expansion of education to this constituency was much debated in class terms.

A number of themes and tensions can be identified within and between these various definitions. Class conflict has taken place over the forms of workers' education so that educational initiatives developed by middle-class philanthropists have been challenged and contested by workers. For instance, in early nineteenth-century Britain the notion of 'really useful knowledge', linked to collective social emancipation, was used to counter middle-class notions of 'useful knowledge' related to individual workplace skills and compliance. Over time, such informal tendencies coalesced into more formal working-class movements that would develop their own forms of education.

A related issue has been the thorny relations between workers' education and the state. Workers' organisations have argued for access to state education while attempting to influence the content and nature of that education. Independent forms of workers'

education have often utilised state funding, but this has been scrutinised in terms of inducing compliance and loss of autonomy. In some countries funding through the state and other bodies has meant that workers' education may be carried out by salaried employees of universities and local government in the form of industrial relations courses, trade union studies or university extension. In former communist countries under the influence of the Soviet Union, workers' education was conceived as closely inter-related with state education itself. From a different perspective, in parts of the developing world, such as newly independent African countries, workers' education was also connected to wider nation-building developments. For instance, in 1962 ten workers' colleges were established in Ghana.

The content and purpose of workers' education varies considerably. The discrete educational initiatives of workers' movements have often been directed at leaders and those who play a role in trade union bureaucracies. In this context education may be technical and specific. In countries strongly influenced by social democratic ideas, such as Germany and Sweden, workers have been trained to participate in workplace decisions and have sat on boards of companies. Elsewhere, day release and paid time off for workers to study has been negotiated by unions. The content of workers' education has also been debated in terms of whether it should relate to social change and activism or should be little different from mainstream education. For instance, in early twentieth-century Britain, the Workers' Educational Association championed the notion of liberal education modelled on the university degree, a position actively contested by the Plebs League and labour colleges, organisations which emphasised the role of education in the class struggle. In reality, these conflicts clouded a considerable overlap in approach and a competition for similar students.

Issues of gender, race, sexuality and disability can also be identified in the history of workers' education, although they have not always been openly faced by such movements themselves. More recent social movements have not always located themselves within a class framework. The notions of 'transformatory education' and 'radical' or 'critical pedagogy' have aimed to appeal to a wider diversity of people and have drawn upon the ideas of Paolo Freire. Groups of poor and marginalised people from countries in the South, such as the Self-Employed Women's Association in India, have also impacted upon a growing global network of social movements fostering change. Western labour movements have worked with partners in Latin American, African and Asian countries through various networks as well as the International Labour Organisation, International Confederation of Free Trade Unions and International Federation of Workers' Education Associations. Recent invocations of 'lifelong learning' have embraced diverse forms of 'learning' that encompass parts of workers' education, especially its informal aspects, although the political motivations and sense of social movement tend to be absent from such accounts.

See also: adult education; lifelong learning; recurrent education; vocational education; work-based/work-located/workplace/work-related learning; Workers' Educational Association (WEA)

Further reading

London, S. H., Tarr, E. R. and Wilson, J. F. (eds) (1990) *The Reeducation of the American Working Class*, Westport CT: Greenwood Press.
Woodin, T. (2007) 'Working class education and social change in nineteenth and twentieth century Britain', *History of Education*, 36.

TOM WOODIN

WORKERS' EDUCATIONAL ASSOCIATION (WEA)

The Workers' Educational Association (WEA) is a voluntary association with chari-

table status that provides and promotes adult education in the United Kingdom. Over 5,000 courses are organised each year, which attract 110,000 adult learners. The WEA aims to influence policy and campaign on behalf of adult learners, and supports the development of learning, particularly among excluded groups and those who previously missed out on education. It is committed to the notion of lifelong learning as enhancing a democratic society.

Learners play a role in the planning and provision of courses, as well as governance. Membership is free and open to those who support the principles of the organisation. There are approximately 19,000 members, divided into over 650 local branches, with nine regions in England as well as a Scottish Association.

Examples of courses include literacy and numeracy, family learning, literature, art, history, yoga, music, social sciences, computing courses, people's history, women's studies and community training. Workplace learning is delivered in partnership with employers and trade unions. Provision is developed locally, sometimes in partnership with community groups and organisations. The WEA is partly funded by the Learning and Skills Council, the Scottish Executive, and other sources such as local authorities, the European Union and the National Lottery.

It was set up in 1903 by a number of activists, most notably Albert Mansbridge, an employee of the Cooperative Movement. It pioneered three-year tutorial classes based on the university degree and targeted working-class people, although it has always attracted a broad range of students. Many classes chose their subject of study, rejected certification and emphasised non-vocational liberal learning. Some of the first classes were run by R. H. Tawney.

Workers' educational associations developed in a number of other countries, including New Zealand and Canada. In 1945 the WEA played a pivotal role in the creation of the International Federation of Workers' Education Associations, which now has over 100 affiliated organisations spread across the world. It facilitates discussions and networks which critically engage with and stimulate the development of workers' education.

See also: adult education; extra-mural class; lifelong learning; Tawney, R. H.; university extension; workers' education

TOM WOODIN

WORLD BANK

The World Bank came into existence on 27 December 1945 and began operating six months later from its headquarters in Washington DC. It comprises two unique institutions, currently owned by 184 member countries: the *International Bank for Reconstruction and Development* (IBRD) and the *International Development Association* (IDA). As well as the IBRD and IDA, three further organisations make up the World Bank Group: the *International Finance Corporation* (IFC), the *Multilateral Investment Guarantee Agency* (MIGA) and the *International Centre for Settlement of Investment Disputes* (ICSID).

The primary responsibility of the Bank is to provide finance and advice to countries to further enhance their economic development, reducing poverty and improving standards of living. This is done mainly by providing low-interest loans, interest-free credit, technical assistance and grants to developing countries in order to bring about levels of sustainability in areas such as education, health, infrastructure and communications.

The Bank's day-to-day operations are spearheaded by a president, appointed for five years, who is nominated by the country that holds the largest shares in the Bank, i.e. the United States of America, holding a 16.4 per cent share in 2006, ahead of Japan's 7.9 per cent, Germany's 4.5 per cent and the 4.3 per cent each held by France and the United Kingdom. The World Bank's president heads a board of governors comprising the ministers of finance or development in the member countries, who meet annually.

The Bank's educational work has financed research, consultancies and published reports – many of which may be accessed at www.worldbank.org – on such topics as early childhood development, primary, secondary and tertiary education, vocational education, the economics of education, educational policy and planning, educational technology and distance education. The Bank's website states that:

> Education is central to development and a key to attaining the Millennium Development Goals. It is one of the most powerful instruments for reducing poverty and inequality and lays a foundation for sustained economic growth. The World Bank's strategic thrust is to help countries integrate education into national economic strategies and develop holistic education systems responsive to national socio-economic needs. The World Bank is committed to help countries achieve Education For All (EFA) and, through Education for the Knowledge Economy (EKE), build dynamic knowledge societies.

A frequent criticism of the World Bank is that, while exercising its role in good governance, it influences the domestic politics of the countries that it serves and may deny these countries a sense of self-worth, self-determination and self-sufficiency. Caufield (1997) argues that the present structure of the World Bank harms economically poor nations, forcing them to abandon cultural practices and adopt Western values in order to benefit from financial assistance or expertise.

See also: economics of education; Education for All (EFA); international education

Further reading

Caufield, C. (1997) *Masters of Illusion*, New York: Henry Holt.
McClure, P. (ed.) (2003) *A Guide to the World Bank*, Washington DC: World Bank.
McLellan, E. P. (ed.) (2003) *The World Bank: Overview and Current Issues*, New York: Nova Science Publishers.

CARLTON MILLS

WORLD EDUCATION FELLOWSHIP (WEF)

The World Education Fellowship (WEF) is a voluntary association and UNESCO non-governmental organisation. Its purpose is to discuss and promote progressive education and is open to individuals. Although the Fellowship is committed to plurality in educational thinking, the main focus has been on child-centred education, world citizenship, international understanding and promoting world peace. It aims to influence policy, promote social and economic justice, foster social responsibility and build communication among diverse groups of people. It holds international conferences and publishes books and pamphlets, while national sections organise workshops, meetings and projects. Its journal is called *The New Era in Education*, previously *New Era*.

WEF was established in 1921 as the New Education Fellowship by Beatrice Ensor and a group of progressive educationists who were associated with the British Theosophical Society. It grew into an international organisation and was renamed the World Education Fellowship in 1966. An English section of the Fellowship was founded in 1927 and included amongst its members such leading educationists as Fred Clarke, Joseph Lauwerys, Percy Nunn, Michael Sadler and R. H. Tawney. The English section was also instrumental in the establishment of the Home and School Council and the English Association of New Schools. More recently it has been involved in a partnership which aims to use the internet to support the professional development of those providing lifelong learning.

See also: child-centred education; progressive education; United Nations Educational, Scientific and Cultural Organization (UNESCO)

TOM WOODIN

WRANGLER/WOODEN SPOON

At the University of Cambridge, England, a student who passes the final stage of the undergraduate mathematics degree with first-class honours is known as a wrangler. Historically, the student heading the pass list is the 'senior wrangler' and the second-placed student is 'second wrangler'. The specific title and also the prestige involved in winning it date from the nineteenth century, and reflect the significance and wider esteem of Cambridge mathematics. It was originally open only to male undergraduates: in 1890 Philippa Fawcett (1868–1948) was placed 'above the Senior Wrangler' at a point when women were not eligible to receive the Cambridge bachelor of arts degree. The term 'wooden spoon' was, by contrast, traditionally applied to the person who gained the lowest exam marks while still passing the Cambridge mathematics degree, and this usage has now become popular in a wide range of fields including sports and games, to denote the last person or team in a competition.

See also: excellence; underachievement

GARY McCULLOCH

WRITING

Writing and reading are key components of literacy which cannot easily be separated out from one another. The ancient Mesopotamians are usually credited with developing the first writing systems which allowed language to be directly written down as opposed to earlier pictorial forms of representation. It has been claimed that writing is a marker of the beginning of history as opposed to 'prehistory' and its development has been associated with the expansion of communication, trade and culture. Writing has also been linked with historical change and development, with progress and modernisation, especially economic expansion and political enlightenment. According to this line of thinking, more 'backward' societies tend to be characterised by a lack of literacy and more limited uses of writing. Histories of literacy have often been accounts of such growth illustrated with quantitative evidence. Jack Goody (1977) has argued that writing as a system involved a change in cognition which facilitated the growth of complex societies. Similarly, Walter Ong (1986) claimed that writing, in so far as it was 'interiorized' by people, became a 'technology that restructures thought'.

However, others have argued that the relationship between literacy and development is more confused and complex. Often the use of writing has been enmeshed with power relationships and used to reinforce existing inequalities. Ethnographic evidence has revealed the complexities of 'oral' cultures; the oral and written are conceived as closely interrelated rather than there being a great divide between the two. For instance, Brian Street (1984) rejected the 'autonomous' view of literacy as a neutral technology with power in and of itself, and instead posited the idea that all literacy practices are inherently 'ideological' and must be understood in their specific context.

Teaching writing is a key element of educational systems, and institutions tend to promote it as a value system in itself. One of the functions of schooling is to produce educated people able to use writing competently in order that they will be able to participate in society. Learning to write is a social activity that may help to develop cultural communication, promote acceptance and loyalty to a set of norms and values, and develop individuality. Different approaches can be discerned within the teaching of writing. According to one perspective it may be seen as a mechanical skill which must be learned through an apprenticeship, especially in terms of grammar, syntax and other rules. Following this approach, models of 'correct' writing must be taught to students, including genres, styles and conventions. This has been compared with those approaches which see writing as closely connected to the development of personal identity, personal expression and empowerment. Quality of expression, exploration of ideas and personal growth may be given greater prominence. In reality, these contrasting priorities often overlap and can be found, to varying degrees, in most curricula across national boundaries.

Since the 1970s writing has increasingly come to be viewed as a process rather than a product. It has been connected to problem-solving in which writers must engage iteratively in planning, representation, editing and evaluation. According to Bereiter and Scardamalia (1987) more advanced writers may be involved in 'knowledge transformation' rather than 'knowledge telling', have a clearer sense of their audience and focus on the 'global' rather than particular. Proponents of the 'new literacy studies' have emphasised the social context of writing in understanding the community contexts that students may bring with them into educational institutions. Radical approaches have examined how writing can both include and exclude and is interconnected with wider social and political activities. Multi-modal analyses have begun to examine the multiple communicative contexts within which writing takes place.

See also: grammar; literacy; reading; spelling

Further reading

Bereiter, C. and Scardamalia, M. (1987) *The Psychology of Written Composition*, London: Lawrence Erlbaum.

Clarke, R. and Ivanic, R. (1997) *The Politics of Writing*, London: Routledge.

Gee, J. P. (1996) *Social Linguistics and Literacy*, London: Taylor and Francis.

Goody, J. (1977) *Domestication of the Savage Mind*, Cambridge: Cambridge University Press.

Heath, S. B. (1983) *Ways with Words*, Cambridge: Cambridge University Press.

Ong, W. J.(1986) 'Writing is a technology that restructures thought'. In G. Baumann (ed.) *The Written Word: Literacy in Transition*, Oxford: Clarendon Press.

Street, B. (1984) *Literacy in Theory and Practice*, Cambridge: Cambridge University Press.

Vincent, D. (2000) *The Rise of Mass Literacy*, Cambridge: Polity Press.

TOM WOODIN

Y

YOUNG, MICHAEL (1915–2002)

A British social entrepreneur, Young was influenced by the positive experience he had as a boy at Dartington Hall, the progressive school in Devon, England. He developed ideas about the Open School, viewed as a laboratory for learning, involving pupils, teachers and parents. He became director of research for the British Labour Party aged twenty-nine, and personally wrote *Let Us Face the Future*, the manifesto which brought the Attlee government to power in 1945. He became internationally famous with the publication of *The Rise of the Meritocracy* (1958) a satirical account of the way that IQ measurements and academic certification had replaced wealth in the reproduction of social inequalities. For Young, equal access to schooling was a basic human right. During this period he was also the founder of the British consumer rights organisation the Consumers' Association and its magazine *Which?*. His 1957 study (with Peter Willmott) *Family and Kinship in East London* linked schooling, income, housing and health in an account of the poor. Even though it was more in the tradition of Booth, Rowntree and Mayhew than of modern social science, it became a standard text within teacher training for many years. Young founded the Advisory Centre for Education in 1960. From small beginnings Young developed and expanded the idea of the Open University and the National Extension College, which institutionalised the idea of distance learning through broadcasting and correspondence. In his later years Young continued to create education organisations linking consumer power and open access.

See also: distance education/learning; meritocracy; Open University

STEVEN COWAN

YOUTH CLUB/WORK

The practices we now know as 'youth work' emerged during the third quarter of the nineteenth century. Various types of philanthropic leisure-time provision for young people were on offer before this, including Sunday Schools, ragged schools, young men's prayer groups, Bible study and social action groups that preceded the formation of the Young Men's Christian Association (YMCA) in 1844. However, with the growth of philanthropic and associational activity, new approaches developed and, by the end of that century, 'work among youth' had established its typical forms: clubs, uniformed troupes, fellowship, and outreach to those not initially attracted to such groups.

The first clubs and institutes for youths appeared in Britain in the mid-nineteenth century. The formation of lads' and boys' clubs, and girls' clubs and groups gathered pace during the 1880s and 1890s, both in Britain and the United States of America. Uniformed groups, offering a mix of formal and informal activity, grew quickly following the establishment of the Boys' Brigade by William Alexander Smith (1854–1914) in 1883, and exploded after the formation of the Scouts by Robert Baden-Powell (1857–1941) in 1908. At the same time, a range of fellowship groups associated with churches and religious organisations was flourishing, one of the most significant being the Girls' Friendly Society. Outreach work had its origins in district and parish visiting schemes and the like, which were a key feature of local Victorian life in many areas.

During the first decades of the twentieth century, much of the growth in work with young people still took the form of single-sex provision. There were some notable exceptions, including the development of 4-H (Head, Heart, Hands, and Health) clubs around agricultural renewal in the United States of America, and many local church groups in Britain. It was when mixed club work became the norm, from the 1940s, that the terms 'youth work' and 'youth club' came into common usage. In Britain, Josephine Macalister Brew (1904–57) authored the first account of 'modern' youth work, while Grace Coyle (1892–1962) pioneered group work in the USA. Literature and practices enabled youth work to gain its classic characteristics:

- attention to the needs, experiences and contribution of young people and the offer of a sanctuary or a second home;

- the appointment of workers of character and integrity to guide and befriend young people;
- the fostering of fellowship and associational life;
- opportunities for reflection and learning in friendship groups;
- freedom for young people to participate on the basis of choice, namely 'the voluntary principle'.

Church and community-oriented youth work continues to feature strongly, but an alternative model of 'youth development' work, featuring targeted, individualised, programmatic and accreditation-oriented forms of working, emerged in the late twentieth century, extending beyond the USA to other countries.

See also: church; community education; informal/nonformal learning; peer group; Scout Association; social capital

Further reading

Brew, J. Macalister (1943) *In The Service of Youth: A Practical Manual of Work among Adolescents*, London: Faber.
Delgado, M. (2002) *New Frontiers for Youth Development in the Twenty-first Century*, New York: Columbia University Press.
Jeffs, T. and Smith, M. K. (2007) *Youth Work*, Basingstoke: Palgrave.

MARK K. SMITH

Z

ZONE OF PROXIMAL DEVELOPMENT

An important concept in his cultural-historical theory of learning and human development, Lev Vygotsky used the term 'zone of proximal development' (ZPD) to distinguish maturing (developing) cognitive processes from matured (developed) cognitive processes in children. When describing or assessing a child's mental development, Vygotsky believed psychologists should take into account incipient higher-order thinking skills which, in his view, appropriate pedagogical practices could promote. The boundaries of ZPD were thus defined by a child's zone of independent performance (developmental level) on one side, and her/his zone of assisted performance on the other.

Vygotsky was primarily concerned with the acquisition and use of language, both as a mental tool in its own right, and as a means to cognitive development. According to Vygotsky's dynamic view of learning and human development, children develop higher-order thinking skills by mastering external materials of cultural reasoning through a 'cognitive apprenticeship' involving 'social speech'. External materials are thereby internalised as mechanisms of thought, first through 'inner speech' and ultimately through 'verbal thinking'. Vygotsky did not include teachers in his definition of ZPD, yet his oft-quoted distinction between a child's independent problem-solving ability and a child's problem-solving ability with adult guidance has generated controversial interpretations of ZPD that include tasks a child completes with the assistance of teachers and/ or peers. Although it is unclear whether Vygotsky considered himself a social constructivist, his ZPD concept has become a major component of constructivist theories of education.

See also: constructivism; social constructivism; Vygotsky, Lev

JASON BLOKHUIS

ZONING

School zoning is the process of identifying geographic areas for the purpose of assigning school-age children living in that area to a public school appropriate to their age and/or some social goal supported by the polity or proffered by elites. In the United States, school zoning is not only the racially neutral student assignment technique it generally is in the rest of the world, but also a means of maintaining, or eliminating, school segregation. Neighbourhood school attendance zones, still the dominant assignment rule in the US during and after more than fifty years of school desegregation, are constructed by drawing a line around a school to create a geographic area that will contain the appropriate number of students for the school's size and grade structure and minimise distance from the school for the students. Before the US Supreme Court decision, *Brown v. Board*

651

of *Education* (1954), the South maintained a dual neighbourhood school system with one set of schools for black students and another set for white students. The North, by contrast, had a single set of neighbourhood schools with some schools racially isolated because of the racial composition of their neighbourhoods.

Brown II required in 1955 that school districts dismantle the dual school system and adopt a single set of neighbourhood schools. By the late 1960s, most Southern school districts had adopted a single set of neighbourhood school zones. For the smaller school districts, this was usually sufficient to desegregate all, or almost all, of their schools. For the larger school districts, it usually was not.

As a result, the Supreme Court turned *Brown* on its head in *Green v. New Kent County* (1968) and opined that Southern school districts had to achieve racially balanced schools. Within a few years, black civil rights groups outside the South began filing lawsuits in Northern school districts alleging that actions by school administrators that maintained racially isolated neighbourhood schools constituted 'intentional segregation' on a par with the de jure segregation of the South. Many federal district courts accepted this argument and racial balance zoning plans were being ordered in many school districts in the North by the early 1970s.

The specific zoning techniques used during this era to racially balance schools included pairing and clustering, satellite zoning, and contiguous rezoning. Pairing and/or clustering plans draw a line around two or more opposite race schools and change the grade structure of the two schools so that half the grades are in one school for the early grades (e.g. K–2) and half in the other school for the later grades (e.g. 3–5).

If the assignment of opposite race zones to two schools does not include a grade change, however, it is either satellite zoning if there are non-contiguous zones or contiguous rezoning if there are contiguous zones. The 1975 Boston school desegregation plan is an example of satellite zoning because the school system was divided into hundreds of non-contiguous geographic codes assigned to schools so as to racially balance them, with the schools keeping the grade configuration they had before desegregation.

The success of these zoning tools in actually producing desegregated schools has been mixed. Zoning to produce racial balance in the schools did indeed produce racial balance – that is, the schools reflected the racial composition of the school district. However, it also produced so much white flight that, within about five years of the implementation of one of these plans, the absolute level of exposure of minority students to whites was usually less than before the plan (Armor 1980; Armor and Rossell 2002; Rossell 2002). Nor did these plans reduce the black–white achievement gap in the school districts they were implemented in (Armor and Rossell 2002). As a result, there is little impetus to maintain zoning for racial balance once a school district is no longer under a court order to desegregate. And the Supreme Court of the USA will decide in 2007 whether this is even legal.

See also: catchment area; neighbourhood school; parental choice; segregation/desegregation

Further reading

Armor, D. J. (1980) 'White flight and the future of school desegregation'. In W. G. Stephan and J. R. Feagan (eds) *School Desegregation: Past, Present and Future*, New York: Plenum Press.
Armor, D. J. and Rossell, C. H. (2002) 'Desegregation and resegregation in the public schools'. In A. Thernstrom and S. Thernstrom (eds) *Beyond the Color Line*, Palo Alto CA: Hoover Institution Press.
Rossell, C. H. (2002) 'The effectiveness of desegregation plans' In C. H. Rossell, D. J. Armor and H. J. Walberg (eds) *School Desegregation in the 21st Century*, Westport CT: Praeger.

CHRISTINE H. ROSSELL

Index

abacus **1**;
  see also arithmetic; Italy
Abelard, Peter **1**, 333, 357;
  John of Salisbury 1, 333–34;
  University of Paris 1;
  Yes and No 1;
  see also Aristotle; church; John of Salisbury; lecture/
    lecturer; Plato; scholasticism; Aquinas, Thomas
ability **1–4**, 268, 385–86;
  ability tests 2–3;
  analytic ability 3;
  children's abilities 53;
  cognitive ability 2, 3–4, 31;
  definition 2;
  development of 3, 4;
  educational abilities 64;
  and effort 2, 3–4;
  innate and learned 2, 3–4;
  linguistic ability 2, 3;
  logical ability 2;
  mathematical ability 2, 3;
  mental 2, 3;
  verbal and non-verbal abilities 2–3;
  see also ability grouping; aptitude; Binet, Alfred;
    cognition; excellence; Gardner, Howard;
    giftedness; intelligence/intelligence tests;
    merit; mixed-ability teaching; selection;
    Spearman, Charles; skills; streaming/tracking;
    test/testing; underachievement; Vygotsky,
    Lev; zone of proximal development
ability grouping **4–5**;
  differential access to the curriculum 4, 5;
  effects 4–5;
  grouping systems 4;
  teachers' attitude towards 5;
  see also ability; attainment; giftedness; high-stakes
    testing; intelligence/intelligence tests; mixed-
    ability teaching; selection; setting; streaming/
    tracking; underachievement; whole-class
    teaching
academic/academic profession **5–7**;
  academic community 5, 7;
  academic identity 5–6;
  causes of dispute 5–6;

'proletarianization' 6;
  see also dean; don; higher education; lecture/
    lecturer; profession/professionalism/
    professionalisation; professor; reader; scholar;
    scholarship; specialisation; university
academic freedom **7–8**;
  academic self-government 7–8;
  boundaries 8;
  definition 7;
  'four essential freedoms' 8;
  individual academic freedom 8;
  institutional autonomy 8;
  principles 7–8;
  see also academic/academic profession;
    autonomy; university
academy **8–9**, 441;
  as higher education 9;
  women in the ethos of 9;
  see also higher education; Plato; university; urban
    education
accountability 6, **9–10**, 21, 83, 194, 291;
  accountability data 10;
  aims of educational accountability systems 10;
  Canada 68;
  challenges 10;
  educational accountability systems 9–10;
  effects on evaluated units 10;
  elements 9;
  performance expectation 9;
  standards 21;
  see also accreditation; assessment; benchmarking;
    high-stakes testing; inspection; mission statement;
    monitor; performance indicators; profession/
    professionalism/professionalisation; restructuring;
    standardised tests; summative assessment;
    systemic reform; underperforming/failing school
accreditation **10–11**;
  accrediting body 11;
  definition 10–11;
  requirements for 11;
  spurious providers 11;
  see also accountability; accreditation of prior
    achievement/learning; inspection; qualifications
accreditation of prior achievement/learning **11–12**;

advantages for skilled workers 11–12;
alternative terminology for 11;
benefits 12;
definition 11;
dual role 11;
see also accreditation; higher education; recruitment;
  university; work-based/work-located/
  workplace/work-related learning
action research **12–14**;
  action researchers 13;
  advantages 13;
  aims of 13;
  conceptual development 12–13;
  disadvantages 13–14;
  definition 13;
  Elliott's model 13;
  Kolb's cyclical model 12;
  Lewin's cyclical model 13;
  models 13;
  uses 13;
  see also educational research; ethnography;
    experiential learning; practitioner research;
    qualitative research; reflective practitioner;
    Schön, Donald; Stenhouse, Lawrence; teacher
activity theory **14–15**;
  activity systems networks 15;
  beginnings 14;
  components of activity systems 15;
  historical development 14–15;
  key ideas 14;
  uses 15;
  see also action research; psychology; social
    constructivism; Vygotsky, Lev
Addams, Jane **15–16**;
  see also equality of opportunity
adult education **16–17**, 149;
  beginnings 16;
  college 109;
  Cuba 147;
  definition 16;
  Greece 282;
  institutions providers of 16;
  liberal adult education 16–17;
  Sweden 577;
  tendencies 16–17;
  University of the Third Age (U3A) 17;
  see also andragogy; athenaeum; continuing
    education; extra-mural class; International
    Council for Adult Education (ICAE); liberal
    education; lifelong learning; Lyceum;
    mechanics' institute; university extension;
    workers' education; Workers' Educational
    Association (WEA)
adult literacy 22, 78, 127–28, 197, 210, 230, 261,
  607, 619;
  see also adult education
Africa 16, **17–20**, 25, 94, 162;
  African educational history 17–19;
  African Union (AU) 17, 19;
  brain drain 59;

and British Council 61;
  challenges 19;
  children's literature 89;
  colonial education 18–19;
  curriculum 18;
  DuBois, William E. B. 181–82;
  educational gender parity 19, 39;
  extra-mural class 247;
  indigenous knowledge systems (IKS) 18;
  key ideas for future education policies 19–20;
  Mandela Rhodes Foundation 495;
  mission schools networks 18;
  New Economic Partnership for Africa (NEPAD)
    17, 19;
  Pan-African movement 182;
  Rhodes Scholars' Southern Africa Forum
    (RSSAF) 495;
  University of East Africa 582;
  vocational education 634;
  see also Education for All; globalisation; indigenous
    education; literacy; Nigeria; rural education;
    South Africa; Tanzania; World Bank
alternative education **20–21**;
  alternative school 20;
  curriculum 21;
  definition 20;
  diplomas 21;
  General Educational Development (GED) 21;
  principles 20;
  programs 21;
  recidivism rate 21;
  school structures key 21;
  settings for 20;
  standards 21;
  target population 20;
  see also autodidact; charter school; delinquency;
    discipline; dropouts; emotional and behavioural
    difficulties (EBD); exclusion/expulsion; home
    schooling; informal/nonformal learning; magnet
    school; school culture; suspension; truancy
alumni **21–22**;
  alumni associations 21–22;
  definition 21;
  see also endowment; graduate/graduation;
American Educational Research Association
  (AERA) **22–23**, 314;
  awards programme 23;
  communication role 22–23;
  goals 22;
  governance structure 23;
  members 22;
  beginnings 22;
  publications 22;
  structure 22;
  see also educational research
American Women's Educational Association 47
andragogy **23–24**;
  definitions 23;
  etymology 23–24;
  beginnings and development 23–24;

throughout the world 24;
see also adult education; distance education/
learning; further education; learning; lifelong
learning; pedagogy
anthropology of education **25–26**;
key ideas 25;
development of the project 25;
Council on Anthropology and Education (CAE) 25;
publications 26;
supporting organisations 25–26;
see also classroom observation; comparative
education; cultural transmission; culture;
ethnography; indigenous education;
informal/nonformal learning; learning;
Mead, Margaret; sociology of education
antiracist education **26–28**;
DuBois, William E. B. 181–82;
and monocultural education 26–27;
and multicultural education 25;
UK Race Relations (Amendment) Act 27;
United States 622–23, 652;
see also equality of opportunity; multicultural
education; Washington, Booker T.; zoning
apprenticeship **28–30**, 159;
Britain 28, 29–30, 33;
definitions 28–29;
dual system 29, 30;
functions 29;
German-speaking states 235;
Germany 28, 272;
in the Middle Ages 28;
in modern times 28;
around the world 29–30;
see also crafts; day release; dual system; industrial
training; skills; technical education/school/
college; training; vocational education;
Vocational and Technical Education (VET);
work-based/work-located/workplace/work-
related learning
approved school **30–31**;
see also delinquency
aptitude **31–32**;
aptitude tests 31–32;
definition 31;
innate or acquired 31;
and intelligence 31;
see also ability; intelligence/intelligence tests;
selection; skill; standardised tests;
underachievement
Aquinas, Thomas 1, 32, 75, 249, 601;
Summa Theologiae 511;
see also Abelard, Peter; scholasticism
Aristotle 1, **32**, 43, 96, 215, 334, 364, 372, 441;
and equity 231;
and moral education 390;
see also Lyceum; Plato; scholasticism
arithmetic **32**;
the 'three Rs' 32, 46, 130, 615;
see also mathematics; numeracy
Armed Forces **33–34**;

centres of technical and higher education 33;
education activities 33;
history of Armed Forces' education 33–34;
naval schools 33;
see also professional education; technical
education/school/college
Arnold, Matthew **34**, 149, 151, 532;
Culture and Anarchy 34, 151;
see also Arnold, Thomas; culture; inspection
Arnold, Thomas **34–35**, 452, 614;
Tom Brown's Schooldays 34, 64;
see also Arnold, Matthew; boarding school/
education; Forster, William Edward; prefect;
public school; secondary school/education
art **35–36**;
current strands 36;
curriculum 36;
International Society for Education through Art 35;
programmes 35, 36;
Read, Herbert Edward 35;
schools of art 40;
as a subject 35–36;
see also crafts; creativity; subjects
Ascham, Roger **36**;
The Scholemaster 36;
Toxophilus 36;
see also Elyot, Sir Thomas; Mulcaster, Richard
Asperger's syndrome 42;
see also special education/special educational
needs/special needs
assessment 17, **37–38**, 56, 77, 277;
Brazil 59–60;
England 291;
etymology 37;
fairness 37;
as inquiry 37–38;
intended purposes 37;
Japan 291;
means 37;
portfolio assessment 610;
self-assessment 37, 38;
United States 291;
see also accountability; continuous assessment;
coursework; criterion-referenced tests;
diagnostic assessment; evaluation; examinations;
formative assessment; grades; norm-referenced
tests; marking; multiple-choice tests;
psychometrics; standardised tests; standards;
summative assessment; test/testing; Tyler, Ralph
athenaeum **38**;
see also adult education; mechanics' institute;
public library
attainment **38–39**;
child's attainment 53;
definition 38;
England 38;
grades, marks 38;
level of 38;
ranking tables 38–39;
variables affecting attainment 39;

see also accountability; core curriculum/national curriculum; marking; qualifications; pupil mobility; school effectiveness; school improvement; standards; streaming/tracking; value added

Attention Deficit Disorder (ADD) 183;
   Hyperactivity Disorder (AD/HD) 183;
   see also hyperactivity

Australia **39–41**;
   Australian Association for Research in Education (AARE) 41;
   British colony 39;
   career guidance 69;
   chancellor 81;
   children's literature 89, 90;
   church schools 39, 40;
   Commonwealth of Australia 39;
   comparative education 113;
   crèche 139–40;
   cultural diversity and immigration 395;
   diploma 170;
   distance education/learning 40, 176;
   educational broadcasting 201;
   educational issues 40;
   educational leadership and management 202;
   further education (FE) 264;
   high school 290;
   kindergarten 339;
   mass education and credential inflation 141;
   mechanics' institutes 40;
   mentoring 380;
   merit 381;
   middle school 319;
   Monash University 368;
   numeracy 409;
   Open Learning Australia 416;
   Open University Australia 416;
   pastoral care 428;
   performance indicators 431;
   population 39;
   privatisation/marketisation 455;
   Recognition of Prior Experiential Learning (RPEL) 11;
   religious schools 94;
   School of the Air 201;
   schools of art 40;
   state schools 39;
   supply/substitute teaching 574;
   suspension 575;
   Sydney University 114;
   travelling teachers 40;
   universities 40;
   urban education 629;
   vocational education 40;
   Vocational Education and Training (VET) 40;
   see also indigenous education; multicultural education; Oceania; Polynesia

Australasia, multicultural education 26

Australian Association for Research in Education (AARE) **41**;

awards 41;
   definition 41;
   history 41;
   publications 41;
   see also Australia; educational research

autism **41–42**;
   autistic spectrum disorder (ASD) 41;
   average age of diagnosis 41–42;
   definition 41;
   diagnosis criteria 42;
   features 41;
   IQ scores 42;
   particular abilities 42;
   theories on 42;
   triad of impairments 41;
   see also emotional and behavioural difficulties/disorders (EBD); inclusive education; learning disabilities; special education/special educational needs/special needs

autodidact **42–43**;
   autodidactic learning 297;
   definition 42;
   working-class autodidacts 43, 644;
   see also adult education; home schooling; informal/nonformal learning; self-directed learning

autonomy **43–44** 135;
   concerns of in educational philosophy 43–44;
   as educational goal 43;
   etymology 43;
   Mill's ideal 44;
   see also Aristotle; correspondence theory; indoctrination; Locke, John; Mannheim, Karl; Mill, John Stuart; philosophy of education; Plato; profession/professionalism/professionalisation; training

baseline assessment (BA) **45–46**;
   challenge 46;
   definition 45;
   findings from research on 46;
   purposes 45;
   statutory BA 45;
   strengths 45;
   see also assessment; literacy; numeracy; primary school/education; special education/special educational needs/special needs; value added

basic skills **46–47**, 138;
   concept 46;
   the 'three Rs' 32, 46, 130, 615;
   see also arithmetic; literacy; numeracy; reading; skills; spelling; writing

Beecher, Catharine 47;
   American Women's Educational Association 47;
   The Moral Instructor for Schools and Families: Containing Lessons on the Duties of Life 47;
   A Treatise on Domestic Economy 47;
   see also health education; physical education/training

behaviourism 14, **47–48**;
   behaviour therapy 47;

classical behaviourism 47;
criticism of 47–48;
definition 47;
neo-behaviourism 47;
stimulus–response model 47;
see also hyperactivity; psychology; Skinner,
  Burrhus Fredric; Thorndike, Edward Lee
bell curve **48**;
definition 48;
see also elitism; intelligence/intelligence tests;
  meritocracy
benchmarking **48–49**;
basis of 49;
beginnings 48;
deficiencies 49;
definition 48;
types 48;
United Kingdom 48–49;
uses 48–49;
see also economics of education; educational targets;
  performance indicators; school effectiveness;
  school improvement; underachievement
Bernstein, Basil **49–50**, 116, 429;
Pedagogy, Symbolic Control and Identity 50;
see also Bourdieu, Pierre; pedagogy; school
  knowledge; sociology of education
bicultural education **50**;
see also bilingual education; indigenous
  education; multicultural education
bilingual education **50–51**;
aims 50;
Canada 50–51;
definition 50;
'dual language immersion' 50;
factor in success 51;
programmes 50;
Proposition 227 (California) 51;
'transitional bilingualism' 50;
United States 51;
see also bicultural education; curriculum;
  indigenous education; literacy; modern
  languages; multicultural education; Singapore
binary system **52–53**, 627;
in astronomy 52;
in British higher education 52;
Education Reform Act (1988) 52;
in mathematics 52;
Robbins Committee 52;
see also dual system; higher education;
  mathematics; polytechnic
Binet, Alfred 2, **53**, 317–18;
Mentally Defective Children 53;
see also giftedness; intelligence/intelligence tests;
  psychology; psychology of education
biology **53–54**;
aims 53;
basis 53;
definition 53;
etymology 54;
historical roots 54;

molecular and genetic biology 54;
sub-disciplines 54;
theory of evolution 54;
tools 54;
see also chemistry; curriculum; medicine; nature
  study; science/science education; sex education;
  subjects
blind, teaching of **54–56**;
On Blindness 55;
Braille, Louis 55;
Braille type 55, 56;
Britain 55;
France 55;
Germany 55;
International Council for Education of People
  with Visual Impairment (ICEVI) 56;
Royal National Institute for the Blind (RNIB) 55;
see also inclusive education; learning disabilities/
  difficulties; special education/special
  educational needs/special needs
Bloom, Benjamin **56**;
Developing Talent in Young People 56;
message 56;
Problem-Solving Processes of College Students 56;
Taxonomy of Educational Objectives 56;
see also assessment; continuous assessment;
  individualised instruction/personalised learning
boarding school/education **56–58**, 304;
'boarding need' 57;
Boarding School Association (BSA) 57;
Britain 57;
Cuba 147;
ethos 57;
essential feature 56;
historical and cultural precedents 56–57;
influence on state schools 57;
model for analysing boarding schools 57–58;
statistics 57;
see also Arnold, Thomas; independent/private
  school/education; public school
Bologna Framework of Qualifications 476
Bologna Process 235, 372, 388, 422, 504
Bourdieu, Pierre **58**, 147–48, 150, 397, 545–46;
cultural capital 58;
habitus 58;
see also Bernstein, Basil; cultural capital; cultural
  studies; educational theory; habitus; social
  capital; sociology; sociology of education
brain drain **58–59**;
causes 58–59;
common usage of the term 58;
definition 58;
see also globalisation; knowledge economy;
  recruitment
Brazil **59–60**, 276;
children's literature 89;
economy 59;
educational problems 60;
educational system history 59;
educational system structure 59;

Freire, Paolo 16, 18, 112, 243, 261, 355, 366, 430, 645;
higher education 59, 60;
illiteracy 60;
long-distance education 60;
national system of assessment 59–60;
Plan for the Development of Education 60;
population 59;
private sector schools 59;
public sector schools 59;
school reform 524–25;
special needs 60;
see also Latin America
British Council **60–62**;
aim 60;
beginnings 61;
definition 60;
Foreign Office 61;
impact of political developments on work of 61;
Leeper, Sir Reginald 61;
Strategy 2010 61;
works abroad 60–61;
working fields 60–61;
World War II 61;
see also culture; international education
British Educational Research Association (BERA) **62–63**;
activities 62;
aim 62;
awards 62;
beginnings 62;
definition 62;
governance structure 63;
members 62;
meetings 62;
publications 62;
research fields 62;
similar associated societies 62;
see also charities, educational; educational research
British Open University *see* United Kingdom Open University
Bruner, Jerome **63**, 86, 175, 213, 430;
The Culture of Education 63;
and early childhood education 186;
Man: A Course of Study (MACOS) 63;
The Process of Education 63;
Toward a Theory of Instruction 63;
see also Gardner, Howard; pedagogy; psychology of education; spiral curriculum; Vygotsky, Lev
bullying 4–5, **63–64**, 174;
definition 63;
in higher education 63;
motivations 63;
in schools 63;
stereotype bully 63–64;
students: responsible for and victims 63;
teachers: responsible for and victims 63;
see also discipline; emotional and behavioural difficulties/disorders (EBD); pastoral care; school security; school violence; truancy

Burt, Cyril **64**, 318;
Intelligence and Fertility 64;
intelligence: inherited/socially determined 64, 318;
IQ tests 64;
The Subnormal Mind 64;
The Young Delinquent 64;
see also Galton, Francis; giftedness; intelligence/intelligence tests; psychometrics; selection; Spearman, Charles
business school/education **64–65**;
case study 65;
definition 64;
Master of Business Administration (MBA) degrees 64;
purpose 65;
secondary education 64–65;
see also economics; higher education; Master's; secondary school/education; specialisation

Cambridge University 104, 225, 246; 372, 456, 510, 541, 628, 632, 647
Canada **67–68**;
accountability 68;
Act of Union (1841) 67;
bilingual education 50–51;
British North America Act (1867) 67;
career guidance 69;
chancellor 81;
charter school 83;
child guidance 87;
comparative education 113,
compulsory education 121;
cultural diversity and immigration 395;
curriculum standards/programmes of study 157–8;
early childhood education (ECE) 185;
educational broadcasting 201;
educational leadership and management 202;
educational history 67–68;
educational system structure 68;
graduation ceremony 278;
high school 290;
home schooling 298;
investment in education 68;
junior high school 319;
language minorities 67–68;
minorities rights 67;
motives for challenges in education 68;
normal school 406;
performance indicators 431–32;
rural education 501;
supply/substitute teaching 574;
urban education 629;
Workers' Educational Association (WEA) 645;
see also Catholic school/education; church; indigenous education; multicultural education
career guidance **69**;
definition 69;
tools 69;
United Kingdom 69;
United States 69;

see also counselling; lifelong learning; work
    experience
Caribbean **70–71**;
    Caribbean Advanced Proficiency Examinations
        (CAPE) 71;
    Caribbean Examinations Council (CXC) 70–71;
    colonial education system 70;
    education system and class system 70;
    geo-cultural division 70;
    higher education 70;
    nationalisation of education system 71;
    University College of the West Indies (UCWI)
        70–71;
    see also Latin America
Carnegie Foundation for the Advancement of
    Teaching **71–72**, 221, 338, 496;
    aims 71;
    beginnings 72;
    definition 71;
    governance 72;
    holistic education system 71–72;
    partnerships 71;
    publications 72;
    strands 72;
    teacher education 72;
    see also academic/academic profession; profession/
        professionalism/professionalisation; teacher;
        teaching/teaching methods; teaching profession
case study 64, **73–74**, 103, 104, 238;
    advantages 74;
    classification 73;
    definition 73;
    methods or tools 73–74;
    relatability, generalisability, validity 74;
    see also classroom observation; educational research
catchment area **74–75**, 536;
    definition 74;
    see also comprehensive school/education;
        parental choice; privatisation/marketisation;
        pupil mobility; urban education; zoning
catholic school/education **75–76**;
    educational role of the church throughout history
        75;
    France 257;
    quadrivium 75, 96, 233–34, 532;
    staff 76;
    statistics 76;
    trivium 75, 96, 233–34, 532;
    Vatican II 76;
    see also church; Italy; Jesuit education; religious
        education; scholasticism
centralisation/decentralisation **76–78**, 155, 424;
    advantages of decentralisation 77;
    centralisation; definition 76;
    decentralisation: definition 77;
    Eastern Europe 77;
    key issues in decentralisation 77;
    Latin America 77;
    modes of decentralisation 77;
    role of the state in education 77;

South Asia 77;
    see also accountability; educational policy;
        educational reform; marketisation/privatisation;
        core curriculum/national curriculum; parental
        choice; Russia; school-based management;
        school reform; standards; Tanzania; technocrat/
        technocratic/technocracy
Centre for Educational Research and Innovation
    (CERI) **78–79**, 420;
    audience 79;
    beginnings 78;
    criticism 79;
    definition 78;
    programmes 78–79;
    publications 79;
    working themes 78;
    see also educational research; globalisation;
        Organisation for Economic Co-operation
        and Development (OECD)
certificate/certification 17, **79–80**;
    certificate: definition 79;
    certification requirements in education 80;
    common path of obtaining certification as
        teacher 80;
    licence 80;
    non-traditional paths to teacher certification 80;
    renewal of certificates 80;
    revoking of certificates 80;
    value and uses 79–80;
    see also diploma; examinations; postgraduate;
        qualifications; teacher education/training;
        training
chancellor **81**;
    Commonwealth countries 81;
    United States 81;
    see also rector; university; vice-chancellor
charities, educational **81–82**;
    applications for funding 82;
    definition 81;
    history 81;
    Oxfam 82;
    Rockefeller Foundation 82;
    Rhodes Trust 82;
    supported areas 82;
    United Nations Children's Fund (UNICEF)
        82;
    see also church; endowment; Rhodes Trust;
        scholarship; student finance/loans; United
        Nations Children's Fund (UNICEF);
        voluntarism
charity schools 109, 304;
    see also charities, educational
charter school **83–84**, 120;
    Canada 83;
    curricular focus 83;
    definition 83;
    history 83;
    opponents and supporters views 83;
    sponsors 83;
    United States 83;

see also alternative education; magnet school;
marketisation; parental choice; specialisation;
vouchers

chemistry **84–85**;
alchemy 84–85;
basis 84;
Dalton, John 85;
definition 84;
historical roots 84;
Mendeleev, Dmitri 85;
Moseley, H. G. J. 85;
unifying theme 85;
see also biology; curriculum; science/science
education; subjects

child development **85–87**, 651;
cognitive development 86, 651;
constructivist theories 86;
impact of culture and context on 86;
interrelation of all domains of development 86;
learning theories 86;
moral development 86;
physical development 86;
previous conceptions 85;
psychoanalytic theory 86;
Rousseau's view 498;
socialisation 86;
see also Bruner, Jerome; cognition;
constructivism; Freud, Sigmund; Isaacs,
Susan; Kohlberg Lawrence; Mead, Margaret;
Montessori, Maria; Piaget, Jean; psychology;
reception class; Rousseau, Jean-Jacques;
Vygotsky, Lev; zone of proximal
development

child guidance **87–88**;
beginnings 87;
child guidance nowadays 88;
child guiders 87;
definition 87;
institutional base of 87;
juvenile crime 87;
Juvenile Psychopathic Institute 87;
parent problem 88;
parent training 88;
teacher education 88;
see also behaviourism; child development;
delinquency; emotional and behavioural
difficulties/disorders (EBD); family; Locke,
John; psychology of education

child-centred education **88–89**, 166, 261;
aims 88;
criticism 89, 175;
and discovery method/learning 175;
see also Dewey, John; Neill, Alexander
Sutherland; progressive education; project
method; Rousseau, Jean-Jacques; United
Nations Children's Fund (UNICEF); United
Nations Educational, Scientific and Cultural
Organization (UNESCO); Rousseau, Jean-
Jacques; Rugg, Harold; World Education
Fellowship (WEF)

children's literature **89–90**;
in behaviour shaping 89;
courses on 90;
in cultural and political education 89;
first books for children 89;
in language teaching 89;
and literacy 90;
nowadays 90;
see also Comenius, Johann Amos; literacy;
reading

China 89, **90–93**, 275, 276;
ancient China 1, 90;
brain drain 59;
Buddhism 90;
centralisation 91;
Chinese abacus 1;
Chinese education traditions 90;
Chinese education traditions/China's modern
development 93;
Communist Party 91;
compulsory education 92;
concerns about current Chinese education 92;
Confucian approach to knowledge 90, 91;
Confucian tradition 90, 91, 92, 93, 96;
cramming 138;
cultural function of education 91;
Cultural Revolution 91;
current education system 92;
diploma 170;
economic function of education 91;
education for all 191;
Education Law 92;
educational innovation 191;
educational reform 92;
first recorded use of examinations 240;
Higher Education Law 92;
history (subject) 294;
imperial examination system 91;
independent/private school/education 303, 304;
indoctrination 310;
influences on Chinese education 91, 92;
inspection system 315;
knowledge economy 341;
Mandarin Chinese 92;
mass education and credential inflation 141;
May 4th Movement (1919) 91;
mentoring 380;
Open Learning Hong Kong 416;
Open University Hong Kong 416;
philosophical principles of education throughout
Chinese history 90–91;
political function of education 91;
polytechnic 446;
psychometrics 468;
Revolution of 1911 91;
standardisation 91;
statistics 92;
selective schools 536;
sixth form 543;
educational innovation 191;

Soka Gakkai International 367;
Taoism 90;
textbook 598–99;
urban education 629;
see also centralisation/decentralisation; compulsory education; East Asia; Japan; Malaysia; rural education
church 1, 32, **93–94**, 428;
Anglican church 615;
definition 93;
division 93;
education and church 94;
first church schools 94;
grammar school 279–80;
medieval cathedral song schools 94;
missionary activity 93, 94;
oldest institution in Western world 626;
see also charities, educational; Catholic school/education; Colet, John; dual system; Jesuit education; profession/professionalism/professionalisation; religious assembly; religious education; religious school; scholasticism; Sunday school; theology; voluntarism; youth club/work
citizenship/civics **94–96**, 130;
citizenship/civics education 94;
concept 94;
curriculum 94, 95;
dispositions promoted in citizenship/civics education 95;
Japan 95;
learning activities to promote citizenship/civic skills 95;
and liberal education 359;
subject matter 94–95;
subject matter approaches 95;
see also collaborative/cooperative learning; curriculum; education; history; Scout Association; social studies
class size **96**;
advantages of small classes 96;
statistics 96;
see also classroom
classical education **96**;
different denotations 96;
quadrivium 75, 96, 233–34, 532;
trivium 75, 96, 233–34, 532;
see also classical studies; grammar; Italy; liberal education; Socratic method; vocational education
classical studies **97–99**, 271;
Altertumswissenschaft 97–99;
America 97, 99;
current popularisation 99;
curriculum 97, 98;
definition 97;
distinguishing feature of 97;
epistemological crisis of 98;
Germany 97, 98;
Great Britain 97;

Gymnasium 97, 271, 272;
influences on contemporary classical studies 98;
organisations promoting classical studies 99;
philology and textual criticism 97–98;
see also classical education; curriculum; grammar school; Greece; Jowett, Benjamin; liberal education; modern languages; scholarship; subject
classroom **99–101**;
beginnings and development 99–100;
classroom life 100, 101;
definition 99;
different arrangements of 101;
teachers autonomy in 100–101;
see also class size; classroom management; hidden curriculum; monitorial system; open plan; practitioner research; reflective practitioner; visual aids; whole-class teaching
classroom management **101–2**, 174, 183;
classroom management strategies for managing dyslexia 183;
crucial time for 101–2;
definition 101;
implementation phase 102;
maintenance phase 102;
phases of 101;
preparation phase 101;
principle for effective implementation of 102;
student perspectives on 102;
see also classroom; collaborative/cooperative learning; corporal punishment; discipline; hyperactivity; practitioner research; school culture; whole-class teaching
classroom observation **102–4**;
description 102;
involvement of the observer 103–4;
structure 103;
validity and reliability 103, 104;
see also case study; anthropology of education; educational research; ethnography; qualitative research; quantitative research; Rice, Joseph Mayer
coeducation **104–5**;
advantages and disadvantages 105;
definition 104;
England 104;
single-sex education 104–5;
United States 104;
see also equality of opportunity; feminist theory
cognition **105–6**;
cognitive abilities 2, 3–4, 318;
cognitive development 86, 106, 341, 440;
cognitive diagnosis 169;
cognitive growth 3;
cognitive levels 56;
cognitive processes 105, 106;
cognitive psychological research and education 106;
cognitive revolution 63;
cognitive science 3;
cognitive strategies 106;

cognitive theory of learning 31, 430;
definition 105;
development 651;
hierarchy of knowledge 563;
individual differences in human cognition 105;
linguistic and paralinguistic areas of 268;
major issues in understanding human cognition 105;
microgenetic method 106;
see also Bruner, Jerome; child development;
excellence; intelligence/intelligence tests;
Kohlberg, Lawrence; learning; Piaget, Jean;
psychology; psychology of education;
situated cognition/learning; Spearman,
Charles; Vygotsky, Lev; zone of proximal
development
Colet, John **106–7**;
translation of the Bible 106;
see also church; public school; theology
collaborative/cooperative learning **107–8**, 351;
cognitive elaboration 108;
condition to be effective 108;
description 107;
development perspective 108;
motivational theories 107;
social cohesion theories 107–8;
theoretical perspectives or theories 107;
see also classroom; cognition; experiential learning;
Freinet, Celestin; individualised instruction/
personalised learning; learning; learning
community; learning styles; Makarenko,
Anton Simeonovitch; motivation; peer group;
Piaget, Jean; Vygotsky, Lev
college **108–9**, 159;
adult education 109;
definition 108;
examinations 278;
extracurriculum 246;
further education 109, 159, 264;
higher education 108–9;
tertiary education 109;
United States 622;
see also adult education; further education; higher
education; lecture/lecturer; mission statement;
public school; sandwich course; school;
semester/term; tertiary education; university
colonial education 18, 59, 70, 345;
see also church; cultural imperialism; indigenous
education; religious schools
Comenius, Jan Amos 89, **109**, 323, 338, 461;
Didactica Magna 109;
Janua Linguarum Reserata 109;
Moravian Movement 109;
Orbis Sensualium Pictus 89, 109,
see also children's literature; progressive education
common school **109–10**, 370;
aim 109;
characteristics 110;
precursor to elementary and secondary
education 110;
resistance to 110;

United States 109–10, 621;
see also comprehensive school/education;
elementary school; Mann, Horace; secondary
school/education
Commonwealth of Learning 177
community education **110–13**;
community: main areas of meaning 111;
contributions 112;
curriculum and methods 111;
definition 110;
Freire's perspective 112;
radical and reformist traditions 110;
traditional origins 110–11;
see also adult education; culture; Dewey, John;
franchising; Freire, Paolo; further education;
lifelong learning; rural education; travellers,
education of; workers' education; youth
club/work
comparative education 25, **113–15**;
beginnings 113;
comparative education-of-action 114;
comparative education of the professional
societies 114;
examples of 'comparative thinking' 114;
importance 115;
new emphases 114;
Organisation for Economic Co-operation and
Development (OECD) 114;
'policy-driven' comparative education 114;
theoretical work on 114–15;
World Bank 114;
see also anthropology of education; education;
education/educational studies; International
Bureau of Education (IBE); international
education; International Institute for
Educational Planning; Sadler, Michael
Ernest; Organisation for Economic
Co-operation and Development (OECD);
Weber, Max; World Bank
compensatory education **115–17**;
aim 115;
'cultural deprivation' 115–16;
Education Action Zones (EAZs) 116;
Educational Priority Areas (EPAs) 116;
positive discrimination/affirmative action 116;
Project Head Start 116;
see also Bernstein, Basil; educational priority
areas; equality of opportunity; positive
discrimination/affirmative action; secondary
school/education
comprehension **117–18**;
brain functioning in constructing meaning 117;
brain theory 117;
comprehension/comprehending 118;
constructing meaning 117;
definition 117;
and language 117;
memory-prediction model 117;
reading 117–18;
proficient reading 118;

see also cognition; English; Piaget, Jean; literacy; reading; writing

comprehensive school/education 74, **118–21**, 280, 428, 447, 536;
aims 118;
beginnings 118–19;
criticism 119, 120;
description 118;
Europe 119;
Finland 254;
Germany 119;
Israel 328;
New Zealand 403;
Nordic countries 235;
Scandinavia 508;
Southern Europe 235;
United Kingdom 119, 386, 615;
United States 118–19;
uncertain future 120;
see also common school; grammar school; high school; secondary school/education; selection

compulsory education **121–23**;
beginnings 121;
Canada 121;
China 92, 122;
criticism 122;
compulsory schooling 121;
definition 121;
deschoolers 122;
economical benefits 122;
England 121;
free-schoolers 122;
sociological benefits 122;
starting/leaving ages 121;
United Kingdom 484;
United States 121, 122, 622;
see also deschooling; Education for All; educational system structure; educational targets; equality of opportunity; home schooling; Illich, Ivan; primary school/education; Sadler, Michael; travellers, education of; truancy; United Nations Children's Fund (UNICEF); universal education/mass education; voluntarism

compulsory schooling 121;
see also compulsory education; home schooling

computer-assisted learning (CAL) **123**, 175;
definition 123;
Information and Communication Technology (ICT) 123;
modern CAL 123;
multimedia systems 123;
see also educational technology; e-learning; learning; technology; virtual learning; Web-based learning

computer studies **123–24**;
application software 124;
computer system 124;
database 124;
definition 123;

hardware 124;
history and development of computing 124;
operating system 124;
software 124;
see also computer-assisted learning; curriculum; educational technology; e-learning; subjects; technology; virtual learning; Web-based learning

Comte, Auguste 125, 212, 554, 594

Conant, James Bryant **124–25**;
The Comprehensive High School 125;
Education and Liberty 125;
meritocracy 125;
Several Lives 125;
Slums and Suburbs 125;
see also higher education; meritocracy; metropolitanism

Condorcet, Marie-Jean **125**;
Essay on the Application of Analysis to the Probability of Majority Decisions 125;
Report and Decree on the General Organisation of Public Education 125;
Sketch of the Intellectual Progress of Mankind 125;
see also France

consciousness 14;
education as consciousness raising 144;
see also cognition; Freire, Paolo

constructivism **125–27**, 429;
contributions about learning 126;
epistemic relativism 126;
'knowing rather than knowledge' 126;
mental activity in learning 126;
radical constructivism 126;
reception/construction views 125–26;
principle of 125;
see also accreditation of prior achievement/learning; child development; correspondence theory; experiential learning; learning; postmodernism; Vygotsky, Lev; zone of proximal development

continued/continuing professional development (CPD) **127**, 128;
definition 127;
functions 127;
main focuses 127;
see also continuing education; in-service education; lifelong learning; mentor/mentoring; professional education; progression; teacher; teacher education/training; work-based/work-located/workplace/work-related learning

continuing education **127–28**;
beginnings 128;
continuing vocational education (CVE) 127, 128;
definitions 127;
economic functions 128;
Finland 128;
Germany 128;
institutional forms 128;
Italy 128;

'Madison idea' 128;
UNESCO 128;
United States 128;
United Kingdom 128;
see also adult education; compulsory education;
continued/continuing professional
development; extra-mural class; informal/
nonformal learning; lifelong learning;
progression; recurrent education; university
extension; vocational education
continuous assessment **129–30**;
advantages 129;
assessment of content/assessment of processes 129;
basis 129;
definition 129;
as diagnostic tool 129;
differences between continuous and terminal
assessment 129;
disadvantages 129–30;
fairness 129;
strategies and forms 129;
terminal assessment 129;
in tertiary education 129;
uses 129;
see also assessment; examinations; formative
assessment; summative assessment; work-based/
worklocated/ workplace/work-related learning
core curriculum/national curriculum 77–78, 101,
130, 156, 234, 291;
definition 130;
citizenship/civics 130;
traditional model of 130;
United Sates 291;
see also citizenship/civics; curriculum; curriculum
development; curriculum differentiation;
curriculum policy and implementation;
curriculum standards; extracurriculum;
hidden curriculum; science/science
education; subjects; systemic reform
core skills/core competences **130–32**;
core competencies around the world 131;
core competencies in the United Kingdom 131;
core skills 130;
definition 130;
difficulties in expanding the core skills and
competencies 131–32;
functional skills 131;
German concept of skills 131;
key skills 130;
a socially constructed concept 131;
see also knowledge economy; lifelong learning;
literacy; numeracy; situated cognition/
learning; skills
corporal punishment **132–33**, 174, 337, 363;
countries where corporal punishment has been
banned 133;
definition 132;
forms of 132;
impact of corporal punishment on children's
behaviour and health 132;

physical discipline 132;
physical punishment 132;
statistics 132;
United States 132;
uses 132;
a violation of children's rights 132–33;
see also classroom; classroom management;
discipline; Locke, John; school violence
correspondence course **133**;
Cuba 147;
definition 133;
description 133;
see also distance education/learning; Open
University; Web-based learning
correspondence theory **133–35**;
beginnings 133;
definition 133–34;
education as a mirror of the hierarchical division
of labour 134;
New Sociology of Education 133;
Rikowski's criticism or 'debilitating
problematics'134–35;
Rikowski's solution to the dilemas of 135;
Schooling in Capitalist America (SCA) 133, 134;
see also autonomy; educational theory; sociology
of education
counselling **136–37**;
American Counselling Association 136;
beginnings 136;
Choosing a Vocation 136;
counsellors' functions 136;
definition 136;
need for counselling nowadays 137;
setting of work 136;
United States 136;
see also career guidance; pastoral care; suspension;
tuition/tutor/tutorial
coursework **137**;
definition 137;
different from homework 137;
forms of 137;
plagiarism 137;
use of 137;
see also assessment; examinations; homework;
plagiarism; standards
crafts **137–38**;
definition 137;
priority of basic skills programmes over crafts
programmes 138;
prominence in post-compulsory and adult
education 138;
subjects in former times 137;
see also art; creativity
cramming **138**;
Britain 138;
China 138;
cram schools 138;
definition 138;
Greece 281;
Japan 138;

South Korea 138;
see also examinations
creativity **138–39**, 179;
    and cultural development 139;
    current boom in education 138–39;
    definition 138;
    as divine inspiration 138;
    and economic competitiveness 139;
    England 139;
    problems to solve 139;
    in psychology 138;
    see also art; culture; curriculum; drama; Gardner,
        Howard; giftedness; literacy; Maslow,
        Abraham Harold; psychology
crèche **139–40**;
    definitions 139–40;
    description 140;
    see also nursery school
credential society **140**;
    The Credential Society 140, 141;
    see also credentials/credentialing; diploma
        disease; meritocracy; United States
credentials/credentialing **140–41**;
    concerns about 141;
    The Credential Society 140, 141;
    definition 140;
    forms of 140;
    in higher education 140–41;
    mass education and credential inflation around
        the world 141;
    see also certificate/certification; credential society;
        degree; diploma; examinations; higher
        education; knowledge economy; plagiarism
criterion-referenced tests (CRTs) **141–43**;
    CRTs items and formats 142;
    CRTs' other names 143;
    CRT score interpretation 142;
    cutscores 143;
    definition 141–42;
    differences between CRTs and NRTs 142;
    norm-referenced test (NRT) score
        interpretation 142;
    uses 143;
    see also examinations; multiple-choice tests; norm-
        referenced tests; standardised tests; test/testing
critical pedagogy 16, **143–45**;
    aim 143;
    Brazil 144;
    Freire, Paolo 144;
    particularism/universalism in 144;
    The Pedagogy of the Oppressed 144;
    reproduction theories 143;
    resistance theories 143–44;
    versions 144;
    see also culture; Freire, Paolo; pedagogy;
        postmodernism; social reconstructionism
critical theory **145–46**;
    beginnings 145;
    conceptual broadening 145;
    definition 145;

education as criticism 146;
    Foucault's view 145;
    influences 145;
    method 145;
    supradisciplinary approach 145;
    see also educational theory; feminist theory;
        Foucault, Michel; Habermas, Jürgen;
        sociology; sociology of education
Cuba **146–47**;
    adult education 147;
    boarding schools 147;
    correspondence courses 147;
    distance education 147;
    education and economy 146–47;
    education and health: priorities since the 1959
        revolution 146;
    educational history 146;
    educational system criticism 147;
    educational system structure 146;
    geographical location 146;
    higher education 147;
    literacy campaign 146;
    Ministry of Education 146;
    Ministry of Higher Education 147;
    Nationalisation of Education Law 146;
    popular education 147;
    population 146;
    statistics 146;
    vocational skills 146–47;
    see also Caribbean
cultural capital 58, **147–48**, 370;
    Bourdieu's four capitals 147;
    Degrees of Choice 147;
    The Field of Cultural Production 148;
    function of 148;
    An Invitation to Reflexive Sociology 147–48;
    Knowledge and Control 147;
    Reproduction in Education, Society and Culture 147;
    theoretical context 147;
    use of 148;
    Which Way Is Up? 147;
    see also Bourdieu, Pierre; habitus; Mannheim,
        Karl; social capital; social reproduction;
        sociology of education
cultural deprivation 25, 115–16
cultural imperialism 61, 94, 150, 151, 345, 383;
    Culture and Imperialism 151;
    Latin America 345;
    see also culture; cultural transmission
cultural studies **149**;
    Britain 149;
    Centre for Contemporary Cultural Studies 149;
    Culture and Society 149;
    cultural studies nowadays 149;
    definition 149;
    interdisciplinary study 149;
    Making of the English Working Class 149;
    The Uses of Literacy 149;
    see also culture; discipline; subjects
cultural transmission **149–50**;

common means of 149;
cultural capital perspective 150;
cultural identity 149;
cultural imperialism 150, 151;
definition 149;
and globalisation 150;
in a multicultural society 150;
politics of culture 151;
schooling as agent of 149;
social interactions as agents of 149;
youth cultures as agents of 149–50;
see also cultural capital; culture; family;
multicultural education; museum education;
Stenhouse, Lawrence; textbook
culture 149, **150–51**;
Clifford Geertz's definition of 151;
counter-culture 150;
cultural identity 149, 151;
cultural imperialism 150, 151;
cultural transmission 150;
and curriculum 153;
definitions 151;
high culture 150;
Matthew Arnold's notions of 149, 151;
politics of culture 151;
youth culture 150;
see also British Council; creativity; cultural
transmission; hidden curriculum; multicultural
education; museum education; reading;
school culture; teacher cultures; travellers,
education of
curriculum 18, 19, 77–78, **152–54**, 487;
alternative education curriculum 21;
curricular specialisation 235;
curriculum-in-use 152;
and culture 153;
definitions 152;
difference between concept and practice 152;
European liberal curriculum 18;
Frederick Rudolph's definition 153;
formal curriculum 152;
geography 270;
at Harvard 125;
hidden curriculum 152–53;
kinds of 152;
mediating factors in implementing the
curriculum 152;
organisation and selection 153;
persistent issues around curriculum 153–54;
physical exercise as part of 47;
process of curriculum making 153–54;
received curriculum 152;
rhetorical curriculum 152;
and society 153;
unorthodox curriculum 20;
Wilfred Carr's perspective 152–53;
see also core curriculum/national curriculum;
curriculum development; curriculum
differentiation; curriculum policy and
implementation; curriculum standards;

extracurriculum; health education; hidden
curriculum; history of education; law; lesson;
literacy; mathematics; modern languages;
music; nature study; physical education/
training; physics; primary school/education;
reflective practitioner; religious education;
school knowledge; science/science education;
sex education; specialisation; spiral
curriculum; Stenhouse, Lawrence; syllabus;
subjects; textbook; vocational education
curriculum development **154–56**;
definition 154;
evaluation of educational programmes 155;
identifying educational experiences 155;
levels of occurrence 155;
main tasks of 154–55;
organisation of educational purposes 154–55;
participants in 155;
selection of educational purposes 154;
see also assessment; centralisation/
decentralisation; curriculum; curriculum
policy and implemen-tation; evaluation;
subjects; test/testing
curriculum differentiation **156–57**;
levels 156;
main areas commonly adapted in 156;
non-state funded schools 156;
pupils with learning difficulties or disabilities
156–57;
state funded schools 156;
see also ability grouping; curriculum; curriculum
policy and implementation; individualised
instruction/personalised learning; learning
disabilities; learning styles; mixed-ability
teaching; pedagogy; setting; specialisation;
streaming/tracking
curriculum policy and implementation **157**;
interrelation between curriculum policy and
implementation 157;
see also curriculum; education policy; profession/
professionalism/professionalisation; reflective
practitioner
curriculum standards/programmes of study 156,
157–58;
definition 157–58;
see also core curriculum/national curriculum;
curriculum; standards; subjects
Curtis, Sir William 130

day release **159**;
common areas for 159;
description 159;
see also apprenticeship; college; training; work-
based/work-located/workplace/work-
related learning
dean **159**;
deanship 159;
definition 159;
supporters 159;
see also faculty; higher education

degree **159–60**, 277, 325, 388, 626;
   bachelor's degrees 160, 325;
   definition 159;
   doctorates 160;
   master's degrees 160;
   see also doctorate; foundation degree; graduate/
      graduation; higher education; master's;
      postgraduate; qualifications; sandwich course;
      student; thesis/dissertation; undergraduate;
      university; undergraduate
delinquency **160–61**;
   acts of 160;
   age-crime curve 160;
   causes and correlates 161;
   crime prevention 161;
   definition 160;
   gender differences in delinquent involvement 160;
   juvenile crime 87;
   lifelong criminals 161;
   non-delinquent troublesome child 87;
   pre-delinquent 87;
   through life 160–61;
   see also child guidance; disaffection; emotional
      and behavioural difficulties/disorders (EBD);
      exclusion/expulsion; Lane, Homer; social
      exclusion/inclusion; suspension
department **161–62**;
   examples of 161;
   education department 161–62;
   see also college; faculty; higher education; school;
      subjects; university
Department for International Development (DfID)
   162–63, 405;
   aims 162;
   criticism 163;
   and distance education/learning 177;
   in higher education 162;
   Millennium Development Goals 162;
   see also globalisation; international education;
      Millennium Development Goals; United
      Nations Educational, Scientific and Cultural
      Organization (UNESCO); World Bank
deschooling 122, **163–64**;
   Compulsory Miseducation 164;
   Crisis in the Classroom 163;
   criticism of deschooling argument 164;
   Deschooling Society 163;
   Everitt Reimer's School is Dead 164;
   Illich, Ivan's criticism of schooling 163;
   see also compulsory education; alternative
      education; Illich, Ivan; informal/nonformal
      learning; school; project method; Rogers,
      Carl
design *see* art
detention **164–65**;
   definition 164;
   detention centres 164;
   uses of detention period 164;
   see also approved school; discipline; exclusion/
      expulsion; suspension

development plan **165**;
   educational development plans 165;
   in English educational history 165;
   see also economics of education; education
      policy; school change; school reform;
      Tanzania
Dewey, John 89, 91, 111, **165–68**, 190, 213, 215,
   243, 310, 376, 461–62, 463, 464, 550, 551, 622;
   aim of education 166;
   The Child and the Curriculum 166;
   democracy 167–68;
   Democracy and Education 166, 175;
   Experience and Education 166;
   four influences in Dewey's theory of education
      166–68;
      biological basis of mind 166, 167;
      dualism 166–67;
      practice and theory of education 166;
      social constructivism 167;
   habit 167;
   How We Think 166, 175;
   Human Nature and Conduct 167;
   influences of in education 168;
   inquiry 166–67;
   instrumentalism 166;
   John Dewey Society 168;
   language in the coming out of the mind 167;
   Logic: The Theory of Inquiry 166;
   method/subject matter 167;
   My Pedagogic Creed 166;
   progressive education 165;
   three moral traits of character 95;
   The School and Society 166;
   see also child-centred education; educational
      theory; experiential learning; Hall, Granville
      Stanley; indoctrination; learning; Mead,
      George Herbert; philosophy of education;
      progressive education; social constructivism;
      social reconstructionism
diagnostic assessment **168–69**;
   an alternative to traditional test 169;
   definition 168;
   diagnostic frameworks 168–69;
   facets 169;
   interpretation 168;
   psychometric models 169;
   purposes 168;
   semi-dense item 169;
   see also assessment; cognition; formative assessment;
      psychometrics; standards; test/testing
didactics/didacticism **169–70**;
   bildung 170;
   definitions 169–70;
   didactics research 170;
   didactics studies 170;
   die Didaktik 169–70;
   etymology 169;
   Germany 169–70;
   see also curriculum; learning; pedagogy;
      teaching/teaching methods

diploma **170–71**, 277;
  definition 170;
  description 170;
  German education system 170;
  see also certificate/certification; degree; graduate/
    graduation; postgraduate; qualifications
diploma disease **171–72**;
  Britain 171;
  Dore, Ronald 171;
    Diploma Disease 171;
  Dore's thesis' advocates 171–72;
  educational inflation 171;
  qualification inflation 171;
  see also certificate/certification; credentials/
    credentialing; diploma; examinations;
    meritocracy; qualifications
disaffection **172–73**, 380;
  causes and possible solutions 173;
  definition 172;
  forms of 172;
  major cause of educational underachievement 173;
  RHINOs 172;
  United Kingdom 173;
  see also delinquency; learning; learning
    disabilities/difficulties; motivation; truancy;
    underachievement
discipline **173–74**;
  definitions 173–74;
  Mill, John Stuart 174;
  in school context 174;
  in vocational training context 173–74;
  see also bullying; classroom; classroom
    management; corporal punishment;
    exclusion/expulsion; hyperactivity; Mill,
    John Stuart; school security; school violence;
    suspension
discovery method/learning **174–75**;
  benefits 174;
  Bruner, Jerome 175;
  criticism 175;
  definition 174;
  Democracy and Education 175;
  Dewey, John 175;
    How We Think 175;
  Froebel, Friedrich 174–75, 215;
  Montessori, Maria 175;
  and new technologies 175;
  Pestalozzi, Johann Heinrich 174;
  Piaget, Jean 175;
  Rousseau, Jean-Jacques 174;
    Emile 174;
  supporters and advocates 175;
  see also Bruner, Jerome; child-centred education;
    Dewey, John; learning; progressive
    education; Rousseau, Jean-Jacques; Spencer,
    Herbert; teaching/teaching methods
distance education/learning 17, 40, **175–78**, 201;
  alternative terminologies 176;
  Australia 176;
  beginnings and development 176;

benefits 177;
Brazil 59–60;
communication technology as prerequisite of 177;
criticism 177;
Cuba 147;
distance education theories 176;
distance learning master's programmes 372;
France 176;
Germany 176;
International Council for Distance Education
  and Open Learning (ICDE) 177;
mass education as main promoter of 176–77;
Millennium Development Goals 177;
New Zealand 176;
Oceania 415;
second-rate system of education 177;
Soviet Union 176;
supporting agencies and organisations 177;
  Commonwealth of Learning 177;
  Department for International Development
    (DfID) 177;
  UNESCO 177;
  World Bank 177;
Sweden 176;
role of information and communication
  technologies (ICTs) 178;
United Kingdom 176;
UK's Open University 176;
United States 176;
worldwide success 177;
see also andragogy; correspondence course;
  educational broadcasting; educational
  technology; e-learning; home schooling;
  master's; open learning; Open University;
  rural education; Web-based learning; Young,
  Michael
doctorate **178–79**;
  common pathways 178;
  definition 178;
  etymology 178;
  higher doctorate 178;
  honorary doctorate 179;
  professional doctorate 178–79;
  research doctorate 178;
  thesis 178, 179;
  see also coursework; degree; examinations;
    higher education; oral examinations;
    professional education; qualifications; thesis/
    dissertation; university
don **179**;
  decline of the donnish hierarchy 179;
  definition 179;
  see also higher education; meritocracy; university
drama **179–80**;
  after-school drama clubs 179;
  in colleges and universities 180;
  cross-curricular subject 179;
  etymology 179;
  extracurricular subject 179;
  plays 179–80;

and public examinations 179–80;
in secondary schools 170;
as subject 179;
see also creativity; extracurriculum; music;
   physical education
drawing 35;
observational drawing 35;
technical drawing 35;
see also art
dropouts 20, 119, **180**, 188–89;
causes and correlates 180;
consequences 180;
definition 180;
Italian universities 329;
Latin America 346;
misrepresent or frame-up 188–89;
see also early school leaving; grade retention;
   higher education; pupil mobility; retention;
   secondary school/ education
dual system **180–81**;
definition 180;
Germany 180–81;
United Kingdom 180, 615;
United States 181;
see also apprenticeship; binary system; church;
   religious education; training; vocational
   education; voluntarism
DuBois, William E. B. **181–82**;
Historical Studies 181;
National Association of the Advancement of
   Coloured People (NAACP) 182;
pioneer of American sociology 182;
see also antiracist education; multicultural education
Durkheim, Emile **182**, 198, 212;
anomie 182;
Année Sociologique 182;
see also functionalism; moral education; social
   control; sociology of education
dyslexia **182–84**;
acquired dyslexia 182;
classroom management and pedagogical
   strategies for managing dyslexia 183;
definition 182;
developmental dyslexia 182;
gender parity 183;
and learning problems 183;
phonic languages and dyslexia 183;
a processing difficulty 182;
statistics 182;
UK-based Dyslexia Institute 183;
see also cognition; learning disabilities/
   difficulties; psychology of education; reading;
   special education/special educational needs/
   special needs; spelling; underachievement

early childhood education (ECE) **185–88**, 231;
benefits of ECE according to:
   longitudinal studies 187;
   monitoring studies 187;
   neurological studies 186–87;

causes of expansion of in developed countries 185;
childhood skills and competencies valued in:
   African countries 186;
   Indian subcontinent 186;
   UK 186;
early childhood institutions 186;
early childhood period 185;
'educare' 185;
main ideas on childhood that inform ECE's
   purpose 185;
   child as the product of science 185;
   Locke's view 185;
   Rousseau's view 185;
main influences on the form and content of 186;
Oceania 413;
pro and contras 485;
Sweden 576;
see also Bruner, Jerome; child development;
   crèche; Froebel, Friedrich; Isaacs, Susan;
   kindergarten; Locke, John; McMillan,
   Margaret; Montessori, Maria; nursery school;
   Owen, Robert; Pestalozzi, Johann Heinrich;
   Piaget, Jean; reception class; Rousseau, Jean-
   Jacques; Steiner, Rudolf; Vygotsky, Lev
early school leaving **188–90**;
causes of early school leaving 189;
concept 189;
dropouts 188;
dropouts frame-up 188–89;
United Kingdom 484;
universal provision 188, 189;
see also compulsory education; pupil mobility;
   retention; underachievement; universal
   education/mass education
East Asia 138, **190–92**;
definition 190;
globalisation 191;
China:
   education for all 191;
   educational innovation 191;
   socialistic and market socialism philosophy 191;
   common educational issues and problems 192;
   cultural idioms in educational practice 191;
   cyclical view of time 192;
   keyu examination system 191;
   spatial and national sense of being 191–92;
   inequality in educational opportunities 192;
Japan:
   current market philosophy 190–91;
   democratisation through education 190;
   neo-liberal philosophy 190;
   nineteenth century modernisation 190;
   post-war educational systems 190;
   subject-centred instead of child-centred
      curriculum 190;
   US post war educational missions in Japan 190;
Korea:
   free primary compulsory education 191;
   modernisation of educational policies 191;
   textbook 598–99;

vocational training 190;
Western influences on educational ideas 190, 191;
see also China; Indonesia; Japan; Malaysia; Singapore
economics **192–93;**
definition 192;
Marshall, Alfred 192;
microeconomics 192–93;
The Principles of Economics 192;
Smith, Adam 192;
The Wealth of Nations 192;
see also curriculum; economics of education; subjects
economics of education **193–94;**
accountability 194;
applied work 193;
economic rate of return to education 193;
empirical work 194;
endogenous growth theory 193;
external efficiency 194;
former and current conceptions of 193;
household datasets 193;
human capital revolution 193;
internal efficiency 194;
Millennium Development Goals 193;
school voucher schemes 193, 194;
statistical techniques 194;
topics in applied research and discussion 193–94;
see also economics; education/educational studies; globalisation; Mill, John Stuart; privatisation/marketisation; quantitative research; Robbins, Lionel; school effectiveness; student finance/loans; voluntarism; vouchers; World Bank
Edgeworth, Maria **194–95;**
Letters to Literary 195;
The Parent's Assistant 195;
Practical Education 195;
progressivism 195;
see also progressive education
education **195–97;**
citizenship 197;
curriculum 196, 197;
definition 195;
education aims 195–97;
mass/elite 5;
'proletarianization' 6;
unresolved philosophical issues 197;
unresolved practical issues 197;
upbringing:
definition 196;
developmentalist/liberationist views on upbringing 195–96;
in a liberal–democratic society 196–97;
see also curriculum; educational research; education/educational studies; educational theory; indoctrination; sociology of education; subjects
Education Action Zones (EAZs) 116, 205, 427, 616, 630;

see also Bernstein, Basil; compensatory education; educational priority areas; equality of opportunity; positive discrimination/affirmative action; secondary school/education
Education Acts (Canada):
Act of Union (1841) 67;
British North America Act (1867) 67;
see also law
Education Acts (Ireland):
Irish Education Act (1998) 302;
Irish Equal Status Act (2000) 302;
see also law
Education Acts (Malaysia):
1961 367;
see also law
Education Acts (New Zealand/Aotearoa):
Native Schools Act (1867) 402;
1877 Education Act 402, 403;
1914 Education Act 403;
Conditional Integration of Private Schools Act (1975) 403;
1989 Education Act 403;
1990 Education Amendment Act 403;
1991 Education Amendment Act 403;
see also law
Education Acts (United Kingdom):
1840 (Grammar School Act) 280;
1886 (Idiots Act) 353;
1870 (Elementary School Act) 55, 180, 256, 484, 491, 615;
1893 55;
1902 180, 491, 506, 615;
Indian Universities Act (1904–5) 307;
1944 55, 165, 180, 386, 425, 442, 488–89, 490, 491, 535, 615;
1962 569;
1981 55, 302, 560;
Education Reform Act (1988) 52, 291, 447, 489, 490, 491, 525, 616;
School Standards and Framework Act (1998) 488–89, 490, 491;
Special Educational Needs and Disability Act (2001) 302;
UK Race Relations (Amendment) Act 27;
see also law; United Kingdom
Education Acts (United States):
1837 370;
1944 569;
Education of All Handicapped Children Act (1975) 302;
Individuals with Disabilities Act (1997) 302;
Goals 2000 (1994) 525;
No Child Left Behind Act (2001) 9, 10, 121, 291, 310, 493, 525, 550, 579, 623;
Education Science Reform Act (2002) 238;
see also law; United States
education in democratic societies 195, 196;
aim 221;
citizenship/civics 95;
educational leadership and management 203;

teacher unions 588;
see also community education; education;
    indoctrination; social reconstructionism
Education for All (EFA) 19, **197–98**, 209–10, 230,
    302, 396, 618–19, 625;
    achievements 198;
    compulsory elementary education 122;
    Dakar World Education Forum 19, 177, 209,
        210, 302, 320, 618–19;
    Fast Track Initiative (FTI) 197;
    definition 197;
    goals 197;
    Millennium Development Goals 197–98;
    see also compulsory education; educational
        targets; equality of opportunity; inclusive
        education; international education;
        International Bureau of Education (IBE);
        international education; Millennium
        Development Goals; multigrade education;
        Nigeria; Polynesia; primary school/
        education; Tanzania; United Nations
        Children's Fund (UNICEF); United
        Nations Educational, Scientific and
        Cultural Organization (UNESCO);
        universal education/mass education; World
        Bank
education policy **198–99**;
    critical policy analysis 198–99;
    Durkheim, Emile 198;
    Foucault, Michel 198–99;
    policy analysis 198;
    policy definition 198;
    see also Durkheim, Emile; education; Foucault,
        Michel; history of education; politics of
        education; privatisation/marketisation;
        restructuring; sociology of education
education in totalitarian societies:
    citizenship/civics 95;
    teacher unions 588;
    see also indoctrination
education/educational studies **199–200**;
    Britain 200;
    criticism of current educational studies 200;
    definition 199;
    foundation disciplines of education 199;
    undergraduate courses 200;
    in the university context 199;
    see also education; educational publishing;
        educational theory; history of education;
        philosophy of education; psychology of
        education; sociology of education; teacher
        education/training
educational broadcasting 94, 133, 177, 178,
    200–2;
    beginnings 201;
    Britain 201;
    British Broadcasting Corporation (BBC) 201;
    definition 200;
    digital technologies 201–2;
    distance education 201;

European Broadcasting Union 201;
    Open University 201;
    schools broadcasting services 201;
    UK's Open University 201;
    United States 201;
    see also correspondence course; distance
        education/learning; educational publishing;
        home schooling; Open University; visual aids
educational gender parity 105, 123, 193, 197, 454;
    Africa 19;
    Egypt 219;
    and hidden curriculum 290;
    higher education 293;
    Italian higher education 330;
    Japanese higher education 332;
    Latin America 290;
    Nigeria 405;
    Tanzania 582;
    United Kingdom 615;
    United States 623;
    see also equality of opportunity; feminist theory
educational leadership and management **202–4**;
    Changing Leadership for Changing Times 203;
    Changing Our Schools 203;
    Critical Perspectives on Educational Leadership 204;
    educational administration or management 202;
    Educational Administration and the Social Sciences
        202;
    Effective School Management 202;
    headteachers and principals in 203;
        as transformational leaders 203;
        work of headteachers and principals as
            transformational leaders 203;
    Leaders 202;
    leaders/managers 202–3;
    Leading Learning 204;
    Towards a Philosophy of Administration 202;
    transformational leadership 203–4;
        criticism 203–4;
    Troubling Women 204;
    in Western-style democracies 203;
    see also head teacher/principal; managerialism;
        school-based management; school change;
        school effectiveness; school improvement;
        school leadership
educational priority area (EPA) **204–5**;
    beginnings 204;
    boundaries 204;
    definition 204;
    positive discrimination 204;
    United Kingdom 205;
    United Sates 204;
    see also partnerships, educational; positive
        discrimination/affirmative action; systemic
        reform; urban education
educational provision 50, 51, 115, 182, 187, 217,
    222, 229–30;
    for gifted children 273;
    see also history of education
educational publishing **205–6**;

academic journals 205–6;
description of the term 205;
impact of publishing industry on 205;
see also educational broadcasting; educational
    research, Educational Resources Information
    Center (ERIC); education/educational
    studies; educational technology; reader;
    specialisation; textbook
educational research **206–9**;
areas of, according to practice-focused
    orientation 206–7;
complexity and tensions:
    conflicts between different disciplinary
        methods and theories 207;
    educational practice view/academic discipline
        view 206–7;
    lack of disciplinary integration within 207;
definitions 206;
different focuses of 208;
and gate-keeping 269;
history 206;
tasks 206;
see also action research; American Educational
    Research Association; Australian Association
    for Research in Education; British Educational
    Research Association; classroom observation;
    critical theory; educational publishing;
    European Educational Research Association;
    evaluation; evidence-based policy/practice;
    experimental research; history of education;
    International Association for the Evaluation
    of Educational Achievement (IEA); Mead,
    Margaret; Nordic Educational Research
    Association (NERA)/Nordisk Förening för
    Pedagogiska Forskning (NFPF); objective tests;
    philosophy of education; practitioner research;
    qualitative research; quantitative research
Educational Resources Information Center
    (ERIC) **209**;
definition 209;
sponsors 209;
users 209;
see also educational publishing; educational
    research; public library
educational system structure 597;
Brazil 59;
Canada 68;
China 92;
Cuba 146;
Egypt 218;
Finland 254;
France 258;
Germany 272;
Greece 281–82;
Indonesia 311, 312;
Iran 324–25;
Iraq 325;
Israel 327–28;
Italy 329;
Japan 331;

Malaysia 367–68;
New Zealand 402–3;
Nigeria 405;
Russia 504;
Scandinavia 508;
Singapore 541;
Sweden 576–77;
Tanzania 581;
United Kingdom 614;
    four key stages 616;
    reception class 484–85;
    sixth form 543;
United States 622;
see also compulsory education; elementary school;
    primary school/education; secondary school/
    education; universal education/mass education
educational targets **209–10**;
access to and completion of primary education
    209–10;
adult literacy 209–10;
criticism 210;
Dakar targets 209–10;
definition 209;
Education For All 209–10;
elimination of gender disparities 209, 210;
expansion de early childhood education 209–10;
Millennium Development Goals 210;
reducing illiteracy 209;
UNESCO 209;
universal primary education (UPE) 209–10;
uses for planning 209–10;
see also compulsory education; Education for All
    (EFA); Millennium Development Goals;
    performance indicators; school effectiveness;
    school improvement; standards; universal
    education/mass education
educational technology **210–11**;
etymology 210–11;
Homer 211;
pen and paper: the oldest technology 211;
Plato 211;
subservient to educational tasks 210;
    orientation for educational tasks 211;
see also computer-assisted learning; distance
    education/learning; educational publishing;
    e-learning; learning; open learning;
    technology; virtual learning; visual aids
educational theory **211–14**;
beginnings and development 212;
a contested term 212;
education as human science 213–14;
    analytic philosophy of education 213–14;
    Bourdieu, Pierre 213;
    critical pedagogy 213;
    Freire, Paolo 213;
    phenomenological, existential and
        hermeneutical inquiry 213;
education as science 212;
    Bruner, Jerome 213;
    Comte, August 212;

Descartes, René 212;
Dewey, John 213;
educational psychology 213;
empiricism 212;
experimental psychology 213;
Hume, David 212;
Locke, John 212;
Mill, John Stuart 212;
Piaget, Jean 213;
moral sciences 212;
positivism 212, 213;
rationalism 212;
Saint Simon 212;
scientia 212;
sociology/sociology of education 212;
Thorndike, Edward Lee 213;
Vygotsky, Lev 213;
foundation discipline of education 199;
humanities approach to 212;
Plato 212;
reasons for lack of unified theory of education 211;
structuralism and post-structuralism 214;
see also activity theory; constructivism;
    correspondence theory; critical theory; Dewey,
    John; education; educational research; feminist
    theory; Foucault, Michel; globalisation;
    pedagogy; philosophy of education;
    postmodernism; progressive education; social
    capital; social control; social reproduction
educationist/educationalist **214–16**;
Aristotle 215;
Britain 215;
definition 214;
Dewey, John 215;
and educator 214;
Froebel, Friedrich 215;
Locke, John 215;
Neill, Alexander Sutherland 215;
Plato 215;
    Republic 215;
Rousseau, Jean-Jacques 215;
    Emile 215;
    The Social Contract 215;
The World Library of Educationalists series 215;
see also education; teacher education/training
egalitarianism **216–17**, 222;
Finland 254;
and meritocracy 216, 217;
parental liberty 216;
principle of educational equality 216;
    challenges of 216;
see also elitism; equality of opportunity; equity;
    meritocracy; moral education; parental
    choice; Scandinavia; underachievement
Egypt **217–19**, 379;
Ain Shams University 218;
Al-Azhar 217, 218;
American University in Cairo 218;
Cairo 217;
Cairo American College 218;

Cairo University 218;
challenges in education:
    additional educational costs 219;
    adult illiteracy 218;
    inflexible centralised education system 218–19;
    gender disparity 218;
    no satisfactory quality of education 219;
educational system structure 218;
free and compulsory education 218;
geographic location 217;
hieroglyphic alphabet 217;
Islamic education 218;
kuttab 217;
military school system 218;
modernisation 217–18;
Muslim religious schools 218;
population 217;
statistics 218;
University of Alexandria 218;
see also dropouts; Israel; literacy; Mediterranean;
    religious school; World Bank
e-learning **219–20**, 260;
basis 219;
definition 219;
e-universities 219;
internet 219–20;
m-learning 219;
t-learning 219;
uses 219;
see also computer-assisted learning; distance
    education/learning; educational technology;
    learning; open learning; technology; virtual
    learning; Web-based learning
elementary school **220**;
definition 220;
see also educational system structure;
    intermediate/middle school; primary
    school/education; public school; scholarship;
    school
eleven-plus examination 3, 280, 425, 426, 535,
    609, 616;
see also examinations
Eliot, Charles William **221**;
American high school curriculum 221;
Harvard University 221;
see also higher education; university
elitism **221–22**;
definition 221;
description 222;
educational elitism 222;
equality 222;
fairness/'same-ness' 222;
French higher education 258;
intellectual elitism 221–22;
perpetuation of 221;
supporters 222;
see also egalitarianism; equality of opportunity;
    excellence; giftedness; independent/private
    school/education; technocrat/technocratic/
    technocracy

Elyot, Sir Thomas **222–23**;
The Boke Named the Governour 222;
The Castel of Helth 223;
development of standard English 223;
Elyot's curriculum 223;
see also Ascham, Roger; scholar; scholarship
emotional and behavioural difficulties/disorders
(EBD) **223–24**;
categories 223;
causes 224;
conceptual differences 223;
definition 223;
difficulties/disorders 223;
incidence 223–24;
inclusive schooling 224;
literature about 224;
maladjustment 223;
treatment, therapies 224;
see also autism; bullying; delinquency; hyperactivity;
learning; learning disabilities/difficulties;
psychology of education; special education/
special educational needs/special needs
endowment **224–25**, 279, 280, 568;
definition 224;
endowment fund 225;
see also charities, educational; grammar school;
student finance/loans
engineering **225**;
first engineering faculties 225;
future challenges 225;
German engineering 275;
Industrial Revolution 225;
medieval beginnings 225;
see also physics; science/science education;
subjects; technical education/school/college;
technology
English 61, **225–27**, 393;
definition 225–26;
English grammar 278;
English language arts programmes 226;
English Language Centre 61;
English prose 36;
Growth through English 226;
International Federation for the Teaching of
English 226;
subject matter 226;
content 226;
standard English 223, 393;
teaching of English 226;
see also bilingual education; curriculum; Elyot,
Sir Thomas; literacy; phonics; reading;
spelling; writing
English National Curriculum 36, 101, 226–27;
see also United Kingdom
environmental education **227**;
activities and campaigns 227;
aims 227;
higher education 227;
interdisciplinary field 227;
in schools curricula 227;

see also biology; chemistry; geography; school
journeys; nature study; science/science
education
equality of opportunity 176, 222, **227–30**, 276, 454;
advocates' approaches 228;
conflictual issues: class, race, gender, disability
and sexuality 229;
Education For All 230;
and educational policy priorities 229–30;
and hidden curriculum 290;
Latin America 346;
meaning 228;
Millennium Development Goals 230;
Nordic countries 235;
right-wing libertarian approach 228–29;
school improvement 230;
Universal Declaration of Human Rights 228;
see also antiracist education; distance education/
learning; educational gender parity;
egalitarianism; elitism; equity; inclusive
education; learning disabilities/difficulties;
Mann, Horace; merit; meritocracy; Mill, John
Stuart; multicultural education; parity of esteem;
positive discrimination/affirmative action; social
exclusion/inclusion; sociology of education;
Tawney, Richard Henry; Washington, Booker
T.; Wollstonecraft, Mary; zoning
equity **230–32**;
Aristotle 231;
definition and implications 230–31;
equity or adequacy? 231;
public schools 231;
United States 623;
see also Aristotle; egalitarianism; equality of
opportunity; meritocracy; positive
discrimination/affirmative action; segregation/
desegregation; social exclusion/inclusion;
Erasmus of Rotterdam 99, 106, 194, 222, 378, 511
ethnography 13, 35, **232–33**;
Beachside Comprehensive 232;
Deviance in Classrooms 232;
ethnography research features 232;
later genders, topics and styles included in 233;
Life in Classrooms 232;
methods of data collection 232;
methodological triangulation 232;
origins and development 232;
qualitative criticism 233;
quantitative criticism 232–33;
Social Relations in a Secondary School 232;
see also action research; anthropology of
education; classroom observation; educational
research; museum education; qualitative
research; sociology; sociology of education
Europe **233–36**;
andragogy 24;
Armed Forces 33;
art 35;
blind, teaching of 55;
Bologna Framework of Qualifications 476;

Bologna Process 235, 372, 388, 422, 504;
British Council 61;
business school 64;
classical studies 98;
comprehensive school 119;
cultural and traditional influences 233;
educational charities 81;
Erasmus/Socrates programme 510;
European Broadcasting Union 201;
European curriculum 18;
European languages 35;
European Union 235–36;
first European schools 233–34;
German-speaking states 235;
history (subject) 294;
home schooling 298;
influences on Chinese education 91;
Jesuits 234;
mentoring 380;
national curricula and assessment 234;
national education systems 234;
Nordic countries 235;
popular literacy 234;
primary school/education 452;
scholasticism 234;
Southern Europe 234–35;
see also European Educational Research
  Association; Finland; France; Germany; Greece;
  Italy; Mediterranean; Sweden; United Kingdom
European Broadcasting Union 201
European Educational Research Association
  (EERA) **236**, 406;
aims 236;
European Research Journal 236;
members 236;
network groups 236;
origins 236;
see also educational research
European Union 28, 233, 346, 347, 414, 422, 645;
Erasmus/Socrates programme 510;
European Union Continuing Education
  Network (EUCEN) 128;
and modern languages 387;
see also Europe; Mediterranean
evaluation **236–38**;
definition 236;
dissemination and reporting 237;
evaluation/action 237;
goal 237;
methods 238;
models and types:
  democratic/non-democratic 236–37;
  engineering/enlightenment model 237;
  formative/summative 237;
  scientific/anthropological 237;
political and economic dimension 237;
purposes 238;
see also case study; educational research;
  evidence-based policy/practice; experimental
  research; International Association for the

Evaluation of Educational Achievement
  (IEA); qualitative research; quantitative
  research; Tyler, Ralph
Every Child Matters 310
evidence-based policy/practice **238–39**;
concept 238;
expert and expert panels 239;
methodology requirements 238–39;
systematic methods 239;
see also educational research; evaluation
examinations **239–41**, 277–78;
cramming and coaching 239–40;
description 239;
'eleven-plus' examination 3, 280, 425, 426, 535,
  609, 616;
examination marking 240;
  marks, grades, reports 240;
  pass/fail 240;
  statistical procedures in examination marking
    240;
fairness, bias and other issues 240;
first recorded use in China 240;
traditional examinations 239;
types:
  onscreen e-assessments 240;
  open book examinations 240;
  portfolio of evidence 240;
written examinations 240;
  multiple-choice tests 240;
see also assessment; continuous assessment;
  coursework; criterion-referenced tests
  (CRTs); doctorate; formative assessment;
  grades; grammar school; high-stakes testing;
  marking; matriculation; norm-referenced
  tests; oral examination; plagiarism; proctor;
  qualifications; scholarship; secondary school/
  education; selection; standards; summative
  assessment; subjects; syllabus; test/testing
excellence **241–42**, 280;
definition 241, 242;
developing of 241–42;
different perspectives on 241;
education for wisdom 242;
etymology 241;
excellence of character 241;
excellent individuals 242;
expertise 241;
genetic inherited ability 241;
in institutions 241;
see also ability; behaviourism; cognition; elitism;
  Gardner, Howard; giftedness; grammar school;
  intelligence; moral education; psychology of
  education; wrangler/wooden spoon
exclusion/expulsion 164, 174, **242**;
description 242;
duration 242;
United Kingdom 242;
United States 242;
see also delinquency; discipline; pupil mobility;
  school security; school violence; suspension

experiential learning 12, **242–242**;
  beginnings and correlates 243;
  as classroom strategy 243;
  definition 242;
  Dewey, John 243;
  essence of 243;
  learning 242–43;
  experiential learning/traditional and rote learning 242, 243;
  Rogers, Carl 243;
  role of the teacher in 243;
  students engagement 243;
  see also accreditation of prior achievement/ learning; collaborative/cooperative learning; constructivism; Dewey, John; learning; learning styles; Piaget, Jean; reflective practitioner; Rogers, Carl; social constructivism
experimental research **244–45**;
  criticism 245;
  experimental research and RCT main issues 244–45;
  the 'gold standard' in education and medical research 244, 245;
  naturalistic approach's main features 244;
  randomised and controlled trial (RCT) 244–45;
  see also educational research; qualitative research; quantitative research; vouchers
extracurriculum **245–46**;
  description 245–46;
  in secondary schools, colleges and universities 246;
  see also drama; music; summer school; school journeys
extra-mural class **246–47**;
  adult education 246;
  beginnings and development 246;
  Britain 246–47;
  continuing education 247;
  definition and uses of the term 246;
  generic use of the term 247;
  Oxford Delegacy for Extra-Mural Studies 247;
  Tawney, Richard Henry 246;
  tensions in university extra-mural classes 246–47;
  United States 247;
  Workers' Educational Association (WEA) 246;
  see also adult education; continuing education; Sadler, Michael Ernest; Tawney, Richard Henry; university extension; workers' education; Workers' Educational Association (WEA)

faculty **249**;
  definitions 249;
  first faculties in University of Paris 249;
  governance 249;
  United States 249;
  see also dean; department; faculty psychology; mission statement; professor; university
faculty psychology **249–50**;
  basis 249;

The Modularity of Mind 249;
  origins and development of the concept 249;
  phrenology 249–50;
  see also faculty; phrenology; psychology; psychology of education
family **250–52**;
  as agent of cultural transmission 251;
  divorce 250;
  as households 250;
  ideological concept 250;
  lack of intergenerational view of family life and consequences 250–51;
  as networks of kin relations 250;
  as sites of social relations 251;
  structural change 251;
  see also child guidance; cultural transmission; feminist theory; home schooling; social capital
feminist theory **252–53**, 290;
  aim 252;
  Civil Rights Movement 252–53;
  definition 252;
  gender inequality 252;
  Marxist feminism 253;
  National Organisation for Women 252;
  phases of development 252–53;
    first wave 252;
    The Second Sex 252;
    second wave 252;
    The Feminine Mystique 252;
    third wave 253;
  themes and topics explored 252;
  see also critical theory; Edgeworth, Maria; educational gender parity; educational theory; family; gender studies; postmodernism; Wollstonecraft, Mary
Ferry, Jules François Camille **253–54**;
  banning of clerics from teaching 253;
  and French language and culture 253–54;
  see also France; politics of Education
financial support *see* scholarship
Finland **254–55**;
  apprenticeship 30;
  best school system in the world 254;
  child nutrition 288;
  comprehensive school 254;
  continuing education 128;
  didactics/didacticism 170;
  educational system structure 254;
  egalitarian system 254;
  geography 270;
  higher education 254;
  industrialisation 254;
  population 254;
  polytechnic 254, 447;
  teacher training 254;
  universities 254;
    University of Turku 486;
  vocational education 254;
  see also comprehensive school/education; Nordic Educational Research Association (NERA)/

Nordisk Förening för Pedagogiska Forskning (NFPF); polytechnic; Scandinavia; tertiary education; vocational education

formative assessment 169, **255–56**;
'Assessment for Learning' 255;
distinction between formative and summative assessment 255;
Inside the Black Box 255;
main focuses 255–56;
purpose 255;
United Kingdom 255;
see also assessment; continuous assessment; diagnostic assessment; examinations; high-stakes testing; learning; summative assessment; test/testing

Forster, William Edward **256**, 363;
beginning of the provision of universal schooling 256;
Elementary School Act (1870) 256;
see also Arnold, Thomas; politics of education

Foucault, Michel 198–99, **256–57**, 397;
The Archaeology of Knowledge 257;
Madness and Civilization 256;
The Order of Things 256;
postmodernism 257, 450;
see also critical theory; educational theory; postmodernism

foundation degree **257**;
aim 257;
American association degree 257;
definition 257;
level 257;
value 257;
see also degree; further education; higher education; lifelong learning; qualifications; undergraduate; university; work-based/work-located/workplace/ work-related learning

France **257–59**, 275;
Abelard, Peter 1, 333, 357;
Binet, Alfred 2, 53, 317–18;
blind, teaching of 55;
Bourdieu, Pierre 58, 147–48, 150, 397, 545–46;
Catholic education 257;
children's literature 89;
classroom 99;
comparative education 113,
Condorcet, Marie-Jean 125;
cultural diversity and immigration 393–94;
distance education/learning 176;
Durkheim, Emile 182, 198, 212;
education system 257–58;
education system development 257–58;
educational system structure 258;
educational charities 82;
Ferry, Jules François Camille 253–54;
Foucault, Michel 198–99, 256–57, 397;
Freinet, Celestin 260–61, 366;
French Revolution 125, 257, 498;
Guizot, François Pierre Guillaume 282–83;
Guizot Law 257–58, 283;

higher education 258;
home schooling 298;
influences on Latin America 345;
Jesuits 257;
major current issues 258–59;
mass education and credential inflation 141;
military education 33,
naval schools 33;
normal school 406;
polytechnic 446;
power struggle between state and church 257–58;
private education 258;
religious assembly 488;
religious education 490;
Rousseau, Jean-Jacques 89, 109, 174, 185, 190, 195, 215, 262, 338, 363, 433, 461, 464, 466, 497–98;
secularisation 258;
Sorbonne 53, 182, 257, 283, 440, 512;
technical education/school/college 592;
traditionalism 258;
training 604;
travellers, education of 607;
University of Paris 1, 99, 249, 626;
Validation de l'Experience (VAE) 11, 12;
see also Catholic school/education; Europe; International Baccalaureate; Mediterranean; multicultural education

franchising **259–60**;
benefits 259;
description 259;
in educational context 259;
McDonaldisation 259;
Outward Collaborative Provision (OCP) 259;
quality assurance and regulation 260;
see also community education; further education; higher education

Frankfurt School *see* critical theory

Freinet, Celestin **260–61**, 366;
Public Educators' Cooperative (PEC) 260;
texte libre approach 260;
see also child-centred education; collaborative/cooperative learning; Makarenko, Anton Simeonovitch; writing

Freire, Paolo 16, 18, 112, 243, **261**, 355, 366, 430, 645;
critical pedagogy 144;
Freire's learning process approach 261;
Latin American Liberation theology 261, 601;
The Pedagogy of the Oppressed 144, 261, 430;
see also adult education; critical pedagogy; informal/nonformal learning; pedagogy; progressive education

French Revolution 125, 257, 498;
see also France

Freud, Sigmund 86, **261**;
Jung, Carl 261;
mental system structure:
ego 261;
id 261;
superego 261;

Oedipus complex 261;
psychoanalysis 261;
see also child development; psychology;
    psychology of education
Froebel, Friedrich 109, 174–75, 190, **262**, 287,
    338–39, 461, 465;
and early childhood education 186, 262;
The Education of Man 262;
kindergarten 174–75, 215, 262;
Mother Play 262;
and nursery schools 411;
Universal German Education Institute 262;
see also early childhood education;
    kindergarten; nursery school; Pestalozzi,
    Johann Heinrich; progressive education;
    Rousseau, Jean-Jacques
functionalism **262–63**;
description 262;
Durkheim, Emile 262;
Merton, Robert K. 263;
    Puritanism, Pietism and Science 263;
Parsons, Talcott 262–63;
    The School Class as a Social System 263;
Smelser, Neil J. 263;
    *Social Change in the Industrial Revolution: An
        Application of Theory to The British Cotton
        Industry* 263;
socialisation 262;
Spencer, Herbert 262;
structural-functionalism 262–63;
see also Durkheim, Emile; social capital; social
    control; social reproduction; sociology;
    sociology of education; Spencer, Herbert
further education (FE) **263–65**;
college 109;
description 263;
ethos 264;
United Kingdom 263–64, 615;
see also community education; foundation degree;
    franchising; higher education; lifelong
    learning; secondary school/education; sixth
    form; technical education/school/college;
    tertiary education; vocational education

Galton, Francis **267**, 273, 468, 559;
differential schooling 267;
eugenics 267;
Hereditary Genius 267;
Inquiries into Human Faculty 267;
Natural Inheritance 267;
see also Burt, Cyril; giftedness; intelligence/
    intelligence tests; psychology of education;
    psychometrics; Skinner, Burrhus Fredric;
    Spearman, Charles
Gandhi, Mohandas Karamchand (Mahatma) **267–68**;
anti-colonialist stance 268;
'basic education' 267–68;
Gandhi's educational ideas 267;
see also India
gap year 505

Gardner, Howard 3, **268**, 318, 356;
The Arts and Human Development 268;
Frames of Mind 268, 318, 356;
Man: A Course of Study (MACOS) 268;
multiple intelligences 268, 318, 356, 357, 430;
Multiple Intelligences 268;
Project Zero 268;
The Unschooled Mind 268;
see also Bruner, Jerome; cognition; creativity;
    excellence; intelligence/intelligence tests;
    learning styles; psychology of education
gate-keeping **268–69**;
description 268;
and higher education 268–69;
and research 269;
see also educational research; selection
gender studies **269**;
feminism 269;
higher education 269;
see also feminist theory; postmodernism
geography **269–70**;
central concepts 269;
challenges 270;
definition 269;
educators 270;
Finland 270;
Germany 270;
International Geographical Union (IGU) 269;
*International Research in Geographical and
    Environmental Education* 270;
role of in a person's education 269–70;
United Kingdom 270;
United States 270;
see also curriculum; environmental education;
    subjects
Germany **271–72**, 275, 276;
Abitur 271, 272;
apprenticeship 29, 272;
Bamberg University 24;
Bildung 271;
blind, teaching of 55;
career guidance 69;
child guidance 87, 88;
children's literature 90;
classical studies 97, 99, 271;
Comenius, Jan Amos 89, 109, 323, 338, 461;
comparative education 113;
comprehensive school 119;
continuing education 128;
core skills/core competences 131;
critical theory 145–46;
church and private schools 272;
church's role in education 271;
current challenges in education 272;
cultural diversity and immigration 393–94;
didactics/didacticism 169–70;
diploma 170;
distance education/learning 176;
dual system 180–81, 275;
East Germany's education system 271, 272;

educational system development 271;
educational system structure 272;
engineering 275;
federal educational legislation 271;
Froebel, Friedrich 109, 174–75, 190, 262, 287,
    338–39, 461, 465;
geography 270;
German 278;
German university model 626–27;
German university traditions 7;
Göttingen University 486;
Gymnasium 97, 271, 272;
Habermas, Jürgen 145, 199, 285;
Herbart, Johann Friedrich 190, 289;
Humboldt, Karl Wilhem von 97, 289, 370, 532,
    626;
history (subject) 294;
home schooling 298;
indoctrination 310;
Jena University 289;
Kant, Immanuel 43, 103, 190, 390;
kindergarten 262, 271–72;
Montessori schools 272;
polytechnic 446;
religious education 490;
technical education/school/college 592–93;
training 604;
Universal German Education Institute 262;
Universität 271;
university 272, 292;
University of Berlin 114, 626;
vocational qualification 272;
Waldorf schools 272;
Weber, Max 114, 212, 640;
West Germany's education system 271, 272;
see also Europe; multicultural education
giftedness **272–74**;
Binet, Alfred 273;
education provision 273;
Galton, Francis 273;
Gardner's *multiple intelligences* 273;
Intelligence Quotient (IQ) 273;
meanings: French, English and Non-Western
    perspectives 272–73;
related terms 272;
see also ability; ability grouping; Binet, Alfred; Burt,
    Cyril; creativity; elitism; excellence; Galton,
    Francis; individualised instruction/personalised
    learning; intelligence/intelligence tests; special
    education/special educational needs/special
    needs; streaming/tracking; Terman, Lewis M.
globalisation 17, 19, 77, 78, 114, 128, 137, 150, 171,
    191, 192, **274–77**, 307, 322, 340, 420, 427;
Brazil 276;
Britain 276;
China 275, 276;
Germany 275, 276;
global labour markets 274–75;
global skill strategies of multinational companies
    (MNCs) 274, 276;

human capital theory (HCT) 274–75, 276;
India 275, 276;
and managerialism 369;
processes related to 275–76;
Russia 276;
skills capture theory (SCT) 274, 275, 276;
skill formation theory (SFT) 274, 275, 276;
United States 276;
Vietnam 276;
see also economics of education; educational
    theory; international education; knowledge
    economy; learning society; lifelong
    learning; Organisation for Economic
    Cooperation and Development (OECD);
    skills; United Nations Children's Fund
    (UNICEF); United Nations Educational,
    Scientific and Cultural Organization
    (UNESCO)
grades 38, **277**;
definition 277;
classes 277;
in higher education 277;
numerical and alphabetical scores 277;
marks 38, 277;
percentages 277;
see also assessment; examinations; marking
graduate/graduation **277–78**, 379;
Canada 277;
graduation 277;
    ceremony 278;
    ceremonial fee 278;
    prior to graduation 277–78;
graduate: definition 277;
    as a verb 277;
United States 277;
see also alumni; degree; diploma; high school;
    higher education; university
grammar **278–79**;
ancient Greek 278;
definition 278;
in classical education 96;
English grammar 278;
German 278;
Latin grammar 278;
parts of speech 278;
rules of grammar 278;
traditional grammar 278;
see also grammar school; literacy; spelling;
    standards; writing
grammar of schooling **279**;
definition 279;
standard institutional template 279;
see also pedagogy; school; school change; school
    reform
grammar school 57, **279–81**, 426;
cultural excellence 280;
development into elite public schools 280;
'eleven-plus' examination 279;
endowment 279;
England 279–80;

first American Latin Grammar School 279;
'going comprehensive' 280;
Latin 279;
origins and development 279–80;
revival or final extinction 280;
scola grammatice 279;
School Certificate accreditation 280;
see also church; classical studies; comprehensive
  school/education; endowment;
  examinations; excellence; grammar; parity of
  esteem; public school; scholarship; school;
  secondary school/education; selection;
  technical education/school/college
Greece 115, **281–82**;
  ancient Greece 1, 96, 233, 380, 466, 470, 512;
  ancient Greek education 281, 512;
  Aristotle 1, 32, 43, 96, 215, 334, 364, 372, 441;
  centralisation 282;
  centralised curriculum 282;
  cramming 281;
  culture 282;
  education system structure 281–82;
  ethnic identity 282;
  gymnasium 281;
  Hellenic Open University 281;
  history (subject) 294;
  initial vocational training (IEKs) 281;
  main problems 282;
  Organisation for Economic Cooperation and
    Development (OECD) 282;
  Plato 1, 8, 35, 43, 211, 212, 215, 233, 334, 358,
    372, 373, 441–44;
  religious education 490;
  Spartan model 281;
  special schools 281;
  unified lyceum 281;
  see also classical education; classical studies;
    Europe; Mediterranean; Organisation for
    Economic Cooperation and Development
    (OECD); Socratic method
Greek 38;
  ancient Greek 278;
  ancient languages 387;
  grammar 278;
  translations from 106;
  see also Greece; classical education; classical studies
Guizot, François Pierre Guillaume **282–83**;
  Guizot Law 257–58, 283;
  Manuel général de l'instruction primaire codifié 283;
  Pauline Meulan 283;
  see also France; politics of education

Habermas, Jürgen 145, 199, **285**;
  Knowledge and Human Interests 285;
  Theory of Communicative Action 285;
  see also critical theory
habitus 58, 148, **285–86**;
  agent 286;
  Bourdieu, Pierre 285–86;
  Bourdieu and Education 286;

Class Strategies and the Education Market 286;
  definition 285–86;
  dispositions 286;
  female habitus 286;
  Leaders and Leadership in Education 286;
  Leading Learning 286;
  The Logic of Practice 285;
  In Masculine Domination 286;
  In Other Words 285;
  Pascalian Meditations 285;
  schemes of perception 286;
  thinking tool 285, 286;
  see also Bourdieu, Pierre; cultural capital;
    learning career; sociology of education
Hall, Granville Stanley **287**, 462–63, 466;
  Adolescence 287;
  American Psychological Association 287;
  Child Study Association of America 287;
  The Contents of Children's Mind 462;
  educational psychology 287;
  *The Study of Children and The Content of
    Children's Minds* 287;
  see also Dewey, John; progressive education;
    psychology of education
Harris, William Torrey **287**;
  Alcott, Amos Bronson 287;
  first kindergarten in the USA 287;
  Journal of Speculative Philosophy 287;
  The Psychologic Foundations of Education 287;
  *Webster's International Dictionary of the English
    Language* 287;
  see also kindergarten
Harvard University 118, 124–25, 179, 181, 221,
  225, 262, 287, 466;
  Historical Studies 181
head teacher/principal **287–88**;
  deputy or assistant head 288;
  duties and responsibilities 287–88;
  see also educational leadership and management;
    Reddie, Cecil; school-based management;
    school leadership
health education **288–89**;
  Abbotsholme School 487;
  Britain 288;
  child nutrition 288;
  cross-curricular way of teaching 288;
  Finland 288;
  health education programmes 288–89;
  United Nations Children's Fund (UNICEF) 288;
  United States 288;
  virtuous circle 'education-health' 288;
  see also curriculum; home economics/domestic
    science; McMillan, Margaret; physical
    education/training; sex education; subjects;
    United Nations Children's Fund (UNICEF)
Herbart, Johann Friedrich 190, **289**;
  *Aesthetic Revelation of the World as the Chief Work
    of Education* 289;
  *General Pedagogy Deduced from the Purpose of
    Education* 289;

von Humboldt 289;
see also Pestalozzi, Johann Heinrich; psychology
    of education; teacher education/training
hidden curriculum 152–53, **289–90**;
    definition 289;
    higher education 290;
    Ireland 289–90;
    Latin American 290;
    neo-Marxist theories 289;
    see also classroom; culture; curriculum
high school **290–91**;
    comprehensive high school 119;
    extracurriculum 246;
    Indonesia 312;
    Iran 325;
    Israel 291;
    sections or types 291;
    United States 290–91, 620, 623;
    see also graduate/graduation; intermediate/
        middle school; secondary school/education
high-stakes testing **291–92**;
    accountability 291;
    consequences for poor high-stakes testing
        outcomes 291–92;
    England 291, 292;
    Japan 291, 291;
    low-performing schools 292;
    purposes 291;
    Singapore 292;
    United States 291–92;
    see also ability grouping; accountability;
        curriculum; examinations; formative
        assessment; social promotion; streaming/
        tracking; test/testing
higher education 179, **292–94**, 446–47;
    aims of higher education 402;
    American comprehensive university 292;
    Caribbean 70–71;
    changing nature 292, 293;
    and church 94;
    computer studies 123;
    credentials/credentialing 140–41;
    Cuba 147;
    day release 159;
    dean 159;
    degree 159–60;
    Department for International Development
        (DfID) 162;
    dual system 181;
    education/educational studies 199–200;
    Egypt 218;
    environmental education 227;
    expansion 292, 293;
        credentialist theories 293;
        critical theories 293;
        human capital theories 293;
        institutionalist theories 293;
        political theories 293;
    Finland 254;
    foundation degree 257;
    France 258;
    gate-keeping 268–69;
    gender equity 293;
    gender studies 269;
    geography 270;
    Germany 272, 292;
    governance 293;
    grades 277,
    graduation ceremony 278;
    hidden curriculum 290;
    Italian higher education 330;
    Japanese higher education 332;
    k-16 norm 293;
    Latin America 346;
    lecture/lecturer 357;
    lifelong learning 293;
    mass higher education 5, 6, 292, 293;
    medieval roots 292;
    modular/module 388;
    Nigeria 405;
    Oceania 415;
    oral examinations 419;
    performance indicators 431;
    polytechnics 592;
    post-secondary systems 292–93;
        degree-granting 292–93;
        vocational sectors 292–93;
    restructuring 493;
    Russia 503, 504;
    Singapore 541;
    Tanzania 582;
    technological education 592;
    types 292;
    United Kingdom 615–16;
    United States 221, 621;
    see also academic/academic profession; Carnegie
        Foundation for the Advancement of
        Teaching; Conant, James Bryant; credentials/
        credentialing; degree; doctorate; don;
        economics; franchising; further education;
        graduate/graduation; Kerr, Clark; knowledge
        economy; lifelong learning; master's;
        Newman, John Henry; polytechnic;
        postgraduate; professor; rector; retention;
        Riesman, David; Robbins, Lionel; sabbatical;
        sandwich course; secondary school/
        education; semester/term; student finance/
        loans; teaching assistant; technical education/
        school/college; tertiary education; tuition/
        tutor/tutorial; university; vocational
        education; undergraduate; work-based/
        work-located/workplace/work-related
        learning
history **294–95**;
    as curriculum subject 294;
    England 294;
    history's place in the curriculum: causes of
        international differences 294;
        debates over the subject's nature and purpose
            294–95;

different forms of curriculum 294;
internal organisation of the subject 294;
organisation within school structure 294;
new history 294, 295;
Schools Council History Project (SCHP) 295;
United States 294;
see also citizenship/civics; Condorcet, Marie-Jean; curriculum; core curriculum/national curriculum; John of Salisbury; museum education; social studies; subjects
history of education **295–96**;
compulsory mass schooling 296;
definition 295;
foundation discipline of education 199, 214, 296;
historical debates 295–96;
questions about the future of 296;
societies and journals 296;
see also curriculum; education policy; educational research; education/educational studies
home economics/domestic science **296–97**;
or food technology 297;
Frederick, Christine 296–97;
objectives 297;
origins 296–97;
in school curriculum 297;
see also curriculum; health education; subjects
home schooling **297–98**;
Canada 298;
debate about 298;
definition 297;
educational broadcasting 201;
Europe 298;
France 298;
Germany 298;
legislation and policies 298;
Oceania 298;
physical and social settings 297;
structure 297;
United Kingdom 298;
United States 298;
see also compulsory education; deschooling; distance education/learning; family; independent/private school/education; individualised instruction/personalised learning; informal/nonformal learning; Locke, John; Neill, Alexander Sutherland; parental choice
homework **298–300**;
classification 299;
amount 299;
choice for the student 299;
completion deadline 299;
degree of individualisation 299;
level of difficulty 299;
purpose 299;
skill area 299;
social context 299;
definition 298;
value 299;
see also coursework; project method; pupil; student

human capital theories (HCT) 217, 230, 274–75, 276, 420;
in adult education 17;
China 91;
in continuing education 128;
see also globalisation; Organisation for Economic Cooperation and Development (OECD);
Humboldt, Karl Wilhem von 97, 289, 370, 532;
University of Berlin 114, 626
Hume, David 212, 237, 249;
A Treatise of Human Nature 212
hyperactivity 183, **300**;
Attention Deficit Disorder (AD/HD) 183, 300;
definition 300;
diagnostic criteria 300;
subtypes 300;
predominantly hyperactive-impulsive subtype 300;
predominantly inattentive subtype 300;
combined subtype 300;
see also behaviourism; classroom management; discipline; emotional and behavioural difficulties/disorders (EBD); learning disabilities/difficulties; special education/special educational needs/special needs

Illich, Ivan 122, 163–64, 243, **301**, 355;
The Alphabetization of the Popular Mind 301;
Deschooling Society 163, 301;
Vineyard of the Mind 301;
see also deschooling; Latin America; school
illiteracy 209;
Brazil 60;
East Asia 192;
Egypt 218;
India 308;
traveller communities 607;
see also compulsory education; Education For All (EFA); literacy
inclusive education 224, **301–3**;
basis 302;
definition 301;
disabled students as main focus for legislation 302;
Education For All 302;
legislation 302;
origins of the term 301–2;
Salamanca Statement 301–2;
therapeutic school 224;
United Nations Educational, Scientific and Cultural Organization (UNESCO) 301–2;
see also Education for All (EFA); equality of opportunity; integration; learning disabilities/difficulties; special education/special educational needs/special needs; United Nations Educational, Scientific and Cultural Organization (UNESCO)
independent/private school/education **303–5**;
boarding schools 304;
Britain 303, 304, 305;
challenges 305;

China 303, 304;
churches and charities support 303;
current diversity 304–5;
defining characteristic 305;
definition 303;
elite independent schools 305;
kinds:
  independent schools 303, 304;
  for-profit or proprietary schools 303, 304;
  religious-affiliated schools 303, 304;
Republic of Ireland 303, 304;
Sweden 303;
United Kingdom 615;
United States 303, 304, 305;
see also boarding school/education; Catholic
  school/education; elitism; endowment;
  home schooling; privatisation; public school;
  religious school; Reddie, Cecil; vouchers
India 275, 276, **305–8;**
Buddhist education 306–7;
  monasteries 306;
compulsory education 122;
diploma 170;
education policies and current problems 307;
Gandhi, Mohandas Karamchand (Mahatma)
  267–68, 307;
higher education 307;
illiteracy 308;
immigration 394;
Indian Universities Act (1904–5) 307;
Islamic education 306;
  maktabs, madrasahs, mosques, *khanqahs* 306;
  patshalas 306;
kindergarten 339;
knowledge economy 341;
liberation theology 601;
mass education and credential inflation 141;
modern system of education 307;
monitorial system 389;
religious education 490;
Soka Gakkai International 367;
universities 307;
urban education 629;
Vedic education 305–6;
  Aryans schools 306;
  Hindu castes 306;
  Vedic scriptures 306;
  vocational education 634;
see also Pakistan
indigenous education 162, **308–9;**
*Coolangatta Statement on Indigenous Rights on
  Education* 308;
impact and effects of colonialism and imperialism
  308;
indigenous population 308;
indigenous knowledge systems (IKS) 18;
rights of indigenous peoples to indigenous
  education 308–9;
see also Africa; anthropology of education;
  bicultural education; bilingual education;

culture; equality of opportunity;
  metropolitanism; multicultural education
individualised instruction/personalised learning
  156, **309–10;**
aim 309;
definition 309;
United Kingdom 309;
United States 309;
see also accountability; curriculum
  differentiation; giftedness; home schooling;
  instruction; learning; learning styles;
  Parkhurst, Helen; progressive education;
  project method; special education/special
  educational needs/special needs; teaching/
  teaching methods; Thorndike, Edward Lee
indoctrination **310–11;**
aims and methods of religious and political
  indoctrination 310, 311;
China 310;
De Doctrina Christiana 310;
definitions 310, 311;
Dewey, John 310;
etymology 310;
Germany 310;
ongoing debates 311;
purpose 310–11;
see also autonomy; Dewey, John; education;
  philosophy of education; progressive
  education; religious education; social
  reconstructionism; theology
Indonesia **311–12;**
decentralisation 312;
educational system structure 311, 312;
expansion of national, secular schools 312;
geographical notions 311;
high school 312;
International Monetary Fund 312;
Islamic madrasahs 311;
public/private schools 311;
universal primary education 312;
World Bank 312;
see also centralisation/decentralisation; East Asia;
  privatisation/marketisation; religious school;
  school improvement
industrial training **313–14;**
categories:
  continued skill 313;
  initial training 313;
  retraining 313;
general/specific 313;
main focus 313;
on-the-job/off-the-job 313;
training: definitions 313;
see also apprenticeship; skills; training; vocational
  education; work-based/work-located/
  workplace/work-related learning; work
  experience
industrial revolution 33, 35, 137, 225, 263, 271,
  294, 307, 439, 462, 573, 590, 625
informal/nonformal learning 18, **314–15;**

definition 314;
genealogy of the term 314;
lifelong learning 314;
Resnick's 'learning in school and out' 314;
workers' education 643–44;
see also alternative education; Freire, Paolo;
home schooling; International Council for
Adult Education; learning; learning career;
learning society; lifelong learning; museum
education; public library; workbased/work-
located/workplace/work-related learning;
youth club/work
Information and Communication Technology
(ICT) 123, 124;
see also computer-assisted learning; e-learning;
technology
in-service education **315**;
criticism 315;
definition 315;
teacher associations 315;
see also continued/continuing professional
development; professional education;
teaching profession; workers' education
inspection **315–16**;
China 315;
contextualisation of findings 316;
definition 315;
high stakes inspections 316;
New Zealand 315;
process of inspection:
collection of evidence 316;
interpretation 316;
reporting of inspection findings 316;
United Kingdom 315, 316;
Office for Standards in Education (Ofsted)
316, 526;
United States 315;
see also accountability; Arnold, Matthew;
attainment; Kay-Shuttleworth, Sir James;
monitor; performance indicators; school
effectiveness; school improvement; standards;
underperforming/failing school
instruction **317**;
definitions 317;
public instruction 317;
religious instruction 317;
teacher-centred 317;
see also individualised instruction/personalised
learning; lecture/lecturer; lesson; pedagogy;
teaching/teaching methods; training; tuition/
tutor/tutorial; visual aids
integration **317**;
description 317;
inclusive education 317;
mathematics and calculus' context 317;
outcome of desegregation 317;
see also inclusive education; mathematics;
pastoral care; segregation/desegregation;
social exclusion/inclusion
intelligence/intelligence tests 182, **317–18**;

Binet, Alfred 317–18;
Burt, Cyril; 318;
cognitive ability 318;
definition 317;
Gardner, Howard 318;
kinaesthetic, verbal, logical, natural and
spatial 318;
multiple intelligences 318, 430;
inherited or socially determined? 64, 318;
intelligence scale 317;
IQ 53, 273, 596, 611, 612, 649;
IQ tests 64, 318;
IQ scores 42, 48, 469, 596, 611;
Spearman, Charles 318;
uses of the term:
Middle Ages 318;
seventeenth century 318;
current uses 318;
The Mismeasure of Man 318;
Terman, Lewis 318;
types of 3;
Weschler, David 318;
see also ability; ability grouping; aptitude; Binet,
Alfred; Burt, Cyril; cognition; excellence;
Galton, Francis; Gardner, Howard;
giftedness; learning styles; Mead, George
Herbert; merit; meritocracy; phrenology;
psychometrics; recruitment; selection;
Spearman, Charles; Terman, Lewis Madison;
test/testing; Thorndike, Edward Lee;
underachievement
Intelligence Quotient (IQ) 53, 273, 596, 611, 612,
649;
IQ scores 42, 48, 469, 596, 611;
IQ tests 64, 318, 612;
see also intelligence/intelligence tests; merit;
meritocracy; Terman, Lewis Madison;
underachievement
intermediate/middle school **319**;
Australia 319;
Canada 319;
description 319;
England 319;
Iran 324–25;
Japan 319;
junior high school 319;
New Zealand 319;
Scandinavia 508;
United States 319;
see also elementary school; high school; primary
school/education; secondary school/ education
International Association for the Evaluation of
Educational Achievement (IEA) **319**;
activities 319;
definition 319;
headquarters 319;
origins and development 319;
United Nations Educational, Scientific and
Cultural Organization (UNESCO) 319;
see also educational research; evaluation

International Baccalaureate 322, 368, 475, 541; technical baccalaureate 592
International Bureau of Education (IBE) **319–20**, 323, 619, 620;
activities 320;
definition 319–20;
governance 320;
oldest UNESCO institute 320;
origins 320;
Piaget, Jean 320;
publications 320;
see also comparative education; Education for All (EFA); international education; Piaget, Jean; United Nations Educational, Scientific and Cultural Organization (UNESCO)
International Council for Adult Education (ICAE) 17, **320**, 620;
Convergence, an International Journal of Adult Education 320;
description 320;
goals 320;
governance 320;
Voices Rising 320;
see also adult education; informal/nonformal learning; lifelong learning; United Nations Educational, Scientific and Cultural Organization (UNESCO)
International Council for Education of People with Visual Impairment (ICEVI) 56
international education **321–23**;
activity 323;
advocacy 321, 322–23;
organisations 322–23;
analysis:
contribution of education to development 321–22;
education, dependency and globalisation 322;
educational borrowing and lending 321;
international education comparisons 322;
international education practices and organisations 322;
multilateral agencies 322;
'other' education systems, policies, practices and philosophies 321;
categories of work: analysis, advocacy, activity 321–23;
and comparative education 321;
internationalisation in Japan 190;
United Nations Educational, Scientific and Cultural Organization (UNESCO) 322, 323;
see also Department for International Development (DfID); comparative education; Education for All (EFA); globalisation; International Bureau of Education (IBE); Organisation for Economic Co-operation and Development (OECD); United Nations Children's Fund (UNICEF); United Nations Educational, Scientific and Cultural Organization (UNESCO); World Bank

International Institute for Educational Planning (IIEP) **323–24**;
activities 323–24;
aim 323;
consortia 324;
description 323;
United Nations Children's Fund (UNICEF) 324;
United Nations Educational, Scientific and Cultural Organization (UNESCO) 324;
World Bank 324;
see also comparative education; United Nations Children's Fund (UNICEF); United Nations Educational, Scientific and Cultural Organization (UNESCO); World Bank
Ireland:
hidden curriculum 289–90;
see also Education Acts (Ireland)
Iran **324–25**;
education history:
pre-Islamic era 324;
early Islamic era 324;
current era 324;
educational system structure 324–25;
Jondi-Shapour University 324;
konkour 325;
private education 325;
universities 325
Iraq **325–26**;
'brain drain' 326;
educational system structure 325;
Great National Religious Campaign 326;
modern educational projects: Arabisation, Islamisation, militarisation 326;
Civic Ethics 326;
National and Social Education 326;
National Education 326;
Pan-Arab Culture 326;
Sunni Islamisation of the education system 325;
Tanzimāt 325;
teacher training 326;
University of Baghdad 326;
universities 326
Isaacs, Susan Sutherland **326–27**, 463;
The Children We Teach 327;
and early childhood education 186;
Froebel, Friedrich 327;
Intellectual Growth of Young Children 327;
and nursery school 411;
Social Development in Young Children 327;
see also child development; Froebel, Friedrich; nursery school; progressive education
Israel **327–28**;
boarding school 57;
changes from the 1970s 328;
comprehensive junior schools 328;
current challenges 328;
current educational system 328;
educational system structure 327–28;
expansion of educational system 327;
Hebrew as language of instruction 327;

Jewish-Zionist education 327;
  pastoral care 428;
  religious education 327;
  State Education Law (1957) 327;
    state schools 327;
    state-religious schools 327;
    Arab state schools 327;
  see also Mediterranean
Islamophobia 27;
  see also antiracist education; equality of
    opportunity; multicultural education
Italy **328–30**;
  comparative education 113;
  continuing education 128;
  current educational system 329;
    istituto professionale 329;
    istituto tecnico 329;
    liceo 329;
  current problems 329–30;
  education and language 329;
  educational system structure 329;
  inclusive education 302;
  modern educational system 329;
  Montessori, Maria 156, 175, 389–90, 426, 463;
  Roman empire's educational system 328–29;
    ludus 328–29;
    grammaticus 329;
    rethor 329;
  universities 329;
  university educational system 329;
  see also abacus; Catholic school/education;
    classical education; corporal punishment;
    dropouts; Europe; Mediterranean

Japan **331–32**, 395;
  alumni associations 22;
  blind, teaching of 55;
  child guidance 87, 88;
  citizenship/civics education 95;
  classroom 100;
  cramming 138;
  current educational system 331;
  current market philosophy 190–91;
  Dalton schools 426;
  democratisation through education 190;
  diploma disease 171;
  educational broadcasting 201;
  educational achievements 331;
  educational issues 331;
  educational system structure 331;
  Fundamental Law (1947) 330, 331;
  gender gap in higher education 332;
  global knowledge economy 332;
  history (subject) 294;
  influences on Chinese education 91;
  junior high school 319;
  kindergarten 339;
  Kyoiku Chokugo 331;
  Makiguchi, Tsunesaburo 366–67;
  mentoring 380;

  neo-liberal philosophy 190;
  nineteenth century modernisation 190;
  post-war educational systems 190;
  Rinkyoshin 331–32;
  schooling 25;
  Soka Gakkai International 367;
  subject-centred instead of child-centred
    curriculum 190;
  textbook 598–99;
  United Nations University, Tokyo 486;
  US post-war educational missions 190;
  see also China; East Asia
Jesuit education 94, 234, **332–33**;
  Cuba 146;
  current profile 333;
  educational system and curricula 332;
  first educational system in the Western world 333;
  gifted men with Jesuit formation 332;
  France 257;
  girls' education 332;
  Jesuit schools 332;
  Jesuit university 332;
  Latin America 345;
  prefect of studies and prefect general 332;
  Ratio Studiorum 332, 333;
  restoration of Jesuits 333;
  'schoolmasters of Europe' 333;
  Society of Jesus 332;
  suppression of Jesuits 333;
  see also Catholic school/education; church;
    religious education; religious school; theology
John of Salisbury 1, **333–34**;
  and Aristotle's work 334;
  Metalogicus 334;
  Policraticus 334;
  and the study of history 333–34;
  see also Abelard, Peter; Aristotle; grammar; scholar
Jowett, Benjamin **334**, 632;
  Essays and Reviews 334;
  see also classical studies; university extension;
    vice-chancellor
Jung, Carl Gustav 261, 467
junior school **334–35**;
  junior years of schooling 334;
  organisation in year groups 335;
  see also elementary school; primary school/education

Kant, Immanuel 43, 103, 190, 390
Kay-Shuttleworth, Sir James **337**;
  Department of Education 337;
  Four Periods of Public Education 337;
  Moral and Physical Condition of the Working Class
    in Manchester in 1832 337;
  Public Education 337;
  school inspection system 337;
  teacher training 337;
  see also inspection; teacher education/training
Keate, John **337–38**;
  Arnold, Thomas 337;
  Eton College 337;

see also Arnold, Thomas; corporal punishment;
  public school
Kenya 19, 321, 495, 581, 634;
  diploma disease 171;
  urbanisation 629
Kerr, Clark **338**;
  University of California-Berkeley 338;
  The Uses of the University 338;
  see also higher education; university
kindergarten 174–75, 185, 215, **338–39**;
  banning of 339;
  Canada 68;
  China 92;
  Cuba 146;
  etymology 339;
  first kindergarten 262, 338–39;
  Froebel, Friedrich 339–40;
  Germany 271–72;
  key elements:
    gifts 339;
    occupations 339;
    songs and games 339;
  kindergartners 339;
  Marenholtz-Bülow, Baroness Bertha von 339;
  McMillan, Margaret 339;
  Montessori, Maria 339;
  United States 287;
  see also early childhood education; Froebel,
    Friedrich; nursery school
King, Martin Luther, Jr. 511;
  compulsory education 121
knowledge economy **339–41**, 420;
  definition 340;
  de-institutionalisation of knowledge 12;
  development of the term 340;
  education as key role 340;
  global agencies investing in education 340;
  globalisation 340;
  issues regarding the link education – knowledge
    economy 340–41;
  power and control over knowledge 6–7;
  and university 627–28;
  see also credentials/credentialing; core skills/core
    competences; globalisation; learning society;
    lifelong learning; Organisation for Economic
    Co-operation and Development (OECD);
    qualifications; skills; university; work-based/
    work-located/workplace/work-related
    learning; World Bank
Knox, John **341**;
  Book of Discipline 341;
  national educational system 341;
  see also church
Kohlberg, Lawrence 86, **341–42**;
  child's moral development 341–42;
  Just Community Approach 342;
  Moral Discussion Approach 342;
  The Philosophy of Moral Development 342;
  The Psychology of Moral Development 342;
  see also cognition; moral education

Lancaster, Joseph **343**, 406;
  Improvements in Education 343;
  monitorial system of schooling 343;
  teacher training 343;
  see also monitor; monitorial system; normal
    school; pedagogy; religious school
Lane, Homer **343–44**;
  Little Commonwealth 343, 344;
  progressive education 344;
  Talks to Parents and Teachers 344;
  youth club 343;
  see also delinquency; progressive education;
    youth club/work
language teaching 109;
  computer-assisted learning 123;
  oral examinations 419;
  see also English; modern languages
Latin 38, 109, 279;
  ancient languages 387;
  Latin grammar 278;
  learning 36;
  translation 36;
  see also classical education; classical studies
Latin America **344–47**;
  arielism 345;
  and British Council 61;
  Catholic church 345;
  centralisation/decentralisation 77;
  Chile 425;
  critical pedagogy 345–46;
  current problems in Latin American education 346;
  Dewey, John 345;
  colonial universities 345;
  cultural imperialism 345;
  education in colonial times 345;
  educational gender parity 39;
  educational reforms:
    rationales for these reforms 346;
  Freire, Paolo 346;
  French influences on education 345;
  hidden curriculum 290;
  historical, economical, political and cultural brief
    account 344;
  Illich, Ivan 346;
  Inter-American Development Bank 346;
  Jesuit education 345;
  liberation theology 601;
  Organisation of American States 346;
  school reform 524;
  statistics 346;
  United States' influences 344, 345;
  World Bank 346;
  see also Brazil; Freire, Paolo; Illich, Ivan
law **347–48**;
  as academic/curricular course of study 347–48;
    law-related education 347–48;
    United Kingdom 347;
    United States 347;
    street law programme 348;
  as key element in educational system 348;

countries with written constitutions 348;
countries without written constitutions 348;
Italy 329;
Fundamental Law (Japan 1947) 331, 332;
inclusive education 302;
United Kingdom 347;
United States 348;
see also curriculum; Education Acts (Ireland);
Education Acts (United Kingdom);
Education Acts (United States); positive
discrimination/affirmative action; profession/
professionalism/professionalisation;
professional education; subjects
learning 348–50;
cognitive theory of learning 31;
contemporary understanding 348;
definition 348;
dimensions: content, incentive, interaction 349;
incentive for 36;
influential conditions of learning 349;
learner attitudes to education 173;
learning defence 349;
learning types:
accommodative 349;
assimilative 349;
cumulative 349;
transformative 349;
resistance to learning 349;
see also constructivism; Dewey, John;
disaffection; discovery method/learning;
e-learning; emotional and behavioural
difficulties/disorders (EBD); experiential
learning; formative assessment; individualised
instruction/personalised learning; informal/
nonformal learning; learning career; learning
community; learning curve; learning society;
learning styles; lifelong learning; motivation;
pedagogy; phonics; programmed learning;
psychology; self-directed learning; situated
cognition/learning; Socratic method;
teacher; virtual learning
learning career 350–51;
concept 350;
four main constituent parts 350;
criticism 350–51;
personal dispositions and learning 350;
see also habitus; informal/nonformal learning;
learning; learning society; progression;
social promotion; student; transition
education
learning community 351–52;
Action Learning Set 352;
classroom settings 351;
collaborative learning 351;
definition 351;
key features 352;
learning and teacher forums 352;
schools 351;
school councils 351;
Virtual Learning Environments (VLEs) 352;

see also collaborative/cooperative learning;
learning; practitioner research; situated
cognition/learning; teaching/teaching
methods; virtual learning
learning curve 352–53;
definition 352;
Ebbinghaus, Hermann 353;
forgetting curve 353;
steep learning curve 352;
see also learning; progression
learning disabilities/difficulties 353–54;
definition 353;
disabilities or difficulties 353;
dyslexia 353;
Idiots Act of 1886 353;
mentally handicapped 353;
specific learning disabilities/difficulties 353;
uses of the term 353;
see also blind, teaching of; dyslexia; hyperactivity;
inclusive education; social exclusion/inclusion;
special education/special educational needs/
special needs; underachievement
learning process 106, 357;
see also cognition; learning styles
learning society 354–56, 512;
characteristics 354;
a contested concept 354, 355, 356;
diagnosis and prognosis 356;
creation of 355;
European Commission (EC) 354, 355;
formal provision 354–55;
informal/nonformal learning 354, 355;
knowledge economy 355;
Learning To Be 354, 620;
Organisation for Economic Co-operation and
Development (OECD) 354, 355;
United Nations Educational, Scientific and
Cultural Organization (UNESCO) 354;
skills renewal and continuous learning 355;
see also globalisation; informal/nonformal
learning; knowledge economy; learning;
learning career; lifelong learning; Schön,
Donald; work-based/work-located/
workplace/work-related learning
Learning to Be 354, 360, 620
learning theory:
child development 86;
see also learning; learning career
learning styles 356–57, 386;
Gardner, Howard 356, 357;
Frames of Mind 356;
multiple intelligence theory 356, 357;
Kolb, David 356;
vocational help through learning styles
questionnaires and profilers 356–57;
see also experiential learning; Gardner, Howard;
individualised instruction/personalised
learning; learning; intelligence/intelligence
tests; learning
lecture/lecturer 357;

Abelard, Peter 357;
critics as outdated method 357;
definition 357;
description 357;
origins 357;
video and Web-based technology 357;
see also Abelard, Peter; college; higher education;
instruction; seminar; teaching/teaching
methods; tuition/tutor/tutorial; university;
visual aids
lesson **357–58**;
double lessons 357;
definition 357;
in home 358;
lesson plan 589;
one-to-one basis 358;
planning and timing 357–58;
private lessons 358;
and special educational needs 358;
see also curriculum; instruction; school; subjects;
teacher; teaching/teaching methods; tuition/
tutor/tutorial
Lewin, Kurt 12, 13
liberal education 96, 98, 127, 128, **358–59**;
and citizenship 359;
criticism 358;
elitism 358;
ideal of 358;
liberal/technical education 358–59;
origins 358;
Pring, Richard 358–59;
Whitehead, Alfred North 358;
see also classical education; classical studies; Plato;
technical education/school/college;
university extension; vocational education
lifelong learning 19, 127, 275, 293, 315, 320,
359–60;
aim 360;
concepts 359–60;
humanistic perspective 360;
socio-political perspective 359–60;
criticism 360;
education-real life/knowledge-driven economy
360;
Japan 190;
Learning To Be 360, 620;
Organisation for Economic Co-operation and
Development (OECD) 360;
United Nations Educational, Scientific and
Cultural Organization (UNESCO) 360;
see also adult education; andragogy; core skills/
core competences; foundation degree;
further education; globalisation; higher
education; informal/nonformal learning;
International Council for Adult Education;
knowledge economy; learning; learning
society; mature student; recurrent education;
skills; social exclusion/inclusion; transition
education; university extension; work-based/
work-located/workplace/work-related

learning; workers' education; Workers'
Educational Association (WEA)
linguistics 50, 58, 268;
see also bilingual education; Habermas, Jürgen;
phonics
literacy 18, 191, **360–62**;
adult literacy 127–28, 261;
basic skills of education 360;
continuing education 127–28;
definitions 360–61;
etymology 360;
literacy campaign 146;
psychological studies developments:
modes of reading and writing processes 361;
school literacy attainment as indicator of
effectiveness 361;
use of systematic reviews of evidence 361;
role of missionary activity in developing literacy 94;
sociological studies of literacy 361;
'autonomous' concept 361;
'social practice' concept 361–62;
see also basic skills; bilingual education;
comprehension; core skills/core
competences; creativity; curriculum;
grammar; illiteracy; numeracy; phonics;
primary school/education; public library;
reader; reading; spelling; travellers, education
of; writing
Locke, John 43, 185, 212; 215, 249, **362–63**, 461;
British empiricism 362;
On the Conduct of the Understanding 362;
corporal punishment 363;
educational theory 362;
Essay Concerning Human Understanding 362;
instruction 363;
moral education 362–63;
physical education 363;
religious education 362–63;
Some Thoughts Concerning Education 215, 362;
Some Thoughts Concerning Reading and Study for a
Gentleman 362;
tabula rasa 185, 362;
theory of knowledge 362;
Two Treatises on Government 362;
see also child guidance; corporal punishment;
home schooling; moral education;
philosophy of education; progressive
education; Rousseau, Jean-Jacques
Lowe, Robert **363–64**;
see also accountability; Forster, William; politics
of education
Lyceum **364**;
Greek school 364;
United States 364;
see also adult education; Aristotle; mechanics'
institute; Plato; United States

madrasah 306, 311, 367, 423, 424, 491, 541;
see also religious education; religious school
magnet school **365–66**;

definition 365;
magnet structures 365;
origins 365;
and school of choice 365;
statistics 366;
see also parental choice; segregation/
    desegregation; vouchers; zoning
Makarenko, Anton Simeonovitch **366**;
A Book for Parents 366;
The Road to Life 366;
see also collaborative/cooperative learning;
    Freinet, Celestin; progressive education;
    Russia; youth club/work
Makiguchi, Tsunesaburo **366–67**;
Jinsei Chirigaku (Geography of Human Life) 367;
Soka Gakkai International 367;
Soka Kyoiku Gakkai (the Value-Creation Education
    Society) 367;
Soka Kyoikugaku Taikei (The System of Value-
    Creation Pedagogy) 367;
see also Japan
Malaysia **367–68**;
corporatisation 368;
education and economic growth 367;
education and nation-building project 367;
Education Act of 1961;
educational system structure and curricula 367–68;
ethnic selection 536;
higher education 368;
madrasahs 367;
missionaries 367;
Soka Gakkai International 367;
United Malays National Organisation (UMNO)
    367;
university 368;
see also China; East Asia
managerialism **368–70**;
central tenet 369;
definition 368–69;
developments and complications 369;
and globalisation 369;
see also educational leadership and management;
    performance indicators; performance-related
    pay; privatisation/marketisation; profession/
    professionalism/professionalisation;
    restructuring; school-based management;
    school improvement; technocrat/
    technocratic/technocracy
Mann, Horace **370**;
Common School Journal 370;
common schooling for all 370;
see also common school; equality of opportunity
Mannheim, Karl **370–71**;
cultural capital 370;
Ideology and Utopia 370;
Man and Society 370;
see also autonomy; cultural capital; sociology of
    education
marking **371**;
computer software applications 371;

definition 371;
marking of essays 371;
see also assessment; examinations; grades;
    summative assessment; teaching/teaching
    methods; test/testing
Marx, Karl 14, 145, 212, 446, 481, 568;
Capital 135;
Marxism 134, 145, 199, 228, 263, 295, 322,
    449, 548, 640;
Marxist educational theory 134;
Marxist feminism 253;
Marxist sociology of education 135, 263;
neo-Marxist theories 289, 344;
polytechnic education 446;
see also correspondence theory; critical theory;
    Freire, Paolo
Maslow, Abraham Harold **371**;
Farther Reaches of Human Nature 371;
hierarchy of human needs 371;
Motivation and Personality 371;
'third force' 371;
Towards a Psychology of Being 371;
see also creativity; motivation; psychology of
    education; Thorndike, Edward Lee
Master's **371–72**;
distance learning master's programmes 372;
higher education 371–72;
Master of Arts (M.A.) 372;
Master of Business Administration (MBA)
    degrees 64;
master's degrees 64;
Master of Education (M.E.) 372;
Master of Philosophy (M.Phil.) 372;
Master of Science (M.Sc.) 372;
programme 372;
see also degree; distance education/learning;
    higher education; oral examinations;
    postgraduate; qualifications; student; thesis;
    university
mathematics **372–75**;
classical Greek view 372;
changes introduced by computing technology 374;
core of primary and secondary school
    mathematics 372, 373;
current issues 374;
curriculum 373–74;
importance 372–73;
International Commission on Mathematical
    Instruction (ICMI) 373;
International Commission on the Teaching of
    Mathematics (ICTM) 373;
L'Enseignement Mathématique 373;
'mathematics for all' 372;
mathematics teaching 373, 374;
see also arithmetic; curriculum; integration;
    numeracy; physics; subjects
matriculation **375**;
definition 375;
prerequisites 375;
see also examinations; qualifications; university

mature student **375**;
  definition 375;
  and family commitments 375;
  motivations 375;
  and retention 494;
  United Kingdom 375;
  see also lifelong learning; Open University;
    polytechnic; postgraduate; student
McMillan, Margaret 339, **375–76**;
  The Child and the State 376;
  and early childhood education 186;
  The Nursery School 376;
  nursery schools 411;
  Nursery Schools Association 376, 411;
  school clinics 376;
  see also health education; nursery school
Mead, George Herbert **376**;
  Chicago School of sociology 376;
  Dewey, John 376;
  Mind, Self and Society 376;
  The Philosophy of the Act 376;
  Philosophy of the Present 376;
  self-consciousness and intelligence 376;
  see also Dewey, John; intelligence/intelligence
    tests; philosophy of education; psychology of
    education
Mead, Margaret 25, **376–77**;
  Coming of Age In Samoa 376;
  Growing Up in New Guinea 376;
  see also anthropology of education; child
    development; educational research
measurement see assessment
mechanics' institute 364; **377** 422;
  athenaeum 377;
  Australia 40;
  beginnings 377;
  Birkbeck, George 377;
  Glasgow Mechanics' Institute 377;
  London Mechanics' Institute 377;
  University of London 377;
  Workers' Educational Association (WEA) 377;
  see also adult education; athenaeum; Lyceum;
    university extension; workers' education;
    Workers' Educational Association (WEA)
medicine **377–78**;
  ancient cultures and medicine 378;
  definition 377;
  historical roots 378;
  homeostasis 377;
  modern day medicine 377;
  see also biology; profession/professionalism/
    professionalisation; professional education;
    science/science education; subjects
Mediterranean 61, 233, **378–79**, 394;
  Al-Azhar University 379;
  ancient Mediterranean cultures and education 378;
  countries 378;
  educational system structure 379;
  Erasmus and Eureka 378;
  European Union (EU) 378;

geographical description 378;
  gymnasium 379;
  lyceum 379;
  networks and communities 378–79;
  paideia 378;
  population 378;
  statistics 379;
  universities 378, 379;
  vocational/technical sector 379;
  see also Egypt; Europe; France; Greece; Israel; Italy
mentor/mentoring **379–81**, 386;
  and coaching 379;
  definition 379;
  nature of mentoring 380;
  peer mentoring schemes 380;
  in teacher education 380;
  youth mentoring 380;
  see also continued/continuing professional
    development; peer group; profession/
    professionalism/professionalisation; teaching
    profession
merit **381–82**;
  Merit Certificate 381;
  meritocracy 381;
  selection 381;
  tests and recognition of merit 381;
  Young, Michael 381, 382;
  see also ability; equality of opportunity;
    intelligence/intelligence tests; meritocracy;
    psychology of education; selection; test/
    testing; Young, Michael
meritocracy 125, 216, **382–83**;
  criticism 383;
  definition 382;
  The Rise of the Meritocracy 382, 649;
  Russia 503;
  selection by merit 382;
  Young, Michael 381, 382;
  see also don; elitism; equality of opportunity; equity;
    examinations; excellence; merit; phrenology;
    Russia; selection; sociology; technocrat/
    technocratic/technocracy; Young, Michael
metropolitanism **383**;
  cultural imperialism 383;
  definition 383;
  Lawrence Cremin's set of meanings 383;
  metropolis 383;
  see also Conant, James Bryant; indigenous
    education; urban education
Middle East 61, 94, 327, 344;
  see also Egypt; Iran; Iraq; Israel
Mill, John Stuart 174, 212, **384**;
  On Liberty 384;
  moral sciences 212;
  Principles of Political Economy 384;
  Representative Government 384;
  The Subjection of Women 384;
  System of Logic 384;
  see also autonomy; economics of education;
    equality of opportunity; politics of education

Millennium Development Goals 162, 177, 193, 197–98, 210, 230, 405, 446, 618, 625, 646; *see also* United Nations Children's Fund (UNICEF); United Nations Educational, Scientific and Cultural Organization (UNESCO)

mission statement **384–85**; criticism 385; definition 384; effective mission statement 385; origins 385; uses 384; *see also* accountability; college; faculty; school; university

mixed-ability teaching **385–87**; ability 385–86; benefits 386; definition 385; mixed findings in research 386; *see also* ability; ability grouping; curriculum differentiation; setting; streaming/tracking; whole-class teaching

modern languages **387–88**; aims and objectives 387; ancient languages 387; Communicative Language Teaching (CLT) 387–88; curriculum 387–88; learning of: acquisition of skills and content knowledge 387; methodology 387–88; new technologies in teaching and learning 388; rationales 387; *see also* bilingual education; classical studies; curriculum; subjects

modular/module **388**; aim 388; definitions 388; *see also* degree; higher education

monitor **388–89**; Bell, Andrew 389; definition 388; Lancaster, Joseph 389; monitored entities 388–89; monitorial system 389; pupil monitors 389; school monitors 389; *see also* accountability; inspection; Lancaster, Joseph; monitorial system; prefect

monitorial system 343, **389**, 406; Bell, Andrew 389; description 389; Lancaster, Joseph 389; *see also* classroom; Lancaster, Joseph; normal school; monitor; prefect

monocultural education 27; *see also* antiracist education; equality of opportunity; multicultural education

Montessori, Maria 156, 175, **389–90** 426, 463; *Advanced Montessori Method* 389; *Casa dei Bambini (Children's House)* 389;

and early childhood education 186; 'First educate the senses, then educate the intellect' 390; 'Follow the child' 390; kindergarten 339; *The Montessori Method* 389; Montessori schools 272, 560; and nursery school 411; *see also* child development; early childhood education; Italy; nursery school; Parkhurst, Helen; progressive education

moral education 341–42, 362–63, **390–91**; aim 390; Aristotle and Plato 390; beginnings and development 390; Durkheim, Emile 390; Freud, Sigmund 390; Kant, Emmanuel 390; Kohlberg, Lawrence 390; moral education trends 390; Piaget, Jean 390; psychological behaviourists 390; *see also* Aristotle; Durkheim, Emile; excellence; Kohlberg, Lawrence; Locke, John; pastoral care; philosophy of education; Piaget, Jean; Plato; religious education; training

motivation **391–93**; *de*-motivation 392; educational factors 391–92; external motivation 391; hygiene and psychological factors 391; internal motivation 391, 392; keys in internal motivation 392; KITA motivation 392; push-pull learning motivation 392; *see also* disaffection; learning; Maslow, Abraham Harold; performance-related pay; philosophy of education; psychology; psychology of education; underachievement

Mulcaster, Richard (c.1530–1611) **393**; Ascham, Roger 393; *The Elementaries* 393; *The Positions* 393; *see also* Ascham, Roger; public school

multicultural education **393–96**; aims 393, 394; cultural diversity and immigration: France 393–94; Germany 393–94; United Kingdom 393–94; United States 393–94; definition 393; dimensions of 394–95; content integration 394–95; empowering school culture 395; equity pedagogy 395; knowledge construction process 395; prejudice reduction 395; emphasis 394; intercultural education 393;

see also anthropology of education; bilingual
    education; cultural transmission; DuBois,
    William E. B.; indigenous education; social
    exclusion/inclusion
multiculturalism 26, 27, 35, 150, 253, 549;
    see also cultural transmission; multicultural
    education; social exclusion/inclusion
multigrade education **396**;
    definition 396;
    Education For All 396;
    Escuela Nueva 396;
    monograde classes 396;
    Nigeria 405;
    see also Education for All (EFA); progression;
        social promotion
multiple-choice tests **396–97**;
    criticism and problems of 397;
    definition and description 396;
    guessing 397;
    popularity 397;
    uses 397;
    see also assessment; criterion-referenced tests
        (CRTs); objective tests; test/testing
museum education **397–99**;
    as agent of social change 398;
    constructivist museum 398;
    as cultural regenerator 398;
    and curators 397, 398;
    educational role of the museum 397–98;
    interpretive educational strategies 398;
    see also cultural transmission; culture; ethnography;
        history; informal/nonformal learning
music 179, **399–400**;
    debate about aims, methods and curriculum in
        music education 399;
    diversity in music education provision 399–400;
    informal music education 399, 400;
    music education and state education systems 399;
    musical tuition 399;
    universities, colleges and conservatories 400;
    see also curriculum; drama; extracurriculum;
        subjects

national curriculum *see* core curriculum/national
    curriculum
nature study **401**;
    definition 401;
    historical roots 401;
    see also biology; curriculum; environmental
        education; science/science education; subjects
Neill, Alexander Sutherland 156, 215, **401–2**;
    home schooling movement 402;
    That Dreadful School 401;
    The Problem Parent 401;
    Summerhill 401;
    Summerhill School 401–2;
    see also child-centred education; home
        schooling; progressive education
Netherlands 38, 235, 236, 304, 439;
    andragogy 24;

career guidance 69;
child guidance 87;
continuing education 128;
corporal punishment 133;
immigration 393, 394;
religious education 490;
religious school 491;
sex education 539;
training 604
Newman, John Henry **402**;
    aims of higher education 402;
    Apologia pro Vita Sua 402;
    British Critic 402;
    The Idea of a University Education 402;
    Tracts for the Times 402;
    see also higher education; religious education;
        religious school; theology; university
New Zealand/Aotearoa 50, **402–4**;
    chancellor 81;
    charter school 84;
    comprehensive education 403;
    crèche 139–40;
    current issues in New Zealand education 403;
    distance education/learning 176;
    early childhood education (ECE) 185;
    Education Acts:
        Native Schools Act (1867) 402;
        1877 Education Act 402, 403;
        1914 Education Act 403;
        Conditional Integration of Private Schools
            Act (1975) 403;
        1989 Education Act 403;
        1990 Education Amendment Act 403;
        1991 Education Amendment Act 403;
    education in Maori language 403;
    educational system development 402–3;
    inspection system 315, 316;
    intermediate school 319;
    Maori Tertiary institutions 403;
    Maori schools 402–3;
    marketisation 455;
    mentoring 380;
    National Certificate of Educational
        Achievement (NCEA) 403;
    New Zealand Curriculum Framework 403;
    New Zealand Qualifications Authority (NZQA)
        403;
    pastoral care 428;
    secondary school 403;
    supply/substitute teaching 574;
    Tertiary Education (TEC) Commission 403;
    Workers' Educational Association (WEA) 645;
    see also Oceania; Polynesia
Nigeria **404–5**;
    British Department for International
        Development (DFID) 405;
    continuing education 127;
    educational system development 404–5;
    extra-mural class 247;
    fundamental unresolved issues 405;

geographical features 404;
girls' education project 405;
higher education 405;
Millennium Development Goals 405;
Muslim and Christian missionary education 404;
pastoral care 428;
political history 404;
population 404;
statistics 405;
travellers, education of 607–8;
United Nations Children's Fund (UNICEF) 405;
see also Africa; Department for International
   Development (DFID); Education for All
   (EFA); educational targets; multigrade
   education; United Nations Children's Fund
   (UNICEF)
No Child Left Behind (NCLB) 121, 291, 310,
   493, 525, 550, 579, 623;
see also Education Acts (United States); United
   States
Nordic Educational Research Association
   (NERA)/Nordisk Förening för Pedagogiska
   Forskning (NFPF) **405–6**;
activities 405;
description 405;
European Educational Research Association
   (EERA) 406;
members 405;
Nordisk Pedagogik (Nordic Educational Research) 405;
see also educational research; European
   Educational Research Association (EERA);
   Finland; Scandinavia; Sweden
normal school **406–7**;
Canada 406;
France 406;
   Ecole Normale Supérieure 406;
origins and development of the term 406;
Russia 406;
Scotland:
   Methods of Teaching 406;
teacher training 406–7;
United States 407;
see also Lancaster, Joseph; monitorial system;
   seminary; teacher education/training
norm-referenced tests **407–8**;
criticism 408;
examples of in the United States 407;
norm group 407;
objectives 407;
parallel forms 407–8;
scales and score interpretation 408;
test score norms 408;
uses 407;
see also criterion-referenced tests (CRTs);
   examinations; standardised tests; test/testing
Norway 236, 620;
apprenticeship 30;
corporal punishment 133;
didactics/didacticism 170;
dual system 30;

religious education 490;
see also Nordic Educational Research Association
   (NERA)/Nordisk Förening för Pedagogiska
   Forskning (NFPF); Scandinavia
numeracy **408–10**;
Australia: numerate 409;
British Open University: informed numeracy 409;
critical numeracy 408, 409–10;
definition 408, 409;
Mathematics Counts 409;
origins and development of the term 409;
United Kingdom 409;
see also arithmetic; core skills/core competences;
   literacy; mathematics; primary school/
   education; standards
nursery school **410–12**;
administrative variants 410;
custodial care and educational work 411–12;
curriculum 412;
definition 410;
Froebel, Friedrich 411;
Isaacs, Susan 411;
McMillan, Margaret 411;
Montessori, Maria; 411;
Nursery Schools Association 376, 411;
origins and development 410–11;
Owen, Robert 410–11;
United Kingdom 410, 11, 12;
   Sure Start 412;
United States 411, 412;
   Head Start 412;
see also early childhood education; Froebel,
   Friedrich; Isaacs, Susan; kindergarten;
   McMillan, Margaret; Montessori, Maria;
   Owen, Robert; reception class; Steiner, Rudolf

objective tests **413**;
common forms of 413;
description 413;
uses 413;
see also multiple-choice tests; test/testing
Oceania **413–16**;
distance education 415;
early childhood education 413;
French University of the Pacific 415;
higher education 415;
   challenges 415;
home schooling 298;
National University of Samoa.415;
Pacific Island countries (PICs) 413–16;
primary education 413–14;
secondary education 414–15;
   challenges 414–15;
   curriculum 414;
statistics 414;
teacher training 414;
University of the South Pacific (USP) 413, 414,
   415, 445;
universities 415;
University of Guam and Papua New Guinea 415;

see also Australia; distance education/learning;
New Zealand/Aotearoa; Polynesia; teacher
education/ training; universal education
open learning **416–17**;
British Open University 416–17;
a contested term 416;
definition 416;
distance education 416;
Open Learning 417;
uses of the term 416, 417;
see also distance education/learning; educational
technology; e-learning; Open University;
technology
open plan **417–18**;
definition 417;
Finmere school 417;
Medd, David 417;
Medd, Mary 417;
origins 417;
progressive education 418;
United Kingdom 417–18;
United States 417;
see also classroom; progressive education;
teaching/teaching methods
Open University **418–19**;
definition 418;
distance learning methods 418;
educational broadcasting 201;
Hellenic Open University 281;
Open University Australia 416;
Open University Hong Kong 416;
United Kingdom 176, 409, 416–17;
Young, Michael 418;
see also correspondence course; distance
education/learning; educational
broadcasting; mature student; open learning;
summer school; university; web-based
learning; Young, Michael
oral education 17;
'oral' cultures 648;
see also writing
oral examinations **419**;
definition 419;
foreign language teaching 419;
origins 419;
see also doctorate; examinations; grades; master's;
thesis/dissertation
Organisation for Economic Cooperation and
Development (OECD) 114, 340, **419–22**, 486,
613;
activities 419;
aims 420;
Centre for Educational Research and Innovation
(CERI) 420;
definition 419;
educational work 420;
Forum on Trade in Educational Services 422;
globalisation 420;
Greece 282;
human capital theory 420;

indicators 421–22;
Italy 330;
Japan 332;
knowledge economy 420, 422;
and learning society 354, 355;
lifelong learning 360;
neo-liberal policy agenda 420–21;
Organisation for European Economic Co-
operation (OEEC) 419;
origins and development 419;
programmes 421;
UNESCO 421, 422;
Unit for Education Statistics and Indicators 421;
Education at a Glance 421;
see also Centre for Educational Research and
Innovation (CERI); globalisation; human
capital; international education; knowledge
economy; standards
Oxfam 82
Oxford University 31, 34, 82, 114, 179, 225, 246,
334, 402, 456, 495, 506, 509, 510, 626, 632
Owen, Robert 410–11, **422**;
New Lanark school 422;
New View of Society 422;
Owenite Halls of Science 422;
see also early childhood education; nursery school;
politics of education; workers' education

Pakistan **423–24**;
education infrastructure development 423–24;
educational goals (1949) 423;
Education Sector Reforms Action Plan 2001–4
424;
Implementation Programme 424;
Islam and education 423, 424;
madrasah 423, 424;
National Education Policy 424;
New Education Policy 423;
parallel private system 423;
see also India
parental choice 74, **424–25**, 486;
advocates' arguments 424–25;
criticism 425;
neo-liberalism ideology and education 424;
variety of choice schemes 425;
voucher programme 425;
see also catchment area; centralisation/
decentralisation; home schooling; magnet
school; privatisation/marketisation; school
reform; urban education; vouchers; zoning
parity of esteem 4–5, 280, **425–26**;
definition 425;
eleven-plus examination 425, 426;
grammar school 426;
selection 425–26;
United Kingdom 425;
Education Act 1944 425;
see also equality of opportunity; grammar school;
selection
Parkhurst, Helen 309, **426**;

Dalton schools 426;
Education on the Dalton Plan 426;
Exploring the Child's World 426;
Montessori, Maria 426;
Work Rhythms in Education 426;
see also individualised instruction/personalised
learning; Montessori, Maria; progressive
education
partnerships, educational **426–28**;
benefits and liabilities 427;
description 426;
forms of 426–27;
and non-government organisations (NGOs) 427;
see also educational priority area; privatisation/
marketisation; urban education; voluntarism
pastoral care **428–29**;
aims 428;
Christian Church 428;
comprehensive system 428;
definitions 428;
The Educational Year Book 428;
National Association for Pastoral Care in
Education (NAPCE) 429;
origins and development of the term 428;
Pastoral Care in Education 429;
perspectives on 428–29;
see also bullying; counselling; integration; moral
education; teacher; truancy
pedagogy 183, **429–30**;
Bernstein, Basil 429;
Bruner, Jerome 430;
criticism 429–30;
definitions 429;
Freire, Paolo:
The Pedagogy of the Oppressed 144, 261, 430;
learner-centred pedagogy 243;
multiple intelligences 430;
pedagogical models 430;
Bernstein, Basil 429;
Stones, Edgar 429;
pedagogical strategies for managing dyslexia 183;
post-modern pedagogies 430;
and theories of learning 429–30;
see also andragogy; Bernstein, Basil; Bruner,
Jerome; critical pedagogy; Freire, Paolo;
grammar of schooling; instruction;
Lancaster, Joseph; learning; progressive
education; school knowledge; teacher;
teacher cultures; teaching/teaching
methods; textbook
peer group **430–31**;
benefits 430;
definition 430;
peer group pressure 430;
trainee and probationary teachers groups 430–31;
see also collaborative/cooperative learning;
mentor/mentoring; pupil; social promotion;
student; youth club/work
performance indicators (PIs) **431–32**;
Australia 431;

Canada 431–32;
characteristics 431;
definition 431;
in higher education 431;
United States 431;
US News and World Reports 431;
uses 431;
see also accountability; benchmarking;
educational targets; inspection;
managerialism; performance-related pay;
school improvement; standards; value
added
performance-related pay (PRP) **432–33**;
criticism 433;
description of the process 433;
payment as motivation 432, 433;
payment by results 432;
performance management 432;
in private sector 432;
see also managerialism; motivation; performance
indicators
Pestalozzi, Johann Heinrich 109, 174, 190, 262,
289, 338, **433–34**, 461, 464;
holistic education 434;
How Gertrude Teaches Her Children 434;
*Investigations in the Course of Nature in the
Development of the Human Race* 434;
Rousseau, Jean-Jacques 433;
see also early childhood education; Froebel,
Friedrich; Herbart, Johann Friedrich;
progressive education
philosophy of education **434–35**;
areas:
epistemology 435;
learners and their minds 434–35;
other related areas 435;
definition 434;
foundation discipline of education 199, 214;
see also Dewey, John; educational research;
education/educational studies; educational
theory; indoctrination; Locke, John; Mead,
George Herbert; moral education; Plato;
Socratic method
phonics **435–36**;
definition 435;
DISEC teaching 435–36;
DISEC teaching criticism 436;
phonemes 435, 482;
phonemic or phonological awareness 435;
spelling 435, 436;
see also learning; literacy; reading; spelling;
teaching/teaching methods
phrenology **437**;
aims 437;
definition 437;
intelligence 437;
see also faculty psychology; intelligence/
intelligence tests; meritocracy
physical education/training (PE) 47, 179, 363,
437–38, 562;

definition 437;
Health and Physical Education (HPE) 438;
learning to move 437;
key for success:
  physical activities 438;
  quality physical education 438;
moving to learn 437;
in school curricula 437;
see also curriculum; drama; health education;
  playground; subjects
physics **438–39**;
beginnings as a discipline 439;
current decline and ideas for recovery 439;
in different educational systems 439;
Institute of Physics/Schlumberger 439;
see also curriculum; engineering; mathematics;
  science/science education; specialisation;
  subjects
Piaget, Jean 86, 106, 108, 117, 175, 213, 243, 268,
  320, 341, **439–40**;
and early childhood education 186;
cognitive development 440;
The Language and Thought of the Child 440;
The Origins of Intelligence in Children 440;
teacher training courses 439;
theory on the stages of childhood and
  adolescence 440;
see also cognition; early childhood education;
  International Bureau of Education (IBE);
  moral education; psychology of education;
  spiral curriculum; Vygotsky, Lev
plagiarism **440–41**;
cheat detection and software programmes 441;
and convergence 440;
cryptomnesia 440;
definition 440;
etymology 440;
new modes: internet 441;
'term paper mill industry' 441;
see also coursework; credentials/credentialing;
  degree; examinations; learning;
  qualifications; student; writing
Plato 1, 8, 35, 43, 211, 212, 215, 233, 334, 358,
  372, 373, **441–44**;
Academy 441;
aporia 443;
Aristotle 441;
dialogues 441, 443;
elenchus 443;
Euthyphro 557;
Lysis 557;
Meno 557;
and moral education 390, 442, 443;
myth of the cave 442–43;
Plato's views on education 442–43;
Republic 215, 358, 442, 443, 556–57;
schooling 442;
Socrates 441, 442, 443, 556–57;
Symposium 557;
Theaetetus 557;

see also academy; Aristotle; Greece; liberal
  education; Lyceum; moral education;
  philosophy of education; Socratic method
playground **444**;
description 444;
and timetabled physical education and games
  444;
traditional playground games 444;
see also physical education/training
policy makers 10, 22, 28, 41, 62, 71, 79, 143, 156,
  165, 194;
curriculum policy 157;
see also education policy
politics of education **444**;
definition 444;
educational politics/ politics of education
  444;
see also education policy; Mill, John Stuart;
  Owen, Robert; religious education;
  sociology of education; Tawney, Richard
  Henry; Washington, Booker T.
Polynesia **445–46**;
Australia 445, 446;
Education For All (EFA) 446;
European missionaries 445;
formal schooling 445;
Millennium Development Goals 446;
New Zealand involvement in educational
  systems 445;
teachers 445;
state schooling 445;
tertiary education 445;
University of the South Pacific (USP) 445;
see also Education For All (EFA); New Zealand/
  Aotearoa; Oceania; World Bank
polytechnic 12, 52, 146, 292, **446–47**;
Education Reform Act (1988) 447;
Finland 254, 447;
Marx, Karl 446;
New Zealand 403;
origins 446;
polytechnic training 446;
United Kingdom 446–47;
  A Liberal Vocationalism 447;
  The Polytechnic Experiment 446–47;
see also binary system; Finland; higher education;
  mature students; sandwich course; technical
  education/school/college; university;
  vocational education
popular education 147, 190, 192, 234, 401, 437;
see also Education For All (EFA); equality of
  opportunity; equity
positive discrimination/affirmative action 116,
  205, **448–49**;
definitions 448;
distinction between positive discrimination and
  affirmative action 448, 449;
and law 448;
United Kingdom 448;
Unites States 448;

uses of the term 448;
see also educational priority area (EPA); equality
    of opportunity; equity; law
postgraduate **449**;
    definition 449;
    a mature student 449;
    status 449;
    see also certificate/certification; diploma; higher
        education; degree; master's; mature student;
        teaching assistant; university; undergraduate
postmodernism 135, **449–50**;
    Baudrillard, Jean 450;
    deconstruction 450;
    definition 449;
    Derrida, Jacques 450;
    feminism 449;
    Foucault, Michel 450;
    impact on education 450;
    Lyotard, Jean François 449;
    opposites 449, 450;
    rejection of metanarratives and universals 449–50;
    and school change 516;
    see also critical pedagogy; educational theory;
        feminist theory; Foucault, Michel; gender
        studies
practitioner research **450–52**;
    definition 450;
    long-term learning process 451;
    participants 451;
    the researcher 451;
    roots 450–51;
    Schön, Donald 451;
    Stenhouse, Lawrence 451;
    see also action research; classroom; educational
        research; learning community; qualitative
        research; quantitative research; Schön, Donald;
        Stenhouse, Lawrence; work-based/work-
        located/workplace/work-related learning
prefect 389, **452**;
    Arnold, Thomas 452;
    definition 452;
    see also Arnold, Thomas; monitor; monitorial
        system; sixth form
primary school/education **452–54**;
    challenges 454;
    current issues 454;
    description 452;
    first compulsory stage of mass education 452;
    functions:
        children's physical, emotional and social
            welfare 453;
        classification 453–54;
        numeracy and literacy 452;
        socialisation 453;
    provision of in Europe and North America 452;
    United Kingdom 614–15;
    United States 452, 621–22;
    universal primary education 454;
    see also compulsory education; curriculum;
        educational system structure; elementary

school; intermediate/middle school; literacy;
    numeracy; reception class; school; secondary
    school/education; universal education/mass
    education
privatisation/marketisation **454–56**;
    Australia 455;
    Britain 455;
    debates around 455;
    definition 454;
    distinction between privatisation and
        marketisation 454–55;
    New Zealand 455;
    types and forms 455;
    see also economics of education; education
        policy; Indonesia; managerialism; parental
        choice; partnerships, educational; Russia;
        voluntarism; vouchers; zoning
proctor **456**;
    definitions 456;
    duties 456;
    see also examinations
profession/professionalism/professionalisation
    456–59;
    classic professions 456;
    control of knowledge 457;
    deprofessionalisation 458;
    distinction between professionalism and
        professionalisation 456;
    feminisation of teaching 457;
    negotiation of attributes for the occupation
        457;
    new professionalism 458;
    professional autonomy 457;
    'proletarianization' 6;
    Schön, Donald 456–57;
    teaching as profession 456;
    types of teacher professionalism 457;
    United Kingdom 457;
    United States 457;
    see also accountability; autonomy; church; law;
        managerialism; medicine; mentor/
        mentoring; professional education; reflective
        practitioner; scholar; Schön, Donald; teacher
        education/training; teaching profession;
        teacher unions; teaching profession
professional education **459**;
    description 459;
    off-the-job learning 459;
    see also continued/continuing professional
        development; doctorate; in-service
        education; law; medicine; profession/
        professionalism/ professionalisation;
        reflective practitioner; Schön, Donald;
        specialisation; vocational education; work-
        based/work-located/workplace/work-
        related learning
professor **459–60**;
    description 459;
    emeritus professorship 459;
    professoriate 459;

status 459;
stereotype of 459–60;
United States 459;
see also higher education; reader; university
programmed learning **460**;
definition 460;
difficulties of 460;
Skinner, Burrhus Fredric 460;
theory of operant conditioning 460;
see also learning; Skinner, Burrhus Fredric
progression **460–61**;
in age-grade/multi-grade teaching arrangements 460;
definition 460;
through curriculum or syllabus 460;
uses and forms of 460;
see also continued/continuing professional development; continuing education; learning career; learning curve; multigrade education; retention
progressive education 165, 344, 418, **461–64**;
basic assumptions about education 461, 462;
child-centred education 461–62;
criticism as elitist 463;
definition 461;
educational theories:
Comenius, Johann Amos 461;
Dewey, John 461–62, 463;
Froebel, Friedrich 461;
Locke, John 461;
Pestalozzi, Johann Heinrich 461;
Rousseau, Jean-Jacques 461;
experimental schools 462;
Hall, G. Stanley 462–63;
The Contents of Children's Mind 462;
Isaacs, Susan 463;
learning by doing 462;
Montessori, Maria 463;
New Education Fellowship 463;
new ideas about education 462;
Parker, Francis W. 462;
project method 463;
Progressive Education Association 463;
universities associated with 462–63;
see also child-centred education; Comenius, Johann Amos; Dewey, John; educational theory; discovery method/learning; Edgeworth, Maria; Freire, Paolo; Froebel, Friedrich; Hall, Granville Stanley; individualised instruction/personalised learning; indoctrination; Isaacs, Susan; Lane, Homer; Locke, John; Makarenko, Anton Simeonovitch; Montessori, Maria; Neill, Alexander Sutherland; open plan; Parkhurst, Helen; pedagogy; Pestalozzi, Johann Heinrich; project method; Reddie, Cecil; Rice, Joseph Mayer; Rogers, Carl; Rousseau, Jean-Jacques; Rugg, Harold; social reconstructionism; World Education Fellowship (WEF)

project method **464–65**;
description 464;
Dewey, John 464;
Froebel, Friedrich 465;
Heard Kilpatrick, William 464–65;
changes in schooling 465;
definition of project 464;
purposeful act 464–65;
wholehearted purposeful activity 464–65;
'learning by doin' 464;
Pestalozzi, Johann Heinrich 464;
Rousseau, Jean-Jacques 464;
Soviet Union 465;
see also child-centred education; deschooling; homework; individualised instruction/personalised learning; progressive education
psychoanalysis 14, 467, 488;
see also Freud, Sigmund
psychoanalytic theories:
child development 86;
see also Freud, Sigmund; psychoanalysis
psychology **465–66**;
constructivist psychology 175;
cultural psychology 14;
definition 465;
different approaches:
clinical psychology 466;
cognitive psychology 466;
developmental psychology 466;
educational psychology 466;
experimental psychology 466;
social psychology 466;
Ebbinghaus, Hermann 353, 466;
etymology 465;
James, William 465–66;
Principles of Psychology 466;
Russian psychology 14;
see also child development; cognition; creativity; faculty psychology; Freud, Sigmund; learning; motivation; psychology of education; Sarason, Seymour; Spearman, Charles; Vygotsky, Lev
psychology of education 287, **466–68**;
Britain 467;
definition 466;
distinction between psychology of education and educational psychology 466;
foundation discipline of education 199, 214;
Hall, Granville Stanley 466;
history and development 466;
influences on 467;
James, William 466;
literature:
British Journal of Educational Psychology (UK) 468;
Contemporary Educational Psychology (USA) 468;
Journal of Educational Psychology (USA) 468;
School Psychology International (UK) 468;
and other disciplines 468;
Rousseau, Jean-Jacques 466;
United States 466–67;

see also Binet, Alfred; educational studies; excellence; faculty psychology; Freud, Sigmund; Galton, Francis; Gardner, Howard; Hall, Granville Stanley; Herbart, Johann Friedrich; Maslow, Abraham Harold; Mead, George Herbert; merit; motivation; Piaget, Jean; psychology; psychometrics; Rogers, Carl; Rousseau, Jean-Jacques; Spearman, Charles; spiral curriculum; Terman, Lewis M.; Thorndike, Edward Lee; Vygotsky, Lev

psychometrics 318, **468–69**;
    definition 468;
    in examination marking 240;
    Galton, Francis 468;
    and intelligence testing (IQ) 469;
    origins and development 468;
    psychometric models 169;
    psychometric principles 469;
    psychometric tests categories 468–69;
    Spearman, Charles 468;
    uses 469;
    see also assessment; Burt, Cyril; Galton, Francis; intelligence/intelligence tests; psychology of education; Spearman, Charles

public library **469–71**;
    activities and services 470–71;
    books and other contents 470;
    definition 469–70;
    libraries 469–70;
    mobile libraries 470–71;
    national libraries 470;
    origins and development 470;
    United Kingdom 470;
    United States 470;
    see also Educational Resources Information Center (ERIC); informal/nonformal learning; literacy

public school 57, **471**;
    British public school 471;
    definition 471;
    see also elementary school; grammar school; independent/private school/education; Keate, John; Mulcaster, Richard; Reddie, Cecil; school

pupil **471**;
    definition 471;
    pupil-teacher system 471;
    see also homework; peer group; student

pupil mobility **471–73**;
    definition 471–72;
    impact on pupil 472;
        factors conditioning the impact 472;
    types 472;
    see also attainment; dropouts; early school leaving; exclusion/expulsion; school

quadrivium 75, 96, 233–34, 532;
    see also classical education

qualifications 422, **475–76**;
    Bologna Framework of Qualifications 476;

certificate 475;
    hierarchy in acquisition of 475;
    higher-level qualifications 475–76;
    initial school level qualifications 475;
    International Baccalaureate 475;
    over-qualification 340;
    Qualifications and Curriculum Authority (UK) 476, 491;
    vocational 475;
    see also attainment; certificate/certification; degree; diploma; doctorate; examinations; foundation degree; knowledge economy; master's; matriculation; plagiarism; sandwich course; skills; subjects; training; vocational education

qualitative research 207, **476–77**;
    areas 476;
    common features 477;
    criteria 477;
    distinction between quantitative and qualitative research 477–78;
    qualitative data/qualitative analysis 476–77;
    Qualitative Studies in Education 477;
    research paradigms 476;
    strands 476;
    see also action research; classroom observation; educational research; ethnography; evaluation; experimental research; quantitative research

quantitative research 207, **477–79**;
    definition 477;
    distinction between quantitative and qualitative research 477–78;
    paradigm 478;
    population data 479;
    regression 478;
    sampling theory 478–79;
    statistical modelling 478;
    statistics 478;
    uncertain future 479;
    see also classroom observation; educational research; evaluation; experimental research; practitioner research; qualitative research; value added

Quintilian **479**;
    Institutio Oratoria 479;
    see also classical education

racism 27, 120, 181–82;
    racialisation 536;
    see also antiracist education; Durkheim, Emile; equality of opportunity; multicultural education

Read, Herbert Edward 35

reader **481**;
    different meanings in educational contexts 481;
        academic title 481;
        children motivation for reading 481;
        set text 481;
    see also academic/academic profession; educational publishing; literacy; professor; reading

reading 117–18, **481–84**;
definition 481, 482–83;
education as means of spreading reading 483;
impact on human culture 482;
methods of teaching 483;
modes of reading processes 361;
proficient reading 118;
rationale in educational context 482;
reading complex process 483;
reading standards 483–84;
and writing 343, 483;
written language: origin and development 482;
see also basic skills; comprehension; culture; literacy;
phonics; reader; spelling; standards; writing
reception class **484–85**;
definition 484;
pro and contras of 485;
United Kingdom 484–85;
admission policies 484;
Curriculum Guidance for the Foundation Stage
484–85;
see also child development; early childhood
education; nursery school; primary school/
education
recidivism 87, 575;
alternative school 21;
see also alternative education; delinquency
recruitment **485–86**;
definition 485;
and selection 486;
teachers recruitment 485–86;
students recruitment 486;
see also career guidance; intelligence/intelligence
tests; selection
rector **486**;
chancellor, president 486;
definition 486;
see also chancellor; higher education; university;
vice-chancellor
recurrent education **486**;
definition 486;
*Recurrent Education: A Strategy for Lifelong
Learning – A Clarifying Report* 486;
see also continuing education; lifelong learning;
workers' education
Reddie, Cecil **486–87**;
Abbotsholme School 487;
Fellowship of the New Life 487;
Modern Mis-education 487;
see also head teacher/principal; independent/
private school/education; progressive
education; public school
reflective practitioner **487–88**;
curriculum 487;
professional education 488;
Schön, Donald 487–88;
see also action research; curriculum; experiential
learning; profession/professionalism/
professionalisation; professional education;
Schön, Donald; teacher education/training;

work-based/work-located/workplace/work-
related learning
reform school *see* approved school
religious assembly **488–89**;
aims 488;
alternative approaches to one-faith assemblies 489;
definition 488;
description 488;
Education Act 1944 488–89;
Education Reform Act (1988) 489;
School Standards and Framework Act (1998)
488–89;
Standing Advisory Council for Religious
Education (SACRE) 489;
teachers and parents 489;
see also church; religious education; religious
school; theology
religious education 181, 234, 362–63, **490–91**;
in Africa 17–18;
Albania 490;
banning of clerics from teaching 253;
definition 490;
Denmark 490;
in formal setting 490;
France 490, 491;
Germany 490;
Great National Religious Campaign 326;
Greece 490;
Greek Orthodox religion 282;
India 490;
missions 18;
mission schools networks 18;
Muslim religious schools 218, 306, 311, 324;
in national curriculum 130;
Netherlands 490, 491;
Norway 490;
Pakistan 423, 424;
Religious Studies 490;
Slovakia 490;
Sweden 490;
United Kingdom 490–91;
Agreed Syllabus Conference (ASC) 490;
Education Act (1870) 491;
Education Act (1902) 491;
Education Act (1944) 488–89; 490, 491;
Education Reform Act (1988) 489, 490;
local education authority (LEA) 490, 491;
School Standards and Framework Act (1998)
488–89, 490, 491;
United States 490, 491;
see also curriculum; church; dual system; India;
indoctrination; Indonesia; Iraq; Jesuit
education; moral education; Newman, John
Henry; politics of education; religious
assembly; religious school; scholasticism;
seminary; subjects; theology
religious school 234, **491–92**;
advocates' and opponents' claims 492;
church and state separation 491;
Denmark 490, 491;

examples of 491;
France 490, 491;
Jewish religious schools 327;
Muslim religious schools 217, 306, 311, 324,
    367, 423, 424;
    Islamia Primary School 491;
Netherlands 490, 491;
role in worldwide schools 491;
United Kingdom 490–91;
    Agreed Syllabus Conference (ASC) 490;
    Education Act (1870) 491;
    Education Act (1902) 491;
    Education Act (1944) 488–89; 490, 491;
    Education Reform Act (1988) 489, 490;
    local education authority (LEA) 490, 491;
    School Standards and Framework Act (1998)
        488–89, 490, 491;
    voluntary aided schools 491;
United States 490, 491;
see also academy; church; dual system;
    independent/ private school/education;
    Indonesia; Iraq; Jesuit education; Lancaster,
    Joseph; madrasah; Newman, John Henry;
    religious assembly; religious education;
    seminary; Sunday school; theology; voluntarism
restructuring **492–93**;
    definition 492;
    higher education 493;
    primary and secondary school levels 492–93;
    United States 493;
        No Child Left Behind Act (NCLB) 493;
    university 493;
    see also accountability; education policy; school-
        based management; school change; school
        improvement; school reform; systemic reform
retention **494–95**;
    African retention rates 19;
    definition 494;
    factors favouring dropping out 494;
    factors favouring retention 494;
    mature students 494;
    non-traditional students 494;
    see also dropout; higher education; progression;
        student
Rhodes Trust 82, **495**, 510;
    aims 495;
    beneficiary countries 495;
    definition 495;
    Mandela Rhodes Foundation 495;
    origins 495;
    Oxford University 495;
    Rhodes Scholars' Southern Africa Forum
        (RSSAF) 495;
    see also charities, educational; scholarship
Rice, Joseph Mayer **495–96**;
    Forum magazine 495;
    The People's Government 496;
    Scientific Management in Schools 496;
    see also classroom observation; progressive
        education

Riesman, David **496**;
    The Academic Revolution 496;
    Constraint and Variety in American Education 496;
    The Lonely Crowd 496;
    see also higher education
Robbins, Lionel **496**;
    The Financial Times 496;
    London School of Economics 496;
    Robbins Report 496;
    The University in the Modern World 496;
    see also economics of education; higher education
Rogers, Carl 243, **497**;
    On Becoming a Person 497;
    Client-centered Therapy 497;
    The Clinical Treatment of the Problem Child 497;
    Counselling and Psychotherapy 497;
    Freedom to Learn: A View of What Education Might
        Become 497;
    see also deschooling; experiential learning;
        progressive education; psychology of education
Rome 1, 32, 115, 233, 328, 389, 426, 440, 470, 479;
    see also classical education; classical studies; Italy
Rousseau, Jean-Jacques 89, 109, 174, 185, 190,
    195, 215, 262, 338, 363, 433, 461, 464, 466,
    497–98;
    child development 498;
    Confessions 497;
    Consideration on the Government of Poland 497;
    Discourse on the Arts and the Sciences 497;
    Emile 174, 215, 461, 497–98;
    French Revolution 498;
    The New Heloise 497;
    Political Economy 497;
    Rousseau's educational theory 497–98;
    The Social Contract 215, 497;
    see also child-centred education; Froebel,
        Friedrich; Locke, John; progressive education
Royal Academy of Arts, London 9
Royal National Institute for the Blind (RNIB) 55
Rugg, Harold **498–99**, 551;
    The Child-Centred School 499;
    Rugg's Social Science Pamphlets 499;
    Statistical Methods Applied to Education 499;
    The Teacher in School and Society 499;
    see also child-centred education; progressive
        education; social reconstructionism;
        Thorndike, Edward Lee
rural education 92, **499–502**;
    Canada 501;
    characteristics 499–500;
    definitions 499–500;
    emerging trends 501;
    organisations supporting rural education around
        the world 501;
    qualitative definition 499–500, 501;
    quantitative definition 499, 500, 501;
    South Africa 501;
    United Nations 500;
    United Nations Educational, Scientific and
        Cultural Organization (UNESCO) 499–500;

United States 500–501;
see also Africa; community education; distance education/learning; Russia; United Nations Educational, Scientific and Cultural Organization (UNESCO); urban education; virtual learning
Russia 276, **502–4**;
boarding school 57;
children's literature 89;
educational reforms 503, 504;
educational system development:
imperial age 502, 503;
Enlightenment 502;
1917 October revolution 502, 503;
Stalin's rule 502–3;
Gorbachev's and Yeltsin's governments 503;
educational system restructuring (1991–2007) 504;
educational system structure 504;
geographical features 502;
higher education 503, 504;
kindergarten 339;
knowledge economy 341;
Makarenko, Anton Simeonovitch 366;
meritocracy 503;
normal school 406;
secondary school 504;
statistics 504;
technocracy 503;
universities 504;
University of Moscow 637;
Vygotsky, Lev 86, 108, 213, 440, 547, 636–37;
see also centralisation/decentralisation; meritocracy, privatisation; rural education; Soviet Union

sabbatical **505**;
description 505;
distinction between sabbatical and gap year 505;
higher education 505;
see also higher education; semester/term; university; work experience
Sadler, Michael **505–6**;
An Apology for the Methodists 505;
On the Distress of the Agricultural Labourer 505;
The Factory Girl's Last Day 505;
see also compulsory education; workers' education
Sadler, Michael Ernest **506**;
Continuation Schools in England and Elsewhere 506;
Education Act (1902) 506;
secondary education 506;
see also comparative education; extra-mural class; summer school
sandwich course **506–7**;
definition 506;
official support 506–7;
in public sector 507;
types 506;
United Kingdom 506–7;
see also college; degree; higher education; polytechnic; qualifications; university;

vocational education; work-based/work-located/workplace/work-related learning
Sarason, Seymour **507**;
The Case for Change 507;
The Clinical Interaction 507;
The Culture of the School and the Problem of Change 507;
The Preparation of Teachers: an Unstudied Problem 507;
Psychological Problems in Mental Deficiency 507;
Psychology in Community Settings 507;
Teaching as a Performing Art 507;
see also psychology; special education/special educational needs/special needs; teaching/teaching methods
Save the Children 89
Scandinavia **507–9**;
common features of Scandinavian countries 507–8;
comprehensive school 508;
educational system structure 508;
egalitarian structure 508;
Lutheran religious heritage 508;
middle school 508;
private sector 507, 508;
secondary school 507;
training 604;
upper secondary education 507;
see also egalitarianism; Finland; Nordic Educational Research Association (NERA)/Nordisk Förening för Pedagogiska Forskning (NFPF); Norway; Sweden
scholar **509**;
Britain 509;
broad sense of the term 509;
definition 509;
scholarship 509;
visiting scholar 509;
see also academic/academic profession/professionalism/professionalisation; scholarship; scholasticism; student
scholarship **509**;
as a grant of money to support a student 509;
as learning and erudition 509;
requirement for public financial support 11;
Rhodes Scholarships 510;
scholarship programmes 510;
United Kingdom 509–10;
United States 510;
see also academic/academic profession; charities, educational; classical studies; elementary school; examinations; grammar school; Rhodes Trust; scholar; scholasticism; secondary school/education; student finance/loans; theology; university
scholasticism 1, 32, 75, 234, **510–12**;
Calvin, John 511;
definition 510;
Duns Scotus, John 511;
Erasmus 511;
etymology 510;
influences on 510–11;

Wycliffe, John 511;
Luther, Martin 511;
main themes of disputes 511;
scholastic method:
  disputatio 511;
  lectio 511;
Aquinas, Thomas 511;
  Summa Theologiae 511;
Vatican II 512;
William of Ockham 511;
see also church; religious education; scholar;
  scholarship; theology; Aquinas, Thomas
Schön, Donald 451, 456–57, 487–88, **512**;
Beyond the Stable State 512;
Displacement of Concepts 512;
double loop learning 512;
Invention and the Evolution of Ideas 512;
learning society 512;
reflection in action 512;
The Reflective Practitioner 512;
reflective practitioner 512;
Technology and Change 512;
see also action research; practitioner research;
  profession/professionalism/professionalisation;
  reflective practitioner
school **512–13**;
as agent of cultural transmission 149;
alternative school 20;
community schools 513;
definition 512;
national systems of schooling 513;
origins 512;
therapeutic school 224;
types 512, 513;
see also deschooling; elementary school; grammar
  of schooling; Illich, Ivan; lesson; mission
  statement; primary school/education; public
  school; pupil mobility; secondary school/
  education; semester/term; teaching assistant
school-based management **513–15**;
aim 514;
definition 513;
educational policies related to 513–14;
managerialism 514;
and neo-liberalist market forces 514;
school administration era 514;
school management era 514;
see also centralisation/decentralisation; educational
  leadership and management; head teacher/
  principal; managerialism; restructuring;
  school improvement; school reform
school change **515–16**;
conditions promoting school change 515;
criticism 516;
definition 515;
factors conditioning school change 515, 516;
a local process 515;
South Africa 516;
United Kingdom:
  School Effectiveness and School Improvement 515;

United States:
  A Nation at Risk 515;
see also educational leadership and management;
  grammar of schooling; restructuring; school
  effectiveness; school improvement; school
  leadership; school reform
school culture **516–17**;
basis 516;
description 517;
definition 516;
norms and values 516;
relationships: foundation for school culture 517;
vision and purpose 516;
see also classroom management; culture; school
  knowledge; sociology of education; teacher
  cultures; underperforming/failing school
school effectiveness **517–19**, 631;
criticism 518;
origins 517;
school effectiveness research (SER) 517–18;
school factors affecting outcomes 517–18;
United Kingdom 517, 518, 616;
United States 517, 518;
see also educational leadership and management;
  educational targets; inspection; school
  change; school improvement; school
  leadership; school reform; underperforming/
  failing school; value added
school improvement 230, **519–20**;
basic assumptions 519;
challenges 520;
contributions 520;
definition 519;
distinction between school effectiveness and
  school improvement 519–20;
origins 519;
see also educational leadership and management;
  educational targets; Indonesia; inspection;
  performance indicators; restructuring; school
  change; school effectiveness; school leadership;
  school reform; sociology of education;
  underperforming/failing school; value added
school journeys **520–21**;
as the daily two-way journey home-school 520;
as organised school trip or visit 520–21;
see also extracurriculum; school
school knowledge **521–23**;
Bernstein, Basil 522–23;
and curriculum 521, 522;
knowledge of the powerful 521–22;
main focus 522;
origins of the term 521;
powerful knowledge 521–22;
school and non-school knowledge 521, 522, 523;
see also Bernstein, Basil; curriculum; pedagogy;
  school; school culture; sociology of
  education; subjects
school leadership **523–24**;
and economic markets 524;
framework 524;

school leaders 524;
see also educational leadership and management;
    head teacher/principal; school change; school
    effectiveness; school improvement;
    underperforming/failing school
school reform **524–25**;
    focus 524;
    Latin America 524;
    market-based reform efforts 525;
    school choice 525;
    United Kingdom 524–25;
    United States 524–25;
        A Nation at Risk 524;
    vouchers 525;
    see also centralisation/decentralisation; Education
        Acts (United Kingdom); Education Acts
        (United States); grammar of schooling;
        restructuring; school change; school
        effectiveness; school improvement; school-
        based management; standards; systemic reform
school reports **525–26**;
    about schools 526;
    about students or report card 525–26;
        Office for Standards in Education (Ofsted)
            316, 526;
    see also inspection
school security **526–27**;
    intervention programmes 526;
    a growing business 526–27;
    prevention programmes 526;
    United States 526;
    see also bullying; discipline; exclusion/expulsion;
        school violence; suspension; truancy
school violence **527–28**;
    definition 527, 528;
    examples 527;
    forms of 527, 528;
    violence:
        definition 527;
        motive 527;
    see also bullying; corporal punishment; discipline;
        exclusion/expulsion; school security;
        suspension; truancy
science/science education **528–31**;
    current issues 530–31;
    debates on science curriculum 528;
        curriculum according to abilities and
            attainment 529;
        integration/separation 529;
        investigational work 529;
        process/content 528–29;
        purpose of 529–30;
    history 528;
    see also biology; chemistry; core curriculum/
        national curriculum; curriculum; engineering;
        medicine; nature study; physics; subjects;
        technocrat/technocratic/technocracy
Scout Association **531**, 650;
    aims 531;
    Baden-Powell, Lord Robert 531, 650;

Scouting for Boys 531;
    guides: World Association of Girl Guides and
        Girl Scouts (WAGGGS) 531;
    members and age groups 531;
    origins 531;
    United Kingdom 531;
    see also citizenship; youth club/work
secondary school/education 506, **531–34**;
    Arnold, Matthew 532;
    Business school/education 64–65;
    comprehensive secondary school 118–20;
    current issues:
        curriculum 533;
        elite functions/mass purposes 532–33;
        terminal phase/preparatory stage 533;
    definition 531–32;
    extracurriculum 246;
    and higher education 533;
    lessons, double lessons 357;
    as mass institution 532;
    origins and development 532;
    Russia 504;
    Sweden 576–77;
    United Kingdom 615;
    United States 622;
    see also Arnold, Matthew; educational system
        structure; grammar school; high school;
        intermediate/middle school; primary school/
        education; scholarship; school; selection; sixth
        form; specialisation; subjects; Tawney, Richard
        Henry; technical education/school/college;
        tertiary education; vocational education
secularising of education 253;
    banning of clerics from teaching 253
segregation/desegregation **534–35**;
    definitions 534;
    dual system of neighbourhood schools 534;
    school desegregation plans 534–35;
    United States 534–35;
    see also catchment area; equity; integration;
        magnet school; zoning
selection 381, **535–36**;
    definition 535;
    ethnic selection 536;
    forms of 535;
    levels of the education system at which selection
        takes place 535–36;
    private schools 536;
    selective forms of education 536;
    United Kingdom 425–26, 535, 536;
    United States 536, 622–23;
    see also ability; ability grouping; aptitude; Burt,
        Cyril; examinations; gate-keeping; grammar
        school; intelligence/intelligence tests; merit;
        parity of esteem; recruitment; secondary
        school/education; secondary school/
        education; setting; streaming/tracking
self-directed learning **537**;
    description 537;
    factors related to success 537;

practice of 537;
  see also autodidact; learning
semester/term **537**;
  definition 537;
  organisation 537;
  summer break 537;
  see also college; higher education; school;
    sabbatical; summer school; university
seminar **537–38**;
  description 537;
  forms 537–38;
  see also lecture; Socratic method; tuition/tutor/
    tutorial
seminary **538**;
  Catholic seminaries 538;
  definition 538;
  minor seminaries 538;
  secular seminaries 538;
  see also Jesuit education; normal school; religious
    education; religious school
setting **538**;
  non-traditional 20;
  non-standard 20;
  and streaming 538;
  target-setting 538;
  traditional 20;
  uses of the term 538;
  see also ability grouping; mixed-ability teaching;
    selection; streaming/tracking
sex education **539–40**;
  aims 539;
  best provision for 540;
  controversial subject 539;
  Netherlands 539;
  Sex Education 540;
  United Kingdom 539;
  United States 539;
  and values 539;
  see also biology; curriculum; health education;
    textbook
Simon's task 2
  see also ability test *under* ability; test/testing
Singapore **540–42**;
  assessment, streaming and sorting of students 540;
  bilingual policy 540;
  educational system development 540;
  educational system structure 541;
  exporter of high-quality higher education 541–42;
  higher education 541;
  International Baccalaureate 541;
  madrasahs 540–41;
  National University of Singapore 541;
  Nanyang Technological University 541;
  role of Ministry of Education (MOE) 540;
  Singapore Management University 541;
  Soka Gakkai International 367;
  The University of New South Wales 541;
  see also bilingual education; East Asia
single-sex education *see* coeducation
situated cognition/learning **542–43**;

basis of the situated cognition thesis 542;
  conditions for transferring cognition 542–43;
  principles 542;
  see also cognition; core skills/core competencies;
    learning; learning community
sixth form **543**;
  British post-compulsory education 543;
  definition 543;
  description 543;
  prefects 543;
  see also further education; prefect; secondary
    school/education; work experience
skills 153, 274, **543–45**;
  cognitive/practical-vocational skills 544–45;
  common associations 544;
  different approaches and definitions 544;
  and gender 545;
  German concept of skills 131;
  global skill strategies of multinational companies
    (MNCs) 274, 276;
  and human capital theory 544;
  skills capture theory (SCT) 274, 275, 276;
  skill formation theory (SFT) 274, 275, 276;
  skill in the job/skill in the individual 544;
  transferable skills 544;
  see also ability; apprenticeship; core skills/core
    competences; globalisation; industrial
    training; knowledge economy; lifelong
    learning; qualifications; training; transition
    education; work-based/work-located/
    workplace/work-related learning
Skinner, Burrhus Fredric 47, 460, **545**;
  Beyond Freedom and Dignity 545;
  The Technology of Teaching 545;
  see also behaviourism; Galton, Francis;
    programmed learning; Thorndike, Edward Lee
social capital **545–47**;
  Bourdieu, Pierre 545–46;
  Coleman, James S. 545, 546;
  main issues 546;
  principles 545;
  Putnam, Robert 546;
  types 546;
  see also Bourdieu, Pierre; cultural capital;
    educational theory; family; functionalism;
    sociology; sociology of education; youth
    club/work
social constructivism **547**;
  concept 547;
  national identity 547;
  sociology of education 547;
  Vygotsky, Lev 547;
  see also activity theory; Dewey, John; experiential
    learning; Vygotsky, Lev; zone of proximal
    development
social control **547–48**;
  definition 547;
  development of the concept 547–48;
  Durkheim, Emile 547–48;
  and functionalists 548;

and Marxists 548;
and sociologists 547;
strengths of 548;
see also Durkheim, Emile; educational theory;
    functionalism; sociology of education
social exclusion/inclusion **549–50**;
definition 549;
and developing countries 549;
dimensions 549;
social inclusion 11, 12;
United Kingdom 549;
United States 549;
see also accreditation of prior achievement/
    learning; equality of opportunity; equity;
    delinquency; integration; learning
    disabilities/difficulties; lifelong learning;
    multicultural education; multiculturalism;
    truancy; underachievement
social promotion 12, **550**;
definition 550;
grade retention 550;
    United States 550;
see also high-stakes testing; learning career;
    multigrade education; peer group
social reconstructionism **550–52**;
Brameld, Theodore 551;
Counts, George 550–51;
    Dare the Schools Build a New Social Order? 550;
curriculum 551;
Dewey, John 550, 551;
educational programme 551;
indoctrination 551;
reconstructionist 550;
Rugg, Harold 550, 551;
The Social Frontier 551;
origins and development 550–51;
see also critical pedagogy; Dewey, John;
    indoctrination; progressive education; Rugg,
    Harold
social reproduction 148, **552–53**;
functionalist approach 552;
a key function of education 552;
policies relates to 552–53;
ways in which education reproduces social
    ideas 552;
    inequalities 552;
    schooling and occupational hierarchy 552;
Willis, Paul:
    Learning to Labour 552;
see also cultural capital; educational theory;
    functionalism; sociology of education
social studies **553–54**;
benefit for students 554;
citizenship education 553, 554;
Dewey, John 553;
main features of 553;
Progressive Education 553;
The Social Studies in Secondary Schools 553;
subjects included in 553;
United States 553;

see also citizenship/civics; sociology
sociology 212, **554**;
Chicago School of sociology 376;
Comte, August 554;
definition 554;
Durkheim, Emile 182;
origins 554;
see also critical theory; Durkheim, Emile;
    functionalism; social capital; social studies;
    sociology of education; subjects; Weber, Max
sociology of education 25, 212, **555–56**;
definition 555;
empirical work 555–56;
foundation discipline of education 199, 214;
gap between theoretical ideas and empirical
    studies 555;
Marxist sociology of education 135, 263;
Parsons, Talcott 262–63;
    The School Class as a Social System 263;
recent growth and promising future 556;
sociological perspective on education 555;
theories applied by sociologists of education 555;
see also correspondence theory; critical theory;
    cultural capital; Durkheim, Emile; education
    policy; education; educational studies;
    equality of opportunity; functionalism;
    habitus; Mannheim, Karl; politics of
    education; school culture; school
    improvement; school knowledge; social
    capital; social constructivism; social control;
    social reproduction; sociology
Socratic method 96, 233, **556–57**;
conceptual framework 556–57;
definition 557;
Plato 556–57;
    Euthyphro 557;
    Lysis 557;
    Meno 557;
    Republic 556, 557;
    Symposium 557;
    Theaetetus 557;
psyche 556–57;
Socratic questioning 557;
see also Greece; learning; philosophy of
    education; Plato; seminar
South Africa 61, 536, **557–59**;
apartheid 558;
Apartheid and Education 558;
beginnings and development of formal schooling
    557–58;
black schooling 557–58;
Curriculum 2005 558;
liberation theology 601;
Mandela Rhodes Foundation 495;
post-apartheid period 558–59;
racial schooling policies 557;
racialisation 536;
racially integrated educational system 558;
Recognition of Prior Experiential Learning
    (RPEL) 11, 12,

Rhodes Scholars' Southern Africa Forum
(RSSAF) 495;
rural education 501;
school change 516;
see also Africa; equality of opportunity; equity
Soviet Union 61;
counselling 136;
distance education/learning 176;
history (subject) 294;
influence on Chinese education 91;
Makarenko, Anton Simeonovitch 366;
project method 465;
Vygotsky, Lev 86, 108, 213, 440, 547, 636–37;
see also Russia
Spearman, Charles 2, 318, 468, **559**;
The Abilities of Man 559;
*General Intelligence Objectively Determined and
Measured* 559;
*The Nature of Intelligence and the Principles of
Cognition* 559;
see also ability; Burt, Cyril; cognition; Galton,
Francis; intelligence/intelligence tests;
psychology; psychometrics; psychology of
education; Thorndike, Edward Lee
special education/special educational needs/special
needs 224, **559–60**;
Asperger's syndrome 42;
Brazil 60;
description 559;
England 559–60;
main focus of work 560;
Sweden 576;
see also autism; blind, teaching of; dyslexia;
emotional and behavioural difficulties/
disorders (EBD); giftedness; hyperactivity;
inclusive education; individualised
instruction/personalised learning; learning
disabilities/difficulties; Sarason, Seymour;
Steiner, Rudolf; Thelwall, John
special interest groups (SIGs) 22, 41, 62
specialisation **560–61**;
definition 560;
forms of 560;
reasons for 560–61;
England:
specialist schools programme 561;
see also academy; business school; curriculum;
curriculum differentiation; educational
publishing; physics; professional education;
secondary school/education
speech 50, 58, 167, 440, 651;
in autism 41;
educational speech therapy 600;
parts of 278;
see also Bernstein, Basil; linguistics; phonics;
reading, spelling; Thelwall, John
spelling **561–62**;
approaches to word learning 561, 562;
English spelling 562;
The Essential Spelling List 561–62;

Franklin, Benjamin:
*A Scheme for a New Alphabet and Reformed Mode
of Spelling* 562;
Shaw, George Bernard 562;
Spelling Bee 562;
spelling competitions 562;
see also basic skills; dyslexia; grammar; literacy;
phonics; reading; standards; writing
Spencer, Herbert **562–63**;
Essays on Education 562;
hierarchy of knowledge 563;
physical education 563;
see also discovery method/learning;
functionalism;
spiral curriculum **563**;
Bruner, Jerome 563;
criticism 563;
description 563;
see also Bruner, Jerome; curriculum; Piaget, Jean;
psychology of education; subjects
sponsored and contest mobility **563–64**;
Turner, Ralph H. 563;
United Kingdom 563–64;
United States 563–64;
see also meritocracy
Sri Lanka 390;
diploma disease 171
standardised tests **564–65**;
categories:
achievement tests 564–65;
aptitude tests 564;
criterion-referenced tests 565;
description 564;
United States 564–65, 623;
see also accountability; aptitude; assessment;
criterion-referenced tests; norm-referenced
tests; test/testing
standards 77, **565–66**;
common contexts and uses 565–66;
comparative studies about educational standards
566;
impact of 566;
see also assessment; coursework; curriculum
standards/programmes of study; diagnostic
assessment; educational targets; examinations;
grammar; inspection; numeracy;
Organisation for Economic Co-operation
and Development (OECD); performance
indicators; reading; school reform; spelling;
systemic reform; underachievement
Steiner, Rudolf 156, 412, **566–67**;
and early childhood education 186;
anthroposophy 567;
The Story of My Life 567;
Waldorf Schools 272, 462, 567;
see also nursery school; special education/special
educational needs/special needs
Stenhouse, Lawrence 451, **567**;
Authority, Education and Emancipation 567;
Culture and Education 567;

Curriculum Research and Development in Action 567;
   teachers 567;
   see also action research; cultural transmission;
      curriculum; practitioner research; subjects
streaming/tracking 292, **567–68**;
   definition 567;
   setting 568;
   see also ability; ability grouping; attainment;
      giftedness; high-stakes testing; mixed-ability
      teaching; selection; setting;
      underachievement
student **568**;
   benefits 568;
   definition 568;
   distinctions in university context 568;
   non-traditional student 494;
   see also degree; homework; learning career;
      master's; mature student; peer group;
      plagiarism; pupil; retention; scholar; student
      finance/loans; teacher; university
student finance/loans **568–69**;
   cost-sharing 569;
   endowment 568;
   higher education 567–68;
   state contributions to 569;
   student finance system 568;
   United Kingdom 569;
   United States 569;
   see also charities, educational; economics of
      education; endowment; higher education;
      scholarship; student; tuition/tutor/tutorial
subjects **569–71**;
   definition 569–70;
   distinct traditions related to subjects:
      academic 570;
      pedagogic 570;
      utilitarian 570;
   social and political nature 570;
   subject departments 570;
   see also classical studies; curriculum; engineering;
      examinations; geography; health education;
      home economics/domestic science; law;
      lesson; mathematics; medicine; modern
      languages; music; nature study; physical
      education/training; physics; qualifications;
      religious education; school knowledge;
      science/science education; secondary school/
      education; sociology; spiral curriculum;
      Stenhouse, Lawrence; teacher; textbook;
      theology
summative assessment 255, **571–72**;
   characteristics 571;
   costs 571–72;
   coursework 572;
   current concerns related to 572;
   description 571;
   distinction between summative and formative
      assessment 255, 571;
   see also assessment; examinations; formative
      assessment; marking; test/testing

summer school **572**;
   definition 572;
   different forms of 572;
   purposes 572;
   see also extracurriculum; Open University;
      Sadler, Michael Ernest; semester/term
Summerhill School 401–2;
   see also Neill, Alexander Sutherland
Sunday school 94, **572–74**;
   and children's literature 89;
   description 572;
   and mass schooling 573;
   origins and development 573;
   Raikes, Robert:
      Gloucester Journal 573;
   United Kingdom:
      socialist movements 573;
      Proletarian Song Book 573;
      *The Red Dawn: A Book of Verse for
         Revolutionaries and Others* 573;
      The Socialist Commandments 573;
   United States 573;
   see also church; religious school
supply/substitute teaching **574**;
   Australia 574;
   Canada 574;
   definition 574;
   New Zealand 574;
   United Kingdom 574;
   United States 574;
   see also teacher; teaching
suspension 164, 174; **574–76**;
   Australia 575;
   data on rates of 575;
   description 574;
   exclusion from classroom activities 574–75;
   exclusion from the school 574;
   suspension data interpretation 575;
   United States 575;
   see also counselling; delinquency; detention;
      discipline; exclusion/expulsion; school
      security; school violence; truancy
Sweden **576–77**;
   adult education 577;
   beginnings of education system 576;
   compulsory schooling 575;
   current challenges 577;
   different schools 575;
   distance education/learning 176;
   early years' education 576;
   educational system structure 576–77;
   equality of opportunity 230;
   history (subject) 294;
   independent/private school/education 303, 576;
   religious education 490;
   secondary education 576–77;
   special educational needs 576;
   tertiary education 577;
   textbook 599;
   Uppsala University 256;

see also Europe; Nordic Educational Research
Association (NERA)/Nordisk Förening för
Pedagogiska Forskning (NFPF); Scandinavia
Switzerland 24, 235, 236, 567;
apprenticeship 29;
multicultural education 394;
Pestalozzi, Johann Heinrich 109, 174, 190, 262,
289, 338, 433–34, 461, 464;
Piaget, Jean 86, 106, 108, 117, 175, 213, 243,
268, 320, 341, 439–40;
see also Europe
syllabus 75, **577**;
definition 577;
main features 577;
see also curriculum; examinations; textbook
systemic reform **577–79**;
definition 577;
standards-based reforms 577, 578;
technical, normative and political means 578;
United States 578;
Chicago 578;
No Child Left Behind Law (NCLB) 579;
Philadelphia 578–79;
San Diego 578;
see also accountability; core curriculum;
educational priority area; restructuring;
school reform; standards; urban education

Tanzania 18, **581–82**;
compulsory education 581, 582;
educational system structure 581;
gender disparity 582;
geographical features 581;
higher education 582;
primary education 581, 582;
private schools 582;
secondary education 581, 582;
statistics 582;
University College of Tanganyika 582;
University of East Africa 582;
see also Africa; centralisation/decentralisation;
development plan; Education for All (EFA);
standards; voluntarism
Tawney, Richard Henry 246, **582–83**;
The Education of the Adolescent 583;
Equality 583;
Religion and the Rise of Capitalism 583;
Secondary Education for All 583;
Workers' Educational Association (WEA) 583;
see also equality of opportunity; extra-mural class;
politics of education; secondary school/
education; Workers' Educational Association
(WEA)
teacher **583–84**;
commitments and rewards 584;
definition 583;
effectiveness 584;
a profession 583;
professionalism 583;
shortage of in United Kingdom 486;

sources of knowledge 584;
workplace 583;
see also action research; Carnegie Foundation for
the Advancement of Teaching; continued/
continuing professional development; learning;
lesson; pastoral care; pedagogy; Stenhouse,
Lawrence; student; subjects; teacher cultures;
teacher union; teaching/teaching methods;
teaching assistant; teaching profession; teacher
unions; teaching profession;
teacher cultures **584–85**;
content of 585;
forms 585;
Lortie, Dan 584–85;
research about 585;
Schoolteacher: A Sociological Study 585;
see also culture; pedagogy; school culture; teacher;
teaching/teaching methods; teaching profession
teacher education/training 289, 343, 439, 486,
585–87;
concurrent courses 586;
consecutive courses 586;
elements of the programmes 585;
factors influencing type and quality of 586;
Finland 254;
a high-status occupation 586;
Iraq 326;
Italy 329;
mentoring 380;
Oceania 414;
role of teacher educators 586;
see also continued/continuing professional
development; education/educational studies;
Herbart, Johann Friedrich; in-service education;
Kay-Shuttleworth, Sir James; normal school;
Oceania; profession/professionalism/
professionalisation; recruitment; reflective
practitioner; teaching profession
teacher unions **587–88**;
common debates and issues engaged with 587–88;
purpose 587;
relations with the state 588;
teachers' labour rights 587;
see also profession/professionalism/
professionalisation; teacher; teaching profession
teaching/teaching methods **589**;
classroom teaching methods 589;
definition 589;
lesson plan 589, 637;
pedagogy 589;
see also action research; Comenius, Jan Amos;
discovery method/learning; individualised
instruction/personalised learning; instruction;
learning community; lecture/lecturer;
lesson; marking; open plan; pedagogy; phonics;
Sarason, Seymour; teacher; teacher cultures;
teaching assistant; teaching profession; visual aids
teaching assistant **589–90**;
foreign language teachers 589–90;
in higher education institutions 589;

in schools 589;
United Kingdom 375, 589;
see also higher education; postgraduate; school;
teacher; teaching/teaching methods; teaching
profession
teaching profession **590–91**;
autonomy conflict 590;
definition 590, 593;
and neo-liberal restructuring of schooling 591;
profession: definition 590;
see also in-service education; mentor/mentoring;
profession/professionalism/
professionalisation; teacher; teacher cultures;
teacher education/training; teacher unions;
teaching/teaching methods
technical education/school/college 18, **591–93**;
aims 591;
apprenticeship 591, 592;
France 592;
Germany 592–93;
Greece 281;
in higher education 592;
origins and development 591–92;
polytechnics 592;
in secondary education 592;
target population 592–93;
technological baccalaureate 592;
United Kingdom 591–92, 593;
vocational education and training (VET) 593;
see also apprenticeship; engineering; further
education; grammar school; higher education;
liberal education; polytechnic; secondary
school/education; vocational education;
work-based/work-located/workplace/work-
related learning; workers' education
technocrat/technocratic/technocracy **593–95**;
technocrat: definition 593;
technocratic: definition 593;
technocracy:
definition 594;
etymology 594;
goal 594;
literature about 593;
origins and development of the movement 594;
technodeterminism 594;
Russia 503;
see also centralisation; democracy; elitism;
ideology; managerialism; meritocracy;
science/science education; technology
technology **595–96**;
definition 595;
and education 595;
in curriculum 595–96;
post-modernist view 595;
technology of the self 595;
etymology 595;
as a system of practice 595;
as a tool 595; 596;
see also computer-assisted learning; computer
studies; educational technology; e-learning;

engineering; open learning; technocrat/
technocratic/technocracy; virtual learning
Terman, Lewis Madison 318, **596–97**;
Genetic Studies of Genius 596;
intelligence quotient (IQ) 596;
The Measurement of Intelligence 596;
see also giftedness; intelligence/intelligence tests;
psychology of education; Thorndike,
Edward Lee
tertiary education 18, 120, 263, **597–98**;
Caribbean 71;
college 109;
continuous assessment 129;
definition 597;
distinction between tertiary and further
education 597;
in the educational system structure 597;
Finland 254;
Greece 281–82;
New Zealand 403;
Maori Tertiary institutions 403;
Tertiary Education Commission (TEC) 403;
Polynesia 445;
in post-industrial societies 597;
Sweden 577;
see also college; further education; higher
education; secondary education; university;
vocational education; work-based/work-
located/workplace/ work-related learning
test/testing 9, 37, **598**;
ability tests 2–3;
definition 598;
intelligence testing 598;
types 598;
uses 598;
see also ability; assessment; criterion-referenced
tests; diagnostic assessment; examinations;
formative assessment; high-stakes testing;
intelligence/intelligence tests; marking;
merit; multiple-choice tests; norm-
referenced tests; objective tests; standardised
tests; summative assessment; Tyler, Ralph
textbook **598–99**;
pedagogical function 598;
East Asian societies 598–99;
Sweden 599;
United States 599;
textbook market and official approval 599;
textbook research 599;
see also curriculum; educational publishing;
pedagogy; sex education; subjects; syllabus
Thelwall, John **600**;
educational speech therapy 600;
Letter to Henry Cline 600;
see also special education/special educational
needs/special needs
theology **600–601**;
definition 600;
distinction between theology and religious
studies, comparative religion;

etymology 600;
liberation theologies 261, 601;
philosophy of religion 600;
sub-disciplines 600;
theological methods 600–601;
see also church; indoctrination; Jesuit education;
    Newman, John Henry; religious assembly;
    religious education; religious school;
    scholarship; scholasticism; subject
thesis/dissertation **601–2**;
description 601–2;
at doctorate level 602;
length 602;
at master's and undergraduate levels 602;
see also degree; doctorate; master's; oral examination
Thorndike, Edward Lee 47, 213, 371, 498–99, **602**;
The Fundamentals of Learning 602;
Human Nature and the Social Order 602;
The Principles of Teaching: Based on Psychology 602;
The Teacher's World Book 602;
see also individualised instruction/personalised
    learning; intelligence/intelligence tests; Maslow,
    Abraham Harold; psychology of education;
    Rugg, Harold; Skinner, Burrhus Fredric;
    Spearman, Charles; Terman, Lewis Madison
the 'three Rs' 32, 46, 130, 615;
see also arithmetic; basic skills; literacy;
    numeracy; reading; skills; spelling; writing
training **602–5**;
apprenticeship 603–4;
and conditioning 602–3;
development of training systems 603–4;
France 604;
Germany 604;
mechanics' institutes 604;
Netherlands 604;
portfolio assessment 610;
role of training in education 603;
Scandinavia 604;
United Kingdom 604–5;
United States 604–5;
vocational training 605;
see also apprenticeship; autonomy; day release;
    dual system; industrial training; instruction;
    moral education; qualifications; skills;
    transition education; vocational education;
    work-based/work-located/workplace/work-
    related learning
transition education **605–6**;
education-work transition 606;
individual transitions 605–6;
Learning and Work in the Risk Society 606;
societies and educational systems transitions 605,
    606;
studies of 605;
see also learning career; lifelong learning; skills;
    training
transmission pedagogy 174;
see also Rousseau, Jean-Jacques
travellers, education of **606–8**;

European Federation for the Education of the
    Children of Occupational Travellers
    (EFECOT) 607;
mismatch between educational provision and
    learner mobility 607;
travellers response 607;
educational system response 607;
organisations supporting traveller education 607–8;
traveller education 607;
Traveller Education Support Service (TESS) 607;
travellers 606–7;
see also community education/school/college;
    compulsory education; culture; literacy
travelling teachers 40;
see also travellers, education of
trivium 75, 96, 233–34, 532;
see also classical education
truancy 380, **608–9**;
and child labour 608–9;
and crime 608;
definition 608;
factors and reasons for truancy 609;
United States:
    Manual to Combat Truancy 608;
see also bullying; compulsory education; pastoral
    care; school security; school violence; social
    exclusion/inclusion; suspension
tuition/tutor/tutorial **609**;
definitions 609;
higher education tutorials 609;
tuition/tuition fees 609;
see also counselling; higher education;
    instruction; lecture/lecturer; seminar; student
    finance/loans
Tyler, Ralph **610**;
Basic Principles of Curriculum Instruction 610;
Centre for Behavioural Sciences 610;
portfolio assessment 610;
see also assessment; evaluation; test/testing

underachievement **611–12**;
educational achievement 611;
    psychological perspective 611, 612;
    sociological perspective 611;
factors determining underachievement 612;
meanings 611–12;
see also ability; aptitude; intelligence/intelligence
    tests; learning disabilities/difficulties;
    motivation; social exclusion/inclusion;
    standards; streaming/tracking; wrangler/
    wooden spoon
undergraduate **612**;
definition 612;
degree 612;
freshman/fresher 612;
sophomore 612;
see also degree; foundation degree; higher
    education; postgraduate; university
underperforming/failing school 292, **613–14**;
definition 613;

external policy consequences 613;
general goals for underperforming/failing school 614;
identification of 613;
judgement criteria 613;
Organisation for Economic Cooperation and Development (OECD):
Combating Failure at School 612;
origins of the term 613;
United Kingdom 613;
United States 613;
see also accountability; high-stakes testing; inspection; school culture; school effectiveness; school improvement; school leadership
United Kingdom 25, 113, 276, **614–16**;
Accreditation of Prior Experiential Learning (APEL) 11–12;
Anglican church 615;
apprenticeship 28, 29–30, 33;
approved school 30–31;
Arnold, Matthew 34, 149, 151, 532;
Arnold, Thomas 34–35, 452, 614;
Ascham, Roger 36;
athenaeum 38;
attainment 38–39;
autism 42;
baseline assessment 45–46;
benchmarking 48–49;
Bernstein, Basil 49–50, 116, 429;
binary system 52–53;
blind, teaching of 54–56;
boarding school 57;
Bradford University 81;
British Council 60–62;
British Broadcasting Corporation (BBC) 201;
British Educational Research Association (BERA) 62–63;
Burt, Cyril 64, 318;
Business school/education 64–65;
Cambridge University 104, 225, 246; 372, 456, 510, 541, 628, 632, 647;
career guidance 69;
catchment area 74–75;
chancellor 81;
charter school 84;
child guidance 87, 88;
children's literature 89–90;
classical studies 97, 98;
classroom 99, 101;
coeducation 104;
Colet, John 106–7;
comparative education 113,
comprehensive school 119, 386, 615;
compulsory education 121;
continuing education 128;
core skills/core competences 130–32;
cramming 138;
creativity in education 139;
crèche 139–40;
cultural diversity and immigration 393–94;

cultural studies 149;
curriculum standards/programmes of study 158;
Curtis, Sir William 130;
Dalton schools 426;
day release 159;
Department for International Development (DfID) 162–63;
development plan 165;
diploma disease 171;
disaffection 173;
discovery method/learning 75;
distance education/learning 176;
dual system 180, 181, 615;
early childhood education (ECE) 185, 186, 187;
Edgeworth, Maria 194–95;
Education Action Zones (EAZs) 116, 205, 427, 616, 630;
education/educational studies 200;
educational broadcasting 201;
educational charities 81–82;
educational leadership and management 202, 203;
educational priority areas (EPAs) 116, 205;
educationist/educationalist 215;
educational system origins and development 614–16;
educational system structure 614, 616;
elementary school 220, 614–15;
Elyot, Sir Thomas 222–23;
endowment 224;
engineering 225;
English National Curriculum 36, 101;
Eton College 109, 337, 393, 471, 641;
Every Child Matters 310;
evidence-based policy/practice 239;
exclusion/expulsion 242;
Exeter University 246, 628;
extracurriculum 246;
extra-mural class 246–47;
Foreign Office 61;
formative assessment 255;
Forster, William Edward 256, 363;
foundation degree 257;
franchising 259–60;
further education 263–64, 615;
Galton, Francis 267, 273, 468, 559;
gender parity 615;
geography 270;
grammar school 279–80;
health education 288;
high-stakes testing 291–92;
higher education 615–16;
history (subject) 294, 295;
home schooling 298;
Hume, David 212, 237, 249;
independent/private school/education 303, 304, 305, 615;
individualised instruction/personalised learning 309–10;
in-service education 315;
inspection system 315;

John of Salisbury 1, 333–34;
Jowett, Benjamin 334, 632;
junior school 334–35;
Kay-Shuttleworth, Sir James 337;
Keate, John 337–38;
key stages 616;
King's College 337, 393, 641;
kindergarten 339;
Knox, John 341;
Lancaster, Joseph 343, 406;
law 347–48;
learning disabilities/difficulties 353;
Leeds University 246, 247;
Liverpool University 64;
Locke, John 43, 185, 212; 215, 249, 362–63, 461;
Lowe, Robert 363–64;
London Challenge 205;
mature student 375;
McMillan, Margaret 339, 375–76;
mass education and credential inflation 141;
mechanics' institute 364;
mentor/mentoring 380;
merit 381;
middle school 319;
Mill, John Stuart 174, 212, 384;
mixed-ability teaching 386;
monitorial system 389;
Mulcaster, Richard 393;
national educational system 341;
naval schools 33;
Neill, Alexander Sutherland 156, 215, 401–2;
normal school 406;
numeracy 409;
nursery school 410, 411, 412, 614;
Office for Standards in Education (Ofsted) 316, 526;
open learning 416–17;
open plan 417–18;
Open University 176, 409, 416–17;
Oxford University 31, 34, 82, 114, 179, 225, 246, 334, 402, 456, 495, 506, 509, 510, 626, 632;
Owen, Robert 410–11, 422;
parental choice 425;
parity of esteem 425–26;
partnerships, educational 427;
pastoral care 428, 429;
polytechnic 446–47;
prefect 452;
privatisation 455;
proctor 456;
progressive education 463;
psychology of education 466, 467–68;
public library 470;
public school 471, 615;
pupil referral union 242;
Qualifications and Curriculum Authority (UK) 130, 476, 491;
reception class 484–85;
Reddie, Cecil 486–87;
religious assembly 488;

religious education 490;
religious schools 94,
Rhodes Trust 82;
Robbins, Lionel 496;
Royal Academy of Arts, London 9;
Sadler, Michael 505–6;
Sadler, Michael Ernest 506;
sandwich course 506–7;
scholar 509;
scholarship 509–10;
school change 515;
Schools Council History Project (SCHP) 295;
school effectiveness 517, 518, 616;
school reform 524–25;
Scout Association 531;
secondary school/education 615;
sex education 539;
Sheffield University 246, 628;
sixth form 543;
social exclusion/inclusion 549;
Spearman, Charles 2, 318, 468, 559;
special education/special educational needs/ special needs 559–60;
specialist schools programme 561;
sponsored and contest mobility 563–64;
St Andrews University 215, 384;
starting/leaving age 484;
state primary schools 615;
state sector 615;
Stenhouse, Lawrence 451, 567;
Summerhill School 401–2;
Sunday school 94, 573;
supply/substitute teaching 574;
Tawney, Richard Henry 246, 582–83;
teaching assistant 375, 589;
technical education/school/college 591–92, 593;
textbook 599;
Thelwall, John 600;
the three Rs 130, 615;
training 604–5;
travellers, education of 607, 608;
tuition/tutor/tutorial 609;
underperforming/failing school 613;
UK-based Dyslexia Institute 183;
University College, London 50, 64, 70, 267, 318, 496, 559;
University of Durham 26;
University of Glasgow 225, 583;
University of London 40, 50, 70, 96, 97, 113, 187, 200, 327, 363, 370, 377, 463, 582;
University of Manchester 25, 81, 326, 447, 506;
University of Nottingham 128, 246, 368, 628;
University of York 81;
urban education 629, 630;
vice-chancellor 632;
vocational education 634;
voluntarism 635;
whole-class teaching 640;
William of Wykeham 641;
Wollstonecraft, Mary 641;

work-based/work-located/workplace/work-related learning (WBL) 642;
working-class autodidact tradition 43;
Workers' Educational Association (WEA) 377, 645–46;
World Education Fellowship (WEF) 89, 647;
wrangler/wooden spoon 647;
Young, Michael 381, 382–83, 418, 649;
youth club/work 649–50;
see also antiracist education; Education Acts (United Kingdom); English; Europe; multicultural education
United Kingdom Open University 176, 409, 416–17;
educational broadcasting 201;
see also correspondence course; distance education/learning; educational broadcasting; mature student; open learning; Open University; summer school; university; web-based learning; Young, Michael
United Nations 17, 162, 197, 210;
compulsory elementary education 122;
see also Millennium Development Goals; United Nations Children's Fund (UNICEF); United Nations Educational, Scientific and Cultural Organization (UNESCO)
United Nations Children's Fund (UNICEF) 82, 89, 288, 322, 323, 324, 405, **617–18**;
1946–2006: Sixty Years for Children 617;
aims 617;
Convention on the Rights of the Child 617;
Education For All 618;
healthcare 617;
origins 617;
The State of the World's Children 618;
see also compulsory education; Education for All (EFA); globalisation; health education; international education; United Nations Educational, Scientific and Cultural Organisation (UNESCO); universal education/mass education
United Nations Convention on the Rights of the Child 132–33, 302, 617, 618;
see also United Nations Children's Fund (UNICEF)
United Nations Educational, Scientific and Cultural Organisation (UNESCO) 89, 322–23, **618–21**;
civic education 619;
and continuing education 128;
definition 618;
and distance education/learning 177;
Education for All 618–19;
official partners 619;
educational targets 209;
Global Monitoring Report 619;
inclusive education 301–2;
International Bureau of Education 619, 620;
International Council for Adult Education 620;
key documents and policies 618;
and learning society 354;
Learning to Be 620;
lifelong learning 360;
member countries 620;
Millennium Development Goals 618;
origins and development 620;
promotion of cultural diversity 619;
reaching the unreached 619;
Salamanca Statement 301–2;
scientific programmes 619;
Teaching: the Treasure Within 618;
tensions between members countries 620–21;
United Nations Girls' Education Initiative (UNGEI) 619;
see also Department for International Development; Education for All; globalisation; inclusive education; International Bureau of Education; International Council for Adult Education; international education; International Institute for Educational Planning; Millennium Development Goals; rural education; United Nations Children's Fund (UNICEF); universal education/mass education; World Bank; World Education Fellowship (WEF)
United States 61, 276, **621–24**;
Addams, Jane 15–16;
alumni associations 22;
American association degree 257;
American Counselling Association 136;
American Educational Research Association (AERA) 22–23, 314;
American Psychological Association 287;
American sociology 182;
American Women's Educational Association 47;
andragogy 23–24;
apprenticeship 30;
art 35;
assessment system 291;
athenaeum 38;
Atlanta University 181–82;
Beecher, Catharine 47;
bell curve 48;
bilingual education 51;
blind, teaching of 55;
Bloom, Benjamin 56;
Brown University, Rhode Island, 370;
Brown v. Board Education 622;
Bruner, Jerome 63, 86, 175, 213, 430;
Business school/education 64–65;
career guidance 69;
Carnegie Foundation for the Advancement of Teaching 71–72, 221;
certificate/certification 80;
chancellor 81;
charter school 83;
child guidance 87–88;
Child Study Association of America 287;
children's literature 89–90;
Civil Rights Movement 622, 623;
Clarke University, Massachusetts 507, 596;
classical studies 97–99;
coeducation 104;
colleges 622;

Columbia University 166, 215, 371, 376, 463, 464, 495, 496, 497, 499, 602;
common school 109–10, 621;
comparative education 113,
comprehensive school/education 118–19;
compulsory education 121, 122, 622;
Conant, James Bryant 124–25;
continuing education 128;
Cornell University 213;
corporal punishment 132, 133;
counselling 136;
credential society 140;
cultural diversity and immigration 393, 395;
current challenges 623;
curriculum standards/programmes of study 157–58;
educational broadcasting 201;
educational charities 82;
educational missions in Japan 190;
Dewey, John 89, 91, 111, 165–68, 190, 213, 215, 243, 310, 376, 461–62, 463, 464, 550, 551, 622;
distance education/learning 176;
dropouts 180;
DuBois, William E. B. 181–82;
educational leadership and management 202;
educational priority area (EPA) 204;
educational system origins and development 621–23;
educational system structure 622;
educationist/educationalist 215;
elementary school 220;
Eliot, Charles William 221;
engineering 225;
equality of opportunity 230, 623;
evidence-based policy/practice 239;
exclusion/expulsion 242;
extracurriculum 246;
extra-mural class 247;
faculty 249;
feminist theory 252–53;
Fisk University 181;
formal schooling 621;
franchising 259–60;
Frederick, Christine 296–97;
further education (FE) 264;
Gardner, Howard 3, 268, 318, 357;
gender parity 623;
geography 270;
Georgetown University 348;
graduation ceremony 278;
grammar school 279;
Hall, Granville Stanley 287, 462–63, 466;
Harris, William Torrey 287;
Harvard University 118, 124–25, 179, 181, 221, 225, 262, 287, 466;
head teacher/principal 287–88;
health education 288;
high school 290–91, 622, 623;
high-stakes testing 291–92;
higher education 221, 621;
high school dropout rate 20;

history (subject) 294;
home schooling 298;
Illinois State Normal University 407;
independent/private school/education 303, 304, 305;
individualised instruction/personalised learning 309–10;
influences on Chinese education 91;
influences on Latin America 344, 345;
inspection system 315;
Isaacs, Susan Sutherland 326–27, 463;
Johns Hopkins University 97, 287;
junior high school 319;
Kerr, Clark 338;
kindergarten 287, 339;
Kohlberg, Lawrence 86, 341–42;
Lane, Homer 343–44;
law 347–48;
Lyceum 364;
magnet school 365–66;
Mann, Horace 370;
Maslow, Abraham Harold 371;
mass education and credential inflation 141;
Mead, George Herbert 376;
Mead, Margaret 25, 376–77;
mentor/mentoring 380;
military education 33;
Millikin University, Illinois 498;
mixed-ability teaching 386;
multicultural education 26;
multiversity 627;
Nation at Risk 121, 515, 524, 623;
national curriculum 291;
National Organisation for Women 252;
nature study 401;
No Child Left Behind Act (2001) 9, 10, 121, 291, 310, 493, 525, 550, 579, 623;
normal school 407;
norm-referenced tests 407;
nursery school 411, 412;
Ohio State University 497;
open plan 418;
parental choice 425;
Parkhurst, Helen 309, 426;
partnerships, educational 427;
pastoral care 429;
performance indicators 431;
primary school/education 452, 621–22;
Prior Learning Assessment (PLA) 11;
professor 459;
Project Head Start 116;
psychology of education 466, 467;
public library 470;
religious assembly 488;
religious education 490;
religious schools 94,
Rice, Joseph Mayer 495–96;
Riesman, David 496;
Rockefeller Foundation 82;
Rogers, Carl 243, 497;

Rugg, Harold 498–99;
rural education 500–501;
Sarason, Seymour 507;
scholarship 510;
Schön, Donald 451, 456–57, 487–88, 512;
school change 515;
school effectiveness 517, 518;
school reform 524–25;
school security 526–27;
secondary school 622;
segregation/desegregation 534–35, 622–23;
sex education 539;
social exclusion/inclusion 549;
social studies 553–54;
sponsored and contest mobility 563–64;
Soka Gakkai International 367;
standardised tests 564–65, 623;
Stanford University 72, 596, 610;
Sunday school 573;
supply/substitute teaching 574;
suspension 575;
Terman, Lewis Madison 318, 596–97;
textbook 599;
Thorndike, Edward Lee 47, 213, 371, 498–99, 602;
training 604–5;
travellers, education of 608;
Tyler, Ralph 610;
underperforming/failing school 613;
university 627;
    new curriculum 626–27;
University of Buffalo 96, 496;
University of California-Berkeley 338;
University of Chicago 133, 166, 376, 498, 541, 610;
University of Iowa104;
University of Madison, Wisconsin 128;
University of Michigan 166, 215, 376;
urban education 628–30;
vocational education 633–34;
voluntarism 635;
Washington, Booker T. 639;
Wesleyan University, Connecticut 602;
Yale University 507;
youth club/work 649–50;
see also Education Acts (United States);
    multicultural education; progressive education
Universal Declaration of Human Rights 122, 228, 618, 625
universal education/mass education 176, 259, **624–25**;
beginnings and development 624–25;
concepts related to 624;
criticism 625;
Education for All 625;
equality of access 624;
mass higher education 5, 6;
mass/elite 5;
Millennium Development Goals 625;
and the modern state 624;
in the modern world 624;

'proletarianization' 6;
secular ideology of universal progress 625;
Universal Declaration of Human Rights 625;
university massification 627;
see also compulsory education; distance
    education/learning; Education for All;
    educational system structure; educational
    targets; equality of opportunity; Oceania;
    primary school/education; United Nations
    Children's Fund (UNICEF); United Nations
    Educational, Scientific and Cultural
    Organization (UNESCO)
universal provision 188, 189;
see also universal education/mass education
university 234, 446, 447, **625–28**;
Ain Shams University 218;
Al-Azhar 217, 218, 379;
American comprehensive university 292;
Atlanta University 181–82;
Australia 40;
Bamberg University 24;
binary system 52–53, 627;
Bologna 626;
Bradford University 81;
Brandeis University 371;
Brown University, Rhode Island, 370;
Cairo University 218;
Cambridge University 104, 225, 246; 372, 456, 510, 541, 628, 632, 647;
Canada 68;
Catholic University, Dublin 402;
China 92;
and church 94;
Clarke University, Massachusetts 507, 596;
classical studies 98;
coeducation 104;
college 108–9;
Columbia University 166, 215, 371, 376, 463, 464, 495, 496, 497, 499, 602;
comparative education 113, 115;
Cornell University 213;
current challenges 627;
definition 625, 626;
degree 159–60, 626;
e-universities 219;
and economy 627;
Edinburgh University 401, 486;
education/educational studies 199–200;
endowments 225;
examinations 278;
Exeter University 246, 628;
extracurriculum 246;
extra-mural class 246–47;
faculty 249;
Finland 254;
Fisk University 181;
France 258;
French University of the Pacific 415;
gate-keeping 268–69;
Georgetown University 348;

German university model 626–27;
Germany 272, 292, 626;
and globalisation 276;
Göttingen University 486;
Greece 281–82;
Harvard University 118, 124–25, 179, 181, 221, 225, 262, 287, 466;
Helenic Open University 281;
Illinois State Normal University 407;
Indian Universities Act (1904–5) 307;
intellectual work of 625–26;
Iran 325;
Islamic Azad University 325;
Islamic theology 424;
Italy 329, 330;
Jena University 289;
Jesuit university 332;
Johns Hopkins University 97, 287;
Jondi-Shapour University 324;
Kerr, Clark 338;
knowledge economy 627–28;
Latin America 345, 346;
lecture/lecturer 357;
Leeds University 246, 247;
liberal university 626;
Liverpool University 64;
massification 627;
master's 371–72;
matriculation 375;
medieval university 32, 626;
Mediterranean 378, 379;
Millikin University, Illinois 498;
mission statement 385;
modern university 626;
Monash University 368;
multiversity 627;
Nanyang Technological University 541;
National University of Dar es Salaam 582;
National University of Rwanda 486;
National University of Samoa.415;
National University of Singapore 541;
New Zealand 403;
Nigeria 405;
Ohio State University 497;
oldest institution in Western world 626;
Open University Australia 416;
Open University Hong Kong 416;
origins and development 626–27;
Oxford University 31, 34, 82, 114, 179, 225, 246, 334, 402, 456, 495, 506, 509, 510, 626, 632;
performance indicators 431;
and polytechnic education 446–47;
post-war changes 627;
proctor 456;
research 626, 627;
restructuring 493;
Rome University 389;
Russia 504;
scholarships 384;
Sheffield University 246, 628;

Singapore 541;
Singapore Management University 541;
and society 627;
Sorbonne 53, 182, 257, 283, 440, 512;
St Andrews University 215, 384;
Stanford University 72, 596, 610;
stratified system 627;
Sydney University, Australia 114;
United Kingdom Open University 176, 409, 416–17;
United Nations University, Tokyo 486;
United States 627;
  new university curriculum 626–27;
University of Alexandria 218;
University of Baghdad 326;
University of Berlin 114, 626;
University of Buffalo 96, 496;
University of California-Berkeley 338;
University of Chicago 133, 166, 376, 498, 541, 610;
University College, London 50, 64, 70, 267, 318, 496, 559;
University College of Tanganyika 582;
University College of the West Indies (UCWI) 70–71;
University of Durham 26;
University of East Africa 582;
University of East Anglia 567;
University of Geneva 320;
University of Glasgow 225, 583;
University of Guam and Papua New Guinea 415;
University of Havana 146;
University of Iowa104;
University of London 40, 50, 70, 96, 97, 113, 187, 200, 327, 363, 370, 377, 463, 582;
University of Madison, Wisconsin 128;
University of Manchester 25, 81, 326, 447, 506;
University of Michigan 166, 215, 376;
University of Moscow 637;
University of New South Wales 541;
University of Nottingham 128, 246, 368, 628;
University of Paris 1, 99, 249, 626;
University of the South Pacific (USP) 413, 414, 415;
University of the Third Age (U3A) 17;
University of Turku, Finland 486;
University of York 81;
Uppsala University 256;
vice-chancellor 632;
Wesleyan University, Connecticut 602;
Yale University 507;
see also academic/academic profession; academic freedom; chancellor; degree; doctorate; don; foundation degree; graduate/graduation; higher education; knowledge economy; master's; Newman, John Henry; Open University; postgraduate; professor; progressive education; rector; sabbatical; sandwich course; scholarship; semester/term; student; tertiary education; undergraduate

university extension 16, **628**;
  lifelong learning 628;
  origins 628;
  subjects covered by early university extension 628;
  United States 628;
  see also adult education; continuing education;
    extra-mural class; Jowett, Benjamin; liberal
    education; lifelong learning; mechanics' insti-
    tute; Workers' Educational Association
    (WEA)
University of the Third Age (U3A) 17;
  see also adult education; andragogy; further
    education; globalisation; higher education;
    informal/nonformal learning; International
    Council for Adult Education; knowledge
    economy; learning; learning society; lifelong
    learning; mature student; recurrent
    education; skills; social exclusion/inclusion;
    transition education; university extension
urban education **628–30**;
  Education Action Zones 630;
  non-urban schools 628–29;
  process of urbanisation 629–30;
    Australia 629;
    Canada 629;
    China 629;
    India 629;
    Kenya 629;
    Soviet Union 629;
    United Kingdom 629, 630;
    United States 628–30;
  uniqueness of 628–29;
  see also academy; catchment area; educational
    priority area; metropolitanism; parental
    choice; partnerships, educational; rural
    education; systemic reform; zoning

value added **631–32**;
  common complications 631–32;
  definition 631;
  earliest examples 631;
  school effectiveness 631;
  and status-based presentations 631;
  see also baseline assessment; performance
    indicators; quantitative research; school
    effectiveness; school improvement
vice-chancellor **632**;
  definition 632;
  duties 632;
  see also chancellor; Jowett, Benjamin; rector;
    university
virtual learning **632–33**;
  artificial intelligence 632–33;
  computer-assisted learning 123;
  content 632;
  definition 632;
  simulation 632;
  virtual learning environments (VLEs) 633;
  see also computer-assisted learning; educational
    technology; e-learning; learning community;

    rural education; technology; web-based
    learning
visual aids **633**;
  definition 633;
  effective use of 633;
  examples 633;
  see also classroom; educational broadcasting;
    instruction; lecture/lecturer; lesson;
    teaching/teaching methods
vocational education 96, **633–34**;
  Africa 634;
  Australia 40;
  continuing vocational education (CVE) 127, 128;
  criticism 634;
  description 633;
  Finland 254;
  and liberal education 633;
  portfolio assessment 610;
  and secondary education 634;
  United Kingdom 634;
    Technical and Vocational Education Initiative
    (TVEI) 634;
  United States 633–34;
  vocational guidance 137;
  vocational qualification 272;
  vocational skills 146–47;
  vocational training 190;
  vocationalism 633–34;
  see also adult education; apprenticeship;
    curriculum; dual system; further education;
    higher education; industrial training; liberal
    education; polytechnic; professional education;
    qualifications; sandwich course; secondary
    school/education; technical education/school/
    college; tertiary education; training;
    workbased/work-located/workplace/work-
    related learning; workers' education
Vocational and Technical Education (VET) 19, 92;
  apprenticeship 28, 30;
  Australia 40;
  see also adult education; apprenticeship; dual
    system; vocational education
voluntarism **634–35**;
  American Founding Fathers 635;
  broad sense 635;
  England 635;
  philosophical perspective 634;
  United States 635;
  volunteering 635;
  see also charities, educational; compulsory
    education; church; dual system; economics of
    education; partnerships, educational;
    privatisation/marketisation; religious school;
    Tanzania; work experience
vouchers 525, **635–36**;
  characteristics of voucher schemes 635;
  Chile 425, 635–36;
  description 635;
  effects of 636;
  school voucher scheme 193, 194;

targeted voucher programmes 636;
United States 425, 636;
universal voucher programmes 635–36;
see also charter school; experimental research;
   independent/private school/education;
   magnet school; parental choice; privatisation/
   marketisation;
Vygotsky, Lev 86, 108, 213, 440, 547, **636–37**;
and early childhood education 186;
planned teaching 637;
Thought and Language 637;
see also activity theory; Piaget, Jean; psychology;
   psychology of education; social constructivism;
   Russia; zone of proximal development

Waldorf Schools 272, 462, 567;
see also Steiner, Rudolf
Washington, Booker T. **639**;
Tuskegee Institute 639;
Working with the Hands 639;
see also equality of opportunity; politics of education
Web-based learning 133, **639–40**;
benefits 639–40;
computer-assisted learning 123;
description 639;
educational broadcasting 201–2;
see also correspondence course; distance
   education/learning; e-learning; Open
   University; virtual learning
Weber, Max 114, 212, **640**;
Economy and Society 640;
The Protestant Ethic and the Spirit of Capitalism 640;
see also comparative education; sociology
whole-class teaching **640–41**;
description 640;
modern information technology 640–41;
United Kingdom 640;
see also ability grouping; classroom; mixed-ability
   teaching
widening participation 11, 16, 128, 165, 264, 398,
   569, 642;
of disabled children 302;
strategies 494;
see also compulsory education; educational
   targets; equality of opportunity; inclusive
   education; international education;
   International Bureau of Education (IBE);
   international education; multigrade
   education; Nigeria; Polynesia; primary
   school/education; Tanzania; United Nations
   Children's Fund (UNICEF); United Nations
   Educational, Scientific and Cultural
   Organisation (UNESCO); universal
   education/mass education
William of Wykeham **641**;
see also public school
Wollstonecraft, Mary **641**;
Thoughts on the Education of Daughters 641;
Vindication of the Rights of Man 641;
Vindication of the Rights of Women 641;

see also equality of opportunity; feminist theory
work-based/work-located/workplace/work-
   related learning (WBL) **641–43**;
assessment 642;
benefits 642–43;
description 641–42;
forms 642;
higher education 642;
sandwich courses 642;
supporting of 642;
United Kingdom 642;
and universities 642;
work experience 642;
see also accreditation of prior achievement/
   learning; continued/continuing professional
   development; day release; foundation degree;
   higher education; industrial training;
   informal/nonformal learning; knowledge
   economy; learning society; lifelong learning;
   practitioner research; professional education;
   reflective practitioner; sandwich course;
   skills; technical education/school/college;
   tertiary education; training; vocational
   education; workers' education
work experience 642, **643**;
aim 643;
description 643;
for students 643;
for unemployed people 643;
see also career guidance; industrial training;
   sabbatical; sixth form; voluntarism
workers' education 377, **643–45**;
content and purpose 645;
Freire, Paolo 645;
informal learning 643–44;
issues regarding workers' education 644–45;
social movements related to 645;
uses of the term 643–44;
   labour education 643;
   vocational education 644;
   working-class educational activities,
      organisations, institutions 643–44;
see also adult education; day release; extra-mural
   class; in-service education; lifelong learning;
   mechanics' institute; Owen, Robert;
   recurrent education; Sadler, Michael;
   technical education/school/college;
   vocational education; work-based/work-
   located/workplace/work-related learning;
   Workers' Educational Association (WEA)
Workers' Educational Association (WEA) 377,
   645–46;
aim 645;
courses 645;
description 645;
International Federation of Workers' Education
   Associations 645–46;
membership 645;
origins and development 645;
supporters 645;

see also adult education; extra-mural class;
   lifelong learning; mechanics' institute;
   Tawney, Richard Henry; university
   extension; workers' education
World Bank 17, 19, 114, 162, 312, 322, 323, 340,
   646;
   aims 646;
   beginnings 646;
   criticism 646;
   and distance education/learning 177;
   governance 646;
   International Bank for Reconstruction and
      Development (IBRD) 646;
   International Centre for Settlement of
      Investment Disputes (ICSID) 646;
   International Development Association (IDA) 646;
   International Finance Corporation (IFC) 646;
   Latin American education 346;
   Multilateral Investment Guarantee Agency
      (MIGA) 646;
   responsibilities 646;
   see also Department for International
      Development (DfID); economics of
      education; Education for All (EFA);
      international education; knowledge
      economy; Polynesia; United Nations
      Educational, Scientific and Cultural
      Organization (UNESCO)
World Education Fellowship (WEF) 89, **647**;
   aims 647;
   definition 647;
   The New Era in Education, previously New Era 647;
   origins 647;
   purpose 647;
   see also child-centred education; progressive
      education; United Nations Educational,
      Scientific and Cultural Organization
      (UNESCO)
World Health Authority 55
World War I 2, 15, 39
World War II 2, 39, 61, 68, 508;
   and computing 124;
   and counselling 136;
   and educational broadcasting 201;
   and universal education 625
wrangler/wooden spoon **647**;
   definitions 647;
   University of Cambridge 647;
   see also excellence; underachievement
writing 117, 118, **647–48**;
   first writing system 647;
   history/pre-history 647;
   modes of writing processes 361;
   'oral' cultures 648;
   as a process 648;
   and progress/power 647–48;

and reading 343, 647;
   teaching writing 648;
      different approaches 648;
   written language 481–82;
      origin and development 482, 647;
   see also comprehension; Freinet, Celestin;
      grammar; literacy; plagiarism; reading;
      spelling

xenophobia 27;
   see also antiracist education; equality of
      opportunity; multicultural education

Young, Michael 381, 382–83, 418, **649**;
   Advisory Centre for Education 649;
   distance learning 649;
   Family and Kinship in East London 649;
   Let Us Face the Future 649;
   Open University 649;
   The Rise of the Meritocracy 382, 649;
   Which? 649;
   see also distance education/learning; merit;
      meritocracy; Open University;
youth club/work 343, **649–50**;
   characteristics 650;
   origins and development 649–50;
   United Kingdom 649–50;
   United States 649–50;
   see also church; community education/school/
      college; informal/nonformal learning; Lane,
      Homer; Makarenko, Anton Simeonovitch;
      peer group; Scout Association; social capital
youth culture 150;
   as agent of cultural transmission 149–50;
   see also cultural transmission; culture; youth club/
      work

zone of proximal development 3, **651**;
   child development 651;
   definition 651;
   Vygotsky, Lev 651;
   see also child development; cognition;
      constructivism; social constructivism;
      Vygotsky, Lev
zoning **651–52**;
   definition 651;
   results of 652;
   United States 651–52;
      Brown v. Board of Education (1954) 651–52;
      Brown II (1955) 652;
      Green v. New Kent County (1968) 652;
   zoning techniques 652;
   see also antiracist education; catchment area;
      equality of opportunity; magnet school;
      parental choice; privatisation/marketisation;
      segregation/desegregation; urban education